COMMUNICATIONS REGULATION

By

Glen O. Robinson
David and Mary Harrison Distinguished Professor of Law, Emeritus
University of Virginia School of Law

Thomas B. Nachbar
Professor of Law
University of Virginia School of Law

AMERICAN CASEBOOK SERIES®

THOMSON
WEST

Mat #40585443

610 Opperman Drive
St. Paul, MN 55123
1-800-313-9378

Printed in the United States of America

ISBN: 978-0-314-18024-7

TEXT IS PRINTED ON 10% POST CONSUMER RECYCLED PAPER

For Kay

— GOR

For Jamie, Amelia, Alex, and Jack

— TBN

*

Preface

There is no need to describe in detail what this book is about. A glance at the table of contents will reveal that. But a few comments may be appropriate to explain why these particular contents have been chosen. As the title indicates, our subject is communications *regulation*. More specifically it is about regulation of *electronic* media—both mass media and telecommunications media. The most salient legal characteristic that separates electronic from other media is the fact that the former are the subject of specialized administrative regulatory regimes. The one exception to this feature of regulation is the Internet, which is not (as yet) subject to the same kinds of regulation as its more traditional kin, television and telephony. Our treatment of Internet-based communications is selective, however, and deals only with those aspects of the Internet closely related to those provided by traditional, regulated media. As we shall see, it is still an open question how far the Internet will remain free of regulation, but at present it remains largely outside the shadow of governmental supervision. This raises an obvious question whether traditional forms of regulation for the other electronic media can continue if the same services are provided by an unregulated Internet. Be that as it may, in those areas where the same services are being provided (half regulated, half "free" so to speak), we have chosen to include them within our subject.

By choosing *regulated* communications law as our subject, we naturally invite the question how much knowledge of administrative law is presumed. The answer is simple: none. In the opening chapter we provide a summary of some general features of administrative law, along with an explanation of the institutional structure and procedures of the principal agency with which we are dealing, the Federal Communications Commission. No more background is needed, nor in our view would it be very useful.

More useful perhaps would be a background in constitutional law, specifically First Amendment law. Communications regulation is, virtually by definition, a subject that implicates the First Amendment. Indeed, the First Amendment is invoked at almost every turn in controversies dealing with both mass media and telecommunications media alike. For this reason we thought it would be useful to provide a very general overview of First Amendment principles and doctrine that that are pertinent to the course. Nevertheless, for all their pervasive presence in this field, one should be careful not to exaggerate the importance of constitutional principles. They establish a limit on policy options, but those limits only occasionally determine the outcomes, either at the FCC or in the courts. The regulatory issues we examine here are shaped more by an interaction between economics, technology, politics, and non-constitutional legal rules than they are by the contours of the First Amendment or other constitutional principles.

Because our subject is about *electronic* media, it is also necessarily about technology. As it happens, electronic media technology is at the cutting edge of applied science. Suspecting that there is something here that is beyond the ken of those with a basic arts-and-science background, our students often ask whether this course is designed for "techies." The answer is, no. If it were, the authors of this book would not be teaching it; our own arts-and-sciences educations would have left us woefully unprepared. While we have had some prior background in the subjects at hand, we make no claim to technical expertise, and we suspect that the same will be true of most of those who teach this subject. To be sure, there is, as you will quickly see, a lot of jargon in this book, most of it consisting of acronyms like CLECs (competitive local exchange carriers) or UNEs (unbundled network elements). On first hearing the jargon is annoying. One always has the sense that the practitioners of the subject are deliberately creating some kind of special code in order to create barriers to entry from outsiders who might want to venture into the field without the appropriate investment in a new vocabulary. But all specialized subjects have their own "codes," and communications law is not really all that different from, say, intellectual property, or securities regulation, or tax.

Just as our subject deals with cutting edge technology, so too it deals with an ever-changing set of legal rules. A glance at the date of the materials in the book says it all. More than half of the cases or reports bear dates no more than a decade old. The authorial challenge should be obvious: how do you keep a book like this up to date? The challenge is made all the more difficult by the fact that being "up to date" is not simply a matter of including the latest case or report on a particular subject because in a field such as this it is extremely difficult to understand the latest case or rule without some knowledge of what preceded it. You'll notice that many chapters of the book begin with an historical overview to place the current materials in perspective. As will quickly become apparent the history of communications regulation is not a simple linear progression; in fact it is often circular. It seems to be a truism of this field that there is no idea so old that it is forgotten and none so moribund that it cannot be revived.

Beyond the challenge of keeping up with the times, a field as complex and controversial as this presents a special challenge of being both accurate and well balanced. Many years ago a distinguished economist introduced his new text in industrial economics by saying, tongue in cheek, that half of what he had written was probably wrong; he just didn't know which half. Anyone who tries to explain the law, economics, and politics of communications regulation has to be sympathetic with that sentiment. Sadly, it is not possible to begin with a *second* edition in which all errors of the first have been corrected before they have been exposed to public scrutiny. So, we plunge ahead, expecting—hoping, indeed—that all of the errors in this edition will be brought to our attention (but will not also be of such a magnitude as to preclude a second edition!). As for being well balanced, we have to admit up front that we have not been bashful about stating our opinions, though we should also caution that in some cases our opinions are, one, not always shared between the two authors, and two, not always as firmly grounded in knowledge as they may appear from the manner in which expressed. Be that as it may, we have generally preferred to give our views in a way that does not mask them in transparently rhetorical questions. (This is not always the case; old habits of legal pedagogy die hard.) We trust, however, that no one embarking on a course like this will be intimidated by our pretense of oracular authority or provocative assertiveness.

Finally, it is customary to acknowledge others who have contributed to an effort such as this. We have had so many conversations with so many individuals regarding this book that such a list would run to several pages, so we will limit our thanks to one: Professor Tim Wu. Tim not only provided tremendous substantive feedback but, as our first adopter, displayed either supreme pedagogical courage or foolhardy trust (or both) by agreeing to teach out of our casebook as we were in the process of writing it. We hope his—and all our readers'—reliance on our efforts will have been worthwhile.

GOR & TBN

August, 2008

*

Copyright Acknowledgements

We would like to thank the following for their permission to reprint portions of the their copyrighted works:

Portions of Thomas A. Hazlett, *The Wireless Craze, The Unlimited Bandwidth Myth, The Spectrum Auction Faux Pas, and The Punchline To Ronald Coase's "Big Joke": An Essay On Airwave Allocation Policy*, 14 HARV. J.L. & TECH. 335 (2001), Yochai Benkler, *Some Economics of Wireless Communications*, 16 HARV. J.L. & TECH. 25, (2002), and Christopher S. Yoo, *Beyond Network Neutrality*, 19 HARV. J.L. & TECH. 1 (2005) are reprinted with permission from the *Harvard Journal of Law and Technology*.

Portions of Mark A. Lemley & Lawrence Lessig, *The End of End-to-End: Preserving the Architecture of the Internet in the Broadband Era*, 48 UCLA L. REV. 925 (2001) are reprinted with permission from the authors.

Portions of Tim Wu, *Why Have a Telecommunications Law?: Anti-discrimination Norms in Communications*, 5 J. ON TELECOM. & HIGH TECH. L. 15 (2006) are reprinted with permission from the author.

*

Summary of Contents

Table of Contents

*

Table of Cases

The principal cases are in bold type. Cases cited or discussed in the text are roman type. References are to pages. Cases cited in principal cases and within other quoted materials are not included.

COMMUNICATIONS REGULATION

*

PART I

THE REGULATORY ENVIRONMENT

Chapter 1

INTRODUCTION

Historically, the United States was almost unique in the world in relying on private enterprise to provide electronic media services.[1] Until very recent times, most of the electronic media of most countries were owned and managed by public enterprises or government agencies. Over the past three decades, most developed countries have moved toward privatization, though many retain some public enterprise in parts of the electronic media. In the United States our political DNA seems to code against reliance on public enterprise to provide ordinary economic goods and services. To be sure there are even today some pockets of local public entities providing an array of services, and there is the example of the U.S. Post Office, which until its transformation into a quasi-private, quasi-public entity was a government agency. But these have never been regarded as suitable models for exporting public ownership into other sectors—not even electronic communications—which virtually every other country treated as public from the beginning.

Electronic media in the United States have not been publicly owned (with the unimportant exception of some non-commercial radio and television stations and a few municipally owned cable systems), but they have been pervasively regulated. Neither telecommunications nor electronic mass media were born into a regulated environment, but regulation was imposed before either of them reached economic maturity. In recent years there has been much ado about relying on market forces

1. A word about semantics. As will become clear later, the field of "communications regulation" encompasses two very different industries: On one side are electronic "mass media" (broadcasting, cable, satellite), and on the other are "telecommunications" services (conventional telephone and data services). We will use those respective terms to describe them. The word "telecommunications" is occasionally used by others to refer to all electronic media, but we will not use the term in that way. Rather, we will use the terms "electronic communications" or "electronic media" to refer to the more general set of communications technologies that are used in mass media and telecommunications and consequently fall within the ambit of "communications regulation." The increasing convergence of electronic media may soon make this conventional distinction obsolete—a matter that we will return to in the last chapter of this book. But the lines that separate mass media services like television from individualized telecommunications services like voice and data still have legal as well as economic significance and justify retaining some of the traditional verbal distinctions for the purposes of our inquiry into communications regulation.

and competition rather than regulation as the model for delivery of electronic media to the public. Competition is clearly on the rise across all communications sectors. So is regulation, perverse as it might seem to say so. Conventional economic theory holds that competition and regulation are alternatives: if you have the first, you don't need the second. Economic theory is not a reliable guide to economic history, however, as the history of regulated communications reveals. We cannot explore here the reasons for the persistence of regulation in the face of increased competition, but some of them will become apparent as we proceed through the book.

As we examine the different components of electronic communications policy, we will encounter countless individual questions about regulation. We can lump them into three large categories: Why regulate? Who regulates? How do we regulate? A more complete explanation awaits you in the chapters that follow; we cannot answer these questions fully now (if ever), for they will require an examination of the entire field before we can even understand them. But we can provide a few general observations, which is the purpose of this introductory chapter. We begin with a few brief observations about regulatory purpose, or we should more precisely say, regulatory purposes, for the only policy objective that covers the entire field is the impossibly banal directive to provide for the "public interest, convenience and necessity" (the statutory lodestar of the Communications Act of 1934). Thereafter we will take up the second question, which in turn requires a short introduction to regulatory history. There is a lot of history in this book; it is impossible to understand the current legal regime without knowing where it came from. Our opening history just sets the stage for introducing the Federal Communications Commission and some other regulatory actors. The third question, "how we regulate," is the subject of the remainder of the book, so again, our purpose in this chapter is limited to exploring, first, the structure of the Communications Act—the basic charter for American communications regulation—and second, a summary of key features of administrative law that provide the procedural framework for regulation.

We conclude the introductory chapter with an overview of the industries generally subject to "communications regulation".

A. WHY REGULATE

Regulation of electronic communications draws on different rationales. The earliest regulatory program we examine, telecommunications, is a form of common carrier regulation that has ancient common law roots. In modern times the usual explanation for why we regulate common carriers is cast in terms of controlling monopoly—protecting consumers against monopolistic abuses (overcharge, discrimination, poor service, etc.). Modern economic theory teaches that the concerns about ensuring equal service on fair terms is largely a product of market imperfections—notably the absence of effective competition among service providers. But the monopoly rationale is historically incomplete in both the traditional common-carriage and telecommunications contexts. The law of common carriage has not been historically rationalized as control of monopoly, and, when federal regulation was first established for telephone and telegraph carriers in 1910, there was significant competition between AT&T and independent telephone companies in most large cities. (AT&T had previously enjoyed a legal, patent monopoly over telephone communications, but those patents had long expired and that expiration had allowed competitive entry.) However, there were doubts at the time whether competition was either desirable or sustainable in the long run. Telephone and telegraph services were widely regarded as a classic example of natural monopoly. We will spend some time later with natural monopoly theory; for present purposes the simplest of definitions is sufficient: A natural monopoly is said to exist where a single firm can serve the market more efficiently (more cheaply) than two or more firms. In the course of the last thirty years the natural monopoly argument for regulation of telecommunications has been discredited. Competition has now been officially proclaimed to be the order of the day. This has not meant an end to regulation but a repurposing of it. The traditional role of protecting end consumers has been largely displaced by a new role of enabling the transition to full competition. In a loose sense, you could say that regulation is now predominantly concerned about regulating the competitive process between the legacy monopolists and the new competitors. Some critics have decided this new regulatory focus as protecting not competition but rather competitors, but we can defer that issue until later.

The regulation of mass media has followed an entirely different path than the regulation of telecommunications. The regulation of mass media grew out of the regulation of radio (that is, the use of the radio spectrum), and radio regulation was never based on either common carrier traditions or natural monopoly theory. Rather, radio regulation was premised on the need to prevent multiple users from attempting to transmit radio signals on the same frequency—to utilize the same portion of the electromagnetic spectrum—at the same time and in the same place. When two users in the same locale attempt to use the same spectrum at the same time, the result is interference, which degrades both uses. This translates into the label of "spectrum scarcity": the radio spectrum is a finite resource that needs to be rationed. Contemporary critics have argued that the asserted scarcity is much exaggerated and in any case not a sufficient condition for regulation. All physical resources are scarce, the argument runs, but we usually allocate them through property rights and markets, not by government licenses, so what is different about the "scarce" spectrum? When regulation was imposed (the first comprehensive statutory scheme was enacted in 1927), however, the prevailing view discounted the relevance of market controls. In 1927 it would have been difficult to find much support even among economists for relying entirely on property rights and markets as the sole solution to the scarcity problem. Today, the idea of spectrum scarcity does much less work than it did then, but it is still often invoked in support of imposing "public interest" obligations on broadcasters (there are few public interest requirements for non-broadcast spectrum users). The scarcity *qua* interference rationale has always been glossed with a conception of the spectrum as an inherently *public* resource. Where modern economic analysts appeal to property models, others insist that if the spectrum is property it is not *private* property but *public*. The analogy is to navigable waters. As we shall discuss in the next chapter, this is a metaphor, for although the spectrum can be described by geography or physical boundaries, it is not a lake, not a stream, not a thing at all. It is an artifact of the propagation of electromagnetic energy in open space. To the extent, then, that "ownership" claims usually imply claims of possession, there is nothing to be possessed. Nevertheless, metaphors are important in public, as in private, discourse, and there is no question that this metaphor has shaped public thinking about the radio spectrum, and this in turn has influenced political action.

The regulation of cable television—on which we will spend considerable time—calls for additional explanations. When the FCC first undertook to regulate cable television in the early 1960s, cable fit neither of the two regulatory paradigms mentioned above. Cable television operators did not hold themselves out to be common carriers, and in any case the FCC did not seek to have them treated as such under the common carrier provisions of the 1934 Act. Equally they did not use the radio spectrum in open space, so they could not fit within the category of radio spectrum users contemplated by the same act.[2] (Again, in any case the FCC did not seek to license cable operators as radio stations.) The FCC invented a new rationale for regulation. Essentially, the core of the FCC's rationale was that cable television threatened to interfere with the regulatory policies that the FCC itself had earlier put in place for over-the-air broadcast stations. It was also based, as we shall see, on policy concerns about "unfair competition" (since cable depended—continues to depend—heavily on retransmitted broadcast signals) and property rights. In time the FCC would also worry about the market power of local cable television monopolies, but in the early years cable struggled against high odds just to be a viable independent service provider so the monopoly justification would be a later rationale.

No modern story of communications regulation can ignore the Internet. The FCC has not yet undertaken to regulate the Internet as such, so the question of why regulate may at first seem moot. But to say that the Internet is not regulated is somewhat misleading, for, as we shall see, the Internet is dependent on the infrastructure of telecommunications networks—the transport system by which Internet services are delivered—that are regulated. To the extent that the infrastructure of

2. Technically, of course, cable television systems do use radio frequencies, as do wired telephone carriers, but since they transmit them over shielded conduit the problem of interference that was the core justification for regulating wireless radio users does not arise.

the Internet is regulated, so too is the Internet itself. But there are issues beyond regulation of the Internet's infrastructure—its "pipes". In the early years of the Internet, some argued that it was a unique information and communications mechanism that was impossible to regulate because of its dispersed character. Few people believe this "impossibility theorem" today, but there remains a question whether the exceptional character of the Internet should exempt it from regulation when it provides services that are inseparable from those that are regulated when provided by conventional communications systems. For example, voice over Internet ("VoIP"—voice over Internet Protocol) is fast becoming a main stream competitor to traditional wireline telephone service ("POTS"—plain old telephone service). To the extent that telephone carriers (including not only traditional telcos but cable systems and companies like Vonage) provide VoIP, is there any reason not to apply the same regulatory requirements (price and service controls, universal service charges, etc.) that apply to POTS? The same question could be asked on the mass media side. A broadcaster may be sanctioned for presenting an "indecent" program over the air. Suppose clips of the same program show up on YouTube. What then? The FCC's indecency rules do not apply to subscription-based services, which presumably would exclude YouTube to the extent it is delivered by a wired or wireless service for which a charge is made. Further, the FCC currently classifies Internet services as "information services," which it forbears from regulating. But the exclusion for subscription services and information services is a matter of the agency's reasonable discretion, not a matter of limited jurisdiction. Direct regulation of the Internet may be one FCC rulemaking away.

B. WHO REGULATES

Electronic communications is a creature of a peculiar regulatory regime. It is a regime that is defined neither by a particular industry, since the various branches of communications are carried out in multiple industries, nor by a technology, since different forms of communications are carried out in technically diverse ways, nor by a regulatory ideal, since the different branches of the statute have seemingly divergent goals. Rather, communications law is an amalgam of regulatory approaches applied by a mix of regulators to several different technologies carried out by varied industry players. Until recently, the domestic world of electronic communications was roughly divided between a broadcast industry, dominated by three commercial networks, and telecommunications industry, dominated by a single national carrier, AT&T. This is something of an oversimplification, for there were many other players (thousands of broadcast stations, hundreds of independent telephone companies), but, for most purposes, the industry actors who counted were three broadcast networks in one industry and a single telecommunications carrier in a completely separate one.

On the other hand, although there are many government regulators involved in communications, including state public utility commissions and even local city councils who grant cable franchises or issue permits for the construction of wireless communications towers, regulation of both mass media and telecommunications has been historically dominated for the last seventy years by the Federal Communications Commission. The FCC's regulatory ambition has waxed and waned over time (and has been periodically adjusted by Congress), but the FCC's pervasiveness as both a mass media and telecommunications regulator merits some attention to exactly how one federal administrative agency became such a major influence in two seemingly distinct industries and how it used its authority through its history.

1. Historical Background of the FCC

The roots of federal regulation of electronic communications date back to the Mann-Elkins Act of 1910, which first subjected telephone-telegraph service to the Interstate Commerce Commission's regulatory jurisdiction. It was a somewhat casual if not exactly accidental extension of the ICC's traditional jurisdiction. Mann-Elkins was intended by its sponsors to give the ICC expanded power over railroads. The provisions to give the ICC jurisdiction over telephone and telegraph carriers were added on the floor of the House and Senate, over the opposition of the two named sponsors, both of who believed that communications regulation should be addressed separately, not simply as a tack-on to the ICC's regulation of railroads. Despite Congress's willingness to entrust telephone and telegraph regulation to the ICC, the Commission did not entirely welcome the additional burden imposed upon it by the Act, and for the next fourteen years largely ignored the telephone and telegraph business.[3]

For all practical purposes the origins of mass media regulation, on the other hand, began seventeen years after the Mann-Elkins Act, with the 1927 Radio Act. The standard story of the 1927 Act describes it as a product of radio spectrum chaos—the unsupervised, uncontrolled use of radio frequencies that resulted in interference among users. To manage use, Congress created the Federal Radio Commission, with power to assign radio spectrum use rights through licensing. Congress was not only concerned with technical interference problems, though. The FRC

3. Three years after Mann-Elkins the Department of Justice entered into a consent decree to settle the first of what was to be three major government antitrust actions against AT&T. The most important provision required AT&T to interconnect its long distance network with independent carriers, in order to provide end-to-end long distance service for independent subscribers. Another provision required AT&T to divest itself of a controlling interest in Western Union, the dominant telegraph carrier. Still another required AT&T to obtain ICC and DOJ approval for acquisitions of independent companies. The latter provision was terminated by the Willis-Graham Act of 1921, which gave to the ICC power to approve telecom mergers and to immunize them from antitrust challenge. None of these moves prevented AT&T from expanding, however, and by the time of the FCC's creation in 1934, AT&T's dominance had been firmly established.

An intermediate regulation on the broadcast side, the Wireless Act of 1912, provided a kind of skeletal licensing system for radio users, but it did not provide an adequate framework on which to construct a mechanism for managing the use of the radio spectrum, in particular the broadcasting services that emerged in the 1920s.

was directed to oversee the responsible use of the assigned frequencies under the rubric of the "public interest" (a phrase borrowed from earlier public utility regulatory schemes). The original plan of the 1927 Act was that all policy making functions would shift after a year to the Department of Commerce, and the FRC would become essentially as an independent "quasi-judicial" body to hear licensing and other disputes. That never happened. The FRC's temporary regulatory charter was continued for want of congressional resolution of how precisely to allocate responsibilities for administration, adjudication, and policy making in mass media. In 1934 the issue was made moot when Congress merged the radio regulatory functions with the telecommunications regulatory functions into a new Federal Communications Commission.

The FCC's early years were relatively quiet. On the telecommunications side, regulation was largely an informal affair. The primary task was regulating interstate telephone rates, and it was handled by informal negotiations with AT&T (a process the FCC labeled "continuing surveillance"), while state regulators were given the task of regulating local telephone monopolies that interconnected in the interstate AT&T network. Not until the late 1960s would the FCC launch a comprehensive rate proceeding to examine AT&T's overall revenue requirements. On the broadcasting side, the primary activity was licensing of radio stations, although the Commission also adopted a number of structural rules governing ownership and relationships between stations and networks.

The quiet years became a little less quiet when the advent of television broadcasting in the 1940s and 1950s forced the FCC to develop a new system to control licensing of the new medium. Embedded in the FCC's plan for licensing television channels were a series of value judgments and regulatory imperatives—most of them targeted at assuring the primacy of local broadcasters—that would have profound effects on the character of the television industry. Those regulatory values would also bring in train a slew of problems that would occupy the FCC for more than a decade, and spectrum planning was only the beginning. Matters would become more complicated with the emergence of an independent cable television industry in the 1960s, a development that threatened the local broadcasters, whose continued existence was central to the FCC's regulatory designs for television. The FCC's initial response was to attempt to contain cable television by treating it purely as a supplement to broadcasting. Ultimately, that strategy failed, and by the mid 1980s, cable had emerged as the dominant distributor of television programs and would begin to distribute new program content as well, with cable networks being formed to compete with the traditional broadcast networks. Then, in the 1990s, satellite broadcasting would add additional complications. With service areas covering the entire country (or at least significant portions of it) with a single broadcast, satellite carriers further threatened the FCC's locality-based regulatory paradigm. And with all these technical innovations came new inter-industry rivalries that the FCC would be called on to consider.

On the telecommunications side, the quiet life lasted a little longer. Not until the 1960s did the FCC face fundamentally new challenges. The beginning of its first formal rate investigation of AT&T presented a challenge, since the FCC was beginning from scratch, but it was still part of the familiar regulatory paradigm that dated back to 1910. Ironically, however, just as the FCC was proceeding to formalize rules for operating within the framework of a telephone monopoly, the framework itself began changing. Competitors began knocking on the FCC's door seeking entry into specialized long distance service and into telephone equipment markets. The FCC allowed limited entry beginning in the 1970s, and by the end of the decade, competition would be established throughout both equipment and interstate long distance service markets. In 1980 the Commission would completely deregulate equipment markets and so-called "enhanced" service markets (a classification that would later be replaced by the category of "information" services—under which most Internet-based services are currently classified). Four years later, AT&T would be broken up, and the telecommunications world would be completely transformed. As late as 1996, when Congress restructured telecommunications regulation with the Telecommunications Act of 1996, monopoly continued to dominate regulatory thinking, even as Congress directed that the FCC promote competition in all markets, including local exchange service markets, which had been the last bastion of officially sanctioned natural monopoly. The wireless explosion of the 1990s may have even more completely undermined the regulatory framework of natural monopoly for telephone service. Competition is now the reigning paradigm. It isn't completely the reigning reality. Basically, the last decade of telecommunications regulatory energies have been devoted to managing the transition from monopoly to competition. It is still a work in progress.

2. The FCC and Its Regulatory "Partners"

The FCC is currently comprised of five commissioners, no more than three of whom can be members of the same political party. The commissioners are appointed by the President with the approval of the Senate for five years, the terms being staggered. The President names one of the Commissioners as Chairman, to serve in that capacity at the pleasure of the President. The Chairman is the general administrator of the Commission's activities, although certain functions are delegated to bureaus and staff units. Over the years the FCC's internal organization has changed; new bureaus have been created, eliminated, modified, and merged—all to reflect changes in the regulatory agenda of the time. However, the basic structure and character of the agency is the same as it was in 1934. Like its predecessor agencies, the FCC is an independent regulatory agency located outside the traditional framework of the executive branch.[4]

As previously noted, the direct precedent for federal regulation of communications was federal regulation of railroads, and the Mann-

4. For what it means to be an "independent" agency, see section C(2)(a) below.

Elkins Act (and later the Communications Act) carried forward some important characteristics of its regulatory ancestor, the 1887 Interstate Commerce Act, most importantly the distinction between interstate and intrastate service, a distinction that continues to this day. The divided jurisdiction has produced recurrent conflicts over policy and in turn a number of jurisdictional turf battles. In 1996, Congress made far-reaching changes in the telecommunications regulatory structure that, among other things, strengthened the FCC's control over national policy. That did not, however, end the conflicts and turf battles between federal and state regulators over the shape and character of telecommunications regulation.

With respect to the mass media, the conflict between federal and state regulators was avoided in the first thirty years of regulation. The Communications Act gave the FCC exclusive jurisdiction over all uses of the radio spectrum other than those by the federal government itself, which preempted all state regulation of broadcasting services.[5] As part of its authority over spectrum use, the FCC licenses all private broadcasting[6] and a great diversity of other radio uses, from aeronautical and maritime communications and radiolocation to land mobile communications to radio astronomy to microwave ovens. The FCC does not regulate other federal users of the radio spectrum; that responsibility is reserved to the President, who in turn has delegated it to the National Telecommunications and Information Administration (NTIA) within the Department of Commerce, whose jurisdiction extends to all use by the U.S. Government.[7]

The FCC's exclusive control over mass media ended with the rise of cable television. Cable initially was not part of the regulatory scheme for the simple reason that it didn't exist in 1934. When cable first appeared (as "community antenna television service," commonly referred to as "CATV") it did so purely as a supplement to broadcasting (by capturing broadcast signals that most household antennas could not receive and transmitting those signals to individual subscribers over a cable). It was accordingly ignored by the FCC until the early 1960s, when the FCC first asserted jurisdiction over it based on what can only be described as a creative interpretation of Title I of the Communications Act, which is

5. Broadcast licensees are subject to state laws of general applicability, of course; they simply aren't subject to state control of those matters regulated by the FCC: program services and related practices.

6. It does not license a group of broadcasters operated or sponsored by the federal government that are aimed at audiences outside the United States, including Voice of America, Radio Free Europe/Radio Liberty, Radio-TV Marti, Alhura and others. They are operated under the general direction of an independent federal agency, the Broadcasting Board of Governors (BBG), that acts more like a broadcaster than a regulator.

7. Allocation of the spectrum between federal government use and private (including state and local government units) use is a matter of coordination and agreement between the NTIA and the FCC. In practical reality the NTIA is more a coordinator than a regulator of federal users, coordination that is a product of negotiation and consensus among the agencies under the auspices of a so-called Interdepartment Radio Advisory Committee (IRAC) whose members include representatives of all the important federal users. (The FCC is a nonmember participant in IRAC meetings.)

basically a declaration of the general jurisdiction of the FCC over all interstate communications by wire and radio. The FCC reasoned that Title I conferred on it an "ancillary" jurisdiction over all forms of communications that, while not directly covered by the regulatory grants in Title II (on telecommunications carriers) or III (on radio broadcasters), nevertheless impacted such regulated communications in such a way as to require regulatory intervention. Because CATV directly impacted broadcast, a Title III service, the FCC could regulate it under Title I. For the next twenty years, the FCC would construct an increasingly elaborate system of cable regulation based on this ancillary jurisdiction. Not until 1984, with the Cable Communications Policy Act, would Congress explicitly confirm that jurisdiction—by adding Title VI to the Act—and in doing so would basically ratify the Commission's policies. In 1992 and again in 1996 Congress would provide additional policy directives.

In contrast to pure broadcasting, the FCC's jurisdiction over cable was shared, to a degree. From the earliest times cable television systems have been subject to local government franchise regulations because they required the use of public rights of way to run the cable that carried their signals. States, too, sometimes are involved; absent any express preemption, states could assert their inherent sovereign powers to regulate cable. Most of them did not, but left the task of regulation to local governments. Local governments in turn exercised (and continue to exercise) a degree of regulation by means of franchises. The franchises are simply contracts that specify certain service conditions (along with fees) in return for the right to use public roads and rights of way, but they serve as mechanisms for imposing regulatory requirements.

Like the federal-state relationship with respect to telecommunications, the federal-local relationship with respect to cable television has not been a smooth one. In the early years of regulation, the FCC set certain limits on the power of local governments to exact what it considered to be extortionate demands (and fees) from cable television. Congress subsequently confirmed the FCC's preeminent authority in 1984 and again in 1992 while nevertheless recognizing a limited regulatory role for local regulation (and that of states, should they choose to assert it[8]). However, ambiguities concerning the boundaries between what was, and was not, within the province of local regulators have continued to be a matter of controversy. See, e.g., *AT&T Corp. v. Portland*, 216 F.3d 871 (9th Cir. 2000) (city had no power to regulate cable modem service).

In more recent times, the appearance of the Internet has raised the question of the extent to which the FCC has jurisdiction over Internet-based services. As we mentioned earlier, the emergence of the Internet

8. Note that local governments have no inherent sovereignty. Residual sovereignty (all power not delegated to Congress) resides in the states, and all government entities below the state level are, so far as the U.S. Constitution is concerned, mere agents of the states. Community Communications Co., Inc. v. City of Boulder, 455 U.S. 40, 53–54 (1982).

as a platform for communications services—data, voice, video—has posed something of a conundrum for communications regulators, a matter we shall discuss in greater detail below. In its early years at least, the Internet was the quintessence of anarchy, and even now the conjunction of the words "Internet" and "regulation" prompts gastric distress among those who thought that the information superhighway was the yellow brick road to a glorious (and unregulated) future. But the yellow brick road has now intersected the traditional highways of regulated communications, presenting the FCC with a stark choice between continuing the regulatory business as usual or reinventing or rethinking some venerable (and still cherished) rules.

Given that much of communications regulation is premised on the regulation of monopolies, it is necessary to also consider the role of antitrust law. Antitrust lawyers do not like to think of antitrust as a form of regulation. Indeed, that is to put it mildly; antitrust practitioners and scholars alike are taught to think that regulation is the enemy of antitrust. This is due to a perception that regulation is either the enemy of competition (the promotion of which is the purpose of antitrust law) or an indifferent onlooker of the competitive scene. Historically, regulation has been seen as the alternative to competition; regulation was instituted where it was perceived competition could not succeed, either because of natural monopoly or other market imperfections. In fact, it has never been that simple, and the use of politically arranged, industry-driven regulation as a means of preempting competition is sufficiently notorious that every budding antitrust lawyer is inoculated against the "disease" of regulation. Putting political motivation to one side, further separating antitrust and industry regulation are their divergent enforcement models: The classic model of antitrust is one of occasional intervention tailored to the circumstances presented by a particular controversy; get in and get out is the traditional *modus operandi*. In contrast, industry regulation takes the form of sustained intervention by administrative agencies that proceed by means of regulatory planning; more get in and stay in.

These contrasting conceptions of antitrust and regulation are very stylized, and can be quite misleading. The notion that antitrust operates only occasionally is correct; the notion that the intervention is limited to the correction of some particular anti-competitive behavior is sometimes not. Perhaps the best example is the 1982 antitrust consent decree that broke up the Bell System. The break-up was not a simple one-off event; rather the consent decree provided a plan for a long-term program of judicial superintendence of the operations of a substantial portion of the telecommunications industry. As we shall see much later, the consent decree was not an alternative *to* regulation; it was an alternative *form* of regulation. For the twelve years it was in effect (until terminated by Congress in 1996), the antitrust divestiture established a program of judicial regulation running parallel to that of the FCC.

The 1982 consent decree is remarkable for its large impact on the course of regulatory policy over a sustained period of time (indeed, to a degree its effects are still evident). Antitrust plays an occasional role in other corners of communications policy. For example, all mergers between major telecommunications companies are subject to review by the Department of Justice and well as by the FCC.[9] However, antitrust merger review generally has not been a significant factor in shaping communications policy simply because it is duplicated by the FCC's own review authority under a regulatory power that is more extensive, and usually more suited to imposing particular restrictions that require ongoing monitoring of the firms involved. As we shall see, though, the changing face of electronic communications may lead to business combinations that elicit more concern from antitrust regulators than communications regulators. As the old industry distinctions diminish, antitrust may come to play more of a role in regulating the communications industry, as reflected by recent interest by antitrust enforcers in major media mergers. As we shall see, however, the Supreme Court has recently warned that *regulatory* obligations are not necessarily enforceable by antitrust remedies. See *Verizon Communications, Inc. v. Law Offices of Curtis V. Trinko*, 540 U.S. 398 (2004) (refusing to incorporate FCC unbundled access requirements into antitrust monopolization law).

C. HOW WE REGULATE

1. The Communications Act of 1934

The Communications Act of 1934, codified at 47 U.S.C. §§ 151–615b, establishes the basic statutory framework for federal regulation of electronic media. It is broken down into seven "titles"[10] as follows:

Title I—General Provisions—47 U.S.C. §§ 151–161, describes the purpose of regulation and establishes the FCC, its jurisdiction and its basic structure and contains various other administrative provisions. Title I does not contain any substantive directives (even the regulatory mantra to regulate in the "public interest, convenience and necessity" appears only in later titles), but Title I's broad grant of jurisdiction over all "interstate and foreign commerce in communications by wire and radio" has been used to extend the reach of regulation to activities not otherwise specifically designated in the Act. As we noted earlier, the FCC originally used Title I to support regulation of cable television even though the Act at the time contained no mention of cable television; Title I also continues to be cited to support a limited FCC jurisdiction over the Internet.

9. The Department of Justice and the Federal Trade Commission have overlapping antitrust jurisdiction, but they have long coordinated their enforcement effort to avoid duplicative effort. "Clearances"—assignment of responsibility—are primarily done by allocating industries to the DOJ or to the FTC. However, some clearances are based on ad hoc negotiations. Under the current agreement executed in 2002, enforcement responsibility for telecom and mass media is assigned to the Department of Justice, although, for non-merger actions, an agency may seek a clearance to proceed with an enforcement action.

10. In the U.S. Code these titles appear as six subchapters, but it is conventional to refer to the original titles of the Act.

Title II—Common Carriers—47 U.S.C. §§ 201–276, contains the provisions for regulating telecommunications common carriers. The original 1934 version of Title II was carried over from the Interstate Commerce Act without substantive change and for the next six decades remained largely the same. The 1996 Telecommunications Act made sweeping changes as part of a radical policy shift, from traditional monopoly-based regulation toward competition-enabling regulation both in interstate and intrastate services. In passing we should note that the 1996 Act also made some important changes in various definitions contained in Title I but affecting the content of Title II. The 1996 Act also added one important substantive provision to Title I exclusively relevant to Title II: a provision directing the Commission to forbear from regulating telecommunications carriers or services whenever regulation is determined to be unnecessary. See 47 U.S.C. § 160.

Title III—Provisions Relating to Radio—47 U.S.C. §§ 301–399b, establishes the framework and detailed rules for regulating use of the radio spectrum by means of FCC licenses. As we observed earlier, the FCC's control over the use of radio extends to all private and non-federal government users. Unlike common carrier regulation, where regulation is divided between federal and state authorities, the FCC's control of all non-federal government radio use is exclusive. Title III has been extensively amended over the years. The basic requirements for obtaining a license are essentially the same as in the original act. The duration of licenses has been extended (the terms vary among different services), but, more importantly, the means of licensing have been radically changed. In cases involving competing applications for the same facilities, the original merit-based licensing procedures (essentially a proceeding to determine which of the competing potential licensees would best serve the "public interest") was replaced with a system for auctioning licenses in 1993 (for non-broadcast radio services) and 1997 (for broadcasting). See § 309. Title III is long on procedure but short on substantive direction. There are a few substantive requirements applicable to broadcast licensees (e.g., a mandate to provide equal opportunities to political candidates, and to provide a certain minimum number of hours per week of children's television), but for the most part the "public interest" mandate remains undefined.

Title IV—Procedural and Administrative Provisions—47 U.S.C. §§ 401–416, contains provisions for enforcement and judicial review of FCC decisions. Since judicial review is also governed by the Administrative Procedure Act, we will cover the relevant portions of Title IV immediately below.

Title V—Penal Provisions–Forfeitures—47 U.S.C. §§ 501–509 prescribe sanctions for "willfully and knowingly" violating the Act, rules of the Commission, treaty obligations, or specified other provisions of 18 U.S.C. (most notably § 1464 proscribing obscene, indecent, or profane language by means of radio communications). The conventional sanction administered by the Commission is a so-called "penalty forfeiture," which is applicable only to persons subject to the Commission's licensing authority. As we shall see later, forfeitures have become a major (and controversial) tool for enforcing the Commission's indecency policy in broadcasting. The main purpose of the forfeiture is to punish activities by licensees that do not warrant revocation of a license (the so-called "death penalty").

Title VI—Cable Communications—47 U.S.C. §§ 521–573 governs cable regulation. It was added by the Cable Communications Policy Act of 1984 and was significantly amended by the Cable Television Consumer Protection and Competition Act of 1992 and more recently still by the Telecommunications Act of 1996. As we noted earlier, Congress was slow to move in this field; for roughly 20 years the FCC had been regulating on its own initiative and discretion based on an assertion of so-called "ancillary" jurisdiction grounded largely in Title I. The 1984 Act largely confirmed what the FCC had already put in place as part of its "common law" powers. In contrast to the federal exclusivity of Title III, Title VI not only sets the basic terms for federal regulation but also for state and local regulation. Title VI is not limited to cable television. It also contains some provisions that are applicable to others in the more general category of "multi-channel video distributors" ("MVPDs"), most notably direct satellite broadcasters like DirecTV and Dish Network.[11]

Title VII [originally Title VI until the 1984 Cable Act]—Miscellaneous Provisions—47 U.S.C. §§ 604–615b, is as the name implies a grab-bag of provisions. They range from provisions forbidding unauthorized reception of communications by wire or radio to provisions for closed captioning for the deaf to provisions authorizing the President to take control of electronic communications in times of war.

2. Administrative Law Fundamentals

Since most of this book deals with administrative regulation, it is appropriate to say a little about the structure and forms of administrative action. A "little" will have to suffice. Not wanting to incorporate the corpus of administrative law, we confine ourselves to a summary of three subjects: (1) the structure of the agency itself, and more particularly what it means to be an "independent" agency; (2) the basic procedures by which agencies make decisions; and (3) judicial review of agency action. For those already familiar with federal administrative law, this section will serve entirely as a refresher.

a) Agency Structure

The FCC is an independent regulatory agency. As an independent agency, the FCC does not formally report to the President (even though its members are presidential appointees). This means that it is beyond the bounds of direct presidential direction, though perhaps not entirely

11. Not all of the terms that govern MVPD regulation are contained in Title VI. The close connection between MVPDs and over-the-air broadcasters requires regulatory linkage as well. For example, the important requirement that a broadcast signal cannot be retransmitted without the consent of the broadcast station is contained in Title III, § 325.

beyond the pale of his influence.[12] The relationship to Congress is somewhat more complicated. Congressmen frequently assert that all independent agencies are "arms of Congress." However, as a matter of elementary separation of powers principles, Congress may not constitutionally exercise either executive or adjudicatory powers, see, e.g., *Bowsher v. Synar*, 478 U.S. 714 (1986) (Congress may not delegate executive powers to Comptroller General, an agent of Congress), so the conceit that the agencies are "arms of Congress" must be considered a kind of constitutional oxymoron. Of course, independent agencies are bound to execute laws duly (and constitutionally) enacted by Congress, but that does not distinguish them from the President himself, or the courts. By the same token, the agencies—like Congress itself—must answer to the rule of law, as declared by the courts. No one, it seems, is entirely independent; that, of course, is the point of the checks and balances that is the corollary to separation of powers.

Whatever their formal constitutional status, there is no room for doubt that independent agencies are subject to political pressures. Within the breathing space allowed by congressional mandates and judicial enforcement of the rule of law, agencies can and do respond to politics. This will not come as any surprise to modern students of government, but it should be said that it departs from the original ideal on which independent agencies like the FCC were constructed (or at least politically proffered to the public). These agencies were suppose to be independent of the other political branches (the Executive and Congress) precisely so that they would be able to exercise expert judgment that was politically unbiased. Given the political implications of something as potentially contentious as regulating media outlets to ensure they serve the "public interest" or deciding how much interstate telephone service should cost, one might doubt whether the ideal of apolitical experts is even an appropriate ideal. Either way, the ideal of a *neutral* expert has never been fully realized. Some would doubt whether the *expert* part has been realized either, but expert or not, no one worth listening to would assert that an agency like the FCC is unaffected by political influence. The only room for dispute is in how agency members respond to such influences, that is, to what extent do members respond to their "constituencies," to what extent do they respond to their own "inner voices," and to what extent are they constrained by externally imposed *legal* constraints. The last point is crucial: at the end of the day agents must operate within four legal constraints: the jurisdictional limits set by the enabling legislation (in the FCC's case, the enabling (or "organic") legislation is the Communications Act); procedural constraints set by the enabling legislation and by the Administrative Procedure Act (APA); an ill-defined standard of rational administrative action set by the same enabling legislation and the Administrative Procedure Act; and judicial review to enforce the first three constraints.

12. For a brief commentary on the practical issue of executive influence see Glen O. Robinson, *Independent Agencies: Form and Substance in Executive Prerogative*, 1988 Duke L.J. 238.

b) Agency Procedures

The Administrative Procedure Act prescribes procedures for two types of agency action: adjudication and rulemaking. Administrative adjudications broadly resemble judicial trials without a jury. The decision is based exclusively on an evidentiary record adduced in a formal hearing. The presiding officer is an administrative law judge (ALJ) who is separated from other agency officials. The ALJ's decision is appealable to the head of the agency, although some agencies, including the FCC, use an intermediate "review board" to hear appeals, from which further appeal is made the agency members and thence to the courts. Formal agency adjudications are rarely the vehicle of important policy formation or enforcement at the FCC. While some federal agencies (for example, the National Labor Relations Board or the Federal Trade Commission) regularly formulate policy by means of agency adjudications, the FCC does not. It relies primarily on rulemaking procedures.

For substantive (as opposed to interpretive or procedural) rules, the APA provides for two types of rulemaking: formal and informal. Formal rulemaking occurs in the relatively few instances when a statute specifically requires a rule to be based on the record of an agency hearing. It plays no significant role at the FCC. In contrast to formal rulemaking on a record, informal—or "notice-and-comment" rulemaking as it is also called—does not involve oral hearings (though the FCC does sometimes provide for oral arguments) or an evidentiary record. The "record" is rather a compilation of comments filed by interested parties, including records of ex parte communications where they are permitted.[13] The APA requires that the agency promulgating rules give public notice of the proposed rules and an opportunity for the public to comment on it. The final rules must be accompanied by "a concise statement of their basis and purpose."[14] The rules, and their rationales, are subject to judicial review under the Communications Act and the APA, as discussed below.

While the APA frames its procedural requirements as either adjudication or rulemaking, it is a commonplace among students of the administrative process that regulatory agencies typically perform an

13. As a general rule of administrative law, parties are permitted in informal rulemaking proceedings to make ex parte contacts with agency members and decision-making staff. However, as a result of some controversial decisions involving ex parte communications in cases that were borderline between informal and formal proceedings, the FCC adopted limitations and conditions on such contacts. The details are complicated, but, put broadly, the rules specify three kinds of proceedings: "exempt" proceedings, in which ex parte presentations may be made freely, "permit-but-disclose" proceedings, in which ex parte presentations to Commission decision-making personnel are permissible but subject to certain disclosure requirements and "restricted" proceedings in which ex parte presentations to and from Commission decision-making personnel are generally prohibited. Most informal rulemaking proceedings at the FCC come within the permit-but-disclose category. Disclosure in such cases requires placing copies of written presentations, or written summaries of oral communications, in the public docket record for the proceedings to which they pertain.

14. The FCC does not treat the word "concise" as a requirement; most FCC rulemaking statements (labeled "reports and orders") are anything but. A typical report and order on a significant rule can run to several hundred pages (presenting a daunting challenge to casebook editors to distill them down to their minimal essence).

array of functions that do not fit within either category. Administrative lawyers call this "informal action" simply because there are usually no procedural formalities prescribed for it, either by the APA or by the agency's enabling statute. Despite the absence of statutory formalities, informal action comprises a large and important part of the FCC's work agenda. For example, most of the FCC's licensing of radio uses (including its conduct of spectrum auctions) is conducted "informally." Most of its enforcement actions consist of warning letters, or proposed fines or forfeitures followed by settlement. (We will see examples when we look at the FCC's enforcement of broadcast content controls, notably its regulation of broadcast indecency). At any given time, FCC staff members may be engaged in giving advice, interpreting rules, reviewing proposed mergers of regulated firms, or otherwise performing informal administrative chores that never result in either a formal adjudication or the promulgation of a new rule. While informal action may not be procedurally constrained, it is nevertheless subject to judicial review (subject to finality and other limitations discussed below).

c) Judicial Review

A longstanding canon of American administrative law is that final federal administrative action is presumptively reviewable in court. There are standing limitations on who can seek review (a person must show injury in fact that is redressable by the relief sought). There are timing limitations on when review can be sought (agency action must be final or ripe for review, and available administrative remedies must be exhausted). The enabling statutes governing federal regulatory programs typically call for most formal agency decisions to be appealable directly to a United States Court of Appeals. The Communications Act so provides, although it provides alternative venues depending on the type of action being appealed. Section 402(a) authorizes review of any order of the Commission (except those appealable under 402(b)) to be brought as prescribed by title 28 U.S.C., which in turn allows appeals in any of the courts of appeals (see 28 U.S.C § 2342(1)). Section 402(b) provides for exclusive review by the Court of Appeals for the District of Columbia Circuit in licensing cases (those in which a license has been denied, revoked or modified).

The scope of review is governed by the Administrative Procedure Act. Section 706 of the APA provides:

> To the extent necessary to decision and when presented, the reviewing court shall decide all relevant questions of law, interpret constitutional and statutory provisions, and determine the meaning or applicability of the terms of an agency action. The reviewing court shall
>
> (1) compel agency action unlawfully withheld or unreasonably delayed; and
>
> (2) hold unlawful and set aside agency action, findings, and conclusions found to be

> (A) arbitrary, capricious, an abuse of discretion, or otherwise not in accordance with law;
>
> (B) contrary to constitutional right, power, privilege, or immunity;
>
> (C) in excess of statutory jurisdiction, authority, or limitations, or short of statutory right;
>
> (D) without observance of procedure required by law;
>
> (E) unsupported by substantial evidence in a case subject to section 556 and 557 of this title [provisions governing formal adjudication] or otherwise reviewed on the record of an agency hearing provided by statute; or
>
> (F) unwarranted by the facts to the extent that the facts are subject to trial de novo by the reviewing court.
>
> In making the foregoing determinations, the court shall review the whole record or those parts of it cited by a party, and due account shall be taken of the rule of prejudicial error.

Before considering what is implied by these review standards, we should first observe the crucial role played by the requirement that the agency explain its decisions. The requirement comes in two parts: In adjudicatory cases and formal rulemaking cases heard upon a formal record, section 557(c) of the APA requires that the agency's decision must be accompanied by a statement of "findings and conclusions and the reasons or basis therefore, on all the material issues of fact, law, or discretion presented on the record." For informal, notice-and-comment rulemaking cases section, 553(c) requires that the agency provide a concise statement of the basis and purpose of the rules adopted. Although these "findings and reasons" requirements appear in the APA's procedural sections, they are really intrinsic to the review process. (Indeed, their origin is in the pre-APA law of judicial review. See *SEC v. Chenery Corp.*, 318 U.S. 80 (1943).) As such they are applicable to informal action as well. See *Citizens to Preserve Overton Park, Inc. v. Volpe*, 401 U.S. 402 (1971).

The findings requirement is very basic to the entire judicial review process in ways that sometimes elude the lay person. The lay observer is used to thinking of successive layers of decision makers. Although lawyers are used to the concept of layers of review, and consequently layers of deference to subsidiary decisionmakers, in order to understand how review works in administrative law, one needs to understand that a reviewing court does not simply decide whether the agency decision was reasonable or not. Rather it decides whether the agency's *reasoning* was sound. In order to decide that question the court demands that the agency first explain what it did and why it did it. At least in theory, the court is not passing judgment on the end product but on the agency's explanation thereof. This might at first glance appear to be a more searching inquiry than simply reviewing the outcome for reasonableness, but if you stop to think about it, you will see that this is rather more *deferential* than simply deciding whether the end decision was correct or reasonable. Reviewing the process rather than just the outcome means that the agency gets to frame the pertinent scope of the inquiry in the first instance; a court may tell the agency that it is addressing the wrong question—that its findings are irrelevant to the key issue raised by its decision—but the court's review is shaped by the way in which the agency presents (and explains) its findings and reasons.

Because most review typically focuses on the adequacy of the findings and reasons, it typically does not produce a simple reversal but instead a remand for further proceedings. This is important, because the remand will often allow the agency to generate a new rationale for an old result, or perhaps some modifications that in turn invite further review. The result is that some controversies go back and forth between agency and court over a fairly long period of time. This is a very common pattern in communications law. We will see some particularly good illustrations in the making of telecommunications policy after 1996, where the FCC and the courts (including the Supreme Court) have engaged in what might fairly be called a ten-year "dialogue" over the proper interpretation of Congress's 1996 mandate to promote competition in local telephone markets.

Let's return to the question of review standards. In addition to general standards that would be applicable to lower courts (unconstitutionality, beyond jurisdiction, procedurally improper, and contrary to the facts), the above quoted provisions of section 706 mention two distinct standards: section 706(2)(A) establishes an "arbitrary-capricious" standard that is generically applicable to all agency action and section 706(2)(E) establishes a more specific "substantial evidence" test applied to formal proceedings decided on an evidentiary record. In practical effect there is not much difference between the non-arbitrariness test and the substantial evidence test other than the fact that they look at the agency decision in a somewhat different way. Substantial evidence is a matter of testing the factual, evidentiary basis of the decision while arbitrariness goes to the logical inferences. However, even that is somewhat misleading, since all agency decisions must have some factual basis; even a non-adjudicatory, rulemaking decision that is not made on the basis of a formal evidentiary record must be based on enough factual support as to be non-arbitrary, which entails something like a substantial evidence test.

Both the substantial evidence and arbitrary-capricious standards are deferential; the court is not entitled to substitute its own judgment for that of the agency but must respect the agency's judgment if it is reasonable (even if the court thinks it is not correct). Explaining what that means in practical terms has been one of the chief occupations of generations of administrative law scholars. The issue of deference plays out in two contexts. One involves review of agency interpretations of statutes whose mandates it is required to enforce. The other involves review of agency action under a general power granted by some statute.

With respect to the first, section 706(2)(C) seems on its face to create a non-deferential standard for reviewing such questions. However, in the context of regulatory statutes that delegate broad discretion to agencies, the questions of what a statute means is not easily separated from the question whether an agency's policy judgment is reasonable. The question therefore becomes one of first determining how much leeway the statute gives to the agency and then asking whether the agency exercised its power reasonably. Basically, this is what the Supreme Court decided in *Chevron, U.S.A., Inc. v. Natural Resources Defense Council, Inc.*, 467 U.S. 837 (1984), involving review of an EPA regulation governing stationary "sources" of air pollution. The question was whether the statutory term "source" could be construed to allow an agency to aggregate all the different emission points at an industrial site or whether it was required to determine emission levels for each point separately. The agency regulations took the former view, and the question was whether a reviewing court should give deference to that interpretation. The Court responded as follows:

> When a court reviews an agency's construction of the statute which it administers, it is confronted with two questions. First, always, is the question whether Congress has directly spoken to the precise question at issue. If the intent of Congress is clear, that is the end of the matter; for the court, as well as the agency, must give effect to the unambiguously expressed intent of Congress. If, however, the court determines Congress has not directly addressed the precise question at issue, the court does not simply impose its own construction on the statute, as would be necessary in the absence of an administrative interpretation. Rather, if the statute is silent or ambiguous with respect to the specific issue, the question for the court is whether the agency's answer is based on a permissible construction of the statute.

Determining whether the statute has a clear meaning is now referred to as "*Chevron* Step One." If the court determines the statute does not have a clear meaning, it then must determine whether the agency's interpretation is reasonable, which is referred to as "*Chevron* Step Two."

The Court's rationale for the deference is noteworthy (and also controversial among some administrative law scholars):

> In this case, the [EPA] Administrator's interpretation represents a reasonable accommodation of manifestly competing interests and is entitled to deference: the regulatory scheme is technical and complex, the agency considered the matter in a detailed and reasoned fashion, and the decision involves reconciling conflicting policies. Congress intended to accommodate both interests, but did not do so itself on the level of specificity presented by this case. Perhaps that body consciously desired the Administrator to strike the balance at this level, thinking that those with great expertise and charged with responsibility for administering the provision would be in a better

position to do so; perhaps it simply did not consider the question at this level; and perhaps Congress was unable to forge a coalition on either side of the question, and those on each side decided to take their chances with the scheme devised by the agency. For judicial purposes, it matters not which of these things occurred.

The end result of all this is that, at *Chevron* Step Two, the deference owed to statutory interpretation looks a lot like the reasonableness test that is incorporated into the arbitrary or capricious standard applicable to *all* agency action. At this point *Chevron* can be seen as just another version of another leading case on deference decided a year earlier, *Motor Vehicle Mfrs. Ass'n v. State Farm Mutual Automobile Ins. Co.*, 463 U.S. 29 (1983), a review of agency action in which the focus was not on any particular term of the governing statute but rather on whether the agency had engaged in reasoned decision making as it held was required by the "arbitrary-capricious" standard. Since all agency action must find support in a statute, one might argue it involves statutory "interpretation" in some sense. Thus, what issues prompt the invocation of *Chevron* and what prompts invocation of *State Farm* is not an easy one to decide. In the end, it may not matter to the extent that *Chevron* Step Two is the same as the arbitrary-capricious test. Subsequent Supreme Court *Chevron* decisions have tended to reinforce this convergence of *Chevron* and a general reasonableness standard by holding that *Chevron* deference only applies to statutes the agency is empowered to administer, and only in proceedings where the agency has been given a substantive power to make the kind of decision for which the agency claims deference. *United States v. Mead Corp.*, 533 U.S. 218 (2001). That implies that deference for statutory interpretation will be applied only in cases where there are issues of substantive discretion of a kind that would be subject to *State Farm* review as well.

D. OVERVIEW OF ELECTRONIC MEDIA

The framework we use in this book is heavily shaped by conventional industry and legal structuring. It is a commonplace that communications is converging. The convergence thesis has been propounded for twenty years, but until the past few years it was more visionary than descriptive. However, there can no longer be any doubt that the historic separation between mass media and telecommunications is breaking down. At the very least it is breaking down as a matter of industry structure. Cable service providers are starting to sell telecommunications service and telephone service providers are now distributing television over phone lines. This convergence presents a challenge to regulators who have to work with legal structures and rules that were put in place in an earlier time when the regulated industries were separate. For our purposes, though, convergence presents a challenge to anyone who wants to provide a coherent framework for studying communications regulation. Should the subject matter be organized in terms of traditional industry or service categories (e.g., broadcast, cable, wireline telecommunications, etc.) or should it be along functional lines that cross industry boundaries, (e.g., competition, ownership, service regulation, etc.)? The latter appears more in line with the convergence thesis. Unfortunately, it is out of line with the still-extant legal structure. The Communications Act, as demonstrated by the structure of Titles II and III, is still organized primarily along the lines first set in place in 1934. Moreover, most of the issues we examine are still tied importantly to particular technologies or industry structures. Thus, an understanding of competition policy in local exchange telephone service is not significantly aided by studying, say, cable-broadcast competition—or vice versa. Consequently, we will largely maintain the traditional distinctions in this book, and the following description of the communications industry lays out those traditional distinctions.

1. Mass Media

a) Conventional Broadcasting

In the beginning was broadcasting—radio in the 1920s, television in the late 1940s and early 1950s. Today, with cable television, satellite broadcasting and, most recently the Internet, it is sometimes difficult to appreciate the fact that for most of the history of electronic media, conventional broadcasting defined electronic mass media. Today television and radio are ubiquitous. More households have televisions than have telephones, and even in the age of the ubiquitous cellphone, they use it more. In the average household, a television set is on 8 hours and 11 minutes per day according to the latest survey.

The basic components of the broadcast industry are: (a) advertisers who provide the financial support for the industry through purchase of advertising time over stations; (b) advertising agencies that manage or assist the advertiser's advertising campaign; (c) networks that provide substantial programming to an interconnected chain of affiliated stations over which the advertiser can simultaneously reach a nationwide audience; (d) program producers (including both the major Hollywood film studios and independent producers); (e) syndicators that sell both network rerun and, increasingly, first-run programs not appearing on the networks; and (f) individual broadcast stations. The heart of commercial broadcast operations is advertising.

Programming is provided through several sources. It may be produced by the station itself which then seeks advertising support. This is the common pattern for radio, where programming consists largely of inexpensively produced music, commentary, and news. (Many radio stations have begun to carry nationally syndicated talk-show programs; however, this is still a small part of overall radio programming.) In the case of television, except for local news and some public affairs programs, individual stations produce negligible programming. The sources of television programming are networks, film studios, independent program producers, and film syndicators. Traditionally, most entertainment programming has been produced by film studios and independent producers, which supply a variety of programming: original, live or film programs produced chiefly for networks or advertisers; "syndicated" films for individual stations—original programs and (more usually) "reruns" of network programs whose syndication rights have been purchased by a program producer or distributor; and "feature film" movies originally produced for movie theaters.

From the earliest days of radio, the commercial networks (originally two), then three, then four—ABC, CBS, Fox, NBC—have been the dominant element in broadcasting.[15] This is no longer true for radio, and with the growing importance of multi-channel cable and satellite service it is becoming less true for television. Non-broadcast channels now account for more than 50% of the viewing share in prime time and in all-day viewing. (Admittedly a large amount of the non-broadcast programming is simply old broadcast programs—usually old broadcast network programs—that are syndicated to non-broadcast networks, but this doesn't alter the fact that the broadcast networks no longer dominate television as they once did.)

The noncommercial sectors of radio and television broadcasting encompass a variety of academic, civic and general programming formats, united only by the non-profit status of the licensees. The vast majority of noncommercial facilities are owned and operated by state and municipal governments and educational institutions. In 1967, Congress laid the cornerstone for the present system of noncommercial broadcasting with the passage of the Public Broadcasting Act. The Act authorized the formation of a non-profit Corporation for Public Broadcasting (CPB) to provide financial assistance to local facilities and to national program producers, and to establish an interconnection service among local stations for the distribution of programming. CPB joined with industry representatives in 1970 to create the Public Broadcasting System (PBS) and National Public Radio (NPR). Both PBS and NPR are governed by representatives of member broadcast facilities. NPR, however, produces programming for national distribution using CPB allocated funds while PBS obtains the programs it distributes from its member stations and does not engage in program production as an independent body. Since the passage of the Public Broadcasting Act, the government has supported licensees, through the CPB, with grants which are periodically reviewed by Congress. These government grants, however, are conditioned on licensee generation of matching funds, forcing those noncommercial licensees not under state or private educational control to appeal to private industry and the public for support.

Although the major commercial networks still dominate the television broadcast industry, the regulatory structure has always stressed the importance of local television stations providing programming that was responsive to local community needs. To that end the FCC in 1952 planned television allotments (in regulatory jargon an "allotment" of channels implies a fixed geographic location) in such a way as to provide

15. CW, jointly owned by CBS and Time Warner, is not counted here because it has yet to develop into a full-service network on a par with the big four. CW was formed in 2006 by combining UPN and WB, subsidiaries of CBS and Time Warner respectively.

local stations to as many communities as possible, consistent with the first priority of ensuring that everyone could receive at least one television service. The allotments are subject to spacing requirements designed to prevent undue interference (e.g., co-channel television stations must be separated by a specified mileage, which varies according to the frequency and the geographic region of the station).

Individual stations are licensed by the FCC for renewable terms of eight years (the duration of the license term has been extended several times; originally it was a mere three years). Since 1997, if there are competing applications for a new license, the license is assigned by auction (applications for renewal of existing licenses are not subject to the auction). Currently, as part of a plan to aid transition from analog to digital format, all television stations have two separate channels to permit simulcast operations in both analog and digital format during the period of transition; however, when conversion to digital is completed in 2009, one of the two channels will be returned to be used for wireless services. (In advance of its return, the spectrum used by the second channel was auctioned to wireless providers in early 2008).

Broadcast licensees are subject to a variety of "public interest" obligations, but the obligations have become quite nominal for the most part. The FCC no longer exercises routine supervision of programming except for the special case of children's programming where Congress has directed a certain minimum amount of such programming. In other cases, such as political broadcasts (the equal time and reasonable access requirements) and indecent or offensive programming, the Commission acts only on complaints. Station licenses are subject to a variety of fixed constraints, most notably limitations on multiple ownership of media.

b) Multi-channel Television: Cable and Satellite

Forty years ago, when over the air broadcasting was virtually the only means of receiving television, a typical television household would count itself lucky if it could receive three commercial channels and one non-commercial channel. In larger cities viewers might receive an independent commercial channel not affiliated with one of the three commercial networks. Today, thanks to cable and satellite the number of channels can exceed two hundred. What the FCC now calls "multichannel video programming distributors"(MVPD) dominates the viewing market. In 2005 nearly 86% of television households subscribed to MVPD service. The largest share was held by cable systems, accounting for just under 70% of the MVPD market, compared to just under 28% held by satellite broadcasters.[16] In addition to cable and satellite there are other MVPD distributors—wireless cable, home satellite dishes, and, most recently local exchange telephone carriers.

16. For these and other statistics—more than almost anyone wants to know—see the FCC's annual reports on the *Assessment of the Status of Competition in the Market for the Delivery of Video Programming.*

Cable was the first MVPD. It began as a supplement to broadcast service in the earliest days of television. In the early 1960s it began to emerge as a separate industry, at which time it came under heavy regulation at the behest of the broadcast industry. Not until the late 1970s did it acquire a position of political and economic strength that allowed it to compete fully with broadcasting, and ultimately (by the mid 1980s) to supplant broadcasting as the dominant distributor of television service. Originally almost all of the programs were retransmitted broadcast programs, originating in a local or non-local broadcast station.[17] However, cable now obtains many programs directly from cable networks (many of them affiliated with the major cable operators) which operate very similarly to broadcast networks. Cable systems offer the programs in different packages or "tiers" of service; for regulatory purposes three general tier packages are recognized—"basic" (containing all broadcast programs that are retransmitted from local or distant stations other than so-called "superstations" which are delivered directly to the cable system by satellite); "cable channels" (including superstations, like TBS, and special channels designed for cable such as CNN, C-Span, ESPN, MTV, Nickelodeon, Discovery, Home Shopping Network, etc.); and pay channels (such as HBO or Showtime, and including pay-per-view channels). The industry is now dominated by a handful of multiple system operators ("MSOs")—most notably, Comcast, Time Warner Cable, Charter Communications, Cox, and Cablevision.

Cable television, unlike broadcasting, is the subject of local regulation—typically by local franchising authorities (city or county).[18] Franchise awards are not exclusive (exclusive franchises have been banned since the Cable Act of 1984); however, most cable systems have a *de facto* monopoly within the area of their franchise. Very few cable systems face competition from other conventional cable systems ("overbuilds" as they are called). At one time there was some modest competition from "wireless" cable systems—multichannel delivery systems employing microwave frequencies instead of coaxial cable—however, this service has declined to a point that is not regarded as a significant competitor. The more important competition in the broadband television market comes from satellite broadcasting.

Broadcast satellites operate from a geo-stationary position in space, about 22,300 miles above the Equator. (The position is said to be geostationary because at that distance the satellite's rotation is the same as the Earth's, which keeps it approximately in a fixed position relative to the Earth.) The service most commonly associated with satellite broadcasting is Direct Broadcast Satellite Service (DBS). The FCC authorized

17. As we shall see, cable systems are required to carry all local broadcast signals on demand of the local broadcast station—the so-called "must carry" rules. Alternatively the local stations can exercise their retransmission consent rights which allows them to demand compensation for carrying the local station's signal. The stations cannot claim both must-carry and retransmission consent rights for the same signal.

18. Some states exercise state-wide jurisdiction over cable, usually through the state's public service commission. In some states, state regulation preempts local regulation, in others it is shared with local franchise regulation.

DBS in 1988 but service was not begun until 1993. DBS describes a direct-to-home service operating within a region of the spectrum allocated to the Broadcast Satellite Service ("BSS") in the upper range of what is styled the "Ku-band" (12.2–12.7 GHz), utilizing high power satellites and small (18–24 inches in diameter) receiving dishes. Pursuant to an international allotment plan for the Broadcast Satellite Service, the United States is allotted eight orbital slots, each with 32 satellite channels/transponders, in the Ku-band. (With current compression techniques a satellite channel can yield between four and eight program channels depending on the nature of the programming—live action sports requiring more channel capacity than, say, movies). A second type of direct-to-home service, commercially indistinguishable from DBS, and usually classified as such, uses medium power satellites which operate in a region of the Ku-band that is allocated to the Fixed Satellite Service. Because of the lower power, this service requires a somewhat larger receiving dish (up to 32 inches). A third type of direct-to-home service is provided by C-band satellites, operating with low power satellites and large receiving dishes (approximately 62 inches). This latter service is an incidental feature of what is designed as a system for television signal relay to terrestrial distributors.

Two systems presently dominate the DBS market: DirecTV (formerly owned by General Motors, now owned by News Corp, which is the parent of the Fox media empire) and EchoStar (marketed as "The Dish Network"). A third firm, Dominion Video Satellite, Inc. (marketed as "Sky Angel") serves fewer than one million subscribers and provides 20 family and religion-oriented channels by means of transponders leased from EchoStar and DirecTV. As we noted above, the growth of satellite broadcasting has made it a significant competitor to cable in virtually all major markets. It has been aided by increased transponder capacity which has enabled it to retransmit local channels into local markets, which in turn allows the satellite carriers to offer the major broadcast networks.[19]

2. Telecommunications

a) Wireline Telecommunications

Historically both telephone and telegraph services—now treated as a single "telecommunications" service—were dominated by two companies, AT&T and Western Union. Western Union long ago ceased to have economic importance. AT&T, on the other hand dominated telephone service for roughly a century until its breakup in 1984 (a product of antitrust litigation, not communications law). Before 1984, AT&T con-

19. As with cable the retransmission of signals requires consent of the stations whose signals are retransmitted. There are also separate copyright licenses involved; the Copyright Act has provisions for compulsory licensing for both cable and satellite transmissions, though the conditions are somewhat different. In the case of satellites a special provision that requires that any carrier seeking to retransmit one local station must retransmit all upon demand. It is similar but not identical to the must-carry requirement imposed on cable systems.

trolled almost the entire telephone infrastructure and had monopolies as a provider of both local and long distance telephone service and the equipment used on those networks, including that in consumers' homes and businesses.[20] The object of the 1984 consent decree was to split the local and long distance markets, leaving several regional monopolies (the Bell Operating Companies, or BOCs) in the local market while opening up the long distance and equipment markets to competition. (The equipment markets had already been deregulated (in 1980) and by the time of the breakup they no longer figured as an important part of the regulatory scheme.) In the years since 1984 the telecommunications industry has been transformed in ways that could scarcely have been imagined twenty years earlier. Today, telecommunications is a commodity; the number of suppliers is equal to that of any fully competitive product market.

After the 1984 breakup, the long distance service markets was dominated by three companies: AT&T, MCI (later Worldcom, then back to MCI when Worldcom was reorganized in Chapter 11) and Sprint. The local exchange carriers after the breakup were dominated by seven Bell Operating Companies that had existed as subsidiaries of the old Bell System: Pacific Telesis, Bell Atlantic, NYNEX, SBC (Southwestern Bell), Ameritech, U.S.West (later Qwest), and Bell South.

The industry structure created by the breakup didn't last long. In the 1990s, the industry was transformed again, this time by mergers and reorganizations.

First, AT&T has morphed countless times, entering and leaving businesses repeatedly, largely through merger and divestiture. After the break-up, AT&T (voluntarily) split up again, spinning off its manufacturing and research arms (Western Electric and Bell Labs) into a separate company, Lucent Technologies, and its computer company (acquired earlier), NCR. AT&T had given its wireless service to the BOCs as part of the break-up, but it eventually acquired another wireless network from McCaw Cellular, which was spun off as an independent company in 2001 and then in 2004 merged with Cingular Wireless. (Cingular was then jointly owned by SBC and BellSouth but after the later mergers of AT&T and SBC and then AT&T and BellSouth it became a part of AT&T again!) In 1999–2000 AT&T made an attempt to enter the cable television business by acquiring two of the largest cable operators (TCI and MediaOne), becoming for a time the largest cable operator in the country. However, after spinning this business off

20. There was a period of competition lasting roughly from the period after the Bell patents expired in 1893 and 1894 until 1921. The latter date marks enactment of the Willis-Graham Act, which terminated a 1913 antitrust consent decree (the so-called "Kingsbury Commitment"). The termination of that decree was more or less an official recognition that monopoly was the correct ("natural") order of things. That policy would not be challenged until the late 1960s and even then would be challenged only with respect to some parts of the telecommunications industry. A complete repudiation of the natural monopoly model in telecommunications would not come until the Telecommunications Act of 1996.

as a separate subsidiary (AT&T Broadband), it sold it to Comcast in 2002.

Second, the BOCs remade themselves: SBC merged with Pacific Telesis, then Ameritech. Bell Atlantic merged with NYNEX and later acquired the largest non-Bell company, GTE, and became Verizon. The latest in the moves towards reconsolidation came in 2006 when AT&T (the old SBC after it merged with and took AT&T's name) acquired BellSouth, reducing the original seven BOCs to three: AT&T, Verizon, and Qwest—in order of market capitalization. (Actually, in market-cap terms Qwest is almost a niche player, despite the fact that it is the dominant provider in some 14 western and midwestern states.)

Third, the separation of local and long distance sought by the 1984 consent decree was eliminated by the Telecommunications Act of 1996, which terminated the 1982 consent decree. The Act allowed local telcos to provide long distance service subject only to a showing that local markets were opened to competition. In time all of the BOCs were allowed to provide long distance service, as in the old days of the integrated Bell System. Once that happened, the way became clear for a reintegration of local and long distance providers. For all practical purposes, long distance as a separate market has disappeared. AT&T, the largest long distance carrier after the breakup was merged with SBC and ceased to be a separate long distance company. The next largest long distance carrier, MCI, was acquired by Verizon and ceased to be a separate long distance company. Sprint, the third largest long distance carrier spun off its wireline business to become a wireless carrier. Today, long distance service is provided either by the local wireline carriers—most notably the BOCs—or by wireless carriers (two of the largest of which are owned by BOCs).

b) Mobile Wireless

Mobile telecommunications cover a large number of different services, both public and private.[21] Mobile radio for public use is largely the creature of technological developments in two-way radio after World War II. Before the war, the only regular users of mobile two-way radio were police, firefighters and other emergency users. Today mobile telephones are ubiquitous thanks to the development of cellular radio in the 1970s. The cellular concept is a means of using radio frequencies more effectively by confining their use to small areas (a "cell") and then reusing them. The idea is to employ low power transceivers which transmit and receive mobile signals within a particular cell from a wireline switch; as a mobile unit passes out of the cell signals are "passed off" to the channel allotted

21. The different services include: Air-Ground Radiotelephone Service, Amateur Radio Service, Aviation Radio Service, Basic Exchange Telephone Radio Service, Cellular Radiotelephone Service, General Wireless Communications Service (GWCS), Location and Monitoring Services, Maritime Mobile Services, Microwave Services, Offshore Radiotelephone Service, Paging Services, Personal Communications Service (PCS), Personal Radio Service, Private Land Mobile Radio Services, Public Safety Radio Services, Rural Radiotelephone Service, Specialized Mobile Radio Service (SMR), to that cell. With particular frequencies combined, so to speak, within a particular area the potential for interference is limited; accordingly the same frequency can be reused a short distance away—say, two cells away. As growing traffic increases the need for frequencies, the cells can be divided into smaller cells, which increases available frequencies by increasing their reuse.

The invention of the cellular concept revolutionized mobile communications; today mobile telecommunications (classified by the FCC under the label CMRS—commercial mobile radio service) is one of the most dynamic elements of the electronic communications sector.[22] In less than two decades it has grown from a subscribership of about 340,000 in 1985 to more than 241.8 million by the end of 2006 (the total U.S. population at that time was about 300 million). The industry is competitive. There are presently four national service providers AT&T; Sprint-Nextel, Verizon Wireless (co-owned with Vodaphone), and T-Mobile. In addition there are a number of large regional providers (e.g., U.S. Cellular and Alltel) as well as smaller, more local providers (e.g., nTelos).[23] For many Americans, wireless has become a substitute in whole or in part for wireline telephony.

c) Internet

The Internet defies simple classification. The FCC, with the blessing of the Supreme Court, classifies the Internet as primarily an information service. This label has some important regulatory implications, but it is quite ambiguous. Exactly what is an "information service" and how does it differ from plain old communications? As we noted earlier, the Internet reflects a true convergence of mass media and telecommunications services. As a provider of news and entertainment "content" the Internet is hardly distinguishable from television except that, in its present stage of development, Internet delivery facilities do not deploy sufficient bandwidth to support the quality of picture available from conventional television services. At the same time the most common use of the Internet is electronic mail, which puts it more in the category of a telecommunications medium. In fact the Internet is being increasingly

and Wireless Communications Service (WCS).

22. Technically there are three different types of CMRS systems, cellular, broadband PCS, and Specialized Mobile Radio (SMR—a system using two-way radio and a repeater to expand range), but today they all operate on the basis of the cellular network design. Analog cellular systems were first licensed beginning in 1982; PCS was developed in the mid 1990s as a digital service (operating in a different frequency band); SMR were first developed at about the same time as cellular and were initially intended to be used for dispatch radio service, which unlike cellular and PCS is not typically connected to the public switched network (think about taxi cabs). However, the SMR systems later morphed into public switched service similar to cellular and PCS when Nextel acquired SMR operators and developed them into a public service—with dispatch functionality (the push-to-talk feature) as well as the regular switched telephony functionality. In recent years a number of cellular and PCS providers have emulated Nextel in providing this dispatch functionality in addition to regular switched service.

23. More data on the wireless industry can be obtained from the FCC's annual reports on commercial mobile services. See, e.g., Annual Report and Analysis of Competitive Conditions with Respect to Commercial Mobile Radio Services, 23 FCC Rcd. 2241 (2008).

used for voice telephony. Then, of course, there is the use of the Internet as a kind of electronic library (the most traditional, and limited sense of "information service").

The present Internet is the legacy of a network constructed for the Defense Department (the "ARPANET"), for research purposes that linked universities, research institutions and the military.[24] The military connection disappeared in the 1980s though the federal government continued to support the network for a growing population of civilian users through the auspices of the National Science Foundation. The NSF role has now been eliminated. The network today functions without any central direction or control (though there is a central directory of addresses); the basic communications backbone is provided by several commercial carriers—e.g., Verizon, Sprint-Nextel, AT&T—but the real glue that holds the system together as a system is a set of protocols for allowing computers to communicate with one another, and none of the commercial players seem to have any real control over that.

Unlike the other electronic media, which have been extensively regulated from infancy if not from birth, the Internet has grown into a mature medium with little government regulation. However, saying that it is largely unregulated requires some elaboration. First, it is necessary to define "regulation." It can, and in some usages does, mean almost any form of legal constraint on an activity or on those who conduct the activity. It would not, for instance, be a semantic mistake to say that being subject to the general laws that govern all citizens is a form of regulation. In this sense the Internet is regulated. Commercial entities engaged in e-commerce are subject to the same laws that govern commerce generally: they pay the same tax (if, uncharacteristically, they operate at a profit), file the same forms with the SEC, etc. They are even subject—within yet undefined limits—to the same general laws governing intellectual property, libel, fraud, etc. However, when communications lawyers speak of media "regulation" they usually have in mind a set of legal controls that go beyond enforcement of legal norms that apply indifferently to all citizens. The model for this kind of regulation is the set of controls that specially govern electronic media, most notably

24. ARPANET was designed and developed in 1969 by Bolt, Beranek, and Newman under contract to the Advanced Research Projects Agency of the U.S. Department of Defense (ARPA). One of the defense needs was to permit researchers to access supercomputers remotely, hence at lower cost. Another need was security: the need for military command and control networks that could survive a nuclear war, a need that led to the development of "packet switching" which would be less vulnerable to destruction from attack or sabotage. Unlike traditional circuit switching used for conventional voice telephony, packet switching moves "bits" of digitalized data in small chunks or "packets," each of which is routed independently of the others. Each packet contains header information which guides it to the ultimate route and gives instructions as to how it is to fit with other packets. Computers on the network (routers) examine these headers and move the data packet to another site towards the ultimate destination. This decentralized and flexible transmission makes packet-switched communications less vulnerable to outages in the transmission lines. It is also provides a more efficient means of transmitting data than the circuit-switched mode used for conventional telephony. (Packet switching is not necessarily better for high-bandwidth, time-critical uses like voice or video, however.)

(but perhaps not exclusively) the set of controls administered by the FCC and counterpart state regulators, and even in some cases (e.g., cable television) local government.

Second, although the Internet has so far been free of special media regulation, the kind of anarchy that has characterized Net activities in its early developmental period is probably unsustainable. Technologically and functionally the Internet is flanked by regulated media—telecommunications on one side, electronic mass media on the other. Telecommunications services are regulated by the FCC and state regulatory commissions; broadcast (terrestrial and satellite) media are regulated exclusively by the FCC, cable media are regulated by the FCC and local franchise authorities. The Internet right now is somewhere between these media; it is not quite a full fledged telecommunications medium like the telephone, and not quite a mass medium like cable television. But the distinctiveness of the Internet as not quite this and not quite that is rapidly disappearing. In fact all the media are converging, as we previously noted, and they are converging around the Internet. Already the Internet is being touted as a future medium for delivering full-motion video (not just "streamers" from newly released films or incidental information about current television programs). Internet voice telephony ("voice over Internet protocol" or "VoIP") is a present reality. In short the Internet is becoming both a telecommunications medium and a mass medium—our telephone and our television. As the Internet moves into the mainstream of these traditional modes of communication, there are political and economic pressures to extend some of the traditional forms of regulation to it.

Precisely what types of regulation is still hard to say. As something of a combination of mass and interactive media, the Internet presents the possibility of being regulated both to control content (as has been the case in broadcast) and the terms of access (as has been the case in telecommunications). When Congress enacted its sweeping reforms of both mass media and telecommunications media in 1996, the Internet was sufficiently new that Congress could not foresee the ways in which it would affect these traditional modes.

Congress did make one foray in the direction of Net regulation with the Communications Decency Act (CDA), part of the Telecommunications Act of 1996, albeit a somewhat distinctive part. The CDA attempted to apply one small regulatory precedent from the model of broadcast regulation to control of indecency on the Net. That measure was short lived thanks to the Supreme Court's 1997 decision in *Reno v. ACLU*, 521 U.S. 844 (1997), striking down the attempt on First Amendment grounds. Congress, undaunted, tried another attempt with the Child Online Protection Act (COPA). This time Congress essentially incorporated the traditional standards of obscenity law (which in theory deny any protection to speech that is found to be "obscene"). The constitutional status of COPA remains in litigation. A lower court decision invalidating it in 2002 was reversed and remanded by the Supreme Court because of a misapplication of the relevant standards. On remand it was struck down again, whence the case returned to the Supreme Court a second time. This time the Court held the statute invalid on the ground that the government had not shown COPA to be the least restrictive means of combating indecency/obscenity. The Court remanded to update the record on the effectiveness of filtering as a less restrictive alternative to censorship, *Ashcroft v. ACLU*, 542 U.S. 656 (2004). On remand, the court concluded that the government had not satisfied its burden of proof on this issue. ACLU v. Mukasey, 2008 WL 2801759 (3d Cir. 2008) (affirming district court).

Despite the concern about Internet indecency and a few other special concerns such as Internet gambling, there has not been any serious attention given to whether the emergence of the Internet as a medium for distributing news, information, and entertainment should entail content regulation of the kind traditionally associated with broadcasting. The prevailing assumption appears to be that any such regulation would be impossible given the diffuse nature of the content and the difficulty of controlling its dissemination. It might not much matter since, as noted above, the traditional regulation of broadcast content has disappeared except for a handful of special concerns.

There has been a growing concern about non-content regulation, however. For example, there is now a raging debate over whether the providers of broadband service (the wireline telephone and cable service providers) should be subject to rules ensuring non-discriminatory access by different types of service (the so-called "network neutrality" issue that is now the topic *de jour* in this field). The emergence of VoIP[25] has raised questions of whether providers should be subject to the same obligations as conventional telephone service providers, such as 911 emergency service, universal service subsidies, and access charges (charges paid by long distance carriers/users to local exchange carriers for interconnection with the local exchange). Some of these issues have not yet been resolved.

25. VoIP is now marketed as part of broadband services provided by wireline and wireless telephone companies and by the major cable companies. It is offered by others, such Vonage, as a special software to be used in connection with broadband transmission service provided by wireline and cable. In addition providers such as Skype (now owned by eBay) provide a peer-to-peer VoIP service that, for some subscribers (those who subscribe to "Skype-Out"), is interconnected with the regular telephone network.

Chapter 2

SPECTRUM MANAGEMENT

A. THE RADIO SPECTRUM AND THE INTERFERENCE PROBLEM

At the outset, it is important to take note of the elementary physics of the radio spectrum. What we call the radio spectrum is only a slice of what is more precisely the electromagnetic spectrum, which encompasses a spectrum from subsonic frequencies at one end to cosmic rays at the other. The following chart illustrates.

The Electromagnetic Spectrum

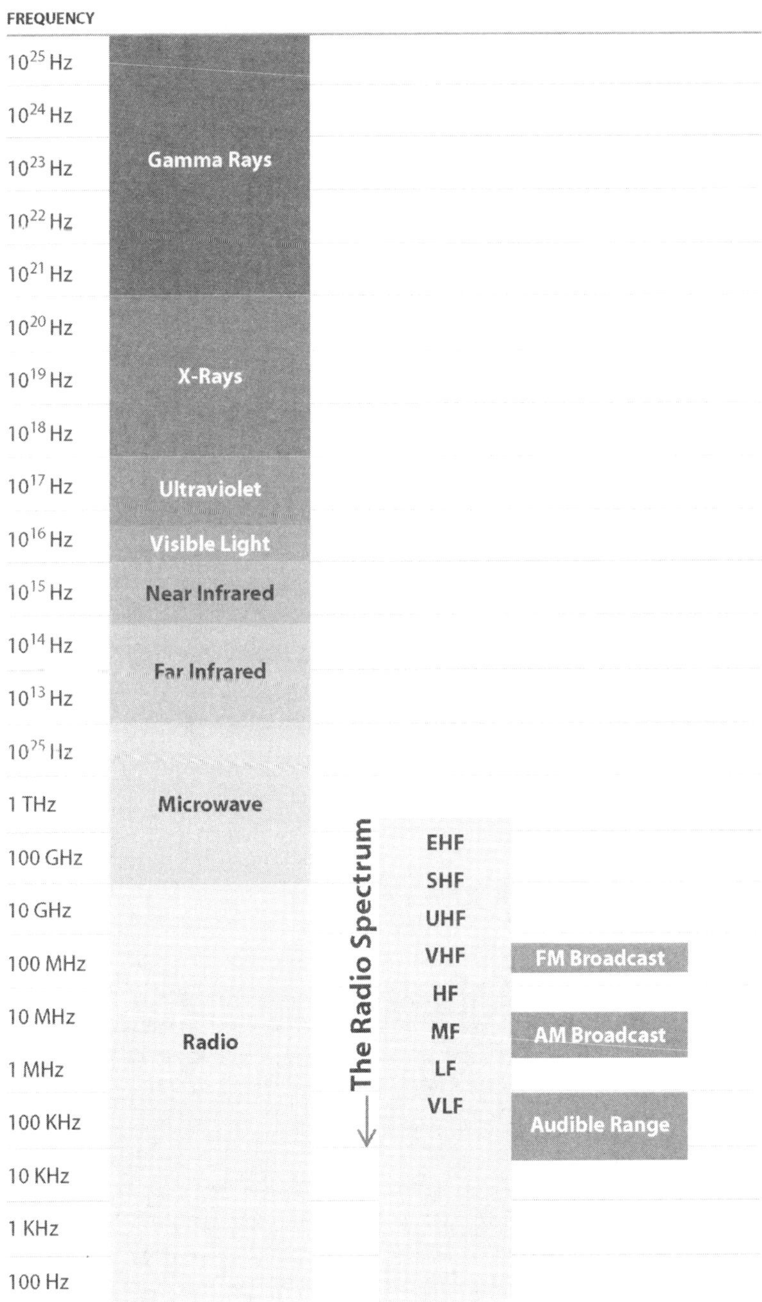

While it is common to refer to the spectrum as a "resource," that locution can be misleading insofar as it suggests that the spectrum represents some physical presence in space. What we call the spectrum is a phenomenon of nature created by the propagation of radio or sound or light waves. (Scientists used to think that these waves were a product of a physical substance—an "ether." Michelson & Morley's famous experiment in 1887 disproved the existence of ether, but, ironically, neither Michelson nor Morley accepted that conclusion, and for many years after they and other scientists continued to believe that there was some ethereal substance out there that accounted for the propagation of wave forms in space. It remained for Einstein to show that the assumption of an ethereal substance was unnecessary and confusing.)

There is, for example, a ubiquitous habit of referring to spectrum regulation as derived from its being "owned" by the public (and managed by the government on the public's behalf), but the conception of spectrum as a "thing" to be "owned" is a product of, not a justification for, regulation, which is to say that the trope of ownership is a function of the government's regulating its use. Does it matter whether the spectrum is a physical thing or just an artifact of transmitting electromagnetic energy in space? Possibly not, though it may help to avoid confusion in how we think about the regulation of spectrum use. Consider the color red. That color is also part of the spectrum, and it is intuitive to us that "red" is not a thing but rather a quality—a frequency of electromagnetic radiation with a particular appearance that, unlike most of the spectrum, is perceptible to the human eye. No one would say that the government "owns" the frequencies that cause redness even though people readily say that it owns lower frequencies used for radio transmission. There are, of course, very practical reasons for the different treatment. There is no need to regulate use of the color red because one person's use of it doesn't *interfere* with another's use. But, unlike the use of red, two simultaneous attempts to transmit information on the same frequency will interfere with each other. If the frequency that produces the color red were to be used for open transmission of communications, perhaps it too will be regulated![1]

Interference arising from uncontrolled frequency use is what underlies the common term "spectrum scarcity," which is the phrase most often invoked to explain government regulation of radio. It is important to bear in mind a couple of elementary things about scarcity *qua* interference.

First, the term "spectrum scarcity" is not a law of physical limits or boundaries. Spectrum scarcity is simply a way of describing the limits on practical use that arise from interference. Interference itself is a product of the technology and the type of use, as well as the way in which spectrum is allocated among users. The human ear is only a mediocre differentiator of simultaneously transmitted sound waves, so two different transmissions at relatively distinct frequencies can easily drown each

1. Such regulation is not as far-fetched as it may sound. Red, or more precisely infrared, is used for electronic communications, so called FSO (free-space-optics). Its usage is not regulated because the beamwidths are so narrow (milli radians) as to obviate the risk of interference. Its power is regulated, but only for eye safety.

other out. Compare that to wireless telephone networks, which use technologies that allow networks carry dozens or hundreds of calls on the same frequency essentially simultaneously. On the other hand, audible sound waves carry over such a short distance that the occupants of a single building can engage in dozens or hundreds of simultaneous conversations without interfering with each other—the interference of audible sound can be managed through the technology of walls.

Second, interference between radio transmissions is not a matter of two radio waves interacting in space and somehow destroying each other, like a particle of matter encountering a particle of anti-matter. Interference arises when one user's receiver cannot differentiate among different signals. What is "destroyed" is not the signal but the information that is carried by it. Moreover, typically the information is not destroyed but rather degraded. The degree to which the degradation destroys the usefulness of the information is not uniform or absolute across all communications. Some communications are more sensitive than others to interference degradations depending on the type of service involved, the nature of the information, and the purposes of the particular signal. Even within a particular type of service, the effects of interference are likely to be quite varied, depending on whether one is watching a live sports event or a cartoon show.

Third, whether one talks in terms of "scarcity" of the spectrum or more specifically about the interference caused by unregulated or uncoordinated use of frequencies, the problem is not constant over time or technology. Technology has improved to the point that the scarcity that existed in 1934 is not a meaningful constraint today. That does not mean we don't still face interference problems; rather we have graduated to new levels of problems (more and different equipment, more and different radio uses) and to new levels of solutions (ability to exploit higher frequency bands, ability to develop new means of transmitting and receiving that minimize interference).

Consider the ever-expanding range of usable frequencies. The size of a slice of spectrum is measured as the difference between the highest frequency and the lowest frequency, so a license to transmit between 1 MHz and 1.1 MHz is a set-aside of 100 KHz of spectrum—the 100 KHz between 1 MHz and 1.1 MHz. At the time of the first regulatory statute, the Radio Act of 1912, only 1500 KHz (or 1.5 MHz) of spectrum was deemed to be usable. By 1930, the Federal Radio Commission defined its jurisdiction to cover 60 MHz. This grew to 300 MHz in 1936 and to 30 GHz in 1944. Today, the range of frequencies designated as "the radio spectrum" stretches to 300 GHz. A glance at the labels used in the earlier spectrum chart illustrates. The so-called "high frequency" band was so designated because at the time the label was coined, that range of the spectrum was considered by spectrum use planners to be functionally "high." As higher frequencies were opened up, new labels had to be invented to differentiate the new higher bands: "very high" and "ultra high" came next, and then "super high" and "extra high." (Virtually all licensed private and governmental uses are below 30 GHz at the present time, but bands above that limit are being actively considered for future exploitation. But we are running out of superlatives. Perhaps the FCC's spectrum planners will need some help from commercial product marketers for the next category of bigger and better!)

Expanding the range of the spectrum has mitigated the "scarcity problem" but not eliminated it, because our growing uses of the spectrum have proved to be insatiable. The fact that every American over age 14 seems to have a cell phone says it all.[2] Happily, it is not simply a matter of putting higher spectrum bands to use. Technology is constantly finding new ways to use and reuse old spectrum. The best example of this is the development of cellular technology, which made possible the aforementioned explosion in wireless telephones. But there are others. Digitalization technology and signal compression technology similarly enhance the use of existing frequencies, allowing more information to be disseminated while also reducing interference problems. Wideband spectrum techniques allow for reduced interference, as do so-called "cognitive radio" devices that allow a kind of dynamic spectrum allocation as part of the design of the transmitting and receiving equipment. We will examine all of these examples further below.

B. ALLOCATING SPECTRUM

At the outset, a note about regulatory semantics: it is common to use the term "allocation" to refer indifferently to any assignment of rights to use spectrum. However, spectrum managers employ a specialized argot that distinguishes three levels of distribution. In that vernacular, the word "allocation" refers not to the assignment of spectrum to a user but rather to a type of use: the distribution of frequencies among various *classes of service*. For example, in the United States the frequencies between 54 and 72 MHz are allocated to television broadcasting (channels 2–4); the frequencies between 50 and 54 MHz are allocated to amateur radio. Once the frequency bands are broken out to types of service, they are further "assigned" to individual users by means of individual licenses. Because the spectrum is first "allocated" to a particular service before it is "assigned" to a particular user, licensees are limited to using their licensed spectrum to provide the FCC-defined service. (There are some exceptions to this in-service limitation, but for now we can ignore them.). In some classes of service there is an intermediate distribution to particular geographic locations, a distribution that spectrum planners call an "allotment." For example, television channel 29 is "allotted" to specific cities, one of which is Charlottesville, Virginia, and the cities close enough to Charlottesville to interfere with channel 29 are allotted different television channels. We will discuss below the television allotment plan (confusingly sometimes also called an "allocations plan"). Not all services have an allotment plan, but television and FM radio are prominent examples of ones that do.

2. As we saw earlier the FCC's most recent report puts the number of U.S. cellphone subscribers at 241.8 million at the end of 2006, approximately 80% of the population at that time. That is approximately the entire population over the age of 14.

Allocation among services begins at the international level. International responsibility for spectrum allocation (allocation of the spectrum among broad classes of service, such as broadcasting, mobile radio, astronomy, amateur, satellite broadcasting, telephony etc.), is a function of the International Telecommunications Union (ITU), a specialized agency of the U.N. Based on international conferences, the ITU maintains, and periodically revises, an international table of allocations. The international table is not uniform among all countries. There are three separate international regions (the U.S. is in Region two, covering North and South America) and the geographic separation allows a degree of non-uniformity between regions for those frequency bands that have limited range (e.g., terrestrial broadcasting channels).

Within the framework of international allocations, the U.S. table of allocations is constructed by two agencies, the FCC and the NTIA. As we noted in Chapter One, the FCC regulates all non-Federal Government users (including state agencies), and the NTIA manages (or at least coordinates) all use by federal government agencies. Allocation of the spectrum between Federal Government use and private (including state and local government units) use is a matter of coordination and agreement between the NTIA and the FCC.

Below is a sample page from the allocations table showing international and national (both FCC and federal government) allocations for a segment of the VHF band. (A color diagram of all U.S. allocations is available on the NTIA's web site at: http://www.ntia.doc.gov/osmhome/allochrt.pdf)

<table>
<tr><td colspan="3">Table of Frequency Allocations</td><td colspan="2">42-137 MHz (VHF)</td><td>Page 17</td></tr>
<tr><td colspan="3">International Table</td><td colspan="2">United States Table</td><td rowspan="2">FCC Rule Part(s)</td></tr>
<tr><td>Region 1 Table</td><td>Region 2 Table</td><td>Region 3 Table</td><td>Federal Table</td><td>Non-Federal Table</td></tr>
<tr><td colspan="3">40.98-41.015
FIXED
MOBILE
Space research
5.160 5.161</td><td colspan="2">(See previous page)</td><td></td></tr>
<tr><td colspan="3" rowspan="2">41.015-44
FIXED
MOBILE
5.160 5.161</td><td rowspan="3">42-46.6</td><td>42-43.69
FIXED
LAND MOBILE
NG124 NG141</td><td>Public Mobile (22)
Private Land Mobile (90)</td></tr>
<tr><td rowspan="2">43.69-46.6
LAND MOBILE
NG124 NG141</td><td rowspan="2">Private Land Mobile (90)</td></tr>
<tr><td colspan="3" rowspan="2">44-47
FIXED
MOBILE
5.162 5.162A</td></tr>
<tr><td>46.6-47
FIXED
MOBILE</td><td>46.6-47</td><td></td></tr>
<tr><td rowspan="4">47-68
BROADCASTING
5.162A 5.163 5.164 5.165 5.169 5.171</td><td rowspan="2">47-50
FIXED
MOBILE</td><td rowspan="2">47-50
FIXED
MOBILE
BROADCASTING
5.162A</td><td>47-49.6</td><td>47-49.6
LAND MOBILE
NG124</td><td>Private Land Mobile (90)</td></tr>
<tr><td>49.6-50
FIXED
MOBILE</td><td>49.6-50</td><td></td></tr>
<tr><td colspan="2">50-54
AMATEUR
5.162A 5.166 5.167 5.168 5.170</td><td rowspan="4">50-73</td><td>50-54
AMATEUR</td><td>Amateur (97)</td></tr>
<tr><td>54-68
BROADCASTING
Fixed
Mobile
5.172</td><td>54-68
FIXED
MOBILE
BROADCASTING
5.162A</td><td rowspan="2">54-72
BROADCASTING
NG115 NG128 NG142 NG149</td><td rowspan="2">Broadcast Radio (TV)(73)
Auxiliary Broadcasting (74)</td></tr>
<tr><td rowspan="4">68-74.8
FIXED
MOBILE except aeronautical mobile
5.149 5.174 5.175 5.177 5.179</td><td>68-72
BROADCASTING
Fixed
Mobile
5.173</td><td rowspan="4">68-74.8
FIXED
MOBILE
5.149 5.176 5.179</td></tr>
<tr><td>72-73
FIXED
MOBILE</td><td>72-73
FIXED
MOBILE
NG3 NG49 NG56</td><td>Public Mobile (22)
Aviation (87)
Private Land Mobile (90)
Personal Radio (95)</td></tr>
<tr><td>73-74.6
RADIO ASTRONOMY
5.178</td><td colspan="2">73-74.6
RADIO ASTRONOMY US74
US246</td><td></td></tr>
<tr><td>74.6-74.8
FIXED
MOBILE</td><td colspan="2">74.6-74.8
FIXED
MOBILE
US273</td><td>Aviation (87)
Private Land Mobile (90)</td></tr>
</table>

C. ALLOTMENTS

Originally, the FCC licensed frequencies without prefixed geographic locations for their use. An applicant applying for, say, a new AM radio broadcast license would be required to show that its proposed frequency could be used in its proposed community of license without creating unacceptable interference to other stations operating on the same or adjacent frequencies. Although the FCC had (and still has) fixed standards for evaluating acceptable and unacceptable interference levels, the process of applying them was purely ad hoc. Over time, the ad hoc process turned out to be unsatisfactory. The AM radio band became seriously congested and interference levels—particularly for daytime broadcasts—were intolerable. When television broadcasting emerged as a new service, the FCC decided on a different approach. It would allot the television channels to fixed locations in order to avoid judging the interference potential in individual cases. License applicants could only apply for channels that had been allotted to their community of license. A person could petition for a change in channel allotments—and this was frequently done—but this required a special rulemaking proceeding. The channel allotment scheme was later applied to FM licensing, though, interestingly, the old AM licensing system was never changed. By the time the allotment system had taken hold, it was considered too late to rectify the damage done by the old ad hoc licensing of AM stations.

The television allotment plan was adopted in 1952 in the Sixth Report and Order on Television Allocations. The Commission had licensed television stations in the 1940s under a preliminary table of allotments that proved inadequate. In 1948, it froze all licensing until a new plan could be engineered. The 1952 plan established a scheme of rather elaborate engineering rules governing the maximum power, antenna height, and geographical separations between co-channel and adjacent-channel stations. To give a very oversimplified description, take this example of how the plan is constructed: Allot channel 9 to Washington, D.C., and specify certain height and power limits that will give it a service area coverage adequate to serve the market with a viewable signal. Specify a mileage separation, in Washington's case 170 miles. (In general, mileage limits vary based on the frequency—different frequencies carry, or "propagate" differently over space—and the geography, which also affects propagation.) Next draw a circle around Washington with a 170-mile radius. Within the area defined by that circle, channel 9 is preempted by the allotment to Washington. One then calculates distance separations for immediately adjacent channels. Here the required separation for the same region is 60 miles, resulting in circles where channels 7 and 8 are excluded. Complete the process east coast to west, and you have a plan.

The allotment scheme was more than a simple engineering construct. Underlying the technical rules governing allocations, power and antenna height limitations, was a system of priorities designed to maximize both the number of signals and the number of local signals. To do this the Commission established the following priorities: Priority No. 1—to provide television service to all parts of the United States. Priority No. 2—to provide each community with at least one television station. Priority No. 3—to provide a choice of at least two television services to all parts of the United States. Priority No. 4—to provide each community with at least two television stations. Priority No. 5—Any channels remaining unassigned under the foregoing priorities were to be assigned to the various communities on the basis of the size of the population of each city, its geographic location, and the number of TV services available from stations in other communities.

The plan was both technically complex and deeply flawed. First, the conflict between providing service writ large and providing local outlets for that service was more significant than the Commission recognized. Focusing on localism led the FCC to allot local channels to cities that were much too small to financially support them, wasting frequencies in a manner that failed to promote either localism or the availability of more services. Second, to compound that problem the FCC decided to use both VHF and UHF channels.[3] Prior to the 1948 freeze, the Commission had concluded that the television system ultimately "must find its lodging in UHF," because only in the UHF band was there enough unallocated spectrum to fill the needs of television. But in 1952, the Commission decided not to disrupt either existing viewer habits or the investments made by some 108 VHF stations established prior to 1948, so the plan used both bands. That decision proved to be a dreadful mistake, made worse by the fact that the Commission chose to intermix VHF and UHF frequencies in the same market. Holding power and antenna height constant, UHF signals have a more limited range than VHF and therefore cannot provide comparable service area coverage (at least not without incurring additional costs to increase power and antenna height). This means that UHF stations were economically disadvantaged in competing with VHF stations in the same market. To compound the problem, at that time some television sets did not even have built-in UHF tuners, and those that did had non-detent tuners that would have challenged Willie Sutton in dialing to a usable signal.[4]

To deal with that problem, the FCC in the 1950s and into the 1960s pursued a couple of strategies, neither of which produced very good

3. The VHF channels allocated to television are channels 2–13 on the television set; channel 1 had been previously transferred to non-broadcast, government use. The UHF channels allocated to broadcasting at the time of the *Sixth Report* were channels 14–82; however, the top 12 channels were reallocated to land mobile radio in the 1970s. The conventional channel numbering is quite deceptive because the actual frequencies are not continuous. There is, most notably, a huge frequency difference between VHF channel 13 and UHF channel 14. That difference translates quite directly into relative signal strength which in turn affects service range, quality of signal and, ultimately, comparative economic strength in providing service.

4. The problem was particularly vexing for ABC, which at that time had the weakest affiliate structure of the three major commercial networks. In markets with only two VHF channels, the VHF stations affiliated with CBS and NBC, leaving ABC with the UHF runts of the local litter of stations.

results. First, it tried to segregate VHF and UHF (or "deintermix" in FCC-ese) some of the markets to equalize competition. That effort mostly failed; the VHF stations that were asked to trade in their superior VHF channels for UHF put up a fight that basically prevented the FCC from deintermixing more than a handful of markets. Second, the FCC tried so-called "drop in" allotments—putting in VHF channels at mileage separations that were less than the *Sixth Report* had specified. Again, there was industry opposition, ostensibly because of the additional interference potential, but that was mostly just a disguise for opposition to new VHF competition. In 1962, Congress tried to lend a hand by directing that all TV receivers have UHF capability, which removed one source of competitive disparity between UHF and VHF. What really "solved" the problem, though, was cable television, for which the VHF/UHF distinction is immaterial. Once cable television was established in a market, all a UHF station needed was to get carried on the cable and all technical disparities between its signal and VHF station signals were removed.

As noted above, the allotments system for television channels was extended to FM radio channels, but none of the above problems of television channel planning are applicable to FM radio, and so the FM allotment system raised no issues worth noting. Satellite television also relies on the allotment system, but it is by necessity international. By international agreements (under the auspices of the ITU), every country is given certain frequencies for use in direct-to-home satellite broadcasting along with fixed orbital positions to be occupied by the satellites. Incidentally, this international allotment plan is specific to broadcasting. Frequencies and orbital positions used for so-called "fixed" satellite service (those used for *telecommunications* services) are not bound by predetermined allotments; use by the various countries is coordinated on an ad hoc basis.

D. ASSIGNMENTS TO INDIVIDUAL USERS

1. Basic Licensing Requirements

Within the allocations regulated by the FCC (and, in the important cases of FM radio and television broadcasting and all satellite broadcasting, within the geographic allotments just discussed), "assignments" of frequencies are made to individual users by means of licenses. The particular requirements for a license vary somewhat depending on the service, but the basic rules for licensing are common across all radio. For convenience, we will focus on broadcasting services.

For uncontested applications, processing of the application is fairly routine. An applicant first files for a construction permit to build a transmission facility. If the construction permit is granted, the permittee files for the final license. The latter is usually a formality designed only to give the Commission an opportunity to ensure that the station has been built according to the construction permit and the Commission's regulations—the important step is the construction permit application.

To receive a construction permit, the applicant must show that it (in most cases "it" is a corporate entity) is legally, financially, and technically qualified. Legal qualifications include being a citizen (in the usual case, an entity that is controlled by citizens), compliance with pertinent regulations governing multiple ownership (of which more in Chapter 4), and the absence of any other disqualification by reason of bad character. Financial qualifications include the ability to construct and operate the licensed station. Technical qualifications include compliance with all the engineering requirements for the particular station, including, of course, the absence of interference with other licensed users or, in the case of FM and TV stations, consistency with the allotment plan.

Public notice is given for all applications for a license with an opportunity for persons to file a petition to deny the application or file a competing application. If a petition to deny states credible grounds for denying the application, the Commission must designate the application for a full adjudicatory hearing.

In the case of competing applications, until recent times the course of action was to designate all competing applications for a so-called "comparative hearing" in which the respective merits of the applicants' proposed services would be compared. We will say more of the comparative hearing in a moment. Suffice it here to say that, in the mid–1990s, comparative hearings were replaced with an auction system.

Licenses are transferable with FCC approval. To obtain approval for either an assignment of the license or transfer of ownership control of the licensed entity, an application is filed showing that the proposed assignee or transferee is legally, financially, and technically qualified to hold the license. Approval is routinely granted. At one time the FCC enforced a policy against "trafficking" in licenses—the practice of obtaining a license only for the purpose of trading it. The policy is still nominally in effect, with a presumption of trafficking in the case where a licensee seeks to assign the license or transfer control within one year of its issuance.

Unlike the certificate of public interest, convenience, and necessity that is used for permitting public utility services, the FCC's radio spectrum licenses are for limited terms, with provision for renewal. The current terms vary across services. For broadcast services the current license is eight years. The theory underlying the limited-term, renewable license is that renewal allows the agency to evaluate the licensee's performance to ensure it is "in the public interest." In the case of non-broadcast licenses, the theory has always been empty, since there are no real "public interest" service obligations beyond making effective use of the radio (i.e., using it to provide the service for which it is authorized). Thus, the FCC does not concern itself with whether the taxi company or the tugboat operator (historically, radios used by dispatchers have required licenses, making taxi companies and tugboat operators FCC licensees) is providing good service with its radio. So long as the radio is used for the general purpose for which the frequency was assigned to that service, there is no further regulatory inquiry. The same holds for virtually all users other than broadcasters. In such cases, then, the periodicity of the license is purely an administrative formality.

In the case of broadcasting, the theory has a more plausible purpose—at least to the extent that renewal is in fact used for the purpose of evaluating the licensee's performance. The history of renewal proceedings for evaluating performance is complicated and controversial. At one time in the early years of radio, it appeared that the FCC would give serious scrutiny to a radio stations' performance on the occasion of renewal—which in those days was every three years (a period that remained in place well into the television era; in 1981 the term was extended to five years for television and seven for radio; in 1996 Congress made it a uniform eight years for both). It soon became apparent that such a close scrutiny was both administratively burdensome and politically unpalatable insofar as it made licensees feel very insecure. The FCC responded by assuring licensees that they could expect renewal in all but unusual circumstances. What constituted "unusual" for these purposes was to become the subject of an intensely controversial set of cases in the 1970s and 1980s. The cases all involved comparative hearings where, at the time of an incumbent licensee's renewal, a new applicant filed a competing application for the same license. Under its rules the FCC was required to put down both the renewal application and the new application for a hearing. At this point we need to interrupt the story in order to say something more about the comparative hearing process itself.

2. Comparative Hearings

If two or more applications are timely filed for the same facility, the traditional mode for choosing between them was the comparative hearing in which the respective merits of the applicants are comparatively evaluated according to some set of criteria. In the case of non-broadcast users there is very little to compare since, as we noted, earlier there are no public service obligations to evaluate. For all practical purposes, therefore, which of two applicants gets a mobile radio license is a matter of regulatory indifference. In the case of broadcasting there was ostensibly a "public interest" to consider as part of the licensing process. One could examine, say, the different program proposals of contesting applicants, or the different facilities they proposed to construct. Unfortunately, trying to implement this public interest proved to be extremely vexing. It became particularly troublesome with television licensing in the 1950s and 1960s.

The heart of the problem was the difficulty of devising clear and coherent standards for picking the winner. In the mid 1960s, the Commission settled on two general criteria: (1) which applicant proposed the best practicable service and (2) which application would best promote diversification of control of mass media. See *Policy Statement on Comparative Broadcast Hearings*, 1 F.C.C.2d 393 (1965). "Best practicable service" was a kind of portmanteau that embraced several lesser criteria:

integration of ownership and management, past broadcast experience, local residence of owners, civic participation. At one time the Commission made some attempt to compare program-related proposals, but it gave that up because it was fraught with obvious First Amendment problems to the extent that it entailed inquiry into the comparative merits of particular programs. It was also unreliable, since the applicants' program proposals were tentative and subject to change. Instead of looking at actual program proposals, therefore, the Commission looked at secondary factors that might serve as a kind of proxy for probable performance. One of the key factors was integration of ownership and management, which the Commission imagined to be a way of ensuring high-level executive responsibility for programming decisions. In 1993 the integration criterion was overturned by the D.C. Circuit on the ground that it was not shown to be related to performance; nor was it effectively enforced as a policy after the comparative process was over:

> While the Commission makes it a central focus of allocation, the Commission takes no interest whatever in the matter when it comes to transfers or even in the continuing conduct of the original licensee. The Commission appears to have no evidence that the preferred structure even survives among the winners, much less that it does so among especially outstanding broadcasters. Because of applicants' incentive to create a facade of integration, and the difficulty of identifying sound business practices, even the preference's touted objectivity proves an illusion. Though we owe substantial deference to the Commission's expertise, we are forbidden to suspend our disbelief totally. We find the integration policy arbitrary and capricious.

Bechtel v. FCC, 10 F.3d 875, 887 (D.C. Cir. 1993).[5]

By eliminating the integration criterion, the court effectively undermined the best practicable service standard,[6] and this in turn left the

5. On the point about not being effectively enforced, one may take judicial notice of this by just noting that the majority of television stations are owned by large public corporations. In the context of a public corporation, it is the most transparent of fictions to assume that the "owners" of such a corporation would be "integrated" with management. Are GE stockholders "integrated" with the management of NBC's television stations? And, for that matter, how much does the management of GE or even NBC-Universal really control the operations of NBC's owned-and-operated local television stations (whose ability to broadcast is the actual object of the license)?

6. The integration criterion included a "plus" factor for minority ownership. The Commission first initiated a minority preference in 1978 as a twofold policy aimed at increasing minority ownership of broadcast stations. The first part of the policy entailed consideration of minority ownership as an affirmative factor in comparative hearings for *new* broadcast licenses, provided the minority owner proposed to participate actively in station management. The second aspect of the policy was designed to aid minority opportunities to purchase licenses by permitting "distress sales" to minorities by licensees whose licenses were in jeopardy because of violations of FCC regulations. The Commission's twofold policy was upheld against a constitutional (equal protection) challenge in Metro Broadcasting, Inc. v. FCC, 497 U.S. 547 (1990). However, the status of *Metro Broadcasting* was put in doubt by Adarand Constructors, Inc. v. Peña, 515 U.S. 200 (1995), in which the Court held that racial preferences in government contracting must be examined with "strict scrutiny" and in doing so disapproved *Metro Broadcasting*'s application of a less exacting standard for federal and state programs. But the particular preference policies at issue in *Metro Broadcasting* were not involved in *Adarand*, leaving open comparative hearing process empty. The ownership diversification criterion had already been rendered ineffectual by the Commission itself, when it previously decided that it would enforce ownership diversity by means of fixed rules rather than in individual licensing proceedings.

Quite apart from the artificial criteria that the Commission used, the comparative hearing process was costly, both in terms of administrative and private resources. The comparative process itself was the modern equivalent of trial by ordeal as each applicant desperately sought to prove itself worthier than its competitor(s) in terms of its financing, its studio location, its ascertainment of local interests, the experience of its managers and so forth. The evaluation process was one that would tangle the head of the most skilled administrative law judge. One applicant would prevail over a competitor on one criterion, but not another, which then made it necessary to assign weights to each criterion in order to derive at some final sum. That was difficult enough in the case of two applicants, but often there were three or four, which compounded the problem. In such cases, it was necessary to construct a complicated matrix by which each applicant was compared against each other on the various criteria.

The ultimate embarrassment for the comparative hearing process, however, was the fact that the entire point of the contest could be undone by a simple assignment of license or transfer of entity ownership by the winner to the loser, and under Section 310(d) of the Act the Commission is expressly denied the power to deny such an assignment or transfer on the ground that the assignee/transferee was inferior to either the transferor or any other person. The result was that, if A, B and C were competing for a license and the Commission evaluated their comparative merits in the order A > B > C, A could assign its license to C even though C was judged inferior to both A and B.

As bad as the initial comparative licensing process was, after the original wave of television licensing in the 1950s and 1960s it looked like the problem would resolve itself in time. Everyone thought that, after most of the valuable frequencies were licensed in major markets, there would be fewer competitive contests, and the problem would disappear. Unfortunately, it did not. In the later 1960s it reappeared in the context of renewal licensing. As previously mentioned, the Commission had assured licensees they could expect renewal in all but unusual cases, and unusual meant some egregiously poor performance record. Though the Act gave the FCC no way to avoid such a comparative hearing should a challenger come forward at renewal, the FCC sent a signal in several early cases that such challengers could not hope to displace even a

the status of the FCC's minority ownership policies. Further complicating matters, in the context of comparative hearings credit for minority ownership subsumed under the integration criterion (with credit being given only where minority owners were integrated with management). Remember that *Bechtel* struck integration generally, leaving the minority preference an orphan in comparative licensing cases. The replacement of comparative licensing with auctions rendered the problem moot, though as we shall see below, there is a residue of the original preference criterion in the "designated entities" program used today in spectrum auctions.

mediocre incumbent. For a time it appeared that would prevent the problem from arising in the television licensing era.

But it did, largely through the FCC's own mistake. It came about because one of its television licensees was found to have committed improprieties in the course of a comparative hearing over an *original* license. The case involved WHDH-TV in Boston and the improprieties had to do with some ex parte contacts between one of the principals of the winning applicant (the Herald-Traveler newspaper in Boston) and the chairman of the Commission. The FCC chose to deal with those improprieties not by vacating the original decision but by designating its renewal application for a hearing and inviting other competing applicants (including but not limited to the original competing applicants) to file on top of it. Several challengers did so and, *mirabile dictu*, one of them carried home the license. See *Greater Boston Television Corp. v. FCC*, 444 F.2d 841 (D.C. Cir. 1970) (affirming the FCC's *WHDH* decision). It was the first time that a television licensee had lost to a challenger in the context of a renewal proceeding. In fact it was not quite a renewal proceeding, since the FCC had indicated that the incumbent was to be treated as if it were an original applicant, but this exceptional feature of the case did not prevent it from becoming a source of industry anxiety. It is fair to say that the FCC had not intended to create such anxiety, and quickly set about to restore the industry's security by emphasizing just how extraordinary the case was. The subsequent history is interesting for what it teaches about the ups and downs of licensing policy, about the relationships between courts and agency, and not least about the rich possibilities for irony in administrative law and politics.

While the *WHDH* case was pending on appeal, the broadcast industry sought and obtained considerable congressional support for reversal of the case, but the effort was abated when the FCC itself retreated by issuing its *Policy Statement Concerning Comparative Hearings Involving Regular Renewal Applicants*, 22 F.C.C.2d 424 (1970). The FCC announced that henceforth it would not conduct a comparative hearing on renewal cases unless it had been first shown that the incumbent had not warranted an expectation of renewal. Challengers would be heard for the limited purpose of calling attention to the incumbent's failings. However, if an incumbent licensee showed a record of "substantial" service to the community, without serious deficiencies, it would be entitled to renewal notwithstanding the promise of superior performance by a challenger. Only upon a refusal to renew because of the incumbent's past failure to provide substantial service (viewed in isolation) would a full comparative hearing be held. This policy statement was overturned by the court of appeals in *Citizens Communications Center v. FCC*, 447 F.2d 1201 (D.C. Cir. 1971) on the ground that it effectively denied a challenger's application without a hearing in violation of Section 309(e) of the Communications Act. The court did not preclude the Commission from giving significant weight to the past broadcast performance of an incumbent licensee; it specifically recognized that "*superior*" performance should be a "plus" of major significance in renewal proceedings.

Following the court's decision, the Commission conducted a further inquiry in which it attempted to clarify its earlier policy announcement by emphasizing that its concept of "substantial performance" meant something more than "minimal performance." However, it refused to embrace the court's standard of superior service, thinking that "superior" literally meant something above average, which would force a kind of race to the top that could not be tolerated. The Commission, apparently lacking familiarity with contemporary academic grading standards, did not believe it possible for every broadcaster to be graded above average. It reasoned that applying the "superior" standard therefore put at risk half of all licensees seeking renewal who, by the depressing property of the bell curve, must be at or below average. For several years following there was an ongoing contest between the FCC and the court of appeals as to the implementation of the "substantial" versus "superior" performance standard. As a practical matter it came to very little, since the Commission refused to unseat even "average" performing incumbents, and the court essentially capitulated (though not without a few harrumphs and remands for more clarification).

Then, to the bewilderment of all, the Commission did unseat an incumbent after a comparative renewal hearing. The incumbent was a one-man classical music radio station in Gloucester, Massachusetts that refused to air any news or public affairs programming. That was too much for the Commission, and in 1982 it awarded his license to a competing applicant. In a curious role reversal, the Commission's newly found vigor in enforcing public service standards was too much for the court of appeals. It reversed the FCC for *over*valuing the past performance of incumbent seeking renewal, and for *under*valuing the incumbent's comparative merit on the issue of diversification and integration (recall the *Bechtel* case): the incumbent here had no other media interests and was about as fully integrated (the owner was the sole employee) as is possible. *Committee for Community Access v. FCC*, 737 F.2d 74 (D.C. Cir. 1984). On remand the FCC renewed the incumbent, *Simon Geller*, 59 P. & F. Radio Reg.2d 579 (1985). Five years later, the *pas de deux* between Commission and court over comparative renewals was repeated but with yet another reversal of roles. The Commission refused to unseat an incumbent despite serious deficiencies, and the court of appeals reversed. See *Monroe Communications Corp. v. FCC*, 900 F.2d 351 (D.C. Cir. 1990); *Harriscope of Chicago, Inc.*, 5 FCC Rcd. 6383 (1990) (on remand, removing the incumbent).

All of this gave renewed energy to the industry's efforts to get more security against the risk that a complete default in a station's performance might actually cost the station its license. In 1996 it was successful. Among the many reforms of the 1996 Telecommunications Act was a provision designed to eliminate the threat that had hung like Damocles' sword since the *WHDH* case. Under this provision, only after the incumbent's performance in the prior license period is first determined to be so deficient as to be not entitled to renewal can the FCC conduct a comparative hearing on the renewal application. The 1996 reform solved the renewal conundrum, but it did not itself abolish comparative hearings. That step came a year later when Congress decided to adopt for broadcast licensing an auction system that it had adopted in 1993 for competing applications in non-broadcast services.

3. Lotteries and Auctions

Auctions were not the first choice of an alternative to comparative licensing. Congress and the FCC first turned to lotteries. In 1981, Congress authorized the use of a lottery for choosing among competing applications whenever the Commission determined such a lottery to be in the public interest. The use of the lottery in mass media was, however, limited by a requirement that it give weighted odds in favor of any group that was "under-represented" in the ownership of communications facilities. The legislative history indicated that this included not only minorities, but also labor unions and community organizations. The 1981 legislation also required the Commission to determine all applicant qualifications *before* the lottery was held. The FCC found the conditions so cumbersome that they effectively precluded a meaningful use of the lottery. In 1982 a new statute was passed that limited preferences in mass media cases to "minority groups"—defined as "Blacks, Hispanics, American Indians, Alaska Natives, and Pacific Islanders." (In non-mass-media services no preferences were given.) The new statute also provided that a full qualifications determination was not required until *after* the lottery, thereby saving the FCC the burden of a detailed check of qualifications of thousands of unsuccessful applicants. The FCC implemented the new lottery, but only in selected radio services, most notably cellular telephone service, which had only recently emerged from the development stage. In 1989, the FCC proposed to adopt a rule that would have extended the use of the lottery to regular radio and television applications in lieu of the comparative hearing. However, it quickly backed off in the face of political opposition that claimed that lotteries would undermine the idea that broadcasters had special public interest responsibilities and that the traditional licensing system was an important means of enforcing them. The latter was dubious, as the experience with comparative licensing had shown, but in the end it did not matter. The use of lotteries in assigning cell phone licenses turned out to be costly and inefficient. The FCC was flooded with applications from persons who had no intent to build and operate systems but sought only to obtain a valuable asset—the license—in order to sell it to others. Not only did this add unanticipated costs to running the lottery, but it also potentially delayed the ultimate deployment of the service.

Responding to the failure of the lottery system, Congress in 1993 authorized the Commission to employ auctions but limited their use to licensees that charged users, a limitation that excluded broadcast users. In 1997, however, Congress mandated the agency to use auctions for broadcast licenses where there were competing applications for the license. The extension to broadcasting has not had a very important impact for the simple reason that, in the "high rent district" of television, most of the major markets were fully licensed under the old system, and the auction system only applies to original licensing—not to renewals.

The approval of auctions was both a practical and conceptual breakthrough in licensing—what Thomas Kuhn would call a "paradigm shift." The idea antedated the reality by several decades. The seminal argument for use of an auction market for broadcast facilities was made by Ronald Coase, *The Federal Communications Commission*, 2 J. Law & Econ. 1 (1959), which was inspired by an earlier proposal set forth by Leo Hertzel, *Public Interest and the Market in Color Television Regulation*, 18 U. Chi. L. Rev. 802 (1951). But the idea never gained public acceptance until Congress's authorization of auctions in 1993 and in 1997. We examine next the basic mechanics of auctions, and then turn to more far-reaching concerns about spectrum management generally.

a) Auction Mechanics

Although the basic idea of an auction is familiar to everyone, the design of auctions for different purposes can be extremely complicated. The economics literature on auction design is vast, as a cursory scan of the bibliography in one recent theoretical work will show. See Paul Milgrom, *Putting Auction Theory to Work* (2004) (Milgrom is one of the leading auction theorists and was one of many economists advising the FCC how to design its spectrum auction system). For our purposes, only a general outline of how the FCC's process works is necessary (or, indeed, possible).

At the outset it is important to understand that, while it is common to talk about auctioning the spectrum, what is auctioned is not just a band of frequencies for any and all uses. Rather what is auctioned is a license that that is bound by the same conditions and limitations that have always controlled licensees. Among other things, that means that a licensee may use or transfer (with the FCC's approval) its license only within the service class to which it has been allocated. Broadcast licensees may use their frequencies for broadcasting but not for, say, wireless telephony. (There are some exceptions to this in-service limitation, but for now we can ignore them.). It also means that the licensee must meet all of the regular legal, financial, and technical criteria for holding a license in the particular service.

In order to bid at an auction, applicants must submit a so-called short-form application that contains certain information including certification that the applicant is legally, technically, and financially qualified to hold a license. (If the applicant is a successful bidder, it must then submit a more detailed, long-form application.) Before an auction, each bidder must submit an upfront payment that determines its bidding eligibility in the auction. During each round of the auction, each bidder is required to bid on a specified portion of its maximum eligibility. If a bidder does not meet this requirement, it uses an activity rule waiver (if available) or loses eligibility. Round results are released within approximately 15 minutes after each round closes. They are available for downloading, both to bidders and to the general public. Interested parties may perform detailed analysis by loading these data files into a spreadsheet program or the Auction Tracking Tool, which is provided by the FCC for most auctions.

Most auctions have used a simultaneous, multiple-round system in which groups of related licenses are auctioned simultaneously over many rounds of bidding. It is in form basically an English auction (the kind of increasing-bid auction we're all used to seeing in movies) except that multiple objects are put up for auction at the same time. That is, the bidder can bid on groups of frequencies, which gives the bidder more flexibility in moving among licenses as prices change. As one license gets bid up, a bidder can shift to an alternative that represents a better value. The number of licenses varies hugely. For example, in 2002 an auction for licenses for paging system frequencies involved some 15,514 licenses. By contrast an auction in 2000 was held for a single broadcast station license. (Details on all of the auctions, past and planned, are available online at http://wireless.fcc.gov/auctions.)

To encourage broad participation in wireless communications, the Commission created a program for so-called "designated entities"—defined as small business, firms owned by minorities or women, and rural telephone companies. Designated entities are qualified to receive bidding credits of varying amounts depending on the size of the firm, effectively inflating their bid prices by the amount of the credit.

The FCC specifies minimum bid increments between rounds, with increments being adjusted in response to bidder behavior. In the early rounds, when bid activity is high, the FCC sets larger bid increments; in the later rounds, when bid activity is low, the FCC sets smaller bid increments. Typically, the bid increments are between 5 and 20 percent. Depending on the auction design, number of bidders, and the number of licenses being offered, an auction might run anywhere from one day to several weeks. The first day of an auction generally opens with long bidding periods, typically two bidding rounds lasting one or two hours each, followed by round results. As the auction continues, the Commission generally increases the number of rounds per day and decreases the duration of the rounds. Bidders gradually drop out of the auction as prices rise. The auction typically continues until all bidding activity stops. Again, the number of rounds varies enormously from auction to auction. An auction in 1996–97 for broadband PCS frequencies currently holds the record for the most rounds at 276. At the other extreme an auction for direct broadcast satellite service in 2004 involved just two rounds.

At the conclusion of the auction, the Commission issues a public notice declaring the auction closed, identifying winning bidders, and specifying the amounts of down payments due. At that time, winning bidders are typically given ten business days to supplement their upfront payments to satisfy the license down payment requirement and to file the required long-form application to the appropriate licensing bureau.

The FCC's auction program has been widely regarded as successful on several counts. First, it is efficient. In contrast to administrative selection, auctions do not involve artificial criteria for selection, they involve a fraction of the time used to conduct administrative hearings (days or weeks at most instead of months or years), and they are administratively simple to conduct (they are conducted electronically through the Commission's website). Second, it simulates the market by putting frequencies into the hands of the highest valued user.[7] Third, it has turned out (unexpectedly) to be a very lucrative source of revenue for the U.S. Treasury. Through 2008, spectrum auctions have yielded a net of over $47 billion.

b) Designated Entities

We noted earlier that the comparative hearing process gave additional consideration (a "plus factor") for minority ownership. The short-lived lottery system similarly required the Commission to give special weights to minority groups wherever the lottery was used to assign licenses to mass media. When Congress approved an auction system, it expanded on this preference policy by directing the Commission to implement rules to "ensure that small businesses, rural telephone companies, and businesses owned by members of minority groups and women are given the opportunity to participate in the provision of spectrum-based services." Included in the means to be considered for this purpose are the possible use of tax certificates, bidding credits, alternative payment schedules and methods of calculation, and other procedures. In 1994 the Commission adopted several measures for promoting these so-called "designated entities" to be selected on an auction-by-auction basis. The primary method is a set of special bidding credits that can be used in bidding for identified blocks of frequencies.[8] In some cases the FCC may set aside certain blocks for designated entities exclusively, and it may also authorize installment payments for the winning bidder. (Both of these latter methods were involved in the *NextWave* case, excerpted in the next section).

Subsequently, the Commission became uncomfortable with the minority and gender preferences. The discomfort with the minority category arose from the Supreme Court's 1995 decision in *Adarand Constructors, Inc. v. Peña*, 515 U.S. 200 (1995), holding that racial preferences must be reviewed under a strict scrutiny standard, one that requires both a compelling state interest and the least discriminatory means

7. This requires qualification: it awards the frequencies to the highest valued user only within a predetermined service classification.

8. The size of the credit is scaled to the bidder's average gross revenues for the preceding 3 years: Businesses with an average gross revenue not exceeding $3 million are eligible for bidding credits of 35 percent; those with revenues not exceeding $15 million are eligible for bidding credits of 25 percent; and those not exceeding $40 million are eligible for bidding credits of 15 percent. 47 C.F.R. § 1.2110(f).

available. While *Adarand* did not directly challenge the Commission's earlier minority preference policy in the case of comparative hearings, it did raise doubts about it. As to gender preferences, the Commission's gender preference standard had been found invalid by the court of appeals in *Lamprecht v. FCC*, 958 F.2d 382 (D.C. Cir. 1992) even under an intermediate scrutiny test; and more recently the Supreme Court apparently raised the bar of scrutiny for gender preferences generally to something close to a strict scrutiny test in *United States v. Virginia*, 518 U.S. 515 (1996). Based on these precedents, the FCC invited public comments on whether to treat minorities and women as designated entities. Remarkably, it received no comments on the issue. It therefore decided that it had no basis for treating minority and women as discrete classes of designated entity. Entities owned by minorities or women entities are thus favored only insofar as they independently qualify as small businesses. *Competitive Bidding Procedures*, 15 FCC Rcd. 21520 (2000).

Is the designated entity program a sensible one? The idea of promoting small business has long been a popular social policy in all sectors of the American economy. But whatever the political and social merits of such a policy generally, is it realistic to expect to promote small enterprise in a sector of the economy that has become increasingly dominated by giants? Bear in mind that we are not for the most part talking about small radio broadcast stations (although some FM channels have been auctioned). As the billions of dollars that have been bid in most auctions to date make clear, this is "big business" by any measure. The Commission's rules sets the definition of a small business on a service-specific basis, taking into consideration the characteristics and capital requirements of the particular service. However, the rules award bidding credits only to entities with a 3-year average gross revenue of $40 million or less. For most auctions that means there is a very large disparity between the capital resources of the favored entity and the amount it will need to make a competitive bid.

Of course, we have banks and other financial intermediaries to supply capital. The question is whether they will supply it based only on the strength of the small business's expectation of success or whether they will do so only in the expectation that the frequencies will be profitably sold to a larger enterprise. Indeed, in some cases it appears that the small businesses are simply pseudo entities that are put together by investors in order to obtain bidding credits with which to garner frequencies. See *United States ex rel. Taylor v. Gabelli*, 345 F. Supp. 2d 313 (S.D.N.Y. 2004) ("qui tam" action under False Claims Act claiming that winning bidders had falsely claimed eligibility and were simply fronts for an investment banker that had financially supported the bids; allegations sufficient to state a claim). In some cases the designated entities are effectively fronts for other, large telecommunications firms to whom the frequencies will be transferred. In 2006 the Commission moved to address the problem.

IMPLEMENTATION OF THE COMMERCIAL SPECTRUM ENHANCEMENT ACT AND MODERNIZATION OF THE COMMISSION'S COMPETITIVE BIDDING RULES AND PROCEDURES

Second Report and Order and Second Further Notice of Proposed Rule Making

Federal Communications Commission, 2006.
21 FCC Rcd. 4753.

BY THE COMMISSION:

* * *

II. BACKGROUND

* * *

9. The Commission's primary method of promoting the participation of designated entities in competitive bidding has been to award bidding credits—percentage discounts on winning bid amounts—to small business applicants. The Commission also has utilized other incentives, such as installment payments and, in the broadband Personal Communications Services [auction] ("broadband PCS"), a license set-aside, to encourage designated entities to participate in spectrum auctions and in the provision of service. In order to qualify for these benefits, an applicant must demonstrate that its gross revenues (and, in some cases, its total assets), in combination with those of its "attributable" interest holders, fall below certain service-specific financial caps. Thus, in determining eligibility for size-based benefits, it is critical to decide which investors' gross revenues (and total assets) must be attributed.

* * *

III. SECOND REPORT AND ORDER

* * *

B. Material Relationship

15. As discussed fully below, we revise our Part 1 rules to consider certain relationships as factors in determining designated entity eligibility. In so doing, we seek to improve our ability to achieve Congress's directives with regard to designated entities and to ensure that, in accordance with the intent of Congress, every recipient of our designated entity benefits is an entity that uses its licenses to directly provide facilities-based telecommunications services for the benefit of the public. Specifically, except as grandfathered below, an applicant or licensee has "impermissible material relationships" when it has agreements with one or more other entities for the lease (under either spectrum manager or de facto transfer leasing arrangements) or resale (including under a wholesale arrangement) of, on a cumulative basis, more than 50 percent of its spectrum capacity of any individual license. Such "impermissible

material relationships" render the applicant or licensee (i) ineligible for the award of designated entity benefits, and (ii) subject to unjust enrichment on a license-by-license basis. Furthermore, except as grandfathered below, an applicant or licensee has an "attributable material relationship" when it has one or more agreements with any individual entity, including entities and individuals attributable to that entity, for the lease (under either spectrum manager or de facto transfer leasing arrangements) or resale (including under a wholesale arrangement) of, on a cumulative basis, more than 25 percent of the spectrum capacity of any individual license that is held by the applicant or licensee. The "attributable material relationship" with that entity will be attributed to the applicant or licensee for the purposes of determining the applicant's or licensee's (i) eligibility for designated entity benefits, and (ii) liability for unjust enrichment on a license-by-license basis. * * *

C. Unjust Enrichment

* * *

37. We adopt the following ten-year unjust enrichment schedule for licenses acquired with bidding credits. For the first five years of the license term, if a designated entity loses its eligibility for a bidding credit for any reason, including but not limited to, entering into an "impermissible material relationship" or an "attributable material relationship," seeking to assign or transfer control of a license, or entering into a de facto transfer lease with an entity that does not qualify for bidding credits, 100 percent of the bidding credit, plus interest, is owed. For years six and seven of the license term, 75 percent of the bidding credit, plus interest, is owed. For years eight and nine, 50 percent of the bidding credit, plus interest, is owed, and for year ten, 25 percent of the bidding credit, plus interest, is owed. If a designated entity loses its eligibility for the same level of bidding credit that it originally received for any reason, including but not limited to, entering into an "impermissible material relationship" or an "attributable material relationship," seeking to assign or transfer control of a license, or entering into a de facto transfer lease with an entity that does not qualify for the same level of bidding credits, this unjust enrichment schedule will be applied to the difference between the original bidding credit and the bidding credit for which the designated entity, assignee, or assignor is eligible.

38. In addition to revising the unjust enrichment payment schedule, we will impose a requirement that the Commission must be reimbursed for the entire bidding credit amount owed, plus interest, if a designated entity loses its eligibility for a bidding credit for any reason, including but not limited to, entering into an "impermissible material relationship" or an "attributable material relationship," seeking to assign or transfer control of a license, or entering into a de facto transfer lease with an entity that is not eligible for bidding credits prior to the filing of the notification informing the Commission that the construction requirements applicable at the end of the license term have been met. For example, if a designated entity seeks to assign a license with a

bidding credit to an entity that is not eligible for bidding credits eight years after the grant of the license and prior to the filing of the construction notification, 100 percent of the bidding credit, plus interest, will be owed, rather than the 50 percent unjust enrichment payment that would have been due had the construction notification been on file with the Commission, pursuant to the revised unjust enrichment schedule, above. * * * [The Commission also issued a further notice of proposed rulemaking to consider, among other things, whether to make further modifications in the bidding rules governing benefits reserved for designated entities.]

Impermissible Relationships. Is the Commission's rule for recapturing the bidding credit (with interest) in cases where the designated entity loses its eligibility sufficient to deter the practices that prompted the rule? If a designated entity enters into an "impermissible relationship" with another entity, would it not be reasonable to presume that this was done purposefully? If so why does the Commission permit the winning bidder to retain the license? Recall that one of the conditions for holding a license is good character. Not every violation of FCC rules is the basis for a character disqualification, but intentional fraud on the Commission certainly is. The same would be true of the other firm with which the bidder had an impermissible relationship, so it would seem to follow that, if the license were transferred, both the transferor and the transferee should be disqualified.

c) When Winner's Fail

A familiar paradox of auctions is the "winner's curse," when the winning bidder overpays for the auctioned asset. Sometimes the curse is simply a psychological pain, as with buyer's remorse with which we are all familiar. Sometimes, however, the curse is a financial reality. By its nature, the designated entity program creates a heightened risk of financial failure by inviting participation by small entities in a very high-stakes enterprise. Of course, in every sector of the economy businesses fail; telecommunications firms are no exception as the famous telecommunications bust of the early 2000s demonstrates. Is this a problem for regulators? Certainly if regulatory policies themselves create special risks of business failure, it is. Whether one can say this about the FCC's auction system in general, or its designated entities program in particular, is a fit subject for debate, but that is not the immediate issue. The immediate issue is what can or should the FCC do to protect the integrity of its auctions when a winning bidder declares bankruptcy before it pays for the frequencies it has won at auction.

FCC v. NEXTWAVE PERSONAL COMMUNICATIONS INC.

Supreme Court of the United States, 2003.
537 U.S. 293.

JUSTICE SCALIA delivered the opinion of the Court.

In these cases, we decide whether § 525 of the Bankruptcy Code, 11 U.S.C. § 525, prohibits the Federal Communications Commission (FCC or Commission) from revoking licenses held by a debtor in bankruptcy upon the debtor's failure to make timely payments owed to the Commission for purchase of the licenses.

I

In 1993, Congress amended the Communications Act of 1934 to authorize the FCC to award spectrum licenses "through a system of competitive bidding." It directed the Commission to "promot[e] economic opportunity and competition" and "avoi[d] excessive concentration of licenses" by "disseminating licenses among a wide variety of applications, including small businesses [and] rural telephone companies." In order to achieve this goal, Congress directed the FCC to "consider alternative payment schedules and methods of calculation, including lump sums or guaranteed installment payments ... or other schedules or methods ..."

The FCC decided to award licenses for broadband personal communications services through simultaneous, multiple-round auctions. In accordance with [the statute,] it restricted participation in two of the six auction blocks (Blocks "C" and "F") to small businesses and other designated entities with total assets and revenues below certain levels, and it allowed the successful bidders in these two blocks to pay in installments over the term of the license.

Respondents NextWave Personal Communications, Inc., and NextWave Power Partners, Inc. (both wholly owned subsidiaries of NextWave Telecom, Inc., and hereinafter jointly referred to as respondent NextWave), participated, respectively, in the FCC's "C-Block" and "F-Block" auctions. NextWave was awarded 63 C-Block licenses on winning bids totaling approximately $4.74 billion, and 27 F-Block licenses on winning bids of approximately $123 million. In accordance with FCC regulations, NextWave made a downpayment on the purchase price, signed promissory notes for the balance, and executed security agreements that the FCC perfected by filing under the Uniform Commercial Code. The security agreements gave the Commission a first "lien on and continuing security interest in all of the Debtor's rights and interest in [each] License." In addition, the licenses recited that they were "conditioned upon the full and timely payment of all monies due pursuant to ... the terms of the Commission's installment plan as set forth in the Note and Security Agreement executed by the licensee," and that "[f]ailure to comply with this condition will result in the automatic cancellation of this authorization."

After the C-Block and F-Block licenses were awarded, several successful bidders, including NextWave, experienced difficulty obtaining financing for their operations and petitioned the Commission to restructure their installment-payment obligations. The Commission suspended the installment payments, and adopted several options that allowed C-Block licensees to surrender some or all of their licenses for full or partial forgiveness of their outstanding debt. It set a deadline of June 8, 1998, for licensees to elect a restructuring option, and of October 29, 1998, as the last date to resume installment payments.

On June 8, 1998, after failing to obtain stays of the election deadline from the Commission or the Court of Appeals for the District of Columbia Circuit, NextWave filed for Chapter 11 bankruptcy protection in New York. It suspended payments to all creditors, including the FCC, pending confirmation of a reorganization plan. NextWave initiated an adversary proceeding in the Bankruptcy Court, alleging that its $4.74 billion indebtedness on the C-Block licenses was avoidable as a "fraudulent conveyance" under § 544 of the Bankruptcy Code because, by the time the Commission actually conveyed the licenses, their value had declined from approximately $4.74 billion to less than $1 billion. The Bankruptcy Court agreed—ruling in effect that the company could keep its C-Block licenses for the reduced price of $1.02 billion—and the District Court affirmed. The Court of Appeals for the Second Circuit reversed, holding that, although the Bankruptcy Court might have jurisdiction over NextWave's underlying debts to the FCC, it could not change the conditions attached to NextWave's licenses. The Second Circuit also held that since, under FCC regulations, "NextWave's obligation attached upon the close of the auction," there had been no fraudulent conveyance by the FCC acting in its capacity as creditor.

Following the Second Circuit's decision, NextWave prepared a plan of reorganization that envisioned payment of a single lump sum to satisfy the entire remaining $4.3 billion obligation for purchase of the C–Block licenses, including interest and late fees. The FCC objected to the plan, asserting that NextWave's licenses had been canceled automatically when the company missed its first payment deadline in October 1998. The Commission simultaneously announced that NextWave's licenses were "available for auction under the automatic cancellation provisions" of the FCC's regulations. NextWave sought emergency relief in the Bankruptcy Court, which declared the FCC's cancellation of respondent's licenses "null and void" as a violation of various provisions of the Bankruptcy Code. Once again, the Court of Appeals for the Second Circuit reversed. Granting the FCC's petition for a writ of mandamus, the Second Circuit held that "[e]xclusive jurisdiction to review the FCC's regulatory action lies in the courts of appeals" under 47 U.S.C. § 402, and that since the reauction decision was regulatory, proclaiming it to be arbitrary was "outside the jurisdiction of the bankruptcy court." The

Second Circuit noted, however, that "NextWave remains free to pursue its challenge to the FCC's regulatory acts."

NextWave filed a petition with the FCC seeking reconsideration of the license cancellation, denial of which is the gravamen of the cases at bar. NextWave appealed that denial to the Court of Appeals for the D.C. Circuit pursuant to 47 U.S.C. § 402(b), asserting that the cancellation was arbitrary and capricious, and contrary to law, in violation of the Administrative Procedure Act, 5 U.S.C. § 706, and the Bankruptcy Code. The Court of Appeals agreed, holding that the FCC's cancellation of NextWave's licenses violated 11 U.S.C. § 525: "Applying the fundamental principle that federal agencies must obey all federal laws, not just those they administer, we conclude that the Commission violated the provision of the Bankruptcy Code that prohibits governmental entities from revoking debtors' licenses solely for failure to pay debts dischargeable in bankruptcy." We granted certiorari.

II

* * * Respondent contends, and the Court of Appeals for the D.C. Circuit held, that the FCC's revocation of its licenses was not in accordance with § 525 of the Bankruptcy Code.

Section 525(a) provides, in relevant part:

"[A] governmental unit may not . . . revoke . . . a license . . . to . . . a person that is . . . a debtor under this title . . . solely because such . . . debtor . . . has not paid a debt that is dischargeable in the case under this title. . . ."

No one disputes that the Commission is a "governmental unit" that has "revoke[d]" a "license," nor that NextWave is a "debtor" under the Bankruptcy Act. Petitioners argue, however, that the FCC did not revoke respondent's licenses "solely because" of nonpayment, and that, in any event, NextWave's obligations are not "dischargeable" "debt[s]" within the meaning of the Bankruptcy Code. They also argue that a contrary interpretation would unnecessarily bring § 525 into conflict with the Communications Act. We find none of these contentions persuasive, and discuss them in turn.

A

The FCC has not denied that the proximate cause for its cancellation of the licenses was NextWave's failure to make the payments that were due. It contends, however, that § 525 does not apply because the FCC had a "valid regulatory motive" for the cancellation. In our view, that factor is irrelevant. When the statute refers to failure to pay a debt as the sole cause of cancellation ("solely because"), it cannot reasonably be understood to include, among the other causes whose presence can preclude application of the prohibition, the governmental unit's motive in effecting the cancellation. Such a reading would deprive § 525 of all force. It is hard to imagine a situation in which a governmental unit would not have some further motive behind the cancellation—assuring the financial solvency of the licensed entity, or punishing lawlessness, or even (quite simply) making itself financially whole. Section 525 means nothing more or less than that the failure to pay a dischargeable debt must alone be the proximate cause of the cancellation—the act or event that triggers the agency's decision to cancel, whatever the agency's ultimate motive in pulling the trigger may be.

Some may think (and the opponents of § 525 undoubtedly thought) that there ought to be an exception for cancellations that have a valid regulatory purpose. Besides the fact that such an exception would consume the rule, it flies in the face of the fact that, where Congress has intended to provide regulatory exceptions to provisions of the Bankruptcy Code, it has done so clearly and expressly, rather than by a device so subtle as denominating a motive a cause. There are, for example, regulatory exemptions from the Bankruptcy Code's automatic stay provisions. And even § 525(a) itself contains explicit exemptions for certain Agriculture Department programs. These latter exceptions would be entirely superfluous if we were to read § 525 as the Commission proposes—which means, of course, that such a reading must be rejected.

B

Petitioners contend that NextWave's license obligations to the Commission are not "debt[s] that [are] dischargeable" in bankruptcy. First, the FCC argues that "regulatory conditions like the full and timely payment condition are not properly classified as 'debts' " under the Bankruptcy Code. In its view, the "financial nature of a condition" on a license "does not convert that condition into a debt." This is nothing more than a retooling of petitioners' recurrent theme that "regulatory conditions" should be exempt from § 525. No matter how the Commission casts it, the argument loses. Under the Bankruptcy Code, "debt" means "liability on a claim," and "claim," in turn, includes any "right to payment," We have said that "[c]laim" has "the broadest available definition," and have held that the "plain meaning of a 'right to payment' is nothing more nor less than an enforceable obligation, regardless of the objectives the State seeks to serve in imposing the obligation," In short, a debt is a debt, even when the obligation to pay it is also a regulatory condition. * * *

C

Finally, our interpretation of § 525 does not create any conflict with the Communications Act. It does not, as petitioners contend, obstruct the functioning of the auction provisions of 47 U.S.C. § 309(j), since nothing in those provisions demands that cancellation be the sanction for failure to make agreed-upon periodic payments. Indeed, nothing in those provisions even requires the Commission to permit payment to be made over time, rather than leaving it to impecunious bidders to finance the full purchase price with private lenders. What petitioners describe as a conflict boils down to nothing more than a policy preference on the FCC's part for (1) selling licenses on credit and (2) canceling licenses rather than asserting security interests in licenses when there is a default. Such administrative preferences cannot be the basis for denying respondent rights provided by the plain terms of a law. " '[W]hen two statutes are capable of co-existence, it is the duty of the courts, absent a clearly expressed congressional intention to the contrary, to regard each as effective.' " There being no inherent conflict between § 525 and the Communications Act, "we can plainly regard each statute as effective." And since § 525 circumscribes the Commission's permissible action, the revocation of NextWave's licenses is not in accordance with law. * * *

Subsequently, the FCC and NextWave agreed on a compromise: NextWave kept licenses in several major markets but returned the rest for reauctioning. In 2005, the frequencies were reauctioned for a little over $2 billion. As Justice Scalia suggests, the NextWave problem could have been eliminated (for the FCC) by eliminating installment payments and requiring full payment upfront. Why hasn't the FCC done that?

d) Auctions With Strings Attached

We noted earlier that an auction system does not confer broad property rights in the spectrum. Rather, it assigns *licenses* to use the frequencies in specified ways, with specified responsibilities. Except for broadcasting services, the obligations consist simply of a requirement to build out the planned system expeditiously and to provide the service defined by the general service classification to which the frequencies have been allocated. (Frequencies allocated to land mobile services cannot be use for maritime mobile, etc.) This does not mean that the user is not subject to regulatory obligations. Quite the contrary. Many licensees have obligations imposed on them by the nature of the service they provide. A wireless commercial common carrier such as Verizon, for instance, may be subject to a set of regulatory obligations for the service its licenses pertain to. But those obligations are usually defined uniformly for all providers of that particular service outside of the licensing process. Thus, when the auction process was adopted for selecting among competing applicants, it was not generally conceived as a process for defining or redefining the obligations—public interest, common carrier, or otherwise—imposed on licensees.

The Commission made an important exception to this general policy in designing an auction of frequencies in the 700 MHz band (the "700 MHz auction"). The band has been used by television broadcasters in order to permit simulcast programming during the transition from analog to digital format. The frequencies are scheduled to be returned to the FCC in 2009 for reallocation to advanced mobile wireless services. In advance of the formal return, the spectrum was auctioned to wireless service providers in early 2008. Under the auction plan, one block of frequencies that are allocated for advanced wireless broadband services are subject to a condition that consumers of the service be allowed to use a handset and applications of their choice subject to some carrier restrictions reasonably designed to protect the network. There is no such current requirement on mobile wireless providers, who specify what handsets can be used and place restrictions on the kinds of uses. We will examine this special condition in Chapter 10. Here we mention it only to illustrate the point that the auction is a means of distributing licenses, not open-ended property rights. This does raise a question, though, about policy-making generally. If open access is a good idea, why impose it on just those providers who use this particular block of frequencies? Is it ever a good idea to impose specific restrictions on specific licensees without applying them to the service (which is itself defined mostly by the obligations imposed on a *set* of licensees) more generally?

E. REFORMING SPECTRUM POLICY

The use of auctions worked a radical change in assignments of licenses to particular users, but they have not altered the structure of allocations policy for the reason noted above: the auction awards a license to use particular frequencies only within prescribed service categories. Although there is some movement toward auctioning some bands for use in multiple services, auctions to date have generally been service-specific. That means that one of the major benefits of auctioning spectrum—assuring it is put to its most valuable use—is short circuited by the service restrictions imposed on licensees. The auctions may change *who* gets to provide a specific service, but they do not directly affect the way in which allocations among general types of services are made. Those allocations continue to be made the "old fashioned way," which is to say by traditional administrative processes (rulemaking) in which the government decides where and how the frequencies will be used and allocates specified frequencies—usually large bands of frequencies—for those specific purposes and no other. In recent years, however, this approach to spectrum allocation has come under increasing scrutiny and criticism. The direction of frequency uses by government fiat now goes by the epithet "command and control," a term that is almost always used with a tone of disapproval. But exactly how command and control regulation should be modified, or what should take its place, is a matter of considerable debate. In the material that follows, we first review some general models of spectrum allocation policy, and then we turn to more specific proposals.

1. Spectrum Management Models

REPORT OF THE SPECTRUM RIGHTS AND RESPONSIBILITIES WORKING GROUP

FCC Spectrum Policy Task Force.
November 15, 2002.

* * *

SPECTRUM USAGE MODELS AND INCENTIVES FOR EFFICIENT USE OF SPECTRUM

* * *

"Command-and-Control" Model

The traditional process of spectrum management in the United States is referred to by some as the "command-and-control" model because of the strict control and oversight exercised by the government. The command-and-control model process involves four steps: allocation, adoption of service rules, assignment, and enforcement. In the allocation process, the Commission decides what types of uses it will permit in particular spectrum bands. Next, the Commission establishes service rules that specify the power limits, build-out requirements, and other rules for the service allocated in this band. The Commission then assigns licenses for use of the spectrum to specific parties through mechanisms such as first-come-first served licensing, lotteries, comparative hearings, or auctions. Finally, the Commission enforces its allocations, service rules, and assignments against the licensees and other users of the spectrum.

The Commission's task in applying the command-and-control model is enormous. The Commission must continually decide and revisit difficult technical questions concerning spectrum allocation, geographical coverage, system configuration, channelization, power flux density, coding, out-of-band emissions, and innumerable other technical criteria at discrete points in time. For allocations that cross international borders, the Commission must work with the National Telecommunications and Information Administration (NTIA), the Department of State, and the International Telecommunication Union (ITU) to coordinate domestic commercial proposals with government and multi-national uses. Meanwhile, rapid technological advances, changing consumer demands, and new market developments steadily erode the utility of spectrum-management decisions that the Commission made years prior to deployment.

Most commenters and workshop participants stressed the costs imposed by the command-and-control approach on licensees and the public, and argued that these costs could be substantially reduced by adopting a more market-oriented approach. One of these commenters characterized the traditional policy as "ultra-conservative," arguing that the Commission gives too much weight to the potential for interference, which burdens new entrants with restrictions and delays the introduction of new technology and competition to the public. Some questioned the Commission's ability to allocate resources efficiently even under the best of circumstances. In addition, various parties argued that, while the Commission has a process to consider transfers and assignments, the current approach is overly burdensome and makes it difficult for spectrum to move to its highest-valued use. These commenters contended that a well-functioning market for resources offers a level of efficiency that a centralized, bureaucratic approach can never match.

Several commenters, however, argued in favor of retaining a command-and-control approach to allocation for certain services on the grounds that more market-based alternatives, such as the exclusive use model, would undervalue or thwart the provision of some important services. Advocates for public-safety organizations contended that the benefits from providing their services cannot be measured in economic terms—arguing that one cannot put a price on safety or human life—and that the spectrum necessary for such services should not be subject to market mechanisms. Some private radio operators argued that they support the nation's industrial and commercial infrastructure, and therefore they should not have to face the greater risk that would accompany a move away from the status quo. Radio astronomy advocates feared that an allocation mechanism that does not include a significant government role will undervalue long-term scientific research projects that may offer significant social benefits but also require dedicated spectrum bands. Similarly, several satellite operators argued that moving to an exclusive use model may give too little weight to the public interest benefits of serving remote and rural areas and providing an alternative communications infrastructure for use in case of disasters. Broadcast commenters asserted that statutory public interest considerations and the free over-the-air nature of broadcasting service have limited applicability to market-based spectrum licensing models.

In other cases, parties asserted that transaction costs associated with assembling the spectrum for a communications network might make providing service prohibitively expensive. Satellite interests, for example, stated that the transaction costs of acquiring spectrum or landing rights through hundreds of seriatim rounds of competitive bidding around the globe would prevent the deployment of international satellite systems. Other parties asserted that specific spectrum bands are needed, and losing the rights to even a few bands could make international harmonization difficult or impossible. These commenters added that an exclusively market-based approach might create perverse incentives to game the international regulatory processes by encouraging nations to make disruptive "paper filings" for spectrum and orbital resources at the International Telecommunications Union. Accordingly, some of these commenters asserted the need for government involvement in overcoming market failures and prohibitively high transaction costs.

Finally, some have argued the physical properties of spectrum, combined with the peculiarities of network industries in general and wireless telecommunications in particular, may require a certain level of "command-and-control" in any spectrum model to avoid inefficient allocation. This argument maintained that characteristics such as consumption externalities that require a critical mass before a technology becomes useful, high switching costs that tend to "lock in" consumers to existing technologies, and large economies of scale all increase the potential for market failure and thus necessitate a higher level of regulatory involvement.

"Exclusive Use" Model

The "exclusive use" model, as discussed in this report, refers to a licensing model in which a licensee has rights that are exclusive, flexible, and transferable, and has specific responsibilities that come with this interest. Under an exclusive use model in its purest form, licensees acquire an interest in a frequency band that is similar to a fee simple interest in the spectrum, with the right granted being exclusive and perpetual, or nearly so. Few or no restrictions exist on the commodification of the spectrum, which allows for secondary market trading, with the spectrum holder's rights transferring with the sale or lease. In short, an exclusive use model provides that the licensee obtains rights to do everything within its assigned frequencies not expressly prohibited under the license. Finally, responsibilities also accompany rights to the spectrum, including technical rules that establish power and out-of-band emission limits. These responsibilities are the flip side of rights, indicating the level of power and potential interference licensees must tolerate from other operators, which corresponds to the rights of these other parties.

Parties who advocated granting exclusive rights to licensees argue that such an approach encourages investment. They indicated that business enterprises view any potential for interference as a danger, and that incumbents are deterred from investing in new technologies if they do not have exclusive rights to spectrum and do not know who might interfere with them in the future. Some economists favored the exclusive use model because it is built on the assumption that there is scarcity in the spectrum, at least at some times and some places. They asserted that this scarcity may be the result of limited access, or an excess of spectrum use relative to capacity. They explained that the exclusive use model promotes economic efficiency because its key characteristics—clearly defined rights, exclusivity, flexibility and transferability—are necessary for efficiently allocating any scarce resource among competing uses.

Participants representing parties interested in trading spectrum rights noted that transferability of rights would be critical in order to achieve efficient use of the spectrum. They claimed that the right to trade this resource would allow it to be moved to its highest valued use, which would help rectify the imbalance between spectrum shortages in some areas and surpluses in others. Rural carriers make similar arguments, noting that secondary markets may improve spectrum efficiency and enable providers to gain access to spectrum for use in rural markets.

Parties that opposed an exclusive use model argued that allocation based on giving exclusive interests to licensees in particular bands may not be the most efficient policy. These parties stressed the benefits of an approach based on shared use under a commons approach, with less emphasis on a purely exclusive use model. Other commenters argued that an exclusive use approach deters innovation because technology advances at least in part out of a need to make better use of resources, and licensees with exclusive use rights have guaranteed access to the spectrum resource. Several even challenged the assumption of scarcity, upon which the exclusive use model is built. Some commenters further opposed any creation of a quasi-property right in spectrum, arguing that such a step would be contrary to the Communications Act, detrimental to free speech, and a threat to economic competitiveness in communications markets.

Finally, some parties raised concerns about market failure that could accompany a strict application of an exclusive use model. Some feared that such a model might encourage commercial hoarding of spectrum rights that would exclude innovative, non-profit, public-service or other uses of the spectrum that benefit society as a whole. Also, they asserted that spectrum users who require immediate, but infrequent access to spectrum, such as public safety agencies, might be unable or unwilling to pay for commercially available services that could provide the same level of reliability in times of peak demand that their current services offer. In addition, they were concerned that spectrum users that require simultaneous operation over global geographic areas, such as satellite service providers, might not obtain internationally harmonized spectrum due to holdout by individual spectrum owners. Additionally, they observed that spectrum users that require the simultaneous use of large segments of spectrum, such as ultra wideband (UWB), or the short-term use of portions of a wide range of spectrum, such as software-defined radio (SDR), might never overcome the transaction costs necessary to gain access to spectrum to operate. They argue that SDR and similar technologies shrink the "frequency/time/space dimension that a user must occupy exclusively in order to communicate without interference," which in turn creates units "so small as to make the transaction costs involved in negotiating allocation of exclusive property rights to them prohibitive."

"Spectrum Commons" Model

In a spectrum commons model, spectrum is available to all users that comply with established technical "etiquettes" or standards that set power limits and other criteria for operation of unlicensed devices to mitigate potential interference. Usage rights are flexible, with minimal or no restrictions placed on the types of use of the spectrum. As is the case under the regulatory regime currently governing unlicensed Part 15 spectrum, there are no licenses and the primary allocation method for using the spectrum is akin to "first come, first served."

Supporters of the commons model argued that this approach leads to greater technological innovation and spectral efficiency than exclusive access: because no spectrum is exclusively held, spectrum commons users have incentives to create spectrally efficient frequency-hopping technologies, whereas licensed spectrum typically sits idle when the license-holder is not transmitting. Commons supporters also stressed that this model precludes warehousing of spectrum, which can create artificial scarcity and is a potential disadvantage of an exclusive use model. Furthermore, proponents of an open, commons approach claimed that spectrum scarcity might actually be reduced under such a regime because of the efficiency enhancing possibilities of new technologies (e.g., ad hoc networks) and the fundamentally different spectrum demands of architectures such as mesh networks.

Although there is some indication that a commons regime may not attract the same level of investment as an exclusive rights system, proponents also argued that the need for long-term capital investments in networks is reduced with this model because the innovation cycle is faster. In addition, attracting major amounts of financing may be less of an issue for systems such as mesh networks because capital costs are distributed among users (through smart receivers, for example) rather than being concentrated at central points of transmission as in traditional architectures. However, various parties noted that industries that do require large fixed investments might have trouble attracting capital or be hesitant to invest further because of the lack of guarantees against future interference. * * *

Other commenters argued that unlicensed spectrum should not be seen as a replacement for licensed spectrum, but akin to a public park, free for anyone to use. Under this approach, the Commission would use market-based mechanisms to sell exclusive use licenses, but also preserve some spectrum as an unlicensed spectrum commons for new or emerging technologies. Many commenters supporting this balanced approach also supported the allocation of additional unlicensed spectrum. Other parties support maintaining a licensed regime with the right of non-interfering technologies (such as spread spectrum, or UWB devices) to operate within the same band, rather than allocating separate unlicensed spectrum.

Application of the Three Models: The Story So Far

In most bands, the Commission has historically used variations of the traditional command-and-control approach to defining rights, in which spectrum is allocated and assigned for specific uses that are limited, often very narrowly, by regulation. More recently, the Commission has developed rules for certain bands that approximate the exclusive rights model, and rules for other bands that approximate the commons model, but it has not applied either model to significant portions of the spectrum, and has not used either model in a pure form.

The command-and-control approach has taken different forms over time. In many cases the Commission has arrived at a regulatory structure through an ad hoc process of accretion over the years, while in other cases it has used a less ad hoc process and has adopted an overall plan for all services in a band at the same time. Moreover, some usage regimes that have command-and-control features have allowed for considerably more usage flexibility than others. And, many licensing regimes involve "exclusive use" licenses of a more restricted form than the exclusive use model involving flexible usage rights discussed in [the section on the exclusive use model] above. * * *

The Commission has begun to move away from command-and-control to more flexible spectrum policies in recent years. In addition, the Commission has amended a variety of service rules to increase the flexibility of existing services. Among the many examples that could be cited are the Paging and Radiotelephone Services rules. Early technological and regulatory restrictions regarding the provision of one-way paging service have been eliminated and paging licensees are free to develop and implement new technologies and uses, including one-way messaging, two-way messaging, mobile data, and fixed wireless services. The Commission has also amended certain Part 15 rules several times in the last fifteen years to accommodate technological developments in spread spectrum technology. Nonetheless, broad applications of flexible rights policies have been adopted for only relatively limited portions of the spectrum.

To the extent that the Commission has adopted a flexible exclusive use approach to spectrum licensing, there is general consensus that the Commission's most successful application of this approach to date in terms of deployment of service has been broadband Personal Communications service (PCS), operating in the 1850–1910 MHz and 1930–1990 MHz bands. The PCS rules follow the exclusive use model quite closely: the Commission granted PCS licensees rights to large blocks of spectrum and allowed substantial flexibility in terms of technology and usage rights, subject only to interference parameters to protect neighboring geographic areas and adjacent spectrum blocks. There are no other users of the band other than fixed microwave incumbents, which are subject to mandatory relocation requirements. However, unlike the "pure" exclusive use model, the PCS rules do not allow for unrestricted flexibility of use, because the allocation precludes use of this spectrum for broadcasting. * * *

The Commission has also applied rules to several spectrum bands that resemble the commons model. The 2.4 GHz band (2402–2450 MHz), for example, is used on an open access, unlicensed basis by thousands of unlicensed consumer and industrial devices, including cordless phones, microwave ovens, and wireless LANs such as those using 802.11b and Bluetooth technology. The proliferation of Wi-Fi and similar technologies was not anticipated when the Commission's rules for unlicensed devices were established, but the open access and technical flexibility afforded by these rules (the primary constraint being the limitation of Part 15 devices to very low power) has allowed significant market-driven innovation. The popularity of the unlicensed 2.4 GHz band makes it clear that there is demand for a commons-type usage model for some spectrum, and that this model can work for several different sorts of services. The parallel to the "pure" commons model is not perfect, however, because the types of equipment used must be registered and operate under certain rules such as those regarding primary use rights and equipment standards. * * *

An examination of the flexible exclusive use and commons models as they have been applied to date suggests that each model has led to different types of technical and economic efficiencies. In broadband PCS, for example, licensees have developed centrally managed wireless networks that cover large geographic areas and accommodate large numbers of mobile customers. The licensing of multiple users has also led to significant competitive benefits in the CMRS market. Parties that have noted the success of PCS disagree about what has driven the innovations that we have seen in that service; some think they have been driven by investments in exclusive use, while others said that they had developed because of competition. It seems likely that in fact both factors have played an important role in the development of PCS. In any event, it does not appear that flexible exclusive use models have deterred the development of technologies and service in this instance. Although some commenters argue that exclusive use will not lead to technical innovations such as Wi-Fi, the PCS rules do not preclude licensees from developing low power Wi-Fi networks if they choose to. The fact that PCS licensees have not done so to date is likely due to the fact that (1) the PCS rules provide for flexibility and interference protection that enables licensees to develop higher-power system architectures, and (2) licensees face a higher opportunity cost with respect to their spectrum that makes such architectures a higher valued use.

In the Part 15 bands, where there are strict power limits and no interference protection, the opportunity cost of spectrum is reduced to a very low amount approaching zero, which forces spectrum users to channel their investment exclusively into developing robust low power technology that can function in this environment and continue to function as the environment grows more congested. The initial technologies that evolved in these bands were low power devices such as cordless phones and garage door openers. More recently, the Part 15 bands have been host to the emergence of "smart" low power devices that can support more sophisticated applications, including peer-to-peer networking. This has resulted in a significant surge of economic investment in these bands. However, the commons model may not offer sufficient certainty or reliability for other types of spectrum uses. For example, services requiring large upfront capital investments or users promising a certain standard of service to paid subscribers may not wish to take the risk of not knowing exactly where, when, and next to whom on the spectrum they can operate. Therefore, it is unlikely that a uniform approach to spectrum management can meet the very different needs of all spectrum users.

Looking Ahead: Applying Spectrum Use Models to the Future

"One Size Does Not Fit All"

* * *

In general, as the comments suggest, we recommend that the Commission base its spectrum policy on a balance of the three basic spectrum rights models outlined ... above: an exclusive use approach, a commons approach, and a command-and-control approach. We further recommend that the Commission fundamentally alter the existing balance among these models—which is dominated by legacy command-and-control regulation—by expanding the use of both the exclusive use and commons models throughout the radio spectrum, and limiting the use of the command-and-control model to those instances where there are compelling public policy reasons to continue using it. * * *

---

2. Beyond Models: Implementing Real Reforms

a) The Persistence of Command and Control

Although the FCC's Spectrum Rights and Responsibilities Working Group talks about balancing the three models, there appears to be a very strong consensus among participants in this debate that command and control needs to be dramatically reduced if not eliminated altogether. Yet after all that has been said and done about this, more has been said than done; the present system is still overwhelmingly command and control. The "spectrum task force report" points to examples of regulated flexibility in the case of PCS, where the service category allows some different uses; it also points to unregulated use in the case of very low power part 15 devices (in this connection the most noteworthy example would be WiFi and cordless phones). However, these and other examples of flexible or unregulated use are very modest exceptions to the rule of command and control, which prevails at virtually all levels of spectrum management. It continues to govern allocations among services in all but minor instances; it is the underpinning for retaining all licensing requirements, including auctioned licenses; it governs the allotments scheme for FM and television broadcasting (as well as satellite broadcasting).

What accounts for this persistence of a model that has been so widely criticized by those within and outside government? One answer might be that command and control protects existing licensees (and their investment in existing technology) against the threat posed by moving to a different regime. That answer seems to fit the conventional narrative of public-choice, but it is incomplete. Consider, for example, proposals to give existing licensees a full property right to use—or transfer—their currently licensed spectrum to *any* use. Surely that would enhance the rights of existing licensees, no? Consider a broadcast licensee operating a marginal UHF station in a large market. Presumably it is a profitable operation, but not necessarily a profit maximizing use of its 6 MHz channel. Alternative non-broadcast uses could very easily bring more reward—but under the current regime, which prevents the licensee from changing the service (or transferring the licenses to someone who will), the licensee cannot realize that extra value. Why wouldn't a rational commercial entity seek to maximize its profit by seeking a more expanded property right? Why wouldn't the entire television broadcast industry march arm-in-arm in support of expanded property rights?

Of course, there is the risk that in this case the broadcasters might also let the cat out of the bag: Broadcasters' free licenses are premised on the need for free television. How better to demonstrate that maintaining these frequencies for broadcasting really isn't a vital national interest than to have the broadcasters clamoring for the right to sell off their spectrum, much less to buyers who would change the service? At that point, someone (the FCC?) might get the idea that the broadcasters do not deserve to have a property right (or do not deserve to have one for zero payment). Conventional television broadcasters in particular occupy a huge swath of channels in the heartland of the VHF and UHF bands—more than 400 MHz of prime real estate. The broadcast industry has always fought any move to take away even *unused* portions of these allocations[9] and the core of its argument has always been that it is an imperative goal of communications policy to preserve free local television broadcast service. The fact that only about 14% of television households now rely on conventional broadcasting (more of this in Chapter 5 when we take up cable and satellite media) has put some strains on this argument, but both Congress and the FCC have continued to accept it. Could that argument be sustained if broadcasters were given (and exercised) the right to transfer their channels to non-broadcast services?

Too, a departure from the status quo of command and control might not lead to robust exclusive property rights; it might lead to an open access commons. It probably goes without saying that, for existing licensees—including especially broadcast licensees sitting on premium frequency space—would not be thrilled at the prospect of having to share their space with others. We consider this shortly.

9. The broadcasters haven't always been successful. In the 1970s, the uppermost 12 UHF television channels were reallocated to land mobile, where they provided the frequency foundation for cellular telephony. Most recently, another block of UHF television channels (channels 52–69) are to be reallocated from television to wireless systems in 2009. What is perhaps most remarkable, however, is not that these channels are being reallocated, but that for more than four decades this block of frequencies was basically held in limbo with only the slimmest chance that they would ever find an economically viable use in television. Not until plans were made in the 1990s to shift from analog to digital were these frequencies licensed, and then only as a means of allowing existing television stations to broadcast on two separate channels while they transitioned to digital.

b) Expanded Property Rights vs. Expanded Commons

While command and control continues to dominate the practice of spectrum management, most of the debate has shifted to choosing between the alternatives of exclusive use/private property rights (expanded to cover rights to the spectrum itself and not to limited licenses) and commons. These alternatives are rarely presented as one-step leaps, but rather as alternative directions for a series of moves. A sample of the debate about which direction to take is provided in the following two excerpts.

THOMAS W. HAZLETT, THE WIRELESS CRAZE, THE UNLIMITED BANDWIDTH MYTH, THE SPECTRUM AUCTION FAUX PAS, AND THE PUNCHLINE TO RONALD COASE'S "BIG JOKE": AN ESSAY ON AIRWAVE ALLOCATION POLICY

14 Harv. J.L. & Tech. 335, 544–53 (2001).

The possible scenarios for spectrum liberalization are diverse, so this paper offers a series of reforms in three doses: Small, Medium, and Large. All are advanced as normative policy improvements; implementation strategy and international considerations are beyond the scope of this essay.

A. Small

1. Spectrum Registry

It is difficult to ascertain how spectrum is used in the United States. This is somewhat surprising; given the regulatory rigidities of the block allocation system, one might think that the precise nature of each band would be easily discernible. Just the reverse is true. The official log maintained by the FCC, the "Table of Frequency Allocations," offers only a vague zoning guide. It lists broad classifications, which often overlap, and does not indicate actual uses, intensity of traffic, or other operational information. Hence, it does not reveal unoccupied or underutilized frequency space. Legal and engineering firms specializing in researching spectrum allocation exist, but costs deter innovation.

Firms specialize in the investigation of allocation information. These firms, and others, ought to be given the opportunity to bid to create a spectrum registry that actually reveals what the Spectrum Inventory Table purports to contain—"information on how the radio spectrum is used in the United States so that you can select the most appropriate spectrum to support your needs and determine the impact of your proposed deployment on existing operations." Computerized and accessible online, this would lower the costs of entrants seeking to use radio waves in innovative applications. The registry created by the Guatemalan Superintendent of Telecommunications might serve as a model. The system should be so transparent, user-friendly, and rich in detail that journalists could access the database and report on spectrum allocation trade-offs to the general public. It is not necessary to devise such a system a priori. Competing vendors would bid to design and operate the mapping function.

2. Privatize Public Safety Communications

Vital radio services could best be provided by market mechanisms, improving both the communications available to selected groups *and* the resources available to such groups. These added resources could fund further advancements in telecommunications or other services of value to constituents.

A remedy is to cede title to radio bands to public safety agencies. Local and state agencies, removed from block allocation restrictions, would be free to innovate. Quality improvements via re-allocation, similar to that engineered on the SMR band by Fleet Call/Nextel in 1991, would naturally follow. Federal, state or local governments could also invite private firms to submit bids to meet particular public safety needs. Competitive bidding lowers costs, thereby introducing efficient technologies. * * *

3. Create a Federal Spectrum Budget

A vast portion of available radio space is consumed by federal (including military) use. There is little disagreement that public sector spectrum use is inefficient because no incentives exist to make it otherwise. If an agency manages to save bandwidth, it is not rewarded. Indeed, the agency budget is taxed because investments in spectrum-saving technology are costly. The result is that governmental units do not economize on scarce spectrum inputs. Hence, equipment used in various public operations could be improved to deliver better service while making spectrum available for alternative uses.

In recent years, Congress has directed the Department of Commerce to identify various quantities of bandwidth to transfer to the FCC for re-allocation from federal to private use. For instance, the PCS allocation of 140 MHz came from the so-called Emerging Technologies Band, 220 MHz transferred to the FCC's jurisdiction by legislation. This ad hoc method, in which an act of Congress orders agencies to transfer a politically mandated quantity of bandwidth, is a mechanism for identifying underutilized frequencies. It is extremely cumbersome, political, and ad hoc. A more systematic method of evaluating government-controlled spectrum bands would deliver very substantial public benefits.

Privatizing radio spectrum rights would remedy this situation. Government would buy (or rent) the spectrum it desires to use at market prices. The government chooses to purchase all manner of vital inputs—from nuclear reactors, to labor, to Air Force fighter jets—rather than procure them by force. Mission critical supplies are not only available from the private sector, they are more efficiently obtained when competitively produced. The logic extends to radio services. * * *

B. MEDIUM

1. Overlay Rights—Use the Pressler Plan to Liberate the TV Band

The 1996 Pressler proposal prescribed full flexibility for existing licensees coupled with the issuance of exhaustive overlay licenses in the TV band. Overlay rights, patterned after PCS licenses, would permit entrants to use the TV band so long as existing wireless communications were respected. The approach builds on existing rules and standards, but it effectively frees bandwidth for uses valued by consumers. The components of this plan are as follows:

Grant existing wireless licensees complete flexibility. Since implicit interference contours have already been created in the allocation used to license broadcasters, deregulation is most straightforward here. The FCC will simply allow existing licensees to provide any service via any technology as long as the interference parameters currently in place are not abrogated. The transition to new services will lead users to request clarifications, as well as to demand new emission boundaries. These are analogous to emission boundary questions raised by a de novo entrant. The existence of licensed operators, however, should allow negotiated settlements among adjacent users. The Commission should implement arbitration procedures to facilitate efficient adjudication of disputes.

Overlay rights exhaustively license TV band. The TV band encompasses 402 MHz of prime, VHF/UHF radio spectrum (sixty-seven channels allocated 6 MHz each). The average U.S. television market (weighted by households) receives thirteen analog TV station broadcasts. Each television station received an additional channel for DTV in 1997. Analog channel licenses are scheduled for return to the FCC in 2006. [Eds. Now slated for February 2009.] The transition (and analog return) is delayed, however, wherever less than 85% of the local households are unable to receive DTV. Given this, it is likely that the transition will be delayed some years beyond 2006 because only 200,000 households (of over 100 million TV households) had purchased DTV-compatible sets as of mid–2000. If TV stations keep both their analog and digital channel licenses indefinitely, only twenty-six 6 MHz channels will be occupied in the average U.S. market. That leaves forty-four (67–23) channels available for reallocation. Still, that process, when done by the FCC's central planning mechanism, takes years and results in prolonging the rigidities found in block allocation. A superior solution is to auction a number of national licenses—say five—with overlay rights. High bidders would win the right to use an 80.4 MHz band to provide any non-interfering service, from broadcast TV or radio to subscription telephone or Internet access. This would unleash an enormous swath of productive radio spectrum into the marketplace and allow the United States to begin catching up (in particular) in the global race to 3G.

2. Underlay right—use an innovative scheme to unleash UWB

The overlay rights concept has a corollary. Underlay rights could give entrants the right to conduct low-power emissions beneath existing users. These operators would utilize the untapped communications capacity in the "noise floor" as sophisticated systems filter out background interference. Rights could be exclusive over a particular frequency block, or be non-exclusive. In the latter instance, a finite number of operators could co-exist in a band, communicating underneath preexisting high-power emissions. Power limits would be set such that existing high-power communications proceed without material degradation. Underlay users co-existing in the same band, or across bands, could coordinate and partition capacity, subject to antitrust oversight.

The shared arrangement would differ from open access in that underlay rights would be limited in number, with each controlling access to a fixed level of low-power emissions within a band. Unrestricted entry makes user coordination problematic. Lacking spectrum rights, actions taken by parties to economize on available spectrum are threatened. Free riders can appropriate the benefits of efficient resource management. Underlay rights could remedy this by allowing owners to determine how a given low-power space is used. Technologies and services could then be crafted such that optimal band use would be achievable; under- and over-exploitation both represent wealth losses to rights holders. With rights fully flexible and transferable, such rights would likely be acquired by UWB technology owners and licensed to manufacturers and/or service operators by contract.

Incumbent operators could yet deter UWB by raising the specter of interference. Under the public interest standard, the argument is essentially free. The only cost-benefit weighting is political, and the politics favor incumbents. UWB has, in fact, been delayed for over a decade while various interests (including NASA and the Federal Aviation Administration) complain that the technology will interfere with important public safety communications. In a more liberal regime, interference is resolved by entrant liability. Proof of financial viability—sufficient to indemnify for potential damages—would substitute for FCC adjudication of interference disputes. Entry would be permitted upon issuance of a credible guarantee that existing users in a band would not suffer material harm as per the transmissions of a UWB entrant. Such operators would compensate parties that do, in fact, suffer harm. Such an approach encourages private testing and the emergence of a competitive certification market. Insurers, contracting with laboratories and engineering firms, would engage in due diligence before assuming liabilities. Products would need to satisfy scientific scrutiny, establishing credibility with investors guaranteeing that UWB use does indeed fit *under* existing communications.

C. Large

1. Abolish the FCC and replace it with a Spectrum Court

* * * The FCC's marketplace is increasingly dominated by the likes of Intel, Cisco, Microsoft, Qualcomm, Nokia, Lucent, Compaq, H–P,

AT&T, Sun, AOL, Nortel Networks, Oracle, Sycamore, Akamai, and Motorola. These are the most unpredictable network builders on the planet, and the economic structures they (and a multitude of competitors to be named later) are constructing will not conform to the guidelines of an FCC rule making. The long-run equilibrium is clear: The FCC will cease to exist. The questions are when and how.

"Soon" and "In favor of a Spectrum Court" are the *A*+ answers. Once a spectrum registry is established, the next step is to invite new entrants into whatever vacant spectrum space they can find. Of course, abolition of FCC spectrum regulation would eliminate the public interest standard for gaining access to radio waves. It should be superceded by a statutory declaration that all non-interfering entry is lawful and that private property rights to radio waves may be registered with the Spectrum Court. The common law rule of priority-in-use, building on institutions and practices of wireless providers under the existing regime, would govern spectrum allocation. The following measures are appropriate:

Grant de novo entrants a presumptive right to use unoccupied frequencies. Remove any burden for establishing a "public interest" in enhanced competitive entry. Allow new competitors to access unoccupied, or underutilized, bands by petitioning the regulatory authority and claiming an interest in such usage. The Commission would have a fixed (short) time to allow responses and a fixed (short) time to resolve interference disputes by binding arbitration. (No other opposition is allowed.) Wherever multiple requests are made for the same bandwidth, auctions will assign rights. Strict time limits will again apply.

Local area wireless devices are permissible. As long as low-power devices are localized, creating material signal degradation only within the user's immediate jurisdiction, unregulated use is permissible. Manufacturers should be liable for damages, but the ability of an individual household or office to internalize damage to alternative uses of the spectrum removes the necessity for imposing truly local spectrum ownership rights.

Grant complete flexibility to existing licensees. Remove regulatory constraints on licensees. The implied bandwidth contours remain. Any service the licensee can profitably supply is legal, as long as transmissions stay within the implied emission boundaries of the original radio station authorization.

Pure interference adjudication. As FCC experience has shown, the degree to which parties can agree on interference standards is surprising when it is not profitable to quibble. The United States now has a long history of technical rulings establishing the substance of reasonable protections in spectrum use, and this body of precedent can form the basis of spectrum property law. The essential reform is to abandon administrative authorizations to operate "radio stations" in favor of private ownership of frequencies. Band owners will have profit incentives to maximize the competitive value of their airspace. Included in that maximization calculus will be proper incentives to protect against interference, presenting cogent arguments to courts as to what degree of protection is warranted. A technically sophisticated Spectrum Court, perhaps initially composed of administrative law judges from a defunct FCC, could serve as the venue for such claims. An important aspect of such proceedings is that entrants could gain a right to proceed with allegedly interfering transmissions before final adjudication wherever they assume liability for damages. Indeed, parties indemnifying themselves against damage claims should be given wide latitude to provide service, as liability will privatize interference adjudication, increasing efficiency. * * *

YOCHAI BENKLER, SOME ECONOMICS OF WIRELESS COMMUNICATIONS

16 Harv. J.L. & Tech. 25, 47–68 (2002).

While it is common to talk about optimizing "spectrum use," a more neutral definition of what we should optimize is *the capacity of users to communicate information without wires*. Focusing on "spectrum" leads one to measure how many bits-meters are being transmitted per hertz. As Part III explains, this is only one relatively simple and inefficient way of describing the problem of how to allow people to communicate information without wires. The question that must be answered is whether there are any systematic reasons to believe that markets in property rights in spectrum will be better at delivering this desideratum, or whether it would better be served by markets in equipment that does not depend on secured rights to specified bands.

The answer is, fundamentally, that we do not know, but we have very good reasons to think that open wireless networks will be more efficient, all things considered, than networks based on a spectrum property rights approach. Now, this is saying both a lot and a little. It is saying a lot because much of current economic commentary on spectrum policy and the *zeitgeist* at the FCC assumes with certainty that we do know the answer—that is, that property rights in spectrum allocations are the optimal approach to attain wireless communications efficiency. This is false, and to say that the reigning conception of current policy debates is false is saying a lot. It is saying a little, however, because we do not yet have a good enough understanding, either theoretical or practical, of the limits on the scalability, efficiency, and growth rate potential of open wireless networks, and so we cannot be certain that at some point introducing a pricing element tagged to the bandwidth used will not improve on a purely commons-based approach. We can, however, outline a series of considerations that tend to suggest that open wireless networks will be more efficient than wireless systems that must be designed around property rights in bands of frequencies. We can also suggest why even if pricing would sometimes be useful, it will only be useful if designed to provide for peak utilization overload relief rather than as a baseline attribute of all wireless communication.

Ironically, the most important reason to doubt the efficacy of property rights in spectrum is rooted in the work of Ronald Coase, the very economist whose incisive critique of the spectrum-licensing regime gave birth to the economists' critique of the old model of spectrum regulation. Coase's Nobel Prize in economics was founded on his introduction of the concept of transaction costs. He explained that using markets to solve problems—like organizing labor and resources into productive combinations, or deciding who among different possible claimants should use a given resource—is a costly exercise. One has to define the rights in resources, collect information about who is doing what, and how much they value things; one has to get parties together to transact; and one has to enforce both rights and agreements. When these costs make market transactions too expensive to solve a resource allocation problem, other mechanisms must do so. Firms and managers who decide which worker uses which raw materials and which machines and judges deciding who among competing parties should get an entitlement are instances he used in his two most important articles to show how institutions emerge to allocate resources when markets are too expensive to use for this purpose. * * *

Overhead: transaction costs and administrative costs. The most important transaction costs associated with open wireless networks are expressed as the network management overhead that devices need to use in order to coordinate their communications. The most important transaction costs associated with spectrum property-based markets are those entailed by the need to negotiate clearance of permissions to transmit in a specified bandwidth. The primary administrative costs of the property system are the definition and judicial enforcement of the property rights. The primary administrative costs of the open wireless system are the standards setting processes and the administrative enforcement of equipment compliance with them. * * *

There are two primary reasons for the central importance of dynamic adaptation to the efficiency of wireless communications systems. First, wireless communications capacity is mostly determined by local conditions, such as who is trying to communicate in a relatively small geographic space, or whether there are leafy trees between two nodes, and which way they are swaying, etc. Second, human communications are highly variable, even over large-scale networks and time frames, and certainly where the relevant demand exists in geographically small areas and for brief time frames. The capacity of a system will be heavily dependent on whether it can design its wireless communications network dynamically to take advantage of changing conditions, or whether it adapts more slowly. To the extent that dynamic adaptation is important, open wireless networks are likely to outperform networks that rely on proprietary spectrum, because the dynamic adaptability of the latter is more limited by transaction costs.

As I explained in the technical description, open wireless approaches rely on intelligent devices that constantly reconfigure the network architecture, the power used, and the frequency bands used—both in terms of total bandwidth used and in terms of specific frequencies used—to fit the dynamically changing environment and usage patterns. Property rights and pricing mechanisms that are attached to spectrum allocations–that is, to a particular band of frequencies—burden this dynamic adaptation of wireless networks by making the bandwidth parameter "sticky." That is, bandwidth is one parameter that, unlike computation, architecture, and power, cannot be changed unilaterally and locally by the network of intelligent devices. It requires a transaction. A shift to a different range of frequencies or a different bandwidth entails identifying who the owner is, finding the lowest cost frequency set that would fulfill the needs of the system at that moment, negotiating a transaction, and shifting to the new spectrum for the specified time slot. * * *

In the most technologically sophisticated version of the property rights argument, Faulhaber and Farber[*] recognize the fact that transaction costs (which they call direct) of a spectrum property system are higher than the transaction costs of an open wireless approach, or a spectrum commons. Indeed, it is to solve this problem that they propose a modified property system, rather than one based on perfect rights of exclusion. Their preferred regime implies into all property rights in spectrum a public "easement" that permits anyone, anywhere, to transmit at any frequency as long as they do not interfere with the owner of the right to transmit in that frequency. This modified property regime is intended to permit very wide-band communications that are "below the noise floor" given the operating parameters of the devices that operate with the property owner's permission in the frequencies they utilize, as well as agile radios that occupy frequencies only when their owner is not using them, and as soon as the owner wants to transmit, hop to a different, unused frequency. While Faulhaber and Farber agree that direct transaction costs are likely to be higher in either of the property-based approaches than in a commons-based approach, they do not attempt to specify the effect of these transaction costs. It is important to emphasize that these transaction costs go precisely to limit the capacity of the spectrum property system to do the one thing that potentially could make it more efficient than open wireless networks—that is, to identify accurately competing values that users place on communications, and to adjust the price of bandwidth accordingly. The important measure of the transaction costs is the extent of the deviation they cause from efficient pricing in the spectrum property-based system. The more that transaction costs cause the spectrum property system to utilize prices that reflect statistical judgments about competing usage patterns, rather than actual real-time bids, the less of a value there is in these systems as compared to an open wireless system that treats all communications equally and will drop high and low value communications with equal probability, but will drop fewer communications in total.

* Eds. Gerald R. Faulhaber and David J. Farber, *Spectrum Management: Property Rights, Markets, and the Commons*, in RETHINKING RIGHTS AND REGULATIONS: INSTITUTIONAL RESPONSES TO NEW COMMUNICATIONS TECHNOLOGIES (L. Cranor And S. Wildman, eds 2003).

Faulhaber and Farber are also quite cognizant not only of the internal limits that the transaction costs associated with spectrum property rights impose on that system's own efficiency, but also of the externalities that implementing such a system would cause, in terms of the constraints it would place on the technological evolution of efficient open wireless networks. Recall, the problem is that the number of rights holders that a transmitter-receiver pair must negotiate with in order to pull together the right to transmit in a band, say, 10 GHz wide, is so great that as a practical matter this mode of communication will be unavailable under a pure spectrum property rights approach. They recognize this as a problem akin to what has come to be known as the "anticommons" problem, that is, a particularly virulent version of the Coasian problem of inefficient design or allocation of rights in the presence of high transaction costs. Rights are so fragmented relative to the efficiently usable contours of a resource that the transaction costs of assembling a usable resource out of these fragments are too high to permit any assembling to occur, causing stasis. Faulhaber and Farber offer two types of solutions to this problem. First, they claim that because of the easement they postulate in their modified property regime, that is, the right of anyone to transmit in any frequency as long as that person is not interfering with the licensed user/owner, anyone will be able to transmit the 10 GHz wide signal as long as that person is "below the noise floor." Second, to the extent that communications that would interfere with other devices are desired, those communications should be permitted in bands purchased for this purpose by the federal or even state or local governments, or perhaps by manufacturers of open wireless network equipment who are seeking to make the market in their equipment more attractive to consumers. * * *

The level of non-cooperating radiation in any given band affects the extent to which a system needs processing and cooperation gain to achieve a certain rate of information delivery through an open wireless network. The more radiation there is, the greater the complexity of the solution to the problem of communicating information through the channel. The greater the complexity of a system, the greater the cost of the equipment needed to implement it. Holding all other things equal, if you permit *only* open wireless systems to operate in a given range of frequencies, they will be able to achieve a given throughput at lower cost than they could if they need to achieve the same throughput in the presence of high-powered communications. Therefore, while the modified property right is much better than the perfect property rights regime in that it does not completely prohibit open wireless systems, it still imposes a burden on the development of those systems. Perhaps the proponents of spectrum property rights are correct, and that burden is socially justified given the relative value of both types of approaches—the proprietary and the open—to wireless communications. But the modified property right does not allow us to have our cake and eat it too. We must still choose how much of each type of wireless communications facility we will have.

The suggestion that federal, state, or local government bodies will buy spectrum to create parks is a surprisingly naïve proposal from two such sophisticated authors. If one were to think that Congress and the federal government were rational decision makers who operate to optimize the public good with the same efficiency as, say, any large corporation maximizes the benefits to its shareholders, this might not fundamentally be a mistaken approach. But the notion that Congress is equally likely to appropriate *x* dollars already in the Treasury as it is to forgo potential revenue by refraining from auctioning the spectrum, particularly under the politically palatable heading of reserving it for a public trust, is surprising. As a matter of treating the government as a rational agent responding to real costs, forgoing *x* millions of dollars by refraining from auctioning the spectrum is identical to spending that amount of money after the spectrum is sold. As a matter of practical politics, they are not similar in the least. I suspect that the rationale behind this aspect of the Faulhaber and Farber proposal has more to do with the integrity of the transition policy—that is, with the Big Bang auction that is intended to launch the property system. But this is a transition policy that would result in substantially lower public investment in space for open wireless networks than might a differently-framed public debate, and the transition policy should not be allowed to preempt the outcome of such a controversial policy question.

As for administrative costs, or what Faulhaber and Farber call "indirect transaction costs," they suggest that the open wireless approach has the highest indirect costs, because uncertainty as to what equipment is "interfering" or complying with the open protocols and what is not will be confusing and difficult (and hence costly) for courts to sort out, and will lead to much litigation. They claim that the pure property regime will have the lowest indirect costs because courts are most adept at solving property rights disputes. And they see their own preferred modified property regime as having higher administrative costs than pure property because the boundary between the easement and the property rights will lead to difficult litigation. However they see their preferred modified property regime as having lower administrative costs than those of open systems because courts, familiar with property disputes, will find a property framework easier to design and enforce than an open system.

This view of the administrative costs takes a somewhat more rosy view of property litigation and a more dim view of administrative equipment certification and private standard setting than I would. All one need do is look at the decades-long history of some of the cases that I teach every year in my first-year property course to see that courts do indeed resolve property disputes—but to say that they will do so efficiently because of their experience with real property is somewhat optimistic. It is important in this regard to see that disputes about use of open wireless networks will occur not with regard to property-type claims, but with regard to equipment compliance with standards. Here, standards can be set for whole industries by open processes like the

Institute of Electrical and Electronics Engineers ("IEEE") or World Wide Web Consortium ("W3C") standard-setting processes. The FCC can then certify equipment as it does now on a Part 15 model. In all these cases, the administrative costs are incurred, but once incurred apply industry wide, and can be enforced against non-complying equipment fairly simply by engineering tests of the equipment. This is by no means a costless exercise for dispute resolution, but it is vastly cheaper and more certain than relying, say, on the owner of property rights in 724–744 MHz in Des Moines, Iowa, to sue the owner of 745–747 MHz in one neighborhood there for using a particular antenna configuration, with the owners of 748–768 MHz and 712–723 MHz as third-party intervenors, and then on courts of appeal to resolve conflicts between how the Iowa court and another court, say adjudicating similar claims in the 2 GHz band in Memphis, Tennessee, decided the case by applying the *sic utere tuo ut alienum non laedaes* maxim rather than *damnum absque injuria*.

More generally, others who have written in favor of property rights in spectrum have treated "property" as being anti-regulation, and commons as being regulation by the back door. The dichotomy between the two in this regard is, however, overstated. In order to have efficient property rights, it is necessary to define, enforce, and update the definition of the content of property rights. These are all functions that require thoughtful institutional design, initially through Congress, and later through enforcement agencies or courts. * * * Property rights can be defined or interpreted in an inefficient and corrupt manner, as can commons-oriented regulatory processes. The trick in setting up either arrangement will be to make sure that they are designed so as not to allow the re-creation of command-and-control regulation through the back door. In the case of commons, the way to do this is probably by improving the Part 15 model of equipment certification so that any sharing protocol and design that is approved by an open standard-setting process gets fast-track approval, and these designs can in turn provide reasonably well-known benchmarks against which to measure proprietary standards that seek certification.

B. Pricing, Block Allocations, QoS, and the Big Bang

The transaction costs analysis suggests three additional observations with regard to the policy implications of the potential value of pricing. Recall that the efficiency with which open wireless networks can provide wireless communications capacity does not necessarily mean that there will never be situations where pricing of bandwidth can improve the efficiency of communication. It is possible that when demand exceeds capacity of a given network of devices, as deployed in a given locale at a given time, introducing pricing will improve allocation of whatever capacity is attainable by the network of devices in place. Three points need to be made with regard to this observation, however. First, the introduction of pricing does not itself support the creation of property rights in blocks of spectrum, as compared to a single fluid market exchange in spectrum on the model proposed by Eli Noam. Second, even if some quality of service ("QoS") assurance is attainable through the introduction of pricing, that still does not mean that the game is worth the candle—that is, that the cost and implications of introducing a pricing system for assuring QoS is worth the social cost of setting up the pricing system. The experience of wired networks suggests otherwise. Whether it is or is not is a question that is most likely to be determined empirically over time, as we get better information about wireless network usage and capacity given the presence of open wireless networks. Third, whatever the possible merits of pricing, they do not merit, based on our present knowledge, a "Big Bang" auction of all spectrum, but at most the dedication of some bands to provide pricing to handle peak utilization periods. * * *

---

c) *Brave New Worlds of Technology*

Somewhere between a full-throated exclusive property rights regime on the one hand and an open access commons on the other is the possibility of what Hazlett and others have called "overlay" and "underlay" rights and others, most notably Faulhaber and Farber, have called a "non-interfering easement," a proposal to which Benkler responds in the above excerpt. There are different versions of how these easements/overlay/underlay rights would be implemented, but the common idea underlying all of them is to make all frequency licenses—whether or not they are labeled property rights—subject to use by others on a non-interfering basis.

Overlay rights involve re-assigning unused spectrum in a way that avoids interference, not only to unlicensed uses but also licensed users. In fact the Commission has sometimes allowed channel sharing on such a basis. For example, land mobile users have been licensed to use UHF frequencies that were allocated to the broadcast service but were not allotted to a particular city; in that city the FCC licensed the mobile users. Overlay rights present new options for more efficient use of the spectrum, but they rely on continued regulatory coordination between primary and secondary uses. Underlay rights present the more radical departure from command and control.

The typical conception of an underlay right is the use of low-power devices that have technological constraints designed to minimize interference—wideband or cognitive radio devices (on which more below) are the usual examples. Overlay rights would be similarly used on a non-interference basis. However, the usual conception of underlay rights is the use of unlicensed devices—so-called "part 15" devices because their un-licensed status is regulated by Part 15 of Title 47 of the Code of Federal Regulations—so low-powered that they operate below the noise floor of, and thus avoid interfering with, high-powered, licensed uses. Unlike overlay rights, a central part of the argument presented for underlay rights is the use of new technologies designed to minimize interference in radio users sharing common frequency bands, and so an understanding of the various technologies underlying the underlay concept is helpful.

One set of technologies that involve new means of transmitting signals over wideband channels. Conventional transmissions involve "narrowband" emissions in which the signal is confined to a discrete band of contiguous frequencies dedicated to that transmission. Interference is avoided by segregating signals, through channel separation, power limitations, and geographic separations. In the case of wideband transmissions, the signal is spread out over a broad band of frequencies at low powers that cannot be detected by narrow-band receivers.

Wideband is really two related but distinct methods of transmission: spread spectrum and ultra-wideband (UWB). Spread spectrum technology has been in use since the early 1940s. It was first invented (and patented by actress Hedy Lamarr) as a means of enabling secure communications in wartime by spreading the information of a signal over a broad range of frequencies. There are two spread spectrum modes, frequency-hopping spread-spectrum (FHSS) and direct-sequence spread spectrum (DSSS). In the former, an information signal modulates a radio frequency carrier that hops from frequency to frequency in concert with a receiver according to a preset code. In direct sequence systems, the information data stream is combined with a high speed digital spreading code that produces a radio signal that is spread over a bandwidth broader than required by the signal. These engineering distinctions between the two modes are irrelevant for our purposes, however. What is important is that spreading the information over a broad frequency band allows transmissions at very low energy levels that cause the signals to be indistinguishable from background noise. That was what makes them secure for military communications. The same feature also reduces the possibility of interference (at most they appear to other receivers as background noise). Ultra-wideband is a cognate technology. It too spreads the information over a wide band of frequencies, but in different fashion. In conventional spread-spectrum techniques, the signals are continuous-wave forms that are modulated with a fixed carrier frequency. In UWB communications, on the other hand, there is no carrier frequency; the signal to be transmitted is converted to very short pulses that are transmitted over an extremely wide bandwidth. (The spread of the bandwidth used is much greater for UWB—several gigahertz as opposed to a megahertz for spread spectrum.) UWB is used for short-range radar and imaging as well as for communications. As with spread spectrum, the power density of the pulses is so low that, to non-wideband receivers, it appears as background noise.

The potential for interference-free transmissions is bi-directional: wideband transmitters do not cause direct interference with narrowband transmissions and in turn do not suffer interference from them. In ideal conditions, then, by minimizing interference, wideband facilitates sharing of frequency bands, which in turn promises more complete utilization of the spectrum. The operative phrase is "in ideal conditions." In fact, all transmitted energy can increase the "noise floor," which eventually degrades the communications environment. For this reason, there has been a resistance to the idea of building spectrum commons structure on the basis of these technologies. The Commission has authorized unlicensed use under part 15 of its rules for a variety of wideband devices. These include familiar communications devices such as wireless LANs (or WiFi), Bluetooth, and cordless telephones (which now commonly use use spread spectrum), as well as non-communications devices such as imaging and radar devices (for UWB).[10] However, the FCC places strict limits on scope of the commons in order to protect licensed users against interference. The power limits on unlicensed devices place very stringent limitations on their ability to provide a fully competitive alternative to narrow-band communications. They can serve an important complementary role, as anyone who has struggled to find WiFi "hot spots" to surf the Internet knows.

The use of unlicensed WiFi can be enhanced by so-called "mesh networks." A mesh network operates somewhat in the fashion of a cell phone network. Low power signals are relayed among multiple nodes (which might be either computers or smart phones) until they reach a network access point. The mesh network has some obvious drawbacks. First, since the WiFi devices use very low power, its effective use depends on a high density of devices in the area. Second, the users of the devices must be willing to leave their devices on when not otherwise in use for the purpose of enabling the relay. Third, there are security problems (though these are present with any wireless communications).

Another technology that has been frequently touted is so-called "cognitive radio" or "smart radio" or "software defined radio." Conventional radio devices are designed with fixed hardware that governs their operating parameters, including the radio frequencies they can use to transmit and receive. Cognitive radio devices allow these parameters to be altered to allow the device to make dynamic adjustments in frequency use, power or other operating features. This adaptive functionality may be hard-wired into the device by the manufacturer or the manufacturer may allow the user to install it. To date, the FCC's focus has been certification requirements for software defined radio. It first authorized certification of software defined radio in 2001 and since then has made some modest changes in its certification rules, dealing with security issues (prevention of unauthorized modification of devices by users) and restrictions on the frequencies that can be selected, power limits, and other technical parameters. See *Facilitating Opportunities for Flexible, Efficient, and Reliable Spectrum Use Employing Cognitive Radio Technologies*, 20 FCC Rcd. 5486 (2005). Again, the underlying concern is to prevent interference. Cognitive radio is sometimes described as "opportunistic" in allowing users to search for open frequencies. The upside of this opportunism is that it can increase utilization of the spectrum; the

10. Note that spread spectrum is also commonly used in licensed radio devices, notably cell phones using CDMA.

downside is that it can also increase the possibility of interference to other users—the more they can "surf" the spectrum, the greater the range of possible interference. Not least of the problems here is the difficulty of locating these "opportunistic" users, particularly if they are operating unlicensed cognitive radio devices that permit the user to select frequencies outside those that are designated for unlicensed use.

The FCC has further sought to facilitate the use of smart radio by means of what it calls "private commons." The concept is linked to various procedures designed to introduce more flexibility into the ability of licenses to transfer use of their licensed frequencies by means of leases. The following subsection explores the Commission's latest efforts to soften command and control mechanisms.

d) Facilitating Secondary Markets Through Leasing and "Private Commons"

PROMOTING EFFICIENT USE OF SPECTRUM THROUGH ELIMINATION OF BARRIERS TO THE DEVELOPMENT OF SECONDARY MARKETS Report and Order and Further Notice of Proposed Rulemaking

Federal Communications Commission, 2003.
18 FCC Rcd. 24817.

BY THE COMMISSION:

* * *

II. EXECUTIVE SUMMARY

A. Report and Order

8. In this Report and Order, we take several steps to facilitate the ability of most Wireless Radio Services licensees that hold "exclusive use" licenses to lease spectrum usage rights to third parties seeking access to spectrum.

9. *General overview of spectrum leasing policies.* We make clear that, subject to the conditions set forth in this Report and Order, licensees in the Wireless Radio Services covered herein may lease some or all of their spectrum usage rights to third parties, for any amount of spectrum and in any geographic area encompassed by the license, and for any period of time within the term of the license. In granting spectrum lessees and licensees the greatest amount of flexibility within the bounds of current law, we first replace the existing standard for assessing de facto control with an updated standard for spectrum leasing that better accommodates recent evolutionary developments in the Commission's spectrum policies, technological advances, and marketplace trends, consistent with statutory requirements. We then provide parties to spectrum lease transactions two different approaches based on the scope of

the rights and responsibilities to be assumed by the lessee when leasing spectrum. Under the first leasing option—"spectrum manager" leasing—we enable parties to enter into spectrum leasing arrangements without the need to obtain prior Commission approval so long as the licensee retains both de jure control of the license and de facto control over the leased spectrum pursuant to the updated de facto control standard for leasing. Under the second option—"de facto transfer" leasing—we provide parties additional flexibility in structuring spectrum leasing arrangements by permitting them, pursuant to a streamlined approval process, to enter into leasing arrangements whereby licensees retain de jure control of their licenses while de facto control over the use of the leased spectrum, and associated rights and responsibilities, are transferred for a defined period to spectrum lessees.

10. *The updated de facto control standard for spectrum leasing.* In order to facilitate spectrum leasing arrangements for which we find no public policy reason to require prior Commission approval, we replace our prior standard for interpreting de facto control under Section 310(d), as set forth in the 1963 *Intermountain Microwave* decision, with an updated standard that has been refined to reflect more recent evolutionary developments in the Commission's spectrum policies, technological advances, and marketplace trends. This new standard is generally based on our "band manager" model that the Commission first employed in 2000 in the 700 MHz Guard Band and recently extended (in a modified form) to the 1390–1392 MHz, 1670–1675 MHz, and 2385–2390 MHz bands and the paired 1392–1395 and 1432–1435 MHz bands. The *Intermountain Microwave* standard imposes significant constraints on the development of efficient spectrum use through secondary markets because it is essentially a "facilities-based" standard that requires licensees to exercise close working control over many different aspects associated with the operation of all of the station facilities using the licensed spectrum. This standard has become increasingly out of step with the flexible, market-based spectrum policies that Congress and the Commission have developed in recent years, and it imposes unnecessary barriers to efficient and effective access to spectrum resources.

11. The refined standard that we adopt provides additional flexibility to licensees and potential spectrum lessees in that it enables these parties to enter into leasing transactions that are not deemed transfers of de facto control under Section 310(d) so long as licensees continue to exercise effective working control over the use of the spectrum they lease. As set forth herein, licensees may lease spectrum usage rights to spectrum lessees, without the need for prior Commission approval, to the extent that the licensees (1) maintain an active, ongoing oversight role to ensure that the lessee complies with all applicable Commission policies and rules, (2) retain responsibility for all interactions with the Commission required under the license related to the use of the leased spectrum (including notification requirements), and (3) remain primarily and directly accountable to the Commission for any lessee violation of these policies and rules.

12. *"Spectrum manager" leasing.* Under the "spectrum manager" leasing option, licensees and spectrum lessees may enter into spectrum leasing arrangements—for any amount of spectrum, in any geographic area, and for any period of time within the scope and term of the license—without the need for prior Commission approval, provided that licensees retain de facto control, as newly defined, over the leased spectrum. Under this leasing option, the licensee acts as a "spectrum manager" with regard to the spectrum rights it chooses to lease.

The requirements of the "spectrum manager" leasing option include—

- The licensee must retain both de jure control of the license and de facto control of the leased spectrum. As noted above, exercising de facto control requires the licensee to maintain an active, ongoing oversight role to ensure that the spectrum lessee complies with the Communications Act and all applicable Commission policies and rules. The licensee must also engage in all interactions (including filings) with the Commission that are directly related to the use or uses of the spectrum, whether by the licensee or the lessee. (The licensee may employ agents in helping to carry out these responsibilities, but remains fully responsible for their performance.) The licensee will be held directly and primarily responsible for both maintaining its eligibility as a licensee and ensuring that each of its spectrum lessees complies with the relevant provisions of the Act and all applicable Commission policies and rules.

- The technical and interference-related services rules applicable to the particular spectrum-based service or frequency band(s) will also apply to the spectrum lessee as if it were a licensee in the service or band(s). In addition, as a general policy matter, the eligibility and qualification rules and the use restrictions applicable to the licensee in a particular service will be applied to spectrum lessees. For example, to address any potential national security, law enforcement, foreign policy, or trade policy concerns, we will require spectrum lessees to certify to foreign ownership criteria analogous to those applicable to Commission licensees. Further, leases associated with "designated entity" and "entrepreneur" licenses will be subject to applicable attribution and affiliation rules as well as our leasing rules, with the attribution and affiliation rules controlling in the event of conflict.

- In enforcing the Act and its policies and rules, the Commission will look primarily to the licensee to exercise its licensee responsibilities and ensure lessee compliance with the particular technical and service rules applicable to the particular spectrum-based service or frequency band(s). To the extent that a licensee fails to ensure such compliance, it potentially will be subject to enforcement action, such as admonishments, monetary forfeitures, and/or license revocation, as appropriate. Although spectrum lessee accountability is generally secondary under this option, the Commission will also hold spectrum lessees independently accountable for complying with the Act and the Commission's policies and rules, potentially subjecting them to enforcement action, such as admonishments, monetary forfeitures, and other administrative sanctions. However, to the extent a lessee provides a communications service over the leased spectrum, the regulatory treatment of the lessee's provision of such service will depend on the nature of the service, and the licensee would not necessarily be responsible for the lessee's compliance with the regulatory responsibilities arising out of the provision of such services (e.g., lessees providing common carriage will be primarily responsible for compliance with applicable Title II requirements).

- The licensee will be required to provide notification and other relevant information and certification to the Commission with regard to each spectrum lease into which it has entered. Such notice must be provided within 14 days of the entering into the lease, and at least 21 days in advance of operation of facilities by the lessee. (For leases of up to one year, the licensee must provide notice at least 10 days in advance of operation.) In particular, licensees must submit information on the spectrum lessee, the specific spectrum leased (amount, frequency, geographic area of operation), and term of the lease. In addition, the lessee will be required to indicate whether it holds interests in other spectrum (through licenses or leases) in the geographic areas covered by the lease. The submission will be placed on an informational public notice on a weekly basis and publicly available in our Universal Licensing System (ULS) database.

- Although prior Commission approval is not required under this leasing option, the Commission retains the right to investigate and obtain additional information regarding particular leasing arrangements, post-notification, and to terminate such arrangements to the extent it determines that an arrangement raises significant public interest concerns (e.g., an arrangement constitutes an unauthorized transfer of de facto control under the new leasing standard or raises foreign ownership or competition concerns) or violates any notification certifications.

13. *"De facto transfer" leasing.* Under this option, licensees and spectrum lessees may enter into spectrum leasing arrangements—for any amount of spectrum, in any geographic area, and for any period of time within the scope and term of the license—in which de facto control of the leased spectrum is transferred to the spectrum lessee(s) for the duration of the lease pursuant to streamlined procedures. For ease of reference, this option is termed the "de facto transfer" leasing option. Policies and procedures under this option will differ somewhat depending on whether the parties enter into "long-term" arrangements (leases with individual or combined terms of longer than 360 days) or "short-term" arrangements (leases of 360 days or less).

The requirements of the "long-term" de facto transfer leasing option include—

- The spectrum lessee, rather than the licensee, exercises de facto control of the leased spectrum. In addition to accepting the rights conveyed from the licensee pursuant to the terms of the lease, the lessee must exercise all associated responsibilities inherent in such control. The licensee retains de jure, or legal, control of the leased spectrum and may impose other terms and conditions on the lessee, as agreed to by the parties. The lessee assumes general responsibility for interacting with the Commission with respect to the leased spectrum (including making associated filings). The spectrum lessee will be held directly and primarily responsible for ensuring that it complies with the Communications Act and all applicable Commission policies and rules.

- All of the particular service rules and policies applicable to the licensee under its license authorization—both interference and non-interference related—will apply to the lessee. Accordingly, the eligibility rules (e.g., foreign ownership restrictions, designated entity/entrepreneur requirements), qualification rules, and use restrictions applicable to licensees will apply to lessees under this option.

- In enforcing the Act and its policies and rules, the Commission will look primarily to the spectrum lessee for compliance. The lessee will be subject to enforcement action, including admonishments, monetary forfeitures, and/or lease revocation, as appropriate. Although the licensee will retain some residual responsibility for ensuring compliance, this will generally be limited to instances in which it has knowledge or should have knowledge about a lessee's ongoing failure to comply, or instances that otherwise constitute a violation of the terms and conditions of the lease agreement. The Commission will not be involved in any disputes between licensees and their lessees to the extent that such disputes are not directly related to compliance with the Communications Act and applicable Commission policies and rules. We would expect that any violations of the terms and conditions of the lease agreement that are also directly related to compliance with the Act or rules would be handled in the first instance by the licensee as a private contractual enforcement matter and that the Commission would independently determine if additional regulatory enforcements steps would be warranted.

- A lease application must be filed with the Commission and prior Commission approval is required. If substantially complete, the application will be placed promptly on public notice. Petitions to deny filed in accordance with Section 309(d) of the Communications Act will be due within 14 days. Within 21 days of the public notice, the Wireless Telecommunications Bureau will either affirmatively consent to the transfer or "offline" the application to the extent that public interest concerns are raised (e.g., the lessee's qualifications, competition concerns) that require further examination.

The requirements of the "short-term" de facto transfer leasing option include—

- As under the long-term leasing arrangements described above, the spectrum lessee exercises de facto control of the leased spectrum, and must exercise all associated responsibilities inherent in such control. The spectrum lessee will be held directly and primarily responsible for compliance with the Communications Act and all applicable Commission policies and rules.

• Due to the short-term nature of these leasing arrangements, we provide some additional flexibility with regard to the particular service rules and policies applicable to the spectrum lessee. While the interference-related rules will apply to the lessee, we will not require that certain service rules applicable to the licensee—including certain use restrictions, designated entity and entrepreneur policies, and policies related to spectrum aggregation—be applied to short-term lessees.

• Short-term leasing arrangements that meet the specified conditions will be approved within 10 days pursuant to our special temporary authority (STA) procedures.

* * *

The following year the Commission adopted a second report and order clarifying and extending the first report in several aspects, including further streamlining of procedures for approval of leasing arrangements, extending leasing policies to some additional wireless services (including public safety services), clarifying leasing policies with respect to designated entities, and facilitating use of "smart radio" devices by means of a so-called "private commons."

PROMOTING EFFICIENT USE OF SPECTRUM THROUGH ELIMINATION OF BARRIERS TO THE DEVELOPMENT OF SECONDARY MARKETS
Second Report and Order, Order on Reconsideration, and Second Further Notice of Proposed Rulemaking

Federal Communications Commission, 2004.
19 FCC Rcd. 17503.

BY THE COMMISSION:

* * *

B. POLICIES TO FACILITATE ADVANCED TECHNOLOGIES

1. Background

85. In the *Further Notice*, we observed that the *Secondary Markets Policy Statement* and the *Spectrum Policy Task Force Report* emphasized the benefits of "smart" or "opportunistic" technologies, especially the potential for increased access to unused spectrum. In addition, the *Spectrum Policy Task Force Report* and the Commission's recently issued *Cognitive Radio NPRM* on the use of advanced technologies describe how they may enable devices to search across many bands, sense the level of emissions, and then operate in spectrum that is either not in use by other parties or below a certain level of emissions. The *Further Notice*

sought comment on the use of advanced technologies in licensed bands in the context of secondary markets and, in particular, requested comment on the *Spectrum Policy Task Force Report* recommendation that the Commission focus on advancing and improving access to spectrum by opportunistic devices through a secondary markets approach, at least in the near term. The *Further Notice* also inquired as to whether the *Report and Order* provided sufficient flexibility for more "dynamic" leasing arrangements made possible by opportunistic devices.

2. Discussion

86. Because we believe that smart or opportunistic technologies hold significant potential to promote access to and more efficient use of the spectrum, we clarify our existing spectrum leasing rules, and introduce an additional means, to help facilitate the development of arrangements involving the use of these new and evolving technologies in services for which spectrum leasing is permitted. Opportunistic use technologies facilitate many dynamic ways of sharing spectrum. For example, smart or cognitive radio devices can potentially sense and adapt to their spectrum environment, find and use spectrum in locations or during time intervals that will not cause interference to other users, and operate across multiple bands and using different protocols. Such devices may also have networking capability, either on a peer-to-peer (device-to-device) basis or by interacting with available wide-area or local-area networks. The spectrum access capabilities of these technologies can be achieved by a variety of potential cooperative approaches, such as secondary markets arrangements, in which users of licensed spectrum arrange access with licensees under mutually agreeable terms. With smart or cognitive radios, for example, it is possible to reconfigure the performance parameters of the individual devices to allow more opportunistic uses of the spectrum. As these capabilities become available on a broader basis, the Commission can facilitate these additional forms of spectrum access by ensuring that our licensing and technical rules do not inadvertently impose barriers to the deployment of such capabilities if and when licensees (or spectrum lessees) seek to take advantage of such capabilities. These cooperative uses of these capabilities would also complement other approaches to promoting spectrum access, *e.g.*, facilitating access for advanced technologies on an unlicensed basis. The approaches considered in this order are cooperative in nature—avoiding placing regulatory barriers on licensees (or spectrum lessees) that wish to provide for opportunistic uses of spectrum pursuant to the terms and conditions that they set—so long as they fall within the licensee's spectrum usage rights and are not inconsistent with applicable technical and other regulations imposed by the Commission to prevent harmful interference to other licensees.

87. Recognizing the variety of ways in which advanced technologies enhance opportunities for more parties to gain access to and share the use of the same spectrum, we seek to provide licensees and spectrum lessees the flexibility to enter into mutually beneficial access and use

arrangements that take fuller advantage of what these new and innovative technologies may make possible. To that end, we clarify below some of the types of spectrum leasing and other arrangements that could allow for use of advanced technologies, including opportunistic devices. The value of this increased flexibility is reflected in the comments received on this issue. Commenters that addressed this issue maintained that licensees should be permitted to engage in dynamic spectrum leasing arrangements, and generally should be free to weigh the potential benefits and costs of allowing access to licensed spectrum. We also introduce an additional mechanism, which we call a "private commons," that will allow cooperative use arrangements not explicitly recognized within the Commission's policies or rules, and we seek comment in the Second Further Notice on how we can distinguish between these and other arrangements, such as spectrum leasing or end-user arrangements, to avoid unintended and unnecessary barriers to the deployment and use of advanced technologies.

a. Facilitating advanced technologies within existing regulatory frameworks, including dynamic spectrum leasing arrangements

88. We clarify that our spectrum leasing policies and rules permit parties to enter into a variety of dynamic forms of spectrum leasing arrangements that take advantage of the capabilities associated with advanced technologies. Such a clarification generally accords with comments we received. For example, one commenter specifically recommended that the Commission's secondary markets policies and rules be expanded to accommodate "dynamic" spectrum leasing arrangements, and other commenters also endorsed adoption of spectrum leasing policies in which licensees could take fuller advantage of technological advances, including opportunistic use devices, through secondary markets arrangements. Consistent with these views, we clarify that parties may enter into spectrum leasing arrangements in which licensees and spectrum lessees share use of the same spectrum, on a non-exclusive basis, during the term of the lease. For example, a licensee and spectrum lessee may enter into a spectrum manager or de facto transfer lease in which use of the same spectrum is shared with each other by employing opportunistic devices. In another variation, a licensee could enter into a spectrum manager lease with one party that has access to the spectrum on a priority basis, while also leasing use of the same spectrum to another party on a lower-priority basis, with the requirement that the lower-priority spectrum lessee employ opportunistic technology to avoid interfering with the priority lessee. Of course, the licensee may not lease spectrum usage rights that exceed the rights it currently holds and, as these examples illustrate, the licensee may choose to lease a more restricted bundle of usage rights.

89. Significantly, these arrangements could facilitate opportunistic use by parties operating at the same power level and under similar technical parameters as the licensee, or they could promote such use at

lower power levels. We also emphasize that neither scenario would affect unlicensed operations to the extent they are permitted in that particular licensed band pursuant to Commission rules under Part 15. For example, as set forth in section 15.209 of the Commission's rules and augmented on a band-by-band basis, Part 15 users (*e.g.*, Ultra-Wide Band operators) can operate pursuant to applicable technical and operational rules whether or not opportunistic use or other advanced technologies are employed or authorized by the licensee. We would also expect that new and innovative radiofrequency devices would be agile enough to function on an unlicensed basis or as part of licensed operations. Moreover, the examples discussed here do not provide an exhaustive list of all the possible arrangements that could involve the use of opportunistic devices and be consistent with secondary markets and service rules already in place. Accordingly, in the Second Further Notice, we seek comment on the types of additional commercial or sharing arrangements that would further exploit the benefits of new and innovative technological advances.

90. We recognize that, in some cases, under the current framework for spectrum manager and de facto transfer lease arrangements, these options may not be economically or technically feasible due to the transaction costs associated with coordinating many users in a single band, or many users employing advanced technologies to access multiple bands by frequency-hopping. Nonetheless, we do not believe that these should be insurmountable barriers and we concur with the *Spectrum Policy Task Force Report* that "a secondary markets approach by opportunistic devices does not necessarily require the prospective opportunistic user to negotiate individually with each affected licensee," and that band managers, clearinghouses, and other intermediaries could facilitate these transactions. We also agree with the *Spectrum Policy Task Force Report* finding that a "secondary market approach has significant potential to foster opportunistic technologies, such as agile frequency-hopping radios, software-defined radios, and adaptive antennas, at reasonable transaction costs." In short, while the existing spectrum leasing options may not meet all types of spectrum access needs, we have great confidence in the ability of market participants to find innovative means of enhancing spectrum access and lowering transaction costs, and we therefore expect the market for spectrum usage rights to become increasingly efficient. At the same time, licensees and spectrum lessees may wish to make spectrum available in ways not anticipated by the Commission's current rules, and such innovative efforts may be a driving force in promoting the development of advanced technologies and the efficient use of the spectrum. We therefore introduce a new concept under our current exclusive-use licensing models that may foster the experimentation and new uses of licensed spectrum without unnecessary regulatory intervention.

b. Private Commons

91. To facilitate the use of advanced technologies, and thus better promote access to and the efficient use of spectrum, we expand the

spectrum licensing framework by identifying an additional option that may be utilized by current and future licensees and spectrum lessees. This concept, which we call a "private commons," will allow licensees and spectrum lessees to make spectrum available to individual users or groups of users that do not fit squarely within the current options for spectrum leasing or within the traditional end-user arrangements associated with the licensee's (or spectrum lessee's) subscriber-based services and network infrastructures. New technologies enable users, through use of advanced devices, to engage in a wide range of communications that do not require use of a licensee's (or lessee's) network infrastructure. To facilitate the use of these technologies, we adopt the private commons option, which will permit, and be restricted to, peer-to-peer communications between devices in a non-hierarchical network arrangement that does not utilize the network infrastructure of the licensee (or spectrum lessee).

92. The private commons option provides a cooperative mechanism for licensees (or lessees) to make licensed spectrum available to users employing these advanced technologies in a manner similar to that by which unlicensed users gain access to spectrum to suit their particular needs, and to do so without the necessity of entering into individual spectrum leasing arrangements under our existing rules. In the 2.4 GHz and 5 GHz bands, for instance, users gain access and use of the spectrum with specified types of low-power communications devices provided they comply with technical requirements established by the Commission and set forth in our Part 15 rules. In these bands, users then can create their own networks—such as those that are ad hoc or "mesh" in nature—using equipment that complies with Commission-established requirements. The private commons option provides a potentially complementary access model, in which licensees (or spectrum lessees) would determine to make access available to a similar class of users, and would do so under technical requirements for sharing use of the licensed band established and managed by the licensee (or lessee). The nature of these types of users' access to spectrum under this private commons option thus differs qualitatively from the nature of access provided to spectrum lessees under the Commission's spectrum leasing policies and procedures. In the private commons, the licensee (or lessee) authorizes users of devices operating at particular technical parameters specified by the licensee (or lessee) to operate on the licensed frequencies, consistent with the applicable technical requirements and use restrictions under the license authorization, using peer-to-peer (device-to-device) technologies. In spectrum leasing arrangements, individually negotiated spectrum access rights are provided to entities that traditionally obtained licenses and that would then provide traditional network-based services to end-users.

93. This approach is consistent with the kinds of additional flexibility many commenters sought. Several commenters supported providing licensees the option of allowing opportunistic use of the licensed spectrum through secondary market mechanisms, and asserted advantages

to empowering licensees to establish the technical parameters and interference rules instead of government-established access rules. Commenters also asserted that enabling licensees to determine the technical parameters of such use would minimize interference concerns relating to other users in the band, and would have the necessary incentives to be innovative and efficient in enabling users to access the licensed spectrum through use of such devices.

94. These private commons arrangements may take a variety of forms, but will share a number of defining characteristics, as described herein. The private commons option will allow for flexible uses of licensed spectrum rights in which the licensee or lessee does not necessarily offer services (in whole or part) over its own end-to-end physical network of base stations, mobile stations, and other elements. The licensee or spectrum lessee, as a manager of a private commons, will set terms and conditions for use in the private commons by users (consistent with the terms of the license and applicable service rules), and retain both de facto control of the use of the spectrum within the private commons and direct responsibility for compliance with the Commission's rules. And, while private commons arrangements will not be subject to the same notification requirements that are required by our spectrum leasing rules, licensees (or spectrum lessees) managing the commons will be required at this time to notify the Commission about any private commons they establish prior to users being permitted to operate within that private commons.

95. We anticipate at least two types of private commons that licensees (or spectrum lessees) could make available to individuals or groups of users. In the first example, a private commons could be created by a licensee (or spectrum lessee), which may or may not otherwise have a network infrastructure to provide services, by granting access for a fee (*e.g.*, on a transaction, usage, fixed, or other basis) to users who employ smart or opportunistic wireless devices that conform to the terms and conditions established by the licensee (or lessee), such as a requirement that devices operating in the licensed band use a particular technology, hardware, or software. The users' devices may be used to engage in peer-to-peer (device-to-device) communications, such as by becoming part of compatible ad hoc or "mesh" wireless networks. Such users may need access to a particular licensed spectrum band in lieu of (or perhaps in addition to) gaining access to other bands that may be more heavily used or that do not allow for the quality of service necessary for a particular application. This type of private commons might be particularly valuable to users that find existing bands that provide for unlicensed operations to be crowded or otherwise less desirable.

96. Under a second potential type of private commons arrangement, the licensee (or spectrum lessee) would not charge an ongoing access fee or otherwise have any direct relationship with the users. For instance, manufacturers of smart or opportunistic devices, or the developers of software or hardware used within such devices, may wish, as licensees or spectrum lessees, to provide spectrum access to anyone who

purchases their devices, or devices with their hardware or software. This type of arrangement might be particularly effective in promoting new technologies or new uses by providing an opportunity for equipment developers to capitalize on their investments and innovations without having to get a license directly from the Commission, but could arrange for users of the equipment to access the spectrum usage rights from an existing licensee. Because a licensee (or spectrum lessee) could offer to private commons users the interference protection rights of its license, this arrangement could provide some additional benefits as compared with possible lower-powered, unlicensed operation in the same or other bands.

97. We will require licensees and spectrum lessees that seek to allow spectrum access on a private commons basis to notify the Commission of the arrangement at this time. This notification will be similar to, but simpler than, the notification required for spectrum manager leases. It would provide certain information and certifications regarding the general terms and conditions for spectrum access to users in the private commons, including the term and coverage area of the arrangement, general information on the technical requirements and the equipment that the licensee or spectrum lessee has approved for operation in the private commons, as well as a description of the types of uses that are allowed. Consistent with our approach to Part 15 devices, we will not require the notification to include specific information about each individual user. We examine this notification requirement, and the continued need for the notification, in the Second Further Notice, below. We also recognize the need to clearly identify the distinguishing elements of spectrum leases, managed private commons, and end-user arrangements, respectively, as means to create spectrum access. Accordingly, in the Second Further Notice, we seek comment on the specifications necessary to make such distinctions consistent with the Commission's regulatory and enforcement objectives, and we seek comment on other arrangements and regulatory changes that may facilitate spectrum access and that should be considered within a private commons framework.

98. We believe that a private commons will provide an important complement to the spectrum leasing policies we have already adopted to facilitate spectrum access, as well as to unlicensed access to spectrum. We expect the combination of spectrum leasing arrangements, private commons, and the various ways in which licensees currently may utilize advanced technology will further enhance this move towards greater spectrum access, and we are optimistic about the potential benefits that are likely to emerge as licensees and other users find more ways to promote access to and the efficient use of spectrum. We note that the flexibility afforded by a private commons may help make possible a number of new means to apply advanced radio technologies, including such concepts as "policy radio," an emerging approach that would allow use that is even more dynamic than that described above.

99. We also envision this approach as part of a balance between license-based access mechanisms, such as the spectrum leasing and

private commons models that allow licensees and spectrum lessees to define access rights based on market forces, and unlicensed access mechanisms that allow free access by non-interfering devices pursuant to regulation. We recognize that there is an ongoing and important debate on spectrum policy, with some parties stressing the merits of unlicensed and shared uses, both within a free and open "spectrum commons" and in licensed bands under private control, and other parties arguing for the merits of "exclusive" licensed use of spectrum. We are not here taking sides in that debate. Rather, we expect that existing and new licensees and spectrum lessees in various services and spectrum bands will consider the market potential of a private commons and other arrangements and seek opportunities to lower transaction costs and provide multiple avenues of spectrum access and a range of devices to consumers, businesses and other entities. In addition, we anticipate that, as unlicensed use becomes more popular, users of unlicensed devices that operate under the Part 15 rules may have an incentive to seek access to a managed private commons in licensed bands that may be less susceptible to overcrowding and, because of the benefit of interference protection, may be a way to avoid the potential risks associated with the "tragedy of the commons." Licensees and spectrum lessees in turn will have an incentive to provide private commons through a variety of means, with terms and conditions that are most valued by users. We expect these users will choose the most efficient means of spectrum access for their particular needs, considering the costs and benefits of all options, including private commons and unlicensed use. * * *

What, if anything, can we actually take away from the FCC's treatment of the licensing (and non-licensing) alternatives? The different alternatives all look good, and the FCC proposes to use them in a mix of different arrangements. Are our regulatory problems solved? Does that mean that the FCC can now move into smaller digs in Washington?

One could be forgiven for wondering whether the FCC has made any real progress at all. Other than altering the method for actually granting licenses (through auction), the FCC's approach to licensing has changed little since the heyday of command and control. Is the FCC likely to give up the power it has in assigning frequencies to particular services? And recall that different frequencies are inherently more valuable (because of their propagation characteristics) than others. Who decides which type of licensing regime is applied to prime spectrum? Similarly, if the U.S. relies on a mix of licensing regimes, who is going to choose among them when they represent such different values and uses? Is adding an additional layer of essentially unreviewable discretion (the choice of type of license for a particular frequency) likely to improve communications policy or lessen the FCC's administrative deadweight? *Plus ça change*...

PART II

MASS MEDIA

Chapter 3

REGULATING MEDIA CONTENT

A. FIRST AMENDMENT FRAMEWORK

1. Introduction

Communications is speech, whether it is expressed in electronic form, print, or even in symbols. As such, the First Amendment plays an important role in communications law. With respect to electronic communications, the First Amendment was not a prominent concern in the early years of regulation. To be sure, everyone was fully aware that direct content regulation raised First Amendment implications. Even in the case of such direct regulation, though, it was not until 1969 that the Supreme Court was prompted to address what those implications were. This relative neglect might reflect an assumption that electronic speech is constitutionally different from other speech—a proposition that *Red Lion Broadcasting Co. v. FCC*, 395 U.S. 367 (1969), which we will examine below, famously, and controversially, confirmed. But it also reflects the fact that First Amendment jurisprudence itself is quite a recent development. Most of the leading First Amendment cases that would have any direct bearing on communications regulation are products of the last half century; for all practical purposes the modern First Amendment has co-evolved with communications regulations themselves. But there is no longer any reticence about introducing the First Amendment into regulatory controversies. The vast legal literature that has emerged in the last four decades on the subject bears witness; it would be pointless to attempt even a short bibliography.[1]

There is almost no issue in communications regulation that has not at some point attracted First Amendment claims. As military strategists might put it, communications regulation has become a target rich environment for First Amendment attacks. We will see examples throughout this book, but the present chapter in particular features

1. However, two books in particular provide excellent introductions. One is part of a three-volume treatise on communications law generally, Harvey L. Zuckman, et al., MODERN COMMUNICATIONS LAW (1999, with updated pocket parts). The other is a book on broadcast regulation, Thomas G. Krattenmaker & Lucas A. Powe, REGULATING BROADCAST PROGRAMMING (1994).

some of the prominent targets. We start with a brief primer on some First Amendment fundamentals. We do so mindful that a few pages of such a complicated topic may be more dangerous than useful, but our experience has been that some students of communications law have only nodding acquaintance with the elements of First Amendment doctrine necessary to understand how it is being applied to electronic communications. We hope only to provide the necessary background for the aspects of First Amendment law implicated by communications regulation, and our coverage will be so limited. The discussion that follows focuses on three very basic questions. The first is a question about the values protected by the First Amendment. The second is a question of breadth: what types of speech are protected? The third is a question of the degree of protection, which is usually translated into a question of the intensity of judicial review of regulation affecting speech.

2. Values of the First Amendment

We begin with a brief comment on free-speech values because they provide the necessary starting point for any critical understanding of the First Amendment's role. Every liberal society puts a high value on free speech, but there seems to be no country that has invested it with such legal authority as the United States. The First Amendment is ubiquitous in our legal system. It applies to governments at all levels. Despite its being nominally addressed only to Congress, the First Amendment was long ago incorporated into the Fourteenth Amendment, whence it applies to states and all subordinate levels of government. And while the Amendment speaks only of "laws" of Congress—legislation—virtually every form of official action falls within its reach, including, in at least some cases, judicial enforcement of private rights. See, e.g., *New York Times v. Sullivan*, 376 U.S. 254 (1964) (libel action by public official barred); *Gertz v. Robert Welch, Inc.*, 418 U.S. 323 (1974) (libel action by private individual; First Amendment applicable to the extent of barring strict liability); *Hustler Magazine v. Falwell*, 485 U.S. 46 (1988) (action for intentional infliction of emotional distress barred).

The Amendment addresses "speech," but that term has been interpreted to include "expressive conduct" ranging from symbolic gestures and wearing apparel to nude dancing,. See, e.g., *Texas v. Johnson*, 491 U.S. 397 (1989) (flag burning in protest is protected "speech"); *Tinker v. Des Moines School District*, 393 U.S. 503 (1969) (wearing black armbands as a protest is protected); *Schad v. Mount Ephraim*, 452 U.S. 61 (1981) (nude dancing in a coin-operated "peep show" protected).

Finally, the sensitivity of the Amendment is very finely tuned. The literal language of the Amendment is "abridge," which Webster's defines as "to shorten in duration or extent." But courts have liberally construed what literally reads as "shorten" to include the imposition of cost or other burdens that might "chill" the vigor of speakers. See, e.g., *Sullivan, supra.*

To what end and to what purpose? Scholars have proffered a number of theories of free speech in general, and the First Amendment in general. An admirable, critical survey of the theories of free speech generally (and, indirectly, a theory of First Amendment values) is Frederick Schauer, *Free Speech: A Philosophical Inquiry* (1982). Schauer identifies three major arguments for free speech (that is, for giving free speech a privileged position in the legal order): the argument from truth, the argument from democracy, and the argument from "the good life"—roughly, individual fulfillment. Each of these three arguments contains a range of more nuanced arguments, and none are necessarily exclusive of the others.

At the level of general values, the promotion of truth is perhaps the oldest theory for privileging free speech. John Milton and John Stuart Mill were among its foremost advocates. In more recent times Justice Holmes gave this theory its now canonical formulation with his "marketplace of ideas" metaphor:

> But when men have realized that time has upset many fighting faiths, they may come to believe even more than they believe the very foundations of their own conduct that the ultimate good desired is better reached by free trade in ideas—that the best test of truth is the power of the thought to get itself accepted in the competition of the market and that truth if the only ground upon which their wishes safely can be carried out. That at any rate is the theory of our constitution."

Abrams v. United States, 250 U.S. 616, 630 (1919). Holmes' "theory of our constitution" has not held up very well. Today it is widely criticized as unrealistic by commentators across the political spectrum, but especially from those on the left, who believe that modern public speech is dominated by giant media. The latter point has a special salience in the case of electronic media which, perhaps because of their modernity, have never enjoyed the respect given the traditional print media.

Holmes' marketplace of ideas was intended to create a large constitutional sanctuary for speech. Too large, according to some modern critics, who argue that the realm of constitutional protection for speech is more properly confined to political and public discourse. The central aim of constitutional protection for public speech, under this approach, is to promote the democratic process, or "self-government." Alexander Meiklejohn, a political scientist, first advanced this view in the 1940s, see Alexander Meiklejohn, *Free Speech and Its Relation to Self–Government* (1948). The theory has been endorsed, at least in part, by a number of contemporary theorists such as Robert Bork, *Neutral Principles and Some First Amendment Problems*, 47 Ind. L.J. 1 (1971) and Lillian BeVier, *The First Amendment and Political Speech: An Inquiry Into the Substance and Limits of Principle*, 30 Stan. L. Rev. 299 (1978). The argument from democracy or self-governance seeks to draw a line between public and private speech, which is to say that it puts all the value on protecting those things that have general public importance—

particularly political importance—as opposed to mere cultural or social value.

The omission of a concern (at least at the level of constitutional protection) for non-political speech has led others to advance a broader theory of speech that is grounded in the values of liberal society generally—one that protects and promotes individual autonomy and self-fulfillment. The original articulation of this conception is usually attributed to Thomas Emerson, *Towards a General Theory of the First Amendment* (1966), but it now has many adherents. See, e.g., C. Edwin Baker, *Human Liberty and Freedom of Speech* (1989). And it has its critics, who point out that free-speech protection with as broad a purpose as maximizing autonomy is not readily confined. As the English historian Thomas Macaulay once famously wrote of the entire American constitution: "it is all sail and no anchor."

It is not necessary that free-speech protection be reduced to a single theory, of course. Each of the above theories can, and does, have some explanatory and some normative power. One way to think about the First Amendment is to see it as a point on which an array of very important social values converge. Even allowing such an eclectic approach, though, the tendency of most First Amendment scholars has been to seek a hierarchy of speech values, distinguishing between those that are at the "core" and those that are at the "periphery." The Supreme Court itself has recognized such a hierarchy, distinguishing between, for example, political speech (at the core), commercial advertising (periphery), and obscenity (traditionally considered beyond the pale).

3. Breadth of Protection

The Supreme Court has recognized distinctions among different types of speech. It has, for example, distinguished between speech about matters of public importance and purely private speech. (See, e.g., *Dun & Bradstreet, Inc. v. Greenmoss Builders*, 472 U.S. 749 (1985) in which the Court held that a defamation action based on an allegedly false private credit report was "far from the core of the First Amendment" and warranted only limited constitutional scrutiny.) It has also distinguished advertising, or so-called "commercial" speech. At one time, the Court refused to assign any constitutional value to commercial advertising. That position was reversed in *Virginia Pharmacy Board v. Virginia Citizens Consumer Council*, 425 U.S. 748 (1976), in which the Court held that commercial product speech was protected but did not necessarily warrant the same degree of protection granted for other speech. Subsequent decisions have been uncertain and varied as to the level of protection owed commercial speech.

If commercial speech is at the periphery of protection, obscenity has been beyond it since *Roth v. United States*, 354 U.S. 476 (1957), in which the Court declared obscene speech to be outside the area of constitutionally protected speech on the ground that it was "utterly without redeeming social importance." The decision to place an entire category of speech beyond the range of constitutional protection had the effect of making everything turn on the definition of the category—what is "obscene." (Recently, however, the Supreme Court indicated that, at least in the context of the Internet, obscenity may not be completely beyond the pale of protected speech. See *Ashcroft v. ACLU*, 542 U.S. 656 (2004)). In *Roth* itself a majority of the Court agreed on a formula that defined obscenity as material that the average person, applying contemporary community standards, would regard as "prurient." However, subsequent decisions would reveal sharp divisions among the justices in the definition and application of the standard. In *Miller v. California*, 413 U.S. 15 (1973), the Court formulated a three-part definition of obscenity that is now the accepted doctrinal framework: (a) whether the average person, applying contemporary community standards would find that the work, taken as a whole, appeals to the prurient interest, (b) whether the work depicts or describes, in a patently offensive way, sexual conduct specifically defined by the applicable state law, and (c) whether the work, taken as a whole, lacks serious literary, artistic, political or scientific value. The *Miller* standard remains authoritative, but, because so much "adult" material does not satisfy the obscenity standard, the Court has found itself having to consider the regulation of speech that is vulgar but not necessarily obscene. Some of the cases involved not bans but zoning regulations, which were not aimed at suppressing pornographic or "adult" material, but simply putting it in its place, so to speak. See *Young v. American Mini Theatres, Inc.*, 427 U.S. 50 (1976). As we shall see, this idea of channeling adult content to adults has come to play an important—and very controversial—role in the regulation of so-called "indecent" program content in broadcasting, see *FCC v. Pacifica Foundation*, 438 U.S. 726 (1978). The Court has also given special attention to the effect of pornography on children, in one way particularly relevant to communications regulation. In *Ginsberg v. New York*, 390 U.S. 629 (1968), the Court held that a state could prohibit making indecent (non-obscene) material available to children. When combined with the "zoning" concept of channeling rather than banning speech, the protection of children from indecent materials has proven to be a particularly strong justification for the regulation of broadcast speech.

There remains to be considered one final category of speech based on technology, but we will defer considering this special category until a bit later.

4. Degree of Protection

The purpose of classifying categories of speech obviously is to determine the degree of constitutional protection to be accorded, the weight to be placed on the speech interest. But the value of the speech is only one part of the analysis. One must also look at how the speech is affected and the nature of the government's purpose. These entail another order of classification.

The traditional classification here is between restrictions that are justified by the harms posed by the speech itself and those justified by ancillary harms. Speech restrictions premised on the idea that the speech itself is harmful are "content-based"; those that are justified by ancillary harms are "content-neutral". The first category is fairly easy to identify (and includes obscenity and indecency restrictions). The second category is not, largely because speech that is likely to create secondary harms is itself often disfavored by the government.

Content-neutral restrictions break down into two types, only one of which truly ignores the content of speech. The first type are cases in which the harm is completely unrelated to the content—the prototypical example is a prohibition against the use of sound trucks to broadcast speech. See *Kovacs v. Cooper*, 336 U.S. 77 (1949). The harm in such cases has nothing to do with the content, just the way it is presented. The harder cases are those in which regulation of the secondary harm selectively impacts certain speech based on its content. The latter category covers a broad set of cases, some easier to explain than others. The (relatively) easier cases involve things like draft-card burning, which the Court held in *United States v. O'Brien*, 391 U.S. 367 (1968), was not constitutionally protected because the regulation was said to be simply a measure to prevent the destruction of government property (the draft cards); any restriction on the burner's expression was "incidental" to the regulatory goal of preserving draft cards. The harder cases have been the zoning cases, in which regulation has been justified by the "secondary harms" of having adult theaters in the same neighborhoods as residences. See *City of Renton v. Playtime Theatres, Inc.*, 475 U.S. 41 (1986). As one can imagine, such cases are rife with possibilities for pretextual discrimination based on the content itself, as many dissenting Justices have pointed out, including in *Renton*. In these types of cases, the term "content-neutral" is somewhat misleading, because the secondary harm is tied to a particular form of content. The question is whether the content's control is the justification for the regulation. Consequently, legislative purpose takes on great importance in determining whether a restriction is content-neutral or content-based.

The distinction between content-based and content-neutral matters a great deal to case outcomes. Content-based regulation receives "strict scrutiny" while content-neutral regulation receives "intermediate scrutiny," which is one step up from minimal scrutiny, or as it is commonly styled, "minimal rationality"—the standard of constitutional review applied to general social and economic legislation. Strict scrutiny requires that the government show that it has a "compelling" government purpose for regulating speech and that it has chosen a means that is least burdensome and most carefully tailored to serve that purpose. It is a high standard. There are only a few accepted "compelling" reasons for government to discriminate against speech based on its content. The tailoring standard is even tighter, especially in recent years. Indeed, it is so tight that even obscene materials may get protection from ill-tailored restrictions. In *Ashcroft v. ACLU*, 542 U.S. 656 (2004), the Court struck down provisions of the Child Online Protection Act, which attempted to ban content on the World Wide Web that was "harmful to minors." The

Court held that the government had failed to show that the ban was the least restrictive method of achieving its objective: protecting children. The Court included the availability of non-governmental alternatives, such as Internet filtering software, as more narrowly tailored means of protection. Since the Act's definition of "harmful to minors" tracks the *Miller* definition of obscenity in all important respects, the effect of the Court's decision is to give obscenity a degree of constitutional protection hitherto unrecognized. We shall return to the case in Chapter 10, where we take up Internet communications.

Intermediate scrutiny applied to content-neutral restrictions requires only a "substantial" government interest, such as restricting camping and keeping crowds out of public parks, keeping public noise down, and shielding churchgoers from having to pass adult theaters on their way to the pews. The government also has more latitude with regard to means under the intermediate scrutiny standard. Under intermediate scrutiny, the means are valid if they are "not substantially broader than necessary to achieve the government's interest." Unlike the narrow tailoring requirement of the strict-scrutiny test, a less-restrictive alternative is not necessarily the death knell for a restriction considered to be content-neutral. See *Ward v. Rock Against Racism*, 491 U.S. 781, 800 (1989).

Unfortunately, the distinction between compelling and substantial government interest does not lend itself to ex ante specification. We don't have any well-defined list of things that are "compelling" and things that are merely "substantial." And the tailoring inquiry is completely ad hoc since there is no way of fixing on a single rule that would account for the indefinite range of legislative purposes and alternative means of achieving those purposes. Nevertheless the effect of the classification is often outcome deciding. There are few laws that survive strict scrutiny, which is why advocates usually go to heroic efforts to put the law into one classification or the other.

In addition to the vagaries of the classifications and the indeterminacy born of relying on legislative purpose, the content-based/content-neutral classification presents additional challenges to First Amendment enthusiasts. First, there is a considerable confusion about what constitutes "content." In its narrowest meaning content would be something that affected a particular message. A law that forbade one from yelling "America is the Great Satan" would be message specific. But now suppose the law does not discriminate among particular messages but simply discriminates among more general types of content. For instance, suppose it bans commercial "For Sale" signs in a residential neighborhood based on concern about "white flight" from the neighborhood. See *Linmark Associates, Inc. v. Township of Willingboro*, 431 U.S. 85 (1977) (a township ordinance prohibiting the posting of real estate "For Sale" and "Sold" signs for the purpose of stemming what the township perceived as the flight of white homeowners from a racially integrated community violates the First Amendment). Or suppose it bans all but commercial signs as a means of regulating residential appearances. See

City of Ladue v. Gilleo, 512 U.S. 43 (1994) (city ordinance banning all residential signs but those falling within one of ten exemptions was unconstitutional). Or all commercial ads that contain price information about a commodity that the government wants to restrict. See *44 Liquormart, Inc. v. Rhode Island*, 517 U.S. 484 (1996). In each of these cases, the ban is not message specific but the Court has held it to be "content" based and as such requires strict scrutiny as to the government's objectives in regulating the speech and whether there are adequate alternatives.

Take a still broader classification: a restriction based on the character of the medium—for example, whether it is broadcast or electronic. As we shall see, the Court has routinely allowed restrictions on electronic speech that it has not allowed for print, but that is something of a special case. How about a regulation that favors speech according to whether it is locally originated? This describes the situation in cable must-carry regulations that we shall examine in detail later. See Turner Broadcasting System, Inc. v. FCC, 512 U.S. 622 (1994). Interestingly, in that case a majority of the Court ruled that the restriction (which was justified in part by providing an outlet for local content)was not content-based. So how do we know what level of classification to apply in deciding whether something is "content" based or not?

B. AFFIRMATIVE CONTENT REGULATION

1. Constitutional Foundations of Broadcast Regulation

There is a lot we don't know about the Framers and how they thought about this and that. This obviously presents some difficulty in translating their views about the social order into our social order. For originalists—or for anyone who thinks that contemporary constitutional law should be at least partly anchored in original understandings—the translation problem is a vexing one. It exists across a range of constitutional values, whether we are trying to comprehend what is a "cruel and unusual punishment" (Eighth Amendment) or an "unreasonable search and seizure" (Fourth) or "taking of property" (Fifth), etc. But, as one would naturally expect, the problem of relating our world to the world of the Framers is greatest in those areas where cultural and social values have been altered by technology. It is not difficult to imagine what James Madison might have thought about the *New York Times* or the *Wall Street Journal*. Although the scale of their reach and impact no doubt exceeds that of any comparable newspapers in his time, it is unlikely that this would have caused him, or his fellow Framers, to think about the "freedom of the press" in a different light. On the other hand, to imagine Madison in front of a radio receiver or a television set forces one to engage in an altogether more free-ranging thought experiment.

Or does it? The question cannot even be properly addressed without asking another: To what extent are First Amendment values dependent on the technologies of speech? To put it somewhat differently, to what extent do technologies affect the underlying values we associate with speech? Is all "speech" the same, whether it is uttered orally, broadcast over a loud speaker, printed in a newspaper, broadcast over a television set, or distributed over the Internet?

RED LION BROADCASTING CO. v. FCC

Supreme Court of the United States, 1969.
395 U.S. 367.

JUSTICE WHITE delivered the opinion of the Court.

The Federal Communications Commission has for many years imposed on radio and television broadcasters the requirement that discussion of public issues be presented on broadcast stations, and that each side of those issues must be given fair coverage. This is known as the fairness doctrine, which originated very early in the history of broadcasting and has maintained its present outlines for some time. It is an obligation whose content has been defined in a long series of FCC rulings in particular cases, and which is distinct from the statutory requirement of § 315 of the Communications Act that equal time be allotted all qualified candidates for public office. Two aspects of the fairness doctrine, relating to personal attacks in the context of controversial public issues and to political editorializing, were codified more precisely in the form of FCC regulations in 1967. The two cases before us now, which were decided separately below, challenge the constitutional and statutory bases of the doctrine and component rules. *Red Lion* involves the application of the fairness doctrine to a particular broadcast, and [*United States v. Radio Television News Directors Association* (*RTNDA*)] arises as an action to review the FCC's 1967 promulgation of the personal attack and political editorializing regulations, which were laid down after the *Red Lion* litigation had begun.

The Red Lion Broadcasting Company is licensed to operate a Pennsylvania radio station, WGCB. On November 27, 1964, WGCB carried a 15-minute broadcast by Reverend Billy James Hargis as part of a "Christian Crusade" series. A book by Fred J. Cook entitled "Goldwater—Extremist on the Right" was discussed by Hargis, who said that Cook had been fired by a newspaper for making false charges against city officials; that Cook had then worked for a Communist-affiliated publication; that he had defended Alger Hiss and attacked J. Edgar Hoover and the Central Intelligence Agency; and that he had now written a "book to smear and destroy Barry Goldwater." When Cook heard of the broadcast he concluded that he had been personally attacked and demanded free reply time, which the station refused. After an exchange of letters among Cook, Red Lion, and the FCC, the FCC declared that the Hargis broadcast constituted a personal attack on Cook; that Red Lion had failed to meet its obligation under the fairness doctrine as expressed in Times-Mirror Broadcasting Co., 24 P & F Radio Reg. 404 (1962), to send a tape, transcript, or summary of the broadcast to Cook and offer him reply time; and that the station must provide reply time whether or not Cook would pay for it. On review in the Court of Appeals for the District of Columbia Circuit, the FCC's position was upheld as constitutional and otherwise proper. Not long after the *Red Lion* litigation was begun, the FCC issued a Notice of Proposed Rule Making, with an eye to making the personal attack aspect of the fairness doctrine more precise and more readily enforceable, and to specifying its rules relating to political editorials. After considering written comments supporting and opposing the rules, the FCC adopted them substantially as proposed. Twice amended, the rules were held unconstitutional, in the *RTNDA* litigation by the Court of Appeals for the Seventh Circuit, on review of the rulemaking proceeding, as abridging the freedoms of speech and press.

> As they now stand amended, the regulations read as follows:
>
> Personal attacks; political editorials.
>
> (a) When, during the presentation of views on a controversial issue of public importance, an attack is made upon the honesty, character, integrity or like personal qualities of an identified person or group, the licensee shall, within a reasonable time and in no event later than one week after the attack, transmit to the person or group attacked (1) notification of the date, time and identification of the broadcast; (2) a script or tape (or an accurate summary if a script or tape is not available) of the attack; and (3) an offer of a reasonable opportunity to respond over the licensee's facilities.
>
> (b) The provisions of paragraph (a) of this section shall not be applicable (1) to attacks on foreign groups or foreign public figures; (2) to personal attacks which are made by legally qualified candidates, their authorized spokesmen, or those associated with them in the campaign, on other such candidates, their authorized spokesmen, or persons associated with the candidates in the campaign; and (3) to bona fide newscasts, bona fide news interviews, and on-the-spot coverage of a bona fide news event (including commentary or analysis contained in the foregoing programs, but the provisions of paragraph (a) shall be applicable to editorials of the licensee)* * *
>
> (c) Where a licensee, in an editorial, (i) endorses or (ii) opposes a legally qualified candidate or candidates, the licensee shall, within 24 hours after the editorial, transmit to respectively (i) the other qualified candidate or candidates for the same office or (ii) the candidate opposed in the editorial (1) notification of the date and the time of the editorial; (2) a script or tape of the editorial; and (3) an offer of a reasonable opportunity for a candidate or a spokesman of the candidate to respond over the licensee's facilities: Provided, however, That where such editorials are broadcast within 72 hours prior to the day of the election, the licensee shall comply with the provisions of this subsection sufficiently far in advance of the broadcast to enable the candidate or candidates to have a reasonable opportunity to prepare a response and to present it in a timely fashion.

Believing that the specific application of the fairness doctrine in *Red Lion*, and the promulgation of the regulations in *RTNDA*, are both authorized by Congress and enhance rather than abridge the freedoms of speech and press protected by the First Amendment, we hold them valid and constitutional, reversing the judgment below in *RTNDA* and affirming the judgment below in *Red Lion*.

The history of the emergence of the fairness doctrine and of the related legislation shows that the Commission's action in the *Red Lion* case did not exceed its authority, and that in adopting the new regulations the Commission was implementing congressional policy rather than embarking on a frolic of its own. * * *

There is a twofold duty laid down by the FCC's decisions and described by the 1949 Report on Editorializing by Broadcast Licensees, 13 F.C.C. 1246 (1949). The broadcaster must give adequate coverage to public issues and coverage must be fair in that it accurately reflects the opposing views. This must be done at the broadcaster's own expense if sponsorship is unavailable. Moreover, the duty must be met by programming obtained at the licensee's own initiative if available from no other source. * * *

When a personal attack has been made on a figure involved in a public issue, both the doctrine of cases such as *Red Lion* and Times–Mirror Broadcasting Co., 24 P & F Radio Reg. 404 (1962)and also the 1967 regulations at issue in *RTNDA* require that the individual attacked himself be offered an opportunity to respond. Likewise, where one candidate is endorsed in a political editorial, the other candidates must themselves be offered reply time to use personally or through a spokesman. These obligations differ from the general fairness requirement that issues be presented, and presented with coverage of competing views, in that the broadcaster does not have the option of presenting the attacked party's side himself or choosing a third party to represent that side. But insofar as there is an obligation of the broadcaster to see that both sides are presented, and insofar as that is an affirmative obligation, the personal attack doctrine and regulations do not differ from preceding fairness doctrine. The simple fact that the attacked men or unendorsed candidates may respond themselves or through agents is not a critical distinction, and indeed, it is not unreasonable for the FCC to conclude that the objective of adequate presentation of all sides may best be served by allowing those most closely affected to make the response, rather than leaving the response in the hands of the station which has attacked their candidacies, endorsed their opponents, or carried a personal attack upon them.

The statutory authority of the FCC to promulgate these regulations derives from the mandate to the "Commission from time to time, as public convenience, interest, or necessity requires" to promulgate "such rules and regulations and prescribe such restrictions and conditions * * * as may be necessary to carry out the provisions of this chapter * * *." The Commission is specifically directed to consider the demands of the public interest in the course of granting licenses, renewing them, and modifying them. Moreover, the FCC had included among the conditions of the Red Lion license itself the requirement that operation of the station be carried out in the public interest. This mandate to the FCC to assure that broadcasters operate in the public interest is a broad one, a power "not niggardly but expansive." *National Broadcasting Co. v. United States*, 319 U.S. 190, 219 (1943), whose validity we have long upheld. It is broad enough to encompass these regulations.

The fairness doctrine finds specific recognition in statutory form, is in part modeled on explicit statutory provisions relating to political candidates, and is approvingly reflected in legislative history. * * *

III

The broadcasters challenge the fairness doctrine and its specific manifestations in the personal attack and political editorial rules or conventional First Amendment grounds, alleging that the rules abridge their freedom of speech and press. Their contention is that the First Amendment protects their desire to use their allotted frequencies continuously to broadcast whatever they choose, and to exclude whomever they choose from ever using that frequency. No man may be prevented from saying or publishing what he thinks, or from refusing in his speech or other utterances to give equal weight to the views of his opponents. This right, they say, applies equally to broadcasters.

Although broadcasting is clearly a medium affected by a First Amendment interest, differences in the characteristics of new media justify differences in the First Amendment standards applied to them. For example, the ability of new technology to produce sounds more raucous than those of the human voice justifies restrictions on the sound level, and on the hours and places of use, of sound trucks so long as the restrictions are reasonable and applied without discrimination.

Just as the Government may limit the use of sound amplifying equipment potentially so noisy that it drowns out civilized private speech, so may the Government limit the use of broadcast equipment. The right of free speech of a broadcaster, the user of a sound truck, or any other individual does not embrace a right to snuff out the free speech of others.

When two people converse face to face, both should not speak at once if either is to be clearly understood. * * * The lack of know-how and equipment may keep many from the air, but only a tiny fraction of those with resources and intelligence can hope to communicate by radio at the same time if intelligible communications is to be had, even if the entire radio spectrum is utilized in the present state of commercially acceptable technology.

It was this fact, and the chaos which ensued from permitting anyone to use any frequency at whatever power level he wished, which made necessary the enactment of the Radio Act of 1927 and the Communications Act of 1934. * * * It was this reality which at the very least necessitated first the division of the radio spectrum into portions reserved respectively for public broadcasting and for other important radio uses such as amateur operation, aircraft, police, defense, and navigation; and then the subdivision of each portion, and assignment of specific frequencies to individual users or groups of users. Beyond this however, because the frequencies reserved for public broadcasting were limited in number, it was essential for the Government to tell some applicants that they could not broadcast at all because there was room for only a few.

Where there are substantially more individuals who want to broadcast than there are frequencies to allocate, it is idle to posit an unabridgeable First Amendment right to broadcast comparable to the right of every individual to speak, write, or publish. If 100 persons want broadcast licenses but there are only 10 frequencies to allocate, all of them may have the same "right" to a license; but if there is to be any effective communication by radio, only a few can be licensed and the rest must be barred from the airways. It would be strange if the First Amendment, aimed at protecting and furthering communications, prevented the Government from making radio communication possible by requiring licenses to broadcast and by limiting the number of licenses so as not to overcrowd the spectrum. * * *

This is not to say that the First Amendment is irrelevant to public broadcasting. On the contrary, it has a major role to play as the Congress itself recognized in § 326, which forbids FCC interference with "the right of free speech by means of radio communication." Because of the scarcity of radio frequencies, the Government is permitted to put restraints on licensees in favor of others whose views should be expressed on this unique medium. But the people as a whole retain their interest in free speech by radio and their collective right to have the medium function consistently with the ends and purposes of the First Amendment. * * * It is the purpose of the First Amendment to preserve an uninhibited marketplace of ideas in which truth will ultimately prevail, rather than to countenance monopolization of that market, whether it be by the Government itself or a private licensee. * * * It is the right of the public to receive suitable access to social, political, esthetic, moral, and other ideas and experiences which is crucial here. That right may not constitutionally be abridged either by Congress or by the FCC. * * *

In terms of constitutional principle, and as enforced sharing of a scarce resource, the personal attack and political editorial rules are indistinguishable from the equal-time provision of § 315, a specific enactment of Congress requiring stations to set aside reply time under specified circumstances and to which the fairness doctrine and these constituent regulations are important complements. That provision, which has been part of the law since 1927, has been held valid by this Court as an obligation of the licensee relieving him of any power in any way to prevent or censor the broadcast, and thus insulating him from liability for defamation. The constitutionality of the statute under the First Amendment was unquestioned.

Nor can we say that it is inconsistent with the First Amendment goal of producing an informed public capable of conducting its own affairs to require a broadcaster to permit answers to personal attacks occurring in the course of discussing controversial issues, or to require that the political opponents of those endorsed by the station be given a chance to communicate with the public. Otherwise, station owners and a few networks would have unfettered power to make time available only to the highest bidders, to communicate only their own views on public issues, people and candidates, and to permit on the air only those with whom they agreed. There is no sanctuary in the First Amendment for unlimited private censorship operating in a medium not open to all. "Freedom of the press from governmental interference under the First Amendment does not sanction repression of that freedom by private interests."

It is strenuously argued, however, that if political editorials or personal attacks will trigger an obligation in broadcasters to afford the opportunity for expression to speakers who need not pay for time and whose views are unpalatable to the licensees, then broadcasters will be irresistibly forced to self-censorship and their coverage of controversial public issues will be eliminated or at least rendered wholly ineffective. Such a result would indeed be a serious matter, for should licensees actually eliminate their coverage of controversial issues, the purposes of the doctrine would be stifled.

At this point, however, as the Federal Communications Commission has indicated, that possibility is at best speculative. The communications industry, and in particular the networks, have taken pains to present controversial issues in the past, and even now they do not assert that they intend to abandon their efforts in this regard. It would be better if the FCC's encouragement were never necessary to induce the broadcasters to meet their responsibility. And if experience with the administration of those doctrines indicates that they have the net effect of reducing rather than enhancing the volume and quality of coverage, there will be time enough to reconsider the constitutional implications. The fairness doctrine in the past has had no such overall effect.

That this will occur now seems unlikely, however, since if present licensees should suddenly prove timorous, the Commission is not powerless to insist that they give adequate and fair attention to public issues. * * *

We need not and do not now ratify every past and future decision by the FCC with regard to programming. There is no question here of the Commission's refusal to permit the broadcaster to carry a particular program or to publish his own views; of a discriminatory refusal to require the licensee to broadcast certain views which have been denied access to the airways; of government censorship of a particular program contrary to § 326; or of the official government view dominating public broadcasting. Such questions would raise more serious First Amendment issues. But we do hold that the Congress and the Commission do not violate the First Amendment when they require a radio or television station to give reply time to answer personal attacks and political editorials.

It is argued that even if at one time the lack of available frequencies for all who wished to use them justified the Government's choice of those who would best serve the public interest by acting as proxy for those who would present differing views, or by giving the latter access directly to broadcast facilities, this condition no longer prevails so that continuing control is not justified. To this there are several answers. Scarcity is not entirely a thing of the past. Advances in technology, such as microwave transmission, have led to more efficient utilization of the frequency spectrum, but uses for that spectrum have also grown apace. * * *

Even where there are gaps in spectrum utilization, the fact remains that existing broadcasters have often attained their present position because of their initial government selection in competition with others before new technological advances opened new opportunities for further uses. Long experience in broadcasting, confirmed habits of listeners and viewers, network affiliation, and other advantages in program procurement give existing broadcasters a substantial advantage over new entrants, even where new entry is technologically possible. These advantages are the fruit of a preferred position conferred by the Government. Some present possibility for new entry by competing stations is not enough, in itself, to render unconstitutional the Government's effort to assure that a broadcaster's programming ranges widely enough to serve the public interest.

In view of the scarcity of broadcast frequencies, the Government's role in allocating those frequencies, and the legitimate claims of those unable without governmental assistance to gain access to those frequencies for expression of their views, we hold the regulations and ruling at issue here are both authorized by statute and constitutional. The judgment of the Court of Appeals in *Red Lion* is affirmed and that in *RTNDA* reversed and the causes remanded for proceedings consistent with this opinion.

Electronic vs. Print Media. In *Miami Herald Pub. Co. v. Tornillo,* 418 U.S. 241 (1974), the Court considered the validity of a Florida statute, modeled on the FCC rules upheld in *Red Lion*, providing a right of reply access to newspapers. In striking down the statute, the Court discussed arguments that were meant to show that the newspaper "spectrum" is at least as scarce as the broadcasting one:

> The appellee and supporting advocates of an enforceable right of access to the press vigorously argue that government has an obligation to ensure that a wide variety of views reach the public.* * * It is urged that at the time the First Amendment to the Constitution

was ratified in 1791 as part of our Bill of Rights the press was broadly representative of the people it was serving. While many of the newspapers were intensely partisan and narrow in their views, the press collectively presented a broad range of opinions to readers. Entry into publishing was inexpensive; pamphlets and books provided meaningful alternatives to the organized press for the expression of unpopular ideas and often treated events and expressed views not covered by conventional newspapers. A true marketplace of ideas existed in which there was relatively easy access to the channels of communication.

Access advocates submit that although newspapers of the present are superficially similar to those of 1791 the press of today is in reality very different from that known in the early years of our national existence. In the past half century a communications revolution has seen the introduction of radio and television into our lives, the promise of a global community through the use of communications satellites, and the specter of a "wired" nation by means of an expanding cable television network with two-way capabilities. The printed press, it is said, has not escaped the effects of this revolution. Newspapers have become big business and there are far fewer of them to serve a larger literate population. Chains of newspapers, national newspapers, national wire and news services, and one-newspaper towns, are the dominant features of a press that has become noncompetitive and enormously powerful and influential in its capacity to manipulate popular opinion and change the course of events. Major metropolitan newspapers have collaborated to establish news services national in scope. * * *

The elimination of competing newspapers in most of our large cities, and the concentration of control of media that results from the only newspaper's being owned by the same interests which own a television station and a radio station, are important components of this trend toward concentration of control of outlets to inform the public.

The result of these vast changes has been to place in a few hands the power to inform the American people and shape public opinion. Much of the editorial opinion and commentary that is printed is that of syndicated columnists distributed nationwide and, as a result, we are told, on national and world issues there tends to be a homogeneity of editorial opinion, commentary, and interpretive analysis. The abuses of bias and manipulative reportage are, likewise, said to be the result of the vast accumulations of unreviewable power in the modern media empires. In effect, it is claimed, the public has lost any ability to respond or to contribute in a meaningful way to the debate on issues. * * *

The obvious solution, which was available to dissidents at an earlier time when entry into publishing was relatively inexpensive, today would be to have additional newspapers. But the same economic factors which have caused the disappearance of vast numbers of

> metropolitan newspapers, have made entry into the marketplace of ideas served by the print media almost impossible. It is urged that the claim of newspapers to be "surrogates for the public" carries with it a concomitant fiduciary obligation to account for that stewardship. From this premise it is reasoned that the only effective way to insure fairness and accuracy and to provide for some accountability is for government to take affirmative action. The First Amendment interest of the public in being informed is said to be in peril because the "marketplace of ideas" is today a monopoly controlled by the owners of the market.

Nevertheless, the Court invalidated the statute:

> We see that * * * the Court has expressed sensitivity as to whether a restriction or requirement constituted the compulsion exerted by government on a newspaper to print that which it would not otherwise print. The clear implication has been that any such a compulsion to publish that which "reason tells them should not be published" is unconstitutional. A responsible press is an undoubtedly desirable goal, but press responsibility is not mandated by the Constitution and like many other virtues it cannot be legislated.
>
> Appellee's argument that the Florida statute does not amount to a restriction of appellant's right to speak because "the statute in question here has not prevented the Miami Herald from saying anything it wished" begs the core question. Compelling editors or publishers to publish that which "reason tells them should not be published" is what is at issue in this case. The Florida statute operates as a command in the same sense as a statute or regulation forbidding appellant to publish specified matter. * * * The Florida statute exacts a penalty on the basis of the content of a newspaper. The first phase of the penalty resulting from the compelled printing of a reply is exacted in terms of the cost in printing and composing time and materials and in taking up space that could be devoted to other material the newspaper may have preferred to print. It is correct, as appellee contends, that a newspaper is not subject to the finite technological limitations of time that confront a broadcaster but it is not correct to say that, as an economic reality, a newspaper can proceed to infinite expansion of its column space to accommodate the replies that a government agency determines or a statute commands the readers should have available.
>
> Faced with the penalties that would accrue to any newspaper that published news or commentary arguably within the reach of the right-of-access statute, editors might well conclude that the safe course is to avoid controversy. Therefore, under the operation of the Florida statute, political and electoral coverage would be blunted or reduced. Government-enforced right of access inescapably "dampens the vigor and limits the variety of public debate," *New York Times Co. v. Sullivan*, 376 U.S., at 279. * * *

> Even if a newspaper would face no additional costs to comply with a compulsory access law and would not be forced to forgo publication of news or opinion by the inclusion of a reply, the Florida statute fails to clear the barriers of the First Amendment because of its intrusion into the function of editors. A newspaper is more than a passive receptacle or conduit for news, comment, and advertising. The choice of material to go into a newspaper, and the decisions made as to limitations on the size and content of the paper, and treatment of public issues and public officials—whether fair or unfair—constitute the exercise of editorial control and judgment. It has yet to be demonstrated how governmental regulation of this crucial process can be exercised consistent with First Amendment guarantees of a free press as they have evolved to this time.

The Court's opinion in *Tornillo* nowhere cites *Red Lion* even to distinguish it. Why? Was it simply avoiding the awkwardness of trying to distinguish it? The immediate explanation for the different treatment of print and broadcast media in regard to the right of reply is the "scarcity" rationale. But is scarcity a credible rationale? Even in 1968 it was a commonplace that in virtually every American city there are far more radio and television broadcast stations than newspapers. One response that *Red Lion* supporters have offered is that scarcity of broadcast media is imposed by government decree (licensure) whereas the limit on newspapers is a matter of economics. Is that a relevant distinction?

The particular subject of *Red Lion*—the fairness doctrine— has now been eliminated by the FCC, as we discuss in the next section. *Red Lion* has never been overturned and is still the canonical reference on the supposed special character of broadcasting. But as the number of electronic media outlets have increased, the scarcity rationale has become thinner and thinner. Even the FCC repudiated it in the late 1980s as the basis for regulating fairness, but the rationale continues to be invoked from time to time in support of other types of content regulation.

Electronic Culture. Scarcity to one side, electronic media clearly are different from print in one respect: they were born into a regulated environment. Except for a very short period in the early 1920s before the Radio Act of 1927, the electronic media have always been regulated. Government control of the media quickly came to be a social norm in a way that was never the case for print media.[2] Indeed, in most countries around the world until recent times, the major broadcast entities were government owned. Explaining the difference between electronic and

2. This cultural difference and its effect on free speech values is the subject of a well-known book, Ithiel De Sola Pool, TECHNOLOGIES OF FREEDOM (1983). Pool worried that the increased dominance of the electronic media threatened First Amendment values because of the regulatory baggage they brought with them. For a critical review of this thesis, see Glen O. Robinson, *The Electronic First Amendment: An Essay for the New Age*, 47 DUKE L.J. 899 (1998) (arguing, inter alia, that in some respects the electronic media has resulted in an *expanded* scope for the First Amendment insofar as it has brought constitutional scrutiny into many areas of routine economic regulation).

print media in terms of "culture" is frustratingly question-begging: in a country otherwise steeped in a liberal tradition of unregulated speech, how did a tradition of regulation become so firmly entrenched? In the context of indecency, the argument takes the form of a particular concern about the pervasive and intrusive character of radio and television. However, it is relatively straight forward to enlarge this concern into a more general one about the social and cultural impact of radio and television, from which one then constructs an argument for treating the electronic media differently: they are too important to be left entirely to their own devices.

Is this a plausible justification for media content regulation? Would Madison approve? It depends, presumably, on what you think the First Amendment is all about. Is it just about protecting speakers—including, of course, the "press"—against government? Or is it also about protecting speech itself against excessive control by "big media"? The concern about media concentration is an old one. And, despite the proliferation of new media, it is a persistent one. Whether it is a justified concern is a matter we will explore further when we take up structural controls—regulation of broadcast and cable ownership, television networks and their affiliations, and related matters. However, the concern about giant media conglomerates clearly has an effect on popular and political attitudes towards content controls. To be sure, media moguls are found outside the radio and television industry—as witness the concentration of book publishing in a handful of giant companies (e.g., Wolters-Kluwer; Bertelsmann AG; Thomson-West) or the concentration among newspaper chains (e.g., The New York Times Company, Gannett, The Tribune Company; McClatchy). However, these publishing giants do not receive the same popular attention as those found in radio and television (e.g., the four major broadcast networks; independent group owners such as Sinclair Broadcasting; cable MSOs such as Comcast, Time Warner and Cablevision, radio station group owners, such as Clear Channel and Viacom—to name a few of the more prominent).

2. Public Issues and Political Broadcasting

We noted above that the Commission terminated its fairness doctrine based on a conclusion that the underlying scarcity rationale no longer required it and on the ground that it did have a potential chilling effect on broadcast speech, finding that the agency's own regulation was not only bad policy, it also violated the First Amendment. The FCC's decision to terminate the doctrine was reviewed by the D.C. Circuit in the following case, which lays out the nature of the fairness doctrine's obligations and examines the broader First Amendment values the doctrine was originally thought to advance (and later thought to impede).

SYRACUSE PEACE COUNCIL v. FCC

United States Court of Appeals, District of Columbia Circuit, 1989.
867 F.2d 654.

WILLIAMS, CIRCUIT JUDGE:

Under the "fairness doctrine," the Federal Communications Commission has, as its 1985 Fairness Report explains, required broadcast media licensees (1) "to provide coverage of vitally important controversial issues of interest in the community served by the licensees" and (2) "to provide a reasonable opportunity for the presentation of contrasting viewpoints on such issues." *Report Concerning General Fairness Doctrine Obligations of Broadcast Licensees*, 102 F.C.C.2d 143, 146 (1985). In adjudication of a complaint against Meredith Corporation, licensee of station WTVH in Syracuse, New York, the Commission concluded that the doctrine did not serve the public interest and was unconstitutional. Accordingly it refused to enforce the doctrine against Meredith. Although the Commission somewhat entangled its public interest and constitutional findings, we find that the Commission's public interest determination was an independent basis for its decision and was supported by the record. We uphold that determination without reaching the constitutional issue.

I.

In the summer of 1982 Meredith ran a series of advertisements over WTVH arguing that the Nine Mile II nuclear power plant was a "sound investment for New York." Syracuse Peace Council complained to the Commission that Meredith had failed to give viewers conflicting perspectives on the plant and had thereby violated the second of the fairness doctrine's two requirements.

In its initial decision the Commission agreed with Syracuse that Meredith had failed to fulfill its obligations under the doctrine and demanded that the station within 20 days give notice of how it planned to meet those obligations.

Meredith filed a petition for reconsideration in which it argued that the fairness doctrine was unconstitutional. Before ruling on Meredith's petition, the Commission completed its 1985 Fairness Report, the culmination of a separate inquiry into both the wisdom and constitutionality of the fairness doctrine.

On the issue of whether the doctrine continued to promote the public interest, the 1985 Report said that the Commission was "firmly convinced that the fairness doctrine, as a matter of policy, disserves the public interest ..." In reaching that conclusion the Commission invoked essentially the same grounds as it has in the present action—chiefly, that growth in the number of broadcast outlets reduced any need for the doctrine, that the doctrine often worked to dissuade broadcasters from presenting any treatment of controversial viewpoints, that it put the government in the doubtful position of evaluating program content, and that it created an opportunity for incumbents to abuse it for partisan purposes. Despite all this, it declined to eliminate the doctrine, expressing concern that it might be statutorily mandated.

The 1985 Report also raised serious doubts about the continuing constitutionality of the fairness doctrine, but, saying that it was "the province of the federal judiciary—and not this Commission—to interpret the Constitution," the Commission refused to make a constitutional ruling.

After issuing the 1985 Report, the FCC in due course considered Meredith's petition for reconsideration. In that context it again refused to address the constitutional issue—not on the ground that Meredith had raised the defense belatedly but solely on the theory that issue should he left to Congress and the courts. It invoked its 1985 Report in support of this view.

On appeal, this court reversed and remanded the case to the Commission. We noted the principle that regulatory agencies cannot invalidate an act of Congress, but said that an agency could not blind itself to a constitutional defense to a "self-generated" policy. In the meantime, we observed, this court had in another decision found that the fairness doctrine was *not* mandated by statute. *Telecommunications Research & Action Center v. FCC*, 801 F.2d 501, *reh'g en banc denied*, 806 F.2d 1115 (D.C.Cir. 1986) ("TRAC"), cert. denied, 107 S. Ct. 3196 (1987). Thus on remand the Commission would have to resolve Meredith's constitutional defense, *unless* it determined in light of the 1985 Report that enforcement of the doctrine was contrary to the public interest. We explicitly noted that the 1985 Report had concluded that indeed the doctrine no longer served the public interest standard of the Communications Act, and that in the Report the Commission had "largely undermined the legitimacy of its own rule" and "eviscerate[d] the rationale" for the doctrine.

On remand, the Commission expanded the scope of the Meredith proceeding by soliciting comments from the public on the general questions whether "in light of the 1985 Fairness Report, enforcement of the fairness doctrine is constitutional and whether enforcement of the doctrine is contrary to the public interest." In its *Memorandum Order and Opinion in Syracuse Peace Council*, 2 FCC Rcd. 5043 (1987), *recon. denied*, 3 F.C.C.2d 2035 (1988), the Commission ruled in favor of Meredith.

The FCC relied heavily on the conclusions drawn in the 1985 Fairness Report, and in fact incorporated that Report into the record and "(reaffirmed) [its] findings and conclusions." After reciting and endorsing the 1985 Fairness Report's conclusions, the Commission declared that "the fairness doctrine chills speech and is not narrowly tailored to achieve a substantial government interest." Consequently, the FCC concluded "under existing Supreme Court precedent, as set forth in *Red Lion* [*Broadcasting Co. v. FCC*, 395 U.S. 367 (1969)] and its progeny, that the fairness doctrine contravenes the First Amendment and thereby disserves the public interest."

II.

At no time during the long and intricate proceedings in this case has any party suggested that the fairness doctrine is constitutionally compelled. Nor can it be claimed here, in view of this court's *TRAC* decision, that the doctrine is statutorily mandated. Accordingly, the Commission has the authority to reject the doctrine if it concludes, without being arbitrary or capricious, that it no longer serves the public interest. The Commission has slightly complicated the issue, however, by asserting that "the policy and constitutional considerations in this matter are inextricably intertwined." If that were true, we could resolve the case only by addressing the constitutional issue.

But it is an elementary canon that American courts are not to "pass upon a constitutional question ... if there is also present some other ground upon which the case may be disposed of." We applied the maxim in this litigation's prior appearance here, and it is obviously no less compelling today. Further, if an agency relies on two grounds for a decision, a court may sustain it if one is valid and if the agency would clearly have acted on that ground even if the other were unavailable.

Thus, if we are persuaded that the Commission would have found that the fairness doctrine did not serve the public interest even if it had foregone its ruminations on the constitutional issue, we must end our inquiry without reaching that issue. In fact, as we explain in part III [omitted], we have no doubt that even in the absence of constitutional problems the Commission would have reached the same outcome. We then turn in part IV to petitioners' objections to the Commission's policy decision, and in part V to issues relating to the Commission's withdrawal of the doctrine's "first prong," the requirement of coverage of controversial issues. * * *

IV.

The FCC's decision that the fairness doctrine no longer serves the public interest is a policy judgment. There is no real dispute that fostering fair, balanced and diverse coverage of controversial issues is a good thing. Nor, so far as we can tell from the record or briefs, is there any question that discouraging any coverage at all, having government officials second-guess editorial judgments, or allowing incumbents an opportunity for abuse of power are things to be avoided, all other things being equal. The Commission's problem was to make predictive and normative judgments about the tendency of the fairness doctrine to produce each of these things, about how bad the bad effects were and how good the good ones, and ultimately about whether bad effects outweighed good. * * *

In this situation, we owe great deference to the Commission's judgment. * * *

The Commission's factual judgments here are almost entirely predictive—statements about the overall effects of a policy on licensees and others. The Supreme Court has observed that "In such cases complete factual support for the Commission's ultimate conclusions is not required since 'a forecast of the direction in which the future public interest lies necessarily involves deductions based on the expert knowledge of the agency.'" Although we do not suppose for a minute that experience without the fairness doctrine will quell dispute—the same problems of measuring the immeasurable will remain—we bear in mind Judge Leventhal's point that for resolution of dispute over "legislative" as opposed to "adjudicative" facts, "a month of experience will be worth a year of hearings."

Of course, an agency can act arbitrarily or capriciously in the exercise of a policy judgment, and we must assure ourselves that did not happen here. The challengers' primary claims are that the supporting evidence was insufficient, that the Commission failed to consider the whole record or to consider alternative solutions adequately, and that its decision in the present case was an arbitrary departure from its 1985 decision to retain the doctrine.

Before addressing those specific attacks, we must describe two core findings of the 1985 Report—that the fairness doctrine often operated to chill broadcaster speech on controversial issues and that recent increases in broadcasting outlets undercut the need for the doctrine—on which the Commission relied heavily in the present decision. It found that the doctrine produced chilling effects by placing burdens on stations which chose to air numerous programs on controversial issues—including the fear of denial of license renewal due to fairness doctrine violations, the cost of defending fairness doctrine attacks and of providing free air time to opposing views if a fairness violation is found, and the reputational harm resulting from even a frivolous fairness challenge. While the FCC recognized that to a degree the first prong of the fairness doctrine offset this effect by requiring broadcasters to present some controversial issues, it nonetheless found that broadcasters were encouraged to air only the minimal amount of controversial issue programming sufficient to comply with the first prong. By restricting the amount and type of controversial programming aired, a broadcaster minimizes the potentially substantial burdens associated with the second prong of the doctrine while remaining in compliance with the strict letter of its regulatory obligations. Therefore, despite the first prong obligation, in net effect the fairness doctrine often discourages the presentation of controversial issue programming.

The 1985 Fairness Report also noted that paradoxically the chilling effect often fell on the expression of unorthodox or "fringe" views on controversial issues. Since the doctrine compelled coverage only of "major" or "significant" opinions, the FCC claimed that in assessing fairness doctrine compliance, the Commission was called upon to evaluate broadcasters' decisions concerning the importance of given viewpoints. The Report expressed its fear that the fairness doctrine thus had the potential "to interject the government, even unintentionally, into the position of favoring one type of opinion over another."

In assessing whether any need for the doctrine persisted, the 1985 Report found a dramatic increase in broadcasting outlets since the 1974 Fairness Report (48 F.C.C.2d 1). This expansion in broadcasting capacity was found to have been spread widely across American society. The FCC found that by 1984 96% of television households received five or more over-the-air (non-cable) television signals, compared with 83% in 1972. Those receiving nine or more signals had tripled, from 21% of TV households in 1972 to 64% in 1984. Of course some signals may for one reason or another be unable to function as serious alternative sources. But the new signals are plainly not trivial in the aggregate, as they have driven the networks' audience share down from 90% in 1982 to 76% in 1984.

The Commission also found significant growth in radio outlets since the 1974 Fairness Report. The number of radio stations grew by 30% between 1974 and 1985. The subset of FM service increased during the same period by 60%, leading the FCC to proclaim that "there has also been a fundamental change in the structure of the radio market. Once predominantly an AM only service, radio is now composed of two very competitive services." The Commission noted that radio expansion impacted smaller communities as well as larger urban areas; "the number of radio voices available in each local market has grown." Looking at substitute electronic media such as low power television, video cassette recorders, satellite master antenna systems, and so forth, the Commission found that the gains in radio and television accessibility and diversity actually understated the true development of broadcast media available to the viewing public. The Report also noted that print media coverage of controversial issues offered Americans exposure to the type of information which the fairness doctrine was designed to foster. We now turn to the specific objections to the Commission's conclusions. * * * [The court here reviews and rejects various claims of insufficiency of evidence supporting the Commission's findings of a chilling effect, failure to consider the benefits of the fairness doctrine and failure to consider alternative methods of enforcement.]

V.

Several parties attack the Commission's repeal of the so-called "first prong" of the fairness doctrine—the requirement that broadcasters provide coverage of important controversial issues of interest to the community they serve. First, they contend that they were not adequately notified of the Commission's intent to reconsider the first prong in this proceeding. Second, petitioners argue that the FCC's abandonment of the first prong was arbitrary and capricious. * * * [The court rejects both arguments.]

CONCLUSION

We conclude that the FCC's decision that the fairness doctrine no longer served the public interest was neither arbitrary, capricious nor an abuse of discretion, and are convinced that it would have acted on that finding to terminate the doctrine even in the absence of its belief that the doctrine was no longer constitutional. Accordingly we uphold the Commission without reaching the constitutional issues. The petition for review is denied.

STARR, CIRCUIT JUDGE, concurring:

* * * With all respect to the court's view enunciated today, I am convinced that the record in this case simply will not, fairly read, yield the conclusion that the agency has based the specific decision before us independently on non-constitutional grounds. There is, therefore, no proper basis for skirting the Commission's constitutional analysis (unless we were to conclude, as I do not, that the Commission erred in even considering that issue); in short, the constitutional justifications for the Commission's action must, alas, be considered. * * *

In short, the record establishes beyond cavil (1) that the FCC based its Order on the premise that the First Amendment questions and public interest issues are "inextricably intertwined" and (2) that the Commission engaged in a *Red Lion* analysis. It follows from [*SEC v. Chenery Corp.*, 318 U.S. 80 (1943),] that this court is wanting in authority to wave all that pesky constitutional analysis away and pretend that what we have before us, in effect, is the 1985 Report. *Meredith* has unleashed *Red Lion*, and it will not do to pretend, with cheery bravado, that *Red Lion* is still secure in its pre-*Meredith* cage. *Red Lion* is now out on the streets, released by a deliberate and careful FCC decision. * * *

Personal Attacks and Political Editorializing. There remained for a decade uncertainty about particular parts of the fairness principle, concerning personal attacks and political editorializing that were involved in *Red Lion*. The Commission kept those rules on the books, but did not enforce them. In 1996 it was petitioned to decided whether the rules were in effect or not. However, a vacancy on the Commission at the time left a membership of four, and they divided on whether to terminate the two regulations. Eventually the question was decided by the court of appeals, which declared the rules to be a non-severable part of the repudiated fairness doctrine, and hence no longer valid. *Radio-Television News Directors Ass'n v. FCC*, 229 F.3d 269 (D.C. Cir. 2000).

Equal Time and Candidate Access. One of the arguments made by two commissioners for retaining the personal attack and political editorializing rules was that the rules did not depend on the fate of the general fairness doctrine, but was complementary to two other rules governing political broadcast that were contained in the Communications Act itself and hence unaffected by *Syracuse Peace Council*.

The first of these is the equal time (aka "equal opportunity") rule. Section 315 of the Communications Act requires that, whenever a licensee permits the "use" of a broadcast station's facilities by "a legally qualified candidate for any public office," it shall afford "equal opportunities to all other candidates for that office." Equal opportunity has been interpreted to mean time on the same terms, conditions, and rates as the initial use. This does not require that free time be given (unless the original use was free). See, e.g., *Carter/Mondale Reelection Comm.*, 81 F.C.C.2d 409 (1980). However, § 315 does require that stations sell time to political candidates at the lowest unit time charge charged for comparable commercial users. Section 315 is triggered only when one candidate is allowed to use the station; there is no initial obligation to allow such use. The second rule is a provision assuring that candidates for federal office have a limited right of access. Section 312(a)(7) prohibits "willful or repeated failure to allow reasonable access or sell reasonable amount of time for use" by such a candidate.

Neither Section 315 nor 312(a)(7) has engendered the kind of controversy generated by the fairness doctrine in its heyday, though the constitutionality of each has been challenged, unsuccessfully. Section 312(a)(7) was upheld against a First Amendment challenge in *CBS v. FCC*, 453 U.S. 367 (1981). The Supreme Court has never spoken to the constitutionality of Section 315, but the court of appeals has rejected such a challenge, relying on *CBS v. FCC*. See *Branch v. FCC*, 824 F.2d 37 (D.C. Cir. 1987).

The principal implementation issue raised by § 315 has centered on what constitutes a "use" by a candidate so as to trigger equal opportunity by an opposing candidate. The FCC has interpreted "use" to include virtually any appearance by the candidate whether or not the appearance is related to the candidacy. At one time the Commission's policy was so mechanical that it counted "appearances" that were not authorized or sponsored by the candidate. For instance in *Adrian Weiss*, 58 F.C.C.2d 342 (1976), the Commission ruled that a station's announced intention to show Ronald Reagan's old movies (most notably "Bedtime for Bonzo") during the period he was a candidate for President would constitute a "use" by him that would trigger equal time responsibilities on the part of the station. (Reagan declared that if the movies were aired he would demand equal time.) The Commission has since overruled *Weiss*; it now requires that the use be authorized, controlled, or sponsored by the candidate or campaign committee. *Political Programming Policies*, 7 FCC Rcd. 4611 (1992). But any authorized appearance still counts as a use even if the use is unrelated to his campaign—as in the case of a newscaster who is running for office while also serving as a newscaster. *Branch v. FCC*, *supra*. The same held true for Fred Thompson, a star of the NBC drama "Law & Order," during his brief run for the Republican presidential nomination in 2007–08. NBC pulled episodes featuring Thompson off the air after he declared his candidacy (but not during the extensive "testing the waters" period permitted under federal election law prior to declaring a candidacy and appearing on state ballots). The equal time rules have been applied to cable, but only to content originated by the local cable operator, 47 C.F.R. § 76–205, so cable channel TNT continued airing L & O episodes, allowing Thompson fans to be able to continue enjoying him in re-runs.

Appearances on "bona fide news" programs are an exception to the equal time requirements. Congress added that exception in 1959 in response to a Commission ruling that evening newscast footage of Chicago Mayor (and candidate for reelection) Richard Daley greeting the president of Argentina triggered an obligation to give equal time to a competing candidate (the perennial fringe, and famously loony, candidate, Lar Daly). It isn't clear what Congress found more disturbing about the ruling, whether it was the fact that the Mayor's appearance was on a routine newscast or whether it provided the occasion for giving exposure to a person whose candidacy was more a stunt than a serious run for office. Be that as it may Congress made no exception for the latter; as long as they satisfy the requisite formalities for being a candidate, it doesn't matter whether they are certifiable nut cases. (Imposing a seriousness threshold would have opened up a can of worms.) Importantly, though, Congress did exempt candidate appearances on a bona fide news program. What constitutes "bona fide news" has been a matter of recurrent controversy, most notably in connection with televised presidential debates. For the first televised debate in 1960, Congress suspended the equal time rule in order to permit televised debates among the two principal party candidates without burdening the stations (networks) with equal time obligations. In 1975, the FCC cured the problem by ruling that the debates could be set up as a separate "news event" and televised as such within the news exemption. See *Chisholm v. FCC*, 538 F.2d 349 (D.C. Cir. 1976) (affirming FCC ruling). Later, the Commission interpreted the exemption to apply even if the debate is sponsored by the broadcasters, making the "news" classification a pure formality. *Henry Geller*, 95 F.C.C.2d 1236 (1983), aff'd, 731 F.2d 995 (D.C. Cir. 1984).

Unlike § 315, the candidate access rule, § 312(a)(7) is limited to allowing candidates for federal office the right to purchase airtime at "reasonable" times and in reasonable amounts. What "reasonable" requires has been a sore subject for the broadcasters. In 1994, the National Association of Broadcasters obtained a declaratory judgment from the FCC that reasonable access only required stations to sell candidates the same standard time intervals (e.g., five minutes) that the stations either offered commercial advertisers or used for programming during a preceding year. On reconsideration, however, the Commission retreated from that ruling and held that stations must evaluate each request for time on individualized basis, taking into account: (1) how much time was previously sold to the candidate; (2) the potentially disruptive impact on the station's regular programming; (3) the likelihood of equal opportunities requests by opposing candidates; (4) the timing of the request. *People for the American Way and Media Access Project*, 1999 WL 688352 (FCC).

3. "Public Interest" Programming

Regulating the content of electronic communications has always been a sometime thing. In the heyday of broadcasting, the regulation of broadcast programming ranked high on the FCC's regulatory agenda, or at least it ranked high on the agenda of policy concerns about which the agency *claimed* to be concerned. Ostensibly these requirements were enforced through the licensing process at renewal time. Renewal applicants were required to show that they had provided diverse and balanced programming. At one time, the applicants filled out detailed programming reports that contained boxes for reporting on the amount of programming in different program classifications ranging from agriculture to public affairs. The Commission would look askance at any very low percentage in such key categories as local news or public affairs. If a zero showed up, the FCC would convey signs of disapproval to the licensee. Rarely, however, was a licensee seriously threatened with loss of license for failure to meet the expectations of the FCC (which were very modest in all events). The detailed reporting of program types gave way to a requirement that the renewal applicant undertake special efforts to learn the needs of its community and then report on how it met those needs. This so-called "ascertainment process" was soon abandoned, but stations are still required to prepare a quarterly report of how their programming has responded to community issues, and the Commission recently standardized this reporting to facilitate public scrutiny. *Standardized and Enhanced Disclosure Requirements for Television Broadcast Licensee Public Interest Obligations*, 23 FCC Rcd. 1274 (2008).

Apart from reporting, however, the public interest responsibilities have become largely aspirational. Though the FCC continues to insist that some vague public interest obligations still inhere in the broadcaster's license, it has no specific mechanism or standard for actively enforcing them. The renewal of licenses has become so routine as to be almost pro forma. The decline of these regulatory requirements reflects a combination of factors. Most immediately it reflects a change in the technology of communications. The primary impetus for regulating broadcast programming came from the fact that broadcasters were privileged to use a scarce resource, the radio spectrum. The scarcity rationale was always controversial on a variety of grounds, but it became particularly stressed as new technology brought on stream a vast new capacity for content delivery—cable, satellites, Internet. Today, the scarcity rationale has been virtually abandoned by all but the most die-hard advocates of regulation. As we saw, the FCC itself repudiated scarcity as a rationale for enforcing the fairness doctrine, though nothing prevents the FCC from repudiating its own prior repudiation.

There are still those who argue for a return to the old days of enforcing "public interest" obligations (the conventional code word for enforcing content regulation on broadcasters). In 1997, a presidential advisory commission (nicknamed, however, after the vice president in recognition of the fact that it was his creation) was established to consider what obligations were owed by broadcasters in the new age of "digital broadcasting." The "Gore Commission" recommendations were something of a muddle, reflecting the fact that the members of the Commission represented a wide range of views about the efficacy or appropriateness of content regulation—from those who wanted more or less a full throttle approach to those who wanted nothing at all. In response to the Gore Commission's report, which made four specific recommendations, the FCC issued the following notice of inquiry.

PUBLIC INTEREST OBLIGATIONS OF TV BROADCAST LICENSEES

Notice of Inquiry

Federal Communications Commission, 1999.
14 FCC Rcd. 21633.

I. Introduction

1. Television is the primary source of news and information to Americans, and provides hours of entertainment every week. In particular, children spend far more time watching television that they spend with any other type of media. Those who broadcast television programming thus have a significant impact on society. Given the impact of their programming and their use of the public airwaves, broadcasters have a special role in serving the public. For over seventy years, broadcasters have been required by statute to serve the "public interest, convenience, and necessity." Congress has charged the Federal Communications Commission with the responsibility of implementing and enforcing this public interest requirement. Indeed, this is the "touchstone" of the Commission's statutory duty in licensing the public airwaves. Under the Communications Act of 1934, the Commission may issue, renew, or approve the transfer of a broadcast license only upon first finding that doing so will serve the public interest.

2. There has been considerable debate over the years about how the Commission should carry out this statutory mandate. Currently, broadcasters must comply with a number of affirmative public interest programming and service obligations. For example, broadcast licensees must provide coverage of issues facing their communities and place lists of programming used in providing significant treatment of such issues in their public inspection files. Broadcasters must also comply with statutory political broadcasting requirements regarding equal opportunities, charges for political advertising, and reasonable access for federal candidates. In addition, television broadcasters must provide children's educational and informational programming under the Children's Television Act of 1990. The Commission enacted new rules implementing this statute in 1996. In terms of programming obligations, broadcasters are also prohibited from airing programming that is obscene, and restricted from airing programming that is "indecent" during certain times of the day. Similarly, broadcasters also have obligations regarding closed captioning, equal employment opportunity, sponsorship identification, and advertisements during children's programming.

3. The discussion of television broadcasters' public interest obligations has been renewed by their transition from analog to digital television (DTV) technology. This is due in part to the new opportunities DTV provides. DTV holds the promise of reinventing free, over-the-air television by offering broadcasters new and valuable business opportunities and providing consumers new and valuable services. DTV broadcasters will have the technical capability and regulatory flexibility to air high definition TV (HDTV) programming with state-of-the-art picture clarity; to "multicast" by simultaneously providing multiple channels of standard digital programming and/or HDTV programming; and to "datacast" by providing data such as stock quotes, or interactive TV via the DTV bitstream.

4. In establishing the statutory framework for the transition to DTV, Congress directed the Commission to grant any new DTV licenses to all existing television broadcasters. Congress stated in section 336 of the Communications Act that "[n]othing in this section shall be construed as relieving a television broadcasting station from its obligation to serve the public interest, convenience, and necessity." Likewise, in implementing section 336, the Commission reaffirmed that "digital broadcasters remain public trustees with a responsibility to serve the public interest," and stated that "existing public interest requirements continue to apply to all broadcast licensees."

5. The Commission also indicated, however, that "[b]roadcasters and the public are also on notice that the Commission may adopt new public interest rules for digital television." Commenters in the DTV proceeding adopted different views on this issue, with some arguing that broadcasters' public interest obligations in the digital world "should be clearly defined and commensurate with the new opportunities provided by the digital channels broadcasters are receiving," while others contended that "current public interest rules need not change simply because broadcasters will be using digital technology to provide the same broadcast service to the public." The Commission declined to resolve this issue in the DTV proceeding, instead choosing to issue a "Notice to collect and consider all views" on this subject at a later date.

6. We undertake that task with this *Notice of Inquiry*. In doing so, we are guided by several proposals and recommendations made in recent years. Among the most significant of these are the recommendations of the President's' Advisory Committee on the Public Interest Obligations of Digital Television Broadcasters ("Advisory Committee"). The Advisory Committee was comprised of a broad cross-section of interests, consisting of twenty-two members chosen by the President from "the commercial and noncommercial broadcasting industry, computer industries, producers, academic institutions, public interest organizations, and the advertising community." On December 18, 1998, the Advisory Committee submitted a report, which contains ten separate recommendations on the public interest obligations digital television broadcasters should assume. These range from enhanced disclosures of existing public interest activities to wholly new approaches and theoretical frameworks

toward the public interest obligations of TV broadcasters. Implementation proposals range from asking the broadcast industry to make voluntary commitments in some areas, to suggesting that the Commission regulate in other areas, and that Congress legislate in still others. On October 20, 1999, Vice President Gore submitted a letter to Chairman Kennard asking that the Commission focus on several of the Advisory Committee's recommendations in particular. We discuss below some of the Advisory Committee's ten recommendations that envision a role for the Commission.

7. In addition to the Advisory Committee's recommendations, on June 3, 1999, People for Better TV filed a petition for rulemaking and a petition for notice of inquiry. People for Better TV also includes a number of diverse groups. People for Better TV argues that the Telecommunications Act of 1996 requires the Commission to determine the public interest obligations of DTV broadcasters, that the advent of DTV requires the Commission to consider public interest obligations anew, and to clarify whether existing guidelines apply, and that both broadcasters and the public need a basic set of public interest standards. * * *

II. Areas of Inquiry and Request for Comments

* * *

A. Challenges Unique to the Digital Era

* * *

11. In implementing section 336, the Commission required that broadcasters air "free digital video programming service the resolution of which is comparable to or better than that of today's services, and aired during the same time period that their analog channel is broadcasting." In doing so, the Commission stated that "broadcast licensees and the public are on notice that existing public interest requirements continue to apply to all broadcast licensees." It is thus clear that DTV broadcasters must air programming responsive to their communities of license, comply with the statutory requirements concerning political advertising and candidate access, and provide children's educational and informational programming, among other things. But as People for Better TV ask, how do these obligations apply to a DTV broadcaster that chooses to multicast? Do a licensee's public interest obligations attach to the DTV channel as a whole, such that a licensee has discretion to fulfill them on one of its program streams, or to air some of its public interest programming on more than one of its program streams? Should, instead, the obligations attach to each program stream offered by the licensee, such that, for example, a licensee would need to air children's programming on each of its DTV program streams? The Advisory Committee Report contemplates that, under certain circumstances, a digital broadcaster should not have nonstatutory public interest obligations imposed on channels other than its "primary" channel. A majority of the members of the Advisory Committee believe that the FCC should prohibit broadcasters from segregating candidate-centered programming to sepa-

rate program streams, because they believe that would violate candidates' reasonable access and equal opportunities. We seek comment on these approaches. In addition, how should we take into account the fact that DTV broadcasters can choose either to multicast multiple standard definition DTV program streams or broadcast one or two HDTV program streams during different parts of the day? In addressing these issues, commenters should discuss the requirements of section 336(d) of the Act, which states that a "television licensee shall establish that all of its program services on the existing or advanced spectrum are in the public interest."

12. People for Better TV propose several other ways that digital broadcasters might better serve the nation's children, such as setting aside a minimum number of hours each week to provide educational programs or services, which might include data transmission for schools. In addition, PBTV suggests that the increased information capability of digital technology could improve the current voluntary ratings system. We seek comment on these ideas. In addition, should the ratings of programs promoted by broadcasters be consistent with the rating of the program during which the promotions run? We also ask commenters to address how the policies set forth in the Children's Television Policy Statement should be applied in the digital environment.

13. By definition, ancillary and supplementary services, such as datacasting or paging, are services other than free, over-the-air services. Do a licensee's public interest obligations apply to its ancillary and supplementary services? In addressing these issues, commenters should discuss the relevance of several sections of section 336. People for Better TV contends that "the public interest standard attends to all DTV uses of the spectrum," and points out that section 336(a)(2) states that the Commission "shall adopt regulations that allow the holders of [DTV] licenses to offer such ancillary and supplementary services on designated frequencies as may be consistent with the public interest, convenience, and necessity." We note that section 336(e) requires the Commission to collect fees from DTV broadcasters that offer ancillary and supplementary services, which fees must "recover for the public an amount that, to the extent feasible, equals but does not exceed (over the term of the license) the amount that would have been recovered had such services been licensed pursuant to the provision of section 309(j) of this Act and the Commission's regulations thereunder." In addition, section 336(b)(3) simply requires the Commission to "apply to any other ancillary and supplementary service such of the Commission's regulations as are applicable to the offering of analogous services by any other person." The Advisory Committee Report recommends that "[b]roadcasters that choose to implement datacasting should transmit information on behalf of local schools, libraries, community-based organizations, governmental bodies, and public safety institutions." The Advisory Committee Report suggests that "[t]his activity should count toward fulfillment of a digital broadcaster's public interest obligations," without indicating which regulations are applicable to ancillary and supplementary services. We seek

comment on this proposal. How would datacasting count toward the DTV broadcasters' public interest obligations? We also seek comment more generally on whether the public interest obligations should apply to ancillary and supplementary services, and if so, how.

B. Responding to the Community

14. One of a broadcaster's fundamental public interest obligations is to air programming responsive to the needs and interests of its community of license. Another of its most basic obligations in responding to the public's informational needs is to air emergency information. Technological advances, including digital technology, may allow broadcasters to fulfill these obligations better. For example, digital technology enables broadcasters to track storms house by house. In addition, broadcasters might make information about their programming more accessible, and therefore more responsive, to their communities of license through posting such information on websites on the Internet. As broadcasters move forward with their transition to digital technology, we seek to find ways to help them serve their communities better and more fully.

1. Disclosure Obligations

15. People for Better TV states that DTV broadcasters should "disclose their public interest programming and activities on a quarterly basis, matched against ascertained community needs," gathered by reaching out to "ordinary citizens and local leaders" and sought through "postal and electronic mail services as well as broadcast announcements." The Advisory Committee Report recommends that DTV broadcasters "should be required to make enhanced disclosures of their public interest programming and activities on a quarterly basis, using standardized check-off forms that reduce administrative burdens and can be easily understood by the public." The Advisory Committee Report explains that effective self-regulation requires broadcasters to make available to the public adequate information about what they are doing. The Committee notes that the Commission already requires all TV broadcasters to place in their public files separate quarterly reports on their non-entertainment programming responsive to community needs and on their children's programming, and recommends that the Commission require broadcasters to augment these reports. The enhanced disclosures "should include but not be limited to contributions to political discourse, public service announcements, children's and educational programming, local programming, programming that meets the needs of underserved communities, and community-specific activities." The Committee also recommends that digital TV broadcasters take steps to distribute public interest information more widely, through newspapers and websites.

16. We seek comment on the above recommendations. Our rules currently require commercial TV broadcasters to include in their public file, among other things, citizen agreements, records concerning broadcasts by candidates for public office, annual employment reports, letters

and e-mail from the public, issues/programming lists, records concerning children's programming commercial limits, and children's television programming reports. Should broadcasters provide the additional types of public service information proposed by the Advisory Committee Report and People for Better TV? Should they provide information in addition to, or in lieu of, that proposed by the Committee and People for Better TV? Should the public file contain information on what programming has closed captioning and video description? We seek comment on the extent to which the Advisory Committee's and People for Better TV's proposals parallel the Commission's previous ascertainment requirements, which the Commission repealed in the 1980s, and we ask parties to address whether the Commission's reasons for eliminating those requirements apply to our consideration of these proposals. These ascertainment guidelines set forth specific standards for broadcasters on consulting with community leaders, identifying and responding to community needs and problems through programming, and maintaining and making available various records on their ascertainment procedures. * * *

2. Disaster Warnings

18. The Advisory Committee Report recommends that "[b]roadcasters should work with appropriate emergency communications specialists and manufacturers to determine the most effective means to transmit disaster warning information. The means chosen should be minimally intrusive on bandwidth and not result in undue additional burdens or costs on broadcasters. Appropriate regulatory authorities should also work with manufacturers of digital television sets to make sure that they are modified to handle these kinds of transmissions." The Advisory Committee Report explains that digital technology will provide innovative and new ways to transmit warnings, such as pinpointing specific households or neighborhoods at risk, and suggests that DTV broadcasters take advantage of these technological advances. The Advisory Committee Report also states that most of these innovations will require only minimal use of the 6 MHz bandwidth allocated to digital broadcasters. * * *

21. We seek comment on the Advisory Committee Report's recommendations regarding minimum public interest requirements. Many members of the Advisory Committee were concerned that not all television broadcasters would adopt voluntary measures, while other members strongly opposed Commission-imposed minimum public interest requirements as unnecessary, preferring to give television broadcasters maximum flexibility and discretion in meeting their public interest obligations. This issue has previously generated strong debate. Some television broadcasters have previously opposed increasing or making more specific their public interest obligations, reasoning that the marketplace is sufficient to produce adequate local programming and meet community needs. Indeed, many television broadcasters have demonstrated a strong record of community service. Other parties have argued in our

DTV proceeding that the Commission should adopt more specific public interest programming requirements given the new opportunities broadcasters will have in converting to DTV. They also express the concern that television broadcasters are not airing a sufficient amount of public interest programming, including local public affairs programming.

22. We invite comment on this debate. Should the Commission establish more specific minimum requirements or guidelines regarding television broadcasters' public interest obligations? Would this make the license renewal process more certain and meaningful by spelling out the public interest standard in more detail? How would such minimum requirements be defined? What additional costs, if any, would those requirements impose? Are there sufficient marketplace incentives to ensure the provision of programming responsive to community needs, obviating the need for additional requirements?

C. Enhancing Access to the Media

23. One of the Commission's long-standing goals in the area of broadcast regulation is to enhance the access to the media by all people, including people of all races, ethnicities, and gender, and, most recently, disabled persons. Congress emphasized this goal when it amended section 1 of the Communications Act in 1996 to refine this agency's mission as making available "to all people of the United States, without discrimination on the basis of race, color, religion, national origin, or sex, a rapid, efficient, Nation-wide, and world-wide wire and radio communication service...." It further highlighted this goal when it added provisions to the Act concerning people with disabilities, such as section 713 relating to closed captioning and video description. Given the efficiencies of digital technology, DTV broadcasters will be able to "multicast" and air several programs at the same time, as well as provide more information within the signal of each programming stream. We seek comment on the ways broadcasters can use this technology to provide greater access to the media.

1. Disabilities

* * *

25. In urging that the Commission issue this NOI, People for Better TV ask that the Commission emphasize, among other things, the "expansion of services to person with disabilities." The group specifically suggests that a "digital broadcast station should provide closed captioning and description services for the blind of PSAs, public affairs programming, and political programming." It urges that "[c]aptioning and descriptions in these areas should be phased in over the first 4 years of a station's digital broadcasts, but should be completed no later than 2006." Similarly, the Advisory Committee Report recommends that digital TV broadcasters "take full advantage" of new digital technologies to provide "maximum choice and quality for Americans with disabilities, where doing so would not impose an undue burden on the broadcasters." The Committee specifically enumerates closed captioning, video descrip-

tion, and disability access to ancillary and supplementary services. The Committee asks broadcasters to take full advantage of digital closed captioning technology that will enable viewers to change the size of captions to see both the caption and text otherwise behind the caption, and also calls on broadcasters to expand gradually captioning on PSAs, public affairs programming, and political programming. The Committee also requests digital broadcasters to allocate sufficient bandwidth among their multiple audio channels to make expanded use of video description technology feasible. The Committee further suggests that any digital broadcaster that provides ancillary and supplementary services not impinge on the 9600 baud bandwidth currently set aside for closed captioning, and encourages broadcasters to explore new digital technologies to expand access to such services to persons with disabilities, such as offering text options for material presented orally and an audio option for material presented visually. The Committee finally recommends that the Commission and other regulatory authorities work with set manufacturers to ensure that modifications in audio channels, decoders, and other technical areas are designed to ensure the most efficient, inexpensive, and innovative capabilities for disability access * * *

2. Diversity

29. Diversity of viewpoint, ownership, and employment have long been and continues to be a fundamental public policy goal in broadcasting. In section 309(j) of the Act, Congress directed the Commission to prescribe competitive bidding rules to promote "economic opportunity for a wide variety of applicants, including small businesses, rural telephone companies, and businesses owned by members of minority groups and women." In part, to fulfill that mandate, we offered a bidding credit to new entrants in our recent auction of broadcast licenses. Prior to the adoption of section 309(j), and throughout its history, the Commission has also pursued a number of initiatives to diversify broadcast station ownership and employment. For example, the Commission identified "diversification of control of the media of mass communications" as "a factor of primary significance" in its comparative licensing processes, and adopted diversity and minority "preferences" in certain of its random selection processes. In addition, we are currently conducting a number of studies to evaluate the barriers to acquisition of broadcast licenses, and barriers to entry or growth, that small, minority-, and women-owned businesses face, as well as to examine the impact of our multiple ownership rules on broadcast station ownership, and the impact of small, minority, and women ownership of broadcast stations on service. The Commission has also adopted equal opportunity rules that are designed to foster opportunity in the broadcast industry for minorities and women. The outreach portion of these rules was struck down on constitutional grounds by the D.C. Circuit. However, last November, we issued a *Notice of Proposed Rulemaking* proposing new EEO rules, and expect to issue an order in the near future.

30. Broadcasters have voluntarily pursued a number of initiatives to foster diversity. Most recently, broadcasters created an investment fund, with current initial cash commitments of $175 million and ultimate purchasing power of possibly $1 billion, to spur ownership of television and radio by minorities and women. In addition, many broadcasters have made voluntary commitments to abide by equal opportunity principles, whether required by law to do so or not.

31. People for Better TV ask that DTV broadcasters exploit digital technology to reflect the diversity of their communities, through any number of practices. The group explains that network programming cannot respond to diverse needs of each community, and so local stations must come to know and provide service to diverse communities. It asks that broadcasters support the goal of diversity and report quarterly on their efforts.

32. The Advisory Committee Report states that "[d]iversity is an important value in broadcasting, whether it is in programming, political discourse, hiring, promotion, or business opportunities within the industry." As such, it recommends that "broadcasters seize the opportunity inherent in the digital television technology to substantially enhance the diversity available in the television marketplace." Many of the Advisory Committee's other recommendations bear on its goal of diversity in broadcasting. For example, the Advisory Committee Report advocates flexibility in multiplexing so that broadcasters can create new opportunities for minority entrepreneurship through channel-leasing arrangements, partnerships and other creative business arrangements. In addition, the Advisory Committee Report recommends that, out of the returned analog spectrum one new 6 MHz channel for each viewing community be reserved for noncommercial purposes, including educational programming directed at minority groups and other underserved segments of the community. The Committee also recommends that "broadcasters voluntarily redouble their individual and collective efforts during the digital transition to encourage effective participation by minorities and women at all levels of the industry," including hiring and promotion policies that result in significant representation of minorities and women in the decision-making positions in the broadcast industry. The Committee hopes that all of the recommendations will help independent producers provide new programming. We note that several major civil rights organizations, including NAACP and La Raza, have raised similar concerns about the lack of cultural diversity on network programming.

33. The Advisory Committee Report generally does not contain separate, stand-alone recommendations on how to achieve diversity in broadcasting; its recommendations are largely contained within other portions of the report on which we have sought comment above. In addition, as indicated above, the Commission currently has a number of initiatives underway designed to diversify broadcast ownership and employment. What other ways could and should the Commission encourage diversity in broadcasting, consistent with relevant constitutional stan-

dards? We seek comment on innovative ways unique to DTV that the Commission could use to encourage diversity in the digital era, and encourage commenters to submit specific proposals.

D. Enhancing Political Discourse

34. The Commission has long interpreted the statutory public interest standard as imposing an obligation on broadcast licensees to air programming regarding political campaigns. * * *

35. We note that some broadcasters have devoted many hours of program time to political coverage. According to a report recently issued by the National Association of Broadcasters ("NAB Report"), in the 1996 election cycle broadcasters valued the time they voluntarily devoted to political campaigns at $148.4 million. This programming took the form of coverage of debates, conventions and issue fora. Many more hours of news programming not accounted for in these figures have been dedicated to covering local and national campaigns. In addition, during the 1996 elections, the Fox, PBS, and ABC networks voluntarily provided free airtime to the major presidential candidates using a variety of formats. For example, during the last six weeks of the 1996 presidential campaign the Fox television network offered each major presidential candidate free airtime, including the opportunity to make ten one-minute position statements that were broadcast in prime time. The PBS and ABC television networks also set aside free airtime for presentations by the major presidential candidates, and the A.H. Belo Corporation provided free airtime in selected federal congressional elections and gubernatorial races. The Commission exempted these efforts from the equal opportunity requirements, finding that the proposals qualified as on-the-spot coverage of a bona fide news event. We seek comment on what the Commission can do to encourage these kinds of voluntary efforts by television broadcasters.

36. On the other hand, we note that there are indications that many television broadcasters are providing scant coverage of local public affairs, and what coverage there is may be shrinking. For instance, a 1998 study by the University of Southern California Annenberg School for Communication found that only 0.31% of local news focused on the California governor's race, compared to a figure of 1.8% in 1974. Similarly, an April 1998 Joint Report by the Media Access Project and the Benton Foundation found that, in the markets examined, 35% of the stations provide no local news, and 25% offer neither local public affairs programming nor local news.

37. The Advisory Committee Report recommends that television broadcasters provide five minutes each night between 5:00 p.m. and 11:35 p.m. (or the appropriate equivalent in Central and Mountain time zones) for "candidate-centered discourse" thirty days before an election. The Committee envisions maximum flexibility for broadcasters, allowing them to choose the candidates and races—federal, state, and local—that deserve more attention. The Committee envisions that stations could

choose formats, which might include giving candidates one minute of airtime, conducting mini-debates, or doing brief interviews, or including the "discourse" in newcasts. We seek comment on this idea. More generally, are there steps the Commission can take to promote voluntary efforts to enhance political debate and the information the public receives concerning candidates?

38. Others have proposed that the Commission adopt rules requiring broadcast licensees to provide time to candidates. Although the Advisory Committee Report proposed voluntary efforts, thirteen members of the Committee—a majority—contend that the Committee's recommendations do not go far enough, and that the Commission should, among other things, require television broadcasters to provide some airtime for national and local candidates. In addition, former FCC General Counsel Henry Geller, on behalf of himself and others, ask the Commission to require television broadcasters to provide political candidates a reasonable amount of time each day in advance of a gereral election. More specifically, Geller et al. propose that the Commission require television broadcasters to provide twenty minutes of airtime each day thirty days before a general election in even-numberered years, and fifteen days before in odd-numbered years, when there are fewer elections. Geller et al. suggest that the Commission give television broadcasters the flexibility to decide how to provide the total of twenty minutes, except that the time should be provided between 6:00 a.m. to midnight, with at least five minutes in prime time. Geller et al. further suggest that the Communications Act requires the Commission to leave the selection of the races to be covered to the licensee. Geller et al. contend that the Commission's public interest authority extends to requiring broadcasters to provide time. We seek comment on these approaches, and on the Commission's authority to require broadcasters to provide airtime to political candidates. We also seek comment on the Advisory Committee's recommendation that the Commission should prohibit television broadcasters from adopting blanket bans on the sale of airtime to state and local candidates. * * *

COMMISSIONER HAROLD FURTCHTGOTT-ROTH, Concurring in Part and Dissenting in Part

I believe today's Notice of Inquiry is a significant step in implementing Section 336's directives regarding the transition from analog to digital broadcast services. The birth of digital television raises discrete issues regarding application of our existing public interest requirements during the transition period and beyond. I concur in the Commission's decision to utilize the flexibility afforded by a Notice of Inquiry to develop a record on these narrow issues.

However, I am both surprised and disturbed by many aspects of the Notice. First, the majority has crafted a document of vast breadth, often musing about public interest mandates that have no discernible nexus to the transition to digital technology. Rather, it appears that special interests have seized on this opportunity to wring as many concessions as possible out of broadcasters. For example, the NOI considers proposals that broadcasters fund solutions to such diverse problems as minority access to capital and the quality of our political discourse. I believe even suggesting such broad policies in this deregulatory and competitive age is pure folly.

Second, this NOI is remarkably out-of-step with today's communications marketplace. The Notice seems to reflect a vintage 1960s' big-government pro-regulation philosophy based on the fundamental factual premise that broadcast television is the sole, dominant media outlet. Yet the new millennium is a vastly different time. The Commission's rules should be moving towards deregulation, not further burdening the emergence of one nascent mass media competitor: digital television (DTV).

Third, I am uncomfortable with this independent agency taking its "guidance" and "focus" from an executive branch Committee and the Vice President on issues that are exclusively within our jurisdiction. Moreover, the timing of today's Inquiry—only weeks after the arrival of a letter request for such action by the Vice President—casts unfortunate doubt on our independence as an agency.

Based on these three factors, I respectfully dissent in part from this Notice of Inquiry.

I. A Limited Inquiry

As noted above, I do believe that this proceeding will assist the Commission in applying our current public interest obligations to DTV. As acknowledged by the Notice, Section 336(d) of the Act states "[n]othing in this section shall be construed as relieving a television broadcasting station from its obligation to serve the public interest, convenience and necessity." That section also requires that "[i]n the Commission's review of any application for renewal of a broadcast license for a television station that provides ancillary or supplementary services, the television licensee shall establish that all of its program services on the existing or advanced television spectrum are in the public interest." Thus, the statute supports the Commission's application of its current public interest obligations to DTV and an assessment of the role of these obligations, if any, to ancillary or supplementary services.

Therefore I believe this NOI rightly addresses such issues as how the public interest obligations apply in a multicast environment (¶ 11), the public interest obligations (if any) that should apply to ancillary and supplementary services provided by DTV broadcasters (¶ 13), and the closed captioning obligations of DTV under Section 305 (f) (¶ 23). Unfortunately, the NOI does not stop there. Instead it goes on (and on) with a laundry list of potential opportunities for "freebies" to be extracted from broadcasters for various "public" purposes—most of questionable utility and legality.

II. The Great DTV Society?

The NOI transforms this proceeding into a roving mandate to seek out "good" things that we can make broadcasters do. The item does not appear to require any particular linkage between the proposals and the transition to DTV. In some cases, there is little connection to broadcasting at all. Moreover, there seems to be little regard for the nature of our statutory authority in this area or the limits imposed by the Constitution.

The proposals are breathtaking in scope. The NOI postulates that broadcasters may: be forced to provide subsidized datacasting to schools and libraries (¶ 13), face new minimum standards for satisfying their public interest obligation (¶ 19), and be required to set up Internet chat rooms to discuss their public interest obligations (¶ 17). The NOI also details a proposal to carve out a channel in cleared analog spectrum for minority educational broadcasting (¶ 29) and searches for ways broadcasters can be used so that "the quality of political discourse might be improved" (¶ 31). Apparently the Notice dreams of creating a new Great DTV Society.

Even if the proposals contained in this Notice had merit—which I believe most of them do not—it eludes me as to why this NOI has become the vehicle for so many big government causes designed to cure virtually every social ill through the mandated largesse of broadcasters. To be sure, there was an argument to be made that broadcasters should pay for their DTV spectrum. Indeed that argument was made in the proper time and place: during the legislative process in Congress. That debate has now been settled through passage of Section 336. It is not for us to backdoor that process by now extracting our pound of flesh for this spectrum.

The vast number of ideas set forth in the Notice makes it difficult to address them all in any detail. However, I discuss below two prominent examples that illustrate these misguided applications of our "public interest" authority.

A. Improving Political Discourse?

In paragraphs 31–34, the Notice sets forth various proposals to grant candidates "free" air time. Congress has repeatedly debated and refused to adopt such a requirement. This legislative activity makes it all the more difficult to assert the legal argument that we have had "public interest" authority to adopt such a requirement all along. Indeed, I have trouble imagining how we could explain, as the Supreme Court has consistently required, that "free" time is " 'reasonably ancillary to the effective performance of the Commission's various responsibilities for the regulation of television broadcasting.' "

Free air time is also just bad policy—a bad policy that has no relationship to the stated purpose of the NOI. First, just who would pay for all of this "free" air time? Broadcasters would, through lost advertising revenue. What this proposal thus amounts to is a painful and targeted tax on their industry in order to fund a general public benefit. This proposal would merely shift the costs of political air time from those who willingly donate to political candidates to the broadcast industry and American consumers, whose resultant funding of this speech could hardly be considered voluntary. In addition, it is not at all clear that free airtime would advance the majority's apparent goals of "promot[ing] democracy" and "better educating the voting public."

B. New Minimum Obligations?

I am also troubled by the portion of the item that asks whether we should specify and quantify broadcasters' public interest obligations. Of course, the closer the Commission gets to outright mandates of type and time for broadcast programming, the more perilously near protected First Amendment ground one gets.* * *

I also believe that it is simply better policy to leave broadcasters with discretion to define and implement their public interest programming, especially local programming. Broadcasters have every reason to serve their local communities and, if they do not meet that challenge, they will go out of business. Ultimately, it is the broadcaster who seeks and finds the local public interest. To my mind, that is a "public interest" standard that has worked well. Indeed I am quite skeptical of government's ability to substitute its judgment for the broadcasters in order to "help [broadcasters] serve their communities better and more fully."

III. The Wrong Direction

Fundamentally, the NOI is out-of-step with today's market and regulatory landscape. In an age where Americans receive information from an increasing diversity of sources, including cable television and the Internet, it seems increasingly anachronistic to saddle broadcasters with additional unique regulatory burdens. Even without such diversity, in a purportedly deregulatory era at the Commission, vast new obligations on broadcast licensees untethered to any technological change seems bizarre. Although I am heartened that this is only an NOI, the mere presence of these notions troubles me greatly.

The primary rationale for broadcasters' public interest obligations has been the theory that broadcast spectrum is a peculiarly scarce resource. Absent spectrum scarcity, however, the justification for affording broadcasters less First Amendment protection than persons engaged in other modes of communication becomes difficult to discern. As I explained in the Biennial Review of Mass Media Ownership Rules, I believe that the Commission must review the empirical basis of "spectrum scarcity" in that proceeding. Should we conclude in that docket that spectrum scarcity is no longer viable as a factual matter, then the instant effort to engage in additional regulation will be highly problematic in constitutional terms.

Even beyond the questionable legitimacy of the scarcity rationale, the NOI seems to signal a willingness by the Commission to return to the highly regulatory policies of the past to achieve tangential policy goals. For example, in the 1980s we eliminated our ascertainment requirements as an unnecessary burden on broadcasters. Yet this NOI describes enhanced disclosure requirements including that "digital TV broadcasters take steps to distribute public interest information more widely, through newspapers and websites." Now broadcasters would apparently not only be forced to use their own mediums to advance general public policy goals, but also required to spend funds on other media. Apparently intoxicated by the opportunity presented by the NOI, the majority seems to have imposed no limits on "goodies" to be extracted from broadcasters for their DTV spectrum. * * *

The Obligation to Talk About the Public Interest Obligation. Much to Commissioner Furtchtgott-Roth's chagrin, the conversation over public interest obligations was initiated within the context of a specific proceeding: the FCC's rules for the transition from analog to digital television. The transition was mandated by Congress, and the FCC had to do something definite to make the transition happen. It eventually did, through a series of orders specifying how and when the transition would take place, but the public interest obligation did not necessarily have to be part of the digital transition, and conversation over the public interest obligations of broadcasters fell out of the FCC's agenda about the same time that Al Gore left the Vice Presidency. Since the 1999 NOI, the FCC has given little more than lip service to reinvigorating the public interest obligations of broadcasters, frequently in response to specific inquiries from legislators regarding particular issues (such as assuring adequate coverage of their own political campaigns). But, in addition to the new regulations for stations to report on how their programming responds to local community discussed above, in 2004 the FCC, in response to concerns raised by its relaxation of broadcast ownership rules (on which more later), issued a new notice of inquiry on broadcast localism responsibilities. See *In the Matter of Broadcast Localism*, 19 FCC Rcd. 12425 (2004).

Should the FCC be doing more with public interest obligations? Many of the same arguments we've considered above apply. Media sources are at once exploding (with new media such as the Internet allowing many new sources) and contracting (with consolidation of much "old" media into conglomerates). The FCC itself creates scarcity in broadcast through its restrictive licensing rules, outlined in the previous chapter. If the government takes it upon itself to restrict a form of communication—essentially creating scarcity—isn't its judgment constrained by the First Amendment? Perhaps the problem is somewhat obviated by the use of auctions, but so long as the government exercises its discretion to favor certain speakers by granting them exclusive licenses to broadcast their speech, doesn't the First Amendment mandate that public rather than private interests be furthered by the license? As we shall see below, the question of government subsidization of some forms of speech through regulation is a complicated one, and one primarily hashed out not in the arena of broadcast licensing but, perhaps ironically, in cable television.

The FCC, spurred by Congress, has been most active with regard to providing programming for children.

4. Children's Broadcast Programming

CHILDREN'S TELEVISION PROGRAMMING
Report and Order

Federal Communications Commission, 1996.
11 FCC Rcd. 10660.

BY THE COMMISSION:

I. INTRODUCTION

1. In this Order, we take action to strengthen our enforcement of the Children's Television Act of 1990 ("CTA"), which requires the Commission, in its review of each television broadcast license renewal application, to "consider the extent to which the licensee . . . has served the educational and informational needs of children through the licensee's overall programming, including programming specifically designed to serve such needs." * * *

2. As explained in greater detail below, we conclude that our initial regulations implementing the CTA have not been fully effective in prompting broadcasters "to increase the amount of educational and informational broadcast television programming available to children." Our review of the record in this proceeding reveals several problems. First, because of their imprecision in defining the scope of a broadcaster's obligation under the Children's Television Act, our rules have led to a variation in the level and nature of broadcasters' compliance efforts that is incompatible with the intent of the CTA. In so doing, our rules fail to adequately counterbalance the marketplace disincentives as Congress intended when it enacted the CTA. Indeed, some broadcasters are carrying very little regularly scheduled standard length programming specifically designed to educate and inform children. Second, some broadcasters are claiming to have satisfied their statutory obligations with shows that, by any reasonable benchmark, cannot be said to be "specifically designed" to educate and inform children within the meaning of the CTA. Third, parents and others frequently lack timely access to information about the availability of programming in their communities specifically designed to educate and inform children, exacerbating market disincentives. Therefore, as proposed in the *Notice of Proposed*

Rule Making (*"NPRM"*) we released in April 1995, we refine our policies and rules implementing the CTA to remedy these problems.

3. First, we adopt a number of proposals designed to provide better information to the public about the shows broadcasters air to fulfill their obligation to air educational and informational programming under the CTA. Such information will assist parents who wish to guide their children's television viewing and, if large numbers of parents use that information to choose educational programming for their children, increase the likelihood that the market will respond with more educational programming. In addition, better information should help parents and others have an effective dialogue with broadcasters in their community about children's programming and, where appropriate, to urge programming improvements without resorting to government intervention.

4. Second, we adopt a definition of programming "specifically designed" to educate and inform children (or "core" programming) that provides better guidance to broadcasters concerning programming that fulfills their statutory obligation to air such programming. In order to qualify as core programming a show must have serving the educational and informational needs of children as a significant purpose. The Commission will ordinarily rely on the good faith judgments of broadcasters as to whether programming satisfies this test and will evaluate compliance of individual programs with this definition only as a last resort. Our new definition of core programming includes other objective elements. A core program must be a regularly scheduled, weekly program of at least 30 minutes, and aired between 7:00 a.m. and 10:00 p.m. The program must also be identified as educational and informational for children when it is aired and must be listed in the children's programming report placed in the broadcaster's public inspection file.

5. Third, we adopt a processing guideline that will provide certainty for broadcasters about how to comply with the CTA and facilitate our processing efforts. As described more fully below, under this guideline, broadcasters will receive staff-level approval of the CTA portion of their renewal applications if they air three hours per week of core programming or if, while providing somewhat less than three hours per week of core programming, they air a package of programming that demonstrates a level of commitment to educating and informing children that is at least equivalent to airing three hours per week of core programming. Broadcasters that do not meet this guideline will be referred to the full Commission for consideration, where they will have a full opportunity to demonstrate compliance with the CTA, including through efforts other than "core" programming and through nonbroadcast efforts.

6. By publishing our guideline for processing television renewal applications, and by identifying in advance those broadcasters who clearly are in compliance with the CTA and those who may not be in compliance, a processing guideline will help ensure that broadcasters who wish to provide an ample amount of children's educational programming will not find themselves at an unfair disadvantage in the market

relative to competing broadcasters who do not, and will not find themselves facing competitive pressure to forgo airing educational programs. A processing guideline will also facilitate speedy and consistent application processing by Commission staff. In short, a processing guideline is a clear, fair and efficient way to implement the Children's Television Act.

7. With regard to the constitutional arguments that have been raised in this proceeding, we conclude, as Congress did when it enacted the CTA, that requiring broadcasters to serve the educational and informational needs of their child audience is clearly within the scope of the long recognized obligation of broadcasters to serve the public interest. We further conclude that the regulations we adopt today directly advance the government's substantial, and indeed compelling, interest in educating America's children. At the same time, the regulations are appropriately tailored to provide flexibility for broadcasters.

8. Congress has enlisted the creativity of broadcasters to advance the nation's powerful interest in educating its youth. As Congress stated, "[i]t is difficult to think of an interest more substantial than the promotion of the welfare of children who watch so much television and rely upon it for so much of the information they receive." We believe that this Report and Order advances that interest. * * *

79. We will retain, with a slight modification, our existing definition of "educational and informational programming" to provide a description of the broad variety of programs that can serve to comply with a licensee's overall requirement to air programming that meets children's educational and informational needs. Our existing definition states that "educational and informational television programming is any television programming which furthers the positive development of children 16 years of age and under in any respect, including the child's intellectual/cognitive or social/emotional needs." In order to track more closely the express language of the CTA, we will modify this definition somewhat so that the broad category of "educational and informational television programming" is defined as "any television programming that furthers the educational and informational needs of children 16 years of age and under in any respect, including children's intellectual/cognitive or social/emotional needs."

80. The definition of core programming that we adopt is designed to provide licensees with clear guidance regarding how we will evaluate renewal applications. The elements of our proposed definition are also designed to be as objective as possible so that they are more easily understood by licensees and the Commission staff and to avoid injecting the Commission unnecessarily into sensitive decisions regarding program content. As we stated in the *NPRM*, programming specifically designed to serve children's educational and informational needs is the only category of programming the CTA expressly requires each licensee to provide. Adopting a definition of such programming will promote this statutory objective by more precisely defining the programming that qualifies and, consequently, provide appropriate incentives to increase

the amount of such programming. We further believe that the definition we adopt today will continue to provide broadcasters ample discretion in designing and producing such programming. We emphasize that the test of whether programming qualifies as core does not depend in any way on its topic or viewpoint. The test is whether it is "specifically designed" to serve the educational and informational needs of children. * * *

VII. First Amendment Issues

* * *

147. *Discussion*. The First Amendment arguments raised by opponents of our proposed CTA regulations essentially fall into two categories—arguments that attack the CTA obligation and arguments that attack the quantification of the CTA obligation. To the extent that some commenters argue that the CTA is unconstitutional, Congress itself addressed that issue. It specifically concluded that "it is well within the First Amendment strictures to require the FCC to consider, during the license renewal process, whether a television licensee has provided information specifically designed to serve the educational and informational needs of children in the context of its overall programming." As the Senate Report noted, broadcasters, in exchange for "the free and exclusive use of a valuable part of the public domain," can be expected to serve as a public fiduciary, obliged to serve the needs and interests of their viewers. That obligation includes the obligation to serve the needs of children. Even more specifically, as the FCC, the courts, and Congress have concluded, a broadcaster's public interest obligation properly includes an obligation to serve the educational and informational needs of children. The question in this proceeding is not *whether* the Commission should give effect to the CTA, but *how* it should do so. * * *

149. The course we adopt today—defining what qualifies as programming "specifically designed" to serve the educational needs of children and giving broadcasters clear but nonmandatory guidance on how to guarantee compliance—is a constitutional means of giving effect to the CTA's programming requirement. "It does not violate the First Amendment to treat licensees given the privilege of using scarce radio frequencies as proxies for the entire community, obligated to give suitable time and attention to matters of great public concern." *Red Lion Broadcasting Co. v. FCC*, 395 U.S. 367, 394 (1969). Congress's authority to order "suitable time and attention to matters of great public concern" includes the authority to require broadcasters to air programming specifically designed to further the educational needs of children. The airwaves belong to the public, not to any individual broadcaster. As the Supreme Court observed in *CBS, Inc. v. FCC*, "a licensed broadcaster is 'granted the free and exclusive use of a limited and valuable part of the public domain; when he accepts that franchise it is burdened by enforceable public obligations.'" The fact that Congress elected to retain public ownership of the broadcast spectrum and to lease it for free to private licensees for limited periods carries significant First Amendment consequences.

150. In *CBS v. FCC* the Supreme Court upheld a challenge to the statute (47 U.S.C. § 312(a)(7)) that requires broadcasters to provide reasonable access to individual candidates seeking federal elective office. Similarly, here, the CTA requires broadcasters to serve the educational and informational needs of children through programming specifically designed for those needs. Both provisions require broadcasters to air certain types of programming they might not otherwise choose to provide. However, the obligation imposed by Section 312(a)(7) appears to be significantly more burdensome than the obligation imposed by the CTA. Under Section 312(a)(7), broadcasters have no control over the content of the political advertising. In contrast, under the CTA broadcasters are obligated to provide children's educational programming, yet they retain wide discretion in choosing what programs to provide, a fact little changed by the clarifying measures we adopt today.* * *

152. Our new regulations, like the CTA itself, impose reasonable, viewpoint-neutral conditions on a broadcaster's free use of the public airwaves. They do not censor or foreclose speech of any kind. They do not tell licensees what topics they must address. They provide only that broadcasters report the educational objective of the program and the expected educational effects. Moreover, they expressly provide that broadcasters need not describe the viewpoint of the program or the opinions expressed on the program.

153. The CTA and our regulations directly advance the government's substantial, and indeed compelling, interest in the education of America's children. As Congress recognized, "[i]t is difficult to think of an interest more substantial than the promotion of the welfare of children who watch so much television and rely upon it for so much of the information they receive." In other contexts, the courts and commentators have recognized the government's "compelling" interest in "safeguarding the physical and psychological well being" of minors.

154. A recent case, *Action for Children's Television v. FCC*, affirms the vitality of the government's interest in ensuring that television programming is consistent with the needs of America's children. In Action for Children's Television, the court of appeals echoed the Supreme Court's recognition of the "well nigh universal belief that good books, plays and art ... improve the mind, enrich the human personality, and develop character." It then concluded that a legislature may regulate the exposure of children to indecent material on the corollary assumption that indecent material may "exert a corrupting and debasing impact." If Congress and the Commission may rely on this corollary to ban broadcast of certain material during specified hours, even under standards of strict scrutiny, it should follow that the Commission's adoption of less restrictive measures to encourage the airing of material beneficial to children is consistent with the First Amendment. That is particularly true because the Children's Television Act is designed to promote programming that *educates and informs* children. The framers of the First Amendment understood that "the greatest menace to freedom is an inert people," as Justice [Brandeis] wrote. It is entirely

consistent with the First Amendment to ask trustees of the public airwaves to pursue reasonable, viewpoint-neutral measures designed to increase the likelihood that children will grow into adults capable of fully participating in our deliberative democracy."

155. Such a requirement also is supported by the Supreme Court's decision in *FCC v. Pacifica Foundation*. In that case the Court recognized that "broadcasting is uniquely accessible to children" and that the "broadcast media have established a uniquely pervasive presence in the lives of all Americans." Both of those factors support Congress' decision to require broadcasters to serve the educational needs of children. As stated previously, television has an influence on children in our society rivalled only by family and school. It would be accurate to blend the two factors noted in *Pacifica* and conclude that television has a pervasive presence in the lives of American children. The Court in *Pacifica* upheld restrictions on the broadcast of indecent material. As stated above, the government's interest in the intellectual development of our nation's children is at least as significant as its interest in protecting them from exposure to indecent material, an interest the Supreme Court "has often found compelling."

156. The measures we adopt today to advance the Nation's interest in the intellectual development of our children are sustainable under the *Pacifica* analysis as they are significantly less burdensome than the measure upheld there. *Pacifica* upheld a complete ban on a particular type of programming (indecent programming) during hours when children are likely to be in the audience, a period which the Commission was later upheld in defining as 16 hours per day (6:00 a.m.–10:00 p.m.) in *Action for Children's Television*. The measures we adopt today do not ban programming of any type, they simply notify broadcasters that compliance with the CTA can be achieved with, on average, less than half an hour a day of programming expressing any viewpoint on any topic that broadcasters desire.

157. For those reasons, our implementing rules are constitutional under the traditional First Amendment standard. But even if evaluated under a heightened standard, our rules would pass muster because the interest advanced is compelling and our regulations are narrowly tailored. As detailed above, our regulations are no more burdensome than necessary to ensure that children will be able to watch educational and informational programming. Like the CTA, our regulations require broadcasters to air children's educational and informational programming, but do not "exclude any programming that does in fact serve the educational and informational needs of children; rather the broadcaster has discretion to meet its public service obligation in the way it deems best suited." Specifically, the processing guideline that we adopt today does not limit this discretion. It provides a means by which a broadcaster can be certain that our staff will be in a position to process its renewal application without further review of the broadcaster's CTA efforts. As we explain above, any programming specifically designed to meet the educational and informational needs of children can "count" for pur-

poses of meeting the processing guideline. In addition, a broadcaster can rely on other more general programming and related non-programming efforts to satisfy its CTA obligation—albeit after full Commission review.* * *

Bargaining with the Government. From reading the Commission's report you would never know that the three hour "processing guideline" adopted by the Commission was the product of an agreement between the Commission and the NAB and major broadcast networks. Glen O. Robinson, *The Electronic First Amendment*, 47 Duke L.J. 899 (1998), gives a summary account and brief critique:

> In 1990 Congress intervened with two directives. The first was a specific limitation on the number of commercial minutes that could be broadcast in children's programming. The second was a directive to the FCC to promulgate specific rules requiring television licensees to present educational programming designed for children. To implement the latter, the FCC sought a voluntary commitment from the industry. The National Association of Broadcasters (NAB) and the major television networks refused to give one. They refused, that is, until the issue became intertwined with the FCC's plan for conversion to digital television.
>
> The digital television story is fascinating in its own right, but it is too complicated to relate here. It is enough simply to summarize those parts that are directly pertinent to children's television. As part of a plan to convert present analog signals to digital, the FCC developed a plan calling for all existing broadcast stations to get a second channel on which to begin simulcasting in digital format for a transitional period, during which there would be a gradual shift from analog to digital. As this plan was being developed, the returns from the FCC's newly authorized auctioning of unassigned frequencies (outside the broadcast channel allocations) were coming in, and they were stunning. When the FCC announced its plan to give a second television channel to broadcasters to facilitate a move to digital television, eyebrows everywhere lifted. The Commission's staff had itself roughly estimated that the new channel would bring between $11 and $70 billion at open auction.
>
> The FCC could not, at that time, auction the second channel to broadcasters. In 1993, when Congress gave the Commission authority to auction unassigned radio frequencies, it stipulated that those frequencies were to be used in services for which the licensee was to, or was likely to, receive compensation from subscribers. This stipulation precluded the FCC from auctioning channels into use for conventional, free, television service. The law could be changed, however, and deliberations on the Telecommunications Act of 1996 provided a timely occasion for doing so. Timely, but as it turned out, not politically convenient. The FCC's chairman sought to mollify

critics of this "giveaway" by insisting that the broadcasters ought to give something in return for the new channel—specifically, educational children's television and free air time for political candidates. The first was forthcoming. Faced with the possibility of having to buy the second channel, the major networks agreed to provide at least three hours per week of children's educational programs.

To date, the children's television episode appears not to have raised any First Amendment concerns, even though the FCC's role in persuading the networks to commit to three hours of children's television is strikingly redolent of the family viewing hour episode of the mid–1970s which did generate such concerns. The family viewing hour was an effort to provide a kind of viewing sanctuary in the early part of the prime time viewing period when parents and their children could watch television together without encountering adult programming deemed unsuitable for family viewing. After exhortation by the FCC's chairman, the NAB and the networks agreed to adopt a self-regulatory restraint on the presentation of such adult programming. The policy was challenged by a group representing Hollywood program writers and a program producer (Tandem Productions, which produced "All in the Family"). This group claimed that the "voluntary" policy was in fact the product of unconstitutional influence by the FCC's chairman. The District Court for the Central District of California found that the FCC chairman's actions implicated the entire Commission, and violated the First Amendment, giving rise to an action for damages. The Court of Appeals for the Ninth Circuit vacated and remanded on the ground that, for reasons of primary jurisdiction, the claim should have been first addressed to the FCC, for it to determine whether the chairman's actions went beyond legitimate persuasion to become coercive censorship. On remand, the NAB Code was dropped, and the FCC found the (former) chairman innocent of coercion.

The constitutional issues raised by the family hour controversy and its more recent avatar, the children's hour(s), seem to be the same. The fact that the former was negatively articulated in terms of what should not be in prime time, whereas the latter is affirmatively articulated in terms of what should be on the air, is purely a semantic matter. Insofar as each policy influences program choices, each has affirmative and negative effects. The important question for both is whether the fact that the government has produced the influence by means of bargaining, rather than by simple command, eliminates the First Amendment problem with government influence over program choices.

This is a hard question. At the outset, notice that the distinction between "bargaining" and "commanding" is conceptually malleable in a context where regulatory commands are linked to the regulator's control of a valuable resource. For instance, suppose the FCC directs a broadcast licensee to present, or not present, a particular type of program as a condition of its receiving (or keeping) its license to use assigned radio frequencies. Some would see this directive as simply an exercise of ownership, part of a lease or sale agreement governing the disposition of the frequencies. I said earlier that this way of rationalizing the regulatory power is analytically flawed. The government should not be allowed to finesse questions of public rationality and legitimacy by hiding behind a metaphor of ownership.

5. Public Interest Obligations of MVPDs

When cable television emerged as an important medium in the early 1960s, the FCC imposed on it an elaborate set of regulations. It did not, however, attempt to impose on cable a general public interest mandate comparable to the one for broadcasters. Whether it could have done so given the absence of any clear statutory authority is a moot point. It was not in any case a key purpose of regulating cable. The purpose of regulating cable in the early years (and to a considerable degree even today) was to protect the broadcast media and the service that they provided, notably locally-based, free television. The Commission asserted what it labeled an "ancillary" jurisdiction to regulate cable as a means of controlling cable's impact on free, over-the-air, broadcast service. This has led to regulations that affect cable programming—notably requirements mandating carriage of local broadcast programming, requiring consent for retransmission of broadcast signals, restrictions on duplicating local programming, and the provision of public access channels. In a sense these could all be considered as a kind of regulation of content. Indeed, that was exactly the claim that the cable industry made, unsuccessfully, in launching a First Amendment challenge to the local must-carry requirements. We examine these regulations in Chapter 5. As we'll see in that chapter, the line distinguishing regulations that indirectly affect programming and those that directly regulate program content can be quite thin.

Today, of course, cable systems offer a mixture of both retransmitted broadcast programming (both local and distant stations) and their own programming provided by cable networks. There has been no attempt to undertake any general regulatory monitoring of cable-originated programming. No doubt the absence of a convenient scarcity rationale would make it difficult to assert general program authority over cable programming, but what about specific obligations such as the equal time rule? In 1972 Congress amended § 315 to make the equal time rules applicable to cable systems. Only those programs originated by the local cable operator and under its exclusive control are subject to the obligation, see 47 C.F.R. § 76.5(p), which gives § 315 very little room for application to cable television. But what is the basis for imposing it at all?

With new forms of media subject to FCC regulation, though, have come new opportunities for considering the public interest obligation, and Congress got into the act in a very big—and very specific—way, substantially limiting the Commission's discretion to take a pass on DBS public interest obligations. As part of the 1992 Cable Act, Congress directed the FCC to impose general public interest obligations on DBS providers, necessarily including the "access to broadcast time requirement of section 312(a)(7) of this title and the use of facilities requirements of section 315 of this title to providers of direct broadcast satellite service". 47 U.S.C. § 335(a). The Act also imposed a new form of public interest obligation suited specifically to the multi-channel nature of satellite service: requiring that DBS providers "reserve a portion of its channel capacity equal to not less than 4 percent nor more than 7 percent, exclusively for noncommercial programming of an educational or informational nature." 47 U.S.C. § 335(b)(1). The D.C. Circuit upheld the new requirements against constitutional challenge in *Time Warner Entertainment Co. v. FCC*, 93 F.3d 957 (D.C. Cir. 1996), ostensibly as a straightforward application of *Red Lion*'s scarcity rationale. It then fell to the FCC to determine exactly which aspects of the public interest obligation (other than the mandated political access, equal time, and the set asides) to impose on DBS providers.

DIRECT BROADCAST SATELLITE PUBLIC INTEREST OBLIGATIONS
Second Order on Reconsideration of First Report and Order

Federal Communications Commission, 2004.
19 FCC Rcd. 5647.

BY THE COMMISSION:

I. INTRODUCTION

* * *

2. In this *Memorandum Opinion and Order*, we consider petitions for reconsideration and other pleadings filed in response to our *First Report and Order* implementing Section 25 of the Cable Television Consumer Protection and Competition Act of 1992 ("1992 Cable Act"). For the reasons discussed below, we conclude that the Commission's interpretation and implementation of Section 25 of the 1992 Cable Act was generally correct, but that clarification and codification of political broadcasting rules for Direct Broadcast Satellite service providers is in order. In addition, we find that revision of our conclusion regarding advertising limits for children's programming is warranted. Therefore we grant in part and deny in part the petitions for reconsideration.

3. At this time DBS providers are complying with the public interest obligations specified in the *First Report and Order*. In response to Commission inquiry, the three operating DBS providers, DirecTV, Inc., EchoStar Satellite Communications Corporation, and Dominion Video Satellite, Inc., state that each has set aside at least four percent of its channel capacity to satisfy the public interest obligation and is

providing a broad range of informational and educational programming, including programming relating to international news, public affairs, family life, foreign language instruction, and academic instruction on various levels.

II. Background

4. In 1992, Congress directed the Commission to initiate a rule-making to impose certain public interest obligations on direct broadcast satellite ("DBS") providers, including political broadcasting rules. In 1998, the Commission adopted the *First Report and Order*, which implements these statutory obligations.

5. The Commission's rules apply to "providers of direct broadcast satellite service." These include entities licensed pursuant to Part 100 of the Commission's rules; entities licensed pursuant to Part 25 of the Commission's rules to provide fixed-satellite service ("FSS"), via the Ku-band, that sell or lease transponder capacity to a video program distributor who offers direct-to-home FSS ("DTH-FSS") to consumers; and non-U.S. licensed satellites providing DBS or DTH-FSS services in the United States. As required by statute, the rules require DBS providers to comply with certain statutory political broadcasting requirements granting candidates for federal office reasonable access to a licensee's facilities on an equal basis with other federal candidates at the lowest rate available. DBS providers must also comply with statutory equal opportunities provisions. As part of the public interest obligations, Congress also mandated that DBS providers set aside channel capacity for noncommercial programming and offer access to educational programmers at reasonable prices, terms and conditions. To implement that requirement, the rules impose program carriage obligations on DBS providers, requiring them to set aside four percent of their channel capacity exclusively for noncommercial educational and informational programming and to make the capacity available at reasonable prices. Access to the noncommercial and informational capacity is limited to bona fide noncommercial national educational programming suppliers, and access is limited to one channel per supplier as long as demand for such capacity exceeds the available supply. The rules allow a DBS provider initially to select qualified, noncommercial programmers, but prohibit a DBS provider from altering or censoring the content of the programming aired on the noncommercial channels. Finally, the rules require that each DBS provider maintain a public file containing a complete and orderly record concerning its compliance with both the political broadcasting and the noncommercial educational and informational programming requirements.

6. Nine petitions for reconsideration and related pleadings were filed in response to the *First Report and Order*. The petitioners raise concerns regarding whether the Commission has correctly determined what entities are defined as DBS providers, whether it has properly implemented the Commission's political broadcasting requirements for DBS providers, and whether it has adequately addressed the issue of

localism. Petitioners also assert that the Commission should have applied certain additional obligations to DBS providers, should have taken steps to protect children from harm associated with over-commercialization, should have prohibited DBS providers from meeting their public service obligation with existing programming, and challenge the Commission's determination to limit access to capacity reserved for educational and informational programming to one channel per national educational programming supplier.

III. Discussion

7. Reconsideration is appropriate only where the petitioner either shows a material error or omission in the original order or raises additional facts not known or existing at the petitioner's last opportunity to present such matters. A petition for reconsideration of a final rule-making proceeding must state with particularity the respects in which the petitioner believes the action taken by the Commission should be changed. We find that some of the petitioners' requests warrant reconsideration and therefore we grant in part some of the petitions and deny the remaining petitions. We also clarify some aspects of the DBS public interest obligations.

A. Definition of Providers of DBS Service

8. Several petitioners assert that the Commission erred when it defined the term "providers of DBS service" to include satellite operators licensed pursuant to Part 25 of the Commission's rules. In the *First Report and Order*, the Commission found that the term included both Part 100 licensees and Part 25 licensees. * * *

14. At the notice phase of this proceeding, the Commission acknowledged that Section 335's definition of a DBS provider was broad enough to apply to a number of different entities, including the FSS satellite licensee and lessees of FSS capacity that distribute video programming directly to subscribers. We agree with petitioners that the definition of DBS provider could include lessees of FSS capacity that distribute video programming to subscribers. We are not, however, persuaded that Congress intended that the ultimate responsibility for complying with public service obligations rests with non-licensees. The petitioners proffer many of the same arguments that were considered in the *First Report and Order*. For the reasons set forth in the *First Report and Order*, we remain convinced that the statute's requirement to make capacity available, its definition of a provider of DBS service, and inclusion of entities licensed under Part 25 of the Commission's rules, clearly indicates that Congress intended that Part 25 Commission licensees be subject to the requirements of Section 335. This interpretation facilitates the Commission's orderly administration of the public interest obligations. It also enables the Commission to apply the same public interest regulatory requirements to both Part 100 and FSS Part 25 satellite operators. Moreover, because the Commission maintains ownership information for satellite licensees, and does not have similar records

for lessees or program distributors, monitoring licensees is easier and enforcement is more effective.

15. We are also not persuaded that forfeitures and cease-and-desist orders or other enforcement remedies arising from the Commission's general authority to regulate interstate communications are as effective as the Commission's broad range of defined powers over its licensees. In addition, it is the satellite licensee, not the Commission, which has the closest connection to its lessee that is the distributor of programming to subscribers. Recognizing, however, that satellite licensees may not be ideally suited to monitor and enforce the public interest requirements, the Commission developed a procedure to permit FSS Part 25 licensees to delegate their responsibility for Section 335 compliance to the programming distributors. The Commission permitted licensees to demonstrate compliance with the public service obligations by relying on certifications from distributors that the obligations are being fulfilled, provided the licensee's reliance is reasonable. * * *

B. Political Broadcasting Requirements

* * *

20. Section 335 of the Act requires that the Commission establish rules applying the political broadcasting provisions of Sections 312(a)(7) and 315 of the Act to providers of DBS service. Section 312(a)(7) requires that a candidate for federal elective office be provided "reasonable access" to broadcast facilities. Section 315 requires that a candidate for any public office be allowed the same opportunities to use broadcast facilities that are afforded all other candidates for the same office ("equal opportunity"), including rates that do not exceed the lowest unit charge ("LUC") paid by the station's most favored commercial advertisers.

21. In formulating rules to apply the requirements of Sections 312 and 315 to DBS, the Commission recognized that there are fundamental differences between DBS systems and traditional terrestrial broadcast stations. Unlike broadcasters, DBS licensees, at the time the *First Report and Order* was adopted, did not originate programming, sell advertising, or generally transmit localized programming. Given these differences, the Commission decided that it was appropriate that the DBS political broadcasting rules afford DBS providers flexibility to meet their obligations in a practical and meaningful way, consistent with the intent of the law. The *First Report and Order* also required that DBS providers maintain a public file of requests for broadcast time and political advertising and the disposition of these requests in order to assist in evaluations of compliance with the political broadcasting rules and to enable competing candidates to review other candidates' advertising access and rates.

22. In general, in its Petition for Reconsideration, DAETC [Denver Area Educational Telecommunications Consortium, Inc.] objected to the manner in which the political broadcasting requirements were imple-

mented in the *First Report and Order* and urged the Commission to adopt specific rules and policies to facilitate the enforcement of Sections 312(a)(7) and 315, as well as to clarify that DBS providers have the same political broadcast advertisement obligations as do terrestrial broadcasters. We reconsider aspects of that decision here, as discussed in detail below, and conclude that it is now appropriate to adopt political broadcast rules that will expressly apply to DBS providers. We will derive the new rules for DBS providers from the existing rules that apply to terrestrial broadcasters or to cable operators, whichever is most appropriate.

23. *Reasonable Access*. Because DBS systems generally provide service on a nationwide basis, as opposed to terrestrial broadcast stations that principally serve the area in or near the communities in which the stations are licensed, the Commission found that presidential and vice presidential candidates were the federal candidates most likely to undertake the expense for national exposure on DBS systems and, thus, deferred a decision on whether and under what circumstances a candidate for a congressional office would be entitled to access. The *First Report and Order* noted also that the number of congressional candidates nationally is large, and the potential technical and financial burden on a national DBS provider to provide access to all federal candidates could be substantial and thus access could be inherently unworkable. Thus, the Commission determined that any public benefit that might be realized from requiring coverage of congressional races might not justify the technical and financial burdens that the obligation would entail.

* * *

28. Although we have received no reasonable access complaints from any federal candidates, including congressional candidates, in connection with DBS providers, we believe that the DBS industry has matured and expanded in the ways described below that warrant imposing more detailed political broadcasting rules. In particular it appears that DBS providers are now capable and willing to sell advertising time on their DBS facilities. In addition, the introduction of spot beam technologies is making DBS a more flexible service with greater potential to serve individual markets or regions. Although this flexibility to date has been used almost entirely for the carriage of local television broadcast signals (each individually subject to the political broadcasting requirements), there is now a greater potential for the introduction of other local services. These changes will have to be factored into providers' responses to federal candidate access requests and into our determination of whether these responses are reasonable.

29. We therefore adopt rules now to clarify our implementation of Section 312(a) (7) for all qualified federal candidates. These rules are modeled on the rules that apply to broadcast licensees. In applying these rules, we will use the rationales and interpretations of terrestrial broadcasting precedent to determine what is reasonable under the particular circumstances of a specific federal candidate's request for DBS access.

This extensive precedent in terrestrial broadcasting will be instructive in resolving controversies that may arise in the context of DBS compliance. * * *

30. *Equal Opportunity*. The *First Report and Order* incorporated Section 315 equal opportunity provisions into the Commission's rules, as well as the policies delineated in previous Commission orders on the subject, and stated that compliance with these provisions will be determined on a case-by-case basis. The Commission stated unequivocally that the equal opportunities provisions of the statute and the Commission's rules, as well as related policies delineated in prior Commission orders, will apply to DBS providers. * * *

C. Opportunities for Localism

36. Section 335(a) requires the Commission "to examine the opportunities that the establishment of direct broadcast satellite service provides for the principle of localism under [the] Act, and the methods by which such principle may be served through technological and other developments in, or regulation of, such service." There is no legislative guidance for the Commission to rely upon in defining "localism" in the context of DBS service. For example, there is no indication of whether localism refers to special programming for individual localities or if it refers to local broadcast channel carriage. In the First Report and Order the Commission noted that DBS providers lack the channel capacity to serve all localities in the country. At the same time, the Commission acknowledged that the Satellite Home Viewer Act of 1988 ("1988 SHVA") severely limited DBS providers' retransmission of local programming, but deferred an in-depth study of localism until the technical and legal issues were resolved through pending legislation that eventually became the Satellite Home Viewer Improvement Act of 1999 ("1999 SHVIA").

37. ACA [American Cable Association] (formerly the Small Cable Business Association) contends that the Commission has not given serious consideration to the manner in which DBS can serve the principle of localism. ACA states that the Commission has failed to meet its statutory obligation under Section 335(a). According to ACA, the Commission's failure is due to the fact that its analysis is based on a stale record. ACA submits that the Commission has not taken into account advances in technology that will enable DBS providers to offer widespread local programming, or recent legislative activity foreshadowing changes to the 1988 SHVA. Moreover, ACA adds that, since the release of the First Report and Order, two significant events have taken place affecting the implementation of localism on DBS. In its comments ACA points out that several major DBS mergers have been approved, raising the prospect of a significantly restructured DBS industry. In addition, ACA explains that the two largest DBS providers have announced intentions to offer local-into-local broadcast stations to subscribers. ACA filed a second Petition for Reconsideration of the *First Report and Order*'s Final Regulatory Flexibility Analysis, claiming generally that the

Commission failed to properly take into account the harm that would be caused to small cable operators by the lack of rules requiring DBS providers to carry all local broadcast programming.

38. ACA is correct in noting that since the *First Report and Order* the DBS industry has experienced a number of significant changes. Many of the legal and technical impediments to the transmission of local television broadcasts are now eroding. The 1999 SHVIA has become law, permitting "satellite carriers" to offer subscribers local-into-local service in markets across the country. On the technical side, advancements have been made in signal compression technology that give DBS providers additional capacity and the ability to carry local broadcast stations. DBS providers are taking advantage of these opportunities. According to the major DBS providers' websites, DirecTV offers local television service packages to subscribers in 64 markets with 59 more announced for 2004 and EchoStar offers similar packages in 104 markets. It also appears that the expansion in local-into-local service may have contributed to the over 8 million, 57%, increase in DBS subscribership between June 2000 and June 2003, making DBS the country's fastest growing competitor in the multichannel video programming distribution ("MVPD") marketplace.

39. The 1999 SHVIA has significantly enhanced the programming offered by DBS providers. In addition to traditional satellite and cable programs, many DBS subscribers are now receiving retransmissions of local terrestrial broadcast stations. These local stations are proving popular and DBS systems are devoting a portion of their system channel capacity to locally originated programming. The statutory requirement to comply with carriage obligations in the 1999 SHVIA has been implemented through a separate Commission proceeding, and DBS providers are now required to carry all local broadcast stations that request carriage, within each local market that the carriers choose to serve through reliance on the Section 122 statutory copyright license. Because it is not clear to what degree the satellite channel capacity may be limited by technical constraints, or whether market demand will result in local-into-local service in all parts of the country, we do not believe it will serve the public interest to impose additional requirements to "further the principle of localism" at this time. We also find that although the Final Regulatory Flexibility Analysis issued in conjunction with the *First Report and Order* was adequate, in any event the intervening adoption of broadcast signal carriage rules for DBS, similar to those imposed on cable systems, has alleviated the concerns articulated by ACA. * * *

E. Guidelines Concerning Commercialization of Children's Programming

44. In our April Order on Reconsideration in this proceeding, we determined not to adopt rules on children's advertising because we concluded that there was insufficient evidence of a problem. Having reconsidered this issue sua sponte, however, we conclude that a different

approach is warranted. We have decided that it is better to take action to protect children from excessive commercialization before we are presented with evidence of abuses. Although Section 335(a) does not require commercialization guidelines for children's programming on DBS, such guidelines are consistent with our public interest programming authority in this section. Accordingly, we conclude that prophylactic rules should be adopted that will protect children while imposing minimal burdens on DBS providers. The rules we adopt in this regard are described in the following paragraphs.

45. In the *First Report and Order*, the Commission found that Section 335(a) provides authority for the Commission to impose other public interest programming requirements on DBS providers, including guidelines concerning the commercialization of children's programming. The Commission declined, however, to take any action, principally because it felt that any additional obligations imposed on the DBS industry at that stage in its development would be burdensome and could prevent DBS from realizing its potential as a robust competitor to cable. Nevertheless, the Commission said that the issue of additional public interest programming requirements will be reexamined if it becomes evident that regulatory intervention is needed to ensure that the needs of children are not overlooked.

* * *

48. Based on the growth, penetration level, and technological advances of DBS, as described below, we find CME's arguments persuasive and that reconsideration is warranted. We agree with CME that the benefits of imposing commercial limits on children's programming outweigh the potential burdens. Therefore upon reconsideration, we will require DBS providers to comply with the rules regarding commercial limits on children's programming that apply to cable operators. As of June 2002, DBS subscribership stood at over 20 million households, representing 20% of all subscribers to multichannel video programming. Given this penetration level, we believe it is now timely and appropriate to exercise our authority under Section 335(a) to ensure that children in DBS households are protected from excessive commercialism on television. A blanket exemption for DBS would expose a significant number of children to the risk of over-commercialization, contrary to Congress' intent in enacting the Children's Television Act of 1990. While the Children's Television Act specifically applies to broadcasters and cable operators, we do not believe that this was intended as a specific and permanent exemption for DBS, which was not yet a commercial service in 1990. Consequently, we shall amend Part 25 of the Commission's rules to include the commercial limits on children's programming that apply to cable operators.

49. We do not believe that compliance with the children's television rules on commercial limits will be burdensome. Many of the programming services carried by DBS providers are the same as are carried by cable systems around the country and thus this programming

already complies with the commercial restrictions. In addition, as we did in the cable context, we will relieve DBS providers from compliance with our rules where a specific statutory scheme prevents a DBS provider from controlling the programming involved. Thus, for example, where a DBS provider passively retransmits a broadcast signal pursuant to statute, it will not be held responsible for compliance with the commercial limits on the channel.

F. Programming on Reserved Capacity

50. Section 335(b)(1) specifies that the Commission must require that a DBS provider reserve a portion of its channel capacity, "equal to not less than 4 percent nor more than 7 percent, exclusively for noncommercial programming of an educational or informational nature." In response to this mandate, the Commission selected four percent as the capacity reservation percentage.

51. Time Warner asserts that DBS providers should not be allowed to fulfill the four percent reservation obligation by carrying noncommercial, educational and informational programming that was already being offered to subscribers before the *First Report and Order* was adopted. Time Warner argues that allowing DBS providers to do so would defeat the purpose of having a separate reservation obligation. Time Warner asserts that Congress intended that a DBS provider's reserved capacity should be available exclusively for programmers that represent interests that are not currently being served. Time Warner is supported by comments from DAETC and CME [Center For Media Education] that contend that prohibiting DBS providers from satisfying the reservation requirement with existing programming will result in greater diversity of media sources on DBS systems.

52. We decline to amend the rule as requested by Time Warner. If the programming is of the type that fulfills the statutory requirement for noncommercial programming of an educational or informational nature, there is no reason to deny a DBS operator credit solely because it carried the programming voluntarily before the set-aside went into effect. We believe that the amendment that Time Warner advocates would unfairly penalize those DBS providers that complied with the requirement before they were obligated to do so. * * *

The Relevance of Scarcity. What of the scarcity rationale? As a powerful dissent from the D.C. Circuit's denial of rehearing en banc in *Time Warner* explains, the scarcity that drove *Red Lion* does not exist in a world with either cable or DBS, much less both of them. See *Time Warner Entertainment Co. v. FCC*, 105 F.3d 723 (D.C. Cir. 1997). Since *Red Lion*, the explosion of cable and satellite service has made household reception of hundreds of channels ubiquitous. With everyone receiving so many channels, how can the original scarcity justification apply to terrestrial broadcasters (its original object), much less the expanded provider base of cable providers and satellite carriers? And, given that cable has been exempted from this type of broad public interest obligation, what justification can Congress (and the FCC) have for imposing it on only one type of MVPD and not the other? Does the 2004 *DBS Order* signal a possible reinvigoration of the public interest obligation for terrestrial broadcasters, too?

Should satellite providers be subject to public interest obligations because they are nationwide, or because they have the ability to "spot beam" their signals into particular markets? The FCC's answer seems to be "Yes," simply scaling the obligation from the local to the national market as the satellite broadcasters' signals scale. Are the interests the same, or is there something special about local markets that demands more (or less) of a subsidy for public interest programming than in national markets?

C. OFFENSIVE BROADCAST CONTENT

1. Obscenity

At the outset, observe that in dealing with obscenity we enter into an area of law that has been developed almost entirely outside the world of electronic communications. There is a separate criminal statute prohibiting the transmission of obscene, indecent, or profane matter by radio (18 U.S.C. § 1464) that the FCC is empowered by § 503 of the Communications Act to enforce by "forfeiture penalties" in addition to the criminal penalties prescribed by the criminal statute itself. However, nothing in the statute indicates that the standards for defining obscenity by radio are different from those applicable to, say, print. Should they be? Consider that question in light of the following, one of the rare cases involving FCC enforcement of radio obscenity.

ILLINOIS CITIZENS COMMITTEE FOR BROADCASTING v. FCC

United States Court of Appeals, District of Columbia Circuit, 1975.
515 F.2d 397.

LEVENTHAL, CIRCUIT JUDGE:

This controversy arises from the response of the Federal Communications Commission to certain radio call-in programs on sex-related topics. On March 27, 1973, the FCC announced an inquiry into the broadcast of obscene, indecent, or profane material. On the following day, FCC Chairman Dean Burch, in a speech before the National Association of Broadcasters, urged licensees to exercise self-restraint. A Notice of Apparent Liability proposing a forfeiture of $2,000 against one licensee was issued on April 11. The forfeiture was paid by the licensee, but Petitioners, Illinois Citizens Committee for Broadcasting and the Illinois Division of the American Civil Liberties Union, filed an Application for Remission of the Forfeiture and a Petition for Reconsideration as representatives of the listening public. The Commission, in a Memorandum Opinion and Order, refused to grant the relief requested by Petitioners but discussed at some length its purpose in instituting the Inquiry and in assessing the forfeiture. We affirm the Commission's action.

I. Statement of Facts

In response to increasing complaints from listeners, the Commission, in January of 1973, asked its staff to tape certain radio call-in programs that focused on sexual topics. The staff taped 61 hours of programs, 22 minutes of which were culled for presentation to the Commissioners on March 21. The Commissioners also heard an 11–minute segment that included an on-the-air complaint from a listener.

On March 27, the Commission released a Notice of "Inquiry into alleged broadcasts and cablecasts of obscene, indecent or profane material by licensees, permittees or cable systems." The inquiry was to be a nonpublic fact-finding proceeding to determine whether certain television, cable, and radio licensees had broadcast material in violation of 18 U.S.C. § 1464 (1970).

On the day of the release, the National Association of Broadcasters, at its annual convention, adopted a resolution condemning sexually oriented radio call-in shows. In his address to the Association on the following day Chairman Burch approved that step and urged the broadcasters to exercise self-restraint in order to avoid intrusions by the Commission, the Congress, and the courts.

After listening to the taped excerpts on March 21, 1973, the FCC instructed its staff to prepare a Notice of Apparent Liability under sections 503(b)(1)(E) and 503(b)(2) of the Communications Act of 1934, as amended, against Sonderling Broadcasting Corporation (Sonderling) for violations of § 1464. The Notice specifically cited Sonderling's "Femme Forum," a call-in show that ran Monday through Friday, from 10 a.m. to 3 p.m. on WGLD–FM, Oak Park, Illinois. The Commission focused on two programs that had been excerpted in the tapes—one, on February 23, 1973, was on the topic of oral sex; the other, on February 21, 1973, discussed "How do you keep your sex life alive?" and included specific descriptions of the techniques of oral sex. The Notice "concluded" that these broadcasts called for the imposition of a forfeiture of $2,000 against Sonderling because they contained "obscene or indecent matter." It also informed Sonderling of a licensee's statutory right to refuse to pay the forfeiture voluntarily and thus to require the FCC to seek to recover it in a trial de novo before a court. Despite its belief that the Commission's action was illegal, Sonderling decided to pay the fine because of "the tremendous financial burden involved."

Asserting that the public had an interest in seeking review of the FCC action despite Sonderling's acquiescence, Petitioners filed an Application for Remission of Forfeiture and a Petition for Reconsideration. They allege that their members and contributors include many numbers of the Chicago area who are being deprived of listening alternatives in violation of their rights under the First Amendment. On July 6, the Commission released the Memorandum Opinion and Order now under review. Although it expressed doubts as to Petitioners' standing to seek remission or reconsideration of the forfeiture, the FCC agreed to clarify its intentions in order to rectify misunderstandings regarding the Notice of Inquiry and the Notice of Apparent Liability. The Commission did not discuss the Chairman's speech, stating that it was not a Commission action. * * *

V. THE FCC'S DETERMINATION THAT THE BROADCAST IS OBSCENE

In its Memorandum Order and Opinion the Commission asserted that Sonderling's broadcast was a clear-cut violation of the law, "well within the constitutional boundaries [for obscenity] established by the Supreme Court," and therefore not entitled to protection under the First Amendment.

The excerpts cited by the Commission contain repeated and explicit descriptions of the techniques of oral sex. And these are presented, not for educational and scientific purposes, but in a context that was fairly described by the FCC as "titillating and pandering." The principles of *Ginzburg v. United States*, 383 U.S. 463 (1966), are applicable, for commercial exploitation of interests in titillation is the broadcaster's sole end. It is not a material difference that here the tone is set by the continuity provided by the announcer rather than, as in *Ginzburg*, by the presentation of the material in advertising and sale to solicit an audience. We cannot ignore what the Commission took into account—that the announcer's response to a complaint by an offended listener and his presentation of advertising for auto insurance are suffused with leering innuendo. Moreover, and significantly, "Femme Forum" is broadcast from 10 a.m. to 3 p.m. during daytime hours when the radio audience may include children—perhaps home from school for lunch, or because of staggered school hours or illness. Given this combination of factors, we do not think that the FCC's evaluation of this material infringes upon rights protected by the First Amendment.

The FCC found Sonderling's broadcasts obscene under the standards of *Roth v. United States*, 354 U.S. 476 (1957), and *Memoirs v. Massachusetts*, 383 U.S. 413 (1966). The Supreme Court subsequently reformulated those standards in *Miller v. California*, 413 U.S. 15 (1973), which sets out the following "basic guidelines for the trier of fact":

> (a) whether "the average person, applying contemporary community standards" would find that the work, taken as a whole, appeals to the prurient interest ... (b) whether the work depicts or describes, in a patently offensive way, sexual conduct specifically defined by the applicable state law, and (c) whether the work, taken as a whole, lacks serious literary, artistic, political, or scientific value.

The Commission reasonably concluded that the dominant theme of the material broadcast by Sonderling was addressed to the prurient interest and was therefore condemnable under that element of the *Memoirs* test. *Miller*, however, requires that the material depict or describe "in a patently offensive way, sexual conduct specifically defined by the applicable ... law." Although Petitioners filed a reply brief after the Court's decision in *Miller*, they did not challenge the possible lack of the requisite statutory specificity. Rather, they assert that *Miller* retained the first two tests of *Memoirs* and that these tests were misapplied by the Commission. We see no point in pursuing in the abstract the question whether the finding of obscenity here survives the narrowing of the second test that was accomplished in *Miller*, especially since we have the additional elements of titillation and probable exposure to children, which even some of the dissenting Justices in *Miller* thought sufficient to permit condemnation. *Paris Adult Theatre I v. Slaton*, 413 U.S. 49, 114 (1973) (Brennan, J., dissenting). Moreover, *Miller*'s specificity requirement is designed to "provide fair notice to a dealer," and it is not clear whether it is a requirement that may be insisted upon by the public when waived by the licensee. Petitioners' goal is to determine what material is withdrawn from censorship on grounds of obscenity because of the protections of the First Amendment, and that turns primarily on the nature of the social purpose that may redeem material that otherwise stands condemned. In this respect *Miller* narrows the protection afforded by *Memoirs* in a manner that undercuts the most important feature of Petitioners' claim.* * *

We conclude that, where a radio call-in show during daytime hours broadcasts explicit discussions of ultimate sexual acts in a titillating context, the Commission does not unconstitutionally infringe upon the public's right to listening alternatives when it determines that the broadcast is obscene.

Topless Radio. As the court's opinion indicates the Sonderling program was part of a larger trend in radio programming, known in the trade at the time as "topless radio." It is interesting to speculate why this obscenity problem surfaced primarily in the context of radio instead of television, though as we will see the "problem" is now arising on cable television. Is there some special characteristic of radio (or cable television) that encourages greater boldness than is found in free, over-the-air television ? Be that as it may, the legal criteria for defining obscenity are not different for radio and television. Nor are they different for radio/television on the one hand and print media on the other. Or are they? Does Judge Leventhal suggest a greater tolerance for regulatory interference in the former than in the latter?

Judge Bazelon seemed to suggest as much in a dissent from a denial of rehearing en banc in *Illinois Broadcasting*. Among other things Judge Bazelon criticized the majority of the court and the FCC for not actually applying the Supreme Court's *Miller* standards for defining obscenity. He argued that the FCC did not apply the local community standard, nor did it judge the material as a whole. Moreover, under the *Miller* criteria it could not be said that the material was without redeeming social value. (Judge Bazelon found "potential redeeming social interest in these materials" in their discussion of "adjustment to changing social mores on sexual relations and in the discussion of sexual problems as a means of solving personal 'hang-ups.' ") Is Bazelon correct? Anent the local community standard in particular, is it inappropriate for a federal agency to be making this judgment? Regardless of who makes that determination, how much weight should be given to the fact that the local community liked "Femme Forum" enough to make it one of the most popular radio shows in Chicago?

2. Indecency and Other Offenses

The criminal statute applied in the *Illinois Broadcasting* case proscribes the broadcast of "indecent" as well as "obscene" material. The court did not reach the question of whether the statute could be constitutionally applied to material that was not obscene. The Supreme Court in the context of another criminal provision, 18 U.S.C.A. § 1461, not involving radio held that, in order for the statute to pass constitutional muster, it was necessary to construe "indecency" as incorporating the same elements as obscenity; in other words "indecency" could have no independent meaning. See *Hamling v. United States*, 418 U.S. 87, 112–14 (1974) (generic terms of § 1461 must be construed to be limited to the sort of "patently offensive representations or descriptions of that specific 'hard core' sexual conduct given as examples in *Miller v. California*."). The question that would have been presented by the FCC's indecency finding, had the *Illinois Broadcasting* court not avoided it, was whether § 1464 should have the same construction. Since the only difference between § 1461 and § 1464 is the fact that the latter involves radio communications, the question is whether that fact has constitutional significance. Should it? On what theory? Is spectrum scarcity à la *Red Lion* relevant to this question? Are there other differences between electronic media and other media (print, theaters, billboards) that justify different constitutional treatment? The next case offered a partial answer, one that has proved to be enduringly controversial.

FCC v. PACIFICA FOUNDATION

Supreme Court of the United States, 1978.
438 U.S. 726.

JUSTICE STEVENS delivered the opinion of the Court (Parts I, II, III, and IV–C) and an opinion in which THE CHIEF JUSTICE and JUSTICE REHNQUIST joined (Parts IV–A and IV–B).

This case requires that we decide whether the Federal Communications Commission has any power to regulate a radio broadcast that is indecent but not obscene.

A satiric humorist named George Carlin recorded a 12-minute monologue entitled "Filthy Words" before a live audience in a California theater. He began by referring to his thoughts about "the words you couldn't say on the public, ah, airwaves, um, the ones you definitely wouldn't say, ever." He proceeded to list those words and repeat them over and over again in a variety of colloquialisms.[*] The transcript of the recording, which is appended to this opinion, indicates frequent laughter from the audience.

At about 2 o'clock in the afternoon on Tuesday, October 30, 1973, a New York radio station, owned by respondent Pacifica Foundation, broadcast the "Filthy Words" monologue. A few weeks later a man, who stated that he had heard the broadcast while driving with his young son, wrote a letter complaining to the Commission. * * *

The complaint was forwarded to the station for comment. In its response, Pacifica explained that the monologue had been played during a program about contemporary society's attitude toward language and that, immediately before its broadcast, listeners had been advised that it included "sensitive language which might be regarded as offensive to some." Pacifica characterized George Carlin as "a significant social satirist" who "like Twain and Sahl before him, examines the language of ordinary people. * * * Carlin is not mouthing obscenities, he is merely using words to satirize as harmless and essentially silly our attitudes towards those words." Pacifica stated that it was not aware of any other complaints about the broadcast.

On February 21, 1975, the Commission issued a declaratory order granting the complaint and holding that Pacifica "could have been the subject of administrative sanctions." The Commission did not impose formal sanctions, but it did state that the order would be "associated with the station's license file, and in the event that subsequent complaints are received, the Commission will then decide whether it should utilize any of the available sanctions it has been granted by Congress."

In its memorandum opinion the Commission stated that it intended to "clarify the standards which will be utilized in considering" the

* Eds. In part the transcript of the record is as follows: "I was thinking one night about the words you couldn't say on the public, ah, airwaves, um, the ones you definitely couldn't say, ever, cause I heard a lady say bitch one night on television, and it was cool like she was talking about, you know, ah, well, the bitch is the first one to notice that in the litter Johnie right (murmur) Right. And, uh, bastard you can say, and hell and damn so I have to figure out which ones you couldn't and ever and it came down to seven but the list is open to amendment, and in fact, has been changed, uh, by now, ha, a lot of people pointed things out to me, and I noticed some myself. The original seven words were, shit, piss, fuck, cunt, cocksucker, motherfucker, and tits. * * * Now the word shit is okay for the man. At work you can say it like crazy. Mostly figuratively, Get that shit out of here, will ya? I don't want to see that shit anymore. I can't cut that shit, buddy. I've had that shit up to here. I think you're full of shit myself. (laughter) He don't know shit from Shinola (laughter) you know that? (laughter) Always wondered how the Shinola people felt about that. (laughter) Hi, I'm the new man from Shinola. (laughter) Hi, how are ya? Nice to see ya. (laughter) How are ya? Boy, I don't know whether to shit or wind my watch. (laughter) Guess, I'll shit on my watch. (laughter) Oh, the shit is going to hit de fan. (laughter) Built like a brick shit-house. (laughter) Up, he's up shit's creek. (laughter) He's had it. (laughter) He hit me, I'm sorry. (laughter) Hot shit, holy shit, tough shit, eat shit, (laughter) shit-eating grin. Uh, whoever thought of that was ill. (murmur laughter) He had a shit-eating grin! He had a what? (laughter) Shit on a stick. (laughter). * * * "

growing number of complaints about indecent speech on the airwaves. Advancing several reasons for treating broadcast speech differently from other forms of expression, the Commission found a power to regulate indecent broadcasting in * * * 18 U.S.C.A. § 1464 (1976 ed.), which forbids the use of "any obscene, indecent, or profane language by means of radio communications." * * *

The Commission characterized the language used in the Carlin monologue as "patently offensive," though not necessarily obscene, and expressed the opinion that it should be regulated by principles analogous to those found in the law of nuisance where the "law generally speaks to channeling behavior more than actually prohibiting it.* * * [T]he concept of 'indecent' is intimately connected with the exposure of children to language that describes, in terms patently offensive as measured by contemporary community standards for the broadcast medium, sexual or excretory activities and organs, at times of the day when there is a reasonable risk that children may be in the audience."

Applying these considerations to the language used in the monologue as broadcast by respondent, the Commission concluded that certain words depicted sexual and excretory activities in a patently offensive manner, noted that they "were broadcast at a time when children were undoubtedly in the audience (i.e., in the early afternoon)," and that the prerecorded language, with these offensive words "repeated over and over," was "deliberately broadcast." In summary, the Commission stated: "We therefore hold that the language as broadcast was indecent and prohibited by 18 U.S.C.A. § 1464."

After the order issued, the Commission was asked to clarify its opinion by ruling that the broadcast of indecent words as part of a live newscast would not be prohibited. The Commission issued another opinion in which it pointed out that it "never intended to place an absolute prohibition on the broadcast of this type of language, but rather sought to channel it to times of day when children most likely would not be exposed to it." The Commission noted that its "declaratory order was issued in a specific factual context," and declined to comment on various hypothetical situations presented by the petition. It relied on its "long standing policy of refusing to issue interpretive rulings or advisory opinions when the critical facts are not explicitly stated or there is a possibility that subsequent events will alter them." * * *

II

The relevant statutory questions are whether the Commission's action is forbidden "censorship" within the meaning of 47 U.S.C.A. § 326 and whether speech that concededly is not obscene may be restricted as "indecent" under the authority of 18 U.S.C.A. § 1464 (1976 ed.). The questions are not unrelated, for the two statutory provisions have a common origin. Nevertheless, we analyze them separately.

Section 29 of the Radio Act of 1927 provided:

Nothing in this Act shall be understood or construed to give the licensing authority the power of censorship over the radio communications or signals transmitted by any radio station, and no regulation or condition shall be promulgated or fixed by the licensing authority which shall interfere with the right of free speech by means of radio communications. No person within the jurisdiction of the United States shall utter any obscene, indecent, or profane language by means of radio communication.

The prohibition against censorship unequivocally denies the Commission any power to edit proposed broadcasts in advance and to excise material considered inappropriate for the airwaves. The prohibition, however, has never been construed to deny the Commission the power to review the content of completed broadcasts in the performance of its regulatory duties. * * *

A single section of the 1927 Act is the source of both the anticensorship provision and the Commission's authority to impose sanctions for the broadcast of indecent or obscene language. Quite plainly, Congress intended to give meaning to both provisions. Respect for that intent requires that the censorship language be read as inapplicable to the prohibition on broadcasting obscene, indecent, or profane language.

There is nothing in the legislative history to contradict this conclusion. * * *

III

The only other statutory question presented by this case is whether the afternoon broadcast of the "Filthy Words" monologue was indecent within the meaning of § 1464. Even that question is narrowly confined by the arguments of the parties.

The Commission identified several words that referred to excretory or sexual activities or organs, stated that the repetitive, deliberate use of those words in an afternoon broadcast when children are in the audience was patently offensive, and held that the broadcast was indecent. Pacifica * * * does not quarrel with the conclusion that this afternoon broadcast was patently offensive. Pacifica's claim that the broadcast was not indecent within the meaning of the statute rests entirely on the absence of prurient appeal.

The plain language of the statute does not support Pacifica's argument. The words "obscene, indecent, or profane" are written in the distinctive, implying that each has a separate meaning. Prurient appeal is an element of the obscene, but the normal definition of "indecent" merely refers to nonconformance with accepted standards of morality. * * *

IV

Pacifica makes two constitutional attacks on the Commission's order. First, it argues that the Commission's construction of the statutory language broadly encompasses so much constitutionally protected speech that reversal is required even if Pacifica's broadcast of the "Filthy Words" monologue is not itself protected by the First Amendment. Second, Pacifica argues that inasmuch as the recording is not obscene, the Constitution forbids any abridgment of the right to broadcast it on the radio.

A

The first argument fails because our review is limited to the question whether the Commission has the authority to proscribe this particular broadcast. As the Commission itself emphasized, its order was "issued in a specific factual context." That approach is appropriate for courts as well as the Commission when regulation of indecency is at stake, for indecency is largely a function of context—it cannot be adequately judged in the abstract. * * *

It is true that the Commission's order may lead some broadcasters to censor themselves. At most, however, the Commission's definition of indecency will deter only the broadcasting of patently offensive references to excretory and sexual organs and activities. While some of these references may be protected, they surely lie at the periphery of First Amendment concern. Cf. *Bates v. State Bar*, 433 U.S. 350, 380–81. *Young v. American Mini Theaters Inc.*, 427 U.S. 50, 61. * * *

B

When the issue is narrowed to the facts of this case, the question is whether the First Amendment denies government any power to restrict the public broadcast of indecent language in any circumstances. For if the government has any such power, this was an appropriate occasion for its exercise.* * *

The question in this case is whether a broadcast of patently offensive words dealing with sex and excretion may be regulated because of its content. Obscene materials have been denied the protection of the First Amendment because their content is so offensive to contemporary moral standards. *Roth v. United States*, 354 U.S. 476. But the fact that society may find speech offensive is not a sufficient reason for suppressing it. Indeed, if it is the speaker's opinion that gives offense, that consequence is a reason for according it constitutional protection. For it is a central tenet of the First Amendment that the government must remain neutral in the marketplace of ideas. * * * These words offend for the same reasons that obscenity offends. Their place in the hierarchy of First Amendment values was aptly sketched by Mr. Justice Murphy when he said: "[S]uch utterances are no essential part of any exposition of ideas, and are of such slight social value as a step to truth that any benefit that may be derived from them is clearly outweighed by the social interest in order and morality."

Although these words ordinarily lack literary, political, or scientific value, they are not entirely outside the protection of the First Amendment. Some uses of even the most offensive words are unquestionably protected.* * *

In this case it is undisputed that the content of Pacifica's broadcast was "vulgar," "offensive," and "shocking." Because content of that character is not entitled to absolute constitutional protection under all circumstances, we must consider its context in order to determine whether the Commission's action was constitutionally permissible.

C

We have long recognized that each medium of expression presents special First Amendment problems. And of all forms of communication, it is broadcasting that has received the most limited First Amendment protection. * * *

The reasons for these distinctions are complex, but two have relevance to the present case. First, the broadcast media have established a uniquely pervasive presence in the lives of all Americans. Patently offensive, indecent material presented over the airwaves confronts the citizen, not only in public, but also in the privacy of the home, where the individual's right to be left alone plainly outweighs the First Amendment rights of an intruder. Because the broadcast audience is constantly tuning in and out, prior warnings cannot completely protect the listener or viewer from unexpected program content. To say that one may avoid further offense by turning off the radio when he hears indecent language is like saying that the remedy for an assault is to run away after the first blow. * * *

Second, broadcasting is uniquely accessible to children, even those too young to read. * * * Other forms of offensive expression may be withheld from the young without restricting the expression at its source. Bookstores and motion picture theaters, for example, may be prohibited from making indecent material available to children. We held in *Ginsberg v. New York*, 390 U.S. 629, that the government's interest in the "well-being of its youth" and in supporting "parents' claim to authority in their own household" justified the regulation of otherwise protected expression. The ease with which children may obtain access to broadcast material, coupled with the concerns recognized in *Ginsberg*, amply justify special treatment of indecent broadcasting.

It is appropriate, in conclusion, to emphasize the narrowness of our holding. This case does not involve a two-way radio conversation between a cab driver and a dispatcher, or a telecast of an Elizabethan comedy. We have not decided that an occasional expletive in either setting would justify any sanction or, indeed, that this broadcast would justify a criminal prosecution. The Commission's decision rested entirely on a nuisance rationale under which context is all-important. The concept requires consideration of a host of variables. The time of day was emphasized by the Commission. The content of the program in which the language is used will also affect the composition of the audience, and differences between radio, television, and perhaps closed-circuit transmissions, may also be relevant. As Mr. Justice Sutherland wrote, a "nuisance may be merely a right thing in the wrong place—like a pig in the parlor instead of the barnyard." * * *

The judgment of the Court of Appeals is reversed.

JUSTICE BRENNAN, with whom JUSTICE MARSHALL joins, dissenting. * * *

I

For the second time in two years, see *Young v. American Mini Theaters*, 427 U.S. 50 (1976), the Court refuses to embrace the notion, completely antithetical to basic First Amendment values, that the degree of protection the First Amendment affords protected speech varies with the social value ascribed to that speech by five Members of this Court. Moreover, as do all parties, all Members of the Court agree that the Carlin monologue aired by Station WBAI does not fall within one of the categories of speech, such as "fighting words," *Chaplinsky v. New Hampshire*, 315 U.S. 568 (1942), or obscenity, *Roth v. United States*, 354 U.S. 476 (1957), that is totally without First Amendment protection. This conclusion, of course, is compelled by our cases expressly holding that communications containing some of the words found condemnable here are fully protected by the First Amendment in other contexts. See *Cohen v. California*, 403 U.S. 15 (1971). Yet despite the Court's refusal to create a sliding scale of First Amendment protection calibrated to this Court's perception of the worth of a communication's content, and despite our unanimous agreement that the Carlin monologue is protected speech, a majority of the Court nevertheless finds that, on the facts of this case, the FCC is not constitutionally barred from imposing sanctions on Pacifica for its airing of the Carlin monologue. This majority apparently believes that the FCC's disapproval of Pacifica's afternoon broadcast of Carlin's "Dirty Words" recording is a permissible time, place, and manner regulation. Both the opinion of my Brother Stevens and the opinion of my Brother Powell rely principally on two factors in reaching this conclusion: (1) the capacity of a radio broadcast to intrude into the unwilling listener's home, and (2) the presence of children in the listening audience. * * *

A

Without question, the privacy interests of the individual in his home are substantial and deserving of significant protection. * * * However, I believe that an individual's actions in switching on and listening to communications transmitted over the public airways and directed to the public at large do not implicate fundamental privacy interests, even when engaged in within the home. Instead, because the radio is undeniably a public medium, these actions are more properly viewed as a decision to take part, if only as a listener, in an ongoing public discourse. Although an individual's decision to allow public radio communications into his home undoubtedly does not abrogate all of his privacy interests, the residual privacy interests he retains vis-à-vis the communication he voluntarily admits into his home are surely no greater than those of the people present in the corridor of the Los Angeles courthouse in *Cohen* who bore witness to the words "Fuck the Draft" emblazoned across Cohen's jacket. Their privacy interests were held insufficient to justify punishing Cohen for his offensive communication.

Even if an individual who voluntarily opens his home to radio communications retains privacy interests of sufficient moment to justify a ban on protected speech if those interests are "invaded in an essentially intolerable manner," the very fact that those interests are threatened only by a radio broadcast precludes any intolerable invasion of privacy; for unlike other intrusive modes of communication, such as sound trucks, "[t]he radio can be turned off," *Lehman v. Shaker Heights*, 418 U.S. 298, 302 (1974)—and with a minimum of effort. * * *

The Court's balance, of necessity, fails to accord proper weight to the interests of listeners who wish to hear broadcasts the FCC deems offensive. It permits majoritarian tastes completely to preclude a protected message from entering the homes of a receptive, unoffended minority. No decision of this Court supports such a result. Where the individuals constituting the offended majority may freely choose to reject the material being offered, we have never found their privacy interests of such moment to warrant the suppression of speech on privacy grounds. * * *

B

Most parents will undoubtedly find understandable as well as commendable the Court's sympathy with the FCC's desire to prevent offensive broadcasts from reaching the ears of unsupervised children. Unfortunately, the facial appeal of this justification for radio censorship masks its constitutional insufficiency. Although the government unquestionably has a special interest in the well-being of children and consequently "can adopt more stringent controls on communicative materials available to youths than on those available to adults," the Court has accounted for this societal interest by adopting a "variable obscenity" standard that permits the prurient appeal of material available to children to be assessed in terms of the sexual interests of minors. *Ginsberg v. New York*, 390 U.S. 629 (1968). * * *

Because the Carlin monologue is obviously not an erotic appeal to the prurient interests of children, the Court, for the first time, allows the government to prevent minors from gaining access to materials that are not obscene, and are therefore protected, as to them. It thus ignores our recent admonition that "[s]peech that is neither obscene as to youths nor subject to some other legitimate proscription cannot be suppressed solely to protect the young from ideas or images that a legislative body thinks unsuitable for them." The Court's refusal to follow its own pronouncements is especially lamentable since it has the anomalous subsidiary effect, at least in the radio context at issue here, of making completely unavailable to adults material which may not constitutionally be kept even from children. * * *

III

It is quite evident that I find the Court's attempt to unstitch the warp and woof of First Amendment law in an effort to reshape its fabric to cover the patently wrong result the Court reaches in this case dangerous as well as lamentable. Yet there runs throughout the opinions of my Brothers Powell and Stevens another vein I find equally disturbing: a depressing inability to appreciate that in our land of cultural pluralism, there are many who think, act, and talk differently from the Members of this Court, and who do not share their fragile sensibilities. It is only an acute ethnocentric myopia that enables the Court to approve the censorship of communications solely because of the words they contain. * * *

Today's decision will thus have its greatest impact on broadcasters desiring to reach, and listening audiences comprised of, persons who do not share the Court's view as to which words or expressions are acceptable and who, for a variety of reasons, including a conscious desire to flout majoritarian conventions, express themselves using words that may be regarded as offensive by those from different socio-economic backgrounds. In this context, the Court's decision may be seen for what, in the broader perspective, it really is: another of the dominant culture's inevitable efforts to force those groups who do not share its mores to conform to its way of thinking, acting, and speaking. * * *

To Infinity and Beyond. Despite the Supreme Court's approval of its newly minted indecency doctrine, the FCC did not rush forth like Buzz Lightyear to do battle with the evil empire of radio smut. Immediately after *Pacifica* the FCC rejected a petition by Morality in Media to deny a license renewal for one of the foremost educational stations in the country on the ground that it had consistently broadcast "offensive, vulgar and otherwise harmful material to children." *WGBH Educ. Found.*, 69 F.C.C.2d 1250 (1978). The Commission held that the Court's decision "affords this commission no general prerogative to intervene in any case where words similar or identical to those in Pacifica are broadcast over a licensed radio or television station. We intend strictly to observe the narrowness of the *Pacifica* holding." To underscore the point then-Chairman Charles Ferris announced that another case like *Pacifica* was "about as likely to occur again as Halley's Comet." *Speech by FCC Chairman Charles D. Ferris to New England Broadcasters Assoc.*, Boston Mass., July 21, 1978.

Ferris was an optimist. Halley's Comet makes a periodic appearance about every 76 years; indecency reappeared before the FCC in just nine. In 1987, the FCC was drawn back into the indecency issue by the appearance of "shock radio" that was designed to push the envelope of provocative programming beyond anything attempted a decade earlier. Howard Stern and his syndicator, Infinity Broadcasting (owned by CBS's then-parent, Viacom), became the new reigning provocateurs. Still, the

FCC responded moderately. It revised its 1978 policy of limiting enforcement policy to the precise seven words of Carlin's "dirty words" monologue, and returned to the original "generic" policy announced in *Pacifica*, which evaluated the total context of the expression. The Court of Appeals for the District of Columbia affirmed the FCC's policy, albeit not without reservation. *Action for Children's Television v. FCC*, 852 F.2d 1332 (D.C. Cir. 1988) ("*ACT I*").

The court's decision was to be the first act of a three-*ACT* play[3] in which the FCC, Congress and courts took turns exploring the permissible limits of the new indecency regime. In the ruling leading to *ACT I*, the Commission had indicated that the late-night hours of midnight to 6:00 AM could serve as a "safe harbor," a period during which indecent material could be broadcast without sanction. Congress disagreed and attempted in 1989 to eliminate the safe harbor period, imposing a 24–hour ban on indecent speech. In the second "act," *Action for Children's Television v. FCC*, 932 F.2d 1504 (D.C. Cir. 1991) ("*ACT II*"), the court struck down Congress's absolute ban as unconstitutional. In the third act, the court partially reversed an attempt to distinguish between commercial and non-commercial stations concerning the period of the ban. After *ACT II*, Congress directed the FCC to reinstate the safe harbor, but directed that the FCC should provide a wider window for for non-commercial stations (from 10:00 PM to 6:00 AM instead of the standard midnight to 6:00 AM safe harbor for commercial stations). Finding no basis for discriminating between commercial and non-commercial indecency, the court held that all stations should be treated alike; the safe harbor was set for 10:00 PM to 6:00 AM for all. *Action for Children's Television v. FCC*, 58 F.3d 654 (D.C. Cir. 1995) ("*ACT III*").

In the aftermath of the *ACT* cases, the Commission continued to view indecency as a problem of controlling a small number of rogue broadcasters and broadcast personalities like Howard Stern, whose talk show was responsible for a very large percentage of all fines paid for indecent broadcasting over the past score years. (In 1995, Infinity Broadcasting paid a then-record sum of $1.7 million to settle indecency complaints over a series of Howard Stern Shows.) Except for Stern and fellow "shock jocks," the Commission basically left mainstream broadcast programming alone. All that changed beginning in 2004, when the Commission accelerated enforcement, increased fines, and expanded the scope of what constituted indecency. For instance, it ruled that a single spontaneous and ephemeral use of the F-word was a violation of its policy. *Complaints Against Various Broadcast Licensees Regarding Their Airing of the "Golden Globe Awards" Program*, 19 FCC Rcd. 4975 (2004) (Bono accepting a Golden Globe Award with the exclamation that it was "fucking brilliant."). Consistent with its focus on a single exclamation (as opposed to the repeated utterances so heavily emphasized in *Pacifi-*

3. There was a fourth *ACT* case, but it dealt only with a constitutional and statutory challenge to the procedures for enforcing 18 U.S.C. 1464. Action for Children's Television v. FCC, 59 F.3d 1249 (D.C. Cir. 1995) ("*ACT IV*"). The court rejected the challenges.

ca), the FCC magnified the impact of its increased regulation by now deciding that each utterance of a forbidden word may be counted as a separate violation instead of looking at a particular program as a single, integrated unit. *In the Matter of Clear Channel Broadcasting Licensees, Inc.*, 19 FCC Rcd. 6773 ¶ 15 (2004). The Commission also moved beyond the traditional targets—radio talk shows that deliberately and repeatedly followed a pattern of provocative programming—for indecency enforcement. In its new phase, the Commission has undertaken a close inspection of movies, regular television series, live events, and even educational documentaries, to locate objectionable language or images. See, e.g., *Complaints Regarding Various Television Broadcasts Between February 2, 2002 and March 8, 2005*, 21 FCC Rcd. 2664 (2006) ("Omnibus Order") (finding violations for use of the "F-word" or "S-word" in, e.g., a documentary program (¶¶ 72–86), a movie (¶¶ 87–99), a live interview (¶¶ 137–144), and a regular television series (¶¶ 125–136)). The most celebrated of its new enforcement actions came as a consequence of Janet Jackson's performance at half time during SuperBowl XXXVIII, in which she revealed (more or less—the exposure was very brief) a bare breast. It proved to be a costly entertainment, at least for CBS, which was ordered to pay the largest fine that had been assessed for a single episode of indecency: $550,000. *Complaints Against Various Television Licensees Concerning Their February 1, 2004 Broadcast of the Super Bowl XXXVIII Halftime Show*, 21 FCC Rcd. 2760 (2006) rev'd, CBS Corp. v. FCC, 2008 WL 2789307 (3d Cir. 2008). Up to this point, the broadcast industry had chosen to pay the forfeitures (as they are technically called) quietly; until the Commission began its aggressive enforcement moves most of the mainstream broadcasters could understandably think they didn't have a dog in the fight. The Omnibus and Super Bowl orders in 2006 showed otherwise.

The litigation over the Omnibus Order provides an excellent view to not only the constitutional complexities of the FCC's approach to indecency but also the impact of administrative law on the FCC's new regulatory emphasis.

FOX TELEVISION STATIONS, INC. v. FCC

United States Court of Appeals, Second Circuit, 2007.
489 F.3d 444.

POOLER, CIRCUIT JUDGE:

Fox Television Stations, Inc., along with its affiliates FBC Television Affiliates Association (collectively "Fox"), petition for review of the November 6, 2006, order of the Federal Communications Commission ("FCC") issuing notices of apparent liability against two Fox broadcasts for violating the FCC's indecency and profanity prohibitions. Fox, along with other broadcast networks and numerous amici, raise administrative, statutory, and constitutional challenges to the FCC's indecency regime. The FCC, also supported by several amici, dispute each of these challenges. We find that the FCC's new policy regarding "fleeting expletives" represents a significant departure from positions previously taken by the agency and relied on by the broadcast industry. We further find that the FCC has failed to articulate a reasoned basis for this change in policy. Accordingly, we hold that the FCC's new policy regarding "fleeting expletives" is arbitrary and capricious under the Administrative Procedure Act. The petition for review is therefore granted, the order of the FCC is vacated, and the matter is remanded to the Commission for further proceedings consistent with this opinion. Because we vacate the FCC's order on this ground, we do not reach the other challenges to the FCC's indecency regime raised by petitioners, intervenors, and amici.

Background

The FCC's policing of "indecent" speech stems from 18 U.S.C. § 1464, which provides that "[w]hoever utters any obscene, indecent, or profane language by means of radio communication shall be fined under this title or imprisoned not more than two years, or both." The FCC's authority to regulate the broadcast medium is expressly limited by Section 326 of the Communications Act, which prohibits the FCC from engaging in censorship. In 1960, Congress authorized the FCC to impose forfeiture penalties for violations of Section 1464. The FCC first exercised its statutory authority to sanction indecent (but non-obscene) speech in 1975, when it found Pacifica Foundation's radio broadcast of comedian George Carlin's "Filthy Words" monologue indecent and subject to forfeiture. * * *

Pacifica appealed the FCC's order to the Court of Appeals for the D.C. Circuit. While that appeal was pending, the FCC issued a "clarification" order in which it specifically noted that its prior order was intended to address only the particular facts of the Carlin monologue as broadcast, and acknowledged the concern that "in some cases, public events likely to produce offensive speech are covered live, and there is no opportunity for journalistic editing." The FCC stated that in such a situation, "we believe that it would be inequitable for us to hold a licensee responsible for indecent language."

Although acknowledging the FCC's additional clarification, the D.C. Circuit nevertheless concluded that the FCC's indecency regime was invalid. Labeling the Commission's actions censorship, the court found the FCC's order both vague and overbroad, noting that it would prohibit "the uncensored broadcast of many of the great works of literature including Shakespearian plays and contemporary plays which have won critical acclaim, the works of renowned classical and contemporary poets and writers, and passages from the Bible."

The Commission appealed this decision to the Supreme Court, which reversed in a plurality opinion. In its brief to the Supreme Court, the FCC stressed that its ruling was a narrow one applying only to the specific facts of the Carlin monologue. The Court took the Commission at its word and confined its review to the specific question of whether the Commission could find indecent the Carlin monologue as broadcast.

The Court first rejected Pacifica's statutory argument that "indecent" in Section 1464 could not be read to cover speech that admittedly did not qualify as obscenity. Finding that obscene, indecent, and profane have distinct meanings in the statute, the Court held that the FCC is permitted to sanction speech without showing that it satisfied the elements of obscenity. The Court then rejected Pacifica's constitutional challenges. The Court stated that "of all forms of communication, it is broadcasting that has received the most limited First Amendment protection" because the broadcast medium is a "uniquely pervasive presence in the lives of all Americans" that extends into the privacy of the home and is "uniquely accessible to children, even those too young to read." The Court therefore found that the FCC could, consistent with the First Amendment, regulate indecent material like the Carlin monologue. The Court then once again "emphasize[d] the narrowness of our holding ... We simply hold that when the Commission finds that a pig has entered the parlor, the exercise of its regulatory power does not depend on proof that the pig is obscene."

Justices Powell and Blackmun, who concurred in the judgment and supplied two of the votes necessary for the 5–4 majority, also emphasized in their concurring opinion that the Court's holding was a narrow one limited to the facts of the Carlin monologue as broadcast. Foreshadowing the question now before us, they explicitly noted that "[t]he Commission's holding, and certainly the Court's holding today, does not speak to cases involving the isolated use of a potentially offensive word in the course of a radio broadcast, as distinguished from the verbal shock treatment administered by respondent here." Furthermore, citing the FCC's brief to the Court, Justice Powell stated that he did not foresee an undue chilling effect on broadcasters by the FCC's decision because "the Commission may be expected to proceed cautiously, as it has in the past."

The FCC took the *Pacifica* Court's admonitions seriously in its subsequent decisions. Shortly after the *Pacifica* ruling, the FCC stated the following in an opinion rejecting a challenge to a broadcaster's license renewal on the basis that the broadcaster had aired indecent programming:

> With regard to 'indecent' or 'profane' utterances, the First Amendment and the 'no censorship' provision of Section 326 of the Communications Act severely limit any role by the Commission and the courts in enforcing the proscription contained in Section 1464. The Supreme Court's decision in *FCC v. Pacifica Foundation*, 46 U.S.L.W. 5018 (1978), No. 77–528, decided July 3, 1978, affords this Commission no general prerogative to intervene in any case where words similar or identical to those in Pacifica are broadcast over a licensed radio or television station. *We intend strictly to observe the narrowness of the Pacifica holding*. In this regard, the Commission's opinion, as approved by the Court, relied in part on the repetitive occurrence of the 'indecent' words in question. The opinion of the Court specifically stated that it was not ruling that 'an occasional

expletive ... would justify any sanction ...' Further, Justice Powell's concurring opinion emphasized the fact that the language there in issue had been 'repeated over and over as a sort of verbal shock treatment.' He specifically distinguished 'the verbal shock treatment [in *Pacifica*]' from 'the isolated use of a potentially offensive word in the course of a radio broadcast.'

The FCC also specifically held that the single use of an expletive in a program that aired at 5:30pm "should not call for us to act under the holding of *Pacifica*." A few years later, the Commission again rejected a challenge to a license renewal that complained the broadcaster had aired indecent programming in violation of Section 1464. The FCC acknowledged the complaint that the broadcaster on three separate occasions had aired programming during the morning hours containing language such as "motherfucker," "fuck," and "shit," but nevertheless concluded that "it is clear that the petitioner has failed to make a prima facie case that [the broadcaster] has violated 18 U.S.C. 1464" since the language did not amount to "verbal shock treatment" and the complainant had failed to show this was more than "isolated use."

It was not until 1987 that the FCC would find another broadcast "indecent" under Section 1464. * * * The Infinity Order affirmed on reconsideration three decisions issued simultaneously by the FCC in April 1987 that found certain programs indecent. The FCC explained in the Infinity Order that it would no longer take the narrow view that a finding of indecency required the use of one of the seven "dirty words" used in Carlin's monologue. The FCC instead would use the generic definition of indecency it had articulated in connection with its prior decision in *Pacifica*. Under the Commission's definition, "indecent speech is language that describes, in terms patently offensive as measured by contemporary community standards for the broadcast medium, sexual or excretory activities and organs. Such indecent speech is actionable when broadcast at times of the day when there is a reasonable risk that children may be in the audience." The FCC also reaffirmed, however, the prevailing view that a fleeting expletive would not be actionable. Notably, in *Pacifica Foundation*, the Commission declined to make a finding of indecency against a radio broadcast of the program "Shocktime America," which had contained words and phrases such as "eat shit," "mother-fucker" and "fuck the U.S.A," in part because, without a transcript or tape of the program, the FCC was unable to determine "whether the use of patently offensive speech was isolated." * * *

This restrained enforcement policy would soon change. During NBC's January 19, 2003, live broadcast of the Golden Globe Awards, musician Bono stated in his acceptance speech "this is really, really, fucking brilliant. Really, really, great." Individuals associated with the Parents Television Council filed complaints that the material was obscene and indecent under FCC regulations. The FCC's Enforcement Bureau, however, denied the complaints on the basis that the expletive as used in context did not describe sexual or excretory organs or activities and that the utterance was fleeting and isolated. The Bureau accordingly found that the speech "does not fall within the scope of the Commission's indecency prohibition," and reaffirmed FCC policy that "fleeting and isolated remarks of this nature do not warrant Commission action."

Five months later, the full Commission reversed the Bureau's decision. First, the FCC held that any use of any variant of "the F–Word" inherently has sexual connotation and therefore falls within the scope of the indecency definition. The FCC then held that "the 'F–Word' is one of the most vulgar, graphic, and explicit descriptions of sexual activity in the English language" and therefore the use of that word was patently offensive under contemporary community standards. The Commission found the fleeting and isolated use of the word irrelevant and overruled all prior decisions in which fleeting use of an expletive was held not indecent.

The FCC then held that the material in question was also "profane" under Section 1464. The Commission acknowledged that prior decisions interpreting "profane" had defined that term as blasphemy, but found that nothing in its prior decisions limited the definition of profane in such a manner. The Commission, however, declined to impose a forfeiture because "existing precedent would have permitted this broadcast" and therefore NBC and its affiliates "necessarily did not have the requisite notice to justify a penalty." The Commission emphasized, though, that licensees were now on notice that any broadcast of the "F–Word" could subject them to monetary penalties and suggested that implementing delay technology would ensure future compliance with its policy.

NBC, along with several other parties including Fox, filed petitions for reconsideration of the *Golden Globes* order, raising statutory and constitutional challenges to the new policy. NBC, Fox, and Viacom Inc. also filed a joint petition to stay the effect of the *Golden Globes* order. These petitions have been pending for more than two years without any action by the FCC. Nevertheless, the FCC has applied the policy announced in *Golden Globes* in subsequent cases.

On February 21, 2006, the FCC issued an order resolving various complaints against several television broadcasts. Through this order, the FCC intended to "provide substantial guidance to broadcasters and the public about the types of programming that are impermissible under our indecency standard." In Section III.B of the Omnibus Order, the Commission found four programs—Fox's broadcast of the 2002 Billboard Music Awards, Fox's broadcast of the 2003 Billboard Music Awards, various episodes of ABC's NYPD Blue, and CBS's The Early Show—indecent and profane under the policy announced in *Golden Globes*. The factual situations at issue are as follows:

- **2002 Billboard Music Awards:** In her acceptance speech, Cher stated: "People have been telling me I'm on the way out every year, right? So fuck 'em."

• **2003 Billboard Music Awards:** Nicole Richie, a presenter on the show, stated: "Have you ever tried to get cow shit out of a Prada purse? It's not so fucking simple."

• **NYPD Blue:** In various episodes, Detective Andy Sipowitz and other characters used certain expletives including "bullshit," "dick," and "dickhead."

• **The Early Show:** During a live interview of a contestant on CBS's reality show Survivor: Vanuatu, the interviewee referred to a fellow contestant as a "bullshitter."

In finding these programs indecent and profane, the FCC reaffirmed its decision in *Golden Globes* that any use of the word "fuck" is presumptively indecent and profane. The Commission then concluded that any use of the word "shit" was also presumptively indecent and profane. Turning to the second part of its indecency test, the FCC found that each of the programs were "patently offensive" because the material was explicit, shocking, and gratuitous. Citing *Golden Globes*, the Commission dismissed the fact that the expletives were fleeting and isolated and held that repeated use is not necessary for a finding of indecency. The FCC, however, declined to issue a forfeiture in each case for the express reason that the broadcasts in question occurred before the decision in *Golden Globes*, and thus "existing precedent would have permitted this broadcast."

Fox and CBS filed a petition for review of the Omnibus Order in this court. ABC filed a petition for review in the D.C. Circuit, which was then transferred to this court and consolidated with the petition for review filed by Fox and CBS. Before any briefing took place, however, the FCC moved for a voluntary remand in order to give the Commission the first opportunity to address petitioners' arguments and "ensure that all licensees are afforded a full opportunity to be heard before the Commission issues a final decision." On September 7, 2006, this court granted the FCC's request for remand and stayed enforcement of the Omnibus Order. The Commission was given sixty days to issue a final or appealable order, at which time the pending appeal would be automatically reinstated.

The FCC promptly issued a public notice soliciting comments on its decision in the Omnibus Order. Numerous parties, including those who have participated in the briefing in this appeal, submitted comments raising various statutory and constitutional arguments against the FCC's indecency regime. The FCC then issued a new order on November 6, 2006. In the Remand Order, the FCC reaffirmed its finding that the 2002 and 2003 Billboard Music Award programs were indecent and profane, but reversed its finding against The Early Show. It also dismissed on procedural grounds the complaint against NYPD Blue.

With regard to the 2003 Billboard Music Awards, the Commission found that it would have been actionably indecent even prior to the decision in *Golden Globes* because the potentially offensive material was "repeated," since Nicole Richie used "two extremely graphic and offensive words," and was "deliberately uttered" because of "Ms. Richie's confident and fluid delivery of the lines." With regard to the 2002 Billboard Music Awards, the Commission "acknowledge[d] that it was not apparent that Fox could be penalized for Cher's comment at the time it was broadcast." In both cases, the FCC rejected Fox's argument that fleeting expletives were not actionable, now characterizing its prior decisions on that issue as "staff letters and dicta." The Commission, however, declined to impose a forfeiture for either broadcast.

Turning to The Early Show, the FCC reversed its finding that the expletive used was indecent or profane because it occurred in the context of a "bona fide news interview." The Commission stated that in light of First Amendment concerns, "it is imperative that we proceed with the utmost restraint when it comes to news programming," and found it "appropriate ... to defer to CBS's plausible characterization of its own programming" as a news interview. Given this context, the FCC declined to find the comment indecent or profane.

In accordance with our September 6th order, this appeal was automatically reinstated on November 8, 2006. Fox then filed a petition for review of the Remand Order and moved to consolidate that appeal with the one already pending before this court. We granted the motion for consolidation as well as motions to intervene by CBS Broadcasting Inc. ("CBS") and NBC Universal Inc. and NBC Telemundo License Co. (collectively, "NBC"). We have also received several briefs from various amici.

Discussion

Fox, CBS, and NBC (collectively, "the Networks"), supported by several amici, raise a variety of arguments against the validity of the Remand Order, including: (1) the Remand Order is arbitrary and capricious because the Commission's regulation of "fleeting expletives" represents a dramatic change in agency policy without adequate explanation; (2) the FCC's "community standards" analysis is arbitrary and meaningless; (3) the FCC's indecency findings are invalid because the Commission made no finding of scienter; (4) the FCC's definition of "profane" is contrary to law; (5) the FCC's indecency regime is unconstitutionally vague; (6) the FCC's indecency test permits the Commission to make subjective determinations about the quality of speech in violation of the First Amendment; and (7) the FCC's indecency regime is an impermissible content-based regulation of speech that violates the First Amendment. The FCC, also supported by several amici, dispute each of these contentions. We agree with the first argument advanced by the Networks, and therefore do not reach any other potential problems with the FCC's decision.

I. Scope of Review

Before turning to the merits of the Networks' arguments, we first note that we reject the FCC's contention that our review here is narrowly confined to the specific question of whether the two Fox broadcasts of the Billboard Music Awards were indecent and/or profane. The Remand Order applies the policy announced in *Golden Globes*. If that policy is invalid, then we cannot sustain the indecency findings against Fox. Thus, as the Commission conceded during oral argument, the validity of the new "fleeting expletive" policy announced in *Golden Globes* and applied in the Remand Order is a question properly before us on this petition for review. As the D.C. Circuit explained in rejecting this precise argument in another proceeding, "the agency may not resort to adjudication as a means of insulating a generic standard from judicial review."

II. Administrative Procedure Act

* * * The Networks contend that the Remand Order is arbitrary and capricious because the FCC has made a 180–degree turn regarding its treatment of "fleeting expletives" without providing a reasoned explanation justifying the about-face. We agree.

First, there is no question that the FCC has changed its policy. As outlined in detail above, prior to the *Golden Globes* decision the FCC had consistently taken the view that isolated, non-literal, fleeting expletives did not run afoul of its indecency regime. This consistent enforcement policy changed with the issuance of *Golden Globes*. * * *

Agencies are of course free to revise their rules and policies. Such a change, however, must provide a reasoned analysis for departing from prior precedent. See *Chevron U.S.A., Inc. v. Natural Res. Def. Council, Inc.*, 467 U.S. 837, 863 (1984) ("An initial agency interpretation is not instantly carved in stone."). Such a change, however, must provide a reasoned analysis for departing from prior precedent. * * * See also *Motor Vehicle Mfrs. Ass'n of U.S., Inc. v. State Farm Mut. Auto. Ins. Co.*, 463 U.S. 29, 41–42 (1983). ("A settled course of behavior embodies the agency's informed judgment that, by pursuing that course, it will carry out the policies committed to it by Congress. There is, then, at least a presumption that those policies will be carried out best if the settled rule is adhered to." (internal quotation marks omitted)). * * *

Our evaluation of the agency's reasons for its change in policy is confined to the reasons articulated by the agency itself. The primary reason for the crackdown on fleeting expletives advanced by the FCC is the so-called "first blow" theory described in the Supreme Court's *Pacifica* decision. In *Pacifica*, the Supreme Court justified the FCC's regulation of the broadcast media in part on the basis that indecent material on the airwaves enters into the privacy of the home uninvited and without warning. The Court rejected the argument that the audience could simply tune-out: "To say that one may avoid further offense by turning off the radio when he hears indecent language is like saying that the remedy for an assault is to run away after the first blow." Relying on this statement in *Pacifica*, the Commission attempts to justify its stance on fleeting expletives on the basis that "granting an automatic exemption for 'isolated or fleeting' expletives unfairly forces viewers (including children) to take 'the first blow.' "

We cannot accept this argument as a reasoned basis justifying the Commission's new rule. First, the Commission provides no reasonable explanation for why it has changed its perception that a fleeting expletive was not a harmful "first blow" for the nearly thirty years between *Pacifica* and *Golden Globes*. More problematic, however, is that the "first blow" theory bears no rational connection to the Commission's actual policy regarding fleeting expletives. As the FCC itself stressed during oral argument in this case, the Commission does not take the position that any occurrence of an expletive is indecent or profane under its rules. For example, although "there is no outright news exemption from our indecency rules," the Commission will apparently excuse an expletive when it occurs during a "bona fide news interview." Certainly viewers (including children) watching the live broadcast of The Early Show were "force[d] ... to take the 'first blow' "of the expletive uttered by the Survivor: Vanuatu contestant. Yet the Commission emphasized during oral argument that its news exception is a broad one and "the Commission has never found a broadcast to be indecent on the basis of an isolated expletive in the face of some claim that the use of that language was necessary for any journalistic or artistic purpose." The Commission further explained to this court that a broadcast of oral argument in this case, in which the same language used in the Fox broadcasts was repeated multiple times in the courtroom, would "plainly not" be indecent or profane under its standards because of the context in which it occurred. The Commission even conceded that a re-broadcast of precisely the same offending clips from the two Billboard Music Award programs for the purpose of providing background information on this case would not result in any action by the FCC, even though in those circumstances viewers would be subjected to the same "first blow" that resulted from the original airing of this material. Furthermore, the Commission has also held that even repeated and deliberate use of numerous expletives is not indecent or profane under the FCC's policy if the expletives are "integral" to the work. See *Complaints Against Various Television Licensees Regarding Their Broadcast on November 11, 2004, of the ABC Television Network's Presentation of the Film "Saving Private Ryan"*, 20 F.C.C.R. 4507, at ¶ 14 (2005) ("Saving Private Ryan") (finding numerous expletives uttered during film Saving Private Ryan not indecent or profane because deleting the expletives "would have altered the nature of the artistic work and diminished the power, realism and immediacy of the film experience for viewers"). In all of these scenarios, viewers, including children who may have no understanding of whether expletives are "integral" to a program or whether the interview of a contestant on a reality show is a "bona fide news interview," will have to accept the alleged "first blow" caused by use of these expletives. Thus, the record simply does not support the position that the Commission's new policy was based on its concern with the public's mere exposure to this language on the airwaves. The "first blow" theory, therefore, fails to provide the reasoned explanation necessary to justify the FCC's departure from established precedent.

* * *

The Commission's new approach to profanity is supported by even less analysis, reasoned or not. The Commission sets forth no independent reasons that would justify its newly-expanded definition of "profane" speech, aside from merely stating that its prior precedent does not prevent it from setting forth a new definition. To the extent the Commission believes its arguments for expanding its indecency enforcement support its new policy regarding profanity, those arguments are rejected for the reasons stated above. Furthermore, the Commission fails to provide any explanation for why this separate ban on profanity is even necessary. Prior to 2004, the Commission never attempted to regulate "profane" speech. In fact, the Commission took the view that a separate ban on profane speech was unconstitutional. The Commission again has not provided this court with a reasoned analysis of why it has undertaken this separate regulation of speech. Finally, the Commission provides no explanation of what harm this separate enforcement against profane speech addresses that is not already addressed by the FCC's indecency and obscenity enforcement. Particularly considering that the scope of the FCC's new profanity definition appears to be largely (if not completely) redundant with its indecency prohibition, see infra Part IV, this would seem to be an important question for the Commission to consider. The Remand Order, however, provides no indication that the Commission has engaged in any such analysis.

Accordingly, we find that the FCC's new policy regarding "fleeting expletives" fails to provide a reasoned analysis justifying its departure from the agency's established practice. For this reason, Fox's petition for review is granted, the Remand Order is vacated, and the matter is remanded to the FCC for further proceedings consistent with this opinion. Because we have found that the FCC's new indecency regime, announced in *Golden Globes* and applied in the Remand Order, is invalid under the Administrative Procedure Act, the stay of enforcement previously granted by this court in our September 6th order is vacated as moot.

III. Constitutional Challenges

"A fundamental and longstanding principle of judicial restraint requires that courts avoid reaching constitutional questions in advance of the necessity of deciding them." Thus, we refrain from deciding the various constitutional challenges to the Remand Order raised by the Networks. We note, however, that in reviewing these numerous constitutional challenges, which were fully briefed to this court and discussed at length during oral argument, we are skeptical that the Commission can provide a reasoned explanation for its "fleeting expletive" regime that would pass constitutional muster. Because we doubt that the Networks will refrain from further litigation on these precise issues if, on remand, the Commission merely provides further explanation with no other changes to its policy, in the interest of judicial economy we make the following observations.

As an initial matter, we note that all speech covered by the FCC's indecency policy is fully protected by the First Amendment. With that backdrop in mind, we question whether the FCC's indecency test can survive First Amendment scrutiny. For instance, we are sympathetic to the Networks' contention that the FCC's indecency test is undefined, indiscernible, inconsistent, and consequently, unconstitutionally vague. Although the Commission has declared that all variants of "fuck" and "shit" are presumptively indecent and profane, repeated use of those words in "Saving Private Ryan," for example, was neither indecent nor profane. And while multiple occurrences of expletives in "Saving Private Ryan" was not gratuitous, a single occurrence of "fucking" in the Golden Globe Awards was "shocking and gratuitous." Parental ratings and advisories were important in finding "Saving Private Ryan" not patently offensive under contemporary community standards, but irrelevant in evaluating a rape scene in another fictional movie. The use of numerous expletives was "integral" to a fictional movie about war, but occasional expletives spoken by real musicians were indecent and profane because the educational purpose of the documentary "could have been fulfilled and all viewpoints expressed without the repeated broadcast of expletives." *Omnibus Order*, 21 F.C.C.R. 2664, at ¶ 82 (finding Martin Scorsese's PBS documentary "The Blues: Godfathers and Sons" indecent). The "S-Word" on The Early Show was not indecent because it was in the context of a "bona fide news interview," but "there is no outright news exemption from our indecency rules," We can understand why the Networks argue that the FCC's "patently offensive as measured by contemporary community standards" indecency test coupled with its "artistic necessity" exception fails to provide the clarity required by the Constitution, creates an undue chilling effect on free speech, and requires broadcasters to "steer far wider of the unlawful zone."

The Networks' position is further buttressed by the Supreme Court's decision in *Reno v. ACLU*, 521 U.S. 844 (1997), which struck down as unconstitutionally vague a similarly-worded indecency regulation of the Internet. The Court found that the statute's use of the "general, undefined terms 'indecent' and 'patently offensive' cover large amounts of nonpornographic material with serious educational or other value. Moreover, the 'community standards' criterion as applied to the Internet means that any communication available to a nation wide audience will be judged by the standards of the community most likely to be offended by the message." Because of the "vague contours" of the regulation, the Court held that "it unquestionably silences some speakers whose messages would be entitled to constitutional protection," and thus violated the First Amendment. Because *Reno* holds that a regulation that covers speech that "in context, depicts or describes, in terms patently offensive as measured by contemporary community standards, sexual or excretory activities or organs" is unconstitutionally vague, we are skeptical that the FCC's identically-worded indecency test could nevertheless provide the requisite clarity to withstand constitutional scrutiny. Indeed, we are hard pressed to imagine a regime that is more vague than one that relies entirely on consideration of the otherwise unspecified "context" of a broadcast indecency.

We also note that the FCC's indecency test raises the separate constitutional question of whether it permits the FCC to sanction speech based on its subjective view of the merit of that speech. It appears that under the FCC's current indecency regime, any and all uses of an expletive is presumptively indecent and profane with the broadcaster then having to demonstrate to the satisfaction of the Commission, under an unidentified burden of proof, that the expletives were "integral" to the work. In the licensing context, the Supreme Court has cautioned against speech regulations that give too much discretion to government officials. In succeeding on this challenge, the Networks need not prove that the FCC "has exercised [its] discretion in a content-based manner, but whether there is anything in [its policy] preventing [it] from doing so."

Finally, we recognize there is some tension in the law regarding the appropriate level of First Amendment scrutiny. In general, restrictions on First Amendment liberties prompt courts to apply strict scrutiny. Outside the broadcasting context, the Supreme Court has consistently applied strict scrutiny to indecency regulations. At the same time, however, the Supreme Court has also considered broadcast media exceptional. "[B]ecause broadcast regulation involves unique considerations, our cases . . . have never gone so far as to demand that such regulations serve 'compelling' governmental interests." Restrictions on broadcast "speech" have been upheld "when we [are] satisfied that the restriction is narrowly tailored to further a substantial governmental interest."

The Networks contend that the bases for treating broadcast media "different[ly]" have "eroded over time," particularly because 86 percent of American households now subscribe to cable or satellite services. As the Networks argue, this and other realities have "eviscerated" the notion that broadcast content is, as it was termed in *Pacifica*, "uniquely pervasive" and "uniquely accessible to children." Whatever merit these arguments may have, they cannot sway us in light of Supreme Court precedent.

Nevertheless, we would be remiss not to observe that it is increasingly difficult to describe the broadcast media as uniquely pervasive and uniquely accessible to children, and at some point in the future, strict scrutiny may properly apply in the context of regulating broadcast television. In light of this possibility, the Networks rightly rest their constitutional argument in part on the holding of [*United States v. Playboy Entertainment Group*, 529 U.S. 803 (2000), excerpted below] which involved a challenge to a statute requiring cable operators who provide channels primarily dedicated to sexually explicit or otherwise indecent programming to either fully scramble these channels or limit their transmission to the 10pm to 6am safe harbor period. The Supreme Court, applying strict scrutiny, invalidated the statute because a less restrictive alternative to the prohibition existed: "One plausible, less restrictive alternative could be found in another section of the [Telecommunications] Act [of 1996]: § 504, which requires a cable operator, 'upon request by a cable service subscriber ... without charge, [to] fully scramble or otherwise fully block' any channel the subscriber does not wish to receive." The Court held: This "targeted blocking is less restrictive than banning, and the Government cannot ban speech if targeted blocking is a feasible and effective means of furthering its compelling interests." In so holding, the Court suggested its decision might go beyond the mechanistic application of strict scrutiny, and rely in part on a notional pillar of free speech-namely, choice:

> When a student first encounters our free speech jurisprudence, he or she might think it is influenced by the philosophy that one idea is as good as any other, and that in art and literature objective standards of style, taste, decorum, beauty, and esthetics are deemed by the Constitution to be inappropriate, indeed unattainable. Quite the opposite is true. The Constitution no more enforces a relativistic philosophy or moral nihilism than it does any other point of view. The Constitution exists precisely so that opinions and judgments, including esthetic and moral judgments about art and literature, can be formed, tested, and expressed. What the Constitution says is that these judgments are for the individual to make, not for the Government to decree, even with the mandate or approval of a majority. Technology expands the capacity to choose; and it denies the potential of this revolution if we assume the Government is best positioned to make these choices for us.

The Court specifically rejected the arguments that parents' ignorance of this option, its underutilization, or its inability to be 100% effective rendered targeted blocking an ineffective alternative: "It is no response that voluntary blocking requires a consumer to take action, or may be inconvenient, or may not go perfectly every time. A court should not assume a plausible, less restrictive alternative would be ineffective; and a court should not presume parents, given full information, will fail to act."

The Networks argue that the advent of the V-chip and parental ratings system similarly provide a less restrictive alternative to the FCC's indecency ban. The FCC counters that the V-chip is an ineffective alternative because, in its view, few televisions feature a V-chip, most parents do not know how to use it, programs are often inaccurately rated, and fleeting expletives, such as those witnessed at the programs at issue here, could elude V-chip blocking even if the show during which they occurred was otherwise accurately labeled. The FCC's arguments are not without merit, but they must be evaluated in the context of today's realities. The proliferation of satellite and cable television channels-not to mention internet-based video outlets-has begun to erode the "uniqueness" of broadcast media, while at the same time, blocking technologies such as the V-chip have empowered viewers to make their own choices about what they do, and do not, want to see on television. *Playboy* distinguished *Pacifica* on the grounds that "[c]able systems have the capacity to block unwanted channels on a household-by-household basis" and thus "[t]he option to block reduces the likelihood, so concerning to the Court in *Pacifica*, that traditional First Amendment scrutiny would deprive the Government of all authority to address this sort of problem." The FCC is free to regulate indecency, but its regulatory powers are bounded by the Constitution. If the *Playboy* decision is any guide, technological advances may obviate the constitutional legitimacy of the FCC's robust oversight.

IV. The FCC's Construction of Profane

The Networks also argue that the FCC employed an improper definition of "profane" under Section 1464. Although we need not reach this argument to dispose of this appeal, on remand, the FCC may desire to explain its gloss on the definition of "profane." In the Remand Order, the FCC applied its new definition of "profane" as set forth in *Golden Globes*. The FCC now defines "profane" as "those personally reviling epithets naturally tending to provoke violent resentment or denoting language which under contemporary community standards is so grossly offensive to members of the public who actually hear it as to amount to a nuisance." The FCC, noting that "shit" and "fuck" fall within this definition, ruled that Cher's and Nicole Richie's fleeting expletives were "profane," as well as indecent. Most dictionaries interpret the term "profane" to denote something that pertains to the irreligious, and since 1927, courts-as well as the FCC itself-have assumed that "profane" in the broadcast context refers to sacrilege, and nothing more.* * *

But the FCC's definition of "profane" here, would substantially overlap with the statutory term "indecent." This overlap would be so extensive as to render the statutory term "indecent" superfluous. Because our canons of statutory construction do not permit such an interpretation, we do not believe the FCC has proffered a reasonable construction of the term "profane." While we may owe Chevron deference to the FCC's construction, the FCC must still demonstrate that its construction is reasonable, particularly in light of Congressional intent, the canons of statutory construction, and the historical view of the plain meaning of this term.

Conclusion

As the foregoing indicates, we are doubtful that by merely proffering a reasoned analysis for its new approach to indecency and profanity, the Commission can adequately respond to the constitutional and statutory challenges raised by the Networks. Nevertheless, because we can decide this case on this narrow ground, we vacate and remand so that the Commission can set forth that analysis. While we fully expect the Networks to raise the same arguments they have raised to this court if the Commission does nothing more on remand than provide additional explanation for its departure from prior precedent, we can go no further in this opinion. Accordingly, we grant the petition for review, vacate the order of the FCC, and remand the case for further proceedings consistent with this opinion. The stay previously granted by this court is vacated as moot.

In March 2008, the Supreme Court granted certiorari. Four months later, the Third Circuit reversed a decision by the FCC fining CBS for Janet Jackson's "costume reveal," cited in the note preceding *Fox*.

Reasoning About Change. The Second Circuit devoted considerable attention to the history of the FCC's regulation of indecency, particularly the period of inaction following *Pacifica*. Although, as the court explains, previous agency interpretations are not "set in stone," what kind of "reasoned analysis" can the FCC offer in favor of changing its interpretation of the statute? Is it possible to state the decision to clamp down on salacious broadcasts as the product of reasoned analysis? What kind of reasoned analysis could have led the Commission to reject their predecessors' preference for hearing swear words on the radio?

Reasoning About Context. The FCC purports to consider the context in which the indecent language was used. As the court notes, the FCC gave a pass to "Saving Private Ryan," in which "fuck" and "shit" are used with considerable regularity, on the ground that the expletives were "integral" to the work. No such pass was given NYPD Blue. Apparently words like fuck and shit are not "integral" to the work of a cop show but are integral to a war film. Does this not suggest that the real issue that the Supreme Court should address when it decides this case is not whether the indecency policy applies to fleeting expressions (such as the exclamations by Bono or Cher) but whether the FCC's criteria for applying it are too subjective to be capable of "reasoned" analysis? Or maybe it suggests that the regulation of indecency is inherently laden with cultural values that are not susceptible to the usual standards of rational government purpose that are used to evaluate speech restrictions. If so, what should the Court do about it? How does one apply a means-ends rationality review to what is, in effect, a *Kulturcamp*? See Glen O. Robinson, *The Electronic First Amendment: An Essay for the New Age*, 47 Duke L. J. 899, 964–65 (1998).

3. Indecency Regulation in Cable Television

In one other area, the absence of scarcity presents no problem. Recall that the *Pacifica* indecency doctrine does not rest on scarcity, but on intrusiveness. If broadcast television is "intrusive" is cable television any less so? Why would one care whether an offensive program appeared by cable or by broadcast? Consider the following.

UNITED STATES v. PLAYBOY ENTERTAINMENT GROUP, INC.

Supreme Court of the United States, 2000.
529 U.S. 803.

JUSTICE KENNEDY delivered the opinion of the Court.

This case presents a challenge to § 505 of the Telecommunications Act of 1996. Section 505 requires cable television operators who provide channels "primarily dedicated to sexually-oriented programming" either to "fully scramble or otherwise fully block" those channels or to limit their transmission to hours when children are unlikely to be viewing, set by administrative regulation as the time between 10 p.m. and 6 a.m. Even before enactment of the statute, signal scrambling was already in use. Cable operators used scrambling in the regular course of business, so that only paying customers had access to certain programs. Scrambling could be imprecise, however; and either or both audio and visual portions of the scrambled programs might be heard or seen, a phenomenon known as "signal bleed." The purpose of § 505 is to shield children from hearing or seeing images resulting from signal bleed.

To comply with the statute, the majority of cable operators adopted the second, or "time channeling," approach. The effect of the widespread adoption of time channeling was to eliminate altogether the transmission of the targeted programming outside the safe harbor period in affected cable service areas. In other words, for two-thirds of the day no household in those service areas could receive the programming, whether or not the household or the viewer wanted to do so.

Appellee Playboy Entertainment Group, Inc., challenged the statute as unnecessarily restrictive content-based legislation violative of the First Amendment. After a trial, a three-judge District Court concluded that a regime in which viewers could order signal blocking on a household-by-household basis presented an effective, less restrictive alternative to § 505. Finding no error in this conclusion, we affirm.

I

Playboy Entertainment Group owns and prepares programs for adult television networks, including Playboy Television and Spice. Playboy transmits its programming to cable television operators, who retransmit it to their subscribers, either through monthly subscriptions to premium channels or on a so-called "pay-per-view" basis. Cable operators transmit Playboy's signal, like other premium channel signals, in scrambled form. The operators then provide paying subscribers with an "addressable converter," a box placed on the home television set. The converter permits the viewer to see and hear the descrambled signal. It is conceded that almost all of Playboy's programming consists of sexually explicit material as defined by the statute.

The statute was enacted because not all scrambling technology is perfect. Analog cable television systems may use either "RF" or "baseband" scrambling systems, which may not prevent signal bleed, so discernible pictures may appear from time to time on the scrambled screen. Furthermore, the listener might hear the audio portion of the program.

These imperfections are not inevitable. The problem is that at present it appears not to be economical to convert simpler RF or baseband scrambling systems to alternative scrambling technologies on a systemwide scale. Digital technology may one day provide another solution, as it presents no bleed problem at all. Indeed, digital systems are projected to become the technology of choice, which would eliminate the signal bleed problem. Digital technology is not yet in widespread use, however. With imperfect scrambling, viewers who have not paid to receive Playboy's channels may happen across discernible images of a sexually explicit nature. How many viewers, how discernible the scene or sound, and how often this may occur are at issue in this case.

Section 505 was enacted to address the signal bleed phenomenon. As noted, the statute and its implementing regulations require cable operators either to scramble a sexually explicit channel in full or to limit the channel's programming to the hours between 10 p.m. and 6 a.m. Section 505 was added by floor amendment, without significant debate, to the Telecommunications Act of 1996(Act), a major legislative effort designed "to reduce regulation and encourage 'the rapid deployment of new telecommunications technologies.'" *Reno v. American Civil Liberties Union*, 521 U.S. 844, 857 (1997). "The Act includes seven Titles, six of which are the product of extensive committee hearings and the subject of discussion in Reports prepared by Committees of the Senate and the House of Representatives." Section 505 is found in Title V of the Act, which is itself known as the Communications Decency Act of 1996(CDA). Section 505 was to become effective on March 9, 1996, 30 days after the Act was signed by the President.

On March 7, 1996, Playboy obtained a temporary restraining order (TRO) enjoining the enforcement of § 505 and brought this suit in a three-judge District Court pursuant to § 561 of the Act. Playboy sought a declaration that § 505 violates the Constitution and an injunction prohibiting the law's enforcement. The District Court denied Playboy a preliminary injunction, and we summarily affirmed. The TRO was lifted, and the Federal Communications Commission announced it would begin enforcing § 505 on May 18, 1997. When the statute became operative, most cable operators had "no practical choice but to curtail [the targeted] programming during the [regulated] sixteen hours or risk the penalties imposed ... if any audio or video signal bleed occur[red] during [those] times." The majority of operators—"in one survey, 69%"—complied with § 505 by time channeling the targeted programmers. Since "30 to 50% of all adult programming is viewed by households prior to 10 p.m.," the result was a significant restriction of communication, with a corresponding reduction in Playboy's revenues.

In March 1998, the District Court held a full trial and concluded that § 505 violates the First Amendment. The District Court observed that § 505 imposed a content-based restriction on speech. It agreed that the interests the statute advanced were compelling but concluded the Government might further those interests in less restrictive ways. One plausible, less restrictive alternative could be found in another section of the Act: § 504, which requires a cable operator, "[u]pon request by a cable service subscriber . . . without charge, [to] fully scramble or otherwise fully block" any channel the subscriber does not wish to receive. As long as subscribers knew about this opportunity, the court reasoned, § 504 would provide as much protection against unwanted programming as would § 505. At the same time, § 504 was content neutral and would be less restrictive of Playboy's First Amendment rights.

* * * The United States filed a direct appeal in this Court pursuant to § 561. The District Court thereafter dismissed for lack of jurisdiction two post-trial motions filed by the Government. We noted probable jurisdiction, and now affirm.

II

Two essential points should be understood concerning the speech at issue here. First, we shall assume that many adults themselves would find the material highly offensive; and when we consider the further circumstance that the material comes unwanted into homes where children might see or hear it against parental wishes or consent, there are legitimate reasons for regulating it. Second, all parties bring the case to us on the premise that Playboy's programming has First Amendment protection. As this case has been litigated, it is not alleged to be obscene; adults have a constitutional right to view it; the Government disclaims any interest in preventing children from seeing or hearing it with the consent of their parents; and Playboy has concomitant rights under the First Amendment to transmit it. These points are undisputed.

The speech in question is defined by its content; and the statute which seeks to restrict it is content based. Section 505 applies only to channels primarily dedicated to "sexually explicit adult programming or other programming that is indecent." The statute is unconcerned with signal bleed from any other channels. ("[Section 505] does not apply when signal bleed occurs on other premium channel networks, like HBO or the Disney Channel"). The overriding justification for the regulation is concern for the effect of the subject matter on young viewers. Section 505 is not " 'justified without reference to the content of the regulated speech.' " It "focuses only on the content of the speech and the direct impact that speech has on its listeners." This is the essence of content-based regulation.

Not only does § 505 single out particular programming content for regulation, it also singles out particular programmers. The speech in question was not thought by Congress to be so harmful that all channels were subject to restriction. Instead, the statutory disability applies only to channels "primarily dedicated to sexually-oriented programming." One sponsor of the measure even identified appellee by name. Laws designed or intended to suppress or restrict the expression of specific speakers contradict basic First Amendment principles. Section 505 limited Playboy's market as a penalty for its programming choice, though other channels capable of transmitting like material are altogether exempt.

The effect of the federal statute on the protected speech is now apparent. It is evident that the only reasonable way for a substantial number of cable operators to comply with the letter of § 505 is to time channel, which silences the protected speech for two-thirds of the day in every home in a cable service area, regardless of the presence or likely presence of children or of the wishes of the viewers. According to the District Court, "30 to 50% of all adult programming is viewed by households prior to 10 p.m.," when the safe-harbor period begins. To prohibit this much speech is a significant restriction of communication between speakers and willing adult listeners, communication which enjoys First Amendment protection. It is of no moment that the statute does not impose a complete prohibition. The distinction between laws burdening and laws banning speech is but a matter of degree. The Government's content-based burdens must satisfy the same rigorous scrutiny as its content-based bans.

* * * Our precedents teach these principles. Where the designed benefit of a content-based speech restriction is to shield the sensibilities of listeners, the general rule is that the right of expression prevails, even where no less restrictive alternative exists. We are expected to protect our own sensibilities "simply by averting [our] eyes." Here, of course, we consider images transmitted to some homes where they are not wanted and where parents often are not present to give immediate guidance. Cable television, like broadcast media, presents unique problems, which inform our assessment of the interests at stake, and which may justify restrictions that would be unacceptable in other contexts. See *Denver Area Educational Telecommunications Consortium, Inc. v. FCC*, 518 U.S. 727, 744 (1996) (plurality opinion); *FCC v. Pacifica Foundation*, 438 U.S. 726 (1978). No one suggests the Government must be indifferent to unwanted, indecent speech that comes into the home without parental consent. The speech here, all agree, is protected speech; and the question is what standard the Government must meet in order to restrict it. As we consider a content-based regulation, the answer should be clear: The standard is strict scrutiny. This case involves speech alone; and even where speech is indecent and enters the home, the objective of shielding children does not suffice to support a blanket ban if the protection can be accomplished by a less restrictive alternative. * * *

There is, moreover, a key difference between cable television and the broadcasting media, which is the point on which this case turns: Cable systems have the capacity to block unwanted channels on a household-by-household basis. The option to block reduces the likelihood, so concerning to the Court in *Pacifica*, *supra* at 744 that traditional First

Amendment scrutiny would deprive the Government of all authority to address this sort of problem. The corollary, of course, is that targeted blocking enables the Government to support parental authority without affecting the First Amendment interests of speakers and willing listeners-listeners for whom, if the speech is unpopular or indecent, the privacy of their own homes may be the optimal place of receipt. Simply put, targeted blocking is less restrictive than banning, and the Government cannot ban speech if targeted blocking is a feasible and effective means of furthering its compelling interests. This is not to say that the absence of an effective blocking mechanism will in all cases suffice to support a law restricting the speech in question; but if a less restrictive means is available for the Government to achieve its goals, the Government must use it.

III

The District Court concluded that a less restrictive alternative is available: § 504, with adequate publicity. No one disputes that § 504, which requires cable operators to block undesired channels at individual households upon request, is narrowly tailored to the Government's goal of supporting parents who want those channels blocked. The question is whether § 504 can be effective.

When a plausible, less restrictive alternative is offered to a content-based speech restriction, it is the Government's obligation to prove that the alternative will be ineffective to achieve its goals. The Government has not met that burden here. In support of its position, the Government cites empirical evidence showing that § 504, as promulgated and implemented before trial, generated few requests for household-by-household blocking. Between March 1996 and May 1997, while the Government was enjoined from enforcing § 505, § 504 remained in operation. A survey of cable operators determined that fewer than 0.5% of cable subscribers requested full blocking during that time. The uncomfortable fact is that § 504 was the sole blocking regulation in effect for over a year; and the public greeted it with a collective yawn.

The District Court was correct to direct its attention to the import of this tepid response. Placing the burden of proof upon the Government, the District Court examined whether § 504 was capable of serving as an effective, less restrictive means of reaching the Government's goals. It concluded that § 504, if publicized in an adequate manner, could be.

The District Court employed the proper approach. When the Government restricts speech, the Government bears the burden of proving the constitutionality of its actions. When the Government seeks to restrict speech based on its content, the usual presumption of constitutionality afforded congressional enactments is reversed. "Content-based regulations are presumptively invalid," and the Government bears the burden to rebut that presumption. * * *

With this burden in mind, the District Court explored three explanations for the lack of individual blocking requests. First, individual blocking might not be an effective alternative, due to technological or other limitations. Second, although an adequately advertised blocking provision might have been effective, § 504 as written did not require sufficient notice to make it so. Third, the actual signal bleed problem might be far less of a concern than the Government at first had supposed.

To sustain its statute, the Government was required to show that the first was the right answer. According to the District Court, however, the first and third possibilities were "equally consistent" with the record before it. As for the second, the record was "not clear" as to whether enough notice had been issued to give § 504 a fighting chance. The case, then, was at best a draw. Unless the District Court's findings are clearly erroneous, the tie goes to free expression.

The District Court began with the problem of signal bleed itself, concluding "the Government has not convinced us that [signal bleed] is a pervasive problem." The District Court's thorough discussion exposes a central weakness in the Government's proof: There is little hard evidence of how widespread or how serious the problem of signal bleed is. Indeed, there is no proof as to how likely any child is to view a discernible explicit image, and no proof of the duration of the bleed or the quality of the pictures or sound. To say that millions of children are subject to a risk of viewing signal bleed is one thing; to avoid articulating the true nature and extent of the risk is quite another. Under § 505, sanctionable signal bleed can include instances as fleeting as an image appearing on a screen for just a few seconds. The First Amendment requires a more careful assessment and characterization of an evil in order to justify a regulation as sweeping as this. Although the parties have taken the additional step of lodging with the Court an assortment of videotapes, some of which show quite explicit bleeding and some of which show television static or snow, there is no attempt at explanation or context; there is no discussion, for instance, of the extent to which any particular tape is representative of what appears on screens nationwide. * * *

Nor did the District Court err in its second conclusion. The Government also failed to prove § 504 with adequate notice would be an ineffective alternative to § 505. Once again, the District Court invited the Government to produce its proof. Once again, the Government fell short. There is no evidence that a well-promoted voluntary blocking provision would not be capable at least of informing parents about signal bleed (if they are not yet aware of it) and about their rights to have the bleed blocked (if they consider it a problem and have not yet controlled it themselves).

The Government finds at least two problems with the conclusion of the three-judge District Court. First, the Government takes issue with the District Court's reliance, without proof, on a "hypothetical, enhanced version of Section 504." It was not the District Court's obligation, however, to predict the extent to which an improved notice scheme would improve § 504. It was for the Government, presented with a plausible, less restrictive alternative, to prove the alternative to be ineffective, and § 505 to be the least restrictive available means. Indeed, to the extent the District Court erred, it was only in attempting to implement the less restrictive alternative through judicial decree by requiring Playboy to provide for expanded notice in its cable service contracts. The appropriate remedy was not to repair the statute, it was to enjoin the speech restriction. Given the existence of a less restrictive means, if the Legislature wished to improve its statute, perhaps in the process giving careful consideration to other alternatives, it then could do so.

The Government also contends a publicized § 504 will be just as restrictive as § 505, on the theory that the cost of installing blocking devices will outstrip the revenues from distributing Playboy's programming and lead to its cancellation. This conclusion rests on the assumption that a sufficient percentage of households, informed of the potential for signal bleed, would consider it enough of a problem to order blocking devices-an assumption for which there is no support in the record. it should be noted, furthermore, that Playboy is willing to incur the costs of an effective § 504. One might infer that Playboy believes an advertised § 504 will be ineffective for its object, or one might infer the company believes the signal bleed problem is not widespread. In the absence of proof, it is not for the Court to assume the former.

It is no response that voluntary blocking requires a consumer to take action, or may be inconvenient, or may not go perfectly every time. A court should not assume a plausible, less restrictive alternative would be ineffective; and a court should not presume parents, given full information, will fail to act. If unresponsive operators are a concern, moreover, a notice statute could give cable operators ample incentive, through fines or other penalties for noncompliance, to respond to blocking requests in prompt and efficient fashion.

Having adduced no evidence in the District Court showing that an adequately advertised § 504 would not be effective to aid desirous parents in keeping signal bleed out of their own households, the Government can now cite nothing in the record to support the point. The Government instead takes quite a different approach. After only an offhand suggestion that the success of a well-communicated § 504 is "highly unlikely," the Government sets the point aside, arguing instead that society's independent interests will be unserved if parents fail to act on that information.

Even upon the assumption that the Government has an interest in substituting itself for informed and empowered parents, its interest is not sufficiently compelling to justify this widespread restriction on speech. The Government's argument stems from the idea that parents do not know their children are viewing the material on a scale or frequency to cause concern, or if so, that parents do not want to take affirmative steps to block it and their decisions are to be superseded. The assumptions have not been established; and in any event the assumptions apply only in a regime where the option of blocking has not been explained. The whole point of a publicized § 504 would be to advise parents that indecent material may be shown and to afford them an opportunity to block it at all times, even when they are not at home and even after 10 p.m. Time channeling does not offer this assistance. The regulatory alternative of a publicized § 504, which has the real possibility of promoting more open disclosure and the choice of an effective blocking system, would provide parents the information needed to engage in active supervision. The Government has not shown that this alternative, a regime of added communication and support, would be insufficient to secure its objective, or that any overriding harm justifies its intervention.

There can be little doubt, of course, that under a voluntary blocking regime, even with adequate notice, some children will be exposed to signal bleed; and we need not discount the possibility that a graphic image could have a negative impact on a young child. It must be remembered, however, that children will be exposed to signal bleed under time channeling as well. Time channeling, unlike blocking, does not eliminate signal bleed around the clock. Just as adolescents may be unsupervised outside of their own households, it is hardly unknown for them to be unsupervised in front of the television set after 10 p.m. The record is silent as to the comparative effectiveness of the two alternatives. * * *

[Concurring opinions by Justice Stevens and Justice Thomas are omitted, as is a separate dissenting opinion by Justice Scalia, who also joined in the following dissent by Justice Breyer.]

JUSTICE BREYER with whom THE CHIEF JUSTICE, JUSTICE O'CONNOR, and JUSTICE SCALIA join, dissenting.

* * *

II

The majority first concludes that the Government failed to prove the seriousness of the problem-receipt of adult channels by children whose parents did not request their broadcast. Ante, at 1889–1891. This claim is flat-out wrong. For one thing, the parties concede that basic RF scrambling does not scramble the audio portion of the program. For another, Playboy itself conducted a survey of cable operators who were asked: "Is your system in full compliance with Section 505 (no discernible audio or video bleed)?" To this question, 75% of cable operators answered "no." Further, the Government's expert took the number of homes subscribing to Playboy or Spice, multiplied by the fraction of cable households with children and the average number of children per household, and found 29 million children are potentially exposed to audio and video bleed from adult programming. Even discounting by 25% for systems that might be considered in full compliance, this left 22 million children in homes with faulty scrambling systems. And, of course, the record contains additional anecdotal evidence and the concerns expressed by elected officials, probative of a larger problem.

I would add to this empirical evidence the majority's own statement that "most cable operators had 'no practical choice but to curtail' " adult programming by switching to nighttime only transmission of adult channels. If signal bleed is not a significant empirical problem, then why, in light of the cost of its cure, must so many cable operators switch to nighttime hours? There is no realistic answer to this question. I do not think it realistic to imagine that signal bleed occurs just enough to make cable operators skittish, without also significantly exposing children to these images.

If, as the majority suggests, the signal bleed problem is not significant, then there is also no significant burden on speech created by § 505. The majority cannot have this evidence both ways. And if, given this logical difficulty and the quantity of empirical evidence, the majority still believes that the Government has not proved its case, then it imposes a burden upon the Government beyond that suggested in any other First Amendment case of which I am aware. * * *

---

4. Children, Sex, Violence and the V-chip

In recent years the emphasis has shifted somewhat away from direct imposition of content standards toward mandating "filters" that can be used by parents to control their children's exposure to content. One such scheme, the so-called "V-chip" device which is part of a scheme mandated by Congress in 1996 in the Communications Decency Act (part of the Telecommunications Act of 1996). The device is a piece of software code that parents can use to block material they deem inappropriate (for their children) by reason of its violent ("V") or other offensive content. The V-chip, like any filtering device, requires some classification system—some means of identifying the various content. The Communications Decency Act also directed that the television industry (or in default of the industry's cooperation, the FCC) adopt a ratings code to be used with the V-chip device. The industry did adopt such a ratings code, which was approved by the FCC in the following proceeding.

VIDEO PROGRAMMING RATINGS
Report and Order

Federal Communications Commission, 1998.
13 FCC Rcd. 8232.

BY THE COMMISSION:

I. INTRODUCTION

1. In the Telecommunications Act of 1996 (the "1996 Act"), Congress determined that parents should be provided with timely informa-

tion about the nature of upcoming video programming and with the technological tools that would allow them to easily block violent, sexual, or other programming they believe is harmful to their children. Congress also provided that distributors of video programming should be given the opportunity to develop a voluntary system to provide parents with ratings information. In response to the 1996 Act, the National Association of Broadcasters ("NAB"), National Cable Television Association ("NCTA") and Motion Picture Association of America ("MPAA") (the "Industry") jointly submitted to the Commission on behalf of their members, a system of voluntary parental guidelines ("TV Parental Guidelines") adopted and implemented by television broadcasters and networks, cable networks and systems, and television program producers. Section 551(e) of the 1996 Act requires the Commission to determine whether video programming distributors (1) have established acceptable voluntary rules for rating video programming that contains sexual, violent or other indecent material about which parents should be informed before it is displayed to children and (2) have agreed voluntarily to broadcast signals that contain such ratings.

2. In this Report and Order, we find that the Industry's TV Parental Guidelines establish acceptable voluntary rating rules and that the concomitant agreement to voluntarily broadcast signals containing ratings pursuant to the TV Parental Guidelines are in compliance with the specific requirements of Section 551(e). In a companion item being issued today we adopt technical rules that require television receivers with picture screens 33 cm (13 inches) or greater to be equipped with features to block the display of television programming with a common rating, commonly referred to as the "v-chip" technology. Although we chose to approach the v-chip and ratings proceedings separately, our deliberations in both proceedings have focused on Congress' goal of achieving an effective method by which the rating system, when used in conjunction with the v-chip technology, will provide parents with useful tools to block programming they believe harmful to their children.

II. Background

* * *

5. Following enactment of the 1996 Act, and over the course of the next year, the broadcasting, cable and program production industries worked together to develop a rating system, which they implemented in early January 1997. Details of the rating system were submitted to the Commission on January 17, 1997. Following the January 17, 1997 Submission, the Commission sought comment from interested parties on the TV Parental Guidelines. Parents groups, public health organizations, members of Congress, public interest groups and others expressed concern about some aspects of the rating system. Discussions between the Industry and certain advocacy groups continued and on August 1, 1997, the Industry submitted to the Commission revisions to the guidelines. The Industry states that the TV Parental Guidelines, as modified, are supported by nine family and child advocacy groups, as well as television

broadcasters, cable systems and networks, and television production companies. The revised TV Parental Guidelines were implemented on October 1, 1997.

III. The TV Parental Guidelines

6. According to the Industry, the TV Parental Guidelines are designed so that "category and program-specific content indicators will provide parents with information that will help them make informed decisions about what their children should watch on television." The TV Parental Guidelines describe a voluntary rating system consisting of six descriptive labels designed to indicate the appropriateness of television programming to children according to age and/or maturity; content indicators concerning sexual situations, violence, language or dialogue; transmission of the ratings information over line 21 of the Vertical Blanking Interval ("VBI"); display of on-screen rating icons and indicators; and the establishment of an Oversight Monitoring Board.

7. The Industry states that the TV Parental Guidelines will apply to all television programming except for news, sports, and unedited MPAA rated movies on premium cable channels. The TV Parental Guidelines (labels and content indicators, and respective meanings) are:

For programs designed solely for children:

TV-Y (All Children—This program is designed to be appropriate for all children). Whether animated or live-action, the themes and elements in this program are specifically designed for a very young audience, including children from ages 2–6. This program is not expected to frighten younger children.

TV-Y7 (Directed to Older Children—This program is designed for children age 7 and above). It may be more appropriate for children who have acquired the developmental skills needed to distinguish between make-believe and reality. Themes and elements in this program may include mild fantasy or comedic violence, or may frighten children under the age of 7. Therefore, parents may wish to consider the suitability of this program for their very young children. Note: For those programs where fantasy violence may be more intense or more combative than other programs in this category, such programs will be designated TV-Y7-FV.

For programs designed for the entire audience,
the general categories are:

TV-G (General Audience—Most parents would find this program suitable for all ages). Although this rating does not signify a program designed specifically for children, most parents may let younger children watch this program unattended. It contains little or no violence, no strong language and little or no sexual dialogue or situations.

TV-PG (Parental Guidance Suggested—This program contains material that parents may find unsuitable for younger children). Many parents may want to watch it with their younger children. The theme itself may call for parental guidance and/or the program contains one or more of the following: moderate violence (V), some sexual situations (S), infrequent coarse language (L), or some suggestive dialogue (D).

TV-14 (Parents Strongly Cautioned—This program contains some material that many parents would find unsuitable for children under 14 years of age). Parents are strongly urged to exercise greater care in monitoring this program and are cautioned against letting children under the age of 14 watch unattended. This program contains one or more of the following: intense violence (V), intense sexual situations (S), strong coarse language (L), or intensely suggestive dialogue (D).

TV-MA (Mature Audience Only This program is specifically designed to be viewed by adults and therefore may be unsuitable for children under 17). This program contains one or more of the following: graphic violence (V), explicit sexual activity (S), or crude indecent language (L).

8. As proposed by the Industry, rating icons and associated content symbols appear for 15 seconds at the beginning of all rated programming and through the use of a display button on a remote control device thereafter. Under the TV Parental Guidelines, the rating guidelines will typically be applied to television programs by broadcast and cable networks and producers, while television stations retain the right to substitute the rating they deem appropriate for their audience. The Industry notes that cable networks and television stations will provide rating information to newspapers and publishers of printed and electronic program guides, and will request that these publishers include the appropriate information in their guides.

9. According to the Industry, the TV Parental Guidelines will work with the v-chip technology to permit parents to block programming with a certain rating from coming into their home. The v-chip, which will be installed in television sets, or available through set-top boxes, will read information encoded in the program and block based on the overall age category or by the S, L, V, or D rating assigned to the program, or by a combination of the two.

10. The Industry has established an Oversight Monitoring Board to ensure that the rating guidelines are applied accurately and consistently to television programming. The Board is comprised of a chairman and 23 members, including 6 members each from the broadcast television industry, the cable industry, and the program production community, and 5 non-industry members selected by the Chairman from the advocacy community, for a total of 24 members. The Oversight Monitoring Board will provide information to producers and other program distributors concerning the TV Parental Guidelines, as well as address complaints and requests from the public about the TV Parental Guidelines and their implementation. The Oversight Monitoring Board will explore attitudes about the TV Parental Guidelines and the way in which they are being applied to programming, conduct focus groups and commission quantitative studies to determine whether the TV Parental Guidelines are

providing useful information to parents, and consider any needed changes to them. The Industry has also committed to independent, scientific research and evaluation of the rating system once the v-chip is in place.

IV. Review of the Voluntary Proposal

* * *

19. Section 551 requires that the Commission determine whether the TV Parental Guidelines are acceptable. As a preliminary matter, we must determine what it means for the rating system to be "acceptable." The term is not defined in the statute, nor are we aware of any statutory interpretation of the term that would be relevant to our determination here. Applying the general meaning of the term, we believe that it is reasonable to interpret the statute to mean that the rating system is acceptable if it meets both the specific requirements of Section 551(e) and the overall goals of Congress in enacting Section 551.

20. Section 551(e)(1)(A) states that the rating system must provide information about programming that contains sexual, violent or other indecent material about which parents should be informed before it is displayed to children. The TV Parental Guidelines provide a comprehensive system for rating programming that contains violent, sexual, or other indecent material, with specific rating information for programs designed solely for children. Programming designated solely for children is age-based to indicate programming appropriate for all children (including ages two to six), programming for older children (ages seven and above) with a more specific content indicator for fantasy violence. Programming for the entire audience is also age-based and supplemented by content indicators for sex, violence, adult language and suggestive dialogue. Morality in Media argues that the categories are subjective. We agree with the majority of commenters, however, who believe that the age-based, content supplemented system adopted by the Industry is sufficiently objective to provide parents with information necessary to make informed decisions. We do not agree with commenters who argue that we cannot find the system "acceptable" absent the inclusion of more specific details about varying degrees of violent, sexual, or other indecent materials found in the programming. The TV Parental Guidelines provide for weighing of each of the descriptors depending on which of the age-based categories it is associated with, i.e., the "V" in TV–PG–V means "moderate violence" while the "V" in TV–14–V means "intense violence." As a result, we do not believe that additional descriptors are necessary to meet the goals of Congress in adopting Section 551. Congress required that the rating system be sufficient to advise parents of the appearance of sexual, violent or indecent material in certain programming. We find that the TV Parental Guidelines meet this goal.

21. Some commenters raise concerns that the TV Parental Guidelines do not rate sports, news, commercials or promotions. Parties argue that these programs contain sexual or violent material that may be

harmful to children. As an initial matter, we note that the EIA standard that we are adopting in the V-chip Proceeding accommodates the rating of programs, including commercials within the program. Since advertisers target specific audiences reached by particular programming, it is not unreasonable for the Industry to rely on the program blocking mechanism to also filter commercials that appear in the program. While it appears that commercials that are not encoded may be passed through, such as locally inserted advertisements, we do not think that failure to rate advertisements individually will defeat the purpose of Congress in enacting Section 551. We also think it is important to recognize that the decision to exclude these categories of programming was made with the support of the advocacy groups that negotiated revisions to the Industry proposal. Similarly, we think it is not unreasonable for the Industry to exempt sports and news programming. In addition to the practical limitations in rating such programming, we note that Congress recognized the danger in requiring rating of political programming, which is often an integral element in news programming. As a result, we conclude that the TV Parental Guidelines are acceptable even though the Industry has decided not to rate these programs as a general rule. * * *

Rating the Ratings. By virtually every account the V-chip program has failed to achieve its intended purpose. In a 2007 report to Congress, *In the Matter of Violent Television Programming and Its Impact on Children*, 22 FCC Rcd. 7929 (2007) the FCC concluded:

> 29. Based on the studies and surveys conducted to date, we believe that the evidence clearly points to one conclusion: the V-chip is of limited effectiveness in protecting children from violent television content. In order for V-chip technology to block a specific category of television programming, such as violent content, it must be activated. However, many parents do not even know if the television sets in their households incorporate this technology and, of those who do, many do not use it. In 2004, the Kaiser Family Foundation conducted a telephone survey of 1,001 parents of children ages 2–17. The results showed: (1) only 15 percent of all parents have used the V-chip; (2) 26 percent of all parents have not bought a new television set since January 2000 (when the V-chip was first required in *all* sets); (3) 39 percent of parents have bought a new television set since January 2000, but do not think it includes a V-chip; and (4) 20 percent of parents know they have a V-chip, but have not used it. According to a 2003 study, parents' low level of V-chip use is explained in part by parents' unawareness of the device and the "multi-step and often confusing process" necessary to use it. Only 27 percent of parents in the study group could figure out how to program the V-Chip, and many parents "who might otherwise have used the V-Chip were frustrated by an inability to get it to work properly." A March 2007 Zogby poll indicates, among other things,

that 88 percent of respondents did not use a V-chip or cable box parental controls in the previous week, leading the Parents Television Council to call the television industry's V-chip education campaign "a failure."

30. In addition to mandating inclusion of V-chip technology in television sets, the Act provides cable subscribers with some ways to block unwanted programming. These provisions of the Act, however, do not benefit households receiving their television programming via over-the-air broadcasting or satellite. Further, similar to the V-chip, to take advantage of these measures a cable subscriber first must be aware of and then affirmatively request that such measures be employed. Finally, to receive these protections, a cable subscriber must take several steps and incur some costs. * * *

33. In addition, any successful viewer-initiated blocking regime with respect to violent programming would depend upon the adoption and successful implementation of an effective ratings system. Currently, to facilitate operation of the V-chip and other blocking mechanisms, broadcast, cable, and satellite television providers, on a voluntary basis, rate programming using the industry-devised TV ratings system guidelines and encode programs accordingly. Most television programming, except for news and sports programming, carries an age-based TV rating set by program networks and producers, and most include content-based ratings as well.

34. Studies and surveys demonstrate, however, that the voluntary TV ratings system is of limited effectiveness in protecting children from violent television content. In the 2004 Kaiser survey discussed above, 50 percent of all parents surveyed stated that they have used the TV ratings. But about 4 in 10 parents (39 percent) stated that most programs are not rated accurately, and many parents did not fully understand what the various ratings categories mean. For example, only 24 percent of parents of young children (two-six years old) could name any of the ratings that would apply to programming appropriate for children that age. Only 12 percent of parents knew that the rating FV ("fantasy violence") is related to violent content, while 8 percent thought it meant "family viewing." One in five (20 percent) parents said that they had never heard of the TV ratings system, an increase from 14 percent in 2000 and 2001. A more recent survey indicates that only 8 percent of respondents could correctly identify the categories.

35. And, of course, ratings can only be effective in protecting children from inappropriate content if the parent understands the ratings information, and such information is accurate. In a study published in the journal *Pediatrics*, parents concluded that half of television shows the industry had rated as appropriate for teenagers were in fact inappropriate, a finding the study authors called "a signal that the ratings are misleading." * * *

45. In response to the specific questions posed, we draw the following conclusions. First, with respect to the evidence of harm to children from viewing violent television content, there is strong evidence that exposure to violence in the media can increase aggressive behavior in children, at least in the short term.

46. Second, although there are constitutional barriers to directly limiting or time channeling the distribution of violent television programming, the Supreme Court's *Pacifica* decision and other decisions relating to restrictions on the broadcast of indecent content provide possible parallels for regulating violent television content. Third, while there are legal, evidentiary, analytical, and social science obstacles that need to be overcome in defining harmful violence, Congress likely has the ability and authority to craft a sustainable definition.

47. Finally, we note that the 109th Congress was considering an extensive bill, introduced by Senators Rockefeller and Hutchinson, designed to protect children from excessive violence on television. The bill also proposed that the Commission consider and report on the effectiveness of the current technology and of consumer understanding of the technology and ratings system. This *Report*, in essence, serves the purpose contemplated in the bill. Our analysis above indicates that the current technology "fix," including but not limited to consumer understanding of the technology and voluntary ratings system, is not effective in protecting children from violent programming. Given the findings in this *Report*, we believe action should be taken to address violent programming. Industry could on its own initiative commit itself to reducing the amount of excessively violent programming viewed by children. Broadcasters could adopt a family hour at the beginning of prime time, during which they decline to air violent content. Multichannel video programming providers (MVPDs) could provide consumers greater choice in how they purchase their programming so that they could avoid violent programming. Under such an approach, consumers could select the channels they want to pay for, and opt out of those that they do not. In short, an a la carte regime would enable viewers to buy their television channels individually or in smaller bundles. In this manner, consumers could avoid purchasing those channels that tend to air more violent programming. Cable and DBS operators could implement a la carte in a variety of ways. For example, it could be limited to digital cable customers who would be permitted to "opt out" of cable programming, requesting not to receive certain cable channels and having their package price reduced accordingly ("channel blocking and reimbursement").

48. Alternatively, customers could be allowed to "opt in" to particular cable programs. This is how premium channels are offered today. In Hong Kong, for example, consumers can select and pay for only the channels they want. A family that wants to watch sports, movies, news and children's programming can receive 15 free chan-

nels plus a selection of 11 additional digital channels including ESPN, HBO, CNN Headline News, National Geographic, Animal Planet, and Discovery for $27.50 per month. To get the same channels in Washington, DC, it would cost $82.00 per month. Another option would be to allow consumers to choose a specific number of channels from a menu of available programming for a fixed price—e.g., 10 channels for $20, 20 channels for $30, etc. Customers then would be able to receive—and pay for—only that programming that they are comfortable bringing into their homes. For example, in Canada, digital subscribers can buy channels individually or enjoy significant savings on a "5 pack," a "10 pack" or a "15 pack" of their own choosing.

49. In sum, Congress could implement a time channeling solution, as discussed above, and/or mandate some other form of consumer choice in obtaining video programming, such as the provision by MVPDs of video channels provided on family tiers or on an a la carte basis (e.g., channel blocking and reimbursement).

Family-Friendly Viewing—Déjà vu. The FCC's "a la carte" proposal will be discussed in Chapter 6. The time channeling idea has traditionally been the FCC's primary solution for "indecent" content, as we discussed above. The specific proposal for a "family hour" is noteworthy for the Commission's failure to mention that a similar concept adopted by the National Association of Broadcasters in the mid 1970s was found by a California federal district court to be a violation of the First Amendment to the extent it was adopted in response to threats and intimidation ("jawboning" as it was popularly labeled in that era) by the FCC's chairman. The court acknowledged that a purely voluntary undertaking by the broadcast industry would not constitute government action and therefore not run afoul of the First Amendment, but it found the informal pressures by the chairman were sufficient to remove it from the category of private action. On appeal the Ninth Circuit reversed and remanded on the ground that the complaints should have been first presented to the Commission itself under a primary jurisdiction referral. The court did acknowledge that informal pressure might raise both procedural issues under the Administrative Procedure Act and substantive constitutional questions, but these should have been presented formally to the FCC before instituting a private action in the district court. *Writers Guild of America, West, Inc. v. American Broadcasting Co., Inc.*, 609 F.2d 355 (9th Cir. 1979). The case was subsequently abandoned after the NAB terminated the family viewing hour.

Chapter 4

MEDIA STRUCTURE

A. INTRODUCTION

The FCC has long followed a tripartite policy toward media ownership, one focused on diversity, economic competition, and localism. Restrictions on the ownership or control of mass media have been an important element of that policy, with promoting diversification of ownership of mass media as a means of enforcing diversity of viewpoints. Promoting economic competition independent of viewpoint diversity has also been a factor, albeit one secondary to diversity. Diversity has also been tied to the policy of localism, as we shall see.

In the case of broadcast licensees, diversification is an element of the Commission's general licensing process, but the principal means of enforcement have been fixed restrictions on the ownership or control of mass media. In the case of broadcast ownership rules in particular, the FCC's attachment to uniform national rules has created a considerable challenge, since they require a single set of ownership restrictions to be applied uniformly in different market environments. The Commission does, from time to time, allow waivers of the rules, but usually such waivers have been for the purpose of giving a particular owner time to adjust to a change in rules or to provide a temporary accommodation for ownership changes. For the most part, the FCC does not attempt to tailor its ownership or other structural regulations to the conditions of individual markets. However, it should be kept in mind that insofar as a media firm is licensed to use radio spectrum, it must obtain Commission approval for any transfer of licenses. Thus, the Commission has the power to exact special conditions or impose special restrictions as a condition of such approval independently of its fixed ownership rules.

Borrowing from antitrust principles, for purposes of examining economic concentration, we generally distinguish two types of relationships: horizontal and vertical. Horizontal relationships involve firms within the same market, firms that are, or could be, direct competitors; vertical relationships involve firms operating in distinct markets, firms that operate at different levels of the market, as with manufacturer and a retailer. These categories are generally applicable to communications firms, but the FCC's rules do not fit perfectly within them. For instance, at the horizontal level the Commission has rules restricting common ownership of media in local markets—where the firms would be, more or less, competitors. But it also has rules restricting the number of broadcast or cable firms that can be held under common control nationwide even though they operate in different markets. In addition to these types of "horizontal" restrictions, there are rules regulating vertical relationships between broadcast stations and program suppliers and between cable operators and program suppliers.

We begin with horizontal restrictions, focusing first on rules governing multiple ownership of broadcast stations in local markets, next examining national ownership limits on both broadcast and cable systems, and finally examining rules governing the relationship between program networks (both broadcast and cable) and stations or cable systems. At one time the FCC also reached further back in the distribution chain to regulate the vertical integration of program producers (film studios in particular) and the broadcast networks. The Commission's rules restricting vertical integration of broadcast networks and program producers were eliminated in the 1990s, but they still warrant examination because they provide some important insights into the structure of broadcasting. Restrictions on vertical relationships in cable, which we will also examine, are still a matter of regulatory controversy.

One final point that is pertinent to all ownership rules: for both local-market and national limits on common ownership it obviously is necessary to define what constitutes a relevant "ownership" interest. The FCC has "attribution rules" that determine when an ownership interest counts for this purpose. Basically (the details are somewhat more complicated) the attribution rules count both active (voting stock interests) and passive (nonvoting interests—e.g., ownership by mutual funds or banks etc.) but weight the interests differently. (For active interests the threshold is 5%; for passive interests it is 20%.) There are several supplemental standards for special situations involving both equity and debt interests.

B. BROADCAST LOCAL OWNERSHIP

For most of its history, the Commission has had some limit on common ownership of media within a single market. Originally the rule took the simple form of a so-called "duopoly rule," which banned common ownership of more than one station within each service—AM, FM, TV—in the same market. The duopoly rule was later revised and made more restrictive. One change, in 1970, was the so-called "one-to-a-market" rule, which banned a combination of AM-FM radio or AM/FM-TV stations. More important than the one-to-a-market rule, which was limited to common ownerships within the broadcast service, were a couple of so-called "cross ownership" bans that applied *across* media. The first of these was a ban in 1970 of common ownership of broadcast stations and cable systems in the same local market. This ban was prompted by a concern that a cable operator that owned a local broadcaster might discriminate against other local broadcasters. (The ban is no longer in effect; it was eliminated as a consequence of the *Fox* decision, *infra*, in 2002). The most important, and most controversial move towards tightening local media ownership came in 1975, when the FCC forbade common ownership of a local broadcast station (of any kind) and a local newspaper—the current "cross ownership" rule.

In the 1980s, the Commission began a course of retrenchment. It was part of a general mood of deregulation that by the end of the decade left the broadcast industry essentially free of any meaningful public interest obligations (most notably including the famous fairness doctrine and the local program needs ascertainment rules) other than those specifically mandated by Congress (such as the equal time rule). In 1989, the Commission eased its one-to-a-market rule by allowing (indeed, practically inviting) requests for waiver of the rules in the top 25 markets. In 1992, the Commission relaxed local radio ownership restrictions and adopted a tiered approach to radio concentration that allowed a single entity to own more radio stations in the largest markets (up to three AM and three FM stations, subject to a local audience reach limitation of 25%).

Congress ratified these deregulatory moves in the Telecommunications Act of 1996. Although the Act was primarily concerned with telecommunications policy, the broadcast industry lent its political support for telecommunications reform in return for a number of broadcast-friendly amendments. Among these was further relaxation of the multiple ownership rules. With respect to local ownership, Congress significantly relaxed the duopoly rule as applied to radio stations, permitting multiple ownership of radio stations with caps pegged to the size of the market. It also directed the FCC to conduct rulemaking proceedings to consider whether to retain, modify, or repeal its television duopoly rule and directed it to extend its 1989 policy of granting waivers of the one-to-a-market rule to the top 50 markets instead of just the top 25. Finally, and perhaps most importantly, it directed the FCC to review all broadcast ownership rules every two years with a view to repealing any rules it deems no longer "necessary" in the public interest.

The Commission's initial responses to the 1996 directive to review the multiple ownership rules did not fare well in the D.C. Circuit. The details are described in the *Prometheus* opinion excerpted below and need not be repeated. Suffice it to say that while the FCC did liberalize the local ownership rules for television, the court of appeals, in *Sinclair Broadcast Group, Inc. v. FCC*, 284 F.3d 148 (D.C. Cir. 2002), held that the FCC had not given a reasoned basis for the modified rules. Another decision, *Fox Television Stations, Inc. v. FCC*, 280 F.3d 1027 (D.C. Cir. 2002), found the same deficiency in the FCC's failure to make any changes in the *national* television ownership rules. The remand proceedings in *Sinclair* and *Fox* were consolidated with the FCC's then-pending third biennial review of media ownership rules. The resulting report—called the 2002 Biennial Report even though it appeared in 2003—made a number of changes, partly in response to the court decisions and partly on independent policy and political grounds. The primary changes were: (1) the local multiple ownership rules were liberalized to allow a few more common ownerships in very large markets; (2) the national television multiple ownership rule was relaxed somewhat: the previous rule that restricted common ownership to stations with a collective audience no greater than 35% of national television households was increased to 45%; (3) the ban on television-newspaper ownership was lifted in favor of a more targeted limitation based on size of market. We will cover the national ownership rules below, in section C.

The changes were greeted with boos from all sides. Congress denounced the liberalization of the ownership rules (in apparent disregard of the fact that it had virtually demanded such liberalization in 1996), and public interest groups denounced them as a sell out to "big media." Even some segments of the broadcast industry were unhappy. Station owners affiliated with the major networks condemned the liberalization of the national ownership rules because it would allow the networks to buy more stations (which, as we will explain later, could reduce network dependence on independently owned stations and thereby give the nets greater leverage in bargaining over network affiliation arrangements). In short, everyone was unhappy. (Even the commissioners were not uniformly satisfied: two commissioners dissented, and the chairman let it be known that he would have gone further in the direction of deregulation.)

The response from Congress turned out to be high in decibels but low in content. Although some congressional leaders wanted to overturn the new rules in their entirety, they didn't have the votes for it, and they faced a threatened presidential veto in any case. Congress made one change in the national ownership cap. The Commission had raised the audience cap on television households that could be reached by commonly owned stations from 35% (where Congress had previously set it) to 45%. Congress knocked it down to 39%. On the choice of this magic percentage more will be said later. The remainder of the rules were challenged in an appeal to the Third Circuit, which found some deep flaws in the Commission's reasoning, most notably in its construction of a so-called "diversity index" which had provided a foundation for the new local ownership rules.

PROMETHEUS RADIO PROJECT v. FCC

United States Court of Appeals, Third Circuit. 2004.
373 F.3d 372.

AMBRO, CIRCUIT JUDGE:

In these consolidated appeals we consider revisions by the Federal Communications Commission to its regulations governing broadcast media ownership that the Commission promulgated following its 2002 biennial review. On July 2, 2003, the Commission announced a comprehensive overhaul of its broadcast media ownership rules. It increased the number of television stations a single entity may own, both locally and nationally; revised various provisions of the regulations governing common ownership of radio stations in the same community; and replaced two existing rules limiting common ownership among newspapers and broadcast stations (the newspaper/broadcast cross-ownership rule and the radio/television cross-ownership rule) with a single set of "Cross-Media Limits." See *Report and Order and Notice of Proposed Rulemaking*, 18 F.C.C.R. 13,620 (2003) (the "Order").* * *

For the reasons stated below, we affirm the power of the Commission to regulate media ownership. In doing so, we reject the contention that the Constitution or § 202(h) of the 1996 Act somehow provides rigid limits on the Commission's ability to regulate in the public interest. But we must remand certain aspects of the Commission's Order that are not adequately supported by the record. Most importantly, the Commission has not sufficiently justified its particular chosen numerical limits for local television ownership, local radio ownership, and cross-ownership of media within local markets. Accordingly, we partially remand the Order for the Commission's additional justification or modification, and we partially affirm the Order. The stay will continue pending our review of the Commission's action on remand. * * *

I. Background

* * *

C. The Telecommunications Act of 1996

In 1996 Congress overhauled the Communications Act by enacting the Telecommunications Act of 1996. The 1996 Act contemplated a "pro-competitive, deregulatory national policy framework designed to accelerate rapidly private sector development of advanced telecommunications and information technologies and services to all Americans by opening all telecommunications markets to competition." The 1996 Act eliminated all limits on national radio ownership and raised the national television audience reach cap from 25% to 35%. 1996 Act §§ 202(a), (c)(1)(B). Congress also eased local radio ownership limits, establishing a four-tier sliding scale limit of numerical caps that allowed for as many as eight co-owned radio stations in the largest markets.

The 1996 Act did not contain a new local television rule, but it directed the Commission to "conduct a rulemaking proceeding to determine whether to retain, modify, or eliminate" its existing local television ownership limitations. It also expanded the applicability of the one-to-a-market radio/television cross-ownership restriction waiver to the fifty largest markets.

Finally, the 1996 Act instructed the Commission to review biennially its broadcast ownership rules "to determine whether any of such rules are necessary in the public interest as the result of competition." Section 202(h) also required the Commission to "repeal or modify any regulation it determines to be no longer in the public interest."

D. Regulatory Review Since 1996

In 1999 the Commission responded to Congress's directive under § 202(c) of the 1996 Act to review its local television rule and announced that it would relax its prohibition on the common ownership of television stations with overlapping signals. The Commission's new rule would allow two commonly owned television stations (a television station "duopoly") in the same Designated Market Area ("DMA" or "market") as long as (1) neither station was ranked among the four largest ("top-four") stations in the market and (2) eight independently owned stations remained in the market post-merger. In the same rulemaking, the Commission also relaxed the one-to-a-market radio/television cross-ownership restriction and allowed radio/television station combinations to exist within three-tiered limits that depend on the size of the market.

Meanwhile, in 1998 the Commission began the first biennial review of its broadcast ownership regulations as required under § 202(h). In 2000 it announced that it would retain the national television ownership rule (the 35% limit provided in the 1996 Act) and its cable/broadcast cross-ownership rule after determining that both rules remained "necessary in the public interest." On appeal, however, the United States Court of Appeals for the D.C. Circuit held that the Commission had not sufficiently explained its reasons for retaining either of these rules. *Fox Television Stations v. FCC*, 280 F.3d 1027, 1043–44, 1051–52 (D.C.Cir. 2002) ("*Fox I*"), *modified on reh'g*, 293 F.3d 537 (D.C.Cir.2002) ("*Fox II*"). As for the national television ownership rule, the Court determined that the agency had taken a "wait and see" approach in evaluating its competition and diversity effects, which was impermissible in light of § 202(h)'s mandate to repeal or modify rules found no longer necessary in the public interest. It remanded the rule to the Commission for additional justification. The Court vacated the cable/broadcast cross-ownership rule, however, finding that the Commission's decision to retain it was arbitrary and capricious and contrary to § 202(h).

A few months later, the same Court reviewed the local television multiple-ownership rule. *Sinclair Broad. Group, Inc. v. FCC*, 284 F.3d 148 (D.C.Cir.2002). The petitioner challenged the "eight independent voices" exception, contending that it lacked foundation or connection to the Commission's goal of promoting diversity in local markets. The Court determined that the Commission had adequately justified its decision to retain the local television rule under the APA and § 202(h), but that it had not provided a rational basis for the exclusion of non-broadcast media from the eight voices exception. It remanded the rule for the Commission's further justification.

E. The Commission's 2003 Report and Order

In September 2002 a Notice of Proposed Rulemaking (the "Notice") announced that the Commission would review four of its broadcast ownership rules pursuant to § 202(h): the 35% national audience reach limit remanded in *Fox*; the local television rule remanded in *Sinclair*; the radio/television cross-ownership rule; and the dual network rule. The Notice also advised that the Commission was incorporating into its biennial review pending proceedings on two additional rules: its rule limiting radio station ownership in local markets and its rule prohibiting newspaper/broadcast cross-ownership. * * *

F. The Order's Modification of Broadcast Media Ownership Rules

After reaffirming the Commission's three traditional policy objectives in promoting the public interest—competition, diversity, and localism—the Commission considered whether each of the six rules remained in the public interest and proposed modifications where it believed necessary. With respect to each of the rules, the Commission determined as follows.

1. Local Television Ownership

The existing local television ownership rule allowed television station duopolies, so long as at least one of the stations was not ranked among the market's four largest stations and so long as at least eight independently owned and operated full-power television stations would remain in the market post-merger. The Order modified this rule to permit television station triopolies in markets with 18 or more television stations and television station duopolies in markets with 17 or fewer television stations. These limits are subject to the restriction (effectively a ban subject to a waiver provision) that a single firm may not own more than one top-four station in a market. This restriction forecloses common station ownership in markets with fewer than five television stations. The existing rule effectively precludes duopolies in most markets; only the largest 70 markets of the nation's 210 DMAs could comply with the "eight voices" test. The new rule would allow triopolies in the nine largest DMAs, which represent 25.2% of the population. Duopolies could exist under the new rule in the largest 162 markets, representing 95.4% of the nation's population.

2. Local Radio Ownership

Although the Order retained the existing numerical limits on radio ownership that Congress established in § 202(b) of the 1996 Act, it modified other aspects of the rule. First, it changed the method for determining radio markets by replacing the "contour-overlap" method (described in detail in Part VI.B infra) with the geography-based market delineations created by Arbitron, a company that generates market data for radio advertisers. Additionally, the Commission would now include noncommercial stations in the station count for each market. The Commission grandfathered any existing radio station combinations rendered noncompliant under the newly defined markets, but generally restricted transfer of these combinations. The Commission also changed the local radio ownership rule by deciding to attribute "Joint Sales Agreements" (agreements under which a licensee sells advertising time on its station to a broker station for a fee) toward the brokering entity's numerical limit.

3 & 4. Newspaper/Broadcast and Radio/Television Cross–Ownership

The Commission has prohibited common ownership of a full-service television broadcast station and a daily public newspaper in the same community since 1975. The Order announced the Commission's decision to repeal both cross-ownership rules (television/newspaper, radio/television) and replace them with a single set of Cross-Media Limits. The Commission determined that neither cross-ownership prohibition remained necessary in the public interest to ensure competition, diversity, or localism. The new Cross-Media Limits prohibit newspaper/broadcast combinations and radio/television combinations in the smallest DMAs, i.e., those with three or fewer full-power commercial or noncommercial television stations. In contrast, in the largest markets-those with more than eight television stations-common ownership among newspapers and broadcast stations is unrestricted. In medium-sized markets-those with between four and eight television stations-one entity may own a newspaper and either (a) one television station and up to 50% of the radio stations that may be commonly owned in that market under the local radio rule or (b) up to 100% of the radio stations allowed under the local radio rule.

In structuring its Cross-Media Limits, the Commission drew upon a methodological tool named the "Diversity Index," which the Commission developed as a measure of viewpoint diversity in local markets to identify those "at-risk" markets where consolidation would have a deleterious effect. The Diversity Index, explained more fully in Part IV.D.1 below, is a highly modified version of the formula for measuring market concentration—the Herfindahl-Hirschman Index—applied by the Department of Justice and Federal Trade Commission to analyze mergers.

5. National Television Ownership

The national television ownership rule prohibits entities from owning television stations that in the aggregate reach a certain percentage of our country's households. Section 202(c) of the 1996 Act directed the Commission to delete the then-existing twelve-station cap and raise the audience reach limit from 25% to 35%. After the D.C. Circuit Court remanded the Commission's decision in the 1998 biennial review to retain the limit at 35%, the Commission decided to increase the audience reach limit to 45%. The Commission also declined to repeal or modify its existing 50% discount for UHF stations' audiences as counted toward the audience reach limit.

6. Dual Network Rule

Under the dual network rule, a television station may affiliate with more than one network except that it may not affiliate with more than one of the four largest networks, ABC, CBS, Fox, and NBC. The rule effectively permits common ownership of networks to the exclusion of the top four. The Commission determined that the dual network rule remained necessary in the public interest, and thus did not repeal or modify it. [The retention of the dual network rule was unchallenged.] * * *

H. Subsequent Legislation

In January 2004, while the petitions to review the Order were pending in this Court, Congress amended the 1996 Act by increasing from 35% to 39% the national television ownership rule's audience reach cap in § 202(c). The legislation also amended § 202(h) in two ways: (1) making the Commission's biennial review obligation quadrennial; and (2) insulating from § 202(h) review "rules relating to the 39 percent national audience reach limitation." Prior to oral argument, Petitioners filed letter briefs addressing the effect of these amendments on their challenges to the Order. [The court later ruled that Congress's action made the national ownership rule moot even though some parties had raised constitutional objections to it.] * * *

IV. Cross-Ownership Rules

The Commission's decision to repeal its newspaper/broadcast cross-ownership rules in favor of new Cross-Media Limits has been attacked on all fronts. Some petitioners support the repeal but argue that the Cross-Media Limits are too restrictive. Others challenge the repeal decision and argue that the new limits are too lenient. We conclude that the Commission's decision to replace its cross-ownership rules with the Cross-Media Limits is not of itself constitutionally flawed and does not violate § 202(h). But we cannot uphold the Cross-Media Limits themselves because the Commission does not provide a reasoned analysis to support the limits that it chose.

A. Regulatory Background and the 2002 Biennial Review

Since the 1970s, the Commission has enforced two separate limits on the common ownership of different-type media outlets in local markets. One cross-ownership rule prohibits the common ownership of a full-service television broadcast station and a daily public newspaper in the same community. The other limits the number of television and radio stations to the following combinations: (1) in markets where at least 20 independently owned media voices would remain post-merger, two television stations and six radio stations or one television station and seven radio stations; (2) in markets where at least 10 independent voices would remain, two television stations and four radio stations; and (3) in other markets, two television stations (subject to the local television ownership rule) and one radio station.

The Commission considered both cross-ownership rules during its 2002 biennial review under § 202(h). In the Order, the Commission announced that because neither rule remained necessary in the public interest, it was repealing them and replacing them with a single set of Cross-Media Limits. The three-tiered Cross-Media Limits regulate common ownership depending on the size of the market: small (those with three or fewer full-power commercial or noncommercial television stations), mid-sized (between four and eight television stations), and large (more than eight television stations). In small markets, newspaper/broadcast combinations and radio/television combinations are prohibited. In medium-sized markets, an entity may own a newspaper and either (a) one television station and up to 50% of the radio stations that may be commonly owned in that market under the local radio rule or (b) up to 100% of the radio stations allowed under the local rule. In large markets, cross-ownership is unrestricted.

B. The Commission's decision not to retain a ban on newspaper/broadcast cross-ownership is justified under § 202(h) and is supported by record evidence.

The Commission determined that the rule prohibiting newspaper/broadcast cross-ownership was no longer necessary in the public interest for three primary reasons: (1) the ban is not necessary to promote competition in local markets because most advertisers do not view newspapers and television stations as close substitutes, (2) the ban undermines localism by preventing efficient combinations that would allow for the production of high-quality local news, and (3) there is not enough evidence to conclude that ownership influences viewpoint to warrant a blanket cross-ownership ban, thus making it unjustifiable on diversity grounds, (and moreover, the presence of other media sources-such as the Internet and cable-compensate for the viewpoint diversity lost to consolidation). The Citizen Petitioners object to the localism and diversity components of the Commission's rationale. We conclude differently, as reasoned analysis supports the Commission's determination that the blanket ban on newspaper/broadcast cross-ownership was no longer in the public interest. * * *

1. Continuing to regulate cross-media ownership is in the public interest.

The Commission's finding that a blanket prohibition on newspaper/broadcast cross-ownership is no longer in the public interest does not compel the conclusion that no regulation is necessary. As described above, the Commission found evidence to undermine the premise that ownership always influences viewpoint, but it did not find the opposite to be true. And while the Commission found that other media sources contributed to viewpoint diversity in local markets, it could not have found that the Internet and cable were complete substitutes for the viewpoints provided by newspapers and broadcast stations. Given the Commission's goal of balancing the public's interests in competition, localism, and diversity, it reasonably concluded that repealing the cross-ownership ban was necessary to promote competition and localism, while retaining some limits was necessary to ensure diversity. * * *

[The court here rejected two constitutional challenges to the ownership rules, one based on the Takings Clause the other on the First Amendment.]

D. The Commission did not provide reasoned analysis to support the specific Cross-Media Limits that it chose.

The Commission concluded that cross-ownership limits were necessary in specific situations to guard against "an elevated risk of harm to the range and breadth of viewpoints that may be available to the public." But recognizing that ownership limits impede the speech opportunities for both broadcasters and newspapers, the Commission endeavored to craft new limits "as narrowly as possible." In that vein, the Commission sought to identify "at risk" local markets—those with high levels of viewpoint concentration—where continued regulation was necessary. By focusing its regulation on those markets, the Commission hoped to avoid needlessly overregulating markets with already ample viewpoint diversity.

But for all of its efforts, the Commission's Cross-Media Limits employ several irrational assumptions and inconsistencies. We do not object in principle to the Commission's reliance on the Department of Justice and Federal Trade Commission's antitrust formula, the Herfindahl-Hirschmann Index ("HHI"), as its starting point for measuring diversity in local markets. In converting the HHI to a measure for diversity in local markets, however, the Commission gave too much weight to the Internet as a media outlet, irrationally assigned outlets of the same media type equal market shares, and inconsistently derived the Cross-Media Limits from its Diversity Index results. For these reasons, detailed below, we remand for the Commission to justify or modify further its Cross-Media Limits.

1. Overview of the Commission's Diversity Index Methodology

The Commission designed a methodology called the Diversity Index to identify "at risk" markets where limits on cross-media ownership should be retained. The Diversity Index was "inspired by" the HHI, which the Department of Justice and the Federal Trade Commission use to measure proposed mergers' effect on competition in local markets. A market's HHI score is the sum of market shares squared. A highly competitive market will have a lower HHI score than a concentrated one. For example, compare the HHI score of a market with 10 equal-sized competitors (10 [competitors] x 10 [each competitor's market share percentage] = 1000) to the HHI score of a market with only five equal-sized competitors (5 x 20 = 2000). The Department of Justice and the Federal Trade Commission categorize markets with HHI scores above 1800 as "highly concentrated." If a proposed merger would exceed that level of concentration, the agencies believe that it would be harmful to the competition in that market. At its core, the Diversity Index here uses the same sum of market share-squared formula.

Next, the Commission selected many sample markets for which it would determine a Diversity Index score. In each of those markets, it counted the number of outlets within each media type and assigned each outlet an equal market share. (For example, the New York City market has 23 television stations, so each one was attributed an equal 4.3% market share.) The Commission calculated the ownership share by multiplying the number of outlets owned by an entity by the market share. (Univision owns three television stations in New York, so its ownership share was 3 x 4.3% = 13.0%.) Each ownership share was then given its relative weight by media type. (Univision's 13.0% share was thus subject to the 33.8% multiplier for television stations). The Commission then squared all of the weighted ownership shares; their sum was the market's total Diversity Index score. But in markets with cross-owned shares (outlets of different media types owned by the same entity) the entity's weighted ownership shares were summed together before they were squared. (ABC owned one television station and four radio stations in New York, so the Commission added its weighted ownership share for the television station (4.3% x 33.8% = 1.45%) to its weighted ownership share for the radio stations (6.7% x 24.9% = 1.67%) for a combined ABC ownership share of 3.12%. The square of 3.12 was included in the summation).

After the Commission calculated Diversity Index scores for markets of different sizes, it determined how those scores would change in several different consolidation "scenarios." To illustrate, the Commission determined that markets with five television stations had an average Diversity Index score of 911. If a newspaper and television station combined in a market of that size, that score would increase by 223, to 1134. The other combination scenarios were: (1) one television station and all of the radio stations allowed to be commonly owned under the local radio rule; (2) one newspaper and all of the radio stations allowed to be commonly owned under the local radio rule; (3) one newspaper, one television station, and half of the number of radio stations allowed to be commonly owned under the local radio rule; (4) two television stations; (5) one newspaper and two television stations; and (6) one newspaper, two television stations, and all of the radio stations allowed under the local radio rule.

Finding that all of the consolidation scenarios resulted in relatively high increases to the average Diversity Index scores for the smallest markets (those with three or fewer television stations), the Commission prohibited newspaper/television, newspaper/radio, and radio/television combinations in those markets. In the large markets (nine or more stations), all of the consolidation scenarios resulted in acceptable increases to the average Diversity Index scores, so the Commission imposed no limits on cross-media ownership in those markets. In the mid-sized markets (between four and eight television stations), the Commission found that all of the scenarios, except the two involving a newspaper and television duopoly, should be allowed, based on their modest increases to the average Diversity Index scores for those markets.

2. The Commission did not justify its choice and weight of specific media outlets.

Petitioners from both sides of the regulatory spectrum attack the Commission's selection of media outlets for inclusion in the Diversity Index formula. The Citizen Petitioners argue that the Commission gave too much weight to the Internet at the expense of television and daily newspapers, thereby understating the level of concentration and overstating the level of diversity in a market. The Deregulatory Petitioners, on the other hand, argue that the Diversity Index understates the actual amount of diversity in a market by ignoring important media outlets, primarily cable television. As explained below, we affirm the Commission's reasoned decision to discount cable. But we think that the same rationale also applies to the Internet. Therefore, its decision to count the Internet as a source of viewpoint diversity, while discounting cable, was not rational.

The Commission properly excluded cable because of serious doubts as to the extent that cable provided independent local news–the Commission's recognized indicator of viewpoint diversity in local markets. While the responses to one question in the Commission's survey suggested that cable is a significant source of local news, the Commission did not find this credible because the responses to other survey questions suggested that respondents were counting broadcast signals that are transmitted as cable channels as sources of local news on cable. The survey's indication that cable is an independent source of local news was also undercut by external evidence, including Neilsen ratings, that local cable channels are the least watched of any broadcast or cable stations in the market. Furthermore, the Commission noted that local cable channels are not available everywhere, but only in select markets. Thus, the Commission justifiably excluded cable from its Diversity Index calculations.

Similarly, the responses to one of the Commission survey questions suggested that the Internet is a source of local news. But the survey did not identify which websites respondents used as sources of local news. There is a critical distinction between websites that are independent sources of local news and websites of local newspapers and broadcast stations that merely republish the information already being reported by the newspaper or broadcast station counterpart. The latter do not present an "independent" viewpoint and thus should not be considered as contributing diversity to local markets. Accordingly, the Commission should have discounted the respondents who primarily rely on these websites from its total number of respondents who indicated that they use the Internet to access local news.

Furthermore, just as the Commission discounted responses indicating that cable was an independent source of local news because this finding conflicted with other record evidence, it should have discounted the Internet responses as well. The Commission does not cite, nor does the record contain, persuasive evidence that there is a significant presence of independent local news sites on the Internet. According to the record, most sources of local news on the Internet are the websites for newspapers and broadcast television stations. And the examples the Commission does cite—the Drudge Report and Salon.com—have a national, not local, news focus. * * *

The Commission attempts to justify different treatment for cable and the Internet by suggesting that local cable news channels are only available in select markets, while the Internet is available everywhere. Not only is this distinction demonstrably false (as even the Commission acknowledged that almost 30% of Americans do not have Internet access), it is irrelevant. That the Internet is more available than local cable news channels does not mean that it is providing independent local news. On remand the Commission must either exclude the Internet from the media selected for inclusion in the Diversity Index or provide a better explanation for why it is included in light of the exclusion of cable.

3. The Commission did not justify its assumption of equal market shares.

* * * The Commission's decision to assign equal market shares to outlets within a media type does not jibe with the Commission's decision to assign relative weights to the different media types themselves, about which it said "we have no reason to believe that all media are of equal importance." It also negates the Commission's proffered rationale for using the HHI formula in the first place—to allow it to measure the actual loss of diversity from consolidation by taking into account the actual "diversity importance" of the merging parties, something it could not do with a simple "voices" test. Finally, assigning equal market shares to outlets that provide no local news almost certainly presents an understated view of concentration in several markets, thus contravening the Commission's goal of making "the most conservative assumption possible" about viewpoint diversity. * * *

4. The Commission did not rationally derive its Cross-Media Limits from the Diversity Index results.

After the Commission calculated the average Diversity Index scores for markets of various sizes, it set out to determine whether the increase in those scores resulting from different consolidation scenarios would have an acceptable or unacceptable effect. * * *

Although the Commission is entitled to deference in deciding where to draw the line between acceptable and unacceptable increases in markets' Diversity Index scores, we do not affirm the seemingly inconsistent manner in which the line was drawn. As the chart above illustrates, the Cross-Media Limits allow some combinations where the increases in Diversity Index scores were generally higher than for other combinations that were not allowed. Consider the mid-sized markets (four to eight stations), where the Commission found that a combination of a newspaper, a television station, and half the radio stations allowed under the local radio rule would increase the average Diversity Index scores in those markets by 408 (four stations), 393 (five), 340(six), 247 (seven), and 314 (eight) points respectively. These permitted increases seem to belong on the other side of the Commission's line. They are considerably higher than the Diversity Index score increases resulting from other combinations that the Commission permitted, such as the newspaper and television combination, 242 (four stations), 223 (five), 200(six), 121 (seven), and 152 (eight). They are even higher than those resulting from the combination of a newspaper and television duopoly—376 (five stations), 357(six), 242 (seven), and 308 (eight)—which the Commission did not permit. The Commission's failure to provide any explanation for this glaring inconsistency is without doubt arbitrary and capricious, and so provides further basis for remand of the Cross-Media Limits. * * *

V. Local Television Ownership Rule

Both the Citizen Petitioners and the Deregulatory Petitioners challenge the Commission's modification to the local television ownership rule, which would allow triopolies in markets of 18 stations or more and duopolies in other markets, subject to a restriction on combinations of the four largest stations in any market. We uphold the top-four restriction but remand the numerical limits for the Commission to harmonize certain inconsistencies and better support its assumptions and rationale. We also remand for the Commission to reconsider or justify its decision to expand the rule's waiver provision—applicable to sales of failed, failing, or unbuilt television stations—by eliminating the requirement that waiver applicants notice the station's availability to out-of-market buyers.

A. Regulatory Background and the 2002 Biennial Review

* * * The Commission consolidated *Sinclair*'s remand order with its 2002 biennial review under § 202(h). The Order announced the Commission's decision to abandon the duopoly rule in favor of a rule that would permit common ownership of two commercial stations in markets that have 17 or fewer full-power commercial and noncommercial stations, and common ownership of three commercial stations in markets that have 18 or more stations. Both limits are subject to a restriction on the common ownership of stations ranked among the market's largest four based on audience share. The Commission also decided to expand its criteria for waiving the rule's ownership restrictions for proposed combinations that involve failed, failing, or unbuilt stations by eliminating the requirement that waiver applicants provide notice of the sale to out-of-market buyers. * * *

C. We uphold the Commission's decision to retain the top-four restriction.

Though the Commission recognized that the combination of television stations within the same market could yield efficiencies that benefit consumers, the Commission also recognized that station combinations only have an overall public "welfare-enhancing" effect when the consolidation does not create a "new largest" entity. Thus, the Commission determined that it had to limit allowable station combinations to those that would not create excessive market power in a "new largest" entity. Finding that a significant "cushion" of audience share percentage points generally separates top-four stations from the fifth-ranked stations, the Commission decided that a top-four restriction would ensure that station consolidations did not lead to excessive market power. The Commission also recognized that efficiencies are less prevalent when financially strong stations merge with each other. For example, top-four stations are already more likely to be originating local news and to have made the transition to digital television.

The Deregulatory Petitioners assert that the top-four restriction prevents small-market stations from yielding any of the benefits of consolidation. They argue that by effectively precluding any consolidation in markets with fewer than five stations, the Commission deprives the benefit of consolidation from stations—those in small markets—who need it most. But the Commission's local television rule is protective of small-market stations. The numerical limits already allowed, in effect, extra concentration to ensure that small-market stations would realize the efficiency benefits of consolidation. As for the smallest markets with fewer than five stations—where the top-four restriction operates to preclude any consolidation—it was not unreasonable for the Commission to conclude, as it did, that the detriment of concentrated market power—e.g., reduced incentive to improve programming of mass appeal—outweighed the efficiency benefits. And, while we recognize that the Commission "cannot save an irrational rule by tacking on a waiver procedure," we note that the modified rule allows the Commission to waive the top-four restriction in small markets where those consolidations would be beneficial overall. * * *

Thus we conclude that the Commission's decision to retain the top-four restriction is supported by record evidence. Accordingly, we extend deference.

D. We remand the specific numerical limits for the Commission's further consideration.

The Commission decided to construct its numerical limits to ensure that most markets would have six equal-sized competitors because the HHI score of a six-member market—1667 (6 x (100 / 6))—is below the Department of Justice and Federal Trade Commission's 1800 threshold for highly concentrated markets for antitrust purposes. Thus the Commission decided to allow triopolies in markets of 18 stations or more (18 / 3 = 6 equal-sized competitors) and duopolies in markets of 17 or fewer (both limits subject to the restriction on a combination of top-four stations).

The Commission's assumption of equal market shares received flak from both ends of the objecting spectrum. The Citizen Petitioners point out that television stations' market shares vary widely and argue that it is arbitrary for the Commission to base its numerical limits on a rudimentary station "head count" of outlets. The Commission's rationale for its triopoly rule requires that we accept a combination of the first, fifth, and sixth-ranked stations as the competitive equal of a combination of the 16th, 17th, and 18th-ranked stations, just because each combination consists of the same number of stations. While the Citizen Petitioners demonstrate the Commission's flawed rationale with examples of what the modified rule allows, the Deregulatory Petitioners demonstrate the same flaw by pointing out what the modified rule forbids. There is no logical reason, they argue, why it should be impermissible to have five duopolies and one triopoly (a total of six competitors) in a market with 13 stations when it is possible that the triopoly could have a lower combined market share than any or all of the duopolies.

The Commission defends its equal market shares approach with the suggestion that market share, which varies with each season's new programs, is too "fluid" to be the basis for its regulations. But elsewhere in the local television ownership rule the Commission found that the market share was stable enough to rely on for support of its top-four restriction. And not only is the Commission's "market share is too fluid" rationale inconsistent with other aspects of the rule, it is unsupported. The Order cites no evidence to support its assumption that market share fluctuates more in television broadcasting than in other industries. Nor does it refute the Citizen Petitioners' suggestion that this is unlikely to be the case because, unlike most other industries, television station owners face a barrier to market entry (requirement of a license) and the number of market participants (television station owners) is in decline. * * *

VI. Local Radio Ownership Rule

Petitioners challenge the Commission's decision to modify its local radio ownership rule, which limits the number of commercial radio stations that a party may own in local markets of different sizes, by, among other changes, adopting a new method for determining the size of local markets. They also argue that the Commission failed to justify its decision to retain the rule's specific numerical limits. We affirm the Commission's decision to modify the rule (including modifying its method for determining local market size), but we agree that its decision to retain the numerical limits was arbitrary and capricious, and hence remand for the Commission's further consideration. * * *

B. We uphold the Commission's new definition of local markets.

Both the Deregulatory Petitioners and the Citizen Petitioners object to the Commission's changes to the way in which it defines a local radio market. Predictably, the Deregulatory Petitioners object to the modification that decreases the size of local markets (using Arbitron Metro markets instead of the contour-overlap methodology)—which potentially lowers the applicable numerical limit in a given market—while the

Citizen Petitioners object to the modification that increases the size of local markets (inclusion of noncommercial stations)—which potentially raises the applicable numerical limit in a given market. But we conclude that the Commission has justified these changes under § 202(h) and they are not arbitrary and capricious under the APA. * * *

E. We remand the numerical limits to the Commission for further justification.

In the Order, the Commission announced its decision to retain the existing numerical limits on radio ownership that Congress established in § 202(b) of the 1996 Act. The existing limits preclude the common ownership of radio stations with overlapping principal community contours, except that: (1) in a radio market with 45 or more commercial radio stations, a party may own up to eight commercial radio stations, not more than five of which are in the same service (that is, AM or FM); (2) in a radio market with between 30 and 44 commercial radio stations, a party may own up to seven commercial radio stations, not more than four of which are in the same service; (3) in a radio market with between 15 and 29 commercial radio stations, a party may own up to six commercial stations, not more than four of which are in the same service; and (4) in a market with 14 or fewer commercial radio stations, a party may own up to five commercial radio stations, not more than three of which are in the same service, except that a party may not own more than 50 percent of the stations in that market.

First, the Commission defended its use of numerical limits from those commenters who argued that there should be no limits at all on local radio station ownership. The Commission explained that radio is a closed-entry market, i.e., all available radio frequency spectrum has been licensed. So the only way to develop market power is to buy existing stations. Thus, the Commission says, numerical limits are a reasonable way of preventing available capacity from being "locked up" in the hands of a few owners.

The Commission then explained that the specific numerical limits that it currently employs are effective to this end. Citing economic literature, the Commission suggested that a market with five equal-sized competitors is a sufficiently competitive market. The existing limits allow for roughly five equal-sized firms in each market. (For example, the eight-station limit for markets of 45 or more stations allows for five eight-station combinations). The Commission concluded that the existing limits ensure sufficiently competitive local markets. The Commission also concluded that the existing limits are not overly restrictive based on data showing that the top-four stations in each metro market are thriving in terms of revenue and audience share. * * *

VII. Conclusion

Though we affirm much of the Commission's Order, we have identified several provisions in which the Commission falls short of its obligation to justify its decisions to retain, repeal, or modify its media ownership regulations with reasoned analysis. The Commission's derivation of new Cross-Media Limits, and its modification of the numerical limits on both television and radio station ownership in local markets, all have the same essential flaw: an unjustified assumption that media outlets of the same type make an equal contribution to diversity and competition in local markets. We thus remand for the Commission to justify or modify its approach to setting numerical limits. * * *

Competition and Diversity. Conventional antitrust economic theory teaches that the greater the concentration among service providers, the greater the likelihood of non-competitive behavior, leading to higher service rates (in this case rates for advertising) and lower output. The standard theory of communications media predicts a similar effect on the diversity of ideas and sources of information. The latter has not gone undisputed, though. There is a theory that, under some conditions, monopoly ownership may actually produce greater diversity of programming than competition. The canonical study is Peter O. Steiner, *Program Patterns and Preferences and the Workability of Competition in Radio Broadcasting*, 66 Q.J. Econ. 194 (1952). Steiner's argument makes the following assumptions: (1) there are a limited number of channels, (2) programs are divided neatly into distinctive types, (3) listeners/viewers only listen to or view their preferred type, and (4) broadcasters seek to maximize their audience because that maximizes advertising revenues. In such a model, competing stations will seek to orient their programming only to the central preferences. For example, suppose three channels and three competing stations operating on them. Assume further that in prime time 75% of the audience has a preference for A (dramatic series, sitcoms, lives sports and popular movies); 15% prefers type B (history and nature shows); 10% prefers type C (Masterpiece Theater-type "serious" drama). Under Steiner's theory, all three competing stations will program A-type content, because taking 1/3 of the 75% of the market that prefers A still allows them to take 25% of the total market, which is a larger audience than any of them would get by taking all of either the B—or C—preference viewers. However, if a monopolist owned all three channels, it would devote one channel to A, one to B and one to C, which would both maximize audience and produce greater diversity. The Steiner theory is highly stylized and limited by its assumptions, in particular the assumption of binary preferences (that people only choose their top preference or tune out) and the assumption of limited channels/stations. For example, if you drop the unrealistic assumption of binary preferences and assume that viewers will watch lesser choices if their first choice isn't available, and if you increase the number of channels, it can be shown that a competitive market will provide more diversity and greater aggregate viewer satisfaction. See Jack H. Beebe, *Institutional Structure and Program Choices in Television Markets*, 91 Q.J. Econ. 15 (1977).

Another limitation of Steiner's model is that it assumes the objective function is maximizing audience satisfaction—i.e., entertainment preferences. However, regulatory policy is less driven by market preferences than by social policy preferences: diversity means not merely maximizing viewer preferences but promoting pluralism of ideas and different sources of information. This does not fit easily into the assumptions of the Steiner model, which may be why Steiner's model has been largely ignored in the regulatory policy arena.

The Role of Localism in Prometheus. Although most cable providers do not provide original local programming, the sheer number of channels they carry dramatically increases program diversity. But the Commission was so heavily invested in localism that it discounted cable entirely as a medium for enhancing diversity. The court of appeals accepted the localism rationale without question and even built upon the FCC's pro-localism preference by discounting the Internet as a source of diverse content because the Internet is not necessarily a good source (or, rather, a separate source) of *local news*. Is there more to diversity than local news? There is plenty of local content on the Internet for virtually any market, even if most of it isn't in the form of news. And what counts as diverse content if not YouTube, even though it may not have a local focus? Isn't there a point at which localism becomes the enemy of diversity?

The New Rules. On remand from the Third Circuit's decision (and an unsuccessful petition for certiorari), the FCC gave up on most of its proposed multiple ownership reforms. But it did reinstate a part of its newspaper-cross ownership rule, allowing such ownership in the top markets and it changed its radio ownership rules in rationale only.

2006 QUADRENNIAL REGULATORY REVIEW—REVIEW OF THE COMMISSION'S BROADCAST OWNERSHIP RULES
Report and Order and Order on Reconsideration

Federal Communications Commission, 2008.
23 FCC Rcd. 2010.

BY THE COMMISSION:

I. INTRODUCTION

1. In this Report and Order and Order on Reconsideration ("Order"), we conclude our 2006 Quadrennial Review of the broadcast ownership rules. Our review encompasses the newspaper/broadcast cross-ownership rule, the radio/television cross-ownership rule, the local television ownership rule, the local radio ownership rule, and the dual network rule. We review these rules under Section 202(h) of the Telecommunications Act of 1996 ("1996 Act"), which requires the Commission to review its ownership rules (except the national television owner-

ship limit) every four years and "determine whether any of such rules are necessary in the public interest as the result of competition." Under Section 202(h), the Commission "shall repeal or modify any regulation it determines to be no longer in the public interest." We modify the newspaper/broadcast cross-ownership rule, and we generally retain the other broadcast ownership rules currently in effect. We also address petitions for reconsideration of the Commission's Report and Order in its 2002 biennial review of its broadcast ownership rules (the "*2002 Biennial Review Order*") and the remand of that Order by the U.S. Court of Appeals for the Third Circuit in *Prometheus Radio Project, et al. v. FCC* ("*Prometheus*").

II. Background

2. *History of the Proceeding.* We initiated this 2006 Quadrennial Review proceeding with the *Further Notice of Proposed Rule Making* ("*Further Notice*"). In addition to inviting comment on whether the ownership rules remain "necessary in the public interest as the result of competition," under the Section 202(h) standard, the *Further Notice* invited comment on how to address the issues raised by the U.S. Court of Appeals for the Third Circuit in its *Prometheus* decision and those raised by the U.S. Court of Appeals for the District of Columbia Circuit in *Sinclair Broadcast Group, Inc. v. FCC.* This Order addresses all of those issues. * * *

III. Newspaper/Broadcast Cross-Ownership

13. In this section we address the newspaper/broadcast cross-ownership rule to determine whether it is necessary in the public interest. The 1975 cross-ownership ban is the only Commission media ownership rule that has remained in effect without modification for over three decades. Today, we make a modest change in the rule that has the primary effect of presuming that certain limited combinations of newspaper and broadcast facilities in the largest markets are in the public interest. In this order, we take a modest step in loosening the complete ban on cross-ownership. We adopt a presumption, in the top 20 Designated Market Areas ("DMAs"), that it is not inconsistent with the public interest for one entity to own a daily newspaper and a radio station or, under the following limited circumstances, a daily newspaper and a television station, if (1) the television station is not ranked among the top four stations in the DMA and (2) at least eight independent "major media voices" remain in the DMA. In all other instances, we adopt a presumption that a newspaper/broadcast station combination would not be in the public interest, with two limited exceptions, and therefore emphasize that the Commission is unlikely to approve such transactions. Taking into account these respective presumptions, in determining whether the grant of a transaction that would result in newspaper/broadcast cross-ownership is in the public interest, the Commission will consider the following factors: (1) whether the cross-ownership will increase the amount of local news disseminated through the affected

media outlets in the combination; (2) whether each affected media outlet in the combination will exercise its own independent news judgment; (3) the level of concentration in the Nielsen DMA; and (4) the financial condition of the newspaper or broadcast outlet, and if the newspaper or broadcast station is in financial distress, the proposed owner's commitment to invest significantly in newsroom operations. Our cautious approach addresses the need to support the availability and sustainability of local news while not significantly increasing local concentration or harming diversity.

* * *

B. Discussion

* * *

39. *Policy Goals.* In the *2002 Biennial Review Order*, the Commission concluded that efficiencies from the common ownership of two media outlets may increase the amount of diverse, competitive news and local information available to the public. We continue to find evidence that cross-ownership in the largest markets can preserve the viability of newspapers without threatening diversity by allowing them to spread their operational costs across multiple platforms. In doing so, they can improve or increase the news offered by the broadcaster and the newspaper. Numerous media owners provide examples of cost savings and shared resources leading to more local coverage and better quality news coverage. * * *

52. We replace the blanket ban on newspaper/broadcast cross-ownership with a rule that establishes clear presumptions as to the limited circumstances when we will presume a newspaper/broadcast transaction will be in the public interest and thus a waiver of the ban should be granted. Establishing presumptions, as opposed to a bright line, will allow for the evaluation of proposed newspaper/broadcast combinations under defined circumstances on a case-by-case basis. In limited cases, we will presume that a proposed combination would be in the public interest. In the vast majority of cases, we will presume that a proposed combination would not be in the public interest, and we therefore would not permit the combination. Nevertheless, no matter which presumption applies, we will consider specific factors in determining whether permitting a particular combination in a particular market would be in the public interest. In addition, our case-by-case approach should partially alleviate the concerns of the newspaper industry commenters who believe the revised rule is too modest in scope to provide sufficient opportunities for cross-ownership and that it fails to recognize the marketplace changes since 1975. Moreover, because our rule presumes combinations are not consistent with the public interest in markets 21 and below and because we will continue to scrutinize combinations of newspapers and the top four television stations in markets 1–20, our rule will not harm diversity or localism, as discussed below.

1. Presumption Favoring Certain Combinations in Top 20 Markets

* * *

56. We find notable differences between the top 20 markets and all other DMAs, both in terms of voices and in terms of television households. We evaluated the range of media outlets available in the top 20 DMAs, and conclude that diversity in those largest markets is healthy and vibrant in comparison to all other DMAs. For example, while there are at least 10 independently owned television stations in 18 of the top 20 DMAs, none of the DMAs ranked 21 through 25 have 10 independently owned television stations. Additionally, while seventeen of the top 20 DMAs have at least two newspapers with a circulation of at least 5 percent of the households in that DMA, four of the five DMAs ranked 21 through 25 have only one such newspaper. Moreover, the top 20 markets, on average, have 15.5 major voices (independently owned television stations and major newspapers), 87.8 total voices (all independently owned television stations, radio stations, and major newspapers), and approximately 3.3 million television households. Markets 21 through 30, by comparison, have, on average, 9.5 major voices, 65.0 total voices, and fewer than 1.1 million television households, representing drops of 38.5 percent, 25.9 percent, and 56.3 percent from the top 20 markets, respectively. Markets 31 through 40 and 41 through 50 have average numbers of voices for each category similar to markets 21 through 30, and even fewer television households on average, 837,800 and 679,200, respectively. Markets 50 through 210 show even more dramatic drops, with on average, 6.7 major voices, 31.2 total voices, and approximately 231,000 television households, representing drops of 56.4 percent, 61.7 percent, and 90.7 percent from the top 20 markets, respectively. The diversity in the number and types of traditional media outlets in the largest markets ensures that the public is well served by antagonistic viewpoints. Markets outside of the top 20 DMAs do not feature diversity to such an extent.

* * *

2. Presumption Against All Other Combinations

63. In adopting our new newspaper/broadcast cross-ownership rule, we presume that it is not inconsistent with the public interest for an entity to own, operate or control, in one of the top 20 DMAs, a daily newspaper and one commercial AM or FM radio station or one TV broadcast station under certain circumstances. As discussed above, we base this presumption on the vibrancy and number of voices in the top 20 DMAs. In all DMAs ranked 21 and below, we adopt a presumption that it is inconsistent with the public interest for an entity to own newspaper and broadcast combinations. * * *

65. *Reversal of Negative Presumption.* In two special circumstances, we will reverse the negative presumption that applies to those proposed combinations that do not otherwise qualify for a positive presumption. First, we adopt a failed/failing station model, based upon

the same criteria that we apply in the local television waiver criteria. Although this standard was not formalized until 1999, the Commission has been applying this type of analysis for over 25 years in evaluating waivers of ownership limits. Under this model, if a newspaper or broadcast outlet is failed or failing, we would apply a positive presumption. * * *

67. Second, we also will reverse the negative presumption when a proposed combination results in a new source of a significant amount of local news in a market. Specifically, we will presume that a proposed newspaper/broadcast combination is not inconsistent with the public interest when it initiates local news programming of at least seven hours per week on a broadcast outlet that otherwise was not offering local newscasts prior to the combined operations. In reviewing whether broadcasters have carried out their obligations to serve the public interest with responsive programming, the Commission has historically considered their news and public affairs programming to be uniquely and particularly important. * * *

68. *Rebutting the Presumption.* To the extent that a proposed combination does not qualify for a positive presumption, it will have a high hurdle to cross to win Commission approval. Similarly, parties objecting to a transaction with a positive presumption will have a high hurdle to persuade the Commission that the transaction should not be approved. We will require any applicant attempting to overcome a negative presumption about a major newspaper and television station combination to demonstrate by clear and convincing evidence that, post-merger, the merged entity will increase the diversity of independent news outlets (e.g., separate editorial and news coverage decisions) and increase competition among independent news sources in the relevant market. Our analysis of the following four factors will inform this determination: (1) the extent to which cross-ownership will serve to increase the amount of local news disseminated through the affected media outlets in the combination; (2) whether each affected media outlet in the combination will exercise its own independent news judgment; (3) the level of concentration in the Nielsen DMA; and (4) the financial condition of the newspaper or broadcast station, and if the newspaper or broadcast station is in financial distress, the owner's commitment to invest significantly in newsroom operations. * * *

69. *Increased Local News.* * * * The record suggests that some entities operating both a newspaper and a broadcast television station may have achieved superior news operations that benefit local audiences. * * * Given the record, we believe it is appropriate that we evaluate whether a proposed newspaper/broadcast combination will increase the amount of local news disseminated and thereby further the goal of localism.

71. *Independent News Judgment.* In adopting the newspaper/broadcast cross-ownership ban in 1975, the Commission stated that, "it is unrealistic to expect true diversity from a commonly owned

station-newspaper combination. The divergence of their viewpoints cannot be expected to be the same as if they were antagonistically run." Today's record now reveals, however, that some co-owned newspaper/broadcast facilities are capable of maintaining separate editorial operations. * * * We adhere to the Commission's long-standing view that independence of news sources is important to civic life and the public welfare. Therefore, in evaluating this factor, the Commission will analyze whether applicants have demonstrated that their respective media outlets will exercise independent news and editorial judgment. * * *

72. *Market Concentration.* The third factor in our public interest determination is the level of concentration in the Nielsen DMA, that is, the extent to which media outlets in a particular market compete in the provision of local news and information to consumers within that market and the impact that the proposed combination would have on such concentration. * * *

73. In evaluating this factor, we will conduct a fact-specific inquiry into the characteristics of the market in question as well as characteristics of the proposed combination. * * * We will not employ any single metric, such as the Diversity Index, because, as the Commission has learned from experience, there are too many qualitative and quantitative variables in evaluating different markets and combinations to reduce the task at hand to a precise mathematical formula. Measuring concentration across platforms in the local news and information market for the purposes of preserving diversity is not akin to measuring concentration in the market for automobiles or washing machines for antitrust purposes. Moreover, the record does not reveal any "silver bullet" formula in this regard. We stress, however, that in future adjudicative proceedings addressing proposed combinations parties are free to point to any metric of their choosing in arguing that a proposed combination either should or should not be approved. * * *

74. *Financial Condition.* We will evaluate whether a newspaper or a broadcast station in a proposed combination is in financial distress. To show financial distress, the applicant will have to show that either the newspaper or the broadcast station is operating at a loss. * * * To the extent that our newspaper/broadcast cross-ownership rule forecloses a viable avenue for a struggling newspaper or a broadcast station to prevent the loss of a source of local programming, our rule would be undermining, rather than promoting, our goals of competition, localism, and diversity. Allowing a struggling newspaper or broadcast station to combine with a stronger outlet can, under certain circumstances, improve its ability to provide local news and information, thus benefiting the public interest. * * *

IV. Radio/Television Cross-Ownership Rule

80. As explained in more detail below, we retain the current radio/television cross-ownership rule. The radio/television cross-

ownership rule limits the number of commercial radio and television stations an entity may own in the same market, with the degree of common ownership permitted varying depending on the size of the relevant market. In contrast to the newspaper/broadcast cross-ownership ban, this rule has been substantially relaxed over the years. * * *

B. Discussion

82. We retain the radio/television cross-ownership rule currently in effect to provide protection for diversity goals in local markets and thereby serve the public interest. Our conclusion in the *2002 Biennial Review Order* that the radio/television cross-ownership rule was no longer necessary to ensure viewpoint diversity was based in large part on our adoption of the cross-media limits in that proceeding. Now that the court has invalidated the cross-media limits, we must adopt diversity protection provisions to act in their place, and therefore retain the current radio/television cross-ownership rule. In doing so, we reaffirm the Commission's conclusion that "fostering the availability of diverse viewpoints remains an important policy goal, and that diversity of ownership promotes diversity of viewpoints." * * *

V. Local Television Ownership Rule

* * *

90. The Commission decided in the *2002 Biennial Review Order* to revise the local television ownership rule to permit an entity to own up to two television stations in markets with 17 or fewer television stations, and up to three television stations in markets with 18 or more television stations. The Commission retained the prohibition on combinations involving more than one station ranked among the top four in the market, thus prohibiting combinations in markets with four or fewer television stations. The Commission eliminated consideration of overlapping Grade B contours, however, and decided to look instead only at whether a station is assigned by Nielsen to a DMA. The *2002 Biennial Review Order* also modified the Commission's criteria for waiver of the local television ownership rule. Although the Commission stated that it would continue to allow entities to seek a waiver if at least one of the stations in the proposed combination is failed, failing, or unbuilt, it removed the requirement that the waiver applicant demonstrate that there is no buyer outside the market willing to purchase the station at a reasonable price.

91. *The Prometheus Decision*. On review in *Prometheus*, the court upheld the Commission's determination that "broadcast media are not the only media outlets contributing to viewpoint diversity in local markets." In light of its decision to remand the Commission's numerical limits, the court found that it need not decide "the degree to which non-broadcast media compensate for lost viewpoint diversity to justify the modified [local television] rule." In addition, in light of evidence in the record, including evidence that "commonly owned television stations are more likely to carry local news than other stations" and studies showing

that "consolidation generally improved audience ratings," the court rejected petitioners' contention "that the Commission's finding of localism benefits from consolidation was unsupported." The court also upheld the Commission's decision to retain the top four-ranked station restriction, stating that it "must uphold an agency's line-drawing decision when it is supported by evidence in the record." It found "ample evidence in the record" to support the Commission's reliance on a "cushion" of audience share percentage points between the fourth-and fifth-ranked stations in most markets to restrict combinations among the top four-ranked stations "as opposed to the top three or some other number."

92. Nonetheless, the court remanded the numerical limits in the new rule for further justification. The limits were premised on the need to ensure six equal-sized competitors. The size of an owner was tied to the number of stations owned, rather than the audience shares of those stations. The court held that the Commission had unreasonably failed to consider the audience shares of stations in setting its numerical limits, finding that "[n]o evidence supports the Commission's equal market share assumption, and no reasonable explanation underlies its decision to disregard actual market share." Further, although the court recognized that the Commission did not intend the numerical limits to be a mechanical application of the *DOJ/FTC Merger Guidelines*, it concluded that the rule was unreasonable because it would allow levels of concentration exceeding the 1800 HHI benchmark relied upon by the Commission in setting its numerical limits. * * *

B. Discussion

96. ... [W]e are persuaded from the evidence in the record that the current rule is consistent with the public interest. Therefore, we will continue to allow an entity to own two television stations in the same DMA if: (1) the Grade B contours of the stations do not overlap; or (2) at least one of the stations in the combination is not ranked among the top four stations in terms of audience share, and at least eight independently owned and operating commercial or non-commercial full-power broadcast television stations would remain in the DMA after the combination. To determine the number of voices remaining after the merger, the Commission will continue to count those broadcast television stations whose Grade B signal contours overlap with the Grade B signal contour of at least one of the stations that would be commonly owned. With respect to the waiver standard for the local television ownership rule, we will reinstate our requirement that a waiver applicant demonstrate that there is no buyer outside the market willing to purchase the station at a reasonable price. * * *

105. *Issues Raised by the Prometheus Court on Remand.* We find that with one exception, the issues remanded by the *Prometheus* court all regarded the new local television ownership rule adopted in 2003. Because we reject that rule and instead retain the eight-voices rule, those issues are moot. The one exception is the court's criticism that the

Commission did not consider the potential impact on minority owners when it eliminated the out-of-market buyer requirement for the waiver standard. To ensure that we do not negatively impact minority owners, we now reinstate that requirement in the waiver standard. * * *

VI. Local Radio Ownership Rule

110. ... [W]e conclude that the current local radio ownership rule, including the market definition as revised in the *2002 Biennial Review Order*, remains "necessary in the public interest" to protect competition in local radio markets. As directed by the *Prometheus* court, we also provide a reasoned justification for our decision to retain the existing numerical limits on local radio ownership. In addition, we deny or dismiss a number of pending petitions for reconsideration of the Commission's action concerning the local radio ownership rule in the *2002 Biennial Review Order*. Accordingly, an entity may own, operate, or control (1) up to eight commercial radio stations, not more than five of which are in the same service (i.e., AM or FM), in a radio market with 45 or more full-power, commercial and noncommercial radio stations; (2) up to seven commercial radio stations, not more than four of which are in the same service, in a radio market with between 30 and 44 (inclusive) full-power, commercial and noncommercial radio stations; (3) up to six commercial radio stations, not more than four of which are in the same service, in a radio market with between 15 and 29 (inclusive) full-power, commercial and noncommercial radio stations; and (4) up to five commercial radio stations, not more than three of which are in the same service, in a radio market with 14 or fewer full-power, commercial and noncommercial radio stations, except that an entity may not own, operate, or control more than 50 percent of the stations in such a market. * * *

116. We reaffirm our conclusion in the *2002 Biennial Review Order* that the ownership tiers in the current rule represent a reasonable means for promoting the public interest as it relates to competition, and that numerical limits on radio station ownership help to keep the available radio spectrum from becoming "locked up" in the hands of one or a few owners, thus helping to prevent the formation of market power in local radio markets.

117. We also conclude that retention of the existing numerical limits in the local radio ownership rule is necessary in the public interest. In so concluding, we depart from the Commission's rationale in the *2002 Biennial Review Order* that the existing limits are appropriate because they allow for roughly five equal-sized firms in each market. Instead, we rest our decision on our conclusion that relaxing the rule to permit greater consolidation would be inconsistent with the Commission's public interest objectives of ensuring that the benefits of competition and diversity are realized in local radio markets. Making the numerical limits more restrictive would be inconsistent with Congress' decision to relax the local radio ownership limits in the 1996 Telecommunications Act and would disserve the public interest by unduly

disrupting the radio broadcasting industry. Based on our examination of the record, we are persuaded that the current numerical limits strike the appropriate balance.

118. The evidence in the record indicates that retaining the numerical limits at the current level is necessary to protect against excessive market concentration. Prior to 1992, our radio ownership rules prohibited most radio mergers. In 1992, we relaxed our local radio ownership rules in recognition of the fact that our rules prevented some firms from achieving the economies of scale that they needed to survive financially. Congress further relaxed the local radio ownership limits in the 1996 Telecommunications Act. Congress's 1996 radio ownership rules revisions have had a substantial effect on the market structure of radio broadcasting, resulting in further consolidation of radio station ownership at both the national and the local level. By maintaining the current numerical limits, we seek to guard against additional consolidation of the strongest stations in a market in the hands of too few owners and to ensure a market structure that fosters opportunities for new entry into radio broadcasting. The number of commercial radio station owners declined by 39 percent between 1996 and 2007, with most of the decline occurring during the first few years after the 1996 Act. Although the average number of commercial owners across all Arbitron radio markets currently is 9.4, the largest commercial firm in each Arbitron Metro market has, on average, 46 percent of the market's total radio advertising revenue, and the largest two firms have 74 percent of the revenue. In 111 of the 299 Arbitron Metro markets, the top two commercial station owners control at least 80 percent of radio advertising revenue. The top four commercial firms also dominate audience share. And evidence in the record indicates that the increase in concentration in commercial radio markets has resulted in appreciable, albeit small, increases in advertising rates. All of this data in the record supports the conclusion that the current numerical limits are not unduly restrictive and that additional consolidation would not serve the Commission's competitive goals.

119. We also conclude that making the numerical limits more restrictive is not justified based on examination of the current record. Prior to 1992, the local radio ownership rules did not effectively recognize that a certain level of consolidation can be efficient. Given the generally difficult economic conditions at the time, the inability of stations to seek efficiencies through consolidation may have contributed to the industry's financial difficulties. We do not seek to undermine the benefits that consolidation has brought to the financial stability of the radio industry.

120. In addition, further tightening of the local radio ownership rule would disrupt the marketplace by necessitating widespread divestitures. In this regard, the Future of Music Coalition cites data showing that at least one radio station owner was at the ownership cap in 194 of 297 Arbitron Metro markets. Requiring widespread divestitures would undermine settled expectations in a market where broadcasters needed regulatory relief to achieve the economies of scale necessary to compete

just 10 years ago. Many broadcasters incurred significant financial risks by acquiring the additional stations permitted under this rule and are creating business development plans for the future based on these current economies of scale. Decreasing the limit would thus be a significant shock to the market. Moreover, it could undermine efficiency gains that such firms otherwise might realize from their current economies of scale, efficiency gains that could bolster the stations' financial standing and increase their ability to provide their local communities with quality programming. We should not cause such a disruption absent persuasive evidence that further tightening of the local radio ownership rule would serve the public interest more effectively than the current rule.

121. Of course, we recognize that the need for widespread divestitures could be avoided by grandfathering existing station combinations, as the Commission chose to do in the *2002 Biennial Review Order*. Again, however, doing so here would involve negative policy consequences that must be avoided if possible. Grandfathering existing combinations would exacerbate competitive imbalances enjoyed by current group owners—those that assembled combinations under the current rules—and would disfavor those that cannot assemble competing combinations because of new ownership restrictions. In other words, grandfathering would "lock in" the competitive advantage of the largest group owners and permanently disadvantage those who have not yet consolidated. Although the Commission previously chose to grandfather existing station combinations based on countervailing considerations, we find that doing so now is not in the public interest.

122. Furthermore, we cannot conclude that tinkering with the existing numerical limits is warranted merely to rationalize the specific numerical limits that Congress chose in 1996 in light of the strong countervailing considerations set forth above. Congress adopted the existing limits in 1996, and mandated that the Commission periodically examine whether they remain necessary in the public interest. The *Prometheus* court rejected the Commission's attempt to rationalize the limits that Congress chose based on game theory and the *DOJ/FTC Horizontal Merger Guidelines*. Had the Commission initially established its own numerical limits, of course, it might have chosen different tiers and/or different caps. Nevertheless, we believe that it would be inconsistent with the public interest, as well as with the deference that we owe to Congress's line-drawing, to modify those limits merely to suit a new rationale, given the negative policy consequences associated with such tinkering. Instead, we believe that retaining the current numerical limits strikes the appropriate balance between protecting competition in local radio markets and enabling radio owners to achieve efficiencies through consolidation of facilities. * * *

VII. Dual Network Rule

139. The Commission's dual network rule provides: "A television broadcast station may affiliate with a person or entity that maintains two or more networks of television broadcast stations unless such dual

or multiple networks are composed of two or more persons or entities that, on February 8, 1996, were 'networks' as defined in Section 73.3613(a)(1) of the Commission's regulations (that is, ABC, CBS, Fox, and NBC)." Thus, the rule permits common ownership of multiple broadcast networks, but prohibits a merger between or among the "top four" networks. In this Order, we conclude that the dual network rule remains necessary in the public interest as a result of competition and localism, and we therefore retain the rule without modification. * * *

The Diversity Index. Explaining its abandonment of the Diversity Index, the Commission states: "We will not employ any single metric, such as the Diversity Index, because, as the Commission has learned from experience, there are too many qualitative and quantitative variables in evaluating different markets and combinations to reduce the task at hand to a precise mathematical formula." What was the "experience" from which it learned between 2003, when the 2003 Biennial Report was released, and 2008 when the new report was issued? It could not have been experience from applying the rules under the DI because *Prometheus* stayed the rules. Putting aside the plea of experience, it may be true that it is difficult to reduce the task to a precise formula, but why isn't that problem solved by simply applying the formula on a market-by-market basis? Note that the Third Circuit did not fault the methodology but faulted the fixed rules that the FCC developed from it. So, why not use the formula (or something like it) to measure diversity on a case-by-case basis? In that way the agency could examine the specific parameters of each market and take into account precisely the variables that the Third Circuit faulted it for overlooking. The FCC has historically been very keen on having bright line ownership rules in order to enable firms to plan their investments and operations. Certainty is surely a valid objective, but is it really all that important in this context? The DOJ and FTC enforce antitrust standards on an ad hoc basis—albeit with the guidance of merger guidelines, which include the Herfindahl-Hirschman index—yet corporate America in general does not seem to be significantly handicapped in its M&A activities. Why would it be any different for media America?

The Radio Rules. The FCC responded to *Prometheus* not by changing the substance of its radio ownership rules but rather the rationale, or rather by abandoning any rationale. In large part, the FCC seems to be explaining (to the court?) why it can't change the rules even if it wanted to, essentially abandoning its own independent attempt to rationalize specific limits by pointing to congressional policy. Is this kind of backward-looking rationale likely to play in the U.S. Courts of Appeals?

The Television Rules. The FCC returned to the pre-2002 rules governing local television ownership, with one modification: it eliminated the Grade B overlap condition. Thus, the rule now allows common ownership of two local television stations if "at least one of the stations in the combination is not ranked among the top four stations in terms of audience share, and at least eight independently owned and operating commercial or non-commercial full-power broadcast television stations would remain in the DMA after the combination" This presumably satisfies the *Prometheus* remand order. There remains the question whether it also removes the problem the *Sinclair* case raised about the eight-station exception before *Prometheus*. In *Sinclair* the court found that the FCC had failed to explain why its eight-station rule considered only television "voices" as alternative sources of local news, when it explicitly considered non-broadcast news sources in crafting the cross-ownership limits. Given the FCC's new rules on cross ownership, is there still a problem of what to count as an alternative "voice" for purposes of measuring diversification of media?

Saving Old Newspapers. The Commission notes the changes in the media marketplace since the original cross-ownership rules were adopted in 1975, most notably the increase in cable competition and the decline in daily newspapers. The latter has been going on for more than just the three decades cited by the Commission. In fact the decline in the number of daily newspapers has occurred with relentless continuity since early in the 20th Century. It is not simply that competing dailies have disappeared in all but 16 cities, 2 *World Press Encyclopedia*, 1020 (2003); the circulation of newspapers has steadily declined as well. For example, between 1970 and 2004 the aggregate circulation of daily newspapers fell by 37 percent—more than twice the decline in the number of newspapers themselves. U.S. Census Bureau, *Statistical Abstract of the United States, 2006*, at p. 738. How does this bear on the cross ownership issue?

The Commission observes that lifting the ban could allow local broadcast-newspaper entities to share operating costs. This observation may be true, but doesn't it involve a curious discrimination against small market media? The FCC states that, in markets below the top 20, entities seeking a waiver of the ban on cross ownership are expected to show, among other things, that the "newspaper and the broadcast outlets each will continue to employ its own news and editorial staff and that each will exercise its own independent news judgment." In other words, efficiency is a value underlying relaxation of the rules, but apparently only for newspapers and broadcasters in large markets; those in small markets must remain as inefficient as they were before in order to receive permission to merge. Moreover, isn't the FCC's notion that requiring "independent" editorial staffs ensures diversity at odds with the underlying assumption of the ownership rules themselves: that *financial ownership* influences viewpoints? To put this in concrete terms, suppose Rupert Murdoch buys the *Wall Street Journal* (this is not hypothetical) but pledges that the editorial board will remain independent of the corporate governance structure of News Corp (the parent of Fox Network et al.). Does that alleviate any concerns we might have about the merger?

C. BROADCAST NATIONAL OWNERSHIP

What are now called national or group ownership rules were first imposed on FM radio in 1940 and thereafter extended to television and AM radio in 1941 and 1943 respectively. The original limits varied by service, six for FM, seven for AM, three for television, but after a series of adjustments each service received a cap of seven, with the condition that, for television at least, two of the stations had to be UHF. The "seven station" rules remained in effect for twenty years. After a major review of the rules, the Commission in 1984 decided they were unnecessary and should automatically sunset after six years. As a transitional measure it raised the limit to twelve stations nationwide. The transition proved to be indefinite. Congress balked at the FCC's decision to open up national ownership, and within six months of the decision, the FCC reversed its decision, eliminating the rule. It did retain the increased limit of twelve, while at the same time supplementing it with an additional limit that prohibited ownership of television stations reaching more than 25% of the country's television households.

Two decades on, congressional opposition to relaxing the multiple ownership rules changed. In 1996 Congress was in a deregulatory mood. While most of that mood concentrated on reforming telecommunications policy, some of it targeted broadcast regulation as well, including several of the broadcast ownership rules. For radio, Congress eliminated the national ownership limit altogether. With respect to television, Congress directed the Commission to eliminate the numerical limit and to raise the audience percentage cap from 25% to 35%. It also directed the FCC to conduct a biennial review of all of its broadcast ownership rules, with the results that we examined above: the Commission in its 2002 Biennial Report raised the ownership cap to 45% only to have Congress adjust it downward to 39%.

If the number 39 appears arbitrary, it is and it isn't. It is not based on any obvious economic principle or policy, and even as a compromise figure, it is odd; the conventional heuristic of splitting the difference between the high and low marks would have produced an audience cap of 40% not 39%. As it happens, however, 39% was just enough to allow two networks, Fox and CBS, to avoid divesting stations that they had acquired in contemplation of a new limit. (The FCC had given them a temporary waiver of the old limit pending the outcome of the rulemaking proceeding to reconsider the limit.)

Of course, to ask why Congress did not split the difference between the old and the new is something of a tangent. It explains the politics of the matter, but it doesn't explain anything about the underlying issue. What is the right cap? Why, indeed, is there any cap at all?

For most of the history of national ownership rules, the Commission avoided a coherent account of just how the national rules affected diversity. When it first promulgated group ownership rules, the FCC explained their purpose as being "[t]o obviate possible monopoly, and encourage local initiative." *Sixth Annual Report* 68 (1941). In 1953, in the course of raising the limit (from three stations in each service—AM, FM and TV—to seven stations) it elaborated on this rationale slightly by saying that the purpose was to "promote diversification of ownership in order to maximize diversification of program and service viewpoints as well as to prevent any undue concentration of economic power contrary to the public interest." *Multiple Ownership of AM, FM and Television Broadcast Stations*, 18 F.C.C. 288, 291–92 (1953), *aff'd sub nom, United States v. Storer Broadcasting*, 351 U.S. 192 (1955). Then, thirty years after its adoption of the "Seven Stations Rule" the Commission concluded that the national ownership was basically irrelevant. In *Multiple Ownership of AM, FM and Television Broadcast Stations*, 100 F.C.C.2d 17 (1984) the Commission found the rules were no longer needed:

> 60. Within the United States, the most important idea markets are local. For an individual member of the audience, the richness of ideas to which he is exposed turns on how many diverse views are available within his local broadcast market. For that individual, whether or not some of those views are also disseminated in other local broadcast markets does not affect the diversity to which he is exposed. Accordingly, national broadcast ownership limits, as opposed to local ownership limits, ordinarily are not pertinent to assuring a diversity of views to the constituent elements of the American public.
>
> 61. It is true, however, that ideas can migrate from one local market to another. Thus it might be argued that there is First Amendment utility in preventing duplication of viewpoints amongst local markets to increase the likelihood that edifying ideas will blossom and spread nationwide. It could be argued that national ownership rules might address this concern for the emergence of good ideas by preventing a single owner from echoing an identical voice in a large number of local markets. However, our concern for this theoretical benefit of the multiple ownership rules is answered by at least three factors. First, the record demonstrates that group owners do not impose monolithic viewpoints on local media outlets; indeed, the record demonstrates the opposite. Therefore, ownership by an entity of a number of broadcast stations located in different markets does not result in fewer viewpoints nationwide. Second, there is such an abundance of idea sources in the aggregate nationwide—more than 10,000 broadcast stations and more than 12,000 newspapers and periodicals—that eliminating the Rule of Sevens would at worst occasion an inconsequential decrease in idea sources nationwide. And even this decrease assumes that group owners will express identical viewpoints in the local markets where they own stations, an assumption contrary to the record.
>
> 62. Third, group ownership likely has offsetting advantages in enriching the variety of information available in the local community. Group owners may be able to devote more resources to newsgathering and other activities which improve the quality of programming presented. There is no evidence in this record suggesting that the

> hypothetical benefits from promoting many sources of ideas outweigh the benefits from new and more expensive programming made possible by allowing broadcasters and other mass media to choose the organizational structures they believe make them most efficient.
>
> 63. In light of the evidence presented by commenters on the irrelevance of national broadcast ownership levels to viewpoint diversity, the discussion above of such factors as the dramatic increase in the number of radio (especially FM) and TV stations since the Rule of Sevens was adopted, the inhibiting effects of the rule in the development of new programming, and the efforts of network and group owners in public affairs programming, the Commission concludes that the public interest, insofar as it relates to encouraging a diversity of viewpoints, would be well served by eliminating the restriction on the number of stations that a single entity may own nationwide. The area from which consumers can select the relevant mass media alternatives is generally the local community in which they work and live. Radio and TV signals are available over the air in generally discrete local markets. Consumers also have recourse to local outlets for other material, such as newspapers, magazines, videocassettes, records, and movies.

Notwithstanding this finding, the Commission decided that an immediate termination of the limit might have some unanticipated effects so it provided for a six year "transition" period at the end of which the cap would be eliminated; meantime it increased the numerical limit from seven to twelve in each broadcast service.

As we saw above, Congress disagreed and voiced its displeasure by providing that no appropriated funds could be spent to implement them prior to April 1985 or after Commission reconsideration. See Pub. L. No. 98-396, § 304, 98 Stat. 1369, 1423 (1984). The FCC took the hint and reconsidered its proposed termination. It adhered to the increase in the numerical cap to twelve, but for television stations it was supplemented with the 25% audience cap. As for a theory of why the caps should continue, the FCC still offered none, instead finding it

> inadvisable to terminate the ownership regulations adopted herein automatically at the end of six years. We continue to believe that it is appropriate to proceed cautiously in relaxing rules that affect such a vital aspect of the broadcasting industry. Virtually all parties on reconsideration agreed that the automatic termination of the multiple ownership rule is not an integral part of relaxing the seven station rule. We agree and find that an automatic sunset of our ownership rules is unnecessary to achieve our policy objectives.

Multiple Ownership of AM, FM and Television Broadcast Stations, 100 F.C.C.2d 74 ¶ 49 (1985).

In 1996, Congress directed the FCC to eliminate the numerical limit and raise the audience cap to 35%. Matters might have remained there but for the biennial review mandated by Congress. Pursuant to that mandate, the FCC again revisited the national ownership rule in 1998. The FCC declined to make any change at that time, but interestingly it discovered a new rationale for national ownership limits: the policy of promoting localism. The idea that national ownership limits might have something to do with localism was not altogether new; in 1941 the FCC had made passing reference to preserving "local initiative." However, it was not explained at the time how the rule did this, and the element of localism faded in subsequent rationalizations of the rule. In 1984, the Commission gave no notice to it. In 1998, however, the Commission explained that a limit on national ownership strengthened the bargaining power of independently owned (specifically non-network owned) stations, which in turn promoted local diversity. Neither the diversity or localism arguments convinced the court of appeals. In *Fox Television Stations, Inc. v. FCC*, 280 F.3d 1027, 1044 (D.C. Cir. 2002), *rehearing granted*, 293 F.3d 537 (D.C. Cir. 2002) the court held that the Commission failed to demonstrate that the national cap advanced competition, diversity, or localism. It pointed to the Commission's conclusion in 1984 that (1) the rule no longer was necessary for national diversity given the abundance of media outlets and (2) a national rule was irrelevant to local diversity. Nor had the Commission demonstrated that the rule strengthens the bargaining power of independently owned affiliates and thereby promotes program diversity. The remanded proceeding in *Fox* was merged into the 2002 biennial review proceeding, and, as we saw above, the Commission responded with an increase in the audience cap (to 45%) only to be partly slapped down (again) by Congress (to 39%).

So the national ownership rule stands. But what theory or purpose is it standing on? Consider the following excerpt from the FCC's 2002 biennial report:

2002 BIENNIAL REGULATORY REVIEW—REVIEW OF THE COMMISSION'S BROADCAST OWNERSHIP RULES
Report and Order and Notice of Proposed Rulemaking

Federal Communications Commission, 2003.
18 FCC Rcd. 13620.

BY THE COMMISSION:

* * *

c. Localism

538. *Introduction*. The Commission's decision in the *1984 Multiple Ownership Report and Order* did not address whether the national TV ownership rule advances its goal of localism. In the *1998 Biennial Review Report*, however, the Commission did address its localism goal, declining to modify the national TV ownership restriction in part because affiliates "play a valuable counterbalancing role" to network programming decisions by exercising their independent programming discretion regarding what programs best serve the needs and interests of

their local communities. In *Fox Television*, the court stated that, although the Commission had failed to present evidence that the cap in fact promoted localism, localism was a legitimate basis for imposing a national ownership cap.

539. Based on our analysis of the extensive record in this proceeding, we conclude that a national television ownership limit is necessary to promote localism on broadcast television. The evidence suggests, however, that the current 35% cap is not needed the protect localism, and may in fact be hindering public benefits that are expected to follow from an increase in the cap. We conclude that a national cap of 45% fairly balances the competing public interest values affected by this rule. We recognize that our decision to retain a national ownership cap is contrary to our conclusion in 1984. We reach this different conclusion principally because we find that a cap is necessary to protect localism by preserving a balance of power between networks and affiliates, a policy objective that was not considered in the 1984 decision. In this section, we detail the localism analysis. Thereafter, we discuss our modified rule.

(i) Whether a National Cap Promotes Localism

540. In this section we examine the effect of a national television cap on the economic incentives for locally responsive programming by television stations. We also consider evidence that a national cap results in behavior by network-affiliated stations that is responsive to the needs and tastes of a station's local community.

(a) Economic Incentives for Localism

541. NAB/NASA contends that the current national cap is needed to preserve affiliates' bargaining power with their networks. NAB/NASA explains that limiting the national audience that networks can reach through their owned stations promotes a balance of power between networks and their affiliates. NAB/NASA also claims that the cap is necessary to counteract the networks' strong financial incentive to promote the widest distribution across the nation of network programming irrespective of the tastes of one or more particular local cities. The widest possible distribution of programming, according to NAB/NASA, increases viewership of network programming, which maximizes network advertising revenues. According to NAB/NASA, maximum national exposure of programming also improves the likelihood that the program owner will realize additional revenues in the program syndication market. NAB/NASA contends that as broadcast networks have ownership stakes in a larger percentage of their prime time programming, their incentive to create programs with syndication value—and their incentive to stifle local preemption—increases.

542. NAB/NASA argues that the incentive of independently-owned affiliates, in contrast to network-owned stations, is to make programming decisions that are more closely aligned with the needs and tastes of their communities of license. A network derives its income from the programming that the network produces (and the syndication revenue

the programs might generate) as well as from its local stations. A local station maximizes its income by providing programming desired by its local community irrespective of national programming preferences. Therefore, the programming interests are not always the same.

(b) Evidence of Localism by Affiliates

543. NAB/NASA contends that the national cap is needed to preserve a body of network affiliates not owned by the network that can influence network programming so that it is more suited to the tastes and needs of the affiliates' communities. In support of this argument, NAB/NASA submitted several examples of the influence independent affiliates can have on network programming:

• When NBC aired a special edition of Fear Factor, featuring Playboy bunnies, during halftime of the Superbowl (airing on Fox), affiliates objected to the network promos, which ran during all hours of the day, and included tag lines such as "who needs football when we've got bunnies?"

• NAB/NASA states that when NBC began a trial program to accept liquor advertisements, so many affiliates opted out of airing the ads due to local concerns that NBC dropped the program.

• CBS had scheduled the Victoria's Secret Fashion Show for 8 p.m. The affiliates objected to the early showing and urged that the program be moved to the 10 p.m. time slot. In response, CBS moved the show to 9 P.M., although some affiliates nonetheless preempted the show as having inappropriate content for their service areas.

• Promotional ads for NBC's Dog Eat Dog included shots of nude contestants promoting the program's challenges such as "strip football" and "strip golf." When affiliates objected to the explicitness of the promos and their airing at all times of day, NBC agreed to eliminate strip stunts from future episodes.

• NYPD Blue was originally designed to include more nudity and graphic language than is currently aired, but after ABC affiliates objected, the amount of nudity and graphic language in the show was reduced. Even so, a number of affiliates initially refused to carry the show.

• Affiliates expressed concerns about the violent and nature content of the series Kingpin, which concerns the life of a drug lord. In response, NBC agreed to allow affiliates to review episodes in advance to ensure the content is appropriate for their local communities.

• In 2002, CBS worked with affiliates to reformat its morning news program, The Early Show. One key issue of affiliate concern was whether they would be permitted to provide local news content during the two-hour time block used by the program, as they had with CBS' prior show, CBS This Morning. Although some local affiliates are permitted to use the blended format with The Early Show, CBS has refused to permit other affiliates to move to the blended local-network news program format.

• NBC affiliates objected to NBC's intention to broadcast the 2002 Olympic Games live, which would have preempted the evening news on the west coast. After initially resisting the requests of the west coast affiliates to air a delayed broadcast during prime time, the network conducted a viewer survey. Results of the survey, however, substantiated the affiliates' assertion that west coast viewers preferred to watch the games during prime time, and the networks complied.

• NBC affiliates initially objected to NBC's decision to require live broadcasting of the XFL games. On the west coast, games substantially preempted both the affiliates' early evening local news and the national network news. In other parts of the country, overruns of the game preempted the late night local news. When affiliates raised similar concerns about Arena Football, claiming that overruns would preempt the 6 p.m. local newscasts on the east coast, the network agreed to work with the sports league to ensure the games do not run over.

• KYTV in Springfield, Missouri, preempted a January 6, 2003 episode of NBC's Fear Factor, which airs at 7 p.m. Central Time, that involved contestants eating horse rectums because it found the material inappropriate for its community.

544. Separate from this "collective negotiation" type of localism, parties also submitted evidence regarding the frequency of station-by-station preemptions for affiliates versus network-owned stations. Preemptions are instances in which local stations, whether they are owned and operated by networks or independently owned but affiliated with these networks, choose to air a program other than the program the network distributes to the station. The networks submitted data comparing prime time preemption rates of network-owned stations versus affiliates for 2001. That data showed that affiliates preempted an average of 9.5 hours of prime time programming per year compared with 6.8 hours per year for network-owned stations. The networks claim that this difference is inconsequential and does not justify retention of a national ownership cap. Affiliates assert that even this hand-picked data by networks confirms that affiliates preempt more than network-owned stations and that a national cap is needed to protect localism.

545. Affiliates seek to explain low preemption rates by arguing that networks have increasingly restricted preemption through their network-affiliate contracts. Cox argues that the networks have been exacting greater concessions from their affiliates, including demands to decrease the number of preemptions. Affiliates complain that they are subject to preemption caps involving financial penalties or loss of affiliation if they exceed the number of network-authorized preemptions, while affiliates' local programs are often "preempted" by network overruns (e.g., network sports overrunning local news). For example, Cox submits information gathered from its television stations in which the stations document their conflicts with the networks over network programming and local tastes and station preemptions. According to NAB/NASA, Fox allows only two preemptions per year, and NBC allows only five hours of

prime-time preemptions per year. Affiliates that exceed their allowable preemption "basket" may be subject to financial penalties or even loss of affiliation. Thus, while a majority of affiliates did not exceed their permitted preemptions, affiliates argue that there are good reasons for that result. In addition, affiliates note that they often maintain a "cushion" of unused preemption time in case it is needed, requiring them to exercise discretion in "spending" their preemption time during the year to avoid contractual financial penalties associated with excessive preemption.

546. *Discussion*. We find that a national television ownership cap is necessary to promote localism. The evidence before us demonstrates both that network affiliates have economic incentives more oriented towards localism than do network-owned stations, and that affiliates act on those incentives in ways that result in networks delivering programming more responsive to their local communities (in the judgment of the affiliate) than they otherwise would. In order for affiliates to continue to serve local community tastes and needs in this way, a national cap is needed to preserve a body of independently-owned affiliates. The two ways in which affiliates can promote localism are by collective negotiation to influence the programming that the networks provide and by preemption by an individual station owner to provide programming better suited to its community. * * *

549. We cannot agree with Fox that network-owned stations provide the same localism value that independently-owned affiliates do. Fox argues that networks listen to the management of network-owned stations as well as to the management of affiliates. It claims that managers of O&Os participate during the networks' program development process and provide more credible input than the management of affiliate stations. Fox also asserts that affiliates have an "inherent economic conflict" with the network regarding the distribution of profits, have no influence in the development of new programs, and learn of the new programs at the same time as do advertisers.

550. We agree with Fox that affiliates have an inherent economic conflict with networks. However, we believe that affiliates' economic incentives actually help explain why affiliates regularly raise programming concerns with networks and why affiliates preempt more network programming, on average, than do network-owned stations. In our view, affiliates' economic incentives to maximize local viewership works to promote localism.

551. In addition, Fox's claim of minimal affiliate influence over programming is overcome by the significant evidence submitted by NAB/NASA that affiliates regularly raise programming concerns with networks and frequently succeed in altering network programming in ways that protect local interests. These numerous instances of the collective influence brought to bear by affiliates on network programming decisions represents a powerful force for the protection of local viewing interests. They represent empirical evidence that affiliates col-

lectively serve as an important counterweight to network programming decisions by influencing networks to deliver programming responsive to local tastes.

552. In sum, we believe that this affiliate/network dynamic is beneficial to viewers and should be preserved. We conclude that eliminating the cap altogether would shift the balance of power with respect to programming decisions toward the national broadcast networks in a way that would disserve our localism policy.

Dealing for Dollars. If the localism explanation is not entirely new, the Commission's emphasis on network power does seem to be a new variable in the ever-changing formula of the public interest. For most of its history, the national ownership rule was not conceived as a means of containing network power. No such rationale appears in the 1984 report, for example. But when the networks became the chief protagonists for eliminating the rule, it became apparent that that one of the primary effects of doing so would be to shift the balance of power of networks *vis-à-vis* independently owned affiliates. The networks wanted to own more stations in order to lessen their dependence on independently owned affiliates for carrying ("clearing") network programs. The independently owned affiliates opposed for the same reason. Interestingly, so did the National Association of Broadcasters. Although the NAB generally purports to represent the entire industry, in this case the "industry" was divided and the association allied with the stations over the networks.

Although the debate over the "affiliate/network" dynamic is addressed solely in terms of program choice, it is unlikely that this was the only point of conflict. Networks and affiliates also bargain over compensation—the rates that networks pay affiliates for clearing network programs. Notice that the same "dynamic" that affects bargaining power with respect to preemption rates must also affect bargaining over those rates. As the networks increase the number of households that can be reached via their owned-and-operated stations, the importance of the marginal market, and the marginal affiliate, decreases. If the Commission is concerned about station autonomy in program choice, should it also be concerned about the distribution of income between networks and stations?

Quality Control by Local Affiliates. The Commission cites a number of examples of the baleful influence of networks in seeking to present program content or advertising that the affiliates believed to be in inappropriate (e.g., Playboy Bunnies, liquor ads, "strip football"). As we shall see in section D, the FCC's regulations are clear that stations cannot surrender their right and responsibility to reject programs they deem unsuitable; the right and the responsibility both come with the license. Would that be changed by allowing networks to own more stations? Is the implicit premise here that network owners are generally less sensitive to audience tastes than local owners? Or is it simply that networks are less sensitive to *special* audience tastes in distinctive markets (e.g., too many liquor ads in Utah)?

D. VERTICAL INTEGRATION IN BROADCASTING

The debate over the effect of the national ownership rules on the affiliate/network relationships and on localism reprises in part a long and complicated history of regulation of vertical relationships in the broadcast industry. The concern expressed about networks dominating stations can be traced to the early days of regulation. The central premise of the Commission's regulatory program was that it was the licensed stations who were answerable for the service they provided on the "public's airwaves." As it quickly developed, however, the networks called most of the program shots, first in radio and later in television. It was simply not economically feasible for local stations to produce their own quality programming. The only way such programming could be financed was to produce it for and distribute it to a national audience. This inevitably meant some kind of national system for developing and distributing programming, and this in turn meant that the effective control of programming choice shifted from stations to central program distributors—principally the networks. (Programs are also distributed via independent syndicators, but syndication arrangements involve particular programs or series of programs. Attention has always been centered on the networks because the continuous affiliation arrangements were seen as giving networks a long-term influence over licensee program choices.)

In 1938 the Commission instituted an investigation into "chain broadcasting" with a view toward promulgating regulations to limit network influence. The result three years later was a series of rules that survive to this day as the backbone of the network regulations. The chain broadcasting rules were primarily concerned about vertical integration of the industry, the control of the stations by the networks. The rules did deal with horizontal concentration in two respects. One, they forbade common ownership of more than one network, and required NBC to divest itself of one of its two networks (the divested network became ABC). Two, they imposed a restriction (one not confined to networks) against ownership of more than one station in any community—the beginning of the national ownership rule we just examined. Beyond these restrictions, the main thrust of the rules was not to regulate indirectly through ownership restrictions but instead to directly regulate the relationship between the networks and their affiliated stations. Before looking at the rules governing the network-affiliate relationship, it is important to know a few things about the structure or the relationship. On the economics of that relationship see Richard E. Caves, *Switching Channels* (2005); Stanley M. Besen, et al., *Misregulating Television* (1984).

Television networks function as both producers and distributors of programs.[1] The networks help to finance the production of programs, obtain advertising support for them and then distribute the product through their own stations ("owned and operated stations") or through independently owned affiliated stations. The affiliation agreements are multi-year agreements. At one time the FCC limited the affiliation agreements to two years, on the premise that longer term agreements gave the networks too much control over the stations. The two-year limit has long been eliminated and today the agreements are typically for 5 to 10 year (renewable) terms. The pattern of network-station affiliations tends to be fairly stable over time. In the early period of television, when most markets had only three stations and there were only three commercial broadcast networks (and no cable television), there was not much opportunity to shift alliances. Basically it was a kind of bilateral oligopoly: in any given market, if a network tired of an affiliate, there was no other station in the market to affiliate with, and *vice versa*. The appearance of the Fox network in the early 1990s destabilized this for a time by giving stations a new option for affiliation. (CBS lost many affiliates who shifted their allegiance to Fox for more attractive affiliation terms.) On the flip side, the increased number of stations in virtually all markets has given the networks new options for downstream partners. For the most part, however, the affiliation partnerships tend to be fairly stable over time.

The terms of the affiliation agreements vary somewhat but all have common features. For regular affiliations, the local station receives the exclusive rights to air the network programs within the designated market area. The exclusive right does not (and by FCC rules may not) preclude the network from offering a program to another station in the market if the affiliate refuses to carry it, but the affiliate has a first call on the programs. It is conventional to describe the arrangement as one in which networks buy "clearances"—air time—for scheduled network programs. One could as easily treat it as one in which the network sells (actually sublicenses) the program under a long term requirements contract. Either way, the agreement sets a series of terms and conditions for this clearance/sale—compensation, advertising breaks, and other terms. Compensation to the affiliate is a share of the national advertising revenue received by the network, as determined by the agreement's formula. However, stations also get revenues from their own advertising slots that are adjacent to those of the network, so advertising time slots are also part of the compensation arrangements. The amount of compensation a station receives obviously depends on the negotiating strength of the parties in the market. This in turn is a function of a number of market-specific variables, such as the size of the market and the strength

1. Historically, the television networks licensed programs produced by the film studios or independent producers. Although the networks helped to finance production, as we will discuss more fully below, they were effectively barred from merging with the studios or independent producers. That ban was removed in the early 1990s and subsequently all of the major networks merged with one of the major studios. Today, most but not all of the programs distributed by the networks are produced at least in part by studios that are affiliated with the network.

of the station (its circulation and ratings), as well as whether the station is owned by a multi-station owner (such as Sinclair Broadcasting or Belo) with affiliates in other markets. See Caves, *supra* at 261–72.

An affiliate may "preempt"—refuse to clear—a scheduled program. Under the FCC's rules (more on this below) the networks may not foreclose this right of preemption altogether. However, the standard affiliation agreements set various other limits on the number of preemptions—with financial or other penalties (including termination of the affiliation agreement) for exceeding the specified limits.[2]

Clearance versus preemption has always been a sore spot in network-station relationships. As we just saw, it was at the core of the dispute over the national/group ownership restrictions. The original limits on group ownerships prevented the networks from owning stations in all but a few markets, which meant they were economically dependent on the affiliated stations to obtain national distribution. As the ownership limits were raised that dependence diminished, and with it the network's leverage over affiliates increased. As we noted, the FCC's rationale for retaining (while raising) the ownership cap was grounded almost entirely on this concern: a relaxed cap would permit networks to own more stations, which would decrease the bargaining power of independently owned affiliates, which would undermine the local control of programming.

Attempting to limit the ability of networks to integrate downstream in order to decrease their dependence on affiliated stations (and also thereby to increase their leverage over affiliated stations) is only the latest in a long history of attempts by the FCC to regulate the networks in order to preserve local station power and prerogatives. We will not attempt to review the full history—which goes all the way back to the beginnings of regulation. Suffice it to say that the FCC began by focusing on the formal contractual relationship between network and affiliate on the (dubious) assumption that regulating the legal arrangements would also regulate the economic relationship.

1. The Network-Affiliate Relationship

The current FCC rules impose a number of restrictions on network affiliation agreements designed to protect the independence of stations in their choice of programming:

47 C.F.R. § 73.658 Affiliation agreements and network program practices; territorial exclusivity in non-network program arrangements.

(a) Exclusive affiliation of station. No license shall be granted to a television broadcast station having any contract, arrangement, or

2. For example the standard CBS agreement currently provides a "preemption penalty" for preemptions exceeding 15 hours of primetime programming annually, and possible termination for exceeding 20 hours. NBC's standard contract provides, among other things, for the station to reimburse the network for loss of gross advertising revenues for primetime preemptions exceeding 18 hours in a year (except for sports programs, where the number is 10). All of the network agreements allow the network to offer any preempted program to other stations in the market.

understanding, express or implied, with a network organization under which the station is prevented or hindered from, or penalized for, broadcasting the programs of any other network organization. (The term "network organization" as used in this section includes national and regional network organizations.)

(b) Territorial exclusively. No license shall be granted to a television broadcast station having any contract, arrangement, or understanding, express or implied, with a network organization which prevents or hinders another broadcast station located in the same community from broadcasting the network's programs not taken by the former station, or which prevents or hinders another broadcast station located in a different community from broadcasting any program of the network organization. This section shall not be construed to prohibit any contract, arrangement, or understanding between a station and a network organization pursuant to which the station is granted the first call in its community upon the programs of the network organization. As employed in this paragraph, the term "community" is defined as the community specified in the instrument of authorization as the location of the station.

(c) [Reserved]

(d) Station commitment of broadcast time. No license shall be granted to a television broadcast station having any contract, arrangement, or understanding, express or implied, with any network organization, which provides for optioning of the station's time to the network organization, or which has the same restraining effect as time optioning. As used in this section, time optioning is any contract, arrangement, or understanding, express or implied, between a station and a network organization which prevents or hinders the station from scheduling programs before the network agrees to utilize the time during which such programs are scheduled, or which requires the station to clear time already scheduled when the network organization seeks to utilize the time.

(e) Right to reject programs. No license shall be granted to a television broadcast station having any contract, arrangement, or understanding, express or implied, with a network organization which, with respect to programs offered or already contracted for pursuant to an affiliation contract, prevents or hinders the station from:

(1) Rejecting or refusing network programs which the station reasonably believes to be unsatisfactory or unsuitable or contrary to the public interest, or

(2) Substituting a program which, in the station's opinion, is of greater local or national importance.

(f) [Reserved]

(g) Dual network operation. A television broadcast station may affiliate with a person or entity that maintains two or more networks of television broadcast stations unless such dual or multiple networks are composed of two or more persons or entities that, on February 8, 1996, were "networks" as defined in § 73.3613(a)(1) of the Commission's regulations (that is, ABC, CBS, Fox, and NBC)

(h) Control by networks of station rates. No license shall be granted to a television broadcast station having any contract, arrangement, or understanding, express or implied, with a network organization under which the station is prevented or hindered from, or penalized for, fixing or altering its rates for the sale of broadcast time for other than the network's programs.

(i) No license shall be granted to a television broadcast station which is represented for the sale of non-network time by a network organization or by an organization directly or indirectly controlled by or under common control with a network organization, if the station has any contract, arrangement or understanding, express or implied, which provides for the affiliation of the station with such network organization: *Provided, however*, That this rule shall not be applicable to stations licensed to a network organization or to a subsidiary of a network organization.

(j) to (*l*) [Reserved]

(m) Territorial exclusivity in non-network arrangements.

(1) No television station shall enter into any contract, arrangement, or understanding, expressed or implied; with a non-network program producer, distributor, or supplier, or other person; which prevents or hinders another television station located in a community over 56.3 kilometers (35 miles) away* * * from broadcasting any program purchased by the former station from such non-network program producer, distributor, supplier, or other person [except in cases of so-called "hyphenated," or large, essentially joint, markets].

(2) Notwithstanding paragraph (m)(1) of this section, a television station may enter into a contract, arrangement, or understanding with a producer, supplier, or distributor of a non-network program if that contract, arrangement, or understanding provides that the broadcast station has exclusive national rights such that no other television station in the United States may broadcast the program.

Local Autonomy and Economic Reality. The ban on time optioning in subsection (d) is noteworthy because it represents the core controversy over the effect of networking on localism, which as we saw earlier is at the heart of the national ownership rules. Option time provisions required the affiliate either to pre-clear the time to the network before the program was identified or to *re*-schedule programming at the network's behest. The FCC's prohibition of option time reflects well the particular tension created by the FCC's insistence on localism in what turned out to be a national market. The assumption underlying the Communications Act and the FCC's implementation of it has always been that program choices would be locally determined. It was, after all, the stations not their program suppliers that were licensed to operate "in the public interest."[3] However, from a very early period it became apparent that the networks were economically the centerpiece of the industry; that is what prompted the chain broadcasting inquiry in 1938. Unfortunately, the economic reality was out of sync with the regulatory ideology. Licensing theory held the individual *stations* responsible for their programming, but the economic reality was that the national networks were basically in charge. While the FCC might stress the importance of its licensees being particularly attuned to local programming needs, the raw democratic fact was that most viewing *preferences*—put to one side local *needs* independent of viewing preferences—were homogeneous across geographic regions. Translating that into economics implies that, the larger the audience, the greater the advertising revenues, and the greater those revenues the more that can be spent on program production ("quality" in an economic, if not aesthetic, sense). This translates quite straight forwardly into a program choice function that is national not local, which in turn explains why programming choices became, *faute de mieux*, those made by the national networks.

Although the FCC saw the centrality of network control as a threat to the basic licensing theory—that local licensee choices were the key—it could not ignore the economic reality that was inherent in a system that depended on maximizing viewer preferences. Hence the dilemma: How to preserve local autonomy but at the same time preserve what had already become established as an economic reality of national determination of what the national audience wanted to see and hear? The networks were eager to secure a national audience so that they could secure the highest advertising revenues (which as we noted are shared with local affiliates according to the affiliation agreement's formula) for programming that was obtained (in this period usually from independent producers). However, for the FCC this was a compromise of the stations' autonomy and hence inconsistent with their license commitment to the FCC to make their own, independent judgment of the kind of programming that would suit the needs of their particular community (the community of license). So the FCC in 1963 banned "option time". 47 C.F.R. § 73.658(d). Question: As we noted above, the networks still impose financial penalties where the affiliates preempt network programs. How can such penalties be squared with the option time rule?

3. Notice in that respect that the FCC's regulations are formally directed to the stations not the networks, for the simple reason that under Title III of the Communications Act the FCC's regulatory power here is derived from its power to license broadcasters, not program producers. Stations are licensed, networks are not (except to the extent they are also licensees). Today, this is a pure formalism, since all the networks also own licensed stations. However, when the regulations were first promulgated, the formalism was considered important.

2. The Network–Supplier Relationship: Fin/Syn and PTAR

The abolition of option time did not significantly reduce the pattern of clearances by stations or the FCC's perception of network dominance. Because clearance rates are determined not simply by the formal contract option but by the underlying economic conditions that shaped the relative bargaining power between networks and stations,[4] the FCC could foreclose some ways by which that power was exercised, but short of a detailed managerial control of all aspects of network-station arrangements, merely controlling some of the contract options was bound to have minimal effect on program choices.

So the FCC shifted gears. Seeing that the abolition of option time did not adequately rein in the networks' control of program selection, the FCC soon turned to another alternative. This time instead of focusing on the networks' power *vis-á-vis* their affiliates—the downstream end of the distribution chain—the Commission directed its attention to the networks' power *vis-á-vis* independent program producers—the upstream connection. In the Commission's view, the networks' buying power—a function of their being the gatekeepers for affiliated stations which at that time dominated all local markets—allowed them to exercise undue control over programming, with consequent loss of diversity. The Commission adopted a twofold strategy.

Part one of the strategy was a set of rules called financial interest/syndication rules ("Fin/Syn," as they came to be called) which forbade the networks from engaging in domestic syndication (distributing programs directly to stations, usually after an initial period of direct network distribution) or from acquiring a permanent financial interest in programs that they licensed from independent producers for network distribution. The purpose here was to keep the networks from leveraging their market power for first-run network distribution into the market for second-run syndication rights. Keeping the networks from syndicating the shows they licensed from independent producers would theoretically enhance the profitability of program producers by giving them all of the "residual" interest in the programming after the initial network run. (There was a particular, though not unique, concern for the smaller independent producers who were less secure than the major film studios.) That added profitability would, the Commission assumed, give the producers greater independence from the networks and that would aid the cause of diversity.

Part two of the strategy was to limit the networks' power over access to the stations. The number of local stations was fixed by the allotment plan that the FCC had adopted in the 1950s, and although there had been some increase in the number of stations with the increased utilization of UHF frequencies, it did not appear at that time there would be any significant growth in the number of local outlets.

4. As we previously mentioned the network affiliation agreements do still provide limits on aggregative levels of station preemption, though they also recite the right of the broadcasters under 47 CFR § 658(e) to preempt.

This meant that the networks would be in a position to block independent program producers from distributing directly to the stations unless they were directly forbidden to control station choices. This in turn led to the second part of the strategy and a set of rules known as "prime time access rules" ("PTAR"). The PTAR rules forbade network affiliated stations from carrying any network programming during one hour of prime time. The expectation was that that this would provide a market for the non-network programs that the Commission expected its Fin/Syn rules to generate, with possibly local programming as an additional bonus.[5] The rules were upheld in *Mt. Mansfield Television, Inc. v. FCC,* 442 F.2d 470 (2d Cir.1971).

In time, the Commission itself gained a new perspective on the matter. The chief reason for the new perspective was that the networks declined in power. The emergence of a fourth network (Fox—which never came under the rules because in those years it did not have a full network schedule) diminished the power of the traditional trioply by giving local stations an alternative source of network programming. More significantly, the growth of cable with its multiple channel offerings took a heavy toll on network viewing. Though many of the viewers who defected from current broadcast network viewing tuned into former network programs now in syndication on cable, the Fin/Syn rules had deprived the networks of any financial gain from viewing old network fare while simultaneously barring them from supplying cable systems directly via syndication. Unless a change was made in the rules to give them better access to the future information superhighway, the networks would be increasingly marginalized as program brokers and distributors. Or so it was concluded. In 1970 the FCC had wanted to curb network power, but it had not contemplated such a decline in network fortunes that the combined force of new competition and Fin/Syn had produced. In 1983, after a lengthy internal staff study recommended abolition of the rules, the FCC tentatively voted to do so, only to back off after President Reagan, on behalf of his Hollywood friends, expressed concern. *Broadcasting,* Nov. 7, 1983, pp. 31–35; Oct. 24, pp. 27–29. In 1990 the FCC returned to the issue but, again, in the face of political pressure (though this time from Congress not the White House), it declined to repeal the rules. Instead, it relaxed some of the limits.

As is often the case with FCC rules, the revised rules were touted as "deregulatory," but to call them that is a somewhat Pickwickean use of the word. The rules did relax some of the old restraints but only by

5. The FCC did not specify any particular hour, but the networks selected, and the FCC informally approved, the first hour of what was then denoted "prime time"—7:00 to 8:00 Eastern and Pacific and 6:00–7:00 in Central and Mountain—as the open period. PTAR quickly developed into a kind of safe harbor for low budget game shows, such as "The Gong Show," "Bowling for Dollars," "The Dating Game," "The Newlywed Game" and others. Those interested in the history of bad television can find further information in Wikipedia. (Some of these programs had originated as network game shows, so they cannot be blamed entirely on PTAR, but it is part of the consensus wisdom that the access rule helped to secure their position in the market by removing competition from current network programs.)

adding new and complicated restrictions that were at least as "regulatory"—in the usual sense of that term—as the old. For example, the new rules removed restrictions on non-entertainment programming, but they forbade the networks from producing more than 40 percent of their own prime-time entertainment schedule. The new rules permitted a network to buy domestic syndication rights from outside producers of prime-time entertainment programming, but they forbade doing so as part of the original negotiations for licensing the programs for first-run viewing. (The theory was to prevent the networks from using the bargaining power they had in negotiating first-run licensing rights to extract second-run syndication rights by divorcing the first-run and second-run negotiations.) Moreover, a network could acquire syndication rights only for programs for which it obtained first-run rights—thus preventing networks from obtaining rights to distribute first-run programming to stations that were not affiliates. Finally, the revised rules forbade the networks from engaging in syndication themselves. They could only exercise their syndication rights by hiring an independent syndication firm to carry out the actual distribution.

As with the 1970 rules, the 1990 revised rules were appealed, but they received a very different reception (from a different court of appeals) than the original rules had twenty years earlier.

SCHURZ COMMUNICATIONS, INC. v. FCC

United States Court of Appeals, Seventh Circuit, 1992.
982 F.2d 1043.

POSNER, CIRCUIT JUDGE.

In 1970 the Federal Communications Commission adopted "financial interest and syndication" rules designed to limit the power of the then three television networks—CBS, NBC, and ABC—over television programming. * * *

Many syndicated programs are reruns, broadcast by independent stations, of successful comedy or dramatic series first shown on network television. Very few series are sufficiently successful in their initial run to be candidates for syndication. Independent stations like to air five episodes each week of a rerun series that originally had aired only once a week or less, so unless a series has a first run of several years—which few series do—it will not generate enough episodes to sustain a rerun of reasonable length. The financial interest and syndication rules thus severely limited the networks' involvement in supplying television programs other than for their own or their affiliated stations.

The concern behind the rules was that the networks, controlling as they did through their owned and operated stations and their affiliates a large part of the system for distributing television programs to American households, would unless restrained use this control to seize a dominating position in the production of television programs. That is, they would lever their distribution "monopoly" into a production "monopoly." They would, for example, refuse to buy programs for network distribution unless the producers agreed to surrender their syndication rights to the network. For once the networks controlled those rights, the access of independent television stations, that is, stations not owned by or affiliated with one of the networks, to reruns would be at the sufferance of the networks, owners of a competing system of distribution. Market power in buying has the same misallocative effects as the more common market power in selling. The relation is especially close in this case because the networks can just as well be viewed as sellers of a distribution service as they can be as buyers of programs—the less they pay for programs, the more in effect they charge for distributing them.

The Commission hoped the rules would strengthen an alternative source of supply (to the networks) for independent stations—the alternative consisting of television producers not owned by networks. The rules would do this by curtailing the ability of the networks to supply the program market represented by the independent stations, and by protecting the producers for that market against being pressured into giving up potentially valuable syndication rights. And the rules would strengthen the independent stations (and so derivatively the outside producers, for whom the independent stations were an important market along with the networks themselves) by securing them against having to purchase reruns from their competitors the networks.

The basis for this concern that the networks, octopus-like, would use their position in distribution to take over programming, and would use the resulting control of programming to eliminate their remaining competition in distribution, was never very clear. If the networks insisted on buying syndication rights along with the right to exhibit a program on the network itself, they would be paying more for their programming. (So one is not surprised that in the decade before the rules were adopted, the networks had acquired syndication rights to no more than 35 percent of their prime-time series, although they had acquired a stake in the syndicator's profits in a considerably higher percentage of cases.) If the networks then turned around and refused to syndicate independent stations, they would be getting nothing in return for the money they had laid out for syndication rights except a long-shot chance—incidentally, illegal under the antitrust laws—to weaken the already weak competitors of network stations. Nor was it clear just how the financial interest and syndication rules would scotch the networks' nefarious schemes. If forbidden to buy syndication rights, networks would pay less for programs, so the outside producers would not come out clear winners—indeed many would be losers. Production for television is a highly risky undertaking, like wildcat drilling for gas and oil. Most television entertainment programs are money losers. The losses are offset by the occasional hit that makes it into syndication after completing a long first run. The sale of syndication rights to a network would enable a producer to shift risk to a larger, more diversified entity presumptively better able to bear it. The resulting reduction in the risks of production would encourage new entry into production and thus give the independent stations a more competitive supply of programs. Evidence introduced in this proceeding showed that, consistent with this speculation, networks in the pre-1970 era were more likely to purchase syndication rights from small producers than from large ones.

Whatever the pros and cons of the original financial interest and syndication rules, in the years since they were promulgated the structure of the television industry has changed profoundly. The three networks have lost ground, primarily as a result of the expansion of cable television, which now reaches 60 percent of American homes, and videocassette recorders, now found in 70 percent of American homes. Today each of the three networks buys only 7 percent of the total video and film programming sold each year, which is roughly a third of the percentage in 1970. (The inclusion of films in the relevant market is appropriate because videocassettes enable home viewers to substitute a film for a television program.) And each commands only about 12 percent of total television advertising revenues. Where in 1970 the networks had 90 percent of the prime-time audience, today they have 62 percent, and competition among as well as with the three networks is fierce. They are, moreover, challenged today by a fourth network, the Fox Broadcasting Corporation, which emerged in the late 1980s.

Notwithstanding the fourth network, which might have been expected to reduce the number of independent stations by converting many of them to network—Fox network—stations, the number of independent stations has increased fivefold since 1970. At the same time, contrary to the intention behind the rules yet an expectable result of them because they made television production a riskier business, the production of prime-time programming has become more concentrated. There are 40 percent fewer producers of prime-time programming today than there were two decades ago. And the share of that programming accounted for directly or indirectly by the eight largest producers, primarily Hollywood studios—companies large enough to bear the increased risk resulting from the Commission's prohibition against the sale of syndication rights to networks—has risen from 50 percent to 70 percent.

The original rules had been supported by the Antitrust Division of the Department of Justice. But as the years passed, antitrust thinking changed. The "leverage" theory, which taught that a firm having economic power in one market would use it to acquire a monopoly of another market, was widely discredited. The evolution of the television industry, sketched above, suggested that the rules, if they were having any effect at all, were working perversely from a competitive standpoint. An extensive staff study ordered by the Commission concluded that the rules were obsolete and recommended that they be abandoned. In 1983 the Commission issued a tentative decision agreeing with the staff, proposing radical revisions in the rules leading to their eventual repeal, but inviting further public comments on the details of its proposals. The networks, the Commission found in the tentative decision, had lost any significant monopoly or market power that they may once have had. The financial interest and syndication rules were hampering the entry of new firms into production by blocking an important mechanism (the sale of syndication rights) by which new firms might have shifted the extraordinary risks of their undertaking to the networks.

Mainly as a result of congressional pressure, there was no follow-up to the tentative decision. The question what to do about the rules remained in limbo until 1990, when the Commission at the request of the Fox network initiated a fresh notice-and-comment rulemaking proceeding. After receiving voluminous submissions from the various segments of the television industry, the Commission held a one-day hearing, after which it issued an opinion, over dissents by two of the five commissioners, including the chairman, promulgating a revised set of financial interest and syndication rules. * * *

The new rules, like their predecessors, appear to harm rather than to help outside producers as a whole (a vital qualification) by reducing their bargaining options. It is difficult to see how taking away a part of a seller's market could help the seller. One of the rights in the bundle of rights that constitutes the ownership of a television program is the right to syndicate the program to non-network stations. The new rules restrict—perhaps, as a practical matter, prevent—the sale of that right to networks. How could it help a producer to be forbidden to sell his wares to a class of buyers that may be the high bidders for them? It is not as if anyone supposed that syndication rights, like babies or human freedom or the vital organs of a living person, should not be salable at all. They are freely salable—except to networks. Since syndication is the riskiest component of a producer's property right—for its value depends on the distinctly low-probability event that the program will be a smash hit on network television—restricting its sale bears most heavily on the smallest, the weakest, the newest, the most experimental producers, for they are likely to be the ones least able to bear risk. It becomes understandable why the existing producers support the financial interest and syndication rules: the rules protect these producers against new competition both from the networks (because of the 40 percent cap [on the amount of prime-time programming the networks may produce themselves]) and from new producers. The ranks of the outside producers of prime-time programming have been thinned under the regime of financial interest and syndication rules. The survivors are the beneficiaries of the thinning. They do not want the forest restored to its pristine density. They consent to have their own right to sell syndication rights curtailed as the price of a like restriction on their potential competitors, on whom it is likely to bear more heavily.

This analysis of risk and its bearing on competition in the program industry is speculative, theoretical, and may for all we know be all wet—though it is corroborated by the increasing concentration of the production industry since the rules restricting the sale of syndication rights were first imposed in 1970. The Commission was not required to buy the analysis. But as the analysis was more than plausible and had been pressed upon it by a number of participants in the rulemaking proceeding—including a putatively disinterested Justice Department that in the past had frequently seen the bogeyman of monopoly lurking everywhere, as well as the Commission's own chairman—the Commission majority was not entitled to ignore it. Not even to consider the possibility that the unrestricted sale of syndication rights to networks would strengthen the production industry (the industry—not necessarily its present occupants) and thereby increase programming diversity by enabling a sharing between fledgling producers and the networks of the risks of new production was irresponsible. For if the argument about risk sharing is correct, the rules are perverse; by discouraging the entry of new producers into the high-risk prime-time entertainment market, they are likely to reduce the supply of programs to the independent stations and so reduce diversity both of program sources and of program outlets. The Commission's stated desiderata are competition and diversity. The rules adopted by the Commission in order to achieve these desiderata have the remarkable property—if the risk-sharing argument that the Commission did not deign to address is correct—of disserving them both.

Central to the Commission's decision to continue restricting the networks' participation in programming is its belief that whether or not they have market power in some antitrust sense they have the power to force producers to sell them programs for less than the programs would be worth in a fully competitive market. The networks call this a contradiction: either they have market power, or they don't; there is no middle ground. A rational commission could disagree. Market power is a matter of degree. Some firms have a lot of it, some a little, some none. It is plausible that each network, even when not colluding with the others (there is no evidence that they are colluding), has some market power and thus can drive a harder bargain with producers than it could do if it had none. Even though each of the three major networks has only about 20 percent of the prime-time audience and a producer who does not sell his program to a network can still hope to distribute it to the public via independent stations and cable networks, or for that matter movie theaters and videocassette dealers, network distribution offers advertisers unique simultaneous access to a large fraction of American households and increases the prospects for successful syndication, which apparently is where the real money in the creation of television entertainment is to be made.

The difficulty is that if the networks do have market power, the new rules (in this respect like the old) do not seem rationally designed to prevent its exercise. A rule telling a person he may not do business with some firm believed to have market power is unlikely to make the person better off. Suppose that in a competitive market a network would pay $2 million for first-run rights to some program and $1 million for syndication rights, for a total of $3 million, but that because of the lack of perfect substitutes for using this network to distribute his program the producer is willing to sell each of these rights to the network for half their competitive-market value (i.e., for $1 million and $500,000 respectively). The producer is made no better off by being forbidden to sell the syndication rights to the network. He gets the same meager first-run license fee ($1 million) and now must cast about for another buyer for the syndication rights. That other buyer is unlikely to pay more than the network would ($500,000); otherwise the producer would have sold the syndication rights to him in the first place. It is no answer that the network would not have given the producer the option of selling it only first-run rights, that it would have insisted on the whole package so that it could control the program supply of the independent stations, which are heavily dependent on reruns and hence on syndication. The producer might indeed be desperate for network distribution, but that desperation would be reflected in the low price at which he was willing to sell the network whatever rights the network wanted. He cannot do better by being forbidden to make such a deal. If he could do better by selling syndication rights to someone else he would not accede to such unfavorable terms as the network offered.

If this is right, the new rules, at least insofar as they restrict network syndication, cannot increase the prices that producers receive. All they can do is increase the costs of production by denying producers the right to share risks with networks. * * *

Reruns. The term "reruns" is commonly used, as in the above case, to refer to programming that is aired on the station after it has completed its network run, i.e., programming that is in syndication. The term is also sometimes used to refer to a repeat of episodes within a first-run network period. These repeats do not involve syndicated distribution; they are part of the original network distribution.[6] In the early years of television the common practice was to produce 39 original episodes, with 13 repeats to fill out a 52 week season. Today, the usual number of original episodes for a traditional series in prime time is 22, interleaved with repeats, over a standard 35 week season.[7] The reduction in originals was driven by supply-side production costs. As program production costs increased for high quality entertainment programming (in significant measure as a function of the impressive salaries com-

6. We are here concerned with post-network syndication of programming. Many programs are produced for first-run syndicated distribution and never intended for network clearance. Sometimes these will be spin-offs of programs first developed for network distribution—as with some of the Star Trek spinoffs (e.g., "Star Trek: Deep Space Nine").

7. Roughly the initial development pattern goes through a sequence of stages, from concept, to script, to pilot (or a handful of episodes), to a test run of the pilot in prime time, to full production. Once a network commits to a series it enters into a licensing agreement with the producer. For a new series a network normally commits to only 13 episodes (a Fall season) with an option on the remaining 9; however, in exceptional cases a commitment may be made for a full season or even more. The terms of the license between the network and the producer vary. The amount of the license fee will depend most importantly on how they share series production costs, and syndication rights. Of course, if the program is produced "in house" by a studio affiliated with the network (Disney-ABC; NBC-Universal; CBS-Paramount; Fox-Fox) these costs and corresponding rights and risks will all be internal to the firm. However, all of the networks continue to work with independent producers; indeed, often the studios themselves partner with independent producers.

manded by star talent[8]), it became that much more costly to produce originals. In recent years, however, increasing the number of repeats in a season has become problematic for the networks because of pressure from the demand side. A combination of competition from cable and satellite providers, and digital video recording devices (e.g., TiVo) has diminished viewer interest in network repeats. Squeezed between increased production costs on the one hand and increased competition on the other, the networks have increasingly looked to other scheduling strategies, including short-run series consisting of all original episodes, but with minimal talent costs. Low-budget "reality" series and game shows, particularly in early prime time, have become a salient part of this strategy.

The economics of syndicated reruns involve some of the same problems. The high cost of producing original programs means that even a successful network series is unlikely to recover its full production costs from the network run alone. Profitability depends on domestic and foreign syndication. Ownership of the syndication rights thus become a critical element in the investment calculus for program production. When the FCC in 1970 denied the networks the right to buy a financial interest in syndication, it did so in the belief that the networks were using their monopsony buying power to force producers (particularly the small independent producers) into selling all or part of their syndication rights to the networks. As Judge Posner points out in *Schurz*, the FCC did not consider the possibility that these rights were simply a deferred compensation for bearing the cost (and the risk) of upfront production costs. If the networks were forbidden to pay that compensation, they would inevitably bear less of the upfront costs. The Fin/Syn rules had not really affected whatever monopsony power the networks had (though PTAR did affect that somewhat); it simply limited the type of financial deals they could make with the producers. If the producers retained all the residuals as the Fin/Syn rules required, they would simply have to bear that much more of the upfront production costs, and the considerable risk that their investment in high-priced programming would not be repaid if the series was a dud in the network run, or in later syndication. For more on the economics of program production, and the Fin/Syn rules see Besen, et al., *Misregulating Television*, *supra*, at chaps. 7–8. (The authors were principal authors and consultants to the FCC's 1980 Staff Study, referred to in *Schurz*: FCC Network Inquiry Special Staff, *New Television Networks: Entry, Jurisdiction, Ownership and Regulation* (1980). Though somewhat dated now, the study is still a valuable source of information on network economics and the history of the FCC's network regulations.)

8. In 2002 Ray Romano broke previous salary records with $1.8 million per episode (a half hour) for the last two years of "Everyone Loves Raymond." When a series has more than one megastar, the numbers really escalate, as with "Friends" where each of the six stars earned $1 million per half-hour episode for their last two seasons. For a 47-year chronology of newsworthy primetime star salaries and salary demands, see Lynette Rice & Jennifer Armstrong, *Deal or No Deal*, Entertainment Weekly, March 30, 2007.

End of an Era. On remand from *Schurz*, the Commission repealed the rules, subject to a two-year transitional period. The court of appeals affirmed the FCC's allowance of a two-year transition over the objection of the networks. *Capital Cities/ABC, Inc. v. FCC*, 29 F.3d 309 (7th Cir. 1994). The repeal of Fin/Syn did not of its own force affect the prime time access rules, but, because PTAR and Fin/Syn were originally conceived as complementary rules it was almost inevitable that the FCC would be asked to repeal PTAR. It was and it did, in 1995. *Prime Time Access Rule*, 11 FCC Rcd. 546 (1995).[9]

The immediate effect of the elimination of the Fin/Syn rules was to spark an interest in vertical integration of Hollywood studios and the major networks. Beginning in 1995 with the merger of Disney and ABC/Cap Cities, each of the major networks soon became integrated with a major Hollywood film studio (Fox was already integrated, but as noted above, it was not at that time treated as a full-schedule network and was thus exempt from the Fin/Syn rules).

E. HORIZONTAL CONCENTRATION IN CABLE OWNERSHIP

Until the 1990s, there was no limit on the number of cable systems that could be held under common ownership. In response to controversies concerning alleged anticompetitive practices by some of the large cable system group owners, Congress adopted section 11(c)(2) of the Cable Communications Consumer Protection and Competition Act of 1992, codified at 47 U.S.C. § 533(f), which mandated the Commission to promulgate both (horizontal) limits on the number of subscribers that could be served by systems under common ownership and (vertical) limits on the number of program channels that could be supplied by affiliated networks.[10]

The Commission responded with two sets of rules. First, on the horizontal aspect it established a 30% limit on the number of homes passed nationwide that any one entity can reach through cable systems in which such entity has an attributable interest. Second, on the vertical aspect, it adopted a 40% limit on the number of channels that can be occupied on a vertically integrated cable system by video programmers in

9. One effect of the PTAR has remained: the networks never attempted to "take back" control of the 7–8pm segment so for network purposes "prime time" now denotes the period 8–11pm.

10. Among other things section 533(f)(1) requires the Commission,

(A) to prescribe rules and regulations establishing reasonable limits on the number of cable subscribers a person is authorized to reach through cable systems owned by such person, or in which such person has an attributable interest;

(B) to prescribe rules and regulations establishing reasonable limits on the number of channels on a cable system that can be occupied by a video programmer in which a cable operator has an attributable interest; and

(C) to consider the necessity and appropriateness of imposing limitations on the degree to which multichannel video programming distributors may engage in the creation or production of video programming.

which the cable operator has an attributable interest.[11] After a long-delayed appeal, the Court of Appeals for the District of Columbia upheld the facial validity of the statute in 2000, deciding that the limits were content-neutral and therefore should be subjected to intermediate scrutiny. See *Time Warner Entertainment Co. v. United States*, 211 F.3d 1313 (D.C. Cir. 2000) (*Time Warner I*). The decision to apply intermediate scrutiny was a fairly straightforward application of earlier Supreme Court precedent, which we will address in the next chapter. Having lost their facial challenge against the statute, the cable operators brought an as-applied challenge against the regulations promulgated by the FCC, and a year later, the court struck down both the horizontal and vertical restrictions, partly as an improper regulation under the statute and partly because they failed the intermediate scrutiny standard adopted in *Time Warner I*. For analytical convenience, we separate the horizontal from the vertical (which we address in the next section), though as we shall see, in some respects both horizontal and vertical restrictions are directed to a common concern in the case of cable—more so than the analogous restrictions adopted in the broadcast context.

TIME WARNER ENTERTAINMENT CO. v. FCC

United States Court of Appeals, District of Columbia Circuit, 2001.
240 F.3d 1126.

WILLIAMS, CIRCUIT JUDGE:

Section 11(c) of the Cable Television Consumer Protection and Competition Act of 1992, ("1992 Cable Act"), amends 47 U.S.C. § 533 to direct the Federal Communications Commission to set two types of limits on cable operators. The first type is horizontal, addressing operators' scale: "limits on the number of cable subscribers a person is authorized to reach through cable systems owned by such person, or in which such person has an attributable interest." The second type is vertical, addressing operators' integration with "programmers" (suppliers of programs to be carried over cable systems): "limits on the number of channels on a cable system that can be occupied by a video programmer in which a cable operator has an attributable interest." The FCC has duly promulgated regulations. Petitioners Time Warner and AT&T challenge the horizontal limit as in excess of statutory authority, as unconstitutional infringements of their freedom of speech, and as products of arbitrary and capricious decisionmaking which violate the Administrative Procedure Act. Time Warner similarly challenges the vertical limit. Together with AT&T, Time Warner also challenges as arbitrary

11. In addition to this limit on vertical integration, section 548 prohibits practices designed to hinder a multichannel video program distributor from providing satellite cable programming or satellite broadcast programming to subscribers or consumers. Among other things this section prohibits discrimination by a satellite cable programming vendor in which cable operators have an attributable ownership interest and satellite broadcast program distributors in the prices or terms and conditions of supplying programs among cable operators or other multichannel video programming distributors.

and capricious the rules for determining what counts as an "attributable interest."[*] Concluding that the FCC has not met its burden under the First Amendment and, in part, lacks statutory authority for its actions, we remand for further consideration of both limits. In addition we vacate specific portions of the attribution rules as lacking rational justification. * * *

The horizontal rule imposes a 30% limit on the number of subscribers that may be served by a multiple cable system operator ("MSO"). Both the numerator and denominator of this fraction include only current subscribers to multichannel video program distributor ("MVPD") services. Subscribers include not only users of traditional cable services but also subscribers to non-cable MVPD services such as Direct Broadcast Satellite ("DBS"), a rapidly growing segment of the MVPD market. The Commission pointed out that under this provision the nominal 30% limit would allow a cable operator to serve 36.7% of the nation's cable subscribers if it served none by DBS. In an express effort to encourage competition through new provision of cable, the Commission excluded from any MSO's numerator all new subscribers signed up by virtue of "overbuilding," the industry's term for cable laid in competition with a pre-existing cable operator. Further, subscribers to a service franchised after the rule's adoption (October 20, 1999) do not go into an MSO's numerator, even if not the result of an overbuild. As a result, the rule's main bite is on firms obtaining subscribers through merger or acquisition.

The vertical limit is currently set at 40% of channel capacity, reserving 60% for programming by non-affiliated firms. Channels assigned to broadcast stations, leased access, and for public, educational, or governmental uses are included in the calculation of channel capacity. Capacity over 75 channels is not subject to the limit, so a cable operator is never required to reserve more than 45 channels for others (.60 x 75 = 45).

As cable operators, Time Warner and AT&T "exercise[ ] editorial discretion in selecting the programming [they] will make available to [their] subscribers," and are "entitled to the protection of the speech and press provisions of the First Amendment," *Turner Broadcasting System, Inc. v. Federal Communications Commission*, 512 U.S. 622 (1994) ("*Turner I*") (*quoting Leathers v. Medlock*, 499 U.S. 439, 444 (1991)). The horizontal limit interferes with petitioners' speech rights by restricting the number of viewers to whom they can speak. The vertical limit restricts their ability to exercise their editorial control over a portion of the content they transmit.

In *Time Warner I* we upheld the statutory provisions against a facial attack, after finding them subject to intermediate rather than, as the

* Eds. The FCC used the broadcasting rules for attribution: a 5% stock ownership interest or an investment interest that exceeds 33% of the total asset value (equity plus debt) of the applicable entity is sufficient to create a common ownership. Except for one minor detail the court affirmed the FCC's attribution rules.

cable firms argued, strict scrutiny. The regulations here present a related but independent set of questions. Constitutional authority to impose some limit is not authority to impose any limit imaginable.

In briefs written before the issuance of *Time Warner I*, petitioners argued here for strict scrutiny. At oral argument they withdrew from this position and said, euphemistically, that they were "happy to stand on intermediate scrutiny." Because of that concession and, in any event, not seeing any distinction between the statute and the regulations for level of-scrutiny purposes, we apply intermediate scrutiny. Under the formula set forth *in United States v. O'Brien*, 391 U.S. 367, 377 (1968), and reaffirmed by *Turner Broadcasting System, Inc. v. Federal Communications Commission*, 520 U.S. 180, 189 (1997) ("*Turner II*"), a governmental regulation subject to intermediate scrutiny will be upheld if it "advances important governmental interests unrelated to the suppression of free speech and does not burden substantially more speech than necessary to further those interests."

The interests asserted in support of the horizontal and vertical limits are the same interrelated interests that we found sufficient to support the statutory scheme in *Time Warner I*: "the promotion of diversity in ideas and speech" and "the preservation of competition." After a review of the legislative history, we concluded that Congress had drawn "reasonable inferences, based upon substantial evidence, that increases in the concentration of cable operators threatened diversity and competition in the cable industry." But the FCC must still justify the limits that it has chosen as not burdening substantially more speech than necessary. In addition, in "demonstrat[ing] that the recited harms are real, not merely conjectural," the FCC must show a record that validates the regulations, not just the abstract statutory authority.

The FCC asserts that a 30% horizontal limit satisfies its statutory obligation to ensure that no single "cable operator or group of cable operators can unfairly impede ... the flow of video programming from the video programmer to the consumer," while adequately respecting the benefits of clustering and the economies of scale that are thought to come with larger size. It interpreted this statutory language as a directive to prohibit large MSOs—either by the action of a single MSO or the coincidental or collusive actions of several MSOs—from precluding the entry into the market of a new cable programmer. In setting the limit at 30%, it assumed there was a serious risk of collusion. But while collusion is a form of anti-competitive behavior that implicates an important government interest, the FCC has not presented the "substantial evidence" required by *Turner I* and *Turner II* that such collusion has in fact occurred or is likely to occur; so its assumptions are mere conjecture. The FCC alternatively relies on its supposed grant of authority to regulate the non-collusive actions of large MSOs. Congress may indeed, under certain readings of *Turner I* and *Turner II*, have the power to regulate the coincidental but independent actions of cable operators solely in the interest of diversity, but "[w]here an administrative interpretation of a statute invokes the outer limits of Congress' power, we expect a clear indication that Congress intended that result." The 1992 Cable Act, as we shall see, instead expresses the contrary intention. * * *

Part VI of [the implementing regulation] lays out the calculations that lead the FCC to the 30% limit. First the FCC determines that the average cable network needs to reach 15 million subscribers to be economically viable. This is 18.56% of the roughly 80 million MVPD subscribers, and the FCC rounds it up to 20% of such subscribers. The FCC then divines that the average cable programmer will succeed in reaching only about 50% of the subscribers linked to cable companies that agree to carry its programming, because of channel capacity, "programming tastes of particular cable operators," or other factors. The average programmer therefore requires an "open field" of 40% of the market to be viable (.20/.50 = .40).

Finally, to support the 30% limit that it says is necessary to assure this minimum, the Commission reasons as follows: With a 30% limit, a programmer has an "open field" of 40% of the market even if the two largest cable companies deny carriage, acting "individually or collusively." A 50% rule is inadequate because, if a duopoly were to result, "[t]he probability of tacit collusion is higher with 2 competitors than 3 competitors." Even if collusion were not to occur, independent rejections by two MSOs could doom a new programmer, thwarting congressional intent as the Commission saw it. A 40% limit is insufficient for the same reason: "two MSOs, . . . representing a total of 80% of the market, might decline to carry the new network" and leave only 20% "open," which by hypothesis is not enough (because of the 50% success rate). Although the Commission doesn't spell out the intellectual process, it is necessarily defining the requisite "open field" as the residue of the market after a programmer is turned down either (1) by one cable company acting alone, or (2) by a set of companies acting either (a) collusively or (b) independently but nonetheless in some way that, because of the combined effect of their choices, threatens fulfillment of the statutory purposes. * * * Assuming the validity of the premises supporting the FCC's conclusion that a 40% "open field" is necessary (a question that we need not answer here), the statute's express concern for the act of "any individual operator" would justify a horizontal limit of 60%. To reach the 30% limit, the FCC's action necessarily involves one or the other of two additional propositions: Either there is a material risk of collusive denial of carriage by two or more companies, or the statute authorizes the Commission to protect programmers against the risk of completely independent rejections by two or more companies leaving less than 40% of the MVPD audience potentially accessible. Neither proposition is sound. * * *

The only justification that the FCC offers in support of its collusion hypothesis is the economic commonplace that, all other things being equal, collusion is less likely when there are more firms. This observation will always be true, although marginally less so for each additional firm; but by itself it lends no insight into the question of what the appropriate horizontal limit is. *Turner I* demands that the FCC do more than "simply 'posit the existence of the disease sought to be cured.'" * * *

That having been said, we do not foreclose the possibility that there are theories of anti-competitive behavior other than collusion that may be relevant to the horizontal limit and on which the FCC may be able to rely on remand. Indeed, Congress considered, among other things, the ability of MSOs dominant in specific cable markets to extort equity from programmers or force exclusive contracts on them. A single MSO, acting alone rather than "jointly," might perhaps be able to do so while serving somewhat less than the 60% of the market (i.e., less than the fraction that would allow it unilaterally to lock out a new cable programmer) despite the existence of antitrust laws and specific behavioral prohibitions enacted as part of the 1992 Cable Act, and the risk might justify a prophylactic limit under the statute. So the absence of any showing of a serious risk of collusion does not necessarily preclude a finding of a sufficient governmental interest in preventing unfair competition. (We express no opinion on whether exploitation of a monopoly position in a specific cable market to extract rents that would otherwise flow to programmers alone gives rise to an "important governmental interest" justifying a burden on speech.) But the FCC made no attempt to justify its regulation on these grounds. * * *

With the risk of collusion inadequately substantiated to support the 30% limit and no attempt to find other anticompetitive behavior, there remains the Commission's alternative ground—that programming choices made "unilaterally" by multiple cable companies, might reduce a programmer's "open field" below the 40% benchmark. The only support the Commission offered for regulation based on this possibility was the idea that every additional chance for a programmer to secure access would enhance diversity:

[T]he 30% limit serves the salutary purpose of ensuring that there will be at least 4 MSOs in the marketplace. The rule thus maximizes the potential number of MSOs that will purchase programming. With more MSOs making purchasing decisions, this increases the likelihood that the MSOs will make different programming choices and a greater variety of media voices will therefore be available to the public.

Petitioners challenge the FCC's authority to regulate for this purpose on both constitutional and statutory grounds.

We have some concern how far such a theory may be pressed against First Amendment norms. Everything else being equal, each additional "voice" may be said to enhance diversity. And in this special context, every additional splintering of the cable industry increases the number of combinations of companies whose acceptance would in the aggregate lay the foundations for a programmer's viability. But at some point, surely, the marginal value of such an increment in "diversity" would not qualify as an "important" governmental interest. Is moving from 100 possible combinations to 101 "important"? It is not clear to us how a court could determine the point where gaining such an increment is no longer important. And it would be odd to discover that although a newspaper that is the only general daily in a metropolitan area cannot be subjected to a right of reply, it could in the name of diversity be forced to self-divide. Certainly the Supreme Court has not gone so far.

We need not face that issue, however, because we conclude that Congress has not given the Commission authority to impose, solely on the basis of the "diversity" precept, a limit that does more than guarantee a programmer two possible outlets (each of them a market adequate for viability). * * *

On the record before us, we conclude that the 30% horizontal limit is in excess of statutory authority. While a 60% limit might be appropriate as necessary to ensure that programmers had an adequate "open field" even in the face of rejection by the largest company, the present record supports no more. In addition, the statute allows the Commission to act prophylactically against the risk of "unfair" conduct by cable operators that might unduly impede the flow of programming, either by the "joint" actions of two or more companies or the independent action of a single company of sufficient size. But the Commission has pointed to nothing in the record supporting a non-conjectural risk of anticompetitive behavior, either by collusion or other means. Accordingly, we reverse and remand with respect to the 30% rule." * * *

After remand the cable ownership cap languished at the Commission for six years. Finally, on the same day that it announced its new broadcast-newspaper rules, the FCC announced a re-adoption of the same 30% cap on cable ownership that had been earlier struck down.

CABLE HORIZONTAL AND VERTICAL OWNERSHIP LIMITS
Fourth Report & Order and Further Notice of Proposed Rulemaking

Federal Communications Commission, 2008.
23 FCC Rcd. 2134.

BY THE COMMISSION:

I. INTRODUCTION

1. In this *Fourth Report and Order*, we set the Commission's cable horizontal ownership limit to prohibit cable operators from owning or having an attributable interest in cable systems serving more than 30 percent of multichannel video programming subscribers nationwide. Our decision implements the statutory directive that we impose a limit designed to ensure that no single cable operator or group of operators,

because of its size, can unfairly impede the flow of programming to consumers. Our action also responds to the court's concerns in *Time Warner Entertainment Co. v. FCC* (*"Time Warner II"*), that the Commission had failed adequately to justify the 30 percent limit.

2. In establishing the 30 percent cable horizontal ownership limit, we rely on a modified "open field" approach to ensure that no single cable operator becomes so large that a programming network can survive only if that operator carries it. To calculate a horizontal limit that meets this test, we first determine the minimum number of subscribers a network needs in order to survive in the marketplace and then estimate the percentage of subscribers a network is likely to serve once it secures a carriage contract. The resulting calculation indicates that an open field of 70 percent and an ownership limit of 30 percent are necessary to ensure that no single cable operator is able to impede unfairly the flow of programming to consumers.

3. In the *Further Notice of Proposed Rulemaking*, we seek further comment on (1) whether to retain the single majority shareholder attribution exemption, which currently applies to the cable and broadcast ownership rules; (2) whether, under the cable attribution rules, a limited partner may sell programming to the partnership and retain insulation; and (3) whether the Commission should clarify certain aspects of the cable Equity Debt ("ED") attribution rule, as it did for the broadcast Equity/Debt Plus attribution rule. We also invite comment in the *Further Notice* on an appropriate channel occupancy limit, because the record evidence so far is inadequate to allow us to set such a limit.

II. Fourth Report & Order

* * *

13. In 2002, the Commission sought to obtain empirical data and information by conducting a programming network survey and an experimental economics analysis, and it sought comment on theoretical analyses designed to determine the relationship between bargaining power and buyer size in a bilateral bargaining environment. * * * While these analyses of bargaining power show that increasing horizontal size imparts increased bargaining power to the largest buyer of video programming, they did not indicate the point at which such increased bargaining power is likely to impede the flow of programming to consumers.

14. In 2005, the Commission again sought comment to update and supplement the record. The Commission observed that three significant events had changed the structure of the media industry since the close of the record on the *2001 Further Notice*: (1) the 2002 Comcast-AT&T cable transaction had resulted in one entity having a share of MVPD subscribers very close to the remanded 30 percent ownership limit; (2) the 2003 News Corp.-Hughes transaction had created the first vertically integrated DBS operator, involving a number of video programming assets; and (3) courts had remanded several media ownership rules, requiring that the Commission more firmly base its rules on empirical data and record

evidence. The Commission sought comment on the proposals in the record, recent developments in the industry, and certain tentative conclusions. It asked commenters to supplement the record where possible by providing new evidence and information to support the formulation of horizontal and vertical limits, and invited parties to undertake their own studies in order to further inform the record. The Commission also sought comment on three analytical frameworks for determining whether, and at what level, a cable operator's size is likely to impede the flow of programming to consumers or diminish effective competition: (1) the open field approach, (2) an approach based on monopsony theory, and (3) an approach based on bargaining power as a source of unilateral anti-competitive action. Finally, the Commission invited comment on Media Bureau Staff Research Paper No. 2004-1, which examined the effect of subscribership on a network's ability to survive in the marketplace.

B. Analytical Framework

1. Background

* * *

a. The Open Field Approach

18. The open field approach determines whether a programming network would have access to alternative MVPDs of sufficient size to allow it to successfully enter the market, if it were denied carriage by one or more of the largest cable operators. The Commission adopted this approach in 1999 to set a 30 percent horizontal limit based on a theory that cable operators at certain concentration levels could effectively prevent programming networks from entering or surviving in the marketplace simply by deciding not to carry them. The Commission found that a new programming network needs access to 15 to 20 million subscribers to be viable and that the typical programming network had only a 50 percent chance of actually serving all available MVPD subscribers. The Commission concluded that a programmer needed to have an "open field" of 40 percent of MVPD subscribers nationwide and that a 30 percent MVPD subscriber limit would assure that a 40 percent open field remained even if the two largest cable operators decided not to carry it. The Commission determined that calculations of the horizontal limit should include all MVPD subscribers, including non-cable MVPD subscribers, to take into account the increased market share of non-cable MVPDs.

* * *

b. Monopsony Framework

21. Monopsony theory examines whether a buyer has sufficient market power to force down the price it pays for a homogenous input by reducing its purchases, and whether this is inefficient, in a market with a single price for all units of the input purchased. A firm acting as a

buyer of an input is said to have monopsony power when it has the ability to establish the price at which input is purchased. * * *

c. Bargaining Theory

26. A branch of game theory, bargaining theory examines the determinants of a bargaining outcome, where outcome is defined in terms of whether a bargain is struck and, if struck, the share of the gains that accrue to each side of the bargain. In 2001, the Commission suggested that excessive bargaining power could enable cable operators to force down the prices they pay to programmers, causing the programmers to curtail their activities and thereby limit the quality and diversity of programming. * * *

2. Discussion

28. Open Field Analysis: We find that a modified open field approach best enables us to implement a horizontal ownership limit designed to prevent a single cable operator from unfairly impeding the flow of programming to consumers in such a way as to undermine the statutory objective to enhance effective competition. Our application of this approach will ensure that no single operator can create a barrier to a programming network's entry into the market or cause a programming network to exit the market simply by declining to carry the network. The *Time Warner II* court acknowledged that the exercise of editorial discretion by a single cable operator can unfairly impede the flow of programming if the operator is so large that its decision not to carry the network seals its fate. The open field approach we adopt here results in a limit that ensures that the success of a programming network does not rely entirely on the carriage decision of a single cable operator. This approach prevents harms to the flow of programming caused by a number of possible factors, discussed below.

29. A cable operator may fail to carry a network valued by consumers for several reasons, including reasons related to market failures. For example, if there is asymmetric information about the costs and value of the network, inefficient trading will result, and negotiations can break down. Thus, a network might not be carried by a cable operator because the parties cannot agree to a price, even though consumers value it and both the programmer and the cable operator would profit from the deal. Second, the cable operator may mistakenly believe that the network will not be popular with consumers. The open field approach ensures that a single operator's mistake in judgment will not prevent a valued network from reaching consumers.

30. Cable operators may also fail to carry programming valued by consumers for reasons unrelated to the dynamics of marketplace competition. For example, a large cable operator may prefer to carry only that programming whose content reflects its viewpoint and tastes. One of the Commission's goals is to maintain diversity of programming in the marketplace. In addition to our competitive analysis, therefore, we have considered how the horizontal limit serves the public interest by promot-

ing diversity of programming in the MVPD market. As the *Time Warner II* court recognized, in promoting this goal, the Commission "is on solid ground in asserting authority to be sure that no single company could be in a position singlehandedly to deal a programmer a death blow." If it can profitably sell its programming to multiple cable operators with different viewpoints and tastes, a network will not be pressured to make changes in the content and viewpoint of its programming to suit the desires of the largest cable operator. Our horizontal limit, and the framework supporting it, ensure that the largest cable operator will not be so large that the operator's failure to carry a network will prevent that network from entering or surviving in the market.

31. We conclude that the traditional models of monopsony and bargaining theories as applied to the available evidence are unable to predict the point at which an increase in cable operator concentration will unduly restrict the flow of programming. We find that the necessary assumptions for a traditional monopsony model do not hold in the programming market and that bargaining theory is inadequate for determining whether specific harms to the programming market are likely to result from an increase in bargaining power by cable operators. Thus while a number of likely harms to the flow of programming can be identified, the traditional economic theories of monopsony power and bargaining are not useful for setting a limit in these circumstances. * * *

32. Monopsony Model: We agree with those commenters who argue that the traditional monopsony model is not useful in analyzing the impact of cable operators' market power on the flow of programming. The usual requirement for a monopsony model to be employed—that the supply of programming for each firm be sensitive to a market price (thus yielding an upward-sloping supply curve)—does not hold here. Under the traditional monopsony model, a monopsonist, because it is the only buyer, has the ability to set the price at which its desired input is acquired. And because of the existence of an upward sloping supply curve, it achieves a lower price by restricting the quantity of that input it acquires. In the market for programming, however, negotiations between programmers and cable operators are bilateral and largely confidential. Thus for every potential purchase that could yield a positive benefit to consumers, the cable operator has an incentive to negotiate a price and purchase the programming. From the perspective of a cable operator, agreeing to a higher price in a particular transaction for programming that has a higher cost may not raise the cost of purchasing programming from other sellers, as would occur in the usual monopsony model. In addition, the negotiated prices are complex and difficult to compare. Thus, there is no market price to be affected, and the usual incentive for a firm to exercise monopsony power does not occur in this market. In any event, even assuming that monopsony theory could be applied to this market, the record before us is inadequate to make a determination of the relevant market price.

* * *

34. Bargaining Theory: Because of its ability to incorporate the key market-specific and transaction-specific factors that typically characterize negotiations for the purchase of programming, bargaining theory may be better able than monopsony theory to describe and model the programming market. We determine that bargaining theory does identify some of the harms likely to occur from the exercise of market power by a large cable operator. In particular, bargaining theory points out that even if both parties have an incentive to negotiate an agreement, and both parties would benefit from an agreement, bargaining can break down if there is asymmetric information (i.e., uncertainty about the cost of the network and its value to consumers), resulting in the programmer failing to gain carriage. Thus the rules we craft to ensure the flow of programming must take into consideration the possibility that a network valued by consumers will fail to gain carriage. In addition, bargaining theory shows that a cable operator with greater bargaining power can obtain lower prices than it would otherwise. This would have the effect of reducing programmers' incentive to enter the market and to invest in high-quality programming.

35. We find, however, that bargaining theory is not useful for setting a horizontal limit, because it cannot be applied specifically to determine at what particular level of concentration these harms are likely to occur. The results of the models used in bargaining theory are very sensitive to the particular circumstances of the transaction. Thus, whether or not a particular programming network is carried depends on a variety of factors specific to its negotiations with each cable operator. This makes it difficult to develop market-wide results relating market concentration and the general flow of programming using a theoretical bargaining model. Indeed, no commenters have proposed a reliable means of using bargaining theory to determine the horizontal limit needed to prevent the harms identified.

* * *

C. Establishing the Horizontal Limit

40. In this section we calculate the ownership limit using the modified open field approach. The resulting limit will ensure that no single operator can, by simply refusing to carry a programming network, cause it to fail. The individual elements of this approach account for the factors that govern a network's ability to obtain subscribers. The basic building block of the calculation is the minimum viable scale of a program network. This value represents the minimum number of subscribers a programming network requires in order to be viable. Because not all of an MVPD's subscribers receive access to all of the networks carried by the MVPD, the minimum viable scale must be modified to determine how many of an MVPD's subscribers will also be subscribers to the program network. The subscriber penetration rate is used to make this determination. The resulting value is the total number of subscribers, to MVPDs that carry the network, necessary in order for the program network to serve the minimum viable scale. This value is then

expressed as a percentage of the total number of MVPD subscribers to determine the fraction of the MVPD market that must agree to carry the program network so that it can serve the minimum viable scale. If there is no coordinated denial of carriage by MVPDs, this value would represent the open field necessary to give a program network a reasonable chance of serving the minimum viable scale. Expressed as a formula, the ownership limit under the open field approach is:

$$Limit = \left(1 - \frac{MVS}{Pen} \cdot \frac{1}{Subs}\right)$$

Three values are required in order to calculate the ownership limit: (1) total MVPD subscribers ("*Subs*"), (2) the minimum viable scale ("MVS"), and (3) the subscriber penetration rate ("*Pen*"). As described below, the resulting calculation indicates that an open field of 70 percent and an ownership limit of 30 percent are necessary to ensure that no single cable operator is able to impede unfairly the flow of programming to consumers. * * *

2. Minimum Viable Scale

49. In 1999, based upon an examination of the number of subscribers that successful networks had acquired, as well as industry comments, the Commission calculated that the minimum viable scale of a programming network was on the order of 15 million subscribers. In 2005, the Commission sought comment on the number of subscribers a programming network requires in order to remain viable. The Commission proposed that viability is partly a function of the time the network has been in the market, and that simply because recently-launched networks tend to have a limited number of subscribers early in the launch, does not mean that those networks will remain viable in the future with a limited number of subscribers. Referring to the comments of programmers that were submitted in other proceedings, the Commission suggested that long term viability may require more than 40 million subscribers.

* * *

52. In order to determine the minimum viable scale (MVS) of a programming network for purposes of calculating the ownership limit in the formula set out above, as previously proposed, we rely upon an analysis that estimates the probability that a programming network will continue to operate based on the number of subscribers it has at a point in time. The Commission previously proposed using the methodology set forth in the *Media Bureau Survival Study* to calculate the minimum viable scale and sought comment on this proposal. That study was based on survival analysis and is a standard method used in the fields of economics, biology, and engineering. The study accounts for all of the revenue sources that maintain the viability of the programming network, including international distribution, and reflects the impact of advertising revenues, which may vary based on the markets where the program-

ming network is carried. It is based on an unbiased sample of networks that have launched service and gained distribution. The data also account for the impact of DBS competition on the carriage decisions of cable operators. For example, any competitive pressure from DBS that makes a cable operator's refusal to carry a particular programming network more costly will be reflected in an increase in the odds of network survival. The study also accounts for the effect of vertical integration with a cable operator on the viability of a network and the value of being associated with a successful network (a "spin-off"). Because the study evaluates the viability of a network over its lifecycle beginning with its inception, it is able to account for the relatively small number of subscribers a network requires to remain viable in its early stages, while accounting for the larger number of subscribers necessary at later stages. * * *

4. Accounting for Coordinated Action

63. In 1999, the Commission implicitly used a coordination index of two because it was concerned that two cable operators could jointly refuse to carry a programming network and therefore prevent the network from becoming viable. The court rejected the Commission's analysis and held that the Commission must present empirical or theoretical evidence that coordinated action is likely in order to sustain a limit based on a theory of joint action.

* * *

66. Accordingly, we do not include an adjustment for coordinated action. While commenters have provided some evidence that large cable operators tend to carry the same programming networks, they have not provided a sufficient set of arguments to demonstrate that it is coordinated action rather than individual action generating the observations. It is not surprising, for example, that nearly every cable MSO carries the most popular networks. Such an observation likely arises from the popularity of the network, not necessarily from collusive action. Thus, we lack evidence to draw definitive conclusions regarding the likelihood that cable operators will behave in a coordinated fashion.

5. The Cable Horizontal Ownership Limit

67. After careful consideration of the evidence before us, including the language and intent of the statute and our understanding of the programming market, we determine that use of the open field approach to set a horizontal limit is the most appropriate means of ensuring that the flow of programming to consumers is not unfairly impeded. The modified open field method that we adopt in this Order yields a horizontal ownership cap that ensures that no cable provider is so large that it can prevent a programmer from serving "the number of viewers needed for viability—independent of concerns over anticompetitive conduct." We apply the first three values discussed above to the ownership limit formula, and reject the fourth value concerning coordinated action. The values we apply are (1) a total MVPD subscriber number of 95,784,478;

(2) a minimum viable scale of 19,030,000; and (3) a subscriber penetration rate of 0.2742. The calculation generates a result of .28, which reflects that as long as the largest cable operator does not serve more than 28 percent of all MVPD subscribers, that operator cannot significantly undermine the viability of a programming network by refusing to carry the network.

68. Based on this calculation, we conclude that a horizontal limit of 30 percent will best serve the public interest. As noted above, the Commission first established a 30 percent horizontal ownership limit in 1993. In 1999, the Commission revised the method by which horizontal ownership was calculated, but retained a 30 percent ownership limit. Although that limit was subsequently remanded by the court, the Commission has continued to apply the 30 percent limit in merger reviews since that time and the media marketplace has continued to operate under this requirement. Therefore, for consistency, we adjust the limit slightly upward, from 28 percent to 30 percent. This small upward adjustment is unlikely to cause harm. We do not believe this minor adjustment will adversely affect our ability to provide the protection the statute requires. Moreover, this adjustment will have no affect on the largest cable operator in the market today because it would satisfy either a 28 percent or 30 percent limit. For these reasons, we set a 30 percent horizontal limit.

* * *

III. Further Notice of Proposed Rulemaking

* * *

B. Vertical Limit

2. Discussion

135. The record developed in response to the *2005 Second Further Notice* remains inadequate to support a specific vertical limit. No commenter proposed a specific limit, provided us with evidence to support a specific limit, advanced any methodology that could help us to determine a specific limit, or demonstrated a link between any of the harms identified and a specific limit designed to prevent these harms. * * *

143. We invite commenters to propose a specific vertical limit, including whether or not the current 75-channel cap is still appropriate and relevant. We tentatively conclude that the 75-channel cap should be eliminated. We ask that commenters provide theoretical or empirical evidence to support any specific proposed limit and discuss how the proposed limit will appropriately balance the potential harms and benefits of vertical integration. Alternatively, we invite commenters to advance a particular methodology and rationale that will help us to determine a specific limit that is supported by record evidence. In either case, we request that commenters demonstrate a link between the

specific harms sought to be prevented and the specific limit proposed to prevent or remedy such harms.

* * *

Dissenting Statement of COMMISSIONER ROBERT M. MCDOWELL

* * *

Today's 30 percent cap has a smaller chance of surviving appeal than did the ill-fated and ill-advised 2001 30 percent cap. In 2001 in *Time Warner Entertainment Co. v. FCC*, the D.C. Circuit rejected the 30 percent cable ownership cap and imposed a heavy burden on the Commission to adopt any new cap on remand. The court found that the Commission lacked an evidentiary basis for a 30 percent cap and, as a result, did not meet its obligation under the First Amendment to show a "real risk" of "non-conjectural harm" to programmers. The court also rejected the Commission's argument that a 30 percent cap was justified in order to "enhance diversity."

Indeed, the court stated that based on the marketplace evidence in 2001, the Commission could justify at most, a 60 percent cap—twice the number the majority adopts today. Specifically, the court maintained that a 60 percent limit "might be appropriate as necessary to ensure that programmers had an adequate 'open field' even in the face of rejection by the largest company" and that the "present record supports no more." In particular, the court found that the Commission had not given sufficient weight to marketplace developments, especially the increasing success of Direct Broadcast Satellite ("DBS"). The court pointed out that because "DBS could be considered to 'pass every home in the country' " its competitive effect is especially significant. The Court admonished the Commission to account for this fact when considering any new ownership cap. The majority's order does not clear this hurdle, not by a mile. How can the same 30 percent limit that insufficiently accounted for DBS in 2001 possibly satisfy the requirements of *Time Warner II* today when DBS is roughly twice as large a competitive presence as it was in 2001, and when other competitors are competing vigorously with cable operators? The answer is that it cannot.

III. THE CAP CREATES REGULATORY DISPARITY AND ASYMMETRY.

Placing a horizontal ownership cap on cable creates regulatory disparity and asymmetry, all at a time when this Commission has been trying to level the regulatory playing field by creating parity. Order after order over the past few years has sought to change the stove-pipe paradigm of old in an attempt to treat similar technologies and services alike, not differently. Today's cap applies only to cable, not to satellite. Furthermore, we don't cap the number of:

- wireline telephone subscribers one company can have;
- wireless subscribers one company can have; or
- websites a company can own.

Even in the era of rapid technological convergence, such asymmetry will only create market distortions that will inhibit investment and innovation. How does that serve the public interest? In a world where cable companies compete directly against telephone companies and others to provide video, voice and data services, restricting the ability of one group of competitors to achieve the economies of scale enjoyed by others undermines years of efforts to spur intermodal competition and violates the well-established principle of competitive neutrality. If the majority sees so many flaws in the cable industry, it should remedy those shortcomings by encouraging competition, as we did with our video franchising order, not through unnecessary and unconstitutional regulation. Likewise, it is ironic that those who are voting today to limit cable company growth have consistently voted to expand telephone company growth. Such a reversal of policy just for this one sector defies logic. * * *

Open Fields . . . Forever. Commissioner McDowell thinks it is an easy bet that the court of appeals will reverse. Notice, though, that this time the Commission has abandoned the assumption of coordinated action, which was central to its earlier decision. Does that make the Commission's chance of success on appeal any greater? How does the FCC arrive at the same 30% limit without assuming coordination or collusion among two cable systems? Under the previous report it was assumed that an open field of 40% was required. Absent collusion, that would imply an ownership cap of 60%—as the court found. The basis on which the Commission originally set the cap at 30% was the assumption that this would leave enough of a field of potential subscribers even if two cable MSOs *coordinated* their purchasing to deny an outlet to an upstream supplier. Obviously if one removes coordinated action, something else has to be done to justify the 30% limit; the FCC responded to the loss of the collusion theory by setting the new open field at 70%! The rule is the constant; the rationale is adjusted to fit the rule!

Putting aside the question of how big the open field needs to be, Commissioner McDowell raises a question whether the open field is also a level field. The Commission places no similar cap on DBS providers who are competitors of cable in the MVPD market. In fact DirecTV is the second largest MVPD provider, just behind Comcast. Should it also be subject to a cap on subscribers reached by its system?

F. VERTICAL INTEGRATION IN CABLE

1. Channel Occupancy Limits

As noted above the 1992 Cable Television Consumer Protection and Competition Act was concerned with horizontal ownership and also with vertical integration, though in a sense both are concerned with vertical integration. Thus, the horizontal ownership cap is really designed to prevent foreclosure in (upstream) programming supply markets that arises only because the MSOs are affiliated with programming suppliers. In other words, Congress and the FCC worried that a very small number of downstream MSOs would be in a position to foreclose retail distribution markets to upstream program suppliers who competed with the MSOs' own affiliated program networks. A hypothetical example would be Cablevision refusing to carry Turner Classic Movies or Fox Movie Channel because they compete with AMC, a programming supplier owned by Cablevision. A similar concern animated the other "vertical" rule addressed by the court in *Time Warner* dealing with channel occupancy limits.

TIME WARNER ENTERTAINMENT CO. v. FCC

United States Court of Appeals, District of Columbia Circuit, 2001.
240 F.3d 1126.

WILLIAMS, CIRCUIT JUDGE:

* * *

The FCC presents its 40% vertical limit as advancing the same interests invoked in support of its statutory authority to adopt the rule: diversity in programming and fair competition. As with the horizontal rules the FCC must defend the rules themselves under intermediate scrutiny and justify its chosen limit as not burdening substantially more speech than necessary. Far from satisfying this test, the FCC seems to have plucked the 40% limit out of thin air.

The FCC relies almost exclusively on the congressional findings that vertical integration in the cable industry could "make it difficult for non-cable affiliated ... programmers to secure carriage on vertically integrated cables systems" and that "vertically integrated program suppliers have the incentive and the ability to favor their affiliated cable operators ... and program distributors." Regulatory limits in response to these consequences would "increase the diversity of voices available to the public." In *Time Warner I* we thought these findings strong enough to overcome the First Amendment challenge to the relevant provision of the 1992 Cable Act. In doing so, we held that such a prophylactic rule was not "rendered unnecessary merely because preexisting statutes [such as the antitrust laws and the antidiscrimination provisions of the 1992 Cable Act] impose behavioral norms." Beyond that we did not assess the appropriateness of the burden on speech. We upheld no specific vertical limit—none was before us.

We recognize that in drawing a numerical line an agency will ultimately indulge in some inescapable residue of arbitrariness; even if 40% is a highly justifiable pick, no one could expect the Commission to show why it was materially better than 39% or 41%. But to pass even the arbitrary and capricious standard, the agency must at least reveal " 'a rational connection between the facts found and the choice made.' "

Here the FCC must also meet First Amendment intermediate scrutiny. Yet it appears to provide nothing but the conclusion that "we believe that a 40% limit is appropriate to balance the goals." What are the conditions that make 50% too high and 30% too low? How great is the risk presented by current market conditions? These questions are left unanswered by the Commission's discussion.

The FCC argued before us that no MSO has yet complained that the 40% vertical limit has required it to alter programming. This is no answer at all, as it says nothing about plans that the rule may have scuttled. Petitioners responded that their subsidiaries frequently must juggle their channel lineups to stay within the cap. Furthermore, it appears uncontested that AT&T's merger with MediaOne brings the vertical limits into play.

In fairness, the FCC does make an attempt to review some relevant conditions. The FCC cites the House Report's conclusion that "some" vertically integrated MSOs favor their affiliates and "may" discriminate against others. But it also notes a report that none of the top five MSOs "showed a pattern" of favoring their affiliates. Indeed, the FCC concludes that "vertical relationships had increased both the quality and quantity of cable programming services." But still it settled on a limit of 40%. There is no effort to link the numerical limits to the benefits and detriments depicted. Further, given the pursuit of diversity, one might expect some inquiry into whether innovative independent originators of programming find greater success selling to affiliated or to unaffiliated programming firms, but there is none.

Quite apart from the numerical limit vel non, petitioners attack the Commission's refusal to exclude from the vertical limit cable operators that are subject to effective competition. The FCC had proposed exempting cable operators who met the definition of effective competition provided by § 623 of the Communications Act of 1934. Of course our decision in *Time Warner I* acknowledged the existence of incentives to use affiliated programming. For example, even where an unaffiliated supplier offered a better cost-quality trade-off, a company might be reluctant to ditch or curtail an inefficient in-house operation because of the impact on firm executives or other employees, or the resulting spotlight on management's earlier judgment. But petitioners argue, quite plausibly, that exposure to competition will have an impact on a cable company's ability to indulge in favoritism for in-house productions. After all, while reliance on in-house suppliers offering an inferior price-quality trade-off will reduce a monopolist's profits, it may threaten a competitive firm's very survival. This analysis is not foreign to the Commission, which endorsed it when proposing the exemption [in a proposed version of the rule]:

> We believe that this proposal is appropriate since effective competition will preclude cable operators from exercising the market power which originally justified channel occupancy limits. Where systems face effective competition, their incentive to favor an affiliated

programmer will be replaced by the incentive to provide programming that is most valued by subscribers.

The FCC makes two arguments to justify its refusal to exempt MVPDs that are subject to effective competition. First, it says that the definition of competition provided by 47 U.S.C. § 543 was "not adopted for this specific purpose" but rather for relief from rate regulation. Indeed, we have recognized that one of the ways in which the statutory standard is met may be surprisingly defective as a mark of real competition. But the Commission is free to carve out subsections that are truly pertinent to competition, as it had proposed. Of course competition that is adequate to justify dispensing with rate regulation could still leave an undue likelihood of improper favoritism for affiliated programmers. But the possible failure of readily available criteria does not itself justify the use of so blunt a blade. Congress expressly directed the Commission to take "particular account of the market structure ..., including the nature and market power of the local franchise." Because competition raises the stakes for a firm that sacrifices the optimal price-quality trade-off in its acquisition of programming, the issue seems to trigger the legislative directive. Yet the Commission seems to ignore its own conclusions about cable companies' incentives and constraints, and the dynamics of the programming industry. If the criteria of § 543(*l*)(1) are unsuitable, the Commission can consider concepts of effective competition that it finds more apt for these purposes.

Second, the FCC comments that if a competing MVPD favored its own affiliated programmers, the presence of competition would have no tendency to create room for independent programmers. But this theory seems contradicted by the Commission's own observation, mentioned earlier, that no vertically integrated MVPD has complained of reaching the 40% limit. Vertically integrated MVPDs evidently use loads of independent programming. Further, although cable operators continue to expand their interests in programmers, "[t]he proportion of vertically integrated channels ... continue[d] to decline" for each of the last two years. Even if competing MSOs filled all of their channels with affiliates' products (as unlikely as that seems), the Commission nowhere explains why, in the pursuit of diversity, the independence of competing vertically integrated MVPDs is inferior to the independence of unaffiliated programmers. In any event, the Commission's point here does not respond to the intuition that competition spurs a firm's search for the best price-quality trade-off.

In its brief the Commission adds the argument that truly effective competition under § 543(*l*)(1) existed only for a tiny fraction of cable systems. Indeed, it said in its *Sixth Annual Report* that of the nation's 33,000 cable community units, only 157 satisfy the definition through being in a market offering more than one wireline MVPD. (In the *Seventh Annual Report* we learn that now 330, or 1% of the total, meet the competition standard through exposure to another MVPD; in this report the qualifier "wireline" is absent. But in determining whether or not the regulations burden substantially more speech than necessary, it is a weak move to point to the paucity of MVPDs facing competition if, as seems the case, it is easy to exempt them from the limit.

We find that the FCC has failed to justify its vertical limit as not burdening substantially more speech than necessary. Accordingly, we reverse and remand to the FCC for further consideration.

The APA or the First Amendment? Why was the court so keen to put its decision on the First Amendment instead of the Administrative Procedure Act? The court finds the FCC's rationale for its vertical rules would not pass muster under the "arbitrary and capricious" standard (the standard prescribed by the APA); why not let it go at that? Is it appropriate to pick a constitutional basis for overturning the agency when there is an adequate non-constitutional basis for doing so? Perhaps the court wants to remind the FCC that there is a First Amendment in the background; but is that not true of the entire field of communications law?

On Remand . . . Forever? The vertical rules are still pending before the Commission on remand. As noted in the 2008 report on the new horizontal cable ownership cap excerpted above, the FCC was unable to reach a decision on the vertical rules and has sought a new round of public comments. It is not uncommon for rulemaking proceedings to last more than six years, but might it not be of some significance that in six years the FCC still has not been able to develop a standard for this particular rule?

2. Program Access Rules

The channel occupancy limits were intended to address one side of the vertically integrated cable firm: the possibility that vertically integrated firms would use their market power as cable operators to freeze out competing program producers. But the other side of the firm also carries the potential for leveraging: vertically integrated cable companies may find themselves controlling valuable content, and may unfairly refuse to license that content to other MVPD operators in order to favor themselves in the subscription market. (To carry forward the previous example, imagine Cablevision refusing to allow DirecTV to carry AMC because DirecTV competes with Cablevision for subscribers.) Thus, in addition to directing the FCC to place reasonable limits on the number of channels that a MSO could devote to affiliated programming, the 1992 Cable Act (in § 19, which added a new § 548 to the Communications Act) also generally prohibited (except with the Commission's approval on a case-by-case basis) exclusive contracts between vertically integrated programming vendors and cable operators.[12]

12. The statute is worded in both general terms of "unfair methods of competition or unfair or deceptive acts or practices" (in § 548(b)) and "minimum contents" of the FCC regulations, which are to prohibit, in most cases, "exclusive contracts for satellite

However, Congress provided for the ban to sunset in ten years unless the FCC made findings that it "continues to be necessary to preserve and protect competition and diversity in the distribution of video programming." The Commission made such a finding in 2002 based on its belief that integrated cable operators had the ability and the incentive to deny their competitors access to programming controlled by the integrated operator/programming vendors. The FCC extended the sunset period for another five years. In 2007 it issued a new notice of proposed rulemaking to consider whether to eliminate the ban or continue the sunset.

IMPLEMENTATION OF THE CABLE TELEVISION CONSUMER PROTECTION AND COMPETITION ACT OF 1992
Notice of Proposed Rulemaking

Federal Communications Commission, 2007.
22 FCC Rcd. 4252.

BY THE COMMISSION:

* * *

5. Congress based the program access provisions on its concern that in the absence of regulation, vertically integrated programmers have the incentive and ability to favor affiliated cable operators over nonaffiliated cable operators and programming distributors using other technologies such that competition and diversity in the distribution of video programming would not be preserved and protected. We ask whether this concern has diminished or increased in today's marketplace.

6. In the [2002] *Sunset Report and Order*, the Commission examined the status of the MVPD market over the decade between the adoption of the program access provisions and the sunset review. The Commission observed that cable's overall market share declined from 95 percent in 1992 to 78 percent at the time of the *Sunset Report and Order*. The Commission also considered DBS, which at the time served 18 percent of MVPD households. Finally, the Commission noted that other competitors such as multichannel multipoint distribution service ("MMDS"), SMATV, and HSD,[*] had not fared as well, comprising less than four percent of all MVPD subscribers. As of June 2005, basic cable subscribers comprised approximately 69 percent of all MVPD households and DIRECTV and EchoStar Communications Corporation ("EchoStar")

cable programming or satellite broadcast programming" (in § 548(c)(2)(C)).

* Eds. MMDS is a sort of "wireless cable," in which a local operator uses short-range transmission to small dishes on subscribers' homes to carry content instead of physical cables. SMATV, or "satellite master antenna television," is also somewhat like cable, but tends to be provided to residents of a single (large apartment) building. It consists of a large antenna connected to a number of subscribers via cable, but one that does not access public rights of way. HSD, or "home satellite dish" was the precursor to the now-ubiquitous DBS, using larger dishes with lower-power satellites.

(marketed as the DISH Network) served approximately 27.7 percent of all MVPD households nationwide. As of June 2005, MMDS, SMATV and HSD operators served less than three percent of all MVPD subscribers. How has the exclusivity prohibition impacted the general state of competition among MVPD operators? We seek comment on the current status of all these current MVPD competitors to cable and their continued viability should the prohibition on exclusivity be permitted to sunset. In addition, how would the absence of an exclusivity prohibition affect the likelihood that potential MVPD competitors will enter the market?

7. We request information as to whether developments in the marketplace since the passage of the 1992 Cable Act and our 2002 sunset review have diminished or increased the need for the exclusivity prohibition. In this regard, we seek comment on three events which have occurred in the multichannel programming market since our 2002 sunset review. First, we seek comment on the increase in the provision of MVPD service by local exchange carriers ("LECs"). For example, AT&T is moving forward with its IP-enabled broadband network called "Project Lightspeed," using both Fiber to the Node ("FTTN") and Fiber to the Home ("FTTH") to deliver video and other services to residential customers. AT&T states that it currently has approximately 3,000 customers, with more projected once it launches beyond San Antonio, Texas. In addition, Verizon is deploying a FTTH network that delivers video, telephony, and high-speed Internet access service. Verizon estimates that it had 100,000 video subscribers at the end of the 3rd quarter, 2006, and that they will have 175,000 video subscribers and pass 1.8 million households by the end of 2006. Second, we seek comment on the impact of the acquisition of control of the assets of Hughes Electronics Corporation by The News Corporation Limited ("News Corp."). Through this transaction, News Corp. placed under common control DIRECTV, the nation's second largest MVPD, and the broadcast and multichannel programming assets of the Fox Entertainment Group. Finally, we seek comment on the recent acquisition by Comcast Corporation and Time Warner, Inc. of the assets of Adelphia Communications Corporation. We seek comment on the extent, if any, to which these specific events should inform our analysis of whether to retain the prohibition on exclusivity. In addition, we seek comment on any other relevant developments in the MVPD market since our 2002 sunset review that we should consider in deciding whether to retain the prohibition on exclusivity.

8. We ask whether competitive MVPDs' access to what some refer to as "marquee" or "must have" vertically integrated programming, such as CNN, HBO, TNT, Discovery and others, remains essential to successful implementation of competitive services. Does satellite-delivered vertically integrated programming remain necessary to the viability of competitive MVPDs because there is no good substitute programming available? We also ask whether the retention of the exclusivity prohibition affects access to national and regional sports programming networks. We seek comment on the effects that the exclusivity prohibition

has had on the development and production of programming for the current MVPD marketplace. We concluded in the *Sunset Report and Order* that the retention of the exclusivity prohibition would not reduce incentives to create new or diverse programming. In support, we noted that the number of national programming services increased from the exclusivity prohibition's inception in 1992 from 87 to 294 in 2001. We also noted that the number of vertically integrated programming services nearly doubled from 56 in 1994 to 104 in 2001 and concluded that the ban did not serve as a disincentive for cable MSOs to develop new cable networks. Since the extension of the exclusivity ban in 2002, has there been a significant overall increase or decrease in the development, promotion, and launch of new and diverse programming services? We note that, our most recent report on the status of video competition found that, as of June 2005, there were 531 satellite-delivered national programming networks. How has the exclusivity prohibition affected investment incentives in the current marketplace for both vertically integrated and independent programming? We also ask if there has been any change in the resources of nonaffiliated cable operators and competitive MVPDs and their ability to develop their own programming, thereby limiting their dependence on "must have" vertically integrated programming. Finally, we ask what effect the retention of the exclusivity ban has had on the launch of local origination programming that may have a more limited geographic appeal.

9. We also ask how the current state of cable system clusters and distribution of regional video programming services affiliated with cable operators should affect our decision regarding the exclusivity prohibition. As the Commission concluded in the *Sunset Report and Order*, "[w]e believe that clustering, accompanied by an increase in vertically integrated regional programming networks affiliated with cable MSOs that control system clusters, will increase the incentive of cable operators to practice anticompetitive foreclosure of access to vertically integrated programming." We seek comment on the continuing validity of this conclusion and whether events since the *Sunset Report and Order* mitigate or exacerbate the impact of clustering. In particular, we seek comment on what impact our recent approval of the acquisition of the assets of Adelphia Communications by Comcast and Time Warner has on this topic. We also seek comment on whether the current state of horizontal consolidation in the cable industry increases incentives for anticompetitive foreclosure of access to vertically integrated programming.

10. We seek comment on whether the exclusivity prohibition continues to be necessary to preserve and protect diversity in the distribution of programming. Our focus in this area is not on programming diversity, but rather on "preserving and protecting diversity in the distribution of video programming—i.e., ensuring that as many MVPDs as possible remain viable distributors of video programming." As the Commission observed in the *Sunset Report and Order*, "[o]ther than the two largest non-cable MVPDs, DirecTV and EchoStar, nonaffiliated cable

operators and competitive MVPDs . . . assert that they lack the resources and ability to develop their own programming and are thus dependent on access to the programming of others, including 'must have' vertically integrated programming.'' Does this continue to be true for nonaffiliated cable operators and competitive MVPDs in today's marketplace? We seek comment on whether retention of the exclusivity prohibition in the current climate helps to ensure that as many MVPDs as possible remain viable distributors of video programming. Would the sunset of the exclusivity prohibition in the current state of the market limit or foreclose access to vertically integrated programming so as to jeopardize a diverse market of existing and potential competitors? * * *

Horizontal vs. Vertical Restrictions in Cable. Both the horizontal and vertical restrictions on cable providers are designed to keep the pipes open for non-affiliated content. But, if the vertical rules are enforced, what work are the horizontal restrictions actually doing?

National Markets vs. Local Markets in Cable. One reason why vertical integration seems like such a pernicious problem in cable television is not because of national markets but because of local ones. Very few people have a choice among multiple cable operators in local markets (although that situation is changing). Even if *national* ownership is diverse, the national market simply doesn't exist for most cable consumers; from their perspective, the ''national'' cable market is simply a collection of monopolistic local markets. Given that local markets are actually less competitive than national ones, do the horizontal restrictions on national ownership actually accomplish anything?

The Nature of both Local and National Markets for MVPDs. Since 1992, the MVPD market has changed considerably, with DBS becoming a viable competitor to cable television for both program providers and consumers. From the programmers' perspective, DBS reaches almost the entire nation, providing an alternative, nation-wide outlet for non-affiliated programming. From the consumers' perspective, there is now frequently a choice between providers, even if the choice is not a perfect one (even today, many markets cannot get the convenience of receiving their local broadcast channels through DBS; the carriage of local channels on cable is a regulatory certainty). Does the existence of DBS as an alternative to cable alter the arguments for imposing either horizontal or vertical restrictions on the cable industry? As we shall see later, some local exchange telephone carriers (most notably Verizon) are entering the television market with the construction of new optical fiber networks. How far into the future should the FCC look in assessing the competitiveness of the market?

G. VERTICAL INTEGRATION IN SATELLITE BROADCASTING

As the 2007 ''Sunset'' Notice of Proposed Rulemaking pointed out, the nation's second-largest MVPD is not an MSO at all but rather a DBS provider: DirecTV. In 2004, that operator became vertically integrated. Is there reason for us to be equally concerned about a vertically integrated satellite operator as we are about vertically integrated MSOs?

IN THE MATTER OF GENERAL MOTORS CORPORATION AND HUGHES ELECTRONICS CORPORATION, TRANSFERORS AND THE NEWS CORPORATION LIMITED, TRANSFEREE
Memorandum Opinion and Order

Federal Communications Commission, 2004.
19 FCC Rcd. 473.

BY THE COMMISSION:

I. INTRODUCTION

1. In this Order, we consider the application ("Application") of General Motors Corporation ("GM"), Hughes Electronics Corporation ("Hughes"), and the News Corporation Limited ("News Corp.") (collectively, the "Applicants") for consent to transfer control of various Commission licenses and authorizations, including direct broadcast satellite ("DBS") and fixed satellite space station, earth station, and terrestrial wireless authorizations held by Hughes and its wholly-or majority-owned subsidiaries to News Corp. The proposed transaction involves the split-off of Hughes from GM, wherein Hughes will become a separate and independent company, followed by a series of transactions through which News Corp., through its majority-held subsidiary, Fox Entertainment Group ("FEG"), will acquire a 34% interest in Hughes. The remaining 66% interest in Hughes will be held by three GM employee benefit trusts (managed by an independent trustee), which combined will hold an approximately 20% interest in Hughes, and by the general public, which will hold an approximately 46% interest in Hughes. * * *

3. Among News Corp.'s video programming assets are 35 owned and operated ("O&O") full-power television broadcast stations, a television broadcast network, ten national cable programming networks, and 22 regional cable programming networks. With 11.4 million subscribers—13% of all multichannel video programming distribution ("MVPD") households—DirecTV is second only to Comcast Corporation in its share of the MVPD market. With its national footprint, DirecTV competes with every single MVPD in the country, in markets of all sizes.

4. Currently, News Corp. supplies programming to DirecTV and other MVPDs, and DirecTV is a buyer of programming content from News Corp. and other programming suppliers. By combining News Corp.'s programming assets with DirecTV's national distribution platform, the proposed transaction creates a vertically integrated content/distribution platform. It thereby changes the nature of News Corp.'s relationship with all other MVPDs from that of solely a programming supplier to that of both a supplier of crucial inputs and a direct

competitor in the end user MVPD market. As discussed more fully below, our analysis of the principal allegations of competitive harm in the record demonstrates that this vertical integration has the potential to increase the incentive and ability of News Corp. to engage in temporary foreclosure bargaining strategies during carriage negotiations with competing MVPDs for two types of "must have" video programming products—broadcast television station signals and regional cable programming sports networks—in order to secure higher prices for its programming. Although News Corp., like other broadcast networks, engages or attempts to engage in this sort of behavior today, ownership of a competing MVPD platform with a national footprint means that News Corp. stands to gain from any subscriber losses the affected MVPD suffers during the period of foreclosure when those subscribers move over to its competing MVPD platform to access the desired programming. The ability to gain revenues via its ownership interest in DirecTV thereby helps offset any temporary losses that News Corp. would suffer from withdrawal of its programming from the competing MPVD in terms of lost advertising and/or affiliate fee revenues. This off-setting revenue gain makes use of the strategy more tolerable to News Corp post-transaction than it was pre-transaction and thereby increases the likelihood and frequency of its use. This lowering of the costs of foreclosure to News Corp. from present levels fundamentally and substantially alters the bargaining dynamic between the program supplier and the competing programming distributor to the benefit of the former at the expense of the latter and its subscribers. To the extent that News Corp. succeeds in using temporary foreclosure strategies to extract supra-competitive prices for its programming, these transaction-specific higher programming costs are likely to be passed through as higher MVPD prices, which in turn would harm consumers.

5. Applicants have alleged, and we have found, various public interest benefits from the transaction, including more potent competition to cable, increased innovation and consumer benefits in terms of programming and services, and increased penetration of local-into-local broadcasting service. Our license conditions described below are designed to lessen the impact of the public interest harms outlined above, while preserving the benefits of the transaction for the public. Based on the record before us, we find that on balance and as conditioned, the subject license transfer approvals will serve the public interest. We therefore grant the Application with the conditions specified below. * * *

VI. Analysis of Potential Harms in the Relevant Markets

A. Introduction

* * *

69. Transactions involving the acquisition of a full or partial interest in another company may give rise to concerns regarding "horizontal" concentration and/or "vertical" integration, depending on the lines of business engaged in by the two firms. A transaction is said to be

horizontal when the firms in the transaction sell products that are in the same relevant markets and are therefore viewed as reasonable substitutes by purchasers of the products. Horizontal transactions are of antitrust concern because they eliminate competition between the firms and increase concentration in the relevant markets. The reduction in overall competition in the relevant markets may lead to substantial increases in prices paid by purchasers of products in the markets.

70. Vertical transactions raise slightly different competitive concerns. At the outset, it is important to note that antitrust law and economic analysis have viewed vertical transactions more favorably in part because vertical mergers, standing alone, do not increase concentration in either the upstream or downstream markets. In addition, vertical mergers may generate significant efficiencies. For example, a vertical transaction may produce a more efficient organization form, which can reduce transaction costs, limit free-riding by internalizing incentives, and take advantage of technological economies. Where both the upstream and downstream firms possess enough market power to set prices above marginal costs, a vertical transaction also may reduce prices through the elimination of this "double marginalization." The reduction occurs because the integrated firm, in determining the costs of producing the downstream product and consequently the final price charged to consumers, will consider the real economic cost of the input rather than the higher price (including the upstream profit margin) previously charged by the unintegrated upstream firm.

71. Nevertheless, as discussed in greater detail below, vertical transactions also have the potential for anticompetitive effects. In particular, a vertically integrated firm that competes both in an upstream input market and a downstream output market, such as post-transaction News Corp., may have the incentive and ability to: (1) discriminate against particular rivals in either the upstream or downstream markets (e.g., by foreclosing rivals from inputs or customers); or (2) raise the costs to rivals generally in either of the markets. We first address potential horizontal harms and then analyze, with respect to each affected product and geographic market, potential vertical harms arising from the proposed transaction.

B. Potential Horizontal Harms

* * *

75. *Discussion*. We agree with the Applicants that the instant transaction does not present horizontal concentration issues. The Commission has previously held that broadcast television is not sufficiently substitutable with the services provided by MVPDs to constrain attempted MVPD price increases, and hence, is not in the same relevant product market. The concern Cablevision raises-access to Fox network programming delivered via television broadcast stations for Cablevision's MVPD product-demonstrates that broadcast signals are an input used to produce a downstream product-MVPD service. We view access to News

Corp.'s broadcast signals not as a horizontal concentration issue, but as a vertical integration issue, and we address it as part of our potential vertical harms discussion below. We therefore conclude that, because the Applicants do not offer the same products or services, the transaction does not present horizontal combination issues.

C. Potential Vertical Harms

1. Background

76. *Background.* In this section, we consider the potential vertical harms of the proposed transaction. In particular, we consider whether, as a result of the transaction, Applicants will have an increased incentive and ability to engage in anticompetitive foreclosure strategies with respect to national and non-sports regional cable programming networks, regional sports cable programming networks, broadcast television station signals, programming-related technologies, including electronic and interactive programming guides and fixed satellite services. * * *

78. With respect to vertical foreclosure, which is the main harm alleged in the record, a vertically integrated firm, as the result of a transaction, may have the incentive and ability (or an increased incentive and ability) to foreclose downstream competitors from important inputs. That is, where a firm that has market power in an input market acquires a firm in the downstream output market, the acquisition may increase the incentive and ability of the integrated firm to raise rivals' costs either by foreclosing supply of the input it sells downstream competitors or by raising the price at which it sells the input to competitors. By doing so, the integrated firm may be able to increase its profits by raising prices in the downstream market, or increasing its market share in that market, or both.

79. The economic literature suggests that an integrated firm will engage in permanent foreclosure only if the present discounted value of the increased profits it earns in the downstream market as the result of foreclosure exceeds the present discounted value of the losses it incurs from reduced sales of the input in the upstream market. If an integrated firm calculates that permanent foreclosure would be unprofitable, it nevertheless might find it profitable to engage in temporary foreclosure in certain markets. In markets exhibiting consumer inertia, among other things, temporary foreclosure may be profitable even where permanent foreclosure is not, because, during the period of foreclosure, downstream customers may switch to the integrated firm's downstream product and, due to inertia, then not immediately switch back to the competitor's product once the foreclosure has ended. Consumers choosing an MVPD are subject to inertia and partial lock-in, because, among other things, there are switching costs associated with changing providers and some MVPDs, including DirecTV generally require one-year contracts. Thus, temporary foreclosure may generate profits that continue for a longer period than the period of upstream losses caused by the reduction in demand for the input.

80. There is an additional reason why temporary foreclosure may be profitable. Specifically, by temporarily foreclosing supply of the input to a downstream competitor or by threatening to engage in temporary foreclosure, the integrated firm may improve its bargaining position so as to be able to extract a higher input price from the downstream competitor than it could have negotiated if it were a non-integrated input supplier. In order for an integrated firm successfully to employ temporary foreclosure or the threat of temporary foreclosure as a strategy to increase its bargaining position, the foreclosure strategy must be credible. This means that competitors must believe that temporary foreclosure is profitable (whether or not it actually is) in order to extract a higher input price. For example, if the vertically integrated firm, by temporarily withholding an input from a competitor, can cause the competitor to lose sufficient revenue or suffer other competitive harms, the competitor might agree to pay a higher price for the input, which could lead to higher prices for the output, thus injuring consumers. Even if the vertically integrated firm suffered a loss in profits from engaging in a specific instance of temporary foreclosure, it might nevertheless find it to be a profitable strategy over the longer run. Specifically, if by temporarily foreclosing certain competitors, the vertically integrated firm may signal to other downstream competitors its willingness to foreclose, which may cause other downstream competitors to agree to a higher price without the vertically integrated firm's having to actually engage in repeated foreclosures. Temporary foreclosure may result in a widespread increase in the input price and thus upstream profits in the longer-run. In addition, if the increase in the input price affects the marginal cost of producing the downstream product, prices in the downstream market will rise as well.

81. The underlying purpose of temporary foreclosure generally is to extract a higher price for the integrated firm's upstream input and thus raise its downstream rivals' costs. It is recognized that this raising rivals' costs strategy may take two forms. First, an integrated firm, if it can, will generally seek to discriminate in the price it charges downstream rivals for its upstream input. Specifically, it will have an incentive to charge a higher input price to its downstream competitors than it charges itself or non-competing firms in ancillary markets. In many cases, however, either legal or regulatory constraints or market forces will limit the ability of the integrated firm to engage in price discrimination.

82. Where the downstream affiliate is wholly owned, the integrated firm can always raise the internal transfer price of an input so that it equals the price charged to downstream competitors. Under these conditions, however, the increase in the internal transfer price is not particularly meaningful, since the integrated firm in making business decisions will consider the real economic cost of the input and not its nominal transfer price. Thus, in the case of a wholly owned downstream affiliate, it may be difficult to detect if price discrimination is occurring and anti-discrimination rules may not function effectively.

83. Where, as in this case, the upstream input supplier holds only a partial ownership interest in the downstream firm, matters become even more complicated. The Applicants note that corporate law generally requires that the transfer price not be set in a manner that disadvantages the other shareholders of the downstream firm. As our discussion of corporate governance in the following section demonstrates, the protections afforded by corporate law are neither absolute nor omniscient. Even when corporate law effectively limits the ability of the upstream firm to enter into arrangements that disadvantage the minority shareholders of the downstream firm, it is equally true that the upstream firm can circumvent this problem if it can effectively compensate the downstream firm and its shareholders for any increase in the transfer price of the input. This compensation is frequently referred to as a "side-payment." As a result, the upstream firm will likely be willing to incur any transaction costs associated with arranging such side-payments if the expected revenues from the uniform input price increase exceed the expected transaction costs of arranging the requisite side payments. If the transaction costs associated with designing the compensation scheme exceed the expected revenues from the uniform price increase, then again, it will not find it profitable to attempt such a strategy.

84. The above discussion confirms that the program access rules (and other non-discrimination safeguards) serve several useful functions with respect to the video programming subject to the vertically integrated firm's control. First, the program access rules prohibit permanent foreclosure with respect to all satellite cable programming. Second, they can prevent overt discrimination in the prices the integrated firm charges for such inputs. Finally, they can also prevent uniform increases in satellite cable programming input prices where the downstream affiliate is partially owned and where the cost of compensating the affiliate exceeds the expected profits resulting from the price increase. Because, under the proposed transaction, News Corp. will acquire only a partial ownership interest in DirecTV, we believe that our program access rules and the Applicants' proposed program access commitments can help prevent permanent foreclosure, discriminatory input price increases and, in some cases, non-discriminatory uniform input price increases with respect to satellite cable programming of general interest. Conversely, the above discussion suggests that these safeguards will not prevent an upstream firm that partially owns the downstream affiliate from uniformly raising the price of its input to both its downstream affiliate and downstream competitors when it has both the economic incentive and ability to do so. Thus, the partially integrated firm may be able to execute a uniform input price increase without running afoul of corporate law and despite such non-discrimination safeguards especially if it is able to profitably arrange a mechanism for side-payments to occur. It would certainly be able to execute such a uniform price increase for video programming inputs not subject to such safeguards and for

which it has significant market power, and may even risk shareholder litigation to do so. * * *

86. Our review of the record, using the approach described above, demonstrates that, with respect to national and non-sports regional cable programming, the program access rules, together with the Applicants' program access-like commitments should adequately protect against permanent foreclosure and overt price discrimination. Further, there is no evidence in the record that significant numbers of customers will shift MVPDs if such programming is temporarily withdrawn from their current MVPD. This suggests that temporary foreclosure will not significantly increase downstream profits of DirecTV or that this increase in profits will exceed the sum of the loss in revenues in the upstream market plus the transaction costs associated with arranging compensation for DirecTV's other shareholders. As a result, we find it unlikely that News Corp. will have an incentive to temporarily withhold such programming in an effort to secure a uniform increase in the price of its general interest cable programming.

87. In contrast, we find substantial evidence in the record that a temporary withdrawal of regional sports programming networks and local broadcast television station signals would cause a significant number of customers to shift from their current MVPD, which is subject to the foreclosure, to DirecTV. In addition, there is significant evidence in the record that the per-subscriber profits generated by each additional DirecTV subscriber are sufficiently large that the increased downstream revenues resulting from temporary foreclosure are likely to exceed the costs of foreclosure in many local markets. Accordingly, we find that, as a result of the transaction, the increased profits accruing to DirecTV and News Corp. as a result of the temporary withdrawal of regional sports programming and broadcast signals will give News Corp. an increased incentive to adopt a strategy of temporary foreclosure in order to uniformly raise the price of its broadcast television and regional sports programming and/or obtain other carriage concessions. News Corp.'s post-transaction ability to act anti-competitively to increase its competitors' programming costs is greater than it would otherwise be due to News Corp.'s post-transaction ability to off-set temporary revenue losses arising from foreclosure with increased profits accruing to DirecTV as subscribers drop the affected MVPD and subscribe to News Corp's affiliated MVPD. This increased ability and incentive to seek and obtain higher programming rates through unilateral temporary foreclosure would likely lead to higher prices to MVPD consumers than would otherwise occur and thereby harm the public interest. To avoid public interest harms that would result from such conduct, we impose several conditions to maintain the balance of bargaining power between News Corp. and other MVPDs at roughly pre-transaction levels. * * *

3. Discrimination Against Unaffiliated Programming

* * *

(ii) Discussion and Condition

107. Applicants have offered that "neither News Corp. nor DirecTV will discriminate against unaffiliated programming services in the selection, price, terms or conditions of carriage." We conclude that Applicants' proposed commitment to allow unaffiliated programmers access to the DirecTV platform on nondiscriminatory terms and conditions adequately addresses concerns raised regarding unaffiliated video programmers' access to the DirecTV platform. We will therefore condition our grant of the Application on compliance with this access commitment. At this time, we will not prescribe standards of conduct pursuant to which DirecTV must act to comply with this condition although we expect DirecTV to act reasonably when dealing with unaffiliated programmers. We note that Applicants' proposed commitment is not unlike the nondiscrimination requirement in the Act and our program carriage rules. Similar to our treatment of the remainder of Applicants' proposed program access commitments in the following section, we clarify that aggrieved programmers and MVPDs may seek relief for any alleged violations of this condition by using the existing enforcement mechanisms found at Section 76.1003 of the Commission's rules.

108. As to broadcast programming, we find it unlikely that, after the transaction, DirecTV would discriminate against competing television broadcast stations. The applicable statutory and regulatory provisions thoroughly address satellite carriage of broadcast television programming. In any market in which DirecTV offers local-into-local service pursuant to the statutory copyright license, it is required to carry all television broadcast stations within that local market that request carriage. The Commission's rules detail the technical terms of carriage, certain anti-discrimination provisions based on SHVIA, [Eds. Satellite Home Viewer Improvement Act, discussed in Chapter 5] and the complaint process by which aggrieved parties can seek Commission redress if DirecTV has failed to meet its carriage obligations. Alternatively, television broadcast stations that provide retransmission consent can negotiate the terms and conditions of carriage. We reiterate that, under the SHVIA, we will, in reviewing carriage complaints against any MVPD, consider any unreasonable terms or conditions or negotiating procedures.

4. Discrimination Against Unaffiliated MVPDs

a. Access to National and Non–Sports Regional Cable Programming Networks

* * *

(ii) Discussion and Conditions

124. We conclude that the program access rules, combined with the Applicants' proposed program access conditions, will be sufficient to eliminate any potential for anti-competitive conduct due to the vertical relationship between News Corp's satellite cable programming networks

and DirecTV's distribution platform with respect to News Corp.'s general national and non-sports regional programming. Accordingly, we adopt the Applicants' proposed conditions and decline to impose additional program access restrictions for this programming.

125. In enacting the program access provisions of the 1992 Cable Act. Congress found that extensive vertical integration between cable operators and cable programming vendors created an imbalance of power, both between cable operators and programming vendors and between incumbent cable operators and their multichannel competitors. Congress determined that this imbalance of power limited the development of competition among MVPDs and limited consumer choice. Congress expressed its concern that unaffiliated MVPDs faced difficulties gaining access to programming required to provide a viable alternative to cable. Congress found that vertically integrated program suppliers had the incentive and ability to favor their affiliated cable operators. In response, Congress imposed specific conduct restrictions, including limits on exclusive contracts, to ensure market entrants could gain access to all vertically integrated satellite cable programming. The competitive concerns, addressed through the program access statute are similar to many of the concerns expressed by commenters regarding fair and non-discriminatory access to News Corp.'s cable programming. That is, Congress essentially recognized that access to all vertically integrated satellite cable programming on non-discriminatory terms and conditions was needed by all MVPDs and that until competitive conditions significantly altered, the Commission must enforce prohibitions on unfair and discriminatory terms and conditions of carriage. Because Congress' focus at the time was the market power in incumbent cable operators, it additionally imposed a prohibition on exclusive carriage arrangements among cable operators and vertically integrated satellite cable programming vendors.

126. In its 2002 examination of whether to permit the exclusivity prohibition to sunset, the Commission reiterated that "access to vertically integrated programming continues to be necessary in order for competitive MVPDs to remain viable in the marketplace," and that "failure to secure even a portion of vertically integrated programming would put a nonaffiliated cable operator or MVPD at a significant disadvantage vis-à-vis a competitor with access to such programming." In addition, the Commission observed that "cable programming—be it news, drama, sports, music or children's programming—is not akin to so many widgets," and explained that complete loss of access to certain highly popular programming networks may harm the foreclosed unaffiliated competitor in the marketplace. The Commission explained, "there is a continuum of vertically integrated programming, ranging from services for which there may be substitutes (the absence of which from a rival MVPD's program lineup would have little impact), to those for which there are imperfect substitutes, to those for which there are no close substitutes at all (the absence of which from a rival MVPD's program lineup would have a substantial negative impact). The Commission concluded that despite the

progress made in the last ten years in terms of the availability of cable programming, "a considerable amount of vertically integrated programming in the marketplace today remains "must have" programming to most MPVD subscribers," such that the program access rules, including particularly the exclusivity provision, continue to be necessary to prevent anticompetitive foreclosure of access to all of the vertically integrated satellite programming covered by the rules. Further, although the Commission recognized that "certain programming services, such as sports programming, or marquee programming, such as HBO, may be essential and for practical purposes, 'must haves' for program distributors and their subscribers," it recognized "the difficulty of developing an objective process of general applicability to determine what programming may or may not be essential to preserve and protect competition." The Commission therefore declined to narrow the scope of the exclusivity prohibition to apply only to certain types of programming that may be considered "essential programming services."

127. *Permanent Foreclosure.* * * * To ensure that the access and non-discrimination requirements of the program access rules will continue to apply to News Corp.'s national and regional cable programming, and to obtain the additional protections encompassed by the Applicants' related commitments, we adopt the following conditions proposed by Applicants:

- News Corp. will not offer any of its existing or future national and regional programming services on an exclusive basis to any MVPD and will continue to make such services available to all MVPDs on a non-exclusive basis and nondiscriminatory terms and conditions.

- DirecTV will not enter into an exclusive distribution arrangement with any Affiliated Program Rights Holder.[*]

* * *

- DirecTV may continue to compete for programming that is lawfully offered on an exclusive basis by an unaffiliated program rights holder (e.g., NFL Sunday Ticket)

- Neither News Corp. nor DirecTV (including any entity over which either exercises control) shall unduly or improperly influence: (i) the decision of any Affiliated Program Rights Holder to sell programming to an unaffiliated MVPD; or (ii) the prices, terms and conditions of sale of programming by any Affiliated Program Rights Holder to an unaffiliated MVPD.

- These commitments will apply to News Corp. and DirecTV for the later of (1) as long as the FCC deems News Corp. to have an Attributable Interest in DirecTV and the FCC's program access rules are in effect (provided that if the program access rules are modified these commitments shall be modified to conform to any revised rules adopted by the

* Eds. As used in the order, an "Affiliated Program Rights Holder" is "a program rights holder in which News Corp. or DirecTV holds a non-controlling 'Attributable Interest' (as determined by the FCC's program access attribution rules)."

FCC) or (2) if these commitments are embodied in a consent decree or other appropriate order issued by or agreement with the DOJ, FTC or FCC, for the term specified by such consent decree, order or agreement.

128. Applicants will be bound by these program access conditions so long as the Commission has program access rules applicable to satellite cable programming vendors affiliated with cable operators. * * *

b. Access to Regional Sports Cable Programming Networks

(i) Background

133. Since the Commission first began tracking regional cable programming networks in 1998, it has repeatedly recognized the importance of regional sports programming to MVPD offerings. This acknowledgement is based, in part, on the finding that for such programming, there are no readily acceptable close substitutes. The basis for the lack of adequate substitutes for regional sports programming lies in the unique nature of its core component: regional sports networks ("RSNs") typically purchase exclusive rights to show sporting events and sports fans believe that there is no good substitute for watching their local and/or favorite team play an important game. The Commission's extension of the sunset date for the exclusivity program access rules last year was intended, in part, to ensure that competing MVPDs would have continued access to the satellite-delivered regional sports programming owned by vertically integrated cable operators. We also have long recognized that the terrestrial distribution of programming-particularly RSN programming-by vertically integrated cable operators could competitively disadvantage competing MVPDs if they were denied access to the terrestrially delivered programming.

134. News Corp. is a major owner of RSNs. It owns or has an attributable interest in 19 RSNs, 12 of which it manages, which reach 79 million television households. According to NCTA's Cable Developments 2003, those RSNs produce over 4,700 live events each year, and carry 65 of the 80 professional Major League Baseball ("MLB"), National Basketball Association ("NBA") and National Hockey League ("NHL") teams. RSNs wholly owned by News Corp. carry 45 of the 80 professional teams, and thus controls a significant amount of professional sports programming on regional sports networks. * * *

(iii) Discussion

147. We conclude that News Corp. currently possesses significant market power with respect to its RSNs within each of their specific geographic regions, and that the proposed transaction will enhance News Corp.'s incentive and ability to temporarily withhold or threaten to withhold access to its RSN programming to increase the fees it receives for the programming, over and above what it could negotiate absent the transaction, to the ultimate detriment of the public. Moreover, we find that in contrast to the situation with respect to access to national and

non-sports regional programming, neither our program access rules nor Applicants' proposed program access commitments are sufficient to protect against these likely transaction-specific harms. * * *

151. In addition to the studies submitted by the parties, Commission staff conducted its own economic analysis. As commenters correctly observe, the increased ability of an RSN owner to credibly threaten to withhold its signal, even if it does not actually do so, changes its bargaining position with respect to MVPDs, and could allow the RSN owner to extract higher prices, which are ultimately passed on to consumers. The staff's economic analysis is premised on the assumption that, if the transaction significantly enhances News Corp.'s incentive and ability to withhold signals of its RSNs by lowering the costs to News Corp. of employing such bargaining tactics, News Corp. will engage in such behavior, and that this will result in an increase of rival MVPDs' programming costs, and ultimately end-user prices. Key to determining the degree to which the transaction lowers News Corp.'s costs of engaging in temporary foreclosure is the number of subscribers that can be predicted to shift from the affected MVPD to competitor DirecTV to access the foreclosed programming, which in turn will increase the profits of the post-transaction company as a whole, over and above levels achievable under today's conditions.

152. *Permanent Foreclosure*. As discussed in greater detail in Appendix D, the technical appendix, the staff's economic analysis examined the potential profitability of both permanent and temporary foreclosure strategies for each of News Corp.'s RSNs. Based upon the staff's analysis, we agree with Applicants that a strategy of permanent RSN foreclosure, assuming that it were permissible under the rules, would be unprofitable for News Corp. and therefore unlikely to be pursued any more frequently post-transaction than it is today. We therefore do not find that permanent foreclosure of RSN programming is likely to be transaction-specific harm.

153. *Temporary Foreclosure*. We also agree with commenters who argue that a temporary foreclosure strategy is likely to be profitable to News Corp. in many instances. The staff's analysis supports the further conclusion that this increase in the profitability of temporary foreclosure to News Corp. will make the threat of withdrawing programming a more credible tactic. By employing this tactic News Corp. will be able to negotiate higher prices than it could absent its control of DirecTV. On this basis, we find it likely that temporary foreclosure will be employed more frequently following News Corp.'s acquisition of control of DirecTV than it is today, and that this would, in turn, lead to greater programming price increases to MVPDs and higher subscription prices to consumers than we would expect to find absent News Corp.'s control of DirecTV. Increased use of temporary foreclosure strategies would thus harm competition and consumers by raising rivals' costs, by amounts greater than those News Corp. could reasonably expect to gain absent the transaction, thereby causing undue increases in MVPD subscription prices. * * *

162. In light of the foregoing analysis, we conclude that neither the Commission's existing rules nor the Applicants' proposed safeguards are sufficient to protect against harms caused by temporary foreclosure. We find, contrary to Applicants' arguments, that the program access rules will not adequately protect against this harm, because they were not intended to regulate or address the level of rates per se. Moreover, we recognize that, even if the program access rules adequately address rate levels (and not just discrimination), News Corp. would still be able to withhold programming pending resolution of a program access complaint. Because we find that the proposed transaction poses likely consumer harms that will not be adequately mitigated by the Commission's existing rules or the Applicants' proposed conditions, we consider whether other conditions can mitigate this harm below.

(iv) Conditions

* * *

172. *Conditions*. Our analysis demonstrates that the primary public interest harm likely to follow from the unique combination of News Corp.'s RSN programming assets and DirecTV's nationwide distribution platform is the competitive harm of an across-the-board MVPD price increase resulting from News Corp.'s ability to extract rents or other unfair carriage concessions from MVPDs for carriage of RSN programming through the more frequent use of threats of withholding or actual withholding of RSN programming during a period of temporary foreclosure. A secondary public interest harm is that MVPD subscribers are deprived of programming that is highly desired during such a period. * * *

175. Thus, our remedy is to allow MVPDs to demand commercial arbitration when they are unable to come to a negotiated "fair" price for the programming. The staff analysis has found that the allure of temporary withholding to News Corp. is substantial, even after the ability invariably to obtain supracompetitive affiliate fee increases is eliminated. Accordingly we do not allow News Corp. to deauthorize carriage of the RSN after an MVPD has chosen to avail itself of the arbitration condition. We also specify that expedited arbitration procedures be used and that the final offers submitted to the arbitrator by each side may not include any compensation for RSN carriage in the form of the MVPD's agreement to carry any video programming networks or any other service other than the RSN. * * *

VII. Other Potential Public Interest Harms

* * * [The Commission here considers and rejects various claims in opposition. Among these were claims that the transaction will reduce diversity. The argument basically reprised the arguments above about News Corp's ability to foreclose other MVPDs' access to Fox's programming. A related claim was that News Corps could bypass its local

affiliates in favor of exclusive distribution through DirecTV. Finally, the Commission rejected as speculative a claim that the transaction would give News Corp. new incentives to collude with other vertically integrated distributors (the large cable MSOs) to the detriment of independent distributors and consumers.]

IX. Balancing Potential Public Interest Harms and Benefits

358. Our task under the Communications Act is to determine whether the "public interest, convenience and necessity will be served" by the granting of the Application. The public interest standard involves a balancing of potential public interest harms of the proposed transaction and the potential public interest benefits. The Applicants bear the burden of proving, by a preponderance of the evidence that the proposed transaction, on balance, serves the public interest. Our options at this stage are to approve the application without conditions, approve it with conditions, or hold a hearing if we are unable to make the findings required for approval. The Application and the substantial record before us make clear that, on balance, the public interest will be served by approval of the application as amended by the conditions that we impose herein. * * *

Structural Limits Through Licensing. Neither the vertical limits based on § 533(f) nor the prohibition against exclusive agreements in § 548(c)(2)(D) applies to DirecTV. (The general unfair competition provision of § 548(b) does apply to Fox, a "satellite broadcast programming vendor"). Rather, the Commission imposed the limits as a condition on the transfer of the necessary licenses to operate the DirecTV satellites (and their ground stations and the terrestrial transmission equipment DirecTV uses to operate its enterprise). On what authority was the FCC regulating? GM/Hughes and Fox accepted rather than challenged the limits, obviating the need for a showdown in the courts, but the parties must have been confident that the FCC could legally deny the transfer in order to have been willing to accept them without a fight. Should the Commission be able to impose such limits as a condition on the transfer of licenses?

The Argument for Vertical Integration. The Commission cites antitrust theory for the argument that vertical integration can often lead to efficiencies. The idea, generally, is that a company may do a better job of managing its suppliers (and retailers) if they are all in the same company, for instance, manufacturers may be able to exercise better control over their sales force (through training, etc.) if they own the retailers than if they rely on independent retailers. What possible economic efficiencies will result from integrating programming with either cable or satellite operations?

The Enemy of My Enemy ... The Commission is concerned about Fox's increased potential for overreaching in negotiating with cable operators for its content now that it has an alternative distribution path. The FCC treats Fox's increased market power as a bad thing, but is that necessarily so? Isn't enlisting Fox's increased market power as a counterbalance to the vertically integrated MSOs a better way of keeping them in check than imposing potentially arbitrary regulatory limits on the MSOs? Indeed, isn't a Fox left unhindered by vertical limits all the better to challenge the MSOs?

Fox as a Broadcaster. One major difference between Fox and the vertically integrated MSOs is the nature of the content they provide. The MSOs are, largely, vertically integrated cable content providers; Fox is largely a vertically integrated broadcast content provider. As we've seen throughout this part, broadcast stations hold a special place in the FCC's institutional heart. Does it matter that Fox owns both a broadcast network and many broadcast stations? If you are a cable operator, are you more worried about making sure you carry CNN or the local broadcast station? Conversely, are you more likely to hold out in negotiations against CNN or the local broadcast station? We will examine the relationship between broadcast and MVPDs in the next chapter.

Chapter 5

INTER-MEDIA COMPETITION

A. INTRODUCTION

In the last chapter we examined a variety of structural rules designed to promote competition and diversity within the broadcasting, cable, and satellite industries. As the DirecTV merger case suggests, though, competition (and the temptation to subvert it) may occur *between* types of media—in that case between cable and DBS. As it happens, inter-media competition has been regulated from its earliest appearance in the 1960s. In this chapter we explore this aspect of mass media regulation. As we have done throughout this book, we begin with some history because it is impossible to understand the present regulatory framework without it. However, as will be become quickly apparent, the rivalry among mass media—first broadcast against cable and eventually broadcast and cable collectively against the upstart DBS providers—remains a centerpiece of regulatory controversy even after nearly 50 years.

The subject here is competition among *video* mass media—different forms for delivering video content. As we noted in the last chapter, the proliferation of radio stations has pretty much eliminated concern about competition in that medium. Moreover, audio programming simply has not undergone as stark a transformation in the way it is delivered. Even in 2008 terrestrial radio still dominates audio mass media.

The video programming market, on the other hand, has changed dramatically from the days when broadcasting was the dominant delivery system. In 1960 the average television household was fortunate to receive three reliably good channels.[1] Today it is an unusual household that does not have access to more than 50 in even the smallest markets, and more than 100 in the larger markets. This, of course, is the result of multi-channel media, cable and satellite—which the FCC now lumps

1. Recall from Chapter 2 that for more than a decade after the seminal television allotment plan in 1952, the Commission struggled to enable smaller markets to receive three competitive viewing options—a problem that had been created as a result of the inability of UHF channel stations to compete effectively with VHF channel stations in markets where only two VHF channels had been allotted.

together as a single product market labeled "multichannel video programming distributors"("MVPD"). About 86% of all households now subscribe to cable or satellite service; cable predominates over satellite by a margin of more than 2 to 1, but the margin has been steadily declining as DBS has increased its subscription at the expense of cable. See *Annual Assessment of the Status of Competition in the Market for the Delivery of Video Programming*, 21 FCC Rcd. 2503 ¶ 8 (2006). For purposes of assessing competition in the MVPD market, the Commission includes a variety of other delivery systems. For example, so-called "wireless cable" systems and large home satellite dishes ("HSD") are included, though both have steadily declined in importance with the growth of wired cable and DBS. A more promising new category is what the Commission calls "broadband service providers" ("BSP"), which are designed to provide video, voice, and data (Internet) services over a single network.[2] This category includes new optical fiber networks being constructed by local exchange telephone service carriers, and cable providers are getting into that business as well. We will have occasion to examine aspects of BSP later when we deal with Internet issues in Chapter 10. In the present chapter we focus on the two principal MVPD systems—cable and satellite—and the longstanding rivalry over the delivery of video content.

B. BROADCASTING AND CABLE

1. The Evolution of Cable Regulation

More than any other sector of regulated communications, cable television regulation has resembled a sine wave of undulating currents of regulation, deregulation, and reregulation. In its first cycle, from the early 1960s to the late 1970s, cable regulation followed a virtually uniform pattern of increased regulation. The next decade, lasting into the late 1980s, saw a considerable downward trend in the cycle, only to be followed by an upturn that lasted for about another decade. Since then, the cyclical swings have been less clearly marked and of shorter duration—a mixture of up and down.

To start at the beginning—of television that is—it must be noted that cable did not figure in the FCC's 1952 national television allocation plan, which as we saw in Chapter 2 provides the basic framework for television regulatory policies to this day. Cable was in those early years a minor service auxiliary to broadcast. The business of early cable television providers was essentially to hook their subscribers up to large broadcast television antennas in order to receive existing broadcast signals. (One frequently sees the acronym "CATV" used to refer to "cable television," but "CATV" originally stood for "community antenna television".) The purpose of cable during this time was merely "fill in

2. Although broadcast stations can and do provide multiple channels with their new digital channels, this "multicast" service does not make them MVPDs. The Commission limits MVPDs to entities that are "engaged in the business of making available for purchase, by subscribers or customers, multiple channels of video programming." 47 C.F.R. § 76.1000. Thus, only those that charge viewers are included.

the gaps" of regular television service, that is, to extend service to areas where, because of geographic remoteness or terrain obstacles, regular television service was unavailable. But, along with the growth of regular television in the 1950s, cable television also expanded. By the early 1960s it had begun to emerge from its auxiliary service role into a service potentially competitive with regular television broadcasting. Its expanding role was enhanced by the use of long distance microwave transmission facilities, which enabled cable systems to not only passively receive existing local broadcast signals but also to transmit signals acquired from "distant" markets and introduce them into local markets—in competition with local television broadcast stations. Local broadcast stations, concerned about the potential economic impact of cable, sought the FCC's protection.

At first the FCC declined to take jurisdiction, based largely on the absence of any demonstrated economic impact. However, the broadcasters kept pressing and the FCC's initial reluctance was soon overcome. Beginning in 1962 and extending for more than a decade into the early 1970s, the FCC would construct one of the most elaborate regulatory regimes constructed without congressional action, which only came much later.

The jurisdictional basis for asserting control over cable was thin. Cable television did not fit the conventional definition of a "broadcast station" which would place it within the Commission's jurisdiction under Title III of the Communications Act. The character of the cable medium (wires) resembles telephony, which might have warranted regulation under Title II of the Communications Act. However, even if cable had been so regarded it would not have served the FCC's purposes. For one thing, cable is provided on a local basis, and as such would primarily have been within the jurisdiction of state and local governments, not the FCC. Moreover, Title II was then primarily concerned with *consumer* regulation, and the FCC was not then interested in protecting consumers; the concern was the competitive impact on local broadcasting and there was nothing in the structure of the classic common carrier regulation contained in Title II that lent itself to that purpose.

Undaunted by the absence of a specific textual or clear functional basis for regulation under either Title II or III, the Commission turned to Title I, which specifies the general purposes of the FCC (most generally that of "regulating interstate and foreign commerce in communications by wire and radio...") but contains no specific terms of regulation—those ostensibly being the function of Titles II and III. The Commission reasoned that Title I conferred a general jurisdiction over all interstate communications by wire and radio and that was at least sufficient to carry out the programmatic functions conferred by the other Titles. In other words it had "ancillary" jurisdiction derived from its overall role as a regulator of electronic communications and on the asserted need to protect the broadcasting system—and the regulatory scheme the FCC had put in place for it—under Title III. To those who think of tight interpretive canons, the jurisdictional theory might seem a bit strained, for there is not even legislative history much less text in the statute itself to support such an open-textured basis for regulation. But as we remarked in Chapter 1, the Communications Act was considered to confer broad powers. In all events, whatever it may have intended in 1934, Congress was disinclined to assert itself through clarification while the FCC was constructing this new regulatory program. Congress would not be heard from on the subject for over two decades, until 1984, when it added Title VI to the Act to deal with cable television. By that time the FCC had not only completed but begun to deconstruct the first generation of cable regulation. Thus Congress came in during the second act, when the plot of the play had taken a radically different tack from where it had started 20 years earlier. It would not be the last time the plot would change, but of this more later.

Needless to say, the FCC perceived cable not as an opportunity but as a threat, and the early regulation reflected that stance. Probably because it was not entirely confident in its ancillary jurisdiction theory, the Commission's initial foray in 1962 was limited to regulating cable where it relied on microwave feeds to re-transmit broadcast signals to the local head-end of the cable system. This use of radio transmission of (previously) broadcast signals gave the FCC a Title III basis to require that no such microwave licensee could transmit programs to a cable system that caused economic injury to a local broadcast station. But the FCC quickly moved beyond this limited purpose and limited jurisdiction. In two seminal rulemaking proceedings in 1965 and 1966, the Commission asserted general jurisdiction over all cable systems (regardless of whether they used radio in any manner) and imposed a variety of restrictions designed to prevent economic harm to local broadcast stations. Among other things this included a requirement that all cable systems carry the signals of all television stations in their community (called "must-carry"), a prohibition against importing any out-of-market signal that duplicated the network programming of the local broadcast stations (called "network non-duplication"), and a set of limitations on the importation of signals from distant markets in certain markets regardless of their content (called "distant signal importation"). The distant signal rules varied by market size. In the top 100 markets cable could not engage in distant signal importation of any out-of-market signals except on a showing in an evidentiary hearing that the importation would not constitute a threat to the development of UHF facilities in those markets. In smaller markets local stations could also challenge importation but the proof burden was reversed (the theory being that smaller markets would not be able to support additional UHF channels anyway). After a few years the FCC gave up on the evidentiary hearing requirement and simply imposed a moratorium on all distant signal importation while the Commission considered a comprehensive regime for dealing with the cable "problem."

Considering that the Commission had spent the previous decade exploring ways to increase the number of local channels that viewers could receive, the identification of cable as a "problem" might appear ironic. After all, cable television offered, even at that early stage, more channels of television than were typically available over the air—and the potential existed for an order of magnitude increase in channels in the near future. From that perspective cable was a solution to a problem that had found no other solution given the relative scarcity of broadcast signals necessitated by the 1952 television allotment plan. However, cable did in fact create a "problem" to the extent that it posed an economic threat to "free" (advertiser supported) television broadcast by local stations serving local needs. Too, the Commission viewed cable as a form of "unfair" competition. The FCC's *Second Report on CATV*, 2 F.C.C.2d 725 (1966), provides a summary.

As to the local service rationale, the FCC explained, at 775:

> (i) CATV does not now serve the rural areas, and it has not been established that it can practically do so. If CATV were to undermine the healthy development of UHF, it would mean that people in the urban or more built up areas would be getting additional service at the expense of those in the rural areas; we think that such a result is patently inconsistent with the public interest and the act's goals.
>
> (ii) CATV is a form of pay TV, in the sense that one must pay to obtain the television service. There are substantial numbers of people who either cannot afford to or do not wish to pay for television. If then the CATV blocks development of UHF broadcasting, it would again mean that some people would be getting additional service at the expense of those who cannot afford or are unwilling to pay for such service.
>
> (iii) Most important, CATV does not serve as an outlet for local self expression. It does not present local discussions, the local ministers or educators, the local political candidates, etc. If events in the major markets should establish that CATV has prevented the healthy maintenance of UHF broadcasting, it would mean that, for example, New York independents would have been substituted for Philadelphia independents. We think that would be contrary to sound allocation principles, long established in section 307(b) of the act.

As to the fairness concern the FCC noted, at 775–76:

> A television station normally obtains the right to exhibit nonnetwork programs by outright payments to program suppliers, from whom the station usually secures the exclusive right to exhibit the programs within a particular geographical area and for a particular length of time. This exclusivity reflects the judgment that presentation by others of a program such as a feature film within the station's market within some period of time obviously reduces the audience and the value of program to the station. * * *
>
> [T]he CATV system presently stands outside of the above program distribution process * * * "it does not compete for network affiliation, nor for access to syndicated programs, feature films or sports events." It is not concerned with bidding against competing broad-

casters for the right to exhibit these programs nor with bargaining with program suppliers for time and territorial exclusivity.

In 1968 the Supreme Court upheld the Commission's regulatory power to promulgate regulations based on the ancillary theory in *United States v. Southwestern Cable Co.*, 392 U.S. 157 (1968).

The regulations promulgated in 1965 and 1966 were not seen as the "final solution" (though from the vantage point of a struggling cable system they might well have appeared to be in the colloquial sense of that term). In fact the FCC itself almost immediately backtracked and began to look for ways of easing the restraints on cable expansion. That task was complicated by the question of copyright. The FCC had regulated cable because of its impact on broadcast television, but another way of skinning the cat would be to grant broadcasters (or the program producers they dealt with) the power to control the distribution of the programs themselves, rather than the broadcast signal. But the Supreme Court refused to impose copyright liability on cable's unauthorized use of broadcast signals. See *Fortnightly Corp. v. United Artists Television, Inc.*, 392 U.S. 390 (1968); see also the later *Teleprompter Corp. v. Columbia Broadcasting System, Inc.*, 415 U.S. 394 (1974)). While the absence of copyright protection did not affect the localism *cum* economic protection rationale, it did strongly affect the "unfair competition" point—it was hard to describe as "unfair" a form of program distribution sanctioned by the Supreme Court. The copyright question was a statutory one, which led the Commission to ask Congress to resolve the copyright question for cable television so that it could reformulate its cable policy. However, copyright liability for cable systems was a small part of a much larger effort to re-write the entire Copyright Act, which at this time was stalled.[3] With no copyright legislation on the horizon, the Commission was unwilling to impose its own regulatory solution without agreement of the major interested parties: the broadcast and cable industries, and the copyright interests (mainly Hollywood film producers and distributors). Under the auspices of the FCC Chairman and the Director of the Office of Telecommunications Policy in the White House, the three major interest groups conducted intensive negotiations culminating in a compromise "Consensus Agreement" in 1971.

With some modifications, the consensus scheme was incorporated into formal FCC rules (following notice and comment rulemaking). See *Cable Television Report and Order*, 36 F.C.C.2d 141 (1972). The regulatory scheme eliminated the freeze on distant signal importation, allowing cable to expand into larger markets. However, the new rules continued the older pattern of tight restrictions on cable operations, most notably: the "must-carry" and "network non-duplication" rules, which were expanded to include protection of non-network, syndicated programs as well (called "syndicated exclusivity" rules). Also included in the scheme

3. A new copyright law would not be enacted until 1976. Part of that new act made unauthorized retransmission of broadcast signals an infringement, but it also provided for a compulsory license. We discuss the provisions in greater detail below.

were various provisions establishing standards for franchising of cable systems by local government authorities along with a variety of technical rules. The 1972 rules had a Byzantine complexity that defies simple summary. For example, the rules were tailored to the types of stations carried (UHF or VHF, auxiliary or regular stations), the size of cable systems, and the size of the television market. The FCC had one set of carriage rules for cable systems operating in the top 50 television markets, another for those operating in the second 50 markets and yet another for markets below the top 100. And so on. Although many of these regulations are relevant only for historical purposes, the must-carry, network non-duplication, and syndicated exclusivity rules lived on and formed the foundation for modern cable regulation.

The next turning point in the FCC's regulatory strategy for cable came as the result of its attempt to restrict the ability of cable systems to offer channels on a paid, subscription basis. Pay television had been the subject of regulatory controversy before the emergence of cable as an important medium of television. The Commission initially authorized over-the-air subscription television on an experimental basis in the late 1950s. The experiment was authorized only after opposition by theater owners and the broadcast industry. The theater owners' opposition was based on the simple threat of competition (that potential theatergoers might pay to watch a movie in the comfort of their own homes rather than travel to a movie theater for the same privilege); that of the broadcast industry also rested on competitive impact but the argument was a bit more complex. The broadcast industry argued that subscription television would cause programming to be "siphoned" away from advertiser-supported broadcasting; subscription television stations could outbid regular broadcasters (including networks) for program rights because they could collect a direct fee from subscription viewers that was greater than advertisers would, or could, pay to reach those same viewers. In order to understand this threat you have to understand that advertisers pay only a couple of cents per viewer expected to be reached by advertiser-supported programs. Given that there are only a limited number of advertising minutes that can be sold to support any given program, this means that very large audiences are needed in order to draw enough advertising revenues to support the production and distribution costs of quality programming. Anheuser–Busch will pay big dollars to buy time spots on Monday Night Football on the assumption that the games draw millions of television viewers, and on that assumption broadcasters will pay the NFL big dollars to license NFL games for "free" broadcast television. But now suppose that the NFL figures that it can derive more revenue by foregoing advertising and charging each subscribing household, say, $2.00 a game. If you compare the $2.00 subscription fee per household to the roughly $.02 that advertisers will pay per viewer, it becomes apparent that subscription television requires only a fraction of the audience to generate equal revenue and thus to be in a position to siphon programming from "free" TV to pay TV.

To prevent this threat to free television, the Commission in 1968 placed stringent restrictions on subscription operations. They were probably unnecessary in the market conditions that then prevailed in *broadcast* television; the opportunity costs were too high. Given their limited number, broadcast television channels were more valuable as advertising media than as subscription media. But with the appearance of cable, and its ability to carry many, many more channels, the economic calculus changed dramatically. The high number of channels that cable could carry made the opportunity cost of devoting one or more channels to pay programming close to zero. With cable, then, the siphoning threat suddenly seemed more serious—at least in the minds of broadcasters. If this obvious fact was not lost on cable entrepreneurs, it was also not lost on a broadcaster-friendly FCC. Two years after its adoption of the restrictive subscription television broadcasting rules, the FCC extended them to pay-cable services. The rules were relaxed slightly in 1975, but somewhat ironically it was the relaxation of the rules that provided a fresh opportunity to challenge them in court (the earlier rules governing subscription broadcasting had been upheld).[4] This time the court in *Home Box Office, Inc. v. FCC*, 567 F.2d 9 (D.C. Cir. 1977), found the rules procedurally defective, substantively unreasonable, and a violation of the First Amendment.[5]

Evaluating the substantive content of the rules under the arbitrary and capricious standards of the Administrative Procedure Act, the court determined that the FCC had not demonstrated that the siphoning threat was even a real problem. The Commission had framed the issue as "how cablecasting can best be regulated to provide a beneficial supple-

4. Here is a summary of the rules; the actual rules are much more detailed, but even from the summary you can discern the agency's penchant for finely tuned rules: First, the rules prohibited four categories of programs to be aired on pay cable channels: (1) feature films more than three, but less than 10, years old; (2) specific sports events (e.g., the World Series) shown on broadcast television within the previous five years; (3) more than the minimum number of non-specific (i.e., regular season) sports events which had not been broadcast in any of the five preceding years, and in some cases only half that number; and (4) all series programs (i.e., programs with interconnected plot or substantially the same cast of principal characters). Second, rules prohibited commercial advertising in conjunction with pay exhibition of programming. Third, the rules limited the overall number of hours of pay operation which could be devoted to sports and feature films to 90% of total pay operations. The prohibited categories represent those categories of programs that were thought to be most vulnerable to siphoning, that is being preempted for *exclusive* distribution by cable. It was for that reason that, on further consideration, the fourth category was eliminated.

5. The court's finding of a procedural defect became a controversial landmark in administrative law. The defect was that interested parties in the rulemaking had been allowed to make ex parte communications to the Commission. Such contacts had been (and to a degree still are) permissible in information (notice-and-comment) rulemaking, though as we observed in Chapter 1, the FCC now routinely places some restrictions on them. In *HBO* the court found the ex parte communications objectionable because it viewed the rulemaking proceeding as similar in substance if not in form to an adjudication of "conflicting private claims to a valuable privilege" between the respective industry interests. A moment's reflection on the regulatory process will reveal that this claim could be made about virtually all agency rulemaking. In a subsequent decision—also involving the FCC—a different panel of the same court gave a very narrow reading of this aspect of *HBO*, substantially undercutting it. Action for Children's Television v. FCC, 564 F.2d 458 (D.C. Cir. 1977).

ment to over-the-air broadcasting without at the same time undermining the continued operation of that 'free' television service." In responding, the court took dead aim on what had been the central premise of all cable regulation: that cable must be confined to a supplemental role. "[T]he Commission has in no way justified its position that cable television must be a supplement to, rather than an equal of, broadcast television. Such an artificial narrowing of the scope of the regulatory problem is itself arbitrary and capricious and is ground for reversal." The court went on to hold that, even if siphoning might work a harm to the public interest, the Commission had produced no substantial evidence that it was a realistic threat.

The most far-reaching aspect of its decision was the court's holding that the pay cable regulations violated the First Amendment, under the standards of *United States v. O'Brien*, 391 U.S. 367 (1968), as content-neutral restraints:

> We have already concluded that the Commission has not put itself in a position to know whether the alleged siphoning phenomenon is a real or merely a fanciful threat to those not served by cable. Instead, the Commission has indulged in speculation and innuendo. *O'Brien* requires that "an important or substantial governmental interest" be demonstrated, however a requirement which translates in the rulemaking context into a record that convincingly shows a problem to exist and that relates the proffered solution to the statutory mandate of the agency. The record before us fails on both scores. Moreover, we doubt that the Commission's interest in preventing delay of motion picture broadcasts could be shown to be important or substantial on any record.

On remand the FCC abandoned its restrictions on pay cable. *HBO* was a noteworthy victory for cable not only because it gave cable a new service to sell, but because it marked a turning point for the industry. For more than a decade regulation had relentlessly moved upwards. But now even the FCC entertained second thoughts about the regulatory straitjacket it had imposed on the industry. It was partly helped in this direction by Congress's enactment in 1976 of a new copyright law that covered cable carriage of copyrighted broadcast programs. Perhaps more important was the fact that, despite all the handicaps, cable had survived, had grown, and yet had not caused significant economic distress to the broadcast industry. With that growth the old model of cable as strictly a supplementary service became increasingly untenable. Finally, political realists will take note of the fact that as cable matured it acquired not only added political strength but also a degree of recognition as a regulatory client. In contrast to the 1960s, when cable was an outsider, cable was now represented within the industry—with its own bureau within the FCC. The most important move to relax the regulatory constraints on cable came in 1980 with the repeal of restrictions on the number of signals that could be imported from distant markets, and a repeal of the syndicated exclusivity rules. Cable systems were free to carry signals without limitation, subject to the requirements that local signals had to be carried on request and *network programming* could not be simultaneously duplicated by distant signals. When the court of appeals affirmed in 1981, *Malrite TV of New York v. FCC*, 652 F.2d 1140, 1147 (2d Cir.1981), it definitively marked the end of the first act of cable regulation. When Congress made its entrance on the scene with the 1984 Cable Act, it essentially confirmed what the FCC had already done.

But nothing lasts forever, and in the field of communications the shelf life of a particular policy is often no more than a few years. No sooner had the FCC made a substantial turn towards deregulation, with Congress's approval, than there arose fresh pressure for reregulation. Cable's rise to dominance stimulated new concerns not only at the FCC but in Congress as well. As cable became more entrenched in local communities and more the dominant medium nationwide, there was audible grumbling. Some of it came from the broadcast industry and some from the general public. In 1992 Congress was galvanized into action, this time to rather different purpose and effect than in 1984. The most important features of the 1992 act were (1) a reinstatement of must-carry rules (which had been invalidated by the court of appeals in the late 1980s); (2) creation of a new requirement that cable providers obtain permission from local broadcasters for carriage of local signals (called "retransmission consent"); and (3) creation of a two-tier regime (with authority split between the FCC and local governments) for consumer rate controls.

Since 1992, the course of cable regulation has been somewhat erratic—a combination of regulation and deregulation in no consistent pattern. But the regulatory landscape for cable has remained both defined and dominated by three major regulations: the old network non-duplication and syndicated exclusivity rules, which were not altered by the 1992 Act (although they were extended to satellite broadcasting, which we address below); the reinstated must-carry rules; and the new retransmission consent rules. (We defer an examination of the rate control provisions of the 1992 Cable Act to the next chapter.)

2. Network Non-duplication and Syndicated Exclusivity

Recall from the brief sketch of cable regulatory history that when the FCC first set out to regulate cable television it was struck by the unfairness of allowing one competitor, cable, to use the property of another, broadcasters, without any form of compensation or consent. At that time the copyright law did not prevent cable systems from retransmitting broadcast programs. The Commission first dealt with the problem by means of its network non-duplication and syndicated exclusivity rules. As we saw earlier, the network non-duplication provisions protect the broadcasters from having their programming distributed to additional viewers without compensation, but, in the early years at least, protection against uncompensated distribution was probably secondary to the FCC's interest in for minimizing economic loss from audience fragmentation—the splitting of audiences to watch the same programming on multiple channels, resulting in an insufficient audience for any one channel to be sustainable.[6] The Commission subsequently extended this type of property rights protection to *non*network programming—programming purchased by the broadcast stations from syndicators. The period of protection is the same for syndicated as for network programs. A local broadcast station can demand that cable systems in its market not duplicate either network or syndicated programs for the same period of time that the broadcaster has exclusive rights from the network or syndicator that supplies it the program. If, for instance, the network-affiliate agreement or the syndicator-station agreement gives the local station an exclusive right to air the program (*vis-à-vis* other broadcast stations) for fourteen days, then the station is entitled to demand exclusivity (*vis-à-vis* the cable system) for that same period in the particular market covered by the agreement.[7] There are various exceptions to this protection for programs of out-of-market broadcast stations that are significantly viewed in the market where protection is demanded.

Unlike network non-duplication, syndicated exclusivity was initially viewed solely in terms of a copyright-type of protection. Thus, after Congress amended the copyright laws to provide copyright protection for broadcast programs carried by cable, the FCC decided, in 1980, to eliminate syndicated exclusivity protection. Before long, however, the FCC changed its mind about syndicated exclusivity and reinstated it. The court of appeals sustained its change of mind in the following case. As you read the opinion consider these questions in particular: (1) To the extent that the exclusivity rule designed to protect broadcast property rights, why is it not preempted by the Copyright Act? What other regulatory purpose is there? (2) What role does the compulsory licensing scheme play here? Is the FCC perhaps responding to a periodic complaint by broadcasters that the compulsory license fees are unfairly low? Should that matter to the FCC?

UNITED VIDEO, INC. v. FCC

United States Court of Appeals, District of Columbia Circuit, 1989.
890 F.2d 1173.

WALD, CHIEF JUDGE:

A syndicated television program is a program marketed from its supplier to local television stations by means other than a television network. In 1988, the Federal Communications Commission reinstated

6. The original network non-duplication rules barred only simultaneously duplication. In that case the ban on duplication involved no loss of viewing choice to the consumer (holding technical quality constant). Thus, the audience fragmentation can be viewed as "customer stealing" without any consumer benefit. Later, when the ban was for a significant period before and after the local broadcast, one could no longer claim that viewer welfare is not affected since the ability to view a program at different times is obviously an important element of consumer welfare, as anyone with a video recorder will confirm.

7. The FCC's rules limit the geographic extent of the exclusivity to a zone not to exceed geographic zone of 35 miles (55 miles for network programming in smaller markets). 47 C.F.R. §§ 76.92; 76.120.

its "syndicated exclusivity" rules. These rules allow the supplier of a syndicated program to agree with a broadcast television station that the station shall be the exclusive presenter of the program in its local broadcast area. A broadcast station with exclusive rights to a syndicated program can forbid any cable television station from importing the program into its local broadcast area from a distant station.

Petitioners, mostly cable television companies whose distant signal offerings will be restricted under the new rules, challenge the rules as arbitrary and capricious, and as violative of the Copyright Act of 1976, the Cable Act of 1984, and the first amendment. We find that the Commission's action is within its authority and is not arbitrary or capricious. Accordingly, we deny the petitions for review.

I. Background

* * *

Prior to the 1976 revision of the copyright laws, two Supreme Court decisions held that the distinction between broadcasting and cable transmission had important copyright law implications. *Fortnightly Corp. v. United Artists Television, Inc.*, 392 U.S. 390 (1968), held that when a cable company posted an antenna high on a hilltop, and ran a cable from the antenna into its subscribers' homes, it did nothing significantly different than an individual television owner does when she puts an antenna on her own roof, and runs a cable from it to her television inside. In particular, the cable company's retransmission was not a "performance" of the television program, and so did not violate the copyright on it. *Teleprompter Corp. v. CBS, Inc.*, 415 U.S. 394 (1974), extended this reasoning to cases where the cable brought a program to a distant market. Accordingly, cable companies were free, as far as copyright law was concerned, to pick up signals aired by broadcasters and retransmit them throughout the country.

The distress felt by originating broadcasters whose signals were retransmitted in this way was matched only by the anger of local broadcasters in the receiving end communities, who watched the cable companies importing into their markets the very programs that they were themselves showing, and to which they had purchased exclusive broadcast rights. Even before the *Fortnightly* decision validated this practice against copyright claims, the FCC decided that it was an unfair form of competition. Beginning in 1965, the Commission promulgated exclusivity rules that protected local broadcasters from the importation into their markets of distant signals that duplicated signals to which they had purchased exclusive rights. These rules provided nonduplication protection for both network and syndicated programs. In 1966, the Commission expanded the rules, which in 1965 covered only microwave cable systems, to all cable systems, and required all cable systems to notify the Commission before carrying any distant signal.

The Commission for some time attempted to review every importation of a distant signal into any of the top one hundred local television markets for consistency with "the establishment and healthy maintenance of television broadcast service in the area." This proved an administrative impossibility, however, and the Commission sought a more workable scheme. In 1972, the Commission adopted an industry "consensus agreement," that provided comprehensive regulation of the relationship between broadcast and cable television. The consensus agreement included syndex rules.

In 1976, Congress finally got around to addressing the question of the copyright liability of cable companies that carried distant signals. Congress provided, in the Copyright Revision Act of 1976, a compulsory licensing scheme whereby cable companies paid an administratively set fee for such carriage. Subsequently, in 1980, the FCC decided that, given the new copyright regime, syndex protection was no longer in the public interest, although network exclusivity was retained. *CATV Syndicated Program Exclusivity Rules*, 79 F.C.C.2d 663 (1980). The Commission stated that the elimination of syndex would cause no significant harm to broadcast stations.

Broadcast stations petitioned the Commission for a reconsideration of its negative position on syndex in 1984, but the Commission refused to budge, saying that there had been no change in circumstances that would justify a change in its position. In 1987, however, the Commission began another review of its 1980 decision to eliminate syndex, and in 1988 it promulgated the rules challenged in this case. The Commission decided that its 1980 decision reflected an imperfect understanding of the role cable was to assume in the ensuing decade as a full competitor to broadcast television. The Commission found that with the enormous growth in cable's audience and advertising revenues, the lack of syndex was harming broadcast stations, and might have been significantly affecting the supply of syndicated programs. The Commission decided to reinstate syndex in view of the changes in the cable television industry that occurred between 1980 and 1988.

II. Arbitrariness and Caprice

A. The Commission's Factual Findings

The Commission's decision to reinstate syndex rests on its finding that syndex rules will promote diversity in syndicated programming. In the report accompanying the rules, the Commission found that unrestricted importation of distant signals (i.e., no syndex protection) leads to duplication of programming in local broadcasting areas; this duplication lessens the value of syndicated programs to broadcast stations; that loss of value in turn lowers the price syndicated program suppliers will receive for their programs; and all of this ultimately reduces the incentive for syndicated program suppliers to produce programs, which translates into a reduction in the diversity of programming available to the public. On the basis of this scenario, the Commission concluded that syndex rules should be reinstated in order to promote diversity of programming.

The petitioners challenge the FCC's rule as arbitrary and capricious, for want of support in the rulemaking record. * * * We will examine each of the links in the Commission's alleged causal chain.

1. Duplication

The petitioners do not challenge the Commission's finding that unrestricted importation of distant signals leads to duplication of programming between broadcast and cable channels. Petitioner Tribune, for instance, itself submitted a study to the FCC showing that the lack of syndex rules leads to substantial duplication. The Commission's report cites several studies that show duplication, and notes that the comments received "basically agree on the fact of substantial duplication." This point therefore seems amply supported by the rulemaking record.

2. Lessening of the Value of Syndicated Programs to Local Broadcast Stations

The petitioners hotly contest the Commission's finding that program duplication lessens the value of syndicated programs purchased by local broadcast stations. However, the Commission's report cites substantial evidence from which it could reasonably draw this conclusion. * * *

B. Effects on Program Supply

* * *

We think the Commission's conclusion about the link between lack of program diversity and lowered broadcast revenues due to lack of exclusivity is sufficiently in accord with accepted economic theory that it can stand without empirical support, particularly since we agree with the Commission that it would be very difficult for it to show the degree to which programs are currently not being produced because of the lack of syndex protection. * * *

C. Change in Agency Course

The petitioners complain that the Commission has not adequately explained why it is reinstating syndex rules only eight years after abandoning them, and only four years after reaffirming its decision to abandon them. However, the Commission's report, which examines in great detail its 1980 decision to eliminate syndex, meets this circuit's standard that an agency changing course must "supply a reasoned analysis indicating that its prior policies and standards are being deliberately changed, not casually ignored."

The Commission's report reviews in detail the history of the regulation of cable, including, in particular, the 1980 decision to eliminate syndex rules. The report notes several ways in which the Commission now feels the 1980 decision to have been inadequate. First, the report discusses how circumstances have changed since 1980. The principal change has been the unforeseen emergence of cable television as a full competitor to broadcast television. As the report documents, cable's audience and advertising revenues have increased dramatically and unexpectedly since 1980. In 1980, cable served 19% of television households, but in 1988 it served 51%, a percentage the FCC projected would rise to 60% by 1996. In 1980, the Commission had predicted that cable penetration would never go beyond 48%. Cable advertising revenues were $45.5 million in 1980, but they grew to over $1 billion in 1988; cable's share of total television advertising revenue climbed from less than 0.5% to more than 6%. This unexpected growth, the Commission notes, substantially undermines its 1980 findings that repeal of syndex would not cause significant audience diversion or otherwise harm broadcast stations. * * *

III. The Commission's Authority

The petitioners also claim that the Commission lacks authority to impose the syndex rules. The rules, petitioners claim, are contrary to § 111 of the Copyright Revision Act of 1976, 17 U.S.C. § 111 (1982) ("the Copyright Act"), to § 624(f) of the Cable Communications Policy Act of 1984, 47 U.S.C. § 544(f) (Supp. III 1985) ("the Cable Act"), and to the first amendment. We consider, and reject, these challenges in turn.

First, however, we inquire as to the source of the Commission's affirmative authority to impose syndex rules. The Commission's report claims authority under its "general authority to regulate the relationships of broadcasters and program suppliers"; an aspect of the Commission's power, under 47 U.S.C. § 303(r), to "make such rules and regulations and prescribe such restrictions and conditions, not inconsistent with law, as may be necessary to carry out the provisions of" the Communications Act, as "public convenience, interest, or necessity requires."

The Commission's power under § 303(r) is broad. Even before the 1984 Cable Act, which explicitly gave the Commission power over cable television, the Commission's § 303(r) powers had already been held to permit it to order a cable television station not to carry the signal of a broadcast station outside the broadcast station's primary market. *United States v. Southwestern Cable Co.*, 392 U.S. 157 (1968). Syndex rules are rules that the Commission has found necessary to carry out its mandate under the Communications Act; they clearly fall within the Act's general authority, the regulation of interstate and foreign communication by wire or radio, 47 U.S.C. § 152(a); and, as we concluded above, the rules were reasonably adopted in furtherance of a valid communications policy goal. Hence, they fall under the Commission's § 303(r) powers unless they are "inconsistent with law." See *FCC v. National Citizens Comm. for Broadcasting*, 436 U.S. 775, 796 (1978). We therefore turn to the provisions of law with which the petitioners claim syndex is inconsistent.

A. The Copyright Act

The 1976 Copyright Act, now Title 17 of the United States Code, struck a balance between the rights of copyright owners and the needs of cable television stations. Under the relevant Supreme Court decisions prior to 1976, it was not a copyright violation for cable television stations to retransmit the signal of broadcast stations. Congress, in 1976, decided that when a cable station carries a broadcast station's signal into a distant market, it ought to pay a fee for the carriage. But Congress also believed that it would be impracticable for cable companies to negotiate individually with every copyright owner whose work they wished to carry. Congress therefore created a compulsory licensing scheme, embodied in § 111 of the Act, that provides for payment to copyright owners without the need for individual negotiations. Under the Act, cable stations may carry copyrighted signals into distant markets upon payment of a fee set by the Copyright Royalty Tribunal ("CRT" or "Tribunal"). The Tribunal distributes these fees to copyright owners.

According to the petitioners, § 111 provides the exclusive means by which copyright owners can seek remuneration from cable companies. The FCC, the petitioners claim, has authority only over communications law and has no power to interfere with copyright matters. Syndex therefore represents, according to the petitioners, an impermissible attempt by the FCC to impose on cable television stations the very copyright liability that Congress decided should not exist. The petitioners claim both that the FCC lacks authority to affect copyright liability at all, and also that it cannot make an administrative decision that will effectively nullify Congress' statutory decision to create a compulsory licensing scheme for cable television. * * *

The fundamental problem with the petitioners' argument is that syndex rules were in place when Congress passed the Copyright Act in 1976. We believe that Congress, in the 1976 Act, directly addressed the issue of the Commission's authority to promulgate syndex rules. Abundant evidence in both the text and history of the Act, discussed in detail below, shows that Congress was fully aware of syndex and chose to let it remain in place until the Commission decided to change it. From this evidence, we are unable to draw any other conclusion than that the 1976 Congress believed syndex regulation to be a permissible accoutrement of a regime of compulsory licensing. Congress delegated to the Commission the question of whether, given compulsory licensing, syndex regulation continued to be wise.

Furthermore, the text and history of the Copyright Act show that the petitioners have fundamentally misconceived the relationship between copyright law and communications law. Insofar as they apply to cable television, the 1976 Congress did not imagine copyright law and communications law to be two islands, separated by an impassable sea. Rather, Congress was aware of the interplay between copyright and communications law, and knew that the FCC would have a role to play in determining the scope of compulsory licensing. Congress intended that the Commission's communications policy decisions concerning which signals cable television could carry would affect the copyright liability of cable television companies. * * *

We must also reject petitioners' claim that syndex effectively nullifies compulsory licensing. The text and history reviewed above show that Congress did not consider syndex regulation to be inconsistent with a compulsory licensing scheme. The petitioners compare syndex to a "retransmission consent requirement" a requirement that a cable station obtain the consent of each broadcaster whose signal it wishes to carry which the Commission concedes would be an impermissible interference with compulsory licensing. It is true that if enough broadcasters take advantage of their ability to obtain exclusive rights in programming, the practical difference between syndex and a retransmission consent requirement may be small. We confess that we find it somewhat surprising that Congress, on the one hand, created a compulsory licensing scheme and, on the other hand, let stand a regulation that could greatly limit the set of signals for which that scheme would be effective. However, we think it clear that that is precisely what Congress did, with full knowledge of what it was about. It is not for us to tell Congress how to create a compulsory licensing scheme. Congress clearly thought in 1976 that compulsory licensing and syndex could peaceably coexist, and whatever changes in the industry have come about since, that is the end of the matter.

We accordingly hold that Congress' intent concerning the question of whether the Copyright Act deprives the FCC of power to impose syndex rules is clear. Under *Chevron* step one, we give effect to that intent: we hold that the Copyright Act does not deprive the FCC of that power. * * *

Localism and Network Non-duplication/Syndicated Exclusivity. What, exactly, are the network non-duplication and syndicated exclusivity rules protecting? Program producers have the copyright system (subject to a compulsory license) to protect their interests. The rules make it *harder* for cable subscribers to receive network and syndicated programming, so the rules can't possibly be to ensure an adequate audience base to support continued provision of "free" network and syndicated programming. The rules seek to protect local broadcasters, but are they anything more than a sop to allow local broadcasters to extract rents (cash or otherwise) from cable operators? No one doubts that local broadcasters can get copyright protection over their own local programming; the network non-duplication and syndicated exclusivity rules don't alter that at all. If it's so important to cable subscribers (and thus to cable operators) to have local broadcast content, why doesn't copyright protection do the trick? Or, does the fact that local broadcasters need protection for importation of network and syndicated content suggest that it's not the local content that cable subscribers want but rather the network and syndicated content for which local broadcasters have traditionally been the gatekeepers? If so, what does that tell us about the value of localism?

3. Cable Must-Carry

a) The Basic Obligation

As with virtually all FCC regulations, the must-carry obligation has a lot of complicated conditions and limitations. The basic requirements can be summarized as follows. Subject to certain capacity limits (for example, in general a cable system with more than 12 usable activated channels is only required to carry local stations up to one-third of its activated capacity), a cable system is required to carry all full-time local broadcast signals. What counts as "local" varies. For non-commercial stations a cable system must carry any station whose Grade B signal encompasses the headend or which is located within 50 miles of it. For commercial stations the cable system must carry stations operating within the same designated market area ("DMA") in which the cable system is located. But these standards of "local" are expanded for stations that are "significantly viewed" in the county where the cable system operates even if the station that is significantly viewed is located outside the DMA. (The FCC has a list of all "significantly viewed" stations, but the list can be updated by special surveys.) The must-carry obligation is qualified in several respects (in addition to the capacity limit). For example, a cable system is not required to carry the signal of a local commercial station that simultaneously duplicates the programming of another local station for more than 50 percent of the broadcast week. And a cable system does not need to carry more than one affiliate of a major commercial network. (In the case a cable operator chooses not to carry duplicating or commonly affiliated local stations, it must carry the station closest to the cable headend.) Finally, of great importance as we shall see, a local broadcast station must make an election between the guaranty of carriage offered by must-carry and the possibility of remuneration offered by retransmission consent.

When must-carry was first adopted in 1965, it was not particularly controversial—perhaps because, when compared to the other burdens imposed on cable, it was fairly innocuous. Most cable systems had every reason to carry local stations; after all, in the very early years local programs were the core content of cable systems. Only later, when the number of local stations increased (a lot of UHF newbies were added to local markets) and cable systems' opportunities for additional programs increased, did the burden become important enough to challenge. That time arrived in the late 1980s. Somewhat surprisingly—given the long unchallenged history of the must-carry requirements—the rules were held unconstitutional in 1987 in *Century Communications Corp. v. FCC*, 835 F.2d 292, 293–97 (D.C.Cir.1987). The court held that the FCC had not offered a sufficient justification for the rules to satisfy the *O'Brien* standard for content-neutral restrictions. The court, however, left open the possibility that Congress might come up with a better reason than the FCC had, and Congress accepted the invitation in the 1992 Cable Act, reinstating the must-carry requirement. Congress anticipated an immediate First Amendment challenge and provided for it to be heard exclusively by a three-judge district court (thereby making any decision appealable directly to the Supreme Court). The challenge was quick to come. A split decision by a three-judge district court granted summary judgment for the United States, holding that the must-carry restrictions satisfy the intermediate scrutiny test of *O'Brien*.

In *Turner Broadcasting System v. FCC*, 512 U.S. 622 (1994), the Supreme Court set the terms of the constitutional debate over must-carry.

TURNER BROADCASTING SYSTEM, INC. v. FCC

Supreme Court of the United States, 1994.
512 U.S. 622.

JUSTICE KENNEDY announced the judgment of the Court and delivered the opinion of the Court.

I

* * *

B

On October 5, 1992, Congress overrode a Presidential veto to enact the Cable Television Consumer Protection and Competition Act of 1992 (1992 Cable Act or Act). Among other things, the Act subjects the cable industry to rate regulation by the Federal Communications Commission (FCC) and by municipal franchising authorities; prohibits municipalities from awarding exclusive franchises to cable operators; imposes various restrictions on cable programmers that are affiliated with cable operators; and directs the FCC to develop and promulgate regulations imposing minimum technical standards for cable operators. At issue in this case is the constitutionality of the so-called must-carry provisions, contained in §§ 4 and 5 of the Act, which require cable operators to carry the signals of a specified number of local broadcast television stations.

Section 4 requires carriage of "local commercial television stations," defined to include all full power television broadcasters, other than those qualifying as "noncommercial educational" stations under § 5, that operate within the same television market as the cable system. Cable systems with more than 12 active channels, and more than 300 subscribers, are required to set aside up to one-third of their channels for commercial broadcast stations that request carriage. Cable systems with more than 300 subscribers, but only 12 or fewer active channels, must carry the signals of three commercial broadcast stations.

* * *

Section 5 of the Act imposes similar requirements regarding the carriage of local public broadcast television stations, referred to in the Act as local "noncommercial educational television stations." A cable system with 12 or fewer channels must carry one of these stations; a system of between 13 and 36 channels must carry between one and three; and a system with more than 36 channels must carry each local public broadcast station requesting carriage. The Act requires a cable operator to import distant signals in certain circumstances but provides protection against substantial duplication of local noncommercial educational stations. * * *

Taken together, therefore, §§ 4 and 5 subject all but the smallest cable systems nationwide to must-carry obligations, and confer must-carry privileges on all full power broadcasters operating within the same television market as a qualified cable system.

* * *

II

There can be no disagreement on an initial premise: Cable programmers and cable operators engage in and transmit speech, and they are entitled to the protection of the speech and press provisions of the First Amendment. Through "original programming or by exercising editorial discretion over which stations or programs to include in its repertoire," cable programmers and operators "see[k] to communicate messages on a wide variety of topics and in a wide variety of formats." By requiring cable systems to set aside a portion of their channels for local broadcasters, the must-carry rules regulate cable speech in two respects: The rules reduce the number of channels over which cable operators exercise unfettered control, and they render it more difficult for cable programmers to compete for carriage on the limited channels remaining. Nevertheless, because not every interference with speech triggers the same degree of scrutiny under the First Amendment, we must decide at the outset the level of scrutiny applicable to the must-carry provisions.

A

We address first the Government's contention that regulation of cable television should be analyzed under the same First Amendment standard that applies to regulation of broadcast television. It is true that our cases have permitted more intrusive regulation of broadcast speakers than of speakers in other media. Compare [*Red Lion*], with [*Miami Herald v. Tornillo*]. But the rationale for applying a less rigorous standard of First Amendment scrutiny to broadcast regulation, whatever its validity in the cases elaborating it, does not apply in the context of cable regulation.

The justification for our distinct approach to broadcast regulation rests upon the unique physical limitations of the broadcast medium. As a general matter, there are more would-be broadcasters than frequencies available in the electromagnetic spectrum. And if two broadcasters were to attempt to transmit over the same frequency in the same locale, they would interfere with one another's signals, so that neither could be heard at all. The scarcity of broadcast frequencies thus required the establishment of some regulatory mechanism to divide the electromagnetic spectrum and assign specific frequencies to particular broadcasters.

In addition, the inherent physical limitation on the number of speakers who may use the broadcast medium has been thought to require some adjustment in traditional First Amendment analysis to permit the Government to place limited content restraints, and impose certain affirmative obligations, on broadcast licensees. As we said in *Red Lion*, "[w]here there are substantially more individuals who want to broadcast than there are frequencies to allocate, it is idle to posit an unabridgeable First Amendment right to broadcast comparable to the right of every individual to speak, write, or publish."

Although courts and commentators have criticized the scarcity rationale since its inception, we have declined to question its continuing validity as support for our broadcast jurisprudence, and see no reason to do so here. The broadcast cases are inapposite in the present context because cable television does not suffer from the inherent limitations that characterize the broadcast medium. Indeed, given the rapid advances in fiber optics and digital compression technology, soon there may be no practical limitation on the number of speakers who may use the cable medium. Nor is there any danger of physical interference between two cable speakers attempting to share the same channel. In light of these fundamental technological differences between broadcast and cable transmission, application of the more relaxed standard of scrutiny adopted in *Red Lion* and the other broadcast cases is inapt when determining the First Amendment validity of cable regulation.

This is not to say that the unique physical characteristics of cable transmission should be ignored when determining the constitutionality of regulations affecting cable speech. They should not. But whatever relevance these physical characteristics may have in the evaluation of particular cable regulations, they do not require the alteration of settled principles of our First Amendment jurisprudence.

Although the Government acknowledges the substantial technological differences between broadcast and cable, it advances a second argument for application of the *Red Lion* framework to cable regulation. It asserts that the foundation of our broadcast jurisprudence is not the physical limitations of the electromagnetic spectrum, but rather the "market dysfunction" that characterizes the broadcast market. Because the cable market is beset by a similar dysfunction, the Government maintains, the *Red Lion* standard of review should also apply to cable. While we agree that the cable market suffers certain structural impediments, the Government's argument is flawed in two respects. First, as discussed above, the special physical characteristics of broadcast transmission, not the economic characteristics of the broadcast market, are what underlies our broadcast jurisprudence. Second, the mere assertion of dysfunction or failure in a speech market, without more, is not sufficient to shield a speech regulation from the First Amendment standards applicable to nonbroadcast media.

* * *

B

At the heart of the First Amendment lies the principle that each person should decide for himself or herself the ideas and beliefs deserving of expression, consideration, and adherence. Our political system and cultural life rest upon this ideal. Government action that stifles speech on account of its message, or that requires the utterance of a particular message favored by the Government, contravenes this essential right. Laws of this sort pose the inherent risk that the Government seeks not to advance a legitimate regulatory goal, but to suppress unpopular ideas or information or manipulate the public debate through coercion rather than persuasion. These restrictions "rais[e] the specter that the Government may effectively drive certain ideas or viewpoints from the marketplace."

For these reasons, the First Amendment, subject only to narrow and well-understood exceptions, does not countenance governmental control over the content of messages expressed by private individuals. Our precedents thus apply the most exacting scrutiny to regulations that suppress, disadvantage, or impose differential burdens upon speech because of its content. Laws that compel speakers to utter or distribute speech bearing a particular message are subject to the same rigorous scrutiny. In contrast, regulations that are unrelated to the content of speech are subject to an intermediate level of scrutiny, because in most cases they pose a less substantial risk of excising certain ideas or viewpoints from the public dialogue.

Deciding whether a particular regulation is content based or content neutral is not always a simple task. We have said that the "principal inquiry in determining content neutrality . . . is whether the government has adopted a regulation of speech because of [agreement or] disagreement with the message it conveys." The purpose, or justification, of a regulation will often be evident on its face. But while a content-based purpose may be sufficient in certain circumstances to show that a regulation is content based, it is not necessary to such a showing in all cases. Nor will the mere assertion of a content-neutral purpose be enough to save a law which, on its face, discriminates based on content.

As a general rule, laws that by their terms distinguish favored speech from disfavored speech on the basis of the ideas or views expressed are content based. By contrast, laws that confer benefits or impose burdens on speech without reference to the ideas or views expressed are in most instances content neutral.

C

Insofar as they pertain to the carriage of full-power broadcasters, the must-carry rules, on their face, impose burdens and confer benefits without reference to the content of speech. Although the provisions interfere with cable operators' editorial discretion by compelling them to offer carriage to a certain minimum number of broadcast stations, the extent of the interference does not depend upon the content of the cable operators' programming. The rules impose obligations upon all operators, save those with fewer than 300 subscribers, regardless of the programs or stations they now offer or have offered in the past. Nothing in the Act imposes a restriction, penalty, or burden by reason of the views, programs, or stations the cable operator has selected or will select. The number of channels a cable operator must set aside depends only on the operator's channel capacity, see; hence, an operator cannot avoid or mitigate its obligations under the Act by altering the programming it offers to subscribers. Cf. *Miami Herald Publishing Co. v. Tornillo*, 418 U.S. 241 (1974) (newspaper may avoid access obligations by refraining from speech critical of political candidates).

In a similar vein, although a broadcast station's eligibility for must-carry is based upon its geographic proximity to a qualifying cable system, the Act permits the FCC to grant must-carry privileges upon request to otherwise ineligible broadcast stations. In acting upon these requests, the FCC is directed to give "attention to the value of localism" and, in particular, to whether the requesting station "provides news coverage of issues of concern to such community ... or coverage of sporting and other events of interest to the community." Again, the District Court did not address this provision, but may do so on remand.

The must-carry provisions also burden cable programmers by reducing the number of channels for which they can compete. But, again, this burden is unrelated to content, for it extends to all cable programmers irrespective of the programming they choose to offer viewers. And finally, the privileges conferred by the must-carry provisions are also unrelated to content. The rules benefit all full power broadcasters who request carriage-be they commercial or noncommercial, independent or network affiliated, English or Spanish language, religious or secular. The aggregate effect of the rules is thus to make every full power commercial and noncommercial broadcaster eligible for must-carry, provided only that the broadcaster operates within the same television market as a cable system.

It is true that the must-carry provisions distinguish between speakers in the television programming market. But they do so based only upon the manner in which speakers transmit their messages to viewers, and not upon the messages they carry: Broadcasters, which transmit over the airwaves, are favored, while cable programmers, which do not, are disfavored. Cable operators, too, are burdened by the carriage obligations, but only because they control access to the cable conduit. So long as they are not a subtle means of exercising a content preference, speaker distinctions of this nature are not presumed invalid under the First Amendment.

That the must-carry provisions, on their face, do not burden or benefit speech of a particular content does not end the inquiry. Our cases have recognized that even a regulation neutral on its face may be content based if its manifest purpose is to regulate speech because of the message it conveys.

Appellants contend, in this regard, that the must-carry regulations are content based because Congress' purpose in enacting them was to promote speech of a favored content. We do not agree. Our review of the Act and its various findings persuades us that Congress' overriding objective in enacting must-carry was not to favor programming of a particular subject matter, viewpoint, or format, but rather to preserve access to free television programming for the 40 percent of Americans without cable.

In unusually detailed statutory findings, Congress explained that because cable systems and broadcast stations compete for local advertising revenue, and because cable operators have a vested financial interest in favoring their affiliated programmers over broadcast stations, cable operators have a built-in "economic incentive ... to delete, reposition, or not carry local broadcast signals," Congress concluded that absent a requirement that cable systems carry the signals of local broadcast stations, the continued availability of free local broadcast television would be threatened. Congress sought to avoid the elimination of broadcast television because, in its words, "[s]uch programming is ... free to those who own television sets and do not require cable transmission to receive broadcast television signals," and because "[t]here is a substantial governmental interest in promoting the continued availability of such free television programming, especially for viewers who are unable to afford other means of receiving programming."

By preventing cable operators from refusing carriage to broadcast television stations, the must-carry rules ensure that broadcast television stations will retain a large enough potential audience to earn necessary advertising revenue—or, in the case of noncommercial broadcasters, sufficient viewer contributions, to maintain their continued operation. In so doing, the provisions are designed to guarantee the survival of a medium that has become a vital part of the Nation's communication system, and to ensure that every individual with a television set can obtain access to free television programming.

This overriding congressional purpose is unrelated to the content of expression disseminated by cable and broadcast speakers. Indeed, our precedents have held that "protecting noncable households from loss of regular television broadcasting service due to competition from cable systems," is not only a permissible governmental justification, but an "important and substantial federal interest."

The design and operation of the challenged provisions confirm that the purposes underlying the enactment of the must-carry scheme are unrelated to the content of speech. The rules, as mentioned, confer must-carry rights on all full power broadcasters, irrespective of the content of their programming. They do not require or prohibit the carriage of particular ideas or points of view. They do not penalize cable operators or programmers because of the content of their programming. They do not compel cable operators to affirm points of view with which they disagree. They do not produce any net decrease in the amount of available speech. And they leave cable operators free to carry whatever programming they wish on all channels not subject to must-carry requirements.

Appellants and Justice O'Connor make much of the fact that, in the course of describing the purposes behind the Act, Congress referred to the value of broadcast programming. In particular, Congress noted that broadcast television is "an important source of local news[,] public affairs programming and other local broadcast services critical to an informed electorate," and that noncommercial television "provides educational and informational programming to the Nation's citizens" We do not think, however, that such references cast any material doubt on the content-neutral character of must-carry. That Congress acknowledged the local orientation of broadcast programming and the role that noncommercial stations have played in educating the public does not indicate that Congress regarded broadcast programming as *more* valuable than cable programming. Rather, it reflects nothing more than the recognition that the services provided by broadcast television have some intrinsic value and, thus, are worth preserving against the threats posed by cable.

The operation of the Act further undermines the suggestion that Congress' purpose in enacting must-carry was to force programming of a "local" or "educational" content on cable subscribers. The provisions, as we have stated, benefit all full power broadcasters irrespective of the nature of their programming. In fact, if a cable system were required to bump a cable programmer to make room for a broadcast station, nothing would stop a cable operator from displacing a cable station that provides all local- or education-oriented programming with a broadcaster that provides very little. Appellants do not even contend, moreover, that broadcast programming is any more "local" or "educational" than cable programming.

In short, Congress' acknowledgment that broadcast television stations make a valuable contribution to the Nation's communications system does not render the must-carry scheme content based. The scope and operation of the challenged provisions make clear, in our view, that Congress designed the must-carry provisions not to promote speech of a particular content, but to prevent cable operators from exploiting their economic power to the detriment of broadcasters, and thereby to ensure that all Americans, especially those unable to subscribe to cable, have access to free television programming-whatever its content.

JUSTICE O'CONNOR, with whom JUSTICE SCALIA AND JUSTICE GINSBURG join, and with whom JUSTICE THOMAS joins as to Parts I and III, concurring in part and dissenting in part.

There are only so many channels that any cable system can carry. If there are fewer channels than programmers who want to use the system, some programmers will have to be dropped. In the must-carry provisions of the Cable Television Consumer Protection and Competition Act of 1992, Congress made a choice: By reserving a little over one-third of the channels on a cable system for broadcasters, it ensured that in most cases it will be a cable programmer who is dropped and a broadcaster who is retained. The question presented in this case is whether this choice comports with the commands of the First Amendment.

I

A

* * *

I agree with the Court that some speaker-based restrictions—those genuinely justified without reference to content—need not be subject to strict scrutiny. But looking at the statute at issue, I cannot avoid the conclusion that its preference for broadcasters over cable programmers is justified with reference to content. The findings, enacted by Congress as § 2 of the Act, and which I must assume state the justifications for the law, make this clear. "There is a substantial governmental and First Amendment interest in promoting a diversity of views provided through multiple technology media." § 2(a)(6). "[P]ublic television provides educational and informational programming to the Nation's citizens, thereby advancing the Government's compelling interest in educating its citizens." § 2(a)(8)(A). "A primary objective and benefit of our Nation's system of regulation of television broadcasting is the local origination of programming. There is a substantial governmental interest in ensuring its continuation." § 2(a)(10). "Broadcast television stations continue to be an important source of local news and public affairs programming and other local broadcast services critical to an informed electorate." § 2(a)(11).

Similar justifications are reflected in the operative provisions of the Act. In determining whether a broadcast station should be eligible for must-carry in a particular market, the Federal Communications Commission (FCC) must "afford particular attention to the value of localism by taking into account such factors as ... whether any other [eligible station] provides news coverage of issues of concern to such community or provides carriage or coverage of sporting and other events of interest to the community." In determining whether a low-power station is eligible for must-carry, the FCC must ask whether the station "would address local news and informational needs which are not being adequately served by full power television broadcast stations." Moreover, the Act distinguishes between commercial television stations and noncommercial educational television stations, giving special benefits to the latter. These provisions may all be technically severable from the statute, but they are still strong evidence of the statute's justifications.

Preferences for diversity of viewpoints, for localism, for educational programming, and for news and public affairs all make reference to content. They may not reflect hostility to particular points of view, or a desire to suppress certain subjects because they are controversial or offensive. They may be quite benignly motivated. But benign motivation, we have consistently held, is not enough to avoid the need for strict scrutiny of content-based justifications. The First Amendment does more than just bar government from intentionally suppressing speech of which it disapproves. It also generally prohibits the government from excepting certain kinds of speech from regulation because it thinks the speech is especially valuable.

This is why the Court is mistaken in concluding that the interest in diversity—in "access to a multiplicity" of "diverse and antagonistic sources,"—is content neutral. Indeed, the interest is not "related to the *suppression* of free expression," (emphasis added), but that is not enough for content neutrality. The interest in giving a tax break to religious, sports, or professional magazines, is not related to the suppression of speech; the interest in giving labor picketers an exemption from a general picketing ban, is not related to the suppression of speech. But they are both related to the *content* of speech—to its communicative impact. The interest in ensuring access to a multiplicity of diverse and antagonistic sources of information, no matter how praiseworthy, is directly tied to the content of what the speakers will likely say.

B

The Court dismisses the findings quoted above by speculating that they do not reveal a preference for certain kinds of content; rather, the Court suggests, the findings show "nothing more than the recognition that the services provided by broadcast television have some intrinsic value and, thus, are worth preserving against the threats posed by cable." I cannot agree. It is rare enough that Congress states, in the body of the statute itself, the findings underlying its decision. When it does, it is fair to assume that those findings reflect the basis for the legislative decision, especially when the thrust of the findings is further reflected in the rest of the statute.

Moreover, it does not seem likely that Congress would make extensive findings merely to show that broadcast television is valuable. The controversial judgment at the heart of the statute is not that broadcast television has some value—obviously it does—but that broadcasters should be preferred over cable programmers. The best explanation for the findings, it seems to me, is that they represent Congress' reasons for adopting this preference; and, according to the findings, these reasons rest in part on the content of broadcasters' speech. To say in the face of the findings that the must-carry rules "impose burdens and confer benefits without reference to the content of speech," cannot be correct, especially in light of the care with which we must normally approach speaker-based restrictions

It may well be that Congress also had other, content-neutral, purposes in mind when enacting the statute. But we have never held that the presence of a permissible justification lessens the impropriety of relying in part on an impermissible justification. In fact, we have often struck down statutes as being impermissibly content based even though their primary purpose was indubitably content neutral. Of course, the mere possibility that a statute might be justified with reference to content is not enough to make the statute content based, and neither is evidence that some legislators voted for the statute for content-based reasons. But when a content-based justification appears on the statute's face, we cannot ignore it because another, content-neutral justification is present.

Scarcity or . . . scarcity? The Court in *Turner I* specifically disavowed applying the admittedly reduced level of First Amendment protection applied to broadcasters in *Red Lion*, ostensibly because the scarcity rationale at work in *Red Lion* did not fit the cable model. But Justice Kennedy also refused to apply the opposing bookend—*Miami Herald v. Tornillo* and its use of strict scrutiny in the newspaper context—largely because the technology of cable necessarily limits the number of sources of (video) information in a given market:

> [T]he asserted analogy to *Tornillo* ignores an important technological difference between newspapers and cable television. Although a daily newspaper and a cable operator both may enjoy monopoly status in a given locale, the cable operator exercises far greater control over access to the relevant medium. A daily newspaper, no matter how secure its local monopoly, does not possess the power to obstruct readers' access to other competing publications-whether they be weekly local newspapers, or daily newspapers published in other cities. Thus, when a newspaper asserts exclusive control over its own news copy, it does not thereby prevent other newspapers from being distributed to willing recipients in the same locale.
>
> The same is not true of cable. When an individual subscribes to cable, the physical connection between the television set and the cable network gives the cable operator bottleneck, or gatekeeper, control over most (if not all) of the television programming that is channeled into the subscriber's home. Hence, simply by virtue of its ownership of the essential pathway for cable speech, a cable operator can prevent its subscribers from obtaining access to programming it chooses to exclude. A cable operator, unlike speakers in other media, can thus silence the voice of competing speakers with a mere flick of the switch.
>
> The potential for abuse of this private power over a central avenue of communication cannot be overlooked. See *Southeastern Promotions, Ltd. v. Conrad*, 420 U.S. 546, 557 (1975) ("Each medium of expression . . . must be assessed for First Amendment purposes by standards suited to it, for each may present its own problems"). The First Amendment's command that government not impede the freedom of speech does not disable the government from taking steps to ensure that private interests not restrict, through physical control of a critical pathway of communication, the free flow of information

and ideas. We thus reject appellants' contention that *Tornillo* ... require[s] strict scrutiny of the access rules in question here.

If the problem in *Red Lion* was that a technological aspect of broadcast (interference) required government-imposed scarcity, does it matter that it is a different technological aspect (natural monopoly) of cable that limits media outputs to cable subscribers? Moreover, what does it mean for the Court to say that it is eschewing "the more relaxed standard of scrutiny" of *Red Lion* in the same case that it is choosing intermediate rather than strict scrutiny for analyzing a speech restriction on cable operators?

Turner II. The difference in standards proved not to be critical to the outcome in *Turner I.* Even applying the less-restrictive standard, the Court found that the government had not adequately justified the must-carry restrictions. Congressional justification rested on essentially two propositions: (1) that unless cable operators are compelled to carry broadcast stations, significant numbers of broadcast stations would be refused carriage on cable systems; and (2) that those non-carried broadcast stations would either deteriorate to a substantial degree or fail altogether. Neither of these predictions had been adequately justified. Nor had the government made any findings concerning the impact of must-carry on the speech of cable operators and cable programmers—i.e., the extent to which cable operators would, in fact, be forced to make changes in their current or anticipated programming selections; the degree to which cable *networks* would have their speech limited by being dropped from cable systems in order to make room for local broadcasters; and the extent to which cable operators could satisfy their must-carry obligations by devoting previously unused channel capacity to the carriage of local broadcasters.

The Court reversed and remanded for further proceedings to consider the justifications for, and the burden of, must-carry. On remand the district court took evidence on these questions, and found—by the same split vote—that the evidence was sufficient to make the case for retaining the rules. The case went back to the Supreme Court.

TURNER BROADCASTING SYSTEM, INC. v. FCC

Supreme Court of the United States, 1997.
520 U.S. 180.

JUSTICE KENNEDY delivered the opinion of the Court, except as to a portion of Part II–A–1.

Sections 4 and 5 of the Cable Television Consumer Protection and Competition Act of 1992 require cable television systems to dedicate some of their channels to local broadcast television stations. Earlier in this case, we held the so-called "must-carry" provisions to be content-neutral restrictions on speech, subject to intermediate First Amendment scrutiny under *United States v. O'Brien*, 391 U.S. 367, 377 (1968). A plurality of the Court considered the record as then developed insufficient to determine whether the provisions were narrowly tailored to further important governmental interests, and we remanded the case to the District Court for the District of Columbia for additional factfinding.

On appeal from the District Court's grant of summary judgment for appellees, the case now presents the two questions left open during the first appeal: First, whether the record as it now stands supports Congress' predictive judgment that the must-carry provisions further important governmental interests; and second, whether the provisions do not burden substantially more speech than necessary to further those interests. We answer both questions in the affirmative, and conclude the must-carry provisions are consistent with the First Amendment.

I

* * * Soon after Congress enacted the Cable Television Consumer Protection and Competition Act of 1992 (Cable Act), appellants brought suit against the United States and the Federal Communications Commission (both referred to here as the Government) in the United States District Court for the District of Columbia, challenging the constitutionality of the must-carry provisions under the First Amendment. The three-judge District Court, in a divided opinion, granted summary judgment for the Government and intervenor-defendants. A majority of the court sustained the must-carry provisions under the intermediate standard of scrutiny set forth in *United States v. O'Brien*, *supra*, concluding the must-carry provisions were content-neutral "industry-specific antitrust and fair trade" legislation narrowly tailored to preserve local broadcasting beset by monopoly power in most cable systems, growing concentration in the cable industry, and concomitant risks of programming decisions driven by anticompetitive policies.

On appeal, we agreed with the District Court that must-carry does not "distinguish favored speech from disfavored speech on the basis of the ideas or views expressed," but is a content-neutral regulation designed "to prevent cable operators from exploiting their economic power to the detriment of broadcasters," and "to ensure that all Americans, especially those unable to subscribe to cable, have access to free television programming—whatever its content." We held that, under the intermediate level of scrutiny applicable to content-neutral regulations, must-carry would be sustained if it were shown to further an important or substantial governmental interest unrelated to the suppression of free speech, provided the incidental restrictions did not "burden substantially more speech than is necessary to further" those interests. Although we "ha[d] no difficulty concluding" the interests must-carry was designed to serve were important in the abstract, a four-Justice plurality concluded genuine issues of material fact remained regarding whether "the economic health of local broadcasting is in genuine jeopardy and need of the protections afforded by must-carry," and whether must-carry A 'burden[s] substantially more speech than is necessary to further the government's legitimate interests.' " Justice STEVENS would have found the statute valid on the record then before us; he agreed to remand the case to ensure a judgment of the Court, and the case was returned to the District Court for further proceedings.

The District Court oversaw another 18 months of factual development on remand "yielding a record of tens of thousands of pages" of evidence, comprised of materials acquired during Congress' three years of preenactment hearings, as well as additional expert submissions, sworn declarations and testimony, and industry documents obtained on remand. Upon consideration of the expanded record, a divided panel of the District Court again granted summary judgment to appellees. The majority determined "Congress drew reasonable inferences" from substantial evidence before it to conclude that "in the absence of must-carry rules, 'significant' numbers of broadcast stations would be refused carriage." The court found Congress drew on studies and anecdotal evidence indicating "cable operators had already dropped, refused to carry, or adversely repositioned significant numbers of local broadcasters," and suggesting that in the vast majority of cases the broadcasters were not restored to carriage in their prior position. Noting evidence in the record before Congress and the testimony of experts on remand, the court decided the noncarriage problem would grow worse without must-carry because cable operators had refrained from dropping broadcast stations during Congress' investigation and the pendency of this litigation, and possessed increasing incentives to use their growing economic power to capture broadcasters' advertising revenues and promote affiliated cable programmers. The court concluded "substantial evidence before Congress" supported the predictive judgment that a local broadcaster denied carriage "would suffer financial harm and possible ruin." It cited evidence that adverse carriage actions decrease broadcasters' revenues by reducing audience levels, and evidence that the invalidation of the FCC's prior must-carry regulations had contributed to declining growth in the broadcast industry.

The court held must-carry to be narrowly tailored to promote the Government's legitimate interests. It found the effects of must-carry on cable operators to be minimal, noting evidence that: most cable systems had not been required to add any broadcast stations since the rules were adopted; only 1.2 percent of all cable channels had been devoted to broadcast stations added because of must-carry; and the burden was likely to diminish as channel capacity expanded in the future. The court proceeded to consider a number of alternatives to must-carry that appellants had proposed, including: a leased-access regime, under which cable operators would be required to set aside channels for both broadcasters and cable programmers to use at a regulated price; use of so-called A/B switches, giving consumers a choice of both cable and broadcast signals; a more limited set of must-carry obligations modeled on those earlier used by the FCC; and subsidies for broadcasters. The court rejected each in turn, concluding that "even assuming that [the alternatives] would be less burdensome" on cable operators' First Amendment interests, they "are not in any respect as effective in achieving the government's [interests]." Judge Jackson would have preferred a trial to summary judgment, but concurred in the judgment of the court.

Judge Williams dissented. His review of the record, and particularly evidence concerning growth in the number of broadcasters, industry advertising revenues, and per-station profits during the period without must-carry, led him to conclude the broadcast industry as a whole would not be " 'seriously jeopardized' " in the absence of must-carry. Judge Williams acknowledged the Government had a legitimate interest in preventing anticompetitive behavior, and accepted that cable operators have incentives to discriminate against broadcasters in favor of their own vertically integrated cable programming. He would have granted summary judgment for appellants nonetheless on the ground must-carry is not narrowly tailored. In his view, must-carry constitutes a significant (though "diminish[ing])," burden on cable operators' and programmers' rights, ibid., and the Cable Act's must-carry provisions suppress more speech than necessary because "less-restrictive" alternatives exist to accomplish the Government's legitimate objectives.

This direct appeal followed. We noted probable jurisdiction, and we now affirm.

II

* * * The congressional findings do not reflect concern that, absent must-carry, "a few voices," would be lost from the television marketplace. In explicit factual findings, Congress expressed clear concern that the "marked shift in market share from broadcast television to cable television services," resulting from increasing market penetration by cable services, as well as the expanding horizontal concentration and vertical integration of cable operators, combined to give cable systems the incentive and ability to delete, reposition, or decline carriage to local broadcasters in an attempt to favor affiliated cable programmers. Congress predicted that "absent the reimposition of [must-carry], additional local broadcast signals will be deleted, repositioned, or not carried," with the end result that "the economic viability of free local broadcast television and its ability to originate quality local programming will be seriously jeopardized."

At the same time, Congress was under no illusion that there would be a complete disappearance of broadcast television nationwide in the absence of must-carry. Congress recognized broadcast programming (and network programming in particular) "remains the most popular programming on cable systems." Indeed, reflecting the popularity and strength of some broadcasters, Congress included in the Cable Act a provision permitting broadcasters to charge cable systems for carriage of the broadcasters' signals. Congress was concerned not that broadcast television would disappear in its entirety without must-carry, but that without it, "significant numbers of broadcast stations will be refused carriage on cable systems," and those "broadcast stations denied carriage will either deteriorate to a substantial degree or fail altogether."

Nor do the congressional findings support appellants' suggestion that legitimate legislative goals would be satisfied by the preservation of a rump broadcasting industry providing a minimum of broadcast service to Americans without cable. We have noted that " 'it has long been a basic tenet of national communications policy that "the widest possible dissemination of information from diverse and antagonistic sources is essential to the welfare of the public." ' " Consistent with this objective, the Cable Act's findings reflect a concern that congressional action was necessary to prevent "a reduction in the number of media voices available to consumers." Congress identified a specific interest in "ensuring [the] continuation" of "the local origination of [broadcast] programming," an interest consistent with its larger purpose of promoting multiple types of media, and found must-carry necessary "to serve the goals" of the original Communications Act of 1934 of "providing a fair, efficient, and equitable distribution of broadcast services." In short, Congress enacted must-carry to "preserve the existing structure of the Nation's broadcast television medium while permitting the concomitant expansion and development of cable television."

Although Congress set no definite number of broadcast stations sufficient for these purposes, the Cable Act's requirement that all cable operators with more than 12 channels set aside one-third of their channel capacity for local broadcasters, refutes the notion that Congress contemplated preserving only a bare minimum of stations. Congress' evident interest in "preserv[ing] the existing structure," of the broadcast industry discloses a purpose to prevent any significant reduction in the multiplicity of broadcast programming sources available to noncable households. To the extent the appellants question the substantiality of the Government's interest in preserving something more than a minimum number of stations in each community, their position is meritless. It is for Congress to decide how much local broadcast television should be preserved for noncable households, and the validity of its determination " 'does not turn on a judge's agreement with the responsible decisionmaker concerning' ... the degree to which [the Government's] interests should be promoted."

The dissent proceeds on the assumption that must-carry is designed solely to be (and can only be justified as) a measure to protect broadcasters from cable operators' anticompetitive behavior. Federal policy, however, has long favored preserving a multiplicity of broadcast outlets regardless of whether the conduct that threatens it is motivated by anticompetitive animus or rises to the level of an antitrust violation. Broadcast television is an important source of information to many Americans. Though it is but one of many means for communication, by tradition and use for decades now it has been an essential part of the national discourse on subjects across the whole broad spectrum of speech, thought, and expression. Congress has an independent interest in preserving a multiplicity of broadcasters to ensure that all households have access to information and entertainment on an equal footing with those who subscribe to cable.

A

On our earlier review, we were constrained by the state of the record to assessing the importance of the Government's asserted interests when "viewed in the abstract." The expanded record now permits us to consider whether the must-carry provisions were designed to address a real harm, and whether those provisions will alleviate it in a material way. We turn first to the harm or risk which prompted Congress to act. The Government's assertion that "the economic health of local broadcasting is in genuine jeopardy and in need of the protections afforded by must-carry," rests on two component propositions: First, "significant numbers of broadcast stations will be refused carriage on cable systems" absent must-carry, Second, "the broadcast stations denied carriage will either deteriorate to a substantial degree or fail altogether."

* * * We have no difficulty in finding a substantial basis to support Congress' conclusion that a real threat justified enactment of the must-carry provisions. We examine first the evidence before Congress and then the further evidence presented to the District Court on remand to supplement the congressional determination.

As to the evidence before Congress, there was specific support for its conclusion that cable operators had considerable and growing market power over local video programming markets. * * * Evidence indicated the structure of the cable industry would give cable operators increasing ability and incentive to drop local broadcast stations from their systems, or reposition them to a less-viewed channel. Horizontal concentration was increasing as a small number of multiple system operators (MSO's) acquired large numbers of cable systems nationwide.

Vertical integration in the industry also was increasing. As Congress was aware, many MSO's owned or had affiliation agreements with cable programmers.

* * * In addition, evidence before Congress, supplemented on remand, indicated that cable systems would have incentives to drop local broadcasters in favor of other programmers less likely to compete with them for audience and advertisers. Independent local broadcasters tend to be the closest substitutes for cable programs, because their programming tends to be similar, and because both primarily target the same type of advertiser: those interested in cheaper (and more frequent) ad spots than are typically available on network affiliates. The ability of broadcast stations to compete for advertising is greatly increased by cable carriage, which increases viewership substantially. * * * Empirical evidence also indicates that demand for premium cable services (such as pay-per-view) is reduced when a cable system carries more independent broadcasters. Thus, operators stand to benefit by dropping broadcast stations.

Cable systems also have more systemic reasons for seeking to disadvantage broadcast stations: Simply stated, cable has little interest in assisting, through carriage, a competing medium of communication.

As one cable-industry executive put it, "our job is to promote cable television, not broadcast television." The incentive to subscribe to cable is lower in markets with many over-the-air viewing options. Evidence adduced on remand indicated cable systems have little incentive to carry, and a significant incentive to drop, broadcast stations that will only be strengthened by access to the 60% of the television market that cable typically controls. Congress could therefore reasonably conclude that cable systems would drop broadcasters in favor of programmers—even unaffiliated ones—less likely to compete with them for audience and advertisers. The cap on carriage of affiliates included in the Cable Act, and relied on by the dissent, is of limited utility in protecting broadcasters.

The dissent contends Congress could not reasonably conclude cable systems would engage in such predation because cable operators, whose primary source of revenue is subscriptions, would not risk dropping a widely viewed broadcast station in order to capture advertising revenues. However, if viewers are faced with the choice of sacrificing a handful of broadcast stations to gain access to dozens of cable channels (plus network affiliates), it is likely they would still subscribe to cable even if they would prefer the dropped television stations to the cable programming that replaced them. Substantial evidence introduced on remand bears this out: With the exception of a handful of very popular broadcast stations (typically network affiliates), a cable system's choice between carrying a cable programmer or broadcast station has little or no effect on cable subscriptions, and subscribership thus typically does not bear on carriage decisions.

It was more than a theoretical possibility in 1992 that cable operators would take actions adverse to local broadcasters; indeed, significant numbers of broadcasters had already been dropped. The record before Congress contained extensive anecdotal evidence about scores of adverse carriage decisions against broadcast stations. Congress considered an FCC-sponsored study detailing cable system carriage practices in the wake of decisions by the United States Court of Appeals for the District of Columbia Circuit striking down prior must-carry regulations. It indicated that in 1988, 280 out of 912 responding broadcast stations had been dropped or denied carriage in 1,533 instances. Even assuming that every station dropped or denied coverage responded to the survey, it would indicate that nearly a quarter (21 percent) of the approximately 1,356 broadcast stations then in existence, had been denied carriage. The same study reported 869 of 4,303 reporting cable systems had denied carriage to 704 broadcast stations in 1,820 instances, and 279 of those stations had qualified for carriage under the prior must-carry rules. A contemporaneous study of public television stations indicated that in the vast majority of cases, dropped stations were not restored to the cable service.

2

The harm Congress feared was that stations dropped or denied carriage would be at a "serious risk of financial difficulty," and would "deteriorate to a substantial degree or fail altogether." Congress had before it substantial evidence to support its conclusion. Congress was advised the viability of a broadcast station depends to a material extent on its ability to secure cable carriage. We hold Congress could conclude from the substantial body of evidence before it that "absent legislative action, the free local off-air broadcast system is endangered."

* * * To be sure, the record also contains evidence to support a contrary conclusion. Appellants (and the dissent in the District Court) make much of the fact that the number of broadcast stations and their advertising revenue continued to grow during the period without must-carry, albeit at a diminished rate. Evidence introduced on remand indicated that only 31 broadcast stations actually went dark during the period without must-carry (one of which failed after a tornado destroyed its transmitter), and during the same period some 263 new stations signed on the air. New evidence appellants produced on remand indicates the average cable system voluntarily carried local broadcast stations accounting for about 97 percent of television ratings in noncable households. Appellants, as well as the dissent in the District Court, contend that in light of such evidence, it is clear "the must-carry law is not necessary to assure the economic viability of the broadcast system as a whole."

This assertion misapprehends the relevant inquiry. The question is not whether Congress, as an objective matter, was correct to determine must-carry is necessary to prevent a substantial number of broadcast stations from losing cable carriage and suffering significant financial hardship. Rather, the question is whether the legislative conclusion was reasonable and supported by substantial evidence in the record before Congress. In making that determination, we are not to "re-weigh the evidence de novo, or to replace Congress' factual predictions with our own." Rather, we are simply to determine if the standard is satisfied. If it is, summary judgment for defendants-appellees is appropriate regardless of whether the evidence is in conflict. We have noted in another context, involving less deferential review than is at issue here, that " 'the possibility of drawing two inconsistent conclusions from the evidence does not prevent ... [a] finding from being supported by substantial evidence.' " * * *

B

The second portion of the *O'Brien* inquiry concerns the fit between the asserted interests and the means chosen to advance them. Content-neutral regulations do not pose the same "inherent dangers to free expression," that content-based regulations do, and thus are subject to a less rigorous analysis, which affords the Government latitude in designing a regulatory solution. Under intermediate scrutiny, the Government may employ the means of its choosing " 'so long as the ... regulation promotes a substantial governmental interest that would be achieved less effectively absent the regulation,' " and does not " 'burden substantially more speech than is necessary to further' " that interest.

The must-carry provisions have the potential to interfere with protected speech in two ways. First, the provisions restrain cable operators' editorial discretion in creating programming packages by "reduc[ing] the number of channels over which [they] exercise unfettered control." Second, the rules "render it more difficult for cable programmers to compete for carriage on the limited channels remaining."

* * * While the parties' evidence is susceptible of varying interpretations, a few definite conclusions can be drawn about the burdens of must-carry. It is undisputed that broadcast stations gained carriage on 5,880 channels as a result of must-carry. While broadcast stations occupy another 30,006 cable channels nationwide, this carriage does not represent a significant First Amendment harm to either system operators or cable programmers because those stations were carried voluntarily before 1992, and even appellants represent that the vast majority of those channels would continue to be carried in the absence of any legal obligation to do so. The 5,880 channels occupied by added broadcasters represent the actual burden of the regulatory scheme. Appellants concede most of those stations would be dropped in the absence of must-carry so the figure approximates the benefits of must-carry as well.

Because the burden imposed by must-carry is congruent to the benefits it affords, we conclude must-carry is narrowly tailored to preserve a multiplicity of broadcast stations for the 40 percent of American households without cable. * * *

Appellants posit a number of alternatives in an effort to demonstrate a less-restrictive means to achieve the Government's aims. * * *

[A]fter careful examination of each of the alternatives suggested by appellants, we cannot conclude that any of them is an adequate alternative to must-carry for promoting the Government's legitimate interests. First among appellants' suggested alternatives is a proposal to revive a more limited set of must-carry rules, known as the "*Century* rules" after the 1987 court decision striking them down, Those rules included a minimum viewership standard for eligibility and limited the must-carry obligation to 25 percent of channel capacity. The parties agree only 14 percent of broadcasters added to cable systems under the Cable Act would be eligible for carriage under the *Century* rules. The *Century* rules, for the most part, would require carriage of the same stations a system would carry without statutory compulsion. While we acknowledge appellants' criticism of any rationale that more is better, the scheme in question does not place limitless must-carry obligations on cable system operators. In the final analysis this alternative represents nothing more than appellants' " '[dis]agreement with the responsible decisionmaker concerning' . . . the degree to which [the Government's] interests should be promoted." * * *

The second alternative appellants urge is the use of input selector or "A/B" switches, which, in combination with antennas, would permit viewers to switch between cable and broadcast input, allowing cable subscribers to watch broadcast programs not carried on cable. Congress examined the use of A/B switches as an alternative to must-carry and concluded it was "not an enduring or feasible method of distribution and . . . not in the public interest." The data showed that: many households lacked adequate antennas to receive broadcast signals; viewers might be required to reset channel settings repeatedly in order to view both UHF and cable channels; and installation and use of the switch with other common video equipment (such as videocassette recorders) could be "cumbersome or impossible." Even the cable industry trade association (one of appellants here) determined that "the A/B switch is not a workable solution to the carriage problem." The group's engineering committee likewise concluded the switches suffered from technical problems and that no solution "appear[ed] imminent."

Congress also had before it "considerable evidence," including two empirical studies, that "it is rare for [cable subscribers] ever to switch to receive an over-the-air signal." A 1991 study demonstrated that even "after several years of a government mandated program of providing A–B switches [to] consumers and a simultaneous education program on their use," and after FCC-mandated technical improvements to the switch only 11.7 percent of all cable-connected television sets were attached to an antenna and had an A/B switch. Of the small number of households possessing the switch, an even smaller number (only 38 percent) had ever used it.

Appellants also suggest a leased-access regime, under which both broadcasters and cable programmers would have equal access to cable channels at regulated rates. Appellants do not specify what kind of regime they would propose, or how it would operate, making this alternative difficult to compare to the must-carry rules. Whatever virtues the proposal might otherwise have, it would reduce the number of cable channels under cable systems' control in the same manner as must-carry. Because this alternative is aimed solely at addressing the bottleneck control of cable operators, it would not be as effective in achieving Congress' further goal of ensuring that significant programming remains available for the 40 percent of American households without cable.* * *

Appellants next suggest a system of subsidies for financially weak stations. Appellants have not proposed any particular subsidy scheme, so it is difficult to determine whether this option presents a feasible means of achieving the Government's interests, let alone one preferable to must-carry under the First Amendment. To begin with, a system of subsidies would serve a very different purpose than must-carry. Must-carry is intended not to guarantee the financial health of all broadcasters, but to ensure a base number of broadcasters survive to provide service to noncable households. Must-carry is simpler to administer and less likely to involve the Government in making content-based determinations about programming. The must-carry rules distinguish between categories of speakers based solely on the technology used to communicate. The rules acknowledge cable systems' expertise by according them discretion to determine which broadcasters to carry on reserved channels, and (within the Cable Act's strictures) allow them to choose broadcasters with a view to offering program choices appealing to local subscribers. Appellants' proposal would require the Government to develop other criteria for giving subsidies and to establish a potentially elaborate administrative structure to make subsidy determinations.

Appellants also suggest a system of antitrust enforcement or an administrative complaint procedure to protect broadcasters from cable operators' anticompetitive conduct. Congress could conclude, however, that the considerable expense and delay inherent in antitrust litigation, and the great disparities in wealth and sophistication between the average independent broadcast station and average cable system operator, would make these remedies inadequate substitutes for guaranteed carriage. The record suggests independent broadcasters simply are not in a position to engage in complex antitrust litigation, which involves extensive discovery, significant motions practice, appeals, and the payment of high legal fees throughout. An administrative complaint procedure, although less burdensome, would still require stations to incur considerable expense and delay before enforcing their rights. As it is, some public stations have been forced by limited resources to forgo pursuing administrative complaints under the Cable Act to obtain carriage. Those problems would be compounded if instead of proving entitlement under must-carry, the station instead had to prove facts establishing an antitrust violation. * * *

III

Judgments about how competing economic interests are to be reconciled in the complex and fast-changing field of television are for Congress to make. Those judgments "cannot be ignored or undervalued simply because [appellants] cas[t] [their] claims under the umbrella of the First Amendment." Appellants' challenges to must-carry reflect little more than disagreement over the level of protection broadcast stations are to be afforded and how protection is to be attained. We cannot displace Congress' judgment respecting content-neutral regulations with our own, so long as its policy is grounded on reasonable factual findings supported by evidence that is substantial for a legislative determination. Those requirements were met in this case, and in these circumstances the First Amendment requires nothing more. The judgment of the District Court is affirmed.

JUSTICE BREYER, concurring in part.

I join the opinion of the Court except insofar as Part II–A–1 relies on an anticompetitive rationale. I agree with the majority that the statute must be "sustained under the First Amendment if it advances important governmental interests unrelated to the suppression of free speech and does not burden substantially more speech than necessary to further those interests." I also agree that the statute satisfies this standard. My conclusion rests, however, not upon the principal opinion's analysis of the statute's efforts to "promot[e] fair competition," But rather upon its discussion of the statute's other objectives, namely " '(1) preserving the benefits of free, over-the-air local broadcast television,'" and "'(2) promoting the widespread dissemination of information from a multiplicity of sources.'" Whether or not the statute does or does not sensibly compensate for some significant market defect, it undoubtedly seeks to provide over-the-air viewers who lack cable with a rich mix of over-the-air programming by guaranteeing the over-the-air stations that provide such programming with the extra dollars that an additional cable audience will generate. I believe that this purpose—to assure the over-the-air public "access to a multiplicity of information sources"—provides sufficient basis for rejecting appellants' First Amendment claim.

I do not deny that the compulsory carriage that creates the "guarantee" extracts a serious First Amendment price. It interferes with the protected interests of the cable operators to choose their own programming; it prevents displaced cable program providers from obtaining an audience; and it will sometimes prevent some cable viewers from watching what, in its absence, would have been their preferred set of programs. This "price" amounts to a "suppression of speech."

But there are important First Amendment interests on the other side as well. The statute's basic noneconomic purpose is to prevent too precipitous a decline in the quality and quantity of programming choice for an ever-shrinking non-cable-subscribing segment of the public. This purpose reflects what "has long been a basic tenet of national communications policy," namely that "the widest possible dissemination of information from diverse and antagonistic sources is essential to the welfare of the public." That policy, in turn, seeks to facilitate the public discussion and informed deliberation, which, as Justice Brandeis pointed out many years ago, democratic government presupposes and the First Amendment seeks to achieve. Indeed, *Turner* rested in part upon the proposition that "assuring that the public has access to a multiplicity of information sources is a governmental purpose of the highest order, for it promotes values central to the First Amendment." * * *

JUSTICE O'CONNOR, with whom JUSTICE SCALIA, JUSTICE THOMAS, and JUSTICE GINSBURG join, dissenting. * * *

I

* * * Much of the principal opinion treats the must-carry provisions as a species of antitrust regulation enacted by Congress in response to a perceived threat that cable system operators would otherwise engage in various forms of anticompetitive conduct resulting in harm to broadcasters. The Court recognizes that appellees cannot show an anticompetitive threat to broadcast television simply by demonstrating that "a few" broadcast stations would be forced off the air in the absence of must-carry. No party has ever questioned that adverse carriage decisions by cable operators will threaten some broadcasters in some markets. The notion that Congress premised the must-carry provisions upon a far graver threat to the structure of the local broadcast system than the loss of "a few" stations runs through virtually every passage in the principal

Turner opinion that discusses the Government interests the provisions were designed to serve. Ostensibly adopting this framework, the Court now asks whether Congress could reasonably have thought the must-carry regime necessary to prevent a "significant reduction in the multiplicity of broadcast programming sources available to noncable households."

I fully agree that promoting fair competition is a legitimate and substantial Government goal. But the Court nowhere examines whether the breadth of the must-carry provisions comports with a goal of preventing anticompetitive harms. Instead, in the course of its inquiry into whether the must-carry provisions are "narrowly tailored," the principal opinion simply assumes that most adverse carriage decisions are anticompetitively motivated, and that must-carry is therefore a measured response to a problem of anticompetitive behavior. We ordinarily do not substitute unstated and untested assumptions for our independent evaluation of the facts bearing upon an issue of constitutional law. * * *

Appellees bear the burden of demonstrating that the provisions of the Cable Act restricting expressive activity survive constitutional scrutiny. As discussed below, the must-carry provisions cannot be justified as a narrowly tailored means of addressing anticompetitive behavior. As a result, the Court's inquiry into whether must-carry would prevent a "significant reduction in the multiplicity of broadcast programming sources" collapses into an analysis of an ill-defined and generalized interest in maintaining broadcast stations, wherever they might be threatened and whatever their viewership. Neither the principal opinion nor the partial concurrence ever explains what kind of conduct, apart from anticompetitive conduct, threatens the "multiplicity" of broadcast programming sources. Indeed, the only justification advanced by the parties for furthering this interest is heavily content based. It is undisputed that the broadcast stations protected by must-carry are the "marginal" stations within a given market, the record on remand reveals that any broader threat to the broadcast system was entirely mythical. Pressed to explain the importance of preserving noncable viewers' access to "vulnerable" broadcast stations, appellees emphasize that the must-carry rules are necessary to ensure that broadcast stations maintain "diverse," "quality" programming that is "responsive" to the needs of the local community. Must-carry is thus justified as a way of preserving viewers' access to a Spanish or Chinese language station or of preventing an independent station from adopting a home-shopping format. Undoubtedly, such goals are reasonable and important, and the stations in question may well be worthwhile targets of Government subsidies. But appellees' characterization of must-carry as a means of protecting these stations, like the Court's explicit concern for promoting " 'community self-expression' " and the " 'local origination of broadcast programming,' " reveals a content-based preference for broadcast programming. This justification of the regulatory scheme is, in my view, wholly at odds with the *Turner* Court's premise that must-carry is a means of preserving "access to free television programming—whatever its content." * * *

II

The principal opinion goes to great lengths to avoid acknowledging that preferences for "quality," "diverse," and "responsive" local programming underlie the must-carry scheme, although the partial concurrence's reliance on such preferences is explicit. I take the principal opinion at its word and evaluate the claim that the threat of anticompetitive behavior by cable operators supplies a content-neutral basis for sustaining the statute. It does not. * * *

A

The principal opinion devotes substantial discussion to the structure of the cable industry, a matter that was uncontroversial in I. As of 1992, cable already served 60 percent of American households. I agree with the observation that Congress could reasonably predict an increase in cable penetration of the local video programming market. Local franchising requirements and the expense of constructing a cable system to serve a particular area make it possible for cable franchisees to exercise a monopoly over cable service. Nor was it ever disputed that some cable system operators own large numbers of systems nationwide, or that some cable systems are affiliated with cable programmers.

What was not resolved in *Turner* was whether "reasonable inferences based on substantial evidence" supported Congress' judgment that the must-carry provisions were necessary "to prevent cable operators from exploiting their economic power to the detriment of broadcasters." Because I remain convinced that the statute is not a measured response to congressional concerns about monopoly power in my view the principal opinion's discussion on this point is irrelevant. But even if it were relevant, it is incorrect. * * *

2

* * * [T]he larger problem with the Court's approach is that neither the FCC study nor the additional evidence on remand canvassed by the Court says anything about the broadcast markets in which adverse carriage decisions take place. The Court accepts Congress' stated concern about preserving the availability of a "multiplicity" of broadcast stations, but apparently thinks it sufficient to evaluate that concern in the abstract, without considering how much local service is already available in a given broadcast market. I address this gap in the Court's discussion at greater length below by examining the reasonableness of Congress' prediction that adverse carriage decisions will inflict severe harm on broadcast stations.

Nor can we evaluate whether must-carry is necessary to serve an interest in preserving broadcast stations without examining the value of the stations protected by the must-carry scheme to viewers in noncable households. By disregarding the distribution and viewership of stations not carried on cable, the Court upholds the must-carry provisions without addressing the interests of the over-the-air television viewers that Congress purportedly seeks to protect. The Court relies on analyses suggesting that, as of 1992, the typical independent commercial broadcaster was being denied carriage on cable systems serving 47 percent of subscribers in its local market, and the typical noncommercial station was denied carriage on cable systems serving 36 percent of subscribers in its local market. The only analysis in the record of the relationship between carriage and noncable viewership favors the appellants. A 1991 study by Federal Trade Commission staff concluded that most cable systems voluntarily carried broadcast stations with any reportable ratings in noncable households and that most instances of noncarriage involved "relatively remote (and duplicated) network stations, or local stations that few viewers watch." * * *

In sum, appellees are not entitled to summary judgment on whether Congress could conclude, based on reasonable inferences drawn from substantial evidence, that " 'absent legislative action, the free local off-air broadcast system is endangered.' " The Court acknowledges that the record contains much evidence of the health of the broadcast industry, including evidence that 263 new broadcast stations signed on the air in the period without must-carry rules, evidence of growth in stations' advertising revenue, and evidence of voluntary carriage of broadcast stations accounting for virtually all measurable viewership in noncable households. But the Court dismisses such evidence, emphasizing that the question is not whether Congress correctly determined that must-carry is necessary to prevent significant financial hardship to a substantial number of stations, but whether "the legislative conclusion was reasonable and supported by substantial evidence in the record before Congress." Even accepting the Court's articulation of the relevant standard, it is not properly applied here. The principal opinion disavows a need to closely scrutinize the logic of the regulatory scheme at issue on the ground that it "need not put [its] imprimatur on Congress' economic theory in order to validate the reasonableness of its judgment." That approach trivializes the First Amendment issue at stake in this case. A highly dubious economic theory has been advanced as the "substantial interest" supporting a First Amendment burden on cable operators and cable programmers. In finding that must-carry serves a substantial interest, the principal opinion necessarily accepts that theory. The partial concurrence does not, but neither does it articulate what threat to the availability of a "multiplicity" of broadcast stations would exist in a perfectly competitive market.

B

* * * In my view, the statute is not narrowly tailored to serve a substantial interest in preventing anticompetitive conduct. I do not understand Justice Breyer to disagree with this conclusion. Congress has commandeered up to one third of each cable system's channel capacity

for the benefit of local broadcasters, without any regard for whether doing so advances the statute's alleged goals. To the extent that Congress was concerned that anticompetitive impulses would lead vertically integrated operators to prefer those programmers in which the operators have an ownership stake, the Cable Act is overbroad, since it does not impose its requirements solely on such operators. An integrated cable operator cannot satisfy its must-carry obligations by allocating a channel to an unaffiliated cable programmer. And must-carry blocks an operator's access to up to one third of the channels on the system, even if its affiliated programmer provides programming for only a single channel. The Court rejects this logic, finding the possibility that the must-carry regime would require reversal of a benign carriage decision not "so prevalent that must-carry is substantially overbroad." The principal opinion reasons that "cable systems serving 70 percent of subscribers are vertically integrated with cable programmers, so anticompetitive motives may be implicated in a majority of systems' decisions not to carry broadcasters." It is unclear whether the principal opinion means that anticompetitive motives may be implicated in a majority of decisions, or in decisions by a majority of systems. In either case, the principal opinion's conclusion is wholly speculative. We do not know which of these vertically integrated systems are affiliated with one cable programmer and which are affiliated with five cable programmers. Moreover, Congress has placed limits upon the number of channels that can be used for affiliated programming. The principal opinion does not suggest why these limits are inadequate or explain why, once a system reaches the limit, its remaining carriage decisions would also be anticompetitively motivated. Even if the channel limits are insufficient, the principal opinion does not explain why requiring carriage of broadcast stations on one third of the system's channels is a measured response to the problem.

Finally, I note my disagreement with the Court's suggestion that the availability of less-speech-restrictive alternatives is never relevant to *O'Brien's* narrow tailoring inquiry. The *Turner* Court remanded this case in part because a plurality concluded that "judicial findings concerning the availability and efficacy of constitutionally acceptable less restrictive means of achieving the Government's asserted interests" were lacking in the original record. The Court's present position on this issue is puzzling.

Our cases suggest only that we have not interpreted the narrow tailoring inquiry to "require elimination of all less restrictive alternatives." Put another way, we have refrained from imposing a least-restrictive-means requirement in cases involving intermediate First Amendment scrutiny. It is one thing to say that a regulation need not be the least-speech-restrictive means of serving an important governmental objective. It is quite another to suggest, as I read the majority to do here, that the availability of less-speech-restrictive alternatives cannot establish or confirm that a regulation is substantially broader than necessary to achieve the Government's goals. While the validity of a Government regulation subject to intermediate First Amendment scrutiny does not turn on our "agreement with the responsible decisionmaker concerning the most appropriate method for promoting significant government interests," the availability of less intrusive approaches to a problem serves as a benchmark for assessing the reasonableness of the fit between Congress' articulated goals and the means chosen to pursue them.

As shown above, in this case it is plain without reference to any alternatives that the must-carry scheme is "substantially broader than necessary," to serve the only governmental interest that the principal opinion fully explains—preventing unfair competition. If Congress truly sought to address anticompetitive behavior by cable system operators, it passed the wrong law. Nevertheless, the availability of less restrictive alternatives—a leased-access regime and subsidies—reinforces my conclusion that the must-carry provisions are overbroad. * * *

I therefore respectfully dissent, and would reverse the judgment below.

Giving Viewers What They Want? For a critique of the Court's analysis see Glen O. Robinson, *The Electronic First Amendment*, 47 Duke L.J. 899 (1998). Putting aside the First Amendment issue and just focusing on the policy, the case for compelling cable systems to carry local broadcast signals is (a) a necessary protection for broadcast stations against the monopoly that local cable systems have over access to those seeking broadband television service or (b) a way of promoting local television service because of its assumed special public interest benefits? Don't both come down ultimately to a question about the benefits of local, as opposed to nonlocal television programs? Consider this unfashionable opinion from the cited article about the benefits of localism:

> The only plausible explanation of localism ties it to information needs rather than preferences, to radio and television as a public good. Radio and television have been supplied mostly by private enterprise, of course, but it has always been supposed that there is a significant public component to the service—hence, the public interest ideology always embraced more than just managing the distribution and enforcement of frequency rights, as the Supreme Court acknowledged in 1943. Regulatory critics have had a field day making fun of this ideology, as well as the Commission's implementation of it, but for present purposes I want to bypass that issue to get to another one—namely, why public service has been tied to localism. The standard explanation is to point to the importance of local news and related information service. If you want the news about Charlottesville's latest zoning decision, tuning into a channel that carries only programs from New York, Chicago and Atlanta will not deliver it. Against the possibility that a local cable system might choose such a menu of entirely nonlocal signals, Congress mandates

> that the cable system carry all local broadcast stations that are significantly viewed. This requirement is not conditioned on local stations presenting any particular quantity of local news (and, as I said earlier, the FCC does not enforce any such obligation on local broadcasters). By the same token, must-carry precludes cable operators themselves from exercising any judgment about the quantity or quality of local news or other local programming by preventing them from selecting the local signals it thinks will attract local subscribers or appeal to local advertisers. * * *
>
> There is not likely to be much dispute (least of all among anyone reading this Essay) that information is a matter of high public importance. However, there is likely to be considerable debate about just how much government involvement is required to sustain its adequate supply. Markets do not seem to be visibly failing to provide information services. I do not want to delve into this debate here, for even if there is a public goods aspect to information that calls for government involvement, it is not obvious that any part of it can be linked to localism. Quite the contrary; most of the current information-age theorizing stresses the importance of national and international networks that are the very antithesis of localism. The "National Information Infrastructure" and to a lesser extent the "International Information Infrastructure" are the banners under which government and industry have pushed for more public investment in information services. So far as I am aware, no one has yet coined the phrase "Local Information Infrastructure." For good reason: in a world where information can be pulled or pushed from every corner of the planet, there is something almost quaint about the idea of linking localism and modern information services.

b) Digital Must-Carry

Turner II settled the basic question of constitutional principle, but there has remained a controversy over scope, in particular how the must-carry rules would be applied to digital television channels. There were two basic questions! The first question concerned dual carriage of analog and digital channels. During the transition to digital (due to be completed by 2009) every broadcast station was given two channels in order to allow simulcast operations in both analog and digital format while the stations make the transition. During the transition does the cable system have to carry both analog and digital channels? The second question concerned only must-carry rights for multicast channels on the digital channel. The digital channel was originally intended as a vehicle for presenting high definition television, but it soon developed that the digital channel could be used to carry multiple channels in a standard definition format in lieu of or in addition to the high definition channel. When a station uses its digital channel to present more than one channel of programming can it claim must-carry rights for all the channels? In a first report and order on the subject in 2001 the FCC tentatively answered no to both questions. Four years on it answered no again to both questions.

CARRIAGE OF DIGITAL TELEVISION BROADCAST SIGNALS
Second Report and Order

Federal Communications Commission, 2005.
20 FCC Rcd. 4516.

BY THE COMMISSION:

* * *

I. INTRODUCTION

1. In this Second Report and Order and First Order on Reconsideration, we consider several petitions for reconsideration of the Commission's *First Report and Order* and the various comments submitted in response to the *Further Notice of Proposed Rulemaking* in the above-captioned proceeding. The actions taken in this order are limited to two significant issues, the resolution of which are essential to the Commission's ongoing efforts to complete the transition from analog to digital television. In the interest of providing certainty on these significant issues at this time, we are deferring resolution of the other issues raised on reconsideration and in the *Further Notice* to a future order. The two issues resolved in this order are: (1) whether cable operators are required to carry both the digital and analog signals of a station during the transition when television stations are still broadcasting analog signals (also generally referred to as the "dual carriage" issue); and (2) how to construe the "primary video" carriage limitation under Sections 614(b)(3)(A) (for commercial stations) and 615(g)(1) (for noncommercial stations) under the Act if a broadcaster chooses to broadcast multiple digital television streams (this issue is generally referred to as the mandatory multicast carriage issue).

2. With respect to the dual carriage issue, we determined in the *First Report and Order* that the statute neither mandates nor precludes the mandatory simultaneous carriage of both a television station's digital and analog signals. Furthermore, we tentatively concluded that, based on the available record evidence, a dual carriage requirement would likely violate the cable operator's First Amendment rights. In order to evaluate the issue more fully, we adopted the *Further Notice* to solicit comment on the constitutionality of imposing a dual carriage requirement. Several members of the broadcast industry seek reconsideration of the Commission's statutory interpretation on this issue, and urge us to conclude that the Act mandates dual carriage. For the reasons provided in this order, we are denying the petitions on this issue and affirm our tentative decision not to impose a dual carriage requirement.

3. With respect to the mandatory multicast carriage issue, the Commission, in the *First Report and Order*, interpreted the statutory term "primary video" to mean only a single programming stream. As a result, if a digital broadcaster elects to divide its digital spectrum into several separate, independent, and unrelated programming streams, the Commission found that only one of these streams is considered primary and entitled to mandatory carriage. Several members of the broadcast industry seek reconsideration of our statutory interpretation. For the reasons provided below, we are also denying the petitions on this issue and thereby affirm our decision in the *First Report and Order*.

* * *

III. Carriage of Digital Broadcast Signals

A. Stations Broadcasting in Analog and Digital

9. A fundamental issue addressed in the *First Report and Order* and in the *Further Notice* is whether cable operators are required to carry both the analog and digital signals of a station during the transition when television stations are broadcasting analog and digital signals. We said therein that if the Commission requires carriage of both analog and digital signals (*i.e.*, "dual carriage"), cable operators could be required to carry double the number of television signals, many of which contain duplicative content, while having to drop or forego carriage of varied cable programming services where channel capacity is limited.

10. In the *First Report and Order*, we examined our authority to impose a dual carriage requirement and determined, after extensive review of Sections 614 and 615 of the Act and the accompanying legislative history, that "the statute neither mandates nor precludes the mandatory simultaneous carriage of both a television station's digital and analog signals." It is precisely the ambiguity of the statute that has driven contentious policy debate on this issue. In order to weigh the constitutional questions inherent in a statutory construction that would permit dual carriage, we determined that it was appropriate and necessary to more fully develop the record in this regard. It was our tentative conclusion, however, that a dual carriage requirement would burden cable operators' First Amendment rights substantially more than necessary to further the government's substantial interests. We issued a *Further Notice* addressing several critical questions concerning the constitutionality of dual carriage, including: (1) whether a cable operator will have the channel capacity to carry the digital television signal of a station, in addition to the analog signal of that same station, without displacing other cable programming or services; (2) whether market forces, through retransmission consent, will provide cable subscribers access to digital television signals; and (3) how the resolution of the carriage issues would impact the digital transition process. Before considering the additional record and finally determining the dual carriage question, we first address the petitions for reconsideration of our preliminary decision on the statutory issue in the *First Report and Order*.

1. Statutory Analysis

* * *

13. The arguments that the parties have presented in support of a statutory reading to require dual carriage essentially are no different from those that have previously been submitted, considered, and rejected in the *First Report and Order*. We therefore affirm our earlier conclusion that the Act is ambiguous on the issue of dual carriage. The statute neither mandates nor precludes the mandatory simultaneous carriage of both a television station's digital and analog signals. Further, we do not believe that mandating dual carriage is necessary either to advance the governmental interests identified by Congress in enacting Sections 614 and 615 and upheld in *Turner II* or to effectuate the DTV transition. Since no evidence or arguments submitted on reconsideration gives us any reason to question our original judgment, we deny the petitions for reconsideration on this point.

2. Constitutional Analysis

14. As indicated above, the *First Report and Order* held that the Act was ambiguous as to the question of dual carriage and that further fact-finding was necessary to determine the appropriate statutory interpretation. We rely on several constitutional principles and cases, in particular the Supreme Court's decisions in *Turner I* and *Turner II*, in addressing the constitutionality of mandatory dual carriage. The Supreme Court has recognized that mandatory carriage directly interferes with the free speech rights of cable operators and cable programmers. Nevertheless, the *Turner II* Court upheld the constitutionality of Sections 614 and 615 under an intermediate scrutiny analysis. A majority of the Court found that the mandatory carriage provisions of the Act furthered two governmental interests: (1) preserving the benefits of free, over-the-air local broadcast television for viewers; and (2) promoting the widespread dissemination of information from a multiplicity of sources. * * *

15. * * * After close examination of the information submitted, we find nothing in the record that would allow us to conclude that mandatory dual carriage is necessary to further the governmental interests identified in *Turner*, or other potential governmental interests put forward by commenters. In addition, even if it could be shown that dual carriage could further any of the governmental interests based on the current record, the burden that mandatory dual carriage places on cable operators' speech appears to be greater than is necessary to achieve the interests that must carry was meant to serve. Mandatory dual carriage would essentially double the carriage rights and substantially increase the burdens on free speech beyond those upheld in *Turner*. As noted, *Turner II* found the benefits and burdens of must carry to be congruent, such that must carry is narrowly tailored to preserve the multiplicity of broadcast stations for households that do not subscribe to cable.

16. *Preserving the benefits of free over-the-air television for viewers.* The first governmental interest identified in *Turner* to support mandatory carriage is the preservation of the benefits of free over-the-air television for non-subscribers. The broadcast industry argues that a slow DTV transition places preservation of over-the-air broadcasting at risk. Commercial Broadcasters assert that the entire premise of the digital transition is for digital signals to replace analog signals. They argue that if viewers are unable to receive digital signals, digital cannot replace analog, and broadcasters will be forced to sustain the operation of two facilities at considerable expense, without any additional revenue. Noncommercial Broadcasters assert that the costs of dual transmissions are overwhelming for smaller television stations. * * *

18. Despite the broadcast parties' assertions, the record as a whole does not demonstrate that television stations would face undue hardship in the absence of dual carriage that would, in turn, threaten the ability of broadcasters to provide service to non-cable households. The critical governmental interest, reflected in the Act, was described by the Supreme Court as the preservation of over-the-air broadcasting. More specifically, the congressionally-adopted governmental interest identified in *Turner* was the protection of the interests of over-the-air television viewers—*i.e.*, viewers whose interests were not reflected in the carriage decisions of cable operators nor in the viewing options available to cable subscribers. Thus, the focus of the government interest in *Turner* is not the economic health of broadcasting per se, but the benefits that broadcasting provides to consumers. In sum, the critical factor in interpreting the intent of the statute and in the constitutional analysis of it is that it is designed "to provide over-the-air viewers who *lack* cable with a rich mix of over-the-air programming by guaranteeing the over-the-air stations that provide such programming with the extra dollars that an additional cable audience will generate" and to assure the over-the-air public "access to a multiplicity of information sources." With respect to mandatory dual carriage, all broadcast stations are required to build a digital facility and broadcast a digital signal. Thus, cable carriage is not needed to ensure that non-cable, over-the-air viewers have access to digital broadcast signals. Broadcasters advocating mandatory dual carriage have not demonstrated that non-cable households would benefit from more or better broadcast programming if stations have mandatory dual carriage. Local analog broadcasters are already carried today—either pursuant to must carry or retransmission consent—on virtually every cable system in their market. We have no evidence that the absence of a dual carriage requirement will substantially diminish the availability or quality of broadcast signals available to non-cable subscribers. A small number of broadcasters that have demonstrated legitimate financial hardship if they were required to build their digital facilities have been granted extensions, but the hardship is not due to lack of cable carriage. The absence of a dual carriage requirement might in fact encourage broadcasters to produce a "rich mix of over-the-air programming" in order to convince cable operators to voluntarily carry

their digital signal. Furthermore, the goal of the DTV transition is not to support the ongoing existence of two 6 MHz channels for each broadcast licensee, but rather to transition from one 6 MHz analog allocation to one 6 MHz digital allocation, with the anticipated return of one 6 MHz allocation.

19. *Promoting the widespread dissemination of information from a multiplicity of sources.* The second of the three interrelated governmental interests identified in *Turner* is "promoting the widespread dissemination of information from a multiplicity of sources." Discovery argues that if the Commission were to mandate dual carriage, it would allow a single broadcaster to use up to 12 MHz of cable capacity. Discovery comments that the second 6 MHz channel requested by broadcasters could instead be used by a cable operator to provide as many as a dozen diverse non-broadcast programming services offered on a compressed digital basis. Cable industry commenters also argue that most broadcast stations are upconverting analog signals to a standard definition digital format, and that such duplicative broadcast programming does not contribute to program diversity. On the other hand, CEA argues that dual carriage assures broadcasters and programmers of carriage for digital programming, thus motivating them to produce original digital programming, that will, in turn, provide consumers with incentive to purchase digital receivers. On balance, we find that the current record fails to demonstrate that dual carriage is needed to further this governmental interest because program diversity is not promoted under a dual carriage requirement, given that it would not result in additional sources of programming and that digital programming largely simulcasts analog programming.

20. *Promoting fair competition in the market for television programming.* The third important governmental interest identified in *Turner* is promoting fair competition in the market for television programming. While a majority of the Court agreed that this is an important governmental interest, only four justices found that this interest was achieved by the must carry statutory requirements. Based on our previous conclusions—*i.e.*, that dual carriage is not needed to further the governmental interests found by a majority of the Court, it is unnecessary to consider this third interest in great detail. * * *

22. In many respects, competition in the MVPD market has increased since 1992, although the market for the delivery of video programming to households continues to be characterized by substantial barriers to entry. The record, however, does not evidence a connection between mandating dual carriage and remedying any allegations of cable operators' anti-competitive action against local broadcast stations. Because operators must carry local broadcaster's analog signal, there is no obvious need for cable operators to carry two signals for each local station, and it has not been proven necessary to guarantee such access for both analog and digital signals to ensure fair competition. We believe the burden is on the advocates of dual carriage to prove this competitive necessity and that speculative allegations in this regard are inadequate

in light of the burden on cable operators and cable programmers competing for cable access.

23. *Advancing the Digital Transition*. Broadcast commenters state that a rapid transition from analog to digital broadcast signals is an important governmental interest that can justify burdening speech protected by the First Amendment. They contend that dual carriage is necessary to achieve a swift and successful DTV transition. * * *

24. A swift digital television transition and the return of the analog spectrum for other uses are important governmental concerns. We find that the imposition of a dual carriage requirement, however, is not necessary to complete the transition. Many factors are necessary for the transition to be successful, such as consumer acceptance of a new type of television service and rapid digital receiver penetration. The top ten cable operators (representing more than 85% of cable subscribers nationwide) have committed to deploying high-definition services and are fulfilling that commitment. More recently, NCTA reports that the HDTV carriage data reflect that more and more cable households are receiving HDTV programming: (1) the number of local TV markets in which consumers can now receive a package of HDTV services from their cable operator has grown to 184 (out of 210), including all of the top 100 DMAs; (2) the number of local digital broadcast stations being carried voluntarily by cable systems increased to 504, up from 304 in December 2003; (3) of the 108 million U.S. TV households today, 92 million are now passed by a cable system that offers a package of HDTV programming; and (4) 18 cable networks now offer HD programming during some or all of their network schedules, in broad genres reflecting movies, sports, and general interest.

25. The voluntary carriage of network television stations by these operators, as well as carriage of high definition digital programming from non-broadcast sources like HBO, are more likely to spur the sale of digital television equipment (thereby, facilitating the transition) than the forced dual carriage of all television stations. We thus decline to impose dual carriage requirements that burden speech in the absence of record evidence showing dual carriage is necessary for a timely completion of the transition.

26. *Fifth Amendment Argument*. NCTA argues that dual carriage would constitute an uncompensated taking of private property in violation of the Fifth Amendment to the Constitution, especially where, as here, Congress has not clearly authorized such a requirement. NAB responds, in part, that the mere fact that a dual carriage rule might exact some financial toll from cable operators would not render mandatory dual carriage a taking. Given that we have declined to impose dual carriage on other grounds, we need not address the cable industry's Fifth Amendment argument.

27. *Conclusion*. We have analyzed the governmental interests identified in *Turner*, additional governmental interests proposed by the broadcast industry, and policy concerns. We find that there has not been

an adequate showing that dual carriage is necessary to achieve any valid governmental interest. Therefore, in the absence of a clear statutory requirement for dual carriage, we decline to impose this burden on cable operators.

B. Primary Video/Multicast Carriage

* * *

29. In the *First Report and Order*, the Commission recognized that "the terms 'primary video' as used in sections 614(b)(3) and 615(g)(1) are susceptible to different interpretations," and that "[t]he legislative history does not definitively resolve the ambiguity regarding the intended application of the term 'primary video' as used in [the multicasting] context." The Commission thus analyzed the term within its statutory context, considered the legislative history, and examined the technological developments at the time the must carry provisions were enacted. As a result of dictionary definitions and legislative history indicating that "must carry provisions were not intended to cover all uses of a signal," the Commission stated that "[b]ased on the record currently before us, we conclude that 'primary video' means a single programming stream and other program-related content." As a result, the Commission held that if a digital broadcaster elects to divide its digital spectrum into several separate, independent, and unrelated programming streams, only one of these streams is considered primary and entitled to mandatory carriage. Under this determination, the broadcaster elects which programming stream is its primary video, and the cable operator is required to provide mandatory carriage only of that designated stream.

* * *

33. After consideration of all the arguments and evidence presented on this issue, we affirm our earlier decision, and decline, based on the current record before us, to require cable operators to carry any more than one programming stream of a digital television. * * *

38. Significantly, there is nothing in the current record to convince us that mandatory carriage of all multiple streams of a broadcaster's transmission is necessary to achieve either of these goals [(1) preserving the benefits of free, over-the-air local broadcast television for viewers, and (2) promoting "the widespread dissemination of information from a multiplicity of sources."] In the analog context, broadcasters could invoke explicit Congressional findings that the benefits of free, over-the-air television for viewers would be jeopardized without must carry. Congress, however, has made no such findings regarding multicast must carry and broadcasters have not made a convincing argument that over-the-air broadcasting would be jeopardized in the absence of mandatory multicasting. Unlike in the analog carriage debate, here broadcasters fail to substantiate their claim that mandatory multicasting is essential to ensure station carriage or survival. Broadcasters argue that carriage of multicast streams is essential to help them develop and support additional programming streams, but they have not made the case on the current

record that these additional programming streams are essential to preserve the benefits of a free, over-the-air television system for viewers. Broadcasters will continue to be afforded must carry for their main video programming stream, which can be in standard definition or high definition, and any additional material that is considered program-related. Broadcasters can also rely on the marketplace working without mandatory carriage in order to persuade cable systems to carry additional streams of programming. There is evidence from the record, as well as news accounts, that cable operators are voluntarily carrying the multiple streams of programming of some broadcast stations, including public television stations, that are currently multicasting. Indeed, the Association of Public Television Stations and the NCTA recently announced an agreement that involves cable operators carrying up to four programming streams of at least one public TV station in a DMA during the transition from analog to digital technology, and *every* public TV station in a DMA after the transition, subject to certain nonduplication contingencies. Under these circumstances, the interests of over-the-air television viewers appear to remain protected.

39. Likewise, based on the current record, there is little to suggest that requiring cable operators to carry more than one programming stream of a digital television station would contribute to promoting "the widespread dissemination of information from a multiplicity of sources." Under a single-channel must-carry requirement, broadcasters will have a presence on cable systems. Adding additional channels of the same broadcaster would not enhance source diversity. Furthermore, programming shifted from a broadcaster's main channel to the same broadcaster's multicast channel would not promote diversity of information sources. Indeed, mandatory multicast carriage would arguably diminish the ability of other, independent voices to be carried on the cable system.

40. Additionally, no persuasive case has been made on the current record that a multicasting carriage requirement will facilitate the digital transition. High quality programming in a digital format is a major factor that will drive this transition. Some broadcasters explain that they are reluctant to invest in additional programming streams absent an assurance of carriage. In response, NCTA states that cable operators "*want* to carry HDTV and other compelling digital broadcast content that is desired by their customers," and that they want to carry local programming to distinguish their offerings from satellite. NCTA also cautions that giving "shelf space" to broadcasters might lead to carriage of "infomercials, home shopping, or other low value content." NCTA therefore suggests that a guaranteed carriage requirement would diminish incentives for broadcast stations to produce high quality programming, which would "reduce incentive for consumers to switch to digital TV."

41. Given the lack of a meaningful showing on the current record that mandatory carriage of more than one programming stream is necessary to achieve any of the goals discussed above, we determine not to impose such a requirement. We thus find it a reasonable construction

of the must-carry provisions of the Act, on the record before us and in light of the Supreme Court's precedent, not to require cable operators to designate capacity or "shelf space" for multicasting programming streams at the expense of other competing interests.

42. We also note that cable operators contend that requiring them to carry more than one programming stream would constitute a taking under the Fifth Amendment. Given that we decline to impose such a requirement, we do not reach this issue. * * *

---

4. Retransmission Consent

There is another form of property rights protection that has become increasingly important in the allocation of economic entitlements between broadcast and cable. In 1992, when Congress restored must-carry it also decided to add some further protection for local broadcasters by means of a so-called "retransmission consent" requirement. Under retransmission consent, cable systems and other multi-channel program providers (including "wireless cable" and DBS systems—with some exceptions[8]) must obtain consent from any broadcast stations whose signals are retransmitted by the system—other than must-carry signals that cable systems must-carry on the demand of an entitled station. (A local station must choose whether it wants to assert its must-carry right or its retransmission consent right; if it chooses retransmission consent and fails to negotiate a successful deal with the cable operator, its signal will not be carried to the cable operator's subscribers.)

Given the existence of copyright protection, and program exclusivity protection, what exactly is the purpose of a retransmission consent? The primary difference is that retransmission consent has nothing to do with particular programs at all; it is not program specific. It provides a property right in the *signal* of any broadcast station that is retransmitted *in addition to* the program network non-duplication and syndicated exclusivity rules and copyright (which in the case of non-local programming will usually be held by someone other than the local broadcaster). This raises an interesting question of the relationship between program copyright and rights in the signal. For network and syndicated programs, the broadcast station normally has only an exclusive license for some specified period of time. The terms of that license are dictated by the distribution contracts with the network or syndicator (which in turn are determined by whatever copyright license the network or syndicator have from the copyright owner). This means that the station's retransmission consent rights may be a matter for negotiation not just between the station and cable systems that retransmit the station's signal, but between the station and the holders of the copyrights for the programs involved. However, in adopting implementation rules for the retransmis-

8. Retransmission consent does not apply to non-commercial television stations, nor does it apply to satellite retransmission of broadcast stations that, as of 1991, were denominated as "superstations." 47 U.S.C. § 325(b)(2).

sion consent requirement the Commission stressed that retransmission consent rights are not necessarily subsumed in copyright licensing arrangements. *See Implementation of Cable Television Consumer Protection and Competition Act of 1992–Broadcast Signal Carriage Issues*, 58 Fed. Reg. 17350 (1993). In sum, while it is the station that has the retransmission consent rights initially, like any other property right it can be transferred to others—e.g., to the networks, to syndicators, to programmers.

As noted, local broadcast stations must elect between must-carry and retransmission rights. The statute calls for elections to be made every three years, but the parties can negotiate for longer terms if they want, and many have done so. One of the most striking things that has emerged from the several rounds of retransmission consent bargaining is that retransmission rights have eclipsed must-carry rights for most local stations. The overwhelming percentage of local stations choose to exercise their retransmission consent rights rather than their must-carry rights. What does that say about the fuss over must-carry? If between 80–90% of all local stations choose retransmission consent (those are the typical current estimates) how important can the must-carry rights be? Was the decade-long litigation over constitutionality just a shadow-boxing contest? How does retransmission consent affect the on-going debate over digital must-carry? More on this below.

An examination of the negotiations over retransmission consent reveals a shifting pattern of bargaining power between stations and cable operators. In the first round the large MSOs staked out a position that they would not pay cash for retransmission consent. Instead of cash what was often negotiated was a kind of barter: an exchange of retransmission rights in return for the cable system carrying a new program series or network owned by the broadcasters. In subsequent negotiations the broadcasters—particularly the large group-owned stations and network owned stations have demanded, and received, cash. Whether the outcome has been barter or cash, the negotiations have produced some acrimonious controversies, particularly between large cable owners (such as Comcast or Time Warner) on the one hand and the large station owners (e.g., Sinclair) and networks on the other. In 1999, as part of the Satellite Home Viewer Improvement Act (discussed later) Congress directed the FCC to promulgate rules to ensure bargaining in good faith. Initially the rules were directed at broadcasters, but were subsequently extended to MVPDs (notably, cable and satellite) as well. The good faith bargaining requirements (patterned after labor law good faith bargaining requirements) have not eliminated the complaints. Cable operators in particular have claimed that they are handicapped in negotiations with local stations because they are essentially prevented by the non-duplication/exclusivity rules from looking to out-of-market stations for an alternative source of programming (particularly network programming). It is not the individual sets of rules (network non-duplication/syndicated exclusivity and must-carry/retransmission consent) that control the cable-broadcast relationship but rather their interplay. It is that interplay among the rules to which we now turn.

5. Bargaining Over Retransmission Consent, Must-Carry, and Exclusivity

Central to the controversy over retransmission consent is the relationship between retransmission consent and non-duplication/exclusivity protection. Cable operators claim that the combination of these rules gives the local broadcasters undue leverage in demanding compensation for carriage of local channels because the non-duplication and exclusivity rules essentially prevent cable operators from turning to out-of-market sources for channels that their subscribers consider essential (so-called "must-have" channels). Cable operators have been particularly vexed that local broadcasters are using this leverage to demand carriage of the multicast digital channels that the FCC has refused to subject to must-carry (as discussed in section 3.b)and that their subscribers do not want. A 2005 FCC report to Congress explains the issue.

RETRANSMISSION CONSENT AND EXCLUSIVITY RULES: REPORT TO CONGRESS

Federal Communications Commission, 2005.
2005 WL 2206070.

I. Introduction

1. The Satellite Home Viewer Extension and Reauthorization Act of 2004 ("SHVERA") directs the Commission, within nine months after enactment, to complete an inquiry and submit a report to Congress "regarding the impact on competition in the multichannel video programming distribution market of the current retransmission consent, network non-duplication, syndicated exclusivity, and sports blackout rules, including the impact of those rules on the ability of rural cable operators to compete with direct broadcast satellite ('DBS') industry in the provision of digital broadcast television signals to consumers." SHVERA also directs the Commission to "include such recommendations for changes in any statutory provisions relating to such rules as the Commission deems appropriate." * * *

III. Discussion

32. The rules examined in this report were adopted to ensure that broadcasters are compensated fairly for MVPDs' retransmission of their signals, that MVPD retransmission of distant signals does not undermine exclusivity protections negotiated by broadcasters and their programming suppliers, and that sports leagues' contractual arrangements for the exhibition of sporting events are preserved. All of these rules have been adapted over time in response to new technologies and changing market conditions, as well as to balance various public policy goals. Since 1992, technological advances, increased channel capacity, and the introduction of DBS as a competitor to cable have been accompa-

nied by revisions in the rules to: (1) enhance the viability of over-the-air broadcasting; (2) promote localism; and (3) advance regulatory parity between cable and DBS, while taking account of their different operational structures.

33. It is essential to bear in mind that the four rules considered in this Report do not operate in a vacuum. They are part of a mosaic of other regulatory and statutory provisions (e.g., territorial exclusivity, copyright compulsory licensing, and mandatory carriage) to implement key policy goals. For example, territorial exclusivity protects localism by preventing local broadcasters from contracting for exclusivity outside their local markets, while network non-duplication and syndicated exclusivity protect localism by facilitating enforcement of contractual arrangements that limit importation of duplicative distant broadcast signals into local markets. Thus, these rules complement one another. Similarly, copyright law and retransmission consent rules operate in a complementary fashion. The statutory compulsory license compensates rights holders for use of their property, while permitting MVPDs to retransmit their programming without costly and time-consuming negotiations with individual copyright holders. Further, the government-established copyright fee for distant signals, which is higher than that for local stations, operates together with the network non-duplication and syndicated exclusivity rules to encourage MVPD carriage of local broadcast signals. Finally, broadcast mandatory carriage rights, which promote localism and ensure the viability of free, over-the-air television, complement the retransmission consent regime. Together, must-carry and retransmission consent provide that all local stations are assured of carriage even if their audience is small, while also allowing more popular stations to seek compensation (cash or in-kind) for the audience their programming will attract for the cable or satellite operator. Must-carry alone would fail to provide stations with the opportunity to be compensated for their popular programming. Retransmission consent alone would not preserve local stations that have a smaller audience yet still offer free over-the-air programming and serve the public in their local areas. Because of the interplay among these various laws and rules, when any piece of the legal landscape governing carriage of television broadcast signals is changed, other aspects of that landscape also require careful examination. * * *

A. Retransmission Consent

35. Of the four rules examined in this report, retransmission consent is the most recent right granted. Prior to 1992, when the policy goal was to ensure the continued viability of local broadcasters and thereby to enable more households to receive local broadcast programming through cable carriage, broadcasters did not have the right to negotiate retransmission consent. In 1992, however, Congress enacted a statutory provision to address broadcasters' longstanding claim for fair compensation for retransmission of their signals by MVPDs. Retransmission consent replaced the pre-1992 free use of the broadcaster's signal

with the post-1992 scheme in which signals may be retransmitted pursuant to the broadcaster's consent in exchange for negotiated compensation. Although retransmission consent does not guarantee that a broadcaster will receive fair compensation from an MVPD for retransmission of its broadcast signal, it does provide a broadcaster with the opportunity to negotiate for compensation. Notably, Congress chose not to "dictate the outcome of the ensuing marketplace negotiations." Many expected that cable operators would compensate broadcasters with cash in return for retransmission consent. In reality, much of the compensation for retransmission consent has been in-kind, including carriage of an affiliated non-broadcast channel, or other consideration such as the purchase of advertising time, cross-promotions, and carriage of local news channels. While many of the comments in this proceeding focus on retransmission consent agreements that involve carriage of affiliated non-broadcast networks as a form of compensation for carriage of network owned and operated stations, little or no information has been provided regarding other types of retransmission consent agreements. As we discuss below, our review of the record does not lead us to recommend any changes to the retransmission consent regime at this time.

* * *

2. Discussion

44. We believe that, overall, the regulatory policies established by Congress when it enacted retransmission consent have resulted in broadcasters in fact being compensated for the retransmission of their stations by MVPDs, and MVPDs obtaining the right to carry broadcast signals. As we previously have stated, the retransmission consent process provides "incentives for both parties to come to mutually beneficial arrangements." The Commission has observed that both the broadcaster and MVPD benefit when carriage is arranged—the station benefits from carriage because its programming and advertising will be carried as part of the MVPD's service, and the MVPD benefits because the station's programming makes the MVPD's offerings more appealing to consumers. Most importantly, consumers benefit by having access to such programming via an MVPD. Thus, as a general rule, the local television broadcaster and the MVPD negotiate in the context of a level playing field in which the failure to resolve local broadcast carriage disputes through the retransmission consent process potentially is detrimental to each side.

45. Nevertheless, we note cable operators' widespread concern that retransmission consent negotiations frequently involve broadcasters tying carriage of their broadcast signals to carriage of numerous affiliated non-broadcast programming networks. This process may produce results that go beyond what Congress envisioned. We note, though, that if Congress views the carriage of several of a broadcaster's non-broadcast programming networks as an unintended consequence of retransmission consent and seeks to address this practice, it is important that Congress also consider changes to other aspects of the broadcast signal carriage framework, specifically the mandatory carriage provisions. As we noted

above, the retransmission consent rules are part of a carefully balanced combination of laws and regulations governing carriage of television broadcast signals, with the must-carry and retransmission consent regimes complementing one another. For example, since the Commission's decision to deny broadcasters the ability to assert dual and multicast must-carry, broadcasters have begun using their retransmission consent negotiations to negotiate carriage of their digital signals, thus furthering the digital transition by increasing the number of households with access to digital signals. If broadcasters are limited in their ability to accept in-kind compensation, they should be granted full carriage rights for their digital broadcast signals, including all free over-the-air digital multicast streams. Should Congress consider proposals circumscribing retransmission consent compensation, we encourage review of such related rules and policies, as well, in order to maintain a proper balance.

B. Exclusivity Rules

1. Network Non-Duplication and Syndicated Exclusivity Rules

a. Comments

46. Cable operators propose that the network non-duplication and syndicated exclusivity rules be made unenforceable with respect to stations that elect retransmission consent. Specifically, NCTA asks the Commission to initiate a rulemaking to exempt cable operators from compliance with these rules with respect to local broadcast stations that elect retransmission consent when the cable operator and broadcaster are unable to reach agreement and the cable operator seeks to carry a duplicating distant signal in lieu of the local broadcast signal. NCTA and ACA argue that local stations can use their exclusivity rights to prevent cable operators from providing their subscribers with network programming from distant affiliates. ACA claims that broadcasters use the exclusivity rules to raise the price of retransmission consent because, without the ability to carry distant signals, cable operators do not have an alternative source of network programming. ACA argues that this problem is exacerbated in smaller and rural markets that are underserved by over-the-air broadcasters.

47. Broadcasters maintain that the network non-duplication and syndicated exclusivity rules are needed to protect programming for which broadcasters have exclusive rights. They state that elimination of the rules would harm localism, jeopardize broadcast networks, and undermine retransmission consent. According to broadcasters, the rules promote the long-standing goal of localism by: (1) providing MVPD subscribers with access to local content produced by broadcasters; and (2) maximizing local viewership and advertising revenues to support the development and airing of local content. They claim that the rules are necessary to permit broadcasters that have negotiated exclusivity rights with their programming suppliers to protect those rights against MVPD importation of duplicating distant signals and assert that the rules are intended to provide broadcasters with an incentive to invest in program-

ming that serves their communities. To support their arguments, broadcasters note that in 1988, the Commission concluded that the exclusivity rules are necessary to preserve broadcasters' ability to compete against cable operators. They further point out that the Commission later rejected proposals to eliminate these rules when retransmission consent was implemented in 1993. NAB argues that the consequences of eliminating exclusivity protection would be especially dire in small and medium sized markets because the rules are needed to protect the audience base of stations in such markets.

48. Broadcasters fear that elimination of the rules with respect to stations that elect retransmission consent would endanger localism by subjecting local broadcasters to competition with out-of-market broadcasters. NAB indicates that many network affiliation agreements refer to the Commission's rules to define the parties' obligations with respect to exclusivity and to define the geographic scope of exclusivity. Thus, NAB argues that exempting some cable operators from application of the rules with respect to stations that elect retransmission consent could cause significant disruption of existing contractual relationships by forcing broadcasters and their programming suppliers to renegotiate existing contracts. NAB further contends that adoption of the proposed regulatory modifications may well lead to unintended consequences that cannot be anticipated on the basis of the existing record.

b. Discussion

49. Whether or not these rules remain in place, cable operators' ability to retransmit duplicative distant broadcast signals is governed in the first instance by the contract rights negotiated between broadcasters and their programming suppliers. If networks and syndicators have entered into contracts with broadcasters that limit broadcasters' exclusivity such that a duplicative distant signal could be imported by an MVPD without blacking out the duplicative programming, the Commission's rules would not prevent that result. Conversely, where exclusivity contracts exist, repeal of the Commission's rules would not necessarily be sufficient to enable the retransmission of duplicative programming. Moreover, to some extent, rural cable operators are already able to import distant signals without blacking out duplicative programming. The exclusivity rules already contain certain exceptions that should ameliorate rural cable operators' need for relief. Significantly viewed signals, for example, are not subject to these rules. The rules also do not apply to small cable systems serving fewer than 1,000 subscribers. According to ACA, approximately half of its members qualify for this exemption.

50. To the extent that cable operators are asking the Commission to modify the network non-duplication and syndicated exclusivity rules such that they would supersede contract arrangements between broadcasters and their programming suppliers that are permitted by the rules, we cannot endorse or recommend such modifications. The legislative history of the 1992 Act indicates that the network non-duplication and

syndicated exclusivity rules were viewed as integral to achieving congressional objectives. Based on this legislative history, the Commission previously has refused to find that the network non-duplication rules do not apply to stations that elect to exercise retransmission consent rights with respect to a cable system. Moreover, the Commission has a longstanding policy favoring the provision of local broadcast service to communities, and the Commission expects and indeed requires broadcasters to serve the needs and interests of their local communities. Except in cases where a contract violates the Commission's rules, we do not deem it in the public interest to interfere with contractual arrangements that broadcasters have entered into for the very purpose of securing programming content that meets the needs and interests of their communities. Such interference would contradict our own requirements of broadcast licensees and would hinder our policy goals.

51. Accordingly, we decline to recommend at this time that the network non-duplication and syndicated exclusivity rules be modified as proposed by NCTA. Rather than risking the major disruption and possible unintended consequences of rendering these rules unenforceable with respect to broadcasters that elect retransmission consent, it may be appropriate to consider whether 1,000 subscribers remains the correct benchmark for defining a small system, but there is no record in this proceeding to make that determination. Any such consideration should be undertaken cautiously in view of the important role these rules play in enabling local broadcasters to provide robust local service. * * *

Bargaining in the Shadow of Regulation. The Commission at one point in its report suggests that the key to the bargaining problem faced by MVPDs is to focus not on the regulations but on the underlying distribution arrangements that provide exclusivity in the first place: "If networks and syndicators have entered into contracts with broadcasters that limit broadcasters' exclusivity such that a duplicative distant signal could be imported by an MVPD without blacking out the duplicative programming, the Commission's rules would not prevent that result. Conversely, where exclusivity contracts exist, repeal of the Commission's rules would not necessarily be sufficient to enable the retransmission of duplicative programming." The first sentence in this quote is surely correct: the station's leverage to prevent importation of out-of-market signals is entirely a function of the exclusivity provisions contained in the distribution contracts between the networks or syndicators on the one hand and the stations on the other. So, does that imply that the MVPDs are bargaining with the wrong persons? What is the driving force behind the exclusivity provisions? Suppose, for example, the networks decided to limit exclusivity to, say, a 48-hour window—24 hours before and after the scheduled time when the program airs. This would then allow cable systems to negotiate with out-of-market stations to retransmit their network programs and show them in the market on a delayed basis. This would then give the local cable operator an alternative source for "must-have" programs in case of stymied retransmission consent negotiations with the local station. Clearly this would eliminate much of the bargaining leverage of the local station. Does the *network* have a reason to care?[9] (Consider that about 86 percent of all television households receive their television from MVPDs—cable and DBS combined.)

The second sentence in the above quote from the Commission is also correct—if one assumes the existence of the retransmission consent right (do you see why this is a necessary assumption?). However, that observation just shifts the question to another: why is the retransmission consent right a necessary element of the public interest? For roughly the first three decades of cable regulation it was not deemed to be an essential element of the regulatory scheme. It was created by Congress in 1992 to give an additional source of income to what was perceived to be an industry in economic distress. What's the justification for that? One answer presumably would be our old friend localism. But if that is the answer, why not require the local stations to actually present local programming?

Of particular interest is the Commission's recommendation that if Congress elects to change the retransmission consent rule it should do so only after an examination of other rules. "If broadcasters are limited in their ability to accept in-kind compensation, they should be granted full carriage rights for their digital broadcast signals, including all free over-the-air digital multicast streams." Why would it be necessary to require carriage rights for all "digital multicast streams"? Can't the stations use their retransmission consent rights to bargain for such carriage (by conditioning carriage of the primary signal on carriage of all multicast content)? Should local broadcasters be prohibited from negotiating in-kind carriage of *distant* multicast streams as part of retransmission consent negotiations? Don't such transactions completely undermine localism as a justification for any of these restrictions?

C. TERRESTRIAL AND SATELLITE MEDIA

1. Origins of Satellite Broadcasting

Following the adoption by the International Telecommunications Union of frequency allocations for DBS service in the 12 GHz band in 1979, and in anticipation of a specific channel and orbital slot allotment plan for the western hemisphere in 1983, the Commission in 1982 adopted a preliminary plan for authorizing DBS services. The authorization of a new competitive technology in the 1980s was an occasion for a reprise of the battle between broadcasting and cable in the 1960s and 1970s. The terrestrial broadcast industry again followed a two-fold

9. The standard CBS affiliation agreement reserves a right to cancel, on 6 month's notice, an affiliate's non-duplication protection in cases where the local station has been "unable to maintain or attain cable carriage" on the local cable system.

strategy: first try to stop the authorization of new competition; second, failing the first objective, try to burden the new medium with as many regulatory restrictions as possible. In contrast to the earlier battle over cable, the FCC was not especially receptive to pleas of incumbent broadcasters to stop or handicap the new DBS competitors. So, the broadcasters did what everyone else in America does when faced with a new competitor: they took their case to court. In reading the resulting decision, notice in particular the NAB's localism arguments and recall the same arguments made against cable operators' importation of distant signals into local markets. Needless to say, signals transmitted from 22,000 miles above the earth are about as "distant" as they get. As we shall see, however, the FCC and Congress managed to create a regulatory structure to promote localism by linking a DBS provider's ability to obtain authorization to carry network programs to their carriage of local broadcast station signals.

NATIONAL ASSOCIATION OF BROADCASTERS v. FCC

United States Court of Appeals, District of Columbia Circuit, 1984.
740 F.2d 1190.

MIKVA, CIRCUIT JUDGE:

Of the technological innovations currently revolutionizing the communications field, the most recent, and potentially the most significant, is direct broadcast satellite service (DBS). DBS involves the transmission of signals from the earth to highpowered, geostationary satellites which then beam television signals directly to individual homes equipped to receive them. Use of satellites massively extends the range of a broadcaster's voice by freeing it from the atmospheric limitations that traditionally limit terrestrial broadcasters to narrow broadcast areas; a single DBS signal will eventually be capable of reaching the entire continental United States. For this reason and others, DBS promises several significant advantages over existing television technology: high-quality service to individuals in rural or remote areas where conventional broadcasting is inefficient; the addition of many more channels even in urban areas already receiving several television signals; "narrowcasting" of programs to specialized tastes through the ability to aggregate small, widely dispersed audiences; the development of higher quality visual and audio signals through use of high-definition-television signals; and television transmission of non-entertainment programming, such as medical data and educational information.

The regulatory approach to DBS taken by the Federal Communications Commission (the FCC or the Commission), which we review today, is as novel as the technology with which it is concerned. In essence, the Commission has chosen to deregulate DBS even before the service is born. Two proceedings are before us today that embody that approach: the Commission's Interim DBS regulations, which delineate the basic contours of the regulatory environment that DBS owners and operators will face when DBS becomes operational, and the approval of an actual application to construct this country's first multi-channel DBS system. We find that, on the whole, the FCC has done a commendable job in assuring that regulation in the communications field not impede new technologies that offer substantial public benefits, and we therefore uphold the major portion of the interim DBS regulations and approve in its entirety the FCC's grant of the application to construct an actual DBS system. * * *

Analysis

I. The FCC's Power to Approve Non-Local Broadcast Service

DBS technology is inherently unsuitable for the provision of traditional local broadcast service. The satellites involved cannot presently be located with the requisite precision nor economically equipped with a sufficiently large antenna to provide a spot beam capable of covering only a traditional size local community. Moreover, many of the benefits of DBS—including narrowcasting and provision of service to less densely populated areas—could not practically be realized by a "local" DBS system. As a result, DBS, as authorized by the FCC, will provide regional or national service. The *STC Decision*, for example, authorizes transmission service to the entire Eastern coast of the United States.

Petitioner NAB argues that the FCC does not have the power to approve a technology that will sever broadcast services from their traditional link to a particular community. NAB seeks to rest this luddite argument on section 307(b) of the Communications Act of 1934, as amended, 47 U.S.C. § 307(b) (the Act), which provides:

> "the Commission shall make such distribution of licenses ... among the several States and communities as to provide a fair, efficient, and equitable distribution of radio service to each of the same."

NAB reads this provision to require that broadcast licenses indeed be "distributed" among the "States" and "communities;" NAB thus concludes that the Act mandates a system of local broadcast licensing and service with which STC's authorization, and DBS in general, is "fundamentally irreconcilable."

We do not think it necessary to ascribe to the framers of the Act an intent so shortsighted as to preclude new technology that offers the promise of substantial public benefit. The plain language of the Act does not compel such impracticable consequences. Instead, the Act emphasizes that the FCC's paramount responsibility is to achieve a "fair, efficient and equitable distribution of radio service ... so as to make available, as far as possible, to all the people of the United States a rapid, efficient, nation-wide, and world-wide wire and communications service." The ultimate touchstone for the FCC is thus the distribution of service, rather than of licenses or of stations; the constituency to be served is people, not municipalities. Moreover, the Commission also has an obligation to "encourage the larger and more effective use of radio in the public interest." Given this obligation to facilitate expansion of this country's communications network and in light of the broad grant of authority delegated to the FCC to deal with "the rapidly fluctuating factors characteristic of the evolution of broadcasting," it would be anomalous to read the Act to prevent the FCC from authorizing an innovative system of technology capable of conferring substantial benefits on all Americans. * * * Just as we have held that the Act does not bestow a vested right on any particular licensee to retention of its license, so too we now hold that the Act does not entrench any particular system of broadcasting: existing systems, like existing licensees, have no entitlement that permits them to deflect competitive pressure from innovative and effective technology.

In so holding we do not denigrate the importance of local programming to a national broadcasting system that is designed to serve the public interest. We need not define the outer limits of the Commission's authority to make this country's broadcasting system a regional or national one, however, for two reasons. First, the *DBS Order* does not by its terms eliminate local programming. Second, the Commission explicitly found that DBS will merely supplement the existing local broadcast system, rather than replace it, and we find no error in that finding. We therefore need not decide how far the Commission may go toward the elimination of local programming to hold that not every communications service approved by the Commission need be tied to a local community. * * *

---

2. Satellite Broadcasting and Media Property Rights

Recall from our earlier discussion of cable that the 1976 Copyright Act gave cable systems a right to obtain compulsory copyright licenses on payment of a prescribed royalty fee. No such right was given DBS systems which, of course, were not then in existence or even under active development. However, some homes obtained broadcast service by means of large earth terminals that were capable of receiving the down-links of satellite relays used by the networks to distribute their programming to station affiliates, essentially engaging in "retail" consumption of network programming by intercepting the "wholesale" signal from network to broadcaster. In response, the major networks began scrambling their feeds to broadcast stations thereby preventing unauthorized reception. In 1988 Congress enacted the Satellite Home Viewer Act, 17 U.S.C. § 119(a) ("SHVA"), to provide a compromise solution. Under SHVA "unserved households" can receive network programs (defined as households that could not receive a Grade B quality service and which had not subscribed to cable for 90 days) upon paying a fee, giving them a compulsory copyright license similar to that given cable systems.

The Satellite Home Viewer Act was not aimed at providing a helping hand to DBS, (contrary to a suggestion made in the case below). DBS was still only in the planning stages, and the legislative history provides no indication that Congress was at all mindful of the need for a general compulsory license in order to make DBS competitive with cable. The disparity between satellite and cable in regard to the ability to carry network signals was partly addressed in 1999 with the Satellite Home Viewer Improvement Act ("SHVIA") SHVIA did several things. First, it imposed on satellite broadcasters non-duplication, syndicated exclusivity, and blackout rules parallel (though not precisely identical in detail) to those imposed on cable. Second, it gave satellite broadcasters a compulsory license to carry *local* network signals. However, as a condition for that license, the satellite must carry *all* local signals in the market (or at least all those that request carriage). Reprising the cable operators' challenges to must-carry rules in *Turner I* and *Turner II*, the satellite carriers challenged the so-called "carry one, carry all" condition.

SATELLITE BROADCASTING AND COMMUNICATIONS ASS'N v. FCC

United States Court of Appeals, Fourth Circuit, 2001.
275 F.3d 337.

MICHAEL, CIRCUIT JUDGE:

Direct broadcast satellite (DBS) service has recently joined cable and broadcast television as a major force in the market for delivering television programming to consumers. In these consolidated cases, representatives of the satellite industry raise various constitutional challenges to Congress's efforts to regulate competition in that market through the Satellite Home Viewer Improvement Act of 1999 (SHVIA). Pub.L. No. 106–113, 113 Stat. 1501A–523. * * * By enacting SHVIA, Congress sought to promote competition between the satellite and cable industries by creating a statutory copyright license that allows satellite carriers to carry the signals of local broadcast television stations without obtaining authorization from the holders of copyrights in the individual programs aired by those stations. The Act also imposes a "carry one, carry all" rule, which was designed to "preserve free television for those not served by satellite or cable and to promote widespread dissemination of information from a multiplicity of sources." H.R. Conf. Rep. No. 106–464, at 101 (1999) (SHVIA Conference Report). The rule, which is scheduled to take effect on January 1, 2002, will require satellite carriers that choose to take advantage of the statutory copyright license by carrying one broadcast station in a local market to carry all requesting stations within that market. We hold, as did the district court, that the carry one, carry all rule does not violate either the First Amendment or the other constitutional provisions cited by the satellite carriers. * * *

I.

A.

Nearly all consumers receive their television programming through one of three delivery systems: broadcast television, cable, or satellite. Broadcast television stations transmit electromagnetic signals over the air, and these signals can be captured by any receiving television antenna within range. Twenty percent of American television households rely exclusively on broadcast stations for their television programming. Viewers pay no fee to receive broadcast signals. Instead, broadcast stations are supported by advertisers who pay for air time at rates determined by the audience sizes for particular programs. The most popular broadcast stations are affiliated with one of the four major television networks (ABC, CBS, NBC, and Fox). The major network affiliates compete for viewers and advertisers with various independent broadcasters, including independent commercial stations, noncommercial stations, and affiliates of emerging networks (UPN, WB, and PAX).

The broadcasters' principal competitors in the television programming delivery market are the cable and satellite industries. Cable and satellite companies now serve around 80 percent of America's television households. Unlike broadcasters, their primary source of revenue is subscription fees. Cable television distributes its signals to subscribers over a local network of wires. It has for many years been the leading provider of television programming to American homes. Roughly 67 percent of television households currently subscribe to cable. Although cable subscribers must pay for the right to receive cable signals, they receive better picture quality and a wider variety of programming options than do television viewers who rely on antennas. Today, 84 percent of cable systems offer their subscribers at least 30 channels, including national non-broadcast channels (such as ESPN, MTV, CNN, and The Weather Channel) and regional non-broadcast channels (such as the New England Sports Channel). Cable operators also retransmit the signals of local broadcast stations to their subscribers.

Providers of DBS (direct broadcast satellite) service deliver television programming by uplinking signals to satellites orbiting in space and then beaming those signals to receiving dishes connected to subscribers' television sets. In the 1980s satellite dishes were 6 to 10 feet in diameter, and satellite carriers primarily served customers in rural areas. During the 1990s satellite carriers such as EchoStar and DirecTV developed much smaller dishes and began to compete with cable for subscribers in urban and suburban areas. Today, satellite carriers provide service in each of the nation's 210 television markets and serve about 13 percent of television households.

Whereas cable systems deliver their signals to subscribers over local wire networks, satellite is primarily a national service. The satellites currently used by DBS providers occupy one of three positions in the Earth's orbit (called full CONUS slots) that allow the satellites to transmit a single beam covering the entire continental United States. The beam from a full CONUS satellite contains multiple frequencies, and compression technology enables multiple television channels to be carried on each frequency. The FCC licenses the use of 32 frequencies at each orbital slot; thus, there are 96 total frequencies that satellite carriers can use to reach satellite subscribers across the United States. Currently, 50 of these frequencies are licensed to EchoStar and 46 to DirecTV. Using their current compression ratios, EchoStar and DirecTV each have the ability to carry between 450 and 500 channels via full

CONUS satellites. Every channel carried on these satellites is beamed to the homes of all subscribers; however, channels that individual subscribers do not pay to receive are blocked by the use of software in the subscriber's home satellite equipment.

Like cable, satellite service is financed by subscription fees, and it offers better picture quality and more viewing options than broadcast television. Satellite carriers can provide their customers with more national and regional non-broadcast channels than most cable systems; yet before SHVIA was passed, satellite carriers had difficulty competing with cable for urban and suburban customers. The root cause of this difficulty was plain. Cable systems, but not satellite carriers, provided their customers with access to the signals of local broadcast stations. This competitive advantage was rooted not only in technology but also in federal copyright law. Unlike satellite carriers, cable operators have never been required to obtain copyright clearances for the broadcast programming they retransmit to their subscribers. To explain the origins of cable's competitive advantage over satellite, we must briefly review the history that produced the current legal regime governing the relationships among cable, broadcast television, and satellite.

In 1965, long before cable became a major force in the television programming delivery market, the FCC imposed "must-carry" rules on cable systems requiring them to retransmit the signal of any requesting broadcast station that was "significantly viewed" in its local market. The FCC feared that cable might undermine free, local broadcasting unless "local broadcasters were assured access to the whole of their allocated audience." Specifically, the must-carry rules were designed to aid newer UHF stations, which lacked the signal quality enjoyed by more established VHF stations. The FCC was concerned that in the absence of carriage obligations cable systems would carry only VHF stations and that non-carried UHF stations would be placed at a competitive disadvantage in the race for advertising dollars.

Copyright law had little effect on cable until Congress passed the Copyright Act of 1976, which provides that owners of copyrights in audiovisual works such as television programs have the exclusive right to authorize public performances of those works. Although the Copyright Act of 1909 had granted copyright holders a similar right to control public performances of copyrighted works, cable operators' secondary transmissions of broadcast programs were not regarded as additional performances of those programs under the 1909 Act and thus did not infringe upon the intellectual property rights of the program copyright holders. *See Fortnightly Corp. v. United Artists Television, Inc.*, 392 U.S. 390, 400–01 (1968). The 1976 Act's legislative history reveals that Congress intended to countermand the result in *Fortnightly* by designating cable's secondary transmissions of broadcast programs as public performances of those programs: "a cable television system is performing when it retransmits the broadcast [of a television program] to its subscribers." As a result, copyright law now generally requires parties seeking to retransmit the signal of a broadcast television station to obtain authorization from those holding copyrights in each of the programs broadcast by that station. Cable operators, however, have never been subject to this general rule. Congress found "that it would be impractical and unduly burdensome to require every cable system to negotiate with every copyright owner whose work was retransmitted by a cable system." As a result, the 1976 Copyright Act granted cable operators a statutory license that allows them to retransmit broadcast television signals without securing authorization from program copyright holders.

As cable grew in popularity, cable operators and cable programmers began to chafe at the FCC's must-carry rules. Eventually, cable interests challenged the rules as an unconstitutional burden on freedom of speech, and the rules were struck down by the D.C. Circuit in 1985. After a period of several years during which cable enjoyed the benefits of a statutory copyright license without the burdens of carriage obligations, Congress reimposed must-carry rules by passing the Cable Television and Consumer Protection and Competition Act of 1992 (Cable Act). Like the FCC's original must-carry rules, the Cable Act's must-carry rules were designed to protect broadcast stations that might be refused carriage in the absence of a must-carry requirement.

The Cable Act must-carry rules were also challenged on First Amendment grounds, but were ultimately upheld by the Supreme Court in *Turner Broadcasting System, Inc. v. FCC*, 512 U.S. 622 (1994) (*Turner I*), and *Turner Broadcasting System, Inc. v. FCC*, 520 U.S. 180 (1997) (*Turner II*). * * *

As the above history indicates, the cable industry developed within a context of extensive FCC regulations, but it has been largely unaffected by copyright considerations. Before 1976, cable retransmissions of broadcast programs were not regarded as additional performances of these programs and therefore did not infringe program copyrights. Since 1976, cable has enjoyed a statutory copyright license. In contrast, the satellite industry has until recently enjoyed relative freedom from FCC oversight, but its history has been shaped by a series of changes in federal copyright law. When the 1976 Copyright Act was passed, home satellite service did not exist, and the statutory copyright license created by 17 U.S.C. § 111(c) was granted only to cable systems. Although early satellite carriers lacked the channel capacity to retransmit the signals of local broadcast stations to the local audiences of those stations (called "local-into-local" service), the carriers did have the capacity and the desire to offer their subscribers some distant network signals. In other words, they had enough capacity to carry the signals of network affiliates in a major city (usually New York) throughout the entire country, but not enough capacity to carry local network affiliates in smaller cities. It was unclear, however, whether satellite carriers' secondary transmissions of the signals of network affiliates infringed the copyrights in the various programs broadcast by those stations. Satellite carriers argued that they might be eligible to use the § 111 copyright license as "cable systems," or that their secondary transmissions of broadcast signals were noninfringing under the exemption for passive carriers in 17 U.S.C. § 111(a)(3). Still, they asked Congress to resolve the uncertainties about their copyright liability by passing new legislation.

Congress responded with the Satellite Home Viewer Act of 1988. Pub.L. No. 100–667, 102 Stat. 3949. Recognizing that the high transaction costs involved in clearing the rights to network signals might impede the growth of the fledgling satellite industry, Congress gave carriers a limited copyright license to retransmit the signals of distant network broadcast stations to unserved households that were unable to receive an adequate over-the-air signal through a conventional rooftop antenna. 17 U.S.C. § 119(a)(2)(B) (1994), *amended by* § 119(a)(2)(B) (Supp. V 1999). "Unserved households" were defined in part as those located outside a station's "Grade B contour," as defined by FCC regulations. Congress limited the copyright license to retransmissions to unserved households in order to respect the terms of network-affiliate contracts, which grant local affiliates the exclusive right to broadcast their networks' programming in their local markets. Congress reasoned that local affiliates would lose the benefits of their bargained-for exclusivity rights if satellite carriers were allowed to import distant network signals into the affiliates' local markets. The limited license created by the 1988 Act spurred the growth of satellite carriers and expanded the viewing options of unserved households, though it did little to help satellite effectively compete with cable in urban and suburban areas where viewers could already receive high quality broadcast signals.

In the late 1990s two problems led Congress to revisit its work in the Satellite Home Viewer Act of 1988. First, cable continued to enjoy a virtual monopoly in subscription television services in metropolitan areas, and as a result cable subscribers were paying too much for those services. Second, the 1988 Act failed to deal adequately with the problems of satellite subscribers who lived within the Grade B contours of network television stations. Although these subscribers were ineligible to receive distant network signals under the 1988 Act's limited copyright licence, many of them were unable to receive satisfactory over-the-air signals from their local network affiliates and thus remained without any meaningful access to network programming. In addition, administrative difficulties in deciding which households were genuinely unserved led to increasingly bitter disputes between satellite carriers and broadcasters, leaving bewildered, angry consumers stuck in the middle. *See, e.g., ABC, Inc. v. PrimeTime 24*, 17 F.Supp.2d 478 (M.D.N.C.1998), *aff'd*, 184 F.3d 348 (4th Cir.1999).

Progress in satellite technology seemed to hold out a solution to both of these problems. Satellite carriers had developed the channel capacity to offer local-into-local service to their subscribers in some markets. Congress recognized that satellite carriers that could offer viewers access to their local broadcast stations could compete effectively with cable and drive down the price of subscription television services. In addition, Congress understood that the difficulties in deciding which households were sufficiently unserved to receive distant network signals would be irrelevant if satellite subscribers could watch their local network affiliates.

In 1997 and 1998 Congress conducted extensive hearings on the possibility of extending the satellite carriers' statutory copyright license to include local-into-local retransmissions. Representatives from the various industries had ample opportunities to state their views. Satellite industry representatives argued that without a statutory copyright license, the high transaction costs of obtaining the rights to retransmit broadcast programs would effectively prevent satellite carriers from offering local-into-local service. The satellite representatives further explained that their inability to carry local broadcast stations placed them at a competitive disadvantage to cable because viewers want to be able to receive all of the televisions channels they watch from a single source: "most people who walk into a satellite dealer's showroom turn around and walk out because they can't get their local TV channels through DBS." The cable representatives stressed the need for regulatory parity, arguing that if satellite carriers were granted a statutory license comparable to that enjoyed by cable, they should also be subject to the must-carry rules and other regulatory constraints imposed on cable. Finally, representatives of the broadcast industry emphasized that mandatory carriage rules were needed to ensure that satellite local-into-local service would not undermine Congress's interest in preserving a vibrant system of free, local broadcast television. They explained that without carriage rules satellite carriers would choose to retransmit only the signals of major network affiliates in most markets and that competing stations in those markets would suffer from the loss of access to a significant (and growing) part of their potential audiences:

No rational doubt may exist that a local station denied access to a portion of its in market audience is injured. Lack of carriage reduces potential audience and, therefore, actual audience. Reduced audiences translate to reduced revenue. Even where revenue reductions are less than fatal, they still affect a station's ability to provide the best practicable service to the public. At best, a local station which a satellite carrier refuses to carry would be placed at a demonstrable disadvantage vis-a-vis competing broadcast television stations which are carried.

Congress sought to balance all of these concerns when it enacted SHVIA on November 29, 1999. The Conference Report explained that the legislation was designed to promote competition between satellite and cable while "preserv[ing] free television for those not served by satellite or cable systems." Two interrelated provisions form the heart of SHVIA. The first provision, codified at 17 U.S.C. § 122, amended the Copyright Act to create a statutory copyright license for satellite carriers similar to that enjoyed by cable operators. The license enables satellite carriers to make secondary transmissions of a broadcast station's signal into that station's local market without obtaining the authorization of those holding copyrights in the individual programs broadcast by that station. 17 U.S.C. § 122(a). Satellite carriers that make use of this license pay no royalties to program copyright holders. The second provision, codified at 47 U.S.C. § 338, amended the Communications Act of 1934 by creating mandatory carriage rules, including the carry one, carry all rule that is the focus of this litigation.

Since SHVIA's passage in late 1999 satellite carriers have enjoyed the benefits of the § 122 license without the burdens of the carry one, carry all rule. In order to phase in satellite carriage obligations, Congress decided that the rule would not become effective until January 1, 2002. As of that date the rule will require all satellite carriers who use the § 122 license to make local-into-local retransmissions in a local broadcast market to "carry upon request the signals of all television broadcast stations located within that local market." In other words, the voluntary decision to carry one local station in a market under the statutory copyright license will trigger an obligation to carry all the requesting stations in that market.

Like the cable must-carry rules, SHVIA's carry one, carry all rule was designed to preserve a rich mix of broadcast outlets for consumers who do not (or cannot) pay for subscription television services. SHVIA adopts much of the machinery of the cable rules. For example, broadcast stations may seek carriage from satellite carriers under either § 338's mandatory carriage requirements, or under the Act's retransmission consent provision, which allows broadcast stations to receive compensation from satellite carriers in exchange for permission to retransmit the broadcast stations' signals. In allowing broadcasters to choose between retransmission consent and mandatory carriage, both SHVIA's carry one, carry all rule and the cable must-carry rules recognize the practical realities of the television marketplace. Major network affiliates have bargaining power and will be carried voluntarily in most instances, so they will normally elect to proceed under the retransmission consent provision. In contrast, independent stations (affiliates of emerging networks, independent commercial stations, and noncommercial stations) may need the protection of must-carry rules and will normally elect mandatory carriage.

The primary difference between § 338 and the cable must-carry rules is that § 338's obligations are conditioned upon the satellite carrier's voluntary choice to make use of the § 122 license in a particular television market, but the cable must-carry rules are mandatory in all markets. This difference reflects the technological dissimilarities between cable and satellite. Cable systems are local, and nearly all have enough channel capacity to carry all the broadcast stations in their local market and still provide an attractive mix of national and regional non-broadcast programming. The satellite carriers, in contrast, currently beam the same 450 to 500 channels throughout the continental United States and thus could not comply with a rule requiring them to retransmit the signals of each of the country's roughly 1,600 local broadcast stations. While Congress recognized that satellite technology continues to improve and that eventually an unconditional must-carry rule might be possible, it still had to decide how to structure the satellite copyright license in the interim.

Although minor variations were possible, Congress had two basic options. It could have decided to give satellite carriers a station-by-station copyright license that could be used free of carriage obligations. Under such a license, satellite carriers could "cherry pick" the stations they wanted in each local market. Congress predicted that in practical terms a station-by-station license would result in satellite carriers using their available local-into-local capacity to carry only the major network affiliates in as many markets as possible, beginning with the largest markets and working toward the smaller ones. The other choice was to impose the carry one, carry all rule in order to create a market-by-market copyright license. This kind of license forces satellite carriers to expand their local-into-local service one market at a time, beginning with the carriage of all requesting local stations in the largest markets and expanding from there. In sum, Congress either could have allowed satellite carriers to cherry pick by retransmitting *some* stations (the major network affiliates) in *many* markets, or it could have allowed satellite carriers to retransmit *all* of the stations in *some* markets. While satellite carriers would have preferred (and now argue for) the first result, Congress chose the second because it feared that cherry picking of major network affiliates within local markets would make it more difficult for non-carried stations in those markets to reach their audiences:

> Although the conferees expect that subscribers who receive no broadcast signals at all from their satellite service may install antennas or subscribe to cable service in addition to satellite service, the Conference Committee is less sanguine that subscribers who receive network signals and hundreds of other programming choices from their satellite carrier will undertake such trouble and expense to obtain over-the-air signals from independent broadcast stations.

Non-carried stations in cherry-picked markets would "face the same loss of viewership Congress previously found with respect to cable noncarriage." Congress therefore concluded that the carry one, carry all rule would protect the ability of all local broadcasters to reach their audiences and thereby "preserve free television for those not served by satellite or cable systems and ... promote widespread dissemination of information from a multiplicity of sources."

* * *

II.

A.

The parties devote the lion's share of their attention to the satellite carriers' First Amendment challenge to the carry one, carry all rule enacted in 47 U.S.C. § 338. Satellite carriers, like cable operators, function primarily as conduits for the speech of others. They transmit programming from a variety of sources (national and regional non-broadcast channels, superstations, and local broadcast stations) to their subscribers "on a continuous and unedited basis." Yet both satellite carriers and cable operators engage in speech protected by the First Amendment when they exercise editorial discretion over the menu of channels they offer to their subscribers. Insofar as the carry one, carry all rule seeks to influence the exercise of that discretion, it is open to challenge under the First Amendment.

It is important to be clear at the outset, however, that some of the speech interests present in the *Turner* cases are absent here. The cable must-carry rules burdened the speech of cable programmers who had to be dropped from some cable systems in order to make room for local broadcast stations. To the extent the First Amendment guarantees viewers and listeners the right to receive information, that right was also burdened by the cable must-carry rules because the voices of dropped cable programmers were effectively lost to entire communities. Here, however, the satellite carriers do not claim that the carry one, carry all rule will force them to drop national or regional non-broadcast programmers in order to carry more local broadcasters. They claim only that they will have to carry independent broadcast stations in larger markets at the expense of major network affiliates in smaller markets. While those major network affiliates would no doubt prefer to be carried on satellite services, the carry one, carry all rule does not deprive those affiliates of the ability to reach their audiences. In fact, they will be in exactly the same position under the carry one, carry all rule that they would have occupied if SHVIA had never been passed. Nor will any voices be completely lost to communities as a result of the carry one, carry all rule. The rule's only negative effect on viewers will be that the major network affiliates in some markets will be available to local viewers through only two mediums (broadcast and cable) rather than three. In sum, the carry one, carry all rule burdens speech only to the extent that it affects satellite carriers' decisions about how to allocate their capacity for offering local-into-local service by inducing them to carry a different set of local broadcasters than the carriers would have preferred.

In considering the satellite carriers' First Amendment challenge, our first task is to determine the appropriate standard of review. *Turner I* provides the starting point. In that case the Supreme Court held that the cable must-carry rules were content-neutral restrictions on speech and were therefore not subject to strict scrutiny. Here, the satellite carriers repeat many of the same arguments for strict scrutiny that were examined and rejected in *Turner I.* Although the satellite carriers labor mightily to distinguish that case, their effort ultimately fails. * * *

B.

O'Brien directs us to uphold a content-neutral regulation of speech if "it furthers an important or substantial governmental interest; if the governmental interest is unrelated to the suppression of free expression; and if the incidental restriction on alleged First Amendment freedoms is no greater than is essential to the furtherance of that interest." * * *

1.

Congress enacted the carry one, carry all rule to "preserve free television for those not served by satellite or cable systems and to promote widespread dissemination of information from a multiplicity of sources." These interests are clearly substantial and unrelated to the suppression of free expression. * * *

Congress's prediction that satellite carriers would become a significant force in the television programming delivery market was supported by substantial evidence. While Congress did not explicitly find that satellite carriers would attain any specific level of market penetration, it obviously projected that satellite carriers would attract enough viewers to put downward pressure on cable rates. Congress created the § 122 copyright license to produce this result, and it cannot be unreasonable for Congress to proceed on the premise that its own legislation will be effective. Moreover, the rapid growth in satellite service since SHVIA's enactment suggests that Congress's prediction will soon come true. The number of DBS subscribers grew by 28 percent between June 1999 and June 2000. DBS providers have attributed much of their growth to the '122 license. In its comments for the FCC's Seventh Annual Report, SBAC predicted that DBS service might have as many as 16 million subscribers (over 15 percent of American television households) by the end of 2000. In sum, Congress's first prediction was entirely reasonable.

Congress's second prediction was that without § 338, satellite carriers would refuse to carry significant numbers of independent broadcast stations in markets where they offered local-into-local service. This prediction was supported by substantial evidence in the record before Congress. In addition, the satellite industry's track record under SHVIA has proven the prediction to be accurate. As of November 5, 2001, DirecTV carried the four major network affiliates in 41 markets (a total of 164 stations), but carried a total of only 13 independent stations in those 41 markets. Similarly, EchoStar carried the four major network affiliates in 35 markets (a total of 140 stations), but carried only 13 independent stations in those markets. Thus, during SHVIA's phase-in period the satellite carriers have confined their local-into-local offerings almost exclusively to major network affiliates. Moreover, they have plainly announced their intention to continue cherry picking the major network affiliates so long as they may lawfully do so. This preference for cherry picking will not simply wither away because it is rooted in the national character of existing satellite technology.

As we have said, satellite carriers currently beam the same signals throughout the nation from satellites orbiting in full CONUS slots. As a result, a carrier who chooses to retransmit the signal of an independent commercial station in Boston beams that station's signal to subscribers nationwide, but blocks out the signal at the homes of all subscribers who do not live in the Boston area. As this example illustrates, local-into-local service is a relatively inefficient use of a carrier's finite channel capacity. National programming uses that capacity more efficiently because it can be expected to draw more viewers across the country as a whole than any local channel, even if the national programming is less popular within individual local markets than the programming of the independent broadcast stations in those markets. As a result, satellite carriers have economic incentives to favor national non-broadcast programming over local broadcast programming. While improvements in satellite technology, such as the deployment of spot beam satellites, may reduce the inefficiencies that result from carrying local broadcast stations, these inefficiencies will continue to exist to some degree so long as the beams from individual satellites cover multiple television markets. Yet satellite carriers also recognize that their product is less attractive to subscribers if they fail to carry the local affiliates of major networks because most people watch these stations about "65 percent of the time" they spend watching television. Under these circumstances, the economically rational choice for satellite carriers is to cherry pick the major network affiliates in markets where the carriers offer local-into-local service. We conclude, then, that both the satellite industry's track record and its economic incentives provide substantial evidence supporting Congress's predictive judgment that satellite carriers will deny carriage to significant numbers of independent broadcast stations if the carriers are not bound by the carry one, carry all rule.

Congress's third prediction was that lack of satellite carriage would harm independent broadcast stations. This general prediction rested on the following series of more specific predictions about the consequences of non-carriage. First, a non-carried station will effectively lose access to satellite subscribers if satellite carriers cherry pick the major network affiliates in its market. Second, a station's loss of access to those subscribers will result in lower ratings, which will in turn lead to lower advertising revenues. Third, lower revenues will lead to a decrease in programming quality, which will then further depress ratings and station revenues, all in a vicious cycle. The record before Congress contains substantial evidence to support these predictions. * * *

So far, we have established that Congress had substantial evidence to support its overall prediction that in a world where satellite carriers enjoyed the benefits of a statutory copyright license without the burdens of the carry one, carry all rule, satellite carriers would become significant competitors to cable and would continue to cherry pick major network affiliates in markets where they offered local-into-local service. In that world, non-carried stations in cherry-picked markets would lose access to significant parts of their local audiences. Again, the harder question is whether this predicted set of consequences is enough to justify imposing the carry one, carry all rule on satellite carriers in order to protect the government's interest in preserving a multiplicity of broadcast outlets for over-the-air viewers. In other words, the question is whether preventing the consequences Congress predicted counts as addressing a real threat to that interest in a material way. * * *

In enacting SHVIA, Congress properly considered the effects of satellite and cable together in deciding to protect over-the-air viewers from any significant reduction in their viewing options. Cable and satellite together currently serve around 80 percent of America's television households, with cable accounting for about 65 percent and satellite about 15 percent. We have already explained that both services pose the same kind of threat to broadcast stations because both—by making selective carriage decisions—threaten to cut off independent broadcast stations from parts of their audiences. Together, cable and satellite would pose an overwhelming threat to independent broadcasters if neither were bound by carriage rules. Congress evidently reasoned that with increasing competition from satellite carriers, the threat to independent broadcasters posed by cable would become a threat jointly posed by cable and satellite. It therefore concluded that it could regulate both contributors to that common threat: "The [Conference Committee] expect[s] that, by January 1, 2002, satellite carriers' market share will have increased and that the Congress'[s] interest in maintaining free over-the-air television will be undermined if local broadcasters are prevented from reaching their viewers *by either cable or satellite distribution systems.*"

The satellite carriers contend that the carry one, carry all rule needlessly restricts their speech because it is not necessary to protect the interests of over-the-air viewers. Again, they claim that those interests are not threatened because broadcasters denied satellite carriage will not lose access to enough of their audiences to suffer substantial deterioration. But if over-the-air viewers are currently safe, that only reflects the fact that cable is *already* bound by must-carry rules. In other words, the satellite carriers' arguments boil down to the claim that even if both cable and satellite jointly contribute to a common threat to the government's interest in protecting a multiplicity of broadcast outlets for over-the-air viewers, Congress may not impose carriage rules on satellite carriers because their contribution to that common threat is smaller and because cable is already regulated. The First Amendment does not require this result. It is more sensible to allow Congress the latitude to view the regulatory landscape as a whole by considering the cumulative effects of cable and satellite without making fine distinctions regarding their relative contributions in creating those effects. Where multiple competitors jointly pose a common threat with a common structure, the First Amendment permits Congress to protect important government interests from that threat by imposing reasonable content-neutral restrictions on every competitor who significantly contributes to that threat.

Under this standard, Congress's factual predictions easily justify the imposition of the carry one, carry all rule. Even if it is debatable whether satellite's *current* market share is sufficient to count as a significant contribution to the common threat posed by cable and satellite, Congress surely had a substantial basis for concluding that satellite would soon become a significant challenger to cable in the television programming delivery market. Accordingly, we hold that Congress reasonably concluded that the carry one, carry all rule addressed a real threat to the government's interest in preserving a multiplicity of broadcast outlets for over-the-air viewers. That interest therefore survives the first part of the *O'Brien* inquiry: it is substantial, and it is genuinely advanced by the carry one, carry all rule.

2.

The FCC argues that the carry one, carry all rule also materially advances a second substantial government interest: the interest in preventing SHVIA's grant of a statutory copyright license to satellite carriers from undermining competition in local markets for broadcast television advertising. This interest is, as we have said, closely related to the interest in preserving a multiplicity of broadcast stations for over-the-air viewers. Both interests are threatened when independent broadcasters lose access to parts of their local audiences as a result of cherry picking by satellite carriers. But although cherry picking threatens both interests in the same way, the interests are nonetheless distinct. The first interest is ultimately an interest in protecting over-the-air television viewers. The second is an interest in protecting the broadcasters themselves, as well as the advertisers who benefit from vigorous competition among the broadcast stations in their local markets.

The satellite carriers attempt to portray the carry one, carry all rule as a self-conscious government attempt to manipulate a previously undistorted marketplace of ideas in order to prop up weak broadcast stations. This portrayal misrepresents the realities of the television market. When Congress considered SHVIA in 1999, that market was already pervasively shaped by government policies: FCC licensing of broadcasters, the cable must-carry rules, copyright law, and the statutory licenses enjoyed by cable and (to a lesser extent) satellite are only a few examples. Against that backdrop Congress explicitly sought ways to improve the competitive position of satellite in relation to cable because it believed that cable rates were too high. Nothing in the text of SHVIA or its legislative history indicates that Congress thought broadcasters enjoyed any unfair advantages in relation to satellite or cable. Recognizing that satellite carriers needed a statutory copyright license to be able to compete with cable, Congress then considered the possible effects on independent broadcasters of the decision to grant that license

As we have explained above, the choice was between offering satellite carriers a station-by-station license and a market-by-market license. Congress understood that allowing satellite carriers to offer local-into-local service by cherry picking network affiliates would deprive non-carried stations of access to significant (and growing) parts of their audiences. We have already discussed at length the possibility that cherry picking would ultimately harm over-the-air viewers by reducing the quality or quantity of broadcast outlets available for those viewers, but here we are concerned with the immediate effects of selective carriage on local television advertising markets. Local broadcasters and cable companies compete with one another in those markets, and their competitive positions are a function of their ratings. Independent stations that lost access to even a small part of their potential audiences would therefore be placed at a competitive disadvantage compared to carried stations in their efforts to attract local advertisers. Congress heard testimony that a station-by-station license would essentially enable satellite carriers to pick winners and losers in local advertising markets, undermining the efforts of emerging television networks to compete with the established broadcast networks: "Nothing could more surely dull the cutting edge of competition from new networks, their local affiliates, and innovative independent stations in local markets." In short, Congress had substantial evidence for the judgment that a station-by-station license copyright license would have boosted competition in one market (the market for subscription television services) by hampering competition in another market (the market for local broadcast advertising). Such a license would have harmed both independent broadcasters and local advertisers. By choosing a market-by-market license, Congress acted to minimize the unintended, disruptive effects of its intervention in the television marketplace.

This interest in preserving a level playing field in local broadcast advertising markets seems to us at least as significant as many interests which the Supreme Court has found to be important or substantial. We therefore conclude that Congress's interest in minimizing the unintended adverse effects of its legislation on local broadcast advertising markets is substantial enough to justify incidental, content-neutral restrictions on speech. The carry one, carry all rule advances this interest in a material way because it preserves a level playing field on which local broadcasters can compete for advertising revenue by preventing satellite carriers from making selective carriage decisions within local television markets. Accordingly, we hold that this interest also satisfies the first part of the *O'Brien* analysis.

3.

We have identified two interests that pass scrutiny under the first part of the *O'Brien* analysis. The second part of the *O'Brien* analysis employed in *Turner II* requires us to ask whether the carry one, carry all rule is a narrowly tailored means of advancing these interests. The government has considerable latitude under this test. It may "employ the means of its choosing so long as the ... regulation promotes a substantial governmental interest that would be achieved less effectively absent the regulation and does not burden substantially more speech than is necessary to further that interest." The parties have devoted relatively little attention to this aspect of the *O'Brien* analysis, and with good reason. Congress enacted the carry one, carry all rule to protect independent broadcast stations from the harm they would suffer if satellite carriers denied them carriage while retransmitting the signals of the major network affiliates in their markets. As we have explained, the rule genuinely advances two important interests: the interest in preserving a multiplicity of local broadcast outlets for those who do not subscribe to cable or satellite and the interest in minimizing the unintended effects of SHVIA's statutory copyright license on local broadcast advertising markets. The satellite carriers concede that without the carry one, carry all rule, they would have chosen to carry only major network affiliates in many local markets and would therefore have threatened independent broadcasters with the very harms that Congress sought to prevent. Accordingly, any legislation that created a statutory copyright license without imposing some form of mandatory carriage requirement would have been significantly less effective—indeed, it would have been completely ineffective—in advancing the government's interests. That is sufficient to satisfy *O'Brien*'s narrow tailoring requirement. Further, the particular form of carriage requirement imposed by SHVIA is not an excessive burden on satellite carriers because it leaves them with the choice of when and where they will become subject to the carry one, carry all rule. As a result, we hold that the rule is a narrowly tailored means of promoting the government's important ends of preserving a vibrant mix of local broadcast outlets for over-the-air viewers and minimizing the unintended side effects of SHVIA's statutory copyright license on local broadcast advertising markets. The carry one, carry all rule is therefore consistent with the First Amendment. * * * [The court goes on to reject other claims, including constitutional claims that the carry one, carry all condition exceeded Congress' powers under the copyright clause, Article I, § 8, cl. 8, and violated the takings clause of the Fifth Amendment, and a non-constitutional claim that the FCC's rules were arbitrary and capricious under the Administrative Procedure Act.]

Local into Local. The carry one, carry all requirement is conditional not mandatory; DBS carriers do not have any obligation to carry any local signals unless they want to obtain a compulsory license to carry the local network programs. But why do DBS carriers need the local signals to carry network programs? Why can't a DBS operator obtain the consent to retransmit the signals of out-of-market network stations, or negotiate with the network itself for such carriage rights?[10] The SHIVA made DBS subject to the non-duplication and syndicated exclusivity rules. Thus, the ability of DBS to bring in distant network signals is constrained by the same rules that we discussed in connection with cable. However, recall from section B(5) that the nonduplication rule is completely dependent on the affiliation agreement between the network and its local affiliate. The local station has protection only against whatever exclusive rights as are specified in that agreement. The network could limit that exclusivity or deny it altogether in order to allow an MVPD to carry a network signal (supplied by itself or by another affiliate outside the local market). It appears from present practice that

10. Recall from our earlier discussion that satellite providers are subject to the same retransmission consent requirements as cable—with a couple of exceptions, most notably the exception for carriage of superstations.

the networks do not do this, and we may assume for good economic reasons. What are those reasons?

Even if there are good reasons for networks to continue their present practice of giving local affiliates an exclusive right (a first-call right) on network programs, there is one other possible arrangement that might be made that would appear to satisfy fully the network's and the affiliate's interest in exclusive distribution rights while also allowing the DBS provider to avoid the carry one, carry all rule. In fact this arrangement seems to be one that would enhance the network and its affiliate at the expense of non-network competition. What is it?

Copyright or Communications Policy? As the court indicates the SHVIA amended both the Copyright Act and the Communications Act in order to yoke the compulsory license under the former to local carriage as part of the latter. This might serve the interest of communications policy's localism, but does it promote copyright policy? In contrast to the cable compulsory license the DBS compulsory license does not provide for any payment to the copyright owners, so what do the copyright owners (who, it should be emphasized, are not the local stations) get out of this arrangement?

Cherry-Picking. The effect of the carry one, carry all is said to prevent DBS from "cherry picking" some stations in local markets and ignoring others. What is wrong with cherry picking? Why isn't cherry picking simply responding to market preferences? Is this a level-playing-field problem (cable operators cannot cherry pick so DBS providers shouldn't be able to either)? Do cable and DBS providers bear the same financial burden with regard to local carriage? The satellite providers argued that the effect of the rule was to preclude bringing network signals by satellite into smaller markets because of capacity limits on their satellites. In effect, carry one, carry all privileges independent stations in larger markets whose carriage in those markets absorbs satellite transponder capacity that precludes the carrier from providing network service in smaller markets. The court's response is that "While those major network affiliates would no doubt prefer to be carried on satellite services, the carry one, carry all rule does not deprive those affiliates of the ability to reach their audiences." The response is puzzling; it is not a question of network affiliates' preferences; it is a question whether viewers in smaller markets should be required to forego satellite-based network service because the transponder capacity to provide it has been preempted by the demands of independent stations in some other market (or, indeed, in the same market). Because carry one, carry all requires the DBS carriers to carry at the station's request, it directly pits the interests of large-market independent *stations* against those of small-market *viewers*. Whose interests more closely reflect "the public interest"?

An Enduring Solution to a Disappearing Problem? The capacity issue that has driven the local-into-local controversy is diminishing as satellite capacity expands. In its 12th annual report on video programming competition, the FCC reported that "In 167 of 210 television markets (i.e., designated market areas, or DMAs), which represent 96 percent of all U.S. television households, at least one DBS provider offers the signals of local broadcast stations (local into local service). EchoStar offers local into local service in 162 DMAs and Puerto Rico, representing approximately 95 percent of U.S. television households. DirecTV offers local into local service in 134 markets, representing 93 percent of U.S. television households." See *Annual Assessment of the Status of Competition in the Market for the Delivery of Video Programming*, 21 FCC Rcd. 2503 ¶ 13 (2006). Of course, the fact that technology might solve the capacity problem does not necessarily mean that it solves it without cost. Presumably there is an extra cost to requiring the satellite to carry enough signals to allow all local signals to be carried in all markets (or in most markets for that matter). Do the benefits of the *additional increment* of local content that is assured by the carry one, carry all rule match the cost? (Who bears those costs?)

Chapter 6

CONSUMER-ORIENTED REGULATION OF CABLE PROVIDERS

A. INTRODUCTION

In the last chapter we examined regulations governing the intermodal competition among mass media, notably competition among traditional broadcasting, cable, and satellite media. In this chapter our focus shifts from the regulation of inter-media relationships to regulation of media-*consumer* relationships. We already considered direct program regulation in Chapter 3. As we noted there, direct regulation of program content does not affect cable operators. They are not licensed by the FCC and are therefore not subject to the affirmative public interest mandate of Title III of the Act. Congress did extend § 315 equal time obligations to cable, but this only affects programming that originates with the cable operator and is under its exclusive control, see 47.C.F.R. § 76.5(p), which is a tiny percentage of the programming on cable. Cable operators have not even been subject to such negative program constraints as indecency controls. In the case of satellite broadcasters, we saw that Congress made them subject to the political broadcast obligations of §§ 315 and 312(a)(7), but it left to the FCC whether to impose other public interest responsibilities, and the FCC has thus far declined to do so. Interestingly, the FCC has declined even to enforce its indecency regulations against satellite broadcasters because the service is provided on a subscription basis. (This enabled the famously potty-mouthed Howard Stern to finally escape from the FCC's indecency regulations by moving to Sirius Satellite Radio.)

If MVPD providers have avoided many of the direct content controls that are—at least formally—imposed on conventional broadcasters, they are still heavily regulated. As we saw in the last chapter, cable operators are subject to a complex array of regulations that affect programming, such as the must-carry rules, the exclusivity rules, sports blackout protection, etc. Satellite television providers are subject to a "conditional" must-carry requirement (carry-one, carry-all) if they want to carry local network programs (and both DBS providers now do in all but the smallest markets). And, as we discussed in the last chapter, all satellite television providers are required to set aside a certain percentage of their capacity for educational and informational programming.

In this chapter we consider some additional regulations governing MVPD services, specifically cable providers. (One of the issues that we will take up—the issue of product bundling—could affect DBS providers if it is ever implemented, but at this point in time it is being considered only for cable service.) The regulatory issues here are in part a matter of divided jurisdiction. In the case of broadcasting (both terrestrial and satellite), public service obligations are exclusively defined and enforced by the FCC. The same is true of the inter-media competition rules we considered in the last chapter. However, regulation of the relationship between cable providers and consumers has always been shared between federal and non-federal governments. Most states, in turn, have ceded to local governments (cities and counties) some power to regulate local cable operators.[1] That power is exercised by means of franchises—a license—that permit the service provider to use the local public rights-of-way to reach consumers. Local franchise regulation does not necessarily displace state regulation; some states have continued to regulate cable television rates and services—within the limits allowed by Congress and the FCC.

This tripartite jurisdiction has consistently produced some degree of regulatory confusion. In the early 1960s the FCC was primarily focused on the cable-broadcast relationship, and particularly ensuring that cable was kept in its "proper place" as an auxiliary, complementary service to broadcasting. However, as it moved towards a comprehensive "solution" to the cable "problem," the FCC confronted the issue of how jurisdictional responsibilities should be allocated.

Unsurprisingly, the two principal industries involved—broadcasting and cable—were sharply divided on how the FCC should proceed. The broadcasters argued for continued local franchising subject to FCC standards. The cable industry sought general preemption of both local and state regulation, particularly regulation of cable rates. For their part the state and local governments, unsurprisingly, opposed preemption. In 1972, in its comprehensive *Cable Television Report and Order*, 36 F.C.C.2d 143 (1972), the Commission established a basic framework for shared jurisdiction. The Commission began by rejecting a program of federal licensing. Even if such a regime could be fit within the "ancillary" theory of jurisdiction over cable—which we discussed in the last chapter—the Commission deemed it an impractical burden. (Why it would be any more impractical than licensing of thousands of local

1. There is no official count of the number of local governments having franchise authority. In 2007 it was estimated that 32,813 communities were served by 6635 cable systems. TV & CABLE FACTBOOK 2008 F-12. However, not all local governments have franchising authority. Local governments possess only such powers as they are given by the states, either by home-rule charters or by specific statutes. Some states have vested exclusive franchising power in state agencies, and a few others have imposed special limitations on local government powers.

broadcast stations was not explained.) But the Commission agreed that there should be federal guidelines on the franchising process, such as the length of the franchise period (generally 15 years was considered appropriate), applicant qualifications (financially and legally qualified) and limits on local powers, such as restrictions on franchise fees (fees above 3% of gross receipts required special justification) and service rate regulation (rates should be "fair to the system and to the subscribing public"). The FCC did keep a hand in, requiring that cable systems in the top 100 markets undertake to provide a minimum 20-channel capacity and devote three channels for free access by the public, educational, and governmental entities. It also required the systems to provide leased access to channels not used for broadcast retransmission or local origination. State and local governments were forbidden to regulate any of the local access channels, other than the local government channel. The access rules were subsequently modified in 1976, but they were found to be in excess of the Commission's jurisdiction in *FCC v. Midwest Video Corp.*, 440 U.S. 689 (1979). In 1984, Congress replaced much of the FCC's regulatory apparatus, albeit placing some of that apparatus in the hands of local franchising authorities.

The 1984 Cable Act's purposes (stated in Section 601 of the Act, now codified at 47 U.S.C. § 521) were:

> (1) Establish a national policy concerning cable communications; (2) Establish franchise procedures and standards which encourage the growth and development of cable systems and which assure that cable systems are responsive to the needs and interests of the local community; (3) Establish guidelines for the exercise of Federal, State, and local authority with respect to the regulation of cable systems; (4) Assure that cable communications provide and are encouraged to provide the widest possible diversity of information sources and services to the public; (5) Establish an orderly process for franchise renewal which protects cable operators against unfair denials of renewal where the operator's past performance and proposal for future performance meet the standards established by this title; and (6) Promote competition in cable communications and minimize unnecessary regulation that would impose an undue economic burden on cable systems.

Although the specified purposes are broad, two things are particularly noteworthy. The first is the reference to minimizing "unnecessary regulation." Recall that by this time cable had developed beyond its fledgling status as a purely auxiliary service. Many of the harsh features of early FCC regulation had been eliminated, and there was now an emphasis on deregulation. The second is the emphasis on setting standards for local franchise regulation. In this respect the Act paralleled the FCC's own regulations, although with a few modifications.

Among other things the Act reinstated the local public-educational-governmental channels, though it did so on a local option basis, authorizing local franchising authorities to require "PEG" or "access" channels (as they are commonly called) rather than mandating them outright. It also required cable systems to allow commercial leasing of a 10 to 15% (depending on the channel capacity of the system) of available (unused) channels. It approved the FCC's regulations on ownership, including cross ownership by broadcast stations or telephone carriers. It placed limits on local franchise fees (limits somewhat more generous than those the FCC had prescribed). It authorized local rate regulation with respect to the basic tier of cable services (the "basic" tier includes local must-carry and access channels and such additional channels as the cable operator chooses to include in this tier) but only on a showing that there was not "effective competition" in the market—as defined by the FCC.

One provision of the Act that will have importance later when we consider broadband communications is § 621 (47 U.S.C. § 541(c)) declaring that "a cable system shall not be subject to regulation as a common carrier or utility by reason or providing any cable service." "Common carrier" and "utility" in this context must be understood in a somewhat Pickwickean sense. After all, cable systems are required to carry, without discrimination, all local channels; they are required to provide free PEG channels, as well as to lease—without discrimination—unused channels to others; they are forbidden to exercise editorial control over any of these PEG or leased channels; and they are subject to rate regulation (though today this is limited to the basic tier of service). These are all classic components of common carrier regulation. We will return to examine this issue in Chapter 10 in the context of attempts by to subject cable to so called "open access" rules concerning the right of Internet service providers to demand access to cable facilities.

The deregulatory climate in which the 1984 Cable Act was enacted did not last. Eight years later, Congress enacted the Cable Television Consumer Protection and Competition Act of 1992, which imposed a series of new regulations on cable. In the last chapter we examined the two most important: the reinstatement of must-carry (which had been struck down in the late 1980s) and the adoption for the first time of retransmission consent regulation. It also enacted a more energized form of rate regulation in response to wide-spread public outcries about rising cable rates.

The old system of rate regulation had not been effective in significant degree because of the Commission's rules. The 1984 Act had limited local rate regulation to markets where there was not effective competition in the delivery of video program service—as determined by FCC rules. The FCC first defined as competitive any market where there were three or more *broadcast* television signals available, ignoring the monopoly position of most cable operators. Since virtually every market had three local television broadcast stations, that effectively eliminated rate regulation of cable in all markets but those that were too small to be able to bear the burden of regulation. Later the FCC raised the number to six services, but this too left all major markets unregulatable. As discussed in greater detail below, the 1992 Act changed all that by changing the entire conception of the relevant market to focus not on broadcast services but the nature of market for MVPDs themselves, displacing local rate regulation in cases in which a privately owned cable operator does not dominate the market.

Under the 1984 Act only local and state governments could regulate rates, and only the rates of the basic service tier. The 1992 Act expanded rate controls by authorizing the FCC to regulate the second tier service—all cable programming channels. A third tier—video programming offered on a per-channel (such as HBO) or per-program (such as pay-per-view) basis—was excluded from any regulation. Local governments had to obtain a certification from the FCC that they had the legal authority and the resources to regulate and that their franchise areas qualify for regulation. With respect to the FCC's own regulation, it was triggered on a case-by-case basis when a subscriber, franchising authority, or other relevant state or local governmental entity files a complaint. The 1996 Telecommunications Act terminated the FCC's rate regulation of the middle tier of cable programming (effective after 1999), but left local or state rate regulation of the basic tier in place. However, local regulation is constrained by an elaborate set of conditions prescribed by the FCC, and also further subject to review by the Commission. The following section illustrates some of the issues in current rate regulation.

B. LOCAL RATE REGULATION

For a franchising authority to regulate cable rates it must be certified by the FCC. To obtain such a certificate, the authority must file with the Commission a certificate that the authority will adopt regulations conforming to FCC regulations, that it has the legal authority to adopt and the personnel to administer regulations governing rates, that its rate regulation proceedings provide reasonable opportunity to consider the views of all interested parties, and that the cable system is not subject to effective competition (as described below). If the FCC does not act on the certificate it becomes effective within 30 days. See 47 C.F.R. § 76.910.

To say the least, the FCC's rules governing local rate regulation are elaborate and detailed—covering more than 50 pages in the Code of Federal Regulations. We shall not even attempt to summarize them. The FCC commonly undertakes two types of review of local cable regulation. First, while the FCC no longer sets rates, it does set the methodology for determining rates and it reviews rate proceedings for consistency with that methodology. While important, such proceedings tend to be both highly technical (they are focused as much on accounting rules as on rate policy) and quite particular to a specific franchise arrangement. For example, a paragraph from a recent proceeding explained:

> Falcon challenges both the City's decision to increase the equipment basket by adding in amounts representing additional contract labor and home wiring maintenance expenses and the City's methodology for calculating the additional home wiring maintenance cost. Falcon argues that the City made the same mistakes in calculating the HSC

and also argues that the City should not have calculated an HSC for the period covered by Falcon's initial FCC Form 1205, which it claims was completed for unbundling purposes only.

In the Matter of Falcon Community Ventures, 20 FCC Rcd. 1678 (2005). Because there is little to be learned from such proceedings that is readily generalizable to other contexts, we mention them only by way of introduction. The second type of proceeding involves review of the question of whether there is "effective competition" in the market. As amended in 1996, the Communications Act contains a rather liberal test for "effective competition" based on the degree to which the MVPD market is controlled by a dominant, private operator. Under this new regime effective competition is defined in terms of four situations: (1) a franchise area in which fewer than 30 percent of the households in the franchise area subscribe to the cable service of a cable system; (2) a franchise area that is both (i) served by at least two unaffiliated multichannel video programming distributors each of which offers comparable video programming to at least 50 percent of the households in the franchise area; and (ii) the number of households subscribing to programming services offered by multichannel video programming distributors other than the largest multichannel video programming distributor exceeds 15 percent of the households in the franchise area; (3) a franchise area in which a multichannel video programming distributor operated by the franchising authority for that franchise area offers video programming to at least 50 percent of the households in that franchise area; or (4) a franchise area in which a local exchange carrier or its affiliate offers video program service comparable to that of the local cable operator. *See* 47 U.S.C. § 543(*l*). In recent years, paragraph (2) has become a common basis for cable operators challenging local regulators because the widespread availability of DBS has at last made it plausible to assert the presence of competing MVPDs in the market.

IN THE MATTER OF COXCOM, INC.

Federal Communications Commission, 2007.
22 FCC Rcd. 4522.

By the Deputy Chief, Policy Division, Media Bureau:

I. Introduction

1. CoxCom, Inc. d/b/a Cox Communications Orange County ("Cox") has filed a petition with the Commission for determinations of effective competition in twenty-one Southern California franchise areas (the "Franchise Areas") pursuant to Section 623(a) of the Communications Act ("Act") [47 U.S.C. § 543(a)] and the Commission's implementing rules. Cox alleges that its cable systems serving these Franchise Areas are subject to effective competition and, therefore, are exempt from cable rate regulation. Specifically, Cox claims that the effective competition present in these Franchise Areas arises from the competing services provided by two unaffiliated direct broadcast satellite ("DBS")

providers, DirecTV, Inc. and EchoStar Satellite, L.L.C. As a result, Cox asserts that it is subject to effective competition in these franchise areas under the "competing provider" test set forth in Section 623(*l*)(1)(B) of the Communications Act. The City of Los Angeles (the "City") has filed an Opposition to Cox's Petition for special relief specific to the community commonly referred to as San Pedro, California ("Area N"). In sum, the City asserts that: (1) finding effective competition based only on Cox's production of DBS penetration data supplied by an industry source would be contrary to the intent of the Act; and (2) accepting DBS penetration data from a private entity would constitute an unlawful delegation of the Commission's authority in the effective competition context. Cox has filed a Reply to the City's Opposition, as summarized below.

II. Discussion

* * *

4. The City asserts that DBS competition is insufficient to curb a cable operator's market power and that DBS is not as effective as wireline-based (i.e., cable overbuilder) video competition in keeping basic cable rates reasonable. Moreover, the City states that the Commission cannot assume that DBS competition offers comparable video programming to cable so long as there is a statistically significant differential between cable rates in DBS-only competitive areas and those areas enjoying wireline competition. Cox argues that the City's subjective view of how effective competition should be defined ignores congressional intent and the express language of the Act and associated Commission regulations.

5. We reject the City's arguments and determine that Cox has satisfied the first prong of the competing provider test. First, Section 623 of the Act does not exclude DBS from the competing provider test and does not expressly authorize us to make "market power" determinations when deciding whether a cable operator faces effective competition. Second, we are not authorized by statute to decide whether one form of video competition is more effective than another in keeping basic service tier rates reasonable. Additionally, the Act does not require us to make an economic determination when applying the program-comparability prong. With respect to the issue of program comparability, we find that the DBS providers' programming satisfies the Commission's program-comparability criterion because DirecTV and EchoStar offer more than 12 channels of video programming, including more than one non-broadcast channel. We further conclude that Cox has demonstrated that the Franchise Areas are served by at least two unaffiliated MVPDs, namely DirecTV and EchoStar, each of which offer comparable video programming to at least 50 percent of the households in the franchise area. Therefore, the first prong of the competing provider test is satisfied.

6. The second prong of the competing provider test requires that the number of households subscribing to MVPDs, other than the largest

MVPD, exceeds 15 percent of the households in a franchise area. Cox's assertion that it is the largest MVPD provider in these Franchise Areas was not disputed by the City.

7. To determine the number of DBS subscribers in the Franchise Areas, Cox first ascertained all of the residential zip codes located either wholly or partially within its franchise areas. Cox also purchased from the Satellite Broadcasting and Communications Association ("SBCA") an Effective Competition Tracking Report ("ECTR") for each Franchise Area. The ECTR reflects the number of DBS subscribers within the zip code(s) associated with a given cable community. Cox then allocated the subscribers reported in the ECTR to Cox's franchise areas using a Commission-approved allocation methodology.

8. The City questions Cox's reliance on SBCA data as support for its Petition. The City states that the Commission has never fully examined SBCA's data collection methodologies for reliability and accuracy and such data should not be the only source of competitive information for a finding of effective competition. It argues that the Commission must consider other relevant data supplied by local franchising authorities ("LFAs") to substantiate a cable operator's findings, such as recent residential growth and whether individuals living in multiple dwelling units may be unable to receive satellite television service. The City additionally asserts that the current system of collecting evidence is burdensome because it must obtain its own SBCA data and conduct lengthy independent investigations to oppose an effective competition filing. It argues that this effectively shifts the evidentiary burden from the cable operator to the LFA in violation of the Act and the Commission's regulations.

9. The City also argues that the Commission's reliance on SBCA's data "essentially delegated to a private entity the regulatory task of determining the facts on which its local regulatory authority depends." The City asserts that this alleged delegation of private authority is unlawful because neither the statutory definition of effective competition nor any other provision of the Act authorizes the Commission to delegate authority to decertify an LFA. According to the City, the Commission's unchallenged acceptance of SBCA data is unsound and improper because there has been no general public participation in the full range of data collection and data accuracy issues.

10. The City also argues that Cox's methodology of using a five-digit zip code to calculate DBS penetration in each franchise area lacks precision. The City faults Cox for not using the SBCA "Zip–plus–4" data, which would produce more accurate results. When using the "Zip-plus–4" data, the City purportedly found that Cox's allocation formula overestimated the DBS penetration rate in the Franchise Area. The City states that the Commission should require the use of Zip–plus–4 data, which results in significantly lower DBS penetration rates.

11. Cox states that the City provides no reasonable basis for the Commission to reject its Petition. Essentially, Cox asserts that: (1) the

Commission consistently has rejected the City's burden-shifting argument; (2) the SBCA's five-digit zip code service is an approved method of demonstrating DBS penetration and, in any case, even if the zip code plus four data were accepted, more than 15 percent of the occupied households in Area N subscribe to a competing MVPD; and (3) the acceptance of SBCA's satellite subscriber data is not an impermissible delegation of authority by the Commission. As to the latter assertion, Cox states that the City's argument fails because the raw subscriber data provided by SBCA does not evaluate, let alone decide, whether a cable operator is subject to effective competition under the Act.

12. For the following reasons, we reject the City's arguments and determine that Cox has satisfied the second prong of the competitive provider test. First, our reliance on SBCA data is not an impermissible delegation of authority. The SBCA has not decided the merits of Cox's Petition; it merely has provided industry subscriber data to the cable operator for use in its Petition. It is the Commission that assesses the reliability of supporting data and decides whether effective competition exists. As Cox observes, we repeatedly have determined that data such as SBCA's, on which the satellite industry relies to conduct business, is sufficiently reliable. With regard to the City's "burden" arguments, we find that the current evidentiary standards for effective competition set forth in our rules are consistent with the Act and pose no undue hardships on either the cable operator or the relevant LFA. Although there may be some costs associated with obtaining the necessary subscriber penetration data, there are very few other expenses associated with establishing or disproving effective competition. Further, cable operators routinely attach the DBS subscriber report they obtained from SBCA, obviating the need for the LFA to purchase its own report. Cox, in fact, did so in this proceeding.

13. We accept the data provided by Cox as establishing a reasonable basis for finding that DBS penetration exceeds 15 percent in the Franchise Areas. * * *

The Future of Cable Rate Regulation under "Effective Competition". Given that the two DBS providers (DirecTV and Dish Network) reach 50% of the population in virtually *every* zip code in the United States, how much longer can local franchise authorities expect to remain in the business for regulating cable rates? Is a market in which three sellers offer what is largely an undifferentiated service "competitive" by any measure? The statute would go much further, obviating local rate regulation in cases in which two MVPDs share the market in an 85/15 split. Applying the HHI methodology discussed in Chapter 4, such a market would have an HHI of 7450 (as a matter of comparison, the Department of Justice Merger Guidelines treat a market with an HHI above only 1800 as severely concentrated). Even if, as is the case in most parts of the U.S., there are two DBS providers (and assuming they share the necessary 15% of subscribers evenly), a qualifying community would have an astronomically high HHI of 7337.5. Can such competition truly be called "effective"? Is there anything about the nature of the U.S. cable industry that mitigates the risk posed by such high market concentration in individual communities?

C. LOCAL FRANCHISE REGULATION OF COMPETITIVE ENTRY

In addition to eliminating federal rate regulation of cable, the 1996 Act made another important deregulatory change by repealing a statutory ban (part of the 1984 Cable Act) on telephone carriers owning cable systems or providing video program services. This prohibition had been held to be a violation of the First Amendment by several courts of appeals in the mid 1990s. *See, e.g., Chesapeake & Potomac Tel. Co. v. NCTA*, 42 F.3d 181 (4th Cir. 1994), vacated as moot, 516 U.S. 415 (1996). The Supreme Court had agreed to hear the issue, but when the 1996 Telecommunications Act repealed the ban, the issue was declared moot. Somewhat curiously, considering how hard they fought for the right to enter video program distribution, the telcos did not at once rush into the business. Rather, the cable systems starting moving toward providing two-way communications—both data (cable modem Internet service) and voice—in addition to video programming. In time, the threat from cable systems induced the telcos to invest in a similar package of services.

As added by the 1996 Act, 47 U.S.C § 571 provides four options for telcos seeking to enter the video programming services market: (1) they can provide program services by radio under the requirements of Title III—in other words as a licensed broadcast station; (2) they can provide transmission services on a common carrier basis under the requirements of Title II—in other words they can provide a "pipe" for *others* to deliver video programming; (3) they can provide program services subject to the requirements of Title VI—in other words as a franchised cable system; (4) they can provide program services as a so-called "open video system" (OVS). The OVS was created in 1996 as a special hybrid system that is subject to some but not all of the provisions governing cable systems but limits the OVS operator to programming no more than one-third of its activated channels, with the rest being leased to independent program providers. OVS operators are certified by the FCC and are not subject to local franchising authority. See 47 U.S.C. § 573.

The entry of telcos into the video distribution market via the third option has revived old controversies concerning local regulation. The telcos have complained that they have been subjected to unnecessary delays and handicaps in obtaining franchises. This complaint echos older complaints by cable systems, but it has a new twist since the traditional cable industry—faced with new entry from the telcos—has now become a *defender* of the local franchising burden. Whatever problems cable operators have had with local regulators over things like franchise fees, local exactions (PEG channels and related demands), they now have a new appreciation of the strategic advantages of restrictive franchise requirements. Again, the (new) complainants have turned to the FCC seeking preemptive protection. The Report and Order below is the FCC's first response to this complaint. Note that it is not limited to telco competitors; the problem can arise for any new "overbuilder"—as new facilities-based competitors are called. However, the primary source of new overbuilder competition happens to be the local telephone carriers.

IMPLEMENTATION OF SECTION 621(a)(1) OF THE CABLE COMMUNICATIONS POLICY ACT OF 1984 AS AMENDED BY THE CABLE TELEVISION CONSUMER PROTECTION AND COMPETITION ACT OF 1992

Report and Order and Further Notice of Proposed Rulemaking

Federal Communications Commission, 2007.
22 FCC Rcd. 5101.

I. Introduction

1. In this Report and Order ("Order"), we adopt rules and provide guidance to implement Section 621(a)(1) [47 U.S.C. § 541] of the Communications Act of 1934, as amended (the "Communications Act"), which prohibits franchising authorities from unreasonably refusing to award competitive franchises for the provision of cable services. We find that the current operation of the local franchising process in many jurisdictions constitutes an unreasonable barrier to entry that impedes the achievement of the interrelated federal goals of enhanced cable competition and accelerated broadband deployment. We further find that Commission action to address this problem is both authorized and necessary. Accordingly, we adopt measures to address a variety of means by which local franchising authorities, i.e., county- or municipal-level franchising authorities ("LFAs"), are unreasonably refusing to award competitive franchises. We anticipate that the rules and guidance we adopt today will facilitate and expedite entry of new cable competitors into the market for the delivery of video programming, and accelerate broadband deployment consistent with our statutory responsibilities.

2. New competitors are entering markets for the delivery of services historically offered by monopolists: traditional phone companies are primed to enter the cable market, while traditional cable companies are competing in the telephony market. Ultimately, both types of companies are projected to offer customers a "triple play" of voice, high-speed Internet access, and video services over their respective networks. We believe this competition for delivery of bundled services will benefit consumers by driving down prices and improving the quality of service

offerings. We are concerned, however, that traditional phone companies seeking to enter the video market face unreasonable regulatory obstacles, to the detriment of competition generally and cable subscribers in particular.

3. The Communications Act sets forth the basic rules concerning what franchising authorities may and may not do in evaluating applications for competitive franchises. Despite the parameters established by the Communications Act, however, operation of the franchising process has proven far more complex and time consuming than it should be, particularly with respect to facilities-based telecommunications and broadband providers that already have access to rights-of-way. New entrants have demonstrated that they are willing and able to upgrade their networks to provide video services, but the current operation of the franchising process at the local level unreasonably delays and, in some cases, derails these efforts due to LFAs' unreasonable demands on competitive applicants. These delays discourage investment in the fiber-based infrastructure necessary for the provision of advanced broadband services, because franchise applicants do not have the promise of revenues from video services to offset the costs of such deployment. Thus, the current operation of the franchising process often not only contravenes the statutory imperative to foster competition in the multichannel video programming distribution ("MVPD") market, but also defeats the congressional goal of encouraging broadband deployment.

4. In light of the problems with the current operation of the franchising process, we believe that it is now appropriate for the Commission to exercise its authority and take steps to prevent LFAs from unreasonably refusing to award competitive franchises. We have broad rulemaking authority to implement the provisions of the Communications Act, including Title VI generally and Section 621(a)(1) in particular. In addition, Section 706 of the Telecommunications Act of 1996 [47 U.S.C. § 157] directs the Commission to encourage broadband deployment by removing barriers to infrastructure investment, and the U.S. Court of Appeals for the District of Columbia Circuit has held that the Commission may fashion its rules to fulfill the goals of Section 706.

II. Background

6. Section 621. Any new entrant seeking to offer "cable service" as a "cable operator" becomes subject to the requirements of Title VI. Section 621 of Title VI sets forth general cable franchise requirements. Subsection (b)(1) of Section 621 prohibits a cable operator from providing cable service in a particular area without first obtaining a cable franchise, and subsection (a)(1) grants to franchising authorities the power to award such franchises.

7. The initial purpose of Section 621(a)(1), which was added to the Communications Act by the Cable Communications Policy Act of 1984 (the "1984 Cable Act"), was to delineate the role of LFAs in the franchising process. As originally enacted, Section 621(a)(1) simply stat-

ed that "[a] franchising authority may award, in accordance with the provisions of this title, 1 or more franchises within its jurisdiction." A few years later, however, the Commission prepared a report to Congress on the cable industry pursuant to the requirements of the 1984 Cable Act. In that Report, the Commission concluded that in order "[t]o encourage more robust competition in the local video marketplace, the Congress should ... forbid local franchising authorities from unreasonably denying a franchise to potential competitors who are ready and able to provide service."

8. In response, Congress revised Section 621(a)(1) through the Cable Television Consumer Protection and Competition Act of 1992 (the "1992 Cable Act") to read as follows: "A franchising authority may award, in accordance with the provisions of this title, 1 or more franchises within its jurisdiction; except that a franchising authority may not grant an exclusive franchise and may not unreasonably refuse to award an additional competitive franchise." In the Conference Report on the legislation, Congress found that competition in the cable industry was sorely lacking. * * *

9. In 1992, Congress also revised Section 621(a)(1) to provide that "[a]ny applicant whose application for a second franchise has been denied by a final decision of the franchising authority may appeal such final decision pursuant to the provisions of section 635." Section 635, in turn, states that "[a]ny cable operator adversely affected by any final determination made by a franchising authority under section 621(a)(1) ... may commence an action within 120 days after receiving notice of such determination" in federal court or a state court of general jurisdiction. Congress did not, however, provide an explicit judicial remedy for other forms of unreasonable refusals to award competitive franchises, such as an LFA's refusal to act on a pending franchise application within a reasonable time period. * * *

III. Discussion

18. Based on the voluminous record in this proceeding, which includes comments filed by new entrants, incumbent cable operators, LFAs, consumer groups, and others, we conclude that the current operation of the franchising process can constitute an unreasonable barrier to entry for potential cable competitors, and thus justifies Commission action. We find that we have authority under Section 621(a)(1) to address this problem by establishing limits on LFAs' ability to delay, condition, or otherwise "unreasonably refuse to award" competitive franchises. We find that we also have the authority to consider the goals of Section 706 in addressing this problem under Section 621(a)(1). We believe that, absent Commission action, deployment of competitive video services by new cable entrants will continue to be unreasonably delayed or, at worst, derailed. Accordingly, we adopt incremental measures directed to LFA-controlled franchising processes, as described in detail below. We anticipate that the rules and guidance we adopt today will facilitate and expedite entry of new cable competitors into the market for

the delivery of multichannel video programming and thus encourage broadband deployment.

A. The Current Operation of the Franchising Process Unreasonably Interferes with Competitive Entry

19. Most communities in the United States lack cable competition, which would reduce cable rates and increase innovation and quality of service. Although LFAs adduced evidence that they have granted some competitive franchises, and competitors acknowledge that they have obtained some franchises, the record includes only a few hundred examples of competitive franchises, many of which were obtained after months of unnecessary delay. In the vast majority of communities, cable competition simply does not exist.

20. The dearth of competition is due, at least in part, to the franchising process. The record demonstrates that the current operation of the franchising process unreasonably prevents or, at a minimum, unduly delays potential cable competitors from entering the MVPD market. Numerous commenters have adduced evidence that the current operation of the franchising process constitutes an unreasonable barrier to entry. Regulatory restrictions and conditions on entry shield incumbents from competition and are associated with various economic inefficiencies, such as reduced innovation and distorted consumer choices. We recognize that some LFAs have made reasonable efforts to facilitate competitive entry into the video programming market. We also recognize that recent state level reforms have the potential to streamline the process to a noteworthy degree. We find, though, that the current operation of the local franchising process often is a roadblock to achievement of the statutory goals of enhancing cable competition and broadband deployment.

21. Commenters have identified six factors that stand in the way of competitive entry. They are: (1) unreasonable delays by LFAs in acting on franchise applications; (2) unreasonable build-out requirements imposed by LFAs; (3) LFA demands unrelated to the franchising process; (4) confusion concerning the meaning and scope of franchise fee obligations; (5) unreasonable LFA demands for PEG channel capacity and construction of I-Nets; and (6) level-playing-field requirements set by LFAs. We address each factor below.

22. *LFA Delays in Acting on Franchise Applications.* The record demonstrates that unreasonable delays in the franchising process have obstructed and, in some cases, completely derailed attempts to deploy competitive video services. Many new entrants have been subjected to lengthy, costly, drawn-out negotiations that, in many cases, are still ongoing. The FTTH Council cited a report by an investment firm that, on average, the franchising process, as it currently operates, delays entry by 8–16 months. The record generally supports that estimate. For example, Verizon had 113 franchise negotiations underway as of the end of March 2005. By the end of March 2006, LFAs had granted only 10 of

those franchises. In other words, more than 90% of the negotiations were not completed within one year. Verizon noted that delays are often caused by mandatory waiting periods. BellSouth explained that negotiations took an average of 10 months for each of its 20 cable franchise agreements, and that in one case, the negotiations took nearly three years. AT&T claims that anti-competitive conditions, such as level-playing-field constraints and LFA demands regarding build-out, not only delay entry but can prevent it altogether. BellSouth notes that absent such demands (in Georgia, for example), the company's applications were granted quickly. Most of Ameritech's franchise negotiations likewise took a number of years. New entrants other than the large incumbent local exchange carriers ("LECs") also have experienced delays in the franchising process. NTCA provided an example of a small, competitive IPTV provider that is in ongoing negotiations that began more than one year ago.

23. These delays are particularly unreasonable when, as is often the case, the applicant already has access to rights-of-way. One of the primary justifications for cable franchising is the LFA's need to regulate and receive compensation for the use of public rights-of-way. However, when considering a franchise application from an entity that already has rights-of-way access, such as an incumbent LEC, an LFA need not and should not devote substantial attention to issues of rights-of-way management. Moreover, in obtaining a certificate for public convenience and necessity from a state, a facilities-based provider generally has demonstrated its legal, technical, and financial fitness to be a provider of telecommunications services. Thus, an LFA need not spend a significant amount of time considering the fitness of such applicants to access public rights-of-way.

24. Delays in acting on franchise applications are especially onerous because franchise applications are rarely denied outright, which would enable applicants to seek judicial review under Section 635. Rather, negotiations are often drawn out over an extended period of time. As a result, the record shows that numerous new entrants have accepted franchise terms they considered unreasonable in order to avoid further delay. Others have filed lawsuits seeking a court order compelling the LFA to act, which entails additional delay, legal uncertainty, and great expense. Alternatively, some prospective entrants have walked away from unduly prolonged negotiations. Moreover, delays provide the incumbent cable operator the opportunity to launch targeted marketing campaigns before the competitor's rollout, thus undermining a competitor's prospects for success.

25. Despite this evidence, incumbent cable operators and LFAs nevertheless assert that new entrants can obtain and are obtaining franchises in a timely fashion, and that delays are largely due to unreasonable behavior on the part of franchise applicants, not LFAs. For example, Minnesota LFAs claim that they can grant a franchise in as little as eight weeks. The record, however, shows that expeditious grants of competitive franchises are atypical. Most LFAs lack any temporal

limits for consideration of franchise applications, and of those that have such limits, many set forth lengthy time frames. In localities without a time limit or with an unreasonable time limit, the delays caused by the current operation of the franchising process present a significant barrier to entry. For example, the cities of Chicago and Indianapolis acknowledged that, as currently operated, their franchising processes take one to three years, respectively. Miami-Dade's cable ordinance permits the county to make a final decision on a cable franchise up to eight months after receiving a completed application, and the process may take longer if an applicant submits an incomplete application or amends its application.

26. Incumbent cable operators and LFAs state that new entrants could gain rapid entry if the new entrants simply agreed to the same terms applied to incumbent cable franchisees. However, this is not a reasonable expectation generally, given that the circumstances surrounding competitive entry are considerably different than those in existence at the time incumbent cable operators obtained their franchises. Incumbent cable operators originally negotiated franchise agreements as a means of acquiring or maintaining a monopoly position. In most instances, imposing the incumbent cable operator's terms and conditions on a new entrant would make entry prohibitively costly because the entrant cannot assume that it will quickly—or ever—amass the same number or percentage of subscribers that the incumbent cable operator captured. The record demonstrates that requiring entry on the same terms as incumbent cable operators may thwart entry entirely or may threaten new entrants' chances of success once in the market.

27. Incumbent cable operators also suggest that delay is attributable to competitors that are not really serious about entering the market, as demonstrated by their failure to file the thousands of franchise applications required for broad competitive entry. We reject this explanation as inconsistent with both the record as well as common sense. Given the complexity and time-consuming nature of the current franchising process, it is patently unreasonable to expect any competitive entrant to file several thousand applications and negotiate several thousand franchising processes at once. Moreover, the incumbent LECs have made their plans to enter the video services market abundantly clear, and the evidence in the record demonstrates their seriousness about doing so. For instance, they are investing billions of dollars to upgrade their networks to enable the provision of video services, expenditures that would make little sense if they were not planning to enter the video market. Finally, the record also demonstrates that the obstacles posed by the current operation of the franchising process are so great that some prospective entrants have shied away from the franchise process altogether.

28. We also reject the argument by incumbent cable operators that delays in the franchising process are immaterial because competitive applicants are not ready to enter the market and frequently delay initiating service once they secure a franchise. We find that lack of

competition in the video market is not attributable to inertia on the part of competitors. Given the financial risk, uncertainty, and delay new entrants face when they apply for a competitive franchise, it is not surprising that they wait until they get franchise approval before taking all steps necessary to provide service. The sooner a franchise is granted, the sooner an applicant can begin completing those steps. Consequently, shortening the franchising process will accelerate market entry. Moreover, the record shows that streamlining the franchising process can expedite market entry. For example, less than 30 days after Texas authorized statewide franchises, Verizon filed an application for a franchise with respect to 21 Texas communities and was able to launch services in most of those communities within 45 days.

29. Incumbent cable operators offer evidence from their experience in the renewal and transfer processes as support for their contention that the vast majority of LFAs operate in a reasonable and timely manner. We find that incumbent cable operators' purported success in the franchising process is not a useful comparison in this case. Today's large MSOs obtained their current franchises by either renewing their preexisting agreements or by merging with and purchasing other incumbent cable franchisees with preexisting agreements. For two key reasons, their experiences in franchise transfers and renewals are not equivalent to those of new entrants seeking to obtain new franchises. First, in the transfer or renewal context, delays in LFA consideration do not result in a bar to market entry. Second, in the transfer or renewal context, the LFA has a vested interest in preserving continuity of service for subscribers, and will act accordingly. * * *

31. *Impact of Build-Out Requirements.* The record shows that build-out issues are one of the most contentious between LFAs and prospective new entrants, and that build-out requirements can greatly hinder the deployment of new video and broadband services. New and potential entrants commented extensively on the adverse impact of build-out requirements on their deployment plans. Large incumbent LECs, small and mid-sized incumbent LECs, competitive LECs and others view build-out requirements as the most significant obstacle to their plans to deploy competitive video and broadband services. Similarly, consumer groups and the U.S. Department of Justice, Antitrust Division, urge the Commission to address this aspect of the current franchising process in order to speed competitive entry.

32. The record demonstrates that build-out requirements can substantially reduce competitive entry. Numerous commenters urge the Commission to prohibit LFAs from imposing any build-out requirements, and particularly universal build-out requirements. They argue that imposition of such mandates, rather than resulting in the increased service throughout the franchise area that LFAs desire, will cause potential new entrants to simply refrain from entering the market at all. They argue that even build-out provisions that do not require deployment throughout an entire franchise area may prevent a prospective new entrant from offering service.

33. The record contains numerous examples of build-out requirements at the local level that resulted in delayed entry, no entry, or failed entry. A consortium of California communities demanded that Verizon build out to every household in each community before Verizon would be allowed to offer service to any community, even though large parts of the communities fell outside of Verizon's telephone service area. Furthermore, Qwest has withdrawn franchise applications in eight communities due to build-out requirements. In each case, Qwest determined that entering into a franchise agreement that mandates universal build-out would not be economically feasible.

34. In many instances, level-playing-field provisions in local laws or franchise agreements compel LFAs to impose on competitors the same build-out requirements that apply to the incumbent cable operator. Cable operators use threatened or actual litigation against LFAs to enforce level-playing-field requirements and have successfully delayed entry or driven would-be competitors out of town. Even in the absence of level-playing-field requirements, incumbent cable operators demand that LFAs impose comparable build-out requirements on competitors to increase the financial burden and risk for the new entrant.

35. Build-out requirements can deter market entry because a new entrant generally must take customers from the incumbent cable operator, and thus must focus its efforts in areas where the take-rate will be sufficiently high to make economic sense. Because the second provider realistically cannot count on acquiring a share of the market similar to the incumbent's share, the second entrant cannot justify a large initial deployment. Rather, a new entrant must begin offering service within a smaller area to determine whether it can reasonably ensure a return on its investment before expanding. For example, Verizon has expressed significant concerns about deploying service in areas heavily populated with [multi-dwelling units] already under exclusive contract with another MVPD. Due to the risk associated with entering the video market, forcing new entrants to agree up front to build out an entire franchise area too quickly may be tantamount to forcing them out of—or precluding their entry into—the business. * * *

38. Although incumbent LECs already have telecommunications facilities deployed over large areas, build-out requirements may nonetheless be a formidable barrier to entry for them for two reasons. First, incumbent LECs must upgrade their existing plant to enable the provision of video service, which often costs billions of dollars. Second, as the Commission stated in the *Local Franchising NPRM*, the boundaries of the areas served by facilities-based providers of telephone and/or broadband services frequently do not coincide with the boundaries of the areas under the jurisdiction of the relevant LFAs. In some cases, a potential new entrant's service area comprises only a portion of the area under the LFA's jurisdiction. When LECs are required to build out where they have no existing plant, the business case for market entry is significantly weakened because their deployment costs are substantially increased. In other cases, a potential new entrant's facilities may already cover most

or all of the franchise area, but certain economic realities prevent or deter the provider from upgrading certain "wire center service areas" within its overall service area. For example, some wire center service areas may encompass a disproportionate level of business locations or multi-dwelling units ("MDUs") with MVPD exclusive contracts. New entrants argue that the imposition of build-out requirements in either circumstance creates a disincentive for them to enter the marketplace. * * *

43. *LFA Demands Unrelated to the Provision of Video Services.* Many commenters recounted franchise negotiation experiences in which LFAs made unreasonable demands unrelated to the provision of video services. Verizon, for example, described several communities that made unreasonable requests, such as the purchase of street lights, wiring for all houses of worship, the installation of cell phone towers, cell phone subsidies for town employees, library parking at Verizon's facilities, connection of 220 traffic signals with fiber optics, and provision of free wireless broadband service in an area in which Verizon's subsidiary does not offer such service. In Maryland, some localities conditioned a franchise upon Verizon's agreement to make its data services subject to local customer service regulation. AT&T provided examples of impediments that Ameritech New Media faced when it entered the market, including a request for a new recreation center and pool. FTTH Council highlighted Grande Communications' experience in San Antonio, which required that Grande Communications make an up-front, $1 million franchise fee payment and fund a $50,000 scholarship with additional annual contributions of $7,200. The record demonstrates that LFA demands unrelated to cable service typically are not counted toward the statutory 5 percent cap on franchise fees, but rather imposed on franchisees in addition to assessed franchise fees. Based on this record evidence, we are convinced that LFA requests for unreasonable concessions are not isolated, and that these requests impose undue burdens upon potential cable providers.

44. *Assessment of Franchise Fees.* The record establishes that unreasonable demands over franchise fee issues also contribute to delay in franchise negotiations at the local level and hinder competitive entry. Fee issues include not only which franchise-related costs imposed on providers should be included within the 5 percent statutory franchise fee cap established in Section 622(b),[*] but also the proper calculation of franchise fees (i.e., the revenue base from which the 5 percent is calculated). In Virginia, municipalities have requested large "acceptance fees" upon grant of a franchise, in addition to franchise fees. Other LFAs have requested consultant and attorneys' fees. Several Pennsylvania localities have requested franchise fees based on cable and non-cable revenues. Some commenters assert that an obligation to provide anything of value, including PEG costs, should apply toward the franchise fee obligation.

* Eds. Section 622(b) of the Communications Act caps the franchise fees charged by an LFA to 5% of the cable operator's gross revenues.

45. The parties indicate that the lack of clarity with respect to assessment of franchise fees impedes deployment of new video programming facilities and services for three reasons. First, some LFAs make unreasonable demands regarding franchise fees as a condition of awarding a competitive franchise. Second, new entrants cannot reasonably determine the costs of entry in any particular community. Accordingly, they may delay or refrain from entering a market because the cost of entry is unclear and market viability cannot be projected. Third, a new entrant must negotiate these terms prior to obtaining a franchise, which can take a considerable amount of time. Thus, unreasonable demands by some LFAs effectively creates an unreasonable barrier to entry.

46. *PEG and I-Net Requirements*. Negotiations over PEG and I-Nets[†] also contribute to delays in the franchising process. In response to the *Local Franchising NPRM*, we received numerous comments asking for clarification of what requirements LFAs reasonably may impose on franchisees to support PEG and I-Nets. We also received comments suggesting that some LFAs are making unreasonable demands regarding PEG and I-Net support as a condition of awarding competitive franchises. LFAs have demanded funding for PEG programming and facilities that exceeds their needs, and will not provide an accounting of where the money goes. For example, one municipality in Florida requested $6 million for PEG facilities, and a Massachusetts community requested 10 PEG channels, when the incumbent cable operator only provides two. Several commenters argued that it is unreasonable for an LFA to request a number of PEG channels from a new entrant that is greater than the number of channels that the community is using at the time the new entrant submits its franchise application. The record indicates that LFAs also have made what commenters view as unreasonable institutional network requests, such as free cell phones for employees, fiber optic service for traffic signals, and redundant fiber networks for public buildings.

47. *Level-Playing-Field Provisions*. The record demonstrates that, in considering franchise applications, some LFAs are constrained by so-called "level-playing-field" provisions in local laws or incumbent cable operator franchise agreements. Such provisions typically impose upon new entrants terms and conditions that are neither "more favorable" nor "less burdensome" than those to which existing franchisees are subject. Some LFAs impose level-playing-field requirements on new entrants even without a statutory, regulatory, or contractual obligation to do so. Minnesota's process allows incumbent cable operators to be active in a competitor's negotiation, and incumbent cable operators have challenged franchise grants when those incumbent cable operators believed that the LFA did not follow correct procedure. According to BellSouth, the length of time for approval of its franchises was tied directly to level-playing-field constraints; absent such demands (in Georgia, for example), the company's applications were granted quickly.

† Eds. "I-Net" refers to "institutional networks that are operated by the cable system and generally available only to non-residential subscribers."

NATOA contends, however, that although level-playing-field provisions sometimes can complicate the franchising process, they do not present unreasonable barriers to entry. NATOA and LFAs argue that level-playing-field provisions serve important policy goals, such as ensuring a competitive environment and providing for an equitable distribution of services and obligations among all operators.

48. The record demonstrates that local level-playing-field mandates can impose unreasonable and unnecessary requirements on competitive applicants. As noted above, level-playing-field provisions enable incumbent cable operators to delay or prevent new entry by threatening to challenge any franchise that an LFA grants. Comcast asserts that MSOs are well within their rights to insist that their legal and contractual rights are honored in the grant of a subsequent franchise. The record demonstrates, however, that local level-playing-field requirements may require LFAs to impose obligations on new entrants that directly contravene Section 621(a)(1)'s prohibition on unreasonable refusals to award a competitive franchise. In most cases, incumbent cable operators entered into their franchise agreements in exchange for a monopoly over the provision of cable service. Build-out requirements and other terms and conditions that may have been sensible under those circumstances can be unreasonable when applied to competitive entrants. NATOA's argument that level-playing-field requirements always serve to ensure a competitive environment and provide for an equitable distribution of services and obligations ignores that incumbent and competitive operators are not on the same footing. LFAs do not afford competitive providers the monopoly power and privileges that incumbents received when they agreed to their franchises, something that investors recognize.

49. Moreover, competitive operators should not bear the consequences of an incumbent cable operator's choice to agree to any unreasonable franchise terms that an LFA may demand. And while the record is mixed as to whether level-playing-field mandates "assure that cable systems are responsive to the needs and interests of the local community," the more compelling evidence indicates that they do not because they prevent competition. Local level-playing-field provisions impose costs and risks sufficient to undermine the business plan for profitable entry in a given community, thereby undercutting the possibility of competition.

50. *Benefits of Cable Competition.* We further agree with new entrants that reform of the operation of the franchise process is necessary and appropriate to achieve increased video competition and broadband deployment. The record demonstrates that new cable competition reduces rates far more than competition from DBS. Specifically, the presence of a second cable operator in a market results in rates approximately 15 percent lower than in areas without competition—about $5 per month. The magnitude of the rate decreases caused by wireline cable competition is corroborated by the rates charged in Keller, Texas, where the price for Verizon's "Everything" package is 13 percent below that of

the incumbent cable operator, and in Pinellas County, Florida, where Knology is the overbuilder and the incumbent cable operator's rates are $10–15 lower than in neighboring areas where it faces no competition. * * *

52. In sum, the current operation of the franchising process deters entry and thereby denies consumers choices. Delays in the franchising process also hamper accelerated broadband deployment and investment in broadband facilities in direct contravention of the goals of Section 706, the President's competitive broadband objectives, and our established broadband goals. In addition, the economic effects of franchising delays can trickle down to manufacturing companies, which in some cases have lost business because potential new entrants would not purchase equipment without certainties that they could deploy their services. * * *

C. Steps to Ensure that the Local Franchising Process Does Not Unreasonably Interfere with Competitive Cable Entry and Rapid Broadband Deployment

* * *

1. Maximum Time Frame for Franchise Negotiations

* * *

a. Time Limit

68. The record shows that the franchising process in some localities can drag on for years. We are concerned that without a defined time limit, the extended delays will continue, depriving consumers of cable competition and applicants of franchises. * * *

71. Based on our examination of the record, we believe that a time limit of 90 days for those applicants that have access to rights-of-way strikes the appropriate balance between the goals of facilitating competitive entry into the video marketplace and ensuring that franchising authorities have sufficient time to fulfill their responsibilities. In this vein, we note that 90 days is a considerably longer time frame than that suggested by some commenters, such as TIA. Additionally, we recognize that the Communications Act gives an LFA 120 days to make a final decision on a cable operator's request to modify a franchise. We believe that the record supports an even shorter time here because the costs associated with delay are much greater with respect to entry. When an incumbent cable franchisee requests a modification, consumers are not deprived of service while an LFA deliberates. Here, delay by an individual LFA deprives consumers of the benefits of cable competition. An LFA should be able to negotiate a franchise with a familiar applicant that is already authorized to occupy the right-of-way in less than 120 days. The list of legitimate issues to be negotiated is short, and we narrow those issues considerably in this Order. We therefore impose a deadline of 90 days for an LFA to reach a final decision on a competitive franchise

application submitted by those applicants authorized to occupy rights-of-way within the franchise area.

72. For other applicants, we believe that six months affords a reasonable amount of time to negotiate with an entity that is not already authorized to occupy the right-of-way, as an LFA will need to evaluate the entity's legal, financial, and technical capabilities in addition to generally considering the applicant's fitness to be a communications provider over the rights-of-way. Commenters have presented substantial evidence that six months provides LFAs sufficient time to review an applicant's proposal, negotiate acceptable terms, and award or deny a competitive franchise. We are persuaded by the record that a six-month period will allow sufficient time for review. Given that LFAs must act on modification applications within the 120-day limit set by the Communications Act, we believe affording an additional two months—i.e., a six-month review period—will provide LFAs ample time to conduct negotiations with an entity new to the franchise area.

73. Failure of an LFA to act within these time frames is unreasonable and constitutes a refusal to award a competitive franchise. Consistent with other time limits that the Communications Act and our rules impose, a franchising authority and a competitive applicant may extend these limits if both parties agree to an extension of time. We further note that an LFA may engage in franchise review activities that are not prohibited by the Communications Act or our rules, such as multiple levels of review or holding a public hearing, provided that a final decision is made within the time period established under this Order.

* * *

77. In the event that an LFA fails to grant or deny an application by the deadline set by the Commission, Verizon urges the Commission to temporarily authorize the applicant to provide video service. In general, we agree with this proposed remedy. In order to encourage franchising authorities to reach a final decision on a competitive application within the applicable time frame set forth in this *Order*, a failure to abide by the Commission's deadline must bring with it meaningful consequences. Additionally, we do not believe that a sufficient remedy for an LFA's inaction on an application is the creation of a remedial process, such as arbitration, that will result in even further delay. * * * Therefore, if an LFA has not made a final decision within the time limits we adopt in this Order, the LFA will be deemed to have granted the applicant an interim franchise based on the terms proposed in the application. This interim franchise will remain in effect only until the LFA takes final action on the application. * * *

2. Build-Out

82. As discussed above, build-out requirements in many cases may constitute unreasonable barriers to entry into the MVPD market for

facilities-based competitors. Accordingly, we limit LFAs' ability to impose certain build-out requirements pursuant to Section 621(a)(1).

* * *

89. Accordingly, we find that it is unlawful for LFAs to refuse to grant a competitive franchise on the basis of unreasonable build-out mandates. For example, absent other factors, it would seem unreasonable to require a new competitive entrant to serve everyone in a franchise area before it has begun providing service to anyone. It also would seem unreasonable to require facilities-based entrants, such as incumbent LECs, to build out beyond the footprint of their existing facilities before they have even begun providing cable service. It also would seem unreasonable, absent other factors, to require more of a new entrant than an incumbent cable operator by, for instance, requiring the new entrant to build out its facilities in a shorter period of time than that originally afforded to the incumbent cable operator; or requiring the new entrant to build out and provide service to areas of lower density than those that the incumbent cable operator is required to build out to and serve. We note, however, it would seem reasonable for an LFA in establishing build-out requirements to consider the new entrant's market penetration. It would also seem reasonable for an LFA to consider benchmarks requiring the new entrant to increase its build-out after a reasonable period of time had passed after initiating service and taking into account its market success.

* * *

3. Franchise Fees

* * *

96. The fundamental franchise fee limitation is set forth in Section 622(b), which states that "franchise fees paid by a cable operator with respect to any cable system shall not exceed 5 percent of such cable operator's gross revenues derived in such period from the operation of the cable system to provide cable services." Section 622(g)(1) broadly defines the term "franchise fee" to include "any tax, fee, or assessment of any kind imposed by a franchising authority or other governmental entity on a cable operator or cable subscriber, or both, solely because of their status as such." Section 622(g)(2)(c), however, excludes from the term "franchise fee" any "capital costs which are required by the franchise to be incurred by the cable operator for public, educational, or governmental access facilities." And Section 622(g)(2)(D) excludes from the term (and therefore from the 5 percent cap) "requirements or charges incidental to the awarding or enforcing of the franchise, including payments for bonds, security funds, letters of credit, insurance, indemnification, penalties, or liquidated damages." It has been established that certain types of "in-kind" obligations, in addition to monetary payments, may be subject to the cap. * * *

4. PEG/Institutional Networks

* * *

112. Section 611(a) of the Communications Act operates as a restriction on the authority of the franchising authority to establish channel capacity requirements for PEG. This Section provides that "[a] franchising authority may establish requirements in a franchise with respect to the designation or use of channel capacity for public, educational, or governmental use only to the extent provided in this section." * * * "[A]dequate" should be given its plain meaning: the term does not mean significant but rather "satisfactory or sufficient." * * *

114. Consumers for Cable Choice and Verizon argue that it is unreasonable for an LFA to request a number of PEG channels from a new entrant that is greater than the number of channels that the community is using at the time the new entrant submits its franchise application. We find that it is unreasonable for an LFA to impose on a new entrant more burdensome PEG carriage obligations than it has imposed upon the incumbent cable operator.

* * *

120. While we prefer that LFAs and new entrants negotiate reasonable PEG obligations, we find that under Section 621 it is unreasonable for an LFA to require a new entrant to provide PEG support that is in excess of the incumbent cable operator's obligations. We also agree that a pro rata cost sharing approach is one reasonable means of meeting the statutory requirement of the provision of adequate PEG facilities. To the extent that a new entrant agrees to share pro rata costs with the incumbent cable operator, such an arrangement is per se reasonable.

5. Regulation of Mixed-Use Networks

121. We clarify that LFAs' jurisdiction applies only to the provision of cable services over cable systems. To the extent a cable operator provides non-cable services and/or operates facilities that do not qualify as a cable system, it is unreasonable for an LFA to refuse to award a franchise based on issues related to such services or facilities. For example, we find it unreasonable for an LFA to refuse to grant a cable franchise to an applicant for resisting an LFA's demands for regulatory control over non-cable services or facilities. Similarly, an LFA has no authority to insist on an entity obtaining a separate cable franchise in order to upgrade non-cable facilities. For example, assuming an entity (e.g., a LEC) already possesses authority to access the public rights-of-way, an LFA may not require the LEC to obtain a franchise solely for the purpose of upgrading its network. So long as there is a non-cable purpose associated with the network upgrade, the LEC is not required to obtain a franchise until and unless it proposes to offer cable services. For example, if a LEC deploys fiber optic cable that can be used for cable and non-cable services, this deployment alone does not trigger the obligation to obtain a cable franchise. The same is true for boxes housing infrastructure to be used for cable and non-cable services.

122. We further clarify that an LFA may not use its video franchising authority to attempt to regulate a LEC's entire network beyond the provision of cable services. We agree with Verizon that the "entirety of a telecommunications/data network is not automatically converted to a 'cable system' once subscribers start receiving video programming." For instance, we find that the provision of video services pursuant to a cable franchise does not provide a basis for customer service regulation by local law or franchise agreement of a cable operator's entire network, or any services beyond cable services. Local regulations that attempt to regulate any non-cable services offered by video providers are preempted because such regulation is beyond the scope of local franchising authority and is inconsistent with the definition of "cable system" in Section 602(7)(C). This provision explicitly states that a common carrier facility subject to Title II is considered a cable system "to the extent such facility is used in the transmission of video programming...." As discussed above, revenues from non-cable services are not included in the base for calculation of franchise fees.

* * *

D. Preemption of Local Laws, Regulations and Requirements

125. Having established rules and guidance to implement Section 621(a)(1), we turn now to the question of local laws that may be inconsistent with our decision today. Because the rules we adopt represent a reasonable interpretation of relevant provisions in Title VI as well as a reasonable accommodation of the various policy interests that Congress entrusted to the Commission, they have preemptive effect pursuant to Section 636(c). Alternatively, local laws are impliedly preempted to the extent that they conflict with this Order or stand as an obstacle to the accomplishment and execution of the full purposes and objectives of Congress. * * *

129. Applying these principles to this proceeding, we find that local franchising laws, regulations, and agreements are preempted to the extent they conflict with the rules we adopt in this *Order*. Section 636(c) expressly preempts state and local laws that are inconsistent with the Communications Act. This provision precludes states and localities from acting in a manner inconsistent with the Commission's interpretations of Title VI so long as those interpretations are valid. It is the Commission's job, in the first instance, to determine the scope of the subject matter expressly preempted by Section 636. As noted elsewhere, we adopt the rules in this *Order* pursuant to our interpretation of Section 621(a)(1) and other relevant Title VI provisions in light of the twin congressional goals of promoting competition in the multichannel video marketplace and promoting broadband deployment. These rules represent a reasonable interpretation of relevant provisions in Title VI as well as a reasonable accommodation of the various policy interests that Congress entrusted to the Commission. They therefore have preemptive effect pursuant to Section 636(c).

130. Alternatively, we find that such local laws, regulations, and agreements are impliedly preempted to the extent that they conflict with this *Order* or stand as an obstacle to the accomplishment and execution of the full purposes and objectives of Congress. Among the stated purposes of Title VI is to (1) "establish a national policy concerning cable communications," (2) "establish franchise procedures and standards which encourage the growth and development of cable systems and which assure that cable systems are responsive to the needs and interests of the local community," and (3) "promote competition in cable communications and minimize unnecessary regulation that would impose an undue economic burden on cable systems." The legislative history to both the 1984 and 1992 Cable Acts identifies a national policy of encouraging competition in the multichannel video marketplace and recognizes the national implications that the local franchising process can have on that policy. The national policy of promoting a competitive multichannel video marketplace has been repeatedly reemphasized by Congress, the Commission, and the courts. The record here shows that the current operation of the franchising process at the local level conflicts with this national multichannel video policy by imposing substantial delays on competitive entry and requiring unduly burdensome conditions that deter entry. And to the extent that local requirements result in LFAs unreasonably refusing to award competitive franchises, such mandates frustrate the policy goals underlying Title VI. The rules we adopt today, e.g., limits on the time period for LFA action on competitive franchise applications, limits on LFA's ability to impose build-out requirements, and limits on LFA collection of franchise fees, are designed to ensure efficiency and fairness in the local franchising process and to provide certainty to prospective marketplace participants. This, in turn, will allow us to effectuate Congress' twin goals of promoting cable competition and minimizing unnecessary and unduly burdensome regulation on cable systems. Thus, not only are Section 636(c)'s requirements for preemption satisfied, but preemption in these circumstances is proper pursuant to the Commission's judicially recognized ability, when acting pursuant to its delegated authority, to preempt local regulations that conflict with or stand as an obstacle to the accomplishment of federal objectives. * * *

Dissenting Statement of Commissioner Adelstein

* * *

According to the Telecommunications Industry Association, "some recent examples of overly-burdensome, and ... 'unreasonable,' extraneous obligations" included: (1) Merton Group's two year negotiations with Hanover, New Hampshire, which concluded in December, 2004; (2) Knology's negotiations with Louisville, Kentucky in early 2000; (3) Knology's franchise negotiations with the greater Nashville, Tennessee area in March 2000; and (4) Grande Communication's negotiations with San Antonio and Corpus Christi, Texas in 2002. Additionally, Fiber-To-The-Home Council cites the efforts of Guadalupe Valley Telephone Cooperative to seek a franchise in the City of Bulverde, Texas in 2004.

The *Order* itself relies on unconfirmed allegations by Verizon and AT&T about unreasonable demands and negotiations being drawn out over an extended period of time; and complaints by U.S. Telecom Association, Qwest, and Bell South about new entrants accepting franchise terms that they considered unreasonable in order to avoid further delay in obtaining the franchise, or, in one case, filing a "friendly lawsuit."

These examples, based on my review of the record evidence, represent the extent to which competitive video providers argue that LFAs are delaying in acting on franchise applications. However, considering the current franchising process has been in place nearly 15 years and there are over 30,000 LFAs, I find these sporadic examples, individually and collectively, wholly insufficient to justify the Commission's quasi-legislative attempt to federalize the local franchising process. These sparse allegations and anecdotal evidence do not rise to a level that warrants today's drastic, substantive measures. The Commission's blind acceptance of a few alleged instances as illustrative of a much broader problem is a poor and unfortunate reflection of the disregard for proper agency process. The Commission neither attempted to conduct any independent fact-finding or due diligence, nor verify the allegations made by parties who have a vested interest in the outcome of this proceeding. Even more shocking, the Commission and the commenters fail to cite to a single actual, present day problem pending with any specific LFA.

Notwithstanding the scant record evidence to justify agency preemption and the creation of a national, unified franchising process in contravention of federal law, the Commission conjures its authority to reinterpret and, in certain respects, rewrite section 621 and Title VI of the Communications Act, on just two words in section 621(a)(1)—"unreasonably refuse." The Commission ignores the verb that follows: "to award." A plain reading of section 621(a)(1) does not provide a wholesale "unreasonable" test for all LFA action. Rather, the statutory language focuses on the act of awarding a franchise. While I agree that the Commission has authority to interpret and implement the Communications Act, including the Commission does not have authority to ignore the plain meaning, structure and legislative history of section 621, and judicial precedent.

While the Commission purports to limit its action today to interpreting "unreasonably refuse," the *Order* stretches section 621 well beyond the meaning that the statute can bear and, consequentially, changes the franchising process in fundamental ways. There are certain salient features of today's *Order* that raise serious legal and policy implications, requiring careful scrutiny. Most notably, the *Order*: (1) imposes a 90-day shot clock on LFAs to render a decision on the franchise application of a competitive applicant with existing rights-of-way; (2) deems a competitive entrant's franchise application granted after 90-days; (3) prohibits the denial of a competitive entrant's application based upon the entrant's refusal to comply with any build-out obligations; (4) prohibits the denial of a competitive entrant's application based upon the entrant's refusal to build and support PEG and I-net; and (5) authorizes a new entrant to refrain from obtaining a franchise when it is upgrading "mixed use" facilities that will be used for the delivery of video content.

The *Order* finds that franchising negotiations that extend beyond the time frames created today by the Commission amount to an unreasonable refusal to award a competitive franchise within the meaning of 621(a)(1). This finding ignores the plain reading of the first sentence of section 621(a)(1), which provides that a franchising authority "may not unreasonably refuse to award an additional competitive franchise." On its face, Section 621(a)(1) does not impose a time limitation on an LFA's authority to consider, award, or deny a competitive franchise. The second and final sentence of section 621(a)(1) provides judicial relief, with no Commission involvement contemplated, when the competitive franchise has been "denied by a final decision of the franchising authority." There is no ambiguity here: Congress simply did not impose a time limit on franchise negotiations, as it did on other parts of Title VI (see discussion infra). Hence, whether you read the first sentence alone or in context of the entire statutory provision or title, its plain and unambiguous meaning is contrary to the Commission's interpretation. Section 621(a)(1) provides an expressed limitation on the nature, not the timing, of the refusal to award a competitive franchise. * * *

The franchising framework established in Title VI does not support the Commission's decision to select 90 days as the deadline for a default grant—another Commission creation—to become effective. Throughout Part III (Franchising and Regulation) of Title VI, when Congress specifically decided to impose a deadline for LFAs to consider sales of cable systems, modification of franchise obligations, and renewals of existing franchises, in all three instances, Congress chose 120 days. In other sections of the Act, the prevalent time frame Congress imposed on LFAs and the Commission is 180 days. Today, the Commission, without authority, cannot take the place of Congress and impose a tighter time frame than Congress ever contemplated to impose on LFAs in the franchising process. This is well beyond Commission "line-drawing" authority, which requires the Commission to operate within the established framework of the authorizing legislation. * * *

Without anything other than the asserted authority to interpret "unreasonably refuse," the Commission creates a regulatory reprimand for an LFA's failure to render a final decision within the Commission-created time limits. The consequences of the failure to reach agreement within 90 days is that the LFA will be deemed to have granted the competitive entrant an interim franchise based on the terms proposed in the entrant's franchise application. In practicality, this will confer rights-of-way access over local property. In selecting this remedy, the Commission purportedly "seeks to provide a meaningful incentive for local franchising authority to abide by the deadlines contained in the *Order*." While the policy goal is understandable and arguably consistent with congressional intent to encourage the award of competitive cable franchises, we do not have legal authority to establish punitive, one-sided consequences, in order to create an "incentive." Moreover, the Commission ignores that by establishing a default grant of franchise applications effectively confers local property rights unilaterally and without regard for inherent local police powers and public health, safety and welfare. * * *

In terms of build-out, the Commission seems to make a deliberate effort to overlook the plain meaning of the statute and to substitute its policy judgment for that of Congress. The Commission concludes that it is unlawful for LFAs to refuse to grant a competitive franchise on the basis of an applicants' refusal to agree to any build-out obligations. The Commission's analysis in this regard is anemic and facially inadequate.

Section 621(a)(4)(A) provides that "[i]n awarding a franchise the franchising authority shall allow the applicant's cable system a reasonable period of time to become capable of providing cable service to all households in the franchise area." Absent express statutory authority, the Commission cannot declare it unreasonable for LFAs to require build-out to all households in the franchise area over a reasonable period of time. The Commission's argument in this regard is particularly spurious in light of the stated objective of this *Order* to promote broadband deployment and our common goal of promoting affordable broadband to all Americans. In the end, this is less about fiber to the home and more about fiber to the McMansion. * * *

How can the majority declare build-out to be an impediment to entry when one of the major incumbent phone companies, AT&T, claims that it does not need a franchise to operate its video service, and the other, Verizon, has agreed to different, but favorable, build-out obligations with various states and localities? Under the federalist scheme of the Act, different jurisdictions can choose models that best suit their specific needs. For example, in New Jersey, the state-wide franchise reform law correlates build-out principally to population density, while build-out obligations in Virginia principally track the entrant's existing wireline facilities. And in New York City, Verizon and the LFA were actively negotiating universal build-out over a period of a few years.

The broad pen with which the majority writes today's *Order* does not stop with build-out. The *Order* also uses the Commission's alleged authority under Section 621(a)(1) to determine that any LFA refusal to award a competitive franchise because of a new entrant's refusal to support PEG or I-Net is per se unreasonable. Although the *Order* purports to provide clarification with respect to which franchise fees are permissible under the Act, it muddles the regime and leaves communities and new entrants with conflicting views about funding PEG and I-Net. Indeed, Congress provided explicit direction on what constitutes or does not constitute a franchise fee, with a remedy to the courts for aggrieved parties. * * *

While my objections to today's *Order* are numerous and substantial, that should not overlook the real need I believe there is for franchise reform. Indeed, there is bipartisan support for reform in Congress, and most LFAs throughout this country are committed to bring video competition to their jurisdictions. My fundamental concern with this *Order* is that it is based on such paper-thin jurisdiction, but it is truly broad in scope. It ignores the plain reading of the section 621, usurps congressional prerogative and pre-empts LFAs in certain important respects that directly contradict the Act. * * *

The FCC's order was upheld on appeal by the U.S. Court of Appeals for the Sixth Circuit. *Alliance for Community Media v. FCC*, 2008 WL 2549008 (6th Cir. 2008).

Accounting for (Local) Public Interests. Commissioner Adelstein accuses the Commission of both exceeding its statutory authority to dictate terms to local franchising conditions and overreacting based on a few examples of abuse. Putting aside the question of authority to preempt, Adelstein's argument about overreacting poses an interesting question about what kind of factual record the Commission needs to support what are essentially prophylactic general standards for local franchise practices. Notice that even Adelstein supports franchise reform; on what ground does he do so if the record before the Commission is as thin as he asserts?

Adelstein's dissent notwithstanding, assume there is reason to be concerned about local franchising barriers to competitive entry into wireline MVPD markets (remember that local authorities have no jurisdiction over satellite MVPDs). Ask yourself why local franchising authorities would want to create such barriers? Of course, incumbent cable operators support onerous franchise restrictions, which might lead one to conclude that this is simply a case of regulatory capture by the local cable companies. Interest group capture is a time-honored explanation for government behavior, but is it the correct explanation here? As between telephone companies and cable companies, is there any theory that predicts which one of them will "capture" local governments?

In recent years simple capture theories are seldom offered by political analysts as monolithic drivers of political action. The emergence of modern public choice theory has emphasized the interests not only of those demanding regulation but also the interests of those supplying it.[2] At every level of government officials have their "preference functions"—as economists describe motivation. Members of Congress, executive officers (including members of independent agencies such as the FCC), state legislators and state executive officers, and last but not least local government officials, all have their "utility maximands" (another label from the economics profession). What do they maximize, and how?

To be more concrete, consider the local franchise regulators. Presumably they, like any other officials, have a mixture of motivations,

2. Specifically with respect to regulation, useful introductions to public choice are George J. Stigler, *The Theory of Economic Regulation*, 2 Bell J. Econ. & Mgt Sci. 3 (1971) and Richard A. Posner, *Theories of Economic Regulation*, 5 Bell J. Econ. & Mgt Sci. 335 (1974). For a survey of public choice theory, and a comprehensive bibliography, Dennis C. Mueller, Public Choice III (2003) is recommended

both public and private spirited. But whatever the mix of those motivations, it is probable that local public opinion has some effect on their decisions, at least to the extent that they want to retain office. This presents a political puzzle. It was a rising tide of public concern over increases in local cable rates that produced Congress's reinvigoration of rate regulation in 1992. While the tide subsided enough to induce Congress in 1996 to eliminate FCC regulation of non-basic-tier services, basic tier rate regulation continued. That continuation of basic tier regulation has not, however, stopped cable rates from rising. For example, an FCC report released in 2005 showed that the overall average monthly rates for cable service—including basic and expanded basic cable programming services and equipment—increased by 5.4 percent over the 12–month period ending January 1, 2004. Of course, some of that increase was surely due to the cost of expanded service (more channels, higher capacity, etc.). However, it seems unlikely that increased costs totally account for the differential increase. The same report compared prices charged by cable operators that face effective competition with the prices charged by operators that do not face such competition. It found that average monthly rate for basic and expanded basic cable programming services and equipment increased by 3.6 percent for the group of cable operators that face effective competition and by 5.6 percent for the group of operators that do not face effective competition. *Statistical Report on Average Rates for Basic Service, Cable Programming Service, and Equipment*, 20 FCC Rcd. 2718 (2005). In light of the foregoing, why isn't the obvious solution to facilitate more competitive entry? And if this is the obvious solution, why would local franchising authorities not make it easy for telcos to enter the market?

One answer is that this is a simple negotiation game in which local regulators are attempting to extract as much of the surplus from the bargain as possible[3] for the benefit of the local community. If that is the answer, is it a good one? Does that answer imply that the local government is indifferent to rising cable rates or simply that it is playing a kind of game of "chicken" to see how much rent can be extracted from the applicant? On the latter possibility, is it a good game to play? The Commission cites examples of a number of demands by local governments for the cable system to provide special public benefits as a condition of the franchise; could they match the benefits of competitive services? (How much of an increase in their monthly subscription fees do you think cable subscribers would pay for an extra PEG channel or two?)

Bargaining with the Government. Notice that some of these special benefits—"exactions" as they are commonly labeled in local government law—are not related to video program service nor to the underlying rationale for giving local government the franchise power. For example, the Commission cites a "request" by one local franchise authority for a new recreation center and pool. The demand for such benefits/exactions

3. The local franchising process is invariably characterized as a matter of contractual negotiation. On this model, the negotiation would be presumably judged by the rules and standards of, say, the Uniform Commercial Code. Is that the right model?

would seem to be a violation of 47 U.S.C § 544, which forbids local authorities from enforcing requirements other than those specified in that statutory section—specifically, for "facilities and equipment" and "broad categories of video programming or other services." Do the restrictions on the types of exactions matter? Suppose the government does ask for a new opera house or a park, or a statue of the late (lamented) Senator J. Fred Muggs. This is just a financial exaction, isn't it? (The cable operator doesn't have to build it, merely pay for it.) As a financial exaction, presumably it should be limited by the statutory cap on franchising fees, but is there any reason to care whether there is a relationship between the exaction and the regulatory purpose?[4]

D. PROGRAM PACKAGING

MVPD services have always been offered in bundled tiers of channels. Different MVPDs break out the bundles in different ways, but the classic cable model includes at least three tiers: (1) A basic tier which includes, at a minimum, all local television broadcast signals required to be carried by the must-carry rules plus any public, educational, or government access channels required by the system's franchise agreement. It may include additional signals chosen by the operator. (2) A cable programming tier (sometimes labeled "enhanced basic") which includes cable-network supplied programming and out-of-market broadcast signals (e.g., from "superstations"). (3) One or more configurations of premium or pay channels and pay-per-view channels.

In an earlier era, no one questioned the practice of bundling MVPD channels, but, of course, in the early era MVPDs did not dominate the market. Today, as we have noted earlier, approximately 86% of all television households receive their television via cable or DBS providers, which means that they buy their service and they buy it in bundles. This is now the subject of a vigorous controversy. Some persons object to paying for channels that they do not want and never watch. The MVPD providers counter that there are cost advantages to bundling and if they were forced to offer channels "a la carte"—as the option is now called—it would actually increase the cost of providing the services to most subscribers. As in all such disputes, the FCC has been urged to do something. Just what that something is, and whether they can do it, has

4. Those familiar with exactions in local land use regulation might see an analogy here to Dolan v. City of Tigard, 512 U.S. 374 (1994) and Nollan v. Cal. Coastal Comm'n, 483 U.S. 825 (1987), in which the Supreme Court found that exactions that did not have a reasonable nexus to the underlying purpose of the government action, and were not reasonably proportionate to that purpose, were unconstitutional conditions when they had the effect of taking the permit applicant's physical property without just compensation. In the franchising case it's "only" money; does that make a difference? Quite apart from its (controversial) application in these cases, the so-called unconstitutional conditions doctrine generally has been famously muddled. For a sample of perspectives see Seth Kreimer, *Allocational Sanctions: the Problem of Negative Rights in a Positive State*, 132 U. Pa. L. Rev. 1293 (1984); Richard A. Epstein, *Foreword: Unconstitutional Conditions, State Power and the Limits of Consent*, 102 Harv. L. Rev. 4 (1988); Kathleen M. Sullivan, *Unconstitutional Conditions*, 102 Harv. L. Rev. 1413 (1989).

been the subject of two conflicting FCC staff studies—conducted under the auspices of two different FCC chairmen (who happened to have different views on the merits of a la carte). The second staff study is excerpted below.

FURTHER REPORT ON THE PACKAGING AND SALE OF VIDEO PROGRAMMING SERVICES TO THE PUBLIC

Federal Communications Commission, 2006.
2006 WL 305873.

I. Introduction and Background

1. In response to requests from several members of the U.S. House of Representative's Committee on Energy and Commerce and, separately, from the Chairman of the U.S. Senate's Committee on Commerce, Science and Transportation, the Media Bureau of the Federal Communications Commission prepared and, on November 18, 2004, released a *Report on the Packaging and Sale of Video Programming Services to the Public* ("First Report") addressing issues relating to "the efficacy of providing a la carte and themed-tier services to cable and satellite subscribers." The First Report addressed both constraints on the ability of multichannel video programming distributors ("MVPDs") to offer such a la carte and themed-tier services, resulting from the contractual agreements entered into with sellers of programming (wholesale issues), and economic and consumer welfare issues associated with the manner in which content distributors package and market such programming (retail issues). The First Report concluded that a la carte regulation would increase operational expenses for MVPDs, increase the marketing costs and reduce the revenues of programming networks, and provide little economic benefit to consumers. The First Report thus implied that a la carte regulation is undesirable and focused its policy recommendations on methods to increase competition and investment in new technologies in the retail MVPD market.

2. The staff has undertaken a Further Report ("Further Report") to respond to questions that have arisen regarding the appropriateness of the assumptions relied upon and the conclusions reached in the First Report. The Further Report concludes that the First Report relied on problematic assumptions and presented incorrect and biased analysis. Based on a more complete analysis of the costs and benefits of bundling and the potential costs and benefits of a la carte, the Further Report concludes that a la carte could be in consumers' best interests. Moreover, it explores several alternatives for increasing consumer choice in purchasing multichannel video programming that could provide substantial consumer benefits.

* * *

II. Assessment of First Report's Analysis and Conclusions

* * *

B. Impact of A La Carte on the Price of Programming

* * *

2) First Report Understates Benefits of A La Carte and Harms of Bundling

* * *

27. In its analysis of bundling, the economics literature typically compares three different regimes for selling goods, in which goods are sold either strictly in a bundle, strictly individually, or both individually and in a bundle. In the retail MVPD market, these alternatives correspond to consumers purchasing programming networks either strictly as part of a bundle ("pure bundling"), individually ("pure a la carte"), or with the choice of buying either bundles or individual channels ("mixed bundling"). As pointed out in the First Report, economists have posited that firms choose to sell their goods in bundles, as opposed to selling them individually, for the following reasons: (1) as a means of price discrimination (rather than charging a single price for each good, the bundle price incorporates the fact that some consumers value some goods more than others do); (2) as a means of reducing production costs (due to economies of scale and economies of scope), reducing transaction and information costs, and improving quality; and (3) as a strategic device for deterring entry of new competitors. Most of the literature focuses on the price discrimination explanation for bundling and why bundling can increase profits for firms in a variety of circumstances.

28. The First Report focuses its economic analysis on the comparison of pure bundling with pure a la carte. The First Report relies on two key economic theories to support its contention that bundling is welfare-enhancing: (1) the non-rivalrous nature of the consumption of programming; and (2) the use of bundling as a means of price discrimination. Careful consideration shows that neither of these theories leads to the First Report's conclusions.

29. First, the First Report claims that bundling is more efficient than a la carte, because the consumption of programming is non-rivalrous. That is, once programming has been produced, everyone can watch it without diminishing others' ability to watch it. While the First Report is correct that efficiency is increased if programming with a positive value is distributed more widely, since this can be done at close to zero marginal cost, it is not correct that pure bundling will better achieve this result than pure a la carte or mixed bundling. As demonstrated below, sales of some desirable networks could be greater under a la carte than under bundling. Moreover, the First Report ignores the impact of such a mechanism on the amount of programming that is produced; i.e., it assumes that because programming is produced it should be widely distributed, without considering whether the appropriate amount of programming is produced.

30. Second, the First Report touts the benefits derived from bundling as an improved means of price discrimination. The First Report

explains that bundling permits MVPDs to recover a larger portion of the cost of a given network from customers who value that network more highly and a lower portion from customers who value it less highly. The First Report contends that such price discrimination facilitates the MVPDs' ability to generate sufficient revenue to cover the cost of offering the networks that consumers want, thereby enhancing welfare. As the economics literature indicates, however, it is unclear whether consumers and society are better off with the use of price discrimination schemes (like bundling of programming) than with the use of single market prices (like offering programming a la carte). Indeed, that literature discusses the potential problems caused by bundling, in some cases finding that bundling can be bad for consumers and can create greater inefficiency than a la carte.

31. Therefore, the First Report's economic arguments are incomplete and thus misleading or at least do not paint a complete picture of whether bundling programming networks is in consumers' and society's best interest. To assess the desirability of switching to a la carte properly, one must also consider the potential harms that bundling may cause. Specifically, as discussed below, bundling may raise consumers' programming costs and provide consumers with programming packages less valuable to them than those they could purchase under a la carte. For many consumers, these harms could outweigh any benefits gained from bundling.

* * *

4) First Report Incorrectly Assesses Impact on Advertising Revenues

44. As described in the First Report, the costs of production of most cable programming networks are recovered from two sources of revenues: (1) network advertising; and (2) license fees paid by MVPDs for the right to distribute the network programming to subscribers. Ultimately, both revenue streams are dependent on the number of subscribers who view the network. The First Report's analysis of the impact of introducing additional choice through a la carte took a pessimistic view of the associated costs and likely consumer responses. Industry commenters projected significant drops in audience share, as well as in advertising revenues and license fees, for programming networks. Many of these projections, however, were based on unproven assumptions about the reactions of consumers to new options. The First Report's analysis of the impact of a la carte on network entry and funding contains conceptual errors and faulty assumptions that are reexamined below.

45. * * * [T]he Booz-Allen-Hamilton Study, on which the First Report relied, predicts a la carte would cause consumers to view almost 25% less television and states that the average household watches on average 9 hours a day. Thus, the Study assumes, without any basis, that a shift to a la carte would cause the average household to watch more than 2 hours less television per day or almost 15 hours less per week.

While the First Report predicts substantial drops in audience shares following the introduction of a la carte, this is not the only possible response. There is little reason to believe that, given enhanced choice, consumers would watch video programming less than they do today, although they may make some changes in what they watch. If this is the consumer reaction, there would be little if any change in overall audience levels. In the absence of a change in audience levels, significant decreases in the advertising revenues of program networks are less likely.

* * *

C. Impact of A La Carte on Programming Diversity

1) Introduction

65. A la carte could be preferable to bundling in providing diverse programming responsive to consumer demand. The First Report implies that bundling gives consumers the programming they desire when it argues that "bundling does not force consumers to pay for programming they do not want." Since no one alleges that consumers are being forced to buy bundles for more than they value them, this argument is a straw man. As the First Report notes, in a free market economy consumers will not purchase goods if the price exceeds the value they place on it. The relevant question concerns not whether consumers are paying for bundles in excess of the bundles' value, but rather whether consumers would prefer the service they could get under a la carte. If bundling, as compared to a la carte, causes consumers to pay more or prevents customers from getting the programming they want, then bundling has made them worse off.

66. To maximize revenue under pure bundling, MVPDs carry networks that either: (1) allow them to raise the price of the bundle; or (2) add to subscribership. This means that the networks that have value to consumers will not always get carriage under pure bundling for two reasons. First, because their goal is to maximize the price and sales of the bundle, there are many circumstances when MVPDs will have an incentive not to provide the networks preferred by some consumers. For example, some mainstream networks may not be added because, unlike niche networks, they do not increase subscribership. Second, bundling can obscure signals regarding consumer valuation of individual networks. Under bundling, consumers provide no information about which networks they like best; while under a la carte, consumers' interest in a network can be measured by its a la carte sales. Thus, it is more difficult to ascertain the relative value of networks under bundling, especially for smaller networks that have no published ratings. The analysis below considers how these factors can affect the availability of diverse programming responsive to consumer demand.

2) Bundling Distorts Incentives to Carry Networks

67. Bundling may create incentives for MVPDs to include or exclude programming in a manner inconsistent with consumer preference.

The First Report assumes that MVPDs will want to carry networks that are preferred by consumers. Because their goal is not to maximize sales of an individual network, but instead to maximize the revenue gained from the bundle, there are circumstances in which MVPDs will not carry the most desired networks. Indeed, consumers may be disappointed with the programming they receive in bundled packages either because it includes programming they find without sufficient value to justify its cost or because it excludes valued networks.

68. First, MVPDs that bundle may find it profitable to include content that some consumers do not watch, potentially forcing those consumers to pay more than they would under a la carte. The First Report takes the view that since programming is non-rivalrous in consumption, it is desirable to distribute all available programming to the largest possible viewing audience. This ignores the possibility that some consumers might find some programming to be without value, so that they would prefer not to pay for the programming as part of the bundle price. Yet, bundling of such programming networks may be profitable to MVPDs, even though some consumers do not watch it.* * *

70. Second, some programming networks that appeal to mainstream consumers might find it more difficult to enter under bundling than under a la carte. As stated above, an MVPD carries a network only if it either expands the base of subscribers willing to pay the bundle price or if it enables the MVPD to increase the price it can charge for the bundle. * * *

71. Third, bundling may induce MVPDs to exclude from their bundles the networks some of their viewers most strongly value. This applies particularly to networks that attempt to serve a programming niche that is already served by one or more other networks. Networks that are less strongly preferred by viewers might better increase MVPD revenues from the bundle and thus gain carriage. The preferred networks could be available under pure a la carte, provided the value to the consumer of the preferred programming network exceeds the network's costs. * * *

3) Bundling Limits Ability to Ascertain Demand

78. Even when the MVPD wants to carry the most-desired networks, it may have difficulty determining which ones are most popular with viewers under bundling. Whether or not a network gets carried depends on an MVPD's guess as to the popularity and profitability of carrying a network. Since consumers are buying a bundle of networks, and since Nielsen does not rate smaller networks, the MVPD may have little information about how much consumers value the ability to watch a particular network, even after carrying it for a while.

79. Under a la carte, consumers indicate their interest by agreeing to pay a fee for receiving the network. This provides the MVPD direct information about how many consumers place a high valuation on the network. Because the consumers who pay for a network are likely to be

watching it a portion of the time, it also provides information to advertisers about the likely number of viewers. Since MVPDs want to carry networks that increase subscribers and revenues per subscriber, and since advertisers want to know which networks have large numbers of viewers, networks with large numbers of viewers might find it easier to get higher license fees and advertising revenues under a la carte than under bundling. Meanwhile networks with few interested viewers will likely get less revenue when it becomes obvious they have few subscribers under a la carte, and they may consequently lose carriage.

80. In addition, under bundling a network may have a reduced incentive to improve its quality, because a moderately higher number of viewers for a network may go unnoticed and unrewarded. Under a la carte, on the other hand, improvements in quality can lead quickly to an increase in the number of paying subscribers and the size of the fees they are willing to pay for the network, thus quickly providing a reward for the investment. The marketplace will thus be able more quickly to shed unpopular networks in favor of popular networks under a la carte than under bundling and in the process become more responsive to consumer demand for better programming. Programmers may also have an increased incentive to improve their programming under a la carte.

III. Additional Options for Introducing Consumer Choice

A. Introduction

81. As Section II of this Report explained, the First Report did not present an accurate or balanced picture of the consequences of increasing consumer choice. In fact, there are significant benefits that may be gained by allowing consumers to choose. For example, a la carte could decrease many consumers' video programming bills. This section examines some alternative options for providing increased consumer choice that the First Report failed to analyze fully. These options are limited to channels currently offered in a digital format, in hopes of minimizing any cost and disruption associated with the transition to increased consumer choice.

82. Below we consider three options for increasing consumer choice. They are: (1) mixed bundling, in which consumers are allowed to choose from all the digital channels on an a la carte basis, in addition to bundles the MVPD may choose to provide; (2) themed tiers, in which MVPDs offer tiers of related digital programming, such as a children's programming tier or sports programming tier; and (3) subscriber-selected tiers, in which customers have the option of purchasing smaller bundles than are currently offered and choosing the channels that go into that bundle from among the MVPDs' digital offerings. All of these options provide consumers increased choice in selecting the programming they wish to pay for and receive. Likewise, all the options permit MVPDs to continue to offer their current bundled and a la carte selections, so that consumers can continue to purchase pre-established bundles if those bundles best meet their needs. The following section

discusses the advantages and disadvantages of each option and the implementation issues they present.

B. Discussion of Options

1) Mixed Bundling

83. Instead of receiving most of their digital channels exclusively in bundles as they do today, consumers could be allowed the choice of purchasing such channels either on an a la carte basis or as part of the bundles an MVPD chooses to provide ("mixed bundling"). That is, under this option, consumers could elect to purchase networks individually, at a set price for each network, or to pay the bundled price.

84. It is worth noting that MVPDs have some experience selling channels and features on an a la carte or smaller bundle basis. For example, consumers are able to purchase premium channels, pay-per-view features, and Video-On-Demand (VOD) programming either individually or as part of small packages, with a variety of approaches being taken for offering these services. In counterpoint to industry claims that the increased complexity of a la carte will harm the market and impose undue costs on their operations, cable operators have been able to absorb the increased marketing and customer care requirements associated with their premium, pay-per-view, and VOD program offerings, which offer their subscribers essentially a la carte programming options. Moreover, many of the network and system costs are already in place to allow for premium, pay-per-view, and VOD offerings.

85. Mixed bundling would provide many benefits over pure bundling. First, consumers who are only interested in a few channels could buy the channels they want, possibly at a considerable cost savings to the bundle price. This could significantly lower these consumers' total bills for video programming. Moreover, a la carte could induce consumers to take MVPD service who would not otherwise be willing to pay the bundle price. Finally, mixed bundling would permit consumers to avoid paying for networks that they do not watch.

86. The fact that consumers could still buy the MVPD-established bundles would provide an additional layer of benefits. If there were significant savings from bundling channels that appeal to different sets of customers, as industry suggests in its comments, then the pre-established bundles should remain an attractive option to consumers. Similarly, any consumers who found the decisions presented by an a la carte programming option overwhelming could purchase bundled programming instead.

87. Increased choice for consumers of this sort could also increase competitive pressures among competing MVPDs, who might feel pressure to match each others' prices and offerings. The current programming packages that MVPDs offer tend to be remarkably similar and few in number, which may limit the strength of competition among MVPDs. Offering consumers additional options in programming packages could

spur increased competition among MVPDs by opening up additional fronts on which MVPDs could compete to satisfy consumer demand.

88. Mixed bundling would also help to provide market signals that reflect the popularity of a network with consumers. Although not fully representative of the number of viewers (because many subscribers may have access through purchase of a bundle), the volume of a la carte sales could represent useful information to advertisers and MVPDs concerning the popularity of a network. This could increase advertising revenues for popular networks, allowing those networks to lower their license fees.

89. The availability of bundles under mixed bundling should also alleviate many of the concerns expressed by networks about the cost of marketing themselves under a pure a la carte regime. Those consumers that like to channel surf could continue to buy the pre-established bundles.

90. As discussed further below, we lack information about what a la carte prices would be for individual networks. Some a la carte network prices could be relatively low, but other network prices could appear relatively high to consumers. In any event, consumers would likely have the opportunity to lower their total programming bill by purchasing fewer channels.

91. Overall, a mixed bundling regime has the potential to provide great flexibility to consumers. Mixed bundling could produce reduced prices for some consumers, as well as make programming available to consumers with a limited interest in MVPD programming and a small budget. While consumers would have the option to purchase channels a la carte, they would retain the option of buying a pre-established bundle if that best suited their needs.

2) Themed Tiers

92. Another possible sales method is the themed-tier model, pursuant to which MVPDs would offer one or more tiers of digital programming with a particular theme. The program networks in this type of tier would still be available in a larger, more general (and more expensive) package if the distributor so chose. A themed tier would allow a consumer to pay a subscription fee only for that genre of programming that he or she finds appealing.

93. Domestic cable operators are technically capable of offering such tiers, as evidenced by the sports, foreign language, and other themed tiers currently offered for sale. Charter, for example, offers a limited basic service tier consisting of broadcast stations and local access channels, an expanded basic tier, and many additional channels on four separate digital tiers (the "Family and Information Tier," the "Movie Tier," the "Sports Tier," and the "Latino Tier"). Bright House Networks has focused on expanding its digital offerings, which include, inter alia, a digital basic tier and a digital sports tier. Cablevision offers seven separate tiers of foreign language programming catering to, among others, Russian, Korean, and Hispanic subscribers, as well as digital tiers

for sports enthusiasts. These examples and others like them demonstrate that such tiers are economically and technically feasible.

94. Under a themed-tiers option, consumers could reap some of the economic benefits that bundling may provide, while still receiving and paying for only the kinds of networks that appeal to their interests. Indeed, consumers could potentially save money by purchasing themed tiers, either because themed tiers could be cheaper than existing bundles or because consumers could avoid purchasing networks they do not watch. * * *

3) Subscriber-Selected Tiers

97. An alternative to MVPD-established themed tiers would be a subscriber-selected tier. That is, the MVPD subscriber, rather than the MVPD, could choose the content of the tier to be purchased. For example, if a subscriber desired a mix of program network types, such as sports, movies, and children's programming, she would be able to select a prescribed number of channels for a set price from among the MVPD's digital offerings. This tier would be smaller than the MVPD's pre-established bundles. Thus instead of being required to purchase perhaps 80 networks as part of a larger bundle, a subscriber could purchase a smaller package of perhaps 20 or 40 or 60 networks for a reduced price, with the subscriber choosing the networks. Subscribers could continue to buy the pre-established programming packages if they so chose.

98. Subscriber-selected tiers would combine the potential benefits of bundling with the potential benefits and greater choice that a la carte could provide consumers and have therefore received some attention in the economics literature. Two FCC economists recommended examining this option in a recently published paper.

99. Moreover, international examples suggest the feasibility of this approach. For example, Videotron, a Canadian cable operator, allows its subscribers to select certain types of digital program networks on an a la carte basis. Videotron customers must buy a basic digital tier that includes 22 government-mandated channels for a monthly fee of $19.48. Customers then have a variety of additional choices. Customers can purchase channels one at a time, in small bundles of five or six, or in larger bundles of 20, 30, 65, or 106 channels.

100. Rogers Cable, another Canadian cable operator, likewise offers subscriber-selected tiers. Subscribers who purchase a 30 channel basic tier for $24.00 and lease a digital converter box for $8.95 can then purchase certain digital networks on an a la carte basis for $2.49 each. Alternatively, subscribers can create their own new digital "5-pack" for $9.95, "10-pack" for $14.95, "15-pack" for $18.75 and so forth. Other Canadian cable operators offer similar packages.

101. Subscriber-selected tiers would allow consumers to purchase the networks they want, while avoiding receiving or paying for other networks that they do not watch. In contrast to themed tiers, with subscriber-selected tiers, consumers would not be restricted to the net-

works the MVPD bundled together in making their choices. The ability of consumers to choose which channels go into their bundles would also provide feedback to MVPDs and advertisers as to which networks are most popular. We would expect MVPDs to monitor closely which networks consumers select, as a yardstick of a network's value to viewers. As discussed above, having this information available about consumer preferences would help make programming more responsive to consumer demand, since networks that are more popular and that have invested in raising their quality would find it easier to demonstrate their success to MVPDs and advertisers under subscriber-selected tiers, as compared to pure bundling.

102. The First Report raises the concern that networks have different costs and thus cannot be lumped together in a single package at a fixed price. The concern is that, because some networks cost more to provide than others, providing a single package with high and low cost networks could be difficult to price. The theory is presumably that consumers should pay more for the high cost networks. Yet this is not how the video programming industry works, either through broadcast television or MVPD bundling. Networks that cost more and provide greater quality would get more viewers and subscribers and thus are compensated with more subscription fees and advertising revenues. In addition, the price of the bundle, and the proportion of the price that goes to each network, could be adjusted to account for the average take rate of the different kinds of networks.

103. Subscriber-selected tiers would present issues, however, regarding how to set the size and price of the bundles. Indeed, the ability of subscriber-selected tiers to generate consumer savings is difficult to determine absent more pricing information. As discussed above, though, the concerns expressed in the First Report are overstated in terms of the difficulties smaller networks might face. Further, the inclusion of networks in bundles would mean that the networks and MVPDs would still get the benefits of bundling in terms of getting contributions from both high-interest and low-interest consumers to cover their costs.

104. In practice, the potential for significant consumer benefits from offering a subscriber-selected tiers option could outweigh any potential difficulties in determining how the size and price of these smaller bundles would be set. This form of increased consumer choice would provide some consumers lower prices and all consumers the ability to avoid paying for networks they do not watch. Meanwhile this option retains any potential benefits of bundling. * * *

The Economics of Bundling. Product bundling is a kind of "tying" arrangement in which one good is offered only with another. It is a very common practice. Everyone who buys an automobile must buy a package of goods—tires, engine, radio, etc.—that are physically distinct and indeed can otherwise be purchased separately but are sold collectively as a car. In the usual case we don't think twice about such bundling or tying because the aggregation of distinctive "things" seems to be part of what the relevant product is: a "car" simply is a collection of parts; shoes and socks only come in pairs. In other cases, it is not so simple. For example, at some stores if you want to buy a pair of socks you have to buy a package of at least three pair even though the product market is conventionally defined as one pair of socks not three. Why do sellers bundle goods that are physically and economically separate units? There are multiple explanations for tying and bundling of goods, some benign, some malign. See generally Dennis W. Carlton and Jeffrey M. Perloff, *Modern Industrial Organization* ch. 10 (3d ed. 2000). The FCC staff report cites these standard explanations:

> [E]conomists have posited that firms choose to sell their goods in bundles, as opposed to selling them individually, for the following reasons: (1) as a means of price discrimination (rather than charging a single price for each good, the bundle price incorporates the fact that some consumers value some goods more than others do); (2) as a means of reducing production costs (due to economies of scale and economies of scope), reducing transaction and information costs, and improving quality; and (3) as a strategic device for deterring entry of new competitors. Most of the literature focuses on the price discrimination explanation for bundling and why bundling can increase profits for firms in a variety of circumstances.

The second staff report generally dismisses the second explanation and does not discuss the third. That leaves the price discrimination explanation. It is a very common explanation, as the report indicates, but is it a benign or a malign result? What is the harm of price discrimination?

Conventional economic theory teaches that price discrimination has ambiguous effects on consumer welfare. Under some conditions it can increase output (which, all else being equal is considered a good thing), but on the other hand it can also produce distortions in production and in wealth distribution. By general agreement, though, price discrimination can yield more profit for the seller under certain conditions. To see how, consider this very simple example, a stylized version of one first formulated by George Stigler, *United States v. Loews, Inc.: A Note on Block–Booking*, 1963 Sup. Ct. Rev. 152 (1963).[5] Assume a monopolist of two goods, X and Y, who sells to two buyers who have different valuations of the two goods. Assume for the moment the marginal cost of X and Y is zero. Buyer 1 values X at \$5 and Y at \$3 for a total of \$8 for both goods. Buyer 2 values X at \$6 and Y at \$2, again for a total of \$8. The seller's Plan A is to bundle X and Y at a price of \$8 and earn a total of \$16. Plan A in this case yields the same result as "perfect price

5. There are many illustrations of Stigler's famous model. For others see, e.g., the *first* FCC staff report on a la carte, FCC Media Bureau, REPORT ON THE PACKAGING AND SALE OF VIDEO PROGRAMMING SERVICES TO THE PUBLIC 82–83 (2004); Carlton & Perloff, *supra* at 307. Our own example varies the numbers slightly to highlight a couple of points.

discrimination'' albeit indirectly.[6] Suppose next that bundling is forbidden, and the seller is also forbidden to discriminate between buyers. The seller turns to a second best option, Plan B: sell X at $5 and Y at $2, which yields $14. If we are sensitive to the welfare of the buyer and the seller, plan B seems to be the best plan. However, this might not always be the case if we factor in a cost condition. Assume that the cost of X is $4 and that of Y is $3. Plan A is still best for the seller, of course, but is B best for the buyer? Plan B puts the price of X at $5, which covers the seller's cost and meets the reservation prices of both buyers. Everyone is happy. What about Y? Buyer 2 will not purchase Y at a price of $3 and the seller won't sell below that price. The result is a deadweight loss of value to both seller and buyer. If X and Y were packaged, buyer 2 would be willing to pay $2 for Y and $6 for X, which would make both him and the seller better off.

The Effect of Competition. An omitted section of the second FCC staff report comments, as did the first report, on the increase in MVPD competition and its likely effect on consumer choice:

> MVPD competition continues to provide consumers with increased choice, better picture quality, and greater technological innovation. The Commission recently found that almost all consumers now have the choice between over-the-air broadcast television, a cable service, and at least two DBS providers. And in some areas, consumers also may have access to video programming delivered by emerging technologies, such as digital broadcast spectrum, fiber to the home, or video over the Internet. Increased choice in providers should foster increased consumer choice.

If MVPD competition is increasing and competition fosters increased consumer choice, what is the point of the Commission forcing MVPD providers to adopt a la carte? Why isn't the *market* forcing them to offer a la carte?[7]

How Much Selection? The first staff report in 2004 made clear that the debate over a la carte only concerns the so-called ''enhanced basic'' or ''cable programming'' tier, not the basic tier which includes (inter alia) all of the local broadcast stations that have must-carry rights. What is the basis for treating the basic tier as special: if consumers should be allowed to select among individual channels, should they not be able to select which (if any) of the local channels they want? Putting aside the basic tier question, how many and what kinds of choices should the FCC

6. Perfect price discrimination involves prices set according to each individual buyer's reservation price for each good. In our example: $5 + $3 + $6 + $2 = $16. Perfect price discrimination is exceedingly rare because the seller has no way of ascertaining the reservation price of each buyer and no practical means of fine tuning the price. Compare, however, the auction strategy in some marketing schemes, such as Priceline.com in which each potential buyer bids for, say, an airline ticket or a hotel room. Obviously, this is not a practical strategy for most mass-marketed goods—including MVPD channels.

7. The staff report does note that some cable and DBS providers have announced plans to launch ''family-friendly'' tiers. This obviously is aimed at viewer groups concerned about indecency and violence, but it does not seem to portend any broader move towards a la carte.

mandate? Should the FCC require that cable operators provide a "family viewing" tier? The above report is cast in terms of monetary costs, but FCC Chairman Martin was quite explicit that one of the reasons to revisit a la carte was that it would be a means of addressing the problem of indecency and violence. (Note in particular the report's discussion of "themed" tiers—which would include "family friendly" packages.) Is a la carte a plausible strategy for dealing with those concerns? Consider the indecency cases that we examined in Chapter 3; how many of those cases involved program choices that would be affected by a la carte choices among program *channels*?

The First Amendment. It is superfluous to ask whether a rule mandating a la carte offerings would raise a First Amendment issue. When it comes to regulating communications—certainly mass media communications—virtually every rule of substance can raise a First Amendment issue. The question always is how serious are the First Amendment concerns, and what standard of judicial scrutiny should be employed in addressing those concerns? The first staff report in 2004 summarized comments by others but reached no conclusion on the First Amendment issue. A key initial question is what standard of review should apply which, of course, depends on whether an a la carte mandate would be considered to be content-based or content neutral regulation. This in turn might depend on whether any a la carte rule included some kind of requirement for "themed tiers"—which appears facially to be a content-specific rule. Assuming no such content requirement, is there any constitutional difference between an a la carte requirement and the must-carry requirements upheld in *Turner Broadcasting System v. FCC*, 520 U.S. 180 (1997), discussed in the last chapter?

Statutory Authority. The issue of statutory authority to impose a la carte was discussed in the 2004 staff report but again with no conclusions being reached. Among the points noted by the 2004 report was the fact that § 541(c) of the Act forbids the imposition of common carrier or utility-type regulation on cable operators. Would that preclude a rule mandating a la carte? Even if § 541(c) does not preclude such a mandate, the FCC would have to locate some provision of the Act that confers affirmative authority to regulate. Title VI does not contain any such affirmative provisions, but recall that the FCC originally grounded its jurisdiction over cable in Title I, based on a theory that cable regulation was reasonably "ancillary" to its regulation of broadcasting. Of course, this theory of regulation preceded enactment of the 1984 Cable Act expressly giving the Commission jurisdiction. Can the Commission still use this ancillary theory to provide authority that Title VI does not provide? There is in any case a question whether this type of regulation could be considered to be within the ambit of ancillary jurisdiction. See *FCC v. Midwest Video Corp.*, 440 U.S. 689 (1979) (holding that a rule mandating local access channels was not within the FCC's ancillary jurisdiction authority). This may be a moot issue; the FCC to date has made no claim of jurisdiction. The FCC's chairman has urged Congress to enact legislation to mandate a la carte, but as of the date this book went to press no legislation has been introduced.

*

Part III

TELECOMMUNICATIONS

Chapter 7

REGULATORY FOUNDATIONS OF TELECOMMUNICATIONS

A. INTRODUCTION TO TELECOMMUNICATIONS[1]

Telephone service starts (of course) with the telephone handset located at the network subscriber's premises (we will assume a residence for simplicity). The telephone is connected by a pair of copper wires to the network interface device ("NID") located in a box outside the residence. The NID marks the interface between the network and inside wiring. From the NID the wires typically run to a telephone box at some point in the immediate vicinity of the residence; this box collects lines from multiple residences into a cable, which runs to a switch located in the service provider's central office ("CO").[2]

The function of the switch warrants brief notice in order to illustrate the trade-off between transmission and switching. In a network without central switching, connectivity would require a direct transmission path between every network subscriber, as shown at left in the illustration below. At a glance it will be seen that such a network would be hopelessly complicated and costly. Central switching, shown at right, greatly simplifies the connectivity problem.

1. There are a number of useful introductions to telecommunications technology. For an overview of technology and law see Jonathan E. Nuechterlein and Philip J. Weiser, DIGITAL CROSSROADS (2005). For a detailed history of telecommunications technology and law see Christopher H. Sterling, Phillis W. Bernt, and Martin B.H. Weiss, SHAPING AMERICAN TELECOMMUNICATIONS: A HISTORY OF TECHNOLOGY, POLICY AND ECONOMICS (2006).

2. The cable may run directly to the telephone company switch or, in more modern times, it may run to a concentrator that combines it with other voice signals (by multiplexing) onto a coaxial or optical fiber cable that connects to the CO. The difference is immaterial for our purposes.

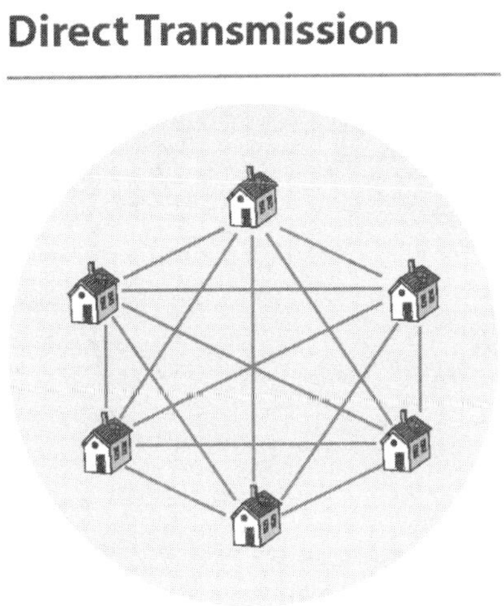

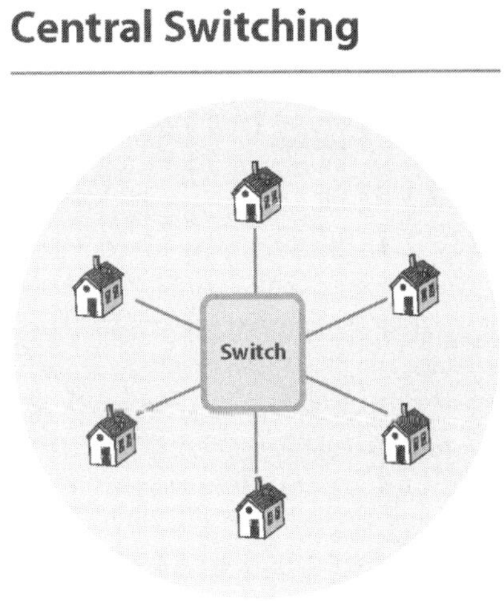

The traditional public switched telephone network ("PSTN") developed in the United States by AT&T was designed as a network hierarchy of switching points for the purpose of concentrating or handling overflow traffic as shown in the illustration below. At the lowest level is the Class 5 office, the CO, commonly called the "end office" or "wire center". The CO is the first point at which the end subscriber is connected to the switched network. The area served by the CO is the local exchange area, which is (also called the "wire center service area" and the "last mile"). Above the CO is the Class 4 or toll office (also commonly referred to as the "tandem office"). The tandem office connects COs where they are not directly connected. The network as initially designed by AT&T included three higher switching points—Class 3 (a so-called "primary office"), Class 2 (a "sectional office") and Class 1 (a "regional office"). The function of each of these was to provide higher level aggregation of lines and to interconnect lower offices. Thus, Class 4 offices would be connected through a Class 3, and so on up the ladder. Modern switching technology has made this hierarchical structure more or less obsolete. Today, multiple calls in a circuit switched network can be aggregated and carried over the same wire (or "multiplexed"). With multiplexing, the required resource switching and trunking capacity is available at the lower levels of the CO and a toll or tandem office. Tandem offices interconnect COs and serve also as the access point of presence ("POP") for "long distance" calls between local access and transport areas ("LATAs").[3]

3. It is important to distinguish the local exchange service area—the area served by a CO—from a LATA. The LATA is a regulatory classification that was created with the breakup of AT&T in 1984 for the purposes of defining the boundary between local service and long distance. However, LATAs include multiple local exchange service areas.

Public Switched Telephone Network

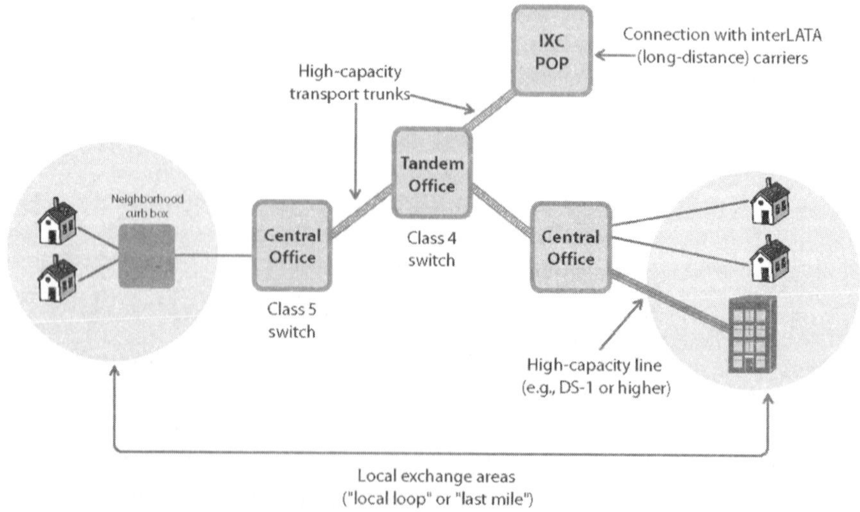

The PSTN is a circuit-switched network based on a dedicated transmission channels connecting the calling parties. In circuit switching, a conversation takes place over single, fixed circuit that is created by connecting a series of wires together from the originating to the receiving party. As shown in the comparison of direction transmission and circuit switching, it would be impossibly expensive and complex to string wires between each telephone on the network, so switches are used to dynamically create circuits between callers. In order to establish a connection, the originator of the call takes the phone "off-hook," which signals the CO to provide a dial tone. An address on the network, in the form of a telephone number is then dialed, and the switch makes a connection by designating a time slot or frequency interval by which the message will be carried over a sequence of wireline paths to the called party.[4] In circuit switching, the routing of the call is performed at the time the circuit is established. At that time, the links on the path between the sender and the receiver are determined by forwarding tables that are hardwired at each switching point. The circuit remains in place for the entire duration of the call and is terminated when the call is completed and the phone goes on-hook. At that time, the various links used by the circuit are freed up for use by new calls.

By allocating a fixed circuit for the conversation, circuit switching allows a high quality of voice communication, because once the circuit is established there is a reserved path for the signals to follow between the parties. But the quality of circuit switching is off-set by its being very resource intensive, since the circuit facility is tied up even when there is

4. Again, today multiplexing plays an important part. With multiplexing, not every call requires its own physical wire; the system maintains a dedicated circuit between the calling and receiving parties over shared wires.

no communication (e.g, when there are pauses in the conversation, one party leaves the phone off the hook while running to get the baby from mischief, etc.). As technology has advanced, it has found new ways to use those "pauses" (when viewed digitally, every conversation is full of tiny pauses, even when the speakers are actually speaking) to transmit other information. The result is that circuit switching has become *relatively* less efficient over time when compared to other technologies. Circuit switching also suffers from some other deficiencies. If no circuit can be established between a sender and a receiver because of a lack of resources, the connection is completely blocked; there is no temporary storage of the message (instead, the caller must repeat the call). Similarly, if there is a failure on one of the circuit links, the communication is interrupted unless a back-up circuit has been pre-programmed into the routing set up.

An alternative form of switched transmission is packet switching. Originally developed for long distance data transmission, it has become familiar to all modern users as an essential feature of Internet communications (the Internet Protocol (or "IP") is optimized for use over packet-switching networks). But packet switching is now widely used as well for regular voice communications in transporting messages between exchanges. The signal is digitalized and broken into segments by a packet assembler-dissembler ("PAD"). Each packet contains part of the information to be transmitted (digitized voice or data) together with a header containing information for routing and sequencing of the data packet and a trailer with additional information such as a framing sequence and error correcting codes. Each packet may proceed separately over different routes, to be reassembled at the end according to the header instructions. Packets from different users may be interleaved together, as shown below.

Packet Switching

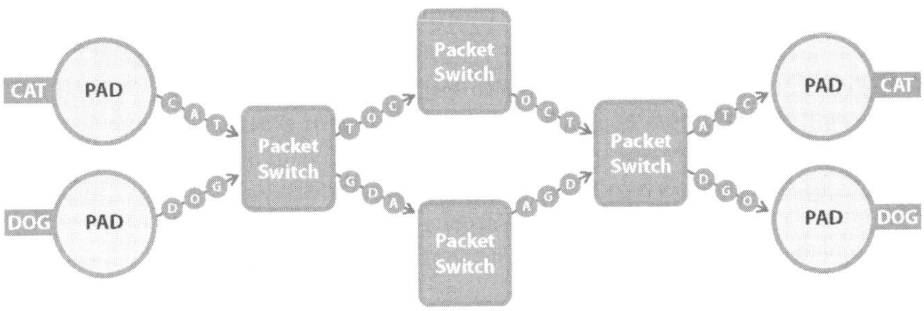

In circuit switching the routing is hardwired at the time the call is established and does not change until the session is terminated; each bit of information exchanged follows the same path.[5] In packet switching, the routing of each packet is dynamic; at each node the router will read the address of the packet and determine the best path to send it to the end destination. In the diagram above, the information from the message "CAT" is broken into three packet segments by the PAD, they are combined with the packet segments from the message "DOG". For simplicity we have shown only a couple of intermediate nodes through which the packets pass en route to their destination.

Notice, that, because different packets in a single communication may follow different paths, they frequently arrive at their destination out of order—neither the path nor the sequencing of the packets is fixed. The packets will be reassembled at their destination in the proper sequence (remember that each packet contains code that describes how the information is to be sequenced). Moreover, because the network does not "reserve" a circuit to carry packets, they may be delayed. For example, the "A" in CAT might have to wait in a queue at the second switch until the router is able to establish a path over the network. This may produce end-to-end latency problems. Such delays are insignificant for most data transmissions but for voice or video, where message continuity is important, the delay was for a time thought to make packet switching (and therefore the Internet) unattractive for voice and video. Advanced switching technology has, however, overcome this problem, and, as we shall see, the Internet has become a viable network for the carriage of telephony (often called "voice over Internet" or "VoIP"). Internet video is still a work in progress because of bandwidth problems, but it too is emerging. Importantly, packet switching can be carried over a variety of physical media; it allows a separation between the form of communication and the physical network it is carried over. Packet switching works equally well over both the dedicated copper wires connecting residences to telcos' COs and the unswitched loops of coaxial cable that connects residences to the local head ends of cable operators. When circuit switching was dominant, a potential competing telephone provider might have to build their own network of switches to provide circuits to carry telephone calls. Now, all that is required for packet-switched communications of any kind is a wire connecting the residence to some head end (such as that used by cable operators, or even electricity providers![6]) and a high-speed connection to the Internet.

Traditionally, the heart of "plain old telephone service" or "POTS" has been based on the copper wire pair, designed to deliver an analog signal suitable for voice communications. However, telcos have long

5. Today, even circuit-switched networks use a form of interleaving through multiplexing, usually time-division multiplexing ("TDM"). The difference between TDM and packet switching is that, in TDM, the assignment of space for interleaving in the shared conduit is synchronous and reserved, while in packet switching it is random (not reserved), so that if there is no packet to send at a particular time, the conduit is not wasted—it can be reallocated to carrying another piece of information.

6. The technology is called "broadband over powerlines" or "BPL" and has seen a number of limited commercial deployments but has yet to see widespread commercial success. The FCC has made BPL a regulatory priority.

provided to business users high-capacity digital transmission lines (e.g., DS1 line or higher).[7] Increased demand for high-speed access to the Internet has stimulated the telcos to deploy high capacity digital service for residential users as well. High speed DSL (digital subscriber line) service is now widely available over traditional copper wire used in the local loop. For technical reasons, though, DSL is available only to subscribers within about three miles of the CO. That limitation—plus the more limited capacity of DSL—has given cable operators a comparative advantage in providing residential broadband service. Cable modems have potentially far greater bandwidth than current DSL technology allows and they are not subject to the same distance limitation, allowing many who live too far from the CO to purchase broadband access (and, by virtue of packet switching, that access includes not only Internet service but can also include VoIP service). Because cable companies have always provided television service, the advent of cable broadband service and VoIP service means that they have been able to offer one-stop shopping for the so-called "triple play" of voice, data, and video. Some telcos, most notably Verizon, have begun to install optical fiber directly to the home ("FTTH") or at least to the neighborhood "box" (the "curb") that connects to the home in order to not only improve their broadband carriage capacity but also to allow them to offer video entertainment programming as well, to finally put them in the position of being able to compete directly with the cable companies on all fronts.

B. THE BELL SYSTEM MONOPOLY

Telecommunications has gone through cycles of monopoly and competition, but until the late 1970s monopoly was the most enduring condition. The initial period of monopoly, though, was a product of intellectual property rather than communications law. Although there is some dispute over who actually invented the telephone, Alexander Graham Bell was the first to the patent office and his initial patent and the ones that followed gave the Bell Telephone Company (the firm that eventually became the American Telephone and Telegraph Company) an initial period of exclusivity that ran from 1876 to 1894. After the expiration of the Bell patents, competition did break out and was quite vigorous for a time. However, by 1910, when telecommunications was placed under the regulatory jurisdiction of the Interstate Commerce Commission, this competition had been diminished, in part by aggressive

7. We will encounter the "DS" designation again. DS (digital signal) describes a hierarchy of speeds used to classify the capacity of telephone lines. DS0 is the basic voice-grade level (64kbs) that is associated with the familiar copper-wire pair. DS1 has a capacity of 1.544 Mbps, equal to 24 DS0s. (DS1 is often used interchangeably with a "T1" line, though technically the latter describes the equipment rather than the speed.) The DS hierarchy goes up to DS4, which is the equivalent of 168 DS1's. In addition to the DS classification there is another classification for optical fiber transmission rates—"OCn" (optical carrier, level n). OCn designations are typically used to describe high capacity lines used in SONET networks (synchronous optical networks) that provides the high traffic backbone for modern data transport. The basic level, OC1, has a capacity of 51.840 Mbps. Higher numbers are direct multiples; for instance, OC48 denotes a SONET channel 48 times that of OC1, or 2.488 Gbps. (The levels rise to a current maximum of OC255, or 13.21 Gbps.)

acquisitions by AT&T and in part by AT&T's refusal to interconnect its long distance network with the local networks of its rivals. Regulation by the ICC proved to be lackluster. In the 24 years that it had regulatory responsibility, the ICC gave almost no attention to telephone and telegraph regulation (which was cited as one of the reasons for eventually transferring jurisdiction to the FCC in 1934).

A short-lived attempt to check AT&T's dominance and enable independent competition came from an other quarter in 1913. The Justice Department filed an antitrust action against AT&T, claiming that its attempted acquisition of an independent long distance competitor in the Pacific Northwest amounted to monopolization under the Sherman Act. The suit was quickly settled by the so-called "Kingsbury Commitment" in which AT&T promised to refrain from acquiring competing telephone companies except with the prior approval of the Justice Department, to permit independent companies to interconnect with its long distance network facilities, and also to sell stock that it had earlier acquired in Western Union. The commitment did not significantly hinder AT&T's path to dominance. The Justice Department routinely approved most of the proposed mergers. In 1921 the Willis-Graham Act gave to the ICC exclusive authority to approve future acquisitions and immunized such approved acquisitions from antitrust challenge. The prohibition against acquiring *non*-competing companies and the required interconnection with independents probably enhanced more than curtailed AT&T's dominance. The expansion in competitive local service resulted in a similar expansion in demand for long distance services, a market in which AT&T faced very little effective competition. The Willis-Graham Act has been often regarded as signaling the end of the competitive era in telecommunications. By 1934, when federal regulation was passed from the ICC to the newly established FCC, AT&T dominated the telecommunications industry. Telephony came to displace telegraphy as the principal medium of electronic communications, and AT&T displaced Western Union as the dominant firm in what could now be described as a single industry. AT&T owned 80 percent of the telephones in the United States. (Until the late 1970s telephones were owned by the service provider and leased to subscribers.) The other 20 percent were owned by a large number of small, generally unintegrated firms that were dependent on AT&T's long distance network.

Monopoly in the telecommunications industry was not an accident. Theodore Vail, architect of the Bell System, had been entirely successful in convincing regulators that a single system was the necessary for system integrity, for efficient service for ... in short, all the elements of the "public interest". Vail called this vision of a single telephone network "universal service," a term he used somewhat differently from its meaning today. Today the term "universal service" is used in the Communications Act to describe a policy of providing service to everyone. See 47 U.S.C. § 254. It does not necessarily imply that we should do so through a *unitary system*, which was Vail's meaning. Universal service does imply universal connectivity—everyone connected to everyone—but this can be (and today is) provided by interconnection requirements. Be that as it may, Vail's vision of a single, unified system became the accepted regulatory paradigm. Telecommunications would soon become a canonical model of the concept of a natural monopoly. (The term was not in common use at that early time, though the concept was known in economics.) That there had once been head-to-head competition among telephone companies did not necessarily teach a contrary lesson to contemporary policy makers. The "law" of natural monopoly does not teach that competition cannot exist, merely that it cannot survive. Economies of scale (and, in more recent economic thinking, economies of scope—involving the integration of related services or products) doomed competition in the long term because a single firm can serve the entire market at the lowest cost.

The traditional policy implication derived from a finding that a market is naturally monopolistic and that the market demand can be most cheaply satisfied by a single firm is that competition is not only unsustainable in the long run but undesirable in the short. The assumption here is that competition would only lead to unstable pricing and wasted investment. In simplest terms this policy amounts to saying that, if a single firm is the cheapest producer, there is no point to competition.[8] Of course, this notion assumes we can reliably determine what the condition of the market not only is at present but will be in the future. As such it represents a rather static view of the market (as well as related technology). More generally, it represents a static view of the nature of competition—as an equilibrium condition as opposed to a dynamic, ever evolving process. It was understood, of course, by the regulators and regulated alike, that a natural monopoly had to be regulated in order to protect the public. That much is unexceptionable, but the same regulation that is used to protect the public is also a vehicle for preventing new competition. Regulation became a two-sided bargain to secure the "natural" monopoly from "unnatural" competition.

While it was widely accepted that natural monopoly was the correct description of telecommunications, there was always some ambiguity about its scope. The 1913 antitrust suit was, in a sense, an attempt to set a boundary on the monopoly. In the event, it did not really succeed in doing so. (The long distance market it sought to keep open was basically shut after 1921.) A second government antitrust suit in 1949 sought to draw a boundary between regulated service and unregulated equipment by seeking to divest AT&T of its manufacturing arm, Western Electric. That case was also settled by consent decree in 1956, in which AT&T was allowed to keep Western Electric subject to the condition that AT&T and Western Electric would be forbidden to enter or sell equipment to unregulated markets. In time, uncertainty about the proper boundaries

8. The economic literature on natural monopoly and its implications is large. Ronald R. Brautigam, *Optimal Policies for Natural Monopolies*, in II HANDBOOK OF INDUSTRIAL ORGANIZATION 1290 (1989) provides a technical economic survey of the economics and regulatory strategies. A less technical legal and economic critique of regulatory policies when natural monopoly was still ascendant is Richard A. Posner, *Natural Monopoly and Its Regulation*, 21 STAN. L. REV. 548 (1969).

of natural monopoly would lead the FCC to allow competition in equipment and long distance service markets. AT&T's opposition to those moves would lead to a third government antitrust suit—"the big one"—brought in 1974 and settled in 1982, which reorganized the Bell System. The boundaries of the natural monopoly were thus not immutable, though the concept was persistent. Natural monopoly would not be officially discarded as a basis for public telecommunications policy until the Telecommunications Act of 1996.

But we are getting ahead of ourselves. Before we look at the restructuring brought about by the antitrust case, we need to back up a bit and look at those early challenges to the monopoly model. We will examine three areas of early competition in telecommunications markets: foreign attachments, the re-sorting of services in the *Computer* inquiries, and the piece that led to the antitrust case itself, competition in long distance services. Although these specific competitive reforms have largely been overshadowed by more recent changes, the arguments behind them—and the categories they created—underlie many of today's debates in telecommunications regulation. Following that, we will examine the 1982 antitrust decree and its immediate aftermath in greater detail.[9]

C. EARLY CHALLENGES

1. Foreign Attachments and Customer Premises Equipment

Of the three areas in which early competition was (re)introduced to telecommunications markets, the simplest was in what was variously called "customer premises equipment" ("CPE") or "terminal equipment." As a soup-to-nuts operation, AT&T controlled every piece of equipment that made up the network, from long distance transmission lines to telephone device sitting on its customers' desks. Even though the telephone was under the physical control of the customer, it was owned by AT&T, which used that control to limit the devices that could be connected to its network. But, with complete physical access to this part of AT&T's empire, consumers (and third-party manufacturers) could not help but come up with ideas about other ways to use CPE or other forms it could take. And so was born the controversy over whether to allow non-AT&T equipment, or "foreign attachments," to be connected to the PSTN.

IN THE MATTER OF USE OF THE CARTERFONE DEVICE IN MESSAGE TOLL TELEPHONE SERVICE

Federal Communications Commission, 1968.
13 F.C.C.2d 420.

COMMISSIONER JOHNSON FOR THE COMMISSION:

This proceeding involves the application of American Telephone and Telegraph Co. tariffs to the use by telephone subscribers of the Carterfone.

9. Some additional details on this era can be found in Glen O Robinson, *The Titanic Remembered: AT&T and the Changing World of Telecommunications*, 5 YALE J. ON REG. 517 (1988).

The Carterfone is designed to be connected to a two-way radio at the base station serving a mobile radio system. When callers on the radio and on the telephone are both in contact with the base station operator, the handset of the operator's telephone is placed on a cradle in the Carterfone device. A voice control circuit in the Carterfone automatically switches on the radio transmitter when the telephone caller is speaking; when he stops speaking, the radio returns to a receiving condition. A separate speaker is attached to the Carterfone to allow the base station operator to monitor the conversation, adjust the voice volume, and hang up his telephone when the conversation has ended.

The Carterfone device, invented by Thomas F. Carter, has been produced and marketed by the Carter Electronics Corp., of which Mr. Carter is president, since 1959. From 1959 through 1966 approximately 4,500 Carterfones were produced and 3,500 sold to dealers and distributors throughout the United States and in foreign countries.

The defendant telephone companies, acting in accordance with their interpretation of tariff FCC No. 132, filed April 16, 1957, by American Telephone and Telegraph Co., advised their subscribers that the Carterfone, when used in conjunction with the subscriber's telephone, is a prohibited interconnecting device, the use of which would subject the user to the penalties provided in the tariff. The tariff provides that:

> No equipment, apparatus, circuit or device not furnished by the telephone company shall be attached to or connected with the facilities furnished by the telephone company, whether physically, by induction or otherwise.[*]
>
> * * *

The examiner found that there was a need and demand for a device to connect the telephone landline system with mobile radio systems which could be met in part by the Carterfone. He also found that the Carterfone had no material adverse effect upon use of the telephone system. He construed the tariff to prohibit attachment of the Carterfone whether or not it harmed the telephone system, and determined that future prohibition of its use would be unjust and unreasonable. He also found that it would be unduly discriminatory under section 202(a) of the Act, since the telephone companies permit the use of their own interconnecting devices. However, he did not find the tariff prohibitions to have

* Eds. In greater detail, the tariff prohibited the attachment of any equipment that was electrically tied to the network or would otherwise present a danger to the network. In addition, the tariff provided that "nothing herein shall be construed to permit the use of . . . a device to interconnect any line or channel of the telephone company with any other communications line or channel of the company or of any other person."

been unlawful in the past, largely because the harmless nature of the Carterfone was not known to the telephone companies, and he did not find that a general prohibition against nontelephone company supplied interconnecting devices was unjust or unwise, because of the risk he saw of "serious harm to the heart of the nation's communications network."

We agree with and adopt the examiner's findings that the Carterfone fills a needs and that it does not adversely affect the telephone system. They are fully supported by the record. We also agree that the tariff broadly prohibits the use of interconnection devices, including the Carterfone. Its provisions are clear as to this. Finally, in view of the above findings, we hold, as did the examiner, that application of the tariff to bar the Carterfone in the future would be unreasonable and unduly discriminatory. However, for the reasons to be given, we also conclude that the tariff has been unreasonable, discriminatory, and unlawful in the past, and that the provisions prohibiting the use of customer-provided interconnecting devices should accordingly be striken.

We hold that the tariff is unreasonable in that it prohibits the use of interconnecting devices which do not adversely affect the telephone system. *See Hush-A-Phone Corp. v. U.S.*, 238 F. 2d 266, 269 (D.C. Cir., 1956), holding that a tariff prohibition of a customer supplied "foreign attachment" was "[a]n unwarranted interference with the telephone subscriber's right reasonably to use his telephone in ways which are privately beneficial without being publicly detrimental." The principle of *Hush-A-Phone* is directly applicable here, there being no material distinction between a foreign attachment such as the Hush-A-Phone and an interconnection device such as the Carterfone, so far as the present problem is concerned. Even if not compelled by the *Hush-A-Phone* decision, our conclusion here is that a customer desiring to use an interconnecting device to improve the utility to him of both the telephone system and a private radio system should be able to do so, so long as the interconnection does not adversely affect the telephone company's operations or the telephone system's utility for others. A tariff which prevents this is unreasonable; it is also unduly discriminatory when, as here, the telephone company's own interconnecting equipment is approved for use. The vice of the present tariff, here as in *Hush-A-Phone*, is that it prohibits the use of harmless as well as harmful devices.

AT&T has urged that since the telephone companies have the responsibility to establish, operate and improve the telephone system, they must have absolute control over the quality, installation, and maintenance of all parts of the system in order effectively to carry out that responsibility. Installation of unauthorized equipment, according to the telephone companies, would have at least two negative results. First, it would divide the responsibility for assuring that each part of the system is able to function effectively and, second, it would retard development of the system since the independent equipment supplier would tend to resist changes which would render his equipment obsolete.

There has been no adequate showing that nonharmful interconnection must be prohibited in order to permit the telephone company to carry out its system responsibilities. The risk feared by the examiner has not been demonstrated to be substantial, and no reason presents itself why it should be. No one entity need provide all interconnection equipment for our telephone system any more than a single source is needed to supply the parts for a space probe. We are not holding that the telephone companies may not prevent the use of devices which actually cause harm, or that they may not set up reasonable standards to be met by interconnection devices. These remedies are appropriate; we believe they are also adequate to fully protect the system.

Nor can we assume that the telephone companies would be hindered in improving telephone service by any tendency of the manufacturers and users of interconnection devices to resist change. The telephone companies would remain free to make improvements to the telephone system and could reflect any such improvements in reasonable revised standards for nontelephone company provided devices used in connection with the system. Manufacturers and sellers of such devices would then have the responsibility of offering for sale or use only such equipment as would be in compliance with such revised standards. An owner or user of a device which failed to meet reasonable revised standards for such devices, would either have to have the device rebuilt to comply with the revised standards or discontinue its use. Such is the risk inherent in the private ownership of any equipment to be used in connection with the telephone system.

The present unlawfulness of the tariff also permeates its past. It has been unreasonable and unreasonably discriminatory since its inception, for the reasons given above.That the telephone companies may not have known prior to the proceedings herein that the Carterfone was in fact harmless is irrelevant, since they barred its use without regard to its effect upon the telephone system. Furthermore, the tariff was the carrier's own. It was not prescribed by the Commission. It has remained subject to complaint and to a finding that it had been unlawful since its inception.

* * *

In view of the unlawfulness of the tariff there would be no point in merely declaring it invalid as applied to the Carterfone and permitting it to continue in operation as to other interconnection devices. This would also put a clearly improper burden upon the manufacturers and users of other devices. The appropriate remedy is to strike the tariff and permit the carriers, if they so desire, to propose new tariff provisions in accordance with this opinion. We make no rulings as to damages since that relief has not been requested. As noted above, the carriers may submit new tariffs which will protect the telephone system against harmful devices, and may specify technical standards if they wish.

Hush-A-Phone. The FCC relied heavily for its outcome on *Hush-A-Phone Corp. v. United States*, 238 F.2d 266 (D.C. Cir. 1956). *Hush-A-Phone* dealt with a different device, a plastic cup that attached to the telephone receiver that allowed the user to close the gap between their mouth and the receiver, ostensibly to prevent others in the same room from hearing what the user was saying. AT&T identified the Hush-A-Phone as a risk to the network, and the FCC concurred, finding that the Hush-A-Phone is "deleterious to the telephone system and injures the service rendered by it," resulting in a "public detriment." (Everyone acknowledged some reduction (13 decibels) in call quality for the individual user.) The court, seeing use of the Hush-A-Phone as a matter of somewhat less gravity, rejected with skepticism the idea that a plastic cup presented a substantial risk to the nation's telephone network:

> To say that a telephone subscriber may produce the result in question by cupping his hand and speaking into it, but may not do so by using a device which leaves his hand free to write or do whatever else he wishes, is neither just nor reasonable. The intervenors' tariffs, under the Commission's decision, are [a]n unwarranted interference with the telephone subscriber's right reasonably to use his telephone in ways which are privately beneficial without being publicly detrimental.

Does the FCC's reversal of policy in the *Carterfone* decision necessarily follow from *Hush-A-Phone*? The question in *Hush-A-Phone* was whether the device harmed the network, but the Carterfone did much more than affect the sound of a call; although it attached at the "end" of the network, it actually interconnected the telephone network with another form of telecommunications (one, radio, that the FCC itself regulates). The tariff at issue in *Carterfone* prohibited not only harmful devices but also devices used for interconnection, regardless of whether or not they harmed the network. Does the question of whether to require interconnection depend solely on the possibility of harm to the network?

The Move to a Competitive Market and Deregulation in CPE. The *Carterfone* decision is correctly hailed as a seminal move toward competitive supply of customer premises equipment, although the decision itself was only a first step in that direction. First, the decision did not pertain to CPE generally but rather to peripheral attachments. Second, the immediate objective was primarily directed at customer convenience not at competition. The latter would develop as a logical outgrowth of the former, but this would take several years to evolve. In response to *Carterfone*, AT&T actually went beyond the specific ruling of the decision, which was to allow the use of non-Bell *peripheral* devices, and altered its tariff to permit the substitution of privately supplied *core equipment* such as telephone handsets or private branch exchange equipment as well. But there was a catch; AT&T's amended tariff required that non-Bell equipment use a so-called "protective connection arrangement" ("PCA"), ostensibly designed to protect the network from harm. The ostensible purpose disguised an anticompetitive one: the connecting arrangements were unnecessarily restrictive and had the effect of imposing a cost handicap on the use of non-Bell equipment. In the mid-1970s, the FCC removed the handicap by establishing a system of registration for CPE based on uniform technical standards applicable to all suppliers, including AT&T. AT&T's initial PCA requirement would be later cited as one of the episodes of anticompetitive conduct underlying the government's antitrust case in 1974.

Following the FCC's adoption of a CPE registration system in the mid-1970s, the supply of CPE became fully competitive, sufficiently so that by the end of the decade the FCC would decide that it should be completely deregulated. In 1980 the Commission ruled that the supply of CPE would be removed from telephone service tariffs as part of the *Computer II* decision, which we cover next. Our principal focus, though, is on a second aspect of the case, dealing with the provision of "enhanced services".

2. Re-sorting the Services: The *Computer* Inquiries

A year before its decision in *Carterfone*, and three years before the first two computers were joined together by what eventually became the Internet, the FCC initiated the *Computer Inquiries*. As the demand for data processing grew through the 1960s, it became clear that the future of data processing was going to be closely tied to the future of telecommunications. After all, what good is data (processed or otherwise) if it cannot be communicated? Data processing companies like IBM wanted to be able to use the telephone network to provide services to their customers, while the telephone companies wanted to be able to move into the data processing business. But the telephone carriers' business had been regulated, which raised the question of how to treat these new services that, while they used the telephone network, were not traditional telephone service. The FCC's regulatory mandate was unclear. These new services challenged the traditional economic model underlying telephone regulation, since there is no way to view data processing as being subject to the type of natural monopoly forces that justified telephone regulation. Having a monopoly like AT&T enter what was widely considered to be a competitive market presented a number of problems. In the course of dealing with those problems, the FCC created a structure that, today, dominates not only the regulation of data-related services (i.e. the Internet) but eventually was backward-migrated to regulation of telephony itself.

The FCC's first cut at the problem came in 1970, when the first *Computer* order was issued. In *Computer I*, the Commission did two remarkable things: First, it separated traditional "communications services," which it would continue to regulate under Title II, from the new "data processing services," which it chose not to regulate. (It also created a grey area, "hybrid services," involving the provision of both communications and data processing services. Some hybrid services would be regulated, some would not. The FCC expressly refused to give an exact definition separating those that would from those that wouldn't.[10]) Second, it decided to allow telephone companies to enter the new data processing business. But there were concerns. The telephone companies' virtual monopolies over carriage meant that they could defeat their (new) data processing competitors by denying them access to the network. Moreover, firms that engage in both a regulated business (as communications services was) and an unregulated business (such as data processing) have the potential to shift some of the profits from the regulated side of the business the competitive side through cross-subsidization. In order to prevent either form of abuse, the FCC required that firms providing communications services form separate subsidiaries to provide data processing services and to follow strict accounting rules to make sure that the relationships between the regulated and unregulated firms remained transparent, a set of safeguards it called "maximum separation". See *In the Matter of Regulatory and Policy Problems Presented by the Interdependence of Computer and Communication Services and Facilities*, 28 F.C.C.2d 267 (1971) ("*Computer I*").

The FCC revisited the question in the late 70s, refining both its distinction between the types of services (renamed "basic services" and "enhanced services") and its rules for how firms could provide them. In doing so, the Commission fleshed out both the theory and practice of its role as a regulator of the information economy.

IN THE MATTER OF AMENDMENT OF SECTION 64.702 OF THE COMMISSION'S RULES AND REGULATIONS (SECOND COMPUTER INQUIRY) Final Decision

Federal Communications Commission, 1980.
77 F.C.C.2d 384.

BY THE COMMISSION:

* * *

I. INTRODUCTION

1. * * * The thrust of this proceeding is threefold: a) to determine whether enhanced services which are provided over common carrier telecommunication facilities should be subject to regulation and, if so, to what extent; b) to examine the competitive and technological evolution of customer premises equipment, with a view toward determining wheth-

10. "Hybrid" services, in turn, were further defined as either "hybrid data processing services" ("a hybrid service offering wherein the message-switching capability is incidental to the data processing function or purpose") and "hybrid communication services" ("a hybrid service offering wherein the data processing capability is incidental to the message-switching function or purpose"). Hybrid communications services were treated in the default as communications services and were regulated; hybrid data processing services were treated in the default as data processing services and were not. The Commission essentially retained the power to change the category on a case-by-case review basis but refused to give any additional guidance ex ante.

er the continuation of traditional regulation of terminal equipment is in the public interest; and c) to determine, consistent with the statutory mandate set forth in the Communications Act of 1934, as amended, 47 U.S.C. § 151, the role of communication common carriers in the provision of enhanced services and customer-premises equipment.

II. Summary of Decision Network Services

* * *

5. Based on the voluminous record compiled in this proceeding, we adopt a regulatory scheme that distinguishes between the common carrier offering of basic transmission services and the offering of enhanced services. Although more simplified terminology is employed, this basic/enhanced dichotomy for network services is consistent with the approach taken in the *Tentative Decision*. We find that basic service is limited to the common carrier offering of transmission capacity for the movement of information, whereas enhanced service combines basic service with computer processing applications that act on the format, content, code, protocol or similar aspects of the subscriber's transmitted information, or provide the subscriber additional, different, or restructured information, or involve subscriber interaction with stored information.

* * *

7. The decision sets forth the regulatory scheme for basic and enhanced services. The common carrier offering of basic transmission services are communications services and regulated as such under traditional Title II concepts. Consistent with the determinations made in the *First Computer Inquiry*, we find that regulation of enhanced services is not required in furtherance of some overall statutory objective. In fact, the absence of traditional public utility regulation of enhanced services offers the greatest potential for efficient utilization and full exploitation of the interstate telecommunications network Significant public benefits accrue to the Commission's regulatory process, providers of basic and enhanced services, and consumers under this approach.

Customer-Premises Equipment

8. In the *Tentative Decision*[*] we proposed a regulatory scheme for carrier-provided customer-premises equipment (CPE) based on whether the CPE performed more than a basic media conversion (BMC) function. We attempted to set forth a structure under which carriers could, separate from their basic transmission services, provide CPE that incorporated various computer processing applications. We sought comment, however, as to whether any regulatory distinction should be made between the various kinds of CPE offered by carriers, and whether all such equipment should be deregulated. We find that the public interest

* Eds. *See Tentative Decision and Further Notice of Inquiry and Rulemaking*, 72 F.C.C.2d 358 (1979).

would not be served by classifying CPE based on whether or not more than a basic media conversion function is performed. We conclude that, in light of increasing sophistication of all types of CPE and the varied uses to which CPE can be put while under the user's control, it is likely that any given classification scheme would impose an artificial, uneconomic constraint on the design and use of CPE. In general, no regulatory distinction should be made between various types of carrier-provided CPE.

9. As to the appropriate regulatory scheme for CPE, we find that the tariffing of CPE in conjunction with regulated communications services has a direct effect on rates charged for interstate services. To the extent rates for interstate services bear costs attributable to carrier-provided CPE regulation serves to thwart the competitive provision of CPE. The continuation of tariff-type regulation over carrier-provided CPE neither recognizes the role of carriers as competitive providers of CPE, nor does it reflect the severability of CPE from transmission services. We conclude that CPE is a severable commodity from the provision of transmission services and that regulation of CPE under Title II is not required and is no longer warranted.

* * *

11. We consider as well whether it is necessary to apply the resale structure set forth in the *Tentative Decision* to all carriers owning transmission facilities. We address whether certain carriers should be required to offer enhanced services on a resale basis through a separate corporate entity and whether CPE should likewise be marketed through an entity separate from that providing basic services.

12. Weighing the public interest benefits of our objectives and the economic tradeoffs inherent in a separate subsidiary requirement, we have determined that limited imposition of the requirement will best serve the communications ratepayer and the public interest more generally. There is little need to subject carriers to the resale structure if such entities lack significant potential to cross-subsidize or to engage in other anticompetitive conduct. We find that only AT&T and GTE present a sufficiently substantial threat such that they should be required to establish separate corporate entities for the provision of enhanced services and customer-premises equipment. We will not require any other underlying carrier to form separate entities for the provision of these services and CPE. * * *

13. Finally, we believe that our action does not preclude AT&T from offering enhanced services and CPE under the provisions of the 1956 Western Electric consent decree.

* * *

V. Discussion

* * *

B. Network Services

Basic and Enhanced Services

* * *

88. The comments generally support distinguishing between basic common carrier services and enhanced services. Questions were raised, however, as to the manner in which we delineated the three categories of service-voice, basic non-voice (BNV), and enhanced non-voice (ENV). The comments raise concerns on two fronts. First, it is argued that use of "voice" and "non-voice" terminology may result in an artificial voice/data service distinction that will eventually fall of its own weight as technology evolves. Second, various parties argue that the definitions of BNV and ENV services should somehow be altered. In this regard, certain regulated carriers seek to have the BNV category expanded so as to not restrict their regulated activities. At the same time various unregulated entities seek a narrow construction of voice and BNV services so as not to unnecessarily expand the scope of regulation.

89. Unnecessary confusion may have resulted in proposing these three service categories using voice/non-voice terminology. Continued use of these terms is not warranted. The same objective is obtainable through use of simplified and more descriptive terminology. We believe that delineating between basic transmission services and enhanced services is consistent with the thrust of the *Tentative Decision* and will remove any conceptual problems as to the technological merging of voice and data.

90. The "voice" and "basic non-voice" categories proposed in the *Tentative Decision* represent nothing more than basic transmission services. The "voice" category was limited, by definition, to telephone service and was intended to distinguish "plain old telephone service" (POTS) from other basic and enhanced services where interaction of the human voice is involved. The "basic non-voice" category was essentially defined in terms of functions necessary to route a message through the network. That nothing more than a basic transmission service was intended by these two categories is evident from our statement that "this structure requires the facilities of the underlying carrier to be transparent to the information transmitted and for a carrier to provide a 'pure transmission' service which forms the basis upon which all 'enhanced' services are provided." *Tentative Decision*, at para. 75. Accordingly, it is consistent with the *Tentative Decision* to refer to services that would fall within the voice and BNV categories as "basic" transmission services. Likewise, the ENV category was intended to encompass those computer offerings which are more than basic services, and it included both voice and data applications. . . .

91. We disagree with the first argument that an artificial distinction is made between voice and data services, or that we are imposing such a separation. The incorporation of voice and data transmission capabilities into the network is inherent in the basic service category. This dual capability is also recognized in the provision of enhanced

services. To the extent confusion may have resulted over the use of "voice" and "non-voice" terminology, it should be alleviated by our use of more descriptive "basic" and "enhanced" terminology in differentiating services falling within the former "voice," "basic non-voice," and "enhanced non-voice" categories.

92. We conclude that the record in this proceeding supports our adopting a basic/enhanced dichotomy for network services. In going forward with a regulatory scheme that distinguishes a carrier's basic transmission services from its enhanced services, it behooves us to make clear our perception of what constitutes a basic service. In so doing we are mindful of the arguments raised by various parties that the basic service category should be broadly construed so as to not limit the scope of regulated services. However, based on our review of the comments and our determination, *infra*, that enhanced services should not be subject to regulation, we conclude that the parameters of a basic service should be dictated by the purposes of the Act and the statutory scheme set forth in Title II for the regulation of common carrier communications services.

93. A basic transmission service is one that is limited to the common carrier offering of transmission capacity for the movement of information. In offering this capacity, a communications path is provided for the analog or digital transmission of voice, data, video, etc. information. Different types of basic services are offered by carriers depending on a) the bandwidth desired, b) the analog and/or digital capabilities of the transmission medium, c) the fidelity, distortion, or other conditioning parameters of the communications channel to achieve a specified transmission quality, and d) the amount of transmission delay acceptable to the user. Under these criteria a subscriber is afforded the transmission capacity to suit its particular communications needs.

94. Traditionally, transmission capacity has been offered for discrete services, such as telephone service. With the incorporation of digital technology into the telephone network and the inclusion of computer processing capabilities into both terminal equipment located in the customer's premises and the equipment making up a firm's "network," this is no longer the case. Telecommunications service is no longer just "plain old telephone service" to the user. A subscriber may use telephone service to transmit voice or data. Both domestic and international networks allow for voice and data use of the same communications path. Thus in providing a communications service, carriers no longer control the use to which the transmission medium is put. More and more the thrust is for carriers to provide bandwidth or data rate capacity adequate to accommodate a subscriber's communications needs, regardless of whether subscribers use it for voice, data, video, facsimile, or other forms of transmission.

95. Accordingly, we believe that a basic transmission service should be limited to the offering of transmission capacity between two or more points suitable for a user's transmission needs and subject only to the technical parameters of fidelity or distortion criteria, or other condition-

ing. Use internal to the carrier's facility of companding techniques, bandwidth compression techniques, circuit switching, message or packet switching, error control techniques, etc. that facilitate economical, reliable movement of information does not alter the nature of the basic service. In the provision of a basic transmission service, memory or storage within the network is used only to facilitate the transmission of the information from the origination to its destination, and the carrier's basic transmission network is not used as an information storage system. Thus, in a basic service, once information is given to the communication facility, its progress towards the destination is subject to only those delays caused by congestion within the network or transmission priorities given by the originator.

96. In offering a basic transmission service, therefore, a carrier essentially offers a pure transmission capability over a communications path that is virtually transparent in terms of its interaction with customer supplied information. It is clear that in defining a basic service in this manner, we are in no way restricting a carrier's ability to take advantage of advancements in technology in designing its telecommunication network. Consistent with our *Tentative Decision*, a carrier maintains its flexibility to structure its communications network such that the network efficiently functions as the basic building block upon which it (in the form of a separate subsidiary in some cases) as well as other service vendors can add computer facilities to perform myriad combinations and permutations of information processing, data processing, process control, and other enhanced services.

97. Under this scenario, the regulatory demarcation between basic and enhanced services becomes relatively clear-cut. An enhanced service is any offering over the telecommunications network which is more than a basic transmission service. In an enhanced service, for example, computer processing applications are used to act on the content, code, protocol, and other aspects of the subscriber's information. In these services additional, different, or restructured information may be provided the subscriber through various processing applications performed on the transmitted information, or other actions can be taken by either the vendor or the subscriber based on the content of the information transmitted through editing, formatting, etc. Moreover, in an enhanced service the content of the information need not be changed and may simply involve subscriber interaction with stored information. Many enhanced services feature voice or data storage and retrieval applications, such as in a "mail box" service. This is particularly applicable in time-sharing services where the computer facilities are structured in a manner such that the customer or vendor can write its own customized programs and, in effect, use the time-sharing network for a variety of electronic message service applications. Thus the kinds of enhanced store and forward services that can be offered are many and varied.

98. * * * At footnote 60 of the *Tentative Decision*, we stated that we are not foreclosing enhanced processing applications from being performed in conjunction with "voice" service. We indicated that "com-

puter processing applications such as call forwarding, speed calling, directory assistance, itemized billing, traffic management studies, voice encryption, etc., may be used in conjunction with 'voice' service." *Id.* The intent was to recognize that while POTS is a basic service, there are ancillary services directly related to its provision that do not raise questions about the fundamental communications or data processing nature of a given service. Accordingly, we are not here foreclosing telephone companies from providing to consumers optional services to facilitate their use of traditional telephone service. Any option that changes the nature of such telephone service is subject to the basic/enhanced dichotomy and their respective regulatory schemes. For example, voice storage or automatic call answering within the network would be enhanced services. Thus any tariffed optional services must not change the nature of traditional telephone service.

* * *

100. We believe that our adoption of a differentiation between basic and enhanced services best furthers the public interest because it comports with the actual development of this dynamic industry. As the market applications of computer technology increase, communications capacity has become the necessary link allowing the technology to function more efficiently and more productively. Transmission networks have benefitted from some of the productive breakthroughs which this relatively new field has made possible. As a result, the computer industry and the communications industry are becoming more and more interwoven. We believe, and the record shows, that this trend will become even more pronounced in the future. As it does, an increasing number of enhanced services will be developed to meet the need of the marketplace. Thus, the pressure on a set of administrative rules which fail to recognize the growth in operational sophistication demanded by our nation's economy will be inexorable.

101. The distinction we adopt today recognizes that development and indeed should encourage its continuation. We believe it will do so in several ways. First, it leaves undisturbed the provision of basic service, whether as a building block supporting the provision of enhanced services or by itself. Second, it allows the provider of these basic services to integrate technological advances conducive to the more efficient transmission of information through the network without the threat of a sudden, fundamental change in the regulatory treatment of that service or firm. Third, it draws a clear and, we believe, sustainable line between basic and enhanced services upon which business entities can rely in making investment and marketing decisions. Fourth, in conjunction with our decision on the regulatory scheme applicable to such services, it removes the threat of regulation from markets which were unheard of in 1934 and bear none of the important characteristics justifying the imposition of economic regulation by an administrative agency.

Enhanced Services: Communications/Data Processing Classification

* * *

103. With the advent of distributed processing, we recognized the need for clearer delineations in order to minimize uncertainties for those making business decisions related to the provision of new and innovative enhanced services. We noted the need for a revised definitional structure to address this environment, rather than attempting to artificially construe the present [definitions adopted in *Computer I*] with the prospect of ambiguity and uncertainty. The existing [distinction drawn in *Computer I*] is inadequate primarily because it was formulated at a time when processing capabilities were limited to large-scale central computers; its inherent deficiencies rest with the fact that it thus does not take into account the type of services marketed in today's environment of distributed processing.

104. We proposed a new definitional structure as a means of classifying enhanced services as either regulated communications or unregulated data processing services. Attention was focused on enhanced services because it is at this level that new and innovative computer services are offered and uncertainty exists as to the communications or data processing nature. The definitional scheme would affect both communications common carriers and unregulated vendors of computer processing services. We noted that, as a practical matter, when Commission findings are made that certain computer services are or are not a communications offering, a guide is provided for service vendors as to what service may be offered without coming under our Title II regulatory umbrella. It is not surprising, therefore, that the definitional scheme advanced was the subject of substantial comment.

* * *

106. While there is some agreement among the parties as to the appropriateness of distinguishing between basic and enhanced services, there is no consensus that adoption of the proposed definitional scheme for distinguishing the communications/data processing nature of enhanced services would be in the public interest. Without exception, every element of the definitional structure we proposed was subject to criticism by one party or another, and various changes were suggested for rewording the definition of such terms as "computer processing," "data processing," "data processing service," and "hybrid data processing." Carriers argued that certain definitions should be altered or expanded to make clear that various computer services were communications services; unregulated service vendors found certain definitions too broad and argued that their adoption would result in regulation of data processing services.

107. After three attempts to delineate a distinction between communications and data processing services and failing to arrive at any satisfactory demarcation point, we conclude that further attempts to so distinguish enhanced services would be ultimately futile, inconsistent with our statutory mandate and contrary to the public interest. In coming to this conclusion we are convinced that pursuing such a course of action would not accomplish the objectives of this proceeding, i.e., "to

(a) foster a regulatory environment conducive to the stimulation of economic activity in the regulated communications sector with respect to the provision of new and innovative communications-related offerings; and (b) enable the communications user to optimize his use of common carrier communication facilities and services by taking advantage of the ever increasing market applications of computer processing technology." *Tentative Decision*, at para. 59. It is apparent that, over the long run, any attempt to distinguish enhanced services will not result in regulatory certainty. At most, reliance on a definitional approach which uses a primary purpose standard is a stop-gap measure, which—even assuming we were able to define the services accurately—would only reflect the differences in these services as they are configured with today's technology. In a market as vibrant as enhanced services, however, this distinction may miss important new developments. Thus, the need for *ad hoc* determinations would continue. As the market applications of computer technology continue to evolve we believe that attempts to distinguish enhanced services either will fail or result in an unpredictable and inconsistent scheme of regulation. This is because a definitional structure is not independent of advances in computer technology and its concomitant market applications. A certain degree of flexibility must be maintained to accommodate these advances. To the extent flexibility is incorporated into the definitions, there is a corresponding degree of uncertainty. Thus the boundary line differentiating enhanced communications and data processing services can vacillate, and confidence in decisions made based on that distinction would be diminished.

108. In addition to the fact that the record in this proceeding does not support the conclusion that greater regulatory certainty would result by adopting the proposed definitional structure, there are other factors which militate against classifying enhanced services for regulatory purposes. Such a regulatory scheme would most likely result in the direct or indirect expansion of regulation over currently unregulated vendors of computer services and deprive consumers of increased opportunities to have services tailored to their individual needs.

* * *

Regulatory Scheme

114. Having concluded that there should be no regulatory distinction between enhanced services, we are left with two categories of services—basic and enhanced. The common carrier offering of basic transmission services are regulated under Title II of the Act. This proceeding does not address the nature and degree of regulation exercised over providers of basic services. Insofar as enhanced services are concerned, there are two options-subject all enhanced services to regulation, or refrain from regulating them *in toto*. We believe that, consistent with our overall statutory mandate, enhanced services should not be regulated under the Act.

115. We find the public interest benefits inherent in distinguishing basic and enhanced services and regulating only the former far outweigh any regulatory scheme that attempts to regulate some enhanced services and not others. Significant public interest benefits accrue to the Commission, carriers and other service providers, and consumers under this regulatory structure. Moreover, we are convinced that such a regulatory scheme offers the greatest potential for efficient utilization and full exploitation of the interstate telecommunications network. The basis for such conviction becomes apparent when the advantages of this structure are compared to the existing regulatory environment or that proposed in the *Tentative Decision*.

116. From the perspective of the regulator, a major benefit in not classifying services within the enhanced category is that the scope of Commission regulation is focused on those services which are clearly within the contemplation of the Communications Act and which serve as the foundation for all enhanced services. Moreover, the extent of our regulatory authority is not automatically expanded with advances in technology and the types of enhanced services that can be offered. Semantic distinctions are avoided as to whether a given service is data processing, information processing, process control, communications processing, or some other category. As such, the potential for the development of an inconsistent regulatory scheme to accommodate these services is eliminated; all enhanced services are accorded the same regulatory treatment. To the extent uncertainty creates a regulatory barrier to entry, that barrier is also removed. With the nonregulation of all enhanced services, FCC regulations will not directly or indirectly inhibit the offering of these services, nor will our administrative processes be interjected between technology and its marketplace applications. This structure enables us to direct our attention to the regulation of basic services and to assuring nondiscriminatory access to common carrier telecommunications facilities by all providers of enhanced services.

117. Service vendors also benefit under this structure. Providers of enhanced services are afforded tremendous flexibility because there is no restriction on the types of services they may provide, except those imposed by the demands of their customers. The boundary between basic and enhanced services raises no such barrier since we believe we have identified a common necessary element in our definition of basic services. The trend in technology is toward new and innovative enhancements that build upon basic services. For computer vendors and entrepreneurs the momentum is away from basic communications services, rather than toward it. As a result, the types of enhanced services they may provide is limited only by their entrepreneurial ingenuity and competitive market constraints. Services need not be artificially structured or limited so as to avoid transgressing a regulatory boundary.

118. The benefit to consumers is that services which depend on the electronic movement of information can be custom-tailored to individual subscriber needs. Moreover, information systems can be programmed so that users dictate the nature and extent of computer processing applica-

tions to be performed on any given amount of information. As greater flexibility is offered consumers to tailor their services, a broader spectrum of the marketplace can be expected to take advantage of information processing services. To the extent regulatory barriers to entry are removed and restrictions on services are lifted there is a corresponding potential for greater utilization of the telecommunications network through greater access to new and innovative service by a larger segment of the populace. Finally, this structure creates the proper economic incentives for vendors to segregate their services such that consumers need pay only for those services necessary for their own information processing requirements.

* * *

130. We appreciate there can be disagreement as to the line we have drawn between basic and enhanced services. Plausible arguments can be tendered for drawing it elsewhere. At the margin, some enhanced services are not dramatically dissimilar from basic services or dramatically different from communications as defined in *Computer Inquiry I.* But any attempt to draw the line at this margin potentially could subject both the enhanced services providers and us to the prospect of literally hundreds of adjudications over the status of individual service offerings. We have noted the danger that such proceedings could lead to unpredictable or inconsistent regulatory definitions. Such proceedings also could consume a very significant proportion of the resources of this agency. The requirement to devote significant resources to try to make individual service distinctions would necessarily reduce the resources available for regulating basic services and ensuring non-discriminatory access to common carrier telecommunications facilities.

131. We have tried to draw the line in a manner which distinguishes wholly traditional common carrier activities, regulable under Title II of the Act, from historically and functionally competitive activities not congruent with the Act's traditional forms. We believe that the Communications Act and the jurisprudence which has grown up around it make it plain that Congress intended that substance not form govern the treatment of services within the Act's reach. We have acted upon the belief by applying traditional Title II regulatory mechanisms to basic services and applying no direct regulatory mechanism for enhanced services.

132. Finally, the nature of enhanced services and their market underscores the reasonableness of our decision. As indicated, we do not believe these are communications common carrier services within the meaning of Title II. We acknowledge, of course, the existence of a communications component. And we recognize that some enhanced services may do some of the same things that regulated communications services did in the past. On the other side, however, is the substantial data processing component in all these services. We never have imposed a scheme of regulation over data processing. Any agency regulatory decision in this area must assess the merits-as we do in this order-of

extending regulation to an activity simply because a part of it is subject to the agency's jurisdiction where such regulation would not be necessary to protect or promote some overall statutory purpose. * * *

Authority to Not Regulate? One objection raised to the Second Computer Inquiry ("*Computer II*") was that, because enhanced services involve transmission, the FCC was therefore *required* to regulate them under the common carriage principles of Title II of the Communications Act. The FCC declined, using the converse of the argument it had invoked in order to justify its regulation of cable television under Title I:

> Because enhanced service was not explicitly contemplated in the Communications Act of 1934, there is no more a requirement to confront it with a specific traditional regulatory mechanism than there was, for example, in the case of cable television, which has formal elements of common carriage and broadcast television, or of specialized mobile radio services, which bears many formal similarities to radio common carriage. Precedent teaches that the Act is not so intractable as to require us to routinely bring new services within the provision of our Title II and III jurisdiction even though they may involve a component that is within our subject matter jurisdiction.

Computer II at para. 121. The FCC used an even stronger form of the argument with regard to its deregulation of customer premises equipment, which, unlike enhanced services, the FCC previously *had* regulated. The FCC suggested that, even though the it had regulated CPE for decades, it had never said that its regulation was premised on Title II. Rather, the FCC concluded, its regulation of CPE had in fact been discretionary regulation under Title I, and therefore the decision to *de*regulate CPE was similarly discretionary. *Id.* at paras. 172–73. Which form of loose use of Title I—its use to expand regulation or its use to contract it—is more troubling? After *Computer II*, is there any point to the distinction between mandatory regulation under Title II or discretionary regulation under Title I?

Because All Good Things Come in Threes. After the breakup of AT&T—on which more below—the *Computer II* rules were applied to the newly separated Bell Operating Companies ("BOCs") as well as AT&T. The separate subsidiary requirement proved to be a costly burden for provision of CPE and enhanced services, which prompted the FCC to seek a substitute in the form of what it called "non-structural safeguards." In 1986, the FCC issued the *Computer III* order (see *In the Matters of: Amendment of Sections 64.702 of the Commission's Rules and Regulations*, 104 F.C.C.2d 958 (1986) ("*Computer III*")) adopting a system of safeguards designed to serve the same purposes of the separate subsidiary requirement but with less cost to the dominant carriers—which at the time comprised just AT&T and the BOCs. *Computer III* allowed them to provide *integrated* enhanced services and CPE (that is, services and equipment bundled with basic telecom services) so long as they allowed competing providers of enhanced services access to their network facilities on terms equal to those enjoyed by AT&T and the BOCs themselves. Initially the scheme was to be deployed in two stages. In the first stage a plan of "comparably efficient interconnection" ("CEI") was to be adopted for each type of service offered. In the second stage the CEI plan was to be supplanted by a plan of "open network architecture" ("ONA") that called for a more comprehensive system of unbundled, leased access to basic network facilities (e.g., transport and switching facilities). The long run objective under ONA was for competing providers of enhanced services to be able to lease the "basic service elements" ("BSEs") of the BOC. Thus, if the BOC wanted to provide enhanced services or customer premises equipment, it would have to provide access to the BSE underlying that enhanced service on terms comparable to that enjoyed by the BOC itself.

The *Computer III* rules were first overturned by the court of appeals in 1990, then modified, then overturned again in 1994. The specific grounds for each reversal are different, but in very general terms the court on both occasions found that the Commission had failed to show that the different iterations of rules answered the concerns that had prompted the original structural separation requirement. See *California v. FCC*, 905 F.2d 1217 (9th Cir. 1990); *California v. FCC*, 39 F.3d 919 (9th Cir. 1994). In 1995 the Commission began a new rulemaking to consider how to correct those shortcomings; more than a dozen years later the docket is still open! In the meantime the same rules remain in effect; after the 1994 decision the FCC granted the BOCs a continuing waiver of the *Computer II* requirements conditional on their compliance with CEI and any ONA plans that had been approved by it. (AT&T at this point was no longer a dominant carrier, but would become one again after its acquisition by SBC in 2005.) As a practical matter the *Computer III* rules probably no longer matter since their function has been largely filled by a new scheme of unbundled access introduced in 1996—the subject of Chapter 8.[11] However, the *Computer III* rules are historically noteworthy as a prototype for the 1996 unbundled access regime.

3. Breaking into Long Distance

Carterfone introduced competition at the ends of the network; the *Computer Inquiries* decreed that new uses of the network would similarly be subject to competition. In 1969, the FCC opened the door to competition in AT&T's core business of carriage itself. The way had been paved for the *MCI* decision a decade earlier. In 1959 the FCC first opened up the possibility of privately supplied microwave transmission facilities. See *Allocation of Frequencies in the Bands Above 890 MHz*, 27 F.C.C. 359 (1959). As in *Carterfone*, the logic of allowing users to do for

11. Interestingly, while the FCC has declined to eliminate the *Computer III* rules, it did recently rule that they would not be applied to one very important type of enhanced services, the provision of broadband Internet service by the BOCs. See Appropriate Framework for Broadband Access to the Internet over Wireline Facilities, 20 FCC Rcd. 14853 (2005), affirmed, 507 F.3d 205 (3d Cir. 2007).

themselves what previously only AT&T could do for them would lead to competitive supply of telephone services. In this instance, that move was first taken by an application in 1963 by Microwave Communications, Inc. (later known as "MCI") to provide private line services between Chicago and St. Louis. After years of delay, the application was approved in the following decision granting a license for a single long distance trunk line between Chicago and St. Louis for select business customers. Note that MCI was not proposing to displace the large telcos at all because they were not proposing to offer their customers a complete connection. One might have thought that the limited nature of the service would ameliorate AT&T's concerns about facing competition, but the limits themselves had exactly the opposite effect.

IN RE APPLICATIONS OF MICROWAVE COMMUNICATIONS, INC.

Federal Communications Commission, 1969.
18 F.C.C.2d 953.

COMMISSIONER BARTLEY for THE COMMISSION:

1. This proceeding involves applications filed by Microwave Communications, Inc. (MCI), for construction permits for new facilities in the Domestic Public Point-to-Point Radio Service at Chicago, Ill., St. Louis, Mo., and nine intermediate points. MCI proposes to offer its subscribers a limited common carrier microwave radio service, designed to meet the interoffice and interplant communications needs of small businesses. Its subscribers would be able to lease microwave channels in varying bandwidths in increments of 2 kc. for either the entire length of its system or any segment thereof. For broadband users, channels may be leased in increments of 48,250, and 1,000 kc. MCI, however, does not plan to provide its subscribers with a complete microwave service. The proposed service would be limited to transmissions between MCI's microwave sites, making it incumbent upon each subscriber to supply his own communications link between MCI's sites and his place of business (loop service).

2. MCI contends that it will offer its subscribers substantially lower rates than those charged for similar services by the established carriers and that subscribers with less than full-time communication needs will be able to achieve additional savings through the channel sharing and half-time use provisions of its proposed tariff. Up to five subscribers will be permitted to share each channel on a party-line basis with a pro-rata reduction in rates. MCI will lease channels for half-time use between 6 a.m. and 6 p.m. with a 25-percent reduction in rates; and between 6 p.m. and 6 a.m. it proposes to combine the channels leased for half-time use into broadband channels of 48, 250, or 1,000 kc. for high-speed data transmission. MCI further asserts that its proposed tariff contains fewer restrictions than those of the existing common carriers, so that greater flexibility of use will be possible, particularly with respect

to channel bandwidth, splitting channels for voice and data transmissions, and in the attachment of customer equipment.

* * *

Need for MCI's Proposals

13. Relying upon a market survey conducted by the Spindletop Research Center of Lexington, Ky., and upon the testimony of witnesses produced at the hearing by MCI, the examiner found that there is a market for microwave service of acceptable quality at lower rates than offered by the existing carriers, that MCI is offering such a service, and he concluded that a need exists for the service proposed by MCI. The carriers challenge these findings and the conclusions of need based thereon upon a number of grounds, including, inter alia, claims that rates will not be lower, that the service proposed is not of acceptable quality or reliability, and that no service not previously available is being offered.

* * *

15. * * * [T]he existing carriers do not offer a 2-kc. voice channel and MCI will; so that a subscriber may achieve a substantial saving in his communications costs by utilizing MCI's services. Further savings may be effected by the sharing and part-time provision of MCI's proposal. MCI will permit up to five subscribers to share one channel with a pro-rata reduction in costs; and for those subscribers with less than full-time needs, use from 6 a.m. to 6 p.m. is offered at a 25-percent reduction in rate. No comparable offerings are made by the existing common carriers. Thus, a grant of the applications under consideration will make microwave service available to potential users who have no need for and cannot afford the full-time, nonsharing, and more sophisticated services to which they are limited under present tariffs.

16. Bell asserts that it had previously marketed 2-kc. voice channels but was forced to abandon the offering because of customer dissatisfaction. Utilizing a 2-kc. voice channel, MCI cannot be expected to match the quality of voice communications offered by Bell with its 4-kc. channels; but the record establishes that MCI's 2-kc. channel will provide an acceptable voice communications service. As a result, MCI will attract users with less stringent requirements as to quality but who are in need of an economic communications service. Subscribers for whom quality of service rather than cost is the primary consideration will continue to utilize existing services rather than those of MCI.

17. Additional advantages to MCI's subscribers are afforded by the flexibility of its system. In contrast to the protesting carriers which will lease no less than a nominal 4-kc. channel for voice use, MCI will lease and subdivide its channel into bandwidths in increments of 2 kc. and permit multiple terminations of channels. Furthermore, MCI imposes fewer restrictions on the nature of the subscribers' terminal equipment and on the use of its channels. The absence of restrictions gives each MCI subscriber the same flexibility to vary its stations' capability and

use as if it were its own private system. Thus, each subscriber may adapt the system to its particular needs and equipment, lease shelter and tower space from MCI, and use the MCI trunk system for the carriage of voice, facsimile, and high speed or lower speed data transmissions, or a combination thereof in a manner which best suits its business requirements. No comparable degree of flexibility is offered by the existing carriers. Thus, while no new technology is involved in MCI's proposal, it does present a concept of common carrier microwave offerings which differs from those of the established carriers. Therefore in determining the question of need, the controlling consideration is not whether existing communications services are being utilized by potential subscribers of MCI, but whether the proposed operation would better meet the particular needs of potential subscribers. We believe that MCI's offering would enable such subscribers to obtain a type of service not presently available and would tend to increase the efficiency of operation of the subscribers' businesses.

* * *

21. The carriers argue that even if lower rates for MCI communications services have been shown, that factor may not properly be considered in resolving the issue of need. They assert that they are required by the Commission to serve both high-density high-profit and low-density low-profit areas and in order to maintain rates which are relatively uniform, all rates are based on a cost averaging principle. Claiming that MCI is "cream skimming," i.e., proposing to operate solely on high density routes where lower fixed costs per channel permit lower rates with higher profits, the carriers state that in order to compete with MCI they will be forced to abandon their cost averaging policies with a resultant increase in rates for subscribers on lightly used routes.

22. MCI is offering a service intended primarily for interplant and interoffice communications with unique and specialized characteristics. In these circumstances we cannot perceive how a grant of the authorizations requested would pose any serious threat to the established carriers' price averaging policies. Lower rates for the service offered is not the sole basis for our determination that MCI has demonstrated a need for the proposed facilities, but the flexibility available to subscribers, and the sharing and the part-time features of the proposal have been considered to be significant factors as well. The case of *WADS*, 35 F.C.C. 149 (1963), cited by Bell is therefore inapposite. Here the potential demand for the new service is not generated solely by reason of lower rates for a like service but because there is a "need for service which, if not met, would result in a serious deficiency in the communication services available to the public" (35 F.C.C. at 155). It may be, as the telephone companies and Western Union argue, that some business will be diverted from the existing carriers upon the grant of MCI's applications, but that fact provides no sufficient basis for depriving a segment of the public of the benefits of a new and different service.

23. Moreover, if we were to follow the carriers' reasoning and specify as a prerequisite to the establishment of a new common carrier service that it be so widespread as to permit cost averaging, we would in effect restrict the entry of new licensees into the common carrier field to a few large companies which are capable of serving the entire Nation. Such an approach is both unrealistic and inconsistent with the public interest. Innovations in the types and character of communications services offered or economies in operation which could not at once be instituted on a nationwide basis would be precluded from ever being introduced. In the circumstances of this case, we find the cream skimming argument to be without merit.

* * *

Reliability of Service

27. While some of MCI's potential subscribers indicated a willingness to compromise on reliability of service in order to obtain the benefits of lower rates, a common carrier communications system will be of little value if it fails to provide its customers with a substantial degree of reliability in the transmission of messages. The carriers argue that MCI will be unable to supply a reliable communications service since its physical plant and facilities, system maintenance, and signal beam clearance are inadequate.

* * *

29. The carriers further argue that MCI's radio equipment will be inadequately housed in unheated metal toolsheds, that its emergency power source (8-hour batteries) will not suffice in the event of a power failure, and that the provisions for service and maintenance are deficient. We recognize that, in order to economize, MCI does not propose to use material and equipment equal in quality to that of the major carriers, but this fact, in and of itself, is not a matter of critical importance. Of course, economy cannot be used as an excuse to justify the use of inferior materials or the elimination of essential safeguards which may result in a degraded service and substantial outages; but, if less expensive equipment will nevertheless provide a competent, reliable, and acceptable common carrier service, its proposed use does not require a denial of the requested authorizations.

30. Despite the strong protests of the existing carriers we are not persuaded that MCI's proposed equipment is technically deficient in any material respect. The sheds to be used for housing the equipment are waterproof and will afford sufficient protection against adverse weather for the microwave transmitting and receiving equipment which has an operational range from -30 degree to 50 degree C. While working conditions in the sheds in case of a breakdown would not be of the best, there is nothing in the record to justify a finding that they are not usable. It may be, as the carriers contend, that reliance upon generators instead of batteries is preferable. Nevertheless, it appears, that batteries will keep the system operational during periods of all but exceptionally

extended power outages; and in that event the batteries will suffice until another power source is made available. We also find that MCI's arrangements for maintenance are adequate. By reason of the relatively limited size of its system, MCI will not employ a fulltime maintenance staff and it would be uneconomical to do so. In lieu thereof, MCI has contracted with two firms, both of which are experienced in installing and maintaining private microwave systems, to periodically inspect the microwave facilities and to perform all necessary repair and maintenance work. Each microwave relay site will be equipped with a fault alarm connected to a 24-hour answering service which, in turn, will contact the appropriate maintenance company. These companies operate on a 24-hour basis and no tower site is located more than 106 miles from one of them. On the basis of this showing, we are satisfied that the steps proposed to be taken by MCI for maintenance and repair of its equipment should keep to a minimum any interruption in service resulting from equipment or power failure.

31. Western Union's criticism that the proposed system is deficient in that no provision is made for alternate routing in the event of damage or outage at any point on the system must be rejected as without merit. The alternate routes maintained by the major carriers serve also as primary routes for other cities and thus have a dual purpose. However, were MCI to construct an alternate route it would lie fallow except during periods of extended outages and such limited use would constitute a waste of frequencies which would not be in the public interest. MCI has available substitute towers and other equipment. It is prepared in case of outages to make repairs expeditiously and, with the possible exception of a major catastrophe, to resume operations with a minimum of delay.

* * *

The Feasibility of Loop Service

35. The testimony of MCI's public witnesses and the findings of the Spindletop survey show that, in general, MCI's potential subscribers have no interest in providing their own communications link between their facilities and MCI's transmitter sites. Therefore, MCI's ability to market its service will be dependent on the ability of its subscribers to secure loop service from the other common carriers serving the service area.

36. We are not unmindful of the fact that the carriers maintain that loop service is not technically feasible and that there is no provision for such service in their tariffs. However, insufficient evidence is contained in this record to support a conclusion that the proposed interconnection is not feasible, and we are not disposed to deny MCI's applications on the basis of the unsubstantiated allegations which have been advanced herein by the telephone companies and Western Union. What seems a more likely obstacle to interconnection is, as the hearing examiner indicated, the "carriers' intransigence, manifested in this case

* * *." In these circumstances, the carriers are not in a position to argue that consideration of the interconnection question is premature. Since they have indicated that they will not voluntarily provide loop service we shall retain jurisdiction of this proceeding in order to enable MCI to obtain from the Commission a prompt determination on the matter of interconnection. Thus, at such time as MCI has customers and the facts and details of the customers' requirements are known, MCI may come directly to the Commission with a request for an order of interconnection. We have already concluded that a grant of MCI's proposal is in the public interest. We likewise conclude that, absent a significant showing that interconnection is not technically feasible, the issuance of an order requiring the existing carriers to provide loop service is in the public interest.

Summary

37. This is a very close case and one which presents exceptionally difficult questions.... We have found, based on the weight of the evidence, that there is a substantial likelihood that the communications of its subscribers will arrive promptly, in accurate form, and without extended interruptions due to failures in the system. We wish to make clear, therefore, that the findings and conclusions reached herein apply only to the frequencies specified, and for the areas described, in the applications now pending before us. Should MCI seek to obtain additional frequencies or to extend its microwave service to new areas, our action on its application will be based on a close scrutiny of its operations, the rules then governing the grant of applications for common carrier microwave frequencies and all other applicable policy considerations. Likewise, in connection with an application for renewal of license, we may deny the application if circumstances so warrant or grant renewal on such conditions as we deem essential to insure that MCI's subscribers receive a reliable transmission service of acceptable quality. However, it would be inconsistent with the public interest to deny MCI's applications and thus deprive the applicant of an opportunity to demonstrate that its proposed microwave facilities will bring to its subscribers the substantial benefits which it predicts and which we have found to be supported by the evidence in this proceeding. We conclude, on the basis of the record as a whole, that the public interest will be served by a grant of MCI's application.

Dissenting Statement of Chairman Rosel H. Hyde

* * *

The decision would authorize the use of a microwave frequency in one of the most critical bands for the benefit of at most 204 private-line customers, according to the applicant's own marketing consultants. The same frequency could ordinarily be used to derive thousands of circuits, predominantly used for the benefit of the ordinary long distance message toll user. There has been no showing here of "* * * reasonable expectation that competition may have some beneficial effect".

Why does the majority condone this obviously grossly inefficient use of the spectrum. Because, they say, of the low cost and flexibility of the facilities proposed by applicants. It should be noted that the socalled flexibility cited by the majority is here, as it was in the TEL PAK case, a mere euphemism connoting lower rates. But how is it that applicant is able to propose lower rates than the existing common carriers for private-line service? For no other reason than that it is proposing a typical "cream-skimming" operation. Thus, it has selected a major route, Chicago to St. Louis, with heavy traffic density characteristics and the concomitant lower unit costs. The existing common carriers, on the other hand have been encouraged by the Commission, primarily for social reasons, to base their rates both for message toll and private-line services on nationwide average costs. Thus the small users in the hinterlands is afforded the same rates as the large users in the major cities. The evidence in this record tends to show, and there is no basis in our experience to believe otherwise, that AT&T and Western Union could offer lower rates for private-line service between Chicago and St. Louis than those proposed by MCI, were they to base such rates on their costs for that route alone.

The chances are, and the record so indicates, that AT&T and Western Union will be constrained to lower their private-line rates to meet the competition of MCI. This, however, means that other users, either the small private-line users who are not so fortunate as to live in large cities, or message toll users, or both, will have to make up the difference if total revenue requirements are to be met. This is in addition to the higher costs which are bound to fall on all communications users by virtue of the inefficient use of the frequency at stake.

The effect of the majority decision is to destroy the principle of nationwide average ratemaking. Perhaps, as some economists have urged, this is a desirable result. But it certainly should not be accomplished through the vehicle of a grant of a radio authorization which represents a wasteful use of our scarce spectrum space. This entire case is a classic example of an inefficient, uneconomic misallocation of resources.

Squeezing Water from a Stone. What's the basis for viewing MCI's entry as increasing competition? Long distance networks may be more amenable to competition than local ones, since there may be enough demand to support more than one line between cities, and once there is enough demand for more than one line, there is room for more than one provider. But, as the FCC points out, MCI did not intend to provide communications in a more efficient way—they were using old technology to provide established services. Rather, MCI's competitive stance seemed to be based on their willingness to provide 2-Kc voice channels instead of the higher-quality 4-Kc channels, more flexible arrangements (in terms of multiplexing and time-sensitive pricing), and their lower reliability standards (using battery backup instead of generators and not providing 24-hour on-site repair support). The former two changes, matters of contract not telecommunications, could easily be provided by AT&T itself, and once they did, AT&T's enormous relative economies of scale would seem to doom MCI's efforts. As for the third difference, is the tradeoff between lower rates and lower reliability a good thing? Given the economics of communications networks, what's the point of allowing MCI to enter the market unless they are either going to introduce some change that allows them to either provide something that AT&T cannot provide or to provide similar service at lower rates? Do consumers really get any benefit by having MCI repackage the long distance component of carriage without adding any additional value?

"Cream skimming," Cross-Subsidization, and the Road to the Break-up. A major concern in the case is the possibility that MCI was "cream skimming." The theory is that some customers were much more profitable to serve than others. Users in densely populated areas are cheaper to serve than those in rural areas, but rate regulation required charging both customers the same amount. MCI would be subject to common carriage obligations, but if they could arrange their basket of services such that they were unattractive for low-profit customers, they could "skim" the high-profit customers away.

But cream skimming is predicated on rate regulation that does not accurately reflect the cost of providing service. Telephone rates were intentionally designed not to reflect the cost of service in a number of ways so that users of one service would subsidize users of another service. Thus, rate averaging subsidized high-cost rural users by charging to low-cost urban customers the same rates. Business customers were charged higher rates than similarly situated residential customers on a theory of raw price discrimination: businesses were willing to pay more for phone service than residential customers. Similarly, long distance service were frequently regulated at rates that subsidized local service. According to the dissent, by serving only business, long distance uses, MCI was doing no more than profiting by thwarting the cross-subsidization goals inherent in telecommunications regulation. As described below, AT&T was limited by the FCC in its ability to lower long distance rates to compete with the new entrants. AT&T fought back in other ways, leading to the antitrust action that eventually broke up its telephone monopoly.

The Road to Competition in Switched Services After MCI. Following its decision in 1969, the Commission conducted a general rulemaking proceeding on the question of competition in private line services (i.e., non-switched services) generally. In 1971, the FCC authorized competitive private line services in *Specialized Common Carrier Services*, 29 F.C.C.2d 870 (1971), *aff'd* 513 F.2d 1142 (9th Cir. 1975), a decision that was to prompt sharp controversy over the intended scope of competition in interstate long distance service. The issue of intent arose specifically in connection with whether the specialized carriers would have access on the same terms as other common carriers to AT&T's foreign exchange

("FX") and common control switching arrangement ("CCSA") services.[12] In 1974 the FCC ordered access, over Bell's vigorous opposition. AT&T's resistance to providing access to these services was to be a key element in the Justice Department's antitrust case against AT&T discussed below.[13] At the time of this authorization, neither AT&T nor the FCC appreciated that a little adroit packaging of these services would allow MCI to provide a basic switched service in direct competition with AT&T's MTS and WATS services. When the FCC learned (from AT&T) that this is what access to FX and CCSA produced, it ruled that MCI's new service (called "Execunet") was unlawful since competition in basic switched service was not part of the "original intent" of its 1971 decision. The court of appeals reversed in two successive decisions, holding that the FCC had failed to rationalize the distinction between private line and switched service. *MCI Telecommunications Corp. v. FCC*, 561 F.2d 365 (D.C. Cir. 1977); *MCI Telecommunications Corp. v. FCC*, 580 F.2d 590 (D.C. Cir. 1978). This in turn prompted a new rulemaking proceeding to consider the scope of competition in AT&T's switched service markets, which led in 1980 to open competition in switched services, and resale of AT&T's services. See *MTS and WATS Market Structure*, 81 F.C.C.2d 177 (1980); *Resale and Shared Use*, 83 F.C.C.2d 167 (1980). At this point, the authorization of competition in interstate long distance service networks, combined with the *Computer II* decisions deregulating interstate enhanced services and CPE, signaled a major curtailment of AT&T's dominance of telecommunications. The next step in that same direction came from another source: as it had twice before, the Justice Department would enter the picture with an antitrust claim.

D. ANTITRUST AND THE MODIFICATION OF FINAL JUDGMENT

In 1974 the Department of Justice filed a wide-ranging antitrust action against AT&T alleging a series of antitrust violations against the firm. The thrust of the case was that AT&T was guilty of monopolization under Section 2 of the Sherman Act. Under Section 2 a firm with monopoly power (which is usually defined as the existence of market power sufficient to set prices or exclude competitors) is guilty of *monopolization* when it engages in anticompetitive misconduct to acquire or

12. FX permits a customer to make or receive local calls through a distant switching center. It has been described as the equivalent of a long extension cord in the form of a dedicated line between the customer's location and a telephone company switching system in the distant location (the foreign exchange). CCSA is, essentially, the equivalent of a miniature long distance network designed for a single, large customer. AT&T had refused to allow MCI to use these services and had also imposed restrictions on the ability of MCI to interconnect with its local network. Without access to these arrangements MCI's initial plan of providing a cheaper long distance link proved to be not a viable business plan.

13. It was also a key element in a private antitrust action against AT&T by MCI, which produced a treble damage recovery of $1.8 billion in 1981—just before the settlement of the government's case. See MCI Communications Corp. v. AT&T, 708 F.2d 1081 (7th Cir. 1983) (affirming lower court decision).

maintain that monopoly power. This very general formulation is invariably translated to require conduct that is designed to exclude rivals and has no justification that promotes consumer welfare. AT&T's alleged misconduct was its use of the legal monopoly it enjoyed in local service markets to preserve its monopolies in both interstate long distance service (service between cities or calling areas) and equipment markets that the FCC had been gradually opening up to competition. After a drawn-out fight, AT&T capitulated at the final hour, giving in to all of DoJ's demands. The result was divestiture, a separation of AT&T's long distance business from its local telephone businesses, which were held in the form of several regional operating companies. For a detailed history of the case, the events leading up to it and the immediate aftermath of the reorganization see Peter Temin & Louis Galabos, *The Fall of the Bell System* (1987).

UNITED STATES v. AMERICAN TEL. AND TEL. CO.

United States District Court, District of Columbia, 1982.
552 F. Supp. 131, *aff'd*, 460 U.S. 1001 (1983).

HAROLD H. GREENE, DISTRICT JUDGE.

These actions are before the Court for a determination whether a consent decree proposed by the parties is in the "public interest" and should therefore be entered as the Court's judgment. * * *

IV

The Divestiture

A key feature of the proposed decree is the divestiture of the Operating Companies from the remainder of AT&T. In order to determine whether that divestiture is in the public interest, the Court must decide first whether it is a remedy that is likely to eliminate anticompetitive conditions within the telecommunications industry. In addition, the Court must assess the efficacy of alternative remedies and it must weigh the effect of the divestiture on the public interest generally, particularly on the level of charges for local telephone service.

A. Conditions Necessitating Antitrust Relief

1. Evidence of Anticompetitive Actions by AT&T

In its complaint and in documents filed thereafter (i.e., the several Statements of Contentions and Proof), the government asserted that AT&T monopolized the intercity telecommunications market and the telecommunications market and the telecommunications product market in a variety of ways in violation of the Sherman Act.

The evidence that was produced during the AT&T trial indicates that, at least with respect to several of the government's claims, this charge may be well taken. It would be inappropriate for the Court at this juncture to draw definitive conclusions with regard either to the sufficiency of the evidence to sustain a finding of liability or to the validity of

AT&T's various legal and factual defenses. The Court is not called upon, in this public interest proceeding, to render a final judgment on this case; indeed, not all the evidence that may bear on the issues has yet been adduced. It is not improper, however, for the Court to consider whether the state of proof at trial was such as to sustain this divestiture as being in the public interest.

In its intercity case, the government alleged that AT&T used its control over its local monopoly to preclude competition in the intercity market. The government proved inter alia that after 1968 AT&T included a "customer premises" provision in its interconnection tariff which deterred potential competitors from entering that market; that it refused to provide FX and CCSA services to specialized common carriers and domestic satellite carriers until 1974 when the FCC specifically ordered it to do so; and that it attempted to prevent competitors from offering metered long distance service that would compete with AT&T's own regular long distance service.

AT&T's basic rationale for these policies was that it was attempting to prevent competitors from "creamskimming." As viewed by AT&T, it would have been able successfully to combat creamskimming if it had priced each of its routes on the basis of the costs for operating that route. However, it concluded that the FCC had rejected this approach when it endorsed national rate averaging in the interest of promoting the goal of universal service. Accordingly, AT&T argued that, since rate averaging is inconsistent with competition, and since the basic rate averaging policy had been required by the FCC as being in the public interest, it was acting reasonably under the Communications Act in preventing competition as best and as long as it could.

What this line of reasoning fails to consider is that, at least by the mid-1970s, the FCC had clearly begun to promote competition in telecommunications. The government contended during the trial—correctly, in the Court's view—that AT&T had an obligation to follow the more recent FCC policy rather than the Commission's previous policies which may have suited it better, particularly since there was never a direct FCC rule against de-averaging. Moreover, even if, because of the lack of definite guidance from the FCC, AT&T's actions were to be regarded as reasonable under the Communications Act standards, it does not at all follow that these same actions were immunized under the standards of the Sherman Act.

What is significant about these events is that AT&T was able to adopt the policies described above in large part because of its control over the local exchange facilities. For example, it was because of its ownership and control of the local Operating Companies—whose facilities were and are needed for interconnection purposes by AT&T's competitors—that AT&T was able to prevent these competitors from offering FX and CCSA services. Similarly, AT&T was able to deter competition by manipulating prices for access to the Operating Company networks.

AT&T's control over the local Operating Companies was central also to the anticompetitive behavior alleged with respect to the second facet of the government's case, that involving customer-provided terminal equipment.

The government proved that AT&T prohibited the attachment of competitors' equipment to the network except through a protective connecting arrangement (PCA). There was evidence that some experts (including a panel of the National Academy of Sciences) believed that such a PCA was necessary if the nationwide telephone network was to be protected from a variety of harms. On the other hand, the government's evidence indicated that AT&T required PCAs for equipment that in all probability could not harm the network; that there were delays in providing PCAs; that the PCAs were over-designed and over-engineered, and, thus, over-priced; that PCAs were required for competitive equipment while identical equipment sold by AT&T did not require their use; and that PCAs could not guard against all four potential harms to the network.

Additionally, the alternative option of certification was available but never seriously pursued by Bell. Moreover, when ultimately certification was directly mandated by the FCC as a substitute for the protective connecting arrangement, the telephone network—AT&T's predictions to the contrary notwithstanding—did not cease to function in its customary fashion. Indeed, AT&T was unable during the trial to prove any actual harm to the network form the elimination of the PCAs.

In its procurement part of the case, the government alleged, and there was proof, that AT&T used its control over the local Operating Companies to force them to buy products from Western Electric even though other equipment manufacturers produced better products or products of identical quality at lower prices. Here, too, AT&T's control of the Operating Companies was central to the allegedly anticompetitive behavior.

Without making definitive findings on any or all of the issues, it is certainly clear that—to the extent that the proposed decree is offered by the government on the premise that it will destroy the basic of past anticompetitive behavior—the Court would not be justified in rejecting it as constituting a remedy for non-existent anticompetitive acts. * * *

VII

Restrictions on the Divested Operating Companies

The proposed decree limits the Operating Companies, upon their divestiture, to the business of supplying local telephone service. In addition to a general prohibition against the provision of "any product or service that is not a natural monopoly service actually regulated by tariff," there are more specific restrictions in Section II(D) which deny the Operating Companies the opportunity to engage in the following activities: (1) the provision of interexchange services; (2) the provision of information services: (3) the manufacture of telecommunications products and customer premises equipment; (4) the marketing of such equipment and (5) directory advertising, including the production of the "Yellow Pages" directories. * * *

The restrictions are based upon the assumption that the Operating Companies, were they allowed to enter the forbidden markets, would use their monopoly power in an anticompetitive manner. It is accordingly necessary for the Court first to determine whether these companies will actually have the incentive and opportunity to act anticompetitively. Second, the restrictions are, at least in one sense, directly anticompetitive because they prevent a potential competitor [the Operating Companies themselves] from entering the market. The Court must accordingly also consider the extent to which the participation of the Operating Companies would contribute to the creation of a competitive market.

In addition, the Court must assess the effect of the restrictions upon other important public policies. Many persons, including particularly the States, claim that these restrictions would have adverse consequences in that they would either undermine the financial viability of the divested Operating Companies, or produce substantial increases in the rates for local telephone service, thus eroding the statutory goal of universal telephone service for all Americans. This factor, to be sure, cannot preclude the imposition of a restriction necessary to preclude the anticompetitive activity; but to the extent that a restriction does not have a procompetitive effect, it may not be imposed if it infringes upon other important public policies.

The Court will examine the various substantive provisions in light of these general principles.

A. Interexchange Services

The proposed decree prohibits the divested Operating Companies from providing interexchange services. This restriction is clearly necessary to preserve free competition in the interexchange market.

Access to the local exchange is essential for all interexchange carriers and, as the evidence in the AT&T action has suggested, there are many ways in which the company controlling the local exchange monopoly could discriminate against competitors in the interexchange market. * * * If the Operating Companies were free to provide interexchange service in competition with the other carriers, they would have substantial incentives to subvert these equal access requirements. The complexity of the telecommunications network would make it possible for them to establish and maintain an access plan that would provide to their own interexchange service more favorable treatment than that granted to the other carriers. Such a result would perpetuate the very inequalities that the proposed decree is designed to eliminate. Finally, the Operating Companies would also have the ability to subsidize their interexchange prices with profits earned from their monopoly services. * * *

B. Information Services

The proposed decree prohibits the Operating Companies from providing information services, an umbrella description of a variety of services including electronic publishing and other enhanced uses of telecommunications. This prohibition is necessary for reasons similar to those justifying the restriction on interexchange services, as well as for additional reasons not relevant to the interexchange problem.

All information services are provided directly via the telecommunications network. The Operating Companies would therefore have the same incentives and the same ability to discriminate against competing information service providers that they would have with respect to competing interexchange carriers. Here, too, the Operating Companies could discriminate by providing more favorable access to the local network for their own information services than to the information services provided by competitors, and here, too, they would be able to subsidize the prices of their services with revenues from the local exchange monopoly. * * *

C. Manufacture of Equipment

The provision in the proposed decree which prohibits the Operating Companies from manufacturing telecommunications equipment and customer premises equipment (CPE) is also an outgrowth of the government's case in the AT&T action. * * *

There is a substantial likelihood that, should the Operating Companies be permitted to manufacture telecommunications equipment, nonaffiliated manufacturers would be disadvantaged in the sale of such equipment and the development of a competitive market would be frustrated. The Operating Companies would have an incentive to subsidize the prices of their equipment with the revenues from their monopoly services as well as to purchase their own equipment, even though it was more expensive and not of the highest quality. In that respect, the Operating Companies lack the competitive restraints that ordinarily prevent the typical vertically-integrated company from engaging in such practices: the absence of competition in the end product market—exchange telecommunications—immunizes these purchasing decisions from competitive pressures. The Operating Companies therefore would be able to pay inflated prices for poor quality equipment and to reflect these costs in their rates without suffering a diminution in revenues.

Moreover, if they were permitted to manufacture CPE, the Operating Companies would have substantial incentives to favor their own manufacturing arms by providing to them information regarding changes in network standards, thus permitting them to gain an advantage over non-affiliated manufacturers. In addition, they could subsidize the price of their equipment with revenues from the exchange monopoly. * * *

D. Marketing of Customer Premises Equipment

The proposed decree would also prohibit the Operating Companies from selling or leasing customer premises equipment. While the Department of Justice's comments and briefs tend to blur the distinction between manufacturing and marketing, in fact the restrictions on the two activities present wholly different considerations. Based upon a realistic assessment, marketing of CPE presents little potential for anticompetitive behavior by the Operating Companies. While the Operating Companies would have the theoretical ability to engage in the types of anticompetitive activities which support the prohibition on manufacturing of CPE, their incentives and their practical ability to do so would be minimal. * * *

E. Directory Advertising

Each Bell Operating Company presently publishes Yellow Pages directories for its service area. The proposed decree would bar the divested Operating Companies from all activities related to directory advertising, including the production of the so-called Yellow Pages. This restriction lacks an appropriate basis and is not in the public interest. * * *

XII

Conclusion

The proposed reorganization of the Bell System raises issues of vast complexity. Because of their importance, not only to the parties but also to the telecommunications industry and to the public, the Court has discussed the various problems in substantial detail. It is appropriate to summarize briefly the major issues and the Court's decisions which are central to the proceeding.

A. The American telecommunications industry is presently dominated by one company—AT&T. It provides local and long-distance telephone service; it manufactures and markets the equipment used by telephone subscribers as well as that used in the telecommunications network; and it controls one of the leading communications research and development facilities in the world. According to credible evidence, this integrated structure has enabled AT&T for many years to undermine the efforts of competitors seeking to enter the telecommunications market.

The key to the Bell System's power to impede competition has been its control of local telephone service. The local telephone network functions as the gateway to individual telephone subscribers. It must be used by long-distance carriers seeking to connect one caller to another. Customers will only purchase equipment which can readily be connected to the local network through the telephone outlets in their homes and offices. The enormous cost of the wires, cables, switches, and other transmission facilities which comprise that network has completely insulated it from competition. Thus, access to AT&T's local network is crucial if long distance carriers and equipment manufacturers are to be viable competitors.

AT&T has allegedly used its control of this local monopoly to disadvantage these competitors in two principal ways. First, it has attempted to prevent competing long distance carriers and competing equipment manufacturers from gaining access to the local network, or to delay that access, thus placing them in an inferior position vis-a-vis AT&T's own services. Second, it has supposedly used profits earned from the monopoly local telephone operations to subsidize its long distance and equipment businesses in which it was competing with others.

For a great many years, the Federal Communications Commission has struggled, largely without success, to stop practices of this type through the regulatory tools at its command. A lawsuit the Department of Justice brought in 1949 to curb similar practices ended in an ineffectual consent decree. Some other remedy is plainly required; hence the divestiture of the local Operating Companies from the Bell System. This divestiture will sever the relationship between this local monopoly and the other, competitive segments of AT&T, and it will thus ensure—certainly better than could any other type of relief—that the practices which allegedly have lain heavy on the telecommunications industry will not recur.

B. With the loss of control over the local network, AT&T will be unable to disadvantage its competitors, and the restrictions imposed on AT&T after the government's first antitrust suit—which limited AT&T to the provision of telecommunications services—will no longer be necessary. The proposed decree accordingly removes these restrictions.

The decree will thus allow AT&T to become a vigorous competitor in the growing computer, computer-related, and information markets. Other large and experienced firms are presently operating in these markets, and there is therefore no reason to believe that AT&T will be able to achieve monopoly dominance in these industries as it did in telecommunications. At the same time, by use of its formidable scientific, engineering, and management resources, including particularly the capabilities of Bell Laboratories, AT&T should be able to make significant contributions to these fields, which are at the forefront of innovation and technology, to the benefit of American consumers, national defense, and the position of American industry vis-a-vis foreign competition. * * *

C. After the divestiture, the Operating Companies will possess a monopoly over local telephone service. According to the Department of Justice, the Operating Companies must be barred from entering all competitive markets to ensure that they will not misuse their monopoly power. The Court will not impose restrictions simply for the sake of theoretical consistency. Restrictions must be based on an assessment of the realistic circumstances of the relevant markets, including the Operating Companies' ability to engage in anticompetitive behavior, their potential contribution to the market as an added competitor for AT&T,

as well as upon the effects of the restrictions on the rates for local telephone service.

This standard requires that the Operating Companies be prohibited from providing long distance services and information services, and from manufacturing equipment used in the telecommunications industry. Participation in these fields carries with it a substantial risk that the Operating Companies will use the same anticompetitive techniques used by AT&T in order to thwart the growth of their own competitors. Moreover, contrary to the assumptions made by some, Operating Company involvement in these areas could not legitimately generate subsidies for local rates. Such involvement could produce substantial profits only if the local companies used their monopoly position to dislodge competitors or to provide subsidy for their competitive services or products—the very behavior the decree seeks to prevent. * * *

Bell's Surrender. Why did AT&T surrender so completely? A decision by the court in 1981, rejecting AT&T's motion to dismiss at the end of the government's case in chief, concluded that there was a prima facie showing of numerous antitrust violations, and that AT&T bore the burden of disproving the government's case. *United States v. AT&T*, 524 F.Supp. 1336, 1381 (D.D.C. 1981). The tenor of the opinion indicated that AT&T could not have sustained that burden. However, the court had given no hint as to the probable remedies for any or all of the conduct offenses, and there is reason to doubt that the court would have ordered the radical restructuring sought by the government. Indeed, the assistant attorney general for antitrust later expressed doubt that the court would have gone beyond "a sort of ceremonial fracturing of Western Electric and a few sacrificial operating companies here and there." See Barry Cole, ed., *After the Breakup: Assessing the New Post–AT&T Divestiture Era* 38 (1991) (comments by Assistant Attorney General William Baxter). AT&T did, however, have one seemingly compelling reason for seeking settlement: it offered relief from the restrictions of an earlier antitrust decree entered in 1956.[14] See *id.* (comments by AT&T CEO Charles Brown). In the case settled in 1956 the government claimed that AT&T had monopolized the telecommunications equipment market and as relief sought divestiture of AT&T's manufacturing subsidiary, Western Electric. The 1956 consent decree allowed Bell to keep Western Electric but precluded AT&T from engaging in any business other than the provision of common carrier communications services and precluded Western Electric from manufacturing equipment other than that used by the Bell System. In 1956, the restriction seemed fairly innocuous for AT&T, but later when it desired to enter the computer and related business, the 1956 decree prevented it from doing

14. This explains the title of the decree: "Modification of Final Judgment" ("MFJ") refers to a modification of the 1956 final judgment.

so.[15] The 1982 decree removed this restriction, allowing AT&T to pursue this and other new ventures. As it later turned out AT&T's decision to enter the computer industry was a business mistake, and it was soon forced to exit after piling up large losses. It was but one of a series of business misadventures by the post-breakup AT&T until its acquisition by SBC in 2005. For a journalist's account, see Leslie Cauley, *End of the Line: The Rise and Fall of AT&T* (2005).

After the Fall. A plan of reorganization was drawn up and submitted to the court which approved it in *United States v. Western Elec. Co.*, 569 F.Supp. 990 (D.D.C. 1983). AT&T's local operating companies (Bell Operating Companies or "BOCs") were separated from AT&T's long distance and manufacturing divisions. The operating companies were divided among seven independent regional holding companies ("RBOCs")—approximately similar to AT&T's former regional divisions. (As noted in Chapter 1, the original seven is now down to three: AT&T (the product of successive mergers of SBC and Pacific Telesis, then SBC and AT&T and, more recently AT&T and BellSouth), Verizon (the product of a merger of NYNEX and Bell Atlantic, and a later acquisition of a non-Bell company, GTE), and Qwest (formerly US West). With the breakup, local exchange service was divided among local exchange and transport areas ("LATAs")—exclusively providing local transport among end users within the LATAs and access to "long distance" service carriers, which exclusively provide interLATA service. Although they define "local exchange service" for purposes of the separation between the BOCs and the interexchange carriers, LATAs do not correspond to the service areas defined by area codes. A LATA will usually contain multiple area codes. (For example, the New York City has five area codes, but is within a single LATA, covering the New York metropolitan area.) The primary criterion for defining the LATA was to create a local service area large enough to attract competitive interexchange service. Thus the size varies with population density; in some cases it will be coextensive with a metropolitan area, in others it will be larger (some LATAs cover an entire state).

The MFJ restrictions on the BOCs were the subject of continued controversy and litigation for a dozen years after the decree. The prohibition against providing unregulated services—carried over from the 1956 decree—was removed by Judge Greene in 1987. The ban on information services was removed in 1991, in response to what was in practical effect a mandate from the court of appeals. The other two restraints, on manufacturing CPE and on providing interLATA long distance service, were terminated by the Telecommunications Act of 1996, subject to regulatory conditions that we will examine later.

15. Recall that in the *Computer II* decision the FCC opined that deregulating enhanced services and CPE did not prevent AT&T from providing them insofar as they were incidental to common carrier communications services for which the 1956 decree contained an exemption. The FCC's opinion was not authoritative since it had no jurisdiction over the decree or its enforcement, but in any case it would not alter the fact that the decree clearly did bar AT&T from engaging in computer and related businesses that were not incidental to common carrier communications services.

Regulating Judges. The government's antitrust case rested not only on the various attempts by AT&T to thwart new competition in equipment and long distance service markets, it also implicitly assumed that the FCC had not been able to prevent AT&T from doing so. AT&T at one point sought dismissal on the ground that it should be immune from antitrust precisely because the FCC was in control. Judge Greene rejected that claim, and gave the rather clear impression to observers that he believed the FCC had not been up to the task of regulating the giant company. Considering his view of the ineffectiveness of regulation (or at least of the FCC), it is a bit ironic that the MFJ itself became an instrument of regulation—by the court. It had not been planned that way. The department's theory was that separating the local exchange service market from the long distance and equipment manufacturing markets and barring the BOCs from entering the latter markets would effectively remove both the incentive and the power to use monopoly control of local exchange (the "bottleneck" through which other services must flow) to bar competition in long distance and equipment markets. It was expected that this simple cutting of the proverbial Gordian knot that tangled monopolistic local with competitive long distance and equipment would be more or less self enforcing. That expectation was mistaken. Interpreting and enforcing the terms of the line of business restrictions proved to be no small task. For twelve years after the breakup, Judge Greene would issue hundreds of rulings on the details of the MFJ.[16] Observers came to call Judge Greene a new "czar" whose regulatory powers over long distance telecom service rivaled those of the FCC. A decree that had seemingly promised a simple solution to a regulatory knot had become just another knot of regulation.

Antitrust practitioners generally have an aversion to what are called "regulatory decrees" in monopolization cases for several reasons. One of the primary reasons is that such decrees involve courts in a business for which they are not well suited. Quite apart from formalist, separation of powers questions, courts are not equipped with the resources to handle the demands of continuing regulatory oversight. A second reason is that regulatory decrees have proven to be vulnerable to obsolescence. Antitrust decrees have been known to remain in force for decades, as was the case with the MFJ. At the time of the MFJ, AT&T was still operating under a 1956 antitrust consent decree administered by a district court in New Jersey. In fact, the Modification of Final Judgment was structured as a modification of the 1956 decree (hence the name). Tacking the period of the 1956 decree to that of the MFJ means that some part of the Bell System was subject to judicial "regulation" for 40 years (until 1996). Perhaps it is needless to say, in a dynamic environment (and even the most stagnant sector of the economy is dynamic over a period of

16. A review of the oversight record in the first eight years reported: "There have been hundreds of new motions, complaints and other requests to enforce, modify, or interpret the decree. The Department of Justice has issued thousands of advisory letters. Some 6,000 briefs have been filed with Judge Greene. Fifteen groups of consolidated appeals have been brought to the D.C. Circuit." Michael K. Kellogg, John Thorne and Peter W. Huber, FEDERAL TELECOMMUNICATIONS LAW 344 (1992).

several decades), this kind of regulation can quickly become out of touch with contemporary economic conditions. The MFJ regime was terminated by the Telecommunications Act of 1996, by which Congress sought to remodel the entire telecommunications regulatory regime. We pick up that story in the next chapter.

E. RATE REGULATION BEFORE AND AFTER THE BREAKUP

Although the telephone industry changed in 1982 with the MFJ, the change happened from without—through antitrust. The MFJ did not signal a change in the FCC's regulatory stance. Telephone regulation continued after 1982 much as it did before 1982, with changes to adjust to the new structure of the industry as mandated by the MFJ. Many of those regulatory policies have analogs under the current regime, which was adopted in 1996, but the cornerstone of those regulatory policies goes back to the initial decision to create, feed, and control a privately operated telephone monopoly.

Historically the central purpose for regulating monopolies was to protect consumers against monopoly overcharge, defined to be prices above the economic cost of providing service—with "economic cost" being understood to include not only cost of operating the telephone network but also "capital costs," the annualized cost of the fixed assets that make up network itself. For most of the history of telecommunications regulation, the FCC and state regulators were concerned primarily with protecting consumers against unreasonably high rates. When competition in long distance emerged in the 1970s, the task of rate regulation became more complicated, for it was now necessary not only to consider the simple case of monopoly *overcharge* but also the possibility that AT&T would use its ability to overcharge in its monopoly local services markets to subsidize (and thus *undercharge*) in competitive long distance markets. This "predatory" pricing theory was one of the claims underlying the antitrust case that eventually led to AT&T's breakup. In the early competitive era, the complicated task of regulating long distance rates fell primarily on the FCC since it was in interstate long distance markets where competition was first introduced (and would remain confined until the late 1990s). The task of rate regulation would become more complicated still in the aftermath of the AT&T breakup in 1984, when it became necessary to create new compensation arrangements for services provided one carrier to another, since local and long-distance service would now be provided by different companies. In the heyday of the AT&T monopoly, inter-carrier services were a matter of either internal transfer payments within the Bell System or settlements between AT&T and independent companies for interconnection services. With the division between local and long distance, these informal arrangements had to be translated into a more formal set of charges—"access charges." To add yet more confusion, the rules have always been shaped by a social policy of subsidizing certain kinds of services to certain classes of users. The policy is labeled a "universal service" policy, though as we shall see that label covers a lot of disparate, if not incoherent, subsidies. In recent years there has been an effort to separate out the subsidy components and make them an explicit charge; however, the effort is incomplete. It is only a mild exaggeration to say that there is almost no *regulated* telecommunications service that does not bear the imprint of redistributive policies.

The changing character of regulatory purpose makes it difficult to get a coherent view of rate regulation. Today rate regulation is partly about protecting end consumers and partly about protecting competitors both in their role as competitors and in their role as buyers of telecommunications services. We take up some of the general background principles in this chapter, but we will return to more recent applications of rate regulation, both as it affects consumers and competitors, in the next.

We begin with a brief summary of classic rate-of-return regulation. This type of regulation has been generally displaced in modern times by so-called "price cap" regulation. However, the classic form of regulation remains important to an understanding of the underpinnings of more modern forms of rate regulation since to some degree all regulation depends on a calculation of the cost of service, which is what rate-of-return regulation was designed to measure in a formal way.

1. Rate of Return Regulation

Although rate-of-return regulation was long the standard means of regulating public utility rates, the FCC's own use of the method came rather late in its career. In its first thirty plus years the FCC relied primarily on informal negotiations with AT&T—a process it called "continuing surveillance." Not until the late 1960s when the agency suddenly realized that it had no reliable information about what AT&T's true cost of service was did it embark on its first comprehensive effort to prescribe a rate of return for Bell's long distance service.

The term "rate of return" is a conventional label for determining the cost of providing service. It is, however, a somewhat misleading label because, properly speaking, the rate of return describes only one component of the cost of service, which includes broadly two categories of cost: operating costs and capital costs. In very rough generality the methodology of cost of service regulation is as follows. For a more detailed discussion see 1 A. Kahn, *The Economics of Regulation: Principles and Institutions*, ch. 2 (1988).

The regulator begins by determining the **revenue requirement** for the regulated enterprise, which is the combination of **operating costs** and the **cost of capital**. This is sometimes called a general revenue proceeding or rate level proceeding. The object is to determine a general level of revenues that will cover all the costs of providing service. Once that is done the overall return level has to be translated into individual rates for specific services. That means that the aggregate of all individual rates cannot exceed the overall return level. For present purposes we want to focus on the rate level issue, that is, what overall return will permit the enterprise to cover the full cost of service.

The first task usually is to determine **operating costs** based on actual expenditures in recent, representative years, of operating the business with some adjustment for known future costs. The operating cost calculation is conceptually straight forward in most cases. But that does not mean it is entirely free from judgment calls, and from some degree of manipulation. One component of operating cost is the yearly depreciation in the value of capital assets, and choosing the right depreciation rate is an exercise in judgment that firms can manipulate. For instance, by choosing unusually low depreciation rates, a regulated business can make operating costs artificially low, and in so doing, make the the book value of the equipment artificially high. That can affect the other component of the calculation: the rate base.

Once the regulator has calculated the operating costs, it is necessary to calculate the **cost of capital**. Capital costs are calculated as a "fair rate of return" on the value of invested capital—the so-called **rate base**. So the first step to calculating the capital cost component of the revenue requirement is to set the rate base. Normally the value assigned to the rate base is simply the book value of the assets—that is, the depreciated cost of the firm's assets.[17] But one needn't rely on book value, especially if there is reason to believe the firm is using unrealistic depreciation rates. It's also possible to rely on other measures of value, such as the value that the firm could sell its assets for (market value) or what it would cost for the firm to replace its assets (replacement value). The difference between methodologies can be substantial; one of the most heavily litigated cases in telecom history was over which measure of value to use for a firm's assets.[18]

At this point we need to introduce a qualifying explanation of what is meant by the "firm." The regulator is rarely concerned with the entire firm; it is concerned only with the investment that has been made in that part of the firm providing the regulated service. This is an important qualification, since a firm may engage in various businesses and only some may be regulated, or assets may be used in multiple markets that are subject to different regulatory regimes. That has been the case with telecom, with the states and the federal government sharing regulatory jurisdiction, the states over intrastate service and the federal government over long distance service. Thus it is necessary to decide how much of the regulated firm's facilities are devoted to the particular

17. At one time, the question of valuation was not automatically identified with costs, at least not with book costs. In 1898 in Smyth v. Ames, 169 U.S. 466 (1898), the Court held that, as a matter of constitutional law, rates not based on the "fair value" of the firm's assets would be deemed "confiscatory." Fair value was not precisely defined in *Smith*; it included an amalgam of different measures—original cost, reproduction cost, and other elements. In 1944 the Court in FPC v. Hope Natural Gas Co., 320 U.S. 591, 603 (1944) repudiated the "fair value" standard, and held that the Takings Clause did not require any single methodology.

18. See Verizon Communications, Inc. v. FCC, 535 U.S. 467 (2001), which we discuss in the next chapter.

regulated business within the jurisdiction of the regulator—in the case of telecommunications, to separate the cost of a carrier between intra- and interstate services. In the jargon of telecommunications regulation this is called "separations." To the extent that costs are variable with the type of service, the task is easy; one simply assigns cost on a causation basis: assign those costs to the service that created them. Unfortunately, most of the costs are not attributable in that way. For example, a caller who wants to call from New York City to San Francisco uses a the same local loop (to reach the CO) and some of the same switching facilities that are used by someone who calls from Manhattan to Brooklyn. There is no cost-causation basis for assigning those costs. One simple way to assign them would be to divide the common cost of transport and switching costs on the basis of relative use: to figure the ratio of interstate to intrastate usage and charge interstate and intrastate customers according to that ratio. Historically, though, the actual allocation was deliberately skewed to place a heavier burden on the interstate service than intrastate service, and in particular to subsidize local exchange service at the expense of long distance service. The amount of this cost shifting increased significantly over time. Under the last plan in effect before divestiture—the so-called "Ozark Plan"—joint and common costs that were not causally attributable to a particular call (local or long distance) were allocated between local, intrastate and long distance interstate services such that for every 1% of unattributable costs born by local service, about 3.3% was born by interstate long distance service. In short, interstate long distance service subscribers were paying more than three times what local service subscribers paid for the joint or common costs of using the network. This implicit subsidy had the effect of keeping interstate long distance rates at costs higher than the cost of service, and this in turn invited other firms to enter to "skim the cream"—in other words to arbitrage the difference between prices and costs in long distance markets. That was what first induced MCI to seek entry into long distance markets in the late 1960s. Ultimately, of course, the ensuing competition made it impossible to sustain the subsidy.

Once the rate base is determined, the next step is to calculate the cost of capital as a *percentage annual return on the rate base*. Capital costs, of course, take two forms: debt and equity.[19] Calculating the debt part is fairly straight forward: the cost of debt is determined by the payments the firm actually makes to its creditors and bond holders. But the equity component is both complicated and necessarily involves substantial judgment on the part of regulators. The objective is to find a rate that matches shareholders' expectations, but identifying shareholder expectations is very hard, and all the more so in telecom, where the regulators' very act of setting rates creates substantial circularity (be-

19. Normally a regulator will take the firm's capital structure as a given, so if it has, say, 40% debt and 60% equity, that is what the regulator will assume. But not necessarily. If a regulator thinks the firm is too thinly capitalized, it may impute a different structure, but this is a complication we can ignore.

cause investor expectations are in turn a function of the rates being determined).[20]

Regulators have used various methodologies for calculating the rate of return on equity. In modern times the so-called discounted cash flow ("DCF") model has been widely used and was the formula used by the FCC. The formula is R = D/P + G, where R is the revenue requirement, D is the dividend, P is the price of the stock and G is the expected future growth of the dividend.[21] The basic intuition of this formula is that the stock price reflects the discounted value of a future stream of earnings. Thus to meet existing investor expectations (and to allow the firm to attract capital in the future) the regulator calculates the level of earnings that will sustain current market values.

Once the overall rate level is determined, the next step is to break out the overall return level among individual services. If only a single service were provided by the firm, this would be a simple task. In such a case the single service customers would pay a rate that was designed to cover the full costs of the firm (or at least regulated part of the firm), i.e., the direct cost of service together with the capital costs. The individual rate would be such as to allow the full fair rate of return allowed in the rate-level determination. However, it is never the case that a utility provides only one service; there will always be different classes of service, based on different functional uses or different categories of users. The provision of different services raises questions about the reasonableness of individual rates in relation to the cost of that service and in relation to other services. At bottom, the problem is how to allocate common and joint costs among the different kinds of services, for instance, between POTS and specialized business services. There is no one correct way to do this. One method is a so-called "fully distributed" cost allocation, in which all common or joint costs are allocated according to their proportion of direct costs or their proportion of revenues. As an alternative one could choose to allocate the costs unevenly so that the burden of the common costs would fall heaviest on a particular group of users. One well-known economic methodology is what is known among regulatory cognoscenti as "Ramsey pricing."[22] In essence Ramsey pricing calls for a two-part pricing regime in which

20. The circularity problem can be ameliorated by looking not simply at the stock prices of the regulated firm in question, but at the prices of other firms which compete in the market for capital. Think about it this way: in order to enable the firm to attract capital (on reasonable terms) it is necessary that the firm be seen by investors as an attractive investment choice relative to other investment opportunities, which is to say that the FCC must examine the **opportunity cost** of capital. That in turn implies that the firm be allowed earnings should be equal to those of comparable firms.

21. Cash flows also result from the ultimate sale of the stock. However, the theory is that the next investor will be willing to buy the stock at a price based on his estimate of future dividends and the price at which he will be able to sell, and so on.

22. The Ramsey pricing model is found in Frank Ramsey, *A Contribution to the Theory of Taxation*, 37 Econ. J. 47 (1927). Ramsey formalized but did not invent the principle—which has long been a staple of public utility regulation under the rubric of "value of service pricing." See William J. Baumol and David Bradford, *Optimal Departures from Marginal Cost Pricing*, 60 Am. Econ. Rev. 265 (1970).

prices are set to cover the direct costs of providing service with common and joint costs distributed to users whose demand is least sensitive to price—those who won't change their demand based on price. Or, in economic terms, allocate shared costs according to the inverse price elasticity of demand. The traditional rationale for this is that it causes the least distortion in the demand for the service, since the burden of the costs falls on those whose demand will be affected the least by having to bear them. Finally, one could allocate costs in such a way as to subsidize a particular group for purposes of achieving some social objective—such as universal service. This form of allocation would in many cases yield the same pattern of cost allocation as Ramsey pricing, though the two are not necessarily the same and do not involve the same social objective.

2. Price Cap Regulation

Classic rate-of-return regulation has been much criticized, for its costly complexity and for the perverse incentives which it created for the regulated firm, notably the disincentive to economize on costs (the predictable consequence of any system of cost-plus pricing), an incentive to invest inefficiently in capital costs (which expand the rate base and thereby increase the allowable earnings levels), and an incentive to manipulate the allocation of costs between competitive services and monopoly services, thereby using the latter to subsidize the former. To correct these problems some state regulators (following a pioneering program by British Telecom) sought a new approach to rate regulation that would decouple price control from cost of service, thereby removing the regulated firm's incentive to manipulate costs. Price cap methodology is directed at *prices* not general earnings.

Most price cap regimes have supplanted a previous regime of rate-of-return regulation. When price caps follow rate-of-return regulation, it is relatively straight forward to set the baseline rates according to what the previous regime has established as fair and reasonable. If the existing rates have been fairly set to enable the firm to cover its full cost of service, then all that is needed is to make forward adjustments in price to account for changes in costs. This is typically done by using some national price index, adjusted by a special productivity factor—which the FCC dubs the "X" factor—to account for the difference between the productivity of the industry and that of the economy generally.

In 1989 the FCC adopted price cap regulation for AT&T as the only "dominant" interstate long distance carrier. (Its two major competitors, MCI and Sprint, had only a fraction of the interstate long distance market at this time.) However, in 1990 and 1991 price cap regulation was extended to dominant local exchange carriers ("LECs"), a category that includes all of the BOCs, with respect to their interstate access services—i.e., services that connect long distance calls to the local exchange network. Non-dominant LECs were allowed to opt for price caps in lieu of traditional rate-of-return regulation.[23] In 1995 AT&T was declared to be no longer "dominant" in long distance and was relieved of price cap regulation. However, because of its subsequent merger with SBC AT&T is now a BOC and as such subject to the FCC's price cap rules for interstate access services. The following excerpt from the Commission's 1989 report explains the general concept and operation of price caps, and also offers a sustained critique of the "traditional" rate-base, rate-of-return regulation described above.

RATES FOR DOMINANT CARRIERS (PRICE CAPS) Report and Order

Federal Communications Commission, 1989.
4 FCC Rcd. 2873.

BY THE COMMISSION:

I. INTRODUCTION

* * *

B. Background and Summary of Order

1. Synopsis of Historical Dominant Carrier Regulation

18. Since this Commission was created in 1934, we have revisited and altered the mix of our regulatory policies and rules on many occasions. At the present time, we employ a regulatory system known as rate base, or rate of return, regulation to ensure that the rates for AT&T and LEC interstate services remain within the zone of reasonableness. This approach requires not only that we establish a carrier's allowable rate of return, but also whether: (1) its investment and cash expenses are properly calculated and efficiently incurred; (2) the level of non-cash expenses such as depreciation and other accruals is properly reflected in rate calculations; and (3) the rates proposed or in effect cover these costs and produce a fair rate of return.

19. This elaborate approach is often thought of as "traditional" regulation. In fact, we did not begin to develop this system until the mid–1960s. Prior to that time, there were no explicit criteria for determining whether Bell System rates were just and reasonable. Instead, we followed a policy of "continuing surveillance" of Bell System earnings levels to ensure that rates remained within the zone of reasonableness. This process operated without regular formal proceedings of any kind, and rate adjustments occurred only if this Commission or Bell System

23. Under the original rules the opt-in choice was irreversible: carriers could not later switch back to rate-of-return regulation. The rationale for this so-called "all-or-nothing" rule was to prevent carriers from switching back and forth for strategic reasons depending on which way their costs were changing. In 2004 the Commission modified the rule to allow some exceptions. Multi-Association Group Plan for Regulation of Interstate Service of Non-Price Cap Incumbent Local Exchange Carriers and Interexchange Carriers, 19 FCC Rcd. 6872 (2004)

representatives initiated "discussions looking toward appropriate rate changes whenever the level of ... total interstate earnings ... appeared to warrant such action."

20. During the period when the "continuing surveillance" policy was in effect, a voice occasionally was raised in complaint that the Bell System's costs and rates might be too high, but only once during this period did this Commission initiate a comprehensive investigation of such matters. This inquiry in the late 1930s cost millions of dollars and occupied approximately 300 researchers for several years. The staff's efforts culminated in the preparation of a voluminous report on Bell System costs and operations, but allegations of inflated costs and rates—and substantial cost shifting between unregulated Western Electric and regulated telephone company operations—were never documented to the Commission's satisfaction. Ultimately, no action was taken on the report's major recommendations, and the investigation produced no significant changes in Commission or Bell System procedures.

21. The use of "continuing surveillance" to assure just and reasonable rates occurred during a period when the Bell System faced little or no competition in the domestic interstate telecommunications market. The absence of competition resulted in large measure from the formidable barriers to entry into telephone markets, including substantial scale economies that operated to the advantage of the incumbent Bell System. These barriers may not have been so great as to impart to the telephone industry the status of a "natural monopoly," but they formed a distinct boundary between that industry and other industries. And, they existed during a time of technological stability.

22. In the 1950s and 1960s, technological developments began to lower economic barriers to entry into the telephone business and to put pressure on the boundary between telephone companies and other firms. The development of microwave technology rendered scale economies insignificant at the "high" end of the telephone market. As a result, entities using large amounts of telephone service, which generally had been telephone company customers, could operate their own telephone systems and, potentially, compete against their former suppliers. The development of satellite technology as a cost-effective method of transmitting messages transformed firms with satellite expertise into potential entrants into the telephone field. Previously unrelated firms, such as aerospace companies and the Bell System, thus came into competitive interaction. Rapid development of digital electronics and transistor technology blurred the line between computers and communications. Computer systems took on the characteristics of telephone systems—i.e., switches linked by transmission lines—while, at the same time, telephone companies were adopting computer technology for use in communications systems and expanding their operations into the domain of computer firms.

23. This Commission was not unmindful of the pressures and changes generated by technological developments. In the face of such

developments, and often following the lead of the courts, we embarked on two paths of regulatory change.

24. The first path consisted of a series of proceedings in which we addressed the impact of technological advances that made it possible for companies outside the Bell System to provide telecommunications equipment and services. The second path consisted of a series of proceedings in which we abandoned the "continuing surveillance" policy and began to construct the regulatory system currently relied upon to regulate dominant carriers. In retrospect, it is easy to see how the two paths of regulatory change were related in major part, with the second coming as a response to the first. Permitting entry into certain segments of telecommunications allowed competition to develop in part, but not all, of that market. New competitors called upon this Commission to police the boundary between the competitive and less competitive portions of the market, and to arbitrate disputes among all competitors. Issues that had been left largely to telephone companies during the period of "continuing surveillance," such as rate structure, became crucial competitive variables. The allocation of telephone company costs among competitive and less competitive services became a subject of intense controversy. * * *

2. The Rate of Return System

29. Our experiences in traveling the second path of regulatory change, in which we developed the existing rate of return structure, illuminate the difficulties of administering rate of return regulation under any circumstances. In theory, rate of return is intended to replicate competitive market results. However, there are many differences in the manner in which rate of return regulation and competitive forces operate. Competition holds each firm to "normal" profit levels as a result of a dynamic process that operates over time—a firm strives to maximize profits and secure advantage over other firms by responding to consumer demand effectively. Under rate of return, however, "normal" profit levels are established in advance by regulatory fiat. The dynamic process that produces socially beneficial results in a competitive environment is strongly suppressed. In fact, rather than encourage socially beneficial behavior by the regulated firm, rate of return actually discourages it.

30. The distorted incentives created by rate of return regulation are easily illustrated. In a competitive environment, where prices are dictated by the market, a company's unit costs and profits generally are related inversely. If one goes up, the other goes down. Rate of return regulation stands this relationship on its head. Although carriers subject to such regulation are limited to earning a particular percentage return on investment during a fixed period, a carrier seeking to increase its dollar earnings often can do so merely by increasing its aggregate investment. In other words, under a rate of return regime, profits (i.e., dollar earnings) can go up when investment goes up. This creates a powerful incentive for carriers to "pad" their costs, regardless of wheth-

er additional investment is necessary or efficient. And, because a carrier's operating expenses generally are recovered from ratepayers on a dollar-for-dollar basis, and do not affect shareholder profits, management has little incentive to conserve on such expenses. This creates an additional incentive to operate inefficiently. Moreover, in situations in which carriers providing more than one service face competition for one or more of such services, rate of return regulation enables carriers to distort the competitive process by manipulating their reported cost allocations.

31. A system that establishes such incentives is unlikely to encourage efficiency. Moreover, administering rate of return regulation in order to counteract these incentives is a difficult and complex process, even when done correctly and well. This is so primarily for two reasons. First, such regulation is built on the premise that a regulator can determine accurately what costs are necessary to deliver service. In practice, however, a regulator may have difficulty obtaining accurate cost information as the carrier itself is the source of nearly all information about its costs. Furthermore, no regulator has the resources to review in detail the thousands of individual business judgments a carrier makes before it decides, for example, to install a new switching system.

32. The second inherent difficulty associated with administering rate of return regulation relates to its requirement that determinations be made about how to allocate a carrier's costs among services that often are provided jointly or in common. Such determinations tend to become more economically problematic as they become more detailed. The history of this Commission's experience in this area over the past several decades reflects the difficulty of implementing cost allocation systems. We recently have been able to implement rational and effective allocation systems for the purpose of allocating costs between regulated and nonregulated activities. It must be recognized, however, that even though cost allocation systems deter anticompetitive activity and assist in its detection, these results may be obtained at a high cost to society. This is so because a cost allocation system can present a strong deterrent to anticompetitive activity and, at the same time, be so detailed and rigid that it imposes on a carrier a complex and inflexible rate structure, one that may have little relation to consumer demand. If such a rate structure is deployed in a competitive environment, it may result in distorted consumption decisions, distorted production decisions, and distortions of the competitive process.

33. Our experiences administering rate of return regulation lead us to conclude that this methodology has certain inherent flaws. As explained above, this type of regulation presents carriers with certain incentives—to pad their rates and forgo efficient innovation, for example—that are perverse when viewed from a public interest perspective. These incentives would exist even if technology and industry boundaries were to remain stable, and the existence of such incentives alone provides sufficient justification to seek alternative regulatory approaches

that are better suited than rate of return to achieving the consumer-oriented goals of the Communications Act. * * *

35. Our concerns about rate of return regulation are shared by many state, federal, and foreign bodies with experience in the telecommunications arena. The National Telecommunications and Information Agency (NTIA) has evaluated the rate of return approach and found it wanting in many respects. Both NTIA and the United States Department of Justice are participating in this proceeding, and both are supportive of the price cap approach, particularly as we have proposed to apply it to AT&T. Regulators in the United Kingdom have administered price cap regulation successfully since 1984. Furthermore, the flight from the rate of return approach by state regulators continues unabated. Only 20 of the 42 states in which AT&T offers service currently regulate AT&T pursuant to a regulatory structure like that employed by this Commission, and the number of states applying some form of incentive regulation to LECs is increasing.

3. The Incentive System

36. The attractiveness of incentive regulation lies in its ability to replicate more accurately than rate of return the dynamic, consumer-oriented process that characterizes a competitive market. In general, such regulation operates by placing limits on the rates carriers may charge for services. In the face of such constraints, a carrier's primary means of increasing earnings are to enhance its efficiency and innovate in the provision of service. Because cost padding and cross-subsidization do not justify higher prices under this system—but instead lower profits—the incentives to engage in such activity are limited. The system also is less complex than rate of return regulation and easier to administer in the long run, which should reduce the cost of regulation.

37. Because cost allocation requirements do not play as central a role under incentive regulation as they do under rate of return, incentive regulation represents a more effective method of policing shifting industry boundaries than rate of return. The restraints on price increases become less significant when competition develops because competitive forces hold prices down. Indeed, a system of pricing restraints offers a means of determining what sectors of the market are becoming competitive, as this will be revealed when carriers voluntarily price below authorized pricing levels. Our ability to obtain such information will enable us to determine more accurately under incentive regulation than we can under rate of return what, if any, further movement should be made regarding regulation of particular dominant carriers. More important, the pricing limitations offer consumers strong protection against attempted exercises of market power.

38. The incentive regulatory approach adopted for tariff review purposes in this Order for AT&T and proposed for the LECs operates according to the following model. A carrier's services are grouped together in accordance with common characteristics, and the weighted prices in

each group are adjusted annually pursuant to formulas designed to ensure that rates are based on the cost of providing service. The formulas provide for adjustments similar to those carriers make to their rates under the current system. For example, all carriers currently adjust their rates in accordance with changes in their input costs. Our formulas accomplish the same result, measuring such changes with reference to the Gross National Product Price Index (GNP-PI), a recognized, government-administered index that reflects broad-based input cost changes experienced by dominant carriers more accurately than the more commonly known Consumer Price Index. We also will continue under price caps the current policy of adjusting rates for known cost changes, such as those caused by regulatory decisions, that are beyond a carrier's direct control. For example, AT&T's rates will be adjusted to reflect regulatory changes, such as changes in the level of access charges, as is the case today.

39. Our incentive system also requires that we add another component to our formula limiting aggregate price increases. Although the GNP-PI already reflects productivity gains for the economy as a whole, it does not reflect the degree of productivity gains experienced by the telecommunications industry historically. A number of studies demonstrate that the telecommunications sector has been more productive than the economy as a whole. In evaluating how large to make the productivity factor, we have examined a number of long term historical studies of pre divestiture Bell System productivity and concluded that, on a long term basis, productivity has been approximately 2.1 percent per year higher than the general economy. Data from the more recent period, i.e., the 1970s and 1980s, have tended to be slightly higher than the number suggested by the long term studies. Our own analysis of AT&T's price changes during the post-divestiture period indicates that AT&T's productivity differential since 1984 has been approximately 2.3 percent per year. Because we are sufficiently impressed with evidence of the more recent trend in telecommunication productivity indicating a productivity level slightly above the long term view, and because we wish to err, if we must, on the side of consumers, we have decided that AT&T's productivity factor under our plan should be 2.5 percent per year.

40. For the LECs, we similarly found that the available data suggest a long term historical productivity differential of slightly over 2 percent per year above the general economy, with a slightly higher differential in the more recent period. Unlike for AT&T, however, we are unable to corroborate to the same degree the LECs' productivity experience since divestiture. Because of this and possible variations in individual LEC productivity around the industry average, we tentatively have decided to proceed with a 2.5 percent productivity factor, while proposing other adjustments to LEC aggregate prices in order to ensure just and reasonable rate levels.

41. The downward pressure on rates exerted by the 2.5 percent productivity offset assures that consumers will be as well off under caps

as they likely would have been under rate of return. Because our goal is to make consumers better off under price caps than they likely would be if we continued rate of return regulation, however, our plan requires carriers to meet goals that exceed the historic productivity of the telephone industry. In addition to the 2.5 percent adjustment noted above, carriers would be required to lower rates by another 0.5 percent—an amount we refer to as the Consumer Productivity Dividend—in order to ensure that consumers receive a guaranteed, up-front share of the additional efficiencies flowing from the improved incentives created by price cap regulation.

42. In effect, the price cap rate adjustment formula establishes a rule of thumb to use in evaluating a carrier's performance for tariff review purposes: a benchmark. The rates filed by carriers are self-initiated, but the relationship of those filed rates to the price cap formula will trigger various types and levels of Commission scrutiny. If a carrier achieves results superior to this benchmark as a result of its own initiative, it is permitted to keep the resulting profits, at least for a while. If a carrier claims that it cannot achieve the benchmark, we will suspend its tariff revisions and examine its proferred justification. Suspension and investigation is a reasonable response to such an event because the benchmark is based in part on a measurement of carriers' past performance, calculated on a long run basis, and failure to achieve that level of performance is legitimate grounds for inquiry. After the fourth year of the plan, the mark is subject to adjustment as a result of our comprehensive review of the price cap system, which will be conducted in light of the information the carrier reveals about itself in the course of operating pursuant to the plan. This ensures that consumers will be the beneficiaries of all achieved efficiencies. And, this Commission will monitor carriers' performance throughout the four-year period to ensure that the system is operating in the public interest and will make adjustments as necessary. Moreover, Section 204 investigations and Section 208 complaint proceedings will continue to be a forum for examining cost and profit data, as appropriate. * * *

II. Dominant Carrier Regulation

A. Current Approach: Rate of Return Regulation * * *

75. In this section, we consider whether the flaws we perceive in rate of return methodology are sufficiently embedded within its structure to warrant our discarding rate of return regulation for AT&T and local exchange carriers in favor of another approach to regulating those carriers. We have also been challenged by commenters to consider whether it is our administration of rate of return, rather than the system itself, that produces the problems we have found. On both counts, we affirm our tentative views set forth in the Further Notice that our existing rate of return regulation system should be replaced where feasible.

76. The flaws we have cited with regard to rate of return appear to us to be no less endemic today than when we initially examined rate of return in the course of this proceeding. Rate of return regulation is a methodology designed to address the problem of constraining market power exercised by monopoly utilities. The principal method by which it constrains market power is through the limitation of a carrier's ability to earn supranormal profit. Viewed at its most elemental level, rate of return requires regulators to limit a carrier's earnings to "normal" levels of profit, thereby preventing the carrier from charging rates that would reveal its true economic position as a monopolist.

77. Unfortunately, rate of return regulation's greatest strength is also its greatest weakness. As we have previously observed, absolute up-front profit constraints, expressed as a prescribed percentage of allowed earnings on investment, do not prevent carriers from increasing their absolute amount of earnings. By expanding its rate base in the course of making investment decisions regarding its regulated activities, a rate of return regulated firm can increase its profits without any change in the allowed rate of return. This phenomenon, known as the Averch-Johnson effect,[*] encourages carriers to make inefficient investment decisions. Furthermore, rate of return does nothing to encourage carriers to limit expenses, since carrier expenses are flowed directly through to revenue requirements, a phenomenon known as "X-inefficiency."[†] * * *

84. Fewer commenters took issue with our tentative findings that rate of return lends itself to cross-subsidization, fails to achieve pricing efficiency, and is difficult to administer. There appears to be little disagreement that, under rate of return, carriers have an incentive to shift the costs of nonregulated, competitive activities onto regulated, less competitive services. In the Further Notice, we reviewed the great strides we have made in recent years in establishing regulatory road-blocks to discourage cross-subsidization. Nevertheless, we tentatively found that the policies of deterrence we established do not eliminate the strong incentives established by rate of return regulation to engage in cross-subsidy. We affirm that tentative decision here.

85. We also find that the administrative burdens imposed by rate of return regulation are significant. The process of acquiring sufficient information to pass judgment on carrier rates requires us to explore

* Eds. See Harvey Averch & Leland L. Johnson, *Behavior of the Firm Under Regulatory Constraints*, 52 AM. ECON. REV. 1052 (1962). The "A-J" effect is sometimes labeled "rate base padding" or "gold plating." The A-J effect does not describe a practice of simply exaggerating rate base costs; what it describes is an incentive for the firm to skew its choice of inputs to favor capital inputs over operating-cost inputs in order to leverage a higher rate of return. The formal conditions of the model are very restrictive, which probably accounts for the fact that, despite a cottage industry of theoretical writing on the subject, the empirical evidence in support of the effect is very thin.

† Eds. See Harvey Leibenstein, *Allocative Efficiency vs. X-Efficiency*, 56 AM. ECON. REV. 392 (1966). X-inefficiency is not a peculiar feature of rate regulation; the idea is simply that monopoly is more conducive to wasteful expenditures than is competition. There are some skeptics. See George J. Stigler, *The Xistence of X-Efficiency*, 66 AM. ECON. REV. 213 (1976).

complex cost allocation methodologies, evaluate demand predictions, and review comprehensive earnings data. If a simpler method of oversight were available, the savings generated would substantially ease the burdens on the carriers of preparing support materials and would eventually result in lower rates. In addition, simpler filings would, over the long term, lessen the burdens on this Commission, which would free our resources to focus on other important regulatory policies, such as the enforcement of market rules that foster competition. We recognize that the process of initiating incentive regulation, while retaining rate of return for some carriers, means that the administrative burdens on this Commission will not decrease substantially in the short term. Nevertheless, some savings will accrue immediately. We acknowledge those comments that would have us streamline our rate of return apparatus to produce administrative savings. We are constantly working to fine tune our regulatory methods so as to alleviate unnecessary burdens. Reduction of rate of return burdens, however, does not address the problems we have identified with that form of regulation. * * *

100. Our interest in formulating an alternative regulatory approach for dominant carriers stems directly from our concern with the drawbacks of rate of return regulation. We therefore tend to measure alternative regulatory methods against our rate of return system and, specifically, the four flaws that we have identified with it: (1) incentives for carriers to be inefficient; (2) insufficient incentives to encourage innovation; (3) tendency to foster cross-subsidization and inability to move toward an optimally efficient set of prices; and (4) high administrative costs. As we did in the Further Notice, we find that incentive regulation comes out ahead on all four fronts. In addition to these four areas, we have added a fifth criterion that we have said must be present for us to embrace incentive regulation—whether consumers will be better off than under rate of return. Therefore, before we decide that incentive regulation is a superior alternative for AT&T and local exchange carriers, we must be satisfied that a new regulatory approach helps solve the problems we have identified with rate of return and ensures that consumers will benefit.

101. The advantages we perceive in adopting incentive regulation are substantial. Most importantly, focusing in the first instance on limiting prices instead of profits dramatically reverses the tendency of rate of return regulated firms to engage in inefficient behavior. Carriers, faced with the inability to raise prices above a pre-set limit, must engage in efficiency-enhancing techniques to generate profits. This is exactly the type of behavior that we observe in firms in the competitive arena, where prices are in effect "set" by the market.

102. Unlike rate of return, incentive regulation is not in conflict with the fundamental consumer welfare-enhancing motivations that are created by competitive forces. Stated differently, the economic basis on which dominant carriers make decisions under incentive regulation is precisely the same as for a fully competitive firm. Once incentive regulation is introduced for dominant carriers, we can expect that more

and more efficiencies will gradually be introduced into carrier operations, thereby lowering a carrier's overall costs. The drop in costs associated with production represents a net benefit to the Nation's economy, since the same output is being produced at less cost. We therefore believe that incentive regulation, right from the start, will sharply reduce the tendency of carriers to engage in the types of behavior that have been labelled and measured in the economic literature as the Averch-Johnson effect and X-inefficiencies.

103. Other significant effects flow from incentive regulation, as well. Carriers are encouraged to engage in innovation to a greater degree than they were under rate of return. Under incentive regulation, the risks that carriers take in underwriting innovation, can be matched by rewards that are not limited by a profit cap. While it is true that some potential innovations may not be undertaken in an incentive-based regulatory structure, the decisions about whether to support the development of an innovative product or service are far more likely to be based on factors that competitive firms face in similar circumstances, which will help protect ratepayers against rate base padding through inefficient innovation. Those factors, such as the level of risk and the likely appeal of the good or service in the market, are better suited to stimulating useful innovation than any incentives that currently exist under rate of return.

104. Furthermore, incentive regulation substantially curtails the economic incentive to engage in cross-subsidization. In an environment of incentive regulation, carriers are limited in their ability to enhance profits by shifting costs from more competitive to less competitive activities, since the cap on prices limits a carrier's ability to raise rates to accommodate the shifted costs. Moreover, incentive regulation eliminates the incentive to shift costs to regulated services from nonregulated services. Under incentive regulation, all that a carrier accomplishes by moving costs to regulated services is to depress earnings, not to increase them. Incentive regulation, coupled with our existing regulatory controls to deter cross-subsidy, should substantially discourage anticompetitive activity involving cost shifting between regulated and nonregulated lines of business. * * *

111. In addition to finding that incentive regulation is capable of eliminating, and even reversing, several significant flaws inherent in rate of return, we also find that incentive regulation is better for consumers. By acting directly on a carrier's costs of providing service, and by increasing a carrier's willingness to innovate, incentive regulation means that telecommunications consumers can look forward to low cost and innovative services that the current regulatory structure would discourage. Furthermore, as will be discussed as part of the implementation sections of this Order, we are introducing substantial ratepayer protections to ensure that consumers will be better off as a group, and in particular, that residential ratepayers receive benefits from our plan. Features such as the Consumer Productivity Dividend (CPD), review and adjustment of the productivity factor beginning three years from the

date of inception, and careful attention to the design of baskets and bands ensures that consumers will benefit from an incentive system. * * *

III. Incentive Regulation For AT&T

* * *

C. Mechanics of Incentive Regulation

1. The Price Cap Index

185. The "price cap" we tentatively selected in the Further Notice consisted of a formula that would track inflation, carrier productivity, access costs, and other costs beyond a carrier's control. * * *

193. None of the commenters in this proceeding have persuaded us to discard the GNP-PI as the measure of inflationary changes faced by dominant carriers. * * *

221. As we stated in the Further Notice, an analysis of productivity must begin with a determination of whether the productivity of the telecommunications industry has exceeded that of the economy as a whole. Only if telecommunications productivity experiences greater gains than does the general economy is it necessary to include a productivity offset in our price cap index. Significantly, no party took issue with our tentative finding that, over the past 40 years, telecommunications productivity has exceeded that of the general economy by about 2 to 3 percent, with slightly lower values characterizing earlier periods of time. Parties did take issue, however, with whether the historical experience is relevant to AT&T's current productivity. In addition, parties are divided over what measure of productivity will best reflect current experience, and concerns are also expressed about our own analysis of AT&T productivity since divestiture. Based on our review of the record, we affirm the tentative findings we made on these issues in the Further Notice, and conclude that AT&T's productivity factor should be set at 2.5 percent, exclusive of the Consumer Productivity Dividend. * * *

248. To ensure that ratepayers are better off under price cap regulation, and to pass on directly to them gains resulting from efficiency improvements that we expect will result under a price cap system, we proposed to add the Consumer Productivity Dividend (CPD) of 0.5 percent to the productivity factor. The CPD ensures that consumers are the first beneficiaries of added efficiency under price caps, since prices will be 0.5 percent lower than otherwise. Only after AT&T achieves this degree of efficiency will it be in a position to reap rewards. As a result, the CPD essentially represents a guarantee that under a price cap system, inflation-adjusted rate reductions will exceed the historical average under rate of return. * * *

359. If our only concern in implementing incentive regulation were economic efficiency, we could establish one basket for all AT&T services, and no bands. In purely economic terms, customers as a whole would be at least as well off as they would be with any other combination of

baskets and bands, because prices in the aggregate could not exceed the cap. This structure also would present to the firm the incentives to pursue price changes that will recover total company costs while concomitantly reducing the loss in consumer surplus. However, economic efficiency is but one of this Commission's concerns. We also undertake to minimize the possibility of cross-subsidization and predation, both to protect residential and small business customers, and to foster competition that benefits all ratepayers. In the Further Notice, we proposed two baskets, one for switched and one for private line services. In employing the two-basket approach, the Further Notice relies heavily on bands to prevent predation. The pleadings in response to the Further Notice suggest that a different combination of baskets and bands would better balance our concerns about economic efficiency, ratepayer protection, and predation. We agree that modifications to our proposal should be made.

* * *

361. We conclude that services used primarily by residential and small business users should be in a separate basket, so that AT&T will not be able to raise prices for these services in order to lower prices for services that larger business customers use. A separate basket also means that residential and small business customers will be assured of their full share of access flow throughs. * * * Finally, we require AT&T to calculate an average residential rate, and we permit this rate to increase no more than one percent per year relative to the price cap index. Since the productivity factor embedded in the PCI operates to exert downward pressure on rates of 3 percent per year, the pricing constraint we place on the average residential rate has the effect of causing AT&T's average residential rate to fall 2 percent per year in real (inflation-adjusted) terms, absent exogenous cost changes. So long as AT&T proposes rates within the cap and band limitations, its tariffs will be given streamlined review.

362. Our decision to separate residential and small business services into their own basket leaves open the regulatory treatment of those services used predominantly by larger business customers. The record demonstrates that substantial barriers to entry remain in the 800 Service market and continue to impede competitive provision of 800 Service. Therefore, we establish a second separate basket for 800 Service with 5 percent upper and lower bands on each service category. We have also examined the remaining AT&T services to determine if further disaggregation is required, and have weighed the arguments for additional baskets against the need to design a system capable of attaining the economic and pricing efficiencies we seek. We find that the remaining services are generally provided to large users, and that much of the competitive activity in the interexchange market involves these services. We therefore conclude that these remaining services should be contained in a single basket, subject to service category banding limitations. * * *

391. Despite the fairly broad consensus on the need for bands, the latest round of comments is of little assistance in setting the numerical value for the percentage limitation. We conclude that the 5 percent upper bands for most service categories, and the 5 percent lower bands for all service categories, strike a reasonable balance between AT&T's ability to price efficiently, and customers' need for rate stability and regulatory protections. * * *

Price Caps for LECs. As we noted, the Commission subsequently adopted the price cap regime for dominant local exchange carriers (a category primarily which includes the three BOCs and other dominant LECs) with respect to their interstate access service. See *Policy and Rules Concerning Rates for Dominant Carriers*, 5 FCC Rcd. 6786 (1990), *on reconsideration*, 6 FCC Rcd. 2637 (1991), *affirmed sub nom. National Rural Telecom Ass'n v. FCC*, 988 F.2d 174 (D.C. Cir. 1993).[24] However, some of the details were changed for dominant LECs. Most notably, the Commission provided for a higher industry productivity offset, or "X factor" as the Commission called it—a total of 3.3% (with consumer dividend) instead of the 3% set in 1989 The "X factor" is subject to periodic adjustment to keep pace with the productivity of the industry compared to that of the economy generally. Currently the X factor is 6.5% (a productivity offset of 6% and a consumer dividend of .5%) See 47 C.F.R. § 61.45. (Carriers subject to price cap regulation are required to file adjustments in the price cap index as part of an annual tariff filing for each service basket.)

Baskets and Bands, Whistles and Bells. The LEC price cap scheme established four service baskets (instead of the three established in the 1989 order): (1) common line services; (2) traffic sensitive services; (3) special access services; and (4) interexchange services. As the Commission's 1989 order explains, the purpose of the baskets is to limit the ability of carriers to engage in unlawful cross subsidization. Within each basket the Commission then places "bands" designed to limit the degree of pricing change for that set of services—which is said to further hinder anti-competitive practices as well as protect the consumer against rapid price fluctuation. Are these whistles and bells necessary? In fact many participants in the LEC proceedings argued for even more detailed regulation—more baskets, tighter banding of prices, and other measures to limit the LECs' pricing flexibility.

And Baselines. Price caps do not themselves contain a mechanism for determining whether the carrier is earning a fair rate of return; they depend on the assumption that the baseline rates are fair. In its 1990 order, the Commission addressed this point (at 5 FCC Rcd. 6814–15):

> Our confidence in July 1, 1990 rates as a starting point for price cap regulation flows from a lengthy, six-year history of regulatory re-

24. Many state regulators also use price caps for regulating intrastate local services.

> form to refine our administration of rate of return regulation. * * * Our confidence in July 1, 1990 rates as a starting point for price cap regulation flows from a lengthy, six-year history of regulatory reform to refine our administration of rate of return regulation. * * * Our conclusion that July 1, 1990 rates are in general the best that rate of return regulation can produce is the result of this Commission's six year long effort at reforming our rate of return methods.

In light of the Commission's own critique of rate-of-return regulation, as exemplified in the 1989 report above, and repeated in the 1990 report, should the Commission have been so confident?

And Consumer "Productivity." The FCC adds a "consumer productivity dividend" on top of the industry productivity factor. Despite the label the Commission presumably isn't referring to a productivity enhancement attributable to actions by the consumer. All it means is that the consumer gets a first claim—a "dividend"—on any savings due to the productivity of the regulated firm. On what theory is the consumer entitled to such a dividend? The consumers already enjoy the benefit of the industry productivity factor, what claim should they have to a cut of savings over and above the industry average? Or perhaps this dividend is just a "fudge factor" designed to protect the consumer against an incorrect assessment of the true productivity savings?

Chapter 8

REMAKING TELECOMMUNICATIONS MARKETS: THE 1996 ACT

A. CONSTRUCTING A NEW REGIME

Modern times in telecommunications law begin in 1996 with the enactment of Telecommunications Act of 1996, the most comprehensive legislation on communications law since the original Communications Act of 1934. While the 1996 Act made a number of important changes in mass media law, its most important elements were in telecommunications, where it had three overarching objectives: (1) promote increased competition in long distance service markets; (2) reform the universal service system by shifting the subsidy burden from intercarrier access charges to explicit charges on long distance services; and (3) open local exchange and exchange access markets to competitive entry.

In addition to a general duty imposed on all carriers to interconnect (see 47 U.S.C. § 251(a)), the 1996 Act sought to accomplish these three general goals through fairly detailed mechanisms. Perhaps counterintuitively, the approach to expanding competition in long distance markets was to focus on local telephone monopolies. In addition to stricter interconnection obligations to make sure that the legacy local telephone monopolies (the "incumbent local exchange carriers," or "ILECs") would not discriminate against new long distance carriers, the statute also provided a set of incentives for BOCs to enter the long distance markets under § 271 of the Act, essentially in exchange for opening up their local monopolies to competition. Reform of the universal service system, too, focused on the interface between local and long distance carriers. Traditionally, long distance services had subsidized local service through implicit subsidies inherent in overcharging for long distance service and consequently undercharging for local service. But the implicit subsidy model would no longer work once the local and long distance services were provided by different companies, as demonstrated by the set of restraints adopted by AT&T that led to the breakup. At the same time, by adding competitive local carriers, the 1996 Act introduced a problem very similar to the access-charge problem: how to handle the billing relationship for calls originating from one LEC's network and terminating on another. Noting the similarity of the revenue flows, the FCC has chosen to handle both the long-distance-to-local and local-to-local sets of relationships under the unified rubric of "intercarrier compensation," while splitting off the subsidy question into its own inquiry on "universal service". In order to facilitate competitive entry at the local level, the Act imposed on ILECs a duty to disaggregate their local telephone service into a series of constituent pieces and to lease those "unbundled network elements" ("UNEs") to the new "competitive local exchange carriers" ("CLECs"). The plan was predicated on the understanding that it might be economically infeasible for CLECs to enter the local service market if they were required to build their own networks from scratch. Instead, entry was to happen by allowing CLECs to provide some elements of the local service and to lease the other elements from the ILEC. The decade since the 1996 Act has seen a running battle between the ILECs and CLECs over both the identity of the elements to be unbundled and the price CLECs should pay for them.

As one might expect, dismantling the national telephone monopoly has led to considerable upheaval and disagreement. We address each set of reforms in the sections that follow.

B. IMPROVING LONG DISTANCE COMPETITION

The 1996 Act repealed the 1982 AT&T consent decree, which had the effect of removing the last two of the line-of-business restrictions—the ban on BOC manufacture of telecom equipment and the ban on long distance service. However, the removal of restraints on long distance service came with some strings attached.[1] First, the Act distinguished between in-region and out-of-region services, that is between long distance service connecting points located in states within the respective home regions of the BOCs (where they offered local exchange service) on the one hand versus long distance service *across* the BOCs' regional boundaries on the other. The distinction between in-region and out-of-region interLATA service was premised on the assumption that, outside its region, a BOC would have no strategic advantage since it did not have a legacy monopoly in local exchange service; thus the bottleneck problem underlying the MFJ would not exist. On this assumption Congress authorized the RBOCs to provide inter-region interLATA service immediately upon enactment and without prior FCC authorization. However, BOC entry into in-region long distance service—service that is in whole

1. Actually there were some strings attached to the removal of the manufacturing ban as well. Among other things, § 272 of the Act required the BOCs to form a separate subsidiary for manufacturing, interLATA telecommunications and information services. However, the separate subsidiary requirement was subject to a sunset provision that terminated the requirement three years after the BOC was authorized to provide telecommunications service or, in the case of information services, four years from the date of the Act. Both conditions are now just history, but they reveal the rather cautious approach of Congress notwithstanding its overriding interest in repealing the MFJ.

or in part within the region where the BOC provides local exchange service—was subject to conditions designed to secure the BOC's cooperation in opening up their local service markets to competition.

In essential outline, § 271(c)(1) of the Act required that, for in-region long distance (that is, interLATA service originating in any state where the BOC provided local service) the BOC must obtain for each such state an authorization by the FCC. Basically the FCC authorization required proof that the BOCs had entered into interconnection and network access agreements with a competing local exchange carrier in its local market or that no competitor had requested such interconnection and access. Section 271(c)(2) further required that the agreement specified in 271(c)(1) comply with a set of detailed requirements set forth in a "competitive checklist" providing, among other things, access to all unbundled service components of the local exchange and interconnection in accordance with sections 251 and 252 (the very complicated provisions of which we take up in the sections below). For now the central point is simple: BOC entry into long distance was held hostage to obtaining their cooperation in enabling competitive entry into the BOC's local exchange markets.

Satisfying the requirements of § 271 for BOC entry into long distance proved to be no easy task. For years the BOCs' applications for FCC authorization were resisted by the existing long distance carriers—AT&T and MCI were then dominant in the market—on the ground that the BOCs had not satisfied the checklist criteria. Of course, AT&T and MCI had a double stake in the fight, since they were seeking both to defend their long distance markets against new competition and to enter into the BOCs' local markets. The battle over long distance authorization was waged on a state-by-state basis until late 2003, by which time the BOCs had secured long distance authority from the FCC for all states in which they offered local exchange service. The conflict over § 271, which consumed countless hours and dominated much of telecommunications legal practice for years, is by now a purely historical matter.

C. INTERCARRIER COMPENSATION

1. Introduction

Among other things, the breakup of AT&T has forced regulators to explicitly consider many aspects of the nation's telephone system that remained implicit so long as it was operated as a monopoly. Implicit in that monolithic structure were a set of revenue flows that served many different policies, policies that were frequently unrelated, occasionally hidden, and almost universally crossed jurisdictional boundaries. Specifically, under the old system, revenues tended to flow from long distance to local service, essentially working a subsidy of local service by charging inflated rates for long distance service. The explicit separation of long distance providers from the local providers made that implicit subsidy both more contentious as a general matter (because it would now be moving between distinct businesses instead of between divisions of a single business) and untenable in its previous form (because it was selectively applied to AT&T but not its competitors like MCI).

Moreover, the 1996 Act, by introducing competition at the local level, created an entirely new set of transactions between local carriers, a possibility that did not exist at the time of local telephone monopolies. Before, whenever a local call was placed, it remained within a single company. After, though, a local call might originate on one company's network and terminate on another's. Thus, the 1996 Act, by splitting the local carriage between carriers, raised the question of how to split the cost of that carriage between two carriers—who should pay for which portion of the call and how? The proliferation of wireless and voice over Internet protocol ("VoIP") service has only exacerbated the problem, as regulators struggle to deal with how differences in the various technologies should (or should not) be accounted for in the method for determining how revenue should flow between originating and terminating carriers.

With these new, essentially wholesale relationships among potential competitors, the emphasis of rate regulation in the modern competitive era has shifted away from protecting end consumers and toward protecting competitors who purchase services or facilities from dominant carriers. This is the central burden of the price cap regime examined in Chapter 7. While state regulators use price caps (or rate of return regulation) for local exchange services provided to end consumers, both state regulators and the FCC's use price caps to regulate the prices that LECs charge *other carriers*—respectively competing local carriers and long distance carriers—for the use of the local exchange facilities.

In an attempt to rationalize the entire system, the FCC has chosen to deal with the many problems presented by all of these revenue flows through a single, comprehensive proceeding, the *Unified Intercarrier Compensation* proceeding, which has been pending since 2001. Our effort to better understand all that is in play in the *Unified Intercarrier Compensation* proceeding is to disaggregate the many questions before considering the FCC's unified approach to reforming intercarrier compensation. We will first consider the question of compensation by long-distance providers for access to local networks—the problem of "access charges"—before moving on to the question of how to handle the local-to-local problem—that of "reciprocal compensation," and, finally, the Commission's unified intercarrier compensation reform agenda.

2. Access Charges

As was discussed in the *MCI* case in Chapter 7, in order for long distance carriers to have anything worth buying, they need to be able to reach individual phones served by the local carriers. Local carriers want to be compensated for that use of their facilities, and long distance carriers pay for that use through the mechanism of "access charges".

The problem of access charges has been enormously controversial and increasingly important with the rise of competition. Unfortunately, to understand the controversy it is necessary to return to a bygone era, when there was, for all practical purposes, a single, vertically integrated telephone system. In that era there were no access charge as such; instead costs were allocated between intra- and interexchange service as a means of accommodating the regulatory divide between intrastate jurisdiction of the states and the interstate jurisdiction of the FCC. The allocation of costs between local and the long distance is called "separations." Where AT&T provided both local and long distance this was basically just a matter of internal bookkeeping. Where AT&T interacted with independent carriers (typically local exchange carriers such as GTE), it involved intercarrier compensation arrangements known as "settlements." The cost/pricing mechanism was deliberately skewed to produce a system of cross subsidies that defies easy summary, but for present purposes we can focus on the central subsidy mechanism, which was to support local exchange service users at the expense of long distance service users; this was and is the core of a policy of "universal service"—the extension of telephone service to all households—that has roots in the early years of regulation.

The advent of competition into long distance markets in the 1970s required a radical overhaul of the traditional mechanisms for cost allocation and intercarrier compensation. If two services were provided by distinct companies, what had been largely a matter of informal account settlements had to be formalized. When, for example, the long distance provider MCI demanded interconnection with AT&T's local exchange network, it was necessary to establish a proper rate for the former's use of the local exchange facilities to complete a call. That was not a major problem, since AT&T had tariffs governing interconnection services. The key problem was how to handle the subsidy. AT&T could no longer be expected to bear the entire burden of supporting local service by keeping its long distance service rates high if MCI could systematically undercut them by not paying the subsidy. If there was to be competition in long distance markets, there had to be a level playing field (more or less): the new competitors would have to make the same proportionate contribution to local service as AT&T. In 1978, after years of debate and litigation between the parties over what that contribution should be, an agreement was reached among AT&T, MCI and other competitive carriers on a set of exchange access fees ("exchange network facilities access" or "ENFIA" fees), which the FCC approved as an interim arrangement. The ENFIA charges called for the competitors to pay more for access to the local exchange than they had been paying for simple interconnection arrangements. The competitors still paid less than the payments made by AT&T to its own local operating companies, so to a considerable degree there was still not a level playing field.

ENFIA was a transitional measure. Within a few years, the breakup of the Bell System would require a new set of access charges. In 1983, the FCC developed a set of access charges to be borne equally by all of the interexchange carriers. The new access charges did not eliminate the subsidy to local exchange service, but spread it proportionately (ostensibly) among the competitive long distance carriers. The new access charges were approved in *Rural Telephone Coalition v. FCC*, 838 F.2d 1307 (D.C. Cir. 1988). However, access charges continued to be controversial, in major part because of claims that AT&T still bore more than a proportional share of the costs. That issue aside, there was a growing concern about the distortion that was created by burdening access charges with the universal service subsidy. That distortion proved to be particularly difficult with the appearance of competitive access carriers, carriers that competed with the BOCs for providing access services to major local users. If major local users contracted with a competitive access carrier, that user would bypass the LECs (and thus bypass the high access charges and its contribution to the universal service subsidy).

When Congress enacted the Telecommunications Act of 1996 directing that local markets be made competitive and that long distance markets be made more competitive, it was forced to recognize that the existing access charge system had to be changed to remove the distorting influence of subsidies. It directed the FCC to reform the access charge system and the universal service system, to make the former cost-based and the latter an explicit, transparent subsidy independent of access charges. It turned out that was a tall order, on both counts. In fact, like local competition, it is still an unfinished task. In order to simplify our inquiry, we will delay discussion of the target of the subsidy—universal service—for the next section.

IN THE MATTER OF ACCESS CHARGE REFORM
First Report and Order

Federal Communications Commission, 1997.
12 FCC Rcd. 15982.

BY THE COMMISSION:

I. INTRODUCTION

1. In passing the Telecommunications Act of 1996 (the 1996 Act), Congress sought to establish "a pro-competitive, deregulatory national policy framework" for the United States' telecommunications industry. With this Order, we begin the third part in a trilogy of actions collectively intended to foster and accelerate the introduction of competition into all telecommunications markets, pursuant to the mandate of the 1996 Act.

2. In the *Local Competition Order*, we set forth rules to implement section 251 and section 252 of the Communications Act of 1934, as amended. As with all of Part II of Title II of the Communications Act, those sections, and the rules implementing them, seek to remove the legal, regulatory, economic, and operational barriers to telecommunications competition. Among other things, sections 251 and 252 provide entrants with the opportunity to compete for consumers in local markets

by either constructing new facilities, leasing unbundled network elements, or reselling telecommunication services.

3. In the *Universal Service Order*, which we adopt in a companion order today, we take steps to ensure that support mechanisms that are necessary to maintain local rates at affordable levels are protected and advanced as local telecommunication markets become subject to the competitive pressures unleashed by the 1996 Act. * * *

A. Background

1. The Existing Rate System

* * *

22. The Commission uses a multi-step process to identify the cost of providing access service. First, the rules require an incumbent LEC to record all of its expenses, investments, and revenues in accordance with accounting rules set forth in our regulations. Second, the rules divide these costs between those associated with regulated telecommunications services and those associated with nonregulated activities. Third, the separations rules determine the fraction of the incumbent LEC's regulated expenses and investment that should be allocated to the interstate jurisdiction. After the total amount of interstate cost is identified, the access charge rules translate these interstate costs into charges for the specific interstate access services and rate elements. Part 69 specifies in detail the rate structure for recovering those costs. That is, the rules tell the incumbent LECs the precise manner in which they may assess charges on interexchange carriers and end users.

23. Determining the costs that an incumbent LEC incurs to provide interstate access services and that, consequently, should be recovered from those services, is relatively straightforward in some cases and problematic in others. Some facilities, such as private lines, can be used exclusively for interstate services and, in such cases, the entire cost of those facilities is assigned to the interstate jurisdiction by the separations rules. Most facilities, however, are used for both intrastate and interstate services. The costs of some of these facilities vary depending on the amount of telecommunications traffic that they handle. The separations rules typically assign these traffic-sensitive (TS) costs on the basis of the relative interstate and intrastate usage of the facilities, as measured, for example, by the relative minutes of interstate and intrastate traffic carried by such facilities. By contrast, the costs of other facilities used for both interstate and intrastate traffic do not vary with the amount of traffic carried over the facilities, i.e., the costs are non-traffic-sensitive. These costs pose particularly difficult problems for the separations process: The costs of such facilities cannot be allocated on the basis of cost-causation principles because all of the facilities would be required even if they were used only to provide local service or only to provide interstate access services. A significant illustration of this problem is allocating the cost of the local loop, which is needed both to provide local telephone service as well as to originate and terminate

long-distance calls. The current separations rules allocate 25 percent of the cost of the local loop to the interstate jurisdiction for recovery through interstate charges.

24. The Commission has recognized in prior rulemaking proceedings that, to the extent possible, costs of interstate access should be recovered in the same way that they are incurred, consistent with principles of cost-causation. Thus, the cost of traffic-sensitive access services should be recovered through corresponding per-minute access rates. Similarly, NTS costs should be recovered through fixed, flat-rated fees. The Commission, however, has not always adopted rules that are consistent with this goal. In particular, the Commission limited the amount of the allocated interstate cost of a local loop that is assessed to residential and business customers as a flat monthly charge, because of concerns that allowing the flat charges to rise above the specified limits might cause customers to disconnect their telephone service. The residual cost of the loop not recovered from end users through the flat charge is recovered through a per-minute-of-use charge assessed to long-distance carriers.

25. Through the end of 1990, the vast majority of access revenues were governed by "cost-of-service" regulation. Under cost-of-service regulation, incumbent LECs calculate the specific access charge rates using projected costs and projected demand for access services. Thus, for example, if an incumbent LEC projects that it will provide 10,000 total minutes of switching for interstate calls and estimates that it must generate $1,000 dollars in revenue in order to recover the costs of switching that are allocated to the interstate jurisdiction by the separations rules, the access charge for local switching would be set at $0.10 per minute ($1,000/10,000 minutes). In 1991, however, we implemented a system of price cap regulation that altered the manner in which the largest incumbent LECs established their interstate access charges. While most rural and small LECs remained subject to all of the Part 69 cost-of-service rules, generally the largest incumbent LECs are now subject to price cap regulations set forth in Part 61 of our rules.

26. Price cap regulation fundamentally alters the process by which incumbent LECs determine the revenues they are permitted to obtain from interstate access charges for access services. Briefly stated, cost-of-service regulation is designed to limit the profits an incumbent LEC may earn from interstate access service, whereas price cap regulation focuses primarily on the prices that an incumbent LEC may charge and the revenues it may generate from interstate access services. Under the Part 69 cost-of-service rules, revenue requirements are based on embedded or accounting costs allocated to individual services. Incumbent LECs are limited to earning a prescribed return on investment and are potentially obligated to provide refunds if their interstate rate of return exceeds the authorized level. By contrast, although the access charges of price cap LECs originally were set at the cost-of-service levels that existed at the time they entered price caps, their prices have been limited ever since by price indices that have been adjusted annually pursuant to formulae set

forth in our Part 61 rules. Price cap carriers whose interstate access charges are set by these pricing rules are permitted to earn returns significantly higher than the prescribed rate of return that incumbent LECs are allowed to earn under cost-of-service rules. Price cap regulation encourages incumbent LECs to improve their efficiency by harnessing profit-making incentives to reduce costs, invest efficiently in new plant and facilities, and develop and deploy innovative service offerings, while setting price ceilings at reasonable levels. In this way, price caps act as a transitional regulatory scheme until the advent of actual competition makes price cap regulation unnecessary.

27. Although price cap regulation eliminates the direct link between changes in allocated accounting costs and change in prices, it does not sever the connection between accounting costs and prices entirely. The overall interstate revenue levels still generally reflect the accounting and cost allocation rules used to develop access rates to which the price cap formulae were originally applied. Price cap indices are adjusted upwards if a price cap carrier earns returns below a specified level in a given year. Moreover, a price cap LEC may petition the Commission to set its rates above the levels permitted by the price cap indices based on a showing that the authorized rate levels will produce earnings that are so low as to be confiscatory. In the past, all or some price cap LECs were required to "share," or return to ratepayers, earnings above specified levels. The new rules adopted in the companion *Price Cap Fourth Report and Order* remove this limit on the maximum returns that can be earned by price cap incumbent LECs.

2. Implicit Subsidies in the Existing System

28. Both our price cap and cost-of-service rules contain requirements that inevitably result in charges to certain end users that exceed the cost of the service they receive. To the extent these rates do not reflect the underlying cost of providing access service, they could be said to embody an implicit subsidy. Some of these subsidies are due to the rate structures prescribed by our rules, which in some cases prevent incumbent LECs from recovering their access costs in the same way they have been incurred. For example, although the cost of the local loop that connects an end user to the telephone company's switch does not vary with usage, the current rate structure rules require incumbent LECs to recover a large portion of these non-traffic-sensitive costs through traffic-sensitive, per-minute charges. These mandatory recovery rules inflate traffic-sensitive usage charges and reduce charges for connection to the network, in essence creating an implicit support flow from end users that make many interstate long-distance calls to end users that make few or no interstate long-distance calls.

29. Several Federal-State Joint Boards have observed that additional subsidies and distortions may be due, not only to the rate structure, but to the separations rules that divide costs between the interstate and intrastate jurisdictions. For example, the current separations rules require larger incumbent LECs to allocate the costs of their

switching facilities between the interstate and intrastate jurisdictions on the basis of relative use (i.e., if 30 percent of the minutes of use handled by the LEC's switching facilities are interstate long-distance calls, 30 percent of the LEC's switching costs are allocated to the interstate jurisdiction and recovered through interstate access charges). Our rules, however, permit smaller incumbent LECs to allocate a greater share of their switching costs to interstate access services than would result from the relative use allocator. These smaller incumbent LECs multiply the interstate use ratio by a factor (as high as 3) specified in the separations rules. In its *Recommended Decision*, the Joint Board on Universal Service observed that these separations rules "shift what would otherwise be intrastate costs to the interstate jurisdiction," thereby allowing such LECs to charge lower prices for intrastate services. Similarly, in the *Marketing Expense Recommended Decision*, another Federal-State Joint Board observed that the separations rules allocate a share of the incumbent LECs' retail marketing expenses to the interstate jurisdiction that is unreasonably high, given that the interstate access services consist primarily of wholesale service offerings. To the extent these and other separation rules do not apportion costs between the jurisdictions in a manner that reflects the costs incurred to provide service in each jurisdiction, they might be viewed as generating subsidies from the interstate to the intrastate jurisdiction. These subsidies effectively require incumbent LECs to charge higher rates for interstate services and lower rates for intrastate services than would otherwise occur if the subsidies were eliminated.

30. This "patchwork quilt of implicit and explicit subsidies" generates inefficient and undesirable economic behavior. For example, a rate structure that requires the use of per-minute access charges where flat-rated fees would be more appropriate increases the per-minute rates paid by IXCs and long-distance consumers, thus artificially suppressing demand for interstate long-distance services. Similarly, the possible overallocation of costs to the interstate jurisdiction may, for some consumers, increase long-distance rates substantially, suppressing their demand for interstate interexchange services. Implicit subsidies also have a disruptive effect on competition, impeding the efficient development of competition in both the local and long-distance markets. For example, where rates are significantly above cost, consumers may choose to bypass the incumbent LEC's switched access network, even if the LEC is the most efficient provider. Conversely, where rates are subsidized (as in the case of consumers in high-cost areas), rates will be set too low and an otherwise efficient provider would have no incentive to enter the market. In either case, the total cost of telecommunications services will not be as low as it would otherwise be in a competitive market. Because of the growing importance of the telecommunications industry to the economy as a whole, this inefficient system of access charges retards job creation and economic growth in the nation. * * *

3. The Telecommunications Act of 1996

32. The existing system of implicit subsidies and support flows is sustainable only in a monopoly environment in which incumbent LECs are guaranteed an opportunity to earn returns from certain services and customers that are sufficient to support the high cost of providing other services to other customers. The new competitive environment envisioned by the 1996 Act threatens to undermine this structure over the long run. The 1996 Act removes barriers to entry in the local market, generating competitive pressures that make it difficult for incumbent LECs to maintain access charges above economic cost. For example, by giving competitors the right to lease an incumbent LEC's unbundled network elements at cost, Congress provided IXCs an alternative avenue to connect to and share the local network. Thus, where existing rules require an incumbent LEC to set access charges above cost for a high-volume user, a competing provider of exchange access services entering into a market can lease unbundled network elements at cost, or construct new facilities, to circumvent the access charge. In this way, a new entrant might target an incumbent LEC's high-volume access customers, for whom access charges are now set at levels significantly above economic cost. As competition develops, incumbent LECs may be forced to lower their access charges or lose market share, in either case jeopardizing the source of revenue that, in the past, has permitted the incumbent LEC to offer service to other customers, particularly those in high-cost areas, at below-cost prices. Incumbent LECs have for some time been claiming that this process has already made more than trivial inroads on their high-volume customer base.

33. Recognizing the vulnerability of implicit subsidies to competition, Congress directed the Commission and the states to take the necessary steps to create permanent universal service mechanisms that would be secure in a competitive environment. To achieve this end, Congress directed the Commission to strive to replace the system of implicit subsidies with "explicit and sufficient" support mechanisms. * * *

34. In the *Universal Service Order*, we establish "explicit and sufficient" support mechanisms to assist users in high-cost areas, low-income consumers, schools, and health care providers. By creating explicit support mechanisms, we establish a system to advance the universal service goals of the 1996 Act that is compatible with the development of competition in the local exchange and exchange access markets. By creating a portable and measurable system of subsidies, we utilize the power of the market to serve universal service goals more efficiently. That order, in short, guarantees that Congress's universal service goals are met in a way that conforms with the pro-competitive and deregulatory goals of the 1996 Act.

B. Access Charge Reform

35. In light of Congress's command to create secure and explicit mechanisms to achieve universal service goals, we conclude that implicit

subsidies embodied in the existing system of interstate access charges cannot be indefinitely maintained in their current form. In this Order, therefore, we take two steps with respect to the rules governing the interstate access charges of price cap incumbent LECs. First, we reform the current rate structure to bring it into line with cost-causation principles, phasing out significant implicit subsidies. Second, we set in place a process to move the baseline rate level toward competitive levels. Together with the *Universal Service Order*, these adjustments will promote the public welfare by encouraging investment and efficient competition, while establishing a secure structure for achieving the universal service goals established by law. Further, the process we set in place to achieve these goals avoids the destabilizing effects of sudden radical change, facilitating the transformation from a regulated to a competitive marketplace. * * *

Having adopted a theory of access charge reform, the FCC set about actually coming up with a set of access charges. That effort culminated in a three-tier set of charges which were challenged in the D.C. Circuit in 2004.

NATIONAL ASSOCIATION OF STATE UTILITY CONSUMER ADVOCATES v. FCC

United States Court of Appeals, District of Columbia Circuit, 2004.
372 F.3d 454.

GINSBURG, CHIEF JUDGE:

The National Association of State Utility Consumer Advocates (NASUCA) petitions for review of an order of the Federal Communications Commission adjusting the manner in which Local Exchange Carriers (LECs) may recover the fixed costs they incur in providing service to residential and single-line business customers. NASUCA claims the approach adopted by the Commission violates the "universal service" provisions of the Telecommunications Act of 1996, results in rates that are unjust and unreasonable, and is arbitrary and capricious, in violation of the Administrative Procedure Act. We hold the Commission acted reasonably and in conformity with the 1996 Act and, accordingly, we deny NASUCA's petition for review.

I. BACKGROUND

This case challenges the Commission's latest attempt to phase out certain "implicit subsidies" resulting from the access fee the LECs charge interexchange carriers (IXCs) in order to recover the expenses the LECs incur to build and operate local loops—the part of the telecommunications network that runs from the LEC's switch to the customer's premises (a/k/a "the last mile"). These implicit subsidies are the means by which the Commission assures the provision of universal service, for without the subsidies many customers in sparsely populated areas would be unwilling to pay the high rates necessary to cover the LECs' cost of serving them. As detailed more fully below, and in accordance with the policy of the 1996 Act, the Commission has been attempting to make the subsidies transparent by replacing implicit subsidies with explicit subsidies. *See* 47 U.S.C. § 254. The order here under review is intended to be a step in that direction.

When AT&T was broken up in 1984, the Commission first issued rules governing the access charges IXCs were to pay LECs for originating and terminating long distance calls. Those charges did not, however, cover the cost of the local loop, which the LECs instead recovered directly from end users through a flat fee per line called the Subscriber Line Charge (SLC); it is flat because the LEC's cost of providing the local loop is not traffic-sensitive. Recovering the cost of the loop from end users, however, raised the prospect that customers in outlying regions, where the cost per line could be quite high, would drop their telephone service and thus compromise the objective of universal service. The Commission therefore decreed that some of the cost of the local loop would be recovered through a per-minute-use charge, known as the Carrier Common Line (CCL) charge, that IXCs would pay LECs for handling their traffic. The Commission initially capped the SLC at $3.50 per line. Because that was significantly below the average fixed cost of the local loop, a substantial portion of the cost had to be recovered through the CCL charge, which worked a large, albeit implicit, subsidy from high-to low-volume long distance callers.

The implicit subsidies inherent in the Commission's rate structure helped to assure access to affordable telecommunication service in rural areas, but they were incompatible with another goal of the 1996 Act, namely, opening local telecommunication markets to competition.... In 1997 the Commission took a step toward "[r]ationalizing" its rate structure by "eliminat[ing] significant implicit subsidies in the access charge system." This it did by allowing greater recovery of fixed costs through flat (as opposed to traffic-sensitive) fees. The Commission did not, however, allow further recovery through the SLC, which remained capped at $3.50 per line, because it was concerned that a higher price for the basic dial tone could cause rural customers to discontinue service—"contrary to [the Commission's] mandate to ensure universal service." Rather than impose an additional charge upon the end user, therefore, the Commission settled upon a "flat, per-line charge assessed on the IXC to whom [sic] the access line is presubscribed," *id.*, known as the presubscribed interexchange carrier charge (PICC).

Not long after introducing the PICC, the Commission realized it was not a complete solution: "Because IXCs have recovered the residential PICCs on a per-account basis, residential customers with only one line pay the same as those with two or more lines, and so pay more than the costs IXCs have incurred for providing them service." *In the Matter of Access Charge Reform; Price Cap Performance Review for Local Exchange Carriers; Low–Volume Long Distance Users; Federal–State Joint*

Board On Universal Service (*CALLS I*) ¶ 19, 15 FCC Rcd 12,962, 12,970 (2000). In order to offset that newly-introduced cross-subsidy, the Commission scheduled incremental increases in the cap on the SLC that LECs charge end users—from $3.50 per line to $4.35 in 2000, to $5.00 in 2001, to $6.00 in 2002, and to $6.50 in 2003. Well, not necessarily. * * * The maximum allowable recovery via the SLC, CCL charge, and PICC combined is equal to the amount the LEC would be allowed to recover under price cap regulation, which is based upon the LEC's historical cost of providing the local loop. * * *

Because a LEC recovers its local loop costs in a "cascading fashion"—first through the SLC, then the PICC, and finally the CCL charge—an increase in the SLC cap reduces by the same amount what the LEC may recover through the CCL charge and the PICC—the Commission's goal being to minimize and then to eliminate those charges. *See In the Matter of Cost Review Proceeding for Residential and Single-Line Business Subscriber Line Charge (SLC) Caps; Access Charge Reform; Price Cap Performance Review for Local Exchange Carriers* (*CALLS II*) ¶ 15, 17 FCC Rcd 10,868, at 10,875–76.

In *CALLS I* the Commission also established the Universal Service Fund, an "explicit interstate universal service support mechanism," in order to help offset the reduction in the implicit subsidies; it is to be funded with $650 million raised through a new element in the rate that LECs charge subscribers....

Finally, in *CALLS I* the Commission undertook to "review any increases to residential and single-line business SLC caps above $5.00 to verify that any such increases are appropriate and reflect higher costs where they are to be applied." In doing that review, the Commission said it would examine "forward-looking cost information" to be provided by the LECs.

The Commission completed its review in September 2001 and issued its findings in June 2002 [in *CALLS II*]. This is what the Commission found:

> [E]ven the most conservative estimate of forward-looking costs [i.e., NASUCA's] shows that a substantial number of lines exceed both the current $5.00 SLC cap, and the ultimate $6.50 SLC cap. Thus, we determine that raising the SLC cap to the levels set forth in [*CALLS I*] is justified by the record in this proceeding. We also find that those increases to the SLC cap are necessary to achieve our access charge reform goals, as stated in [*CALLS I*], of removing implicit subsidies by moving to a more cost-causative rate structure and enabling greater opportunities for SLC deaveraging.

The Commission also pointed out that it had previously found a SLC cap of $6.50 is "affordable" for residential and single-line business customers.... Hence, the Commission concluded, "to achieve the benefits of removing implicit subsidies and allowing SLC deaveraging, while maintaining affordable residential and single-line business rates for consumers," it would allow the SLC cap to increase as scheduled in *CALLS I*.

NASUCA petitions this court for review of the Commission's decision in *CALLS II*.

II. Analysis

NASUCA argues the Commission's decision in *CALLS II* violates several provisions of the 1996 Act and is "arbitrary and capricious," in violation of the [Administrative Procedure Act].

A. 1996 Act Claims

NASUCA first argues the Commission failed to "give effect to the unambiguously expressed intent of Congress," to remove implicit subsidies and to replace them with explicit subsidies, as expressed in §§ 254(b)(5) and 254(e) of the 1996 Act. NASUCA supports the factual predicate of this claim by pointing to its own cost study, which showed nearly 75% of residential and single-line business customers have forward-looking costs less than $5.00 and 86% of those lines have forward-looking costs less than $6.50. NASUCA views any SLC charge exceeding forward-looking costs as an "implicit subsid[y] running from customers with lower cost lines to customers with higher cost lines."

The Commission responds that an implicit subsidy from lower cost to higher cost lines was not immediately ruled out by the 1996 Act and under *CALLS I* is only to be phased out over time; in fact, some subsidization is "inevitable" as long as there is any rate averaging. According to the Commission, the issue in this case, properly understood, is whether its approach is "an improvement over the pre-existing situation and will provide a transition to less subsidization." We agree.

Although the Act charges the Commission with devising "specific, predictable and sufficient Federal and State mechanisms to preserve and advance universal service," 47 U.S.C. § 254(b)(5), it does not decree an immediate revolution; as we have said before, "there is no time limit on *realization* of the reform," The Commission in *CALLS I* put in place a reasonable timetable, recognizing that only by proceeding in steps may all implicit subsidies be eliminated without compromising universal service.

In *CALLS II* the Commission explained that an increase in the SLC cap would help LECs eliminate the PICC, which the Commission had previously found to be an inefficient method of recovering the LECs' fixed costs:

> By eliminating the residential and single-line business PICCs, the CALLS Proposal establishes a straightforward, economically rational pricing structure which enables consumers to make a choice among competing providers through head-to-head comparisons and better promotes competition by sending potential entrants economically correct entry incentives.

Again, an increase in the SLC cap does not increase the LEC's revenue; rather, it merely shifts the source of the LEC's CMT Revenue away from the CCL charge and the PICC....

NASUCA next argues the increase in the SLC cap allows LECs to charge SLC rates that are not "just and reasonable," in violation of 47 U.S.C. §§ 201(b) and 254(b)(1). [A]ccording to NASUCA, the Commission must [under the methodology it committed itself to in *CALLS I*] set rates based upon forward-looking costs. The Commission responds by pointing out that in *CALLS II* it changed only the SLC cap; it did nothing to change the method it uses to set the underlying SLC rates.

The Commission is clearly correct. Nothing in *CALLS I* committed the Commission to the sea change in rate-setting urged by NASUCA, that is, immediately basing all LECs' rates solely upon forward-looking costs. On the contrary, the Commission stated in *CALLS I* that it was "extending for five years" its existing approach, which would over time bring rates "toward forward-looking economic cost." As the Commission reasonably observed in the order under review, the *CALLS* proceedings were "not designed to change the existing method of setting SLC rates, which relies on the application of the price cap formula to CMT revenues." That approach, as mentioned above, is based upon historical, not forward-looking, cost.

Finally, both in arguing the Commission violated the 1996 Act and in arguing its decision is arbitrary and capricious (see Part II.B, below), NASUCA claims no further increase in the SLC cap was necessary due to the "explicit" support provided by the $650 million Universal Service Fund. That Fund, however, is only one part of the Commission's overall approach to eliminating implicit subsidies. Neither in *CALLS I* nor in *CALLS II* did the Commission indicate the Universal Service Fund alone would be sufficient to achieve the Commission's ultimate goal of eliminating all implicit subsidies. Accordingly, NASUCA's invocation of the Fund does nothing to call into question the reasonableness of the Commission's decision.

B. APA Claims

NASUCA argues the Commission's decision in *CALLS II* is "arbitrary and capricious" because it: (1) "runs counter to the evidence" in the record; (2) "failed to articulate any explanation" for its conclusion; (3) departed from precedent upon the basis of irrelevant factors; and (4) failed to explain why it departed from prior FCC policy. For the most part, NASUCA here simply repackages its claims under the 1996 Act as claims the Commission's decision violates the Administrative Procedure Act. We find the Commission's decision no less reasonable when viewed through the lens of the APA. * * *

The Commission is necessarily entitled to substantial deference when it must draw numerical lines in order to balance two congressional policies that cannot both be fully achieved. * * *

In sum, NASUCA's claim that the Commission's decision to raise the SLC cap was arbitrary and capricious simply ignores the Commission's reasoning in *CALLS II* and the facts upon which that decision is based. The Commission's decision striking a balance between competing congressional directives—reducing implicit subsidies and maintaining universal service—was reasonable and was supported by substantial evidence in the record.

III. Conclusion

For the foregoing reasons, NASUCA's petition for review is *Denied.*

Robbing Peter to Pay Paul. As indicated in the *First Report and Order*, there were actually two points to the access charge proceedings: to eliminate the implicit subsidy and to rationalize access charges to reflect true nature of the fixed costs of providing access. But when the FCC actually confronted what the true costs of providing access were, it blinked and supplemented the fixed-cost subscriber line charges with a usage-based CLC. Why? As the court points out in *NASUCA*, the changes to the access charge regime did not increase the total amount that the LECs were receiving, it just shuffled it between fixed and usage-based pricing. What's the point of doing so? The FCC was concerned that some users would drop their local service when faced with high subscriber line charges, but then it shifted those costs to a usage-based measure. Was the theory that those who use more long distance are actually wealthier or just that they are less price sensitive because they are more dependent on their telephones? Is the policy of universal service served if it provides service to people who can afford service but who simply don't value the service as much as it costs to provide it? After the CLC proved inadequate, the FCC adopted the PICC, which was a fixed fee but was assessed on the IXC rather than the user. The PICC might have been truer to cost accounting principles than the CLC, but how would it have appeared to users?

3. Reciprocal Compensation

Reciprocal compensation—payments made by one carrier for the termination of local calls (those not subject to access charges)—is governed by sections 251(b)(5) and 252(d)(2) of the Communications Act. Because they pertain to intrastate calls, reciprocal compensation rates are set by state public utility commissions (or rather through interconnection agreements ratified by state public utility commissions), not the FCC, but they are set according to rules and standards established by the FCC. Like the problem of access charges, reciprocal compensation represents a set of choices that are somewhat confused by a muddled history, albeit a shorter one. Also like the access charge context, it represents both a major policy choice and a set of very detailed implementing rules.

The major problem raised by reciprocal compensation comes from the potential for asymmetries in both the use and cost of the terminating network. When local telephone service was provided by a monopoly, every call both originated and terminated on the same network. In that world, it made sense to simply charge the calling customer for the entire cost of the call. As far as the customers were concerned, there was some intuitive appeal to charging the customer that had chosen to initiate the call and, as far as the carrier was concerned, there was no economic difference between the calling and receiving customers since they were both customers of the monopoly. With the advent of local competition, the second assumption was no longer true. If the calling and receiving carriers split, there needs to be a way to fund both sides (the "originating" and "terminating") of the call. The intuitive, initiator-pays model works fine for the carrier serving the calling party, but there is no easy answer for how to fund the carrier that terminates the call with the receiving party.

Thus, the major policy question in the reciprocal compensation context is how to fund the terminating carrier's carriage, and the major choice is between "calling party network pays" (or "CPNP") and "bill-and-keep" arrangements. CPNP follows the pre-competition model in which the calling party pays for the entire call, and the calling party's carrier compensates the terminating carrier for the portion of the call carried over the terminating carrier's network. Under bill-and-keep, no funds are transferred between carriers and each carrier charges their customers for use of the network, whether placing or receiving calls.

In the wake of the 1996 Act, the Commission adopted CPNP as the standard for most local traffic. Although CPNP was the traditional rule in the United States, there are some segments in which customers are used to paying for calls that they receive in addition to those they place; the best example is probably termination of calls to wireless customers, which operates largely on a bill-and-keep system.

Because CPNP requires payments to flow between (frequently competing) carriers, rate setting is an important issue. Because they are local in nature, reciprocal compensation rates are set locally, either by state-filed tariff or through state-arbitrated interconnection agreements using an FCC-determined standard for setting rates (much as they do in regard to the provision by ILECs to CLECs of unbundled network elements, which we discus in more detail below). Rate setting makes asymmetries even more problematic. Some carriers (especially rural, high-cost ILECs and wireless carriers) have higher costs to terminate than do other carriers. Moreover, some customers generate or receive a disproportionate number of calls. Unless the rates are perfectly calibrated, once asymmetry is a possibility, so is arbitrage.

Asymmetrical advantage was the cause of the first major dispute regarding reciprocal compensation: The heyday of dial-up Internet access corresponded with they introduction of competition in local service, and ISPs receive many calls but rarely place them, setting the stage for a systematic asymmetrical use of the network between calling parties and receiving parties. Looking for reciprocal compensation dollars, many CLECs built their businesses by targeting dial-up ISPs, who receive many calls but rarely place them. ILECs responded by seeking (and obtaining) a ruling limiting the ability of CLECs to collect reciprocal compensation for ISP-bound traffic in 1999. That ruling was twice remanded by the court of appeals, and the status of ISP-bound traffic is still in limbo.[2] At the same time that it issued the still-standing order calling for bill-and-keep in the ISP context, the FCC initiated the inquiry in *Developing a Unified Intercarrier Compensation Regime*, which remains pending as this book goes to press.

4. Intercarrier Compensation Reform

One of the major problems the FCC has identified with the current regime is that it treats access charges and reciprocal compensation differently even though they provide essentially the same function: access to the local network in order to create a connection between one carrier and the customers of another. Thus the FCC's "unified" approach to reform.

DEVELOPING A UNIFIED INTERCARRIER COMPENSATION REGIME
Further Notice of Proposed Rulemaking

Federal Communications Commission, 2005.
20 FCC Rcd. 4685.

BY THE COMMISSION:

* * *

A. THE NEED FOR REFORM

* * *

2. The Current Intercarrier Compensation Regimes Cannot Be Sustained in the Developing Marketplace

a) Introduction

15. The record in this proceeding shows that the three basic principles underlying our existing intercarrier compensation regimes

2. The Commission first ruled that, because the call is for communication that will eventually lead to another source (a computer out on the Internet), ISP-bound traffic was interstate in nature and therefore not subject to reciprocal compensation. See Inter-Carrier Compensation for ISP-Bound Traffic, Declaratory Ruling, 14 FCC Rcd. 3689 (1999). The D.C. Circuit vacated and remanded portions of the ruling, seeking further justification for the Commission's determination that ISP-bound traffic is necessarily interstate in nature. See Bell Atlantic Tel. Cos. v. FCC, 206 F.3d 1 (D.C. Cir. 2000). The FCC responded by finding ISP-bound traffic to be "mixed interstate and intrastate traffic," but should still not be subject to reciprocal compensation arrangements. Instead it established a bill-and-keep system, albeit with a transitional set of compensation rules subject to a cap on the amount that LECs could charge for terminating ISP-bound traffic. Intercarrier Compensation for ISP–Bound Traffic, Order on Remand and Report and Order, 16 FCC Rcd. 9151 (2001). Again, the court reversed and remanded because the FCC's actions were not authorized by the provisions of the Act on which it had relied. However, it did not vacate the new order, noting that many of the petitioners themselves favored the bill-and-keep system and that the FCC possibly had authority to mandate it under other provisions. WorldCom, Inc. v. FCC, 288 F.3d 429 (D.C. Cir. 2002).

must be re-examined in light of significant market developments since the adoption of the access charge and reciprocal compensation rules. First, our existing compensation regimes are based on jurisdictional and regulatory distinctions that are not tied to economic or technical differences between services. As the Commission observed in the *Intercarrier Compensation NPRM*, regulatory arbitrage arises from different rates that different types of providers must pay for essentially the same functions. Our current classifications require carriers to treat identical uses of the network differently, even though such disparate treatment usually has no economic or technical basis. These artificial distinctions distort the telecommunications markets at the expense of healthy competition. Moreover, the availability of bundled service offerings and novel services blur the traditional industry and regulatory distinctions that serve as the foundation of the current rules.[48]

16. Second, our existing compensation regimes are predicated on the recovery of average costs on a per-minute basis. Under average cost pricing, a network can invest in facilities to attract subscribers and recover a share of those costs from subscribers choosing competing networks. As competition has increased, the ability to shift costs to competitors through intercarrier charges increasingly distorts the competitive process. In addition, advancements in telecommunications infrastructure affect the way carrier costs are incurred and call into question the use of per-minute pricing.

17. Third, under the existing regimes, the calling party's carrier, whether LEC, IXC, or CMRS provider, compensates the called party's carrier for terminating the call. Thus, as a general matter, our existing regimes are based on a "calling-party-network-pays" (CPNP) approach to compensation. Developments in the ability of consumers to manage their own telecommunications services undermine the premise that the calling party is the sole cost causer and should be responsible for all the costs of a call. As discussed below, we find that all these developments compel the Commission to move toward a new, unified intercarrier compensation regime that is better suited to a market characterized by competition among multiple types of carriers and technologies.

b. Developments in Service Offerings

18. The telecommunications marketplace has changed dramatically since the Commission adopted the existing intercarrier compensation regimes. For instance, most wireless services were not widely available in the 1980s, when the Commission adopted the access charge regime, and wireless services were only beginning to gain a foothold in the market in 1996. Today, there are at least 160 million wireless subscribers and the numbers continue to increase. Due in part to the Commission's deregulatory approach to these services, wireless providers were able to offer bundled local and long-distance packages, and the availability of these

48. For instance, the Commission has struggled to determine the appropriate regulatory regime for Internet traffic. In this proceeding, the Commission hopes to address the compensation regime for all types of traffic, including ISP-bound traffic.

bundled packages contributed to the astounding growth of wireless services.

19. Prior to 1996, most wireline carriers were limited to providing a single type of service, such as local or long-distance. The 1996 Act fundamentally changed the telecommunications marketplace by opening all market segments to competition and by lifting existing restrictions on the provision of specific services by some classes of carriers. It is undisputed that carriers are taking advantage of the competitive opportunities presented by the 1996 Act. These legal and regulatory changes enable carriers to offer a broad range of services to their customers, including flat-rated "bundles" of two or more services. Carriers such as Verizon, MCI, and AT&T now offer unlimited local, long-distance, and other services in one flat-rated service package. These offerings, which from the customer's perspective do not distinguish between local and long-distance service, are dramatically different than the retail offerings that existed prior to the 1996 Act.

20. In addition to competitive developments within the wireless and wireline sectors, the advent of voice-over-internet protocol (VoIP) technology has introduced another mass market alternative to traditional fixed telephone service. New entrants, such as Vonage, have initiated VoIP services in recent years, and a number of other service providers, including Qwest, Verizon, and a number of cable operators, have begun to use or will soon use Internet protocol to provide voice services. These developments have raised a number of regulatory issues for the Commission to resolve.[*]

21. These bundled offerings and novel services blur traditional industry and regulatory distinctions among various types of services and service providers, making it increasingly difficult to enforce the existing compensation regimes. Moreover, in a market where carriers are offering the same services and competing for the same customers, disparate treatment of different types of carriers or types of traffic has significant competitive implications. For instance, if one type of carrier primarily recovers costs from other carriers, rather than its retail customers, it may have a competitive advantage over another type of carrier that must recover the same costs primarily from its own retail customers.

* * *

c. Developments in Telecommunications Infrastructure

23. Another consideration is how the telecommunications infrastructure has developed, which affects the way carrier costs are incurred and recovered under the intercarrier compensation regimes. Our existing compensation regimes are based largely on the recovery of switching costs through per-minute charges. In a separate rulemaking before the Commission, however, a number of carriers argue that a substantial

* Eds. We will address the relationship between VoIP and intercarrier compensation in Chapter 10.

majority of switching costs do not vary with minutes-of-use (MOU). MCI argues, for example, that vendor contracts for switches establish per-line prices, rather than per-minute prices, and thus LECs do not incur switching costs on a per-minute basis. Similarly, AT&T argues that switches generally have excess capacity so that increases in usage do not increase the cost of a switch. In addition, the overall capacity of telecommunications networks has increased dramatically due to the increased deployment of fiber optic facilities. It appears, therefore, that most network costs, including switching costs, result from connections to the network rather than usage of the network itself. This development in infrastructure calls into question whether intercarrier compensation mechanisms based on per-minute charges remain appropriate or necessary.

24. Exacerbating the issue of inefficient rates is the problem of terminating access monopolies. Even when an end user takes service from two providers, *e.g.*, wireless and wireline, the originating carrier must deliver the call to the terminating carrier with the telephone number dialed by the calling party. Other carriers seeking to deliver calls to that end user have no choice but to purchase terminating access from the called party's LEC. Originating carriers generally have little practical means of affecting the called party's choice of access provider, and the called party's LEC may take advantage of the situation by charging excessive terminating rates to a competing LEC. To address the terminating access monopoly problem, the Commission generally has determined that carriers should not be permitted unilaterally to impose termination charges that are not subject to regulation.

d. Developments in Consumer Control Over Telecommunications Services

25. Finally, there have been major developments in the ability of customers to manage their telecommunications services. Carriers now offer a number of call screening services that permit customers to block unwanted calls, such as telemarketing calls. Screening services such as caller ID, privacy messages, and non-solicitation messages give customers greater control over the calls they receive. The fact that recipients of calls can and do pay for these services indicates that these customers benefit from receiving calls, and indeed benefit more from receiving some types of calls than others. * * *

27. This increased ability of consumers to avoid calls for which they may not perceive a benefit (*e.g.*, telemarketing calls) means that they generally will benefit from calls they choose to accept. As a result, we question the assumption underlying our current rules that the calling party is the primary beneficiary of any given call and therefore should bear all the costs of the call. As the Commission observed in the *Intercarrier Compensation NPRM*, it may be more rational to assume that both the calling and called party benefit from any given call. Indeed, for customer choice in a competitive marketplace to be economically meaningful, customers should bear the cost of the network of their

choosing and avoid the cost of the networks rejected. Similarly, networks should make investment decisions based on whether they can recover costs from the customers that investment will attract.

28. All of these developments warrant a re-evaluation of the existing regimes, and the record confirms the need for comprehensive reform efforts. In addition to the extensive record received in response to the *Intercarrier Compensation NPRM*, industry groups have been negotiating and developing comprehensive reform proposals for consideration in this proceeding. Recognizing that the marketplace has changed significantly since these regimes were established, all of the proposals advocate replacing the existing rules with a more unified approach to intercarrier compensation.

* * *

B. Goals of Intercarrier Compensation Reform

* * *

33. We also agree that any new intercarrier compensation approach must be competitively and technologically neutral. Given the rapid changes in telecommunications technology, it is imperative that new rules accommodate continuing change in the marketplace and do not distort the opportunity for carriers using different and novel technologies to compete for customers. In addition, we favor an approach that provides regulatory certainty where possible and limits both the need for regulatory intervention and arbitrage concerns arising from regulatory distinctions unrelated to cost differences. Similar types of traffic should be subject to similar rules. Similar types of functions should be subject to similar cost recovery mechanisms. We are interested in not only similar rates for similar functions, but also in a regime that would apply these rates in a uniform manner for all traffic. To the extent a proposed regime would preserve distinctions between types of carrier or types of traffic, such distinctions should be based on legitimate economic or technical differences, not artificial regulatory distinctions. An approach requiring minimal regulatory intervention and enforcement is consistent with the pro-competitive de-regulatory environment envisioned by the 1996 Act. Consequently, proposals that rely on negotiated agreements between carriers might be preferable to regimes requiring detailed rules and regulations.

Even if the Commission was truly "seeking comment" and remained uncommitted in the 2005 *Intercarrier Compensation FNPRM*, the staff of the Wireline Competition Bureau displayed a stronger predilection in favor of bill-and-keep.

DEVELOPING A UNIFIED INTERCARRIER COMPENSATION REGIME
Further Notice of Proposed Rulemaking
Appendix C
A Bill-And-Keep Approach to Intercarrier Compensation Reform

Federal Communications Commission, 2005.
20 FCC Rcd. 4685.

An Analysis of Pleadings in CC Docket No. 01–92 by the STAFF OF THE WIRELINE COMPETITION BUREAU.

The following report was prepared by the staff of the Wireline Competition Bureau for inclusion in the record of the *Intercarrier Compensation* rulemaking.... [T]his staff report does not represent the views of, and is not endorsed by, the Commission.

In the *Further Notice* in this proceeding, the Commission concluded that there is an urgent need for comprehensive reform of the existing intercarrier compensation rules. The Commission noted that many parties support moving to a unified compensation regime, but that there is no consensus as to what type of regime the Commission should adopt. As a general matter, parties have advocated two different types of unified regimes—a bill-and-keep regime and a unified calling party's network pays (CPNP) regime. Bill-and-keep can be thought of as a unified compensation regime with a rate of zero. Under a bill-and-keep regime, carriers do not charge each other for the origination and termination of traffic. Rather, carriers recover all their costs from their subscribers. In contrast, under a unified CPNP regime, carriers would continue to compensate each other for the termination of traffic, but the rate charged by any particular carrier would be the same for all types of traffic. In some cases, a unified CPNP regime also would require long distance carriers to continue paying local exchange carriers for the origination of traffic.

In response to the *Intercarrier Compensation NPRM*, many parties submitted comments on the relative merits of bill-and-keep and a unified CPNP approach to intercarrier compensation reform. The following staff analysis of the principle arguments in the record regarding bill-and-keep is offered to aid the Commission and interested parties in further consideration of these issues.

1. BILL-AND-KEEP AND COST CAUSATION

In the *Intercarrier Compensation NPRM*, the Commission sought comment on the assumption underlying its current rules that the calling party is the sole cost causer and sole beneficiary of a call and therefore bill-and-keep makes sense only in certain narrow circumstances. In this section, we re-evaluate the relative benefits of a bill-and-keep approach to intercarrier compensation based on the record developed in this proceeding.

Bill-and-keep provides a mechanism whereby end users pay for the benefit of making and receiving calls. Thus, bill-and-keep is consistent with the assumption that both the calling party and the called party may benefit from any given call, and, therefore, that the originating and the terminating networks should share the costs associated with the call by recovering their costs from their own end-user customers. * * *

[Some] commenters, however, contend that there is an insufficient basis for altering the historical assumption that the calling party is responsible for the costs of the call. * * *

We are not persuaded that principles of cost causation require retention of a CPNP regime. The purpose of a telephone call is to facilitate communications between two or more parties. These communications enable the exchange of information between the parties, not just the relaying of information to a recipient. Although the calling party decides to place the call, the called party must decide to answer and continue the communication. The communication therefore is a two-way joint interaction between the calling party and called party. Each party is capable of taking measures to avoid call-related costs, if any. Moreover, in the current networking environment, consumers are increasingly connected through a number of communications devices and express a desire to be connected with others through these devices. Thus, the need or desire to exchange information causes the communications, rather than the party initiating the communication.

* * *

Some commenters contend that bill-and-keep assumes incorrectly that each party benefits equally from a call and therefore does not capture the relative benefits of a call to the calling and called parties. Regulators cannot realistically institute a regime that perfectly reflects the division of benefits for each and every call. Thus, any approach that the Commission adopts must generalize the relative benefits to some degree. The relevant question is whether, judging from the overarching policy goals discussed in the *Further Notice*, the simplifying assumptions underlying a bill-and-keep regime are preferable to the assumptions underlying a CPNP regime. As one commenter points out, there is no evidence that the prevailing assumption that all the benefits flow to the calling party and none to the called party is more realistic than an assumption that the benefits flow to each party equally. Indeed, because consumers have the incentive and the ability to avoid, or reduce the duration of, unwanted calls, we believe that the better assumption is one that reflects some benefit to both the calling party and the called party.

Commenters opposing a bill-and-keep regime on efficiency grounds often cite the example of unwanted calls, such as telemarketing calls, to demonstrate a case where the called party receives no benefit and must cover some cost of the unwanted call. Intercarrier compensation is neither the source of unwanted calls nor the solution to the unwanted call problem. The most direct and efficient response to the problem of unwanted calls is to empower consumers to manage their own telecommunications services. * * *

Additional arguments opposing bill-and-keep on economic grounds are based on the assumption that costs depend on the number or duration of calls on the network, rather than on connectivity to the network (*i.e.*, that costs are incurred on a per-minute or per-call basis, rather than a per-line basis). * * *

We have two responses to these arguments. First, as explained above, we believe that a CPNP approach is problematic in a competitive marketplace because it allows networks to shift costs to other networks. Consequently, even if additional minutes or calls increase a carrier's costs, there is no reason why each carrier should not recover these costs from its subscribers, rather than from each other. Second, underlying all these arguments is a fundamental presumption that most network costs are incurred on a per-minute or per-call basis, *i.e.*, that a doubling of the number of calls or minutes would double total network costs, and that each call therefore imposes additional costs on recipients. As described by the Commission in the *Further Notice*, it does not appear that minutes-of-use are a significant determinant of costs given developments in telecommunications technologies. * * *

2. Bill-and-Keep and Competitive Neutrality

As the Commission acknowledged in the *Intercarrier Compensation NPRM*, any discrepancy in regulatory treatment that is not based on differences in underlying economic costs is likely to raise regulatory arbitrage concerns. In particular, the Commission observed that "parties will revise or rearrange transactions to exploit a more advantageous regulatory treatment, even though such actions, in the absence of regulation, would be viewed as costly or inefficient." Under the existing regimes, different types of carriers are subject to different rules and pricing methodologies when they provide services with the same or similar costs. For example, according to the Intercarrier Compensation Forum, interexchange carriers pay average interstate access charges ranging from 0.6 cents per minute to 1.8 cents per minute to terminate traffic, depending on the LEC involved, whereas LECs pay average reciprocal compensation rates of 0.2 cents per minute to terminate traffic. Moreover, CMRS carriers are subject to different compensation rules because they have larger local calling scopes than wireline carriers. Thus, based on this evidence, the existing regimes are not technologically or competitively neutral.

A bill-and-keep approach may be more technologically and competitively neutral than the current regimes because it moves the intercarrier compensation system away from traditional regulatory and jurisdictional classifications that are not based on actual economic cost differences. A bill-and-keep approach would free the Commission from the difficult task of making regulatory distinctions that are no longer sustainable. We acknowledge that, as compared to the current regimes, any unified approach would have these benefits. A unified CPNP regime, however, would still afford carriers the opportunity to shift costs to competitors rather than recover these costs from their subscribers. Because this type of regime distorts the pricing signals received by consumers, it does not serve the Commission's goal of competitive neutrality.

Some commenters contend that a bill-and-keep approach is not competitively neutral because it favors carriers with balanced traffic exchanged with interconnected carriers, such as incumbent LECs, and assumes that competitive LECs should have the network architecture, customer base, and customer calling patterns of incumbent LECs. For instance, some commenters claim that, because incumbent LECs have a larger and more diverse customer base than competitive LECs, they will have more opportunities to recover costs across broad classes of customers. We disagree that a bill-and-keep approach necessarily favors incumbent LECs or carriers with characteristics similar to them. As an initial matter, these commenters confuse average costs with incremental costs, and assume that a call actually imposes a measurable incremental cost on the terminating network. Further, concerns about the balance of traffic exchanged reflect the assumption, which we question, that the calling party's network should bear all the costs of a call. As discussed above, an important benefit of a bill-and-keep regime is that it puts all carriers in a position where they must recover their own costs from their own retail customers. Under this regime, success in the marketplace will reflect a carrier's ability to serve customers efficiently, rather than its ability to extract payments from other carriers.

3. Bill-and-Keep and the Deployment of Efficient Technologies

In the *Intercarrier Compensation NPRM*, the Commission observed that an intercarrier compensation regime that involves termination payments, such as a CPNP regime, may create the opportunity for the terminating carrier to exploit undesirable pricing power. The terminating carrier has a monopoly of sorts over the facilities serving the end user who receives calls because any interconnecting carrier attempting to reach that customer must use the terminating carrier's network. If the originating carrier is prohibited from blocking or declining traffic based on the identity of the terminating carrier, and the terminating carrier may unilaterally impose charges (*e.g.*, by filing a tariff), the originating carrier cannot avoid unreasonable termination charges. Moreover, in many cases, the originating carrier is unable to pass these charges on to the end-user customer. Because the end-user customer receives no market signals to avoid these costs, the unreasonable termination charges may persist. There is no market pressure to moderate these rates.

In contrast, under an approach where terminating carriers cannot impose payment obligations unilaterally, such as bill-and-keep, the terminating carrier must recover its costs from its own end-user customers, thereby allowing that customer to compare the prices charged for termination and choose the most efficient carrier. The end user thus controls the decision whether to purchase from the lowest cost provider and may select providers based on considerations of cost and functionality. Bill-and-keep therefore encourages the development of competition by rewarding carriers based on their ability to serve customers efficiently rather than their ability to shift costs to other carriers.

* * *

4. Bill-and-Keep and Regulatory Oversight

In the *Intercarrier Compensation NPRM*, the Commission discussed several potential advantages of a bill-and-keep approach, including the claim that it eliminates the need for regulators to set the level and structure of termination rates. Under a CPNP approach, because of the "terminating monopoly" issue, there is an obvious need to regulate the termination rates that carriers charge each other. Commenters contend that, absent a truly competitive marketplace, ratesetting requires considerable resources from carriers and regulators, leads to litigation, and results in considerable uncertainty in the marketplace. * * *

Other commenters, however, maintain that a bill-and-keep approach would require more regulatory intervention than a CPNP approach. For instance, some commenters contend that converting intercarrier charges to end-user charges would create additional means for incumbent LECs to engage in anticompetitive conduct. They further argue that a bill-and-keep regime would result in new arbitrage issues requiring regulatory intervention, including disputes over interconnection costs and demarcation requirements. Similarly, ALTS argues that bill-and-keep would create even more regulatory uncertainty. Other commenters express general concern over the many implementation issues arising under a bill-and-keep regime, including the potential need to adjust and regulate end-user rates and safeguard against cross-subsidization.

While a bill-and-keep regime would undoubtedly require regulatory oversight, we do not believe it can be reasonably argued that bill-and-keep is somehow "more regulatory" than a CPNP regime. Given that a CPNP regime requires regulation of both retail and wholesale rates, while bill-and-keep requires only retail rate regulation, bill-and-keep would appear to require substantially less regulatory intervention. Indeed, our experience with CPNP regimes demonstrates the need for substantial regulation of terminating charges because of the terminating access monopoly. Because the terminating carrier controls the only line and local switch connecting the called party to the network, that carrier has strong incentives to extract as high a payment as possible from the calling party's carrier. Competition at the retail level has not diminished the terminating access monopoly of the carrier selected by the called party. Even if the called party takes service from two different networks (*e.g.*, a LEC network and a CMRS network), it will have a different telephone number for each service and the originating network has no choice but to terminate the call on the network to which the called number is assigned.

As a result, under a CPNP approach, regulators must ensure that terminating rates are cost-based, and the need for regulation continues indefinitely. If regulators had perfect information at their disposal and easily could set cost-based prices, this constant need for rate regulation might be tolerable. In practice, however, regulators rarely have sufficient information or sufficient resources to establish rates that accurately reflect the cost of providing service. For example, notwithstanding the Commission's extensive experience with circuit switching technology, the issue of what portion of switching costs are traffic-sensitive is highly controversial.

Furthermore, as new technologies and network architectures develop, the challenges associated with setting cost-based rates will only increase. The ratemaking experience of state and federal regulators generally has been limited to incumbent LEC wireline networks. Regulators are far less familiar with the costing of other types of networks, such as wireless networks, that have not previously been subject to cost-based rate regulation. The Commission then would be faced with the choice of examining the costs of these other types of networks, which would be an overwhelming task, or establishing rates based on incumbent LEC networks, which could lead to significant arbitrage issues if the costs of the networks differ. In either case, the inevitable result of maintaining a CPNP regime in the face of these new technologies would be increased litigation and regulatory uncertainty. * * *

The "Termination Monopoly". Note the staff's attention to the "termination monopoly". Given all the competition in service (not only by CLECs and cable operators but also from wireless), how does the terminating carrier have any kind of monopoly? The staff is essentially referring to a "monopoly" of terminating for a *particular customer*. That is, if John Smith has Verizon as his LEC, by the staff's usage, Verizon has a "monopoly" in terminating calls to John Smith. Is control over termination to a single customer a "monopoly" in any meaningful sense of the word? Rather, the staff seems to be pointing to the agency problem inherent in all termination arrangements: the calling party does not have control over costs incurred on the receiving party's side of the call. But, unless there truly is a monopoly in local service for the receiving party, the calling party hasn't ceded control to the carrier, he's ceded it to the receiving party. It's that agency problem, not the normal regulatory concerns over monopoly, that drives the move toward bill-and-keep.

Simplicity as a "Virtue" of Bill-and-Keep. One of the oft-cited advantages of bill-and-keep is that it will be less costly to administer than CPNP (partly because it does not require the same degree of regulatory supervision over rates). But as we saw above, when the FCC was confronted with truly divesting access charges of their subsidy component in inventing the Subscriber Line Charge, the FCC blinked. Can we really expect any different behavior if and when the FCC adopts a bill-and-keep mechanism to "simplify" intercarrier compensation?

D. UNIVERSAL SERVICE

Received wisdom has it that a policy of universal service has been with us since the beginning of telecommunications. Theodore Vail, architect of the Bell System, claimed in 1909 that AT&T was founded on the lines of "One System, One Policy, Universal Service." Twenty-five years later Congress is supposed to have adopted the universal service concept in the opening provisions of the Communications Act of 1934, which give as a central purpose of regulation making available "so far as possible, to all the people of the United States a rapid, efficient, Nation-wide, and world-wide wire and radio communication service...." Recent historical accounts have showed the received wisdom is not quite correct. Vail's original concept was not the same concept articulated today. See Milton L. Mueller, Jr., *Universal Service* 92–103 (1997). Essentially what Vail had in mind was a nationally integrated, that is interconnected, system that would be "universal" in the sense that there was a single ("universal") network by which one user could reach any other user. It must be remembered that when Vail pronounced the need for universal service there was no single, integrated telephone system; many cities had parallel local exchange providers (so-called "dual service") unconnected to each other or to exchanges in other cities. AT&T itself refused to interconnect competitive independent carriers either locally or with its growing long distance network. (In 1913 it agreed, under threat of antitrust liability, to interconnect its long distance lines with independents, but this did not extend to interconnection among competing local carriers.)

In time universal service acquired its present policy gloss of economically promoting basic access to the network by means of internal or external subsidies. The clearest manifestation of this policy was in the separation and settlements that were used to allocate non-traffic-sensitive costs between local and long distance service—which we discussed in the last chapter—which had the effect of shifting a disproportionate percentage of fixed and joint costs from local to interstate long distance. It is noteworthy, however, that these shifts in cost were not loudly proclaimed at the time to be moves to support universal service. So far as the general public was concerned they were not proclaimed at all. Only a relatively small group of telecommunications specialists were aware of the magnitude of the subsidy; it was not until the introduction of competition in the 1970s threatened the entire subsidy scheme that the concept of universal service was invoked in public debate (by AT&T). Thus, it was mostly by way of retroactive characterization—when the whole scheme was threatened by the emergence of competition—that universal service became a clearly articulated policy.

It is ironic that universal service in this modern sense came to be associated with the Bell System and thereby associated with regulated monopoly. In fact the promotion of telephone service owes less to AT&T than popular history imagines. The early growth of telephone service was spurred by competitive rivalry more than monopoly. Until the expiration of Bell's patents in the early 1890s, the growth of telephone service was essentially stagnant; it was the development of an independent and competitive telephone industry, offering lower prices and more aggressive promotion of service, that produced the most rapid expansion of telephone service in the history of the industry. But we can put that irony aside; the ideological battle between competition and monopoly is now finished, at least for the time being. Now that Congress has given its imprimatur on competition, the only debate is over implementation.

This includes, of course, debate over how to implement subsidies to promote universal service objectives now that it is no longer possible to do this as a matter of internal bookkeeping within a single firm. The introduction of competition and the subsequent breakup of the Bell System required a fundamental rearrangement of the traditional means of allocating costs among services, particularly between long distance and local exchange. It did not require elimination of universal service subsidies. The access charges implemented by the FCC in the wake of the AT&T divestiture continue to provide a degree of subsidy to basic local service insofar as the charges are not based on the costs of providing access. However, with the introduction of competition it was inevitable that subsidization of certain classes of user or certain services be made more explicit and overt. In the mid-1980s, the Commission established a Universal Service Fund. Note that that fund was not a direct subsidy to users; it provides special financial assistance to local exchange *carriers* in high-cost markets. The FCC also implemented two programs ("Lifeline" and "Link Up") for direct subsidies to low-income individuals for basic, limited service.

In 1996 Congress planned something more ambitious for the future. No longer content with the vague mandate of the Communications Act of 1934 to make communication by wire and radio available "so far as practicable to all of the people," Congress in 1996 provided a set of explicit principles and instructions with respect to promoting telecommunications service through coordinated federal and state policy. The principles include the traditional support of service to high-cost areas, but for the first time the concept of "service" included more than plain old telephone service. Communications service has now been expanded to include "advanced communications and information services." And the intended beneficiaries now include schools, libraries and rural health care providers. Taking seriously the new information superhighway rhetoric, Congress wanted to ensure that everyone had the means to access and travel it. The 1996 Act directed the Commission and the Joint Board, which coordinates state and federal regulation, to take care of the details.

The Commission's first stab at the problem came in 1997 with a massive Universal Service Order, of which the following is little more than an outline. By way of brief introduction, the order implements Congress' mandate by setting out a detailed scheme for the three classes of explicit support: high-cost support (for carriers serving areas where costs are above average); low-income customers, and the newly minted institutional subsidies for schools, libraries and rural health care providers.

FEDERAL-STATE JOINT BOARD ON UNIVERSAL SERVICE
Report and Order

Federal Communications Commission, 1997.
12 FCC Rcd. 8776.

BY THE COMMISSION:

I. INTRODUCTION

1. In the Telecommunications Act of 1996 (1996 Act), Congress directed the Commission and states to take the steps necessary to establish support mechanisms to ensure the delivery of affordable telecommunications service to all Americans, including low-income consumers, eligible schools and libraries, and rural health care providers. Specifically, Congress directed the Commission and the states to devise methods to ensure that "[c]onsumers in all regions of the Nation, including low-income consumers and those in rural, insular, and high cost areas ... have access to telecommunications and information services ... at rates that are reasonably comparable to rates charged for similar services in urban areas." Congress further directed the Commission to define additional services for support for eligible schools, libraries, and health care providers, and directed the Commission to "establish competitively neutral rules ... to enhance, to the extent technically feasible and economically reasonable, access to advanced telecommunications and information services for all public and non-profit elementary and secondary school classrooms, health care providers, and libraries."

2. This Order sets forth a plan that satisfies all of the statutory requirements, and puts in place a universal service support system that will be sustainable in an increasingly competitive marketplace. Consistent with the explicit statutory principles, our immediate implementation of section 254 is shaped by our commitment to achieve four critical goals. First, we must implement all of the universal service objectives established by the Act, including those for low-income individuals, consumers in rural, insular, and high cost areas, schools, libraries, and rural health care providers. Second, we must maintain rates for basic residential service at affordable levels. We believe that the rates for this service are generally at affordable levels today. Third, we must ensure affordable basic service continues to be available to all users through an explicit

universal service funding mechanism. For the present, we believe we can achieve this goal by maintaining our existing high cost mechanism at current funding levels, picking a platform mechanism by December 1997, and implementing a forward-looking economic cost mechanism for universal service for non-rural carriers starting January 1, 1999. Fourth, we must bring the benefits of competition to as many consumers as possible. To implement this goal, we must, in our access charge reform proceeding, address the implicit subsidies in interstate access charges.* * *

4. This proceeding is part of a trilogy of actions that are focused on achieving Congress's goal of establishing a "pro-competitive, de-regulatory national policy framework designed to accelerate rapidly private sector deployment of advanced telecommunications and information technologies and services to all Americans by opening up all telecommunications markets to competition." The other components of the trilogy are the local competition and access reform rulemakings. Pursuant to the mandate of the 1996 Act, these three proceedings are collectively intended to encourage the development of competition in all telecommunications markets.

5. In the *Local Competition Order*, we set forth rules to implement sections 251 and 252 of the Communications Act. As with all of Part II of Title II of the Communications Act, those sections, and the rules implementing them, seek to remove the legal, regulatory, economic, and operational barriers to local telecommunications competition. Sections 251 and 252 provide entrants with the opportunity to compete for consumers in local markets by either constructing new facilities, purchasing access to unbundled network elements, or reselling telecommunication services.

6. Through this Order and our accompanying *Access Charge Reform Order*, we establish the definition of services to be supported by federal universal service support mechanisms and the specific timetable for implementation. We set in place rules that will identify and convert existing federal universal service support in the interstate high cost fund, the dial equipment minutes (DEM) weighting program, Long Term Support (LTS), Lifeline, Link Up, and interstate access charges to explicit competitively neutral federal universal service support mechanisms. We will provide universal service support to carriers serving rural, insular, and high cost areas through a mechanism based on forward-looking economic cost beginning on January 1, 1999, for areas served by non-rural LECs, and establish the process to determine a forward-looking economic cost methodology for areas served by rural LECs. That mechanism will—based upon cost studies states will conduct during the coming year or, at the state's election, based upon Commission-developed methods—calculate the forward-looking economic cost of providing service to consumers in a particular rural, insular, or high cost area. In this proceeding, we modify the funding methods for the existing federal universal service support mechanisms so that such support is not generated, as at present, entirely through charges imposed on long distance carriers. Instead, as the statute requires, we will require

equitable and non-discriminatory contributions from all providers of interstate telecommunications service. We also take other steps to make federal universal service support mechanisms consistent with the development of local service competition.

7. When it enacted section 254 of the Communications Act, Congress set forth the principles to guide universal service reform. It placed on the Commission the duty to implement these principles in a manner consistent with the pro-competition purposes of the Act. It also emphasized that the preservation and advancement of universal service was to be the result of federal and state action, stating "[t]here should be specific, predictable and sufficient Federal and State mechanisms to preserve and advance universal service." Congress also entrusted the states with a role in universal service, including expressly granting states the authority "to adopt regulations not inconsistent with the Commission's rules to preserve and advance universal service," and requiring every telecommunications carrier that provides intrastate telecommunications services to "contribute, on an equitable and nondiscriminatory basis, in a manner determined by the state, to the preservation and advancement of universal service in that state" when such state establishes universal service support mechanisms. States traditionally have promoted universal service by, among other things, assuring affordable residential access by explicitly and implicitly subsidizing and pricing basic telephone service at levels associated with very high telephone subscribership rates, currently 94.2%.

8. Universal service support mechanisms that are designed to increase subscribership by keeping rates affordable will benefit everyone in the country, including those who can afford basic telephone service. At the simplest level, increasing the number of people connected to the telecommunications network makes the network more valuable to all of its users by increasing its usefulness to them. Increasing subscribership also benefits society in ways unrelated to the value of the network per se. For example, all of us benefit from the widespread availability of basic public safety services, such as 911.

9. Congress also specified that universal service support "should be explicit," and that, with respect to federal universal service support, "every telecommunications carrier that provides interstate telecommunications services shall contribute, on an equitable and non-discriminatory basis, to the specific, predictable, and sufficient mechanisms established by the Commission to preserve and advance universal service." As explained further in the Joint Explanatory Statement of the Committee of the Conference, Congress intended that, to the extent possible, "any support mechanisms continued or created under new section 254 should be explicit, rather than implicit as many support mechanisms are today."

10. Today, universal service is achieved largely through implicit subsidies. The Commission currently has in place some explicit support mechanisms directed at increasing network subscribership by reducing rates in high cost areas (the high cost fund and Long Term Support) and

at making service affordable for low-income consumers (the Lifeline and Link Up programs). The current "system," however, consists principally of a number of implicit mechanisms at the state and, to a substantially lesser extent, federal levels designed to shift costs from rural to urban areas, from residential to business customers, and from local to long distance service.

11. The urban-to-rural subsidy has been accomplished through the explicit high cost fund mentioned above, and through geographic rate averaging. The result of state requirements that local telephone rates be averaged across the state is that high-density (urban) areas, where costs are typically lower, subsidize low-density (rural) areas. State pricing rules have also in many cases created a business-to-residential subsidy. Most states have established local rate levels such that businesses pay more on a per-line basis for basic local service than do residential customers, although the costs of providing business and residential lines are generally the same. In addition, rates charged for vertical services such as touch tone, conference calling and speed dialing, subsidize basic local service rates. Finally, interstate and intrastate access charges are set relatively high in order to cover certain loop costs not recovered through local rates. These usage-based charges are then recovered through higher usage charges for interstate long distance service. Thus, interstate long distance customers—and particularly those with higher calling volumes—indirectly subsidize local telephone rates.

12. Of the three implicit subsidy mechanisms—geographic rate averaging, subsidizing residential lines via business lines, and interstate access charges—only the interstate access charge system has been regulated by the Commission, and this contributes the smallest subsidy of the three. Thus, a number of factors operate today to keep basic local telephone rates low, and Congress ordered that we devise a coordinated federal-state scheme to achieve universal service goals.

13. By our Orders today, we reject the arguments made by some parties that section 254 compels us immediately to remove all universal service costs from interstate access charges. As stated previously, we have met section 254's clear command that we identify the services to be supported by federal universal service support mechanisms, and that we establish a specific timetable for implementation. Under that timetable, we will over the next year identify implicit interstate universal support and make that support explicit, as further provided by section 254(e). Moreover, as with any implicit support mechanism, universal service costs are presently intermingled with all other costs, including the forward-looking economic cost of interstate access and historic costs associated with the provision of interstate access services. We cannot remove universal service costs from interstate access charges until we can identify those costs, which we will not be able to do even for non-rural incumbent local exchange carriers (ILECs) before January 1, 1999.

14. We do not, by our Order today, attempt to identify existing implicit universal service support presently effected through intrastate

rates or other state mechanisms, nor do we attempt to convert such implicit intrastate support into explicit federal universal service support. The Commission, in light of section 2(b) of the Communications Act, does not have control over the local rate-setting process, which generally has aimed at ensuring affordable residential rates. States have maintained low residential basic service rates through, among other things, a combination of: geographic rate averaging, higher rates for business customers, higher intrastate access rates, higher rates for intrastate toll service, and higher rates for vertical features. States, acting pursuant to sections 254(f) and 253 of the Communications Act, must in the first instance be responsible for identifying intrastate implicit universal service support. We further believe that, as competition develops, the marketplace itself will identify intrastate implicit universal service support, and that states will be compelled by those marketplace forces to move that support to explicit, sustainable mechanisms consistent with section 254(f). As states do so, we will be able to assess whether additional federal universal service support is necessary to ensure that quality services remain "available at just, reasonable and affordable rates."

15. Federal universal service support will be distributed based on the interstate portion of the difference between the forward-looking economic cost of providing service and a nationwide revenue benchmark. The amount of support will be explicitly calculable and identifiable by competing carriers, and will be portable among competing carriers, i.e., distributed to the eligible telecommunications carrier chosen by the customer. It will be funded by equitable and non-discriminatory contributions from all carriers that provide interstate telecommunications services. In the *Access Charge Reform Order* that we also adopt today, we direct that federal universal service support received by ILECs be used to satisfy the interstate revenue requirement otherwise collected through interstate access charges. Accordingly, through this Order and the *Access Charge Reform Order*, interstate implicit support for universal service will be identified and removed from interstate access charges, and will be provided through explicit interstate universal service support mechanisms. To the extent that we fail to identify a source of implicit support, we are confident that the marketplace will, as competition develops, highlight it for further Commission attention.

16. We wish to avoid action that directly or indirectly raises the price of the basic residential telephone service that guarantees access to the local telephone network. We also believe, as did the Joint Board, that raising the existing flat-rate charge on every consumer's line for access to interstate telephone service—the subscriber line charge (SLC) on primary residential lines—is not desirable, because it could adversely affect the affordability of local service. Therefore, we decide in today's Order and its companion *Access Charge Reform Order* that we will not permit any increase in the primary residential line SLC and will not order the creation of any additional end-user charges for local service over these lines. Our primary reason for not mandating the recovery of

universal service contributions through basic rates, directly raising charges for basic access through an increase in the primary residence SLC, or adopting any new end-user charge from the local telephone company to the residential consumer for basic access is that we have high subscribership rates today, and therefore believe that current rate levels are "affordable." We see no reason to jeopardize affordability by raising rate levels.

17. At present, the existing system of largely implicit subsidies can continue to serve its purpose, and our current implementation of section 254 relies principally on the continuation of existing mechanisms, with modifications to make them more consistent with the statutory requirements and principles. This system is not sustainable in its current form in a competitive environment. Implicit subsidies were sustainable in the monopoly environment because some consumers (such as urban business customers) could be charged rates for local exchange and exchange access service that significantly exceeded the cost of providing service, and the rates paid by those customers would implicitly subsidize service provided by the same carrier to others. By adoption of the 1996 Act, Congress has provided for the development of competition in all telephone markets. In a competitive market, a carrier that attempts to charge rates significantly above cost to a class of customers will lose many of those customers to a competitor. This incentive to entry by competitors in the lowest cost, highest profit market segments means that today's pillars of implicit subsidies—high access charges, high prices for business services, and the averaging of rates over broad geographic areas—will be under attack. New competitors can target service to more profitable customers without having to build into their rates the types of cross-subsidies that have been required of existing carriers who serve all customers.

18. By this Order, therefore, we will retain, with some limited modifications, the existing explicit high cost and low-income support programs until January 1, 1999, but make collection more equitable and nondiscriminatory and allow carriers other than ILECs to receive support; we will continue to coordinate with the states to determine the appropriate extent of universal service support for high cost areas as competition and related state decisions dictate; and we will fund universal service for eligible schools, libraries, and rural health care providers consistent with the statute. The total amount of federal high cost support (both implicit and explicit) will not decline materially, but will be restructured. * * *

II. Executive Summary

A. Principles

21. Section 254(b) sets forth the principles that are to guide the Commission in establishing policies for the preservation of universal service. These principles include:

(1) quality services should be available at just, reasonable, and affordable rates;

(2) access to advanced telecommunications and information services should be provided in all regions of the Nation;

(3) consumers in all regions of the Nation, including low-income consumers and those in rural, insular, and high cost areas, should have access to telecommunications and information services, including interexchange services and advanced telecommunications and information services, that are reasonably comparable to those services provided in urban areas and that are available at rates that are reasonably comparable to rates charged for similar services in urban areas;

(4) all providers of telecommunications services should make an equitable and non-discriminatory contribution to the preservation and advancement of universal service;

(5) there should be specific, predictable and sufficient [f]ederal and [s]tate mechanisms to preserve and advance universal service; and

(6) elementary and secondary schools and classrooms, health care providers, and libraries should have access to advanced telecommunications services.

In addition, the Commission may consider such "additional principles" as the Commission and the Joint Board determine are necessary and appropriate for the protection of the public interest, convenience and necessity and are consistent with the Act. In addition to the principles specified in section 254(b), we agree with the Joint Board and adopt its recommendation that "competitive neutrality" should be among the principles that guide the universal service support mechanisms and rules. We adopt this principle and the principles enumerated by Congress in section 254(b) to preserve and advance universal service while promoting the pro-competitive goals of the 1996 Act.

B. Definition of Universal Service

22. Section 254(c)(1) requires the Commission to establish a definition of telecommunications services that will be supported by universal service support mechanisms. Based on the principles embodied in section 254, and guided by the recommendation of the Joint Board, we find that the definition of supportable services includes: voice grade access to the public switched network, with the ability to place and receive calls; Dual Tone Multifrequency (DTMF) signaling or its functional equivalent; single-party service; access to emergency services, including in some instances, access to 911 and enhanced 911 (E911) services; access to operator services; access to interexchange services; access to directory assistance; and toll limitation services for qualifying low-income consumers. As recommended by the Joint Board, eligible carriers must offer each of the designated services in order to receive universal service support. We find that, consistent with the Joint Board's recommendation, a carrier that currently is unable to provide single-party service

may petition its state commission to receive universal service support for a designated period of time while the carrier completes the network upgrades needed to offer single-party service. Further, based on the Joint Board's recognition that some carriers currently may be unable to provide access to E911 service and toll limitation services, carriers may receive, for a specified period of time, universal service support while completing network upgrades required for them to offer these services. In addition, all business and residential connections that are currently supported will continue to be supported until the forward-looking methodology for high cost companies is operational. Finally, as recommended by the Joint Board, we will convene a Federal-State Joint Board to review the definition of universal service on or before January 1, 2001.

C. Affordability

23. Based on the Joint Board's recommendation, we conclude that states should monitor rates and non-rate factors, such as subscribership levels, to ensure affordability. We agree with the Joint Board that there is a correlation between subscribership and affordability and we further agree that joint examination by the Commission and the states of the factors that may contribute to low penetration is warranted in areas, such as insular areas, where subscribership levels are particularly low.

D. Carriers Eligible for Universal Service Support

24. We conclude that the plain language of section 214(e)(1) does not permit the Commission or the states to adopt additional criteria as prerequisites for designating carriers eligible telecommunications carriers. Therefore, consistent with the Joint Board's recommendation, we adopt the statutory criteria contained in section 214(e)(1) as the rules for determining whether a telecommunications carrier is eligible to receive universal service support. Pursuant to section 214(e), eligible carriers must offer and advertise all the services supported by federal universal service support mechanisms throughout their service areas using their own facilities or a combination of their own facilities and resale of another carrier's services. We interpret the term "facilities" in section 214(e)(1) to mean any physical components of the telecommunications network that are used in the transmission or routing of the services designated for support under section 254(c)(1). * * *

25. We agree with the Joint Board that the statute affords state commissions the primary responsibility for designating service areas served by non-rural carriers. * * *

E. High Cost Support

26. Consistent with the Joint Board's recommendation, we find that a cost methodology based on forward-looking economic cost should be used to calculate the cost of providing universal service for high cost areas because it best reflects the cost of providing service in a competitive market for local exchange telephone service. We believe that a cost methodology can be designed based upon such consistent assumptions as

economic depreciation, forward-looking cost of capital, and forward-looking outside plant cost, including reasonable profits. We agree with the Joint Board that the cost methodologies presented to us thus far are not sufficiently reliable to be used to determine universal service support at this time. * * *

F. Support for Low-Income Consumers

27. We adopt the Joint Board's recommendations to make three broad categories of changes to the Lifeline and Link Up programs so that they better comport with our universal service principles and the 1996 Act's renewed concern for low-income consumers. First, we agree with the Joint Board's recommendation to expand Lifeline to make it available in all states, territories, and commonwealths of the United States, modify the state matching requirement, and increase the federal Lifeline support amount. We find that these modifications comply with the principles in sections 254(b)(1) and (3), respectively, that rates should be "affordable" and access should be provided to "low-income consumers" in all regions of the nation. Second, we adopt the Joint Board's recommendation to make the contribution and distribution of low-income support competitively and technologically neutral by requiring equitable and nondiscriminatory contributions from all providers of interstate telecommunications services, consistent with sections 254(d) and (e), and allowing all eligible telecommunications carriers to receive support for offering Lifeline and Link Up service. Third, we adopt the Joint Board's recommendation to provide low-income consumers with access to certain services and policies. * * *

G. Support for Schools and Libraries

29. We concur with the Joint Board's recommendation to provide schools and libraries with discounts on all commercially available telecommunications services, Internet access, and internal connections. This program provides schools and libraries with the maximum flexibility to purchase the package of services they believe will meet their communications needs most effectively. We conclude that sections 254(c)(3) and 254(h)(1)(B) authorize us to permit eligible schools and libraries to receive telecommunications services, Internet access, and internal connections at discounted rates from telecommunications carriers. Because we share the Joint Board's preference that we foster competition from non-telecommunications carriers, we encourage those non-carrier providers to enter into partnerships or joint ventures with telecommunications carriers in order to provide services to schools and libraries. In addition, we adopt the Joint Board's recommendation to provide discounts for Internet access and internal connections provided by non-telecommunications carriers. We adopt this recommendation under the authority of sections 254(h)(2)(A) and 4(i). * * *

32. We agree with the Joint Board that all schools falling within the definition contained in the Elementary and Secondary Education Act of 1965 and meeting the criteria of section 254(h), whether public or

private, shall be eligible for universal service support. In light of an amendment to section 254(h)(4), enacted in late 1996, we found it necessary to look anew at the definition of library and adopt a definition that is consistent with the directives of section 254(h). * * *

34. We concur with the Joint Board's finding that Congress intended to require accountability on the part of schools and libraries. We agree, therefore, with the Joint Board's recommendation that eligible schools and libraries be required to: (1) conduct internal assessments of the components necessary to use effectively the discounted services they order; (2) submit a complete description of services they seek so that it may be posted for competing providers to evaluate; and (3) certify to certain criteria under penalty of perjury.

H. Support for Health Care Providers

35. Sections 254(c) and 254(h) add health care providers to the list of entities that may benefit from universal service support. Recognizing that section 254 requires that universal service support mechanisms be specific, predictable, and sufficient, we establish support for health care providers subject to a $400 million annual cap. Section 254(h)(1)(A) provides that a health care provider that serves persons who reside in rural areas shall receive telecommunications services necessary for the provision of health care services in a state at rates that are reasonably comparable to those charged for similar services in urban areas in that state. Because section 254(h)(1)(A) specifies that the calculation of the credit for carriers providing the service is to be based on the difference between rates in "comparable rural areas," and the rates charged to the health care provider, we, consistent with the Joint Board recommendation, provide support under this section for telecommunications services for all public and not-for-profit health care providers located in rural areas. Any telecommunications service of a bandwidth capacity up to and including 1.544 Megabits per second (Mbps) that is necessary for the provision of health care services is eligible for support, but there are limits on the services that each rural health care provider may obtain. Telecommunications carriers must charge eligible rural health care providers a rate for each supported service that is no higher than the highest tariffed or publicly available commercial rate for a similar service in the closest city in the state with a population of 50,000 or more people, taking distance charges into account.

36. Section 254(h)(2)(A) directs the Commission to establish "competitively neutral rules to enhance, to the extent technically feasible and economically reasonable, access to advanced telecommunications and information services for all public and nonprofit health care providers." To meet the goals of this section, and, based on our review of comments filed in response to the Recommended Decision, we adopt mechanisms to provide support for limited toll-free access to an Internet service provider. Each health care provider that lacks toll-free access to an Internet service provider may receive the lesser of the toll charges incurred for 30

hours of access to an Internet service provider or $180 per month in toll charge credits for toll charges imposed for connecting to the Internet.

37. Carriers providing supported telecommunications services to health care providers will be entitled to treat the amount eligible for support as an offset against their annual universal service obligation and receive a reimbursement for any amount by which the support due the carrier exceeds the obligation in any one year. Non-telecommunications providers providing supported services to health care providers will receive direct reimbursement for the eligible amount.

I. Interstate Subscriber Line Charge/Carrier Common Line Charges

38. We adopt the Joint Board's conclusion that LTS must be removed from carrier common line (CCL) charges. This change will be effectuated in the access charge reform proceeding. Consistent with the Joint Board's recommendation, we provide for payments similar to LTS out of the new universal service support mechanisms to rural telephone companies that currently receive LTS or competitors that win subscribers from such carriers. Consistent with the Joint Board's recommendation, we maintain the current $3.50 cap on the SLC for primary residential and single-line business lines.

J. Administration of Support

39. Section 254(d) states that all carriers that provide interstate telecommunications services must contribute to universal service support mechanisms in an equitable and nondiscriminatory manner. To ensure that all providers of similar services make the same contributions to universal service, we adopt the Joint Board's recommendation that all telecommunications carriers that provide interstate telecommunications services must contribute to the support mechanisms and we issue a list of examples of interstate telecommunications services. * * *

41. Because the Joint Board did not address how contributors would recover their universal service contributions, we maintain historic jurisdictional lines and permit recovery of universal service contributions through the contributing carrier's interstate rates. For ILECs subject to price caps, we will permit universal service contributions to be added to the carrier's common line basket, and recovered in the same manner as common line charges. * * *

TEXAS OFFICE OF PUBLIC UTILITY COUNSEL v. FCC

United States Court of Appeals, Fifth Circuit, 1999.
183 F.3d 393.

JERRY E. SMITH, CIRCUIT JUDGE:

This is a consolidated challenge to the most recent attempt of the Federal Communications Commission ("FCC") to implement provisions of the landmark 1996 Telecommunications Act (the "Act"). Petitioners, joined by numerous intervenors, challenge several aspects of the FCC's Universal Service Order (the "Order") implementing the provisions of the Act codified at 47 U.S.C. § 254. We grant the petition for review in part, deny it in part, affirm in part, reverse in part, and remand in part.

I. Background

A. The 1996 Act And The Universal Service Order.

Beginning with the passage of the Communications Act of 1934 (the "1934 Act"), Congress has made universal service a basic goal of telecommunications regulation. As Section 1 of the 1934 Act stated, the FCC was created

> [f]or the purpose of regulating interstate and foreign commerce in communication by wire and radio so as to make available, so far as possible, to all the people of the United States, without discrimination on the basis of race, color, religion, national origin, or sex, a rapid, efficient, Nation-wide, and world-wide wire and radio communication service with adequate facilities at reasonable charges....

47 U.S.C. § 151 (as amended).

Armed with this statutory mandate, the FCC historically has focused on increasing the availability of reasonably priced, basic telephone service via the landline telecommunications network. Rather than relying on market forces alone, the agency has used a combination of implicit and explicit subsidies to achieve its goal of greater telephone subscribership. Explicit subsidies provide carriers or individuals with specific grants that can be used to pay for or reduce the charges for telephone service. This form of subsidy includes using revenues from line charges on end-users to subsidize high-cost service directly and to support the Lifeline Assistance program for low-income subscribers.

Implicit subsidies are more complicated and involve the manipulation of rates for some customers to subsidize more affordable rates for others. For example, the regulators may require the carrier to charge "above-cost" rates to low-cost, profitable urban customers to offer the "below-cost" rates to expensive, unprofitable rural customers.

For obvious reasons, this system of implicit subsidies can work well only under regulated conditions. In a competitive environment, a carrier that tries to subsidize below-cost rates to rural customers with above-cost rates to urban customers is vulnerable to a competitor that offers at-cost rates to urban customers. Because opening local telephone markets to competition is a principal objective of the Act, Congress recognized that the universal service system of implicit subsidies would have to be re-examined.

To attain the goal of local competition while preserving universal service, Congress directed the FCC to replace the patchwork of explicit and implicit subsidies with "specific, predictable and sufficient Federal and State mechanisms to preserve and advance universal service."

Congress also specified new universal service support for schools, libraries, and rural health care providers. It then directed the FCC to define such a system and to establish a timetable for implementation within fifteen months of the passage of the Act.

The Federal–State Joint Board (the "Joint Board"), created by the Act to coordinate federal and state regulatory interests, issued two recommendations on how to implement the universal service provisions. The FCC met the statutory deadline when it issued the Order on May 8, 1997. Since that time, the agency has issued seven reconsideration orders (the last one on May 28, 1999) and has made two reports to Congress regarding the Order.

The FCC designated a set of core services eligible for universal service support, proposed a mechanism for supporting those services, and established a timetable for implementation. Pursuant to the Act, the agency developed rules for modifying the existing system of support for high-cost service areas and created new support programs for schools, libraries, and health care facilities.

1. High-Cost Support.

The FCC's plans for changing the high-cost support system required it to resolve a number of complicated issues, including (1) what methodology to use for calculating high-cost support; (2) how to allocate costs between the states and the federal government; (3) which carriers should be required to contribute to the support system; and (4) when to implement the high-cost support program. The agency resolved the question of how to calculate the proper amount of high-cost support by accepting the Joint Board's second recommendation to identify areas where the forward-looking cost of service exceeds a cost-based benchmark and to provide extra support to any state that cannot maintain reasonable comparability.

Most importantly, the FCC decided to use the "forward-looking" costs to calculate the relevant costs of a carrier serving a given geographical area. In other words, to encourage carriers to act efficiently, the agency would base its calculation on the costs an efficient carrier would incur (rather than the costs the incumbent carriers historically have incurred).

The FCC developed rules for determining which carriers should be required to contribute to the interstate universal service support system and how their contributions should be calculated. It decided to require all telecommunications carriers and certain non-telecommunications carriers to contribute in proportion to their share of end-user telecommunications revenues. The agency determined that to reduce the burden on individual carriers' prices, the carriers' contribution base should be as broad as possible. Therefore, the agency required contributing carriers to include their international telecommunications revenues in their contribution base and rejected claims by certain carriers, which do not receive direct subsidies from the support program, seeking an exemption from making any contributions.

Finally, the FCC adopted a timetable for implementing its high-cost support plan. Because it has not yet developed an accurate assessment of forward-looking costs, it delayed implementation of its support program for non-rural carriers until January 1, 2000. Additionally, because the agency believes it will take even longer to develop accurate forward-looking cost models for rural carriers, it delayed the implementation of its new support plan for rural carriers to "no sooner than January 1, 2001."

During this delay in implementation, the FCC decided that carriers will continue to receive support at the levels generated by existing universal support programs. According to the agency, this gradual, phased-in plan for implementing its new high-cost support system meets the Act's requirement of a "specific timetable for completion."

2. Schools and Libraries.

Pursuant to § 254(h), the FCC adopted rules implementing new programs for schools, libraries, and health care facilities, in particular by providing universal service support for internet access and internal connections in schools and libraries. The agency decided that any entity, including non-telecommunications carriers, that provides internet access or internal connections to schools and libraries will receive universal service support.

To fund the new § 254(h) programs, the FCC accepted the Joint Board's recommendation to assess the interstate and intrastate revenues of providers of interstate telecommunications service. Because many states do not already have similar support programs for schools and libraries, the agency justified its inclusion of intrastate revenues as necessary to ensure adequate funding for § 254(h) programs.

B. Challenges to the Order.

On September 5, 1997, petitioner Celpage Inc. filed a motion in this court to stay the Order. We denied that motion on October 16, 1997, and rejected a similar motion by various rural telephone companies on December 31, 1997. Their petitions, along with challenges to the Order by other petitioners, were consolidated in this court.

There are two sets of challenges to the Order. The first regards the FCC's plan for replacing the current mixture of explicit and implicit subsidies with an explicit universal service support system for high-cost areas. On both statutory and constitutional grounds, petitioners attack (1) the methodology for calculating support under the plan; (2) the allocation of funding responsibilities between the FCC and the states; and (3) the agency's restrictions on how carriers can recover universal service costs.

Other petitioners attack the FCC's high-cost support plan as an encroachment on state authority over intrastate telecommunications regulation because it restricts state eligibility requirements and imposes a "no disconnect" rule for low-income telephone subscribers. Petitioners also challenge, for lack of specificity and for failing to delay implementation of the plan for some rural carriers, the FCC's timetable for implementing the new universal service plan. Additionally, petitioners challenge the FCC's system for assessing contributions, arguing that it improperly includes [wireless telephone] providers and unfairly assesses carriers on the basis of their international and interstate revenues.

The second set of challenges regards the FCC's proposal for implementing § 254(h) programs supporting schools, libraries, and health care providers. Petitioners claim that the FCC impermissibly expanded the scope of § 254(h) support to include the provision of internet access and internal connections. Moreover, they attack the FCC's statutory authority to provide such support to non-telecommunications providers.

Additionally, petitioners charge that the agency encroached on state authority to implement state support programs for schools and libraries and failed to designate which telecommunications services will receive § 254(h) support. They also argue that the FCC exceeded its statutory authority by requiring subsidies for toll-free telephone calls to internet service providers by non-rural health care providers. Finally, they attack the FCC's § 254(h) contribution system because it assesses both the intrastate and interstate revenues of carriers.

We affirm most of the FCC's decisions regarding its implementation of the high-cost support system, concluding, for the most part, that the Order violates neither the statutory requirements nor the Constitution. We remand for further consideration, however, as to the FCC's decision to assess contributions from carriers based on both international and interstate revenues. We also reverse (1) the requirement that ILEC's recover their contributions from access charges and (2) the blanket prohibition on additional state eligibility requirements for carriers receiving high-cost support.

On jurisdictional grounds, we reverse the rule prohibiting local telephone service providers from disconnecting low-income subscribers. We also conclude that the agency exceeded its jurisdictional authority when it assessed contributions for § 254(h) "schools and libraries" programs based on the combined intrastate and interstate revenues of interstate telecommunications providers and when it asserted its jurisdictional authority to do the same on behalf of high-cost support. * * *

III. Analysis.

A. High-Cost Support.

1. Methodology for Calculating Support for High-Cost Areas.

A. Forward-Looking Cost-of-Service Methodology.

GTE and Southwestern Bell (collectively "GTE") and the FCC engage in a fairly complex economic debate over the merits of calculating costs using the forward-looking cost models based on the "least cost, most efficient" carrier. Because incumbent local exchange carriers ("ILEC's") such as GTE will receive their subsidies, under the new system, based on the difference between the costs of providing service to a high-cost region and the revenue that could be derived from that service, GTE fears that using the costs of a hypothetical most-efficient carrier will significantly reduce the amount of universal service support it receives.

i. Statutory Interpretation.

The question, of course, is not whether it is good policy for the FCC to use such cost models, but whether the decision to adopt this methodology conforms to the plain language of the statute. If the language is ambiguous, we must then ask whether the use of forward-looking cost models is reasonable given the terms of the statute and the deference the FCC must be afforded under *Chevron*. Additionally, we must consider whether the agency's actions in reaching its decision are "arbitrary and capricious" under the APA.

We conclude that the plain language is ambiguous as to whether the FCC's cost models are permitted. We then decide that under *Chevron* step-two, the FCC's forward-looking cost models are authorized under their reasonable interpretations of the statutory language. Finally, we do not conclude that the FCC acted in a "arbitrary and capricious" manner in reaching its decision to adopt forward-looking cost models. * * *

To be sure, the FCC's reason for adopting this methodology is not just to preserve universal service. Rather, it is also trying to encourage local competition by setting the cost models at the "most efficient" level so that carriers will have the incentive to improve operations. As long as it can reasonably argue that the methodology will provide sufficient support for universal service, however, it is free, under the deference we afford it under *Chevron* step-two, to adopt a methodology that serves its other goal of encouraging local competition. * * *

c. Limiting the Federal Mechanism to Twenty-Five Percent of Universal Service Costs.

The third step in the FCC's methodology for calculating support to high-cost, non-rural areas allocates 25% of the funding responsibility to the agency, leaving 75% to be provided by the states. In other words, only 25% of the overall funds for the explicit universal support program for high-cost areas will be provided from the funds collected from interstate telephone calls; the rest must be provided by the states, usually through charges on intrastate service. Certain states, GTE, and Kansas and Vermont challenged this allocation on statutory grounds. Specifically, they question the 25% rule for failing to provide "sufficient" support under § 254(e). Kansas and Vermont also challenged the FCC's 25% allocation decision for lack of notice and for failing to ensure reasonable comparability between rural and urban rates.

[W]e do not consider these challenges, because the FCC has accepted the Joint Board's recommendation to scrap the 25%/75% rule. The *Seventh Report and Order* proposes a new methodology that places "no artificial limits on the amount of federal support that is available" when a state cannot by itself maintain reasonable comparability. This new framework is "a different regulation, containing on its face reasoning not previously articulated by the agency as its policy." Therefore, we dismiss the challenges by all of the petitioners as moot. * * *

3. Authority to Prohibit Carriers from Disconnecting Local Service to Low-Income Consumers Who Fail to Pay Toll Charges.

Bell Atlantic and the states challenge the FCC's adoption of a regulation prohibiting carriers receiving universal service support from disconnecting Lifeline services from low-income consumers who have failed to pay toll charges. The petitioners charge that the "no disconnect" rule exceeds the agency's jurisdictional authority under § 2(b) of the 1934 Act, which prohibits FCC regulation of intrastate telecommunications service. * * *

[T]he FCC exceeded its jurisdiction when it imposed the "no disconnect" rule. Because there is no express grant of statutory authority, a proper showing of "impossibility," or a persuasive explanation of how § 254 applies to intrastate service, we reverse, for want of agency jurisdiction, those portions of the Order implementing the "no disconnect" rule.

4. Recovery of Universal Service Contributions.

a. Requiring Incumbents to Recover Contributions Through Access Charges.

GTE and the FCC again wrangle over the meaning of "explicit" in their dispute regarding the rule requiring most ILEC's to recover their universal service contributions through access charges. GTE contends that the rule violates § 254(e)'s command that any support for universal service be "explicit," because recovering contributions through increased access charges is a form of implicit subsidy.

GTE argues that the rule unfairly disadvantages ILEC's because, unlike their potential new competitors, they cannot recover their universal service contributions through explicit charges on their end-users, but, instead, are required by the FCC to increase their access charges on long-distance service providers. Though they do not necessarily lose out in terms of amounts recovered, GTE fears that this recovery method will put them at a competitive disadvantage because, instead of [ ] seeing the costs of universal service on his bill as an explicit surcharge, an ILEC consumer will pay for the costs of universal service through higher rates.

The FCC advances a different understanding of "explicit." "Regardless of how carriers recover their contributions, the FCC's universal service system 'satisfies the statutory requirement that support be explicit' by requiring each carrier to contribute a specific percentage of its end user revenues". As long as carriers know exactly how much they are contributing to the support mechanisms, the subsidies are explicit.

The statute provides little guidance on whether "explicit" means "explicit to the consumer" (as urged by GTE) or "explicit to the carrier" (as urged by the FCC). The statute does state, how ever, that all universal service support should be "explicit." We read "explicit" to mean the opposite of "implicit."

By forcing GTE to recover its universal service contributions from its access charges, the FCC's interpretation maintains an implicit subsidy for ILEC's such as GTE. In fact, requiring carriers to recover their contributions from access charges on interstate calls shifts the costs of intrastate universal service to the interstate jurisdiction. These are precisely the sorts of implicit subsidies currently used by the FCC in its [DEM] weighting program.

We are convinced that the plain language of § 254(e) does not permit the FCC to maintain any implicit subsidies for universal service support. Therefore, we will not afford the FCC any *Chevron* step-two deference in light of this unambiguous Congressional intent. Because the agency continues to require implicit subsidies for ILEC's in violation of a plain, direct statutory command, we reverse its decision to require ILEC's to recover universal service contributions from their interstate access charges.

b. Requiring Interstate Carriers to Reduce Interstate Access Charges by the Amount of Federal High-Cost Support They Receive Under the New Universal Service System.

The states contest an aspect of the Order's effect on interstate access charges, arguing that the requirement that carriers reduce their interstate access charges by the amount of direct federal high-cost support they receive will leave insufficient funds for intrastate universal service. The states make two unconvincing plain-language arguments. First, they point to § 254(b)(5)'s language about "specific, predictable and sufficient" mechanisms to "preserve and advance universal service." As we have observed, § 254(b) identifies a set of principles and does not lay out any specific commands for the FCC. Even § 254(e), which is framed as a direct, statutory command, is ambiguous as to what constitutes "sufficient" support. Therefore, we do not consider the language an expression of Congress's "unambiguous intent" allowing *Chevron* step-one review, and we review its interpretation for reasonability under *Chevron* step-two.

The states argue that § 254(e) does not permit the application of federal universal service funds for the interstate jurisdiction. In essence, they seek to preserve state universal service support by reading the statute to require all high-cost support to remain intrastate. Though this might make compelling policy, nothing in the plain language of § 254(e) unequivocally establishes the states' right to all of the federal universal support funds. The statutory language is at best ambiguous as to

Congress's intent, which, under *Chevron* step-two, leaves it to the FCC's reasonable interpretation.

The FCC has offered good reason to believe that its new explicit support through direct subsidies will replace the amounts lost through the reduction of access charges. To be sure, the states and intervenor NASUCA make a plausible argument that ILEC's will receive less under the new plan than they did through implicit subsidies. As we have determined, however, because the FCC has offered reasonable explanations of why it thinks the funds will still be "sufficient" to support high-cost areas, we defer to the agency's judgment of what is "sufficient."

Under the agency's new universal service plan, it is possible that the states will receive less support for intrastate universal service costs than they did under the old plan. While this may seem unfair as a matter of policy, the states have failed to show that the FCC's interpretation, which may possibly result in a reduction of their level of support, is "arbitrary, capricious, or manifestly contrary to the statute."

B. Subsidization of Services for Schools, Libraries, and Health Care Providers.

Section 254(h) adds a new wrinkle to the concept of universal service by directing the FCC to provide support to elementary and secondary schools, libraries, and health care providers. Thus, the agency has a new statutory mandate to subsidize support for certain beneficiaries, irrespective of whether they are high-cost consumers. GTE raises objections to the agency's implementation of this broad statutory mandate, and Cincinnati Bell and the states challenge the proposal to assess contributions to this new universal service fund.

1. Mandating Support for Internet Access and Internal Connections to Schools and Libraries.

While section 254(h) plainly authorizes the FCC to support discounted telecommunications services to schools and libraries, GTE finds no equivalent statutory authority to support discounted internet access and internal connections. Therefore, GTE argues that the agency exceeded its statutory authority when it mandated support for discounted internet services and internal connections.

Although we agree with GTE that the statute and its legislative history do not support the FCC's interpretation, the language of the statute is ambiguous enough to require deference under *Chevron* step-two. Because, however, the FCC's decision to extend universal service support to internet access and internal connections raises grave doubts as to whether § 254(h) creates an unconstitutional tax, we construe the statute narrowly to avoid raising these constitutional problems.

The FCC concedes that internet access and internal connections cannot be defined as "telecommunications services" for purposes of the section. It argues, however, that the plain language of § 254(h)(1)(B) and (c)(3) authorizes it to require discounted internet access and internal connections to schools and libraries (but not to health care providers).

Subsection 254(h)(1)(B) requires all telecommunications providers to provide to elementary schools, secondary schools, and libraries, on request, discounted services "that are within the definition of universal service under subsection (c)(3) of this section." Subsection (c)(3) authorizes the FCC to designate "additional services for such support mechanisms for schools, libraries, and health care providers for the purposes of subsection (h) of this section." These "additional services" are "[i]n addition to services included in the definition of universal service under paragraph (1)," which defines universal service as an "evolving level of telecommunications services."

The FCC points out that there is no language restricting these "additional" services to telecommunications services. Furthermore, Congress used the limiting term "telecommunications services" in § 254(h)(1)(A) when discussing the provision of universal service support for rural health care providers. The agency argues that "the varying uses of the terms 'telecommunications services' and 'services' in § 254(h)(1)(A) and (B) suggests that the terms were used consciously to signify different meanings." Therefore, the FCC concluded that the term "additional services" is not limited to telecommunications services. It then decided that, based on the legislative history and its understanding of the purposes of the statute, it should require internet access and internal connections support for schools and libraries.

Even though GTE has offered a persuasive reading of the statute, its plain language does not make Congress's intent sufficiently "unambiguous" for *Chevron* step-one review. Therefore, we defer to the FCC's interpretation under *Chevron* step-two and affirm those aspects of the Order providing internet services and internal connections to schools and libraries. * * *

4. Exercising Authority in Deciding That Schools and Libraries Can Obtain Discounts on All Commercially Available Telecommunications Services.

The FCC has also decided that, pursuant to its authority under § 254(c)(3), it will allow schools and libraries to obtain supported discounts on all commercially available telecommunications services. The agency believes that this approach will maximize schools' and libraries' flexibility to purchase whatever package of services they need. * * *

Under *Chevron* step-two, the FCC has reasonably concluded that it can fulfill its statutory duty to "designate" while giving schools and libraries the maximum flexibility to choose which services they need. It is not unreasonable for the FCC to conclude that it could best "take into account ... the particular needs" of schools and libraries by allowing support for all commercially available telecommunications services. Because Congress's use of "designate" in subsection (c)(3) does not unambiguously require the FCC to limit which services may be supported, and because the FCC's decision is reasonable under Chevron step-two, we reject GTE's request and affirm the decision to allow schools and libraries to obtain support for all "commercially available telecommunications services."

5. Authority to Subsidize Toll-Free Telephone Calls to Internet Service Providers by Non-Rural Health Care Providers.

Congress directed the FCC to provide universal service support for "any public or nonprofit health provider that serves persons who reside in rural areas." Congress also instructed the agency "to enhance, to the extent technically feasible and economically reasonable, access to advanced telecommunications and information services for all public and nonprofit ... health care providers." The FCC has seized on the more general language in the second provision as authority for subsidizing telephone calls to internet service providers by both rural and non-rural health care providers. * * *

The FCC has found a way to "enhance access," as authorized by the plain language of § 254(h)(2)(A), so we affirm this portion of the Order.

6. Contribution System to Provide Universal Service Funding for Schools, Libraries, and Rural Health Providers.

The FCC decided to fund the universal support mechanisms for schools, libraries, and rural health care providers by "assessing both the interstate and intrastate revenues of providers of interstate telecommunications services." The uncertainty of state support for the new § 254(h) subsidies and other financial considerations, according to the FCC, justifies assessing both the intrastate and interstate revenues of interstate carriers.

Cincinnati Bell ("CBT"), a small carrier with a mostly intrastate revenue base, attacks the decision as a violation of § 2(b)'s prohibition on federal regulation of intrastate services. The states challenge the FCC's related assertion that it has the authority to require carriers to recover their intrastate contributions from the states. * * *

Without a finding that § 254 applies, the FCC has no other basis to assert jurisdiction, because *Iowa Utilities* explicitly prohibits FCC jurisdiction over intrastate matters stemming from the agency's plenary powers. Therefore, we reverse that portion of the Order that includes intrastate revenues in the calculation of universal service contributions.

b. Authority to Refer Carriers to the States to Seek Recovery of Intrastate Contributions.

Though it stated that it had "the authority to refer carriers to the states to seek authority to recover a portion of their intrastate contribution from intrastate rates," the FCC also declined to exercise this authority. Instead, it directed carriers to recover their contributions from interstate revenues only.

The states and CBT challenge this assertion of authority on the same grounds they question the inclusion of intrastate revenues for universal service contributions. Because the FCC bases its authority on the same provisions it cited on that issue, our decision to deny the agency jurisdiction on that question applies equally to the its claim of authority to assess intrastate rates. * * *

IV. CONCLUSION.

It is difficult to disagree with the Supreme Court's assessment that the Act is "a model of ambiguity or indeed even self-contradiction." As the Court notes, Congress realizes that many of these ambiguities will be resolved by the FCC during its implementation of the statute, and we, like the Court, generally defer to the agency's interpretation of the sometimes-mysterious sections. In this case, we have done so, and we affirm most aspects of the Order implementing the universal service program and dismiss challenges to several parts of the Order as moot.

Still, our deferential approach does not require us to affirm the FCC in every circumstance. In particular, the agency exceeded its statutory authority in (1) prohibiting the states from imposing eligibility requirements and (2) requiring ILEC's to recover their contributions from access charges. Applying the Court's most recent pronouncements on the Act, we also deny the FCC jurisdiction over state control of local service disconnections and universal service contributions based on intrastate revenues. * * *

Debating Universal Service. The post-1996 reform of universal service has created considerable debate over method, that is, how to construct a subsidy that was transparent and not disguised as part of an internal pricing system. For an accessible, and extended critique see Robert W. Crandall and Leonard Waverman, *Who Pays for Universal Service* (2000). What is notable in the debate over universal service is how little debate or even discussion there is about the underlying principle. What is the justification for the subsidy? In the above Joint Board report and order the Commission at paragraph 8 gives a succinct account of the conventional justification: "Universal service support mechanisms that are designed to increase subscribership by keeping rates affordable will benefit everyone in the country, including those who can afford basic telephone service. At the simplest level, increasing the number of people connected to the telecommunications network makes the network more valuable to all of its users by increasing its usefulness to them. Increasing subscribership also benefits society in ways unrelated to the value of the network per se. For example, all of us benefit from the widespread availability of basic public safety services, such as 911." Is this one rationale or two? How much of universal service is due to a theory of value added to the network and its users and how much is due to social benefits independent of specific benefits to telecommunications users? The former involves a question of network effects, the latter a question of social welfare.

Network Effects and Externalities. The concept of a network effect is intuitive to anyone who has ever used a telephone: the value of a network is a function of the number of users. Or, as Alfred Kahn, a leading regulatory economist, once put it succinctly: "if you were the only one who could own a telephone, you would not want it." The idea of a network effect is often equated with that of a "network externality." But a network effect may or may not be an externality depending on whether the effects are captured by a market pricing mechanism. It is only where the external effects are not internalized by market transactions that there is an externality that invites correction by non-market (governmental) attention. If an externality is negative—pollution is the standard example[3]—the usual government policy prescription takes the form of a tax or direct regulatory control. If an externality is positive, the usual government policy prescription is some form of subsidy. In the present context of network externalities the usual assumption is that telecommunications connectivity is a positive effect, thus justifying a subsidy. That assumption rests on two further assumptions: One, the marginal cost of adding the *nth* subscriber exceeds the benefits to that *nth* subscriber,[4] hence that person will not subscribe without some subsidy. Two, the loss of that subscriber is a loss to the existing network subscribers such that they should, in principle, be willing to pay part of the cost of connecting them. If those two assumptions hold, then some kind of subsidy might make sense in order to maximize the value of the network. There are some questions, though, that rarely get asked, let alone answered:

First, who should bear the burden of the subsidy? Universal service charges have always been placed on long distance callers. Why? Is it because they are relatively more affluent? That they get more benefit than local callers? Of course, if the tax were placed on local callers there would have to be a means of exempting those persons for whose benefit the subsidy is imposed. One could do that easily if local calls were metered, but in the U.S. they are not, so one would have to develop some other means of discrimination—such as income. Interestingly, apart from the low-income support program, universal service is not wealth-based; thus we have no reason to think that it is a progressive tax. Distributional equity questions to one side, is this justified in terms of the network effects argument above? Consider, for example, the high-cost support program, which accounts for the lion's share of the fund.[5]

3. In the case of networks, the pertinent example would be congestion. Notice, however, that congestion in the network would normally not be an externality since the subscribers would experience the effects, and those effects would lead either to network management to control the congestion or to pricing changes to account for it.

4. This is put in terms of the *benefits* to that subscriber even though there may also be a problem of ability to pay as the Commission noted. However, the ability to pay is a relative matter that involves the subscriber's estimates of benefits compared to other expenditures.

5. USAC, the Universal Service Administrative Company, which administers uni-

The high-cost support effects a subsidy to rural users (in high-cost routes) at the expense of urban users (in low-cost routes). The implicit assumption is that rural users faced with paying higher costs for service may not subscribe to the network—to the assumed detriment of all network subscribers. But if the higher costs of rural users are shifted to urban users, isn't it possible that some urban users, faced with the higher costs imposed by the universal service charge, will not subscribe? Unless there is some reason to believe that the rural Paul's demand for service is more price sensitive (more "elastic" in economic terms) than the urban Peter's demand, does this redistribution of costs really advance the cause of maintaining the size of the network?

Second, what is the definition of "universal"? Presumably in terms of network effects alone, there must be a point where the costs of extending service are exceeded by the benefits, but how would that be determined? Today, a little over 94% of U.S. households have a telephone—compared, incidentally, to 98% that have television sets. *U.S. Census Bureau, Statistical Abstract of the United States: 2007, Table 1111.* (Subscription rates have been as high as 95.5%, never higher.) How much higher should the government attempt to push subscription rates? Indeed, might it not be the case that they are already too high?[6]

Third, what kinds of services should be supported? Traditional universal service was designed to support voice telephone service. This is still the core target of universal service support, although Congress in 1996 allowed for an evolving category of services, including Internet access. The FCC in 2008 issued a notice of proposed rulemaking seeking comment on a proposal by the Federal-State Joint Board on Universal Service that the high-cost program should be expanded to include support for wireless and broadband facilities in high cost areas. *In the Matter of High-Cost Universal Service Support*, 23 FCC Rcd. 1531 (2008). Do such services fit within the network effects principle or are they based on some broader principle of public goods and social welfare?

Social Welfare. As the FCC's quote above indicates, the benefits of increased subscribership are not necessarily confined to benefits internal to the telecommunications system itself. When Congress broadened universal service to include new information services and users other than households—notably schools, libraries and health clinics—it presumably had in mind a concept of general social welfare. At that point,

versal service, reports the following data on the size and distribution of the fund. In 2006 the total was an estimated $7.3 billion. Of that, the high-cost program accounted for $4.2 billion; low-income, $820 million, rural health care, $45 million; schools and libraries $2.25 million. http://www.usac.org/about/universal-service/fund-facts/fund-facts.aspx.

6. There may be still among us some who feel as Mark Twain, who wrote (at the dawn of the telephone):

> It is my heart-warm and world-embracing Christmas hope and aspiration that all of us, the high, the low, the rich, the poor, the admired, the despised, the loved, the hated, the civilized, the savage, may eventually be gathered together in a heaven of everlasting rest and peace and bliss, except the inventor of the telephone.

"Christmas Greetings," *Boston Daily Globe*, December 25, 1890, p. 3.

the question of purpose becomes rather expansive. It is no longer a matter of network externalities as traditionally defined, but about the provision of public goods generally. What things should be subsidized? As Crandall and Waverman, *supra* at p. 23 ask: "Why is telephone service any different from scores of other household services, such as household plumbing, electricity, refrigeration of household food stocks, or even the services of a television set?" Of course, pressing this question too hard opens a Pandora's box of similar questions for countless other public subsidies that are effected either by explicit appropriations or by tax policy or other measures, such as price supports and other subsidies for agricultural products.

Even accepting that universal service is a given, there still remains the question, how best to manage it. If we are no longer talking about benefits that are internal to the telecommunications system but accrue to society as a whole, is it not a little odd that we should be taxing telecommunications users to provide a subsidy to telecommunications users?[7] Bringing the benefits of modern telecommunications and related information services to schools or rural health clinics, for example, might indeed be a high social priority, but, if so, why not fund these services from general tax revenues, whence the usual questions of distributional equity (including progressivity, etc.) would be more transparent?

Bill-and-Keep and Universal Service. As described in the Wireline Competition Bureau staff report annexed to the *Unified Intercarrier Compensation FNPRM*, one major advantage of bill-and-keep is its regulatory simplicity. But the intercarrier compensation regime has traditionally been a major source of universal service funding. Part of the universal service regime has required funding between carriers, and a bill-and-keep price of zero for interconnection would seemingly make that impossible. The staff addressed the problem in its report advocating for bill-and-keep. Sort of. The immense problem of how bill-and-keep would fit with universal service, prompted this treatment by the staff:

> Many commenters, including carriers, state commissions, and consumer groups, express concern about the potential impact of bill-and-keep on end-user charges. They contend that a bill-and-keep regime is not in the public interest because it would affect the affordability of telecommunications services in rural and remote areas. Several commenters also argue that a bill-and-keep approach would have significant implications for universal service and may necessitate changes to the existing universal service support mechanisms.
>
> We recognize the need to address the universal service consequences of a bill-and-keep regime. As the Commission made clear in the *Further Notice*, it is committed to ensuring the availability of tele-

7. Taxing telephone users to support exogenous social benefits is not unknown, however. In 1898 Congress imposed a 3% tax on telephone service to help support the Spanish American War. It was repealed in 2006, by which time Congress apparently decided it was no longer needed for that purpose.

communications services in rural and high-cost areas at rates that are affordable and reasonably comparable to rates in urban areas, consistent with section 254 of the Act. We acknowledge the many commenters, including carriers, state commissions, and consumer groups, that express concerns that bill-and-keep will raise end-user charges and may affect the affordability of telecommunications services, particularly in rural and high-cost areas. We recognize that addressing these affordability concerns will require further adjustments to the Commission's existing explicit universal service mechanisms and may require additional commitments of universal service funds.

Does the staff's treatment adequately account for the Commission's response to the problems presented by cross-subsidization in the past? Is the Commission likely to completely divorce universal service from the question of intercarrier compensation, as the staff seems to be suggesting it will?

E. PROMOTING COMPETITION IN LOCAL EXCHANGE SERVICE

1. Introduction

A fundamental purpose of the 1996 Act was to promote competition in local exchange service markets where ILECs (a category that includes both the BOCs and incumbent independents) continued to have monopolies. Although promoting additional competition in long distance markets was seen as important, it was always viewed as tied to the purpose of opening up local markets. Opening up those local markets was a complex undertaking from an institutional perspective because the new competition was a carry-over from the old monopoly.

First, since local exchange service (being virtually all intrastate) was within the province of state regulators—who had strongly resisted competition in the past—it was considered necessary to develop a comprehensive federal scheme that in significant degree preempted state regulatory discretion to the extent it might impede the overall congressional policy of promoting competition in local markets.

Second, there were significant economic barriers to new entry to the extent that facilities-based entry required large, upfront investment in infrastructure by the CLECs. While Congress considered facilities-based competition to be desirable, it also thought it might not be practical to expect new entrants to duplicate all of the incumbent network facilities. Thus, it provided for three entry options: (1) entrants could supply their own network facilities; (2) they could buy incumbent services at wholesale rates and resell them (with or without additional services of their own); or (3) they could buy (lease) particular network facilities—e.g., local loops, switches, or transport (which is carriage between switches)—as needed to provide competitive services. These were not mutually exclusive options, of course; new entrants could choose a combination of these strategies. The important thing was to get the ball rolling towards competition in local markets.

The details of the congressional mandate to enable this new entry are dauntingly complex. Section 253 of the 1996 Act destroys the previous state monopolies by authorizing the FCC to preempt state laws that prohibit entities from offering intrastate or interstate telephone services. Section 251 imposes numerous duties on ILECs, most notably a duty to interconnect with other carriers at specified points in their network, a duty to lease to other carriers—on an unbundled basis—individual elements of their network (commonly dubbed "UNEs"—unbundled network elements), and a duty to allow other carriers to resell their services. Section 252 then establishes procedures for negotiating, arbitrating, and approving the agreements under which ILECs would both interconnect with, and provide services to, CLECs. Sections 251 and 252 warrant quoting at length.

Section 251 (emphases added to clarify the different categories of carriers):

(a) General duty of telecommunications carriers

Each telecommunications carrier has the duty—

(1) to interconnect directly or indirectly with the facilities and equipment of other telecommunications carriers; and

(2) not to install network features, functions, or capabilities that do not comply with the guidelines and standards established pursuant to section 255 or 256 of this title. [Eds. These sections prescribe requirements for making equipment and services accessible to disabled persons and for coordinating interconnectivity standards.]

(b) Obligations of **all** local exchange carriers

Each local exchange carrier has the following duties:

(1) Resale

The duty not to prohibit, and not to impose unreasonable or discriminatory conditions or limitations on, the resale of its telecommunications services.

* * * [Other specified duties include arrangements for number portability, dialing parity, sharing access rights of way and reciprocal compensation for carriage of calls originating from another carrier.]

(c) Additional obligations of **incumbent** local exchange carriers

In addition to the duties contained in subsection (b) of this section, each incumbent local exchange carrier has the following duties:

(1) Duty to negotiate

The duty to negotiate in good faith in accordance with section 252 of this title the particular terms and conditions of agreements to fulfill the duties described in paragraphs (1) through (5) of subsection (b) of this section and this subsection. The requesting telecommunications carrier also has the duty to negotiate in good faith the terms and conditions of such agreements.

(2) Interconnection

The duty to provide, for the facilities and equipment of any requesting telecommunications carrier, interconnection with the local exchange carrier's network—

(A) for the transmission and routing of telephone exchange service and exchange access;

(B) at any technically feasible point within the carrier's network;

(C) that is at least equal in quality to that provided by the local exchange carrier to itself or to any subsidiary, affiliate, or any other party to which the carrier provides interconnection; and

(D) on rates, terms, and conditions that are just, reasonable, and nondiscriminatory, in accordance with the terms and conditions of the agreement and the requirements of this section and section 252 of this title.

(3) Unbundled access

The duty to provide, to any requesting telecommunications carrier for the provision of a telecommunications service, nondiscriminatory access to network elements on an unbundled basis at any technically feasible point on rates, terms, and conditions that are just, reasonable, and nondiscriminatory in accordance with the terms and conditions of the agreement and the requirements of this section and section 252 of this title. An incumbent local exchange carrier shall provide such unbundled network elements in a manner that allows requesting carriers to combine such elements in order to provide such telecommunications service.

(4) Resale

The duty—

(A) to offer for resale at wholesale rates any telecommunications service that the carrier provides at retail to subscribers who are not telecommunications carriers; and

(B) not to prohibit, and not to impose unreasonable or discriminatory conditions or limitations on, the resale of such telecommunications service, except that a State commission may, consistent with regulations prescribed by the Commission under this section, prohibit a reseller that obtains at wholesale rates a telecommunications service that is available at retail only to a category of subscribers from offering such service to a different category of subscribers.

* * *

(6) Collocation

The duty to provide, on rates, terms, and conditions that are just, reasonable, and nondiscriminatory, for physical collocation of equipment necessary for interconnection or access to unbundled network elements at the premises of the local exchange carrier, except that the carrier may provide for virtual collocation if the local exchange carrier demonstrates to the State commission that physical collocation is not practical for technical reasons or because of space limitations"

(d) Implementation

(1) In general

Within 6 months after February 8, 1996, the Commission shall complete all actions necessary to establish regulations to implement the requirements of this section.

(2) Access standards

In determining what network elements should be made available for purposes of subsection (c)(3) of this section, the Commission shall consider, at a minimum, whether—

(A) access to such network elements as are proprietary in nature is necessary; and

(B) the failure to provide access to such network elements would impair the ability of the telecommunications carrier seeking access to provide the services that it seeks to offer.

* * *

Section 252

(a) Agreements arrived at through negotiation

* * * [Subsections (a), (b) and (c) provide for voluntary negotiations, for mediation and finally for binding arbitration under the auspices of the state regulatory agency.]

(d) Pricing standards

(1) Interconnection and network element charges

Determinations by a State commission of the just and reasonable rate for the interconnection of facilities and equipment for purposes of subsection (c)(2) of section 251 of this title, and the just and reasonable rate for network elements for purposes of subsection (c)(3) of such section—

(A) shall be—

(i) based on the cost (determined without reference to a rate-of-return or other rate-based proceeding) of providing the interconnection or network element (whichever is applicable), and

(ii) nondiscriminatory, and

(B) may include a reasonable profit.

* * *

(3) Wholesale prices for telecommunications services

For the purposes of section 251(c)(4) of this title, a State commission shall determine wholesale rates on the basis of retail rates charged to subscribers for the telecommunications service requested, excluding the portion thereof attributable to any marketing, billing, collection, and other costs that will be avoided by the local exchange carrier.

The 1996 Act contemplated that competitive entry into local service markets could occur from CLECs providing their own facilities, by reselling ILEC services, or by leasing ILEC facilities on an unbundled basis. The first two strategies have been relatively uncontroversial; most of the battles have occurred over the third, and we will focus principally on it. Broadly speaking, the unbundled access controversy has two major components. One is the scope of unbundling—designating which facilities the ILECs must share with CLECs on an unbundled basis; the other is the price that ILECs may charge for the use of unbundled facilities.

2. Leasing Unbundled Network Elements: Issues of Scope

In many ways, the unbundling of network elements required by the 1996 Act is an outgrowth of interconnection obligations AT&T had under the pre-96 regime. Telecommunications carriers have been long required to interconnect with other carriers. Traditionally interconnection was simply a means of providing end-to-end connectivity among different carriers. For example, an independent local exchange carrier in a market not served by AT&T would interconnect with AT&T's long distance network and receive transport services per an AT&T tariff providing such service to other carriers. AT&T provided a service—long distance—to independent local carriers who then passed through the charges to their customers. There was no competitive aspect to the interconnection relationship, since, by definition, the independent local carriers were in markets not served by AT&T. Even when competition appeared in long distance markets and AT&T was forced to interconnect with competitors, it was on the basis of providing an entire service—e.g., selling a particular service (at wholesale rates) not selling the use of individual network facilities such as loop, transport or switching facilities.

The idea of requiring an incumbent carrier to sell not only its *services* to competitors, but also to sell individual facilities (more precisely the "functionalities" or technical services that the particular elements provide) on a piecemeal basis (i.e., unbundling them from the aggregation of elements that are used to provide an end service) is a distinctly modern concept. It is not completely novel with the 1996 Act. As we saw in the last chapter, the idea of providing access to unbundled elements of the incumbent carrier's network facilities was first developed in the *Computer III* decision, which required BOCs to unbundle and offer to competing enhanced services providers the "basic service elements" necessary to providing those enhanced services to customers. However, *Computer III* was a more restricted regime designed to keep dominant carriers from using their control of the network to handicap enhanced service or equipment providers who need to use the basic network facilities to support their CPE or enhanced services. The 1996 scheme expanded on that concept to use access as a means of promoting competition in the basic telecommunications network itself. CLEC access to UNEs means that they can basically use the facilities of the incumbent in providing their own services.

The 1996 regime of unbundled access presented the FCC with a vexing question as to the scope of unbundled access. Some network facilities are intuitive candidates. For example, a local loop connecting the subscriber's premises to the first switch (the CO) is a preeminent candidate for mandatory access simply because it is likely to be the network component that is most costly for a CLEC to duplicate. But the scope issue becomes progressively more uncertain when one works through other elements. For example, what about switches, which can be purchased on the open market? (Until recently, however, mass market switches were classified as UNEs—for reasons that will be apparent from the case below.) For its part Congress did not provide much guidance on what network facilities had to be shared with CLECs. Section 251(c) provides a dual standard:

> In determining what network elements should be made available for purposes of subsection (c)(3) of this section, the Commission shall consider, at a minimum, whether
>
> (A) access to such network elements as are proprietary in nature is necessary; and
>
> (B) the failure to provide access to such network elements would impair the ability of the telecommunications carrier seeking access to provide the services that it seeks to offer.

The "proprietary" elements provision in sub-paragraph (A) refers to facilities that are protected by intellectual property laws—most notably patents or trade secrets. Such elements only need be provided if they are "necessary" to CLECs. The bulk of network facilities, however, fall into the second category where, it appears, Congress intended to enact a more liberal criterion, "impairment," for forced sharing. But exactly what did it mean to say that the absence of access would "impair" the ability of a CLEC to provide services? For a decade after the Act, that question was the occasion for a battle between the ILECs and the CLECs and between the FCC and the courts. We skip over this history; the salient decisions are summarized in the opinion below, which marks the latest chapter in the saga over what network elements must be leased to CLECs.

COVAD COMMUNICATIONS COMPANY v. FCC

United States Court of Appeals, District of Columbia Circuit, 2006.
450 F.3d 528.

SENTELLE, CIRCUIT JUDGE:

The Federal Communications Commission ("FCC" or "the Commission") has thrice attempted—unsuccessfully—to implement the "unbundling" provisions of the Telecommunications Act of 1996, Pub.L. No. 104–104, 110 Stat. 56 ("the Act" or "the 1996 Act"). This case involves a series of petitions for review of the FCC's fourth attempt. Because we conclude the Commission's fourth try is a charm, we deny all of the petitions for review.

I

The 1996 Act sought to foster a competitive market in telecommunications. To minimize the characteristics of natural monopoly in the market, the Act gave the FCC broad powers to require incumbent local exchange carriers ("ILECs") to make unbundled network elements ("UNEs") available to competitive local exchange carriers ("CLECs"), 47 U.S.C. § 251(c)(3), (d); *see also id.* § 153(29) (defining a "network element" as "a facility or equipment used in the provision of a telecommunications service"). Thus, the Commission may require the ILECs to offer pieces of their networks as unbundled building blocks, which the CLECs can lease, repackage, and use to compete against the ILECs in telecommunications markets across the country.

Congress left to the Commission the choice of elements to be "unbundled," specifying that it must "consider, at a minimum, whether the failure to provide access to such network elements would *impair* the ability of the telecommunications carrier seeking access to provide the services that it seeks to offer." Relying upon the implicit breadth of its "at a minimum" authority and its discretion to interpret the meaning of "impair[ment]," the FCC in this case amended its unbundling determinations for three types of UNEs: "switches" (devices that direct calls to their destinations in the same way switchboard operators once did), "transport trunks" (wires that carry calls between switches), and "local loops" (wires that run from switches over the "last mile" to consumers' telephones). The propriety *vel non* of those determinations is the crux of this case.

A

The basics of unbundling are relatively simple. Suppose a CLEC (such as Covad) wants to serve customers in Washington, D.C. One way of doing so is for Covad to purchase its own switches, trunks, and loops, which it can then use to offer service to its new customers. However, given that the local ILEC (*e.g.*, Verizon) has already deployed switches, trunks, and loops to serve the market, it might be economically impossible for Covad to duplicate competitively Verizon's infrastructure. Through regulatory unbundling, however, Covad might be able to lease Verizon's switches, trunks, and loops as UNEs. Covad could then use combinations of UNEs to cobble together a network and compete against Verizon in Washington.

Under the Act, Covad must pay Verizon for every "facility" and every piece of "equipment" the former requests from the latter on an unbundled basis. After a hard-fought litigation battle, the Commission concluded that UNE prices must be based on each element's Total Element Long–Run Incremental Cost ("TELRIC"). *Verizon Commc'ns, Inc. v. FCC*, 535 U.S. 467, 523 (2002) (upholding the FCC's TELRIC pricing methodology for UNEs as "a reasonable policy" choice). TELRIC rates are akin to wholesale prices because CLECs are supposed to be economically able to rent UNEs and then use them to sell telecom services to their retail customers. The ILECs unsurprisingly dislike seeing their own networks wielded as competitive weapons by CLECs—especially when the CLECs enjoy access to UNEs at TELRIC rates. The ILECs therefore champion the use of substitute products that allow CLECs to compete without demanding access to the ILECs' individual network elements. For our purposes, the only relevant substitute product is the tariffed special access service ("TSAS"). Basically, Covad can purchase TSASs from Verizon (at prices above the TELRIC rates associated with UNEs), and the TSASs allow Covad to complete point-to-point calls over dedicated lines. Thus, instead of purchasing or renting a loop, switch, space in a central office, and a transport trunk to complete a call, a CLEC might simply pay the higher TSAS rate for a dedicated line (which does not require separate switching or transport).

Given the lower cost of UNEs, the CLECs favor widespread unbundling, while ILECs favor fewer UNEs and the greater availability of higher-priced TSASs. This tug-of-war—between CLECs advocating more unbundling and ILECs advocating less—has been the nub of an ongoing, decade-long dispute between incumbents and their would-be competitors. To explain today's unbundling battle, we begin with the skirmishes that preceded it.

B

The ILECs' and CLECs' power struggle over UNEs began shortly after the passage of the 1996 Act. In its first attempt to interpret the Act's "impairment" standard, the Commission concluded that a CLEC was entitled to a given UNE "if the quality of the service the entrant can offer, absent access to the requested element, declines and/or the cost of providing the service rises."

The Supreme Court found this interpretation of "impair" unreasonable in two respects. First, the Commission had erroneously refused to consider whether a CLEC could self-provision or acquire the requested element from a third party. *AT&T Corp. v. Iowa Utils. Bd.*, 525 U.S.

366, 389–92 (1999). Second, the Commission had considered any increase in cost or decrease in quality, no matter how small, sufficient to establish impairment—a result the Court concluded could not be squared with the "ordinary and fair meaning" of the word "impair." The Court admonished the FCC that in assessing which cost differentials would "impair" a new entrant's competition within the meaning of the statute, it must "apply some limiting standard, rationally related to the goals of the Act."

On remand from *Iowa Utilities*, the Commission ruled that a would-be entrant is "impaired" if, "taking into consideration the availability of alternative elements outside the incumbent's network, including self-provisioning by a requesting carrier or acquiring an alternative from a third-party supplier, lack of access to that element materially diminishes a requesting carrier's ability to provide the services it seeks to offer." We held the Commission's "impairment" standard was unlawful because it did not differentiate between those cost disparities that a new entrant in any market would be likely to face and those that arise from market characteristics "linked (in some degree) to natural monopoly ... that would make genuinely competitive provision of an element's function wasteful." *U.S. Telecom Ass'n v. FCC*, 290 F.3d 415, 427 (D.C.Cir.2002) ("*USTA I*"), cert. denied sub nom. *WorldCom, Inc. v. U.S. Telecom Ass'n*, 538 U.S. 940 (2003). *USTA I* concluded that the Commission's broad concept of impairment failed to "balance" the costs and benefits of unbundling.

USTA I also instructed the Commission to make nuanced impairment determinations. Though the Act does not necessarily require the Commission to determine "on a localized state-by-state or market-by-market basis which unbundled elements are to be made available," it does require "a more nuanced concept of impairment than is reflected in findings detached from any specific markets or market categories," Thus, the Commission is obligated to establish unbundling criteria that are at least aimed at tracking relevant market characteristics and capturing significant variation.

On remand from *USTA I*, the Commission determined that a CLEC would

> be impaired when lack of access to an incumbent LEC network element poses a barrier or barriers to entry, including operational and economic barriers, that are likely to make entry into a market uneconomic. That is, we ask whether all potential revenues from entering a market exceed the costs of entry, taking into consideration any countervailing advantages that a new entrant may have.

[*Triennial Review Order*], 18 F.C.C.R. 16978, 17035 (2003). In response to *USTA I's* demand for a more "nuanced" impairment standard, the Commission made an absolute national impairment finding, subject to specific exclusions (i.e., findings of non-impairment) by state public utility commissions.

We invalidated much of the *Triennial Review Order* in *United States Telecom Association v. FCC*, 359 F.3d 554, 576 (D.C.Cir.) ("*USTA II*"), cert. denied sub nom., *Nat'l Ass'n of Regulatory Utility Comm'rs v. United States Telecom Ass'n*, 543 U.S. 925 (2004). We concluded that the Commission's "touchstone" of impairment—"uneconomic" entry—was excessively vague. *See id.* at 572 ("Uneconomic by whom? By *any* CLEC, no matter how inefficient? By an 'average' or 'representative' CLEC? By the most efficient existing CLEC? By a hypothetical CLEC that used the most efficient telecommunications technology currently available?" (emphasis in original) (internal quotation marks omitted)). Moreover, *USTA II* held the FCC could not lawfully implement a more "nuanced" (or "granular") impairment standard by adopting a blanket finding of impairment and then delegating power to state regulatory commissions to make non-impairment exceptions to the FCC's nationwide rule. Instead, the FCC must establish unbundling criteria that take into account "relevant market characteristics," which capture "significant variation," sensibly define the relevant markets, connect those markets to the FCC's impairment findings, and consider whether the "element in question" is "significantly deployed on a competitive basis." The fact that CLECs can viably compete without UNEs—for example, by utilizing the ILECs' TSASs—"precludes a finding that the CLECs are 'impaired' by lack of access to the element under § 251(c)(3)."

On remand from *USTA II*, the Commission issued an interim order and notice of proposed rulemaking. ("*NPRM*") The *NPRM* noted that our decision "called into question certain aspects of the Commission's unbundling framework, including the 'open-endedness' of the Commission's 'touchstone' of impairment-uneconomic entry. . . ." Accordingly, the FCC sought "comment on how to respond to the D.C. Circuit's *USTA II* decision in establishing sustainable new unbundling rules under sections 251(c) and 251(d)(2) of the Act." After receiving and considering comments, the FCC issued a four-part order, which is the subject of this case. *See In the Matter of Unbundled Access to Network Elements, Order on Remand*, 20 F.C.C.R. 2533 (2005) ("*Order*"). We discuss each part of the *Order* in turn.

1

First, the Commission altered its unbundling framework. The FCC clarified that it would find "impairment" where it would be "uneconomic" for a "reasonably efficient" CLEC to compete without UNEs. The Commission explained:

> In analyzing entry from the perspective of the reasonably efficient competitor, we do not attach weight to the individualized circumstances of the actual requesting carrier. Thus, we do not presume that a hypothetical entrant possesses any particular assets, legal entitlements or opportunities, even if a specific competitive carrier in fact enjoys such advantages as a result of its unique circumstances. Similarly, under our approach, impairment does not arise

> due to any errors of business judgment made by an actual requesting carrier.

Id. at 2548 (footnotes omitted).

While the FCC presumes that a reasonably efficient competitor "will use reasonably efficient technologies and take advantage of existing alternative facilities deployment," it need not utilize TSASs in the local exchange markets. *USTA II* held that the FCC "must consider" TSAS-based competition in its impairment inquiry for mobile wireless and long-distance UNEs, because competition in those markets is "robust," In contrast, "[t]he local services market does not share the competitive conditions, observed in the mobile wireless services market and long distance services market, that would support a parallel finding that the costs of unbundling outweigh the benefits." Because the Commission concluded that UNEs are vital to the continued development of competition in the local exchange market, it retained its unbundling requirements, regardless of whether CLECs are currently using TSASs to provide local service.

2

Second, the Commission amended its impairment findings for dedicated interoffice transport. "Dedicated transport facilities" refer to facilities that are dedicated to a particular carrier used for transmission between or among ILEC wire centers. For purposes of this opinion, transport comes in two varieties: "DS1" (which can carry 24 voice calls simultaneously) and "DS3" (which has 28 times the capacity of DS1 facilities and can therefore carry 672 voice calls simultaneously).

CLECs often use DS1 transport as part of an end-to-end circuit, called an "enhanced extended link" ("EEL"), which can be used to serve a single customer (typically a small-or medium-sized business). EELs are often composed of a DS1 loop combined with a DS1 transport link. After noting that it will "measure impairment with regard to dedicated transport on a route-by-route basis," the Commission identified two proxies for determining whether entry into a particular market would be economic without unbundled DS1 or DS3 facilities: (i) the extent of fiber-based collocation and (ii) business line density.

The FCC found that CLECs are not impaired without DS1 transport links when both ends of the transport route terminate in "Tier 1" wire centers (i.e., those with four or more fiber-based collocators or 38,000 or more business lines). Similarly, CLECs are not impaired without access to DS3 transport where both ends of the route terminate in "Tier 2" wire centers (i.e., those with at least three fiber-based collocators or at least 24,000 business lines). The higher impairment threshold for DS1 transport reflects the fact that DS1 facilities have less capacity and generate less revenue (thus making them less likely to be deployed by CLECs).

If a CLEC self-certifies that a transport trunk meets the applicable test, the ILEC is obligated to offer immediate access to the trunk on an unbundled basis. If the ILEC seeks to challenge the propriety of unbundling the trunk, it must first provide the UNE and then raise a challenge through the dispute resolution procedures prescribed by the applicable interconnection agreements (i.e., contracts between ILECs and CLECs).

3

Third, the Commission amended its impairment findings for DS1 and DS3 loops. The Commission noted it is often not economical for a CLEC to deploy its own DS1 loops, given their capacity limitations. However, the FCC explained that to offer DS1 or DS3 service, CLECs "install high-capacity fiber-optic cables [including DS3 loops and "optical carrier level n," or "OCn," facilities] and then use electronics to light the fiber at specific capacity levels, often 'channelizing' these higher-capacity offerings into multiple lower-capacity streams." Thus, the FCC concluded, CLECs are not impaired without DS1/DS3 UNEs in markets where CLECs have deployed—or could economically deploy—higher-capacity facilities that can be "channelized" to provide service at lower levels.

After noting that the relevant market for measuring impairment in DS1 and DS3 loops is the area served by a wire center, the Commission again relied upon fiber-based collocators and business-line density as proxies for predicting impairment in high-capacity loop markets. Specifically, the Commission found that CLECs are not impaired without DS1 loops within the service area of a wire center that has at least four fiber-based collocators and at least 60,000 business lines. Similarly, CLECs are not impaired without access to DS3 loops within the service area of a wire center containing at least four fiber-based collocators and at least 38,000 business lines. The higher impairment threshold for DS1 loops reflects the fact that DS1 facilities have less capacity and generate less revenue (thus making them less prone to deployment by CLECs). Loops are governed by the same implementation procedures that the Commission employed for dedicated transport. *See* [*Order*, 20 F.C.C.R.] at 2665–66 (if CLECs self-certify that a DS1/DS3 loop meets the impairment thresholds, ILECs must offer immediate unbundled access and then litigate the issue before the state commissions).

4

Fourth and finally, the Commission concluded that ILECs no longer need to provide CLECs with unbundled access to mass market local circuit switching ("MMLS"). The FCC adopted transitional rules to wean CLECs off the local circuit switching UNEs that are currently in use. Specifically, the Commission afforded CLECs 12 months to eliminate their reliance on unbundled MMLS, and it increased the rates at which ILECs are compensated for unbundled local switching during the transitional period.

D

Numerous parties filed petitions for review. Our review is governed by the classic two-step framework from *Chevron USA v. Natural*

Resources Defense Council, Inc., 467 U.S. 837 (1984): If Congress "has directly spoken to the precise question at issue," we "must give effect to [its] unambiguously expressed intent"; on the other hand, "if the statute is silent or ambiguous," we must defer to the Commission's interpretation so long as it is "based on a permissible construction of the statute." Ultimately, if the Commission's reading of the statute is reasonable, *Chevron* requires us "to accept the agency's construction of the statute, even if the agency's reading differs from what the court believes is the best statutory interpretation."

Both the Supreme Court and our Court have held that the 1996 Act's use of the term "impair," is ambiguous and should be reviewed under *Chevron*'s second step. Similarly, the Commission's reasonable interpretations of are entitled to deference. Under the Administrative Procedure Act, we will uphold the Commission's policy choices unless they are arbitrary and capricious. *See* 5 U.S.C. § 706(2)(A). To survive review under this standard, the FCC "must examine the relevant data and articulate a satisfactory explanation for its action including a rational connection between the facts found and the choice made." *Motor Vehicle Mfrs. Ass'n, Inc. v. State Farm Mut. Auto. Ins. Co.*, 463 U.S. 29, 43 (1983).

In Part II below, we address and reject the ILECs' two challenges to the *Order*. In Part III, we address and reject the CLECs' three challenges to the *Order*. * * *

II

The ILECs raise two challenges to the *Order*. First, the ILECs argue that the FCC unlawfully failed to consider the relevance of TSASs in its unbundling analysis. Second, the ILECs argue that the Commission imposed impossibly high thresholds for assessing the state of competition in the market for DS1/DS3 loops and transport. We reject both claims.

A

The ILECs first argue that the Commission unjustifiably concluded that it would be "inappropriate" to eliminate UNEs where CLECs are "able to compete using an incumbent LEC's [TSASs]." The ILECs argue that to the extent TSASs allow viable competition, the Act's "impairment" requirement is not met, and unbundling is not required. In the ILECs' view, the Commission's conclusion to the contrary "violates this Court's mandate" from *USTA II*.

We disagree. In *USTA II*, we reversed the FCC's decision to make UNEs available to providers of wireless services where CLECs' use of TSASs had allowed "competition not only to survive but to flourish.". Noting that the use of special access had spawned similarly "robust competition" in the long-distance market, we declared that "the presence of robust competition" by users of special access "precludes a finding" that CLECs are impaired without UNEs in the wireless and long-distance markets. We therefore held that the Commission's impairment analysis must consider the availability of tariffed ILEC special access services when determining whether would-be entrants are impaired.... This of course still leaves the Commission free to take into account such factors as administrability, risk of ILEC abuse, and the like. What the Commission may not do is compare unbundling only to self-provisioning or third-party provisioning, arbitrarily excluding alternatives offered by the ILECs.

Notwithstanding the ILECs' arguments to the contrary, the above-quoted holding does not apply with equal force to the local exchange markets. Unlike the "robust competition" that special access services have spawned in the wireless and long-distance markets, the FCC found that TSAS-based competition in the local exchange markets is much more "limited." Nothing in *USTA II* specified how the Commission should analyze the impact of special access services in markets where competition is less than "robust." Instead, we entrusted that task to the agency's discretion and emphasized that the FCC was "free to take into account such factors as administrability, risk of ILEC abuse, and the like."

On remand, the Commission considered the viability of TSAS-based competition and concluded that "even in cases where [CLECs] currently compete using special access," a case-by-case TSAS-based impairment inquiry "would raise insurmountable hurdles regarding administrability...." The FCC found that such an inquiry "would require the Commission to examine all revenues [a CLEC] might hope to capture using the UNE or special access service at issue in a given market and to compare those potential revenues against every relevant state and federal tariff and every [ILEC] retail and wholesale service offered in every market at issue for every element or service," taking into account all "available term and volume discounts." Adding to the complexity of this endeavor, the prices and terms governing special access vary greatly from market to market. Given the apples-to-oranges nature of comparing TSASs nationwide, the Commission decided that evaluating the effect of special access on impairment in individual local markets "would be excessively complicated" and "utterly impracticable," "requiring resources far beyond those available to this Commission."

Moreover, the FCC found that a rule denying access to UNEs whenever tariffed alternatives are available would create an "unacceptable risk of significant abuse by [ILECs]." *see also* [*USTA II*] (suggesting that "on an appropriate record the Commission might find impairment" where the elimination of UNEs would pose a "risk of ILEC abuse" in the TSAS market). The Commission found record evidence that the availability of UNEs serves to discipline special access rates by exercising "a constraining influence" on the ILECs' ability to increase their TSAS rates. Indeed, in an unrelated proceeding, the ILECs acknowledged this was the case. The Commission therefore found that the "elimination of UNEs would significantly risk increased special access pricing, undermining or destroying the ability to compete using tariffed alternatives."

The Commission's analysis is reasonable. In contrast to the wireless and long-distance markets, "carriers generally make only limited use of special access offerings to provide service in the local exchange services market." *Order*, 20 F.C.C.R. at 2572. Moreover, in accordance with our instructions from *USTA II*, the FCC tempered its consideration of TSAS-based competition by "tak[ing] into account such factors as administrability, risk of ILEC abuse, and the like." Thus, the Commission "consider[ed]" the import of TSASs in its impairment inquiry, and it provided a reasoned explanation for its decision not to eliminate unbundling solely on the basis of limited TSAS-based competition. *Chevron's* second step requires nothing more.[6]

B

The ILECs' second argument is that competition is viable (and hence unbundling is both unnecessary and unlawful) in wire centers that have far fewer business lines and fiber-based collocators than required by the Commission's unbundling thresholds. The ILECs argue that *USTA I* and *USTA II* require the FCC to "deny unbundling not only in markets that are already extremely competitive, but also in markets where the evidence shows that [CLECs] can compete without UNEs." However, in the ILECs' view, the Commission denied unbundling only in those markets that are experiencing "extraordinary levels of competition," without considering "the class of markets in which competition is possible without UNEs...."

Again, we disagree. Notwithstanding the ILECs' arguments to the contrary, the Commission repeatedly justifies its unbundling determinations on the basis of both actual and potential competition. * * *

1

The ILECs complain that the Commission granted "exceedingly narrow transport relief." Ironically, however, the Commission eliminated unbundling for high-capacity transport in more wire centers than the ILECs proposed. Specifically, the ILECs suggested—and the FCC rejected—a proposal to eliminate transport unbundling between wire centers that contain one or more fiber-based collocators. The Commission concluded that the ILECs' proposal would *underestimate* the potential for competitive deployment and that unbundling was warranted for transport between wire centers that contained zero fiber-based collocators.

To be sure, the Commission's chosen business-line thresholds (38,000 for DS1s and 24,000 for DS3s) are higher than the ILECs would

6. The ILECs also challenge the Commission's adherence to its policy of allowing CLECs to convert TSASs to UNEs in markets where other CLECs have access to UNEs. As the Commission explained, "[t]he [ILECs'] arguments against conversions are essentially the same as their arguments for finding non-impairment wherever special access facilities are available," and the Commission rejected both sets of arguments for essentially the same reasons. Given that an agency's policy decisions are entitled to deference so long as they are reasonably explained, and given the FCC's reasoned explanation of the administrability problems that a bar on conversions would cause, we deny the petition for review as to this issue as well.

have liked. However, as the Commission explained, the alternative thresholds proffered by the ILECs were too low—as an empirical matter—to support consistent competitive deployment. Given the fact that the Commission has "wide discretion to determine where to draw administrative lines," and given "the inevitability of some over-and under-inclusiveness in the Commission's unbundling rules," we have been "generally unwilling to review line-drawing performed by the Commission unless a petitioner can demonstrate that lines drawn ... are patently unreasonable, having no relationship to the underlying regulatory problem."

Here, the Commission applied its transport thresholds in a "disjunctive tandem" (that is, there is no impairment if the wire centers meet *either* the business line or the collocation metrics) Because "complementary tests will capture markets [with] significant potential revenues and thus, the potential for further competitive build-out," the Commission concluded that a disjunctive test "will better capture actual and potential deployment than any single measure." This analysis clearly bears *some* "relationship to the underlying regulatory problem." As a result, we deny the ILECs' petition for review of the Commission's transport thresholds.

2

The ILECs' challenge to the Commission's unbundling of high-capacity loops is equally unavailing. Again, the FCC chose to assess loop impairment at the wire-center level because wire centers provide the best evidence of "not only actual competition within a given market, but also *potential* competition within that market." Again, the ILECs complain that the FCC "removed high-capacity loop unbundling obligations only in a tiny subset of wire centers where there is evidence of extreme competition." And again, we disagree.

After surveying the economic realities surrounding loop deployment, the Commission decided to apply its loop thresholds "in conjunction with one another" (that is, there is no impairment if a wire center meets *both* the business line and the collocation metrics). The FCC concluded that a conjunctive application of the loop-impairment thresholds would "best minimize and balance any under-inclusiveness and over-inclusiveness" in its unbundling inquiry. Similarly, after surveying the economic differences between DS1 and DS3 loops, the FCC unbundled fewer of the latter than the former because "economic conditions surrounding competitive deployment of DS3-capacity loops permit [more optimistic] inferences regarding potential deployment in the context of DS3 loops that would not be appropriate in the context of DS1 loops." Moreover, because it is generally economic to self-deploy a DS3 loop "when demand nears two DS3s of capacity to a particular location," the FCC imposed a one-loop limit on DS3s.

By contrast, the Commission ordered wider unbundling of DS1 loops because "[t]he record before us indicates that [CLECs] typically do not provision stand-alone DS1 loops. . . .'' In light of evidence that CLECs generally provide DS1 service by ''channelizing'' a bigger DS3 loop, the Commission ''denie[d] unbundled access to DS1 loops only in the areas served by wire centers where [CLECs] actually have deployed, or will deploy, competitive facilities at the DS3 capacity level or higher, creating the potential for [CLECs] to channelize those facilities to offer service at the DS1 capacity level.'' Because it is generally more efficient for a CLEC to self-deploy a DS3 (and channelize it, if necessary) rather than use ten or more DS1-UNEs, the Commission imposed a ten-loop limit on DS1s.

Instead of attacking the FCC's thresholds or loop caps, the ILECs simply lament that the Commission eliminated unbundling only in those markets that are experiencing ''extraordinary levels of competition.'' Of course, the levels of competition in *non*-impaired areas (where competition is thriving at ''extraordinary levels'') are irrelevant for purposes of the ILECs' petition for review. The real question is whether the Commission ignored evidence of competition (either actual or potential) in *impaired* areas. After conducting a thorough analysis of the economic realities surrounding high-capacity loop deployment, the FCC concluded that some of the wire centers identified by the ILECs' alternative unbundling thresholds exhibit indicia of impairment because they ''do not generally exhibit extensive competitive fiber deployment, and do not offer sufficient revenue opportunities to incent such deployment.'' *Order*, 20 F.C.C.R. at 2637. Tellingly, the ILECs never claim (much less show[7]) that competition exists below the Commission's loop thresholds.

Congress gave the Commission—not the petitioners or this Court—discretion in regulatory line-drawing. The mere fact that the Commission's exercise of its discretion resulted in a line that the ILECs would have drawn differently is not sufficient to make it unlawful. The FCC's loop-impairment thresholds—combined with the loop caps—suggest that the Commission ''confront[ed] . . . the issue'' of the costs and benefits of unbundling and ''ma[d]e reasonable trade-offs'' between allowing unbundling where it is necessary and eliminating unbundling where it is not. We have never required anything more. Nor do we today.

III

While the ILECs want less unbundling of high-capacity loops and transport trunks, the CLECs want more. To that end, the CLECs raise three arguments. First, the CLECs argue that they are universally impaired without unbundled access to DS1 loops, DS3 loops, and DS1 transport. Second, the CLECs argue that they are universally impaired

7. The ILECs attempt to shift the blame for this failure by arguing that the CLECs should suffer an ''adverse inference'' for their failure to disclose evidence within their control regarding deployment vel non of high-capacity loops. Again, however, the ILECs' arguments are misguided. Agreeing with comments filed by the ILECs themselves, the Commission adopted an objective wire-center test, which is based on publicly available data that neither party controls. Because only non-proprietary data were relevant to the Commission's unbundling inquiry, there is no basis upon which to draw an adverse inference against the CLECs.

without unbundled access to mass market local switching. Third, the CLECs argue that the Commission's transitional rules for implementing the *Order* are arbitrary and capricious. We reject all three claims.

A

The CLECs first argue that it is economically impossible (and wasteful) for non-incumbents to supply high-capacity loops and transport trunks where the ILECs have already deployed them. Because "these fundamental economic facts" do not vary across markets, the CLECs argue that the Commission's unbundling thresholds are unlawfully high. The CLECs mount separate challenges to the Commission's analysis for DS1 loops, DS3 loops, and DS1 transport. We address each in turn.

1

In the CLECs' view, the Commission erred by restricting the unbundling of DS1 loops. Given the FCC's finding that CLECs "cannot deploy stand-alone DS1-capacity loops on an economic basis," *Order*, 20 F.C.C.R. at 2628, the CLECs conclude that they must be impaired in (and thus entitled to unbundling of) DS1 loops nationwide.

We disagree. *USTA I* and *USTA II* require a nuanced application of a "granular" impairment standard, which incorporates competitive variations within and across markets. The CLECs appear to recognize this fact. Nonetheless, the CLECs advocate the most un-nuanced and un-granular impairment finding imaginable-namely, a nationwide unbundling decree-notwithstanding the fact that we vacated the CLECs' proffered alternative in *USTA II see also Iowa Utils.*, 525 U.S. at 383 (holding the Commission cannot order blanket unbundling because "the Act requires the FCC to apply *some* limiting standard, rationally related to the goals of the Act"); *USTA I*, 290 F.3d at 422 (criticizing the FCC's decision "to adopt a uniform national rule, mandating [an] element's unbundling in every geographic market").

In the order before us, the FCC rejected a nationwide unbundling rule—and reasonably so. Instead of a blanket impairment finding, the FCC adopted a nuanced standard, which assesses impairment *vel non* at the wire center level and imposes "caps" on unbundling in markets in which the prevalence of UNEs suggests that facilities-based competition is viable. The Commission's standard uses market data to predict when and where the CLECs will be economically able to deploy their own high-speed facilities, thus obviating the need for UNEs. We think this balancing act is reasonable.

As a fallback position, the CLECs argue that impairment should be assessed on a building-by-building (as opposed to a wire center-by-wire center) basis. However, after chronicling extensive record evidence, the Commission concluded that a building-by-building approach would be an administrative nightmare, a font of endless litigation, and an ineffective metric of impairment.

Even if the CLECs' building-by-building approach were not riddled with empirical flaws and administrability problems, "the fact that there are other solutions to a problem is irrelevant provided that the option selected [by the FCC] is not irrational." *Ass'n of Pub.-Safety Commc'ns Officials-Int'l, Inc. v. FCC*, 76 F.3d 395, 400 (D.C.Cir.1996) The FCC need not demonstrate that it has made the only acceptable decision, but rather that it has based its decision on a reasoned analysis supported by the evidence before the Commission." *Id.* at 398. "[I]f the [Commission] has offered a reasoned explanation for its choice between competing approaches supported by the record, the court is not free to substitute its judgment for that of the agency." *Id.*

Here, "the Commission has offered a reasoned explanation." The FCC explained that it chose to focus on wire centers, fiber-based collocation, and business line density because those variables are objective, easily verifiable, and highly correlated with both extant and potential levels of facilities-based competition. This explanation easily qualifies as "rational," "reasonable," and "non-arbitrary."

Even if the FCC explained its standard, the CLECs argue, that standard is nonetheless divorced from economic reality. In the CLECs' view, "[t]here is absolutely no evidence" to substantiate the purported correlation between competition and the level of fiber collocation and business line density within a wire center. Moreover, the CLECs argue that even if fiber-based collocation can reasonably predict competition in enterprise markets, it is still insufficiently "granular" to predict competition for mass-market consumers.

Again, the CLECs' argument is wide of the mark. As we have previously held, "collocation can reasonably serve as a measure of competition in a given market," particularly where it is "superior to the various alternatives proposed by petitioners." *WorldCom, Inc. v. FCC*, 238 F.3d 449, 459 (D.C.Cir.2001). Here, the CLECs "offer *no* alternative save a painstaking analysis of market conditions." For example, the CLECs argue that the FCC's impairment analysis should incorporate "operational or structural impediments," which are "specific to the customer's location *within a building*." Such a suggestion takes the concept of granularity to an unrealistic extreme: It defies common sense—and *USTA II's* mandate—to require the Commission to conduct individualized inquiries into the economic particularities of each floor within each building served by the millions of DS1 loops nationwide. *See USTA II*, 359 F.3d at 577 (holding the FCC is "free to take into account such factors as administrability" in its impairment inquiry). Under these circumstances, the Commission is justified in its reliance upon what is "an admittedly imperfect measure of competition."

Finally, even if the *Order* properly accounts for economic reality, the CLECs claim that the Commission arbitrarily "turn[ed] around and ignore[d]" its own "reasonably efficient competitor" standard in its refusal to unbundle DS1 loops. In the CLECs' view, the *Order* "relies on a [CLEC] holding a fiber transmission network," notwithstanding the fact that the Commission's "reasonably efficient competitor" standard "do[es] not presume that a hypothetical entrant possesses any particular assets."

The CLECs either misunderstand or misconstrue the FCC's ruling. The *Order* does *not* presume that a particular CLEC possesses a fiber transmission network. Rather, the FCC presumes that under certain economic conditions, it would be financially possible and attractive for a "reasonably efficient" CLEC to deploy high-speed facilities. And where a "reasonably efficient" CLEC can economically deploy its own facilities, the FCC concludes, *all* CLECs are not "impaired."

At first blush, it might seem a little harsh to eliminate unbundling for all CLECs where one or more has demonstrated the economic feasibility of competing without UNEs. However, as the Commission explained, CLECs can use TSASs and other wholesale facilities "as a gap-filler" to enter or expand into new markets. And the CLECs' assertion that the wholesale supply of DS1 loops is "extremely limited," is belied by the CLECs' own evidence confirming that they are "able to purchase wholesale capacity to serve a DS1 customer." *Order*, 20 F.C.C.R. at 2628. The ILECs corroborated the CLECs' concessions with respect to the availability of DS1 loops at wholesale prices. In the face of evidence that CLECs can—and do—offer DS1 services without UNEs, there is nothing unlawful about the FCC's well-reasoned refusal to order unbundling.

2

The CLECs next argue that the Commission erred by restricting the unbundling of DS3 loops. In a single footnote, the CLECs attempt to incorporate by reference all of their DS1-related arguments "to apply equally to single DS3 loops." This reference is insufficient to raise the issue.

The CLECs' only viable DS3 challenge is their argument that "the FCC's proxies are an insufficient indicator of competitive deployment." However, the CLECs base their attack entirely on the alleged paucity of *extant* competition. Because we have held that unbundling may be appropriate only after the Commission considers the *potential* for future competition, *see USTA II*, 359 F.3d at 575, the CLECs' complaints that *current* DS3 deployment is "minuscule" are wide of the mark. We therefore deny the petition for review with respect to DS3 loops.

3

The CLECs next argue that the Commission erred by restricting the unbundling of DS1 transport. In light of the same record evidence that informed the Commission's impairment analysis for DS1 loops, the FCC found that CLECs are not impaired without unbundled access to DS1 transport on routes between "Tier 1" wire centers. The CLECs' challenge to this conclusion is feeble: They do not dispute that wire centers provide a perfectly reasonable metric to gauge transport impairment, nor do they dispute that competitive transport is or can be self-provisioned between Tier 1 wire centers. Nor do the CLECs dispute that those competitive transport facilities can be channelized to provide transport at the DS1 level. Instead, the CLECs argue that the Commission's impairment inquiry was based "solely on the unfounded prediction" that a *wholesale* market for DS1 transport might develop.

The CLECs' characterization of the Commission's inquiry is inaccurate. After finding empirical proof that more than two-thirds of wire centers above the business-line threshold can attract four or more fiber-based collocators, the Commission inferred that it was "possible that *competitors can deploy* transport facilities to the remainder of the wire centers above this business line threshold." Thus, the Commission did not focus "solely" on the availability of wholesale transport—in fact, the FCC's impairment inquiry centered on the potential for CLECs to *self-deploy* DS1 transport. We therefore deny the petition for review with respect to DS1 transport.

B

The CLECs' second challenge pertains to the Commission's decision not to require unbundled access to mass-market local switching. "Local switching" is the modern-day equivalent of a switchboard operator: Computerized switches route a signal from a caller to a receiver. "Mass market" switching refers to phone calls made by or to residential consumers (as opposed to "enterprise" switching, which refers to calls made by or to business customers). In the *Order*, the Commission declined to order unbundling in MMLS. The CLECs—joined by National Association of State Utility Consumer Advocates ("NASUCA") and the New Jersey Division of the Ratepayer Advocate ("NJDRA")—petition for review. We discuss and reject each petitioner's claims separately.

1

First, we reject the CLECs' challenge to the Commission's ruling on MMLS. The CLEC petitioners argue that a nationwide non-impairment finding must be vacated because it is insufficiently "granular." However, the mere fact that the Commission eliminated unbundling across the board does not make it unlawful: The "granularity" criterion does not require the FCC to manufacture regulatory variation where the record does not support it. *See USTA II*, 359 F.3d at 570 (holding the Commission need only adopt a granular rule if "there is evidence that markets vary decisively (by reference to [the FCC's] impairment criteria)")

On the record before it, the Commission reasonably concluded that CLECs are not "impaired" without unbundled access to MMLS. In light of the fact that CLECs have deployed their own switches in 86% of the ILECs' wire centers across the country, and in light of the fact that CLECs are deploying high-tech switches that have "higher capacity and wider geographic reach" than the old switches employed by the ILECs, the record suggests that it is neither "uneconomic" nor "wasteful" for CLECs to deploy their own switches. While other parts of the ILECs' networks might remain "bottleneck facilities," the CLECs' widespread deployment of switching technology suggests "competition is possible" without unbundled switches. *See Order*, 20 F.C.C.R. at 4646 (noting that CLECs are currently combining their own switching and the ILECs' unbundled loops to serve mass market customers in 137 of the nation's largest 150 metropolitan statistical areas). Moreover, the Commission's prior impairment finding [in the *Triennial Review Order*] was based solely on the technical difficulties associated with connecting CLECs' switches with the ILECs' networks (a process termed "hot cutting"). Here, however, the Commission found (and the CLECs do not dispute) that the ILECs have made vast improvements in their hot cut procedures, thus making it easier and more financially attractive than ever for CLECs to deploy their own switches.

Confronted with this record of competitive switch deployment, the CLECs failed to offer any explanations or contrary evidence. The CLECs insist that the Commission unduly focused on improvements in hot cuts while ignoring other "impairments faced by CLECs attempting to serve the mass market with their own switches." However, the CLECs do *not* offer an explanation for what these other "impairments" might be. The CLECs also failed to offer evidence that it is "uneconomic" to serve mass market customers with switches that were originally deployed to serve enterprise customers. Moreover, the CLECs did "not rebut[ ] the evidence of commenters showing that [CLECs] in many markets have recognized that facilities-based carriers could not compete with TELRIC-based UNE-P, and therefore have made UNE-P their long-term business strategy." Given that UNE-P is a "completely synthetic" form of competition, the Commission reasonably eliminated switch unbundling. *See USTA II*, 359 F.3d at 572, 581–82 (noting that the FCC may reasonably use its "at a minimum" authority under § 251(d)(2)to encourage CLECs to invest in—and compete through—their own facilities). Therefore, we deny the CLECs' petition for review. * * * [The court goes on to reject arguments by NASUCA and NJDRA.]

Granularity. In *USTA I and II* the court asked for more "granularity," and it appears it got what it asked for. Notice the detail in the criteria for providing access to high capacity loop and transport. For both DS1 and DS3 lines, the FCC applies a "trigger" based on the size of the wire centers (measured by the number of fiber-optic-based collocators or the number of business lines). The triggers serve as a set of proxies for determining when self-supply of facilities is economically practicable. So, for DS1 lines there is *no* impairment if the transport terminates in a wire center with at least 38,000 business lines. Where do the numbers come from? Why not 20,000, or 40,000? What is the underlying economic premise of these "triggers?"

Only high-capacity lines were at issue in *Covad*. There was no dispute over the Commission's earlier decision to mandate unbundled access to all voice-grade lines (which are classified as DS0). Thus, in all cases a CLEC is deemed to be impaired if it does not receive access to the copper wires that form the core of traditional residential service. Implicit in that finding is the assumption that a CLEC will need access to the ILEC's copper wires in the local loop in all markets. This cannot be true of all CLECs, though. In major markets, cable systems are now rolling out telecommunications voice services using their own wired networks. They are not dependent on the incumbent's local loop or transport. So too wireless carriers. Increasingly many telephone users are "cutting the cord" and relying entirely on cellphones. How should the availability of cable and wireless, each with their own self-sufficient networks, be weighed in the implementation of the access rules?[8]

The End of UNE-P. Elimination of access requirements for mass market switches has importance beyond the fact that CLECs must now self-supply their own switches. The ability to demand access to switches, together with loops, and to demand that both be delivered as a combined package, provided the basis for the so-called "unbundled network element-platform," ("UNE-P"), which provided in a single package basically all of the elements necessary to deliver end-to-end local service. ILECs had long maintained that this gave CLECs the equivalent of access to an entire service and therefore was no different from allowing the CLECs to resell an ILEC service. Section 251 provides for resale of services, but the pricing for resale of services is different than it is for leasing unbundled network elements such as UNE-P. Under section 252 a carrier seeking to resell an ILEC's services pays a wholesale rate that is determined by simply taking the retail rates the ILEC charges end consumers and subtracting the costs attributable to the business of running a retail operation (e.g., marketing, billing, and collection costs). UNE rates (as we will discuss in more detail below), however, are determined by a cost formula that typically would yield a lower "wholesale" rate. Thus, a CLEC relying on UNE-P essentially was able to resell the ILEC's service package based on a specially discounted wholesale rate. Despite the fact that switching equipment has long been available in competitive markets, the Commission, prior to the remand in *USTA II*, was loathe to eliminate mass market switching precisely because it was the lynchpin for UNE-P, which the FCC thought was crucial to the success of many fledgling CLECs.[9] Its removal in the remand order sustained in *Covad* marks a significant change in the competitive landscape.

8. Note that where cable systems are capable of providing two-way services, they are capable of supporting VoIP—voice over Internet—which can be provided not only by the cable system but by independent services providers, such as Vonage or Skype. More on VoIP in Chapter 10.

9. Even though CLECs could purchase mass market switches in the open market, the FCC thought that forcing them to do so would put them at a disadvantage because they would incur extra costs in the form of transferring customers from the ILEC to the CLEC. Where the switches are physically the same (shared by ILEC and CLEC) the transfer is simply a matter of computer programming; where they are separate (as when the CLEC supplies its own switch), the transfer requires a manual reconnection (a process called "hot cuts"), which incurs extra costs and some delay.

3. Leasing Unbundled Network Elements: Pricing Issues

Of course, the importance of UNE-P—or for that matter unbundling generally—turns fundamentally on the pricing issue. The dispute over the scope of unbundling presents another case of regulatory arbitrage like the one fought over entry into long distance decades earlier. In fact, that is true of the entire controversy over unbundled access. As a matter of business principle, firms may object to cooperating with competitors, but as the cynical adage goes, "when someone tells you that it's not the money but the principle ... it's the money." Unfortunately, as we mentioned earlier, the Telecommunications Act is a little light on directions about money. The wholesale pricing standards applicable to resale are tolerably clear and relatively simple to implement. With regard to leased access to UNEs, however, all Congress said (in section 252) is that the rates: "shall be (i) based on the cost (determined without reference to a rate-of-return or other rate-based proceeding) of providing the interconnection or network element (whichever is applicable), and (ii) nondiscriminatory, and (B) may include a reasonable profit." The Commission interpreted that to mean that prices should be based on long-run incremental costs. There was widespread agreement on that as a matter of general principle, but—remember—it's the money that counts. At the operational level, controversy immediately broke out about *how to calculate* incremental costs. There was also a contest over *who* would determine the basic pricing methodology. Although states set the prices, the Commission insisted that Congress wanted national uniformity, which required the Commission to determine the basic criteria for setting prices. The Supreme Court, in the 1999 *Iowa Utilities Board* case discussed in *Covad*, affirmed the FCC's general preemptive authority to set pricing standards. That did not end the substantive controversy over the underlying standards, which would produce a second Supreme Court decision three years on.

VERIZON COMMUNICATIONS INC. v. FCC

Supreme Court of the United States, 2001.
535 U.S. 467.

JUSTICE SOUTER delivered the opinion of the Court.

These cases arise under the Telecommunications Act of 1996. Each is about the power of the Federal Communications Commission to regulate a relationship between monopolistic companies providing local telephone service and companies entering local markets to compete with the incumbents. Under the Act, the new entrants are entitled, among other things, to lease elements of the local telephone networks from the incumbent monopolists. The issues are whether the FCC is authorized (1) to require state utility commissions to set the rates charged by the incumbents for leased elements on a forward-looking basis untied to the incumbents' investment....[*]

* Eds. The case also involved a challenge to the FCC rules allowing "combination" of UNEs, which we have addressed in the previous section. The Court upheld the FCC's rule requiring ILECs to combine the elements on request.

* * * Under the local-competition provisions of the Act, Congress called for ratemaking different from any historical practice, to achieve the entirely new objective of uprooting the monopolies that traditional rate-based methods had perpetuated. * * * For the first time, Congress passed a ratesetting statute with the aim not just to balance interests between sellers and buyers, but to reorganize markets by rendering regulated utilities' monopolies vulnerable to interlopers, even if that meant swallowing the traditional federal reluctance to intrude into local telephone markets. The approach was deliberate, through a hybrid jurisdictional scheme with the FCC setting a basic, default methodology for use in setting rates when carriers fail to agree, but leaving it to state utility commissions to set the actual rates.

While the Act is like its predecessors in tying the methodology to the objectives of "just and reasonable" and nondiscriminatory rates, it is radically unlike all previous statutes in providing that rates be set "without reference to a rate-of-return or other rate-based proceeding," § 252(d)(1)(A)(i). The Act thus appears to be an explicit disavowal of the familiar public-utility model of rate regulation presumably still being applied by many States for retail sales. * * *

II

The 1996 Act both prohibits state and local regulation that impedes the provision of "telecommunications service," and obligates incumbent carriers to allow competitors to enter their local markets. Section 251(c) addresses the practical difficulties of fostering local competition by recognizing three strategies that a potential competitor may pursue. First, a competitor entering the market (a "requesting" carrier, may decide to engage in pure facilities-based competition, that is, to build its own network to replace or supplement the network of the incumbent. If an entrant takes this course, the Act obligates the incumbent to "interconnect" the competitor's facilities to its own network to whatever extent is necessary to allow the competitor's facilities to operate. At the other end of the spectrum, the statute permits an entrant to skip construction and instead simply to buy and resell "telecommunications service," which the incumbent has a duty to sell at wholesale. Between these extremes, an entering competitor may choose to lease certain of an incumbent's "network elements," which the incumbent has a duty to provide "on an unbundled basis" at terms that are "just, reasonable, and nondiscriminatory."

Since wholesale markets for companies engaged in resale, leasing, or interconnection of facilities cannot be created without addressing rates, Congress provided for rates to be set either by contracts between carriers or by state utility commission rate orders. Like other federal utility statutes that authorize contracts approved by a regulatory agency in setting rates between businesses, the Act permits incumbent and entering carriers to negotiate private rate agreements. State utility commissions are required to accept any such agreement unless it discriminates against a carrier not a party to the contract, or is otherwise shown to be contrary to the public interest. Carriers, of course, might well not agree, in which case an entering carrier has a statutory option to request mediation by a state commission. But the option comes with strings, for mediation subjects the parties to the duties specified in § 251 and the pricing standards set forth in § 252(d), as interpreted by the FCC's regulations. These regulations are at issue here.

As to pricing, the Act provides that when incumbent and requesting carriers fail to agree, state commissions will set a "just and reasonable" and "nondiscriminatory" rate for interconnection or the lease of network elements based on "the cost of providing the ... network element," which "may include a reasonable profit." In setting these rates, the state commissions are, however, subject to that important limitation previously unknown to utility regulation: the rate must be "determined without reference to a rate-of-return or other rate-based proceeding." In *AT&T Corp. v. Iowa Utilities Bd.*, 525 U.S. 366, 384–385 (1999), this Court upheld the FCC's jurisdiction to impose a new methodology on the States when setting these rates. The attack today is on the legality and logic of the particular methodology the Commission chose.

As the Act required, six months after its effective date the FCC implemented the local-competition provisions in its First Report and Order, which included as an appendix the new regulations at issue. Challenges to the order, mostly by incumbent local-exchange carriers and state commissions, were consolidated in the United States Court of Appeals for the Eighth Circuit.

So far as it bears on where we are today, the initial decision by the Eighth Circuit held that the FCC had no authority to control the methodology of state commissions setting the rates incumbent local-exchange carriers could charge entrants for network elements. * * *

This Court affirmed in part and in larger part reversed. *AT&T Corp. v. Iowa Utilities Bd.*, 525 U.S. 366, 397 (1999). * * *

With the FCC's general authority to establish a pricing methodology secure, the incumbent carriers' primary challenge on remand went to the method that the Commission chose. * * *

As for the method to derive a "nondiscriminatory," "just and reasonable rate for network elements," the Act requires the FCC to decide how to value "the cost ... of providing the ... network element [which] may include a reasonable profit," although the FCC is (as already seen) forbidden to allow any "reference to a rate-of-return or other rate-based proceeding." Within the discretion left to it after eliminating any dependence on a "rate-of-return or other rate-based proceeding," the Commission chose a way of treating "cost" as "forward-looking economic cost," something distinct from the kind of historically based cost generally relied upon in valuing a rate base [as required for determining whether or not a rate is confiscatory in violation of the

Takings Clause. See *FPC v. Hope Natural Gas Co.*, 320 U.S. 591 (1944)].... In Rule 505, the FCC defined the "forward-looking economic cost of an element [as] the sum of (1) the total element long-run incremental cost of the element [TELRIC]; [and] (2) a reasonable allocation of forward-looking common costs," common costs being "costs incurred in providing a group of elements that "cannot be attributed directly to individual elements." Most important of all, the FCC decided that the TELRIC "should be measured based on the use of the most efficient telecommunications technology currently available and the lowest cost network configuration, given the existing location of the incumbent['s] wire centers."

"The TELRIC of an element has three components, the operating expenses, the depreciation cost, and the appropriate risk-adjusted cost of capital." A concrete example may help. Assume that it would cost $1 a year to operate a most-efficient loop element; that it would take $10 for interest payments on the capital a carrier would have to invest to build the lowest cost loop centered upon an incumbent carrier's existing wire centers (say $100, at 10 percent per annum); and that $9 would be reasonable for depreciation on that loop (an 11-year useful life); then the annual TELRIC for the loop element would be $20.

The Court of Appeals understood § 252(d)(1)'s reference to "the cost ... of providing the ... network element" to be ambiguous as between "forward-looking" and "historical" cost, so that a forward-looking ratesetting method would presumably be a reasonable implementation of the statute. But the Eighth Circuit thought the ambiguity afforded no leeway beyond that, and read the Act to require any forward-looking methodology to be "based on the incremental costs that an [incumbent] actually incurs or will incur in providing ... the unbundled access to its specific network elements." Hence, the Eighth Circuit held that § 252(d)(1) foreclosed the use of the TELRIC methodology. In other words, the court read the Act as plainly requiring rates based on the "actual" not "hypothetical" "cost ... of providing the ... network element," and reasoned that TELRIC was clearly the latter. The Eighth Circuit added, however, that if it were wrong and TELRIC were permitted, the claim that in prescribing TELRIC the FCC had effected an unconstitutional taking would not be "ripe" until "resulting rates have been determined and applied."

* * *

Before us, the incumbent local-exchange carriers claim error in the Eighth Circuit's holding that a "forward-looking cost" methodology (as opposed to the use of "historical" cost) is consistent with § 252(d)(1), and its conclusion that the use of the TELRIC forward-looking cost methodology presents no "ripe" takings claim. The FCC and the entrants, on the other side, seek review of the Eighth Circuit's invalidation of the TELRIC methodology.... We granted certiorari, and now affirm on the issues raised by the incumbents, and reverse on those raised by the FCC and the entrants.

III

A

The incumbent carriers' first attack charges the FCC with ignoring the plain meaning of the word "cost" as it occurs in the provision of § 252(d)(1) that "the just and reasonable rate for network elements ... shall be ... based on the cost (determined without reference to a rate-of-return or other rate-based proceeding) of providing the ... network element...." The incumbents do not argue that in theory the statute precludes any forward-looking methodology, but they do claim that the cost of providing a competitor with a network element in the future must be calculated using the incumbent's past investment in the element and the means of providing it. They contend that "cost" in the statute refers to "historical" cost, which they define as "what was in fact paid" for a capital asset, as distinct from "value," or "the price that would be paid on the open market." They say that the technical meaning of "cost" is "past capital expenditure," and they suggest an equation between "historical" and "embedded" costs, which the FCC defines as "the costs that the incumbent LEC incurred in the past and that are recorded in the incumbent LEC's books of accounts." The argument boils down to the proposition that "the cost of providing the network element" can only mean, in plain language and in this particular technical context, the past cost to an incumbent of furnishing the specific network element actually, physically, to be provided.

The incumbents have picked an uphill battle. At the most basic level of common usage, "cost" has no such clear implication. A merchant who is asked about "the cost of providing the goods" he sells may reasonably quote their current wholesale market price, not the cost of the particular items he happens to have on his shelves, which may have been bought at higher or lower prices.

When the reference shifts from common speech into the technical realm, the incumbents still have to attack uphill. To begin with, even when we have dealt with historical costs as a ratesetting basis, the cases have never assumed a sense of "cost" as generous as the incumbents seem to claim. "Cost" as used in calculating the rate base under the traditional cost-of-service method did not stand for all past capital expenditures, but at most for those that were prudent, while prudent investment itself could be denied recovery when unexpected events rendered investment useless. And even when investment was wholly includable in the rate base, ratemakers often rejected the utilities' "embedded costs," their own book-value estimates, which typically were geared to maximize the rate base with high statements of past expenditures and working capital, combined with unduly low rates of depreciation. It would also be a mistake to forget that "cost" was a term in value-based ratemaking and has figured in contemporary state and federal ratemaking untethered to historical valuation.

What is equally important is that the incumbents' plain-meaning argument ignores the statutory setting in which the mandate to use "cost" in valuing network elements occurs. First, the Act uses "cost" as an intermediate term in the calculation of "just and reasonable rates," and it was the very point of *Hope Natural Gas* that regulatory bodies required to set rates expressed in these terms have ample discretion to choose methodology. Second, it would have been passing strange to think Congress tied "cost" to historical cost without a more specific indication, when the very same sentence that requires "cost" pricing also prohibits any reference to a "rate-of-return or other rate-based proceeding," each of which has been identified with historical cost ever since *Hope Natural Gas* was decided. * * *

B

The incumbents' alternative argument is that even without a stern anchor in calculating "the cost . . . of providing the . . . network element," the particular forward-looking methodology the FCC chose is neither consistent with the plain language of § 252(d)(1) nor within the zone of reasonable interpretation subject to deference under *Chevron U.S.A. Inc. v. Natural Resources Defense Council, Inc.*, 467 U.S. 837, 843–845 (1984). This is so, they say, because TELRIC calculates the forward-looking cost by reference to a hypothetical, most efficient element at existing wire-centers, not the actual network element being provided.

1

The short answer to the objection that TELRIC violates plain language is much the same as the answer to the previous plain-language argument, for what the incumbents call the "hypothetical" element is simply the element valued in terms of a piece of equipment an incumbent may not own. This claim, like the one just considered, is that plain language bars a definition of "cost" untethered to historical investment, and as explained already, the term "cost" is simply too protean to support the incumbents' argument.

2

Similarly, the claim that TELRIC exceeds reasonable interpretative leeway is open to the objection already noted, that responsibility for "just and reasonable" rates leaves methodology largely subject to discretion. The incumbents nevertheless field three arguments. They contend, first, that a method of calculating wholesale lease rates based on the costs of providing hypothetical, most efficient elements, may simulate the competition envisioned by the Act but does not induce it. Second, they argue that even if rates based on hypothetical elements could induce competition in theory, TELRIC cannot do this, because it does not provide the depreciation and risk-adjusted capital costs that the theory compels. Finally, the incumbents say that even if these objections can be answered, TELRIC is needlessly, and hence unreasonably, complicated and impracticable.

a

The incumbents' (and Justice Breyer's) basic critique of TELRIC is that by setting rates for leased network elements on the assumption of perfect competition, TELRIC perversely creates incentives against competition in fact. The incumbents say that in purporting to set incumbents' wholesale prices at the level that would exist in a perfectly competitive market (in order to make retail prices similarly competitive), TELRIC sets rates so low that entrants will always lease and never build network elements. And even if an entrant would otherwise consider building a network element more efficient than the best one then on the market (the one assumed in setting the TELRIC rate), it would likewise be deterred by the prospect that its lower cost in building and operating this new element would be immediately available to its competitors; under TELRIC, the incumbents assert, the lease rate for an incumbent's existing element would instantly drop to match the marginal cost of the entrant's new element once built. According to the incumbents, the result will be, not competition, but a sort of parasitic free-riding, leaving TELRIC incapable of stimulating the facilities-based competition intended by Congress.

We think there are basically three answers to this no-stimulation claim of unreasonableness: (1) the TELRIC methodology does not assume that the relevant markets are perfectly competitive, and the scheme includes several features of inefficiency that undermine the plausibility of the incumbents' no-stimulation argument; (2) comparison of TELRIC with alternatives proposed by the incumbents as more reasonable are plausibly answered by the FCC's stated reasons to reject the alternatives; and (3) actual investment in competing facilities since the effective date of the Act simply belies the no-stimulation argument's conclusion.

(1)

The basic assumption of the incumbents' no-stimulation argument is contrary to fact. As we explained, the argument rests on the assumption that in a perfectly efficient market, no one who can lease at a TELRIC rate will ever build. But TELRIC does not assume a perfectly efficient wholesale market or one that is likely to resemble perfection in any foreseeable time. The incumbents thus make the same mistake we attributed in a different setting to the FCC itself. In *Iowa Utilities Board*, we rejected the FCC's necessary-and-impair rule, which required incumbents to lease any network element that might reduce, however slightly, an entrant's marginal cost of providing a telecommunications service, as compared with providing the service using the entrant's own equivalent element. "In a world of perfect competition, in which all carriers are providing their service at marginal cost, the Commission's total equating of increased cost (or decreased quality) with 'necessity' and 'impairment' might be reasonable, but it has not established the existence of such an ideal world."

Not only that, but the FCC has of its own accord allowed for inefficiency in the TELRIC design in additional ways affecting the likelihood that TELRIC will squelch competition in facilities. First, the Commission has qualified any assumption of efficiency by requiring ratesetters to calculate cost on the basis of "the existing location of the incumbent['s] wire centers." This means that certain network elements, principally local-loop elements, will not be priced at their most efficient cost and configuration to the extent, say, that a shorter loop could serve a local exchange if the incumbent's wire centers were relocated for a snugger fit with the current geography of terminal locations.

Second, TELRIC rates in practice will differ from the products of a perfectly competitive market owing to built-in lags in price adjustments. In a perfectly competitive market, retail prices drop instantly to the marginal cost of the most efficient company. As the incumbents point out, this would deter market entry because a potential entrant would know that even if it could provide a retail service at a lower marginal cost, it would instantly lose that competitive edge once it entered the market and competitors adjusted to match its price. Wholesale TELRIC rates, however, are set by state commissions, usually by arbitrated agreements with 3- or 4-year terms, and no one claims that a competitor could receive immediately on demand a TELRIC rate on a leased element at the marginal cost of the entrant who introduces a more efficient element.

But even if a competitor could call for a new TELRIC rate proceeding immediately upon the introduction of a more efficient element by a competing entrant, the competitor would not necessarily know enough to make the call; the fact of the element's greater efficiency would only become apparent when reflected in lower retail prices drawing demand away from existing competitors (including the incumbent), forcing them to look to lowering their own marginal costs. In practice, it would take some time for the innovating entrant to install the new equipment, to engage in marketing offering a lower retail price to attract business, and to steal away enough customer subscriptions (given the limited opportunity to capture untapped customers for local telephone service) for competitors to register the drop in demand.

Finally, it bears reminding that the FCC prescribes measurement of the TELRIC "based on the use of the most efficient telecommunications technology currently available." Owing to that condition of current availability, the marginal cost of a most-efficient element that an entrant alone has built and uses would not set a new pricing standard until it became available to competitors as an alternative to the incumbent's corresponding element. * * *

(2)

Perhaps sensing the futility of an unsupported theoretical attack, the incumbents make the complementary argument that the FCC's choice of TELRIC, whatever might be said about it on its own terms, was unreasonable as a matter of law because other methods of determining cost would have done a better job of inducing competition. Having considered the proffered alternatives and the reasons the FCC gave for rejecting them, we cannot say that the FCC acted unreasonably in picking TELRIC to promote the mandated competition.

The incumbents present three principal alternatives for setting rates for network elements: embedded-cost methodologies, the efficient component pricing rule, and Ramsey pricing. The arguments that one or another of these methodologies is preferable to TELRIC share a basic claim: it was unreasonable for the FCC to choose a method of setting rates that fails to include, at least in theory, some additional costs beyond what would be most efficient in the long run, because lease rates that incorporate such costs will do a better job of inducing competition. The theory is that once an entrant has its foot in the door, it will have a greater incentive to build and operate its own more efficient network element if the lease rates reflect something of the incumbents' actual and inefficient marginal costs. And once the entrant develops the element at its lower marginal cost and the retail price drops accordingly, the incumbent will have no choice but to innovate itself by building the most efficient element or finding ways to reduce its marginal cost to retain its market share.

The generic feature of the incumbents' proposed alternatives, in other words, is that some degree of long-run inefficiency ought to be preserved through the lease rates, in order to give an entrant a more efficient alternative to leasing. Of course, we have already seen that TELRIC itself tolerates some degree of inefficient pricing in its existing wire-center configuration requirement and through the ratemaking and development lags just described. This aside, however, there are at least two objections that generally undercut any desirability that such alternatives may seem to offer over TELRIC.

The first objection turns on the fact that a lease rate that compensates the lessor for some degree of existing inefficiency (at least from the perspective of the long run) is simply a higher rate, and the difference between such a higher rate and the TELRIC rate could be the difference that keeps a potential competitor from entering the market. If the TELRIC rate for bottleneck elements is $100 and for other elements (say switches) is $10, an entering competitor that can provide its own, more efficient switch at what amounts to a $7 rate can enter the market for $107. If the lease rate for the bottleneck elements were higher (say, $110) to reflect some of the inefficiency of bottleneck elements that actually cost the incumbent $150, then the entrant with only $107 will be kept out. Is it better to risk keeping more potential entrants out, or to induce them to compete in less capital-intensive facilities with lessened incentives to build their own bottleneck facilities? It was not obviously unreasonable for the FCC to prefer the latter.

The second general objection turns the incumbents' attack on TELRIC against the incumbents' own alternatives. If the problem with

TELRIC is that an entrant will never build because at the instant it builds, other competitors can lease the analogous existing (but less efficient) element from an incumbent at a rate assuming the same most efficient marginal cost, then the same problem persists under the incumbents' methods. For as soon as an entrant builds a more efficient element, the incumbent will be forced to price to match, and that rate will be available to all other competitors. The point, of course, is that things are not this simple. As we have said, under TELRIC, price adjustment is not instantaneous in rates for a leased element corresponding to an innovating entrant's more efficient element; the same would presumably be true under the incumbents' alternative methods, though they do not come out and say it.

Once we get into the details of the specific alternative methods, other infirmities become evident that undermine the claim that the FCC could not reasonably have preferred TELRIC. As for an embedded-cost methodology, the problem with a method that relies in any part on historical cost, the cost the incumbents say they actually incur in leasing network elements, is that it will pass on to lessees the difference between most-efficient cost and embedded cost. Any such cost difference is an inefficiency, whether caused by poor management resulting in higher operating costs or poor investment strategies that have inflated capital and depreciation. If leased elements were priced according to embedded costs, the incumbents could pass these inefficiencies to competitors in need of their wholesale elements, and to that extent defeat the competitive purpose of forcing efficient choices on all carriers whether incumbents or entrants. The upshot would be higher retail prices consumers would have to pay.

There are, of course, objections other than inefficiency to any method of ratemaking that relies on embedded costs as allegedly reflected in incumbents' book-cost data, with the possibilities for manipulation this presents. Even if incumbents have built and are operating leased elements at economically efficient costs, the temptation would remain to overstate book costs to ratemaking commissions and so perpetuate the intractable problems that led to the price-cap innovation.

There is even an argument that the Act itself forbids embedded-cost methods, and while the FCC rejected this absolutistic reading of the statute, it seems safe to say that the statutory language places a heavy presumption against any method resembling the traditional embedded-cost-of-service model of ratesetting. At the very least, proposing an embedded-cost alternative is a counterintuitive way to show that selecting TELRIC was unreasonable.

Other incumbents say the FCC was unreasonable to pick TELRIC over a method of ratesetting commonly called the efficient component pricing rule (ECPR). ECPR would base the rate for a leased element on its most efficient long-run incremental cost (presumably, something like the TELRIC) plus the opportunity cost to the incumbent when the entrant leasing the element provides a competing telecommunications service using it. The opportunity cost is pegged to the retail revenue loss suffered by the incumbent when the entrant provides the service in its stead to its former customers.

The FCC rejected ECPR because its calculation of opportunity cost relied on existing retail prices in monopolistic local-exchange markets, which bore no relation to efficient marginal cost. "We conclude that ECPR is an improper method for setting prices of interconnection and unbundled network elements because the existing retail prices that would be used to compute incremental opportunity costs under ECPR are not cost-based. Moreover, the ECPR does not provide any mechanism for moving prices towards competitive levels; it simply takes prices as given." In effect, the adjustment for opportunity cost, because it turns on pre-existing retail prices generated by embedded costs, would pass on the same inefficiencies and be vulnerable to the same asymmetries of information in ratemaking as a straightforward embedded-cost scheme.

The third category of alternative methodologies proposed focuses on costs over an intermediate term where some fixed costs are unavoidable, as opposed to TELRIC's long run. The fundamental intuition underlying this method of ratesetting is that competition is actually favored by allowing incumbents rate recovery of certain fixed costs efficiently incurred in the intermediate term.

The most commonly proposed variant of fixed-cost recovery ratesetting is "Ramsey pricing." Ramsey pricing was originally theorized as a method of discriminatory taxation of commodities to generate revenue with minimal discouragement of desired consumption. The underlying principle is that goods should be taxed or priced according to demand: taxes or prices should be higher as to goods for which demand is relatively inelastic. As applied to the local-exchange wholesale market, Ramsey pricing would allow rate recovery of certain costs incurred by an incumbent above marginal cost, costs associated with providing an unbundled network element that are fixed and unavoidable over the intermediate run, typically the 3- or 4-year term of a rate arbitration agreement. The specific mechanism for recovery through wholesale lease rates would be to spread such costs across the different elements to be leased according to the demand for each particular element. Thus, when demand among entrants for loop elements is high as compared with demand for switch elements, a higher proportion of fixed costs would be added as a premium to the loop-element lease rate than to the switch lease rate.

But this very feature appears to be a drawback when used as a method of setting rates for the wholesale market in unbundled network elements. Because the elements for which demand among entrants will be highest are the costly bottleneck elements, duplication of which is neither likely nor desired, high lease rates for these elements would be the rates most likely to deter market entry, as our earlier example showed: if the rate for bottleneck elements went from $100 to $110, the $107 competitor would be kept out. . . .

(3)

At the end of the day, theory aside, the claim that TELRIC is unreasonable as a matter of law because it simulates but does not produce facilities-based competition founders on fact. The entrants have presented figures showing that they have invested in new facilities to the tune of $55 billion since the passage of the Act (through 2000). The FCC's statistics indicate substantial resort to pure and partial facilities-based competition among the three entry strategies: as of June 30, 2001, 33 percent of entrants were using their own facilities; 23 percent were reselling services; and 44 percent were leasing network elements (26 percent of entrants leasing loops with switching; 18 percent without switching). The incumbents do not contradict these figures, but merely speculate that the investment has not been as much as it could have been under other ratemaking approaches, and they note that investment has more recently shifted to nonfacilities entry options. We, of course, have no idea whether a different forward-looking pricing scheme would have generated even greater competitive investment than the $55 billion that the entrants claim, but it suffices to say that a regulatory scheme that can boast such substantial competitive capital spending over a 4-year period is not easily described as an unreasonable way to promote competitive investment in facilities.

b

The incumbents' second reason for calling TELRIC an unreasonable exercise of the FCC's regulatory discretion is the supposed incapacity of this methodology to provide enough depreciation and allowance for capital costs to induce rational competition on the theory's own terms. This challenge must be assessed against the background of utilities' customary preference for extended depreciation schedules in ratemaking (so as to preserve high rate bases); we have already noted the consequence of the utilities' approach, that the "book" value or embedded costs of capital presented to traditional ratemaking bodies often bore little resemblance to the economic value of the capital. See FCC Releases Audit Reports on RBOCs' Property Records, Report No. CC 99–3, 1999 WL 95044 (FCC, Feb. 25, 1999) ("[B]ook costs may be overstated by approximately $5 billion"); [P. Huber, M. Kellogg, & J. Thorne, Federal Telecommunications Law, p.116 (2d ed.1999)] (We now know that "[b]y the early 1980s, the Bell System had accumulated a vast library of accounting books that belonged alongside dime-store novels and other works of fiction.... By 1987, it was widely estimated that the book value of telephone company investments exceeded market value by $25 billion dollars"). TELRIC seeks to avoid this problem by basing its valuation on the market price for most efficient elements; when rates are figured by reference to a hypothetical element instead of an incumbent's actual element, the incumbent gets no unfair advantage from favorable depreciation rates in the traditional sense.

This, according to the incumbents, will be fatal to competition. Their argument is that TELRIC will result in constantly changing rates based on ever cheaper, more efficient technology; the incumbents will be unable to write off each new piece of technology rapidly enough to anticipate an even newer gadget portending a new and lower rate. They will be stuck, they say, with sunk costs in less efficient plant and equipment, with their investment unrecoverable through depreciation, and their increased risk unrecognized and uncompensated.

The argument, however, rests upon a fundamentally false premise, that the TELRIC rules limit the depreciation and capital costs that ratesetting commissions may recognize. In fact, TELRIC itself prescribes no fixed percentage rate as risk-adjusted capital costs and recognizes no particular useful life as a basis for calculating depreciation costs...

c

Finally, as to the incumbents' accusation that TELRIC is too complicated to be practical, a criticism at least as telling can be leveled at traditional ratemaking methodologies and the alternatives proffered.... At bottom, battles of experts are bound to be part of any ratesetting scheme, and the FCC was reasonable to prefer TELRIC over alternative fixed-cost schemes that preserve home-field advantages for the incumbents. * * *

[A partial dissent by Justice Breyer, joined by Justice Scalia, is omitted. The gist of Justice Breyer's dissent is that the TELRIC methodology did not show a reasonable connection between the method and the objectives of the statute. In Breyer's view, the lease rates that TELRIC would require states to implement would be so low that they would discourage CLECs from building their own facilities, which in turn was inconsistent with the competitive, deregulatory purposes of the Act.]

We Never Promised You a Rose Garden. Some critics have argued that by not guaranteeing that incumbent firms would be able to recover their embedded costs, TELRIC violates an implicit regulatory promise that regulated firms would be entitled to earn a fair return on their investment. See Daniel F. Spulber & J. Gregory Sidak, *Deregulatory Takings and the Regulatory Contract: The Competitive Transformation of Network Industries in the United States* (1997). The lesson of cases like *Hope Natural Gas* is that the Fifth Amendment guarantees a "fair return" on investment, but what does that imply? In *Verizon*, the Court found it premature to address the fair return issue in constitutional terms because TELRIC is not a price but a pricing methodology. In fact, the actual prices that are charged for UNEs vary greatly among states, which suggests that it is not quite so rigid as the ILECs claimed. But suppose it were the case that TELRIC prices would systematically produce stranded costs. Would that be a basis for condemning it either as a violation of the constitution or some implicit regulatory promise? Advocates of the regulatory promise theory do not maintain that there was a promise never to introduce competition, so presumably they aren't protected against competitive forces that would drive prices down to the incremental costs that would result from (pure) competition itself. It is a commonplace of competitive economics that sometimes firms are unable to recover full investments—competitors introduce new technology or cost saving measures that force firms with older facilities to write off part of their investment prematurely. Is that different from what is happening here?

ECPR. The principal alternative to TELRIC is the so-called efficient component pricing rule—"ECPR." ECPR is based on the premise that "costs" should be defined as opportunity costs of providing the UNE. The opportunity cost is the direct cost of providing the UNE plus the foregone profit when the CLEC displaces the ILEC in the provision of the service. As noted by the Court, the ECPR is fairly straight-forward: one simply takes the existing retail price of the ILEC service in which the UNE is used and deducts the incremental costs of providing service—the costs that are saved by the ILEC when the CLEC provides the service instead.[10] Putting to one side any question of "just compensation" for taking the ILEC's facilities, the efficiency claim for ECPR is that it would enable competitive entry into the downstream market (the retail market for the service in which the UNE is an input) only where the competitive entrant can provide the downstream part of the service more cheaply than the incumbent. Only in such a case could the CLEC pay the price of entry. But once competition ensues between the CLEC and the ILEC, won't the cheaper provider prevail in any case? For a helpful survey of ECPR, TELRIC and other pricing methods and an extensive bibliography of economic literature see Ingo Vogelsang, *Price Regulation of Access to Telecommunications Networks*, 41 J. Econ. Lit. 830 (2003). See also Jonathan E. Nuechterlein and Philip J. Weiser, *Digital Crossroads* App. A (2005), which provides a helpful summary of the controversy.

Bookkeeping or Bookcooking. The FCC's objection to ECPR, approvingly quoted by the Court, is that "the existing retail prices that would be used to compute incremental opportunity costs under ECPR are not cost-based. Moreover, the ECPR does not provide any mechanism for moving prices towards competitive levels; it simply takes prices as given." If it is true that existing retail prices do not fairly reflect the cost of service, why is it true? The Court suggests it does not matter whether the cost differences are due to management slack, or poor investment opportunities, or unduly long depreciation rates. Whatever the reason, the Court says that "if leased elements were priced according to embedded costs, the incumbents could pass these inefficiencies to competitors in need of their wholesale elements, and to that extent defeat the competitive purpose of forcing efficient choices on all carriers whether

10. Basically this is the pricing model for setting wholesale prices in the case of the resale of entire services: the wholesale prices are the retail prices minus whatever costs are saved by the incumbent carrier not having to provide retail services. This raises an interesting point about congressional intent: if Congress had intended UNE pricing to be based on the same pricing methodology used for resale, why did it not specify the same formula?

incumbents or entrants. The upshot would be higher retail prices consumers would have to pay." Moreover, even if the present costs are economically efficient, the Court says that using embedded costs would tempt the incumbents to manipulate the books by overstating costs, and "perpetuate the intractable problems that led to the price-cap innovation."

The Court assumes that if the embedded book costs are too high the rates must also be too high. Is that necessarily true? As we saw in the last chapter, traditional rate-of-return regulation sets rates so as to cover all current operating expenses, plus depreciation expenses, plus a risk-adjusted return on capital. (Note that the same elements go into the TELRIC formula, as the Court explains, though the way they are calculated is different.) The return on capital is measured as a percentage return on the rate base, which by assumption would be inflated by excessive book costs. However, if book costs are too *high* because depreciation rates are below what sound accounting principles dictate, would that not imply that the service rates must be too *low*? In other words, since the rate base is calculated by taking the purchase value of the equipment and subtracting depreciation, in order for the rate base to be larger than it should be (which would artificially inflate the return component), then annual expenses for depreciation must be lower than they should be. The question of whether rates are too high must depend, therefore, on whether the higher rate of return (on an inflated rate base) exceeds the lower depreciation expense. Accounting symmetry to one side, the assumption of excessively high retail rates presents something of a puzzle. State regulators have always been sensitive to increases in intrastate rates (and in partnership with the FCC have kept them low by shifting some of the costs to interstate services). Why would they allow low depreciation write-offs if the result—as the Court assumes—was to increase retail prices? As the Court mentions in passing, state regulators and the FCC have largely abandoned rate-of-return regulation in favor of price caps that do not determine individual rates by reference to a return on a rate base. How does this affect the Court's assumptions about high retail costs? If the existing retail service rates were set under a price cap regime, would the Court's point still be valid?

In assuming that the traditional rate system has produced higher retail rates than are cost justified the Court does not mention the fact that, while regulated pricing has allowed prices to be out of sync with economic costs, this misalignment of prices and costs is not uniform over all services. In fact, as we discussed in the last chapter, traditional telecommunications pricing was deliberately designed to discriminate among customers in order to subsidize some groups at the expense of others. The usual direction of the subsidies was that business users subsidized residential users, long distance users subsidized local users, urban users subsidized rural. These subsidies are impossible to sustain in the face of competition and many of them have been removed. However, to the extent they have not disappeared, the existence of such subsidies seems to undermine the Court's assumption about retail rates being too high. Under the traditional subsidies, some retail rates would be too high, others would be too low. To the extent that local exchange was a class of service generally favored by these traditional subsidies, would it not be plausible to suppose that, instead of being too high, the rates are too low?

Does it matter? One might argue that it is not important whether present retail prices are distorted up or down because the whole objective of the regulation is to encourage competition in only those markets in which competition pays, so the signals sent by the rates are actually as important as the rates themselves. What matters is that rates are not based on "true" cost, i.e., the cost that would prevail with the kind of competition we seek to establish. But setting rates in a way that encourages entry (and therefore competition) at the "right" time requires a theory about both what kind of competition we should be seeking (or at least what kind is likely to be produced) and how to produce that competition. It is widely agreed that the *ideal* is facilities-based competition, but there is no comparable agreement that giving easy access to existing network facilities is designed to ensure it. Justice Breyer's dissent in *Verizon* (omitted above) argued at some length that the TELRIC standard will produce access and entry for CLECs without the need to build their own facilities, undermining their incentive to invest in new facilities, which in the long run will retard the introduction of "ideal" (i.e. facilities-based) competition.

Competition by Steps. On the other hand, UNE access was assumed to be a means of enabling facilities-based competition by allowing CLECs to enter the market without the need to self-supply network facilities. This is what has come to be known as the "stepping stone" theory of competitive entry (sometimes also referred to as the "ladder of investment" theory). Essentially, the idea is that over time, new entrants will replace leased facilities with self-supplied facilities as their evolving economic strength in the market permits. Some critics have argued that the stepping stone theory hasn't succeeded because CLECs have not in fact evolved from leased facilities to providing their own, even where it is feasible to do so. See, e.g., Jerry A. Hausman & J. Gregory Sidak, *Did Mandatory Unbundling Achieve Its Purpose: Empirical Evidence from Five Countries*, 1 J. Competition Law and Econ. 173 (2005); Robert W. Crandall & Leonard Waverman, *The Failure of Competitive Entry into Fixed-Line Telecommunications: Who Is At Fault*, 2 J. Competition Law & Econ. 113 (2006). We will examine some data pertinent to this question in Chapter 11. For now it is enough to notice that the stepping stone theory logically entails an assumption that the rules governing mandatory leased access do not distort investment incentives, which assumes economically correct pricing rules. If CLECs are able to lease network facilities at a price below what it would cost to construct or obtain them from independent sources, there is little incentive to take steps towards greater investment in ownership. Basically this is the point made by Justice Breyer in his dissent in *Verizon*.[11]

The Future of TELRIC. Despite its victory in the Supreme Court, the FCC appears to have taken to heart some of the criticisms of its methodology—at least some of the practical objections. At the end of the day, the most telling criticisms of TELRIC turned not on theories of cost recovery so much as on the implementing details. In this respect one of the key objections was that sustained by the lower court's decision in *Verizon*, which was that TELRIC rested on artificially constructed costs based on hypothetical rather than actual network design. In other words the "forward looking" element of TELRIC methodology was not merely forward looking but futuristic. See Dennis L. Weisman, *Did the High Court Reach an Economic Low in* Verizon v. FCC*?* 1 Rev. of Network Econ. 90 (2002). The Supreme Court rejected that claim on the ground that cost estimates were based on existing wire centers. Even accepting the existing configuration of wire centers, though, there is considerable room for making assumptions about new and more efficient network design. What that meant, according to critics, is that the FCC's model for implementing TELRIC imputed to the ILECs new, more efficient technology and design features than were actually used or could be readily adopted. The FCC later seems to have conceded as much. In 2003 it began a new rulemaking proceeding to consider possible modifications in the construction of TELRIC-based prices. The proceeding is "detail" oriented. The FCC indicates it will not reconsider its refusal to require that rates cover all embedded costs, or its rejection of ECPR or Ramsey pricing. The key focus of the new proceeding is on the assumptions about network design, and some other details about how to calculate capital costs and operating costs.

THE PRICING OF UNBUNDLED NETWORK ELEMENTS Notice of Proposed Rulemaking

Federal Communications Commission, 2003.
18 FCC Rcd. 18945.

I. INTRODUCTION

1. In this Notice of Proposed Rulemaking (NPRM), the Commission begins its first comprehensive review of the rules applicable to the

11. Pertinent to the pricing *cum* investment incentives issue is the fact that the UNE leases are allowed to be very short term. This permits a CLEC to keep its investment options open as the CLEC obtains information about market conditions. As that information is revealed the CLEC can then choose between investment or continued lease and resale. Economists recognize this ability to defer investment decisions as a valuable option. See, e.g., Avinish K. Dixit, and Robert S. Pindyck, INVESTMENT UNDER UNCERTAINTY ch. 2 (1993). It is labeled a "real" option not to distinguish it from a fictional option but in order to distinguish it from a financial option that is traded in the open market. But traded or not, there is a consensus among economists that this option has "real" value. If TELRIC-based prices do not incorporate the value of this option, that implies that CLECs are underpaying for an element of value that is being supplied by ILECs, which in turn could distort the investment incentives of both the CLEC and the ILEC. See, e.g., Jerry A. Hausman and J. Gregory Sidak, A Consumer–Welfare Approach to the Mandatory Unbundling of Telecommunications Networks, 109 YALE L. J. 417, 458 (1999). The FCC claims that the option value is implicitly part of the cost-of-capital component of TELRIC pricing, but this has been disputed. See Robert S. Pindyck, Mandatory Unbundling and Irreversible Investment in Telecom Networks, 6 REV. OF NETWORK ECON. 274, 293–94 (2007).

pricing of unbundled network elements (UNEs) pursuant to section 252(d)(1) of the Communications Act of 1934 (the "Act"), as amended by the Telecommunications Act of 1996 (the "1996 Act"). The Commission adopted its current UNE pricing rules, which base UNE prices on the Total Element Long Run Incremental Cost (TELRIC) of a UNE, in 1996 in the *Local Competition Order*. The Commission stated at that time that it would continue to review its pricing rules based on the results of state arbitration proceedings and provide additional guidance as necessary. We have not undertaken a comprehensive review of the TELRIC methodology in the seven years since it was adopted, and it is appropriate to conduct such a review at this time. * * *

IV. UNE Pricing

* * *

B. Network Assumptions

1. General Theory

49. Perhaps the most controversial aspect of the TELRIC rules is the assumption that the cost of a UNE should be calculated based on the cost of ubiquitous deployment of the most efficient technology currently available. In implementing this requirement, current TELRIC models typically are designed to answer the following question: If a single carrier were to build an efficient network today to serve all customer locations within a particular geographic area, taking as given only the locations of existing wire centers, how much would it cost to construct and maintain the network?

50. One of the central internal tensions in the application of the TELRIC methodology is that it purports to replicate the conditions of a competitive market by assuming that the latest technology is deployed throughout the hypothetical network, while at the same time assuming that this hypothetical network benefits from the economies of scale associated with serving all of the lines in a study area. In the real world, however, even in extremely competitive markets, firms do not instantaneously replace all of their facilities with every improvement in technology. Thus, even the most efficient carrier's network will reflect a mix of new and older technology at any given time. * * *

52. We tentatively conclude that our TELRIC rules should more closely account for the real-world attributes of the routing and topography of an incumbent's network in the development of forward-looking costs. We seek comment on whether such an approach would address claims that our TELRIC rules currently distort a competitor's decision whether to invest in new facilities or to lease an incumbent's existing facilities. Yet we also wish to ensure that a reformed TELRIC methodol-

ogy does not swing in the other direction and give incumbents undue advantages. We seek comment on this tentative conclusion and, in particular, on how such an approach may differ from the practices of state commissions in UNE pricing proceedings. * * *

55. In the *Local Competition Order*, the Commission defined the term "long run" to mean a period long enough for all of a firm's costs to become variable or avoidable. Does our tentative conclusion compel us to shift from a long-run average cost methodology to a short-run average cost methodology? If so, what are the consequences of such a shift? To the extent the cost of a UNE under such an approach would in part be based on the existing incumbent LEC network, is such an approach consistent with the "heavy presumption" against the use of embedded costs? Would it be more effective to retain a long-run pricing methodology, but provide specific guidance to the states on the appropriate long-run assumptions upon which to base network inputs? * * *

b. Technology

67. Our current rules require states to assume that the "most efficient telecommunications technology currently available" is used throughout the network. The Commission concluded in the *Local Competition Order* that the forward-looking pricing methodology for interconnection and UNEs should be based on a "reconstructed local network [that] will employ the most efficient technology for reasonably foreseeable capacity requirements." At the same time, the Commission recognized a need for "basing prices on efficient, new technology that is compatible with the existing infrastructure."

68. As noted above, it is unlikely that any carrier, no matter how competitive the marketplace, would deploy new technology instantaneously and ubiquitously throughout its network. Even if the objective is to replicate the results of a competitive market, an approach that reconstructs the network over time seems to be more appropriate than one that assumes the instantaneous deployment of 100 percent new technology.

69. We seek comment on how our tentative conclusion above affects the technology assumptions used to develop UNE prices. Of what relevance is the Commission's statement in the universal service context that "[e]xisting incumbent LEC plant is not likely to reflect forward-looking technology or design choices"? How should a state commission determine the price for equipment in the incumbent LEC network that no longer is widely used in the industry, such as analog switches or older versions of digital loops carrier systems? How does an approach that replicates an incumbent LEC's existing technology compare to a "reproduction cost" methodology? * * *

[The rest of the NPRM invites comments on particular details of cost determination, such as how to determine the cost of capital, how to set operating-cost depreciation rates, etc.]

Five years on (as this book goes to press) nothing more has happened on this front. One speculation is that the salience of the TELRC controversy has faded, reducing political pressure for change. Another is that the issue of prices has been somewhat reduced because of changes in the scope of unbundling—as we noted in the previous section.

F. FORBEARANCE

The 1996 Act put in place a complex scheme for managing the shift to competition. In order to prevent them from using their power as established monopolies to block entry by competitors, ILECs were subjected to many rules that CLECs were not, such as the degree of rate regulation and the unbundling requirements discussed above. Theoretically, those special rules would become unnecessary once local markets became fully open to competition, but the concern remained largely theoretical for almost a decade after the 1996 Act, as no local markets became even remotely close to any measure of "competitive" for some time.

As it happens, the 1996 Act gives the FCC the means for dismantling the regulatory regime it is charged with enforcing. Section 10 of the Act (47 U.S.C. § 160) gives the FCC broad power to forbear from applying regulation to specific carriers, largely on the grounds that competition exists.

47 U.S.C. § 160—Competition in provision of telecommunications service

(a) Regulatory flexibility

Notwithstanding section 332 (c)(1)(A) of this title, the Commission shall forbear from applying any regulation or any provision of this chapter to a telecommunications carrier or telecommunications service, or class of telecommunications carriers or telecommunications services, in any or some of its or their geographic markets, if the Commission determines that—

(1) enforcement of such regulation or provision is not necessary to ensure that the charges, practices, classifications, or regulations by, for, or in connection with that telecommunications carrier or telecommunications service are just and reasonable and are not unjustly or unreasonably discriminatory;

(2) enforcement of such regulation or provision is not necessary for the protection of consumers; and

(3) forbearance from applying such provision or regulation is consistent with the public interest.

(b) Competitive effect to be weighed

In making the determination under subsection (a)(3) of this section, the Commission shall consider whether forbearance from enforcing the provision or regulation will promote competitive market conditions, including the extent to which such forbearance will enhance competition among providers of telecommunications services. If the Commission determines that such forbearance will promote competition among providers of telecommunications services, that determination may be the basis for a Commission finding that forbearance is in the public interest.

In 2005, the FCC granted the first petition for forbearance under 47 U.S.C. § 160 (per its usual practice, the FCC refers to the provision throughout the order by its section number in the 1996 Act: § 10). Back in 1996 some expected competition to arrive quickly; some thought it would never come. Certainly no one anticipated the form in which it would eventually arrive: from cable television providers. We will discuss the provision of telephone service by cable TV and other non-traditional means in greater depth in Chapter 10 on Advanced Services. For present purposes, all you need to know is that it exists, a fact all-too-apparent for those of us unlucky enough to be constantly deluged by direct mail advertising by cable operators hoping to sell us home telephone (and Internet) service.

IN THE MATTER OF PETITION OF QWEST CORPORATION FOR FORBEARANCE PURSUANT TO 47 U.S.C. § 160(c) IN THE OMAHA METROPOLITAN STATISTICAL AREA

Federal Communications Commission, 2005.
20 FCC Rcd. 19415.

BY THE COMMISSION:

I. INTRODUCTION

1. Last year, in the midst of intense facilities-based competition in the Omaha Metropolitan Statistical Area (MSA), Qwest Corporation (Qwest) filed a petition for forbearance pursuant to section 10 of the Telecommunications Act of 1996 from many of the statutory and regulatory obligations that apply to it uniquely as the former monopoly telephone company. Today, we grant Qwest substantial relief from many of these obligations, where the level of facilities-based competition ensures that market forces will protect the interests of consumers and regulation is, therefore, unnecessary. Through this Order, we show that we are ready and willing to step aside as regulators and let market forces prevail where facilities-based competition is robust.

2. We grant Qwest forbearance from the obligation to provide unbundled loops and dedicated transport pursuant to section 251(c)(3) in those portions of its service territory in the Omaha MSA where a facilities-based competitor has substantially built out its network. We also are persuaded by the evidence on the record to forbear from applying certain dominant carrier regulation to Qwest's provision of mass market switched access and broadband services in Qwest's service territory. With the exception of minor relief from sections 271 and

251(c)(6) that reflects the relief we grant from section 251(c)(3), we deny Qwest's Petition in all other respects. While each case must be judged on its own merits, and while we adopt herein no rules of general applicability, we expect our Order to provide incentives for facilities-based competitors to expand their deployment and service offerings in Omaha, and we look forward to the day when that competition justifies more of the relief Qwest seeks.[4]

II. Background

3. *Section 251(c) Requirements.* The Act includes a number of provisions designed to promote the development of competitive markets. As noted above, Qwest seeks relief from all section 251(c) obligations, which are the duties to negotiate in good faith the terms and conditions of section 251(b) and (c) agreements; provide interconnection at any technically feasible point to any requesting telecommunications carrier at cost-based rates for the transmission and routing of telephone exchange service and exchange access service; provide UNEs for the provision of telecommunications service; offer for resale at wholesale rates any telecommunications service that the carrier provides at retail; provide reasonable notice of network changes; and provide collocation.

* * *

5. Section 251(c)(3) imposes on incumbent LECs "[t]he duty to provide, to any requesting telecommunications carrier ... nondiscriminatory access to network elements on an unbundled basis ... in accordance with ... this section and section 252." The Act does not identify which network elements are subject to the section 251 (c) (3) unbundling obligations. Instead, Congress directed the Commission to determine what non-proprietary network elements must be unbundled under section 251(c)(3) after considering, at a minimum, whether access to a non-proprietary element on an unbundled basis would "impair" a requesting carrier's ability to provide service. Under section 252, UNEs that must be offered pursuant to section 251(c)(3) must be made available at cost-based rates, as determined using the TELRIC methodology.

* * *

10. *Dominant Carrier Regulation.* Under Title II of the Act, the Commission traditionally has applied a variety of regulations to carriers in order to protect consumers from unjust, unreasonable, and unreasonably discriminatory rates and practices. These regulations include requirements arising under section 214 related to transfer of control and discontinuance, cost-supported tariffing requirements, and price regulation for services falling under the Commission's jurisdiction. The *Competitive Carrier Proceeding* considered revisions to the Commission's

4. This proceeding considers factors unique to the Omaha MSA. It does not consider and does not reach the situation where the incumbent LEC's primary competitor uses unbundled networks elements (UNEs), particularly unbundled loops, as the primary vehicle for serving and acquiring customers in the relevant market. Such a situation necessarily raises different issues with respect to our section 10 analysis. We do not consider or address them here.

regulations to distinguish between carriers that are subject to effective competition in their respective telecommunications markets and those that are not. The Commission found that certain regulations that apply to all carriers under Title II are unnecessary for carriers that are subject to competition and therefore lack sufficient market power to engage in anticompetitive activity.

11. Qwest asks us to forbear from applying dominant carrier regulation to its provision of telecommunications services in its service area within the Omaha MSA. Because the Commission has in the past found that incumbent LECs, including Qwest, have market power in the provision of most services within their service areas, the rates that incumbent LECs may charge for certain services currently are subject to dominant carrier regulation. Dominant carriers are subject to price cap or rate-of-return regulation, and must file tariffs for some services—on a minimum of seven days' notice and often more—and usually with cost support data. Non-dominant carriers, on the other hand, are not subject to rate regulation and may file tariffs, on one day's notice and without cost support that are presumed lawful. In addition, non-dominant carriers are required to wait only 30 days for their applications to discontinue, reduce, or impair service to be granted, as opposed to a 60 day grant period for dominant carriers. Finally, dominant carriers are eligible for presumptive streamlined treatment for fewer types of transfer of control under section 214 than non-dominant carriers.

12. *Regulation as an Incumbent Local Exchange Carrier*. Qwest requests forbearance from regulation as an incumbent LEC "pursuant to section 251(h)(1)." Section 251(h)(1) defines an "incumbent LEC" as:

> with respect to an area, the local exchange carrier that—(A) on the date of enactment of the Telecommunications Act of 1996, provided telephone exchange service in such area; and (B)(i) on such date of the enactment, was deemed to be a member of the exchange carrier association pursuant to section 69.601(b) of the Commission's regulations (47 C.F.R. 69.601(b)); or (ii) is a person or entity that, on or after such date of enactment, became a successor or assign of a member described in clause (i).

III. Discussion

A. Forbearance Standard

13. The goal of the Telecommunications Act of 1996 is to establish "a pro-competitive, de-regulatory national policy framework." An integral part of this framework is the requirement, set forth in section 10 of the 1996 Act, that the Commission forbear from applying any provision of the Act, or any of the Commission's regulations, if the Commission makes certain specified findings with respect to such provisions or regulations. Specifically, the Commission is required to forbear from any statutory provision or regulation if it determines that: (1) enforcement of the regulation is not necessary to ensure that charges and practices are just and reasonable, and are not unjustly or unreasonably discriminato-

ry; (2) enforcement of the regulation is not necessary to protect consumers; and (3) forbearance is consistent with the public interest. In making such determinations, the Commission must also consider pursuant to section 10(b) "whether forbearance from enforcing the provision or regulation will promote competitive market conditions." Section 10(d) specifies, however, that "[e]xcept as provided in section 251(f), the Commission may not forbear from applying the requirements of section 251(c) or 271 ... until it determines that those requirements have been fully implemented."

14. Consistent with our statutory obligations, in this Order we therefore apply the criteria of section 10 to the regulations and statutory provisions from which Qwest seeks relief. As part of our forbearance analysis, and consistent with Qwest's Petition, we look to the Commission's previous caselaw on dominance for guidance. We emphasize, however, that in undertaking this analysis, we do not issue any declaratory rulings, promulgate any new rules, or otherwise make any general determinations of the sort we would properly make in a rulemaking proceeding on a fuller record. Accordingly, our sole task here is to determine whether to forbear under the standard of section 10 from the regulatory and statutory provisions at issue, and we do not—and cannot—issue comprehensive proclamations in this proceeding regarding non-dominance, non-impairment, or section 251(h) status in the Omaha MSA.

B. Dominant Carrier Regulation

* * *

2. Application of Forbearance Criteria to Qwest's Petition

18. Through the *Competitive Carrier Proceeding*, the Commission established a regulatory framework to distinguish between dominant carriers, which have market power, and carriers classified as non-dominant, which lack market power. Under the framework set forth in the *LEC Classification Order*, the Commission determines whether a carrier is dominant by: (1) delineating the relevant product and geographic markets for examination of market power; (2) identifying firms that are current or potential suppliers in that market; and (3) determining whether the carrier under evaluation possesses individual market power in that market. The Commission defines relevant product markets by identifying and aggregating consumers with similar demand patterns. The Commission has also explained that "[a] geographic market aggregates those consumers with similar choices regarding a particular good or service in the same geographical area," and that it would "treat as a geographic market, an area in which all customers in that area will likely face the same competitive alternatives for a product."

19. Applying the section 10 criteria as informed by the dominance analysis, we forbear from applying certain dominant carrier regulations to Qwest's provision of mass market exchange access services, as well as mass market broadband Internet access services, because we find that all

elements of section 10(a) have been satisfied. We decline to forbear from applying these dominant carrier regulations to Qwest's provision of enterprise services because Qwest has failed to demonstrate satisfaction of *any* of the three conjunctive section 10(a) forbearance criteria.

a. Relevant Markets

(i) Product Market

20. Our inquiry is necessarily limited to those dominance regulations and statutory provisions over which the Commission has jurisdiction—dominant carrier regulation of interstate telecommunications services. Any dominant carrier regulation of local exchange service or other intrastate service is not subject to our forbearance authority.

21. Qwest proposes, without further explanation, that the relevant product market "is the market for services provided under Section 251(c) and selected services under Section 271 provided within the boundaries of the Omaha MSA." We find such a wide scope of services in this proposed definition to be unworkable as a single product market, especially because the services offered to mass market customers may not be adequate or feasible substitutes for services offered to business customers. However, consistent with the statute's deregulatory intent, and in an effort to conduct a thorough forbearance analysis that reflects the evidence compiled in the record, we disaggregate the telecommunications services that Qwest provides into more discrete classes.

22. Accordingly, for purposes of evaluating Qwest's request for relief from dominant carrier regulation, we divide these interstate services into the mass market (residential consumers and small business customers) and the enterprise market (medium-sized and large business customers). Our analyses of the mass market and enterprise market are not identical to, but are in accordance with, the Commission's past product market analyses for those services. In addition, we also separate out mass market broadband Internet access services, consistent with the Commission's separate review of that market in prior merger proceedings. Thus, within the mass market we look at both switched access services and broadband Internet access services. For the purposes of assessing forbearance from dominant carrier regulation, we reject suggestions from commenters that our section 251(c)(3) network element unbundling precedent controls our market framework.

* * *

b. Mass Market Services

25. On the basis of the evidence of competition on the record and the application of the section 10(a) statutory criteria, we conclude that enforcement of the listed dominant carrier regulations for mass market exchange access and broadband Internet access services is unwarranted. In particular, we find most persuasive that Cox has acquired a [**REDACTED**] share of the residential access market [**REDACTED**] Qwest, and that Cox has [**REDACTED**] share of the broadband Internet access

market. Our forbearance from the application of the dominant carrier regulations before us today is conditioned upon Qwest's compliance with competitive carrier requirements, and in no instance is Qwest to be subject to less regulation than any competitive LEC. We reach these conclusions by examining the state of competition in Qwest's service territory in the Omaha MSA for mass market services, including market share, demand and supply elasticities, and Qwest's size, resources, and technical capabilities.

* * *

(i) Section 10(a)(1)—Charges, Practices, Classifications, and Regulations

26. Section 10(a)(1) requires that we determine whether enforcement of the regulations at issue is not necessary to ensure that charges, practices, classifications or regulations by Qwest are not unjustly or unreasonably discriminatory. In its Petition, Qwest argues broadly that dominant carrier regulation of Qwest's "local telephone services" in the Omaha MSA is no longer necessary to ensure that Qwest's rates and practices are just, reasonable and not unreasonably discriminatory, and that Qwest therefore satisfies the criteria of Section 10(a)(1) of the 1996 Act. More specifically, it contends that the Omaha MSA telecommunications market has become highly competitive, that no carrier has market power, and that there is no longer any regulatory justification for applying unique regulatory requirements to any single carrier as "dominant." Qwest asserts that requirements other than dominant carrier regulation, such as sections 201 and 202 of the Act, are sufficient to protect consumers from any carrier attempting to charge unreasonable rates.

27. We conclude that the Commission's relevant rules on dominant carrier price caps, rate of return, tariffing, rate averaging, and discontinuance are no longer necessary to ensure that Qwest's rates and practices are just, reasonable, and not unjustly or unreasonably discriminatory for the services in the product market at issue below. We recognize, however, the special problem of carrier's carrier charges—that all LECs have monopoly power over the rates that they charge carriers wishing to terminate calls to LECs' end user customers. Our analysis below discusses the competitive environment in general, and addresses why certain dominant carrier regulations are not necessary to check Qwest rates and practices with regard to its own end users. We address the special problem of carrier's carrier charges separately below.

(a) Market Share

28. *Mass Market Switched Access Service*. For this factor, we find compelling that Qwest has less than [**REDACTED**] percent of the market for residential access lines in Qwest's service territory in the MSA, based upon Qwest's and Cox's own submitted data. To reach a determination with regard to the mass market for switched access services, we find that the data Qwest and Cox have submitted regarding

residential customers are a reasonable proxy for the number of mass market customers served by each carrier. Qwest reports that as of December 2004, it had [**REDACTED**] residential retail access lines. Cox submits that as of May 1, 2005, it had [**REDACTED**] residential lines.

* * *

(c) Specific Forbearance Granted

39. *Price Cap and Tariffing Forbearance for Exchange Access Services.* Due to Qwest's loss of [**REDACTED**] residential access lines and our analysis of the other factors above, we find that, subject to certain conditions, enforcement of our dominant carrier price cap rules is not necessary to ensure that Qwest's charges, practices, or regulations are just, reasonable, and not unjustly or unreasonably discriminatory with regard to the prices Qwest charges to its own end users. We conclude that enforcing price caps is not necessary, and we forbear from those regulations accordingly. We, however, condition our forbearance from applying section 61.41 price caps to Qwest's mass market access service charges on Qwest's compliance with regulations that apply to all competitive LECs, in particular section 61.26 of the Commission's rules.

40. In the *CLEC Access Charge Reform Order*, the Commission found that interexchange carriers are subject to the monopoly power that all competitive LECs wield over access to their end users, and that carriers' carrier charges cannot be fully deregulated. As a result, the Commission has imposed a detariffing regime through section 61.26 that permits the filing of tariffs on one day's notice without cost support (and presumes the access charges that competitive LECs charge their carrier customers to be just and reasonable) where the rates are at or below a benchmark that is "the rate of the competing ILEC." Competitive LECs are subject to mandatory detariffing of any rates that exceed the benchmark; otherwise, the Commission does not regulate the rates charged pursuant to any other arrangement that competitive LECs may reach with interexchange carriers.

41. To ensure that our forbearance today does not result in rates that are unjust or unreasonable, and in light of the "unique nature" of the access market, we therefore condition this forbearance upon the same regime under which competitive LECs currently operate. * * *

42. *Rate of Return and Tariffing Forbearance for Broadband Internet Access Services.* We find that continued application of our section 61.38 cost support and Part 65 rate of return regulations to Qwest's broadband Internet access transmission services is not necessary to ensure that Qwest's charges, practices, or regulations are just, reasonable, and not unjustly or unreasonably discriminatory so long as Qwest is subject to the same treatment as non-dominant carriers under those rules. * * *

(ii) Section 10(a)(2)—Protection of Consumers

44. The second criterion under section 10 requires that we assess whether enforcement of our dominant carrier regulations to mass mar-

ket interstate switched access and mass market broadband Internet access services is unnecessary for the protection of consumers. Qwest claims that it satisfies the criteria of section 10(a)(2) because the "high level of facilities-based competition, the lack of entry barriers, and the vitality of existing competitors will provide all the product, price, service and choice protection that consumers need." It further argues that customers in the Omaha MSA are being deprived of the full benefits of competition because of the continued regulation of Qwest as a dominant carrier.

45. For many of the same reasons that led us to conclude that section 10(a)(1) is satisfied, we also conclude that section 10(a)(2) is satisfied with regard to a limited set of dominant carrier regulation—price caps, rate of return, tariffing and section 214 regulation. Most notably, in light of Cox's capture of [**REDACTED**] residential access lines compared to Qwest's [**REDACTED**], continuing to subject Qwest to these requirements does not enhance consumer protection. * * *

(iii) Section 10(a)(3)—Public Interest

46. The third criterion of section 10 requires that we determine whether forbearance from applying our dominant carrier regulations, including our tariff filing requirements, our section 214 transfer requirements, and our price cap regulations is consistent with the public interest. In making this determination, the Commission shall consider whether forbearance will promote competitive market conditions, including the extent to which forbearance will enhance competition among providers of telecommunications services. Qwest argues that if the Commission continues to regulate it as a dominant carrier in the Omaha MSA telecommunications market, it will "hobble Qwest's ability to compete for customers, and would continue competitive distortions that do not serve the public interest." Qwest also notes that in the *AT&T Non-Dominance Order*, the Commission describes the significant costs of continued asymmetric regulation. Qwest insists that continued dominant carrier regulation of its services in the Omaha MSA will involve these same costs.

47. Similarly, we conclude that forbearing from our dominant carrier regulations that apply to interstate switched access and broadband Internet access services is consistent with the public interest. Specifically, we find that it will enhance the vigorous local exchange competition that has emerged in the Omaha MSA, and will serve the public interest, if we no longer apply to Qwest the dominant carrier regulations that apply to such services, including our tariff filing requirements, our section 214 requirements, and our price cap regulations. As stated above, Qwest serves less than [**REDACTED**] percent of the residential access lines in the interstate exchange access services market in the Omaha MSA—a market with high supply and demand elasticities for end user customers. Qwest's share of the broadband market is [**REDACTED**]. In these environments that are competitive for end users, applying these dominant carrier regulations to Qwest limits its

ability to respond to competitive forces and, therefore, its ability quickly to offer consumers new pricing plans or service packages.

* * *

49. Indeed, as Qwest argues, forbearing from the application to Qwest of these dominant carrier requirements will increase competition in the market by freeing Qwest from unnecessary regulatory burdens. At a minimum, we believe that forbearing from dominant carrier regulation in the Omaha MSA will serve the public interest by increasing the regulatory parity among providers of mass market interstate exchange access services in the Omaha MSA. As a result of our decision today, the playing field between Qwest and Cox will be leveled to the extent Qwest will no longer be the only carrier in its service territory in the Omaha MSA subject to dominant carrier regulations that apply to mass market interstate exchange access services. In light of the fact that Qwest's share of this market, when compared with Cox's share, is [**REDACTED**], we believe this outcome is warranted and serves the public interest. For DSL services, where the market share is approximately 86,000 for Cox compared to [**REDACTED**] for Qwest, the regulatory parity policy is even more compelling."

* * *

D. Forbearance from Section 251(c) Requirements

57. We grant Qwest's Petition in part, and forbear from applying to Qwest the requirements arising under section 251(c)(3) to provide unbundled access to loop and transport elements in certain wire centers in the Omaha MSA based upon the development of sufficient facilities-based competition and other factors we explain below. * * *

58. In the Petition, Qwest contends that the growth of retail competition in the Omaha MSA has given enterprise and mass market customers multiple competitive options to satisfy their telecommunications needs. On the basis of this retail competition, Qwest argues that it is no longer necessary or appropriate that it remain subject to the requirements of section 251(c) in the Omaha MSA. To support its position, Qwest presents evidence that the number of retail lines it uses to serve customers has fallen steadily since 1997, and claims that retail competition from wireline carriers and intermodal competitors accounts for this decline. In particular, Qwest submits that an incumbent cable operator in the Omaha MSA, Cox, uses its own extensive facilities, including its own loop equivalents, to provide telecommunications services in parts of this MSA; has captured significant market share for narrowband voice customers in this MSA; and is actively competing for enterprise customers.

59. As explained below, we find that the substantial intermodal competition for telecommunications services provided over Cox's own extensive facilities is sufficient to grant Qwest forbearance from the application of its section 251(c)(3) obligations with respect to loops and transport, in light of the continued application in the Omaha MSA of

other statutory and regulatory provisions designed to promote the development of competitive markets for telecommunications services and the actual competition these regulations have facilitated. Over two years ago, in the *Triennial Review Order*, the Commission determined that intermodal competition from cable had not "blossomed into a full substitute for wireline telephony." Today, as a result of Cox's investment in network infrastructure in the Omaha MSA, Cox, like Qwest, is providing telecommunications services over its own extensive last-mile facilities. On the basis of this competition, combined with other statutory and regulatory safeguards that facilitate additional competition, we find that the criteria of section 10(a) are satisfied with respect to Qwest's section 251(c)(3) obligation to unbundle loop and transport elements in 9 of Qwest's 24 wire centers in the Omaha MSA where competitive deployment is greatest. Therefore, we forbear from the application of section 251(c)(3) to Qwest to the extent it requires Qwest to provide access to loops in and transport to those 9 wire centers.

60. However, for the remainder of the section 251(c) obligations from which Qwest seeks relief in the present Petition, we find that Qwest has not satisfied any of the criteria of section 10(a) that might allow us to grant its Petition. Except in limited geographic areas, Qwest has not demonstrated that it is subject to significant competition from competitors that do not rely heavily on Qwest's wholesale services. Cox does not have any coverage at all in [**REDACTED**] of Qwest's 24 wire center service areas in the Omaha MSA, and in other wire center service areas has only limited coverage. Cox is not able to provide the same level of competition where it does not have extensive coverage as where it has such coverage. * * *

1. Unbundled Access to Loops and Transport

* * *

62. We tailor Qwest's relief to specific thresholds of facilities-based competition from Cox. Specifically, we grant Qwest forbearance from obligations to unbundle loops and transport pursuant to section 251(c)(3) in wire centers where Cox's voice-enabled cable plant covers at least [**REDACTED**] percent of the end user locations that are accessible from that wire center. Our decision today also is based on other actual and potential competition, which we find either is present, or readily could be present, in 100 percent of Qwest's service area in the Omaha MSA. Carriers are still able to rely on section 251(c)(4) resale and the other market-opening provisions from which we do not forbear today everywhere in Qwest's service area in this MSA. * * *

a. Section 10(a)(1)—Charges, Practices, Classifications, and Regulations

* * *

65. *Competition in the Omaha MSA.* In today's Order, consistent with our prior decisions, we examine the status of competition in the

retail market as well as the role of the wholesale market in the Omaha MSA. We begin by examining the retail market, and in so doing we agree with Qwest that, in evaluating the level of competition in a market, the Commission should not focus exclusively on competition provided using "identical technology that is currently deployed by the incumbent LECs." In accord with this determination, we take account of telecommunications services provided over intermodal facilities to the extent these services compete as substitutes for Qwest's wireline telecommunications service offerings. Of greatest importance in our analysis is competition from Cox, which uses its cable plant to provide circuit-switched local exchange and exchange access services in this market.

66. Cox has extensive facilities in the Omaha MSA capable of delivering both mass market and enterprise telecommunications services. Cox has proven it is capable of competing very successfully using its own network to provide services in the mass market where the revenue potential, compared with the enterprise market, is relatively low. Indeed, in the residential market, Cox has [**REDACTED**] voice customers in this MSA [**REDACTED**] Qwest. In addition, Qwest has provided evidence that Cox is actively marketing itself to enterprise customers, has succeeded in attracting a large number of significant Omaha businesses as customers, and has doubled its enterprise sales in the Omaha MSA each year for five consecutive years. While Cox has captured a larger share of mass market customers to date, in light of record evidence of Cox's strong success in the mass market, its possession of the necessary facilities to provide enterprise services, its technical expertise, its economies of scale and scope, its sunk investments in network infrastructure, its established presence and brand in the Omaha MSA, and its current marketing efforts and emerging success in the enterprise market, we must conclude that Cox poses a substantial competitive threat to Qwest for higher revenue enterprise services as well. In addition, Qwest has provided maps and other evidence that competitors have deployed their own transport facilities primarily concentrated within the boundaries of the 9 wire center service areas where we grant Qwest forbearance.

67. We also examine the role of the wholesale market. The record does not reflect any significant alternative sources of wholesale inputs for carriers in this geographic market. We find, however, that Qwest's own wholesale offerings will continue to be adequate without unbundled loop and transport offerings. * * * Indeed, Qwest's section 251(c)(4) and section 271(c) wholesale obligations remain in place. The very high levels of retail competition that do not rely on Qwest's facilities—and for which Qwest receives little to no revenue—provide Qwest with the incentive to make attractive wholesale offerings available so that it will derive more revenue indirectly from retail customers who choose a retail provider other than Qwest. This gives us enormous comfort that in the mass market, unbundling loops and transport pursuant to section 251(c)(3) is "not necessary to ensure that the charges, practices, classifications, or regulations by, for, or in connection with that telecommunications carri-

er or telecommunications service are just and reasonable and are not unjustly or unreasonably discriminatory."

* * *

69. While our decision today relies on competitive factors other than facilities-based competition from Cox, to the extent our decision today is based on competition from Cox, we find such competition to be sufficient to justify forbearance in wire center service areas where Cox is willing and able within a commercially reasonable time of providing service to [**REDACTED**] percent of the end user locations accessible from that wire center. We believe that requiring that Cox cover at least [**REDACTED**] percent of the end user locations in a wire center service area before Qwest obtains forbearance from section 251(c)(3) unbundling obligations in that wire center will ensure that all of the customers capable of being served by Qwest from that wire center will benefit from competitive rates, terms and conditions. * * *

70. Furthermore, as the record confirms, a facilities-based competitor such as Cox that does not compete through reliance on section 251(c)(3) access to unbundled loops is unlikely to pattern the architecture of its network after wire center service area boundaries. We do not believe that we should require that Cox's network neatly map to Qwest's wire center service area boundaries as a precondition of granting Qwest forbearance relief. In addition, if we were to require Cox's network to cover 100 percent of a wire center before granting Qwest forbearance in that wire center, Cox would be able to prevent Qwest from obtaining forbearance relief (and may have the incentive to do so) by declining to provide telecommunications services to only a relatively small percentage of potential customers in each wire center service area.

71. For the reasons explained above, we disagree with commenters who contend that forbearing from application of unbundling obligations to Qwest will result in a duopoly. In the present context, we believe that the facilities-based competition between Qwest and Cox, in addition to the actual and potential competition from established competitors which can rely on the wholesale access rights and other rights they have under sections 251(c) and section 271 from which we do not forbear, minimizes the risk of duopoly and of coordinated behavior or other anticompetitive conduct in this market. We note that the Commission previously has rejected arguments "that a fully competitive wholesale market is a mandatory precursor to a finding that section 10(a)(1) is satisfied."

72. Apart from intermodal competition from Cox, Qwest contends that it subject to additional intermodal competition from VoIP and wireless providers, and that it is "appropriate and necessary" for the Commission to consider competition from these sources as well. Because Qwest has not submitted sufficient data concerning the full substitutability of interconnected VoIP and wireless services in its service territory in the Omaha MSA, and because the data submitted do not allow us to further refine our wire center analysis, we do not rely here on intermo-

dal competition from wireless and interconnected VoIP services to rationalize forbearance from unbundling obligations.

* * *

2. Other Requirements of Section 251(c)

* * *

85. *Interconnection-Related Obligations.* We decline to grant Qwest forbearance from the application of sections 251(c)(2), (5) and (6) of the Act, with an exception discussed below. Qwest contends that the Commission should forbear from applying the obligations of section 251(c) that are uniquely imposed on incumbent LECs, because competition in the Omaha MSA has developed to the point where Qwest "is just one of several facilities-based competitors." Qwest in this context is using "facilities-based competitor" to mean a competitor that does not rely exclusively on Qwest's facilities to compete. But while a substantial portion of customers within the 9 wire centers at issue receive service from a Qwest competitor not relying on a Qwest loop, a Qwest switch, or Qwest dedicated transport, *all* of its competitors in the Omaha MSA rely extensively on access to Qwest's network in order to exchange telecommunications traffic. Even Cox, which is the competitive LEC with the most extensive facilities-based coverage in Qwest's territory in the Omaha MSA, depends on Qwest for interconnection, collocation, and reasonable notice of changes in Qwest's network in order to exchange telecommunications traffic in the Omaha MSA. Cox reports that approximately [**REDACTED**] percent of all the traffic that it sends and receives in the Omaha MSA depends on section 251(c)(2) interconnection and collocation—the effectiveness of which depends in part on reasonable notice of network changes. Other competitive LECs, which have less network coverage in this geographic market than Cox, presumably depend even more than Cox on Qwest's satisfaction of its section 251(c) obligations.

* * *

Statement of CHAIRMAN KEVIN J. MARTIN

With this Order, we witness the fruits of the Telecommunications Act of 1996. In the nearly 10 years since the passage of this Act, Cox has become a formidable competitor to Qwest in the Omaha MSA. Accordingly, based on the specific market facts that have been placed before us, we are compelled under the "pro-competitive, deregulatory" framework established by Congress, as well as under section 10's forbearance criteria, to grant Qwest relief from the continued application of legacy regulations.

This Order is significant in two respects. First, it is first time that we have forborne from enforcing unbundling requirements under section 251(c). Second, it is the first time that we have relieved an incumbent

LEC of legacy dominant carrier regulation in the mass market. Cox has made a substantial infrastructure investment in the Omaha MSA and has used these facilities to provide competing telephone services to over a hundred thousand residential and business customers.

This success of intermodal competition warrants the Commission's careful exercise of its forbearance authority. Notably, the relief we grant today is balanced and limited to the areas in which Cox has the most significant facilities presence. For example, we grant unbundling relief only in those wire centers where Cox facilities pass a substantial number of end-user locations served by a particular wire center. In those areas where Cox does not have such an extensive presence, no unbundling relief is granted. Accordingly, I believe this Order strikes the right balance.

Concurring Statement of COMMISSIONERS MICHAEL J. COPPS and JONATHAN S. ADELSTEIN

In today's decision, the Commission grants forbearance from certain unbundling and dominant carrier obligations in areas of the Omaha MSA where a facilities-based carrier has extensively built out its network and taken significant market share from the incumbent wireline provider. While we support the outcome in this Order and believe it is clearly superior to an automatic grant of the underlying petition, we have concerns with the analysis in this decision. As a result, we choose to concur.

The goal of the Telecommunications Act of 1996 is to establish a "pro-competitive, de-regulatory national policy framework." Today's decision lives up to this charge only in part. This item certainly reduces regulation by eliminating some incumbent obligations and demonstrates that the Commission can respond to the dynamic marketplace. But we fall short when it comes to promoting competition. The Commission relies on the intermodal efforts of a single alternative provider—a provider with substantially greater resources than other competitors—to conclude that the Omaha MSA is fully competitive and to carve away both retail and wholesale obligations. While we agree that there is especially strong evidence of competition between the incumbent cable and wireline providers in this market, we believe the statute contemplates more than just competition between a wireline and cable provider—and that both residential and business consumers deserve more.

How much competition is "competition"? As in the broadcast context, the FCC appears to be willing to accept an extremely narrow definition of competition. In Omaha, virtually all of the relevant competition came from one party: Cox Cable. The order redacts actual market shares, but even if Cox had 50% of the market, that would reflect an

HHI of 5,000, well above what antitrust enforcers would consider even mildly competitive. Note that, while the FCC is generous with its numerical criteria for competition, it is less generous with its judgment as to types of competition. In particular, the FCC appears adamant that competition come in the form of *facilities-based* competition. Real competition in local phone markets can only come from those who have their own facilities, since, for those who compete with Qwest through resale of UNEs, Qwest would still control the bottleneck of access to the physical network.

Commissioners Copps and Adelstein seem less enthusiastic about competition from cable. Why? Does it matter in what technical form competition comes? Indeed, given that cable providers have their own network, and thus do not depend on wireline ILECs, aren't they likely to be more powerful CLECs than those that depend on leasing ILEC facilities? What about wireless? The FCC did not consider competition from *wireless* providers because it had no data on wireless substitution in the Omaha market. However, the FCC does have data on wireless substitution nationwide. In its *Twelfth Annual Report and Analysis of Competitive Market Conditions With Respect to Commercial Mobile Services*, 23 FCC Rcd. 2241 (2008), excerpted in the next chapter, the FCC reports the following data on wireless substitution: during the second half of 2006, 11.8 percent of all U.S. adults lived in households with only wireless phones; in the same; one in four adults aged 18–24 years and nearly 30 percent of adults aged 25–29 years lived in households with only wireless telephones. Moreover, the *rate* of substitution has been increasing. Isn't that compelling evidence that wireless service providers can provide market discipline to ILECs?

Forbearance has not (to date) resembled the rush to deregulation that followed the first granted § 271 petition back in 2003. As of early 2008, the FCC had granted one additional petition for forbearance and denied another, largely on the grounds that there was inadequate facilities-based competition in the market. Given that the rollout of facilities-based competitors is both comparatively slow (as compared to the ILECs' ability to alter their own networks to satisfy § 271) and happening at very different speeds in different markets, regulation under the 1996 Act's regime is likely to be a fixture for some time to come.

G. A CONTINUING ROLE FOR ANTITRUST?

One of the most significant events in telecommunications regulation—the divestiture of AT&T—was the product not of communications regulation but of generally applicable antitrust law. In 2004, the Supreme Court had occasion to consider how the 1996 Act affects the role of antitrust law in policing telecommunications markets.

VERIZON COMMUNICATIONS, INC. v. LAW OFFICES OF CURTIS V. TRINKO, LLP

Supreme Court of the United States, 2004.
540 U.S. 398.

JUSTICE SCALIA delivered the opinion of the Court.

The Telecommunications Act of 1996, imposes certain duties upon incumbent local telephone companies in order to facilitate market entry by competitors, and establishes a complex regime for monitoring and enforcement. In this case we consider whether a complaint alleging breach of the incumbent's duty under the 1996 Act to share its network with competitors states a claim under § 2 of the Sherman Act.

I

Petitioner Verizon Communications Inc. is the incumbent local exchange carrier (LEC) serving New York State. Before the 1996 Act, Verizon, like other incumbent LECs, enjoyed an exclusive franchise within its local service area. The 1996 Act sought to "uproo[t]" the incumbent LECs' monopoly and to introduce competition in its place. Central to the scheme of the Act is the incumbent LEC's obligation under 47 U.S.C. § 251(c) to share its network with competitors, including provision of access to individual elements of the network on an "unbundled" basis. § 251(c)(3). New entrants, so-called competitive LECs, resell these unbundled network elements (UNEs), recombined with each other or with elements belonging to the LECs.

* * *

Part of Verizon's UNE obligation under § 251(c)(3) is the provision of access to operations support systems (OSS), a set of systems used by incumbent LECs to provide services to customers and ensure quality. Verizon's interconnection agreement and long-distance authorization each specified the mechanics by which its OSS obligation would be met. As relevant here, a competitive LEC sends orders for service through an electronic interface with Verizon's ordering system, and as Verizon completes certain steps in filling the order, it sends confirmation back through the same interface. Without OSS access a rival cannot fill its customers' orders.

In late 1999, competitive LECs complained to regulators that many orders were going unfilled, in violation of Verizon's obligation to provide access to OSS functions. The PSC and FCC opened parallel investigations, which led to a series of orders by the PSC and a consent decree with the FCC. * * *

Respondent Law Offices of Curtis V. Trinko, LLP, a New York City law firm, was a local telephone service customer of AT&T. The day after Verizon entered its consent decree with the FCC, respondent filed a complaint in the District Court for the Southern District of New York, on behalf of itself and a class of similarly situated customers. See App. 12–33. The complaint, as later amended, *id.*, at 34–50, alleged that Verizon had filled rivals' orders on a discriminatory basis as part of an anticompetitive scheme to discourage customers from becoming or remaining customers of competitive LECs, thus impeding the competitive LECs' ability to enter and compete in the market for local telephone service. * * *

II

To decide this case, we must first determine what effect (if any) the 1996 Act has upon the application of traditional antitrust principles. The Act imposes a large number of duties upon incumbent LECs. * * *

That Congress created these duties, however, does not automatically lead to the conclusion that they can be enforced by means of an antitrust claim. Indeed, a detailed regulatory scheme such as that created by the 1996 Act ordinarily raises the question whether the regulated entities are not shielded from antitrust scrutiny altogether by the doctrine of implied immunity. See, *e.g.*, *United States v. National Assn. of Securities Dealers, Inc.*, 422 U.S. 694 (1975). In some respects the enforcement scheme set up by the 1996 Act is a good candidate for implication of antitrust immunity, to avoid the real possibility of judgments conflicting with the agency's regulatory scheme "that might be voiced by courts exercising jurisdiction under the antitrust laws."

Congress, however, precluded that interpretation. Section 601(b)(1) of the 1996 Act is an antitrust-specific saving clause providing that "nothing in this Act or the amendments made by this Act shall be construed to modify, impair, or supersede the applicability of any of the antitrust laws." 47 U.S.C. § 152, note. This bars a finding of implied immunity. As the FCC has put the point, the saving clause preserves those "claims that satisfy established antitrust standards."

But just as the 1996 Act preserves claims that satisfy existing antitrust standards, it does not create new claims that go beyond existing antitrust standards; that would be equally inconsistent with the saving clause's mandate that nothing in the Act "modify, impair, or supersede the applicability" of the antitrust laws. We turn, then, to whether the activity of which respondent complains violates pre-existing antitrust standards.

III

The complaint alleges that Verizon denied interconnection services to rivals in order to limit entry. If that allegation states an antitrust claim at all, it does so under § 2 of the Sherman Act, which declares that a firm shall not "monopolize" or "attempt to monopolize." It is settled law that this offense requires, in addition to the possession of monopoly power in the relevant market, "the willful acquisition or maintenance of that power as distinguished from growth or development as a consequence of a superior product, business acumen, or historic accident."

United States v. Grinnell Corp., 384 U.S. 563, 570–571 (1966). The mere possession of monopoly power, and the concomitant charging of monopoly prices, is not only not unlawful; it is an important element of the free-market system. The opportunity to charge monopoly prices—at least for a short period—is what attracts "business acumen" in the first place; it induces risk taking that produces innovation and economic growth. To safeguard the incentive to innovate, the possession of monopoly power will not be found unlawful unless it is accompanied by an element of anticompetitive *conduct.*

Firms may acquire monopoly power by establishing an infrastructure that renders them uniquely suited to serve their customers. Compelling such firms to share the source of their advantage is in some tension with the underlying purpose of antitrust law, since it may lessen the incentive for the monopolist, the rival, or both to invest in those economically beneficial facilities. Enforced sharing also requires antitrust courts to act as central planners, identifying the proper price, quantity, and other terms of dealing-a role for which they are ill suited. * * *

The leading case for § 2 liability based on refusal to cooperate with a rival, and the case upon which respondent understandably places greatest reliance, is *Aspen Skiing Co. v. Aspen Highlands Skiing Corp.*, 472 U.S. 585 (1985). The Aspen ski area consisted of four mountain areas. The defendant, who owned three of those areas, and the plaintiff, who owned the fourth, had cooperated for years in the issuance of a joint, multiple-day, all-area ski ticket. After repeatedly demanding an increased share of the proceeds, the defendant canceled the joint ticket. The plaintiff, concerned that skiers would bypass its mountain without some joint offering, tried a variety of increasingly desperate measures to re-create the joint ticket, even to the point of in effect offering to buy the defendant's tickets at retail price. The defendant refused even that. We upheld a jury verdict for the plaintiff, reasoning that "[t]he jury may well have concluded that [the defendant] elected to forgo these short-run benefits because it was more interested in reducing competition ... over the long run by harming its smaller competitor."

Aspen Skiing is at or near the outer boundary of § 2 liability. The Court there found significance in the defendant's decision to cease participation in a cooperative venture. The unilateral termination of a voluntary *(and thus presumably profitable)* course of dealing suggested a willingness to forsake short-term profits to achieve an anticompetitive end. Similarly, the defendant's unwillingness to renew the ticket *even if compensated at retail price* revealed a distinctly anticompetitive bent.

The refusal to deal alleged in the present case does not fit within the limited exception recognized in *Aspen Skiing.* The complaint does not allege that Verizon voluntarily engaged in a course of dealing with its rivals, or would ever have done so absent statutory compulsion. Here, therefore, the defendant's prior conduct sheds no light upon the motivation of its refusal to deal—upon whether its regulatory lapses were prompted not by competitive zeal but by anticompetitive malice. The contrast between the cases is heightened by the difference in pricing behavior. In *Aspen Skiing*, the defendant turned down a proposal to sell at its own retail price, suggesting a calculation that its future monopoly retail price would be higher. Verizon's reluctance to interconnect at the cost-based rate of compensation available under § 251(c)(3) tells us nothing about dreams of monopoly.

The specific nature of what the 1996 Act compels makes this case different from *Aspen Skiing* in a more fundamental way. In *Aspen Skiing*, what the defendant refused to provide to its competitor was a product that it already sold at retail—to oversimplify slightly, lift tickets representing a bundle of services to skiers. * * * In the present case, by contrast, the services allegedly withheld are not otherwise marketed or available to the public. The sharing obligation imposed by the 1996 Act created "something brand new"—"the wholesale market for leasing network elements." The unbundled elements offered pursuant to § 251(c)(3) exist only deep within the bowels of Verizon; they are brought out on compulsion of the 1996 Act and offered not to consumers but to rivals, and at considerable expense and effort. New systems must be designed and implemented simply to make that access possible—indeed, it is the failure of one of those systems that prompted the present complaint.

We conclude that Verizon's alleged insufficient assistance in the provision of service to rivals is not a recognized antitrust claim under this Court's existing refusal-to-deal precedents. This conclusion would be unchanged even if we considered to be established law the "essential facilities" doctrine crafted by some lower courts, under which the Court of Appeals concluded respondent's allegations might state a claim. See generally Areeda, Essential Facilities: An Epithet in Need of Limiting Principles, 58 Antitrust L.J. 841 (1989). We have never recognized such a doctrine, see *Aspen Skiing Co.*, *supra*, and we find no need either to recognize it or to repudiate it here. It suffices for present purposes to note that the indispensable requirement for invoking the doctrine is the unavailability of access to the "essential facilities"; where access exists, the doctrine serves no purpose. Thus, it is said that "essential facility claims should . . . be denied where a state or federal agency has effective power to compel sharing and to regulate its scope and terms." P. Areeda & H. Hovenkamp, Antitrust Law, p. 150, ¶ 773e (2003 Supp.). Respondent believes that the existence of sharing duties under the 1996 Act supports its case. We think the opposite: The 1996 Act's extensive provision for access makes it unnecessary to impose a judicial doctrine of forced access. To the extent respondent's "essential facilities" argument is distinct from its general § 2 argument, we reject it.

IV

Finally, we do not believe that traditional antitrust principles justify adding the present case to the few existing exceptions from the proposition that there is no duty to aid competitors. Antitrust analysis must always be attuned to the particular structure and circumstances of the industry at issue. Part of that attention to economic context is an awareness of the significance of regulation. As we have noted, "careful account must be taken of the pervasive federal and state regulation characteristic of the industry." *United States v. Citizens & Southern Nat. Bank*, 422 U.S. 86, 91 (1975). "[A]ntitrust analysis must sensitively recognize and reflect the distinctive economic and legal setting of the regulated industry to which it applies." *Concord v. Boston Edison Co.*, 915 F.2d 17, 22 (1st Cir. 1990) (Breyer, C.J.) (internal quotation marks omitted).

One factor of particular importance is the existence of a regulatory structure designed to deter and remedy anticompetitive harm. Where such a structure exists, the additional benefit to competition provided by antitrust enforcement will tend to be small, and it will be less plausible that the antitrust laws contemplate such additional scrutiny. Where, by contrast, "[t]here is nothing built into the regulatory scheme which performs the antitrust function," *Silver v. New York Stock Exchange*, 373 U.S. 341, 358 (1963), the benefits of antitrust are worth its sometimes considerable disadvantages. Just as regulatory context may in other cases serve as a basis for implied immunity, it may also be a consideration in deciding whether to recognize an expansion of the contours of § 2.

The regulatory framework that exists in this case demonstrates how, in certain circumstances, "regulation significantly diminishes the likelihood of major antitrust harm." * * *

The regulatory response to the OSS failure complained of in respondent's suit provides a vivid example of how the regulatory regime operates. When several competitive LECs complained about deficiencies in Verizon's servicing of orders, the FCC and PSC responded. The FCC soon concluded that Verizon was in breach of its sharing duties under § 251(c), imposed a substantial fine, and set up sophisticated measurements to gauge remediation, with weekly reporting requirements and specific penalties for failure. The PSC found Verizon in violation of the PAP even earlier, and imposed additional financial penalties and measurements with *daily* reporting requirements. In short, the regime was an effective steward of the antitrust function.

Against the slight benefits of antitrust intervention here, we must weigh a realistic assessment of its costs. Under the best of circumstances, applying the requirements of § 2 "can be difficult" because "the means of illicit exclusion, like the means of legitimate competition, are myriad." Mistaken inferences and the resulting false condemnations "are especially costly, because they chill the very conduct the antitrust laws are designed to protect." The cost of false positives counsels against an undue expansion of § 2 liability. One false-positive risk is that an incumbent LEC's failure to provide a service with sufficient alacrity might have nothing to do with exclusion. Allegations of violations of § 251(c)(3) duties are difficult for antitrust courts to evaluate, not only because they are highly technical, but also because they are likely to be extremely numerous, given the incessant, complex, and constantly changing interaction of competitive and incumbent LECs implementing the sharing and interconnection obligations. *Amici* States have filed a brief asserting that competitive LECs are threatened with "death by a thousand cuts," the identification of which would surely be a daunting task for a generalist antitrust court. Judicial oversight under the Sherman Act would seem destined to distort investment and lead to a new layer of interminable litigation, atop the variety of litigation routes already available to and actively pursued by competitive LECs.

Even if the problem of false positives did not exist, conduct consisting of anticompetitive violations of § 251 may be, as we have concluded with respect to above-cost predatory pricing schemes, "beyond the practical ability of a judicial tribunal to control." Effective remediation of violations of regulatory sharing requirements will ordinarily require continuing supervision of a highly detailed decree. We think that Professor Areeda got it exactly right: "No court should impose a duty to deal that it cannot explain or adequately and reasonably supervise. The problem should be deemed irremedia[ble] by antitrust law when compulsory access requires the court to assume the day-to-day controls characteristic of a regulatory agency." Areeda, 58 Antitrust L. J., at 853. In this case, respondent has requested an equitable decree to "[p]reliminarily and permanently enjoi[n] [Verizon] from providing access to the local loop market ... to [rivals] on terms and conditions that are not as favorable" as those that Verizon enjoys. An antitrust court is unlikely to be an effective day-to-day enforcer of these detailed sharing obligations.

The 1996 Act is, in an important respect, much more ambitious than the antitrust laws. It attempts "*to eliminate the monopolies* enjoyed by the inheritors of AT&T's local franchises." Section 2 of the Sherman Act, by contrast, seeks merely to prevent *unlawful monopolization*. It would be a serious mistake to conflate the two goals. The Sherman Act is indeed the "Magna Carta of free enterprise," but it does not give judges *carte blanche* to insist that a monopolist alter its way of doing business whenever some other approach might yield greater competition. We conclude that respondent's complaint fails to state a claim under the Sherman Act.

Accordingly, the judgment of the Court of Appeals is reversed, and the case is remanded for further proceedings consistent with this opinion.

Not Immune, but Regulated. What, exactly, is the basis for the Court's decision? The 1996 Act's antitrust savings clause means that antitrust is not preempted altogether. That leaves open the question whether, and to what extent, there is any room for antitrust enforcement in the domain covered by the Telecommunications Act. Does *Trinko* say, in effect, there isn't any or is it simply saying that there isn't any for this particular type of claim? The Court does cite "the existence of a regulatory structure designed to deter and remedy anticompetitive harm" as one reason not to read the Sherman Act expansively to cover this kind of refusal to deal. But how is that consistent with either the savings clause or the antitrust cases that eventually led to both the regulation and break-up of AT&T? After *Trinko*, what kind of practices by a regulated ILEC could support an antitrust claim?

The Unessential Essential Facilities Doctrine. Although the Court refuses to recognize or repudiate the "essential facilities" doctrine, it has been recognized by federal Courts of Appeals and District courts in every federal circuit. Virtually all of the cases cite an early Supreme Court decision in *United States v. Terminal Railroad Ass'n of St. Louis*, 224 U.S. 383 (1912) as the origin of the doctrine, and a later case, *Otter Tail Power Co. v. United States*, 410 U.S. 366 (1973) as an illustrative application. Neither of those cases purported to formulate a formal doctrine or specify its parameters, but dozens of lower courts are in agreement about the basic contours of the doctrine. Briefly, the idea of the doctrine is to require monopolists who control an essential input to products or services in downstream markets (which the monopolist also serves[12]) to allow competitors in the downstream market to buy or lease that input on reasonable terms if it is feasible to do so. An influential formulation is that of *MCI Communications Corp. v. AT&T*, 708 F.2d 1081, 1132–33 (7th Cir.1983). We mentioned the case briefly in Chapter 7 in connection with the parallel government antitrust suit that eventually led to the break-up of AT&T. The government's antitrust case also produced an intermediate opinion, prior to the MFJ, which applied the essential facilities doctrine.[13] The *MCI* decision set forth four basic elements of a successful essential facilities claim, which have become canonical for the lower courts:

(1) control of the essential facility by a monopolist;

(2) a competitor's inability practically or reasonably to duplicate the essential facility;

(3) the denial of the use of the facility to a competitor; and

(4) the feasibility of providing the facility.

Although the lower courts have been willing to recognize the theory, they have not been generous in finding these restrictive conditions to be satisfied—a recognition that forced sharing among competitors is excep-

12. The doctrine only applies where the firm having monopoly control over the upstream facility also competes in the downstream market. Thus it is a doctrine designed to prevent the upstream monopolist from extending its monopoly power over the facility into other, competitive markets where the facility is a necessary input to some other service or product.

13. See United States v. AT&T, 524 F.Supp. 1336 (D.D.C.1981) (denying AT&T's motion to dismiss). As in *Trinko*, the essential facility in both the *MCI* and government cases was the local switched network. However, unlike in *Trinko*, the facilities to which competitor access was sought in those cases was general interconnection and access to tariffed services (notably FX and CCSA arrangements); it did not involve access to unbundled components of the network as was the case with the later UNE program.

tional, even where one of the firms has monopoly power. See Glen O. Robinson, *On Refusing to Deal with Rivals*, 87 Corn. L. Rev. 1177 (2002) (discussing the antitrust rules for refusals to deal, for the essential facilities doctrine as a special instance of a duty to deal, and applications to regulated communications). The leading critique of the doctrine is the Areeda article cited by the Court in *Trinko*. See also Abbott B. Lipsky & J. Gregory Sidak, *Essential Facilities*, 51 Stan. L. Rev. 1187 (1999).

While *Trinko* rules out using *antitrust* law to enforce a policy of access to network facilities, it does not preclude the possibility that a *regulator* might use the essential facilities doctrine, or something like it, as a model for mandated access. In *Trinko*, the Court refused to allow antitrust enforcement of forced access because any required sharing of network facilities can be accomplished by FCC rules. That, of course, leaves open the question whether the FCC itself might use the essential facilities doctrine as a framework for its rules. That question was in fact earlier presented. In *AT&T v. Iowa Utilities Board*, 525 U.S. 366 (1999), the Court criticized the FCC's standards for mandating unbundled access as being too unlimited in their scope. In a separate opinion, Justice Breyer, joining that criticism, suggested that the essential facilities doctrine might provide a more limiting standard. *Id.* at 428. In a subsequent court of appeals decision on the same point, Judge Williams similarly suggested using the doctrine for the same limiting purpose. *United States Telecom Ass'n v. FCC*, 290 F.3d 415, 428 & n. 4 (D.C. Cir. 2002). While the FCC acknowledged that the essential facilities doctrine might provide some guidance, it declined to accept it as a formal framework. Instead, the FCC interpreted the Telecommunications Act as calling for a more liberal test of access. *Review of the Section 251 Unbundling Obligations of Incumbent Local Exchange Carriers*, 18 FCC Rcd. 16978 ¶ 107 (2003). As we saw earlier (in particular with the *Covad* decision), the FCC did, under the prodding of the courts, move in the direction of more limited standards, but it has continued to resist using the essential facilities doctrine model. Was it wise to do so? How much difference would it make?[14] Consider, as a test case, the proxy rules for determining whether to require unbundled access to, say, high capacity loop or transport lines—as they were approved in the *Covad* case. If one applied the four criteria of the essential facilities doctrine above, how would it affect those UNE rules?

Remaking the Telephone Monopoly? Over the past two decades the number of Bell Operating Companies has gone from seven BOCs to three; the two largest long distance carriers (AT&T and MCI) and the largest non-Bell carrier (GTE) have been consolidated into the two

14. Canadian competition law recognizes the essential facilities doctrine, and the Canadian Radio-television and Telecommunications Commission (CRTC) has used the doctrine as a framework for its rules regarding unbundled network access. See Telecom Decision, CRTC 2008–17 (March 3 2008) (modifying earlier rules dating back to 1997). However, there is debate in Canada over just how faithfully the CRTC's unbundling rules follow the teachings of the essential facilities doctrine—a debate that would no doubt be raised here if the FCC were to adopt it as a basis for its own regulation.

largest BOCs (AT&T and Verizon). In 2007, two of the four remaining BOCs—AT&T (formerly SBC) and BellSouth—merged, with FCC and Justice Department approval. We will discuss that merger decision in Chapter 11, after we learn more about several aspects of telecommunications markets other than the 1996 Act that affected the FCC's decision to approve the merger.

Chapter 9

MOBILE WIRELESS TELECOMMUNICATIONS

A. INTRODUCTION

Until very recently, telecommunication services were overwhelmingly based on wireline facilities. However, a revolution has been taking place over the course of the past 20 years. Thanks to the development of cellular technology, mobile radio—once confined to commercial and specialized users—is now as ubiquitous as the wireline telephone. Like in so many areas of telecommunications regulation, regulation of this now-ubiquitous technology is an outgrowth of regulation of a much more specialized but similar technology with very different uses.[1]

Wireless mobile telecommunication covers a great variety of uses in aeronautical, maritime and land mobile services, as we noted in Chapter 1. Of these, "land mobile radio" uses have received most of the public's attention and have also generated most of the legal controversy. For that reason we shall focus on the varieties of land mobile use, most notably commercial mobile radio services ("CMRS"), of which the two largest categories are cellular radio and Personal Communications Service ("PCS").

Historically, mobile wireless has been divided into "private" and "common carrier" uses. "Private" use simply denotes service not offered for sale to others; it is mostly incidental to business or public service activities: dispatchers for trucking companies, railroads, taxicabs, public safety (police, fire, etc.). Common carriers (the wireline telcos and a

1. We are concerned here only with mobile wireless, but passing mention should be made of fixed wireless, involving radio transmission between fixed points. Historically, fixed wireless has not been extensively used for consumer services. It has been used in some markets for distributing television signals, though it is fast declining into unimportance. In telecommunications, radio transmissions from fixed stations have been generally limited to intermediate relay and have not been a means of delivering local phone service to end users. In recent years there has been talk of using fixed wireless as an alternative to wireline facilities, but it has not yet emerged as an important mode of delivering end-user services. The explosive growth of mobile wireless on the other hand has in fact emerged as a possible competitive alternative to wireline telecommunications.

number of radio common carriers) provided both paging and radio-telephone services. Traditional radio-telephone was sort of a hybrid service in which a mobile user could communicate via radio with a central location that was tied into the public switched telephone network. Thus, a radio user could effectively interconnect with the telephone network to place (or receive) a telephone call over the radio. Users don't just broadcast willy-nilly; instead, radio-telephone systems use a "trunk radio" design in which users request access to the system, and the system dynamically assigns channels to users on demand. It was notoriously expensive and therefore used by relatively few persons. General public use of mobile communications was limited because the technology simply didn't allow inexpensive, mass use of the spectrum. Development of publicly available mobile wireless service has been a product of technological advances that came to fruition in the 1970s with cellular radio.[2]

B. CELLULAR RADIO AND PCS

1. Evolution of Cellular Radio

Cellular technology was born out of a need to make more effective use of the frequencies allocated to land mobile radio use. Land mobile radio uses had been steadily growing, and both the private radio services and the common carrier services were feeling the pinch of limited frequencies to accommodate the growing use. Pressured by land mobile users (and even more by equipment manufacturers), the FCC in 1974 reallocated additional spectrum in the UHF television band to land mobile, most notably the top 12 UHF television channels (a total of 115 MHz) which had been virtually untouched since they were first allocated to television. The Commission divided the newly reallocated frequencies into three blocks: One block of 40 MHz was set aside for a new common carrier service then in development known as "cellular radio service". A second block of 30 MHz was designated for a new private (non-common carrier) service called specialized mobile radio service ("SMRS") and a third block of 45 MHz was held in reserve for future allocations. At the time, the demand for new frequencies was driven more by private, dispatch radio use than by common carrier radio-

2. Between the conventional radio-telephone and emergence of cellular radio came the phenomenon of citizens band radio ("CB"). CB, intended originally as a general purpose mobile radio, emerged in the late 1970s as a cultural phenomenon. The popularity of CB was the source of great vexation to the FCC. The basic problem was that the FCC attempted initially to license CB the way it licenses other radio uses, but the number of users made this a practical impossibility. Eventually the FCC threw in the towel on efforts to regulate CB, though ironically it did so just as the CB craze was about to disappear. In 1983 the Commission delicensed CB entirely. By that time, however, CB was only a shadow of its former self. CB is still around, but it has lost both its economic importance and its sociological status as a sign of the times. Part of CB's decline can be explained as simply the normal cycle of public fads—think hula hoops and "Tickle Me Elmos." In any event, the CB was doomed with the appearance of cellular telephones, which provide a more diverse form of entertainment—and, of course, utility.

telephone use, but that would change, and the 45 MHz in reserve would eventually be allocated to cellular.

In some respects cellular radio was simply an extension of traditional radio-telephone service. However, that traditional service had long been handicapped by spectrum limitations that had made it a very expensive. The cellular concept was then under development as a means of using radio frequencies more effectively by confining their use to small areas (a "cell") and operating with low-power transmitters, permitting channels to be reused. The illustration below shows the basic design.

Cellular systems function in some ways like a trunked radio, telephone system described above. In fact a cellular system comprised of a single cell is in effect a trunked radiotelephone system. The crucial difference arises when the service area is divided into multiple cells. Each set of cells are allocated a set of frequencies that are used by radiotransmitters operating at low power. The diagram below shows seven different cells, each with a distinct frequency (in reality there would be a group of frequencies in each cell). Using distinct frequencies within the set of cells prevents interference between each cell, using low-power radios prevents interference between each set of cells. Because power output is minimized, frequencies can be reused over the service area, as in the diagram below, in which each of the seven frequencies are reused three times to allow for 21 distinct cells. Increased traffic demand can be accommodated without increasing the number of frequencies by instead dividing the cells into smaller cells, increasing the incidence of frequency reuse. (The cells below are shown to be the same size, but they will vary depending on intensity of traffic. Moreover, the hexagonal shape shown here is purely for modeling purposes. The actual configuration of cells is designed by computers based on terrain features and technical parameters of the system.) The primary advantage of cellular over radio-telephone is the small size of the relevant frequency coverage area, which means that, in addition to the management of frequency reuse, cellular service differs from traditional radio-telephone service by its ability to "hand-off" users as they transit from one cell to another, which is no mean feat.

Cellular Radio

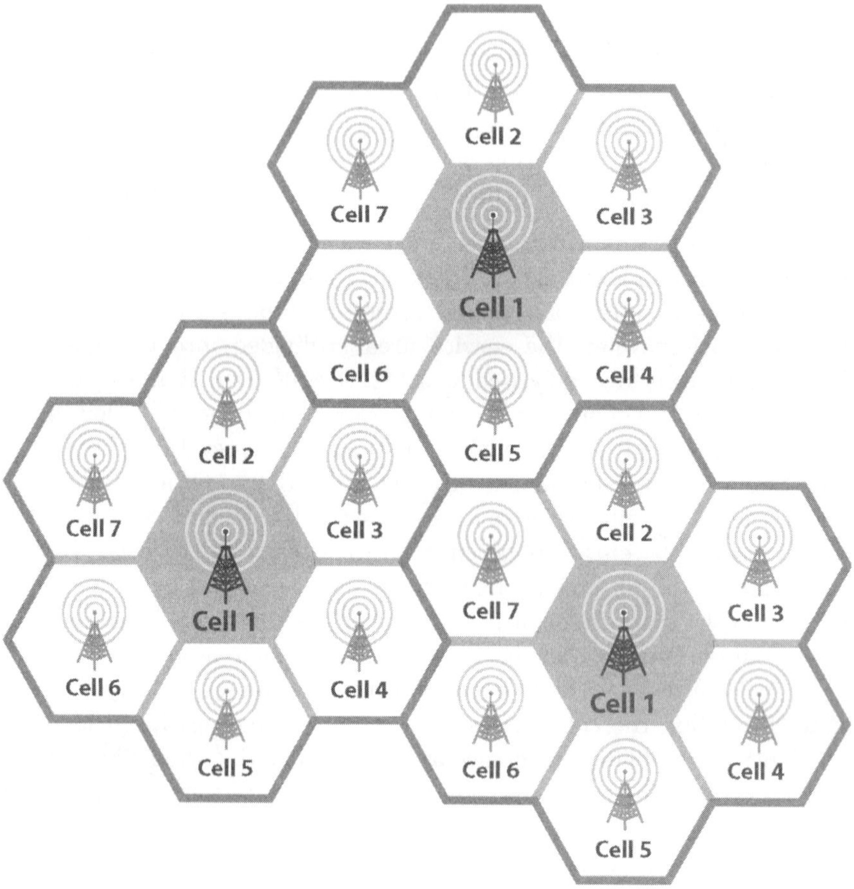

Basically cellular radio operates as follows. A cellular call is initiated by a subscriber when he or she pushes the "send" button on a cellular telephone to place a call. The cellphone emits a radio signal on a specific frequency (channel) and automatically transmits information identifying the subscriber, the specific cellular telephone, and the telephone number the subscriber is trying to reach. Nearby cellular base stations (each consisting of an antenna, transmitter, receiver, and other equipment) receive this signal. One base station sends the call to the nearest mobile telephone switching office, where it is determined, among other things, if the call was placed by a valid subscriber, which base stations will handle the call, and on which of several radio channels the telephone call should be handled. The base station broadcasts information to the subscriber's telephone about which channel the telephone call will be placed on, and ultimately connects the call through the switched telephone network. Each system's cells are connected to each other and to the PSTN by facilities that are either leased from a local telecommunications carrier or are owned and operated by the cellular system itself.

As the call by the subscriber progresses, the base station checks to see if the radio signal remains adequate. If the subscriber moves far enough away from the base station, or if there are obstructing buildings or poor weather conditions, the signal will grow weak. Rather than end the call, the base station hands off the call to a different frequency on another, closer or more suitable, base station, thus allowing the call to continue.

A call from outside the cellular system to a cellular subscriber begins with a caller dialing the telephone number of a cellular subscriber. The network switch recognizes that the exchange is associated with a particular cellular carrier and routes the call to that carrier's network. The cellular network knows, via a database, if the called party's number is a valid subscriber's telephone number. If it is, base stations covering the entire cellular network emit a signal on the designated control channel with the cellular subscriber's unique identifier. If the user has the cellular telephone turned on, the telephone will receive and respond to that signal. From that point on, the call is handled in the same manner as a subscriber-initiated call.

2. Personal Communications Service

The Commission in 1993 created a new category for mobile wireless, the Personal Communications Service ("PCS"). *New Personal Communications Services*, 8 FCC Rcd. 7700 (1993). PCS is not a single service but a collection of distinct services all using digital instead of analog formats. The service is divided into three broad categories, broadband, narrowband, and unlicensed. Broadband services include voice and data service (including Internet access); narrowband is used for paging-like and messaging services; unlicensed PCS includes a variety of services within small areas, such as data networking within office buildings. The main service, PCS broadband, uses the same architecture as the analog cellular systems and provides basically the same functionality to the user, albeit with a digital format that provides better quality of service and more efficient use of radio spectrum (as well as greater security). In fact all of the major cellular providers are now switching to digital.

3. Licensing

Most of the key issues in mobile radio pertain to spectrum and to assigning uses. We have already examined these in Chapter 2. However, there is some additional history that is worth summarizing for the light it sheds on the evolving policies toward mobile radio.

Originally, the FCC intended that cellular radio would be operated as a monopoly; its initial report in 1974 devised a plan that allowed only a single provider per market. The premise was that the service was essentially a natural monopoly and that, in any event, a single system needed the entire block of frequencies that it had allocated (40 MHz) in order to operate efficiently. The decision was viewed with some skepticism but was affirmed by the court in *National Association of Regulatory Utility Commissioners v. FCC*, 525 F.2d 630 (D.C. Cir. 1976). After the successful deployment of experimental cellular systems showed they could operate in 20 MHz bands, the Commission, in 1981, altered its design for cellular service to provide for two systems per market, each operating with 20 MHz. However, the FCC specifically reserved one of the two cellular licenses for the local wireline carrier and the other for a non-wireline carrier for a period of time from the date of the first licensed system (originally the period was 5 years, later reduced to 2). See *MCI Cellular Tel. Co. v. FCC*, 738 F.2d 1322 (D.C. Cir. 1984) (affirming decision).

The FCC's cellular plan would later be criticized for not providing for sufficient competition. However, the number of competitors was more or less fixed by the amount of spectrum made available; according to the best engineering and economic estimates, at least 20 MHz of spectrum was required to support a viable system. With only 40 MHz allocated to the new service, no more than two carriers could be supported. Of course, the Commission might have allocated more spectrum, either by favoring cellular at the expense of other services, like dispatch radio, or by taking a larger chunk of the UHF spectrum from broadcasting. However, cellular telephony at that time was still in the conceptual stage. As mentioned above, the demand for new frequencies was driven primarily by dispatch radio use, and no one foresaw the future of cellular telephony.

As for the two-year set aside, this so-called "head start" was intended to ensure rapid development of the system by providing a period of exclusivity. Part of the reasoning here was that the wireline carriers—AT&T in particular—had both the technological and financial ability to implement cellular systems in what was at the time a very uncertain market for cellular telephony, though perhaps the more compelling reason for the set aside was that it was a means of avoiding the impediments created by the comparative licensing process which we discussed in Chapter 2. The Commission worried that if it held both frequency allocations open for all comers the development of cellular radio would be slowed by the cumbersome comparative hearing process. A wireline set aside solved that problem, since, at that time, there was only one wireline carrier in each market. The Commission acknowledged that the head-start advantage could undermine the competition that the two-per-market policy was intended to promote, but it concluded that the benefits of quick deployment outweighed the harm to competition. See *MCI, supra,* at 1335.

4. Redefining Mobile Radio Services

The Budget Act of 1993 directed the Commission to develop a comprehensive program of classifying and regulating mobile radio. The Budget Act created two broad classifications, "commercial mobile radio services" ("CMRS") and "private mobile radio services" ("PMRS"). The latter were unregulated; the former were classified (generally) as common carrier services, but the Commission was given discretion to "forbear" from traditional common carrier regulation if it could show that it was consistent with the public interest. States were preempted from regulating either service, except by approval of the FCC.

In response to this new statutory mandate, the Commission classified as CMRS all services that offer interconnected service to the general public (or a very substantial segment thereof). This includes all cellular systems and broadband PCS systems and SMRS to the extent they offer services to the general public. The reclassification of SMRS is a somewhat ironic twist given that the Commission originally set up these systems as a private radio service in order to provide a more flexible kind of dispatch service to compete with the radio common carriers ("RCCs"). However, over time SMR systems were acquired and consolidated by a company named Fleet Call, which later became Nextel and is now part of Sprint-Nextel. In this way, the SMR systems were molded into a public, switched network service that is essentially the same as cellular/PCS.

In the early years it was unclear whether the new mobile wireless systems would be competitive with wireline. Certainly the FCC's initial assumption in the 1970s was that mobile wireless would be just a supplementary service. That appears to have been AT&T's assumption as well. In 1984, when AT&T was broken up, its own reorganization plan gave all of its wireless operations to the spun-off BOCs on the assumption that it was an extension of local wireline service. In hindsight, it now seems so clear that mobile wireless was not just the next generation of CB radio, it was the next generation of POTS.There are now more cellphones in use than landline telephones, and the number continues to increase. At present trend rates in a few years the only persons without a cellphone will be very young children and the old order Amish.[4] The following excerpt on the status of competition in CMRS gives a current overview of the industry.

TWELFTH ANNUAL REPORT AND ANALYSIS OF COMPETITIVE MARKET CONDITIONS WITH RESPECT TO COMMERCIAL MOBILE SERVICES

Federal Communications Commission, 2008.
23 FCC Rcd. 2241.

BY THE COMMISSION:

* * *

Mobile Telephone Subscribers

• At the end of 2006, there were 241.8 million mobile telephone subscribers in the United States, up from 213 million at the end of 2005.

4. Actually we are pretty much there already, statistically speaking. As indicated in the following report, approximately 80 percent of the population had a cellphone at the end of 2006. Eighty percent of the population accounts for all persons over the age of 14 in that year.

• The additional 28.8 million subscribers represent the largest absolute yearly increase in the number of subscribers ever.

• The nationwide mobile penetration rate at year end 2006 rose to approximately 80 percent of the approximately 300 million people in the United States.

* * *

International Comparisons

• The U.S. mobile penetration rate is now, for the first time, on par with those in Japan and part of Western Europe.

• U.S. mobile subscribers lead the world in average voice usage by a wide margin, with Western European subscribers averaging 150 minutes and Japanese subscribers averaging 145 minutes, compared to an average of over 700 minutes in the U.S.

• The percentage of mobile subscribers who use their cellphones for web browsing was slightly higher in the United States than in Western Europe, and there were broad similarities in the types of information accessed by American and Western European mobile subscribers.

• Mobile calls were significantly less expensive on a per minute basis in the United States than in Western Europe (where RPM averaged $0.20 in the last quarter of 2006) and Japan ($0.26).

Wireless–Wireline Competition

• During the second half of 2006, 11.8 percent of U.S. adults lived in households with only wireless phones, up from 7.8 percent in the second half of 2005, and triple the percentage (3.5 percent) in the second half of 2003.

• As of the same period, one in four adults aged 18–24 years lived in households with only wireless telephones, and nearly 30 percent of adults aged 25–29 years lived in wireless-only households.

III. Mobile Telecommunications Market Structure

* * *

B. Overview of Service Providers

1. Facilities-Based Mobile Telephone Providers

18. As of year-end 2006, there were four mobile telephone operators in the United States that analysts typically describe as "nationwide": AT&T Inc. ("AT&T") (formerly known as Cingular Wireless), Sprint Nextel Corp. ("Sprint Nextel"), T-Mobile USA ("T-Mobile"), and Verizon Wireless, LLC ("Verizon Wireless"). When an operator is described as being nationwide, it does not necessarily mean that the operator's license areas, service areas, or pricing plans cover the entire land area of the United States. The four mobile telephone carriers that analyst reports typically describe as nationwide all offer facilities-based service in at least some portion of the western, mid-western, and eastern United States. A map of the combined coverage areas of these four

operators can be found in Appendix B. In addition, each of the four national operators has networks covering at least 235 million people (out of 303 million), while the next largest provider covers fewer than 80 million people. In addition to the nationwide operators, there are a number of large regional players, including: Alltel Corp. ("Alltel"), which covers 79 million POPs; Leap Wireless ("Leap"), which covers 48 million POPs; and United States Cellular Corp. ("US Cellular"), which covers 41 million POPs. Moreover, many regional and smaller providers are able to offer pricing plans with nationwide coverage through roaming agreements with other providers.

* * *

2. Resale/MVNO Providers

21. Resellers purchase airtime from facilities-based providers and resell service to the public for profit. Many resellers today are often referred to as MVNOs (Mobile Virtual Network Operators). One commenter argued that "[MVNOs] present even more competition to traditional facilities-based carriers. MVNOs target niche markets by packaging resold airtime with demographic-specific content and features.... MVNOs distinguish themselves via content, but like facilities-based providers, they experiment with a number of business models, such as pre-paid and unlimited plans, some even provide ways for customers to support their favorite charity through monthly usage while receiving information about the cause." According to information provided to the FCC in its ongoing local competition and broadband data gathering program, the resale sector accounted for 7 percent of all mobile telephone subscribers, or 15 million subscribers, at the end of June 2006. Similarly, one analyst estimated that there were 15.1 million wireless subscribers receiving service from a resale provider at the end of 2006, up from 13.4 million customers at the end of 2005.

* * *

3. Broadband Data Providers

25. In addition to the voice and data services offered by mobile telephone providers, other providers offer or plan to offer mobile or portable wireless broadband services using Broadband Radio Service/Educational Broadband Service ("BRS/EBS") or Wireless Communications Systems ("WCS") spectrum.

26. Clearwire Corporation ("Clearwire") offers portable wireless high-speed Internet access and Voice-over-Internet Protocol ("VoIP") services to consumers using spectrum in the 2.5 GHz BRS/EBS band. As of June 2007, the company had launched broadband service in 39 markets, mainly smaller towns and cities, covering approximately 10 million people in portions of 13 U.S. states. In addition, several small wireless broadband providers use BRS/EBS spectrum licenses to offer fixed or portable wireless broadband services. These providers include, for example, Solo Direct Connect in Quad-Cities, IA; Plateau Telecom-

munications in New Mexico and Texas; Info–Link.net in west central Minnesota; Evertek in Iowa; SpeedNet in Michigan; Gryphon Wireless in Kearny, NE; W.A.T.C.H. TV in Lima, OH; BeamSpeed in Yuma, AZ; and Digital Bridge Communications in Rexburg, ID. AT&T is using its 2.3 GHz WCS spectrum licenses to offer fixed wireless broadband Internet access service in eight U.S. markets, including Juneau, AK.

4. Mobile Video Providers

27. Certain wireless licensees have been developing and launching networks dedicated to delivering one-way, IP-based, broadcast or multicast video programming to mobile telephone customers. Because these networks are unidirectional (downlink only), the video services are sold to end users through mobile telephone operators and rely on the mobile telephone operators' networks for any uplink communications. In addition, as currently offered, subscribers must use a device that is compatible with the mobile television network in order to receive programming.

* * *

5. Narrowband Data Providers

31. Several wireless data providers offer messaging and other narrowband mobile data services to enterprise customers using paging and narrowband PCS networks and spectrum. For instance, USA Mobility is the largest U.S. paging company and offers traditional paging and two-way messaging, among other wireless services, to enterprise customers. [FN59] In addition, Space Data Corp. ("Space Data") provides commercial telemetry services across the south-central United States to energy and other industrial companies.

6. Mobile Satellite Providers

32. As discussed in detail in Section VIII of this report, the commercial MSS industry in the United States is currently comprised of five service providers operating in MSS-designated frequency bands, with satellite platforms of differing orbital configurations, and offering multiple products including voice and data services in fixed and mobile environments to a variety of terminal types. The five MSS providers are Globalstar, Inmarsat pic ("Inmarsat"), Iridium Satellite LLC ("Iridium"), MSV, and Orbcomm Inc. ("Orbcomm").

C. Horizontal Concentration

* * *

1. Number of Mobile Telephone Competitors

* * *

37. According to our analysis of American Roamer's July 2007 coverage data of mobile telephone providers, 280 million people, or 99.8 percent of the total U.S. population, have one or more different operators (cellular, PCS, and/or digital SMR) offering mobile telephone service

in the census blocks in which they live. These blocks make up 76 percent of the total land area of the United States (including Alaska), reflecting the nation's uneven population distribution. As one analyst noted: "U.S. carriers have a much more challenging environment in which to build networks. Population density is a mere 50 POPs per square mile compared to an average of 290 per mile in Europe and 370–400 per mile in major European markets like the U.K. and Germany." Based on our definition of rural, roughly 61 million people, or 21 percent of the US population, live in rural counties. These counties comprise 3.1 million square miles, or 86 percent of the geographic area of the U.S. In sum, approximately 79 percent of the U.S. population lives on 14 percent of the land, while 21 percent live on the remaining 86 percent of the land.

* * *

44. As of July 2007, 280 million people, or 98 percent of the total U.S. population, have three or more different operators (cellular, PCS, and/or digital SMR) offering mobile telephone service in the counties in which they live. Roughly 267 million people, or 94 percent of the U.S. population, live in counties with four or more mobile telephone operators competing to offer service.

* * *

E. Entry Conditions and Potential Barriers to Entry

70. Market concentration is necessary but not sufficient for unilateral or coordinated anti-competitive behavior to occur. If entry into a market is easy, then entry or the threat of entry may prevent incumbent operators from exercising market power, either collectively or unilaterally, even in highly concentrated markets. The ease or difficulty of entry generally depends on the nature and significance of entry barriers. Barriers to entry in the mobile telecommunications market may include government regulation of access to spectrum and various non-regulatory entry barriers such as economies of scale. In the following sections, we first address access to spectrum, and then discuss potential non-regulatory barriers to entry.

1. Spectrum Access

71. In this section we first discuss the impact of the Commission's spectrum management policies on entry conditions in the mobile telecommunications market. We then provide an analysis of the outcomes of recent auctions, highlighting the growing number of licensees with near nationwide spectrum footprints. Finally, we identify and discuss the various spectrum bands that can be used for the provision of CMRS.

a. Spectrum Policy and Entry Conditions

72. Government control of spectrum allocation and assignment has the potential to create a barrier to entry into markets for mobile communications services by limiting the amount of spectrum allocated to CMRS and by requiring providers to obtain a government-issued license

in order to use such spectrum for the provision of CMRS. However, the Commission has helped to reduce any potential entry-limiting effects of government-controlled spectrum allocation and assignment through various policies. First, as discussed in greater detail below, the Commission has progressively increased the amount of spectrum available for the provision of CMRS. For example, the allocation of 120 megahertz of spectrum to broadband PCS and the assignment of broadband PCS spectrum licenses through auction ended the cellular duopoly by facilitating the entry of new mobile telephone service providers. More recently, the auction of licenses for spectrum allocated to AWS raised the total amount of spectrum available for CMRS by an additional 90 megahertz. Moreover, the current transition of the BRS/EBS spectrum band and the upcoming auction of commercial spectrum in the 700 MHz band will further increase the amount of spectrum available for CMRS. The impact of the AWS auction, BRS/EBS transition, and 700 MHz band on spectrum-related entry barriers is analyzed in the following section.

* * *

c. Spectrum Bands Potentially Available for Terrestrial CMRS

77. Currently, mobile telephone operators primarily use three types of spectrum licenses to provide mobile voice and, in most cases, mobile data services: cellular, broadband PCS, and SMR. Initially, the Commission authorized up to eight different mobile telephone licenses (two cellular and six broadband PCS) in every geographical area of the country. In addition, there are other bands—including, 700 MHz, 1710–1755/2110–2155 MHz (AWS-1), 2500–2690 MHz (BRS/EBS), 2.3 GHz (WCS), 1670–1675 MHz, and 901–902 MHz (Narrowband PCS)—that are licensed under the Commission's flexible Part 27 or Part 24 rules and can be used to provide CMRS services. Under Commission rules, many licensees may disaggregate (divide the spectrum into smaller amounts of bandwidth) or partition (divide the license into smaller geographical areas) their licenses, or both, to other entities. Many licensees hold more than one license in a particular market. We discuss in more detail below spectrum bands potentially available for terrestrial CMRS. Band plan diagrams for each spectrum band depict where the frequencies are located. Spectrum described in this section may be used for a variety of CMRS products including narrowband data services as well as mobile telephony, broadband data and mobile video services. In addition to the 643 megahertz of terrestrial spectrum described in this section, there is an additional 157.7 megahertz of mobile satellite spectrum available for CMRS voice and data services.

* * *

(i) Cellular

78. The Commission began licensing commercial cellular providers in 1982 and completed licensing the majority of operators by 1991. The Commission divided the United States and its possessions into 734 cellular market areas ("CMAs"), including 305 Metropolitan Statistical

Areas ("MSAs"), 428 Rural Service Areas ("RSAs"), and a market for the Gulf of Mexico. Two cellular systems were licensed in each market area. The Commission designated 50 megahertz of spectrum in the 800 MHz frequency band for the two competing cellular systems in each market (25 megahertz for each system). Initially, cellular systems offered service using analog technology, but today most of the service offered using cellular spectrum is digital.

* * *

(ii) Broadband PCS

79. Broadband PCS is similar to cellular service, except that broadband PCS systems operate in different spectrum bands and have been designed from the beginning to use a digital format. Broadband PCS licenses have been assigned through auction, beginning in 1995. The Commission has set aside the spectrum between 1850 MHz and 1990 MHz for broadband PCS. This spectrum includes 120 megahertz used for mobile telephone services, divided originally into three blocks of 30 megahertz each (blocks A, B, and C) and three blocks of 10 megahertz each (blocks D, E, and F). Two of the 30 megahertz blocks (A and B blocks) are assigned on the basis of 51 Major Trading Areas ("MTAs"). One of the 30 megahertz blocks (C block) and all three of the 10 megahertz blocks are assigned on the basis of 493 Basic Trading Areas ("BTAs").

* * *

(iii) SMR

80. The Commission first established SMR in 1979 to provide for land mobile communications on a commercial basis. The Commission initially licensed spectrum in the 800 and 900 MHz bands for this service, in non-contiguous bands, on a site-by-site basis. The Commission has since licensed additional SMR spectrum through auctions. In total, the Commission has licensed 19 megahertz of SMR spectrum, plus an additional 7.5 megahertz of spectrum that is available for SMR as well as other services. While Commission policy permits flexible use of this spectrum, including the provision of paging, dispatch, mobile voice, mobile data, facsimile, or combinations of these services, the primary use for SMR traditionally was dispatch services. With the development of digital technologies that increased spectral efficiency, SMR providers such as Sprint Nextel (on its iDEN network) and SouthernLINC Wireless, a unit of energy concern Southern Company, became more significant competitors in mobile telephony, while also maintaining dispatch functionality as a part of their service offerings. Furthermore, in apparent response to the dispatch functionality of SMR services, many cellular and broadband PCS providers now offer push-to-talk ("FIT") functionality on their networks, including Verizon Wireless, AT&T, and Alltel. SMR spectrum is also used for certain data-only networks.

* * *

(iv) 700 MHz Bands

82. The 698–806 MHz band (the "700 MHz band") is being reclaimed from use by broadcast services in connection with the transition of the analog television service to digital television ("DTV"). The Digital Television Transition and Public Safety Act of 2005 ("DTV Act") set a firm deadline of February 17, 2009 for the 700 MHz band spectrum to be cleared of analog transmissions and made available for public safety and commercial services as part of the DTV transition. The DTV Act established two specific statutory deadlines for the auction of recovered analog spectrum in the 700 MHz band: (1) the auction must begin no later than January 28, 2008; and (2) the auction proceeds must be deposited in the Digital Television Transition and Public Safety Fund by June 30, 2008. Congress also extended the Commission's auction authority to September 30, 2011. This spectrum is being made available for wireless services, including public safety and commercial services. Although the DTV Act established a date certain for the DTV transition, portions of the 700 MHz band are currently encumbered by television broadcasters, and may remain so until the end of the transition. Nevertheless, there are substantial portions of the band that are not so encumbered and are available for immediate use by new licensees.

* * *

(v) Advanced Wireless Services

85. U.S. mobile providers have the flexibility to deploy advanced wireless technologies, including those commonly called Third Generation or "3G," that allow them to offer high-speed mobile data services using their existing CMRS spectrum. To further the goal of promoting the deployment of advanced services, the Commission has made efforts to allocate and license additional spectrum suitable for offering AWS. As noted in the Eleventh Report, in 2002 the Commission, together with the National Telecommunications and Information Administration ("NTIA"), allocated 90 megahertz of spectrum in the 1710–1755 and 2110–2155 MHz bands that can be used to offer advanced wireless services, including 3G services.

* * *

IV. Provider Conduct in the Mobile Telecommunications Market

111. A concentrated market, in conjunction with significant entry barriers, may lessen competition in the market for commercial mobile services in two distinct ways. First, it may increase the likelihood that a group of competing providers will successfully engage in coordinated interaction aimed at raising prices and lowering output. Second, it may enable an individual provider to profitably raise price and lower output unilaterally. However, neither coordinated interaction nor unilateral action to lessen competition is a necessary consequence of market concentration and entry barriers. For example, unilateral or coordinated action to lessen competition may be thwarted or undermined by the

presence of one or more maverick providers who have the ability and incentive to expand sales by undercutting the prices of rivals, offering innovative service packages and engaging in aggressive advertising and promotional campaigns. The analysis of provider conduct thus focuses on whether incumbent carriers, given the prevailing market structure, engage in intense price and non-price rivalry or instead compete in a less aggressive manner.

A. Price Rivalry

1. Developments in Mobile Telephone Pricing Plans

112. The continued rollout of differentiated pricing plans also indicates a competitive marketplace. In the mobile telephone sector, we observe independent pricing behavior, in the form of continued experimentation with varying pricing levels and structures, for varying service packages, with various handsets and policies on handset pricing. Today all of the nationwide operators, and many smaller operators, offer some version of a national rate pricing plan in which customers can purchase a bucket of minutes to use on a nationwide or nearly nationwide network without incurring roaming or long-distance charges. A more recent example is the introduction and spread of "family plan" packages, in which subscribers sign up for two lines and then have the option of adding additional lines at reduced prices, with all lines sharing the available minutes on the plan jointly. As noted in the *Tenth Report*, all the nationwide carriers also offer some version of a family plan.

113. More recently, a number of operators have been experimenting with "unlimited" calling options. As discussed in the Eleventh Report, some U.S. providers, including Alltel ("My Circle") and T-Mobile ("myFaves"), allow subscribers unlimited free calling to and from a small number of designated numbers, regardless of wireline or wireless carrier. Other providers offer plans that provide for free calls only to customers who use the same wireless provider ("on-net" mobile-to-mobile options). A number of smaller and regional carriers, like Leap and MetroPCS, have been offering unlimited local calling plans for years. Now, first among the nationwide carriers, Sprint Nextel has begun offering unlimited calling plans, for a limited time, in select markets. As of May 2007, Sprint Nextel's bundled plan, Unlimited Access Pack—consisting of unlimited wireless voice, text and data service—was available to residents of the Twin Cities, Philadelphia, San Francisco and Tampa, FL, for $120 per month. The same bundle with unlimited broadband access (via network cards) is offered for $150 per month.

114. While a relatively small number of users subscribe to unlimited calling plans today, one analyst predicts that as many as 20 percent of U.S. wireless users could move to such plans by 2010. Other analysts are less optimistic. One analyst pointed out that several carriers—including Alltel and US Cellular—have experimented with unlimited plans in the

past, but all have eliminated them due to "network capacity, repricing of the base, and ARPU cannibalization issues."

* * *

VI. Mobile Telecommunications Market Performance

* * *

A. Pricing Levels and Trends

1. Pricing Trends

a. Mobile Telephony

195. Wide variations in the non-price terms and features of wireless service plans make it difficult to characterize the price of mobile telephone service, and consequently it is difficult to identify sources of information that track mobile telephone prices in a comprehensive manner. As documented in previous reports, there is ample evidence of a sharp decline in mobile telephone prices in the period since the launch of PCS service. During 2006, however, pricing has been relatively stable, due in part to, as one analyst characterized it, "already very low pricing." However, one analyst saw evidence of more aggressive discounting: "Already, the price per minute is off 10% the past year, 28% over the past two years and 40% over the past three years."

196. Of the three indicators of mobile telephone pricing examined here, one showed the cost of mobile telephone service fell in 2006, another showed no change, and a third showed an increase.

197. According to one economic research and consulting firm, Econ One, mobile telephone prices in the 25 largest U.S. cities increased 5.6 percent in 2006. The average cost of monthly service—which was calculated across four typical usage plans (200, 500, 800 and 1100 minutes)—increased from $44.90 in December 2005 to $47.42 in December 2006.

198. Another source of price information is the cellular telephone services component of the Consumer Price Index ("Cellular CPI") produced by the United States Department of Labor's Bureau of Labor Statistics ("BLS"). Cellular CPI data is published on a national basis only. From 2005 to 2006, the annual Cellular CPI decreased by about 0.6 percent while the overall CPI increased by 3.2 percent. The Cellular CPI has declined 35 percent since December 1997, when BLS began tracking it.

The 700 MHz Auction. Over time, there has been not only an explosion in demand for mobile wireless voice services, but there has also been an explosion in the number of different services that mobile wireless can be used for. Today, CMRS is frequently used for sending email, surfing the World Wide Web, receiving turn-by-turn directions, downloading music, and watching television. With the increased use of spectrum has come increased demand for more. The nationwide switch from analog to digital television (discussed briefly in Chapter 5), has freed up a tremendous amount of spectrum, spectrum that the FCC is free to license—through auction—to CMRS users.

The 700 MHz auction is notable in three respects: First, the auction was major, in terms of the total amount of spectrum up for auction (60 MHz), the size of the individual blocks up for auction (up to 22 MHz), and the ability to aggregate the many geographical licenses into "packages" of virtually nationwide coverage, something that is particularly important for an operator seeking to provide a ubiquitous, nationwide offering. Second, the auction received considerable attention because the FCC decided to impose so-called "open access" rules on one of the larger blocks of spectrum, rules that would end the practice of cell phone operators requiring use of their own devices on the network. We will address the open access rules in greater detail in the next chapter. Third, the FCC chose to impose a 700 MHz Public/Private Partnership on a different block of spectrum. Although the FCC saw the 700 MHz auction as a way to improve CMRS, the politically important issue of radio spectrum for public safety organizations also intruded itself into the auction. The idea was to license one block of the spectrum to a private entity that would both use it for commercial purposes and organize (and make available) the spectrum for use by public safety organizations—essentially to piggyback the development of a public safety radio network on a privately operated commercial network. That part of the auction plan failed. Although the 22 MHz of spectrum subject to the open access rules was auctioned for a total of almost $4.8 billion, the highest bid for the 10 MHz of spectrum subject to the public/private partnership was roughly 10% of that figure. That bid did not meet the reservation price and consequently that license was not sold. As of this writing, the FCC has not yet decided what it will do in response.

The big "winners" in the auction were Verizon and AT&T, who each purchased licenses adequate to establish new, nearly national networks.

Even though the 10 MHz subject to the public/private partnership did not sell, the other 50 MHz of spectrum netted the U.S. Treasury approximately $19 billion. Not a bad haul considering the government was selling neither land nor chattel but rather a "property" of electromagnetic radiation.

5. Regulating CMRS

As we noted above, CMRS providers are classified as common carrier services and as such subject to the array of common carrier obligations specified in Title II. However, Congress expected that the new mobile wireless services would be more competitive than was then the case for local wireline telecommunications providers and made provision accordingly. It specifically gave the FCC authority to forbear from enforcing certain Title II obligations if it found they were not necessary to protect consumers and were otherwise in the public interest. 47 U.S.C. § 332(c)(1)(A). It also forbade all state regulation of rates and services except where they can show, on petition to the FCC, that market conditions are such as to require regulation in order to protect consumers. 47 U.S.C. § 332(c)(3)(A). Congress did specifically preserve the authority of local zoning officials to regulate the placement and construction of personal wireless service facilities (i.e. cell phone towers), although there are limits on the discretion that local zoning authorities may exercise. Most importantly, they may not deny the construction of a tower if doing so has "the effect of prohibiting the provision of personal wireless services." See generally 47 U.S.C. § 332(c)(7)(B). The effective prohibition standard of § 332(c)(7) has been the source of substantial litigation as carriers seek to erect towers and localities deny permission, seeking to keep their backyards free from the blight of cell phone towers. The various United States Courts of Appeals have applied a variety of standards. In the Fourth Circuit, in order to prevail against a local zoning authority, the applicant has to show that the denial means that there are *no* wireless providers in a particular location; in the Ninth it only requires that the denial means that *applicant* cannot provide service in the particular location (even if others can) and their proposal is the least intrusive given the zoning authority's own rules. Others fall in between.

With respect to state preemption, several of the larger states have petitioned the FCC for permission to regulate; they have been uniformly denied. Thus, except for local zoning matters, all regulatory authority for wireless is centralized in the FCC. It is an interesting contrast to the shared regulatory authority for local wireline service. Undoubtedly it reflects the both changes in the understanding of what constitutes "interstate commerce" since the 1934 Act and that, in 1993, Congress foresaw robust competition in wireless service that it did not foresee when it established the line between federal regulation of interstate and state regulation of intrastate wireline service. It also reflects the fact that, in 1993, mobile wireless still was seen largely as a supplement to wireline, not a substitute for it. As to its own jurisdiction, the Commission has forborne from many Title II obligations, notably the requirement for filing of tariffs and the obligation to allow resale. But it has retained the basic obligations of § 201 and § 202 to provide service on a non-discriminatory basis to all customers, as well as certain other obligations, such as a duty of interconnection with other carriers. The following excerpt gives more detail about the scope of regulation/forbearance. Note that this case involves not only § 332(c) but also a more general forbearance provision of the later Telecommunications Act of 1996, codified at 47 U.S.C § 160 (§ 10 in the original statute), which we discussed in the last chapter.

FORBEARANCE FOR BROADBAND PERSONAL COMMUNICATIONS SERVICES
Memorandum Opinion and Order and Notice of Proposed Rulemaking

Federal Communications Commission, 1998.
13 FCC Rcd. 16857.

BY THE COMMISSION:

* * *

III. BACKGROUND

7. The Commission derives its authority to forbear from applying regulations or provisions of the Act from sections 332(c)(1)(A) and 10 of the Act. Section 332(c)(1)(A) provides the Commission with the authority to forbear from enforcing most Title II obligations, but only as to providers of commercial mobile radio service (CMRS). Section 10 provides the Commission with authority to forbear from the application of virtually any regulation or any provision of the Act to a telecommunications carrier or telecommunications service, or a class of carriers or services.

8. The CMRS marketplace in which broadband PCS providers compete is substantially less regulated and more competitive than most telecommunications markets. In 1993, Congress forbade state and local governments from regulating the entry of CMRS providers or the rates charged for CMRS, unless a state successfully petitioned for authority to regulate CMRS rates by showing that market conditions fail to protect subscribers adequately from unjust and unreasonable rates or rates that are unjustly or unreasonably discriminatory, or that such market conditions exist and a CMRS offering is a replacement for land line telephone exchange service for a substantial portion of the telephone land line exchange service within that state. The following year, the Commission forbore under section 332(c)(1)(A) from requiring CMRS providers to comply with the tariff filing obligations of section 203, the domestic market entry and market exit requirements of section 214, and several other provisions of Title II. The Commission also denied the petitions of several states for authority to regulate rates under section 332(c)(3). Taken together, these actions have substantially relieved CMRS providers from the most burdensome aspects of common carrier regulation. We believe these deregulatory actions have contributed significantly to the impressive growth of competition in CMRS markets. As we have recently found, substantial progress has been made towards a truly competitive mobile telephone marketplace, resulting in lower prices and more attractive service offerings for consumers.

* * *

10. The Commission has also had several opportunities to apply section 10 during the two years since the 1996 Act became law. For

example, in the earliest exercise of its section 10 authority, the Commission determined to forbear from requiring or allowing nondominant interexchange carriers to file tariffs pursuant to section 203 of the Act for their interstate, domestic, interexchange services. The Commission found that tariffing in this market was not necessary to ensure against unjust and unreasonable or unjustly or unreasonably discriminatory charges or to protect consumers, and that complete detariffing would be in the public interest because it would "enhance competition among providers of [interstate] services, promote competitive market conditions, and achieve other objectives that are in the public interest." * * * The Commission has also declined to forbear from applying its part 36 jurisdictional separations rules to incumbent LECs subject to its price cap rules, reasoning that forbearance alone would not satisfy the section 10 criteria and that replacing the separations rules with a different apportionment regime, as the petitioner requested, was appropriately addressed in a rulemaking proceeding. * * *.

11. PCIA [Personal Communications Industry Association] now requests that, pursuant to section 10 of the Act, we forbear, with respect to all broadband PCS licensees, from enforcing the following provisions: sections 201 and 202 of the Act (carriers must furnish services upon reasonable request, carriers must establish physical connections with other carriers in accordance with orders of the Commission, and carriers' rates and practices must be just, reasonable, and non-discriminatory), section 214 of the Act (carriers must obtain Commission authorization to provide international telecommunications services), section 226 of the Act (operator service providers and aggregators, with respect to public phones, must comply with certain requirements), and section 20.12(b) of our rules (certain CMRS carriers must not unreasonably restrict the resale of telecommunications services). PCIA argues that forbearance from enforcement of these provisions is warranted under the three-pronged test of section 10 of the Act.

12. Under section 10, we must forbear from applying any regulation or provision of the Act to a telecommunications carrier or service, or class of telecommunications carriers or services, in any or some of its geographic markets if a three-pronged test is met. Specifically, section 10 requires forbearance, notwithstanding section 332(c)(1)(A), if the Commission determines that:

(1) enforcement of such regulation or provision is not necessary to ensure that the charges, practices, classifications, or regulations by, for, or in connection with that telecommunications carrier or telecommunications service are just and reasonable and are not unjustly or unreasonably discriminatory;

(2) enforcement of such regulation or provision is not necessary for the protection of consumers; and

(3) forbearance from applying such provision or regulation is consistent with the public interest.

13. On June 2, 1997, the Wireless Telecommunications Bureau issued a public notice seeking comment on the Petition. Twenty-two parties filed comments on the Petition and thirteen parties filed reply comments. On May 21, 1998, we extended until June 8, 1998, the date on which the Petition would be deemed granted in the absence of a decision that it failed to meet the standards for forbearance under section 10(a). On June 5, 1998, we further extended this deadline until June 23, 1998.

IV. Discussion

A. Sections 201 and 202

14. *Background.* Section 201 of the Act mandates that carriers engaged in the provision of interstate or foreign communication service provide service upon reasonable request, and that all charges, practices, classifications, and regulations for such service be just and reasonable. Section 201 also empowers the Commission to require physical connections with other carriers, to establish through routes, and to determine appropriate charges for such actions. Section 202 states that it is unlawful for any common carrier to make any unjust or unreasonable discrimination in charges, practices, classifications, regulations, facilities, or services, or to make or give any undue or unreasonable preference or advantage to any person or class of persons. Section 332 of the Act requires that the Commission treat all CMRS providers as common carriers for purposes of the Communications Act, except to the extent the Commission determines to forbear from applying certain provisions of Title II. Although section 10 forbearance contains no such restriction, it is notable that, for purposes of forbearance under section 332, the Commission "may not specify any provision of section 201, 202, or 208." PCIA requests section 10 forbearance from the application of sections 201 and 202 of the Act to broadband PCS providers on the ground that market forces, including the competitive presence of other CMRS providers, are sufficient to ensure that rates are just, reasonable and not unjustly discriminatory. PCIA states that forbearance will promote the public interest by enhancing competition, providing consumers with increased choices, driving prices downward, and eliminating compliance costs.

15. *Discussion.* Sections 201 and 202, codifying the bedrock consumer protection obligations of a common carrier, have represented the core concepts of federal common carrier regulation dating back over a hundred years. Although these provisions were enacted in a context in which virtually all telecommunications services were provided by monopolists, they have remained in the law over two decades during which numerous common carriers have provided service on a competitive basis. These sections set out broad standards of conduct, requiring the provision of interstate service upon reasonable request, pursuant to charges and practices which are just and reasonable and not unjustly discriminatory. At bottom, these provisions prohibit unreasonable discrimination by common carriers by guaranteeing consumers the basic ability to

obtain telecommunications service on no less favorable terms than other similarly situated customers. The Commission gives the standards meaning by defining practices that run afoul of carriers' obligations, either by rulemaking or by case-by-case adjudication. The existence of the broad obligations, however, is what gives the Commission the power to protect consumers by defining forbidden practices and enforcing compliance. Thus, sections 201 and 202 lie at the heart of consumer protection under the Act. Congress recognized the core nature of sections 201 and 202 when it excluded them from the scope of the Commission's forbearance authority under section 332(c)(1)(A). Although section 10 now gives the Commission the authority to forbear from enforcing sections 201 and 202 if certain conditions are satisfied, the history of the forbearance provisions confirms that this would be a particularly momentous step.

16. Sections 201 and 202 are enforced through the formal complaint process established in section 208 of the Act. Under section 208, any aggrieved party may file a petition with the Commission complaining of an alleged violation of these provisions. The carrier that is the subject of the complaint must then either rectify the alleged violation or respond to the complaint. The carrier is relieved of liability for any injury if, within a reasonable period specified by the Commission, the carrier rectifies the injury alleged to have been caused. If the carrier does not satisfy the complaint within the specified time or if there appears to be any reasonable ground for investigating the complaint, the Commission shall investigate the alleged violation. Consumers and carriers are protected by this complaint process. Indeed, when we decided to forbear from applying tariff requirements to CMRS, we relied on sections 201 and 202 and the section 208 complaint process as important safeguards to protect consumers in the event of market failure.

17. Consistent with the centrality of sections 201 and 202 to consumer protection, the Commission has never previously refrained from enforcing sections 201 and 202 against common carriers, even when competition exists in a market. In those instances where the Commission has reclassified carriers as "non-dominant" because they lack market power, and reduced those carriers' regulatory burdens, the Commission has continued to require compliance with sections 201 and 202. For example, we concluded in the AT&T Reclassification Order that the prohibitions against unjust and unreasonable rates, practices, and discrimination contained in sections 201 and 202 of the Act apply equally to dominant and non-dominant carriers. We explained that in the absence of section 205 tariff regulation, the substantive obligations imposed under sections 201 and 202, coupled with the complaint and enforcement processes of section 208, would prevent AT&T from engaging in anticompetitive behavior such as prohibition or unreasonable restriction of resale.

18. Based on the record before us, we decline to forbear from enforcing the core common carrier obligations of sections 201 and 202 at this time. The record does not show, as required for forbearance under section 10, that the current market conditions ensure that the charges,

practices, classifications and regulations of broadband PCS carriers are just and reasonable and are not unjustly or unreasonably discriminatory, that market forces are sufficient to protect consumers from discriminatory charges and practices of broadband PCS providers, and that forbearance is in the public interest.

* * *

31. In sum, we find that the record does not permit us, consistent with the three-prong test set out in section 10 of the Act, to forbear from enforcing sections 201 and 202 with respect to broadband PCS providers. First, the record does not show that existing competition in the market in which broadband PCS providers compete has rendered sections 201 and 202 unnecessary to prevent unjust, unreasonable, and unjustly or unreasonably discriminatory practices. Second, the record does not show that sections 201 and 202 are no longer necessary to protect consumers from discriminatory charges and practices by broadband PCS providers. Finally, we do not believe that forbearance from enforcing sections 201 and 202 is consistent with the public interest. The Commission has, pursuant to its authority under section 332(c)(1)(A), forborne from the application of sections 203, 204, 205, 211, 212 and 214 of Title II of the Communications Act to any service classified as CMRS, including broadband PCS. Sections 201 and 202 continue to provide important safeguards to consumers of broadband PCS against carrier abuse in an area that has already been largely deregulated by the Commission. We therefore find that at this time it is necessary to maintain sections 201 and 202, which enable the Commission to ensure that broadband PCS carriers provide service in a just, reasonable, and non-discriminatory manner, and to provide all consumers, including other carriers, with a mechanism through which they can seek redress for unreasonable carrier practices.

Retaining Common Carrier Obligations in Competitive Markets. In its Twelfth Annual Report on CMRS competition, excerpted earlier, the FCC states: "Even with one less nationwide mobile telephone carrier to choose from, U.S. consumers continue to benefit from robust competition in the CMRS marketplace." Accordingly, should the FCC now reconsider the need to retain any common carrier obligations? Is there any basis other than market power for retaining the obligations specified in §§ 201 and 202? There cannot be any doubt about statutory authority. In the above order the Commission concedes that § 10 of the Telecommunications Act (47 U.S.C. § 160) provides authority to forbear from enforcing § 201 and § 202 if it is not needed to protect consumers. Why would it be needed if mobile wireless service is now subject to "robust competition," as the Commission says?

CMRS providers are also still subject to requirements to interconnect with other carriers—the same as with wireline carriers. Is there any reason to *mandate* interconnection in a "robustly competitive" market?

End-to-end interconnection of carriers is conventionally justified on the principle of network effects, that is, interconnection increases the value of the overall communications service by ensuring that users can connect with one another even if they are not using the same carrier. That much is uncontroversial; the question is whether in a competitive marketplace interconnection needs to be legally *mandated*. Doesn't a carrier have an incentive to offer end-to-end connectivity as a means of satisfying its customers? And, if you assume competition, won't all carriers be similarly motivated? Compare the *Qwest* decision in the last chapter where the FCC refused to forbear from mandated interconnection among wireline carriers. Is there any difference between wireline and wireless that might argue for different rules regarding mandatory interconnection?

Chapter 10

THE INTERNET AND ADVANCED SERVICES

A. INTRODUCTION

Although the title of this chapter implies an association between the Internet and "advanced services," they are not necessarily the same. The Internet is a system of interconnected, computer-based networks using digitalized transmission and packet switching technology. "Advanced services," on the other hand, is an imprecise term that the FCC uses to describe both networks and the kinds of services carried over networks. In its former sense, the terminology of "advanced services" was introduced into the policy arena by section 706 of the Telecommunications Act of 1996 (47 U.S.C. § 157), which directs the FCC to study and promote "advanced telecommunications capability," which it defines as follows:

> The term "advanced telecommunications capability" is defined without regard to any transmission media or technology, as high-speed, switched, broadband telecommunications capability that enables users to originate and received high-quality voice, data, graphics, and video telecommunications using any technology.

Put simply, advanced telecommunications capability is about bandwidth (which translates into speed) in any technological form. The FCC defines both "advanced communications capability" and "broadband" as a communications link as having a particular transmission capacity,[1] and the FCC sometimes uses "advanced services" to describe this carriage capability. In its latter sense, "advanced services" correlates roughly, but only roughly, with the *Computer Inquiries*' notion of "enhanced ser-

1. Today, the FCC defines "broadband" in tiers, from 1 to 7, with "Basic Broadband Tier 1" being between 768 kbps and 1.5 Mbps; "Broadband Tier 7" reflects capacity greater than 100 Mbps. From 2000 to 2008, the FCC defined "broadband" as carriage greater than 200 kbps in both directions (the FCC now refers to capacity between 200 kbps and 768 kbps as "1st Generation Data" below the Basic Broadband Tier 1, implying perhaps that its time has come and gone); "high-speed," by contrast, was defined as 200 kbps in *either* direction. Unless specifically noted, we will use terms like "broadband" and "high-speed" in their more generic senses rather than according to the FCC's definition.

vices." The Internet, by virtue of its speed and the massive computer power connected to it, is a potentially unlimited source of such services. That same speed and power, though, also makes the Internet a potential platform for providing both the "basic services" that the *Computer Inquiries* left regulated and—potentially further confusing regulatory categories—mass media services not traditionally provided by telecommunications carriers at all, like video entertainment. The result is a regulatory and policy upheaval unprecedented in the history of the FCC.

Rather than fight the ambiguity in the term "advanced services," we embrace it. The advanced services debate is a many-sided affair, each side advancing its own vision of electronic communications, the technology it relies on, the industry that provides it, and the regulation that necessarily shapes it. "Advanced services" are many things to many people. Advanced services are not synonymous with the Internet, but everyone does seem to agree on two related points: 1) that the Internet architecture will provide the primary platform for delivering advanced services, and 2) that the success of the Internet is dependent on the widespread availability of connections to an inexpensive, high-speed communications network.

We start in this section with an overview of advanced services from the FCC's perspective, as provided by an FCC report prepared in response to Congress's directive in section 706. The report provides both a good overview of the various advanced communications services available and some insight into how the FCC views the advanced services question.

In sections B and C we examine a pair of controversies that have been the centerpiece of on-going debate over how to regulate access to and use of broadband services. The first is the "open access" controversy over whether integrated broadband service providers, cable operators and telephone carriers, must give "open access" to their broadband facilities to other, independent providers. The second is a distinct but related controversy over the degree of control that broadband service providers can exercise over the service they provide—the so-called "network neutrality" question.

In section D we explore issues concerning Internet-based telecommunications services. Broadly speaking these issues concern whether and how to regulate telecommunications services, such as voice services, when they are provided over the Internet instead of through conventional telecommunications technologies. For example, should such voice over Internet ("VoIP") services be subject to universal service obligations? In this section we also look at a recent development in wireless broadband that involves the development of municipally supported Wi-Fi and Wi-Max local networks.

Finally in section E we turn to the mass media side of Internet-based services to examine the regulatory implications of the Internet as a supplement or alternative to conventional mass media. When YouTube presents video clips of, say, "Cowboy Junkies" in concert, it is clear that copyright issues are presented. What if it presents a video of George Carlin's "Dirty Words" monologue: does that present the same kind of indecency issues as those addressed in *Pacifica*?

INQUIRY CONCERNING THE DEPLOYMENT OF ADVANCED TELECOMMUNICATIONS CAPABILITY
Second Report

Federal Communications Commission, 2000.
15 FCC Rcd. 20913.

BY THE COMMISSION:

I. INTRODUCTION

* * *

2. In its most basic form, advanced telecommunications capability allows users to send and receive large amounts of information. More specifically, advanced telecommunications capability is "high-speed, switched, broadband telecommunications capability that enables users to originate and receive high-quality voice, data, graphics, and video telecommunications using any technology." With advanced telecommunications capability consumers can take advantage of advanced services that allow residential and business customers to create and access content, sophisticated applications, and high-bandwidth services. For example, advanced services allow businesses and their customers quickly to exchange data over long distances, doctors to provide real-time diagnosis to patients in remote areas, people with hearing and speech disabilities to communicate through video links using sign language, teachers to create interactive multimedia learning environments for their students, and individuals to have faster, more robust access to the Internet.

* * *

IV. IS ADVANCED TELECOMMUNICATION CAPABILITY BEING DEPLOYED TO ALL AMERICANS?

* * *

A. Overview of the Networks Used to Provide Advanced Services

16. Advanced services are provided using a variety of public and private networks that rely on different network architectures and transmission paths. Some of these networks, like the Internet, are public in the sense that access to the network is open to all users. Other networks, like those built and maintained by corporations for their internal use, are private in the sense that access to the network may be restricted to a particular class of users, often the corporation's employees. Moreover, depending on the network, data may travel from the sender to the recipient over various architectures and transmission paths such as

copper wire, cable, terrestrial wireless radio spectrum, satellite radio spectrum, or a combination of these and other media. In addition, data may be transmitted using different communications protocols that manage and direct traffic at different layers of a particular network.

17. Although advanced services are provided over myriad combinations of public and private networks using a variety of transmission paths and protocols, for the purposes of this report we focus on the physical components of the network infrastructure. For simplicity, we have divided network infrastructure into four general categories: backbone, middle mile, last mile, and last 100 feet. In addition, we refer to the points of connection between these components of the network as connection points.

18. In conceptualizing the categories of network infrastructure identified above, we find it helpful to analogize network infrastructure to a system of roads. In our simplified analogy, each of the categories corresponds to a different type of road:

Backbone—Multi-lane Interstate Highway: Backbone provides a long-distance, high-capacity, high-speed transmission path for transporting massive quantities of data, much like the way a large multi-lane interstate highway allows large amounts of traffic quickly to travel long distances. Most backbone consists of fiber optic lines, either buried in the ground or laid under the sea. In addition, backbone can be provided using satellite systems and radio spectrum.

Middle Mile—Divided Highway: As its name suggests, middle mile facilities provide relatively fast, large-capacity connections between backbone and last mile, similar to the way a divided highway may connect local roads to multi-lane interstate highways. Middle mile facilities can range from a few miles to a few hundred miles. They are often constructed of fiber optic lines, but microwave and satellite links can be used as well.

Last Mile—Local Road: The last mile is the link between the middle mile and the last 100 feet to the end-user's terminal. The last mile is analogous to the local road between a larger, divided highway and a traveler's driveway. A last mile with advanced telecommunications capability provides speeds in excess of 200 kbps in each direction. Last miles may consist of cable modem service, digital subscriber line (DSL) service, terrestrial wireless service, or satellite service. Some last-mile segments—for example those on certain cable systems—provide faster downstream speeds than upstream speeds either because their network configurations will not support the higher upstream speed or because they rely on a telephone return path.

Last 100 Feet—Driveway: The last 100 feet is the link between the last mile and the end-user's terminal, which is similar to the way a driveway connects a traveler's home or office to a local road. The last 100 feet includes the in-house wiring found in a consumer's residence, the wiring in an apartment or office building, the more complex wiring in a wireline local area network, or the wireless links in a local wireless network.

Connection Points—Intersections, On–Ramps, and Interchanges: Connection points are the places at which the various components of the network interconnect, often with the aid of an electronic or optical device (e.g., switches and routers between the middle mile and backbone), so that data can move across the network. Connection points are analogous to the intersections, on-ramps, and interchanges between local roads, divided highways, and multi-lane interstate highways.

B. Components of the Network

19. In this section we examine each of the components of the network described above, both in terms of the technology used and the types of entities providing these components. We focus particularly on the last mile because it is a critical link between existing backbone and middle mile infrastructure on the one hand and the last 100 feet to the end-user's terminal on the other hand. In examining each component of the network, we also attempt to identify any major technological barriers to deployment of advanced telecommunications capability.

1. Backbone Facilities

20. At the core of the physical infrastructure supporting advanced telecommunications capabilities are nationwide backbone transport facilities. Much of the terrestrial fiber optic backbone in this country has been constructed along public rights of way created for railroad, telephone, and electric-utility owned companies. Providers have created additional backbone capacity in the form of undersea cables and satellite systems.

21. National backbone transport providers in the United States include large nationwide providers such as AT&T, WorldCom[*] and Sprint and a number of smaller facilities-based transport providers * * *. There are an additional 35 to 50 wireline, terrestrial wireless and satellite-based national Internet backbone providers, with varying amounts of physical facilities. The major Internet backbone providers transport traffic with capacity ranging from approximately 155 Mbps to over 10 Gbps (OC-3 to OC-192 equivalent speeds).

22. Although the cost of building and maintaining backbone facilities is high, there do not appear to be significant technological barriers to deployment of these facilities. To date, advances in fiber optic and microwave technologies have allowed backbone capacity to keep pace with demand for backbone facilities. While backbone capacity does not appear to present a barrier to deployment of advanced telecommunications capability at this time, the ability to access that capacity presents other questions which are addressed later in this section.

* Eds. WorldCom's backbone network was a legacy of its merger with MCI. After a bankruptcy reorganization, WorldCom changed its name to MCI, which was in turn acquired by Verizon in 2006.

2. Middle Mile Facilities

23. Middle mile facilities provide transport or routing from last mile aggregation points in order to interconnect and exchange traffic with national backbone providers or directly with other middle mile networks. It appears that most fiber optic, middle-mile facilities, like backbone, exist along public rights of way. Other middle miles include fixed wireless and satellite links.

24. Many middle mile facilities were originally built by telephone and cable companies for ordinary telecommunications or cable television services. For example, the fiber optic connections that transport telephone traffic between telephone company central offices can be considered middle mile facilities. * * *

25. Many providers of middle mile transport lease capacity on their networks to non-facilities based Internet service providers (ISPs) and high-speed providers, who find the transport speeds adequate to meet their needs. For example many local exchange carriers (LECs) currently lease the fiber or high-speed lines connecting their central offices. Most cable systems also have fiber or satellite transport facilities to regional and national backbone, which they may lease to other providers. In addition, there are entities known as Global Service Providers providing interLATA transport service.

26. As demand for middle mile facilities has increased, existing providers and new providers have deployed additional facilities. ... [I]n the past five years, the amount of fiber miles deployed in the United States has doubled. Interexchange carriers, incumbent and competitive local exchange carriers, cable television companies and others, including fixed wireless service providers, have invested enormous amounts of money into construction of fiber facilities.

27. We noted in the *First Report* that high capacity fiber connects to almost every local exchange carrier central office. Indeed, significant amounts of unused high capacity fiber, typically referred to as dark fiber, exist within the fiber conduit connecting local exchange carrier central offices. In part because of the lack of ubiquitous alternative middle mile transport, we recently determined that interoffice dark fiber transport qualified as an unbundled network element. This determination allows competitive carriers access to interoffice dark fiber.

3. Last Mile Facilities

28. Last mile facilities provide the connection between middle mile facilities and the last 100 feet to an end-user's terminal. While all components of the network play important roles in the delivery of advanced services, we focus particular attention on the deployment of last mile facilities because they are often the missing link in communities that do not have access to advanced telecommunications capability. The last mile connection to the end-user can take the form of cable modem service, digital subscriber line service (DSL) or some other LEC-provided service, terrestrial wireless service, or satellite service. Some

operators of last mile facilities, like cable providers, transport data entirely over facilities that they own. Others, including many terrestrial wireless providers, lease transport to regional and/or national connection points from local exchange carriers. Last mile facilities called very small aperture terminals (VSATs) may also use satellite links to transport traffic to middle mile facilities or directly to the national backbone networks. In the sections that follow, we examine each of the four major technologies used to provide last mile facilities: cable modem service, DSL and other LEC-provided services, terrestrial wireless, and satellite service. We discuss the types of entities that provide these last mile facilities, from the technology used to deliver advanced services and subscribership rates, to their investments in infrastructure and analysts' forecasts, as well as the significant technological barriers to deployment of each technology.

a. Overview of Cable Modem Service

29. Cable companies offer advanced services, most notably high-speed Internet access services, using cable modem technologies. Cable modem technologies rely on the same basic network architecture used for many years to provide multichannel video service, but with upgrades and enhancements to support advanced services. The typical upgrade incorporates what is commonly known as a hybrid fiber-coaxial (HFC) distribution plant. HFC networks use a combination of high-capacity optical fiber and traditional coaxial cable. Most HFC systems utilize fiber between the cable operators' offices (the "headend") and the neighborhood "nodes." Between the nodes and the individual end-user homes, signals travel over traditional coaxial cable infrastructure. These networks transport signals over infrastructure that serves numerous users simultaneously, i.e., a shared network, rather than providing a dedicated link between the provider and each home, as does DSL technology. As discussed below, the shared architecture of cable networks poses certain challenges for providers that seek to offer high-speed Internet access or other advanced services over cable infrastructure.

30. Before offering high-speed Internet and other two-way high-speed services, most cable providers upgrade their networks. This process often includes extending optical fiber closer to the end-user and improving system quality to reduce signal leakage. Through this upgrade process, cable operators typically increase the system's transmission capacity to 550 MHz or 750 MHz, which allows the operator greater flexibility in allocating bandwidth for two-way high-speed services without reducing the capacity available for existing video services.

31. Upgrading a system for high-speed Internet service typically requires installation of equipment that enables the transmission of digital data packets: routers, switches, and a cable modem termination system. Further, to allow the high-speed transmission of data over the cable infrastructure in both the upstream and downstream directions, operators install amplifiers and optical lasers in both directions. Without such equipment, providers typically can provide high-speed service only

in the downstream direction and must rely on a telephone line return path. Once an HFC network is upgraded, new services are available to all homes passed by the upgraded infrastructure. This contrasts with DSL technologies, where variations in legacy outside plant conditions can limit access to certain end-users even in upgraded areas, and with wireless technologies where line-of-sight requirements may be a factor.

* * *

34. High-speed Internet access over cable is available primarily to the residential market. Several factors may explain this. First, cable operators historically have deployed facilities for video services to the residential market. This leaves them poorly situated to offer service to many business districts. Second, cable's shared network architecture makes it difficult for providers to guarantee the consistent high speeds and secure transmissions that some business customers require. Third, the relatively narrow bandwidth typically allocated to upstream transmission renders cable unable to provide upstream speeds and symmetric transmission capabilities sufficient to support the requirements of some business customers.

b. Overview of Digital Subscriber Line Service

35. Since 1996, local telephone carriers have offered consumers high-speed data service through their digital subscriber line (DSL) service offerings. With the addition of certain electronics to the telephone line, carriers can transform the copper loop that already provides voice service into a conduit for high-speed data traffic. While there are multiple variations of DSL, some of which we discuss below, most DSL offerings share certain characteristics. With most DSL technologies today, a high-speed signal is sent from the end-user's terminal through the last 100 feet and the last mile (sometimes a few miles) consisting of the copper loop until it reaches a Digital Subscriber Line Access Multiplexer (DSLAM), usually located in the carrier's central office. At the DSLAM, the end-user's signal is combined with the signals of many other customers and forwarded though a switch to middle mile facilities.

* * *

38. DSL service is subject to certain limitations that currently prevent it from being deployed as a last mile facility to all potential end-users. First, it is distance sensitive. Currently, an ADSL customer must be within approximately 18,000 feet of the carrier's central office; SDSL customers must be between 10,000 and 12,000 feet of the central office depending on the speed of the service in question. Eighty percent of the subscriber loop plant falls within these distance limitations, and thus is capable of supporting DSL service, but this factor remains an impediment to DSL deployment in more sparsely populated and remote locations. New technologies may allow DSL deployment at substantially greater distances.

39. The second factor limiting the deployment of DSL to some potential customers is the presence on their loops of load coils and

bridged taps, devices that were used to enhance the quality of voice traffic over the copper. While they improve the quality of voice transmission, these devices prevent the deployment of DSL service over a line on which they are installed. Thus, in contrast to an upgraded cable network, which can offer upgraded service to all homes it passes, LECs must "condition" each end-user's line by removing the load coils and bridged taps while increasing the strength of the signal to maintain the quality of the line's voice traffic. Moreover, older loops or loops in need of maintenance, which may occur in poor or inner-city areas, pose additional problems for the deployment of DSL service. Frayed insulation or poorly spliced loops can cause signal leakage, which can result in poor quality transmission.

* * *

c. Overview of Other LEC-Provided Wireline Services

41. In addition to DSL offerings, many local exchange carriers offer more traditional high-speed, circuit switched services like T1 lines, which have been available for some time. The monthly charge for T1 service can range from $150 to $2000, with installation cost ranging from $750 to $5500, depending on the transmission speed desired and equipment purchased. Additionally, local exchange carriers have used fiber technology for many years for their interoffice plant. It is also used to deliver signals at speeds in excess of 45 Mbps directly to certain large business customers. Most residential and smaller business customers currently do not need the transmission speed of fiber, and the cost of fiber service generally makes it prohibitive for all but the largest users. Several fiber-based residential architectures have been devised; however, the high cost associated with deploying this technology makes it economically viable, if at all, only in the most densely populated of residential settings.

d. Overview of Fixed Wireless Service

42. Wireless services and technologies have the potential to deliver high-speed services to residential, rural, and otherwise underserved areas and to increase competition in the last mile in the near future. As discussed below, fixed wireless technologies may offer unique advantages and quick-to-market solutions for the delivery of high-speed services in a number of circumstances. At present, however, technical limitations may constrain the breadth of their overall deployment and their effectiveness in certain settings. At this point, many of these services are in an earlier stage of deployment than the traditional "wired" services, cable-modem and DSL technology, but significant growth is anticipated over the next three to five years, potentially leading to service to millions of households.

* * *

47. Although wireless services can generally be deployed more rapidly and at lower cost than comparable wireline services, they remain

subject to certain technical limitations that may reduce their effectiveness in certain areas and for certain purposes. For example, in addition to requiring access to telecommunications equipment closets and any necessary in-building wiring, wireless providers often must obtain access to rooftops for the placement of antennas. This can become particularly problematic in the case of multi-tenant buildings, in which a building owner may resist permitting access. Also, many, though not all, fixed wireless technologies are subject to line-of-sight restrictions. Thus, there must be an unobstructed path from a wireless provider's antenna to the customer's antenna on the rooftop of a building. While certain advances in wireless technology may help to overcome this limitation in the future, buildings, topographical features, certain adverse weather conditions, and even vegetation can interfere with the provision of service.

* * *

53. *Broadband PCS*. Although cellular and broadband Personal Communications Services (PCS) spectrum technically can support high-speed services, relatively few licensees are currently using their frequencies in this manner. * * *

55. *Unlicensed spectrum*. A handful of companies across the U.S. use unlicensed spectrum in the 2 GHz and 5 GHz spread spectrum bands to offer short-distance high-speed Internet access and other high-speed services, such as wireless wide area network or local area network systems for businesses. As of April 2000, at least eleven companies were reportedly providing these services in twenty-three markets. Unlicensed spectrum, which may be used without a license but is not protected from interference from other services, offers a low-cost means for smaller companies to enter the wireless high-speed market.

e. Overview of Satellite Service

56. Satellite service provides another option for last mile facilities with its own set of unique characteristics. In most current residential satellite-based last mile facilities, only the downstream path is provided by satellite; the upstream path is often provided by a standard dial-up telephone connection. Thus, many current residential satellite offerings are capable of providing speeds in excess of 200 kbps only in the downstream path, and therefore do not meet the definition of advanced telecommunications capability. Nonetheless, satellite-based last mile facilities may provide consumers and small businesses in geographically remote and sparsely populated areas with access to high-speed services that would not otherwise be available. Moreover, several satellite providers have announced plans to begin offering residential service with the downstream and upstream paths both provided by satellite.

* * *

f. Last 100 Feet Facilities

60. The last 100 feet typically refers to the final infrastructure segment from the end of the local access network to the end-user's

terminal. This includes in-building wiring, local area networks and wireless local area networks. There do not appear to be technological barriers for last 100 feet facilities; indeed there are a variety of wireline and wireless options for constructing these facilities. Nevertheless, the cost of some of these facilities may be a significant factor in the deployment of advanced telecommunication capability in the small business or school and library context. Additionally, certain last 100 feet segments may be in poor condition and consequently unable to support advanced services. Unlike a residential setting with a handful of users, small businesses or schools and libraries may have multiple users accessing advanced services simultaneously. This need for simultaneous access may require upgrades to the existing in-building wiring and other last 100 feet facilities, which may have been originally installed only with enough capacity for standard voice telephony services. In addition, access to last 100 feet facilities may be controlled by someone other than the end-user, such as the landlord of a multiple tenant dwelling. This also may create access barriers for these facilities, especially for competitors of the incumbent service provider.

g. Connection points

61. In the preceding discussion, we have examined the various components of the network. In order for advanced services to be delivered to end-users, however, these components must interconnect with each other at the places we loosely describe as connection points—those places at which traffic passes between the various components of networks. High-speed networks exchange traffic at a variety of different places and in a variety of different mechanisms. For example, public telephone networks, including local, long distance and international networks, interconnect at Points of Presence (POPs) or through other interconnection arrangements. Satellite networks exchange traffic with terrestrial networks. Internet backbone service providers exchange traffic at network access points (NAPs), Metropolitan Area Exchanges (MAEs), and through other public and private peering and transit arrangements. National Internet backbone providers report operating commercial exchange points in over 200 cities in the United States and having over 900 POPs where they interconnect with regional networks, private networks and other providers. As usage and demand increase, network operators establish additional arrangements for the exchange of traffic.

* * *

The Local Focus of Federal Regulation of Advanced Services. Note the *Second Report*'s emphasis on the "last 100 feet" and "last mile" portions in the network. Concern over both links is predicated on the lack of viable options for bridging these distances. Lessors may be able to exercise exclusivity over who has access to the last 100 feet. Similarly, in many communities, there will be one or two providers of "last mile" facilities: the ILEC and (recently) the local cable monopoly. The FCC addressed the last-100-feet problem first in 2000, by prohibiting exclusive agreements between telecommunications providers and landlords of commercial buildings; in 2008 the Commission extended the ban to residential buildings. See *Promotion of Competitive Networks in Local Telecommunications Markets, Report and Order*, 23 FCC Rcd. 5385 (2008). Almost all of the regulatory activity with regard to advanced services has been over how to handle the last mile problem, which is the subject of much of this chapter. Given the FCC's focus on the the last 100 feet and last mile, is there anything left of the distinction between interstate and intrastate carriage that originally cabined the FCC's jurisdiction? If the FCC can regulate the last 100 feet, is there still any point in retaining the regulatory authority of states?

Connections. The Internet, as the name itself indicates, is not a single network but a collection of different networks. In order for the Internet to be "inter," it is necessary that the different networks be connected to each other. The Commission's description of the physical architecture of the Internet breaks it down into backbone, middle mile, last mile, and last 100 feet. The last two levels—commonly lumped together as simply the last mile—are familiar from our earlier discussions of the telecommunications network. The first two levels, which are the means by which disparate networks are linked together, warrant brief further explanation, and for expositional convenience we will treat them together under a single category of backbone networks.[2]

2. The middle mile is conceptually distinct as the way that the local ISP connects to larger providers that in-turn can connect it to national backbone providers, but business arrangements for middle-mile carriage—which are largely among ISPs themselves as opposed to being between ISPs and consumers—so closely resemble those for backbone carriage that they can be treated for regulatory purposes as largely interchangeable.

The iconic diagram of Internet architecture depicts an end user connecting to a cloud. At the other end there is a connection from the cloud to another end user.

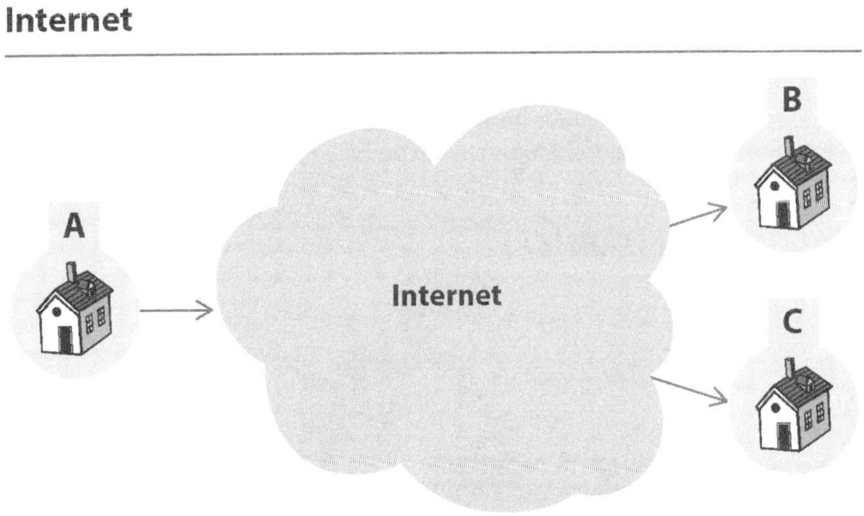

The depiction of a cloud to represent the Internet is symbolically interesting for it not only denotes the diffuse character of the Internet but also suggests a vague if not mysterious set of arrangements by which the bitstreams make their way from point A to points B and C across multiple networks, owned and operated by multiple network providers. For present purposes it is not necessary (nor indeed would it be possible) to explain these mysteries fully, but a few basic features of the backbone architecture may be useful.[3]

Sometimes it is possible to complete an Internet connection on a single network, one in which both end points and the backbone are commonly owned. (Think, for example of a large, national backbone provider such as AT&T that also provides business or residential Internet access to the users at both end points.) More often, though, Internet traffic will flow over more than one network, and this requires both physical interconnection among the networks and an agreement among network providers as to how to handle the exchange. The arrangements among backbone providers are varied and complex. Unlike conventional voice telecommunications traffic, interconnection among Internet backbones is not legally mandated, nor are the contractual arrrangements for handling traffic regulated. As a consequence of being unregulated, the details are made public only as the providers choose, so it is impossible to perfectly describe them. But the basic arrangements fall into two distinct types: "transit" arrangements and "peering."

3. A helpful and more detailed description can be found in an FCC Office of Plans and Policy working paper, Michael Kende, THE DIGITAL HANDSHAKE: CONNECTING INTERNET BACKBONES, http://www.fcc.gov/osp/workingp.html.

In transit arrangements the originating ISP or backbone provider pays another provider to carry its traffic to all end users on the Internet. To take an oversimplified example, consider a hierachical set of connections involving a local ISP that has no backbone (in the artful not the colloquial sense). The ISP will connect to a backbone provider (sometimes called an "upstream ISP") for a fee based on the traffic volume. That backbone provider will provide transit to other broadband providers as necessary to complete the connection. If the broadband provider is a regional ISP, it may have to pass the traffic on to a national provider and typically it will pay a fee to the latter.

Peering and Transit

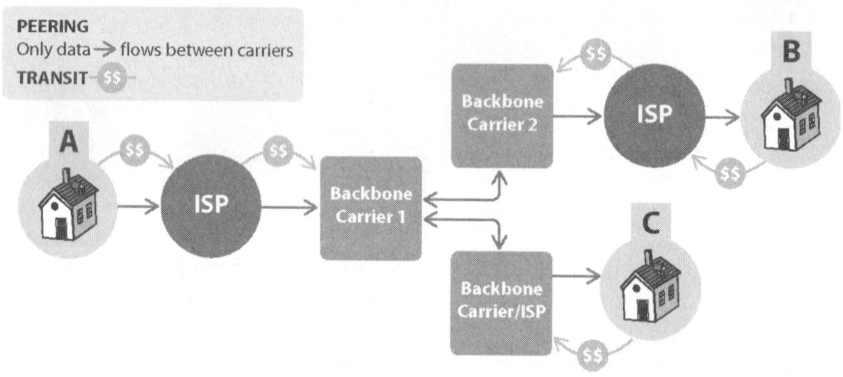

In peering arrangements two providers exchange traffic *without* payment. In contrast to transit arrangements, the exchange only involves each network carrying the traffic that is destined to the end users of that network, not to end users of other networks, and there are no quality of service guarantees. Despite the connotation that the word "peer" suggests, it should not be assumed that peering partners are equal in size, geographic scope, or traffic volume. Providers will peer when each perceives equal benefits from doing so. These benefits could be various, but they are most commonly thought to imply a roughly balanced traffic volume between the peers and a roughly symmetrical cost burden for carrying foreign traffic.[4] In this way, peering somewhat resembles the bill-and-keep arrangements discussed in the last chapter.

4. Note that the volume is sensitive to the type of traffic being carried. For example, a provider that carries an end user's request for content from a web page is not likely to be be the equivalent in volume to the content that is sent in response. Thus the type of traffic carried may be an important criterion in whether one provider will peer with another. Also, important in private peering arrangements is a rough equivalence in interconnection points so as to minimize an asymmetric transport burden. Originally, traffic was exchanged at a handful of designated national access points ("NAPs"). This form of "public peering" has now greatly diminished in favor of "private peering" involving interconnection at points designated by the peers. Under what is called "hot potato" routing, providers exchange traffic at the earliest point of interconnection with the other network, which makes it important to ensure that the peers have mutually convenient points for exchanging traffic.

Backbones vary greatly in terms of geographical scope, number of interconnections, volume of traffic etc. There is no single dimension along which to rank them by size. However, it has become conventional to distinguish between so-called "Tier 1" providers and all others. The prominent Tier 1 providers include the three BOCs—AT&T, Verizon, and Qwest—and a number of other major carriers, such as Sprint, Global Crossing, Genuity and a few others. The exact number is, oddly, uncertain because the definition of a Tier 1 provider depends on the way in which it interconnects with others, which is not a matter of public information. A Tier 1 provider is, by definition, a provider that does not pay transit charges for exchange of traffic but does peer with other Tier 1 providers according to prescribed terms. Tier 1 providers are not necessarily those with the largest volume or even the largest geographic footprint, but they are arguably the most important because of the top-level connectivity they provide both nationally and globally. Does that critical importance argue for regulatory surveillance? The answer from the FCC so far has been no. Some concern has arisen over the assumed ability of backbone, or even middle-mile providers, to use transit and peering arrangements to favor their own network customers. In the next chapter we will examine the the FCC's recent approval of the merger of AT&T and BellSouth which, among other things, considered the impact of the merger on national backbones. The FCC there decided there was no basis for concern given the competition among Tier 1 backbone providers. The problem with that conclusion is that it's not clear on what information it is based. As the FCC itself concedes, it isn't even clear who all the Tier 1 providers are, much less what the market conditions are for peering and transit arrangements, since the they are not publicly available. Given the importance of the backbone, should the FCC be so heavily focused on the last mile?

B. ACCESS TO BROADBAND PLATFORMS

NATIONAL CABLE & TELECOMMUNICATIONS ASS'N v. BRAND X INTERNET SERVICES

Supreme Court of the United States, 2005.
545 U.S. 967.

JUSTICE THOMAS delivered the opinion of the Court.

Title II of the Communications Act of 1934, 48 Stat. 1064, as amended, 47 U.S.C. § 151 et seq., subjects all providers of "telecommunications servic[e]" to mandatory common-carrier regulation, § 153(44). In the order under review, the Federal Communications Commission concluded that cable companies that sell broadband Internet service do not provide "telecommunications servic[e]" as the Communications Act defines that term, and hence are exempt from mandatory common-carrier regulation under Title II. We must decide whether that conclusion is a lawful construction of the Communications Act under *Chevron U.S.A. Inc. v. Natural Resources Defense Council, Inc.*, 467 U.S. 837 (1984), and the Administrative Procedure Act, 5 U.S.C. § 555 et seq. We hold that it is.

I

The traditional means by which consumers in the United States access the network of interconnected computers that make up the Internet is through "dial-up" connections provided over local telephone facilities. Using these connections, consumers access the Internet by making calls with computer modems through the telephone wires owned by local phone companies. Internet service providers (ISPs), in turn, link those calls to the Internet network, not only by providing a physical connection, but also by offering consumers the ability to translate raw Internet data into information they may both view on their personal computers and transmit to other computers connected to the Internet. Technological limitations of local telephone wires, however, retard the speed at which data from the Internet may be transmitted through end users' dial-up connections. Dial-up connections are therefore known as "narrowband," or slower speed, connections.

"Broadband" Internet service, by contrast, transmits data at much higher speeds. There are two principal kinds of broadband Internet service: cable modem service and Digital Subscriber Line (DSL) service. Cable modem service transmits data between the Internet and users' computers via the network of television cable lines owned by cable companies. Cable companies and telephone companies can either provide Internet access directly to consumers, thus acting as ISPs themselves, or can lease their transmission facilities to independent ISPs that then use the facilities to provide consumers with Internet access. Other ways of transmitting high-speed Internet data into homes, including terrestrial- and satellite-based wireless networks, are also emerging.

II

At issue in these cases is the proper regulatory classification under the Communications Act of broadband cable Internet service. The Act, as amended by the Telecommunications Act of 1996, defines two categories of regulated entities relevant to these cases: telecommunications carriers and information-service providers. The Act regulates telecommunications carriers, but not information-service providers, as common carriers. Telecommunications carriers, for example, must charge just and reasonable, nondiscriminatory rates to their customers, design their systems so that other carriers can interconnect with their communications networks, and contribute to the federal "universal service" fund. These provisions are mandatory, but the Commission must forbear from applying them if it determines that the public interest requires it. Information-service providers, by contrast, are not subject to mandatory common-carrier regulation under Title II, though the Commission has jurisdiction to impose additional regulatory obligations under its Title I ancillary jurisdiction to regulate interstate and foreign communications.

These two statutory classifications originated in the late 1970's, as the Commission developed rules to regulate data-processing services offered over telephone wires. That regime, the "*Computer II*" rules, distinguished between "basic" service (like telephone service) and "enhanced" service (computer-processing service offered over telephone lines). *In re Amendment of Section 64.702 of the Commission's Rules and Regulations (Second* Computer Inquiry), 77 F.C.C.2d 384, 417–423, ¶¶ 86–101 (1980) (hereinafter *Computer II Order*). The *Computer II* rules defined both basic and enhanced services by reference to how the consumer perceives the service being offered.

In particular, the Commission defined "basic service" as "a pure transmission capability over a communications path that is virtually transparent in terms of its interaction with customer supplied information." By "pure" or "transparent" transmission, the Commission meant a communications path that enabled the consumer to transmit an ordinary-language message to another point, with no computer processing or storage of the information, other than the processing or storage needed to convert the message into electronic form and then back into ordinary language for purposes of transmitting it over the network—such as via a telephone or a facsimile. Basic service was subject to common-carrier regulation.

"[E]nhanced service," however, was service in which "computer processing applications [were] used to act on the content, code, protocol, and other aspects of the subscriber's information," such as voice and data storage services, as well as "protocol conversion" (i.e., ability to communicate between networks that employ different data-transmission formats). By contrast to basic service, the Commission decided not to subject providers of enhanced service, even enhanced service offered via transmission wires, to Title II common-carrier regulation. The Commission explained that it was unwise to subject enhanced service to common-carrier regulation given the "fast-moving, competitive market" in which they were offered.

The definitions of the terms "telecommunications service" and "information service" established by the 1996 Act are similar to the *Computer II* basic- and enhanced-service classifications. "Telecommunications service"—the analog to basic service—is "the offering of telecommunications for a fee directly to the public . . . regardless of the facilities used." "Telecommunications" is "the transmission, between or among points specified by the user, of information of the user's choosing, without change in the form or content of the information as sent and received." "Telecommunications carrier[s]"—those subjected to mandatory Title II common-carrier regulation—are defined as "provider[s] of telecommunications services." And "information service"—the analog to enhanced service—is "the offering of a capability for generating, acquiring, storing, transforming, processing, retrieving, utilizing, or making available information via telecommunications . . .".

In September 2000, the Commission initiated a rulemaking proceeding to, among other things, apply these classifications to cable companies that offer broadband Internet service directly to consumers. In March 2002, that rulemaking culminated in the *Declaratory Ruling* under review in these cases. In the *Declaratory Ruling*, the Commission concluded that broadband Internet service provided by cable companies is an "information service" but not a "telecommunications service" under the Act, and therefore not subject to mandatory Title II common-carrier regulation. In support of this conclusion, the Commission relied heavily on its Universal Service Report. The *Universal Service Report* classified "non-facilities-based" ISPs—those that do not own the transmission facilities they use to connect the end user to the Internet—solely as information-service providers. Unlike those ISPs, cable companies own the cable lines they use to provide Internet access. Nevertheless, in the *Declaratory Ruling*, the Commission found no basis in the statutory definitions for treating cable companies differently from non-facilities-based ISPs: Both offer "a single, integrated service that enables the subscriber to utilize Internet access service ... and to realize the benefits of a comprehensive service offering." Because Internet access provides a capability for manipulating and storing information, the Commission concluded that it was an information service.

The integrated nature of Internet access and the high-speed wire used to provide Internet access led the Commission to conclude that cable companies providing Internet access are not telecommunications providers. This conclusion, the Commission reasoned, followed from the logic of the *Universal Service Report*. The *Report* had concluded that, though Internet service "involves data transport elements" because "an Internet access provider must enable the movement of information between customers' own computers and distant computers with which those customers seek to interact," it also "offers end users information-service capabilities inextricably intertwined with data transport." ISPs, therefore, were not "offering telecommunications ... directly to the public," and so were not properly classified as telecommunications carriers. In other words, the Commission reasoned that consumers use their cable modems not to transmit information "transparently," such as by using a telephone, but instead to obtain Internet access.

The Commission applied this same reasoning to cable companies offering broadband Internet access. Its logic was that, like non-facilities-based ISPs, cable companies do not "offe[r] telecommunications service to the end user, but rather ... merely us[e] telecommunications to provide end users with cable modem service." Though the Commission declined to apply mandatory Title II common-carrier regulation to cable companies, it invited comment on whether under its Title I jurisdiction it should require cable companies to offer other ISPs access to their facilities on common-carrier terms. Numerous parties petitioned for judicial review, challenging the Commission's conclusion that cable modem service was not telecommunications service. By judicial lottery, the Court of Appeals for the Ninth Circuit was selected as the venue for the challenge.

The Court of Appeals granted the petitions in part, vacated the *Declaratory Ruling* in part, and remanded to the Commission for further proceedings. In particular, the Court of Appeals vacated the ruling to the extent it concluded that cable modem service was not "telecommunications service" under the Communications Act. It held that the Commission could not permissibly construe the Communications Act to exempt cable companies providing Internet service from Title II regulation. * * *

IV

We next address whether the Commission's construction of the definition of "telecommunications service," is a permissible reading of the Communications Act under the *Chevron* framework. *Chevron* established a familiar two-step procedure for evaluating whether an agency's interpretation of a statute is lawful. At the first step, we ask whether the statute's plain terms "directly addres[s] the precise question at issue." If the statute is ambiguous on the point, we defer at step two to the agency's interpretation so long as the construction is "a reasonable policy choice for the agency to make." The Commission's interpretation is permissible at both steps.

A

We first set forth our understanding of the interpretation of the Communications Act that the Commission embraced. The issue before the Commission was whether cable companies providing cable modem service are providing a "telecommunications service" in addition to an "information service."

The Commission first concluded that cable modem service is an "information service," a conclusion unchallenged here. The Act defines "information service" as "the offering of a capability for generating, acquiring, storing, transforming, processing, retrieving, utilizing, or making available information via telecommunications. . . ." § 153(20). Cable modem service is an information service, the Commission reasoned, because it provides consumers with a comprehensive capability for manipulating information using the Internet via high-speed telecommunications. That service enables users, for example, to browse the World Wide Web, to transfer files from file archives available on the Internet via the "File Transfer Protocol," and to access e-mail and Usenet newsgroups. Like other forms of Internet service, cable modem service also gives users access to the Domain Name System (DNS). DNS, among other things, matches the Web page addresses that end users type into their browsers (or "click" on) with the Internet Protocol (IP) addresses of the servers. containing the web pages the users wish to access. All of these features, the Commission concluded, were part of the information service that cable companies provide consumers.

At the same time, the Commission concluded that cable modem service was not "telecommunications service." "Telecommunications service" is "the offering of telecommunications for a fee directly to the public." § 153(46). "Telecommunications," in turn, is defined as "the transmission, between or among points specified by the user, of information of the user's choosing, without change in the form or content of the information as sent and received." § 153(43). The Commission conceded that, like all information-service providers, cable companies use "telecommunications" to provide consumers with Internet service; cable companies provide such service via the high-speed wire that transmits signals to and from an end user's computer. For the Commission, however, the question whether cable broadband Internet providers "offer" telecommunications involved more than whether telecommunications was one necessary component of cable modem service. Instead, whether that service also includes a telecommunications "offering" "tur[ned] on the nature of the functions the *end user* is offered," for the statutory definition of "telecommunications service" does not "res[t] on the particular types of facilities used." See § 153(46) (definition of "telecommunications service" applies "regardless of the facilities used").

Seen from the consumer's point of view, the Commission concluded, cable modem service is not a telecommunications offering because the consumer uses the high-speed wire always in connection with the information-processing capabilities provided by Internet access, and because the transmission is a necessary component of Internet access: "As provided to the end user the telecommunications is part and parcel of cable modem service and is integral to its other capabilities." The wire is used, in other words, to access the World Wide Web, newsgroups, and so forth, rather than "transparently" to transmit and receive ordinary-language messages without computer processing or storage of the message. The integrated character of this offering led the Commission to conclude that cable modem service is not a "stand-alone," transparent offering of telecommunications.

B

* * *

1

Cable companies in the broadband Internet service business "offe[r]" consumers an information service in the form of Internet access and they do so "via telecommunications," but it does not inexorably follow as a matter of ordinary language that they also "offe[r]" consumers the high-speed data transmission (telecommunications) that is an input used to provide this service. We have held that where a statute's plain terms admit of two or more reasonable ordinary usages, the Commission's choice of one of them is entitled to deference. The term "offe[r]" as used in the definition of telecommunications service, is ambiguous in this way.

It is common usage to describe what a company "offers" to a consumer as what the consumer perceives to be the integrated finished product, even to the exclusion of discrete components that compose the product, as the dissent concedes. One might well say that a car dealership "offers" cars, but does not "offer" the integrated major inputs that make purchasing the car valuable, such as the engine or the chassis. It would, in fact, be odd to describe a car dealership as "offering" consumers the car's components in addition to the car itself. Even if it is linguistically permissible to say that the car dealership "offers" engines when it offers cars, that shows, at most, that the term "offer," when applied to a commercial transaction, is ambiguous about whether it describes only the offered finished product, or the product's discrete components as well. It does not show that no other usage is permitted.

The question, then, is whether the transmission component of cable modem service is sufficiently integrated with the finished service to make it reasonable to describe the two as a single, integrated offering. We think that they are sufficiently integrated, because "[a] consumer uses the high-speed wire always in connection with the information-processing capabilities provided by Internet access, and because the transmission is a necessary component of Internet access." In the telecommunications context, it is at least reasonable to describe companies as not "offering" to consumers each discrete input that is necessary to providing, and is always used in connection with, a finished service. We think it no misuse of language, for example, to say that cable companies providing Internet service do not "offer" consumers DNS, even though DNS is essential to providing Internet access. Likewise, a telephone company "offers" consumers a transparent transmission path that conveys an ordinary-language message, not necessarily the data transmission facilities that also "transmi[t] . . . information of the user's choosing" or other physical elements of the facilities used to provide telephone service, like the trunks and switches, or the copper in the wires. What cable companies providing cable modem service and telephone companies providing telephone service "offer" is Internet service and telephone service respectively—the finished services, though they do so using (or "via") the discrete components composing the end product, including data transmission. Such functionally integrated components need not be described as distinct "offerings."

In response, the dissent argues that the high-speed transmission component necessary to providing cable modem service is necessarily "offered" with Internet service because cable modem service is like the offering of pizza delivery service together with pizza, and the offering of puppies together with dog leashes. The dissent's appeal to these analogies only underscores that the term "offer" is ambiguous in the way that we have described. The entire question is whether the products here are functionally integrated (like the components of a car) or functionally separate (like pets and leashes). That question turns not on the language of the Act, but on the factual particulars of how Internet technology works and how it is provided, questions *Chevron* leaves to the Commission to resolve in the first instance. As the Commission has candidly recognized, "the question may not always be straightforward whether, on the one hand, an entity is providing a single information service with communications and computing components, or, on the other hand, is providing two distinct services, one of which is a telecommunications service." Because the term "offer" can sometimes refer to a single, finished product and sometimes to the "individual components in a package being offered" (depending on whether the components "still possess sufficient identity to be described as separate objects"), the statute fails unambiguously to classify the telecommunications component of cable modem service as a distinct offering. This leaves federal telecommunications policy in this technical and complex area to be set by the Commission, not by warring analogies.

We also do not share the dissent's certainty that cable modem service is so obviously like pizza delivery service and the combination of dog leashes and dogs that the Commission could not reasonably have thought otherwise. For example, unlike the transmission component of Internet service, delivery service and dog leashes are not integral components of the finished products (pizzas and pet dogs). One can pick up a pizza rather than having it delivered, and one can own a dog without buying a leash. By contrast, the Commission reasonably concluded, a consumer cannot purchase Internet service without also purchasing a connection to the Internet and the transmission always occurs in connection with information processing. In any event, we doubt that a statute that, for example, subjected offerors of "delivery" service (such as Federal Express and United Parcel Service) to common-carrier regulation would unambiguously require pizza-delivery companies to offer their delivery services on a common-carrier basis.

2

The Commission's traditional distinction between basic and enhanced service also supports the conclusion that the Communications Act is ambiguous about whether cable companies "offer" telecommunications with cable modem service. Congress passed the definitions in the Communications Act against the background of this regulatory history, and we may assume that the parallel terms "telecommunications service" and "information service" substantially incorporated their meaning, as the Commission has held. The regulatory history in at least two respects confirms that the term "telecommunications service" is ambiguous.

First, in the *Computer II Order* that established the terms "basic" and "enhanced" services, the Commission defined those terms functionally, based on how the consumer interacts with the provided information, just as the Commission did in the order below. As we have explained, Internet service is not "transparent in terms of its interaction with customer-supplied information,." the transmission occurs in connection with information processing. It was therefore consistent with the statute's terms for the Commission to assume that the parallel term "telecommunications service" in 47 U.S.C. § 153(46) likewise describes a "pure" or "transparent" communications path not necessarily separately present, from the end user's perspective, in an integrated information-service offering.

The Commission's application of the basic/enhanced service distinction to non-facilities-based ISPs also supports this conclusion. The Commission has long held that "all those who provide some form of transmission services are not necessarily common carriers." For example, the Commission did not subject to common-carrier regulation those service providers that offered enhanced services over telecommunications facilities, but that did not themselves own the underlying facilities—so-called "non-facilities-based" providers. Examples of these services included database services in which a customer used telecommunications to access information, such as Dow Jones News and Lexis, as well as "value added networks," which lease wires from common carriers and provide transmission as well as protocol-processing service over those wires. These services "combin[ed] communications and computing components," yet the Commission held that they should "always be deemed enhanced" and therefore not subject to common-carrier regulation. Following this traditional distinction, the Commission in the *Universal Service Report* classified ISPs that leased rather than owned their transmission facilities as pure information-service providers.

Respondents' statutory arguments conflict with this regulatory history. They claim that the Communications Act unambiguously classifies as telecommunications carriers all entities that use telecommunications inputs to provide information service. As respondent MCI concedes, this argument would subject to mandatory common-carrier regulation all information-service providers that use telecommunications as an input to provide information service to the public. For example, it would subject to common-carrier regulation non-facilities-based ISPs that own no transmission facilities. Those ISPs provide consumers with transmission facilities used to connect to the Internet, and so, under respondents' argument, necessarily "offer" telecommunications to consumers. Respondents' position that all such entities are necessarily "offering telecommunications" therefore entails mandatory common-carrier regulation of entities that the Commission never classified as "offerors" of basic transmission service, and therefore common carriers, under the *Computer II* regime. We doubt that the parallel term "telecommunications service" unambiguously worked this abrupt shift in Commission policy.

Respondents' analogy between cable companies that provide cable modem service and facilities-based enhanced-service providers—that is, enhanced-service providers who own the transmission facilities used to provide those services—fares no better. Respondents stress that under the *Computer III* rules the Commission regulated such providers more heavily than non-facilities-based providers. The Commission required, for example, local telephone companies that provided enhanced services to offer their wires on a common-carrier basis to competing enhanced-service providers. See, e.g., *In re Amendment of Sections 64.702 of the Commission's Rules and Regulations (Third Computer Inquiry)*, 104 F.C.C.2d 958, 964, ¶ 4 (1986) (hereinafter *Computer III Order*). Respondents argue that the Communications Act unambiguously requires the same treatment for cable companies because cable companies also own the facilities they use to provide cable modem service (and therefore information service).

We disagree. We think it improbable that the Communications Act unambiguously freezes in time the *Computer III* treatment of facilities-based information-service providers. The Act's definition of "telecommunications service" says nothing about imposing more stringent regulatory duties on facilities-based information-service providers. The definition hinges solely on whether the entity "offer[s] telecommunications for a fee directly to the public," though the Act elsewhere subjects facilities-based carriers to stricter regulation., see § 251(c) (imposing various duties on facilities-based local telephone companies). In the *Computer III* rules, the Commission subjected facilities-based providers to common-carrier duties not because of the nature of the "offering" made by those carriers, but rather because of the concern that local telephone companies would abuse the monopoly power they possessed by virtue of the "bottleneck" local telephone facilities they owned. The differential treatment of facilities-based carriers was therefore a function not of the definitions of "enhanced-service" and "basic service," but instead of a choice by the Commission to regulate more stringently, in its discretion, certain entities that provided enhanced service. The Act's definitions, however, parallel the definitions of enhanced and basic service, not the facilities-based grounds on which that policy choice was based, and the Commission remains free to impose special regulatory duties on facilities-based ISPs under its Title I ancillary jurisdiction. In fact, it has invited comment on whether it can and should do so. In sum, if the Act fails unambiguously to classify non-facilities-based information-service providers that use telecommunications inputs to provide an information service as "offer[ors]" of "telecommunications," then it also fails unambiguously to classify facilities-based information-service providers as telecommunications-service offerors; the relevant definitions do not distinguish facilities-based and non-facilities-based carriers. That silence suggests, instead, that the Commission has the discretion to fill the consequent statutory gap.

C

We also conclude that the Commission's construction was "a reasonable policy choice for the [Commission] to make" at *Chevron*'s second step.

Respondents argue that the Commission's construction is unreasonable because it allows any communications provider to "evade" common-carrier regulation by the expedient of bundling information service with telecommunications. Respondents argue that under the Commission's construction a telephone company could, for example, offer an information service like voice mail together with telephone service, thereby avoiding common-carrier regulation of its telephone service.

We need not decide whether a construction that resulted in these consequences would be unreasonable because we do not believe that these results follow from the construction the Commission adopted. As we understand the *Declaratory Ruling*, the Commission did not say that any telecommunications service that is priced or bundled with an information service is automatically unregulated under Title II. The Commission said that a telecommunications input used to provide an information service that is not "separable from the data-processing capabilities of the service" and is instead "part and parcel of [the information service] and is integral to [the information service's] other capabilities" is not a telecommunications offering.

This construction does not leave all information service offerings exempt from mandatory Title II regulation. It is plain, for example, that a local telephone company cannot escape Title II regulation of its residential local exchange service simply by packaging that service with voice mail. That is because a telephone company that packages voice mail with telephone service offers a transparent transmission path—telephone service—that transmits information independent of the information-storage capabilities provided by voice mail. For instance, when a person makes a telephone call, his ability to convey and receive information using the call is only trivially affected by the additional voice-mail capability. Equally, were a telephone company to add a time-of-day announcement that played every time the user picked up his telephone, the "transparent" information transmitted in the ensuing call would be only trivially dependent on the information service the announcement provides. By contrast, the high-speed transmission used to provide cable modem service is a functionally integrated component of that service because it transmits data only in connection with the further processing of information and is necessary to provide Internet service. The Commission's construction therefore was more limited than respondents assume.

Respondents answer that cable modem service does, in fact, provide "transparent" transmission from the consumer's perspective, but this argument, too, is mistaken. Respondents characterize the "information-service" offering of Internet access as consisting only of access to a cable company's e-mail service, its Web page, and the ability it provides consumers to create a personal Web page. When a consumer goes beyond those offerings and accesses content provided by parties other than the cable company, respondents argue, the consumer uses "pure transmission" no less than a consumer who purchases phone service together with voice mail.

This argument, we believe, conflicts with the Commission's understanding of the nature of cable modem service, an understanding we find to be reasonable. When an end user accesses a third-party's Web site, the Commission concluded, he is equally using the information service provided by the cable company that offers him Internet access as when he accesses the company's own Web site, its e-mail service, or his personal Web page. For example, as the Commission found below, part of the information service cable companies provide is access to DNS service. A user cannot reach a third-party's Web site without DNS, which (among other things) matches the Web site address the end user types into his browser (or "clicks" on with his mouse) with the IP address of the Web page's host server. It is at least reasonable to think of DNS as a "capability for ... acquiring ... retrieving, utilizing, or making available" Web site addresses and therefore part of the information service cable companies provide. Similarly, the Internet service provided by cable companies facilitates access to third-party Web pages by offering consumers the ability to store, or "cache," popular content on local computer servers. Cacheing obviates the need for the end user to download anew information from third-party Web sites each time the consumer attempts to access them, thereby increasing the speed of information retrieval. In other words, subscribers can reach third-party Web sites via "the World Wide Web, and browse their contents, [only] because their service provider offers the 'capability for ... acquiring, [storing] ... retrieving [and] utilizing ... information.'" "The service that Internet access providers offer to members of the public is Internet access," not a transparent ability (from the end user's perspective) to transmit information. We therefore conclude that the Commission's construction was reasonable.

V

Respondent MCI, Inc., urges that the Commission's treatment of cable modem service is inconsistent with its treatment of DSL service, and therefore is an arbitrary and capricious deviation from agency policy. MCI points out that when local telephone companies began to offer Internet access through DSL technology in addition to telephone service, the Commission applied its *Computer III* facilities-based classification to them and required them to make the telephone lines used to transmit DSL service available to competing ISPs on nondiscriminatory, common-carrier terms. MCI claims that the Commission's decision not to regulate cable companies similarly under Title II is inconsistent with its DSL policy.

We conclude, however, that the Commission provided a reasoned explanation for treating cable modem service differently from DSL service. As we have already noted the Commission is free within the limits of reasoned interpretation to change course if it adequately justifies the change. It has done so here. The traditional reason for its *Computer III* common-carrier treatment of facilities-based carriers (including DSL carriers), as the Commission explained, was "that the telephone network [was] the primary, if not exclusive, means through which information service providers can gain access to their customers." The Commission applied the same treatment to DSL service based on that history, rather than on an analysis of contemporaneous market conditions. The Commission in the order under review, by contrast, concluded that changed market conditions warrant different treatment of facilities-based cable companies providing Internet access. Unlike at the time of *Computer III*, substitute forms of Internet transmission exist today: "[R]esidential high-speed access to the Internet is evolving over multiple electronic platforms, including wireline, cable, terrestrial wireless and satellite." The Commission concluded that "broadband services should exist in a minimal regulatory environment that promotes investment and innovation in a competitive market." This, the Commission reasoned, warranted treating cable companies unlike the facilities-based enhanced-service providers of the past. We find nothing arbitrary about the Commission's providing a fresh analysis of the problem as applied to the cable industry, which it has never subjected to these rules. This is adequate rational justification for the Commission's conclusions.

Respondents argue, in effect, that the Commission's justification for exempting cable modem service providers from common-carrier regulation applies with similar force to DSL providers. We need not address that argument. The Commission's decision appears to be a first step in an effort to reshape the way the Commission regulates information-service providers; that may be why it has tentatively concluded that DSL service provided by facilities-based telephone companies should also be classified solely as an information service. The Commission need not immediately apply the policy reasoning in the *Declaratory Ruling* to all types of information-service providers. It apparently has decided to revisit its longstanding *Computer III* classification of facilities-based information-service providers incrementally. Any inconsistency between the order under review and the Commission's treatment of DSL service can be adequately addressed when the Commission fully reconsiders its treatment of DSL service and when it decides whether, pursuant to its ancillary Title I jurisdiction, to require cable companies to allow independent ISPs access to their facilities. We express no view on those matters. In particular, we express no view on how the Commission should, or lawfully may, classify DSL service.

The questions the Commission resolved in the order under review involve a "subject matter [that] is technical, complex, and dynamic." The Commission is in a far better position to address these questions than we are. Nothing in the Communications Act or the Administrative Procedure Act makes unlawful the Commission's use of its expert policy judgment to resolve these difficult questions. The judgment of the Court of Appeals is reversed, and the cases are remanded for further proceedings consistent with this opinion.

JUSTICE SCALIA, with whom JUSTICE SOUTER and JUSTICE GINSBURG join as to Part I, dissenting.

The Federal Communications Commission (FCC or Commission) has once again attempted to concoct "a whole new regime of regulation (or of free-market competition)" under the guise of statutory construction. Actually, in these cases, it might be more accurate to say the Commission has attempted to establish a whole new regime of *non*-regulation, which will make for more or less free-market competition, depending upon whose experts are believed. The important fact, however, is that the Commission has chosen to achieve this through an implausible reading of the statute, and has thus exceeded the authority given it by Congress.

I

* * *

The Court concludes that the word "offer" is ambiguous in the sense that it has " 'alternative dictionary definitions' " that might be relevant. It seems to me, however, that the analytic problem pertains not really to the meaning of "offer," but to the identity of what is offered. The relevant question is whether the individual components in a package being offered still possess sufficient identity to be described as separate objects of the offer, or whether they have been so changed by their combination with the other components that it is no longer reasonable to describe them in that way.

Thus, I agree (to adapt the Court's example) that it would be odd to say that a car dealer is in the business of selling steel or carpets because the cars he sells include both steel frames and carpeting. Nor does the water company sell hydrogen, nor the pet store water (though dogs and cats are largely water at the molecular level). But what is sometimes true is not, as the Court seems to assume, *always* true. There are instances in which it is ridiculous to deny that one part of a joint offering is being offered merely because it is not offered on a " 'stand-alone' " basis.

If, for example, I call up a pizzeria and ask whether they offer delivery, both common sense and common "usage," would prevent them from answering: "No, we do not offer delivery—but if you order a pizza from us, we'll bake it for you and then bring it to your house." The logical response to this would be something on the order of, "so, you *do* offer delivery." But our pizza-man may continue to deny the obvious and explain, paraphrasing the FCC and the Court: "No, even though we bring the pizza to your house, we are not actually 'offering' you delivery, because the delivery that we provide to our end users is 'part and parcel' of our pizzeria-pizza-at-home service and is 'integral to its other capabilities.' "[1] Any reasonable customer would conclude at that point that his interlocutor was either crazy or following some too-clever-by-half legal advice.

In short, for the inputs of a finished service to qualify as the objects of an "offer" (as that term is reasonably understood), it is perhaps a sufficient, *but surely not a necessary,* condition that the seller offer separately "each discrete input that is necessary to providing ... a finished service." The pet store may have a policy of selling puppies only with leashes, but any customer will say that it *does* offer puppies—because a leashed puppy is still a puppy, even though it is not offered on a "stand-alone" basis.

Despite the Court's mighty labors to prove otherwise, the telecommunications component of cable-modem service retains such ample independent identity that it must be regarded as being on offer—especially

1. The myth that the pizzeria does not offer delivery becomes even more difficult to maintain when the pizzeria advertises quick delivery as one of its advantages over competitors. That, of course, is the case with cable broadband.

when seen from the perspective of the consumer or the end user, which the Court purports to find determinative. The Commission's ruling began by noting that cable-modem service provides *both* "high-speed access to the Internet" *and* other "applications and functions," because that is exactly how any reasonable consumer would perceive it: as consisting of two separate things.

* * *

As the Court acknowledges, DSL service has been similar to dial-up service in the respect that the physical connection to the Internet must be offered separately from Internet functionality. Thus, customers shopping for dial-up or DSL service will not be able to use the Internet unless they get both someone to provide them with a physical connection and someone to provide them with applications and functions such as e-mail and Web access. It is therefore inevitable that customers will regard the competing cable-modem service as giving them *both* computing functionality *and* the physical pipe by which that functionality comes to their computer—both the pizza and the delivery service that nondelivery pizzerias require to be purchased from the cab company.[4]

Since the delivery service provided by cable (the broad-band connection between the customer's computer and the cable company's computer-processing facilities) is downstream from the computer-processing facilities, there is no question that it merely serves as a conduit for the information services that have already been "assembled" by the cable company in its capacity as ISP. This is relevant because of the statutory distinction between an "information service" and "telecommunications." The former involves the capability of getting, processing, and manipulating information. § 153(20). The latter, by contrast, involves no "change in the form or content of the information as sent and received." § 153(43). When cable-company-assembled information enters the cable for delivery to the subscriber, the information service is already complete. The information has been (as the statute requires) generated, acquired, stored, transformed, processed, retrieved, utilized, or made available. All that remains is for the information in its final, unaltered form, to be delivered (via telecommunications) to the subscriber.

This reveals the insubstantiality of the fear invoked by both the Commission and the Court: the fear of what will happen to ISPs that do not provide the physical pathway to Internet access, yet still use telecommunications to acquire the pieces necessary to assemble the information that they pass back to their customers. According to this *reductio*, if cable-modem-service providers are deemed to provide "telecommunica-

4. The Court contends that this analogy is inapposite because one need not have a pizza delivered, whereas one must purchase the cable connection in order to use cable's ISP functions. But the ISP functions provided by the cable company *can* be used without cable delivery—by accessing them from an Internet connection other than cable. The merger of the physical connection and Internet functions in cable's offerings has nothing to do with the " 'inextricably intertwined,' " nature of the two (like a car and its carpet), but is an artificial product of the cable company's marketing decision not to offer the two separately, so that the Commission could (by the *Declaratory Ruling* under review here) exempt it from common-carrier status.

tions service," then so must *all* ISPs because they all "use" telecommunications in providing Internet functionality (by connecting to other parts of the Internet, including Internet backbone providers, for example). In terms of the pizzeria analogy, this is equivalent to saying that, if the pizzeria "offers" delivery, *all* restaurants "offer" delivery, because the ingredients of the food they serve their customers have come from other places; no matter how their customers get the food (whether by eating it at the restaurant, or by coming to pick it up themselves), they still consume a product for which delivery was a necessary "input." This is nonsense. Concluding that delivery of the finished pizza constitutes an "offer" of delivery does not require the conclusion that the serving of prepared food includes an "offer" of delivery. And that analogy does not even do the point justice, since " 'telecommunications service' " is defined as "the offering of telecommunications for a fee *directly to the public*." 47 U.S.C. § 153(46) (emphasis added). The ISPs' use of telecommunications in their processing of information is not offered directly to the public.

The "regulatory history" on which the Court depends so much, provides another reason why common-carrier regulation of all ISPs is not a worry. Under its *Computer Inquiry* rules, which foreshadowed the definitions of "information" and "telecommunications" services, the Commission forbore from regulating as common carriers "value-added networks"—non-facilities-based providers who leased basic services from common carriers and bundled them with enhanced services; it said that they, unlike facilities-based providers, would be deemed to provide only enhanced services. That same result can be achieved today under the Commission's statutory authority to forbear from imposing most Title II regulations. 47 U.S.C. § 160. In fact, the statutory criteria for forbearance—which include what is "just and reasonable," "necessary for the protection of consumers," and "consistent with the public interest," §§ 160(a)(1), (2), (3)—correspond well with the kinds of policy reasons the Commission has invoked to justify its peculiar construction of "telecommunications service" to exclude cable-modem service.

* * *

Finally, I must note that, notwithstanding the Commission's self-congratulatory paean to its deregulatory largesse, it concluded the *Declaratory Ruling* by asking, as the Court paraphrases, "whether under its Title I jurisdiction [the Commission] should require cable companies to offer other ISPs access to their facilities on common-carrier terms." In other words, what the Commission hath given, the Commission may well take away—unless it doesn't. This is a wonderful illustration of how an experienced agency can (with some assistance from credulous courts) turn statutory constraints into bureaucratic discretions. The main source of the Commission's regulatory authority over common carriers is Title II, but the Commission has rendered that inapplicable in this instance by concluding that the definition of "telecommunications service" is ambiguous and does not (in its current view) apply to cable-modem service. It contemplates, however, altering that (unnecessary) outcome, not by changing the law (*i.e.*, its construction of the Title II definitions), but by reserving the right to change the facts. Under its undefined and sparingly used "ancillary" powers, the Commission might conclude that it can order cable companies to "unbundle" the telecommunications component of cable-modem service. And presto, Title II will then apply to them, because they will finally be "offering" telecommunications service! Of course, the Commission will still have the statutory power to forbear from regulating them under § 160 (which it has already tentatively concluded it would do). Such Möbius-strip reasoning mocks the principle that the statute constrains the agency in any meaningful way.

After all is said and done, after all the regulatory cant has been translated, and the smoke of agency expertise blown away, it remains perfectly clear that someone who sells cable-modem service is "offering" telecommunications. For that simple reason set forth in the statute, I would affirm the Court of Appeals.

MCI's concern about the disparate regulatory treatment of cable modem service and DSL service was soon made moot. Although the FCC defended the different treatment of the two broadband services in *Brand X*, it had basically already made a decision to deregulate DSL, which it did immediately after the Supreme Court's decision in *Brand X*. The FCC's decision to deregulate wireline broadband—effectively equalizing its treatment of cable and DSL—was affirmed in the following case.

TIME WARNER TELECOM, INC. v. FCC

United States Court of Appeals, Third Circuit, 2007.
507 F.3d 205.

FUENTES, CIRCUIT JUDGE.

The petition under review arises from an order of the Federal Communications Commission ("FCC"), which substantially limits federal regulation of high-speed Internet access service provided over traditional telephone lines (referred to as "wireline broadband Internet access service"). The dispute centers, in large part, on the FCC's decision to relieve telephone companies of decades-old regulations that required them to grant competing Internet service providers nondiscriminatory access to their wirelines in order to reach consumers. The FCC contends that these regulations "imposed significant costs" on telephone companies, "thereby impeding innovation and investment in new broadband technologies and services." Presumably, the FCC's order now allows telephone companies to enter into individually negotiated arrangements with entities that seek access to their broadband wireline facilities.

Petitioners, who are independent Internet service providers, competing telecommunications service providers, cable modem providers, and various public interest organizations, argue that the FCC's order allows telephone companies to deny competitors access to their wirelines, thereby resulting in decreased competition and consumer choice in the market for broadband Internet service. For the reasons stated below, we conclude that the FCC's order is based on a reasonable interpretation of the Communications Act of 1934, and a proper exercise of agency discretion. Accordingly, we will deny the petition for review.

I. Background

We discuss in some detail the complex technical and regulatory context for the FCC's order, which is set forth at *Appropriate Framework for Broadband Access to the Internet over Wireline Facilities*, 20 F.C.C.R. 14853 (2005) ("*Wireline Broadband Order*").

A. Technical Background

Before the advent of broadband technology, consumers accessed the Internet using "dial-up" connections provided over the interconnected system of telephone wires known as a local exchange. See *Nat'l Cable & Telecomm. Ass'n v. Brand X Internet Svcs.*, 545 U.S. 967, 974 (2005) ("*Brand X*"). With a dial-up connection, consumers use computer modems to make calls which Internet service providers ("ISPs") link to the Internet by providing consumers with a physical connection and "the ability to translate raw Internet data into information they may both view on their personal computers and transmit to other computers connected to the Internet." Dial-up connections, also referred to as "narrowband" connections, transmit data at relatively slow speeds.

By contrast, "broadband" connections, which are increasingly replacing dial-up connections, are much faster and are principally provided by: (1) cable modem service and (2) Digital Subscriber Line (DSL) service. DSL service, the type of transmission at issue in the *Wireline Broadband Order*, involves the use of "[t]wo DSL modems [that] are attached to a telephone loop, one at the subscriber's premises and one at the telephone company's central office." *WorldCom, Inc. v. FCC*, 246 F.3d 690, 692 (D.C.Cir.2001). If the line carries telephone service and high-speed data transmission, the telephone company—also known as the local exchange carrier ("LEC")—separates the streams and sends ordinary voice calls to the telephone network and data traffic to a "packet-switched data network" where it is routed to an ISP. LECs use their transmission facilities to provide consumers with Internet access service, in which case they are referred to as "facilities-based ISPs." They also lease their wires on a wholesale basis to independent ISPs, referred to as "non-facilities-based ISPs," who use the wires to reach their customers.

B. Regulatory Framework

There are three key developments in the regulatory history of telecommunications and data processing services that are significant to this petition for review: (1) Congress's passage of the Communications Act in 1934; (2) the FCC's issuance of its *Computer II* ruling in 1980;

and (3) the passage of the Telecommunications Act in 1996. We discuss each in turn.

1. The Common Carrier Doctrine

The regulatory issues raised in the *Wireline Broadband Order* trace back to the enactment of the Communications Act in 1934, which established the FCC's "broad authority to regulate interstate telephone communications." Title II of the statute heavily regulated the activities of local telephone companies by imposing upon them certain "common carrier" obligations. For example, Title II required telephone companies to charge consumers "just and reasonable" rates and to file and make publicly available their rate schedules (known as "tariffs"); authorized the FCC to set rates if the ones offered by a carrier were not just and reasonable; prohibited carriers from constructing new wirelines without first obtaining a certificate of public convenience and necessity from the FCC; and established liability for carriers that violated the statute. Communications Act. These common carrier provisions remain essentially unchanged, although, as discussed below, Congress has since amended Title II to include additional common carrier obligations.

2. The FCC's Computer Inquiry Proceedings

In 1966, the FCC initiated the *Computer Inquiry* proceedings to address the regulatory issues presented by the growing convergence of traditional telephone communications and data processing services. The FCC issued three important rulings in connection with the proceedings, known as "*Computer I*," "*Computer II*," and "*Computer III*."

* * *

In *Amendment of Section 64.702 of the Commission's Rules and Regulations*, 77 F.C.C.2d 384, ¶ 2 (1980) ("*Computer II*"), . . . [t]he FCC adopted a regulatory framework that distinguished between the offering of "basic transmission service" and "enhanced service"—subjecting only the former to mandatory Title II regulation. * * *

In addition to distinguishing between basic transmission services (subject to Title II) and enhanced services (not subject to Title II), the FCC eliminated the maximum separation regime [first established in *Computer I*] with respect to all telephone common carriers except those under the control of AT&T and GTE, the two dominant carriers that the FCC determined had sufficient market power to engage in anticompetitive activity on a national scale. Thus, telephone companies were no longer required to use separate affiliates to provide enhanced services to consumers. However, the FCC, pursuant to its ancillary jurisdiction under Title I of the Communications Act, required those carriers engaged in the provision of enhanced services to grant competing providers access to their wirelines on a nondiscriminatory basis pursuant to tariffs governed by Title II. The FCC explained the *Computer II* nondiscriminatory access requirements as follows:

> Because enhanced services are dependent on the common carrier offering of basic services, a basic service is the building block upon which enhanced services are offered. Thus those carriers that own common carrier transmission facilities and provide enhanced services, but are not subject to the separate subsidiary requirement, must acquire transmission capacity pursuant to the same prices, terms, and conditions reflected in their tariffs when their own facilities are utilized. Other offerors of enhanced services would likewise be able to use such a carrier's facilities under the same terms and conditions.

These nondiscriminatory access rules are at the center of this petition for review.

* * *

3. Telecommunications Act of 1996

Congress substantially amended the Communications Act of 1934 when it passed the Telecommunications Act of 1996. As one commentator has explained, "the principal goal in the 1996 Act was to open the local telephone market to effective competition." Thus, Title II was expanded to include additional requirements intended to break up the dominance of a small number of LECs over the telecommunications market.

As amended, Title II imposes on LECs the duty not to prohibit or unreasonably restrict resale of their services; to provide number portability so that consumers can switch LECs but still retain their phone numbers; to accord dialing parity so that a LEC customer can reach a customer of another LEC by dialing no more digits than necessary; to permit competing LECs access to their rights of way; and to establish reciprocal compensation with other LECs for the transport and termination of all calls.

In addition, Title II imposes on "incumbent local exchange carriers" ("ILECs"), defined as any LEC that existed as of the date the Telecommunications Act was passed, the obligation to permit nondiscriminatory interconnection with another carrier's facilities at any feasible point in the ILEC's network; provide any other carrier unbundled access to certain elements of the ILEC's network at cost-based rates; establish wholesale rates for the resale of any telecommunications service provided by the ILEC; provide the FCC with notice of any changes to the ILEC's network; and permit the collocation of other telecommunications carriers' equipment on the ILEC's premises.

Crucial to this petition for review, the Telecommunications Act also introduced two new important regulatory classifications that parallel the basic and enhanced services distinction established in *Computer II*: "telecommunications service" and "information service." Only telecommunications service is subject to mandatory regulation under Title II.

C. Regulatory Treatment of Broadband Internet Access Service

1. Cable Modem Broadband Internet Access Service

The FCC first applied the Communications Act's new regulatory classifications to broadband Internet access service in its ruling in *Inquiry Concerning High Speed Access to the Internet Over Cable and Other Facilities*, 17 F.C.C.R. 4798 (2002) ("*Cable Modem Declaratory Ruling*"). In the ruling, the FCC concluded that broadband Internet access service provided by cable companies is an "information service," which does not include a separate "telecommunications service" subject to mandatory Title II common carrier regulation. In addition, the FCC declined to apply the *Computer II* nondiscriminatory access requirements to cable modem broadband operators despite the fact that, at the time, telephone companies engaged in the provision of enhanced services were required to provide non-facilities-based ISPs nondiscriminatory access to their transmission facilities. The Supreme Court upheld the *Cable Modem Declaratory Ruling* in *Brand X*, 545 U.S. at 1002, noting that it "appears to be a first-step in an effort to reshape the way the Commission regulates information-service providers."

2. Procedural Background to the Wireline Broadband Order

* * *

On September 23, 2005, three months after the Supreme Court's *Brand X* decision, the FCC released the order on review, which substantially limited federal regulation of wireline broadband Internet access service through two principal rulings. First, the FCC ruled that wireline broadband Internet access service, like cable modem service, is an information service that does not include a separate "telecommunications service" subject to mandatory common carrier regulation under Title II of the Communications Act, regardless of whether such service is provided by LECs or non-facilities-based ISPs. Second, the FCC eliminated the *Computer II* requirements on grounds that market conditions no longer justify requiring LECs to grant independent ISPs nondiscriminatory access to their wireline transmission facilities. These consolidated petitions for review followed.

Petitioners, who are independent ISPs, competing telecommunications service providers, cable modem providers, and various public interest organizations, challenge the FCC's statutory classification and *Computer II* rulings. * * *

III. Statutory Classification

In the *Wireline Broadband Order*, the FCC rejected the proposition that wireline broadband Internet access service "includes both an information service and a telecommunications. Rather, it found that wireline broadband Internet access service is a functionally integrated "information service." We conclude that this statutory classification is based on a reasonable interpretation of the Communications Act.

* * *

In *Brand X*, the Supreme Court, applying *Chevron*'s familiar two-step analysis, concluded that the term "telecommunications service" is ambiguous as applied to cable modem Internet access service "[b]ecause the term 'offer' can sometimes refer to a single, finished product and sometimes to the individual components in a package being offered." * * *

Applying the same analytical approach used in the *Cable Modem Declaratory Ruling*, the FCC, in this proceeding, concluded that "wireline broadband Internet access service provided over a provider's own facilities is appropriately classified as an information service because its providers offer a single, integrated service (i.e., Internet access) to end users." The parties agree that Internet service is an information service not subject to Title II regulation. Petitioners contend, however, that the FCC erroneously concluded that the wireline transmission component used to provide broadband Internet access is not a "telecommunication service" offering subject to mandatory Title II regulation. * * *

Petitioners attempt to distinguish wireline broadband service from cable modem service on grounds that LECs offer their wireline transmission component on a "stand-alone" basis to other ISPs. That is, LECs lease their transmission facilities to independent ISPs who themselves provide consumers with Internet access service. Therefore, petitioners reason, LECs plainly "offer" a separate telecommunications service. We are not persuaded that this is a basis for distinguishing wireline broadband service from cable modem service.

The fact that LECs have provided independent ISPs with stand-alone transmission capabilities is, as the FCC points out, a function of the very regulatory requirements that the FCC's order seeks to eliminate-that is, wireline providers have been (until the release of the *Wireline Broadband Order*) the only broadband provider required by *Computer II* to offer their transmission component on a stand-alone basis. Indeed, record evidence considered in the *Cable Modem Declaratory Ruling* showed that cable modem providers not only have the capability to offer their transmission facilities on a stand-alone basis, but, in fact, have entered into agreements with independent ISPs to do so. This fact did not prevent the Supreme Court from upholding the FCC's determination that cable modem service is a fully integrated information service. We see no reason why we should reach a contrary decision here.

* * *

[P]etitioners do not provide us with a basis for vacating the FCC's ruling that wireline broadband Internet access service should not be subject to mandatory common carrier regulation under Title II of the Communications Act.

IV. Non Discriminatory Access Under *Computer II*

As discussed, in *Computer II*, the FCC, pursuant to its Title I ancillary jurisdiction, required all LECs to provide competing enhanced service providers nondiscriminatory access to the basic transmission component underlying their enhanced services. Petitioners argue that the FCC's decision to eliminate the *Computer II* requirements was arbitrary and capricious because the FCC: (1) failed to engage in a proper market analysis and (2) failed to properly apply the common carrier test set forth in *National Association of Regulatory Utility Commissioners v. FCC*, 525 F.2d 630, 640 (D.C.Cir.1976) ("*NARUC I*"). In addition, petitioners assert that the FCC decision to relieve LECs of their *Computer II* obligations violates the discontinuance requirements set forth in § 214 of the Communications Act, as well as the Due Process Clause of the Constitution.

A. Market Analysis

Petitioners argue that the FCC's blanket deregulation of wireline broadband Internet access service violates the agency's "well-established regulatory policy for assessing ILEC market power," which "differentiates between services demanded by distinct customer classes." Specifically, petitioners contend, before eliminating the *Computer II* requirements, the FCC was required to consider ILECs' dominance of the business market and certain geographic markets. Accordingly, petitioners request that the Court remand this case to the FCC for a full market analysis. We do not agree that remand is necessary.

To the extent that the FCC's decision not to conduct a traditional market analysis constitutes a departure from past agency practice, it is well-settled that "an agency may change its course so long as it can justify its change with a 'reasoned analysis.'" Here, the FCC argues that it "fully justified its decision to refrain from standard market dominance analysis in order to avoid making highly dubious and 'premature' conclusions about a nascent and dynamic market that is 'rapidly changing.'" * * *

Instead, the FCC considered how the market for broadband services is likely to develop. For example, the FCC predicted based on record evidence that the market penetration of cable modem and wireline broadband service will grow dramatically in the future and that the two services will compete head-to-head; both services will continue to invest in and expand the reach of their services; emerging broadband platforms will exert competitive pressure and gain market share; and demand among consumers for broadband services will only increase. We agree with the FCC that these reasons justified its decision to refrain from a traditional market analysis and to rely instead on larger trends and predictions concerning the future of the broadband services market. * * *

B. The *NARUC I* Common Carrier Test

Petitioners argue that having eliminated the *Computer II* nondiscriminatory access requirements, the FCC was required to determine whether wireline broadband transmission facilities should nevertheless be regulated on a common carriage basis under the test set forth in the D.C. Circuit's decision in *NARUC I*. Under this test, "a carrier has to be regulated as a common carrier if it will make capacity available to the public indifferently or if the public interest requires common carrier operation of the proposed facility." We disagree with petitioners that the FCC failed to properly consider the public interest prong of the *NARUC I* test.

It is well-settled that "the Commission's judgment regarding how the public interest is best served is entitled to substantial judicial deference" because "the weighing of policies under the public interest standard is a task that Congress has delegated to the Commission.". Here, in addition to considering the market conditions discussed above, the FCC explained at length its judgment that continued regulation of wireline broadband providers under *Computer II* would harm consumers by "imped[ing] the development and deployment of innovative wireline broadband Internet access technologies and services."

For example, the FCC credited evidence that showed that wireline broadband providers are unable or unwilling to integrate more efficient equipment into their wireline networks because of the costs of complying with the *Computer II* requirements. Likewise, the FCC noted that "[s]everal parties argue that the *Computer Inquiry* requirements prevent them from altering business priorities in response to changing market demands." Accordingly, the FCC determined that eliminating the *Computer II* rules "will make it more likely that wireline operators will take more risks in investing in and deploying new technologies than they [were] willing and able to take under the [*Computer Inquiry*] regime."

With respect to whether independent ISPs would continue to have reasonable access to ILECs' transmission facilities in the absence of regulatory compulsion, the FCC explained that the record showed that wireline broadband Internet access service providers have business incentives to make their facilities available to competing ISPs on a commercially reasonable basis. In particular, the FCC noted that ILECs have "an economic incentive to spread the costs of [their] network[s] over as much traffic and as many customers as possible regardless of whether such customers are wholesale or retail." In this regard, the FCC implicitly rejected the argument asserted by Time Warner in its brief, that as a result of the elimination of the *Computer II* requirements, "ILECs will now be free to upgrade the transmission inputs they use for their own retail broadband Internet access services, while restricting their competitors' access to the increasingly outmoded transmission services that remain subject to Title II regulation."

C. Section 214 of the Communications Act and the Due Process Clause

Finally, we reject petitioners' argument that the *Wireline Broadband Order* violates § 214 of the Communications Act and the Due Process Clause of the Constitution by granting ILECs a "blanket certification to discontinue providing existing customers [with] common carrier broadband Internet access transmission services." * * *

Eliminating the Computer Inquiry Requirements. In addition to eliminating the non-discriminatory access requirements of *Computer II,* the FCC's *Wireline Broadband Order* also eliminated the non-structural safeguard requirements of *Computer III.* We discussed these in Chapter 7. The only remaining form of mandated access available ISPs are the unbundling requirements of section 251. Of course, only competing *telecommunications carriers* (CLECs) can obtain access under 251. Some ISPs are also CLECs, but by no means all are (AOL and Earthlink being two prominent examples). How much does it matter? As noted by the court, the FCC found that independent ISPs will still be able to get access to wireline broadband by means of tariffed wholesale services provided by the ILECs. Here is what the FCC said in its order:

> Given the nature and history of the broadband Internet access services industry, we expect that wireline broadband transmission will remain available to ISPs and others without any *Computer Inquiry* requirements. Incumbent LECs have represented that they not only intend to make broadband Internet access transmission offerings available to unaffiliated ISPs in a manner that meets ISPs' needs, but that they have business incentives to do so. For example, Qwest offers a tariffed wireline broadband DSL service that enables hundreds of independent ISPs to serve end-user customers over Qwest's broadband facilities. Regardless of the outcome of this proceeding, Qwest has stated it will continue to make available a DSL offering that will enable consumers to reach unaffiliated ISPs because consumers demand the choice, and meeting that demand makes its product more attractive. SBC previously entered into a memorandum of understanding with a trade association representing nearly 300 members of the Internet industry, including many independent ISPs, committing to negotiate private commercial arrangements with unaffiliated ISPs for broadband Internet access. Verizon has similarly indicated its intent to enter into commercially reasonable contracts with unaffiliated ISPs for broadband transmission services because it is in its best interest to do so. Finally, BellSouth has also evidenced a willingness, desire, and incentive to deal with unaffiliated ISPs absent a Commission requirement that compels them to do so. For example, BellSouth has indicated that it will benefit financially from providing DSL transmission to independent ISPs, as it has an economic incentive to spread the costs of its network over as much traffic and as many customers as possible regardless of whether such customers are wholesale or retail.

Wireline Broadband Order at ¶ 74. Should the independent ISPs take comfort in this assurance? Or, put the other way, if carriers are going to sell more carriage by offering it to ISPs at wholesale, is there any reason they won't do so?

Open Access, Applications, and Control. The "open access" debate that eventually led to both *Brand X* and *Time Warner Telecom* was predicated on the idea that consumers should not be forced to accept their carrier's affiliated ISP. But when presented with a choice of ISPs over a given carrier, most consumers have responded with a yawn, viewing ISP services as simply a means for obtaining access to the Internet. If ISP services really are a commodity (and consequently an unlikely source of high profits), then why were independent ISPs fighting so hard for—and cable and telephone companies fighting so hard against—open access? Part of it may have to do with the changing nature of ISPs over time. At the beginning of the open access debates, many ISPs (AOL being a prime example) offered their own organized content and services (generically, "applications") over the network, something of a holdover from the era of dedicated network services like CompuServe, which predated widespread consumer access to the Internet. The concern was that carriers would leverage their (natural) monopolies in carriage into control over the seemingly competitive Internet applications market, exactly the same concern that prompted the split adopted in the *Computer Inquiries*. By the time the debate was resolved, most consumers: 1) had a choice of carriers (between DSL and cable modem), and 2) were relying on web portals like Google or Yahoo! rather than their ISPs as their primary source of organized Internet applications. Attempts by ISPs to direct their customers to favored application providers were antiquated by the time of *Brand X* and *Time Warner Telecom*. But the question of how to handle the relationship between carriers and the Internet applications they carry did not go away with the end of the open access debates. The market, the technology, and the battle over control merely shifted.

C. NETWORK NEUTRALITY

The *Brand X* and *Time Warner Telecom* cases basically ended the long-standing legal controversy over whether integrated broadband service providers—cable operators or LECs—had to provide access to their "pipes" to competing providers of Internet access services. But the ability to control the choice of ISP was always something of a proxy for the ability to control use of the network. The open access contest having been decided in favor of carriers, debate has moved on to the matter of control itself. The conventional label for the issue of control is "network neutrality" (or simply "net neutrality").

The debate is still largely "academic," both because it has primarily been carried out in academic rather than regulatory circles and because it is largely anticipatory—carriers have yet to engage in many practices that would violate network neutrality principles. But that could change, as support for some form of neutrality regulation grows. Congress has actively considered neutrality legislation in recent sessions, and the FCC has already taken the first tentative steps toward imposing neutrality rules on carriers.

1. The Academic Debate

Like so many labels that get picked up in public debate over complex arrangements, net neutrality has come to mean different things to different persons. There are as many different theories about network neutrality are there are ways to exercise control over modern communications networks. Carriers can exercise control over the uses of the network, for example, by charging for different levels of service or imposing conditions and restrictions on different types of use. Whether doing so is problematic depends in large part on one's theory of how the network "should" operate. Such theories are not in short supply.

Conceptually, the network neutrality debate has something in common with the controversies involved in *Brand X* and *Time Warner Telecom* albeit it at a different level of complexity. Both can be said to be about who has what access to the network. But in important respects the two controversies are different. As mentioned above, the question of access for independent ISPs was largely a proxy for underlying concerns about the control that integrated broadband carriers would exercise over the network; the network neutrality debate is more complex in that it directly addresses specific forms of control. Network neutrality also differs from the open access debate because it directly involves additional actors. The open access debate was driven by independent Internet service providers like EarthLink and AOL seeking to use the broadband transport facilities of cable and telco broadband providers. The net neutrality debate is not about giving independent ISPs a right of access to broadband transport facilities in order to provide a competing Internet *access* service. Rather it is about allowing Internet application providers—like Amazon or Vonage—to reach their customers without unreasonable restrictions or discrimination by the telecommunications carriers that own the broadband "pipes." And, at the other end of the line (both figuratively and literally), it is also about allowing end subscribers to access the Internet applications of their choice without unreasonable restriction. For example, AT&T may have an incentive to make it more difficult for its subscribers to access Vonage, whose VoIP technology makes it a competitor to the voice service that AT&T provides over the public switched telephone network. By focusing on what happens at the two ends of the network, some forms of the neutrality argument resemble the old controversy about competitive equipment supply and consumer use of "foreign attachments" that we examined in the *Carterfone* case in Chapter 7, and the FCC has been somewhat receptive to that analogy.

But network neutrality can go beyond control over what happens at the ends of the network to reach the conduct of network providers in the operation of the network itself. Net neutrality advocates seek rules forbidding broadband providers, such as AT&T or Comcast, from either discriminating among application providers, such as Amazon or Vonage, or from reconfiguring their networks to effectively discriminate in favor of some uses and against others. For instance, some Internet applications (such as streaming video) can only work reliably if they receive some priority over non-time-sensitive data. But altering the network to allow such priority carriage to take place would effectively discriminate against non-priority traffic. In its strongest form, net neutrality would prohibit virtually any interference by carriers in what is carried over the network, how it is carried, or for whom it is carried. In furtherance of that claim, the network neutrality movement—as part of an argument first advanced during the open access debate—has enlisted for its regulatory merit a technological argument about how best to design networks: the end-to-end principle.

MARK A. LEMLEY & LAWRENCE LESSIG, THE END OF END-TO-END: PRESERVING THE ARCHITECTURE OF THE INTERNET IN THE BROADBAND ERA

48 U.C.L.A. L. Rev. 925 (2001).

* * *

I. WHY THE ISP MARKET SHOULD REMAIN COMPETITIVE

A. The Architecture of the Internet: End-to-End Network Design

The Internet is the fastest growing network in history. In its thirty years of existence, its population has grown a million times over. Currently, it is the single largest contributor to the growth of the U.S. economy and has become the single most important influence linking individuals, and commerce, internationally.

The Internet is not, however, the first communications network. There have been other networks before the Internet that did not experience the same extraordinary growth. These networks followed different design principles.

It is the view of many in the Internet community, ourselves included, that the extraordinary growth of the Internet rests fundamentally upon its design principles. Some of these principles relate to the openness of the Internet's standards and the openness of the software that implemented those standards. Some are engineering principles, designed to make the Internet function more flexibly and efficiently. But from the very beginning, these principles have been understood to have a social as well as a technological significance. They have, that is, been meant to implement values as well as enable communication. In our view, one aspect of this social significance is the competition in innovation the Internet enables. The tremendous innovation that has occurred on the Internet, in other words, depends crucially on its open nature.

Among the Internet's design principles is one that is particularly relevant to the bundling of broadband cable services. This is the end-to-end design principle that has been latent in system design for many years, but was first articulated explicitly as a principle in 1981 by Professors Jerome Saltzer, David Reed, and David Clark.[11] The e2e argument organizes the placement of functions within a network. It counsels that the "intelligence" in a network should be located at the top of a layered system—at its "ends," where users put information and applications onto the network. The communications protocols themselves (the "pipes" through which information flows) should be as simple and as general as possible.

One consequence of this design is a principle of nondiscrimination among applications. Lower-level network layers should provide a broad range of resources that are not particular to or optimized for any single application—even if a more efficient design for at least some applications is thereby sacrificed. As described in a subsequent paper by Reed, Saltzer, and Clark,

> end-to-end arguments have ... two complementary goals: [(1)] Higher-level layers, more specific to an application, are free (and thus expected) to organize lower level network resources to achieve application-specific design goals efficiently (application autonomy); [(2)] Lower-level layers, which support many independent applications, should provide only resources of broad utility across applications, while providing to applications useable means for effective sharing of resources and resolution of resource conflicts (network transparency).

While the e2e design principle was first adopted for technical reasons, it has important social features as well. E2e expands the competitive horizon by enabling a wider variety of applications to connect to and to use the network. It maximizes the number of entities that can compete for the use and applications of the network. As there is no single strategic actor who can tilt the competitive environment (the network) in favor of itself, or no hierarchical entity that can favor some applications over others, an e2e network creates a maximally competitive environment for innovation.

The e2e design of the Internet has facilitated innovation. As Reed, Saltzer, and Clark argue,

> had the original Internet design been optimized for telephony-style virtual circuits (as were its contemporaries SNA and Tymnet), it would never have enabled the experimentation that led to protocols that could support the World Wide Web, or the flexible interconnect that has led to the flowering of a million independent Internet service providers.... Preserving low-cost options to innovate outside the network, while keeping the core network services and functions simple and cheap, has been shown to have very substantial value.

11. See J.H. Saltzer et al., *End-to-End Arguments in System Design*, available at http://web.mit.edu/Saltzer/www/publications/endtoend/endtoend.pdf (Apr. 8, 1981), reprinted in INNOVATION IN NETWORKING 195–206 (Craig Partridge ed., 1988).

B. The Consequences of These Architectural Principles

The effect of the design of the Internet—including, but not exclusively, e2e—has been profound. By its design, the Internet has enabled an extraordinary creativity precisely because it has pushed creativity to the ends of the network. Rather than relying upon the creativity of a small group of innovators working for companies that control the network, the e2e design enables anyone with an Internet connection to design and implement a better way to use the Internet. Because it does not discriminate in favor of certain uses of the network and against others, the Internet has provided a competitive environment in which innovators know that their inventions will be used if useful. By keeping the cost of innovation low, it has encouraged an extraordinary amount of innovation in many different contexts. By keeping the network simple, and its interaction general, the Internet has facilitated the design of applications that could not originally have been envisioned. To take just a few examples, Internet telephony, digital music transfer, and electronic commerce are all applications far outside the range of expectations of those who designed the Internet (or even those who, much later, created the World Wide Web). Indeed, e-mail itself, the first true "killer app" of the Internet, was an unintended by-product hacked by early users of the network, not the point of the network itself. By keeping the cost of innovation low in the future—especially in the context of broadband media—the design of the Internet should continue to facilitate innovation not dreamed of by those who built it.

E2e design also prevents fears of strategic capture from chilling innovation. Innovation is most likely when innovators can expect to reap rewards in a fair marketplace. Innovation will be chilled if a potential innovator believes the value of the innovation will be captured by those that control the network and have the power to behave strategically. To the extent an actor is structurally capable of acting strategically, the rational innovator will reckon that capacity as a cost to innovation.

If that strategic actor owns the transmission lines itself, it has the power to decide what can and cannot be done on the Internet. The result is effectively to centralize Internet innovation within that company and its licensees. While there is a debate in the economic literature about the wisdom of centralizing control over improvements to any given innovation, we think the history of the Internet compellingly demonstrates the wisdom of letting a myriad of possible improvers work free of the constraints of a central authority, public or private. Compromising e2e will tend to undermine innovation by putting one or a few companies in charge of deciding what new uses can be made of the network.

* * *

E. The Relevance of Legacy Monopolies

* * *

By freeing the telecommunications network from the control of one single actor, the government enabled innovation free from the influences of what one might call "legacy" business models. Companies develop core competencies, and most of them tend to stick to what they know how to do. Companies faced with a potential for radical change in the nature of their market might recoil, either because they do not know how to adapt to changing conditions or because they fear that they will lose dominance in the old market as it becomes a new playing field. Their business planning is, in short, governed by the legacy of their past success. These legacy business plans often affect a company's response to innovation. In a competitive environment, these plans will often disadvantage a company that fails to respond rapidly enough to changed circumstances.

* * *

In a market in which a company has power over the competitive environment itself, however, the rational incentives of a business might be different. If the business has control over the architecture of that competitive environment, then it will often have an incentive to design that architecture to enable better its legacy business models. As Charles Morris and Charles Ferguson describe it,

> Companies that control proprietary architectural standards have an advantage over other vendors. Since they control the architecture, they are usually better positioned to develop products that maximize its capabilities; by modifying the architecture, they can discipline competing product vendors. In an open-systems era, the most consistently successful information technology companies will be the ones who manage to establish a proprietary architectural standard over a substantial competitive space and defend it against the assaults of both clones and rival architectural sponsors.[28]

A company in this position can and will resist change in order to keep doing what it knows best.

This was the problem with the telephone company prior to its breakup by the government. AT&T enjoyed substantial returns from its existing network architecture. Regulators feared that these returns would make AT&T unwilling to experiment with other architectures that might better serve communication needs. As we have said, there is at least some evidence that AT&T in fact resisted the emergence of the Internet because it feared its effect on AT&T's own business model. Certainly it resisted the development and interconnection of other technologies to its telephone network. The regulators who pushed to free the telecommunication network believed that the market would choose differently from how AT&T, as controller of the network, would choose.

Time has proven these regulators correct. Once freed from the strategic control of an entity that had a particular business plan to protect, the communications network has evolved dramatically. The competitive process was enabled by making the network neutral about

28. Charles R. Morris & Charles H. Ferguson, *How Architecture Wins Technology Wars*, HARV. BUS. REV., Mar.–Apr. 1993, at 86, 88–89.

its uses, and by giving competitors access to the network so that they could compete in an effort to put the resources of the network to their best use. The same wires that AT&T used to send only analog voice are now being used to deliver stock quotes, music, fantasy games, reference information—in short, the whole content of the Internet. Left alone, AT&T might have made some content available over the telephone network, but it probably would not have shifted to packet-switched data, and it certainly would not have developed or licensed all of the content that can now be found on the Internet.

The lesson from this explosion of innovation is critically important. An architecture that maximizes the opportunity for innovation maximizes innovation. An architecture that creates powerful strategic actors with control over the network and what can connect to it threatens innovation. These strategic actors might choose to behave in a procompetitive manner; there is no guarantee that they will interfere to stifle innovation. But without competition or regulation to restrict them, we should not assume that they will somehow decide to act in the public interest.

* * *

II. Implications for Broadband Cable

* * *

B. The Costs of Violating Architectural Principles

The costs of undermining the e2e principle are hard to quantify. We simply do not know enough to gauge how sensitive the innovation of the Internet is to changes in this competitive architecture. Obviously, in part the significance turns on how the broadband market develops. But given trends as we can identify them now, the risks are great. In this part, we detail some of these risks.

* * *

The second risk is that legacy monopolies will improperly affect the architecture of the Internet in an effort to protect their own turf. Broadband Internet service is a potential competitor to traditional cable video services. Traditional cable providers might well view this competition as a long-term threat to their business models and might not want to adapt to that competitive threat. By gaining control over the network architecture, however, cable providers are in a position to affect the development of the architecture so as to minimize the threat of broadband to their own video market. For example, a broadband cable provider that has control over the ISPs its customers use might be expected to restrict customers' access to streaming video from competitive content sources, in order to preserve its market of traditional cable video. AT&T has announced just such a policy. When asked whether users of the AT&T/MediaOne network would be permitted to stream video from competing providers across their network, Internet Services President Daniel Somers reportedly said that AT&T did not spend $56 billion to get into the cable business "to have the blood sucked out of our vein."

Even absent a deliberate intent to restrict some forms of innovation, giving the owners of the pipes control over the nature of the network will inherently skew innovation in the network. As Bar and Sandvig observe, "those who control communication networks tend to design communication platforms which support the patterns of interaction that further their interest [and that] reflect their own history and technical expertise." The old Bell System did not design a packet-switched alternative to the telephone system, because it simply did not think in those terms. Similarly, cable companies should be expected to design the systems they control in ways that are consistent with their experience and their interests. But in doing so, they will disadvantage other approaches, even if they do not intend to do so.

The third risk of giving control of the network to a strategic actor is the threat to innovation. Innovators are less likely to invest in a market in which a dominant player has the power to behave strategically against it.

One example of this cost to innovation is the uncertainty created for future applications of broadband technology. One specific set of applications put in jeopardy are those that count on the Internet being always on. Applications are being developed, for example, that would allow the Internet to monitor home security or the health of an at-risk resident. These applications would depend upon constant Internet access. Whether it makes sense as a software designer to develop these applications depends in part upon the likelihood that they could be deployed in broadband cable contexts. Under the e2e design of the Internet, this would not be a question. The network would carry everything; the choice about use would be made by the user. But under the design proposed by the cable industry, AT&T and Time Warner affiliates would have the power to decide whether these particular services would be "permitted" on the cable broadband network. AT&T has already exercised this power to discriminate against some services. It has given no guarantee of nondiscrimination in the future. Thus if cable companies decided that certain services would not be permitted, the return to an innovator would be reduced by the proportion of the residential broadband market controlled by cable companies.

The point is not that cable companies would necessarily discriminate against any particular technology. Rather, the point is that the possibility of discrimination increases the risk an innovator faces when deciding whether to design for the Internet. Innovators are likely to be cautious about how they spend their research efforts if they know that one company has the power to control whether that innovation will ever be deployed. The increasing risk is a cost to innovation, and this cost should be expected to reduce innovation.

Finally, it is worth thinking about how the elimination of ISP competition in broadband markets might affect the architecture of the

Internet as a whole. We have extolled the virtues of decentralization as a spur to innovation. But the decentralization of the Internet has social policy effects as well. It is much harder for the government to censor a vibrant, decentralized ISP market than a market in which only a few ISPs serve all customers. Concentration of the ISP market might make government intervention to control certain forms of speech easier and therefore more likely. Enabling government control could be a good or a bad thing, depending on one's perspective. But for those who doubt the government's motives in regulating speech, it should be a cause for concern.

Is the Internet Neutral? As many have pointed out, there is no such thing as a purely "neutral" network, since the design of any network will naturally favor some applications over others. The public switched telephone network of yesterday was neutral in that AT&T did not prohibit the carriage of particular types of information, but the network was optimized for voice use. For instance, in order to extend the distance that local loops could carry analog voice signals, telephone companies frequently placed "load coils" on the loops. But the same load coils that enabled local loops to carry voice over greater distances rendered the loops incapable of carrying DSL service. The coils improved the transmission characteristics of certain frequencies (the frequencies associated with voice) but at the expense of others (the higher frequencies necessary for DSL). Does the use of load coils violate network neutrality by favoring voice over non-voice transmissions? If so, should telcos be required to build additional central offices so that local loops would not have to be so long as to require load coils, or should they simply refuse to serve anyone far enough from the central office to require a load coil in order to get adequate voice service?

Some networks favor one generation of technological innovation over another. Packet switching was not possible at the time that the telephone network was built; the digital revolution had not yet taken place, making circuit switching the only viable way to build out the network. That circuit-switched network, though, is a very inefficient way of carrying digital information. Was the PSTN "neutral" before the days of packet switching and then suddenly "discriminatory" at the advent of practical packet switching? If so, did the PSTN fall out of neutrality when packet switching was possible or actually demanded by consumers? Does it matter whether AT&T fought the change to packet switching or simply didn't foresee it far enough in advance to prevent a shortage in the face of exploding consumer demand?

Accidental Deadweight Loss. The argument for neutrality differs substantially from the usual reasons for regulating monopolists. Traditionally, monopolists have been regulated (in industries identified as natural monopolies) in order to avoid monopoly over-charge. The argument from neutrality is less about naked rent-seeking than it is about preserving the Internet's ability as an engine of innovation in *other* markets. Viewed in this light, control over the network not only serves to increase the cost of one input to innovation, it also serves to skew innovation in particular directions—directions that seem attractive to the network provider, either in an effort to leverage its control over the network into other markets or simply (as Lemley & Lessig describe with regard to AT&T) as a matter of a corporate blindness to innovations that do not flow directly from the product the monopolist is used to providing. The problem, then, is not the typical problem of monopoly pricing, it is the combination of a monopoly in one market that is so closely related to a developing competitive market. As Professor Tim Wu explains:

> So what do we have today? In terms of market structure, you have a range of diverse and highly competitive markets operating on top of the internet's basic infrastructure. These markets are viciously competitive. Invent a new search engine, like Google did, and in a few years you can be a multi-billion dollar concern. Write a popular blog, and if you're lucky you can have nearly as many readers as the New York Times. Conversely, many more businesses and ideas have failed, like the famed "pets.com," but usually on the merits.
>
> These markets functioning on top of the internet are in many ways an economist's dream. Barriers to entry are low. Startup costs are minimal: many successful business began with just an idea and a good web site. Competition is mostly meritocratic—the best online stores win, not the ones with a famous names or the right connections. Meritocratic competition, in turn, leads to Darwinian or what economists call "Schumpeterian" innovation. That just means that new technologies supplant the old, in a constant process of industrial rebirth. In all, today's markets operating on top of the internet's neutral infrastructure may be some of the best examples of markets working like the free markets are supposed to.
>
> But this thriving market has an Achilles heel. For there's one part of the net which isn't competitive at all: broadband access. The access networks are part of the old telecom world—monopolistic, slow-moving, well-connected in Washington, and prone to anti-competitive behavior.

Network Neutrality: Competition, Innovation, and Nondiscriminatory Access: Hearing Before the Task Force on Telecom and Antitrust of the H. Comm. on the Judiciary, 109th Cong. (2006) (statement of Prof. Tim Wu). The " 'Schumpeterian' innovation" Professor Wu speaks of is what Joseph Schumpeter called "creative destruction". The theory is that real change in product markets happens by virtue of major changes wrought by innovation. See Joseph A. Schumpeter, *Capitalism, Socialism and Democracy* ch. VII (1942). Innovation can force the economy from old models to new ones, but only if there is room for that innovation to take place. On this theory, innovation on the Internet is recursive: innovation in new applications prompts changes in how the network is used, which in-turn opens up the possibility for new applications and the cycle repeats itself. The advent of the World Wide Web dramatically increased demand for residential broadband, which in turn paved the way for high-bandwidth applications like streaming video. Someone exercising control over the network, though, can interrupt the cycle, effectively preventing innovation in either applications or the networks that carry them. It doesn't matter whether the monopolist in question is actively opposed to innovation or simply doesn't see its merits—the harm is the same. Naked rent-seeking, in the form of higher rates for carriage, is a relatively minor concern.

Is the Schumpeterian model the right one? And, if so, can regulators protect it through increased regulation, or do their attempts to replicate the chaos of innovation twist the model beyond recognition? Given the regulatory history of telecommunications, does disruptive innovation adequately explain the explosion of the Internet?

Regulating Innovation. Providing a protective space for innovation is a very different regulatory objective than the usual one of controlling rates. Rate regulators have benchmarks they can look to in the broader economy to determine appropriate rates; how should regulators determining the size (or shape) of the "space" that needs to be provided for innovation? Does the FCC have any experience in evaluating different network models for innovation? Many point to *Carterfone* and *Computer Inquiries* as regulatory precedents for preventing network owners from controlling innovation in uses of the network, but in those cases the FCC focused not on theories of innovation but rather on the nature of the markets for the goods in question, much as Professor Wu does in the above excerpt. Moreover, in both cases, the FCC left the network itself squarely in the hands of the monopolist. The openness of *Carterfone* was predicated on compliance with standards set by AT&T (load coils, for instance, would have been the problem of DSL modem makers—not the network operator), and even in the *Computer Inquiries*, which regulated the network rather than the ends of the network, the choice of services was left up to carriers; the only condition was that they had to be provided to all on equal terms. See Thomas B. Nachbar, *The Public Network*, 17 CommLaw Conspectus ___ (forthcoming 2009). Given its history, is the FCC a likely guardian of network innovation?

In addition to a potentially unlimited number of goals, regulators seeking to ensure neutrality also have a variety of available means. The excerpt from *The End of End-to-End* was written as an argument to prevent vertical integration by cable providers into Internet service and horizontal integration through merger. Both are ways that carriers could achieve the market power that enables control over the nature of the network, but there are others too numerous to mention, such as actively discriminating against certain applications or simply building out the network in such a way that it cannot be used for certain applications. Should regulators simply carry forward the initial design of the Internet (a design chosen for its technical attributes, not its regulatory advantages or even its economic efficiency)? That design decision was made over thirty years ago; doesn't enshrining it in regulation hinder, rather than make room for, innovation?

The need to promote innovation, as it happens, is not only the primary argument for network neutrality. It's also the primary argument against it.

CHRISTOPHER S. YOO, BEYOND NETWORK NEUTRALITY

19 Harv. J.L. Tech 1 (2005).

* * *

III. The Shortcomings of Network Neutrality and the Case for Network Diversity

* * *

This analysis reveals that network neutrality may impair ... efficiency in two ways. First, standardization necessarily reduces economic welfare by limiting product variety. Second, and more importantly for our purposes, network neutrality can impede the emergence of competition in the last mile by reinforcing the economic characteristics that drive markets for telecommunications networks towards natural monopoly (i.e., high up-front costs and network economic effects). To the extent that network neutrality is imposed to limit monopoly or oligopoly power, it can have the perverse effect of entrenching industry concentration by short-circuiting one of the most natural ways to mitigate market failure. Network neutrality is also hamstrung by the practical consideration that the regulatory tools traditionally used to promote ... efficiency are unlikely to work well in industries undergoing rapid technological change. Those tools are also unlikely to be effective when the demands that end users are placing on the network are becoming increasingly heterogeneous in terms of quality of service and content.

* * *

These conclusions suggest that society might be better off if policymakers were to embrace a *network diversity* principle. * * *

A. Network Neutrality and Static Efficiency

* * *

1. The Potential Welfare Gains from Network Diversity and the Inherent Nonneutrality of Network Neutrality

* * * Consumer surplus is created when consumers pay prices that are less than the maximum they would be willing to pay, and producer surplus is created when producers receive prices that exceed the minimum price they would be willing to accept. In a price-theoretic world, then, economic welfare consists solely of the sum of consumer and producer surplus.

A different situation obtains when products are differentiated. The economics of product differentiation acknowledge that utility can also increase by allowing consumers to obtain goods that fit better with their ideal preferences. The welfare benefits from product differentiation are not observable in the classic price-quantity space that dominates economic analysis. They nonetheless remain an important potential source of economic welfare. Conversely, standardization can "prevent the development of promising but unique and incompatible new systems." The concomitant reduction in product variety can represent an important, but often overlooked, source of welfare loss.

These problems appear more acute when the focus is shifted from standardization in the abstract to the particular form of standardization favored by network neutrality proponents. Adoption of any set of protocols has the inevitable effect of favoring certain types of applications and disfavoring others. Even worse, standardization also has the inevitable effect of putting the government in the position of picking technological winners and losers. In addition, to be effective, such intervention would likely be required at an early stage when the underlying technology is still in a state of flux. In short, it appears that the term "network neutrality" is something of a misnomer.

Consider TCP/IP, which remains the de facto standard set of protocols on the Internet. Given the Internet's meteoric success, it is tempting to treat the status quo as the relevant baseline and to place the burden on those who would deviate from it.... As noted earlier, one of the distinguishing features of TCP/IP is that it routes packets anonymously on a "first come, first served" basis without regard to the application with which they are associated. It also transmits packets on a "best efforts" basis without any guarantee of success.

This approach to routing packets was uncontroversial when usage restrictions prohibited commercial use of the Internet and the network was used primarily by technology-oriented academics to share text-based communications that were not particularly sensitive to delays of up to a second. In recent years, however, the environment in which the Internet operates has changed radically. The transformation of the Internet from a medium for academic communication into a mass market phenomenon has greatly complicated the decisions faced by network owners. Indeed, the number of possible connections increases exponentially with network size. The commercialization made possible by the privatization of the Internet has greatly increased the heterogeneity and variability of Internet usage. The shift from text-based applications, such as e-mail, to more bandwidth-intensive applications, such as webpage downloading and file transfers, has dramatically increased the volume of end-user demand. The emergence of applications that are increasingly sensitive to delay (even at the cost of lower accuracy and increased distortion) such as VoIP and streaming video, has created demand for even greater reliability in throughput rates and quality of service and is creating pressure for the deployment of "policy-based routers," which break from TCP/IP by assigning higher priority to packets associated with time-sensitive applications. Furthermore, the unexpected interactions among network components that are the hallmark of complex systems can be quite sensitive to variability of demand. Increases in the variability of network traffic can thus greatly impede network performance even if, on average, utilization of network capacity remains quite low.

Furthermore, the packet anonymity inherent in TCP/IP may be interfering with network owners' attempts to add security features designed to foster e-commerce or to protect against viruses and other hostile elements that are proliferating on the Internet. In addition, the Internet's shift away from academically-oriented users who enjoyed a similar degree of institutional support and shared certain common institutional norms has increased the justification for moving responsibility for system maintenance and management away from end users and towards the network's core.

These considerations make network management quite challenging. Although it is theoretically possible for network owners to respond to some of these demands by expanding bandwidth, the fact that application designers are waiting in the wings with ever more bandwidth-intensive applications dictates that there is no compelling reason to believe that bandwidth will necessarily increase faster than demand, especially in light of the fact that the number of potential connections goes up exponentially with the number of computers added to the system. In addition, decisions about capacity expansion can be difficult when facing uncertainty about the magnitude, heterogeneity, and variability of the demand that will be placed on the network. Decisionmaking is complicated still further by the "lumpiness" of network capacity created by the indivisibility of fixed costs and the fact that increasing network capacity typically takes a considerable amount of time.

In such an environment, it seems counter-productive to tie network owners' hands by limiting the number of ways in which they can manage network demand. * * *

Network neutrality also can restrict the network's functionality. A close analysis of the "end-to-end argument"—often invoked as one of the foundations of network neutrality—demonstrates this point. The end-to-end argument asserts that application-specific functionality should be confined to the hosts operating at the edge of the network and that the core of the network should be as simple and general as possible. The rationale underlying this argument is based in cost-benefit analysis. Increasing the functions performed in the core of the network can improve the functionality of the network, but only at the cost of reduced network performance. The problem is that all applications would have to bear the costs associated with the reduction in performance even if they gain no compensating benefits. This tradeoff can be avoided if the core of the network performs only those functions that benefit almost all applications and if higher-level, application-specific functions are confined to the servers operating at the network's edge.

Although the end-to-end argument is frequently invoked in support of network neutrality, such claims are misplaced. The architects of the end-to-end argument candidly reject calls to elevate end-to-end into a regulatory mandate as "too simplistic." Correct application of the cost-benefit tradeoff lying at the heart of the end-to-end argument requires "subtlety of analysis" and can be "quite complex." Indeed, the architects of end-to-end acknowledge that circumstances exist under which application of end-to-end would do more harm than good. Properly construed, end-to-end calls for implementation on a case-by-case basis rather as a blanket regulatory prohibition.

There is no reason to believe a priori that giving preference to innovations operating at the network's edge over innovations in the network's core will prove to be beneficial in all cases. * * *

Simply put, any choice of standardized protocol has the inevitable effect of favoring certain applications and disfavoring others, just as TCP/IP discriminates against applications that are time sensitive and end-to-end favors innovation at the edge over innovation in the core. As I will subsequently discuss in some detail, whether mandating network neutrality would be socially beneficial is a complicated question that depends on myriad considerations, including the level of aggregate demand, heterogeneity of network uses, the variability in network traffic flows, end users' need for network reliability, and the extent to which technological change is reorganizing the natural boundaries between levels that were previously separated by a natural interface, notwithstanding the many claims to the contrary. In short, the desirability of complete standardization and interoperability is an empirical question that cannot be answered a priori. * * *

2. Network Diversity and the Causes of Market Failure in the Last Mile

a. Supply-Side Determinants of Natural Monopoly: Large, Up-Front Investments

How network neutrality can reinforce the supply-side forces that tend to concentrate markets for network services is best understood in terms of the classic source of scale economies: large, up-front, sunk-cost investments. Although the issue is not free from dispute, the high up-front investments needed to establish the wires and central offices needed to establish telephone service have historically been regarded as turning local telephony into a natural monopoly. The presence of large, up-front capital investments gives the largest firms a decisive economic advantage. The ability to spread those investments over a larger customer base allows them to underprice their smaller competitors. This allows them to capture a still larger share of the market, which in turn causes the cost advantage to widen still further. Eventually, the cost advantage enjoyed by the largest player widens to the point where it is able to drive all of its competitors out of the market. In that case, even markets that are initially competitive are doomed to collapse into monopolies.

* * *

What has been largely overlooked is how allowing networks to differentiate themselves can also alleviate the economies of scale associated with declining average costs. It is the fact that price is the only dimension along which firms can compete that gives the largest players their decisive advantage. A different equilibrium can obtain if competitors are allowed to compete along dimensions other than price. If so, a smaller player may be able to survive notwithstanding lower sales volumes and higher unit costs (and thus higher prices) by tailoring its network towards services that a subsegment of the market values particularly highly. The greater value provided by the differentiation of the network allows a specialized provider to generate sufficient revenue to cover its up-front costs even though its volume is significantly smaller than that of the leading players.

* * *

How could such differentiation occur in the context of broadband? One way is through protocol nonstandardization, such as through the adoption of a different routing protocol. As discussed above, all protocols necessarily favor certain applications over others. If discrete subgroups of end users place sufficiently different valuations on different types of applications, multiple networks will be able to coexist simply by targeting their networks towards the needs of different subgroups. If demand is sufficiently heterogeneous, the greater utility derived from allowing consumers to access consumer services that they value more highly can more than compensate for any cost disadvantages resulting from the reduction in volume. Indeed, it is conceivable that network diversity might make it possible for three different last-mile networks to coexist: one optimized for traditional Internet applications such as e-mail and website access, another incorporating security features to facilitate ecommerce and to guard against viruses and other hostile aspects of Internet life, and a third that prioritizes packets in the manner needed to facilitate time-sensitive applications such as streaming media and VoIP.

* * *

Entering into exclusivity arrangements with respect to content represents another possible means for differentiating one's network. One of the best current examples is the manner in which direct broadcast satellite ("DBS") provider DirecTV is using an exclusive programming package known as "NFL Sunday Ticket" to enhance its ability to compete with cable television. Indeed, it appears that exclusive access to NFL Sunday Ticket constitutes one of the major factors helping DBS emerge as a viable competitor to cable. If regulators were to view this exclusivity arrangement solely in static terms, they might be tempted to appease cable customers who have expressed frustration at their inability to purchase NFL Sunday Ticket by requiring that the package be made available on both platforms. Doing so would reduce DBS's ability to compete by eliminating one of the primary inducements to shift from cable to DBS. In other words, banning exclusivity would only serve to entrench the dominant position that local cable operators have historically enjoyed over multichannel video distribution, which has long represented one of the central policy problems confronting the television industry.

b. Demand-Side Determinants of Natural Monopoly: Network Economic Effects

The other force supposedly driving markets for telecommunications networks toward monopoly is network economic effects. Network economic effects exist when the number of people connected to a network determines the network's value, and the network becomes more valuable as more people become part of it. Because the value of telecommunications networks increase with the number of people attached to them, they have long been regarded as a paradigmatic case in which network economic effects arise. Thus, network economic effects are often described as creating demand-side economies of scale that tend to favor the largest networks. * * *

[D]ifferentiation can ameliorate the demand-side economies of scale created by network economic effects. If the smaller network is optimized for particular functions that a particular group of end users values particularly highly, those end users may be willing to join the smaller network notwithstanding the presence of network economic effects. The increase in value provided by network diversity can more than compensate for any reductions in value resulting from market size. Conversely, network neutrality threatens to preempt this potential solution by narrowing the dimensions along which firms can compete. Mandating the use of standardized protocols threatens to commodify bandwidth and force providers to compete solely on the basis of price and network size, which would in turn reinforce the advantages enjoyed by the largest players. There is thus a real danger that network neutrality could short-circuit one of the most sensible market-based solutions to the problems of market concentration.

3. Implementation Difficulties Caused by the Decommodification of Network Usage

* * *

a. The Limitations of the Regulatory Tools

* * *

[T]he tools needed to implement interconnection, nondiscrimination, rate regulation, and standardization do not function well in industries that are technologically dynamic. The existing approaches for regulating the reasonableness of interconnection rates are based on historical data, from which policymakers must attempt to anticipate and plan for change. It is for these reasons that regulation is thought to place a premium on predictability and continuity. Such an approach is nonsensical when the industry being regulated is undergoing rapid technological change.

The problem is compounded all the more by the fact that improvements in technology can render obsolete an interconnection point that was once a natural boundary between market players. Consider what might happen after regulatory authorities compel interconnection. The forces of competition naturally cause firms operating on either side of the interconnection interface to try to expand into territory occupied by other firms. To the extent that network neutrality forecloses this from occurring, it can stifle an important source of competition. Furthermore, more sweeping technological change can cause what was once a natural interface between two levels to shift or collapse. Requiring network owners to maintain standardized interfaces would have the inevitable effect of locking the existing interfaces into place. This government-imposed interconnection and standardization overlooks the extent to which the network (and not just the servers and applications running on it) can itself represent an important source of innovation. It also has the unfortunate effect of inhibiting the emergence of new technologies that transcend the boundaries that previously separated different segments of the industry.

* * *

In summary, the complexity of the interface, the increasing heterogeneity of end users' demands, and the pace of technological change are reducing the utility of the regulatory tools upon which policymakers have traditionally relied to manage interconnection, nondiscrimination, rate regulation, and standardization.

Whose Side is History On? Both sides of the debate claim that history supports their position. Professors Lemley and Lessig point to *Carterfone*, the *Computer Inquires*, and to the behavior that led to the antitrust case and eventually the MFJ. That much of the history is commonplace. We now have the benefit of some experience that Professors Lemley and Lessig did not have when they wrote *The End of End-to-End*. Which way does it break?

Notwithstanding some well-publicized cases of abuse, we have not seen rampant strategic behavior on the part of network providers since the FCC deregulated both cable modem and DSL service. In perhaps the most frightening case for network neutrality proponents, a LEC entered into a consent decree with the FCC after it reportedly blocked the ability of its DSL customers to use VoIP service, a direct attack by a monopolist on a competing technology. See *In the Matter of Madison River Tele-*

phone Co., 20 FCC Rcd. 19173 (2005). Otherwise, the discrimination landscape has been fairly barren.

But neither have we witnessed the kind of product differentiation of which Professor Yoo writes. To the contrary, the wires that bring cable modem and DSL service to our homes used to carry very distinct services, with cable optimized to carry many channels of one-way, full-motion video and phone lines optimized to carry two-way voice (and limited data) traffic. Rather than further diverging, those services appear to be converging, as both cable providers and telcos seek to offer the "triple play" of video entertainment, Internet access, and voice telephone service. Is there any practical reason to think the path toward convergence will reverse itself and lead to the kind of "network diversity" that Professor Yoo wants to leave room for?

Nondiscrimination as an Alternative. One alternative to achieving neutrality by mandating network design is to simply insist on nondiscrimination. As explained by Professor Tim Wu:

> A third approach focuses on the concept of "like treatment," a concept central to the anti-discrimination rules used in the international trading system. In the international trading system, as in telecommunications, the premise is that distortionary forms of discrimination are principally those which operate on the basis of *identity*. In trade, if a country bans tomatoes from Italy but not from Spain, the result is a distortion of competition in the tomato market. For that reason, the trading system generally bars country from discriminatory treatment of "like products."
>
> In the telecommunications context, the premise is that treating information from one firm or carrier any differently than from another carrier based only on the identity of the carrier will similarly distort the production market for that information. An inefficient provider may dominate the market not because of a superior product but because of preferential access to the network.
>
> Interestingly this approach continues to allow some forms of discrimination on the network. It mandates, however, that the discrimination undertaken must be related to the content in question, and not the source of the information. For example, an internet carrier might decide to speed up the delivery of all video packets on the network, a difference in treatment driven by the differences in the underlying information type. But what the carrier may not do under this approach is to choose favorites, to treat similarly situated packets differently.
>
> A sample of language embodying this approach, as applied to a network carrier, looks as follows: "A carrier may prioritize content,

applications, or services within the operator's networks based only on the type of content, applications, or services and the level of service purchased by the user, without charge for such prioritization."

Tim Wu, *Why Have a Telecommunications Law?: Anti-discrimination Norms in Communications*, 5 J. on Telecom. & High Tech. L. 15, 42–43 (2006).

Would a simple nondiscrimination regime like the one Professor Wu describes solve the same problems as end-to-end proposals while avoiding the problems Professor Yoo raises? Carriers would still be free to modify (and thereby allow diversity in) network offerings; they just wouldn't be able to do so in a way that systematically favored themselves. Or would they? If a carrier is committed to favoring or disfavoring a particular form of content (e.g. a cable carrier that wishes to discriminate against streaming video, which competes with their own traditional cable television offerings), is it the identity of the provider or the application that matters? Note that, unlike mandating particular forms of carriage, the FCC has considerable experience in operating a nondiscrimination regime: *Computer II* and *Computer III* left it up to the carriers to define the services so long as they provided them to all on a nondiscriminatory basis. On the difference between discrimination against uses and discrimination against users, see Nachbar, *The Public Network*, *supra*.

Of course, there is self-serving discrimination and there is discrimination more generally. Professor Wu's proposal would not only prevent carriers from preferring their own service; it would prevent them from offering preferential service to *anyone*. A weaker form of nondiscrimination would be to allow prioritization but require that it be sold on a nondiscriminatory basis to all who can afford it. This form of discrimination—discrimination based on the ability to pay—has a long history in both competitive and regulated markets (think first class rail and airline tickets or "express" package service). What, then, is the problem with applying it to communications markets? According to Professor Lessig, preferential carriage, or "access tiering," can violate the principles underlying network neutrality even if it is applied in a "neutral" way:

> Existing content providers have an incentive to block competitors; access-tiering would be a means to effect that competitive advantage. And while these actions might not rise to the level of an antitrust violation, it is perfectly appropriate for Congress to select a network policy that it believes would maximize innovation and growth for the Nation. Adding toll booths to the Internet may well benefit those who own the roads; but it won't benefit application and content competition on the Internet, both of which drive economic growth.

Net Neutrality: Hearing Before the S. Comm. on Commerce, Science, and Transportation, 109th Cong. (2006) (statement of Prof. Lawrence Lessig), at 58.

Does access tiering present the same types of risks as other forms of network discrimination? Can neutrality regulation prevent it? Many large Internet-based businesses utilize caching services like Akamai that provide faster consumer access to content by storing copies of the content in multiple nodes. Consumers going to a web site that uses one of these services are redirected to another server closer to their location so that the information has a shorter distance to travel and therefore arrives sooner. Given the existence of such services (and their cost), is a speed arms race avoidable simply by regulating carriers? If the point is to keep entry costs low for new companies, won't we have to outlaw such services as well?

Professor Lessig used Google as an example of an existing firm that would benefit from tiering; one of the two examples he used for small entrants who would be harmed by access tiering—YouTube—is now owned by Google. Should the response to access tiering come from the FCC or capital markets?

2. The Regulatory Response

To date the debate between net neutrality proponents and opponents has been essentially stalemated. It has produced an efflorescence of law review commentary as well as some legislative proposals, but very little action. The FCC several years ago produced a brief statement of basic policies, and continued political pressure to do something prompted the following inquiry. General regulation, from either Congress or the FCC, has been lacking. Rather, the FCC has only regulated with neutrality in mind in a few specific cases: The Commission has insisted on agreement to observe some temporary forms of neutrality as a condition for approving two telecom-related mergers (which are discussed in the notice of inquiry below), and it adopted neutrality rules for some of the spectrum it recently auctioned as part of the DTV transition. We consider those license restrictions below.

a) The Four Principles

IN THE MATTER OF BROADBAND INDUSTRY PRACTICES
Notice of Inquiry

Federal Communications Commission, 2007.
22 FCC Rcd. 7894.

BY THE COMMISSION:

* * *

II. Background

2. Over a year ago, the Commission issued a Policy Statement "offer [ing] guidance and insight into its approach to the Internet and broadband" consistent with Congress's direction in sections 230 and 706. In that Policy Statement, the Commission announced the following principles:

- To encourage broadband deployment and preserve and promote the open and interconnected nature of the public Internet, consumers are entitled to access the lawful Internet content of their choice.

- To encourage broadband deployment and preserve and promote the open and interconnected nature of the public Internet, consumers are entitled to run applications and use services of their choice, subject to the needs of law enforcement.

- To encourage broadband deployment and preserve and promote the open and interconnected nature of the public Internet, consumers are entitled to connect their choice of legal devices that do not harm the network.

- To encourage broadband deployment and preserve and promote the open and interconnected nature of the public Internet, consumers are entitled to competition among network providers, application and service providers, and content providers.

3. Since that time, the Commission has had the occasion to review several providers' practices. In several proceedings evaluating wireline mergers, the Commission found that no commenter had alleged that the entities engage in packet discrimination or degradation, and that, given conflicting incentives, it was unlikely that the merged companies would do so. Nonetheless, the Commission specifically recognized the applicants' commitments to act in a manner consistent with the principles set forth in the Policy Statement, and their commitments were incorporated as conditions of their mergers. Likewise, in its review of the Adelphia-Time Warner-Comcast transaction, the Commission found that the transaction was not likely to increase incentives for the applicants to engage in conduct harmful to consumers, and found no evidence that the applicants were operating in a manner inconsistent with the Policy Statement.

4. The Commission, under Title I of the Communications Act, has the ability to adopt and enforce the net neutrality principles it announced in the Internet Policy Statement. The Supreme Court reaffirmed that the Commission "has jurisdiction to impose additional regulatory obligations under its Title I ancillary jurisdiction to regulate interstate and foreign communications." Indeed, the Supreme Court specifically recognized the Commission's ancillary jurisdiction to impose regulatory obligations on broadband Internet access providers.

5. The Commission may exercise ancillary jurisdiction under Title I when: (1) Title I confers subject matter jurisdiction over the service to be regulated; and (2) the assertion of jurisdiction is reasonably ancillary to

the effective performance of the Commission's responsibilities. Both of these conditions are met with respect to the four principles of the Commission's 2005 Policy Statement. Indeed, the Commission found "that both of the predicates for ancillary jurisdiction are likely satisfied for any consumer protection, network reliability, or national security obligation that we may subsequently decide to impose on wireline broadband Internet access service providers."

6. First, as the Commission stated, broadband services are "wire communications" or "radio communications," as defined in sections 3(52) and 3(33) of the Act, and section 2(a) of the Communications Act gives the Commission subject matter jurisdiction over "all interstate and foreign communications by wire or radio."

7. Second, section 1 of the Communications Act confers responsibility on the Commission "to make available ... a rapid, efficient, Nation-wide, and world-wide wire and radio communication service with adequate facilities at reasonable charges." This responsibility is guided by the "policy of the United States ... (1) to promote the continued development of the Internet"; "(2) to preserve the vibrant and competitive free market that presently exists for the Internet"; and "(3) to encourage the deployment of technologies which maximize user control over what information is received by ... [users of] the Internet."

III. Discussion

8. We seek a fuller understanding of the behavior of broadband market participants today, including network platform providers, broadband Internet access service providers, other broadband transmission providers, Internet service providers, Internet backbone providers, content and application service providers, and others. First, we ask commenters to describe today's packet management practices. That is, do providers treat different packets in different ways? How and why? Are these providers operating consistent with the Policy Statement? Are there specific examples of packet management practices that commenters consider reasonable or unreasonable? More specifically, are providers engaging in packet management that is helpful or harmful to consumers? For example, during times of congestion, do providers prioritize packets for latency-sensitive applications such as voice calls, video conferencing, live video, or gaming? Do providers prioritize packets for safety- and security-related applications such as health monitoring, home monitoring, and emergency calls? Do providers block packets containing child pornography, spyware, viruses, or spam? Do providers offer parental controls that block packets containing sexually explicit material? Do providers manage packets to improve their network performance, engineering, or security? Do providers deprioritize or block packets for certain content when the providers or their affiliates offer similar content, or do providers prioritize packets containing their own content over packets containing similar content from unaffiliated providers? Do providers deprioritize or block packets containing material that is harmful to their commercial interests, or prioritize packets relating to applica-

tions or services in which they have a commercial interest? Are any of these packet management practices in place to implement other legal requirements? Are there other packet management practices of which the Commission should be aware? Commenters should provide specific, verifiable examples with supporting documentation, and should limit their comments to those practices that are technically feasible today.

9. Next, we ask commenters to describe today's pricing practices for broadband and related services. Do providers charge different prices for different speeds or capacities? Given the greater availability of bandwidth-intensive applications, do providers charge a premium to download a particular amount of content? Do broadband providers charge upstream providers for priority access to end users? Should our policies distinguish between content providers that charge end users for access to content and those that do not? Do providers currently discriminate in the prices they charge to end users and/or upstream providers? Does behavior vary depending on the number of broadband Internet access service providers offering service in a geographic area? With regard to all practices commenters describe in response to the questions in paragraphs 8 and 9, we ask whether providers disclose their practices to their customers, to other providers, to application developers, and others. Do they offer their subscribers the option to purchase extra bandwidth or specialized processing? How have consumers responded to these pricing practices? How have higher speed broadband networks changed the value proposition for consumers? Are the real prices (i.e., price per Mbps) paid by consumers for broadband nevertheless falling?

10. We next ask whether the Policy Statement should be amended. Do commenters believe that the specific practices described in response to the questions in paragraphs 8 and 9 are helpful or harmful to consumers? In light of the responses to paragraphs 8 and 9, are there specific changes to the Policy Statement that commenters would recommend? We also ask whether we should incorporate a new principle of nondiscrimination. If so, how would "nondiscrimination" be defined, and how would such a principle read? Would it permit any exclusive or preferential arrangements among network platform or access providers and content providers? How would a principle of non-discrimination affect the ability of content and access providers to charge their customers different prices, or to charge them at all?

11. Finally, does the Commission have the legal authority to enforce the Policy Statement in the face of particular market failures or other specific problems? What specific conduct or other factors give rise to any such problems? Does the ever increasing intermodal competition among broadband providers prevent such problems from developing in the first place? If the Commission were to promulgate rules in this area, what would be the challenges in tailoring the rules only to reach any identified market failures or other specific problems, and not to prevent policies that benefit consumers? Would regulations further our mandate to "encourage the deployment on a reasonable and timely basis of advanced telecommunications capability to all Americans"? Assuming it

is not necessary to adopt rules at this time, what market characteristics would justify the adoption of rules?

* * *

Concurring Statement of COMMISSIONER MICHAEL J. COPPS

We live in a world where a very few concentrated broadband providers exercise powerful and not always consumer-friendly control over the pipes that come into our homes and businesses. While we welcome telephone companies and cable providers competing to sell high-speed services, FCC statistics show that together these duopoly operators control some 96 percent of the residential broadband market, with too many consumers lacking a choice even between those two providers. Wireless and broadband over powerline are exciting prospects, but the reality is we are nowhere near seeing the kind of ubiquitous third or fourth player necessary to turn broadband into a vibrantly competitive market.

If eventually we develop a truly competitive marketplace with consumers enjoying broadband speeds like those available to our counterparts in other industrial countries, we can step back and rely on the genius of that marketplace. But in the meantime, the concentrated providers out there increasingly have the ability—and some think the business incentive—to build networks with traffic management policies that could restrict how we use the Internet. I haven't taught history for many years, but I remember enough of it to know that if someone has both the technical capacity and the commercial incentive to control something, it's going to get tried.

Don't take my word for it. It was the *Wall Street Journal* that said large carriers "are starting to make it harder for consumers to use the Internet for phone calls or swapping video files." The more powerful and concentrated our facilities providers grow, the greater their motivation will be to close off Internet lanes and block IP byways. After all, some have already touted their support for segregating Internet traffic by charging premium tolls for passage for favored websites, while consigning everyone else's websites and applications to bumpy travels in steerage.

This brings us to the item before us. It really puts the Commission at a crossroads and the path we choose has the potential to recast and shape the Internet for years to come. At issue is whether a few broadband behemoths will be ceded gatekeeper control over the public's access to the full bounty of the Internet. We have a choice to make.

Down one road lies a FCC committed to honor and preserve the fundamental openness that made the Internet so great—a place of freedom and choice where anyone with a good idea and a little tech-savvy can create an idea or business with global reach. On this road the FCC would adopt policies to ensure that the Internet remains a dynamic technology for creating economic and educational opportunity, a fierce economic engine for innovation and entrepreneurship, and a tool for the sustenance and growth of democracy across the land.

Down the other road lies a FCC that, while it celebrates the Internet, sits idly by as broadband providers amass the power and technical ability to dictate where you can go and what you can do on the Internet. This FCC would see no public interest harms when providers set up gated communities and toll booths on the Internet, altering the openness that has characterized this medium from the very start and endangering the principles of packet equality and non-discrimination. Make no mistake—the practical effect of what is being proposed by some network operators is to invert the democratic genius of the Internet. The original idea was to have neutral dumb networks with intelligence invested at the edges, with you and me and millions of other users. Now some seem bent on making the pipe intelligent and all-controlling even while they make all of us users at the edges dumb. Maybe the Internet entrepreneurs of the future will have to seek permission to innovate from the owner of the broadband pipe. That would be really hard to square with what I think should be our responsibility at the FCC, and that is to do everything we can to preserve the openness that made the Internet so great. You know what? I have enough confidence in this technology and enough confidence in American innovation and creativity to believe we can get to the promised land without that kind of discrimination. * * *

We proceed too leisurely here. Rather than strike out and unflinchingly proclaim this agency's commitment to an open and non-discriminatory Internet, we satisfy ourselves with one tiny, timid step. Let's be frank. Putting out a Notice of Inquiry is not the way to sail boldly forth. History shows that Notices of Inquiry like this have a way of disappearing into the regulatory dustbin, putting off decisions that need to be made now. These are no longer new and novel questions. We adopted our Four Principles of Internet Freedom nearly two years ago. And these issues come back to us in just about every major merger that comes before us—and there have been a lot of those!

We should be building on what we have already approved and going with at least a Notice of Proposed Rulemaking with a commitment to move to an Order within a time certain. These are not esoteric, inside-the-Beltway issues—they go to the very core of what kinds of opportunities are going to be available to all of us in this digital age. We're being left behind in broadband globally, the country is paying a steep cost, and we face the stark challenge to decide if we are going to do something about it or not. We're talking here about the greatest small "d" democratic technology platform that has ever existed. Taking another year or two to decide if we want to keep it that way shortchanges the technology, shortchanges consumers and shortchanges our future. I will not dissent from the one small step forward we take today, but I do lament our not making a Neil Armstrong giant leap for mankind.

Which Way Does the Compass Point? Is it clear from the *Notice of Inquiry* that the FCC is necessarily pro-neutrality? In addition to problematic forms of discrimination, the FCC describes several forms of discrimination that may be beneficial (such as giving priority to time-sensitive applications when congestion is high or blocking content that contains child pornography (recall Professors Lemley and Lessig and their concern about government regulation through discrimination). Given the discussion in paragraphs 3–7, is the question advanced in paragraph 11 about the FCC's authority a serious one? Remember that the FCC removed the common-carrier requirements on both cable modems and DSL; having done so, is it legitimate to undertake "common carrier lite" regulation through Title I? If so, what is the point of having Title II?

Is Commissioner Copps overstating the importance of the Internet as "the greatest small 'd' democratic technology platform that has ever existed"? Given the widely acknowledged "digital divide" separating the wealthy from the poor, is the Internet likely (in the near future) to live up to the promise of the printing press, or radio? Does its potential as an engine for democratic discourse warrant increased or decreased intervention by the government in its operation?

b) Wireless "Open Access"

The FCC's first real foray into network neutrality is in the area of wireless service. The transition to digital television has opened up a major swath of spectrum for reallocation by the FCC. As it is required to by law, the FCC has auctioned the spectrum licenses off, but it included in some of the licenses a form of neutrality mandate (which the FCC has labeled "open access").

IN THE MATTER OF SERVICE RULES FOR THE 698–746, 747–762 AND 777–792 MHz BANDS
Second Report and Order

Federal Communications Commission, 2007.
22 FCC Rcd. 15289.

BY THE COMMISSION:

* * *

(iii) Open Platforms for Devices and Applications

189. Background. In the *700 MHz Further Notice*, we sought comment on a proposal filed by PISC that licenses for at least 30 megahertz of the unauctioned commercial 700 MHz Band spectrum bear a condition requiring a licensee to provide open platforms for devices and applications.[423] PISC described its proposal as including the right of a consumer

423. The *Ad Hoc* Public Interest Spectrum Coalition consists of the Consumer Federation of America, Consumers Union, Free Press, Media Access Project, New America Foundation, and Public Knowledge.

to use any equipment, content, application, or service on a non-discriminatory basis. PISC subsequently expanded its proposal to recommend that these requirements should apply to all 60 megahertz of the unauctioned spectrum.

190. PISC argues that "incumbent wireless carriers ... routinely choke bandwidth to users, cripple features, and control the user experience" in order to protect their wireline broadband offerings (e.g., DSL and cable modem). Supporters offer many examples of such restrictions, including restrictions on the use of Voice Over Internet Protocol (VoIP), webcams, and other media devices. Frontline cites the Apple iPhone device, which is designed to work exclusively on one provider's network....

191. Proponents argue that without mandated open access, wireless broadband service is unlikely to develop into a vigorous competitor for existing wireline broadband services, because incumbent wireless service providers owned by wireline companies will instead limit the quality of their wireless broadband offerings to protect their wireline broadband offerings. These commenters credit the open access model with creating a competitive environment in which independent service and equipment providers flourished in this country under the *Carterfone* decision, the *Computer Proceedings*, and the 1996 Telecommunications Act. They argue that the 700 MHz open access policies they advocate will facilitate competitive entry for both wireless service providers and Internet service providers, which will foster innovation, enhance services, and lower prices. For example, Google maintains that the only way to guarantee new broadband platforms is through open platform requirements: open applications, open devices, open services, and open networks.

192. On the other hand, opponents dispute the need for open access requirements and argue that these requirements could have adverse consequences. They maintain that, unlike the monopoly wireline market in which the *Carterfone* decision was based, there is effective competition in the mobile wireless market and that auction of the remaining commercial 700 MHz Band spectrum will provide opportunities for additional competitors. Opponents assert that open access advocates exaggerate the restrictions wireless providers impose on consumers, and to the extent providers do engage in such practices, such practices are reasonable measures to protect the integrity and efficiency of wireless networks. In addition, some commenters argue that imposing open access requirements would directly contradict Commission findings that bundling mobile handsets with wireless service contracts increases wireless penetration, and that subjecting wireless broadband Internet access service providers to access, price, or unbundling mandates is a disservice to consumers. Verizon Wireless maintains that the "incumbent advantages" cited by Google are not anticompetitive, and result from high-risk capital investments in a competitive market.

193. Opponents also challenge open access requirements as a throwback to an obsolete "command-and-control" regulatory regime, which they see as unnecessarily restricting mobile wireless licensees' flexibility to adapt to market conditions and effectively compete. Verizon Wireless argues that imposing an open access business model undermines the auction process and competitive bidding, which is designed to identify those bidders who place the highest value on the licenses to ensure that this scarce resource is not wasted or underexploited. Verizon Wireless asserts that imposing open access regulations runs contrary to the Commission's "light regulatory touch" for wireless services generally, and is inconsistent with the Commission's prior determinations regarding the regulation of broadband services.... AT&T, on the other hand, maintains that open access requirements for the 700 MHz C Block would enable the introduction of an alternative wireless business model without requiring changes in the business models of AT&T (and others) in the highly competitive wireless industry. According to AT&T, the proposal provides an opportunity for new entrants to bid and test their business models in the marketplace.

* * *

195. Discussion. Although we generally prefer to rely on marketplace forces as the most efficient mechanism for fostering competition, we conclude that the 700 MHz spectrum provides an important opportunity to apply requirements for open platforms for devices and applications for the benefit of consumers, without unduly burdening existing services and markets. For the reasons described below, we determine that for one commercial spectrum block in the 700 MHz Band—the Upper 700 MHz Band C Block—we will require licensees to allow customers, device manufacturers, third-party application developers, and others to use or develop the devices and applications of their choice, subject to certain conditions, as described further below. * * *

197. Wireless service is becoming an increasingly important platform for broadband access. Over the past few years, U.S. service providers have been moving beyond second-generation (2G) wireless network technologies to deploy next-generation, or third-generation (3G), network technologies. These technologies enable them to offer data services at higher data transfer speeds, and to offer mobile broadband services that provide for a variety of new capabilities and services, including broadband Internet access. As part of this evolution, "cell phones" are evolving into multi-media devices capable of surfing the web, sending e-mails, playing songs, taking pictures, playing games, and streaming video. As these devices become more sophisticated, consumers have more opportunities to access broadband services both at home and on the go.

198. Although wireless broadband services have great promise, we have become increasingly concerned that certain practices in the wireless industry may constrain consumer access to wireless broadband networks and limit the services and functionalities provided to consumers by these networks. In our *Wireless Broadband Classification Order*, we recog-

nized that wireless IP-based multimedia content and services are typically sold through a service provider-branded, service provider-controlled portal. We also noted that "in some cases, providers use filters to limit the web sites that a customer can access, and, in other cases, subscribers can enter any URL using a handset but the site may not be viewable due to software, processing, or other constraints of the device." In contrast, wireless broadband Internet access services for laptop computers typically allow consumers to access the same applications that would be available had they chosen a cable or wireline broadband Internet access connection.

* * *

200. The Commission generally relies on the competitive marketplace to deliver the benefits of choice, innovation and affordability to American consumers, and regulates only when market driven forces alone may not achieve broader social goals. The Commission has found that the Commercial Mobile Radio Services (CMRS) market is effectively competitive, and that competitive pressures continue to result in the introduction of innovative pricing plans and service offerings. We have not found, however, that competition in the CMRS marketplace is ensuring that consumers drive handset and application choices, especially in the emerging wireless broadband market. For example, while it is easy for consumers to differentiate among providers by price, most consumers are unaware when carriers block or degrade applications and of the implications of such actions, thus making it difficult for providers to differentiate themselves on this score. As a result, while many commenters assert that market forces require that wireless providers support handsets and applications that consumers want, there is evidence that wireless service providers nevertheless block or degrade consumer-chosen hardware and applications without an appropriate justification.

201. We do not decide in this proceeding whether competition in the CMRS market generally is sufficient to ensure that consumers have the ability to use wireless devices and applications of their choice in the emerging wireless broadband market, especially since these questions are being considered more broadly in other proceedings. Given the nature of this spectrum and the lack of additional similar spectrum capacity that can be made available in the near future, however, what we decide here is important to the evolution of the next generation of wireless technology, industry structure and institutional arrangements. This auction provides a window of opportunity to have a significant effect on the next phase of mobile wireless technological innovation, and on the evolution of market and institutional arrangements—such as arrangements regarding open platforms for devices and applications to the benefit of consumers—that will go along with that innovation. As a result, in light of the evidence suggesting that wireless service providers are blocking or degrading consumer-chosen hardware and applications without an appropriate justification, we believe that it is appropriate to take a measured step to encourage additional innovation and consumer

choice at this critical stage in the evolution of wireless broadband services, by removing some of the barriers that developers and handset/device manufacturers face in bringing new products to market. By fostering greater balance between device manufacturers and wireless service providers in this respect, we intend to spur the development of innovative products and services.

* * *

206. Accordingly, consistent with the broadband principles set out above, we will require only C Block licensees to allow customers, device manufacturers, third-party application developers, and others to use or develop the devices and applications of their choosing in C Block networks, so long as they meet all applicable regulatory requirements and comply with reasonable conditions related to management of the wireless network (i.e., do not cause harm to the network). Specifically, a C Block licensee may not block, degrade, or interfere with the ability of end users to download and utilize applications of their choosing on the licensee's C Block network, subject to reasonable network management. We anticipate that wireless service providers will address this requirement by developing reasonable standards, including through participation in standards setting organizations, as discussed below. Finally, for the reasons noted above, we will not impose additional requirements on the C Block, including wholesale and interconnection requirements.

Wireless Carterfone. Is the FCC's action in the 700 MHz auction a move toward network neutrality or simply consumer-friendly regulation of wireless phone company tactics in tying together service and devices? The wireless industry engages in a litany of practices that are either frustrating or possibly misleading to consumers, such as limiting their customers to a few devices and limiting the features of the ones they do allow. (For a detailed discussion of the problem in a paper cited extensively by the FCC in the 700 MHz auction order, see Tim Wu, *Wireless Net Neutrality: Cellular* Carterfone *on Mobile Networks* (New America Foundation Wireless Future Program Working Paper No. 17, February 2007.)) It is easy to see how allowing carriers to control which devices will connect to their networks can limit the development of phones by companies without agreements with carriers. The harm to innovation may be less sweeping than allowing wireline carriers control the shape of the Internet, but is there any valid reason for the types of restrictions the wireless carriers impose? If not, what's the harm in banning them?

Note that licensees in the 700 MHz auction have almost complete discretion to choose a particular service; there is no requirement, even, that service be two-way. If the service provider chooses to broadcast one-way video, does it matter that consumers can watch it on the device of their choosing? While Verizon argued against the limits, and AT&T for them, Verizon actually won (for approximately $4.7 billion) most of the licenses subject to the open access rules. The imposition of the open access requirement was contingent on bids for the C–Block meeting a reservation price of $4.6 billion, and the only other bidder in the C–Block anywhere close to Verizon was Google, which claimed to have bid up the price past $4.6 billion only for the purpose of triggering the open access rules that will be imposed on Verizon. AT&T, on the other hand, bid for and won (for $6.6 billion, almost $2 billion more) licenses in a less desirable part of the spectrum not subject to the rules. Does Verizon know something we don't? Does Google? Does AT&T?

D. REGULATORY IMPLICATIONS OF INTERNET TELECOMMUNICATIONS

1. VoIP and Related Services

a) Introduction

The business of providing telecommunications services in this country is the subject of complex regulatory apparatus. In addition to positive obligations like rate-setting and nondiscrimination rules, there are a host of other rules that essentially define the business of telecommunications. Interexchange carriers pay access charges to local carriers; local carriers pay each other reciprocal compensation for termination of their calls; all carriers pay into the Universal Service Fund. There are myriad detailed rules we have not discussed to cover things like the ability of customers to keep their phone numbers when they change carriers (number portability) or the now-federally-mandated ability to reach emergency services by dialing "911".

Providing services over the Internet, on the other hand, is not heavily regulated. Amazon, for instance, incurs no particular regulatory obligations by virtue of the fact that it is an Internet, rather than a bricks-and-mortar, retailer.

The question, then, is what to do when a heavily regulated service is provided by a largely unregulated means: digital communication over the Internet. In the following proceeding, the Commission provides an overview of the technological, commercial, and regulatory issues. We consider specific problems that have received regulatory attention in the sections that follow.

IN THE MATTER OF IP-ENABLED SERVICES

Federal Communications Commission, 2004.
19 FCC Rcd. 4863.

BY THE COMMISSION:

I. INTRODUCTION

1. In this Notice of Proposed Rulemaking (Notice), we examine issues relating to services and applications making use of Internet Protocol (IP), including but not limited to voice over IP (VoIP) services (collectively, "IP-enabled services"). We seek comment on the impact

that IP-enabled services, many of which are accessed over the Internet, have had and will continue to have on the United States' communications landscape. As a truly global network providing instantaneous connectivity to individuals and services, the Internet has transcended historical jurisdictional boundaries to become one of the greatest drivers of consumer choice and benefit, technical innovation, and economic development in the United States in the last ten years. We acknowledge that it has done so in an environment that is free of many of the regulatory obligations applied to traditional telecommunications services and networks. Carriers have begun to realize efficiencies associated with utilization of IP in both the backbone and the "last mile" of their networks. Customers are beginning to substitute IP-enabled services for traditional telecommunications services and networks, and we seek comment on the rate and extent of that substitution. Increasingly, these customers will speak with each other using VoIP-based services instead of circuit-switched telephony and view content over streaming Internet media instead of broadcast or cable platforms. By doing so, they will change, fundamentally, their use of these applications and services—consumers will become increasingly empowered to customize the services they use, and will choose these services from an unprecedented range of service providers and platforms. * * *

3. In other proceedings, we have recognized the paramount importance of encouraging deployment of broadband infrastructure to the American people. As broadband facilities have proliferated, communications services and networks have increasingly taken advantage of the efficiencies associated with translating data into IP packets running over the same network infrastructures. As discussed below, enterprises are already relying heavily on IP-based applications to facilitate both internal and external communications. Moreover, providers offering VoIP services are beginning to challenge traditional telecommunications carriers in residential markets—and even today use IP to transport residential interexchange calls, often unbeknownst to end users. The increasing deployment of broadband facilities therefore has prompted the development of services and applications that provide broader functionality and greater consumer choice at prices competitive to those of analogous services provided over the public switched telephone network (PSTN). Many observers predict that, before long, providers will be able to integrate voice and real-time video to provide new capabilities and service offerings. The development of such services is likely to prompt increased deployment of wireline, cable, wireless, and other broadband facilities capable of bringing IP-enabled services to the public, which in turn, we expect, will prompt further development and deployment of such services. This process may challenge the central role that legacy technologies have played in American communications for over 100 years.

4. But VoIP services are not necessarily mere substitutes for traditional telephony services, because the new networks based on the Internet Protocol are, both technically and administratively, different

from the PSTN. Whereas the PSTN is designed to meet the analog communications requirements of two-way voice conversations, IP networks are designed to meet the short-burst digital data communications requirements of computing networks. Whereas the PSTN's design is logically and physically hierarchical, utilizing highly centralized signaling intelligence to connect parties to a communication, IP network design is "flat," distributing network intelligence and permitting highly dynamic and flexible routing that takes into account network delays, changes in loads, and changes in topology. And whereas enhanced functionalities delivered via the PSTN typically must be created internally by the network operator and are often tied to a physical termination point, IP-enabled services can be created by users or third parties, providing innumerable opportunities for innovative offerings competing with one another over multiple platforms and accessible wherever the user might have access to the IP network. The rise of IP thus challenges the key assumptions on which communications networks, and regulation of those networks, are predicated: Packets routed across a global network with multiple access points defy jurisdictional boundaries. Networks capable of facilitating any sort of application that programmers can devise have empowered consumers to choose services they desire rather than merely accepting a provider's one-size-fits-all offering. In this Notice, we seek comment on whether the proliferation of services and applications utilizing a common protocol may permit competitive developments in the marketplace to play the key role once played by regulation.

5. For all these reasons, the changes wrought by the rise of IP-enabled communications promise to be revolutionary. * * * IP-enabled services generally—and VoIP in particular—will encourage consumers to demand more broadband connections, which will foster the development of more IP-enabled services. IP-enabled services, moreover, have increased economic productivity and growth, and bolstered network redundancy and resiliency. Our aim in this proceeding is to facilitate this transition, relying wherever possible on competition and applying discrete regulatory requirements only where such requirements are necessary to fulfill important policy objectives. We expressly recognize the possibility that we ultimately will need to differentiate among various IP-enabled services. For example, much of the telecommunications regulation implemented by the Commission had its roots in seeking to control monopoly ownership of the PSTN. To the extent the market for IP-enabled services is not characterized by such monopoly conditions, we seek comment on whether there is a compelling rationale for applying traditional economic regulation to providers of IP-enabled services. * * * As discussed above, fencing off IP platforms from economic regulation traditionally applied to legacy telecommunications services would not put them beyond the reach of regulations designed to promote public safety and consumer protection (such as E911) or other important public policy concerns. Instead, this proceeding is designed to seek public comment on

future decisions that would start from the premise that IP-enabled services are minimally regulated. * * *

II. Background

7. Our consideration of the critical legal and regulatory questions posed in this Notice is necessarily informed by the specific technological evolution of the services at issue and the specific legal framework under which we exercise our jurisdiction over interstate and international communications. In this section, we first briefly describe the history of IP-enabled services—a history characterized by explosive growth and, recently, the advent of offerings that promise to transform the communications environment—and then discuss the legal context in which we consider the questions posed by those offerings.

A. Technological and Market Evolution of IP-Enabled Services

8. The rise of the Internet has fundamentally changed the ways in which we communicate by increasing the speed of communication, the range of communicating devices, and the platforms over which they can send and receive. This growth has been possible because the Internet employs an open network architecture using a common protocol—the Internet Protocol, or IP—to transmit data across the network in a manner fundamentally different than the way in which signals transit a circuit-switched service. Whereas circuit-switched networks generally reserve dedicated resources along a path through the network, IP networks route traffic without requiring the establishment of an end-to-end path. * * * [T]hese packets may carry any type of information for applications offering widely disparate functions, including those facilitating voice communications.

9. The growth of the Internet has been accompanied by an explosion in consumer access to a growing universe of websites, all relying on IP. Many websites have evolved into content-rich information portals configured to serve the broad commercial, educational, political and entertainment interests of Internet users. In its initial stages, the Internet was primarily utilized for e-mail, file transfer, and—more recently—access to the world wide web. Increasingly, the Internet is being utilized for more sophisticated uses, such as peer-to-peer file sharing, instant messaging, streaming media, online gaming, and virtual private networks (VPNs). In turn, as applications proliferate and demand for Internet access services grows, service providers continue to augment network capacity to offer faster Internet access services. These broadband services have been deployed across multiple platforms, including those of local exchange carriers (LECs), cable operators, direct broadcast satellite (DBS), video programming providers and, increasingly, wireless (including WiFi) providers and electric companies using power lines. In the following sections, we briefly describe a cross-section of the numerous offerings—including not only various sorts of IP telephony, but also new and unique forms of IP-based communication—made possible by these developments.

1. Internet Voice

10. Although several providers carry voice calls over their backbone IP networks, until recently, use of the Internet for the purpose of transmitting voice communications has been limited. Early ventures in peer-to-peer IP telephony were largely unsuccessful in part due to the nature of early IP networks, which offered limited reliability and voice quality. Today, however, as a result of improvements in technology, IP networks are increasingly being used to carry voice communications. For example, private IP networks are used to provide an array of communications services to enterprise customers. Residential users can access VoIP services using phones, laptops, and personal digital assistants. Even many gaming systems now feature VoIP functionality. Also, wireless communications standards have evolved to include IP as a key component. Many manufacturers are concentrating most, if not all, new development and marketing on IP-capable alternatives while merely providing maintenance support for legacy circuit-switched equipment currently in place. Similarly, a recent flood of press announcements reflects that a number of service providers, from residential telephony companies to cable providers, have begun to use or will soon use IP to provide voice services to residential customers.

11. These recent developments, however, must be understood within the context of the development of the technology in recent years, and the myriad services in which it is now used. IP telephony has been offered in various forms since at least 1995. Early experience with the technology, however, appears to have deterred investors and consumers from adopting it because, analysts argue, its reliability and voice quality were below standards that most consumers would tolerate. According to many industry watchers, technology has now overcome prior quality and reliability concerns. These improvements, the creation of new IP services that traditional telephony providers may offer alongside voice service, and increasing penetration of broadband into the residential market have become important market drivers promoting deployment of IP telephony technologies. In addition, market entry by IP service providers such as Vonage appears to have spurred deployment of IP-enabled voice services by established telephony providers.

a. IP Telephony Offerings by Owners of Transmission Facilities

12. As noted above, an IP network transmits IP packets, which may contain data that, when unpacked, forms voice communication. Cable operators, wireline carriers, and wireless providers have announced that they have begun to deploy, or intend to deploy, IP networks to transmit IP telephony services to their subscribers. Cable operators have begun to offer video, broadband Internet, and IP telephony over their hybrid fiber-coaxial cable plant. Time Warner Cable predicts that it will offer IP telephony to all of its subscribers by the end of 2004. To achieve this goal, Time Warner recently entered into an agreement with MCI and Sprint to use those companies' networks to

provide IP telephony to its cable subscribers and to interconnect their calls with the PSTN.

13. AT&T states that it will provide VoIP service in 100 markets by the first quarter of 2004 and expects to enroll over one million customers in the next two years. Other wireline carriers have announced plans to launch IP telephony services in 2004. SBC currently offers IP telephony to small and medium size enterprises (SMEs) in 13 states, and BellSouth plans to rollout service to SMEs in 9 states throughout 2004. Qwest announced that it would offer IP telephony to residential subscribers and SMEs in Minnesota in December 2003. Finally, Verizon intends to offer IP telephony to its DSL subscribers nationwide in the second quarter of 2004, and to businesses in the fourth quarter of 2004.

14. Wireless service providers have also begun providing IP telephony services. Second generation (2G) mobile communications systems solely using circuit-switched networks to provide voice service are now being supplemented by 2.5G and 3G systems providing enhanced multimedia services built on packet switching and IP routing. For example, Verizon Wireless and Sprint PCS have recently launched push-to-talk service, using VoIP technology, and additional carriers are expected to launch push-to-talk service this year. Voice services will also be provided by service providers using WiFi technology.

b. IP Telephony Offerings By Other Providers

15. Providers not owning extensive facilities—or any facilities at all—have also begun to offer IP telephony services to residential end users. For example, pulver.com (Pulver) operates Free World Dialup (FWD), an Internet application that facilitates FWD members engaging in free peer-to-peer communications, exchanging voice, video, or text. FWD subscribers use a Session Initiation Protocol (SIP) phone or personal computer to make "calls" to other FWD members that do not utilize the PSTN. Pulver states that the members' end-user devices establish the actual connection and manage the call, and that the calls are carried by the members' preexisting broadband connection rather than over Pulver-owned facilities. Vonage offers an IP telephony service that permits a subscriber with a broadband connection to place telephone calls to, and to receive calls from, other Vonage broadband subscribers and end users relying on traditional PSTN facilities alike. Vonage does not provide its customers with Internet access or a personal computer. Rather, Vonage supplies software and a multimedia terminal adapter (MTA) that permits its customers to use analog phones to place calls via their broadband Internet connections. Vonage provides each of its customers with traditional telephone numbers so that Vonage customers may be called by PSTN telephone subscribers. When a Vonage customer communicates with a subscriber of ordinary telephone service, Vonage converts its customer's IP packets into the digital TDM (time division multiplexed) format for transfer through a media gateway to the PSTN, and vice versa. If a Vonage customer communicates with another Vonage customer, this transmission does not utilize the PSTN and

Vonage servers use SIP to direct the call to the other customer's personal computer or MTA.

2. Other New and Future IP-Enabled Services

16. As discussed above, software developers expect to introduce IP-enabled data applications that take advantage of broadband speeds. In addition, as telephone service is migrated to an IP network, telephony providers plan to provide new IP-enabled data features that will enhance the telephony experience. Software developers are also upgrading traditional IP-enabled data services, such as instant messaging, e-mail, web surfing, gaming, and virtual private networks, to provide new features and capabilities that capitalize on the availability of higher speeds. As these services—which may integrate voice, video, and data capabilities while maintaining high quality of service—are introduced, it may become increasingly difficult, if not impossible, to distinguish "voice" service from "data" service, and users may increasingly rely on integrated services using broadband facilities delivered using IP rather than the traditional PSTN. Analysts predict the increasing integration of IP-enabled services with devices other than telephones and computers.

17. These new services will likely come in many varieties. For example, analysts predict that high-speed broadband connections will fuel the use of video-conferencing, on-demand conferencing, and collaboration on documents while conferencing. These video calls and conferences may be accompanied by the transmission of data. Some applications that are currently used by enterprise customers, or that may in the future be used by such customers, include distance training, Internet classrooms, IP customer support centers, voice-enabled transactions and content services, subscription video, and telemedicine.

18. With regard to telephone calls, IP-enabled data services might include virtual telephone numbers, directory dialing, automated voice-mail attendants, call pre-screening, and call forwarding of pre-screened calls to other IP enabled devices, such as a computer or wireless phone. Industry analysts also contemplate a unified messaging or a unified mailbox that collects a user's e-mail, voicemail, and faxes, which may be accessed through the web, a telephone or any other IP-enabled device. These services permit users to decide which media they would like to use to respond to a given message. For example, software might read a user's e-mail messages or faxes to him or her over the telephone, allowing the user to respond via e-mail, voicemail, facsimile, or voice telephony.

19. Software developers are embedding traditional IP-enabled data services with voice features. For example, both America Online's and Microsoft Windows XP's instant messaging (IM) clients include a voice feature, as do many chat applications. "Click to talk" services offered by Web- or E-mail-based applications permit customers to click on a web button in order to speak with a service operator or to enter into an instant messaging session with the service operator. Map and navigation services and online gaming services also contain voice components. Many

PC and console games, such as Microsoft's Xbox, permit their owners to play against other players via peer-to-peer Internet connections. Many of these games permit the gamers to speak with each other via the Internet as they play.

20. Applications providers are preparing to provide IP-enabled services over devices other than phones and computers. Microsoft is currently testing its Internet Protocol television (IPTV) product, which it hopes will offer television subscribers more advanced services, such as HDTV, VOD, interactive television, instant channel changing, multiple pictures-in-picture, and a richer multimedia program guide, via their broadband connections. * * *

21. Mobile services have also benefited from technological advances. * * *

22. Thus, as use of IP expands, the technology's transformative effect on the communications landscape will likely become only more prominent, giving rise to a "virtuous circle" in which competition begets innovation, which in turn begets more competition. End users are likely to enjoy greater and greater flexibility in designing or selecting communications packages that suit their individual needs, and can be expected to access those packages over networks of their choosing, on devices of their choosing. Many parties contend that, in all probability, cross-platform competition will sharpen as distinctions between "voice," "video," and "data" services blur. This competition will likely force more innovation and lower prices, resulting in more individual choice and hence even greater competition.

B. Legal Background

23. Our consideration of issues surrounding IP-enabled services and applications takes place within a legal framework comprised of statutory provisions and judicial precedent, prior Commission orders, ongoing Commission proceedings, and state actions relating to IP-enabled services. An understanding of this legal context is important to ensuring full consideration of the issues raised in this Notice.

1. Statutory Definitions and Commission Precedent

24. The Communications Act and prior Commission orders set forth several definitions relevant to our consideration of VoIP and other IP-enabled services. First, the Act defines the terms "common carrier" and "carrier" to include "any person engaged as a common carrier for hire, in interstate or foreign communication by wire or radio." The Act specifically excludes persons "engaged in radio broadcasting" from this definition. Various regulatory obligations and entitlements set forth in the Act—including a prohibition on unjust or unreasonable discrimination among similarly situated customers and the requirement that all charges, practices, classifications, and regulations applied to common carrier service be "just and reasonable"—attach only to entities meeting this definition.

25. Second, the Commission has long distinguished between "basic" and "enhanced" service offerings. In the *Computer Inquiry* line of decisions, the Commission specified that a "basic" service is a service offering transmission capacity for the delivery of information without net change in form or content. Providers of "basic" services were subjected to common carrier regulation under Title II of the Act. By contrast, an "enhanced" service contains a basic service component but also "employ[s] computer processing applications that act on the format, content, code, protocol or similar aspects of the subscriber's transmitted information; provide the subscriber additional, different, or restructured information; or involve subscriber interaction with stored information." The Commission concluded that enhanced services were subject to the Commission's jurisdiction. It further found, however, that the enhanced service market was highly competitive with low barriers to entry; therefore, the Commission declined to treat providers of enhanced services as "common carriers" subject to regulation under Title II of the Act. In separate orders, the Commission also determined that exempted enhanced service providers (ESPs) should not be subjected to originating access charges for ESP-bound traffic.

26. In 1996, the Telecommunications Act codified, with minor modifications, the Commission's distinction between regulated "basic" and largely unregulated "enhanced" services. The 1996 Act defined "telecommunications" to mean "the transmission, between or among points specified by the user, of information of the user's choosing, without change in the form or content of the information as sent and received." The Act then defined "telecommunications service" to mean "the offering of telecommunications for a fee directly to the public, or to such classes of users as to be effectively available to the public, regardless of facilities used." The Commission has concluded, and courts have agreed, that the "telecommunications service" definition was "intended to clarify that telecommunications services are common carrier services." Various entitlements and obligations set forth in the Act—including, for example, the entitlement to access an incumbent's unbundled network elements for local service and the obligation to render a network accessible to people with disabilities—attach only to entities providing "telecommunications service."

27. By contrast, the 1996 Act defined "information service" to mean "the offering of a capability for generating, acquiring, storing, transforming, processing, retrieving, utilizing, or making available information via telecommunications, and includes electronic publishing, but does not include any use of any such capability for the management, control, or operation of a telecommunications network or the management of a telecommunications service." The Act did not establish any particular entitlements or requirements with regard to providers of information services, but the Commission has exercised its ancillary authority under Title I of the Act to apply requirements to information services.

2. Commission Consideration of VoIP

28. While the Commission has not addressed IP-enabled services in a comprehensive and definitive manner, the Commission has discussed issues relating to VoIP. Moreover, there are several petitions relating to this issue currently pending before the Commission. * * *

d. State Regulation

34. We also note that states are beginning to address VoIP issues. Recently, several states have taken actions with regard to VoIP providers that are rapidly changing the regulatory landscape on the state level. Even at this early stage, states have begun to diverge in their approaches to the regulation of VoIP services. For example, some states have required VoIP providers to be certified to provide service in the state, while others have not.

III. Categorizing IP-Enabled Services

35. In this section, we solicit comment regarding how, if at all, we should differentiate among various IP-enabled services to ensure that any regulations applied to such services are limited to those cases in which they are appropriate. As noted above, IP-enabled services are an increasingly available, sophisticated and attractive alternative to consumers. These services have arisen in an environment largely free of government regulation, and the great majority, we expect, should remain unregulated. * * *

V. Appropriate Legal and Regulatory Framework

42. We invite commenters to address the proper legal classification and appropriate regulatory treatment of each specific class of IP-enabled services they have identified in response to the questions posed above. The Act distinguishes between "telecommunications service[s]" and "information service [s]," and applies particular regulatory entitlements and obligations to the former class but not the latter. Thus, our analysis begins with an examination of the statutory definitions as they apply to particular types of IP-enabled service. But, as described more fully, commenters must consider what policy consequences flow from a particular statutory definition. * * *

B. Specific Regulatory Requirements and Benefits

45. We recognize that the nature of IP-enabled services may well render the rationales animating the regulatory regime that now governs communications services inapplicable here, and that the disparate regulatory treatment assigned to providers of "telecommunications services" and "information services" might well be inappropriate in the context of IP-enabled services. We thus ask commenters to address how we might alter the regulatory treatment that might otherwise accompany the statutory classification they urge for various classes of IP-enabled service.

46. As mentioned above, Congress has provided the Commission with a host of statutory tools that together accord the Commission discretion in structuring an appropriate approach to IP-enabled services. Title II of the Communications Act governs the regulation of telecommunications services. Similarly, Title VI governs the regulation of cable services. Title I of the Act confers upon the Commission ancillary jurisdiction over matters that are not expressly within the scope of a specific statutory mandate but nevertheless necessary to the Commission's execution of its statutorily prescribed functions. Section 1 of the Communications Act established the Commission "[f]or the purpose of regulating interstate and foreign commerce in communication by wire and radio," and section 4(i) authorized the Commission to "perform any and all acts, make such rules and regulations, and issue such orders, not inconsistent with this Act, as may be necessary in the execution of its functions." Ancillary jurisdiction may be employed, in the Commission's discretion, where the Commission has subject matter jurisdiction over the communications at issue and the assertion of jurisdiction is reasonably required to perform an express statutory obligation. "Because the Commission's judgment on how the public interest is best served is entitled to substantial deference, the Commission's choice of regulatory tools" when these conditions are met will stand "unless arbitrary or capricious."

47. Second, with regard to telecommunications carriers and telecommunications services, the Commission is required to forbear from applying a particular regulation or statutory provision if it determines that: (1) enforcement of the regulation is not necessary to ensure that charges are just and reasonable, and are not unjustly or unreasonably discriminatory; (2) enforcement of the regulation is not necessary to protect consumers; and (3) forbearance is consistent with the public interest. Use of this forbearance authority might be appropriate if the statutory classification accorded to a particular class of IP-enabled services leads to regulatory consequences that are neither necessary nor appropriate in the context of such services.

48. In light of the statutory prerogatives described above, we ask commenters to describe which particular regulatory requirements and entitlements, if any, should apply to each category of IP-enabled service. In the sections that follow, we set forth particular requirements and benefits that may or may not apply to some or all IP-enabled services. How would the particular statutory classifications urged by the commenter for various IP-enabled services impact the applicability of each of the regulatory obligations and benefits described below? . . . . [There follow a list of discrete regulatory obligations; most of these have been omitted in order to focus on two dominant issues, access charges and universal service charges.]

2. Carrier Compensation

61. The Commission seeks comment on the extent to which access charges should apply to VoIP or other IP-enabled services. If providers of

these services are not classified as interexchange carriers, or these services are not classified as telecommunications services, should providers nevertheless pay for use of the LECs' switching facilities? As a policy matter, we believe that any service provider that sends traffic to the PSTN should be subject to similar compensation obligations, irrespective of whether the traffic originates on the PSTN, on an IP network, or on a cable network. We maintain that the cost of the PSTN should be borne equitably among those that use it in similar ways. Given this, under what authority could the Commission require payment for these services? If charges should be assessed on these services, should they be the same as the access charges assessed on providers of telecommunications services, or should the charges be computed and assessed differently? How should different charges be computed and assessed? By seeking comment on whether access charges should apply to the various categories of service identified by the commenters, we are not addressing whether charges apply or do not apply under existing law.

62. If, on the other hand, VoIP or other IP-enabled services are classified as telecommunications services, should the Commission forbear from applying access charges to these services, or impose access charges different from those paid by non-IP-enabled telecommunications service providers? If so, how should different charges be computed and assessed? If commenters believe charges should be assessed, must carriers pay access charges, or should they instead pay compensation under section 251(b)(5) of the Act? Would assessment of rates lower than access charge rates require increases in universal service support or end-user charges? If no access charges, or different charges, are assessed for VoIP and IP-enabled service providers' use of the PSTN, would identification of this traffic result in significant additional incremental costs?

3. Universal Service

63. We seek comment on how the regulatory classification of IP-enabled services, including VoIP, would affect the Commission's ability to fund universal service. Many of these issues have already been raised in the *Wireline Broadband NPRM*, and we encourage parties to incorporate into this docket prior filings in that proceeding that are relevant to our inquiry here. In the *Wireline Broadband NPRM*, the Commission sought comment on whether facilities-based broadband Internet access providers are required to contribute, pursuant to its mandatory authority, or should be required to contribute to universal service, pursuant to its permissive authority. In this proceeding, we broaden that inquiry by asking commenters to address the contribution obligations of both facilities-based and non-facilities-based providers of IP-enabled services. These questions are also intertwined with issues raised in our separate *Universal Service Contribution Methodology* proceeding, which explores possible ways to reform our current methodology for assessing universal service contributions. We leave questions of whether to reform the current methodology to the separate *Universal Service Contribution Methodology* proceeding.

64. If certain classes of IP-enabled services are determined to be information services, could or should the Commission require *non*-facilities-based providers of such services to contribute to universal service pursuant to its permissive authority? Would such providers "provide" telecommunications? If the Commission were to exercise its permissive authority over facilities-based and non-facilities-based providers of IP-enabled services, how could it do so in an equitable and nondiscriminatory fashion? Would the Commission identify specific services that are subject to its permissive authority? How would providers of IP-enabled services identify the portion of their IP-enabled service revenues that constitute end-user telecommunications revenues? * * *

4. Title III

67. As noted above, IP-enabled services can be provided over any broadband platform, including a wireless platform, and there are numerous examples of wireless providers offering such services. IP-enabled services may also involve the use of wireless technology in combination with other platforms, e.g., a VoIP call may originate from a mobile device and terminate on a wireline or cable platform. To the extent that providers of IP-enabled services use wireless technology to deliver such services, they fall within the ambit of Title III of the Act, which provides the structure for the Commission's regulation of spectrum-based services, including broadcasting and all other services that use radio waves. Moreover, within Title III, Section 332 provides a specific framework for regulation of commercial mobile radio service (CMRS) providers. Section 332 provides that CMRS providers are common carriers subject to the provisions of Title II, but it also authorizes the Commission to forbear from applying Title II provisions it determines are inapplicable. Accordingly, in implementing Section 332, the Commission has forborne from applying most Title II economic regulation to CMRS providers based on the competitive nature of the CMRS marketplace. In addition, Section 332 limits state regulation of CMRS by preempting states from regulating the entry of or rates charged by CMRS providers. * * *

B. Economic Regulation

73. We also seek comment on whether various traditional economic regulations set forth in Title II and Commission rules should be applied to any class of IP-enabled service provider. Among other things, Title II requires all common carriers of interstate or foreign communications by wire or radio to provide those communications upon reasonable request at rates, classifications, and practices that are just and reasonable; prohibits common carriers from unjustly or unreasonably discriminating in "charges, practices, classifications, regulations, facilities, or services" against similarly situated third-party customers; and requires providers of telecommunications service to interconnect directly or indirectly with the facilities and equipment of other such providers. Further, the Act imposes additional requirements upon LECs, including, for example, the obligation to provide number portability. The Act also entitles providers

of telecommunications services to use certain incumbent LEC network elements on an unbundled basis and at cost-based rates. Finally, under the Commission's *Computer Inquiry* decisions, "facilities-based common carriers" are required to provide the basic transmission services underlying their enhanced services on a nondiscriminatory basis pursuant to tariffs. * * *

Starting Premises. The FCC says that it must "start from the premise that IP-enabled services are minimally regulated"? Why should that be the case, or, even if it is descriptively accurate, why should it matter? True, if "retail" is an IP-enabled service, it is "minimally regulated," but no one is suggesting the Commission regulate Amazon. Throughout this area, the notions underlying regulation are being challenged by the fact that a regulated service (telecommunications) may no longer fit the typical economic model (natural monopoly) calling for utility regulation. But if the service and the economic model are diverging, why pay more attention to economics than the service? The most common form of nondiscrimination rule—common carriage—has traditionally been imposed on transportation and communications carriers regardless of their market power, see Thomas B. Nachbar, *The Public Network*, 17 CommLaw Conspectus ___ (forthcoming 2009), and, as described in the last chapter, while it does not impose full Title II regulation on wireless carriers, the FCC has *not* seriously considered relaxing wireless carriers' standard common carrier obligations, in large part because of the service they offer. What is different about IP-enabled services like VoIP?

b) The Regulatory Landscape

The *IP Enabled Services NPRM* describes a general approach to telecommunications provided over the Internet, including VoIP. That inquiry has been percolating at the FCC but has produced no definitive results. Instead, the FCC made some regulatory choices regarding VoIP in the context of specific proceedings. The FCC has still refused to categorically define VoIP, but in the course of rendering specific decisions, it has provided some definition of both how it perceives the service and how it intends to approach its regulation.

At the heart of these decisions is the interplay between four definitions from the 1996 Act: "information service," "telecommunications," "telecommunications carrier," and "telecommunications service." We present them slightly out of (alphabetical and hence statutory) order in order to emphasize the relationship between "telecommunications," "telecommunications service," and "telecommunications carrier".

47 U.S.C. 153—DEFINITIONS

(20) **Information service.**—The term "information service" means the offering of a capability for generating, acquiring, storing,

transforming, processing, retrieving, utilizing, or making available information via telecommunications, and includes electronic publishing, but does not include any use of any such capability for the management, control, or operation of a telecommunications system or the management of a telecommunications service.

(43) **Telecommunications.**—The term "telecommunications" means the transmission, between or among points specified by the user, of information of the user's choosing, without change in the form or content of the information as sent and received.

(46) **Telecommunications service.**—The term "telecommunications service" means the offering of telecommunications for a fee directly to the public, or to such classes of users as to be effectively available directly to the public, regardless of the facilities used.

(44) **Telecommunications carrier.**—The term "telecommunications carrier" means any provider of telecommunications services.... A telecommunications carrier shall be treated as a common carrier under this chapter only to the extent that it is engaged in providing telecommunications services, except that the Commission shall determine whether the provision of fixed and mobile satellite service shall be treated as common carriage.

Two points should jump out: First, the last three definitions build upon each other. A "telecommunications carrier" is "a provider of telecommunications service," which in turn is the "offering of telecommunications for a fee directly to the public." Second, as we discussed earlier, the definitions of "information service" and "telecommunications service" roughly track the *Computer Inquiries* definitions of "enhanced service" and "basic service". The regulatory classifications also track the *Computer Inquiries*' understanding of regulation, with telecommunications services being subjected (by both the FCC and the states) to normal common carriage regulation much like traditional telephone companies and information services being largely unregulated. At issue in most of these cases is whether VoIP should be considered a "telecommunications service" or an "information service" for various regulatory purposes.

The Many Flavors of VoIP. One problem with having a conversation about VoIP is that it is a description of a functionality (voice telephony) provided by a protocol (IP), but it is not necessarily a complete service. There are many ways to carry voice signals over IP, and the first thing the FCC did in this area was to address two easy cases: peer-to-peer VoIP between computers that does not directly involve the PSTN and regular telephone service in which the carrier happens to use the Internet for some portion of the connection.

The FCC excluded purely peer-to-peer VoIP from telephone regulation in *In the Matter of Petition for Declaratory Ruling that pulver.com's Free World Dialup is Neither Telecommunications Nor a Telecommunications Service*, 19 FCC Rcd. 3307 (2004). Adopted the same day as the *IP-Enabled Services NPRM*, *pulver.com* involved a service, "Free World

Dialup" ("FWD"), that provided a way for computers already on the Internet to find each other and to establish connections between them, but it did not actually carry the information itself. Essentially, the system operated as a directory service and, once the two users found each other online, the connection was maintained by the users' computers directly. Importantly, FWD did not involve the use of customer premises equipment (the conversation was carried out through the users' computers, not their phones) and it could not be used to place calls that would interconnect with the PSTN. Any use of the telephone network was simply as a means for carrying the users' Internet traffic, so as far as the Internet was concerned, FWD looked just like any other Internet application, like email, text chat, or the transmission of a web page. The FCC was quick to adopt Pulver's conception of its service, translating it into the statutory classifications by distinguishing whether Pulver provided a telecommunications service or merely used telecommunications in providing a service:

> 9. First, we conclude that FWD is not "telecommunications." Under the statute, the heart of "telecommunications" is transmission.... Pulver neither offers nor provides transmission to its members. Rather, FWD members "bring their own broadband" transmission to interact with the FWD server. * * * FWD provides new information: whether other FWD members are present; at what IP address a member may be reached; or, in some cases, a voicemail or an email response. Finally, the fact that Pulver's server is connected to the Internet via some form of transmission is not in and of itself, as some commenters argue, relevant to the definition of telecommunications. Pulver may "use" some telecommunications to provide its FWD directory service but that does not make FWD itself telecommunications.
>
> 10. We also conclude that FWD is not a "telecommunications service." Section 153(46), the definition of telecommunications service, refers to an "offering of telecommunications." As discussed above, however, FWD does not offer "telecommunications." Therefore, it cannot be a "telecommunications service." In addition, as its name suggests, FWD is free of charge to users and, in order to be a telecommunications service, the service provider must assess a fee for its service. Accordingly, because we determine that FWD is not a "telecommunications service," the common carriage obligations applicable to the provision of such service as set forth in Title II do not apply.
>
> 11. We conclude that FWD is an information service because FWD offers "a capability for generating, acquiring, storing, transforming, processing, retrieving, utilizing, or making available information via telecommunications." * * *

Although Pulver won the battle to avoid being regulated as a common carrier, it lost the war to avoid being regulated. Pulver had actually argued that it was neither a telecommunications service *nor* an information service. The FCC was prepared to give Pulver a lot of slack, but not to let go of the leash entirely:

> 14. We reject Pulver's reading of the definition of "information service." Pulver argues that FWD cannot be an "information service" as that term is defined in the Act because Pulver does not offer transmission to its members. However, the statutory definition of an information service speaks only to the *offering* of various types of computing capabilities *via* telecommunications, not the *offering* of telecommunications itself. The fact that FWD's computing capabilities, as described above, are available to its members via "telecommunications"—*i.e.*, the telecommunications underlying its members' Internet connectivity; the telecommunications connecting Pulver's FWD server to the Internet; and the telecommunications underlying the Internet backbone itself—is sufficient to meet the statutory definition of "information service." In explaining the difference between "enhanced services" and "information services," the Commission previously noted that the former are "limited to services 'offered over common carrier transmission facilities used in interstate communications,' whereas 'information services' may be provided, more broadly, 'via telecommunications.' " The Commission has never required or even suggested that the information service provider must be the entity that provides or offers the telecommunications over which the information service is made available to its members. As described above, FWD members must separately acquire broadband service, as Pulver does not offer transmission to its members.

We previously pointed out that no one is suggesting that the FCC regulate Amazon, but if "the telecommunications connecting Pulver's FWD server to the Internet; and the telecommunications underlying the Internet backbone itself—is sufficient to meet the statutory definition of 'information service,' " then Amazon is surely just as subject to the FCC's regulatory jurisdiction as FWD was. Is that true as a practical matter as well?

Two months after *pulver.com*, the FCC ruled in a case on the opposite extreme: "an interexchange service that: (1) uses ordinary customer premises equipment (CPE) with no enhanced functionality; (2) originates and terminates on the public switched telephone network (PSTN); and (3) undergoes no net protocol conversion and provides no enhanced functionality to end users due to the provider's use of IP technology." See *In the Matter of Petition for Declaratory Ruling that AT&T's Phone-to-Phone IP Telephony Services are Exempt From Access Charges*, 19 FCC Rcd. 7457 (2004). The AT&T service looked exactly like regular long distance service: it originated and ended in normal telephone devices connected to the PSTN and was carried over the AT&T's own network. The only difference was that the middle portion happened to be done using the AT&T's Internet backbone and therefore used IP rather than some other protocol. AT&T argued that its conversion of the conversation from the PSTN to IP and back was "net protocol conversion," which under previous FCC rules would have qualified as enhanced services and therefore were presumptively information services as well (as a statutory matter, presumptively by virtue of the fact that they "transform" the information being carried). The FCC clarified that this type of internal (or "internetworking") protocol conversion did not qualify as "net protocol conversation" and was itself an aspect of providing a telecommunications service.[5]

After *pulver.com*, pure peer-to-peer VoIP looks like it will have no traditional obligations as a telecommunications service, after the *AT&T* case, a PSTN-based phone-to-phone system with IP only in the middle will have all of them. Nether case addressed how to either classify or regulate the intermediate case in which a user places and receives calls over their Internet broadband connection (either using their computer or a specialized box provided by a carrier that allows them to use a telephone instead of a computer) but can either call or receive calls from phones on the PSTN. The FCC eventually *classified* such a service—"services that (1) enable real-time, two-way voice communications; (2) require a broadband connection from the user's location; (3) require IP-compatible customer premises equipment; and (4) permit users to receive calls from and terminate calls to the PSTN"—as "interconnected VoIP services". *IP-Enabled Services*; *E911 Requirements for IP-Enabled Service Providers, First Report and Order and Notice of Proposed Rulemaking*, 20 FCC Rcd. 10245, 10257–58, para. 24 (2005). As to how to *regulate* them, that has been more of a piecemeal affair. The first thing the FCC did, though, was to secure its position as the exclusive government regulator of VoIP.

VoIP and Federalism. Sensing that VoIP looked an awful lot like local telephone service, some state public utility commissions actually attempted to regulate it. In 2003, the Minnesota Public Utilities Commission attempted to regulate the Vonage VoIP service. Unlike FWD, Vonage assigns a regular telephone number to a user, but the service is not dependent on the user actually being in any particular location when using the service. The phone number Vonage assigns to each user is virtual in the sense that it points to the user's account and not to a physical address; anywhere the user is connected to the Internet, they can use the service, both to make and receive calls. Vonage allows both local and interstate calls, rendering it a "jurisdictionally mixed service," with the FCC having the authority to regulate the interstate aspects of

5. *See* In the Matter of Implementation of the Non-Accounting Safeguards of Sections 271 and 272 of the Communications Act of 1934, as Amended, 11 FCC Rcd. 21905, 21957–58, ¶ 106 (1997) ("We note that, under *Computer II* and *Computer III*, we have treated three categories of protocol processing services as basic services, rather than enhanced services, because they result in no net protocol conversion to the end-user. These categories include protocol processing: 1) involving communications between an end-user and the network itself (e.g., for initiation, routing, and termination of calls) rather than between or among users; 2) in connection with the introduction of a new basic network technology (which requires protocol conversion to maintain compatibility with existing CPE); and 3) involving internetworking (conversions taking place solely within the carrier's network to facilitate provision of a basic network service, that result in no net conversion to the end-user).")

the service. But because VoIP service is not location dependent, the Commission reasoned, it would be impossible to separate the intrastate and interstate aspects of the service (the Commission specifically discounted the possibility of using "proxies" for the location of service, such as the billing address of the Vonage user as being "poor fits"), and so it preempted Minnesota's claim to regulation of *any* aspect of the service. The Commission chose not to resolve the question of whether Vonage was a telecommunications service or an information service, arguing instead that, regardless of the classification, the FCC had taken a deregulatory approach to VoIP, which was inconsistent with the Minnesota Commission's attempts to apply traditional telephone regulation to Vonage. See *Vonage Holdings Corporation Petition for Declaratory Ruling Concerning an Order of the Minnesota Public Utilities Commission, Memorandum Opinion and Order*, 19 FCC Rcd. 22404 (2004), *aff'd*, 483 F.3d 570 (8th Cir. 2007).

Having taken the job of regulating VoIP upon itself, the FCC has done so through a variety of proceedings defining particular regulatory obligations of the VoIP providers. Because VoIP providers are not LECs, much less ILECs, they are not even potentially subject to dominant carrier regulation or the obligation to provide either UNEs or wholesale services. Rather, the FCC has focused on the degree to which four different regulations apply to VoIP providers: whether VoIP providers must provide location-specific information as required by so-called "enhanced 911" or "E911" rules, whether they must comply with the requirements of the Communications Assistance for Law Enforcement Act ("CALEA") designed to allow government agencies to intercept communications on digital networks, and, perhaps most importantly, how VoIP figures into the intercarrier compensation scheme or participates in the Universal Service Fund. We address each in turn below.

c) E911

One of the FCC's major policy initiatives is the rollout of so-called "enhanced 911" services. E911 differs from traditional (or "basic") 911 service largely by virtue of the technology it utilizes—it relies on a specialized "selective router" that uses the caller's calling information to route the 911 call to the appropriate dispatch center (in FCC-speak, a "public safety answering point" or "PSAP") via a dedicated wireline 911 network. E911 is largely in place for traditional wireline providers. In 2005, the Commission decided to extend the requirement to some VoIP services—the previously discussed "interconnected VoIP services"—on the theory that consumers who can use their VoIP service to call and receive calls from the PSTN expect their VoIP phones to work in much the same way as traditional telephones do. (Thus, the E911 requirement does not apply to purely virtual, non-interconnected services like FWD.) See *IP–Enabled Services*; *E911 Requirements for IP-Enabled Service Providers, First Report and Order and Notice of Proposed Rulemaking*, 20 FCC Rcd. 10245 (2005). The Commission ordered VoIP providers to implement a solution in which 911 calls from VoIP customers would be routed to the appropriate PSAP along with the caller's call back number and location information. The problem, as the Commission had previously acknowledge in the *Vonage* case, is that there is no particular location for a VoIP call. As the FCC saw it, "our action today is a necessary and logical follow-up to the *Vonage Order* issued late last year." *E911 Order*, 20 FCC Rcd. at 10246. In order to solve the problem, the FCC did not require that the VoIP service send the caller's actual location; instead the would convey the user's "Registered Location," which is a location that the VoIP provider is required to obtain from the user (the location at which the service will first be used, subject to change at will by the user). Even so, because E911 is likely to be far less effective than in the case of geographically fixed phone service, VoIP providers are required to disclose, and receive affirmative acknowledgement from their subscribers of, the limitations of VoIP-based 911 service. The FCC gave VoIP providers only 120 days to comply, pointing to successful tests of the capability and a number of wholesale E911 solutions available to VoIP providers to assist in their transition. Both the requirement and the deadline were upheld on appeal. *Nuvio Corp. v. FCC*, 473 F.3d 302 (D.C. Cir. 2006). In the order, the Commission again refused to classify VoIP as either a telecommunications service or an information service, asserting instead its authority to regulate using its ancillary jurisdiction under Title I of the Act.

d) CALEA

As the nation's telecommunications infrastructure has transitioned toward digital technology, there has been some concern that it would become impossible for law enforcement agencies to monitor communications using the traditional tools of pen registers (which record the telephone numbers dialed by a particular line) or wire taps, both of which have been developed for use on analog phone networks. Congress enacted CALEA in 1994 in order to require that carriers and equipment manufacturers employ technology that would allow law enforcement the continued ability to conduct surveillance on telecommunications traffic. The implementation of CALEA is split between the Department of Justice and the FCC. In 2004, the FBI petitioned the FCC to extend CALEA's coverage to both broadband Internet access providers and VoIP providers.

The proceedings dealing with CALEA have placed considerable pressure on the FCC's attempts to remain noncommittal on the classification of VoIP. CALEA imposes its duties on "telecommunications carriers" and specifically exempts "information services". The Communications Act defines "telecommunications carriers" as those entities that provide "telecommunications services." As demonstrated by the preceding discussion, the FCC has not been willing to define VoIP as a telecommunications service, with all the regulatory baggage that title carries with it. Even more directly, though, prior to the first *CALEA NPRM*, the FCC had already ruled in the *Wireline Broadband NPRM*, *supra*, that broadband Internet access was an "information service" and not a "telecommunications service," which made it seemingly impossible for the FCC to both find CALEA applicable to VoIP and Internet broadband providers while retaining its regulatory flexibility under the Communications Act.

In solving this regulatory conundrum, the FCC relied on some differences between how CALEA and the Communications Act define "telecommunications carrier," most notably how the "Substantial Replacement Provision" ("SRP") expands CALEA's coverage.

IN THE MATTER OF COMMUNICATIONS ASSISTANCE FOR LAW ENFORCEMENT ACT AND BROADBAND ACCESS AND SERVICES
First Report and Order and Further Notice of Proposed Rulemaking

Federal Communications Commission, 2005.
20 FCC Rcd. 14989.

BY THE COMMISSION:

* * *

III. DISCUSSION

* * *

A. Legal Framework

9. In this section, we explain how CALEA's SRP requires us to determine that some providers are subject to CALEA even if they are not telecommunications carriers as defined in the Communications Act. We further explain the relationship between the SRP and CALEA's exclusion for information services. Because the text of CALEA does not provide unambiguous direction, we consider the structure and history of the relevant provisions, including Congress's stated purposes, and interpret the statute in a manner that most faithfully implements Congress's intent. We conclude, as we indicated in the Notice, that the terms "telecommunications carrier" and "information services" in CALEA cannot be interpreted identically to the way those terms have been interpreted under the Communications Act in light of the statutory text as well as Congress's intent and purpose in enacting CALEA.

1. CALEA Definition of "Telecommunications Carrier"

10. We affirm our tentative conclusion that Congress intended the scope of CALEA's definition of "telecommunications carrier" to be more inclusive than the similar definition of "telecommunications carrier" in the Communications Act.[14] Critically, while certain portions of the defini-

14. Prior to the *Notice* in the instant proceeding, the Commission relied exclusively on two subsections of section 102 to identify those entities subject to CALEA's requirements: section 102(8)(A) (Common Carrier Provision), which the Commission

tion are the same in both statutes, CALEA's SRP "has no analogue" in the Communications Act, thus rendering CALEA's definition of "telecommunications carrier" broader than that found in the Communications Act. The SRP directs the Commission to deem certain providers to be telecommunications carriers for CALEA purposes, whether or not they satisfy the definition of telecommunications carrier in sections 102(8)(A) and 102(8)(B)(i). The SRP reflects Congress's intent to "preserve the government's ability to . . . intercept communications that use advanced technologies such as digital or wireless transmission." Under the SRP, a telecommunications carrier is:

> a person or entity engaged in providing wire or electronic communication switching or transmission service to the extent that the Commission finds that such service is a replacement for a substantial portion of the local telephone exchange service and that it is in the public interest to deem such a person or entity to be a telecommunications carrier for purposes of [CALEA]. [47 U.S.C. § 1001(8)(B)(ii).]

11. The SRP contains three components, each of which must be satisfied before the Commission can deem a person or entity a telecommunications carrier for purposes of CALEA. We address each of these components in turn. First, the SRP requires that an entity be "engaged in providing wire or electronic communication switching or transmission service." In the *Notice*, we interpreted the term "switching" in this phrase to include "routers, softswitches, and other equipment that may provide addressing and intelligence functions for packet-based communications to manage and direct the communications along to their intended destinations." We affirm this reading of the statute, which has support in the record. We disagree with commenters who claim that the term "switching" as used by Congress in 1994 did not contemplate routers and softswitches, and thus suggest that the interpretation of this term must forever be limited to the function as it was commonly understood in 1994, namely circuit switching in the narrowband PSTN. Our decision today is reinforced by judicial precedent that has found CALEA to apply to certain packet-switched services. Moreover, limiting the interpretation of "switching" to circuit-switched technology would effectively eliminate any ability the Commission may have to extend CALEA obligations under the SRP to service providers using advanced digital technologies, in direct contravention of CALEA's stated purpose. Our interpretation of the term "switching" is consistent with the Commission's prior recognition that CALEA is a technology-neutral statute that focuses on function, not technology. In today's technological environment, where IP-based broadband networks are rapidly replacing the legacy narrowband circuit-switched network, various types of packet-mode equipment are increasingly being deployed to "originate, terminate, or direct communi-

has interpreted to include those entities covered by the definition of a telecommunications carrier under the Communications Act, and section 102(8)(B)(i) (CMRS Provision), which includes any CMRS carrier, as defined in section 332 of the Communications Act. [Eds.: relocated footnote] cations" to their intended destinations. Interpreting CALEA's inclusion of the word "switching" to describe a function that Congress intended to be covered—regardless of the specific technology employed to perform that function—is, in our view, the interpretation most consistent with the purpose of the statute.

12. Second, the SRP requires that the service provided be "a replacement for a substantial portion of the local telephone exchange service." We conclude that this requirement is satisfied if a service replaces any significant part of an individual subscriber's functionality previously provided via circuit-switched local telephone exchange service. This interpretation of an ambiguous statutory provision is most consistent with the language of section 102(8)(B)(ii), the express purpose of CALEA, and its legislative history. Congress did not enact language consistent with an interpretation offered by some commenters that would require the widespread use of a service before the SRP may be triggered. Instead, the SRP's phrase "substantial portion of the local telephone exchange service" indicates that the appropriate test is a functional one. It is triggered when a service replaces a portion of traditional telephone *service*, *i.e.*, all or some of the components, or functions, of the service. Because the statutory phrase includes the word "substantial," we will require the functions being replaced to be a significant or substantial function of traditional telephone service.

13. As we explained in the *Notice*, the legacy local telephone exchange network served two distinct purposes at the time CALEA was enacted: it provided POTS, which enabled customers to make telephone calls to other customers within a defined local service area; and it was the primary, if not the only, conduit (*i.e.*, transmission facility) used to access many non-local exchange services such as long distance services, enhanced services, and the Internet. The legislative history indicates that Congress intended CALEA to cover both the ability to "make, receive and direct calls" (*i.e.*, the POTS functionality) *and* the transmission facilities that provide access to other services (*i.e.*, the access conduit functionality). In 1994, this transmission function was commonly provided by dial-up Internet access, which shows that Congress did not mean to limit CALEA's scope to voice service alone. We therefore agree with DOJ that the language "substantial portion of the local telephone exchange service" includes both the POTS service and the transmission conduit functionality provided by local telephone exchange service in 1994. Commenters have not persuaded us otherwise.

14. The SRP's third component requires that the Commission find that "it is in the public interest to deem ... a person or entity to be a telecommunications carrier for purposes of [CALEA]" once that entity has met the first and second components of the SRP. We sought comment in the *Notice* on how to define the "public interest" for purposes of CALEA, as the statute does not explicitly define the term. We noted that the *House Report* specifically identified three factors for the Commission to consider, at a minimum, in making its public interest determination under the SRP: whether deeming an entity a telecommu-

nications carrier would "promote competition, encourage the development of new technologies, and protect public safety and national security." Based on the record before us, we conclude that it is appropriate to rely primarily on these three factors when making our public interest determination for purposes of the SRP. We find that consideration of these three factors balances the goals of competition and innovation with the needs of law enforcement.

2. CALEA Definition of "Information Services"

15. As we explained in the *Notice*, the treatment of information services under CALEA is different from the treatment such services have been afforded under the Communications Act. In keeping with the legislative history of the Communications Act, the Commission interprets that Act's definitions of "telecommunications service" and "information service" to be mutually exclusive. Moreover, because the definition of "telecommunications service" focuses on the character of a provider's "offering . . . to the public," the Commission has concluded that the classification of a particular service as a telecommunications service or an information services "turns on the nature of the functions that the end user is offered." Additionally, the Communications Act's definition of "telecommunications" "only includes transmissions that do not alter the form or content of the information sent," a definition that the Commission has found to exclude Internet access services, which "alter the format of information through computer processing applications." For these reasons, the Commission has concluded that a single entity offering an integrated service combining basic telecommunications transmission with certain enhancements, specifically "capabilities for generating, acquiring, storing, transforming, processing, retrieving, utilizing, or making available information," offers *only* an information service, and not a telecommunications service, for purposes of the Communications Act if the telecommunications and information services are sufficiently intertwined. In other words, the Commission does not recognize the telecommunications component of an information service as a telecommunications service under the Communications Act.

16. In contrast with the Communications Act, CALEA does not define or utilize the term "telecommunications service," it does not adopt the Communications Act's narrow definition of "telecommunications," and it does not construct a definitional framework in which the regulatory treatment of an integrated service depends on its classification into one of two mutually exclusive categories, *i.e.*, telecommunications service or information service. As a result, structural and definitional features of the Communications Act that play a critical role in drawing the Act's regulatory dividing line between telecommunications service and information service, and that undergird the Commission's resulting classification of integrated broadband Internet access service as solely an information service for purposes of the Communications Act, are absent from CALEA. Those structural differences between the two statutes have significance, because "statutory language cannot be con-

strued in a vacuum. It is a fundamental canon of statutory construction that the words of a statute must be read in their context and with a view to their place in the overall statutory scheme." Unlike the Communications Act, CALEA's "overall statutory scheme" does not require the Commission to classify an integrated service offering as solely a telecommunications service or solely an information service depending on "the nature of the functions that the end user is offered," and thus the classification of broadband Internet access services under the Communications Act is not controlling under CALEA.

17. The text of the "information services" definition is entirely consistent with this interpretive approach. CALEA defines "information services" as the offering of a capability for manipulating and storing information "via telecommunications," but the statutory definition does not resolve the question whether the telecommunications functionality used to access that capability itself falls within the information service category. Under the Communications Act's similar definition of information service, we have resolved that ambiguity by concluding that the telecommunications component of an integrated information service offering falls within the information service category, but that result is not compelled by the text of CALEA, and thus the Act leaves the Commission free to resolve the definitional ambiguity as appropriate in light of CALEA's purposes and the public interest, without being bound by the approach followed under the Communications Act.

18. We also reach that same conclusion by a separate, and independent, route. CALEA excludes from its definition of telecommunications carrier "persons or entities insofar as they are engaged in providing information services," and the definition of information services in CALEA is similar to the definition in the Communications Act. The SRP, however, adds a third category of services to the mix. A provider of communication switching or transmission service that is not a telecommunications service under the Communications Act is nonetheless deemed to be a telecommunications carrier under CALEA if the Commission finds that the service replaces a substantial portion of local telephone exchange service and it is in the public interest to treat the provider as a telecommunications carrier. To give significance to the SRP, this new category of services must include some aspects of services that may be "information services" under the Communications Act. An "irreconcilable tension" would occur if the Commission rendered Congress's deliberate extension of CALEA's requirements to providers satisfying the SRP insignificant by simply applying its Communications Act interpretation of "information services" to CALEA. Consequently, to resolve that tension in a manner that the Commission determines best reflects Congressional intent under CALEA as well as the text of the statute, a service classified as an "information service" under the Communications Act may not, in all respects, be classified as an "information service" under CALEA.

* * *

22. That conclusion is further supported by CALEA's structure. CALEA establishes a general rule that telecommunications carriers (including those covered by the SRP) are subject to CALEA's assistance capability requirements. Information services are an exception to that general rule. It is a well recognized principle of statutory construction that "[w]here a general provision in a statute has certain limited exceptions, all doubts should be resolved in favor of the general provision rather than the exceptions." Accordingly, it is appropriate to give the Information Services Exclusion a narrow construction in order to give full effect to CALEA's general rule.

23. We thus find that the classification of a service as an information service under the Communications Act does not necessarily compel a finding that the service falls within CALEA's Information Service Exclusion. Decisions about the applicability of CALEA must be based on CALEA's definitions alone, not on the definitions in the Communications Act. Equally important, the classification of a service provider as a telecommunications carrier under CALEA's SRP *does not limit* the Commission's options for classifying that provider or service under the Communications Act.

B. Applicability of CALEA to Broadband Internet Access Services

* * *

1. Broadband Internet Access Service Providers Are "Telecommunications Carriers" Under CALEA

26. *Broadband Internet Access Service Includes Switching or Transmission.* We find that facilities-based broadband Internet access service providers are "engaged in providing wire or electronic communication switching or transmission service" and therefore meet the first prong of the SRP. As discussed above, we interpret the "switching or transmission" component of the SRP broadly to capture not only transmission or transport capabilities, but also new packet-based equipment and functionalities that direct communications to their intended destinations. No commenter suggests that facilities-based broadband Internet access providers do not provide a transmission or transport function. Indeed, commenters providing broadband Internet access service today describe the underlying transport component of their service as "switching and forwarding data."

27. *Broadband Internet Access Service Replaces a Substantial Portion of the Local Telephone Exchange Service.* We next conclude that facilities-based broadband Internet access service providers provide a replacement for a substantial portion of the local telephone exchange service, specifically, the portion of local telephone exchange service that provides subscribers with dial-up Internet access capability. We base this conclusion on Congress's understanding of the reach of CALEA's capability at the time the statute was enacted, the purpose for which the statute was enacted, and the support we find in the record for this conclusion.

28. Broadband Internet access service unquestionably "replaces" a portion of the functionality that the traditional local telephone exchange service provides—namely, the ability to access the Internet. CALEA's legislative history supports our conclusion that broadband Internet access service was intended to be covered by CALEA, as are both dial-up and common carrier DSL transport services. That history explains the distinction between the portion of e-mail service that was subject to CALEA (a service that was accessible only over the Internet) and the portion that was not. The only way that the "transmission of an E-mail message" could have been captured under CALEA in 1994 was through the dial-up facilities and capabilities of narrowband local telephone exchange service. Thus, to the extent that dial-up capabilities are "replaced" today by broadband Internet access service, we ensure that the "transmission of an E-mail message" continues to be subject to CALEA by finding that the SRP covers the transmission component of broadband Internet access service.

* * *

32. *Public Interest Factors Weigh in Favor of Subjecting Broadband Internet Access Service to CALEA.* We further find that it is in the public interest to deem facilities-based broadband Internet access service providers to be "telecommunications carriers" for purposes of CALEA under the SRP. The public interest factors that we consider in reaching this determination—the effect on competition, the development and provision of new technologies and services, and public safety and national security—on balance, support this finding.

33. One of the cornerstones of the Commission's broadband policy is achieving the goal of developing a consistent regulatory framework across all broadband platforms by treating providers in the same manner with respect to broadband services providing similar functionality.[90] Because all facilities-based providers of broadband Internet access services will be covered by CALEA, our finding today will have no skewing effect on competition. In addition, covering all broadband Internet access service providers prevents migration of criminal activity onto less regulated platforms.

* * *

C. Applicability of CALEA to VoIP Services

39. We conclude that CALEA applies to providers of "interconnected VoIP services." As defined in our recent *VoIP E911 Order*, interconnected VoIP services include those VoIP services that: (1) enable real-time, two-way voice communications; (2) require a broadband connection from the user's location; (3) require IP-compatible customer premises equipment; and (4) permit users to receive calls from and terminate calls

90. *Cf.* Wireline Broadband NPRM, 17 FCC Rcd. at 3023, para. 6 ("[T]he Commission will strive to develop an analytical framework [for broadband Internet access] that is consistent, to the extent possible, across multiple platforms.")[brackets in the *CALEA Order*].

to the PSTN. We find that providers of interconnected VoIP services satisfy CALEA's definition of "telecommunications carrier" under the SRP and that CALEA's Information Services Exclusion does not apply to interconnected VoIP services. To be clear, a service offering is "interconnected VoIP" if it offers the *capability* for users to receive calls from and terminate calls to the PSTN; the offering is covered by CALEA for all VoIP communications, even those that do not involve the PSTN. Furthermore, the offering is covered regardless of how the interconnected VoIP provider facilitates access to and from the PSTN, whether directly or by making arrangements with a third party.

* * *

1. Interconnected VoIP Providers Are "Telecommunications Carriers" Under CALEA

41. *Interconnected VoIP Includes Switching or Transmission.* We find that providers of interconnected VoIP satisfy the three prongs of the SRP under CALEA's definition of "telecommunications carrier." First, these providers are "engaged in providing wire or electronic communication switching or transmission services." As we have explained, we interpret the term "switching" in the CALEA definition of "telecommunications carrier" to include "routers, softswitches, and other equipment that may provide addressing and intelligence functions for packet-based communications to manage and direct the communications along to their intended destinations." Interconnected VoIP service providers use these technologies to enable their subscribers to make, receive, and direct calls. The record reflects that any VoIP provider that is interconnected to the PSTN "must necessarily" use a router or other server to do so. Thus, even VoIP providers that do not own their own underlying transmission facilities nonetheless are engaged in providing "switching" services to their customers.

42. *Interconnected VoIP Replaces a Substantial Portion of the Local Telephone Exchange Service.* Second, interconnected VoIP satisfies the "replacement for a substantial portion of the local telephone exchange service" prong of the SRP because it replaces the legacy POTS service functionality of traditional local telephone exchange service. As we explained in the *VoIP E911 Order*, customers who purchase interconnected VoIP service receive a service that "enables a customer to do everything (or nearly everything) the customer could do using an analog telephone." Indeed, the urgency with which the Commission recently addressed 911 requirements for interconnected VoIP was largely related to incidents where consumers had abandoned legacy POTS service in favor of interconnected VoIP. We determine that a service that is increasingly used to replace analog voice service is exactly the type of service that Congress intended the SRP to reach. Moreover, commenters offer no evidence to dispute the use of interconnected VoIP to obtain voice service capability, among other features.

43. *Public Interest Factors Weigh in Favor of Subjecting Interconnected VoIP Providers to CALEA.* Finally, we find that it is in the public interest to deem an interconnected VoIP service provider a telecommunications carrier for purposes of CALEA. In reaching this conclusion, we examine the three prongs of the public interest analysis that the *Notice* proposed to consider: promotion of competition, encouragement of the development of new technologies, and protection of public safety and national security. These three factors compel a finding that CALEA should apply to interconnected VoIP. First, our finding today will not have a deleterious effect on competition because all providers of interconnected VoIP will be covered by CALEA. Singling out certain technologies or categories of interconnected VoIP providers would be more harmful to competition than applying CALEA requirements to all providers of interconnected VoIP services, as we do today. Second, we are confident that our decision today will not discourage the development of new technologies and services. Interconnected VoIP providers are already obligated to cooperate with law enforcement agencies under separate electronic surveillance laws. We have seen no evidence that these requirements have deterred the development of new VoIP technologies and services in the period of time since the Commission issued its tentative conclusion that some types of VoIP service are covered by CALEA. Instead, we have seen an increasing effort on the part of many interconnected VoIP providers to develop CALEA capabilities, and the record indicates that VoIP providers are already modifying their operations to ensure that they are able to comply with CALEA. Industry solutions appear to be readily available.

44. Finally, the protection of public safety and national security compels us to apply CALEA to interconnected VoIP service providers. The *Notice* indicated, and the record confirms, that excluding interconnected VoIP from CALEA coverage could significantly undermine law enforcement's surveillance efforts. The *Notice* explained, and commenters agreed, that broadband Internet access providers alone might not have reasonable access to all of the information that law enforcement needs. Specifically, call management information (such as call forwarding and conference call features) and call set-up information (such as real-time speed dialing information and post-dial digit extraction information) are unlikely to be reasonably available to a broadband Internet access provider. The record thus indicates that the broadband Internet access provider and the interconnected VoIP provider must both be covered by CALEA in order to ensure that law enforcement agencies' surveillance needs are met. These considerations convince us that applying CALEA to interconnected VoIP service providers is in the public interest.

2. CALEA's Information Services Exclusion Does Not Apply to Interconnected VoIP

45. We find that interconnected VoIP service is not subject to the Information Services Exclusion in CALEA. The regulatory classification

of interconnected VoIP under the Communications Act is not determinative with regard to this inquiry. Indeed, the Commission has yet to determine the statutory classification of providers of interconnected VoIP for purposes of the Communications Act, but nowhere does CALEA require such a determination before analyzing a service provider under the SRP. Instead, the appropriate focus is on the meaning of the term in CALEA, and for that, as we have noted, we must again look to the text and legislative history of CALEA for guidance. As we have explained, the legislative history contains much discussion of "information services," but not once did Congress contemplate that any type of voice service would fall into that category. Most significantly, Congress explicitly distinguished between "information services" that are not covered by CALEA and "services or facilities that *enable the subscriber to make, receive or direct calls*," which are covered. Congress intended the capability to make what appear to the consumer to be ordinary voice calls—regardless of the technology involved—to fall outside the category of excluded information services under CALEA. To the extent that commenters question the appropriateness of applying CALEA to interconnected VoIP services because they believe that interconnected VoIP is an information service under the Communications Act, we strongly disagree. Charged with implementing CALEA and given the discretion contained in the public interest prong of the SRP to extend CALEA obligations to service providers that both meet the SRP and provide a service that Congress explicitly understood would be subject to CALEA, we cannot reasonably decline to find interconnected VoIP service providers subject to CALEA simply because these services may, at some future time, be classified as information services under the Communications Act.

The CALEA Test. Isn't the comparative portion of the CALEA SRP definition ("a replacement for a substantial portion of the local telephone exchange service") the right approach not only for the regulation of VoIP in the CALEA context but with regard to regulation more generally under Communication Act? After all, the Commission pledged itself in the *Wireline NPRM*, and reaffirmed in the *CALEA Order*, to like treatment for similar services across multiple platforms; a comparative standard would do just that. Is the FCC precluded under *Chevron* from interpreting the Communications Act's definitions according to a comparative standard like the one used in CALEA?

The D.C. Circuit upheld the distinction drawn in the *CALEA Order* (over a dissent) in 2006. See *American Council on Education v. FCC*, 451 F.3d 226 (D.C. Cir. 2006).

e) Intercarrier Compensation

Perhaps the thorniest regulatory problem the FCC faces with interconnected VoIP services is how to deal with their interconnection with the PSTN, both how to compensate LECs for terminating calls originating on VoIP services and how to compensate VoIP providers for terminating calls originating on the PSTN. On this matter the Commission has done very little. Rather, the FCC has rolled this problem into its *Unified Intercarrier Compensation* inquiry, which we discussed in the last chapter. To date, the FCC gone little beyond offering the following thoughts on the problem:

> 20. In addition to competitive developments within the wireless and wireline sectors, the advent of voice-over-internet protocol (VoIP) technology has introduced another mass market alternative to traditional fixed telephone service. New entrants, such as Vonage, have initiated VoIP services in recent years, and a number of other service providers, including Qwest, Verizon, and a number of cable operators, have begun to use or will soon use Internet protocol to provide voice services. These developments have raised a number of regulatory issues for the Commission to resolve.
>
> 21. These bundled offerings and novel services blur traditional industry and regulatory distinctions among various types of services and service providers, making it increasingly difficult to enforce the existing compensation regimes. Moreover, in a market where carriers are offering the same services and competing for the same customers, disparate treatment of different types of carriers or types of traffic has significant competitive implications. For instance, if one type of carrier primarily recovers costs from other carriers, rather than its retail customers, it may have a competitive advantage over another type of carrier that must recover the same costs primarily from its own retail customers.
>
> 22. Even if there were economic or technical differences among the different types of services that warranted different termination rates, the increased use of alternative services makes it difficult to sustain current regulatory distinctions. Technological alternatives to POTS service that are not tied to a geographic location, such as wireless services and some IP-based services, make regulatory distinctions based on jurisdiction difficult to enforce. Combined with other developments, . . . the availability of these alternatives makes it difficult to identify the geographic end points of a call using telephone numbers. Further, as one commenter notes, services provided via the Internet "neither respect nor reflect most of the traditional boundaries and classifications of service used to define regulatory status." As the demand for these new services and offerings continues to grow, so will the challenges associated with determining the appropriate intercarrier compensation for this traffic under our current rules.
>
> * * *
>
> 80. . . . [U]nder the "mixed use" doctrine, traffic is treated as jurisdictionally interstate if it is impossible or impractical to separate the interstate and intrastate components. We ask parties to

> comment on whether this same analysis applies to other types of traffic, such as calls that originate or terminate with other types of VoIP service or on a CMRS network.... Does the inability to determine the actual geographic end points of a call provide a basis on which to conclude that the intrastate component of certain types of traffic is not severable from the interstate component? If it becomes impossible or impractical to determine the end points of a substantial portion of traffic, would that justify a finding that all traffic should be treated as jurisdictionally interstate for purposes of intercarrier compensation? Do certain characteristics of IP-enabled services counsel interstate treatment for intercarrier compensation purposes, such as the inseverability of multiple features that can be accessed simultaneously, the irrelevance of geography to the provisioning and use of the service, or the lack of service-related reasons to incorporate geographic or jurisdictional tracking systems into the IP network?

Developing a Unified Intercarrier Compensation Regime, Further Notice of Proposed Rulemaking, 20 FCC Rcd. 4685 (2005). In many ways, the compensation problem presents a combination of all the previous cases: an undetermined location combined with a jurisdictional divide between local and long distance service. Perhaps it is no surprise that the FCC has been slow to act in solving the intercarrier compensation problems presented by the wireline and wireless industries. It has not been so hesitant when faced with the same set of problems in the context of Universal Service.

f) Universal Service

The FCC has been somewhat more willing to regulate VoIP providers like traditional telephone companies when it comes to tapping them for contributions to the Universal Service Fund, as the following order demonstrates.

IN THE MATTER OF UNIVERSAL SERVICE CONTRIBUTION METHODOLOGY
Report & Order & Notice of Proposed Rulemaking

Federal Communications Commission, 2006.
21 FCC Rcd. 7518.

BY THE COMMISSION:

* * *

C. Interconnected VoIP Services

34. We require providers of "interconnected VoIP services," as defined by the Commission, to contribute to the federal USF under the existing contribution methodology on an interim basis ... [T]he number of VoIP subscribers in the United States has grown significantly in

recent years, and we expect that trend to continue. At the same time, the USF contribution base has been shrinking, and the contribution factor has risen considerably as a result. We therefore find that extending USF contribution obligations to providers of interconnected VoIP services is necessary at this time in order to respond to these growing pressures on the stability and sustainability of the Fund.

35. The Commission has not yet classified interconnected VoIP services as "telecommunications services" or "information services" under the definitions of the Act. Again here, we do not classify these services. To the extent interconnected VoIP services are telecommunications services, they are of course subject to the mandatory contribution requirement of section 254(d). Absent our final decision classifying interconnected VoIP services, we analyze the issues addressed in this Order under our permissive authority pursuant to section 254(d) and our Title I ancillary jurisdiction. Specifically, we find that interconnected VoIP providers are "providers of interstate telecommunications" under section 254(d), and we assert the Commission's permissive authority to require interconnected VoIP providers "to contribute to the preservation and advancement of universal service" because "the public interest so requires." We also exercise our ancillary jurisdiction to extend contribution obligations to interconnected VoIP providers. We note that both Vonage and the VON Coalition[*] have stated on the record in this proceeding their belief that interconnected VoIP providers should be required to contribute to the Fund, apparently conceding that the Commission has the authority to impose such a requirement. Finally, we address implementation issues related to our requirement that interconnected VoIP providers contribute to the USF.

1. Scope

36. We extend universal service obligations to providers of interconnected VoIP services, as previously defined by the Commission. The Commission has defined "interconnected VoIP services" as those VoIP services that: (1) enable real-time, two-way voice communications; (2) require a broadband connection from the user's location; (3) require IP-compatible customer premises equipment; and (4) permit users to receive calls from and terminate calls to the PSTN. We emphasize that interconnected VoIP service offers the capability for users to receive calls from and terminate calls to the PSTN; the obligations we establish apply to all VoIP communications made using an interconnected VoIP service, even those that do not involve the PSTN. Furthermore, these obligations apply regardless of how the interconnected VoIP provider facilitates access to and from the PSTN, whether directly or by making arrangements with a third party. Finally, we recognize that the definition of interconnected VoIP services may need to expand as new VoIP services increasingly substitute for traditional phone service.

* Eds. The Voice over Net Coalition, a trade group representing VoIP providers.

37. We believe that it is appropriate to require USF contributions from interconnected VoIP providers because this approach is consistent with important principles that the Commission has established in its implementation of section 254 of the Act. Specifically, the Commission has previously found it appropriate to extend universal service contribution obligations to classes of providers that benefit from universal service through their interconnection with the PSTN. In addition, in the *Universal Service First Report and Order*, the Commission established competitive neutrality as a principle to guide the development of universal service policies. As discussed in more detail below, we find that these two principles support our conclusion that extending universal service contribution obligations to this particular category of providers is in the public interest.

2. Authority

a. Permissive Authority Under Section 254(d)

38. Section 254(d) states that the Commission may require "[a]ny other provider of interstate telecommunications" to contribute to universal service, "if the public interest so requires." Pursuant to the Act's definitions, a "provider of interstate telecommunications" provides "the transmission, between or among points specified by the user, of information of the user's choosing, without change in the form or content of the information as sent and received." Unlike providers of interstate telecommunications services, however, providers of interstate telecommunications do not necessarily "offer" telecommunications "for a fee directly to the public." The Commission has previously used this permissive authority to require private carriers and payphone aggregators to contribute to the Fund. In the *IP-Enabled Services Notice*, the Commission sought comment on, among other things, its authority, including mandatory and permissive authority under section 254(d), to require universal service contributions by IP-enabled service providers.

39. *Providers of Interstate Telecommunications.* We find that interconnected VoIP providers are "providers of interstate telecommunications" as required for the use of the permissive authority pursuant section 254(d). Specifically, using the Act's definitions, we find that interconnected VoIP providers "provide" "the transmission, between or among points specified by the user, of information of the user's choosing, without change in the form or content of the information as sent and received." is a service rather than a complete service.

40. First, we must consider whether interconnected VoIP providers "provide" telecommunications. Congress did not define the term "provide" or "provider," but the structure of the Act informs us that "provide" is a different and more inclusive term than "offer." It is settled law that the determination of what is "offered," under the Act's definitions, "turns on the nature of the functions the end user is offered." Had Congress intended us to look at the same factors in analyzing our permissive authority under section 254(d), it would have

referred to "other offerors of telecommunications." Because Congress used a different term—"providers"—we understand Congress to have meant something broader. Common definitions of the term "provide" suggest that we should consider the meaning of "provide" from a supply side, *i.e.*, from the provider's point of view. For example, Black's Law Dictionary defines "provide" to mean "[t]o make, procure, or furnish for future use, prepare. To supply; to afford; to contribute." Transmission is an input into the finished service "offered" to the customer. But from the interconnected VoIP provider's point of view, we believe that the provider "provides" more than just a finished service. We believe that it is reasonable to conclude that a provider "furnishes" or "supplies" components of a service, in this case, transmission.

41. Second, we determine that interconnected VoIP providers provide "telecommunications." As the Commission has recognized, "the heart of 'telecommunications' is transmission." The Commission has previously concluded that interconnected VoIP services involve "transmission of [voice] by aid of wire, cable, or other like connection" and/or "transmission by radio" of voice. Indeed, by definition, interconnected VoIP services are those "permitting users to receive calls from and terminate calls to the PSTN." To provide this capability, interconnected VoIP providers may rely on their own facilities or provide access to the PSTN through others. "Over the top" interconnected VoIP providers generally purchase access to the PSTN from a telecommunications carrier who accepts outgoing traffic from and delivers incoming traffic to the interconnected VoIP provider's media gateway. The telecommunications carrier supplies transmission to or from the PSTN user, or transmits the communication to another carrier that can transmit the communication to the PSTN user. Facilities-based interconnected VoIP providers similarly enter into arrangements with telecommunications carriers to complete communications to and from the PSTN. The telecommunications carriers involved in originating or terminating a communication via the PSTN are by definition offering "telecommunications." Just as the Commission has previously found resellers to be supplying telecommunications to their customers even though they do not own or operate the transmission facilities, we find interconnected VoIP providers to be "providing" telecommunications regardless of whether they own or operate their own transmission facilities or they obtain transmission from third parties. In contrast to services that merely use the PSTN to supply a finished product to end users, interconnected VoIP supplies PSTN transmission itself to end users.

42. Finally, the Commission previously determined that Vonage's interconnected VoIP service is a jurisdictionally mixed service in which part of the service is interstate in nature. We believe that other interconnected VoIP services similarly are jurisdictionally mixed and thus are subject to USF contributions on interstate and international revenues. For these reasons, we conclude that interconnected VoIP providers are "providers of interstate telecommunications" under section 254(d).

* * *

44. We also find that the principle of competitive neutrality supports our conclusion that we should require interconnected VoIP providers to contribute to the support mechanisms. Competitive neutrality means that "universal service support mechanisms and rules neither unfairly advantage nor disadvantage one provider over another, and neither unfairly favor nor disfavor one technology over another." As the Commission has noted, interconnected VoIP service "is increasingly used to replace analog voice service." As the interconnected VoIP service industry continues to grow, and to attract subscribers who previously relied on traditional telephone service, it becomes increasingly inappropriate to exclude interconnected VoIP service providers from universal service contribution obligations. Moreover, we do not want contribution obligations to shape decisions regarding the technology that interconnected VoIP providers use to offer voice services to customers or to create opportunities for regulatory arbitrage. The approach we adopt today reduces the possibility that carriers with universal service obligations will compete directly with providers without such obligations. We therefore find that the principle of competitive neutrality is served by extending universal service obligations to interconnected VoIP service providers.

* * *

b. Ancillary Jurisdiction

46. In addition to permissive authority under section 254(d), we exercise our ancillary jurisdiction under Title I of the Act to extend universal service contribution obligations to interconnected VoIP providers. We conclude that regardless of the statutory classification of these services, the Commission has ancillary jurisdiction to promote universal service by adopting universal service contribution rules for interconnected VoIP services, and commenters largely agree. Ancillary jurisdiction may be employed, in the Commission's discretion, when Title I of the Act gives the Commission subject matter jurisdiction over the service to be regulated and the assertion of jurisdiction is "reasonably ancillary to the effective performance of [its] various responsibilities." Both predicates for ancillary jurisdiction are satisfied here.

* * *

3. Implementation

* * *

51. *Identifying Revenues for Reporting Purposes.* * * *

52. Interconnected VoIP providers must report and contribute to the USF on all their interstate and international end-user telecommunications revenues. To fulfill this obligation, interconnected VoIP providers have three options: (1) they may use the interim safe harbor established in this Order; (2) they may report based on their actual interstate telecommunications revenues; or (3) they may rely on traffic studies, subject to the conditions described below.

53. As we recognized in the *Vonage Order*, it is difficult for some interconnected VoIP providers to separate their traffic on a jurisdictional basis. Indeed, many of these VoIP providers have advocated to us in other proceedings that their services are "inherently interstate." Consistent with this advocacy and based on the conclusions in the *Vonage Order*, we find that it would be reasonable for us to treat the interconnected VoIP traffic as 100% interstate for USF purposes. Indeed, in another context where providers were unable to separate their interstate telecommunications revenues from other revenues, the Commission found a safe harbor of 100 percent to be reasonable. Nevertheless, we establish a safe harbor that is lower than 100 percent as a convenient alternative for interconnected VoIP providers. Our safe harbor is necessarily the product of line drawing. In adopting a safe harbor we consider what would be an appropriate analogue. One industry report has estimated that 83.8 percent of VoIP traffic in 2004 was either long distance or international and only 16.2 percent was local. Thus, it appears that VoIP traffic is predominantly long distance or international. As such, it is much like wireline toll service which similarly offers interstate, intrastate toll, and international services. In fact as stated in paragraph 55 below, VoIP services are often marketed as a substitute for wireline toll service. The percentage of interstate revenues reported to the Commission by wireline toll providers is 64.9 percent. We therefore find that establishing a safe harbor of 64.9 percent is reasonable for purposes of this interim action.

54. Moreover, we believe that setting the safe harbor at 64.9 percent is reasonable pending the completion of the attached NPRM where we seek comment on whether to change or eliminate all of the safe harbors. To set the safe harbor lower would permit providers that actually provide more interstate service to escape universal service contribution obligations for some of their interstate traffic, thus undermining our actions to preserve and advance the goals of universal service. Furthermore, to the extent the safe harbor percentage is higher than some providers' actual interstate use, providers may instead contribute to the fund based on actual revenue allocations or by conducting a traffic study, as described below. We encourage interconnected VoIP providers to explore these more precise avenues for determining the jurisdictional nature of their revenues.

* * *

56. While, as stated above, interconnected VoIP providers may report their actual interstate telecommunications revenues, we recognize that some interconnected VoIP providers do not currently have the ability to identify whether customer calls are interstate and therefore subject to the section 254(d) contribution requirement. Indeed, a fundamental premise of our decision to preempt Minnesota's regulations in the *Vonage Order* was that it was impossible to determine whether calls by Vonage's customers stay within or cross state boundaries. Therefore, an interconnected VoIP provider may rely on traffic studies or the safe harbor described above in calculating its federal universal service contri-

butions. Alternatively, to the extent that an interconnected VoIP provider develops the capability to track the jurisdictional confines of customer calls, it may calculate its universal service contributions based on its actual percentage of interstate calls. Under this alternative, however, we note that an interconnected VoIP provider with the capability to track the jurisdictional confines of customer calls would no longer qualify for the preemptive effects of our *Vonage Order* and would be subject to state regulation. This is because the central rationale justifying preemption set forth in the *Vonage Order* would no longer be applicable to such an interconnected VoIP provider.

57. In lieu of using the interim safe harbor or reporting actual interstate telecommunications revenues, interconnected VoIP providers may rely on traffic studies [to show the percentage of their calls that are intra- vs. inter-state].

A Slender Reed. The *Universal Service Contribution Methodology Order* distinguishes between a "provider of interstate telecommunications" (which is required to contribute to the Universal Services Fund) and a "telecommunications service" (which the FCC has previously refused to classify VoIP) because one "provides" and the other "offers" telecommunications. Note that a "telecommunications carrier" is defined in the Act as a "provider of telecommunications services". Given the (now repeatedly) stated policy of "regulatory neutrality," why is the FCC working so hard to maintain the distinction between VoIP and traditional telephone service? Or, asked differently, if common carrier regulation under the Act is so problematic as applied to VoIP providers, why is it good for LECs? This order, too, was largely upheld on appeal, see *Vonage Holdings Corp. v. FCC*, 489 F.3d 1232 (D.C. Cir. 2007); the court struck only a few provisions of the order applying a higher standard for VoIP compliance and contributions than previously applied to other types of carriers.

2. Municipal Telecommunications Networks

At least in some circles it has been a source of concern that the U.S. lags many other developed countries in the deployment of broadband facilities.[6] It has also been a matter of concern that the deployment of broadband is so dependent on telephone and cable providers. The extensive development of wireless, which we examined in the last chapter, has promised a third competitive alternative, but *broadband* wireless—capable of delivering quality video as well as data and voice—is still a work in progress. To spur the development of broadband and to reduce dependence on established providers, many cities have undertaken to develop

6. In 2007 the U.S. ranked fifteenth among OECD countries in the OECD's measurement of "Broadband subscribers per 100 inhabitants"—behind, Canada, UK, France, Sweden, and Korea, among others, although the U.S. is slightly ahead of the OECD average. See http://www.oecd.org/sti/ict/broadband.

their local public wireless networks based on unlicensed spectrum used in the private Wi-Fi networks that have been widely deployed by both business and residential users.

The prospect of local public wireless networks generated a considerable enthusiasm among those who thought that public investment telecommunications infrastructure would both spur the growth of broadband capability and increase competition in advanced telecommunications services. It also generated hostility and opposition by established service providers—most notably the BOCs—which obtained legislation in a number of states barring or restricting municipally supported or operated systems. The municipalities in turn challenged the legislation on the ground that it was preempted by the Telecommunications Act of 1996, which forbade state or local governments from imposing restrictions on competition in telecommunications markets.

NIXON v. MISSOURI MUNICIPAL LEAGUE

Supreme Court of the United States, 2004.
541 U.S. 125.

JUSTICE SOUTER delivered the opinion of the Court.

Section 101(a) of the Telecommunications Act of 1996, 110 Stat. 70, 47 U.S.C. § 253, authorizes preemption of state and local laws and regulations expressly or effectively "prohibiting the ability of any entity" to provide telecommunications services. The question is whether the class of entities includes the State's own subdivisions, so as to affect the power of States and localities to restrict their own (or their political inferiors') delivery of such services. We hold it does not.

I

In 1997, the General Assembly of Missouri enacted the statute codified as § 392.410(7) of the State's Revised Statutes:

> No political subdivision of this state shall provide or offer for sale, either to the public or to a telecommunications provider, a telecommunications service or telecommunications facility used to provide a telecommunications service for which a certificate of service authority is required pursuant to this section.

On July 8, 1998, the municipal respondents, including municipalities, municipal organizations, and municipally owned utilities, petitioned the Federal Communications Commission (FCC or Commission) for an order declaring the state statute unlawful and preempted under 47 U.S.C. § 253:

> No State or local statute or regulation, or other State or local legal requirement, may prohibit or have the effect of prohibiting the ability of any entity to provide any interstate or intrastate telecommunications service. § 253(a).

> If, after notice and an opportunity for public comment, the Commission determines that a State or local government has permitted or imposed any statute, regulation, or legal requirement that violates subsection (a) or (b) of this section, the Commission shall preempt the enforcement of such statute, regulation, or legal requirement to the extent necessary to correct such violation or inconsistency. § 253(d).

After notice and comment, the FCC refused to declare the Missouri statute preempted, relying on its own earlier order resolving a challenge to a comparable Texas law....

III

A

In familiar instances of regulatory preemption under the Supremacy Clause, a federal measure preempting state regulation in some precinct of economic conduct carried on by a private person or corporation simply leaves the private party free to do anything it chooses consistent with the prevailing federal law. If federal law, say, preempts state regulation of cigarette advertising, a cigarette seller is left free from advertising restrictions imposed by a State, which is left without the power to control on that matter. On the subject covered, state law just drops out.

But no such simple result would follow from federal preemption meant to unshackle local governments from entrepreneurial limitations. The trouble is that a local government's capacity to enter an economic market turns not only on the effect of straightforward economic regulation below the national level (including outright bans), but on the authority and potential will of governments at the state or local level to support entry into the market. Preemption of the state advertising restriction freed a seller who otherwise had the legal authority to advertise and the money to do it if that made economic sense. But preempting a ban on government utilities would not accomplish much if the government could not point to some law authorizing it to run a utility in the first place. And preemption would make no difference to anyone if the state regulator were left with control over funding needed for any utility operation and declined to pay for it. In other words, when a government regulates itself (or the subdivision through which it acts) there is no clear distinction between the regulator and the entity regulated. Legal limits on what may be done by the government itself (including its subdivisions) will often be indistinguishable from choices that express what the government wishes to do with the authority and resources it can command. That is why preempting state or local governmental self-regulation (or regulation of political inferiors) would work so differently from preempting regulation of private players that we think it highly unlikely that Congress intended to set off on such uncertain adventures. A few hypotheticals may bring the point home.

B

Hypotheticals have to rest on some understanding of what § 253 means when it describes subjects of its preemption as laws or regulations that prohibit, expressly or in effect, "the ability of any entity" to provide telecommunications. The reference to "ability" complicates things. In customary usage, we speak simply of prohibiting a natural or legal person from doing something. To speak in terms of prohibiting their ability to provide a service may mean something different: it may mean denying the entity a capacity or authority to act in the first place. But this is not clear, and it is possible that a law prohibiting the ability to provide telecommunications means a law that limits or cuts back on some preexisting authority (under a different law) to go into the telecommunications business.

If the scope of law subject to preemption under § 253 has the former, broader, meaning, consider how preemption would apply to a state statute authorizing municipalities to operate specified utilities, to provide water and electricity but nothing else. The enumeration would certainly have the effect of prohibiting a municipally owned and operated electric utility from entering the telecommunications business (as Congress clearly meant private electric companies to be able to do), and its implicit prohibition would thus be open to FCC preemption. But what if the FCC did preempt the restriction? The municipality would be free of the statute, but freedom is not authority, and in the absence of some further, authorizing legislation the municipality would still be powerless to enter the telecommunications business. There is, after all, no argument that the Telecommunications Act of 1996 is itself a source of federal authority granting municipalities local power that state law does not. * * *

Or take the application of § 253 preemption to municipalities empowered by state law to furnish services generally, but forbidden by a special statute to exercise that power for the purpose of providing telecommunications services. If the special statute were preempted, a municipality in that State would have a real option to enter the telecommunications business if its own legislative arm so chose and funded the venture. But in a State next door where municipalities lacked such general authority, a local authority would not be able to, and the result would be a national crazy quilt. We will presumably get a crazy quilt, of course, as a consequence of state and local political choices arrived at in the absence of any preemption under § 253, but the crazy quilt of this hypothetical would result not from free political choices but from the fortuitous interaction of a federal preemption law with the forms of municipal authorization law.

Finally, consider the result if a State that previously authorized municipalities to operate a number of utilities including telecommunications changed its law by narrowing the range of authorization. Assume that a State once authorized municipalities to furnish water, electric, and communications services, but sometime after the passage of § 253 narrowed the authorization so as to leave municipalities authorized to enter only the water business. The repealing statute would have a prohibitory effect on the prior ability to deliver telecommunications service and would be subject to preemption. But that would mean that a State that once chose to provide broad municipal authority could not reverse course. A State next door, however, starting with a legal system devoid of any authorization for municipal utility operation, would at the least be free to change its own course by authorizing its municipalities to venture forth. The result, in other words, would be the federal creation of a one-way ratchet. A State or municipality could give the power, but it could not take it away later. Private counterparts could come and go from the market at will, for after any federal preemption they would have a free choice to compete or not to compete in telecommunications; governmental providers could never leave (or, at least, could not leave by a forthright choice to change policy), for the law expressing the government's decision to get out would be preempted.

The municipal respondents' answer to the one-way ratchet, and indeed to a host of the incongruities that would follow from preempting governmental restriction on the exercise of its own power, is to rely on § 253(b), which insulates certain state actions taken "on a competitively neutral basis." Respondents contend that a State or municipality would be able to make a competitively neutral change of mind to leave the telecommunications market after deciding earlier to enter it or authorize entry. But we think this is not much of an answer. The FCC has understood § 253(b) neutrality to require a statute or regulation affecting all types of utilities in like fashion, as a law removing only governmental entities from telecommunications could not be. An even more fundamental weakness in respondents' answer is shown in briefs filed by amici City of Abilene and Consumer Federation of America. We have no reason to doubt them when they explain how highly unlikely it is that a state decision to withdraw would be "neutral" in any sense of the word. There is every reason to expect just the contrary, that legislative choices in this arena would reflect the intent behind the intense lobbying directed to those choices, manifestly intended to impede, not enhance, competition. After all, the notion that the legislative process addressing governmental utility authority is susceptible to capture by competition-averse private utilities is fully consistent with (and one reason for) the FCC's position that statutes like Missouri's disserve the policy objects of the Telecommunications Act of 1996. Given the unlikely application of § 253(b) to state or local choices driven by policy, not business failure, the fair conclusion is that § 253(a), if read respondents' way, would allow governments to move solely toward authorizing telecommunications operation, with no alternative to reverse course deliberately later on. * * *

The judgment of the Court of Appeals for the Eighth Circuit is, accordingly, reversed.

The Future of Municipal Wireless and Public Superhighways. In 2006 Pennsylvania enacted a statute similar to Missouri's but with an interesting condition, reflecting a negotiated compromise between Philadelphia—which had adopted an ambitious plan for a public wireless broadband network—and Verizon, which opposed it. The statute essentially prevents local governments from offering advanced services unless it first requests the local exchange carrier to provide such service and the latter does not accept the request and begin service within 14 months. As part of the compromise that produced the legislation, Verizon and Philadelphia agreed that Verizon would not exercise its option to build in Philadelphia. John Cox, *Full speed ahead for Philly's Wi-Fi plan*, Network World, Jan. 17, 2005. After the compromise, Philadelphia entered into a deal with EarthLink to build and operate the system. However, the system has not been, and may not be, completed. In February 2008, EarthLink, which had similar deals with other cities, announced that municipal Wi-Fi was no longer in its "strategic direction." Translation: we can't make money out of it. Apparently other providers that entered into municipal partnerships for local Wi-Fi networks have reached similar conclusions. As a result, construction of municipal Wi-Fi in major cities such as Chicago, San Francisco, Miami, and Portland has been halted. Ian Urbina, *Hopes for Wireless Cities Fade as Internet Providers Pull Out*, New York Times, Mar. 22, 2008, p. A10.

Some observers think it might be possible to salvage municipal Wi-Fi with a different business model, i.e., one that does not insist on stand-alone profitability. Ian Urbina quotes one analyst:

> The entire for-profit model is the reason for the collapse in all these projects," said Sascha Meinrath, technology analyst at the New America Foundation, a nonprofit research organization in Washington.
>
> Mr. Meinrath said that advocates wanted to see American cities catch up with places like Athens, Leipzig and Vienna, where free or inexpensive Wi-Fi already exists in many areas.
>
> He said that true municipal networks, the ones that are owned and operated by municipalities, were far more sustainable because they could take into account benefits that help cities beyond private profit, including property-value increases, education benefits and quality-of-life improvements that come with offering residents free wireless access.

Should Philadelphia catch up with Athens, Leipzig, and Vienna by ditching the for-profit model? Meinrath has a point, does he not? If the system is going to be profitable, why would we need *municipalities* to invest in them? On the other hand, if there is a public goods aspect to these networks that warrants public investment, is it so clear that it is a *local* public good? If the critics are right that the U.S. suffers insufficient broadband infrastructure, maybe it the *U.S.* government that should invest in this business. There is a precedent of sorts: From the late 1950s to the early 1990s the U.S. invested billions of dollars to build the

Interstate Highway System—the original "superhighway." Is it an apt precedent?[7]

As noted in Chapter 8, in response to a proposal by the Federal-State Joint Board on Universal Service, the FCC has recently instituted a rulemaking on whether to add to the high-cost component of universal service, support for broadband and wireless. Notice, though, that this would address only high-cost (rural) routes, whereas the municipal Wi-Fi initiatives imply that we don't even have adequate infrastructure in low-cost urban areas.

E. REGULATORY IMPLICATIONS OF INTERNET MASS MEDIA SERVICES

Until recently the possibility that the Internet would be a means of distributing conventional television programming was at best dimly perceived simply because of the limitations of narrow-band, dial-up transport. But the analog copper wire that holds us hostage to the telephone company technology of yesterday is on its way out. With broadband comes the possibility that the Internet will become a complementary, or even competitive, medium for the delivery of conventional programming. It already happens in small ways: news clips and movie trailers are now common. A variety of providers—including the networks—provide streaming video news and other video features as a supplement to regular television programs. *Movielink*, a joint venture of five major film studios, provides a movie downloading service. Lee Gomes, who writes a column on Internet matters ("Portals") for the Wall Street Journal notes that

> a growing number of big content companies are putting programming from "regular" TV out on the Web. Walt Disney, which also owns ABC and ESPN, has been especially aggressive in this regard. So has the BBC, which already has most of its radio broadcasting online. It announced last week that it would be putting much of its TV up, too—though initially as a very limited test inside the United Kingdom. Sports is another growing source of Internet TV. You can pay $14.95 a month and watch Major League Baseball games at your desk—or even pay-per-view cricket, courtesy of Ireland's Setanta.com.
>
> Don't go rushing over to your PC and expect to see a high-definition picture with Dolby surround sound. Video on a personal computer, while better than the matchbook-sized images of a few years ago, is

7. The Department of Transportation gives a historic cost of $128.9 billion based on a final estimate made in 1991. See http://www.fhwa.dot.gov/interstate/faq.htm#question6. On the occasion of its 50th anniversary, the cost was estimated to be roughly $425 billion in 2006 dollars. Al Neuharth, *Traveling interstates is our sixth freedom*, USA Today, June 26, 2006. An equivalent public investment today in broadband infrastructure would likely put the U.S. at the top of the world's list of broadband superpowers. Of course, this assumes that private investment would remain constant. Is that the answer to the question whether the Interstate Highway example is an apt precedent?

> still confined to a relatively small portion of the screen, and it offers quality levels that would get booed out of most living rooms. But it's slowly getting better. In Asia, connection speeds are already so good that the Web can be used for full-blown, couch-potato-style TV. In Hong Kong, a new breed of Web-TV suppliers gives you a set-top box that lets you plug in an Internet cable; you then watch TV just as you would with cable or satellite. (Incidentally, you don't have any Microsoft software controlling things, despite the strenuous efforts of that company to make its player software a part of all Internet-enabled TV viewing.)

Lee Gomes, *Web TV Is Changing The Way Programming Is Watched and Sold*, Wall St. J. May 10, 2004, at p. B1. As the Internet takes on the shape of a conventional mass medium, the question naturally arises whether delivery of content via the Internet is any different, for regulatory purposes, from programming delivered by broadcasting and cable systems. When ABC streams news into its subscribers' terminals via the Internet, is it doing anything different than when it delivers it by way of a broadcast station or cable system? (Notice, by the way, that the conventional distinction between wireless broadcast and wireline cable may not be significant in a "3G" wireless world in which wireless broadband Internet connections become widely available.) What are the regulatory implications of this change in distribution medium? Consider the following, written when the Internet potential was far less developed than today.

KEVIN WERBACH, DIGITAL TORNADO: THE INTERNET AND TELECOMMUNICATIONS POLICY

FCC/OPP Working Paper March 1997, pp. 40–45.

The provision of real-time, or "streaming" audio and video services over the Internet raises the question of whether some Internet-based services qualify as "broadcasting" subject to Title III of the Communications Act. "Broadcasting" is defined in the Act as:

> (153)(6) Broadcasting.—The term "broadcasting" means the dissemination of radio communications intended to be received by the public, directly or by the intermediary of relay stations.

"Internet radio" services exist today that transmit continuous, real-time audio over the Internet. Many other sites now offer a selection of real-time audio clips that users can choose to listen to, such as news, weather forecasts, and music. Users must access theses sites, generally through a World Wide Web browser, and must have the proper software and hardware to receive and play streaming audio. Although analog modem bandwidth is largely insufficient to support real-time video transmissions over the Internet, such services are already available for users with higher-bandwidth connections. For example, software known as CU-See Me has been available for some time that allows real-time video conferencing over the Internet, and a other products such as

VDOLive will allow real time simultaneous video and audio conferencing. Live video of several events has been broadcast over the MBONE, a service that allows certain users with high-speed connections to receive real-time video feeds through the Internet.

The Commission has never considered whether any of the rules that relate to radio and television broadcasters should also apply to analogous Internet-based services. The vast majority of Internet traffic today travels over wire facilities, rather than the radio spectrum. As a policy matter, however, a continuous, live, generally-available music broadcast over the Internet may appear similar to a traditional radio broadcast, and the same arguments may be made about streaming video applications. The Commission will need to consider the underlying policy principles that, in the language of the Act and in FCC decisions, have formed the basis for regulation of the television and radio broadcast industries. One significant different may be the fact that radio and television broadcasts are subject to the inherent scarcity of the usable electromagnetic spectrum, whereas such transmissions over the Internet are simply a different type of data packets, indistinguishable at any moment from other types of traffic passing through the network.

Similar issues arise in the context of cable television regulations under Title VI of the Communications Act. The Act defines "video programming" as "programming provided by, or generally considered comparable to programming provided by, a television broadcast station." A "cable service" means "the one-way transmission to subscriber of ... video programming." A "cable system" is "a facility, consisting of a set of closed transmission paths ... that is designed to provide cable service," but not "a facility that serves only to retransmit the signals of one or more television broadcast stations; ... a facility that serves subscribers without using any public right-of-way; ... [or] a facility of a common carrier" that does not provide video programming directly to subscribers (except solely to provide interactive on-demand services) or serve as an open video system under section 653 of the Act.

To what extent is real-time video transmitted over the Internet "comparable" to broadcast television? The technology of the current Internet limits video transmission, even for users with relatively high-speed access, to relatively low-quality images. Most Internet users today are able to connect to the network at only 14.4 kbps or 28.8 kbps, which supports only rudimentary video images that can easily be distinguished from broadcast television images. These limitations are not permanent, however. As compression technology develops and end-user access speeds increases, Internet video applications will provide service that increasingly resembles the quality of television broadcast stations. In addition, the number of entities providing real-time video over the Internet is today relatively small, but is certain to increase rapidly over time as bandwidth increases. It seems inevitable that, at some point, consumers will be able to view images that are virtually indistinguishable in quality and equally varied in selection to those provided by television broadcasters. At what point will the threshold of "comparability" be crossed?

A determination about whether Internet-based video applications constitute "video programming" under the Act would not necessarily mean that these services would legally be treated as cable systems. Section 602(7)(B) of the Act states that facilities that do not use any public right-of-way are not considered cable systems. The Internet uses public right-of-way to the extent that it runs over the existing telephone network, and in the future over existing cable company facilities. The provision of video services over the Internet, however, generally requires no additional use of public right-of-way beyond that necessary to provide basic Internet connectivity, or to provide existing telephony or cable services. An additional definitional issue is the extent to which Internet video services provided by common carriers such as telephone companies are considered "interactive on-demand services," and therefore not treated as cable systems, since many Internet-based video concepts require the user to select a specific "program" to view. An Internet-based video service might be considered an "open video system," since the Internet itself is an inherently open platform that allows capacity to be shared among all entities with broadcast capabilities. Finally, certain providers of Internet-based video services could be classified as "multichannel video programming distributors" (MVPDs) under 602(11) of the Act. MVPDs are entities that "make[] available for purchase, by subscribers or customers, multiple channels of video programming."

Policy-makers must consider the policy rationales behind Title VI of the Act, and whether they apply to Internet-based video delivery systems with the same force. It does appear, however, that at some point the Internet may have significant competitive effects. A recent survey suggested that 61% of Internet users watch less television in order to spend more time online. The FCC's 1995 Cable Competition Report notes the possibility that the Internet will affect the video marketplace, "perhaps significantly," but concludes that it is too early to assess the impact of the Internet on this market. At some point, if the Internet continues to grow and greater bandwidth is widely available to end users, the Internet may have even more significant competitive effects on the video marketplace. Moreover, with the deployment of Internet access over cable facilities and digital cable set-top boxes, however, the Internet may exert an influence over the cable market not only as a competitor, but as a component of cable service as well.

The fact that the Internet may affect competition in the video marketplace is not itself a justification for additional regulation. If the Internet enhances competition, it may in fact justify reducing regulation on all video service providers. Moreover, existing regulations for broadcasters and cable operators were never designed with Internet services in mind, and could produce strange results if applied blindly to companies that enable streaming audio or video transmissions over the Internet.

Internet Exceptionalism: The Case of Content. Werbach's caution not to extend existing video regulations "blindly" may be superfluous, since, as we saw in Chapter 3, there is not a very intense regulatory surveillance or control of program content even in the broadcast field. Still, there are a few notable exceptions and they prompt the intriguing question whether they would be (or should be) applied across different delivery platforms.

Consider, as examples, the equal time and political candidate access rules, both specifically mandated by Congress, and rules restricting advertising on children's television, also congressionally required. Suppose the New York Times website streams a video clip of a speech by a political candidate that, if broadcast over conventional television, would be subject to the equal time rule; would this video clip be any different from a broadcast? If the answer is no, on whom does obligation to provide equal time fall—the New York Times as the content provider or the ISP that provided access (or, perhaps the Internet portal or search engine—Yahoo!, Google or MSN)? But if regulation of Internet content is considered to be off the table, how does one justify the continuation of regulation—such as there is—of conventional radio and television? No doubt the question, if asked of the FCC, would be addressed in terms of editorial control. Thus, a broadcast station would be assumed to have more control over program content than would an ISP. That answer might work for ISPs, but isn't it implausible for portals such as Google or services dedicated to content distribution, like YouTube? Or does it not beg the question about the degree to which we expect that the service provider control the content of the service?

Although FCC regulation of content does not look to be a realistic possibility at this time, there have been attempts by Congress to ban content "harmful to minors".

ASHCROFT v. ACLU

Supreme Court of the United States, 2004.
542 U.S. 656.

JUSTICE KENNEDY delivered the opinion of the Court.

This case presents a challenge to a statute enacted by Congress to protect minors from exposure to sexually explicit materials on the Internet, the Child Online Protection Act (COPA). We must decide whether the Court of Appeals was correct to affirm a ruling by the District Court that enforcement of COPA should be enjoined because the statute likely violates the First Amendment.

In enacting COPA, Congress gave consideration to our earlier decisions on this subject, in particular the decision in *Reno v. American Civil Liberties Union*, 521 U.S. 844 (1997). For that reason, "the Judiciary must proceed with caution and ... with care before invalidating the Act." The imperative of according respect to the Congress, however, does not permit us to depart from well-established First Amendment principles. Instead, we must hold the Government to its constitutional burden of proof. * * *

I

A

COPA is the second attempt by Congress to make the Internet safe for minors by criminalizing certain Internet speech. The first attempt was the Communications Decency Act of 1996, 47 U.S.C. § 223 (1994 ed., Supp. II). The Court held the CDA unconstitutional because it was not narrowly tailored to serve a compelling governmental interest and because less restrictive alternatives were available.

In response to the Court's decision in *Reno*, Congress passed COPA. COPA imposes criminal penalties of a $50,000 fine and six months in prison for the knowing posting, for "commercial purposes," of World Wide Web content that is "harmful to minors."

Material that is "harmful to minors" is defined as:

> any communication, picture, image, graphic image file, article, recording, writing, or other matter of any kind that is obscene or that—
>
> (A) the average person, applying contemporary community standards, would find, taking the material as a whole and with respect to minors, is designed to appeal to, or is designed to pander to, the prurient interest;
>
> (B) depicts, describes, or represents, in a manner patently offensive with respect to minors, an actual or simulated sexual act or sexual contact, an actual or simulated normal or perverted sexual act, or a lewd exhibition of the genitals or post-pubescent female breast; and
>
> (C) taken as a whole, lacks serious literary, artistic, political, or scientific value for minors.

"Minors" are defined as "any person under 17 years of age." A person acts for "commercial purposes only if such person is engaged in the business of making such communications." "Engaged in the business," in turn,

> means that the person who makes a communication, or offers to make a communication, by means of the World Wide Web, that includes any material that is harmful to minors, devotes time, attention, or labor to such activities, as a regular course of such person's trade or business, with the objective of earning a profit as a result of such activities (although it is not necessary that the person make a profit or that the making or offering to make such communications be the person's sole or principal business or source of income)."

While the statute labels all speech that falls within these definitions as criminal speech, it also provides an affirmative defense to those who employ specified means to prevent minors from gaining access to the prohibited materials on their Web site. A person may escape conviction under the statute by demonstrating that he

> has restricted access by minors to material that is harmful to minors—
>
> (A) by requiring use of a credit card, debit account, adult access code, or adult personal identification number;
>
> (B) by accepting a digital certificate that verifies age, or
>
> (C) by any other reasonable measures that are feasible under available technology.

Since the passage of COPA, Congress has enacted additional laws regulating the Internet in an attempt to protect minors. For example, it has enacted a prohibition on misleading Internet domain names in order to prevent Web site owners from disguising pornographic Web sites in a way likely to cause uninterested persons to visit them. It has also passed a statute creating a "Dot Kids" second-level Internet domain, the content of which is restricted to that which is fit for minors under the age of 13.

B

Respondents, Internet content providers and others concerned with protecting the freedom of speech, filed suit in the United States District Court for the Eastern District of Pennsylvania. They sought a preliminary injunction against enforcement of the statute. After considering testimony from witnesses presented by both respondents and the Government, the District Court issued an order granting the preliminary injunction. The court first noted that the statute would place a burden on some protected speech. The court then concluded that respondents were likely to prevail on their argument that there were less restrictive alternatives to the statute: "On the record to date, it is not apparent ... that [petitioner] can meet its burden to prove that COPA is the least restrictive means available to achieve the goal of restricting the access of minors" to harmful material. In particular, it noted that "[t]he record before the Court reveals that blocking or filtering technology may be at least as successful as COPA would be in restricting minors' access to harmful material online without imposing the burden on constitutionally protected speech that COPA imposes on adult users or Web site operators."

The Government appealed the District Court's decision to the United States Court of Appeals for the Third Circuit. The Court of Appeals affirmed the preliminary injunction, but on a different ground. The court concluded that the "community standards" language in COPA by itself rendered the statute unconstitutionally overbroad. We granted certiorari and reversed, holding that the community-standards language did not, standing alone, make the statute unconstitutionally overbroad. We emphasized, however, that our decision was limited to that narrow issue. We remanded the case to the Court of Appeals to reconsider whether the

District Court had been correct to grant the preliminary injunction. On remand, the Court of Appeals again affirmed the District Court. The Court of Appeals concluded that the statute was not narrowly tailored to serve a compelling Government interest, was overbroad, and was not the least restrictive means available for the Government to serve the interest of preventing minors from using the Internet to gain access to materials that are harmful to them. The Government once again sought review from this Court, and we again granted certiorari.

II

A

* * *

The District Court, in deciding to grant the preliminary injunction, concentrated primarily on the argument that there are plausible, less restrictive alternatives to COPA. A statute that "effectively suppresses a large amount of speech that adults have a constitutional right to receive and to address to one another ... is unacceptable if less restrictive alternatives would be at least as effective in achieving the legitimate purpose that the statute was enacted to serve." When plaintiffs challenge a content-based speech restriction, the burden is on the Government to prove that the proposed alternatives will not be as effective as the challenged statute.

In considering this question, a court assumes that certain protected speech may be regulated, and then asks what is the least restrictive alternative that can be used to achieve that goal. The purpose of the test is not to consider whether the challenged restriction has some effect in achieving Congress' goal, regardless of the restriction it imposes. The purpose of the test is to ensure that speech is restricted no further than necessary to achieve the goal, for it is important to assure that legitimate speech is not chilled or punished. For that reason, the test does not begin with the status quo of existing regulations, then ask whether the challenged restriction has some additional ability to achieve Congress' legitimate interest. Any restriction on speech could be justified under that analysis. Instead, the court should ask whether the challenged regulation is the least restrictive means among available, effective alternatives.

In deciding whether to grant a preliminary injunction stage, a district court must consider whether the plaintiffs have demonstrated that they are likely to prevail on the merits. As the Government bears the burden of proof on the ultimate question of COPA's constitutionality, respondents must be deemed likely to prevail unless the Government has shown that respondents' proposed less restrictive alternatives are less effective than COPA. Applying that analysis, the District Court concluded that respondents were likely to prevail. That conclusion was not an abuse of discretion, because on this record there are a number of plausible, less restrictive alternatives to the statute.

The primary alternative considered by the District Court was blocking and filtering software. Blocking and filtering software is an alternative that is less restrictive than COPA, and, in addition, likely more effective as a means of restricting children's access to materials harmful to them. The District Court, in granting the preliminary injunction, did so primarily because the plaintiffs had proposed that filters are a less restrictive alternative to COPA and the Government had not shown it would be likely to disprove the plaintiffs' contention at trial.

Filters are less restrictive than COPA. They impose selective restrictions on speech at the receiving end, not universal restrictions at the source. Under a filtering regime, adults without children may gain access to speech they have a right to see without having to identify themselves or provide their credit card information. Even adults with children may obtain access to the same speech on the same terms simply by turning off the filter on their home computers. Above all, promoting the use of filters does not condemn as criminal any category of speech, and so the potential chilling effect is eliminated, or at least much diminished. All of these things are true, moreover, regardless of how broadly or narrowly the definitions in COPA are construed.

Filters also may well be more effective than COPA. First, a filter can prevent minors from seeing all pornography, not just pornography posted to the Web from America. The District Court noted in its factfindings that one witness estimated that 40% of harmful-to-minors content comes from overseas. COPA does not prevent minors from having access to those foreign harmful materials. That alone makes it possible that filtering software might be more effective in serving Congress' goals. Effectiveness is likely to diminish even further if COPA is upheld, because the providers of the materials that would be covered by the statute simply can move their operations overseas. It is not an answer to say that COPA reaches some amount of materials that are harmful to minors; the question is whether it would reach more of them than less restrictive alternatives. In addition, the District Court found that verification systems may be subject to evasion and circumvention, for example by minors who have their own credit cards. Finally, filters also may be more effective because they can be applied to all forms of Internet communication, including e-mail, not just communications available via the World Wide Web. * * *

Filtering software, of course, is not a perfect solution to the problem of children gaining access to harmful-to-minors materials. It may block some materials that are not harmful to minors and fail to catch some that are. Whatever the deficiencies of filters, however, the Government failed to introduce specific evidence proving that existing technologies are less effective than the restrictions in COPA. The District Court made a specific factfinding that "[n]o evidence was presented to the Court as to the percentage of time that blocking and filtering technology is over- or underinclusive." In the absence of a showing as to the relative effectiveness of COPA and the alternatives proposed by respondents, it was not an abuse of discretion for the District Court to grant the preliminary injunction. The Government's burden is not merely to show that a proposed less restrictive alternative has some flaws; its burden is to show that it is less effective. It is not enough for the Government to show that COPA has some effect. Nor do respondents bear a burden to introduce, or offer to introduce, evidence that their proposed alternatives are more effective. The Government has the burden to show they are less so. The Government having failed to carry its burden, it was not an abuse of discretion for the District Court to grant the preliminary injunction.

One argument to the contrary is worth mentioning—the argument that filtering software is not an available alternative because Congress may not require it to be used. That argument carries little weight, because Congress undoubtedly may act to encourage the use of filters. We have held that Congress can give strong incentives to schools and libraries to use them, *United States v. American Library Assn., Inc.*, 539 U.S. 194 (2003), and by promoting the development of filters by industry, and their use by parents. It is incorrect, for that reason, to say that filters are part of the current regulatory status quo. The need for parental cooperation does not automatically disqualify a proposed less restrictive alternative. In enacting COPA, Congress said its goal was to prevent the "widespread availability of the Internet" from providing "opportunities for minors to access materials through the World Wide Web in a manner that can frustrate parental supervision or control." COPA presumes that parents lack the ability, not the will, to monitor what their children see. By enacting programs to promote use of filtering software, Congress could give parents that ability without subjecting protected speech to severe penalties. * * *

B

There are also important practical reasons to let the injunction stand pending a full trial on the merits. First, the potential harms from reversing the injunction outweigh those of leaving it in place by mistake. Where a prosecution is a likely possibility, yet only an affirmative defense is available, speakers may self-censor rather than risk the perils of trial. There is a potential for extraordinary harm and a serious chill upon protected speech. The harm done from letting the injunction stand pending a trial on the merits, in contrast, will not be extensive. No prosecutions have yet been undertaken under the law, so none will be disrupted if the injunction stands. Further, if the injunction is upheld, the Government in the interim can enforce obscenity laws already on the books.

Second, there are substantial factual disputes remaining in the case. As mentioned above, there is a serious gap in the evidence as to the effectiveness of filtering software. For us to assume, without proof, that filters are less effective than COPA would usurp the District Court's factfinding role. By allowing the preliminary injunction to stand and remanding for trial, we require the Government to shoulder its full constitutional burden of proof respecting the less restrictive alternative argument, rather than excuse it from doing so.

Third, and on a related point, the factual record does not reflect current technological reality—a serious flaw in any case involving the Internet. The technology of the Internet evolves at a rapid pace. Yet the factfindings of the District Court were entered in February 1999, over five years ago. Since then, certain facts about the Internet are known to have changed. It is reasonable to assume that other technological developments important to the First Amendment analysis have also occurred during that time. More and better filtering alternatives may exist than when the District Court entered its findings. Indeed, we know that after the District Court entered its factfindings, a congressionally appointed commission issued a report that found that filters are more effective than verification screens. * * *

Remand will also permit the District Court to take account of a changed legal landscape. Since the District Court made its factfindings, Congress has passed at least two further statutes that might qualify as less restrictive alternatives to COPA—a prohibition on misleading domain names, and a statute creating a minors-safe "Dot Kids" domain. Remanding for trial will allow the District Court to take into account those additional potential alternatives.

On a final point, it is important to note that this opinion does not hold that Congress is incapable of enacting any regulation of the Internet designed to prevent minors from gaining access to harmful materials. The parties, because of the conclusion of the Court of Appeals that the statute's definitions rendered it unconstitutional, did not devote their attention to the question whether further evidence might be introduced on the relative restrictiveness and effectiveness of alternatives to the statute. On remand, however, the parties will be able to introduce further evidence on this point. This opinion does not foreclose the District Court from concluding, upon a proper showing by the Government that meets the Government's constitutional burden as defined in this opinion, that COPA is the least restrictive alternative available to accomplish Congress' goal.

* * *

On this record, the Government has not shown that the less restrictive alternatives proposed by respondents should be disregarded. Those alternatives, indeed, may be more effective than the provisions of COPA. The District Court did not abuse its discretion when it entered the preliminary injunction. The judgment of the Court of Appeals is affirmed, and the case is remanded for proceedings consistent with this opinion.

It is so ordered.

JUSTICE SCALIA, dissenting.

I agree with Justice Breyer's conclusion that the Child Online Protection Act (COPA), is constitutional. Both the Court and Justice

Breyer err, however, in subjecting COPA to strict scrutiny. Nothing in the First Amendment entitles the type of material covered by COPA to that exacting standard of review. "We have recognized that commercial entities which engage in 'the sordid business of pandering' by 'deliberately emphasiz[ing] the sexually provocative aspects of [their nonobscene products], in order to catch the salaciously disposed,' engage in constitutionally unprotected behavior."

There is no doubt that the commercial pornography covered by COPA fits this description. The statute applies only to a person who, "as a regular course of such person's trade or business, with the objective of earning a profit," and "with knowledge of the character of the material," communicates material that depicts certain specified sexual acts and that "is designed to appeal to, or is designed to pander to, the prurient interest." Since this business could, consistent with the First Amendment, be banned entirely, COPA's lesser restrictions raise no constitutional concern.

JUSTICE BREYER, with whom the CHIEF JUSTICE and JUSTICE O'CONNOR join, dissenting.

The Child Online Protection Act (Act), seeks to protect children from exposure to commercial pornography placed on the Internet. It does so by requiring commercial providers to place pornographic material behind Internet "screens" readily accessible to adults who produce age verification. The Court recognizes that we should "proceed . . . with care before invalidating the Act," while pointing out that the "imperative of according respect to the Congress . . . does not permit us to depart from well-established First Amendment principles." I agree with these generalities. Like the Court, I would subject the Act to "the most exacting scrutiny," requiring the Government to show that any restriction of nonobscene expression is "narrowly drawn" to further a "compelling interest" and that the restriction amounts to the "least restrictive means" available to further that interest.

Nonetheless, my examination of (1) the burdens the Act imposes on protected expression, (2) the Act's ability to further a compelling interest, and (3) the proposed "less restrictive alternatives" convinces me that the Court is wrong. I cannot accept its conclusion that Congress could have accomplished its statutory objective—protecting children from commercial pornography on the Internet—in other, less restrictive ways.

I

Although the Court rests its conclusion upon the existence of less restrictive alternatives, I must first examine the burdens that the Act imposes upon protected speech. That is because the term "less restrictive alternative" is a comparative term. An "alternative" is "less restrictive" only if it will work less First Amendment harm than the statute itself, while at the same time similarly furthering the "compelling" interest that prompted Congress to enact the statute. Unlike the majority, I do not see how it is possible to make this comparative determination without examining both the extent to which the Act regulates protected expression and the nature of the burdens it imposes on that expression. That examination suggests that the Act, properly interpreted, imposes a burden on protected speech that is no more than modest.

A

The Act's definitions limit the material it regulates to material that does not enjoy First Amendment protection, namely legally obscene material, and very little more. A comparison of this Court's definition of unprotected, "legally obscene," material with the Act's definitions makes this clear.

Material is legally obscene if

> (a) ... 'the average person, applying contemporary community standards' would find that the work, taken as a whole, appeals to the prurient interest ...; (b) ... the work depicts or describes, in a patently offensive way, sexual conduct specifically defined by the applicable state law; and (c) ... the work, taken as a whole, lacks serious literary, artistic, political, or scientific value." *Miller v. California*, 413 U.S. 15, 24 (1973).

The present statute defines the material that it regulates as material that meets all of the following criteria:

> (A) the average person, applying contemporary community standards, would find, taking the material as a whole *and with respect to minors*, [that the material] is designed to appeal to, or is designed to pander to, the prurient interest;
>
> (B) [the material] depicts, describes, or represents, in a manner patently offensive *with respect to minors*, an actual or simulated sexual act or sexual contact, an actual or simulated normal or perverted sexual act, or a lewd exhibition of the genitals or post-pubescent female breast; and
>
> (C) [the material] taken as a whole, lacks serious literary, artistic, political, or scientific value *for minors*.

Both definitions define the relevant material through use of the critical terms "prurient interest" and "lacks serious literary, artistic, political, or scientific value." Insofar as material appeals to, or panders to, "the prurient interest," it simply seeks a sexual response. Insofar as "patently offensive" material with "no serious value" simply seeks that response, it does not seek to educate, it does not seek to elucidate views about sex, it is not artistic, and it is not literary....

The only significant difference between the present statute and *Miller*'s definition consists of the addition of the words "with respect to minors," and "for minors." But the addition of these words to a definition that would otherwise cover only obscenity expands the statute's scope only slightly. That is because the material in question (while potentially harmful to young children) must, first, appeal to the "prurient interest" of, *i.e.*, seek a sexual response from, some group of adolescents or postadolescents (since young children normally do not so respond). And material that appeals to the "prurient interest[s]" of some group of adolescents or postadolescents will almost inevitably appeal to the "prurient interest[s]" of some group of adults as well.

The "lack of serious value" requirement narrows the statute yet further—despite the presence of the qualification "for minors." That is because one cannot easily imagine material that has serious literary, artistic, political, or scientific value for a significant group of adults, but lacks such value for any significant group of minors. Thus, the statute, read literally, insofar as it extends beyond the legally obscene, could reach only borderline cases. And to take the words of the statute literally is consistent with Congress' avowed objective in enacting this law; namely, putting material produced by professional pornographers behind screens that will verify the age of the viewer.

These limitations on the statute's scope answer many of the concerns raised by those who attack its constitutionality. Respondents fear prosecution for the Internet posting of material that does not fall within the statute's ambit as limited by the "prurient interest" and "no serious value" requirements; for example: an essay about a young man's experience with masturbation and sexual shame; "a serious discussion about birth control practices, homosexuality, . . . or the consequences of prison rape"; an account by a 15-year-old, written for therapeutic purposes, of being raped when she was 13; a guide to self-examination for testicular cancer; a graphic illustration of how to use a condom; or any of the other postings of modern literary or artistic works or discussions of sexual identity, homosexuality, sexually transmitted diseases, sex education, or safe sex, let alone Aldous Huxley's *Brave New World*, J.D. Salinger's *Catcher in the Rye*, or, as the complaint would have it, "Ken Starr's report on the Clinton-Lewinsky scandal."

These materials are *not* both (1) "designed to appeal to, or . . . pander to, the prurient interest" of significant groups of minors *and* (2) lacking in "serious literary, artistic, political, or scientific value" for significant groups of minors. Thus, they fall outside the statute's definition of the material that it restricts, a fact the Government acknowledged at oral argument.

I have found nothing elsewhere in the statute's language that broadens its scope. Other qualifying phrases, such as "taking the material as a whole," and "for commercial purposes," limit the statute's scope still more, requiring, for example, that individual images be considered in context. See *Roth v. United States*, 354 U.S. 476, 490 (1957). In sum, the Act's definitions limit the statute's scope to commercial pornography. It affects unprotected obscene material. Given the inevitable uncertainty about how to characterize close-to-obscene material, it could apply to (or chill the production of) a limited class of borderline material that courts might ultimately find is protected. But the examples I have just given fall outside that class.

B

The Act does not censor the material it covers. Rather, it requires providers of the "harmful to minors" material to restrict minors' access to it by verifying age. They can do so by inserting screens that verify age using a credit card, adult personal identification number, or other similar technology. In this way, the Act requires creation of an internet screen that minors, but not adults, will find difficult to bypass.

I recognize that the screening requirement imposes some burden on adults who seek access to the regulated material, as well as on its providers. The cost is, in part, monetary. The parties agreed that a Web site could store card numbers or passwords at between 15 and 20 cents per number. And verification services provide free verification to Web site operators, while charging users less than $20 per year. According to the trade association for the commercial pornographers who are the statute's target, use of such verification procedures is "standard practice" in their online operations.

In addition to the monetary cost, and despite strict requirements that identifying information be kept confidential, the identification requirements inherent in age-screening may lead some users to fear embarrassment. Both monetary costs and potential embarrassment can deter potential viewers and, in that sense, the statute's requirements may restrict access to a site. But this Court has held that in the context of congressional efforts to protect children, restrictions of this kind do not automatically violate the Constitution. And the Court has approved their use.

In sum, the Act at most imposes a modest additional burden on adult access to legally obscene material, perhaps imposing a similar burden on access to some protected borderline obscene material as well.

II

I turn next to the question of "compelling interest," that of protecting minors from exposure to commercial pornography. No one denies that such an interest is "compelling." Rather, the question here is whether the Act, given its restrictions on adult access, significantly advances that interest. In other words, is the game worth the candle?

The majority argues that it is not, because of the existence of "blocking and filtering software." The majority refers to the presence of that software as a "less restrictive alternative." But that is a misnomer—a misnomer that may lead the reader to believe that all we need do is look to see if the blocking and filtering software is less restrictive; and to believe that, because in one sense it is (one can turn off the software), that is the end of the constitutional matter.

But such reasoning has no place here. Conceptually speaking, the presence of filtering software is not an *alternative* legislative approach to the problem of protecting children from exposure to commercial pornography. Rather, it is part of the status quo, *i.e.*, the backdrop against which Congress enacted the present statute. It is always true, by definition, that the status quo is less restrictive than a new regulatory law. It is always less restrictive to do *nothing* than to do *something*. But "doing nothing" does not address the problem Congress sought to address—namely that, despite the availability of filtering software, children were still being exposed to harmful material on the Internet.

Thus, the relevant constitutional question is not the question the Court asks: Would it be less restrictive to do nothing? Of course it would be. Rather, the relevant question posits a comparison of (a) a status quo that includes filtering software with (b) a change in that status quo that adds to it an age-verification screen requirement. Given the existence of filtering software, does the problem Congress identified remain significant? Does the Act help to address it? These are questions about the relation of the Act to the compelling interest. Does the Act, compared to the status quo, significantly advance the ball? (An affirmative answer to these questions will not justify "[a]ny restriction on speech," as the Court claims, for a final answer in respect to constitutionality must take account of burdens and alternatives as well.)

The answers to these intermediate questions are clear: Filtering software, as presently available, does not solve the "child protection" problem. It suffers from four serious inadequacies that prompted Congress to pass legislation instead of relying on its voluntary use. First, its filtering is faulty, allowing some pornographic material to pass through without hindrance. Just last year, in *American Library Assn.*, Justice Stevens described "fundamental defects in the filtering software that is now available or that will be available in the foreseeable future." He pointed to the problem of underblocking: "Because the software relies on key words or phrases to block undesirable sites, it does not have the capacity to exclude a precisely defined category of images." *Ibid.* That is to say, in the absence of words, the software alone cannot distinguish between the most obscene pictorial image and the Venus de Milo. No Member of this Court disagreed.

Second, filtering software costs money. Not every family has the $40 or so necessary to install it.

Third, filtering software depends upon parents willing to decide where their children will surf the Web and able to enforce that decision. As to millions of American families, that is not a reasonable possibility. More than 28 million school age children have both parents or their sole parent in the work force, at least 5 million children are left alone at home without supervision each week, and many of those children will spend afternoons and evenings with friends who may well have access to computers and more lenient parents.

Fourth, software blocking lacks precision, with the result that those who wish to use it to screen out pornography find that it blocks a great deal of material that is valuable. As Justice Stevens pointed out, "the software's reliance on words to identify undesirable sites necessarily results in the blocking of thousands of pages that contain content that is completely innocuous for both adults and minors, and that no rational person could conclude matches the filtering companies' category definitions, such as pornography or sex." Indeed, the American Civil Liberties Union (ACLU), one of the respondents here, told Congress that filtering software "block[s] out valuable and protected information, such as information about the Quaker religion, and web sites including those of the American Association of University Women, the AIDS Quilt, the Town Hall Political Site (run by the Family Resource Center, Christian Coalition and other conservative groups)." The software "is simply incapable of discerning between constitutionally protected and unprotected speech." It "inappropriately blocks valuable, protected speech, and does not effectively block the sites [it is] intended to block."

Nothing in the District Court record suggests the contrary. No respondent has offered to produce evidence at trial to the contrary. No party has suggested, for example, that technology allowing filters to interpret and discern among images has suddenly become, or is about to become, widely available. Indeed, the Court concedes that "[f]iltering software, of course, is not a perfect solution to the problem."

In sum, a "filtering software status quo" means filtering that underblocks, imposes a cost upon each family that uses it, fails to screen outside the home, and lacks precision. Thus, Congress could reasonably conclude that a system that relies entirely upon the use of such software is not an effective system. And a law that adds to that system an age-verification screen requirement significantly increases the system's efficacy. That is to say, at a modest additional cost to those adults who wish to obtain access to a screened program, that law will bring about better, more precise blocking, both inside and outside the home.

The Court's response—that 40% of all pornographic material may be of foreign origin—is beside the point. Even assuming (I believe unrealistically) that *all* foreign originators will refuse to use screening, the Act would make a difference in respect to 60% of the Internet's commercial pornography. I cannot call that difference insignificant.

The upshot is that Congress could reasonably conclude that, despite the current availability of filtering software, a child protection problem exists. It also could conclude that a precisely targeted regulatory statute, adding an age-verification requirement for a narrow range of material, would more effectively shield children from commercial pornography.

Is this justification sufficient? The lower courts thought not. But that is because those courts interpreted the Act as imposing far more than a modest burden. They assumed an interpretation of the statute in which it reached far beyond legally obscene and borderline-obscene material, affecting material that, given the interpretation set forth above, would fall well outside the Act's scope. But we must interpret the Act to save it, not to destroy it. So interpreted the Act imposes a far lesser burden on access to protected material. Given the modest nature of that burden and the likelihood that the Act will significantly further Congress' compelling objective, the Act may well satisfy the First

Amendment's stringent tests. Indeed, it does satisfy the First Amendment unless, of course, there is a genuine alternative, "less restrictive" way similarly to further that objective.

III

I turn, then, to the actual "less restrictive alternatives" that the Court proposes. The Court proposes two real alternatives, *i.e.*, two potentially less restrictive ways in which Congress might alter the status quo in order to achieve its "compelling" objective.

First, the Government might "act to encourage" the use of blocking and filtering software. The problem is that any argument that rests upon this alternative proves too much. If one imagines enough government resources devoted to the problem and perhaps additional scientific advances, then, of course, the use of software might become as effective and less restrictive. Obviously, the Government could give all parents, schools, and Internet cafes free computers with filtering programs already installed, hire federal employees to train parents and teachers on their use, and devote millions of dollars to the development of better software. The result might be an alternative that is extremely effective.

But the Constitution does not, because it cannot, require the Government to disprove the existence of magic solutions, *i.e.*, solutions that, put in general terms, will solve any problem less restrictively but with equal effectiveness.

Otherwise, "the undoubted ability of lawyers and judges," who are not constrained by the budgetary worries and other practical parameters within which Congress must operate, "to imagine *some* kind of slightly less drastic or restrictive an approach would make it impossible to write laws that deal with the harm that called the statute into being." As Justice Blackmun recognized, a "judge would be unimaginative indeed if he could not come up with something a little less 'drastic' or a little less 'restrictive' in almost any situation, and thereby enable himself to vote to strike legislation down." Perhaps that is why no party has argued seriously that additional expenditure of government funds to encourage the use of screening is a "less restrictive alternative."

Second, the majority suggests decriminalizing the statute, noting the "chilling effect" of criminalizing a category of speech. To remove a major sanction, however, would make the statute less effective, virtually by definition.

IV

My conclusion is that the Act, as properly interpreted, risks imposition of minor burdens on some protected material—burdens that adults wishing to view the material may overcome at modest cost. At the same time, it significantly helps to achieve a compelling congressional goal, protecting children from exposure to commercial pornography. There is no serious, practically available "less restrictive" way similarly to further this compelling interest. Hence the Act is constitutional.

Strict Scrutiny for Unprotected Speech? In his dissent Justice Scalia states that the kind of speech reached by COPA could be banned entirely; therefore the strict scrutiny test applied by the Court (and by Justice Breyer in his dissent) is inappropriate. Recall from Chapter 3 that since its foundational decision in *Roth v. United States*, 354 U.S. 476 (1957), it has been conventional doctrine that speech qualifying as "obscene" is not entitled to *any* constitutional protection. As Justice Breyer observes, COPA incorporated nearly verbatim the Court's prevailing definition of obscenity, adjusting it only slightly by adding the words "with respect to minors," and "for minors."[8] So, why isn't Justice Scalia correct that, having defined the offensive content in terms that track the existing law of obscenity, it is beyond the pale of First Amendment protection? What difference does it make whether there are less restrictive alternatives if the speech isn't entitled to protection? Or perhaps the Court is now retreating from its position in *Roth*? If so, should that retreat apply equally to other media—broadcast porn, cable porn, magazine porn?

The Court returned the case again for a further factual inquiry as to whether the availability of less restrictive alternatives warranted a permanent injunction.

AMERICAN CIVIL LIBERTIES UNION v. GONZALES

United States District Court, E.D. Pennsylvania, 2007.
478 F.Supp.2d 775.

LOWELL A. REED, JR. SENIOR DISTRICT JUDGE.

At issue in this case is the constitutionality of the Child Online Protection Act, 47 U.S.C. § 231 ("COPA") and whether this court should issue a permanent injunction against its enforcement due to its alleged constitutional infirmities. COPA provides both criminal and civil penalties for transmitting sexually explicit materials and communications over the World Wide Web ("Web") which are available to minors and harmful to them. After a trial on the merits, for the reasons that follow, notwithstanding the compelling interest of Congress in protecting children from sexually explicit material on the Web, I conclude today that COPA facially violates the First and Fifth Amendment rights of the plaintiffs because: (1) at least some of the plaintiffs have standing; (2) COPA is not narrowly tailored to Congress' compelling interest; (3) defendant has failed to meet his burden of showing that COPA is the

8. Even if these words are taken to broaden the definition of obscenity, the standard would still appear to fall within conventional precedent, allowing a somewhat broader definition of obscenity when it is targeted at minors. See Ginsberg v. New York, 390 U.S. 629 (1968).

least restrictive, most effective alternative in achieving the compelling interest; and (3) COPA is impermissibly vague and overbroad. As a result, I will issue a permanent injunction against the enforcement of COPA.

* * *

III. Findings of Fact

* * *

F. Internet Content Filtering Technology and its Effectiveness

1. In General

67. Internet content filters ("filters") are computer applications which, *inter alia*, attempt to block certain categories of material from view that a Web browser or other Internet application is capable of displaying or downloading, including sexually explicit material. Filters categorize and block Web sites or pages based on their content. By classifying a site or page, and refusing to display it on the user's computer screen, filters can be used to prevent children from seeing material that might be considered unsuitable. In addition, businesses often use filters to prevent employees from accessing on employer controlled computers Internet resources that are either not work related or otherwise deemed inappropriate.

68. Filters can be programmed or configured in a variety of different ways according to, *inter alia*, the values of the parents using them and the age and maturity of their children. As discussed more fully below, filters can be set up to restrict materials available on Web pages and other Internet applications based on numerous factors including the type of content they contain, the presence of particular words, the address of the Web site, the Internet protocol used, or computer application used. Some filters can also restrict Internet access based on time of day, day of week, how long the computer has been connected to the Internet, or which user is logged onto a computer.

69. Some filters can be purchased on a Compact Disc ("CD") or downloaded from the Internet and installed on a personal computer. Some filters are designed to be run on a server in a business, library, or school environment. Other filters are built into the services provided by Internet Service Providers ("ISP").

* * *

2. The Availability and Cost of Filters

87. Filters are widely available and easy to obtain. Numerous filtering products are sold directly to consumers, either in stores or over the Internet. Filters are also readily available through ISPs. Because most ISPs offer filtering products, a parent does not have to do anything to obtain a filter other than to activate it through the ISP's Web site or to call the ISP.

88. Many of the ISPs offer filters to their customers for free. AOL's filter is now even available for free to anyone who wants to use it, even non-AOL subscribers.

* * *

4. The Effectiveness of Filters

* * *

b. Study Results

110. Based upon the testimony of Dr. Cranor, which I accept, I find that filters generally block about 95% of sexually explicit material.

* * *

G. Select Legislative History of COPA and the Limitations of COPA

* * *

130. In discussing COPA, the Commerce Committee dismissed their opponent's concerns that a "domestic legislative solution will not stop material from being sent into the United States" and noted that the amount of foreign harmful to minors material was undocumented while "the fact remains that much of the harmful material is produced and posted in the United States." The Committee further noted that the United States had an eight million dollar adult entertainment industry and concluded that "[c]learly domestic restrictions in the United States will help reduce a child's access to pornography.... To the extent that an international problem exists, the Committee has requested that the Commission on Online Child Protection study the matter and report back to Congress."

131. In a letter dated October 5, 1998, from the Acting Assistant Attorney General to the Chairman for the Commerce Committee, explaining the views of the Department of Justice on COPA, the Assistant Attorney General explained why the Department felt that COPA would be problematic. Specifically, the Assistant Attorney General stated, *inter alia*, that:

> The Department's enforcement of [COPA] could require an undesirable diversion of critical investigative and prosecutorial resources that the Department currently invests in combating traffickers in hard-core child pornography, in thwarting child predators, and in prosecuting large-scale and multi district commercial distributors of obscene materials.

And that:

> We do not believe that it would be wise to divert the resources that are used for important initiatives ... to prosecutions of the kind contemplated under the COPA. Such a diversion would be particularly ill-advised in light of the uncertainty concerning whether the COPA would have a material effect in limiting minors' access to harmful materials. There are thousands of newsgroups and Internet

relay chat channels on which anyone can access pornography, and children would still be able to obtain ready access to pornography from a myriad of overseas web sites. The COPA apparently would not attempt to address those sources of Internet pornography, and admittedly it would be difficult to do so because restrictions on newsgroups and chat channels could pose constitutional questions, and because any attempt to regulate overseas web sites would raise difficult questions regarding extraterritorial enforcement. * * *

H. Statistical Information on Obscenity Prosecutions

132. Existing laws make it illegal to distribute material over the Internet that constitutes obscenity, or child pornography. From 2000 to 2005, defendant initiated fewer than 20 prosecutions for obscenity which did not also accompany charges of child pornography, travel in interstate commence to engage in sex with a minor, or attempting to transfer obscene material to a minor.

133. There have been fewer than 10 prosecutions for obscenity which did not also accompany charges of child pornography, travel in interstate commerce to engage in sex with a minor, or attempting to transfer obscene material to a minor since 2005.

I. The Affirmative Defenses in COPA and Their Availability and Effectiveness

134. It is an affirmative defense to liability under COPA when a Web site owner restricts access by minors to material that is harmful to them by requiring the use of a "credit card, debit account, adult access code, or adult personal identification number", "by accepting a digital certificate that verifies age", or by "any other reasonable measures that are feasible under available technology" in order to attempt to verify that the consumer is not a minor.

* * *

137. In the physical world, assessing the validity of an assertion about a person's age is relatively straightforward because of face-to-face interactions. In a retail establishment, for example, someone seeking to purchase harmful to minors material can be asked to show identification indicating the purchaser's age. The provider can view the buyer face-to-face and compare this identification to the person presenting it. That level of assurance is not available during an Internet purchase because of the absence of face-to-face interactions over the Web.

1. The General Availability of Age Verification Technologies

138. From the weight of the evidence, I find that there is no evidence of age verification services or products available on the market to owners of Web sites that actually reliably establish or verify the age of Internet users. Nor is there evidence of such services or products that can effectively prevent access to Web pages by a minor.

* * *

5. The Economic Burdens and Loss of Web Viewership Associated with the Affirmative Defenses

161. Based upon the below referenced evidence, I find that there are fees associated with all of the affirmative defenses and verification services identified in COPA, as well as all other services that claim to provide age verification. These fees apply any time a user attempts to access material on a Web site, even if there is no purchase. The fees must either be paid by the Web site or passed on to the users. As a result, Web sites such as the plaintiffs' sites, which desire to provide free distribution of their information, will be prevented from doing so.

162. Requiring the use of a payment card to enter a Web site would impose a significant economic cost on Web site owners. In addition to set-up fees and administrative fees, Web site owners would also need to pay fees for processing payment card information for each transaction.

* * *

IV. Conclusions of Law

* * *

B. Strict Scrutiny Applies to this Action

There is no doubt that COPA restricts speech based upon its content. Therefore strict scrutiny applies to the claims in this action.

* * *

C. Defendant Has Failed to Meet His Burden of Proof

1. Defendant Has Failed to Show that COPA Is Narrowly Tailored to Congress' Compelling Interest

a. COPA Is Overinclusive

9. COPA is overinclusive. Due to the broad definitions and provisions of COPA, COPA prohibits much more speech than is necessary to further Congress' compelling interest. 47 U.S.C. § 231. For example, . . . the definitions of "commercial purposes" and "engaged in the business" apply to an inordinate amount of Internet speech and certainly cover more than just commercial pornographers, contrary to the claim of defendant. Moreover, as discussed below in Conclusions of Law 42 and 49, the fact that COPA applies to speech that is obscene as to all minors from newborns to age sixteen, and not just to speech that is obscene as to older minors, also renders COPA over-inclusive.

b. COPA Is Underinclusive

10. COPA is also underinclusive. For example, . . . there is a significant amount of sexually explicit material on the Internet which originates from outside of the United States. As discussed below, unlike Internet content filters which are able to block from view unsuitable material regardless of its origin, COPA has no extra-territorial application. * * *

c. The Affirmative Defenses in COPA Do Not Aid in Narrowly Tailoring It to Congress' Compelling Interest

17. The affirmative defenses cannot cure COPA's failure to be narrowly tailored because they are effectively unavailable. Credit cards, debit accounts, adult access codes, and adult personal identification numbers do not in fact verify age. As a result, their use does not, in good faith, "restrict [ ] access" by minors. * * *

2. Defendant Has Failed to Show that COPA Is the Least Restrictive Alternative for Advancing Congress' Compelling Interest

26. Defendant has failed to successfully defend against the plaintiffs' assertion that filter software and the Government's promotion and support thereof is a less restrictive alternative to COPA. The Supreme Court recognized, upon the evidence before it at the time of the issuance of the preliminary injunction in 1999, that:

> Filters are less restrictive than COPA. They impose selective restrictions on speech at the receiving end, not universal restrictions at the source. Under a filtering regime, adults without children may gain access to speech they have a right to see without having to identify themselves or provide their credit card information. Even adults with children may obtain access to the same speech on the same terms simply by turning off the filter on their home computers. Above all, promoting the use of filters does not condemn as criminal any category of speech, and so the potential chilling effect is eliminated, or at least much diminished. All of these things are true, moreover, regardless of how broadly or narrowly the definitions in COPA are construed.

Ashcroft, 542 U.S. at 667. The evidence at trial shows that this is still the case today. It remains true, for example, that unlike COPA there are no fines or prison sentences associated with filters which would chill speech. Also unlike COPA, ... filters are fully customizable and may be set for different ages and for different categorizes of speech or may be disabled altogether for adult use. As a result, filters are less restrictive than COPA.

27. Moreover, defendant contends that: (1) filters currently exist and, thus, cannot be considered a less restrictive alternative to COPA; and that (2) the private use of filters cannot be deemed a less restrictive alternative to COPA because it is not an alternative which the government can implement. These contentions have been squarely rejected by the Supreme Court in ruling upon the efficacy of the 1999 preliminary injunction by this court. * * * I agree with the Supreme Court and conclude today that the mere fact that filters currently exist does not indicate that they cannot be a less restrictive or effective alternative to COPA nor does it make them part of the regulatory status quo. I also agree and conclude that in conjunction with the private use of filters, the government may promote and support their use by, for example, providing further education and training programs to parents and caregivers,

giving incentives or mandates to ISP's to provide filters to their subscribers, directing the developers of computer operating systems to provide filters and parental controls as a part of their products (Microsoft's new operating system, Vista, now provides such features ...), subsidizing the purchase of filters for those who cannot afford them, and by performing further studies and recommendations regarding filters.

3. Defendant Has Failed to Show that Other Alternatives Are Not at Least as Effective as COPA

28. Defendant has also failed to show that filters are not at least as effective as COPA at protecting minors from harmful material on the Web. The first hurdle in this analysis is that there is no showing of how effective COPA will be. However, the evidence shows that at a minimum, COPA will not reach a substantial amount of foreign source sexually explicit materials on the Web, which filters will reach. * * *

D. Vagueness and Overbreadth

* * *

41. Although ... Congress intended COPA to apply solely to commercial pornographers, ... the phrase "communication for commercial purposes", as it is modified by the phrase "engaged in the business", does not limit COPA's application to commercial pornographers. The lack of clarity in these phrases results in Web sites, which only receive revenue from advertising or which generate profit for their owners only indirectly, from being included in COPA's reach. Since the enforcement of COPA could result in prosecution of the plaintiffs in this case, it is reasonable for the plaintiffs to fear prosecution under COPA. The uncertainty resultant from the vagueness of "communication for commercial purposes" would cause the plaintiffs' speech to be chilled or self censored....

42. As noted above, COPA defines a minor as "any person under 17 years of age." 47 U.S.C. § 231(e)(7). Although the government argues that the term minor should be interpreted to mean an older minor, as the Third Circuit noted, such an interpretation would be "in complete disregard of the text" of COPA. As discussed by the Third Circuit, defining minors as "any person under 17 years of age," creates a serious issue with interpretation of COPA since no one could argue that materials that have "serious literary, artistic, political, or scientific value" for a sixteen-year-old would necessarily have the same value for a three-year old. Likewise, what would be "patently offensive" to an eight-year-old would logically encompass a broader spectrum of what is available on the Web than what would be considered "patently offensive" for a sixteen-year-old. Presumably no material covered by COPA would be "designed to appeal to, or [be] designed to pander to, the prurient interest" of a two or four-year old. As the Third Circuit noted, "[i]n abiding by this definition, Web publishers who seek to determine whether their Web sites will run afoul of COPA cannot tell which of these 'minors' should be considered in deciding the particular content of their Internet post-

ings." Thus, the application of the definition of minors to COPA creates vagueness in the statute.

43. I recognize that state laws prohibiting obscene-as-to-minors material have been upheld by the Supreme Court with no discussion of whether they apply to minors of every age or only to older minors. In a store, the cashier can easily discern if a patron is 10 or 11 years old instead of a claimed age of 17. The same cashier, however, may have trouble discerning whether a patron is 16 years old or 17 years old without some form of photographic identification. Thus, with laws that are concerned with face-to-face transactions, in reality it is only those borderline cases in which a minor is close to the age of majority that are at issue. As a result, in the pre-Internet age, it was not completely necessary to be more specific in delineating what was obscene as to minors of various age groups. However, on the Internet, everyone is faceless and fairly anonymous and, thus, the context is radically changed. The Internet merchant has no viable method of determining whether an individual is 6, 12, 17 or 51 years old. Consequently, we are presented with this novel problem where a general prohibition on materials obscene as to minors creates a vagueness in the context of Internet transactions that is lacking in other situations.

44. COPA does not define the term "as a whole" and the plain language of the statute does not lend itself to a obvious definition of "as a whole" as it might be applied to the Internet. The Third Circuit concluded in a dictum that the language of COPA clearly demonstrated that each individual "communication, picture, image, graphic image file, article, recording, writing or other matter of any kind" should be considered without context. But, as Justice Breyer noted in his dissent, "as a whole" has been traditionally interpreted in obscenity cases to require an examination of the challenged material within the context of the book or magazine in which it is contained. As Justice Kennedy noted in his concurring opinion, "The notion of judging work as a whole is familiar in other media, but more difficult to define on the World Wide Web. It is unclear whether what is to be judged as a whole is a single image on a Web page, a whole Web page, an entire multipage Web site, or an interlocking set of Web sites." Thus, with the disparate views noted above, and as discussed below, in the context of the Web, I conclude that the use in COPA of the phrase "as a whole" without any further definition, is vague.

45. There is no question that a printed book or magazine is finite, and, as a result, it is very easy to discern what needs to be examined in order to make an "as a whole" evaluation. The same is not true for a Web page or Web site since Web pages and sites are hyperlinked to other Web pages and sites. As demonstrated by online magazines such as Nerve and Salon, even the Web sites for online magazines, without considering the hyperlinks to off-site materials, have greater depth and breadth than their counterpart in print. Instead of having a two-hundred page book or an issue of a magazine to look to for context, COPA invokes some undefined portion of the vast expanse of the Web to provide

context for material allegedly violating the statute. As a result, a Web publisher cannot determine what could be considered context by a fact finder, prosecutor, or court, and therein lies the source of the vagueness.

* * *

2. COPA Is Overbroad

* * *

49. As discussed above, because a story that might have "serious literary value" for a sixteen-year-old could be considered to appeal to the "prurient interest" of an eight-year-old and be "patently offensive" and without "serious value" to that child, Web publishers do not have fair notice regarding what they can place on the Web that will not be considered harmful to "any person under 17 years of age." As the Third Circuit stated in ruling on the efficacy of the 1999 preliminary injunction by this court, "[b]ecause COPA's definition of 'minor' therefore broadens the reach of 'material that is harmful to minors' under the statute to encompass a vast array of speech that is clearly protected for adults ... the definition renders COPA significantly overinclusive." * * *

The district court's order was affirmed in *ACLU v. Mukasey*, 2008 WL 2801759 (3d Cir. 2008).

Strict Scrutiny for Obscenity: The Role of Filters. After *Ashcroft* and *Gonzales/Mukasey*, even if general obscenity regulation is constitutional, is there room for its enforcement on the Internet? The district court, in particular, focused on the problem of the "harmful to minors" classification, but how does that relate to the separate issue of filters as a less restrictive means? Doesn't the existence of filtering software suggest a more narrowly tailored means than a prohibition even for content that could be banned outright, like obscenity? Do *Ashcroft* and *Gonzales/Mukasey* have any implication for regulating television? Filtering technology is improving for television as well. The FCC was less-than-successful in its rollout of the V-chip, but doesn't the existence of the technology, and the ratings that now accompany all U.S. broadcast television, at least demonstrate that less restrictive means are available for controlling content, suddenly rendering indecency (or obscenity) prohibitions imposed on broadcast television unconstitutional?

Internet Intrusiveness. Recall that one of the prominent rationales for regulating indecent speech in the case of broadcasting was its supposed intrusiveness. The Court in *Pacifica* emphasized that part of broadcast's pervasiveness was by virtue of listeners' inability to shelter themselves from offensive speech in their own homes "where the individual's right to be left alone plainly outweighs the First Amendment rights of an intruder." How is the Internet any different? Does it matter that it's harder to mistakenly "tune" in offensive speech on the Internet than over the air? *Is* it harder to mistakenly "tune" in offensive speech on the Internet than over the air? How about a mis-typed URL or the not-so-occasional piece of pornographic spam? Why is intrusiveness relevant in any case? After *Pacifica* the canonical argument for regulating offensive electronic content rests on protection of children. Is the concern for protecting children based on the fact that they can't avoid it, or might encounter it by surprise or is it based on their immaturity about the subject matter? If we are protecting children because of their assumed immaturity, should we not protect them from their own immature judgments in actively searching for offensive material?

F. INTERNATIONAL COMPLICATIONS

The ability to provide global access to information sources and to interconnect people across the planet hugely increases the social and cultural impact of the Internet as compared to traditional electronic media. The Internet has internationalized communications and information distribution as no medium has done before. Radio broadcasting has always had some measure of international reach by means of high-frequency radio, and the advent of satellite broadcasting gave a similar international reach to television. But the impact of both of these has been fairly limited. International radio broadcasting has been confined to a small number of government-owned stations (BBC, VOA, etc.), and the international reach of satellite television broadcasting is limited in substantial degree by technical parameters governing the assignment of frequencies and orbital positions.

Even with such limited international reach, international broadcasting has been controversial to the extent it imports from "foreign" sources messages that were unwelcome in the receiving country (unwelcome, that is, by the receiving country's government). At one time non-democratic countries of eastern Europe tried to block international radio broadcasts through "jamming" because of their political messages. It was not only political messages that were matters of concern, however, and not only non-democratic governments that were concerned. When satellite broadcasting appeared on the scene, there were cries of anguish everywhere about the prospect of "cultural invasion" from foreign (mostly American) media. There was even an attempt to get an international law requiring prior consent before signals could be transmitted across national boundaries.

These efforts at direct national censorship of broadcasting have largely ceased over the past twenty years. A handful of countries still jam signals from some international broadcast stations, and there are still efforts to limit if not prevent the importation of foreign program content—for instance, by imposing domestic content quotas on local media or by handicapping access to foreign satellite transmissions. For the most part, however, these efforts have been quite marginal.

With the global growth of the Internet, however, there are some signs of a revived concern about the political, social, economic, and cultural impact of foreign content. As yet there have been relatively few attempts to curb the freedom of Internet communications. Some would say this is because of the futility of attempting to do so given the decentralized character of the Internet—thus Internet activist John Gilmore's statement that "the net views censorship as damage and routes around it." Others point out that governments have over time successfully rebuffed a series of challenges to the territorial model of regulation and have at their disposal not only a number of tools to limit access to the Internet but also traditional tools for regulating the conduct of the people use the Internet. See Jack Goldsmith & Tim Wu, *Who Controls the Internet?* (2006).

The full ability of governments to control, or at least limit, Internet speech has yet to be put to the test. One recent controversy that might have provided such a test arose from efforts by the French government to block its citizens from accessing web sites that sold Nazi memorabilia. Yahoo! was the principal target. In 1999 a French court ordered Yahoo! to devise means that would prevent any French resident from accessing Yahoo! auctions sites selling Nazi memorabilia.

Although Yahoo! subsequently did remove Nazi memorabilia, it insisted that it was not doing so specifically in response to the French order. It also did not capitulate in principle to the assertion of foreign jurisdiction. To affirm the latter point, Yahoo! filed suit in a federal district court in California seeking a declaratory judgment that the French court had no jurisdiction and that its judgment could not be enforced in the United States. What follows is the district court's decision on summary judgment.

YAHOO!, INC. v. LA LIGUE CONTRE LE RACISME ET L'ANTISEMITISME

United States District Court, N.D. California, 2001.
169 F.Supp.2d 1181.

FOGEL, DISTRICT JUDGE.

* * *

II. OVERVIEW

As this Court and others have observed, the instant case presents novel and important issues arising from the global reach of the Internet. Indeed, the specific facts of this case implicate issues of policy, politics, and culture that are beyond the purview of one nation's judiciary. Thus it is critical that the Court define at the outset what is and is not at stake in the present proceeding.

This case is *not* about the moral acceptability of promoting the symbols or propaganda of Nazism. Most would agree that such acts are profoundly offensive. By any reasonable standard of morality, the Nazis were responsible for one of the worst displays of inhumanity in recorded history. This Court is acutely mindful of the emotional pain reminders of the Nazi era cause to Holocaust survivors and deeply respectful of the motivations of the French Republic in enacting the underlying statutes and of the defendant organizations in seeking relief under those statutes. Vigilance is the key to preventing atrocities such as the Holocaust from occurring again.

Nor is this case about the right of France or any other nation to determine its own law and social policies. A basic function of a sovereign state is to determine by law what forms of speech and conduct are acceptable within its borders. In this instance, as a nation whose citizens suffered the effects of Nazism in ways that are incomprehensible to most Americans, France clearly has the right to enact and enforce laws such as those relied upon by the French Court here.

What *is* at issue here is whether it is consistent with the Constitution and laws of the United States for another nation to regulate speech by a United States resident within the United States on the basis that such speech can be accessed by Internet users in that nation. In a world in which ideas and information transcend borders and the Internet in particular renders the physical distance between speaker and audience virtually meaningless, the implications of this question go far beyond the facts of this case. The modern world is home to widely varied cultures with radically divergent value systems. There is little doubt that Internet users in the United States routinely engage in speech that violates, for example, China's laws against religious expression, the laws of various nations against advocacy of gender equality or homosexuality, or even the United Kingdom's restrictions on freedom of the press. If the government or another party in one of these sovereign nations were to seek enforcement of such laws against Yahoo! or another U.S.-based Internet service provider, what principles should guide the court's analysis?

* * *

IV. Legal Issues

A. Actual Controversy

* * *

The threshold question in any declaratory action thus is whether "there is a substantial controversy, between parties having adverse legal interests, of sufficient immediacy and reality to warrant the issuance of a declaratory judgment." * * *

2. Real and Immediate Threat

The French order prohibits the sale or display of items based on their association with a particular political organization and bans the display of websites based on the authors' viewpoint with respect to the Holocaust and anti-Semitism. A United States court constitutionally could not make such an order. The First Amendment does not permit the government to engage in viewpoint-based regulation of speech absent a compelling governmental interest, such as averting a clear and present danger of imminent violence. In addition, the French Court's mandate that Yahoo! "take all necessary measures to dissuade and render impossible any access via Yahoo.com to the Nazi artifact auction service and to any other site or service that may be construed as constituting an apology for Nazism or a contesting of Nazi crimes" is far too general and imprecise to survive the strict scrutiny required by the First Amendment. The phrase, "and any other site or service that *may be construed* as an apology for Nazism or a contesting of Nazi crimes" fails to provide Yahoo! with a sufficiently definite warning as to what is proscribed. Phrases such as "all necessary measures" and "render impossible" instruct Yahoo! to undertake efforts that will impermissibly chill and perhaps even censor protected speech. "The loss of First Amendment freedoms, for even minimal periods of time, unquestionably constitutes irreparable injury."

* * *

Defendants also claim that there is no real or immediate threat to Yahoo! because they do not presently intend to seek enforcement of the French order in the United States. In *Salvation Army v. Department of Community Affairs of the State of New Jersey*, 919 F.2d 183 (3d Cir. 1990), a religious group that operated a family center for disadvantaged persons claimed a state statute regulating boarding houses violated its right to the free exercise of religion. After the group brought suit, the state authorities agreed outside of the judicial proceedings to exempt the group from some of the provisions. The district court then granted summary judgment and dismissed the action. On appeal, the group claimed it still faced uncertainty with respect to future enforcement of the statute because the exemptions were not legally binding and the regulations in their entirety impermissibly intruded upon its First Amendment rights. The Court of Appeals for the Third Circuit agreed with the trial court that there was no immediate threat to the group because the state had provided an express assurance that it would not enforce any of the waived provisions, no criminal penalties could be imposed under the statute unless additional steps were taken by the state, the state could not impose fines without giving notice and opportunity to comply, and there was no evidence that the group's First Amendment rights actually would be affected by the threat of future law suits.

Salvation Army is distinguishable from this case in several significant respects. First, the New Jersey statute's penalties were "enforceable by the defendants only prospectively . . ." The French order permits *retroactive* penalties. Second, while the exemptions granted to the Salvation Army allowed it to maintain the status quo, the French order had the immediate effect of inducing Yahoo! to implement new restrictive policies on its auction site. Third, while the perceived threat to the Salvation Army was the potential withdrawal of the exemptions in the future, the provisions of the French order that require Yahoo! to regulate the content of its websites on Yahoo.com never have been waived, suspended or stayed and apparently remain in full force and effect. Under these circumstances, Defendants' assurances that they do not intend to enforce the order at the present time do not remove the threat that they may yet seek sanctions against Yahoo!'s *present and ongoing* conduct. * * *

4. Comity

No legal judgment has any effect, of its own force, beyond the limits of the sovereignty from which its authority is derived. However, the United States Constitution and implementing legislation require that full faith and credit be given to judgments of sister states, territories, and possessions of the United States. The extent to which the United States, or any state, honors the judicial decrees of foreign nations is a matter of choice, governed by "the comity of nations." Comity "is neither a matter of absolute obligation, on the one hand, nor of mere courtesy and good will, upon the other." United States courts generally recognize foreign judgments and decrees unless enforcement would be prejudicial or contrary to the country's interests.

As discussed previously, the French order's content and viewpoint-based regulation of the web pages and auction site on Yahoo.com, while entitled to great deference as an articulation of French law, clearly would be inconsistent with the First Amendment if mandated by a court in the United States. What makes this case uniquely challenging is that the Internet in effect allows one to speak in more than one place at the same time. Although France has the sovereign right to regulate what speech is permissible in France, this Court may not enforce a foreign order that violates the protections of the United States Constitution by chilling protected speech that occurs simultaneously within our borders.... The reason for limiting comity in this area is sound. "The protection to free speech and the press embodied in [the First] amendment would be seriously jeopardized by the entry of foreign [ ] judgments granted pursuant to standards deemed appropriate in [another country] but considered antithetical to the protections afforded the press by the U.S. Constitution." *Bachchan v. India Abroad Publications, Inc.*, 585 N.Y.S.2d 661, 665 (Sup. Ct. 1992). Absent a body of law that establishes international standards with respect to speech on the Internet and an appropriate treaty or legislation addressing enforcement of such standards to speech originating within the United States, the principle of comity is outweighed by the Court's obligation to uphold the First Amendment.[12]

The Yahoo! case was overturned on appeal on the grounds that the district court did not have personal jurisdiction over the defendants. *Yahoo! Inc. v. La Ligue Contre Le Racisme et L'Antisemitisme*, 379 F.3d 1120 (9th Cir. 2004). Judge Brunetti dissented, arguing that defendants'

12. The Court expresses no opinion as to whether any such treaty or legislation would or could be constitutional.

actions were deliberately and expressly aimed at Yahoo! for the very purpose of having their effects felt in California and were thus sufficient to establish that "they purposely availed themselves of the forum" so as to warrant the exercise of specific jurisdiction. In February 2005 the Ninth Circuit agreed to rehear the case en banc. As of this book's writing, the court has yet to issue an opinion on the rehearing.

Exporting Speech—or Speech Regulation? Is the *Yahoo!* case one of the French exporting their speech regulation to the U.S. or of the U.S. exporting its speech regulation to France? Yahoo! complied with the French order, though the court's holding seems to assume that compliance was coerced. If Yahoo! had refused to comply—and succeeded in getting its content through to French consumers—then those consumers would effectively be able to consume content prohibited under French law because it is permitted under U.S. law. Does Yahoo! have a constitutional right to have its speech heard *in France*?

Technology and Principle. In the French proceeding Yahoo! claimed that it could not comply with the demand to prevent access by French residents alone because it had no way to identify the origin of persons accessing Yahoo!'s U.S. servers. Thus, Yahoo! claimed that the French court's demand required them to remove the offending material from its servers altogether, which would be tantamount to giving world-wide effect to French law. That claim turned out to be wrong if not disingenuous. It was discovered that the Yahoo! material was not even hosted on servers in the U.S. but on mirror sites in Sweden, which were chosen specifically to serve content to European users. This suggested that it was possible to identify the general geographic region from which the server was receiving messages. At this point a panel of experts was convened, and it concluded that Yahoo! could ascertain the source of the requests with about 90% accuracy. (A further corroboration of this came from the fact that Yahoo! addressed French users with French-language advertisements!) Goldsmith and Wu, *supra* at 8–9. The ability of Yahoo! to selectively screen material turned out not to matter since Yahoo! chose to remove the memorabilia from all Yahoo! sites. Yet the appeal continues in the Ninth Circuit. Presumably Yahoo! wants to establish some kind of constitutional principle here, but exactly what principle?

The Multi-national Corporation's Appeal to Localism. Speaking of principle, at the same time that Yahoo! was fighting regulation under French law, it was courting regulation under Chinese law. Yahoo! eventually negotiated an agreement with the Chinese government for access to the Chinese Internet (which is otherwise heavily firewalled). As a condition of that access, Yahoo! agreed to cooperate with Chinese government efforts to regulate Internet access by Internet users in China. The agreement sparked considerable controversy back in the United States, including in Congress, where it was suggested that a U.S. company should not be aiding foreign governments in pursuing repressive speech policies. Yahoo! seems to have avoided the problem for now, partly by having a Chinese company (in which it owns a 40% stake) operate the Chinese version of Yahoo! *in China* and therefore subject to Chinese—rather than U.S.—law. Should U.S. courts be so willing to protect the speech rights of U.S. firms if those firms are effectively free to opt in to more restrictive regimes whenever it serves their financial interests?

*

Part IV

THE FUTURE OF COMMUNICATIONS REGULATION

Chapter 11

THE VIEW AHEAD

A. INTRODUCTION

This book addresses a pair of industries currently undergoing revolutionary change subject to a regulator struggling to change its regulation fast enough to keep up with those changing industries. Having a "conclusion" to such a book would be misleading because we are in the middle, not the end, of the story. Rather than provide a conclusion, then, we can only provide an indication of legal and economic trends—some but not all of which will be driven by technology. The speculation we offer here is not all that visionary. It is little more than a projection of events that have been unfolding over the last two decades in the form of commentary on what we have seen in the earlier chapters. We have organized this commentary under the rubric of four "Cs": "Consolidation, Convergence, Competition, and Complexity."

B. CONSOLIDATION

The trend toward consolidation in electronic media is undeniable. In the mass media sector, broadcast and cable ownership has become steadily more concentrated for several decades. In Chapter 4 we examined the FCC's most recent relaxation of broadcast ownership limits, which was in line with a fairly consistent trend over the preceding twenty years. While Congress intervened to halt part of that trend—in national group ownership—and the court of appeals temporarily limited another part—the local and cross-media ownership rules—it is unlikely that this setback will be the end of the trend. The cable industry, too continues to experience consolidation among the larger systems in particular. In 2005, the four largest MVPDs accounted for 63% of all MVPD subscribers, up 5% from the previous year, although most of the change was in the form of subscribers shifting from (the many) cable operators to (one of only two major) DBS operators. *Annual Assessment of the Status of Competition in the Market for the Delivery of Video Programming*, 21 FCC Rcd. 2503 ¶ 9 (2006).

The more dramatic examples of consolidation have occurred in the telecommunications sector, and they have been through merger. Over the past two decades, the number of Bell Operating Companies has gone from seven to three; the two largest long distance carriers (AT&T and MCI) and the largest non-Bell carrier (GTE) have been consolidated into the two largest BOCs (respectively AT&T and Verizon). Such mergers are reviewed by both the FCC and the Department of Justice, but the DoJ has displayed considerable deference to the FCC. The latest of these consolidations—the merger of AT&T (formerly SBC) and BellSouth—has prompted some to speculate that the former pieces of "MaBell" (as it was known in its salad days) that were put asunder in 1984 have managed to reassemble themselves into a new mother of all telecoms.

IN THE MATTER OF AT&T INC. AND BELLSOUTH CORPORATION
Memorandum Opinion and Order

Federal Communications Commission, 2007.
22 FCC Rcd. 5662.

BY THE COMMISSION:

I. INTRODUCTION

1. AT&T Inc. (AT&T) and BellSouth Corporation (BellSouth) (collectively, the Applicants) have filed a series of applications pursuant to sections 214 and 310(d) of the Communications Act of 1934, as amended (Communications Act or Act) and section 2 of the Cable Landing License Act in connection with their proposed merger. This merger would combine two regional Bell Operating Companies (BOCs). AT&T and BellSouth offer competing services in certain communications markets, and BellSouth supplies wholesale inputs relied upon by AT&T and other competitors in various retail markets. Thus, the proposed merger requires us to examine its effects on competition—which are both horizontal and vertical in nature—in a wide range of significant communications markets.

2. In accordance with the terms of sections 214(a) and 310(d), we must determine whether the Applicants have demonstrated that the proposed transfers would serve the public interest, convenience, and necessity. Based on the record before us, and as discussed more fully below, we find that the transaction meets this standard. After analyzing the record, we conclude that this merger may reduce from two to one the number of competitors with direct connections to a handful of buildings where other competitive entry is unlikely. We further find, however, that AT&T's voluntary commitment to divest at least eight fiber strands in the form of ten-year IRUs [Eds., "IRU" = indefeasible right of use] for these two-to-one buildings where entry is unlikely adequately remedies these potential harms. Moreover, to the extent that the merger increases concentration in those or other relevant markets, we find that the public interest benefits of the merger outweigh any potential public interest harms.

II. Executive Summary

3. As discussed below, our analysis of the competitive effects of the merger, which focuses on the following key services, finds that the merger is not likely, with one exception, to result in anticompetitive effects in relevant markets.

- **Special access competition.** The record indicates that, in a small number of buildings in the BellSouth in-region territory where AT&T and BellSouth are the only carriers with direct connections, and where other competitive entry is unlikely, the merger is likely to have an anticompetitive effect on the market for Type I wholesale special access services.[*] We further find, however, AT&T's voluntary commitment to divest at least eight fiber strands in the form of ten-year IRUs for these two-to-one buildings where entry is unlikely adequately remedies these potential harms. With respect to Type II wholesale special access services, we find that a sufficient number of other competitors with similar types of local facilities will remain post-merger to help mitigate the loss of AT&T as a competitor in BellSouth's region.

- **Retail enterprise competition.** We find that the merger will not likely have anticompetitive effects for enterprise customers, even though we find that the Applicants currently compete against each other with respect to certain types of enterprise services and some classes of enterprise customers. We find that competition for medium and large enterprise customers should remain strong after the merger because medium and large enterprise customers are sophisticated, high-volume purchasers of communications services and because there will remain a significant number of carriers competing in the market. With respect to small enterprise customers, we recognize that AT&T continues its withdrawal from that market in BellSouth's region, and we conclude, after examining the record, that it is not exerting significant competitive pressure with respect to those customers.

- **Mass market voice competition.** We conclude that the merger will not likely have anticompetitive effects on mass market voice services. We find that neither BellSouth nor AT&T is a significant present or potential participant in this market outside of their respective regions. Consequently, we find that neither party was exerting significant competitive pressure on the other in their respective in-region territories. Moreover, we note the rapid growth of intermodal competitors—particularly cable telephony providers (whether circuit-switched or voice over IP (VoIP))—as an increasingly significant competitive force in this market, and we anticipate that such competitors likely will play an increasingly important role with respect to future mass market competition.

- **Mass market Internet competition.** We find that the merger is not likely to result in anticompetitive effects for mass market high-speed

* Eds. "Type I" special access services are defined by the FCC as those offered wholly over a carrier's own facilities. "Type II" use a combination of the carrier's own facilities for two of the segments and the special access services of another carrier for the third segment.

Internet access services. Specifically, we conclude that there are no horizontal effects as a result of the proposed merger for this service because neither BellSouth nor AT&T provides any significant level of Internet access service outside of its respective region. We also conclude that, while the merger may result in some vertical integration, the record does not support commenters' conclusions that the merged entity will have the incentive to act anticompetitively in the mass market high-speed Internet access services market.

• **Internet backbone competition.** Based on the record, we are persuaded that the merger is not likely to result in anticompetitive effects in the Internet backbone market. We find that the Tier 1 backbone market is not likely to tip to monopoly or duopoly, based either on market share or on other factors, such as changes in relative traffic volumes or through targeted de-peering or degraded interconnection. Rather, we expect a number of Tier 1 backbones to remain as competitive alternatives to the merged entity. We also are not persuaded that the merger will increase the Applicants' incentive and/or ability to raise rivals' costs. Given the level of competition we expect to remain in the Tier 1 backbone market, we are not persuaded that such actions would be viable.

• **International competition.** We find that the merger is not likely to result in anticompetitive effects for international services provided to mass market, enterprise, or global telecommunications services customers. Additionally, we find that the merger is not likely to result in anticompetitive effects in the international transport, facilities-based IMTS, or international private line markets.

4. We further conclude that significant public interest benefits are likely to result from this transaction. These benefits, which are likely to flow to consumers, relate to: accelerated broadband deployment; enhancements to Multichannel Video Programming Distributor (MVPD) and programming competition; national security, disaster recovery, and government services; unification of Cingular's ownership; efficiencies related to vertical integration; economies of scope and scale; and cost savings.

5. Accordingly, based on the record, we find that the merger of BellSouth with AT&T is in the public interest and we grant the applications for transfer of control.

* * *

V. Potential Public Interest Harms

A. Analytical Framework

23. In this section, we consider the potential public interest harms, including potential harms to competition, arising from the merger. Because AT&T and BellSouth currently compete with respect to a variety of services and groups of customers, we must consider the potential horizontal effects of this merger. In addition, because both

AT&T and BellSouth provide critical inputs, particularly special access services, to various communications markets, we need to consider the potential vertical effects of the merger—specifically, whether the merged entity will have an increased incentive or ability to injure competitors by raising the cost of, or discriminating in the provision of, inputs sold to competitors.

24. With respect to the horizontal effects, consistent with Commission precedent, we first perform a structural analysis of the merger to examine whether it is likely to result in anticompetitive effects. We begin by defining the relevant product markets and relevant geographic markets. We next identify market participants and examine market concentration and how concentration will change as a result of the merger. We also consider whether entry conditions are such that new competitors could likely enter and defeat any attempted post-merger price increase.

25. If our structural analysis suggests that the merger may have anticompetitive effects, we must then examine in more detail whether and how the merger might affect competitive behavior. In performing this behavioral analysis, we consider whether the merger is likely to have anticompetitive effects either through unilateral actions of the merged entity or through coordinated interaction among firms competing in the relevant market.

26. With regard to potential vertical effects, we will examine how the merger affects the Applicants' incentives and ability to discriminate in provisioning inputs to competitors. In particular, we will consider the effect of the merger on the merged entity's incentives and ability to discriminate in the provision of special access services.

B. Wholesale Special Access Competition

27. In this section, we consider the effects of the proposed merger on the provisioning and pricing of wholesale special access services. As discussed below, wholesale special access service is a critical input for: competitive LECs in providing services to their retail enterprise customers, wireless and competitive LECs in connecting their networks to other carriers, long distance carriers seeking to connect customers to their long distance networks, and entities seeking to connect with Internet backbones. Firms needing dedicated transmission links essentially have three choices: to deploy their own facilities, to buy special access service from incumbent LECs, or to purchase such service from a competing special access provider. As discussed below, we find that AT&T provides special access services in competition with BellSouth's special access services in BellSouth's in-region territory. We further find that AT&T is currently the sole carrier, besides BellSouth, with a direct wireline connection to a number of buildings in BellSouth's region, so that the merger will reduce the number of competitors with direct connections to those particular buildings from two to one. We further find that competitive entry is unlikely in a small number of these buildings and that, as a result, the merger may result in anticompetitive effects with respect to

that subset of buildings. AT&T has, however, voluntarily committed to divest IRUs to those buildings, which we find adequately remedies the potential harms.

2. Competitive Analysis

* * *

a. Horizontal Effects

40. *Unilateral Effects.* Certain commenters claim that the present merger likely would result in increased wholesale special access prices at specific buildings where AT&T currently is offering Type I and Type II special access services. The record suggests that the merger will result in a reduction in the number of competitors offering Type I services in buildings where AT&T is currently connected via its own facilities, and that, of those buildings, there is a small number where AT&T is the sole carrier with a direct connection (besides BellSouth) and where entry is unlikely. The elimination of AT&T as a provider of Type I special access services to these buildings poses a potential competitive harm. AT&T has, however, voluntarily committed to divest IRUs to these buildings and we find that it is in the public interest to accept that commitment. With respect to Type II special access services, we find that the merger is not likely to result in anticompetitive effects in the provision of Type II services. Competing carriers can use their existing collocation facilities in the relevant wire center (or contract with a competitor that has such collocation facilities) and can purchase special access circuits or UNE loops to provide Type II services.

* * *

58. *Coordinated Effects.* We also are not persuaded by opponents' arguments that the merger will increase the likelihood of coordinated interaction. It is generally recognized that the likelihood of coordinated effects depends on a number of factors, including the ease with which firms can reach tacit agreement, the incentive of firms to cheat, and the ability of the remaining firms to detect and punish such cheating. Carriers that purchase wholesale special access services, whether Type I or Type II, are sophisticated customers that often rely on a competitive bid process or negotiate individual contracts, and that enter into long-term contracts. Moreover, as noted above, there will remain numerous competitors that are able to provide Type II wholesale special access services. We find that these factors make it unlikely that the merger will lead to tacit collusion or other coordinated effects in the relevant special access markets in BellSouth's region.

59. *Mutual Forbearance.* Ad Hoc Telecom Users argue that if the present merger is consummated, the merged entity and Verizon will be more likely to "mutually forbear" from competing against each other in the provision of wholesale special access services in the other's service territory. While we recognize that mutual forbearance is possible in theory, we reject commenters' allegations that this merger is likely to

result in anticompetitive effects in Verizon's region. As an initial matter, AT&T has invested billions in its nationwide network, including facilities in Verizon's region. In light of this investment, it is reasonable to expect AT&T to have strong incentives to utilize fully its assets in Verizon's territory. More significantly, however, we find no record evidence to suggest that the competitive conditions in Verizon's territory are significantly different than the competitive conditions in BellSouth's territory. Thus, just as there are numerous competitors with local facilities that will continue to provide competing special access services post-merger in BellSouth's territory, we have no reason to doubt that there similarly will be numerous competitors with local facilities in Verizon's territory that will provide competing special access services post-merger. Thus, we conclude that, even if AT&T/BellSouth forbears from offering competing special access services in Verizon's region, competitive alternatives will remain for those locations where AT&T offered competing special access services.

b. Vertical Effects

60. We disagree with the argument of certain commenters that the merger will increase the Applicants' incentive and/or ability to raise rivals' costs or engage in a price squeeze. As an initial matter, where UNEs are available, they provide an alternative for special access service and might serve to constrain, at least to some extent, special access price increases and other raising rivals' costs strategies. For areas where UNEs are not available, we note that competing carriers have invested heavily in the 11 MSAs where AT&T has local facilities. As described above, we have analyzed the likely impacts of this merger with regard to the provision of special access services and have found that AT&T's voluntary commitment to divest at least eight fiber strands in the form of ten-year IRUs for 31 two-to-one buildings where entry is unlikely is sufficient to address any potential anticompetitive effects. Like other incumbent LECs, BellSouth already is a vertically integrated provider of telecommunications services, including wireless services. The merger therefore is not likely to impact significantly the Applicants' incentives regarding discrimination. As we have found previously, "[t]o the extent that certain incumbent LECs have the incentive and ability under our existing rules to discriminate against competitors" using special access inputs, "such a concern is more appropriately addressed in our existing rulemaking proceedings on special access performance metrics and special access pricing." A voluminous record on industry-wide special access pricing issues (along with specific pricing information) has been submitted to the Commission in one of these proceedings. By addressing these issues in the context of a rulemaking, we will be able to develop a comprehensive approach based on a full record that applies to all similarly-situated incumbent LECs.

* * *

C. Retail Enterprise Competition

62. In this section, we analyze the potential competitive effects of the proposed merger on retail enterprise services. We find that the Applicants compete against each other with respect to certain types of enterprise services and some classes of enterprise customers, and that the merger will lead to increased concentration in certain relevant markets. We conclude, however, that the merger is not likely to result in anticompetitive effects for enterprise customers. We find that competition for medium and large enterprise customers should remain strong after the merger because medium and large enterprise customers are sophisticated, high-volume purchasers of communications services, including in particular high-capacity communications services, and because there will remain a significant number of carriers competing in the market. With respect to small enterprise customers, we recognize that AT&T continues its withdrawal from this customer segment, and we conclude, after examining the record, that it is not exerting significant competitive pressure outside its in-region territory with respect to those customers.

* * *

2. Competitive Analysis

a. Horizontal Effects

71. *Unilateral Effects.* We conclude that, although there is evidence that horizontal concentration will increase as a result of the merger, this increase is not likely to result in anticompetitive effects for medium and large enterprise customers, given the large number of competitors already participating in this market and the high level of sophistication of mid-sized and large enterprise customers. For small enterprise customers, we similarly conclude that the merger is not likely to result in anticompetitive effects, based upon AT&T's withdrawal from this segment of the market, as well as likely increased competition from cable and VoIP providers.

* * *

D. Mass Market Telecommunications Competition

88. In this section, we consider the effects of the proposed merger on local service; long distance service; and bundled local and long distance service provided to mass market customers. As discussed below, we find that AT&T's acquisition of BellSouth is not likely to result in anticompetitive effects for mass market services.

1. Relevant Markets

a. Relevant Product Markets

89. Based on the record in this proceeding and consistent with the *SBC/AT&T Order* and the *Verizon/MCI Order*,[*] we identify three

* Eds. These were the two most recent major mergers of telecommunications carriers. In both cases, the FCC considered similar issues of concentration, but both involved the merger of an RBOC with a long distance provider.

relevant product markets for our mass market analysis: (1) local service; (2) long distance service; and (3) bundled local and long distance service. Also, consistent with those orders, we consider both the demand for "access" and demand for "usage" when defining our relevant product markets.

(i) Local Service

90. Based on record evidence, and consistent with the *SBC/AT&T Order* and the *Verizon/MCI Order*, we define the market for local service to include not only wireline local service, but also facilities-based VoIP service, and circuit-switched cable telephony service to the extent that consumers view these as close substitutes for wireline local service. In addition, the record evidence suggests that, for certain categories of customers, mobile wireless service is viewed as a close substitute to wireline local service.

91. *Competitive LECs.* Competitive wireline carriers in the AT&T and BellSouth franchise areas provide local service to mass market consumers. Most of these carriers provide service using a mix of their own facilities and the incumbent wireline carrier's facilities. Some companies resell communications service provided entirely over the incumbent's facilities.

92. *VoIP.* VoIP services are being provided to consumers in a variety of ways today. The degree to which particular VoIP services are viewed as close substitutes to other local services varies depending upon the characteristics of the VoIP offering. Consistent with the *SBC/AT&T Order* and the *Verizon/MCI Order*, we divide VoIP providers into two general types: (1) facilities-based VoIP providers and (2) "over-the-top" VoIP providers. As discussed below, we find that mass market consumers view facilities-based VoIP services as sufficiently close substitutes for local service to include them in the relevant product market. However, the record is insufficient to determine which over-the-top VoIP services should be included in the relevant product market.

93. Based upon the information in this record, we find that facilities-based VoIP services clearly fall within the relevant service market for local services. Facilities-based VoIP services have many similar characteristics to traditional wireline local service. There is also significant evidence indicating that mass market subscription to cable-based VoIP continues to increase nationwide as cable operators continue to roll out these services throughout their footprints. In addition, the record indicates that the Applicants view cable-based VoIP as their primary competitive threat in the mass market, and consider the prospect of consumer substitution to cable-based VoIP when devising their strategies and service offers.

94. As with the SBC/AT&T and Verizon/MCI proceedings, the record here is inconclusive regarding the extent to which various over-

the-top VoIP services should be included in the relevant product market for local services. The varieties of over-the-top VoIP differ significantly in their service characteristics, including quality of service and price. The extent to which consumers view these services as substitutes for traditional wireline local service may vary based on these differences. In addition, the requirement that a consumer have broadband access to be able to use certain over-the-top VoIP services affects its substitutability. Specifically, for consumers who do not already have broadband access service, the subscription fee to obtain it must be added to the subscription fee for the over-the-top VoIP service when weighing it against the price of traditional wireline local service, which could make substitution uneconomical. Even for consumers who have broadband service, their willingness to subscribe to over-the-top VoIP service instead of wireline local service will vary with the attributes of the service and their willingness to trade service characteristics for lower prices. Although it is likely that some portion of mass market consumers view certain over-the-top VoIP services as substitutes for wireline local service, there is insufficient information in our record to determine which types of over-the-top VoIP services should be included in the product market. For this reason, and in order to be conservative, we decline to include these services for purposes of our product market analysis in this proceeding.

95. *Mobile Wireless Service.* Consistent with the *SBC/AT&T Order* and the *Verizon/MCI Order*, we find that mobile wireless service should be included in the local services product market when it is used as a complete substitute for all of a consumer's voice communications needs. On the one hand, increasing numbers of mass market consumers are subscribing to mobile wireless services, thus providing an additional access option for making local telephone calls. On the other hand, we recognize that the average cost for mobile wireless service appears to be higher than for wireline local service. In addition, while most customers making wireline local calls face a per-minute cost of zero (because they can make unlimited local calls for a flat monthly fee), many wireless customers must pay per-minute fees when making local calls with their wireless phones.

* * *

(ii) Long Distance Services

97. As with the SBC/AT&T and Verizon/MCI proceedings, there is significant evidence in the record that long distance service purchased on a stand-alone basis is becoming a fringe market, including the 2004 decision by legacy AT&T to cease marketing long distance services, the declining proportion of consumers choosing a long distance provider different from their local service provider, and other documentary evidence. Nonetheless, because equal access requirements permit a consumer to choose to subscribe to an alternative carrier's long distance service, we follow Commission precedent and consider long distance services as a separate relevant product market. As discussed below, we find that this market includes not only presubscribed wireline long distance providers,

but also mobile wireless service and transaction services, such as prepaid calling cards and dial-around services.

98. *Mobile Wireless.* We find it appropriate to include mobile wireless services in the relevant market at least to some extent based upon usage substitution between wireless and wireline long distance service, although the precise extent of the substitution is unclear. The Commission previously has noted mobile wireless providers' increased offering of wide-area pricing plans, and that consumers are switching minutes of long distance usage from wireline to mobile wireless services.

* * *

(iii) Bundled Local and Long Distance Services

101. We agree with the Applicants and commenters that it remains appropriate to treat bundled local and long distance services as a separate relevant product market. Because of the varied marketing strategies and limitations in the data, we define a local and long distance service bundle, for purposes of this proceeding only, as a customer's purchase of local and long distance services from the same carrier, regardless of whether these services are purchased together as part of an advertised bundle from a single carrier or whether the consumer creates the bundle by selecting separately-offered local and long distance service plans from the same provider. The evidence indicates that consumers predominantly purchase local and long distance services from a single provider today. This trend is likely to continue, and the stand-alone wireline long distance market is steadily declining in size relative to the bundled services market.

* * *

2. Competitive Analysis

a. Horizontal Effects

106. *Unilateral Effects.* * * *

108. Although we agree with commenters that the Applicants' post-merger market shares for the relevant products are high, we nonetheless find that these numbers significantly overstate the likely competitive impact of the merger. Regardless of the role legacy AT&T played in the past, its withdrawal from the mass market outside of the SBC region means the legacy AT&T infrastructure is not a significant provider (or potential provider) of local service, long distance service, or bundled local and long distance service to mass market consumers in the BellSouth region. The record demonstrates that once legacy AT&T determined that mass market services were no longer a viable business opportunity, it implemented steps to close down its mass market operations. We reject as speculative and unrealistic commenters' suggestion that AT&T is a potential mass market competitor in BellSouth territory on the grounds that it could readily reverse this decision. Thus, we agree with the Applicants that AT&T is not a significant present or potential participant in these markets.

109. Similarly, we find that BellSouth is not a competitor for mass market communications services in AT&T's region. Further, we note that the record evidence indicates that the Applicants' current and future pricing incentives are based more on likely competition from intermodal competitors than from competitive LECs.

* * *

111. *Coordinated Effects.* We also find that AT&T's acquisition of BellSouth is unlikely to result in anticompetitive effects through coordinated interaction among remaining competitors. Given our finding that neither AT&T nor BellSouth is a significant mass market participant outside its region, we find no indication that the proposed acquisition increases the likelihood of coordinated interaction for the relevant products. Moreover, the increasing trend toward bundled service offerings likely decreases the possibility of coordinated interaction. Because of the complexity and variety of the bundled local and long distance service offers, competitors will find it difficult to coordinate on prices.

b. Vertical Effects

112. We also are not persuaded by commenters' claims that the merger will increase the merged entity's incentive and ability to raise the costs of mass market rivals. We discussed these vertical concerns in our analyses of the wholesale special access market and in other sections of this Order.

E. Mass Market High-Speed Internet Access Competition

113. In this section, we consider the competitive effects of the proposed merger in the markets for mass market high-speed Internet access services. * * *

2. Competitive Analysis

a. Horizontal Effects

115. The record demonstrates that AT&T does not actively market mass market Internet access services out-of-region, nor does it plan to implement a major out-of-region marketing initiative. The record also demonstrates that BellSouth does not provide any out-of-region high-speed Internet access service offerings, nor does it appear that it plans to do so. Based on the record evidence, we thus conclude that the proposed merger has no horizontal effects.

b. Vertical Effects

116. Several commenters claim that the vertical integration created by the proposed merger will give the merged entity an incentive to limit consumers' access to unaffiliated content and/or applications on the Internet by either: (a) blocking consumer access; (b) injecting latency into the consumers' high-speed Internet access service; and/or (c) mandating that the consumer pay more for access to unaffiliated content and applications. In addition, several commenters have alleged that the

merged entity will have increased incentive to discriminate against unaffiliated ISPs. For the reasons given below, we conclude that given the competitive nature of the broadband market, the proposed merger is not likely to increase incentives for the merged entity to engage in conduct that is harmful to consumers or competition with respect to the delivery of Internet content, services, or applications.

117. We agree with Applicants that there is substantial competition in the provision of Internet access services. Broadband penetration has increased rapidly over the last year with more Americans relying on high-speed connections to the Internet for access to news, entertainment, and communication. Increased penetration has been accompanied by more vigorous competition. Greater competition limits the ability of providers to engage in anticompetitive conduct since subscribers would have the option of switching to alternative providers if their access to content were blocked or degraded. In particular, cable providers collectively continue to retain the largest share of the mass market high-speed Internet access market. Additionally, consumers have gained access to more choice in broadband providers. Moreover cable modem service and DSL service are facing emerging competition from deployment of cellular, Wi-Fi, and Wi-Max-based competitors, and broadband over power line (BPL) providers. Commission statistics indicate that satellite and wireless broadband lines more than sextupled between December 2004 and December 2005, from 549,621 to 3,809,247, with BPL lines increasing 20 percent between June 2005 and December 2005. Given these alternatives, if the merged entity sought to discriminate against competing content or service providers, it would risk losing customers to competing broadband service providers. Thus, we find that the strong and increasing competition for mass market high-speed Internet access services will limit the incentives and ability of the merged entity to discriminate.

118. Further, there is no record evidence indicating that either of the Applicants has willfully blocked a web page or other Internet content, service, or application via its high-speed Internet platforms. Commenters and petitioners do not offer evidence that the merged entity is likely to discriminate against Internet content, services, or applications after the proposed transactions are complete; nor do they explain how the changes in ownership resulting from the transactions could increase the merged entity's incentive to do so. If in the future, evidence arises that any company is willfully blocking or degrading Internet content, affected parties may file a complaint with the Commission.

119. The Commission also has adopted an *Internet Policy Statement* on broadband access to the Internet. This statement reflects the Commission's view that it has the jurisdiction necessary to ensure that providers of telecommunications for Internet access or Internet Protocol-enabled services operate in a neutral manner. To ensure that broadband networks are widely deployed, open, affordable, and accessible, the Commission adopted four principles embodied in that Internet Policy Statement: (1) consumers are entitled to access the lawful Internet

content of their choice; (2) consumers are entitled to run applications and use services of their choice, subject to the needs of law enforcement; (3) consumers are entitled to connect their choice of legal devices that do not harm the network; and (4) consumers are entitled to competition among network providers, application and service providers, and content providers. The Commission held out the possibility of codifying the *Internet Policy Statement*'s principles where circumstances warrant in order to foster the creation, adoption, and use of Internet broadband content, applications, services, and attachments, and to ensure consumers benefit from the innovation that comes from competition. Accordingly, the Commission chose not to adopt rules in the *Internet Policy Statement*. This statement contains principles against which the conduct of the merged entity and other broadband service providers can be measured. Nothing in the record of this proceeding, however, demonstrates that these principles are being violated by AT&T or BellSouth or that the transactions before us create economic incentives that are likely to lead to violations. Additionally, as noted above, the vigorous growth of competition in the high-speed Internet access market further reduces the chances that the transactions are likely to lead to violations of the principles.

120. With respect to claims that the merged entity will have an increased incentive to discriminate against unaffiliated ISPs, we find that merger of AT&T and BellSouth is not likely to result in anticompetitive effects. The merger will have no impact on the rights and obligations of ISPs as related to wireline facilities-based providers. Further, the fact that there are an increasing number of other broadband competitors should provide new opportunities for ISPs to provide service to customers in the combined AT&T/BellSouth territory.

F. Internet Backbone Competition

* * *

1. Background

122. As the Commission recently explained, the Internet is an interconnected network of packet-switched networks. * * * ISPs provide access to the Internet on a local, regional, or national basis, and most have limited network facilities. In order to provide Internet service to end users, ISPs and owners of other smaller networks interconnect with Internet backbone providers (IBPs), which generally are larger Internet backbone networks. The backbone networks operate high-capacity long-haul transmission facilities and are interconnected with each other. Typically, a representative Internet communication consists of an ISP sending data from one of its customers to the IBP that the ISP uses for backbone services. The IBP, in turn, routes the data to another backbone network, which delivers the data to the ISP serving the end user to whom the data is addressed.

123. IBPs may exchange traffic either through "peering" or "transit" arrangements. Under a peering arrangement each IBP "peer" will

accept and deliver, without charge, traffic destined either for its own network or for one of its own backbone customers. Transit arrangements, by contrast, permit an ISP, small or regional IBP, or other corporate business, to reach the entire Internet using dedicated access lines linking it directly to the transit provider's Internet backbone network. An IBP providing transit service enables the customer to send and receive traffic through the purchaser's IBP to any other network or destination on the Internet. * * *

124. IBPs generally can be categorized into tiers based on their size, geographic scope, and interconnections. "Tier 1" IBPs consist of a small group of the largest IBPs that sell transit and/or dedicated Internet access to substantial numbers of ISPs and corporate customers or other enterprise customers. These Tier 1 IBPs peer with all other Tier 1 IBPs on a settlement-free basis. Lower tier IBPs may peer with each other, but generally must purchase transit from a higher tier IBP to reach those end users that are not customers of the networks of their peers.

* * *

c. Market Participants

127. Based on our prior decisions and the record evidence, we find that there likely are between six and eight Tier 1 Internet backbone providers based on the definition of Tier 1 backbones that has been used in the past: AT&T, Verizon, Sprint, Level 3, Qwest, Global Crossing, and likely SAVVIS and Cogent. These eight providers offer dedicated Internet access and transit services primarily to ISPs and enterprise customers, and they generated **[REDACTED]** in revenues in 2003, the most recent year for which revenue data is available. In choosing an IBP, ISP and enterprise customers seek the lowest price, highest quality, and broadest geographic reach consistent with their needs, and these Tier 1 backbone providers compete vigorously on these bases.

128. The Applicants argue that, based on the above definition of a Tier 1 provider, there may well be other competitively significant, nearly fully peered backbones beyond those listed above. We find no evidence, however, that other networks could provide viable competitive alternatives for customers seeking transit if there were to be a small but significant and nontransitory increase in price by domestic Tier 1 IBPs. We therefore limit our analysis to these eight Tier 1 IBPs.

3. Competitive Analysis

129. For the reasons given below, we find that the merger is not likely to result in anticompetitive effects either through unilateral action by the merged entity or possible tipping of the Tier 1 Internet backbone market to a monopoly or duopoly. We also find it unlikely that the remaining Tier 1 IBPs would engage in coordinated interaction as a result of the merger. Finally, we are not persuaded that the vertical aspects of the proposed merger would increase the merged firm's incen-

tive and ability to raise rivals' costs by discriminating against the IP traffic of its broadband competitors or by raising the price of special access services to its backbone competitors.

a. Horizontal Effects of the Merger

130. As the Commission previously has explained, the Internet backbone market is characterized by "direct network effects," where the value of the network increases with each additional user who joins it." Because of these strong network effects, the Commission and the DOJ have recognized that, if one backbone provider were to become significantly larger than the others, or if it were to develop greater negotiating power, there is a danger that this dominant provider might be able to "tip" the Internet backbone market into monopoly and then raise prices for all transit services. By contrast, in a market where each backbone provider derives roughly equal benefit from settlement-free access to the other backbone providers' customers, the incentive to cooperate will predominate and the market participants will peer with each other. Thus, because of these strong network effects, the Commission and the DOJ have focused on whether a merger between two Tier 1 IBPs is likely to lead the Internet backbone market to tip into a situation in which one or two backbones dominate.

* * *

140. We are satisfied that the proposed merger will not increase horizontal concentration to such an extent that it is likely to result in anticompetitive effects in the Internet backbone market. Examining revenue data, we find that AT&T has a pre-merger share of the Tier 1 IBP services market between **[REDACTED]** percent and **[REDACTED]** percent and, adding BellSouth's IBP revenues to AT&T's, will have a post-merger share between **[REDACTED]** percent and **[REDACTED]** percent. The pre-merger HHI is between **[REDACTED]** and the post-merger HHI is between **[REDACTED]**. The change in HHI is between **[REDACTED]**. Alternatively, looking at traffic data, we find that AT&T has a pre-merger share of **[REDACTED]** percent and, adding BellSouth's traffic to AT&T's, will have a post-merger share of **[REDACTED]** percent. The pre-merger HHI is **[REDACTED]**; the post-merger HHI is **[REDACTED]**; and the change in HHI is **[REDACTED]**. It is noteworthy that, using either set of data, the change in the HHI is relatively small.

141. In addition, we note that BellSouth is not a Tier 1 backbone itself; thus, the merger will not reduce the number of Tier 1 providers. Second, BellSouth currently has peering agreements with both Tier 1 and non-Tier 1 backbones and **[REDACTED]**. **[REDACTED]**.

142. Even if AT&T were to route all of BellSouth's traffic over AT&T's backbone (i.e., both its transit traffic and the traffic currently routed through peering agreements), we find that competition in the Tier 1 IBP market would not be significantly affected. BellSouth is relatively small compared to AT&T (e.g., its Internet revenues that are

only **[REDACTED]** percent of AT&T's). Thus, even if all of its traffic and revenues were added to AT&T's, AT&T's market share would not increase significantly.

143. We further find that the merger does not change the market ranking of the Tier 1 backbones, and that several Tier 1 competitors with significant market shares will remain in the market post-merger. In addition, we note that some backbone providers appear to have higher shares of traffic than of revenue. In particular, we note that the 2004 traffic data show that Level 3's share of Internet traffic had surpassed old AT&T's. Finally, we observe that the market shares for Tier 1 backbones have fluctuated over time, suggesting that the market is both competitive and dynamic. Therefore, we agree with the Applicants that the proposed merger is unlikely to create a single dominant Tier 1 Internet backbone provider with a market share that is overwhelmingly disproportionate to its rivals, which was the key concern in prior backbone mergers.

144. We also conclude that the merged entity will not have sufficient market share and negotiating leverage to engage in targeted de-peering of rival Tier 1 IBPs. We find that AT&T's post-merger market share is too small for it to be able to engage in targeted de-peering of rival Internet backbones, particularly when viewed in light of the significant market shares of other Tier 1 backbones. While AT&T might have some increased negotiating leverage over smaller backbone providers, we conclude that it will lack the ability to target its larger rivals, including Verizon, Sprint, Level 3, and Qwest, all of which command significant revenue shares of the backbone market. These providers each have unique advantages in the backbone services marketplace and likely would provide significant counterweight to the merged entity. For example, as the Commission noted in the *SBC/AT&T Order* and the *Verizon/MCI Order*, the recent merger of Sprint and Nextel created a stronger backbone and wireless competitor. Sprint/Nextel since has teamed with several large cable companies to offer video, broadband Internet access, VoIP and wireless service together (a "quadruple play"). Based on the foregoing, we conclude that there is not a significant risk that AT&T would be able to dominate the Tier 1 IBP service market through a strategy of targeted de-peering.

* * *

b. Vertical Effects (Raising Rivals' Costs)

150. We reject commenters' assertions that the vertical integration resulting from the merger of AT&T and BellSouth could allow the merged entity to raise the costs of its VoIP and retail broadband rivals by: (a) using its backbone to discriminate against IP packets transmitted by its broadband Internet access and VoIP competitors, and other Internet content, service, and application providers; and/or (b) leveraging bottleneck control over special access to gain a competitive advantage in the backbone markets. For the reasons given below, we conclude that the

proposed merger is not likely to have such adverse effects on competition.

151. *Packet Discrimination and Traffic Degradation.* We are not persuaded by commenters' assertions that the merger gives rise to an increased incentive and/or ability for the merged company to use its Internet backbone to degrade or otherwise discriminate against competitors' IP traffic. Commenters claim that the merger increases the potential for three forms of backbone "broadband discrimination" with respect to competing VoIP, IP video, and other IP-enabled services with limited tolerance for latency and packet loss: (i) giving the merged entity's IP packets priority over the packets generated by third party providers; (ii) affirmatively injecting latency or otherwise degrading the packets sent by third-party Internet application providers; and (iii) blocking certain transmissions. Such actions by the merged entity, if undertaken, conceivably could place competing providers at a significant competitive disadvantage as to quality of service.

152. We are not persuaded that commenters' concerns are sufficiently merger specific or that the merged entity is likely to pursue the alleged strategies. First, we note that no commenter has alleged that AT&T (or BellSouth) currently engages in packet discrimination or degradation. Second, to the extent that commenters allege that packet degradation or discrimination could occur using the merged entity's backbone, we find it unlikely that the merged entity would have the incentive to engage in such conduct. We acknowledge that, in theory, the merger could give the merged entity an increased incentive to degrade or discriminate against the IP traffic of its retail competitors. We find, however, that the merged entity will likely have strong incentives to provide VoIP (and to make others' VoIP services available to its broadband customers), in order to retain customers that seek a VoIP alternative to circuit-switched voice service. Consequently, we believe that these countervailing incentives make it unlikely that the merged entity would choose to engage in packet discrimination or degradation of IP traffic over its backbone.

153. Third, as the Commission found in the *SBC/AT&T Order* and the *Verizon/MCI Order*, it is not clear that the merged entity would be able effectively to discriminate or degrade competitors' IP traffic using its Internet backbone. Given the routing of VoIP calls today, for example, it does not appear that the backbone creates a new bottleneck for VoIP providers that use their own backbone or a virtual private network to deliver service to their customers by delivering the traffic directly to the public switched telephone network (PSTN), rather than routing it through the merged entity's backbone. Further, while the merged entity may have an incentive to prioritize its own traffic using queuing or other such differentiated service mechanisms, by recent measures significant excess capacity remains on backbone networks. Given this excess capacity and the number of Tier 1 backbone providers, competing providers of VoIP, IP video, and other IP-enabled services and applications are likely to be able to reroute traffic if discrimination were encountered. Thus, in

the absence of affirmative efforts to degrade a competitor's traffic, queuing and packet prioritization are likely to yield only extremely small increases in latency and packet loss in many cases.

154. *Special Access and the Internet Backbone Market.* We also reject commenter suggestions that the merged entity will have an increased incentive and market power in the special access market to gain a competitive advantage in the backbone and broadband markets. As noted above, the Commission is currently addressing the issue of competition in the special access market in two ongoing rulemaking proceedings, which will allow the Commission to address any competitive issues on a full record on an industry-wide basis.

G. U.S. International Services Competition

155. In this section we consider the competitive effects of the proposed merger in the markets for U.S. international services. We conclude that the merger is not likely to result in anticompetitive effects for international services provided to mass market, enterprise, or global telecommunications customers. Additionally, we find that the merger will not result in anticompetitive effects in the international transport, facilities-based international message telecommunications service (IMTS), or international private line markets.

* * *

VII. Potential Public Interest Benefits

A. Introduction

200. In addition to assessing the potential harms of the proposed transaction, we also consider whether the combination of these companies' operations is likely to generate verifiable, merger-specific public interest benefits. In doing so, we ask whether the combined entity will be able, and is likely, to pursue business strategies resulting in demonstrable and verifiable benefits that could not be pursued but for the combination. As discussed below, we find that the proposed transaction is likely to generate several significant merger-specific public interest benefits, although it is difficult to quantify precisely the magnitude of some of these benefits.

* * *

C. Accelerated Broadband Deployment

204. In section 706 of the 1996 Act, Congress directed the Commission to encourage, without regard to transmission media or technology, the deployment of advanced telecommunications capability to all Americans on a reasonable and timely basis through, among other things, removing barriers to infrastructure investment. By virtue of the voluntary commitments that the Applicants have offered, we are persuaded that consumers will benefit from the deployment of broadband in the merged entity's territory more rapidly than might otherwise have occurred absent the merger.

D. Benefits of Unifying Cingular's Ownership

205. We agree with the Applicants that unifying the ownership of Cingular will result in public interest benefits, such as a quicker rollout of new converged services and enhanced efficiency. Currently, AT&T and BellSouth each have negative control of Cingular. The Applicants explain that the interests of Cingular's parents are not fully aligned, and that "[a]ll of Cingular's key strategic decisions" must be approved by a committee composed of three representatives each from AT&T and BellSouth. Given the facts presented in the record and the well-recognized inefficiencies associated with joint control, we find persuasive Applicants' contentions that unifying the ownership of Cingular will align the Applicants' incentives, facilitating a more efficient decision making structure. In particular, we believe the more streamlined ownership structure will enable the Applicants and Cingular more quickly and efficiently to bring—among other products and services—new IP Multimedia Subsystems (IMS) networks and services to market, which will speed to enterprise and mass market customers the significant improvements in integration of services offered across multiple IP networks that such systems provide.

206. We find that by streamlining the ownership of Cingular, the Applicants' ability to provide converged wireline/wireless services will be enhanced. We are persuaded that as a result of the merger, customers will benefit not only from new services, but also will benefit from the improvements in performance and reliability resulting from the network integration, and will benefit from improved converged offerings sooner.

E. Enhancement of MVPD and Programming Competition

207. We find that the present transaction is likely to hasten competition in the MVPD marketplace in BellSouth's region, bringing to consumers in this territory the benefits of MVPD competition faster and more efficiently than would occur but for the merger. The Applicants contend that BellSouth is investing $2.2 billion over a five-year period to upgrade its broadband access and core network infrastructure—upgrades that will permit BellSouth and the merged entity to offer a wide range of IP-based interactive services, including IPTV. While BellSouth has taken some preliminary steps toward offering IPTV service, AT&T has been at the forefront of telecommunications carriers' efforts to develop and market such video services, and has been a particularly aggressive competitor in this regard. We therefore agree with Applicants and find that the merger likely will enable the combined company to deploy IPTV in BellSouth's territory more quickly and at lower cost than BellSouth could do on its own. The GAO has found that cable rates are from 15 to 41 percent lower where the incumbent cable company faces competition from a wireline video provider. But for the merger, consumers in BellSouth's territory likely would have to wait longer for the benefits of IPTV competition.

F. Enhancements to National Security, Disaster Recovery, and Government Services

* * *

209. We agree with the Applicants and find that the merger will "provide significant benefits to government customers and strengthen national security by creating a stronger, more efficient, U.S.-owned and U.S.-controlled supplier of critical communications capabilities." Both AT&T and BellSouth provide substantial telecommunications and technology services to federal and state government agencies involved in national security. We find that the merger will create a stable, reliable, U.S.-owned company that will provide improved service to government customers. Moreover, we find that the merger will help BellSouth and Cingular improve communications security and network efficiency, which in turn should benefit national defense and homeland security.

* * *

G. Efficiencies Related to Vertical Integration

212. We find that significant benefits are likely to result from the vertical integration of the complementary networks and facilities of AT&T and BellSouth. The Applicants assert that their wireline networks are complementary, with BellSouth and AT&T each providing a non-overlapping extensive local network with substantial amounts of fiber, and AT&T providing a global fiber optic long distance network and global data capabilities. The Applicants claim that the combined company will be able to offer services over a centrally managed network and provide customers with end-to-end communications and comprehensive network management. They further maintain that the combination of their services will benefit large enterprise and wholesale customers by enhancing the merged entity's ability to make available the broad range of communications services and global reach that those customers demand.

213. We find that the merger will permit the integration of the complementary networks and assets of AT&T and BellSouth, giving each carrier facilities it previously lacked, and enabling the merged entity to offer a wider range of services to its broad range of customers.

H. Economies of Scope and Scale

214. We find that the merger of AT&T and BellSouth is also likely to give rise to significant economies of scope and scale, although these are difficult to quantify. While AT&T and BellSouth compete in some of the same markets, the focus and success of their efforts has often come in different segments of these markets. The merger thus not only gives the combined company a larger total customer base, but also significant shares of customers across a wider range of communications markets than either carrier had before the merger. In addition, we agree with the Applicants that, by broadening its customer base, the merged entity will have an increased incentive to engage in basic research and develop-

ment. The Commission has recognized in the past that, when a "transaction enables the parties to combine their R&D efforts and to spread the cost of those R&D efforts over" a more extensive customer base, this "could result in new products and services that would not have been introduced absent the proposed transaction." We further find that continued intense competition from other carriers will provide sufficient incentives for the merged company to continue to invest in more applied research and product development. We also find that BellSouth will benefit from the substantial investment AT&T has made to ensure that its networks, including critical national defense networks, remain robust and technologically advanced. Finally, we agree with the Applicants that the transaction will accelerate service innovations, such as advanced IP services and converged wireline/wireless services.

I. Cost Synergies

215. As discussed below, we credit certain cost reductions as benefits resulting from the merger. The Applicants assert that the merger will result in over $16 billion in savings for both fixed and variable operations costs. They contend that the cost savings would include the elimination of duplicative network facilities, staff, and operation systems; greater utilization of network assets by combining the companies' traffic streams; reduced network center and network planning costs; and elimination of duplicative information technology (IT) projects. * * *

217. After careful examination of the Applicants' synergy model, we find that we cannot credit the $16 billion savings in its entirety. * * *

221. In summary, we find that the proposed transaction is likely to generate several significant public interest benefits, although it is difficult to quantify precisely the magnitude of some of these benefits.

222. In addition, on December 28, 2006, AT&T made a series of voluntary commitments that are enforceable by the Commission and attached as Appendix F. These conditions are voluntary, enforceable commitments by AT&T but are not general statements of Commission policy and do not alter Commission precedent or bind future Commission policy or rules.

VIII. Conclusion

223. We find that several significant public interest benefits are likely to result from the proposed transaction and that, with one exception, the merger is not likely to have anticompetitive effects in any relevant markets. As discussed above, we recognize that there will be an increase in market concentration with respect to certain services, including special access services, retail enterprise services, mass market services, and Internet backbone services. We do not find, however, that these increases in concentration are likely to result in anticompetitive effects. In addition, we find that the merger will result in a reduction from two to one in the number of competitors with direct connections to

31 buildings where other competitive entry is unlikely. We find, however, that AT&T's voluntary commitment to divest at least eight fiber strands in the form of ten-year IRUs for these two-to-one buildings where entry is unlikely, which we accept and make an express condition of our approval of this merger, adequately remedies this potential special access harm.

224. We also find potential public interest benefits from the proposed merger that, taken as a whole, outweigh the relatively limited possible public interest harms. These public interest benefits relate to: accelerated broadband deployment; enhancements to MVPD and programming competition; national security, disaster recovery, and government services; unification of Cingular's ownership; efficiencies related to vertical integration; economies of scope and scale; and cost savings.

225. We therefore conclude that, on balance, the positive public interest benefits likely to arise from this transaction are sufficient to support the Commission's approval of AT&T's and BellSouth's application under the public interest test of sections 214 and 310(d) of the Communications Act.

Reconstructing the Egg. Is the Humpty-Dumpty egg of the late great Bell monopoly being put back together again? Not yet at least. Bear in mind that AT&T the firm is not the only thing that has grown since the 1984 divestiture. Consider, for example, that in 1983 AT&T accounted for 82.3% of the telecommunications service industry's operating revenues of $84.175 billion. *U.S. Statistical Abstract*, Tables 926–27 (1985). In 2005 the industry's revenues were $449.3 billion. http://www.census.gov/svsd/www/services/sas/sas_data/51/2005_NAICS51.pdf In that year the combined revenues of AT&T and BellSouth were $64.5 billion or 14.3% of the industry. http://money.cnn.com/magazines/fortune/fortune500/2006/snapshots/1182.html and http://money.cnn.com/magazines/fortune/fortun500/2006/snapshots/191.html So, even after the AT&T/BellSouth merger AT&T remains a shadow of its former self.

Of course, one response to the last observation might be that the question of "how big" is basically irrelevant. The relevant economic question is, how big compared to what? The conventional answer is, the market. That answer then segues into the next issue: has consolidation led to a reduction of competition in specific markets?

C. CONVERGENCE

The "convergence" of media is both aligned with and provides tension against consolidation. Historically, as we remarked in Chapter 1, there was a sharp divide between mass media on the one hand and telecommunications media on the other. This is rapidly disappearing: the large cable systems are adding voice and data to video services, while telephone carriers are adding video to their traditional voice and data services. The so-called "triple play" option—a marketing term for bundling of voice, video and data (Internet)—has become the mantra of both the cable and telephone carriers. To this trio the telephone carriers have long been invested in what is what the FCC called in the *AT&T/BellSouth Order* a "quadruple play"—which adds wireless. (The two largest wireline carriers—AT&T and Verizon—are also the two largest wireless providers.)

On the one hand, convergence can lead to consolidation, as it did in 1998, when AT&T acquired MediaOne and TCI to become, overnight, the largest cable operator in the country. That consolidation didn't last; AT&T sold its cable operation to Comcast three years later, but merger has historically been a powerful tool for expanding into new markets. If convergence does entail consolidation, should we be concerned? To the extent that firms "buy" their way into other markets it means there are fewer entities out there providing services. But it's generally thought that consolidation of product lines—conglomeration—does not present the same risks as either horizontal or vertical consolidation. In this way, convergence represents a somewhat more benign form of consolidation. Regulatory implications also arise when the different services become bundled. Thus, when cable operators began to offer broadband data (Internet) as part of a bundled service, it immediately raised questions of whether this integrated service would handicap narrow-band Internet service providers. This spawned the controversy over open access that we examined in the last chapter.

On the other hand, convergence can also lead to competition, and has done so, especially in telecommunications markets, as cable operators have provided competition to LECs and vice versa. Currently, the largest providers of residential broadband service are not the LECs but rather cable operators.[1] Similarly, DBS providers have found it necessary to become telecommunications providers in order to effectively compete with their cable competitors in the mass-media market, entering joint marketing arrangements with both LECs and wireless providers. Much of the next section on competition focuses on the competition created as cable, telephone, DBS, and even wireless providers struggle to break into each others' businesses.

D. COMPETITION

1. Telecommunications Competition

Despite the series of BOC mergers since the breakup of AT&T, the old Bell monopoly has not been restored to its former glory. Of course, that does not necessarily establish that the industry is as competitive as it could be. In some sectors, there cannot be much doubt about the vigor of competition. Telecommunications equipment supply, once the preserve of AT&T, has been robustly competitive since the 1980s. Mobile

1. In 2005, coaxial cable accounted for 60.3% of residential broadband access as compared to 37.2% for DSL.

wireless service markets are also very competitive. Local exchange service markets are a more complicated story. More than a decade has passed since the Telecommunications Act directed the FCC and the states to open up local telecommunications markets to competition. How well has it succeeded?

Of course, the question is sensitive to what is meant by "it." Nominally, "it" refers to competition, but that begs a non-obvious question of what counts as "competition" or more precisely what counts as evidence of real competition. If one were to measure competition simply by the number of carriers providing service in local markets, one might conclude that competition is very robust. However, a mere numbers count would be misleading without some further specification about market shares—how much of the market is served by CLECs—and also about the form of service—whether it is resale or facilities based.

Among economists there is general agreement that, all else being equal, facilities-based competition is the first-best objective of competition policy. The FCC itself has endorsed that policy preference. Mandatory resale of services or unbundled network facilities has been explained as a transitional, second-best solution—the "stepping stone" approach to competition discussed in Chapter 8. The stepping stone model was always under-theorized. Congress never expressly articulated it—and the FCC's own statements on this point are fairly casual—but it has been generally assumed that the end-goal was to promote facilities-based competition as fully as possible, and that mandating resale and access was a means toward that goal.

As we noted in Chapter 8, recent economic critiques have argued that the stepping stone approach has failed. See, e.g., Jerry A. Hausman & J. Gregory Sidak, *Did Mandatory Unbundling Achieve Its Purpose: Empirical Evidence from Five Countries*, 1 J. Competition Law & Econ. 173 (2005); Robert W. Crandall & Leonard Waverman, *The Failure of Competitive Entry into Fixed-Line Telecommunications: Who Is At Fault*, 2 J. Competition Law & Econ. 113 (2006). The evidence to date shows, not only here but in other countries, that leasing incumbent facilities has not led to a level of CLEC investment in facilities greater than that which would have obtained otherwise. Some critics (Hausman and Sidak) have argued that the stepping stone was flawed as a theory. That depends on how one specifies what the theory entails. At a level of high generality there is no reason to believe that leased access could not lead to a greater level of facilities-based competition. It depends entirely on the terms of the leasing. If the stepping stone model has failed, it is probably because the terms of leased access undermined the CLEC incentives to construct their own facilities. If the scope of unbundling is very broad and the lease prices are below the risk-adjusted cost of investing in new facilities, any rational CLEC will choose simply to continue leasing, arbitraging the spread between the regulated lease price and the market value of the facilities.

The long term fate of competition based on leased access to UNEs is unclear. As will be seen in the data below the number of CLEC access lines has fallen since the FCC abolished UNE-P (as we discussed in Chapter 8). The two largest CLECs, AT&T (the "original" AT&T) and MCI—which were heavy users of UNE-P—have merged into ILECs. But whatever the future of UNE-lease-based competition, there is evidence that facilities-based competition is succeeding. If it is, though, it would be hard to attribute its success to the stepping stone strategy. The strongest wireline competitors are the cable companies, who have their own networks. Below we present some data from the FCC's Wireline Competition Bureau, *Trends in Telephone Service* (February 2007), which will give some concrete numbers to the foregoing generalizations.

The first table measures comparative access lines—a conventional measure of market shares.

Table 8.1

End–User Switched Access Lines Reported*

Date	ILEC Lines	CLEC Lines	Total	CLEC Share
Dec 1999	181,202,853	8,194,243	189,397,096	4.3%
Jun 2000	179,648,725	11,557,381	191,206,106	6.0
Dec 2000	177,561,022	14,871,409	192,432,431	7.7
Jun 2001	174,752,275	17,274,727	192,027,002	9.0
Dec 2001	171,917,359	19,653,441	191,570,800	10.3
Jun 2002	167,330,006	21,644,928	188,974,934	11.5
Dec 2002	164,386,452	24,863,691	189,250,143	13.1
Jun 2003	158,274,538	26,985,345	185,259,883	14.6
Dec 2003	153,157,843	29,775,438	182,933,281	16.3
Jun 2004	147,993,218	32,033,915	180,027,133	17.8
Dec 2004	144,809,899	32,880,812	177,690,711	18.5
Jun 2005	143,757,708	33,975,336	177,733,044	19.1
Dec 2005	143,773,101	31,387,839	175,160,940	17.9
Jun 2006	142,249,668	29,782,241	172,031,909	17.3

Note the decline in total lines reported since 2000. The percentage of U.S. households having telephone service has been fairly constant at between 94–95% (with some fluctuations that probably reflect surveying problems more than actual changes). The decline in lines no doubt reflects a shift towards wireless. For example, as reported by the FCC in its 2008 annual CMRS report excerpted in Chapter 9, in the last half of 2006 nearly 12 percent of adults lived in wireless-only households, and based on the growth in substitution in the last couple of years, the *rate* of substitution is increasing. (For more on the trend see Stephen J. Blumberg and Julian V. Luke, *Wireless Substitution: Early Release of Estimates Based on Data from the National Health Interview Survey,*

* Only LECs with at least 10,000 lines in a state were required to report through December 2004. Beginning with the June 2005 data all LECs are required to report.

July–December 2006, http://electoral-vote.net/evp2008/Info/cell-phone-only.pdf.) Of particular importance on the question of competition, the FCC's report indicates that 98 percent of the total U.S. population have a choice of three or more different operators and 94% have four or more.

Since facilities-based competition is the first-best objective, the amount of competition that is based on CLEC use of their own facilities is especially important. The following table provides a breakdown of competitive services by whether they are resale, UNE-based or facilities-based.

Table 8.3*

Reporting Competitive Local Exchange Carriers

(End-User Switched Access Lines in Thousands)

Date	CLECs Reporting	Total End-User Lines	Acquired from Other Carriers		CLEC-Owned	Percent		
			Resold Lines	UNEs[1]	Lines[2]	Resold	UNEs	CLEC-Owned
Dec 1999	81	8,194	3,513	1,959	2,723	42.9%	23.9%	33.2%
Jun 2000	78	11,557	4,315	3,201	4,042	37.3	27.7	35.0
Dec 2000	89	14,871	4,114	5,540	5,217	27.7	37.3	35.1
Jun 2001	91	17,275	3,919	7,580	5,776	22.7	43.9	33.4
Dec 2001	94	19,653	4,250	9,332	6,072	21.6	47.5	30.9
Jun 2002	96	21,645	4,478	10,930	6,236	20.7	50.5	28.8
Dec 2002	112	24,864	4,677	13,709	6,479	18.8	55.1	26.1
Jun 2003	125	26,985	4,887	15,728	6,370	18.1	58.3	23.6
Dec 2003	136	29,775	4,842	17,888	7,045	16.3	60.1	23.7
Jun 2004	137	32,034	4,927	19,624	7,483	15.4	61.3	23.4
Dec 2004	149	32,881	5,417	18,961	8,503	16.5	57.7	25.9
Jun 2005	326	33,975	5,826	19,025	9,124	17.1	56.0	26.9
Dec 2005	382	31,388	6,704	14,521	10,163	21.4	46.3	32.4
Jun 2006	399	29,782	6,549	12,546	10,687	22.0	42.1	35.9

Note the steady rise in the use of UNEs through June 2004 followed by a steady decline thereafter. The significant decline after June 2005 presumably reflects the cutback in UNE access by the FCC following the court's remand in *USTA II* (see the decision and discussion in Chapter 8).

The next table, taken from FCC Wireline Competition Bureau, *Local Telephone Competition: Status as of June 30, 2006* (2007), showing type of technology, shows the growing importance of cable systems in provid-

* Before June 2005 only carriers with more than 10,000 lines were required to report to the FCC so the numbers before that are understated by an unknown amount.

1. Includes unbundled network element (UNE) loops leased from an unaffiliated carrier on a stand-alone basis and also UNE loops leased in combination with UNE switching or any other unbundled network element.

2. Lines provided over CLEC-owned "last-mile" facilities.

ing competitive telecommunications services. Note that the far right column, percent of coaxial cable, is a percent of all *CLEC* lines—including those provided by UNE and resale.

Table 5 Competitive Local Exchange Carrier Lines by Type of Technology (End-User Switched Access Lines in Thousands)

Date	**Coaxial Cable**	**Other Technologies**	**Total**	**Percent Coaxial Cable**
Dec 1999	308	7,886	8,194	3.8%
Jun 2000	614	10,943	11,557	5.3
Dec 2000	1,125	13,746	14,871	7.6
Jun 2001	1,876	15,399	17,275	10.9
Dec 2001	2,246	17,408	19,653	11.4
Jun 2002	2,597	19,048	21,645	12.0
Dec 2002	3,071	21,793	24,864	12.4
Jun 2003	3,123	23,863	26,985	11.6
Dec 2003	3,301	26,474	29,775	11.1
Jun 2004	3,338	28,696	32,034	10.4
Dec 2004	3,706	29,174	32,881	11.3
Jun 2005	4,571	29,404	33,975	13.5
Dec 2005	5,100	26,287	31,388	16.2
Jun 2006	5,969	23,813	29,782	20.0

To date the growth of local competition has been based largely on wireline—either traditional copper wire, or coaxial cable, or most recently optical fiber (usually some mix of fiber and cable). In recent years, however, wireless has become ubiquitous, as we saw in Chapter 9.

Competition in long distance has ceased to be a significant policy concern. As the Commission noted in its *AT&T/BellSouth* decision, a separate long distance market has become a fringe market. As a separate market, long distance was n artifact of the line-of-business restrictions contained in the MFJ that kept the separated BOCs out of long distance. The decree was terminated by the Telecommunications Act, substituting the § 271 conditions on entry into long distance, and by 2003 all the BOCs had thereby secured entry into long distance. BOC entry into long distance, combined with increased competition from wireless (as noted in the *AT&T/BellSouth* decision) basically meant the end of long distance as a separate service market. The following table, from FCC, *Trends in Telephone Service* (February 2007) shows the evolution of competition among wireline carriers from just before the 1996 Act to 2005. The 2005 cutoff is before recent mergers that have changed the identify of most of the players. For example, AT&T, SBC and Bell South are now a single firm. Verizon and MCI are a single firm, and Sprint's wireline business was spun off and is now a separate firm, Embarq.

Table 9.5
Residential Household Market Shares %
(1995 - 2005)

	AT&T	MCI	Sprint	BellSouth	Qwest	SBC	Verizon	Other
1995	74.6	13.0	4.2					8.2
1996	69.9	14.1	5.0					11.0
1997	67.2	13.2	5.7					13.8
1998	62.6	15.1	5.7					16.6
1999	62.5	16.0	6.2					15.4
2000	51.1	18.0	6.6	0.1	1.6	1.0	4.6	17.0
2001	42.3	18.5	6.8	0.1	2.9	2.6	6.7	20.0
2002	36.7	15.8	7.6	0.2	2.5	3.8	9.3	24.1
2003	31.7	13.0	7.1	2.2	3.2	7.5	10.8	24.4
2004	23.5	9.9	6.9	4.4	5.7	13.2	12.9	23.5
2005	18.1	7.7	6.2	5.9	5.9	15.9	16.2	24.1

2. Competition in Mass Media Markets

Unlike telecommunications, where competition is still a relatively new policy objective, mass media markets were always supposed to be competitive. They may not have been fully competitive in fact (a system dominated by an oligopoly of three national networks could only be considered weakly competitive), but there was no real debate about whether competition (*cum* diversity) was a component of regulatory policy. But there have always been doubts by some as to whether the FCC was doing all it could to promote and expand it. Those doubts were never expressed more vigorously than they were when the FCC released its *2002 Biennial Regulatory Review of the Commission's Broadcast Ownership Rules*, 18 FCC Rcd. 13620 (2003), reversed and remanded in part in *Prometheus Radio Project v. FCC*, 373 F.3d 372 (3d Cir. 2004), which we examined in Chapter 4. Critics decried the action as the latest in a trend towards increased concentration of media ownership.

The popular perception of increased media concentration no doubt owes much to the fact that the large media owners—both broadcast and cable—have increased in size (i.e., in the number of stations and cable systems owned). This has led to an increase in the concentration in the respective *industries*. The table below shows this increase over three recent time periods, based on U.S. Economic Census data for 1992, 1997 and 2002.

Broadcasting Concentration Figures (% of Industry)			
Year	Top 4 Firms	Top 8 Firms	Top 20 Firms
1992	27.7	39.5	53.9
1997	31.9	50.3	71.9
2002	41.2	57.4	69.9

Cable Concentration Figures (% of Industry)

Year	Top 4 Firms	Top 8 Firms	Top 20 Firms
1992	36.6	50.3	66
1997	42.3	59.4	74.3
2002	63.9	77.7	91.1

While the figures show significant increases in ownership concentration for the *industries*, they do not reveal anything about particular markets. Ultimately, the test of competition and of diversity is the number of independent viewing or listening choices in any particular market. Here the numbers point to a large increase in the number of sources of information and entertainment over the years. The Commission's *2002 Biennial Review* provides some illustrative data based on a comparison of media outlets within 10 selected radio markets. The following table is derived from that Commission's report. We have omitted the data relating to local newspapers. The data on newspapers would show that over the period studied the number of competitive dailies remained essentially constant, and for good reason: the number of competitive dailies had long ago declined nearly to the vanishing point.[2] In contrast the number of competing broadcast media have increased substantially, as the table shows.

Selected Media Outlet Counts for Ten Radio Markets–1960, 1980, 2000

Market	Rank	Years	#Radio Stations	# Owners	#TV Stations	# Owners
New York NY	1	1960	74	52	7	7
		1980	128	100	17	15
		2000	148	84	24	22
Kansas City MO	29	1960	18	15	3	3
		1980	36	27	7	6
		2000	40	22	9	7
Birmingham AL	57	1960	22	19	3	3
		1980	35	27	7	6
		2000	45	25	9	8
Little Rock AR	85	1960	12	12	3	3
		1980	26	23	6	4
		2000	42	21	13	8
Lancaster PA	113	1960	7	5	5	5
		1980	11	7	7	7
		2000	13	11	7	2
Burlington VT/ Plattsburgh NY	141	1960	10	9	2	2
		1980	24	19	10	7
		2000	37	22	11	7
Myrtle Beach SC	169	1960	4	4	1	1
		1980	16	11	4	3
		2000	29	16	6	4
Terre Haute IN	197	1960	9	7	1	1
		1980	18	13	5	5
		2000	24	14	5	5

2. In 2001 only 49 cities had competing daily newspapers, and in 16 of those cities the "competitors" were under common ownership. See 2 World Press Encyclopedia 1020 (2d ed. 2003).

Market	Rank	Years	#Radio Stations	# Owners	#TV Stations	# Owners
Charlottesville VA	225	1960	7	4	0	0
		1980	10	7	1	1
		2000	17	8	2	2
Altoona PA	253	1960	6	5	3	3
		1980	12	7	5	5
		2000	14	7	6	5

Notice that the table only shows the number of local outlets within the relevant markets, not the number of services available from out-of-market stations. Presumably this was because the FCC was primarily interested in measuring local diversity. However, with the development of cable television after 1960, focusing only on local outlets is quite misleading as a measure of diversity of sources of information and entertainment. Indeed, in the modern world of multi-channel media it seems almost quaint to be focusing on broadcasting at all. Consider for example, that in 1960 the percentage of television households subscribing to multi-channel media (in those days, the only MVPD was cable) was less than 2%. Today it is 86%. That is only part of the story. In 1960 a typical cable system offered fewer than a dozen channels; today the average system exceeds 100. Both of the nationwide DBS providers offer almost 300 channels (more if one includes each of the local-into-local channels they carry). *Annual Assessment of the Status of Competition in the Market for the Delivery of Video Programming*, 21 FCC Rcd. 2503 (2006). Given the wide range of programming diversity, is it problematic that most localities only have their choice of two or three MVPDs? Or does the availability of so much content simply increase the market power of the few MVPDs that provide the content? Note that vertical integration may not be major part of the problem; of the top 20 cable networks in 2006, only six are vertically integrated.[3] Eleven different entitles accounted for ownership of those top 20 networks.

E. COMPLEXITY

Common intuition suggests that a law dealing with complex technologies should share some of the complexity of that technology. Senator Clarence Dill, one of the authors of the Radio Act of 1927, recalled a conversation with then-Chief Justice Taft about the first radio case that had reached the calendar of the Court. As reported by Dill, Taft thought that "interpreting the law on this subject is something like trying to interpret the law of the occult." *See* Clarence C. Dill, *Radio Law: Practice and Procedure* x (1938). A reader of one of the FCC's recent reports might well concur, but perhaps not for the reasons Taft had in mind. In fact, the technical complexity of modern electronic media accounts for very little of the complexity of the laws and policies that govern their use. Despite Michelson-Morley's famous experiment that appeared to prove that ether does not exist, the original Radio Act still contained a reference to the "ether." (It was later removed.) But it was

3. Of the 531 national cable networks in 2006, 21.8% of them were vertically integrated, a slightly lower percentage than in the top 20.

harmless error. Nothing in the regulatory system that Congress put in place turned on a scientifically correct knowledge of how radio signals propagated.

Today, most students of telecommunications regulation are bewildered by the complexity of the rules and regulations; the jargon alone is daunting—CLEC, ILEC, IXCs, TELRIC, UNEs, DS0 lines versus DS1 or DS3 lines, VoIP, DSLAMs, etc. One of the most dog-eared texts in the business is *Newton's Telecom Dictionary*. However, much of the complexity lies not in the technology itself (though, admittedly, it can be complicated) but in the manner in which the law implements different economic and social policies. Case in point is modern rate regulation. If Justice Taft thought his first radio case was like conjuring with the occult, one can only imagine that he would have been completely flummoxed by the challenge of understanding TELRIC pricing. Even trying to parse such an apparently simple matter as the FCC's rules governing how local franchising authorities can regulate cable television is enough to send one running for the aspirin bottle.

It was not always that way. In the early years the rules for regulation for telecommunications and for radio communications were quite simple, and they remained that way for many decades. It is hard to pinpoint precisely when things began to acquire the complexity they now possess. However, in telecommunications an important turning point was the emergence of competition in the late 1960s. Competition complicated the FCC's regulatory task, probably in ways the FCC staff did not fully foresee. In the days of unchallenged monopoly, the only significant regulatory task was to regulate rates. Formal rate regulation can be complicated, as we saw in Chapter 7, but until the late 1960s the FCC relied on informal negotiation and settlement (so-called "continuing surveillance") to set rate levels. Some states held formal proceedings, but many did not; in fact many states only lightly regulated at all. Their regulatory responsibilities were lessened by the fact that local rates were subsidized by interstate rates, which threw the political burden of rate control on the FCC. In all events, the dominance of AT&T made it relatively easy to focus: there was really only one entity to worry about. Whatever else might be said about putting everything in one basket, it can simplify things. As Mark Twain (in the guise of "Puddin-Head Wilson") put it:"

> Behold, the fool saith, "Put not all thine eggs in the one basket"—which is but a manner of saying, "Scatter your money and your attention"; but the wise man saith, "Put all your eggs in the one basket and—*watch that basket!*"

Which is just what monopoly allowed the FCC to do.

When competition got started, however, the eggs became scattered: Not only did the number of regulated actors proliferate, but having multiple actors also resulted in a proliferation of issues dealing with their relationships. At first the issues were confined to specialized services and specialized equipment (the original "foreign attachments" problem). In the late 1970s competition spilled over into mainstream, switched (long distance) services and all kinds of equipment. In the 1980s the break-up of AT&T may have eased some of the surveillance burden by making explicit (and therefore visible) the previously implicit revenue flows within AT&T, but it created new regulatory tasks that only complicated matters—the need to regulate the newly independent BOCs. In the 1990s when local markets were opened to competition, the complexity increased by an order of magnitude with the flood of CLECs and the accompanying mandates for access regulation, pricing controls, etc.

One can see a similar progression in the mass media sector. In the case of radio and television, the Commission always had a more varied range of policy issues than it did in regulating AT&T: content controls, spectrum allocation issues, licensing procedures, and multiple ownership limitations offered more opportunity for complexity than ensuring the fairness of AT&T's rates. However, things became really complicated with the rise of cable, which introduced a question that had never been presented before: what should one do with a new technology that undermined the central rationale of regulation? One answer might have been to rethink the old regulatory policies, but the FCC gave no serious thought to that answer. Instead, it created a new regulatory regime especially for cable. The rules grew in complexity throughout the 1960s and early 1970s. In time, many of the rules would be eliminated, but the complexity of the rules has remained. The FCC no longer has rules regulating the number of channels that can be imported from distant markets, but it does have a detailed set of rules that govern the conditions on which they can be—the retransmission consent, non-duplication, syndicated exclusivity, and sports blackout rules. In the end, it is not easy to see that the modern regime is any simpler—indeed, it is arguably more complex—than the old.

Sadly, the trend towards more complexity in communications policy is likely to continue. It seems to be an iron law of regulation that it breeds increased complexity—until regulation ceases. There is no present likelihood of regulation ceasing. It was one of the stated goals of Congress in 1996 to promote deregulation—in all communications. But deregulation doesn't necessarily mean *no* regulation. Even before 1996, the Commission deregulated some activities. There has been a relaxation or elimination of many rules. In the mass media sector, most notably the multiple ownership restrictions, network regulations, content controls, cable rate regulation, etc. In the case of telecommunications there has been significant rate deregulation for non-dominant carriers, and relaxation of the network sharing rules, to name just a couple of the more important recessional moves. And yet, if one looks at the overall regulatory picture, for every deregulatory move there appears to be a new regulatory move. In good Newtonian fashion, for every action there is an equal and opposite reaction.

Certainly this is how it appears if one attempts to measure regulation as a general, undifferentiated activity. Consider FCC appropriations as one measure of overall activity. For fiscal year 1986 the FCC's appropriations were $94.4 million. In 1996, the eve of what was to be a new deregulatory era according to Congress, they were $185.7 million. In 2006 they were $290 million. Adjusting for inflation, the 1986 appropriations would be about $170 million in 2006 dollars, so the agency's funding level has increased by more than 70% in constant dollars in the past 30 years,[4] hardly a sign of decreasing regulatory activity.

Well, so what? Regulation has neither ended, nor to all appearances has it declined in overall magnitude. Some critics of regulation will be disappointed (though likely not surprised if they subscribe to public choice theory). Others will say that the generalities of regulatory *activity* mean nothing. "God is in the details," which in this context we can take to mean that the regulatory activity level is not the proper criterion for social evaluation. One must instead look to the particulars of regulatory activity. After the decline of the Bell monopoly, enormous regulatory energies were invested in encouraging competition rather than protecting monopoly; the same can be said for the ownership and program access rules applied to cable. Some of those energies might have been misdirected, but that cannot be determined simply by the overall magnitude of the regulatory activity.

In all events, for the student of communications law, there cannot be much doubt that the law of communications regulation is growing in magnitude and increasing in complexity. To some, this will merely illustrate the famous Chinese curse about "living in interesting times." For the more engaged communications lawyer, on the other hand, "interesting" is not a curse but a challenge.

4. Which is not to say that the FCC isn't a good investment if measured by a simple comparison of expenses versus revenues. Under the Omnibus Budget Reconciliation Act of 1993 regulatory fees are charged for license processing and related regulatory activities. The fees for fiscal 2006 covered all but $1 million of the Commission's appropriations. See http://www.fcc.gov/Reports/fcc2007budget_complete.pdf. As for auction revenues, the returns to date—almost $50 billion through the spring of 2008—would pay for the FCC many times over.

*

Glossary

This glossary gives a very selective, and abbreviated, definition of some technical or otherwise special terms. A far more comprehensive reference of technical telecommunications terms is *Newton's Telecom Dictionary*. Unfortunately, there is no comparable source for mass media terms.

Access Charge. A charge paid by Interexchange Carriers to Local Exchange Carriers for access to the local exchange network at both ends of the call.

Access Line (or Access Link). A line connecting a customer to the local switch of the PSTN—see Local Loop. Access Line can also refer to the connection between a local exchange switch and an interexchange carrier's Point of Presence.

Access Service. The service that connects an Interexchange Carrier with its customers. Switched Access Service uses the Public Switched Telephone Network. Special Access Service provides dedicated lines either for Private Lines or sometimes to interconnect Switched Services. Special Access Services may be used by CLECs to connect end users with the CLEC's switches without having to go through ILEC switches.

Bandwidth. The maximum data-carrying capability of a point-to-point telecommunications connection as a result of the range of frequencies available to be occupied by signals, usually expressed in terms of Hertz. In digital systems, bandwidth is also affected by the technology used to compress the data and is expressed as the number of bits per second a particular line can carry.

Basic Service. A category of service, created by the Computer Inquiries, consisting of the basic transport of information, as contrasted with Enhanced Service. The term Basic Service was eventually superseded by the term Telecommunications Service in the Telecommunications Act of 1996.

Basic Service Elements (BSE). A term used by the Federal Communications Commission in its *Third Computer Inquiry* to identify optional network features, available on an unbundled basis.

Basic Tier. The lowest tier of cable television service, consisting of public access channels, local broadcast channels, and other channels selected by the cable operator. Rates for basic tier cable can be regulated by local franchising authorities, subject to FCC rules.

Bell Operating Company (BOC). The operating companies of the old Bell System, which were divested from corporate parent and long distance provider AT & T in 1984. BOCs are also sometimes referred to as "RBOCs"—Regional Bell Operating Companies—which are the regional holding companies for the BOCs. Originally, there were seven BOCs/RBOCs. Today there are three: AT & T, Qwest, and Verizon.

Bill-and-Keep. An arrangement between carriers for the exchange of traffic without intercarrier compensation—each carrier bills their own customers and keeps all of that revenue. The arrangement is typically associated with conditions where the cooperating carriers have approximately symmetrical traffic flows between them. Contrasted with Calling Party Network Pays.

Bit. A "binary digit"—the smallest unit of measurement in the transmission of digital data. Bits exist as having a value of 0 or 1.

Bottleneck. A facility or portion of a route where traffic aggregates often, allowing the operator or service provider the opportunity to charge monopoly rates and to engage in anticompetitive practices.

Broadband. Generally a data access link, especially an Internet access link, usually defined in terms of the minimum amount of bandwidth to which the end user has access, and whose characteristics facilitate the use of advanced telecommunications applications and services. The FCC currently defines bandwidth in tiers, from 1 to 7, with "Basic Broadband Tier 1" being between 768 kbps and 1.5 Mbps; "Broadband Tier 7" reflects capacity greater than 100 Mbps. From 2000 to 2008, the FCC defined "broadband" as carriage greater than 200 kbps in both directions (the FCC now refers to capacity between 200 kbps and 768 kbps as "1st Generation Data" below the Basic Broadband Tier 1).

Broadcast Network. An interconnected mass media program service by which programs are transmitted via affiliated local stations.

Bundled. The process by which two or more distinctive facilities or services are offered jointly. For example, basic telephone service generally consists of three bundled elements, an access line (the local loop), switching, and transport.

Byte. An intermediate unit of data transmission capacity comprised of 8 bits.

Cable Modem. A device which provides a dedicated communications link via a coaxial cable (cable television) network, usually using Internet Protocol (IP) at the network layer and interconnecting with the Internet so as to provide the customer with Internet access.

Cable Operator. An MVPD that provides television signals over a closed system of cables (usually coaxial) to its customers using public rights of way. Frequently, one company will own many cable systems, in which case it is a Multiple System Operator.

Cable Program Tier. The set of channels programmed by cable networks. An intermediate set of channel options between Basic Tier and Premium Channels.

Calling Party Network Pays (CPNP). A billing arrangement in which the calling party's telecommunications provider pays the receiving party's provider for termination of the call. CPNP is the dominant model for wireline termination in the United States. Contrasted with Bill-and-Keep.

Carrier Hotel. A building that houses multiple telecommunications carriers, including ILECs and CLECs and IXCs.

Carry One, Carry All. See Satellite Home Viewer Improvement Act.

CDMA: Code Division Multiple Access. A Spread Spectrum wireless protocol that assigns unique code to each user's communication, allowing multiple connections to be carried simultaneously across a shared connection. CDMA is used by a number of U.S. wireless carriers.

Cellular Radio/Telephone. A terrestrial radio service designed primarily for mobile applications using microwave transmitters whose low powered operations enable frequency reuse and integrated service throughout a region.

Central Office (CO). A room or building equipped to provide switching, routing, and line transport functions. It provides the first switching point connecting the end user's Local Loop to the PSTN.

Collocation. Location of lines and equipment owned and operated by different carriers at a common physical location.

Comparably Efficient Interconnection (CEI). The FCC requirement that the Bell Operating Companies provide a plan demonstrating that they would not discriminate against unaffiliated enhanced services providers competing with a BOC that provides similar services. While the *Second Computer Inquiry* required the BOCs to provide enhanced services through a separate subsidiary, the *Third Computer Inquiry* eliminated structural separate subsidiaries if the BOCs filed a CEI plan for each enhanced service.

Competitive Local Exchange Carrier (CLEC). A local exchange carrier other than the incumbent local exchange carrier.

Computer Inquiries. A set of proceedings by the Federal Communications Commission beginning in the 1970s designed to erect a regulatory system that permits facilities-based carriers to enter enhanced services markets without cross-subsidization by users of the carrier's basic services.

Cross Ownership. FCC term for ownership of different classes of media, e.g., ownership of a broadcast station and a newspaper.

Customer Premises Equipment (CPE). Telecommunication equipment, including telephones and Private Branch Exchanges, located on user premises.

Customer Proprietary Network Information (CPNI). Information about a customer's basic services usage.

Dark Fiber. Optical Fiber infrastructure that is in place but is not connected to in-service transmission equipment.

Designated Entity. In spectrum auctions, a class of applicant (or bidder) that is entitled to preferential treatment, typically in the form of bidding credits—percentage discounts on winning bid amounts. Originally the category included minorities, women and small business. Today, only small business entities qualify as Designated Entities.

Digital Subscriber Line (DSL). A specification for dedicated, full-duplex service between customer premise and a service provider's point of presence via a conventional twisted cooper pair's upper 4 KHz to 2.2 MHz frequency band. The capacity of the DSL connection is highly dependent on the length of the connection and, therefore, the distance between the customer premise and the service provider's point of presence.

Digital Subscriber Line Access Multiplexer (DSLAM). Equipment that provides DSL on the telephone service provider end of a twisted pair telephone line.

Direct Broadcast Satellite (DBS). The use of a satellite to transmit programming, including audio and video, directly to end users equipped with small receiving dishes and the necessary electronic components; also known as Direct to Home Broadcasting.

Downlink. The transmission of traffic from a satellite to receiving locations.

DS0. A digital service offering a 64 Kbps high-bandwidth—a voice-grade service.

DS1. A service offering video and data transmission at speeds up to 1.544 Mbps (the capacity of a T–1 line).

DS3. A service offering video and data transmission at speeds up to 44.736 Mbps (the capacity of a T3 line).

Duopoly. The FCC's term for the common ownership of two broadcast stations in the same service (TV, FM or AM) in a single market.

Earth Station. Terrestrial equipment used to transmit and receive satellite telecommunications. Some earth stations (such as DBS dishes) provide receive-only functions.

Enhanced Service. A category of computer-based services that use the telecommunications network, including information retrieval and related services, created by the Computer Inquiries, as contrasted with Basic

Services. The term Enhanced Service was eventually superceded by the term Information Service in the Telecommunications Act of 1996.

Exclusivity Rules. FCC rules that protect a local broadcast station's exclusive distribution rights against duplication by cable or satellite service providers. The exclusivity rules take two forms: network non-duplication, which protects network programming from duplication, and syndicated exclusivity, which does so for syndicated programming.

Fiber. See Optical Fiber.

Fixed Satellite Service. The use of satellites to provide service between users at fixed locations.

Fixed Wireless. A method for provisioning a network segment between two fixed locations using wireless devices or systems.

Footprint. The range of geographical coverage of a satellite transmission.

Forbearance. Refraining from regulating certain telecommunications carriers (usually on a finding that they lack market power), thereby affording greater flexibility in pricing and service offerings.

Fully Distributed Costs. The allocation of all costs, including a portion of fixed and common/joint costs, to all consumers.

Geostationary. A position in space where satellites rotate synchronously with the Earth, making them appear from the ground to be stationary.

GigaHertz (GHz). One billion Hertz.

GSM: Global System for Mobile. A TDMA-based protocol implementation for wireless service and a member of the so-called "second generation" (2G) family of mobile protocols. Outside of the United States, GSM is the dominant standard for wireless mobile communications.

Headend. The part of a cable television system at which satellite signals are received for distribution to cable subscribers.

Herfindahl-Hirshman Index. (HHI) A measure of market concentration, commonly used by antitrust enforcement agencies and courts, and also used by the FCC, especially in merger cases. The HHI is calculated by taking the sum of the squares of the market shares of the firms in the market.

Hertz. A measurement of frequency in cycles per second. One hertz = 1 cycle per second.

Incumbent Local Exchange Carrier (ILEC). As defined by the Telecommunications Act of 1996 the Local Exchange Carrier that, on the date of enactment of the Act, provided telephone exchange service in a particular area.

Independent Broadcaster. A local broadcaster (usually a television broadcaster) that is not affiliated with a National Broadcaster. Such stations are usually at a substantial competitive disadvantage with Network Affiliates and usually have much less bargaining power to negotiate their carriage by Cable Operators.

Information Service. See also Enhanced Service. As defined by the Telecommunications Act of 1996, "the offering of a capability for generating, acquiring, storing, transforming, processing, retrieving, utilizing, or making available information via telecommunications. . . ."

Interconnection. The linking of at least two telecommunications networks at a common physical point, where each interconnected network is managed by a separate party, in such a manner as to allow traffic from one party's network to be transferred onto another party's network.

Interexchange Carrier (IXC). A provider of telecommunications services between local exchange areas—or interLATA service.

International Telecommunications Union (ITU). A specialized agency of the United Nations that formulates policy, regulations, and recommendations for telecommunications, including spectrum allocation, satellite orbital arc registration, telecommunications development, standard setting, and conflict resolution.

Internet. A worldwide, dispersed, decentralized network of computers among which data are transferred in discrete, individually addressed and routed packets. The Internet began as a network of defense and research computers in the United States and is now a worldwide conduit for commerce and communication available to the public at large.

Internet Access Provider. Any service provider, including providers of voice telephony or cable television services, that provides Internet access on a retail or wholesale basis. See also Internet Service Provider.

Internet Backbone. The set of all network connections established between the routing computers that move aggregated end-user IP traffic through the Internet.

Internet Protocol (IP). A connectionless, packet-switched network layer protocol for exchanging data between computers.

Internet Service Provider (ISP). Any service provider, including providers of voice telephony or cable television services, that provides Internet connectivity or an Internet-based applications on a retail or wholesale basis. Internet connectivity services include Internet access and Internet transit.

IP address. A 32–bit number that identifies each sender or receiver of information that is sent in packets across the Internet. Internet IP Addresses are assigned and overseen by The Internet Corporation for Assigned Names and Numbers (ICANN).

KiloHertz (KHz). One thousand Hertz.

Local Access and Transport Area (LATA). A geographical region generally denoting local exchange service. LATAs were originally established by the MFJ to implement the separation of long distance (interLATA) service from local exchange (intraLATA) service. Until the MFJ was terminated in 1996, the BOCs were limited to providing service only within, but not between, LATAs.

Local Area Network (LAN). A localized network of computers linked by wiring installed by the operator or the telephone company or by a wireless application.

Local Calling Area. In voice wireline, the sum of all destinations to which a dialed connection may be established over the PSTN without incurring a toll charge above and beyond the local rate. These destinations may be served by one exchange or, especially where extended area service is provided, by more than one exchange.

Local Exchange Carrier (LEC). The provider of local telecommunications services, often considered a natural monopoly and bottleneck through which most interexchange traffic must pass.

Local Loop. The line that connects end users to a Central Office. Also the geographical area served by the CO. See also Access Line.

Long Run Incremental Cost. A measure of the additional cost incurred over the long term to provide a particular amount of a good or service. Long run denotes a period of time in which the cost of underlying facilities is variable.

Low Power Television (LPTV). A broadcast service that permits program origination, subscription service, or both, via low-powered television translators. LPTV service includes the existing translator service and operates on a secondary basis to regular television stations. Transmitter output is limited to 1,000 watts for normal VHF stations and 100 watts when a VHF operation is on an allocated channel.

MegaHertz (MHz). One million Hertz.

Metropolitan Area Network (MAN). A short-haul network which fills the gap between access and long-haul networks by connecting three or more locations together within a single municipality or adjacent municipalities, and then making private-line capacity available on those network segments in increments whose maximum is no less than 44 Mbps. Larger than a local area network (LAN) but smaller than a wide area network (WAN), a MAN is generally used to provide POP-to-POP digital carrier services such as wavelengths or SONET-based private lines. Buildings interconnected through MANs include carrier hotels, central offices, collocation facilities, terminal rooms in multi-tenant units, and similar sites.

MFJ: Modification of Final Judgment. The consent decree that divested AT & T of the Bell Operating Companies in 1982. So named because the decree was structured as a modification of a 1956 consent decree between the AT & T and the Justice Department.

Modem. Common name for modulator-demodulator, a device that allows digital devices to communicate over analog networks by converting digital signals from a computer into analog signals for transmission over the PSTN and converts analog signals from the PSTN into digital signals usable by a computer.

Multicast. The switch from analog to digital format in television broadcasting enabled broadcasters to provide multiple channels of programming over a single allocated "channel" of 6 MHz–a so-called "multicast" option. The number of additional channels depends on whether the main channel is presented in standard digital format or high definition format.

Multichannel Video Programming Distributor (MVPD). A provider of television services on a multi-channel, subscription basis. The primary MVPDs are cable systems and Direct Broadcast Satellite service providers, although there are a few so-called "wireless cable" providers that qualify as MVPDs.

Multiple System Operator (MSO). A cable operator that owns multiple cable systems. Frequently, these are very large organizations (such as Comcast or Time Warner Cable) that control cable systems in multiple states covering millions of subscribers.

Multiplexing. Subdividing circuits into more than one channel to derive more throughput and capacity.

Must-Carry. Under the Communications Act cable systems are required to carry the signals of television broadcast stations that are "local" to the area served by the cable system.

Narrowband. On a point-to-point data access link, two-way capabilities with speed in either direction not exceeding 128 Kbps.

Natural Monopoly. A condition in which a single firm can supply the entire market more cheaply than multiple suppliers. The conditions are generally identified as those involving economies of scale and scope that allow one firm to supply the entire market at the lowest cost.

Network Access Point (NAP). A location where Internet backbone providers exchange traffic.

Network Affiliate. An independently owned broadcaster that has an ongoing relationship with a national Broadcast Network (such as ABC, CBS, NBC, or Fox) for the broadcast (or "clearance") of network programming. Although much of the programming on affiliate stations is network programming, as the actual holder of the broadcast license, affiliates are required to exercise independent judgment in making broadcast decisions. Broadcast stations that are owned by the networks themselves are called Owned and Operated Stations.

Network Effects. A network effect is a demand-side phenomenon that occurs when increased consumption of a good by one party increases the value of the good to others. Communications networks such as the Public Switched Telephone Network and the Internet commonly display network effects because, taking the example of the PSTN, the value of a telephone increases when others also have (and therefore can be reached via) telephones. The Network Effects displayed by the telephone network are summed up neatly by Alfred Kahn, when he pointed out that "if you were the only one who could own a telephone, you would not want it."

Network Externalities. An externality, generally, is when consumption of a good either increases or harms social value in a way that cannot readily be captured by buyers or sellers of the good. Pollution is a common example of a negative externality. A Network Externality is usually said to occur when the increased value (or potentially the harm) of a Network Effect cannot readily be captured by either customers or operators of the network. The presence of an externality is typically advanced as one justification for government intervention (possibly in the form of subsidies or taxes) in markets.

Network Neutrality. A term of variable definition. In its simplest meaning, a regime in which broadband service providers do not discriminate among content providers or types of traffic. For some proponents network neutrality prohibits the service provider from charging content providers for variable quality of service.

Network Non-duplication Protection. See Exclusivity Rules.

Number Portability. A term used to describe the capability of customers to retain their existing telephone number(s)—and the same quality of service–when switching to a new telecommunications carrier.

One to a Market. A former FCC rule that banned a combination of broadcast stations in different services(AM–FM radio or an AM/FM–TV combination) in the same market. The rule has been relaxed to permit such combinations depending on the number of competing broadcast stations in the market.

Open Network Architecture (ONA). A scheme adopted by the FCC in the Third Computer Inquiry as an alternative to so-called structural separation, which requires dominant carriers (today only the BOCs) to allow competing providers of Enhanced Services to obtain access to Basic Service Elements of the dominant carrier on terms that are equal to those enjoyed by the dominant carrier. ONA was designed to be a more comprehensive development of Comparably Efficient Interconnection rules. It is a precursor to the regime of unbundled network access adopted in the Telecommunications Act of 1996.

Open Video Systems (OVS). An alternative method to provide cable-like video service to subscribers. Basically OVS operators are cable systems that devote a fixed percentage of their channel capacity for leased access by other, unaffiliated program distributors.

Optical Fiber. The medium and technology associated with the transmission of information as light pulses guided over a filament of transparent dielectric material, usually glass or plastic.

OSI Reference Model. A vertical, seven-layer model published by the International Standards Organization (ISO) as a standard for data communication which has become a common reference point as to network protocols and services, ranging from the physical communications medium at the bottom to applications at the top.

Owned and Operated Stations (O & Os). A local broadcast station that is vertically integrated with a Broadcast Network. Unlike Network Affiliate stations, O & Os are owned by the network itself and therefore do not present any of the problems networks sometimes encounter in dealing with independent affiliates (such as negotiating Clearances for network programming or occasional Preemption) The number of O & O stations that any network may have is regulated by national ownership rules.

Ownership Attribution Rules. FCC rules establishing the threshold for having a cognizable interest in a broadcast station or other licensed entity for the purpose of review under national and local ownership limits and designated entity status.

Packet. A unit of data formatted for transmission on a network. Data is broken up into packets for sending over a packet-switched network. Each packet has a header containing its source and destination, a block of data content, and an error-checking code. All the data packets related to a message may not take the same route to get to their destination; they are reassembled once they have arrived.

Packet Switching. A transmission technology that reduces messages and data into individually routed packets and reassembles them before reaching the final destination.

Paging System. A one-way mobile radio service where a user carries a small, lightweight miniature radio receiver capable of responding to coded signals. These devices, called "pagers," emit an audible signal, vibrate, or both when activated by an incoming message.

Peering. A settlement-free Interconnection between two Internet Service Providers for the purpose of ensuring that traffic from the first can reach customers of the second, and vice-versa.

PEG (Public, Educational, and Government) Channels. Cable television franchise requirements for providing free public, educational or governmental access channels on local cable systems.

Personal Communications Service (PCS). Any of several types of wireless, voice or data communications systems, typically incorporating digital technology. PCS licenses are most often used to provide services similar to advanced cellular mobile or paging services. However, PCS can also be used to provide other wireless communications services, including services that allow people to place and receive communications while away from their home or office, as well as wireless communications to homes, office buildings, and other fixed locations.

Point of Presence (POP). A physical location where a Local Exchange Carrier and an Interexchange Carrier interconnect. Also a location where Internet Service Providers exchange traffic.

POTS: Plain Old Telephone Service. Conventional voice telephone services provided to residential and small business users.

Preemption. Preemption occurs when an Network Affiliate refuses to broadcast a particular Broadcast Network program, usually because the Network Affiliate believes that the network program is unsuitable (would be unpopular with) its local viewers. Because the Network Affiliate is the licensed entity, it is required to retain independent judgment and therefore it must be able to engage in Preemption. However, affiliation agreements set benchmarks for the number of times an Network Affiliate may preempt network programming, and Network Affiliates that exceed that number may face reduced compensation or even termination of their affiliation with the network.

Premium Channels. Cable television channels typically marketed on a pay per-channel (e.g., HBO) or per-program basis.

Price Cap. A form of price regulation adopted to replace cost-of-service or rate-of-return regulation. Service rates are capped based on some threshold price that is established as allowing a fair return to the carrier and are subsequently raised or lowered based on an price index, adjusted to the productivity factors applicable to a particular industry.

Private Branch Exchange (PBX). A private voice-communications-capable switching facility located in an end-user organization's premises that provides on-premises connection for internal terminals connected to it, including intercom service, and may provide connections to between those terminals and other communications networks, including the PSTN.

Private Line. Any network segment delivered as a clear communications path that provides its full bandwidth for the user's service and on which no control or signaling is performed by the carrier. A private line may be provisioned as a terrestrial private line, including fiber, copper, or microwave, or it may be provisioned as a satellite private line, in which case the point-to-point link is defined by the two terrestrial points that connect the line, making the satellite portion internal to the network segment. Contrast with Switched Service.

Protocol. A set of formal rules and specifications describing how functional units should interact, especially within a network. For example, a data link protocol is the specification of methods whereby data communications are performed over a data link.

Public Switched Telephone Network (PSTN). The worldwide set of interconnected, switched voice telephone networks that deliver fixed telephone services to the general public and are usually accessed by telephones, key telephone systems, private branch exchange trunks, and certain data arrangements, transmitting voice, other audio, video, and data signals. Completion of a PSTN circuit between the call originator and the call receiver requires network signaling and switching. The PSTN includes local loops; short-haul trunks; long-haul trunks, including international links; exchanges; and switching technology.

Ramsey Pricing. A type of price discrimination in which users are charged prices that are inverse to the elasticity of their demand for service (persons whose consumption is least sensitive to price pay more). In the earlier public utility economics literature, the common term for this pricing was "value of service" pricing. Economists often advocate

Ramsey Pricing as an efficient means of recovering fixed costs when average costs are declining.

Reciprocal Compensation. The payment by local exchange carriers to one another for terminating each other's local exchange traffic. Calling Party Network Pays is a form of reciprocal compensation arrangement.

Regional Bell Operating Company (RBOC). See Bell Operating Company

Resale. The subsequent sale or lease on a commercial basis, with or without adding value, of a distinct telecommunications service or distinct telecommunications facilities provided to the reseller by a supplier on a wholesale basis.

Retransmission Consent. Under the Communications Act cable systems are required—with some exceptions—to obtain the consent of a broadcast station before carrying its signal. The requirement is mutually exclusive with the Must–Carry obligation.

Roaming. The used of a wireless phone outside of the "home" service area defined by a service provider. Higher per-minute rates are usually charged for calls made or received while roaming. Long distance rates and a daily access fee may also apply.

Satellite. A radio relay station that orbits the earth. Satellites that orbit the earth synchronously with the earth's rotation are called geosynchronous, or geostationary. A complete satellite communications system also includes earth stations that communicate with each other via the satellite. The satellite receives a signal transmitted by an originating earth station and retransmits that signal to the destination earth station(s). Satellites are used to transmit telephone, television, and data signals originated by common carriers, broadcasters and distributors of cable TV program material.

Satellite Home Viewer Act (SHVA). An act that that granted a compulsory copyright license (aka "statutory license") to cable systems to retransmit network television programs into "unserved households"—defined essentially as those households unable to receive the programs via over-the-air broadcast service.

Satellite Home Viewer Improvement Act of 1999 (SHVIA). An act that, among other things, gives a compulsory ("statutory") copyright license that enables satellite broadcasters (DBS systems) to retransmit local broadcast signals to all subscribers who reside in the local TV station's market subject to a requirement that the DBS system carry the signals of *all* local broadcasters.

Signal Bleed. The visible or audible portion of a scrambled signal (frequently a premium cable television channel) that is received by non-subscribers due to imperfect scrambling technology.

Signaling System 7 (SS7). A digital data network carrying signaling information that interfaces with the telephone company voice and data network for services using the American National Standards Institute (ANSI) Common Channel Signaling (CCS7) protocol. Also known as CCS/SS7.

Spectrum. The range of electromagnetic radio frequencies used in the transmission of information (including sound, radio, and television).

Spread Spectrum. A technology in which a signal is broken up and spread over a band wider than necessary to carry the signal. The result is that information can be transmitted with very low power, reducing the potential for interference with non-Spread–Spectrum devices.

Subscriber Line Charge (SLC). A monthly fee paid by telephone subscribers that is used to compensate the local telephone company for part of the cost of installation and maintenance of the telephone wire, poles, and other facilities that link customer premises to the PSTN. These wires, poles and other facilities are referred to as the Local Loop. The SLC is one component of Access Charges.

Switch. The portion of the telecommunications infrastructure where traffic is received by a device that identifies the intended destination and selects the routing for delivering traffic onward to that point.

Switched Service. A service in which any user can access any other user on the same network or any other interconnected network by means of a switch. See Public Switched Telephone Network.

Synchronous Optical Network (SONET). A family of Optical Fiber Bandwidth rates ranging from 51.84 Mbps (OC–1) to 39.812 Gbps (OC–768). A network composed of Optical Fibers and used as a backbone network.

Syndicated Exclusivity (Syndex). See Exclusivity Rules.

T1. A transmission link with a capacity equal to 1.544 megabits per second in throughput (the equivalent of DS1)

T3. A transmission link with a capacity equal to 44,736 megabits per second–equal to 28 T1's (the equivalent of DS3).

Tandem Switch. An intermediate switch or connection between an originating telephone call or location and the final destination of the call.

Tariff. A contract setting out the price and other terms on which the carrier will provide regulated service to the public. The tariff, filed with the regulatory agency, is binding on both customer and carrier alike. A carrier may not, for example, deviate from the terms of the filed tariff.

Telecommunications Service. See also Basic Service. As defined by the Telecommunications Act of 1996, "the offering of telecommunications for a fee directly to the public . . . regardless of the facilities used."

TDMA: Time Division Multiple Access. A digital wireless protocol that assigns unique time-slots to each user's communication, allowing real-time separation by the sender and reconstruction by the recipient of each communication, allowing the simultaneous use of on frequency by multiple sessions. TDMA is the protocol that underlies the GSM standard used by the majority of wireless carriers in the world; most non-GSM TDMA implementations are so-called "second generation" (2G) wireless protocols, including the 1900 MHz implementation used to delivered PCS services.

Television Translator Station. A station that retransmits the signal of a television station on a separate channel.

TELRIC: Total Element Long Run Incremental Cost. The FCC's costing methodology for establishing the price at which incumbent telephone companies will make their Unbundled Network Elements available to CLECs. The TELRIC price for a network element is the forward looking cost directly attributable to providing the network element.

Transceiver. A device that transmits and receives radio signals.

Transponder. A satellite transceiver.

Trunk-Side. A Central Office switch connection that connects to another switching entity. (As distinct from "line side," which connects the switch to the subscriber's line).

Ultra-Wideband (UWB). A Spread Spectrum technology in which a Spread Spectrum signal is broken up into very short pulses and transmitted over an extremely wide bandwidth, further increasing the number of signals that can be simultaneously carried and further reducing the potential for interference with non-UWB devices.

Unbundled Network Element (UNE, pronounced "yoo-nee"). Any component of an ILEC's network that must be made available to competitors under the Telecommunications Act of 1996.

Unbundling. The term used to describe the access provided by ILECs that other service providers can buy or lease portions of its network elements, such as interconnection loops, to serve subscribers.

UNE–Line/UNE-Loop. The Local Loop or Access Line component of the network

UNE–P: UNE–Platform. A combination of UNEs, including loop, transport, and switching facilities that provide most of the required functionality of a local exchange network.

Universal Service. The financial mechanism that helps compensate telecommunications carriers for providing access to telecommunications services at reasonable and affordable rates throughout the country, especially in rural, insular, and high costs areas, and to public institutions. Telecommunications Carriers, not consumers, are required by law to contribute to this fund. The law does not prohibit carriers from passing this charge on to customers.

Uplink. The process of transmitting traffic from earth to a satellite.

URL: Uniform Resource Locator. An addressing format for reaching other computers linked on the World Wide Web.

V-Chip. A computer chip integrated into electronic circuitry placed primarily in television sets addressable by signals encoded in nearly all television transmissions to permit the set owner to screen out undesired violent and indecent programs.

Video-over-IP. A one-way telecommunications service that allows video images and audio to be transmitted to one or more locations using the Internet Protocol, or a two-way telecommunications service that allows live video images and speech of participants in a session, such as a conference, to be transmitted between two or more locations using the Internet Protocol.

Voice over Internet Protocol (VoIP). A service or capability utilizing both hardware and software that enables users to employ IP networks, such as the Internet, as the transmission medium for voice communication.

Wide Area Network (WAN). A interconnected network of personal computers and work stations situated in different locations.

Wide Area Telephone Service (WATS). Toll-free calling to the call originator provided by many retailing and service organizations.

Wideband. On a point-to-point telecom link, two-way capabilities with speed in at least one direction of greater than 64 Kbps up to and including 1.544 Mbps.

WiFi. A wireless networking protocol based on the 802.11 family of standards; uses unlicensed spectrum in the 2.4 GHz range, with low power and limited range transmission.

WiMax. A wireless networking protocol based on the 802.16 standard, designed for use by both fixed and mobile wireless services operating in the 2–11 GHz range (which includes both licensed and licensed and unlicensed bands), with ranges between 6 and 30 miles depending on line of sight and other conditions.

Wire Center. The location or building where the LEC terminates and aggregates subscriber lines. Sometimes used synonymously with Central Office; however, a wire center may contain multiple central offices and central office switches.

*

Index

References are to Pages

References are to Pages

†